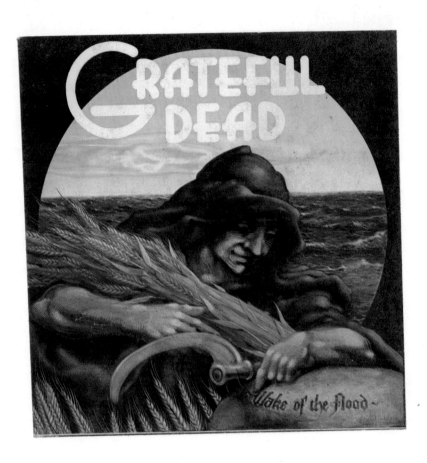

Legal Aspects

of Business

Administration

Third Edition

DOW VOTAW
University of California

Prentice-Hall, Inc. / Englewood Cliffs, N.J.

To
my Mother

13-527531-8

Library of Congress Catalog Card No.: 77-84453

Printed in the United States of America

Current Printing (last digit): 10 9 8 7 6 5 4 3 2

PRENTICE-HALL INTERNATIONAL, INC., *London*
PRENTICE-HALL OF AUSTRALIA, PTY. LTD., *Sydney*
PRENTICE-HALL OF CANADA, LTD., *Toronto*
PRENTICE-HALL OF INDIA PRIVATE LTD., *New Delhi*
PRENTICE-HALL OF JAPAN, INC., *Tokyo*

Preface

A textbook author who feels any sort of responsibility toward his colleagues or his students should never prepare a third or fourth or any later edition of his books without having something really new to say. Perhaps a second edition can usually be justified as an opportunity to correct the mistakes of the first, but thereafter other convincing reasons must be found. Having criticized other authors' later editions on these grounds, I feel more than routinely bound by this golden rule of textbook publishing and more than ordinarily obliged to explain why a third edition of *Legal Aspects of Business Administration* is necessary.

My reason is simple and singular: the well-nigh universal adoption of the Uniform Commercial Code (there is only one hold-out at the time of writing). It seems to me that the Code has now divided business law texts into three eras. First was the era before 1955. The Code was on the horizon, was being experimented with in several states, and had to be reckoned with in any text which purported to be current. During the pre-1955 era, however, anything more than collateral mention gave Code law more immediate importance than it actually enjoyed. The second era, covering the next dozen years, was a transition period, and business law texts had to give equal treatment to the law of the Code and the non-Code states. This era will always be known as the era of the pneumatic texts, which inflated to almost twice their normal size in order to meet the needs of the two distinct markets. The third era has now begun. It requires the deflation of business law texts and permits once more a unified treatment of the areas which the Code has pre-empted.

It seems to me now wholly inappropriate to devote time and space to pre-Code law, except perhaps in a few situations where it may be wise, in the interests of exposition, to trace the ancestry of a Code rule or principle. Consequently, this third edition of *Legal Aspects of Business Administration* treats the Code as the only applicable law in those fields which it occupies. The law of sales, of commercial paper, of secured transactions, and of several other fields is now Code law throughout the country, and the details of what it was like in olden times have been reduced largely to matters of historical interest. Where several states have elected to retain portions of their pre-Code law, however, this is so noted in the third edition. New Code principles of contract law have taken over broad areas of that basic field but, obviously, have not removed the necessity for thorough discussion of the older principles applicable to families of contracts to which the Code does not apply. To put this whole matter another way, this third edition is the Uniform Commercial Code version of *Legal Aspects of Business Administration,* but it is really not necessary to emphasize that any more. The third edition describes business law as it is today, and that means Code law, in the areas covered by the Code, and nothing else.

In addition to working the Code into the fabric of the book, the third edition reworks many of the chapters not affected by the Code and brings up to date those areas which are subject to rapid change and development. The chapter on competitive practices, for example, has been substantially modified by recent developments in antitrust law, particularly with regard to Section seven of the Clayton Act. Two chapters in the second edition have been dropped, the chapters on insurance and patents. Some of the material originally contained in those chapters has been integrated into other portions of the book, but much of it has been omitted entirely as low priority material and in the interests of keeping the third edition within the boundaries of reasonable size.

No major changes are contained in this edition, other than those described by the comments above. The book retains its original format and claims as its distinction a sort of environmental continuity based on the raising of legal problems in the context of the business situations where they normally occur. A real effort has been made to avoid "legalese" and to frame legal rules and principles in terms which are familiar to everybody. The student or the businessman will probably be the best judge of whether that end has been achieved.

Not because they are expected but because they are truly felt, my thanks must go to a number of people who have made major contributions to what is good about this book and have done what they could to help me avoid the bad. My colleagues at Berkeley have been free with their time, advice, and experience. Michael Conant, Edwin Epstein, and Milo Smith, in particular, have advised me on many matters where their knowledge far exceeds mine. My research assistant, John Quigley, performed one of the most thankless tasks of all, in reviewing every word of the book for situations where comment on the Uniform Commercial Code might be appropriate or necessary; I thank him now. Before she moved on to more important responsibilities, Ann Kauth played a crucial role in preparing this large book for revision. Kiyo Noji made her secretarial pool available for typing, and I want to thank them all, especially Norma Hartley, who did most of the final typing, making unbelievably few mistakes and correcting most of mine. For her unlimited sympathy and patience and for her willingness to put in long hours at one of life's least rewarding activities—reading proof—my wife deserves more thanks than I can give her here.

Dow Votaw

Berkeley, California

Contents

part III
Organizing a Business

part IV

Operating a Business

part I

Introduction

THE NATURE OF THE
LEGAL PROBLEMS IN THIS PART

The organization of this book is built around the conclusion that the traditional fields of law related to business are better understood and longer remembered if they are discussed as they arise in the natural course of business events. Legal issues, like social and political issues, are not easy to comprehend if taken out of context or examined outside the normal environment in which they grow, run their natural course, and terminate. No amount of scholarly jargon expounded in a vacuum will elucidate the contrasts between subjective and objective tests of mutual assent, or describe the origins of strict liability in tort, or explain why some debts are discharged in bankruptcy and others not.

Law has a very intimate relationship with the society in which it exists and with the circumstances out of which it arises. In Western Civilization, law is an accurate mirror of the goals, values, institutions, conflicts, problems, and ways of doing things in the society as a whole. Law is also an influence *on* society and an instrument of social change. Law and society are inseparable companions and, like all inseparable companions, have profound effects upon each

1

other. We have antitrust laws because social pressures demanded legislative response to the economic abuses of the late nineteenth century, not because some force or influence outside our society imposed those laws upon us. Once enacted, however, the antitrust laws began to have an effect upon certain aspects of our society and worked major changes in much of our business conduct. In other words, law outside its setting in society and in the business system is meaningless.

These observations have certain implications for the philosophy and organization of even a text in Business Law. Better understanding results if opportunities for the reader to see particular legal issues in their natural surroundings are provided. If the very structure of the book is based on this concept, the learning process is further enhanced. For these reasons, most chapters and major subdivisions thereof are preceded by groups of problems, or variations on a basic problem, which help to set the stage for the discussion of the particular field of law that is the subject matter of the chapter. Thus, the discussion of the law of sales in Chapter 10 is preceded by a detailed business problem which opens up most of the important issues which arise in a sales context, and each major subdivision of the chapter is prefaced by problems focused on the specific material to follow.

In addition, most of the subject matter of the book is allocated among three primary parts depending upon whether the particular topic is most likely to become important during the formation, operation, or termination of a business. In keeping with this basic pattern, matters of dissolution, insolvency, corporate reorganization, and bankruptcy are discussed in a setting characteristic of the termination of a going business, and issues involving sales and competitive practices are considered in the part devoted to the operation of a business. Very few legal issues belong exclusively to any one phase, but most issues are easily located in the phase where they are most important or most appropriate.

Parts I and II do not conform to this pattern based on the phases of business activity. Part I, consisting of Chapters 1 and 2, is devoted to providing the reader with some general background on the nature, origin, and development of law, without particular reference to business, and with some basic understanding of the procedural machinery by which law evolves and is applied. Part II is given over entirely to that field of commercial law which is basic to the discussion of every other field: the contract. Once the reader acquires an understanding of the nature of law and legal procedure and achieves some facility in the use of fundamental contract principles, he is equipped to move ahead in the substantive fields of law associated with actual business practice. In a real sense, of course, contracts play crucial roles in each of the three essential phases, but not just as contracts. They are contracts for sale, or association, or transportation, or security, or transfer of funds, or even restraint of trade, and are examined again in each of these contexts.

Let us begin, then, by looking at the historical and conceptual background of law.

chapter 1

The Background
of the Law

1. IMPORTANCE OF LAW IN BUSINESS ADMINISTRATION

The art of business administration consists largely of making decisions. It will be no surprise to anyone who has been in the habit of making business decisions to learn that the quality of one's decision is a direct function of the quantity and the accuracy of the information that one possesses. This may not be true of the rare intuitive individual who seems to be able to make the correct decisions by using some mysterious internal machinery without any great aid from outside information, but on examination most of these intuitive individuals turn out to possess extensive information plus superior ability to integrate and utilize that information. The better and more thorough the information available, the better the decisions based upon it will be, and the less one must rely on intuition. This is not to imply that better information will tend to minimize the need for intelligence or analytical ability on the part of business managers, or that the able administrator loses his advantage over the less able administrator when information is extensive and of high quality. Quite the contrary; better information gives the more able administrator increased leverage in the exercise of his superior skill.

3

The information utilized in making business decisions comes from a number of different sources, of which experience and education, formal and informal, are among the most important. Much of the necessary detailed information comes from within the business firm itself through reports from subordinates, suggestions from superiors, and from simple observation. It must be recognized, however, that this kind of information is to a business decision pretty much what an artist's paint is to the finished painting. Neither the decision-maker nor the artist can do very much with the charts and graphs or the oil paint unless these things can be combined with completely different types of information. The artist must know something about texture, perspective, brush strokes, and many other things before he can create a good painting. The business manager must know something about economics, marketing, finance, accounting, and human nature before he can make a good decision. He must know something of the social, economic, and legal framework within which he and his business and his customers operate. Thus, a knowledge of the legal aspects of business administration is important to the business manager. The legal ramifications of particular conduct may be just as important as the financial or public relations effects of certain activities. The purpose of this book is to supply the basic legal information that is necessary for good decision-making by business administrators.

It must be noted, however, that one thing this book does not try to do, and properly should not attempt to do, is to train the reader to be his own lawyer. On the contrary, in addition to supplying information about the basic legal framework within which a business must operate, one function of the book is to help *prevent* legal problems and to call attention to the danger signals that indicate the need for expert professional advice. The ability to recognize a legal problem when it is first encountered and before it gets to the irrevocable stage is certainly a useful attribute for a business manager to possess.

Another function the author hopes this book will perform is to reduce the fear most laymen have of things legal. Some degree of familiarity with the more important legal aspects of business administration should go a long way toward allaying the fear with which many of the legal problems of business are regarded when the legal principles surrounding those problems are unknown or unrecognized.

2. NATURE AND PURPOSE OF LAW

A. In General

The fields of law relevant to business administration will be much better understood and can be much more easily utilized if the reader has some knowledge of the background of law and of legal procedure. The first two chapters of this book are devoted to a brief discussion of useful background information and of the court system and legal procedure.

It should be unnecessary in this discussion to argue that law is needed in our society. A moment's reflection makes it obvious that no neighborhood of a half dozen families, or village of a hundred souls, or city of a million, or nation of a hundred million could possibly operate for very long without law. This is even more obvious in the complex social and economic organization of the twentieth century than it would have been, say, in the tenth century. The unquestioned need for law, however, is not a justification for any particular rule or principle of law. There have always been bad laws as well as good ones, and there have always been laws that made it harder for people to get along together as well as laws that made it easier. The nature and purpose of law are discussed below.

In the English language, unlike many other languages, several quite distinct meanings are assigned to the word "law," including *the whole legal system or legal order* and *the specific rule or principle of law*. To say that the legal system is simply the sum of all specific rules or principles would be inaccurate and extremely misleading. Law, in the broader sense, is a basic social institution which employs many tools and devices of which rules are only a part, though an important part. Use and interpret the word "law" with care.

B. What Is Law?

IN GENERAL. There are, no doubt, as many definitions of law as there are people trying to define it. The task is not an easy one. A definition, in order to be effective, must include all of the necessary elements of the thing being defined while leaving out the unnecessary elements. It must be inclusive, but not too inclusive. No definition of law, in anything short of a five-foot shelf of books, can be very informative. Law may be described, however, by calling attention to the functions it performs.

Before an attempt is made to describe law, let us look at some of the ways it has been defined and described through the ages. Law was once looked upon as being of divine origin, as evidenced by the Book of Exodus, which says that Moses "spoke directly to the one and only God and as he descended from Mount Sinai with the holy tablets of the law, thunder and lightning heralded his approach." Men today usually take the responsibility for the law upon themselves. Others have looked upon the law as consisting of abstract and eternal principles that have always existed but which men must discover. Cicero, for example, said: "Law is the highest reason, implanted by nature, which prescribes those things which ought to be done, and forbids the contrary." Modern students of jurisprudence, which is the philosophy of law, take a more realistic view. Justice Oliver Wendell Holmes once said that the "prophecies of what the courts will do in fact, and nothing more pretentious, are what I mean by law."

None of the above suggestions really provides a working description of law that can be used by a student new to the field to improve his understanding of the nature and purpose of law. To describe law as a method of social control is an improvement over the views expressed above, but even that description leaves too much to the imagination. In an ethical sense, law may be described as a process of integrating our knowledge of the physical and social structure of the world so that we may most adequately and happily live in it. This description suggests that human beings make the law in the framework of their own knowledge and experience and do so for the purpose of enabling themselves to live together with a minimum of bloodshed and frustration and at as high a standard of living as is possible under the circumstances. Though providing some useful information, the description is still too general. For our purposes, *law* will be described as the rules by which the force of politically organized society is brought to bear on the individual.

Basically, the law, in order to achieve its objectives, operates as a form of control by society as a whole over the conduct of individuals. Organized society brings pressure on each individual to conform to the rules and patterns which have been determined to be the best for society as a whole. Thus, society has decided that it is best for society as a whole if individual motorists are required to stop for traffic signals when the light is red. It should be noted here that the pressures of society may be brought to bear upon the individual by informal methods, as well as by the formal method, which is law.

INTEGRATION OF LAW AND SOCIETY. It has been said that law is created and imposed by society for the purpose of making organized society possible. It is obvious that in carrying out this purpose the decisions reached as to what the law should be are greatly influenced by the morality and culture of the society itself. One of the best illustrations of this simple principle is the variety of ways in which different societies have resolved the basic conflict between the individual and organized society. The Constitution of the United States, for example, has for its basic objective the preservation of the liberty of the individual rather than the protection of the organized society. It recognizes that the individual cannot be completely free without anarchy resulting, but the orientation of the Constitution is toward limiting the power of the state rather than toward limiting the freedom of the individual. Other societies at other times and at other places have resolved the conflict quite differently.

If, then, law comes from society, it is logical to assume that as society changes the law changes with it. This, of course, is the case. It is not always easy, however, to describe the situation in terms of cause and effect, i.e., to point to a change in society and also to the change in the law resulting from it. One does not have to reflect very long, though, to appreciate the changes in and additions to the law caused by the automobile. Also discussed at various points throughout this book will be changes in the law which can be attributed to particular changes in our economic, cultural, or scientific society.

Sometimes, a change in society or in our knowledge of the world around us would justify a change in the law, yet the change in the law lags so far behind the change in society that the lag becomes noticeable and the law becomes anachronistic and incongruous in its surroundings. Magazines of national circulation have featured some of the simpler and more obvious of these lags in a special column or cartoon series. There are many of these anachronisms in the field of domestic relations, especially the law of divorce, and in the use of scientific evidence in courts of law. In the latter connection, for example, blood tests that prove a particular man could not have been the father of a child whose paternity is at issue may be not be binding on the court or on the jury, which may still make a finding that the person is the father. Some states have by statute made the blood tests conclusive. (Obviously, the tests can prove the negative but not the affirmative of paternity.)

Lags of the type mentioned above are not confined to the law. One does not have to look very far to find lags in education, in business, in government, and even in morals. We find such lags in attitudes toward scientific discoveries without going back to the time of Galileo. Some may recall, not too many years ago, the ridicule, even by some scientists as well as by the public, of Einstein's "crackpot" formula, $e = mc^2$, which helped produce the wonders of nuclear physics. The explanations for the lags are about the same, whatever the field: human inertia and resistance to change, intrenched interests, indifference, and ignorance.

C. Legal Sanctions

RIGHTS AND DUTIES.   The machinery by which individuals are subjected to control for the good of society as a whole is tailored to the premise that there is a natural conflict between the individual and organized society. The conflicts between the objectives of individuals and of society are legally adjusted and reconciled by protecting some of these objectives, by limiting some, and by prohibiting others. The objectives which are protected or merely limited are called *rights* or *interests*. For every legal right there is a corresponding legal duty in other persons not to interfere with the exercise of the right as it is recognized by the law. Thus, a person has a right to be free from offensive bodily contact by other persons, and others have a duty not to cause such contact intentionally; and a party to a contract has a right to have the contract performed by the other party, who has a duty to perform it. Although there is a corresponding duty for every right, there are some duties, known as absolute duties, for which there is really no corresponding right. Most criminal law, for example, imposes absolute duties on everyone not to kill or to rob, but the corresponding right, if there is any, is in society as a whole and takes the form of a right of society to be free of such unsocial conduct. It probably is clear from the discussion in this paragraph that a right may exist against another single person, or against several persons, or against everyone. The rights of a person in his own property fall into the third category, where the owner has rights against the whole world as far as that property is concerned.

ENFORCEMENT OF RIGHTS AND DUTIES.   The rights and duties discussed above are made effective by enforcement or sanction. Theoretically, rights and duties could exist without sanctions, but, practically, this is impossible. A person's right to have his debt paid and the corresponding duty of the debtor to pay the debt would not be very useful or valuable to the creditor unless some provision were made for inducing the debtor to pay. When a person's rights or interests are interfered with, or a person's duties ignored, there must be devices by which society can protect the rights and enforce the duties. These devices are provided formally by the law and informally by society itself. The devices are usually classified into four groups:

1. Punishment. This device is used primarily in connection with violations of absolute duties but is found to a limited extent in other areas as well.

2. Relief or remedy. From a business law point of view, almost all of the sanctions take place in this category. The party whose rights have been interfered with is entitled to some sort of redress for the harm he has suffered. Relief may be *specific,* as where the party under a duty is compelled to do the thing which he ought to have done, or *substitutional,* as where money damages are substituted for the thing which ought to have been done or for the harm which the innocent party has suffered.

3. Prevention. Some sanctions, such as the injunction and many aspects of criminal law, are aimed not at punishment or redress but at preventing breaches of duties or interferences with rights.

4. Informal pressures. Some of the most powerful sanctions are found in the informal acts of society itself, as for example public disapproval or ostracism. These are the only sanctions which are not enforced through formal legal procedures.

D. Classification of Law

For the sake of convenience, law has been classified into a number of categories. One of the reasons for writing this book, however, is to minimize the use of the standard classifications, which are seldom logical and convenient for the student of business administration. Unfortunately for that objective, however, lawyers, judges, lawbooks, and most legal source materials do classify the law in a more or less uniform fashion, and it is necessary, consequently, that even the layman and the student of business be familiar with these classifications.

The two major categories of law are substantive law and adjective law. *Substantive law* is that portion of the law concerned with the creation, limitation, and regulation of legal rights and duties, in contrast with *adjective law,* which is concerned with the procedural machinery by which legal rights and duties are enforced. Substantive law is made up of public law and private law. *Public law* concerns the relations between private persons and the govenment and with the creation and operation of governments. In the field of public law, we find such subcategories as constitutional law and administrative law. *Private law* is the area of the law devoted to the private rights of persons against each other, the most important of all the areas for the business manager and the student of business administration.

Private law, in turn, is divided up into the law of persons, the law of contracts, the law of property, and the law of torts.

The *law of persons* deals with the rights and duties of persons, both human and artificial, and includes such fields of law as agency, partnerships, corporations, and domestic relations. The latter deals with the rights and duties of husbands and wives, parents and children, and guardians and their wards.

The *law of contracts* arises largely from the process of exchange, and is concerned with legal rights and duties that a person voluntarily creates. A contract is a promise or a set of promises enforceable by law. A party to a contract consents to have certain duties imposed upon him in exchange for obtaining certain rights against the other party or parties. Negotiable instruments, bailments, insurance, and secured transactions are specialized branches of the law of contract, as are most of the fields of law mentioned in the paragraph above.

The *law of property* deals with the rights and duties of persons with regard to the ownership, use, possession, and disposition of things. A "thing" may be either *real* property or *personal* property. The former type of property consists of land and other immovables and most interests therein; the latter type is made up of all other property.

The *law of torts* pertains to wrongs of a non-criminal and non-contractual nature, such as libel and slander, assault, battery, deceit, and negligence. In terms of the volume of litigation alone, the law of torts looms very large in the courts. It has been estimated that as much as 80 per cent of all non-criminal litigation is in the tort field. Certain aspects of tort law are discussed elsewhere in this book, and the hypothetical lawsuit set forth in Chapter 2 is based on a tort situation.

There is a growing tendency toward a reclassification of private law so that those aspects of the law that are primarily concerned with business would be grouped separately. Such a classification, however, would embody a very large portion of the private law area.

Adjective or *procedural law* is that area of the law which is the peculiar domain of the lawyer. The substantive fields of law are sometimes difficult to separate from economics, sociology, history, and the other social sciences. The lawyer is not the only one learned in these areas, but when it comes to legal procedure and adjective law, the lawyer is in his own realm. The operation and utilization of the machinery by which rights and duties are enforced are the special functions of the lawyer in our society.

3.　ORIGIN, HISTORY, AND DEVELOPMENT OF LAW

A. Legal Systems in General

Our Western civilization has developed two great systems of law. Under one or the other, most of the civilized world now lives. The older of the two systems is the Roman or Civil Law system, which had its roots in the Roman Empire and finds its descendants in all of the Continental European countries and in those portions of the globe which were colonized or controlled by the nations of Continental Europe. The younger of the two systems is the English or Common Law system, which arose after the Norman conquest of England in 1066. It is the system followed by all of the English-speaking countries of the world and by many of the countries colonized or once controlled by them. The differences between the two systems are often exaggerated, overemphasized, or even found where they do not exist, but at least one basic difference does separate the systems.

The *Civil Law system* is a legislative system based on written codes or statutes whose principles have come down through the generations since the time of Justinian. The codes are changed, of course, but the fundamental legal principles of the codes are more or less continuous. A court operating under the Civil Law system has the task of applying the proper provision of the code to the fact situation which has come before the court. The Civil Law, generally speaking, is made all at once and is then applied to the controversies coming before the courts.

The *Common Law* is largely non-legislative in character and consists of rules and principles on which previous judicial decisions have been based. The Common Law was not devised all at once but developed gradually as new situations and problems came before the courts. Actually, the past tense should not be used in the verbs of the previous sentence because the process is still continuing, and will continue as long as the Common Law system operates. One of the unusual attributes of the Common Law is the fact that each portion of it has resulted from long and careful reasoning, both inductive and deductive, with regard to the problems and issues raised by actual fact situations. It has a preoccupation for concrete statement and individual circumstances which is not found in the Civil Law system, whose origins are general principles laid down outside the context of actual situations. It is sometimes rather startling to note the great similarity between the rules developed by the two systems, in spite of different methods and approaches. Because we live under the Common Law system, it is that system of law with which we will be concerned.

In spite of their different origins, the Civil Law and Common Law systems have much in common. Both are parts of the legal tradition of Western Civilization and have many of the same basic characteristics. Among these is the fundamental idea that, in addition to resolving disputes and performing other obvious functions, the legal system should also provide historical continuity for our society and civilization. Though nations and governments have come and gone many times during the last thousand years, the basic structure of the law has remained unchanged and has, thus, provided the framework within which our civilization has continued to evolve. It should be remembered also that the Civil Law and the Common Law have borrowed extensively from each other and will probably continue to do so in the future.

The Common Law system has the appearance of being more flexible, and, because it is made in a court during the process of deciding actual cases, it has a precision which statutory enactments do not have. The system is based on several assumptions that one should note. It assumes, first, that a court should not try to decide too much at one time and should confine itself to the actual issues raised in the case before it; second, that law is likely to be better if it is made through the active participation of those who are most immediately concerned; and third, that those who are directly concerned are free to challenge the validity of what has previously been decided. While legislation now plays a much more important role in the Common Law fields than it did a century ago, owing in large part to the speed with which some social, economic, and technological changes take place, there is, apparently, no tendency in the Common Law countries to abandon the system. It has been able to preserve its basic characteristics even under the most diverse of modern circumstances.

"Common Law" and "Civil Law" have been capitalized in the above paragraphs for the purpose of emphasis and delineation. The practice will not be followed in the remainder of the discussion and the text.

B. The Common Law

England, the United States, and other areas of the world colonized by the English-speaking peoples use the common law system. Here the term "common law" is used in a broad sense to mean this great system of law. The term is sometimes used to differentiate general law from certain special fields such as admiralty law and the Law Merchant, or to distinguish the general law from equity, which developed in England side by side with the common law, or to distinguish judge-made law from statutory law.

ORIGIN OF COMMON LAW. The common law originated in England's feudal society. At first, the common law was concerned primarily with the problems of feudalism, but spread its coverage to other areas as feudalism declined. Prior to the Norman Conquest, justice in England was administered through a system of local courts, which generally settled controversies by reference to the customs prevailing in the various communities. These courts were scattered and had little communication among themselves. No national law developed in England to any extent until the organizational skill of the Normans pulled England together as one nation.

After the Norman Conquest, a national council of lords was established at Westminster, and was generally referred to as the *curia regis* or King's Council. This body performed both legislative and judicial functions, and through the centuries it gradually evolved into a parliament and into a system of courts.

CUSTOMARY LAW. Under the Normans, the unwritten law, or, as it is often called, the *customary law* of England, together with some elements of the law the Normans brought with them, became unified and highly developed. The customary law evolved into our common law in this manner: The judges not only decided the controversies over which they obtained jurisdiction, but developed the habit of rendering written opinions, usually stating in detail the grounds or rules upon which the decisions were based. The judges' opinions stated the principles of law which the judges believed applicable to the particular case before them. The fact that the court rendered a written opinion setting forth the governing principles would not in itself be significant except for the fact that other judges tended to follow the precedents of the previously decided cases, originally as a matter of self-restraint. Consequently, the idea became established that once a rule of law is announced by a competent court in deciding a controversy, it becomes a precedent for that court and for the subordinate courts of the same jurisdiction, and has persuasive force in other jurisdictions. The rule by which the courts are required to follow prior decisions is referred to broadly as the doctrine of *stare decisis.* Note that a judge, in effect, "makes law." He makes law in the sense that the principles he enunciates will be followed by other judges. The principle that the other judges apply is nothing more than law—the formal principles and rules that govern human conduct. Note also the unusual power and influence of the judiciary upon the development of the law.

It should not be supposed, however, that the doctrine of *stare decisis* makes the law completely rigid, because that is not the case. There is, of course, an effort on the part of the courts to search records of prior decisions and to follow those decisions in deciding later controversies, and this effort does tend to make the common law rather resistant to change in many instances. But built into the common law system are elements of elasticity that keep the common law dynamic and adaptable to changing circumstances:

1. Rarely are two fact situations exactly alike. This gives the judge in a subsequent case leeway to say that the rule of a former case does not apply to the case before him because the facts are different. *Distinguishing the facts* is the name given to this process. It is one of the most important characteristics of the common law system. The process of comparing the facts in order to determine when it will be proper to treat different cases as though they were the same is the method by which the common law evolves and by which it is adapted to changes in the society.

2. The reasons that once existed for a particular rule of law may have changed, and a judge may invoke the legal principle that *cessante ratione legis, cessat et ipsa lex,* or "when the reason for a rule ceases, the rule ceases also."

3. A judge is always entitled to say that a previous decision was wrong. Of course, the level of the court which handed down the original ruling and the level of the court presently considering a case will have some influence on a judge's willingness to find a previous ruling to be wrong.

EQUITY.   *In general.*   Some attempt must be made to explain the place of "equity" in the common law system. Equity is not a complete system of jurisprudence but merely modifies the common law and is a part of it. Equity is virtually impossible to explain in terms of modern usages because the system is largely the result of certain historical accidents. Consequently, we must undertake to review briefly the history of the development of equity.

The development of equity. When an aggrieved party could not get into a court of law, because his problem was not one of the situations with which the courts of law were accustomed to deal, or because he could not afford to pay the necessary fee, or when the remedies available at law were inadequate or inappropriate, he was permitted to turn to the king for special treatment. Although the king could handle these cases himself, and sometimes did, most of them came to be turned over to one of the king's officers, the chancellor. As the number of these special cases increased, the chancellor had to expand his staff to handle the work load and soon found himself at the head of a system of courts completely separated from the ordinary courts of law. These courts were called *chancery courts* or *courts of equity*. The judges in these courts were not bound by precedent and were free, for a long time, to invent all sorts of special remedies to solve special problems. Eventually, the courts of equity began to look to precedent, and the freedom to invent new remedies faded away, but by this time such useful legal devices as the injunction and specific performance had become a part of the system. The equity system never did become as rigid in its methods as the law system, but it did lose much of its flexibility. Historically, the system of law known as "equity" developed in mitigation of the rigors and arbitrary procedure of the courts of law and to provide more adequate remedies in special situations; hence, its name. Although law and equity are now merged in most jurisdictions, the principles and procedures developed centuries ago in the courts of equity still serve as mitigating influences on our whole legal system.

Modern practice. In England, equity remained as a separate system of law until 1873, when all of the higher courts were merged into one, and this court was given jurisdiction over both law and equity. Steps toward merging the two systems began earlier in the United States. In 1848 New York abolished the distinctions between actions at law and suits at equity, and some degree of merger has taken place since that time in all of the states. In many states, the distinctions have been abolished, while in others some of the distinctions are retained, but the two systems are administered by the same court. Even where these differences have been eliminated by special statute, the whole problem of the nature of the remedy available to a particular litigant is bound up in notions of the separation of law and equity. The relief available to the modern litigant often depends on whether he would originally have taken his case to the old court of law or to a court of equity. This concept is sometimes difficult to grasp without a thorough study of the development of the common law.

Contrasts between law and equity. Some of the points of contrast between an action at law and a proceeding in equity should be mentioned. In the former, a party has the right to have a jury determine the truth of the alleged facts. The judge decides the questions of law. A court of equity uses no jury, except on rare occasions in an advisory capacity. Consequently, the judge sitting as a court of equity determines the facts as well as the law. In an action at law, the proceedings are governed by very complex rules of evidence that were developed to insure that the jury considered only proper evidence. The technical rules of evidence are not so strictly applied in an equity proceeding because the judge is not as likely to be misled as a jury.

EQUITABLE REMEDIES. It is the type of remedy available, however, that really distinguishes an equitable proceeding from an action at law. The law courts generally restricted themselves, as far as remedies were concerned, to money damages. Since equity jurisprudence developed largely because this remedy and other legal remedies often were inadequate, it follows that equity procedure offers remedies that are in contrast to those granted by a court of law. Some of the equitable remedies are examined briefly below.

Specific performance. A court of equity, or a court acting in the capacity of a court of equity, has the power to compel a party to a contract to do the thing or perform the act he promised to perform under the terms of the contract. This unusual remedy is discussed in detail in Chapter 3.

Injunction. Another of the equitable remedies is the *injunction,* which is simply a court order directing a particular person to refrain from committing a certain act. In a case involving repeated trespasses to land, for example, the remedy afforded by the law courts is money damages, which is not an adequate remedy where the plaintiff is primarily interested in having the defendant cease his illegal trespasses. In an appropriate case, the court of equity would actually order the defendant to stop doing the thing of which the plaintiff complained or order the defendant not to do a thing which he threatened to do. An injunction is also useful in maintaining the *status quo* between the parties to a dispute until their rights can be determined. In this manner, the injunction may be used to prevent irreparable harm that could not be remedied by mere money damages after the occurrence of the event. Although the injunction is a prohibitive decree phrased in the negative, careful wording of the decree is sometimes used to make the remedy available for compelling affirmative acts as well.

Enforcement of a trust. A court of equity will also enforce a trust. In many cases, legal title to specific property is conveyed to a trustee with direction that he hold the title for the benefit and use of another person called the *beneficiary.* If the trustee fails to perform the terms of the trust, a court of equity will order him to do what he has agreed to do in accepting his trusteeship. A court of equity exercises power over the person himself and may order him to perform, and if he does not do so, the court may fine or imprison him until he does comply with the order.

Reformation. It occasionally happens that a written instrument does not express the intent of the parties concerned. If the evidence is very clear and compelling that the instrument failed to reflect the agreement or transaction of the parties because an error was made when the instrument was drafted or when certain words were chosen, the court of equity may order the instrument changed so that it does properly reflect the intention of the parties. This remedy is called *reformation*. A court of equity may apply this remedy to reform a deed or contract or other document in accordance with the true intention of the parties.

The remedies discussed are not intended to be an exhaustive list of the various remedies available in a court of equity. The remedies discussed are, however, some of the typical and more important remedies available in an equitable proceeding. If a particular litigant desires one or more of these remedies, or other remedies generally not available in a court of law, and feels that he can convince the court of the inadequacy of the remedies at law, the litigant may bring his case to the attention of a court of equity, or under modern practice, ask a court to apply equitable procedures and remedies to his problem.

THE LAW MERCHANT.   Another system of law, which was once separate from but is now a part of the common law, is the Law Merchant. This system of law is of particular importance to those interested in business administration because in it are found the roots of much of the modern law of business, e.g., negotiable instruments, sales, insurance, and partnerships. As has already been mentioned, the early common law was preoccupied with the feudal system and those legal problems, chiefly involving land, that were important in the feudal system. The early common law judges knew little of the rules and principles of commerce and were not interested in them. The result of this indifference was a special system of courts in England, many of them operated by the merchants themselves, that dealt only with commercial matters. Many of these courts, called *piepoudre courts,* "courts of the dusty feet," were in session only intermittently, usually so as to coincide with the great English fairs or markets, most of which were in operation only for short periods of time each year.

The law these courts applied was an almost international customary law that had been developed by the common sense of merchants to enable them to conduct their businesses and to carry out their transactions in a satisfactory manner. Commercial law still shows today the marks of its common sense origins—in its basic simplicity, practicality, and in its lack of unnecessary formality. As feudalism receded, the common law courts became more interested in mercantile matters and gradually usurped the business of the merchant courts. By the seventeenth century, the merchant courts had disappeared. It must be said to the credit of the common law judges, who perhaps had little choice, that they retained the principles of the Law Merchant and made a minimum number of basic changes.

C. The Modern Sources of Law

The judge-made and case-made law of the common law system is still a primary source of law today. Statutes are a much more substantial source of law than they were a hundred years ago, as are the local ordinances of city councils and county boards of supervisors. In the United States, constitutions are also important sources of law. A new and important source has appeared in the last half century in the form of rulings and decisions by administrative bodies whose activities are semi-judicial in nature. The increase in the regulation of business, necessitated by the growth in size and complexity and power of business enterprise and by changes in our economic society, produced a host of semi-legal issues with which the courts had neither the time nor the technical experience to deal. Congress and the various state legislatures created a number of administrative agencies, purportedly consisting of experts in particular fields, which were given the power to perform many judicial and quasi-judicial functions in connection with particular problems or areas of commerce. The Interstate Commerce Commission, the Federal Trade Commission, the Securities and Exchange Commission, and the Federal Communications Commission are examples of these bodies on the federal level.

It must be remembered that court-made law still is extremely important, even where statutes are involved. The ultimate interpretation and enforcement of the statutes are the function of the courts, and, consequently, the judiciary exercises its influence on the making of law here as well as elsewhere.

4. UNIFORM COMMERCIAL CODE

Certainly one of the major legal developments in the United States during this century has been the drafting and the widespread adoption of the Uniform Commercial Code. This development marks not only a substantial step toward uniformity of state law over a broad and basic area but also an acceleration of the trend throughout our legal system toward greater reliance on statutory enactments and codes. Although this trend began early in the 19th century, it did not reach major proportions until the very end of that century. Until that time, legislation served primarily as a means of removing inequities in the case law and of dealing with problems which the courts could not handle efficiently. Such legislation was sporadic and haphazard.

By the beginning of the 19th century, it was becoming obvious to many that 800 years of the common law system had produced, in addition to some marvelously realistic and useful principles, a huge and complicated collection of cases which were, in some areas of the law, confused, contradictory, anachronistic, and inequitable. Partly because it was still based upon social, cultural, and political systems that had long vanished or never existed in the United States, and partly because it was the most pervasive of all the legal fields, procedural law was the first area to be reformed by legislation. Although there had been perfunctory attempts at reform before 1848, the first effective revision in procedural law was the David Dudley Field Code of Civil Procedure in New York in that year. Other states soon followed. Thorough procedural reform did not take place in England until the Judicature Act of 1873. In all states today, procedural law is largely a matter of statute.

Criminal law was the next field to enjoy the effects of legislative revision and reform, and properly so. Before the end of the century, every state had adopted comprehensive criminal codes, and much of the confusion and injustice inherent in the old common law crimes were eliminated. A few states (California, Georgia, Idaho, Louisiana, Montana, North Dakota, and South Dakota) have enacted codes covering much of their substantive law.

In the United States, the problems caused by the sheer weight of numbers of common law cases were not the only problems that were profoundly affecting the administration of justice by the end of the 19th century. The federal system, consisting of the several states and the federal government, resulted in a multiplicity of jurisdictions—each with its own common law. Over the years, the rules and principles arrived at in the various states had drifted rather far apart. As transportation and communication improved and the nation became for the first time a single economic unit, the conflicts and discrepancies among the laws of the different states became serious barriers to commercial intercourse.

Furthermore, the peculiar evolution in the common law system of the principles governing most aspects of commercial conduct had led, even in England, to a great deal of confusion and uncertainty. Conflicting rules of law, equity, and the Law Merchant often came to bear upon the same problem. In 1882, Parliament enacted into law the Bills of Exchange Act, which removed from this confusion an important area of commercial law, that of negotiable instruments.

At about the same time, in this country, the American Bar Association came into existence; one of its expressed objectives was to eliminate contradictory laws and seek uniformity among the states. After an unsuccessful attempt to achieve uniformity through federal legislation, much of the initiative shifted to a new body, organized in 1891, known as the National Conference of Commissioners on Uniform State Laws. This body came into being as a result of cooperative action on the part of several states. Its first efforts were directed at a Uniform Negotiable Instruments Law, patterned on the English statute, which was submitted to the states in 1896 and adopted by all states during the next thirty years. The Commissioners drafted and submitted many uniform acts in the decades that followed: the Uniform Sales Act, the Uniform Conditional Sales Act, the Uniform Partnership Act, the Uniform Limited Partnership Act, and many others. Some of the uniform acts were adopted very widely, while others met with little acceptance.

Unfortunately, the hopes for uniformity did not materialize, for several reasons: some of the uniform acts were adopted by only a few states; many of the states that adopted the uniform acts did so in modified form; most important, the courts of the various states interpreted the uniform acts in different ways. By the time of World War II, the discrepancies among the states in some areas were almost as wide as they had been a generation before. Furthermore, commercial practices had changed to such an extent between the two World Wars that several of the uniform acts were clearly outmoded. Added to these pressures for a reconsideration of the approach to uniform legislation was the realization that many of the uniform acts dealt with essentially similar commercial transactions and relationships in different ways; it was clear that much of the broad area of commercial law could be handled effectively in a single enactment.

Financed by a number of foundations and legal and commercial groups, the Commissioners on Uniform State Laws and the American Law Institute began in 1945 the monumental task of drafting a Uniform Commercial Code. With the help and advice of lawyers, judges, businessmen, and scholars from all over the country, the official draft was completed in seven years and submitted to the states for adoption. Pennsylvania, which has long been in the vanguard of legal reform, was the first to enact the Code into law in 1954. Detailed studies of the Code in other states and actual experience with the Code in Pennsylvania revealed a number of problems in the use of the Code and stimulated many suggestions for improvement. The draft of 1952 was modified to take these into account and resubmitted. At this time of writing, 1968, all but one of the states have adopted the Code, and it appears it will not be long before the enactment is unanimous.

The Code replaces the following uniform acts: the Uniform Negotiable Instruments Law, the Uniform Warehouse Receipts Act, the Uniform Sales Act, the Uniform Bills of Lading Act, the Uniform Stock Transfer Act, the Uniform Conditional Sales Act, the Uniform Trust Receipts Act, and portions of certain others.

Hopes are again high for uniformity, and the chances of success are probably higher than ever before. Although many states have made modifications in their local versions of the Code, there has been much consultation and exchange of views among the states and with the Commissioners, and the variations in the statute itself are not, speaking generally, of major dimensions. Of course, the greatest dangers of a new drift away from uniformity lie in the interpretations of the Code by the courts of each state. For several reasons, expectations are more favorable than in the past. Because the Code gives comprehensive coverage to most areas of commercial practice, there should be less of a tendency for the courts to find inconsistencies between code legislation and applicable non-code statutes. In addition, the provisions of the Code are accompanied by detailed Official Comments by the draftsmen as a guide to interpretation. Obviously, these comments do not have any binding effect upon the courts of the various states, but they do help to remove uncertainties in the meaning of the language and reveal the thought and analysis that lie behind each Code provision.

The enactment of the Uniform Commercial Code imposes upon lawyers and judges in America a greater responsibility than they have ever had before to understand and to appreciate the technique of legal reasoning as applied to statutory law. The cultural habits of 900 years are not easy to break or amend, but the modern lawyer must become as adept at statutory reasoning as he is at case to case reasoning and reasoning by judicial precedent.

Many of the rules, principles, and practices discussed in this book have been affected by the Code, with the result that after widespread adoption of the Code large segments of the book have had to be altered. In some parts, the new Code law has simply been substituted for pre-code law. This was the pattern employed in the chapters having to do with the sale of goods, negotiable instruments, and secured transactions. Because only one state has yet to adopt the Code, there seems to be little purpose in devoting time and space to older rules and principles which now have only very limited application and may soon have none at all. In other parts of the book, the Code has had an impact but has not replaced the law in a whole field or situation. The procedure has been, in these cases, to add discussion of the Code to discussions of pre-code law and to indicate where the Code has or may in the future have influence.

PROBLEMS

1. Compare law with morals and ethics.

2. Give examples of situations where the law appears to have lagged behind changes in society.

3. What are the methods by which legal rights and duties are enforced?

4. Outline the categories into which law has been classified.

5. It is said that a rule of law, having been set forth by a court of competent jurisdiction in deciding a controversy, becomes a precedent for that court and for subordinate courts of the same jurisdiction and that the decision is also persuasive and may tend to influence courts of other jurisdictions to adopt a similar rule.

   a. This doctrine is usually referred to by what name?

   b. Under what legal system would the above statements be true?

   c. Does this doctrine tend to increase or decrease the importance of the judiciary? Explain.

6. Trace the development of equity. What remedies in use today had their origins in equity? Describe those remedies.

7. What is the Law Merchant?

8. What are the modern sources of law?

9. Why did the enactment of a Uniform Commercial Code become necessary in the mid-twentieth century? Trace in your own state the discussions and debates that led up to the enactment of the Code.

chapter 2

Legal Procedure

1. THE COURT SYSTEM

A. In General

The task of administering justice is carried out, primarily, by the courts, although there are other tribunals, such as administrative agencies, which also participate. When persons cannot settle their differences informally, they must resort to the machinery that has been set up for the purpose of resolving those differences. It is the role of the court, when cases come before it, to apply the rules and principles we now know as "law" to the controversies and differences that have arisen, and to determine the rights and duties of the parties involved. Society, through its constitutions and its legislatures, has set up the courts and assigned to them the authority to apply the law and settle disputes. Some courts are limited to particular types of situations or kinds of cases, or to particular stages of legal procedure, or to specified types of enforcement which they may employ. All courts are limited to particular geographical boundaries.

The word *court* is used in a number of different ways. It may be used in place of "judge," or it may refer to all of the personnel necessary to carry on the court's business, e.g., judge, clerk, and jury, or it may be used simply to describe a particular type of legal machinery. Courts are usually organized into systems, where the functions, duties, and jurisdictions are divided up among a number of separate courts. There are fifty-one of these systems in the United States—one in each state and the federal system. Because this book will be read by persons from many states, no detailed effort will be made to discuss or to describe any particular state court system. The systems conform more or less to a pattern, however, of which the federal system is typical. The federal system will be considered in some detail below.

B. Federal Court System

In General. Section 1 of Article III of the Federal Constitution lays the foundation of the federal courts by providing:

> The judicial Power of the United States, shall be vested in one supreme Court, and in such inferior Courts as the Congress may from time to time ordain and establish. The Judges, both of the supreme and inferior Courts, shall hold their Offices during good Behavior, and shall, at stated Times, receive for their Services, a Compensation, which shall not be diminished during their Continuance in Office.

Under the mandate of this clause in the Constitution, the Congress established a system of federal courts, consisting of the District Courts and the Circuit Courts of Appeals, now correctly called the United States Courts of Appeals. The jurisdiction of all of the federal courts is limited by the Constitution, and that of the Supreme Court is described precisely by Section 2, Article III.

District Courts. Congress created the District Courts as the lowest level in the federal court hierarchy. They are trial courts, sometimes spoken of as *courts of original jurisdiction,* which means that they are the courts where most cases that come into the federal system begin. A trial court or a court of original jurisdiction is contrasted with an appellate court, which reviews but does not retry cases that have been tried in the lower court. The District Courts have jurisdiction over the following matters: cases under the bankruptcy, postal, or federal banking laws; all cases of admiralty, which includes all maritime contracts, torts, and offenses; all cases of crimes punishable under the laws of the United States or committed on the high seas; all actions involving a question under the Federal Constitution, or federal laws or treaties; all actions involving controversies between citizens of different states, provided the amount in controversy is in excess of $10,000.

Each state has at least one of these courts. The larger and more populous states have several. New York, for example, has four. The jurisdiction of a District Court does not extend beyond the boundaries of the state in which it is located. The volume of business determines how many judges there will be in each District Court. Where there is more than one judge, as is true of many of the districts, each judge sits as the District Court for that district. The judges, ordinarily, do not sit in groups as do the judges of appellate courts. Theoretically, then, a Federal District Court with four judges could have four sessions of the court operating simultaneously.

It is in the District Courts, because they are trial courts, that testimony is introduced, witnesses are heard, and juries are impaneled. Appellate courts, generally, do not re-examine the facts as determined by the trial court but confine themselves to the accuracy of the law applied and to the propriety of the procedures.

UNITED STATES COURTS OF APPEALS. Congress has divided the United States into eleven judicial circuits, numbered one to ten, with the eleventh being the Court of Appeals for the District of Columbia. Each of these Courts includes several states within its jurisdiction. The Ninth, for example, includes Alaska, Arizona, California, Hawaii, Idaho, Montana, Nevada, Oregon, and Washington. A litigant who feels aggrieved by the treatment he has received in one of the District Courts ordinarily may appeal to the Court of Appeals for the particular area in which the District Court is located.

Each Court of Appeals has at least three judges. Some have many more. The judges sit in groups of three, and decisions are reached by majority vote. An appellate court operating on the level of the Court of Appeals, in between a trial court and a higher appellate court, is called an *intermediate appellate court*. The jurisdiction of the Court of Appeals is almost entirely appellate, but Congress, from time to time, gives it original jurisdiction in special situations.

It is the primary function of this court to hear appeals from the lower courts. An appellate court almost never undertakes to retry the case already tried on the District Court level, but, on the contrary, is content to examine the record of the trial below and to determine whether the proceedings were properly conducted. This is typical of appellate courts. Even in cases where the court might have the inherent authority to order an appropriate remedy, it generally looks only at the record to see that the litigants were properly treated in the court below. If the appellate court believes that the trial judge made certain errors in instructing the jury, perhaps, or in admitting or excluding certain evidence, the appellate court generally sends the case back for a new trial, with instructions to the lower court to conduct the new trial in accordance with the notions advanced by the appellate court in its opinion.

SUPREME COURT OF THE UNITED STATES. The highest appellate court on the federal level is the Supreme Court of the United States, the only court that is expressly provided for in the Constitution of the United States. Although this court has original jurisdiction in a few special cases provided for in the Constitution, its work is primarily appellate. The Supreme Court is not required to hear all of the appeals that are addressed to it, and the Court is very selective in the cases that it will hear. In fact, only rarely will a litigant be able to appeal to the Supreme Court of the United States as a matter of right. Since the court has considerable discretion in selecting its cases, it generally has chosen to assume jurisdiction only in cases that it considers very important, such as those involving basic human rights, basic constitutional rights, or cases wherein a conflict exists between the lower courts. The Supreme Court, like appellate courts generally, restricts its activities to an examination of the record made on the trial level and at the intermediate appellate level, and ordinarily will send the case down for a new trial if convinced that an error was made in the conduct of the proceedings below. The Supreme Court of the United States wields enormous power and has great influence. The principles enunciated by the Supreme Court of the United States are followed by the other federal courts and applied to the various controversies that come before these courts. If the decision of the court involves basic constitutional questions, the court's decision will be followed generally by all of the various courts of the United States, both federal and state.

MISCELLANEOUS FEDERAL COURTS. The basic federal court system is a three-tier system consisting of a trial court, an intermediate appellate court, and the Supreme Court. In addition, there are some specialized federal courts which perform generally, but not exclusively, on the trial level. For example, the Court of Claims is a specially constituted court with authority to hear and pass on matters involving non-tort claims against the government. It operates primarily on the trial level. The Tax Court of the United States is another specialized court with limited jurisdiction to hear cases involving federal taxes. It operates generally as a court of equity on the trial level, within its limited jurisdiction. There are also specialized courts hearing patent matters and customs matters. Some of these "courts" are no more than administrative tribunals.

C. State Court Systems

The basic federal pattern is followed by most of the states of the United States. Most states have the three-tier system, consisting of a trial court, an intermediate appellate court, and the highest appellate court of the jurisdiction in question. These courts perform almost the same functions that the corresponding federal courts perform. It is impossible to determine merely from the name of the court whether it operates on a trial or appellate level, unless this fact is otherwise known. For example, in California, the basic state trial court is known as the Superior Court; in New York, the basic trial court is known as the Supreme Court. Some states have only a two-tier system, omitting the intermediate appellate court. These states, by and large, are the less populous states, for an intermediate appellate court is most useful in screening the volume of appeals going from the trial level to the highest appellate level.

Supplementing the basic trial court, some states have established specialized courts to handle probate, criminal, or other special matters. A state is free to establish those courts deemed necessary and convenient. In most states, a number of inferior courts may also be found, operating even below the trial court level. Some typical courts are Justice of the Peace courts and police courts, which exist in many cities and areas of the United States. These courts are generally concerned with minor matters and generally have extremely limited jurisdiction. The reader should undertake to familiarize himself with the exact pattern of the court system in his particular state.

2. THE JUDICIAL POWER

The power that courts exercise, the judicial power, has certain basic attributes which virtually all courts recognize and apply. We will consider some of these attributes.

CASE-OR-CONTROVERSY RULE. In general, all courts observe the *case-or-controversy* rule. This rule provides that a court will usually refuse to hear and decide a matter unless it involves a genuine contest or conflict of interest between parties having actual adverse interests. The reason for this rule is that trial courts ordinarily hear only such evidence as the parties put before them, and the appellate courts only examine the record of the trial court proceedings. Courts do not make independent investigations of cases coming before them. They depend upon the parties to present all sides of the particular case or controversy. The presence of adverse interests before the court makes for the better presentation of evidence.

The strictness of the rule in its early forms has been somewhat relaxed in modern times to permit declaratory judgments. At one time, the case-or-controversy rule required that no case could be heard or judgment given until a controversy became immediate. For example, if a landlord told a tenant that he would refuse to renew a lease when it expired, despite a provision in the lease which the tenant believed entitled him to a renewal, the tenant could not go to court until the lease expired and the landlord refused to renew it. This might work a special hardship on the tenant who is a businessman operating a business on the premises. Today, most courts will give a declaratory judgment, stating the rights and duties of the parties without requiring them to wait until relationships are disrupted. Notice, however, that there still must be a dispute between the parties as to the meaning of the lease or contract in question. We are talking in very general terms, and the reader should not get the impression that this rule is a hard and fast one. In some states, the courts are permitted to give advisory opinions to public agencies requesting them, even where there is no controversy at all.

Res judicata. All courts observe, to a greater or lesser extent, the rule of *res judicata.* In simple terms, this doctrine means that once a case has been decided by a court of competent jurisdiction, the matter will not ordinarily be reconsidered by the same court or retried by another court. The rule contemplates that the litigant has had every opportunity to prove his case, to appeal the case if appropriate, and that final decision has been entered. Once a decision has become final, the court will not undertake to retry the same matter, nor will any other court undertake to determine the same controversy. The rule is a practical one which foresees the end of litigation and the final determination of a controversy. After all, a litigant should not be allowed to return to court repeatedly until he has won a decision in his favor.

Contempt powers. All courts have the power to punish for contempt of court. They have the inherent power and authority to maintain decorum in the courtroom, to uphold the dignity of the court, and generally to protect and enforce the orderly administration of justice. Acts committed in the presence of the court which in the opinion of the court constitute an interference with orderly legal processes are termed *direct contempts,* and may be punished in summary fashion. By *summary fashion,* we mean that the court has the power to order the offender into custody and to impose a sentence or fine upon that person. The court has the power to do this without trial and without any supplementary proceedings of any kind. The only restriction upon this power of the court is that the court must not act in an arbitrary fashion, and the actions of the judge are subject to review by an appellate court. Contrasted with direct contempt is *constructive contempt,* which arises from matters not occurring in or near the presence of the court. They tend to obstruct the administration of justice and usually consist of a failure or refusal of a party to obey a lawful order or decree by the court. Constructive contempts cannot be punished summarily but may be punished after a proper trial and after a determination of the facts of the alleged contempt. By and large, the court has very broad contempt powers and will not hesitate to use these powers in an appropriate case.

JURISDICTION. *In general.* A court cannot act without *jurisdiction,* i.e., without having the power and authority to act. Every court derives its power and authority from the particular political sovereign creating the court and conferring authority upon it. For the purposes of this general discussion, jurisdiction may be divided into jurisdiction over persons and jurisdiction over certain subject matter.

Jurisdiction over persons. A court acquires jurisdiction over a person when that person appears voluntarily in the court or when he is properly served with judicial process. *Service of process* is a term given to the formal notification of the defendant that he is being sued and that he is required to appear in court and defend himself. The process, as a general rule, must be served upon the individual when he is within the territorital limits of the jurisdiction of the court. For example, a court of the State of New York, operating under the power and authority conferred upon it by the legislature or constitution of that political entity, cannot ordinarily obtain control over a person outside of the boundaries of the state so as to be able to render a judgment or order personally binding that person. The practical result of this principle is that the plaintiff must usually undertake to bring his action against the defendant where the latter may be located and brought into a court having a personal power and authority over him. This means that the plaintiff will have to serve process on the defendant in the particular state or jurisdiction where the defendant may be found. Although this does not mean in every case that the plaintiff must journey to a distant place in order to institute and prosecute his claim against a defendant residing in that locality, it does mean that he must in any event bring his action in that jurisdiction and probably must engage the services of an attorney licensed to practice in that jurisdiction to handle the matter for him, if he wants a personal judgment against the defendant. Even though the plaintiff might have a claim that could be properly heard by a federal court, only the Federal District Court having jurisdiction over the particular geographical area in which the defendant may be located has the power and authority over that person.

Jurisdiction over subject matter. Jurisdiction over the subject matter of a case exists where the subject matter itself is within the territory over which a particular court has jurisdiction. Some things are under the control of a particular court because of their geographical location alone, and without regard to the residence of the parties who may have some interest in the subject matter. For example, a state court generally has power and authority over land located within the boundaries of that particular state. The court can exercise its power to render a judgment affecting the title or disposition of this land even though its judgment may incidentally affect the rights of persons who are not residents of that particular state. The court, after all, has control over the land itself, and, provided proper safeguards are taken to notify the persons who may have an interest in the land so that they may appear and defend their rights, the court can dispose of the land by proper exercise of its jurisdiction. As a further example, a court has jurisdiction to award a divorce if one of the parties of the marriage lives within the court's territory. This is because the subject matter is the marital status, and that status is within the jurisdiction of the court when one of the married persons is domiciled within the territory over which the court has power and authority.

Although all judgments conform to a certain basic pattern, the jurisdiction of the court in a particular case may affect the kind of judgment which the court can hand down. Judgments may be personal, *quasi-in-rem,* or *in rem.* A *personal judgment* is binding and imposes a personal obligation on a specific person or on specific persons. This kind of judgment results when the court handing down the judgment has jurisdiction over the person or persons who are obligated by the judgment. A judgment *quasi-in-rem* affects the interests of specific persons in some particular thing. Whereas in the personal judgment a court has the power to impose a personal obligation on a certain person to pay money or to do or refrain from doing something or other, the *quasi-in-rem* judgment cannot impose these obligations on a person because the court lacks jurisdiction over the person. The *quasi-in-rem* judgment, for example, may affect or destroy a person's interest in a piece of property, but it cannot impose a burden on the person to pay something or to do something. A judgment *in rem* affects the interests of all persons in a specific thing. Where a court has jurisdiction over the thing, like a piece of land, it may hand down a judgment determining the interests of all persons. Such a judgment fixes the status of some subject matter, rather than rights between or among parties, and it is binding against the whole world instead of just among the parties actually involved.

The rule requiring a court to have jurisdiction before it can act has a basis in the Federal Constitution, which requires that no person may be deprived of life, liberty, or property without "due process of law." A defendant is not receiving due process of law unless the court has obtained proper authority and power over him or over the property in question.

Out-of-state motorists. There are some peculiar jurisdictional dilemmas that arise in the application of these general principles. For some of them, practical solutions have been found. One perplexing problem, which formerly existed on a widespread basis throughout the various states of the United States, arose with regard to out-of-state motorists. If a non-resident entered a particular state and injured persons or property within that state and then left the state before he could be served with process, the injured person was often faced with the disheartening prospect of bringing his action in some faraway place and perhaps transporting himself and witnesses to that distant locality for the purpose of the trial, all at very great expense. Often it was completely impractical for the injured person to attempt to bring an action against the non-resident motorist.

Many states have now passed statutes providing that when an out-of-state motorist uses the highways of the particular state, he automatically subjects himself to service of process by registered mail and appoints an agent, usually the Secretary of State of the state in question, to accept service of process in his behalf. In this manner an out-of-state motorist can be brought under the control and authority of the local court and subjected to the judgment of that court, if, when using the highways, he causes injury to the person or property of a resident of the state. This modification of the usual requirements for the service of process can only be justified by the serious problem created by the great mobility of the automobile, the tremendous numbers of automobiles, the widespread practice of Americans of driving frequently from one state into another, and the huge toll of lives and property which the automobile takes each year. Here we have another example of a change in the law resulting from a change in society.

Foreign corporations. A similar problem is posed by corporations which do business in a particular state but have no offices or property there. The courts have worked out the rule that if a corporation does a sufficient amount of business in a particular state, it is deemed to be legally present in the state and subject to the power and authority of the courts of that state.

FULL FAITH AND CREDIT CLAUSE. The Federal Constitution requires that state court judgments be given "full faith and credit" by the courts of the sister states. As a matter of fact, the full faith and credit doctrine applies to all official acts of a sister state. In its simplest terms, the full faith and credit clause would require a California court to recognize a judgment properly rendered by a state court in New York. The California courts would not directly enforce the New York judgment but would grant the plaintiff a California judgment, based upon the New York judgment, without further proceedings. Armed with a California judgment, the plaintiff then may invoke the aid of the California court in seizing property belonging to the defendant in satisfaction of the judgment. The operation of the full faith and credit clause, however, assumes that the judicial act of the state for which recognition is sought in a sister state was a proper exercise of the authority of the state doing the act. It is fundamental, therefore, that a state need not recognize the judicial act of a sister state if that state did not have proper jurisdiction over the matter at hand. A practical application of this latter limitation upon the full faith and credit clause occurs when the authority of a particular state court to render a divorce decree is challenged in another state. A state does not have jurisdiction through its courts to dissolve a marriage unless one of the parties is domiciled in that state. This generally means that the spouse in question must be a resident of that state, having gone to that state intending to remain there as a resident for an indefinite period. Many "quickie" divorces, granted by states which permit residence to be established in very short periods of time, have been challenged on these grounds and held not to be entitled to recognition. This is a complex legal question and a full discussion is far beyond the scope of this book. Mention is made of this situation merely for the purpose of illustrating some of the problems inherent in issues of jurisdiction.

DIVERSITY OF CITIZENSHIP JURISDICTION. It is the primary function of the federal courts to decide controversies or questions arising under the statutes and the Constitution of the United States. Most controversies between individuals will be governed by state law. This is true of the ordinary cases involving questions of torts, contracts, and the like. Unless there is some federal question involved, the federal courts ordinarily do not have jurisdiction in these types of cases.

There is an important exception to this general rule, however. The federal courts do have jurisdiction in cases involving diversity of citizenship. This means that if the litigants are citizens of different states, the federal courts have the power to try the case. Although the rights of the parties may be governed by state law, the federal courts do have jurisdiction based on the incidental fact that the litigants are residents of different states. Many believe that this provision tends to clutter up the federal courts with controversies that could best be decided by the state court systems. Be this as it may, the federal courts in diversity cases generally attempt to follow and apply state law, presumably as it would have been applied by a state court hearing the controversy.

3. THE COURSE OF A LAWSUIT

A. Fundamental Principles

IN GENERAL. In the belief that an understanding of the steps and procedures involved in the prosecution of a lawsuit is a considerable help in the
understanding of the substantive fields of law, a portion of the book is set aside
here for the purpose of leading the reader through a hypothetical, though
typical law suit. It must be borne in mind that the terminology and some of the
details will vary from state to state, but, in essence, legal procedure with regard
to the course of a lawsuit is the same almost everywhere in this country. Thus,
considerable value is attached to the discussion below though it may not apply
specifically to the reader's own state. Before the actual steps involved in a lawsuit are examined, however, it is well to take a brief look at the two basic principles underlying our adversary procedure.

OPPORTUNITY TO BE HEARD. It is probably no surprise to anyone reading
this book to learn that both sides in a controversy must be given the opportunity
to be heard. One does not have to look far around the world, however, to see
legal systems where this concept never arose or has been abandoned in the
interest of compelling unwavering conformity with a national or political point
of view. Note that the requirement is only that there be "opportunity" to be
heard, not that both sides actually be heard. The defendant is not compelled to
appear in the ordinary lawsuit between private parties, but he must be given opportunity to do so. If the opportunity has been provided, the defendant has
only himself to blame if, in his absence, the lawsuit goes badly for him. The
opportunity to be heard is provided by the service of process, discussed previously, where the defendant is notified that an action has been filed against him
and that he has an opportunity to answer the charges and appear in his own
defense.

BURDEN OF PROOF. Another of the basic principles of Anglo-Saxon legal
procedure is that the burden of establishing the facts underlying the claim
rests upon the person making the claim. Rather than compelling the party who is
being brought into court against his will to prove that the initiating party's
claim is without legal support, the burden is put on the initiating party to support and prove his claim. A moment's reflection will reveal to the reader how
much more difficult it usually is to prove the negative of a proposition than it is
to prove the affirmative. Unless the initiating party can present enough facts to
support the claim which he has made, the defendant need not even make an
argument, as will be seen later. In special situations, the courts sometimes shift
part or substantially all of the burden of proof from one party to the other.

CIVIL VERSUS CRIMINAL PROCEDURE. In addition to being used to differentiate the two great legal systems in the world, the term *civil* is also used to differentiate between criminal cases, where society is the initiating party through its "prosecuting" or "district" attorney, and those cases which arise between private parties. The hypothetical case considered below is a civil case involving the rights and duties of two private parties as between themselves, where there is no concern with an offense against society as a whole. Note that if A injures B while A is driving his automobile at forty miles an hour through a twenty-mile zone, both civil and criminal actions may arise. B may sue A for the harm which A caused to B, and the district attorney on behalf of society may prosecute A for the crime of reckless driving or speeding. Our hypothetical case may indirectly involve such a situation, but our concern will be with the civil case and not the criminal.

B. A Hypothetical Civil Lawsuit

THE FACTS.   Assume that P has been struck and seriously injured by D's automobile while that automobile was being operated by D. We will not concern ourselves with what actually took place at the scene of the accident, but will recognize only the fact that P feels that his injury was the result of some fault on the part of D. It should be noted now that liability in this specific case is based upon some fault on the part of the person who is sought to be held liable. If there is no legal fault, there usually is no liability. It will be seen in other portions of the book that liability sometimes arises without fault on the part of the person being held liable, but we will not let that problem concern us here. The case we have here involves the law of torts, which, it will be remembered, is a field of private substantive law. The particular tort involved here is not assault or battery, as it might be if D had driven over P intentionally, but negligence. P feels that D's negligent operation of the car caused P's injury.

A person is said to be negligent when his conduct has fallen below the standard of conduct expected of reasonable, prudent persons under the same circumstances. P, in our case, will claim that D did not exercise the degree of care in the operation of his motor vehicle that a reasonable man would have exercised under the same circumstances. The basic fact which P will ultimately try to prove is that D was negligent. He will also have to prove that D's negligence was the proximate cause of P's injury. But we are getting ahead of our story.

P feels that he has been aggrieved by D. While, actually, P's next step would be to consult an attorney, we will ignore the attorney for the time being and assume that P is taking the various steps himself. P decides to sue D. The party who brings the action is known as the *plaintiff*. The party against whom the action is brought is called the *defendant*.

THE COMPLAINT.   The first step in the initiation of most lawsuits is the drafting and filing of the *complaint,* which sets forth the basis for the plaintiff's suit, the relief which the plaintiff requests, and usually a statement that the court has jurisdiction over the matter. Although "complaint" is probably the most common and is certainly the most descriptive name for this step in legal procedure, it is identified by other names in some states. The statement of the basis for the plaintiff's suit does not include all of the evidence which the plaintiff will hope to introduce at the trial. It contains only a statement of the ultimate facts which the plaintiff will try to sustain with evidentiary facts at the trial. In our hypothetical case, the ultimate facts would be the negligence of *D*, *P's* injury, and that the negligence was the proximate cause of the injury. The evidentiary facts would be those details of the accident which would support the ultimate facts.

There was a time when the complaint, or the step corresponding to the complaint, was surrounded by all kinds of legal formality, but modern practice makes the complaint relatively simple as far as formality is concerned. This is not to say that the drafting of the complaint is always a simple job. It may be not only a difficult task, but also extremely important at later stages of the lawsuit. The complaint is just one of the so-called *pleadings* by which the controversy between the parties is reduced to concrete issues of fact or of law. The issue which the complaint and the other pleadings pose may not be the best issue from the standpoint of one or both of the parties or from the standpoint of the remedy which may later be available, and, as a result of faulty drafting, may not be the issue which the parties actually sought to raise. An issue is simply a point of dispute, on law or fact, which the court may resolve.

What is done with the complaint varies from state to state. In some states the complaint is delivered directly to the defendant. In most states, the complaint is filed with the clerk of the court in which the action is being brought. The clerk is the administrative officer of the court who is responsible for the keeping of records, filing of documents, and acting on behalf of the judge in signing and issuing certain judicial papers.

SUMMONS AND SERVICE. The clerk of the court issues an instrument known as the *summons,* which notifies the defendant of the action being brought against him by the plaintiff and tells the defendant to answer the complaint within a certain specified period of time. As a practical matter, the summons is usually a standard form, the blanks of which are filled in by the plaintiff's attorney, which is simply signed by the clerk on behalf of the court.

The summons and a copy of the complaint are served upon the defendant. *Service,* as has already been learned, is the device by which the jurisdiction of the court is extended to the defendant so that a judgment against him will be personally binding. It is also the device by which he receives notice of the action and, thus, his opportunity to appear and be heard. Service is usually accomplished by handing to the defendant the summons and the copy of the complaint. This function may be performed by the sheriff or the sheriff's deputy or, generally, any other person who is not a party to the suit. The process server reports back to the clerk or to the plaintiff that the papers have or have not been served.

If the papers cannot, after diligent effort, be served on the defendant personally, the plaintiff may seek the permission of the court to serve the papers by some substitute method. Depending upon the state and upon the situation, the court may give the plaintiff permission to serve the process on some member of the defendant's family or on someone at the defendant's place of residence, or by registered mail to the last known address of the defendant, or even by publication in a newspaper. Since substituted service is an abdication of the normally strict principles with regard to notice and jurisdiction, permission of the court to use it usually is required.

Substituted service is necessary to protect a plaintiff from the defendant who seeks to avoid service so as to escape the jurisdiction of the court. A defendant over whom the court has no jurisdiction and over whom the court cannot get jurisdiction by service of process (as, for example, the resident of another state who does not come under any of the special service statutes) may consent to the court's jurisdiction. This consent may be to the jurisdiction of the court for the general purposes of the suit or for some limited purpose not including the merits of the plaintiff's action. An example of such special appearance or consent by the defendant is an appearance for the sole purpose of contesting the jurisdiction of the court.

Service may be accomplished on partnerships by service on a partner or otherwise as provided by the statutes of the separate states. Service on a corporation is usually made by serving an officer of the corporation or some agent especially designated for the purpose. The details vary considerably from state to state.

DEFENDANT'S ALTERNATIVES.   A defendant has several alternative courses of action after he receives the summons and the copy of the complaint. He may settle with the plaintiff, in which case the plaintiff's suit is dropped. He may fail to answer or appear, in which case judgment will be entered against him by the court. This kind of judgment is called a *default judgment*. If the basis for the claim is a promissory note or any other transaction where the amount owed by the defendant is fixed, judgment will be entered automatically for that amount. If the amount is in doubt, as would be the case in our hypothetical lawsuit, trial must be held to determine the amount. Default judgments may be set aside if the defendant can satisfy the court that his failure to appear was caused by circumstances beyond his control. (See Chapter 17 for special protections for those in military sevice.) A defendant may, of course, select his third alternative and make an appearance and plead to the complaint.

Instead of answering the complaint directly, the defendant may use the pleading, known as the *demurrer,* which questions whether the complaint is sufficient on its face to state a cause of action against the defendant. The defendant says, in effect, that even if he admitted all of the charges in the complaint, there would be no legal basis for an action against him. The demurrer, by that name, has been abolished in some states, but comparable procedure remains in a motion to dismiss.

ANSWER.   If the defendant attacks the complaint directly, he does so by means of the *answer*. In this pleading, the defendant may deny all of the allegations of the plaintiff, admit some and deny others, supply new information which constitutes a defense or a claim against the plaintiff, or combine denials with new information. In the hypothetical case, D might deny that he was negligent, or he might admit that he was negligent but deny that his negligence caused the harm to P, or might admit that he was negligent and that his negligence contributed to $P's$ injury but allege that P was negligent also and that $P's$ negligence contributed to his own injury. The common law rule, which is followed in most states, is that *any* negligence on the part of the plaintiff in a tort action which contributes to his injury frees the defendant of liability, even though the defendant's negligence was the primary factor in the plaintiff's injury. A few states have adopted by statute the doctrine of *comparative negligence* whereby the plaintiff is still entitled to recover from the defendant to the extent that the contribution of the defendant's negligence to the plaintiff's injury exceeded the contribution of the plaintiff's own negligence.

If the complaint and the answer create issues of fact or law for the court to consider, and if the answer does not raise any new matter to which the plaintiff must reply, the pleadings come to an end with the answer. If there is no issue or if a reply is called for, there must be further pleading.

PRE-TRIAL PROCEEDINGS.   Before the trial actually begins, a number of other proceedings may take place. A date must be set for the trial. Either of the parties may ask the court for a judgment based on the pleadings alone. This motion usually occurs only where the issues raised by the pleadings are of law and not of fact. A motion for "summary judgment" may be made in similar situations but can also be used where there are issues of fact but the facts are not material. The judge decides what to do about these motions. They are usually refused. If granted, the judge's decision may be appealed to a higher court.

A very useful and important pre-trial proceeding, which in most states should be used a great deal more than it is at present, is the pre-trial conference. This device permits the judge and attorneys to get together for a more or less informal conference at which the issues are clarified and narrowed, unimportant issues of fact and law are settled, the attorneys disclose the witnesses they intend to call and what they expect to gain from each witness, and documentary evidence is discussed and its admission agreed upon. The pre-trial conference tends to make trials shorter, to encourage settlement without trial, to minimize the importance of surprise, and to bring other beneficial results. It is used extensively in the federal courts, but is not yet in general use elsewhere. Some states employ it, and a considerable number of states are toying with the idea.

An important pre-trial device is the *deposition,* which is a written statement made under oath by a person who would have been a witness in a trial had he not been too ill to attend or had his testimony not been in danger of being lost. The taking of the deposition is a judicial proceeding and there must be opportunity for cross-examination.

SELECTION OF THE JURY. Under the law of all states, the parties have a right to a trial by jury, but in most states the parties to a civil case may waive the jury and agree to a trial by the judge alone. In many states, the parties may also agree on a jury of a lesser number than the traditional twelve. If the parties elect to have a jury trial, the selection of the jury is the first step in the trial. It should be noted that the selection of the jury in the ordinary civil case is much less time-consuming and difficult than in a criminal case where the defendant's life or liberty may be at stake. The laws of the various states vary a great deal with regard to the details of drawing up the lists of persons who may serve as jurors and the actual selection of the persons to serve on a particular jury. In general, a list of persons in the county or judicial district who are qualified to serve as jurors is drawn up by a jury commission or commissioner. The qualifications usually involve length of residence, age, citizenship, eligibility to vote, property ownership, or payment of taxes. A person may not be excluded from a jury because of his race, color, or creed. A few states do not permit women to sit on juries, but this quaint idea is rapidly disappearing. Certain persons are given the right to be exempted from jury duty, but the right may be waived. Examples of such persons are: teachers, military officers on active duty, attorneys, ministers, doctors, and dentists.

From the basic jury lists, a certain number of persons are selected to serve as jurors for a particular session or term of court. This group is called the *panel* or the *array*. The jurors on the panel will appear at the beginning of the trial and from among their number will be selected, by lot, the jurors to serve on the particular case. The jurors who take their places in the jury box are questioned by the attorneys for both parties to the case in order to determine whether there are any grounds for dismissing the particular juror from the jury. The process by which a juror is dismissed is called a *challenge*. A challenge may be *for cause or peremptory,* in either of which case an individual juror is challenged, or *to the array,* where the whole jury panel is challenged.

A challenge for cause may be made when the juror is related to one of the parties, has already made up his mind on the case, has a material interest in the case, or is biased or prejudiced in some way or other. If a juror is challenged for cause, the judge decides whether the cause actually exists. Each party has an unlimited number of challenges for cause. The exercise of a peremptory challenge requires no statement of cause, but each party has only a limited number of these challenges. If a prospective juror is successfully challenged, another juror from the panel takes his place. After the parties have exhausted all of their peremptory challenges and are no longer challenging for cause, the jurors are sworn in and are ready to try the issues.

INTRODUCTION OF EVIDENCE. After the parties have made their customary opening statements to inform the jury of the general nature of the issues before the court, the parties proceed to introduce the specific evidence on which their sides of the argument are based. In compliance with the basic rule that requires the plaintiff to sustain the burden of proving his case, the plaintiff presents his evidence first. Note, however, that if the defendant has admitted the allegations of the plaintiff and has introduced new matter into the pleadings, the defendant has, in effect, become the moving party, and the burden of producing evidence will first be on him. There are actually several different types of burden of proof in a lawsuit, but these are of too technical a nature to justify their detailed examination here. Suffice it to say that in addition to the basic burden of proving the case, which rests on the moving party, there is also another burden which passes back and forth from one party to the other. This second burden is called the *burden of going forward,* and comes into existence when one party has presented evidence which, if uncontradicted or unmitigated, would justify a decision in his favor. We can assume in the hypothetical case that the plaintiff has the initial burden, and we will not concern ourselves with the burden of going forward.

Evidence is introduced by means of the testimony of witnesses and by depositions. Weapons, photographs, books of account, and so on, may themselves by introduced as evidence, but the testimony of witnesses is usually required in order to authenticate this physical evidence. In our case, the witnesses called by P will take the stand first and will presumably supply information that is favorable to P's side of the case. This is called *direct examination.* After P, or rather P's attorney, has completed his questioning of his own witness, D, or D's attorney, has an opportunity to "cross-examine" P's witnesses. This is one of the most interesting parts of the trial. Obviously, D is not interested in getting more testimony from the witness which is favorable to P, but is interested in getting testimony favorable to his own side and in testing the veracity of the witness and the truth of the testimony brought out on direct examination. The witness in our case, for example, who testifies on direct examination that D's automobile was moving in the wrong lane at the time of the accident, may be shown to have very bad eyes or to have been looking the other way.

Whatever the evidence, it must comply with the so-called *rules of evidence,* which seek to admit into the trial only that evidence which will aid in reaching a fair and just decision. Simplifying to a considerable extent, these rules of evidence are two: the evidence must be relevant and material; and the evidence must be competent. The first requirement is simply that the evidence must have something material to do with the issues which are before the court. In our case, evidence that D was insured up to $100,000 would be excluded on the ground that it is not relevant to the issue of D's negligence. What frequently takes place, in this connection, is that the materiality or relevance of the evidence is weighed against the prejudicial effect it might have on the jury. Thus, some evidence might be excluded, though somewhat relevant or material, because it would tend to inflame the jury unreasonably against one or the other of the parties.

The requirement of competency is more difficult to explain. Briefly, it means that a witness must testify as to things of his own knowledge, things which he saw or heard or did or felt or knew. Thus, in our case, X would probably not be allowed to testify that W had reported to him some hours after the accident that W had seen D's car driving in the wrong lane at a high rate of speed. As to these facts, W is the proper witness because he saw them. The only fact to which X can testify is the fact that W *said* certain things. What W *said* is usually immaterial and irrelevant to the issue of D's negligence.

NONSUITS AND DIRECTED VERDICTS.   At any time during the course of the trial, either party may ask the court to dismiss the case. If the court grants the motion, the result is called a *nonsuit*. If the plaintiff asks for a nonsuit, he must pay the costs that have been incurred, but the dismissal is without prejudice, which means that the plaintiff can come back into court at another time on the same issue. If the defendant asks for the nonsuit, it is said to be *involuntary* or *compulsory*. Such a nonsuit occurs only at the close of the presentation of the plaintiff's evidence and is a finding by the judge that the jury could not reasonably find for the plaintiff on the basis of the evidence which he introduced. Judgment is entered for the defendant, and the plaintiff may not come back again, but he may, of course, appeal the judge's ruling to a higher court.

When both parties have presented all of their evidence, either may ask the court for a directed verdict, which is a motion asking the judge to tell the jury to return a verdict in favor of the party who made the motion. Such a motion will be granted where the jury could not reasonably find against the party who made the motion.

If these motions are not made or, if made, are not granted, the parties then sum up their cases for the jury. Depending upon the state, the plaintiff will speak first, then the defendant, and then the plaintiff in rebuttal; or the defendant will speak first and then the plaintiff to close.

CHARGING THE JURY.   At this stage of the trial it becomes necessary to differentiate between the function of the judge and the function of the jury. Briefly, the judge decides the issues of law, while the jury decides the issues of fact. The problem is, of course: How are the two types of decision brought together? In some states, under special circumstances, the jury may be asked to report its findings on the issues of fact to the judge, who applies the findings of fact to the law as he has determined it. The jury does not find for one party or the other, but only answers specific questions of fact. This method is called the *special verdict*. It is not widely used. The usual method is for the judge to instruct the jury on the law of the case and to ask the jury to apply this law to the facts as the jury finds them. In a case such as ours, the judge would tell the jury that the law is that if the jury finds the defendant was negligent and that his negligence caused the plaintiff's injury, the defendant is liable and must compensate the plaintiff for the harm he has suffered—the extent of the harm also to be determined by the jury. But if the jury finds that the defendant was not negligent or that his negligence did not cause the plaintiff's injury or that the plaintiff was negligent also, the law is that the defendant is not liable, and the jury must return a verdict for him. This instruction of the jury is called the *charge* and is a part of the second method by which the findings of law and of fact are brought together. When the jury does what it is told and applies the law to facts, it returns what is called a *general verdict*. Although the usual rule is that the jury must agree unanimously on any verdict it returns, many states permit verdicts to be reached in civil cases by a three-fourths majority or other fraction of the jurors.

Motions After Verdict. Several motions may be made by the parties after verdict. Before the judge turns the verdict into a judgment of the court, a party may move for an arrest of judgment or for a judgment in his favor notwithstanding a verdict in favor of the other party. The former motion is made by a defendant when the verdict has been for the plaintiff. It is a sort of late demurrer where the defendant claims, in effect, that the complaint is insufficient and does not support the verdict. If the motion is sustained, the verdict is set aside without prejudice to the plaintiff, who may bring his action again. The latter motion is made by the plaintiff when the verdict is for the defendant. The plaintiff claims that the answer was legally insufficient because it did not state a defense to the complaint. It should be noted that the use of these motions varies markedly from state to state, and the brief discussion above may not be accurate at all for a particular jurisdiction. The purpose of the discussion is simply to give the reader an idea as to the type of motion which follows the verdict.

A party may make a motion for a new trial either before or after the verdict is converted into a judgment. The purpose of such a motion is to obtain a rehearing on the issues which were before the court. The grounds on which the losing party will base his request for a new trial will be errors which he claims were committed during the trial. He may also suggest that the verdict is contrary to the weight of the evidence. The defendant may argue that the damages assessed against him are excessive. The plaintiff may argue that they were inadequate. Arguments are heard by the judge on motions for a new trial. If the motion is granted, a new trial is set. The same judge may preside, but there will be a new jury. If the motion is overruled, judgment is entered by the court in compliance with the verdict. In some states the judge has the power to raise or lower the amount of the verdict before he enters judgment.

If judgment is entered after the overruling of these motions, the party who feels he is aggrieved may appeal his case to a higher court for review. The party who appeals is called the *appellant,* and the other party is called the *appellee.* There are no new pleadings on appeal and no new evidence. The appellate court reviews the trial of the case below and may uphold the previous decision, or may reverse it and enter a contrary judgment, or may send the case back for a new trial or for other proceedings in pursuance of the order of the appellate court. (For a discussion of judgments and proceedings after judgment, see Chapter 17.)

PROBLEMS

1. What is the organization of the courts in your state? Compare it with the system of federal courts.

2. What is the case or controversy rule?

3. What is meant by *res judicata?*

4. What is the contempt power of the court?

5. Describe in detail the meaning of "jurisdiction."

6. What is the significance of the following quotation: "Full Faith and Credit shall be given in each State to the public Acts, Records, and Judicial Proceedings of every other State"?

7. Name and explain the two basic principles underlying our system of legal procedure.

8. Compare the hypothetical lawsuit described in the text with the same type of suit if brought in your state.

9. Harry Hotemper is on trial for the murder of Arthur Agravat. Assume that you are Harry's attorney. What objections would you make and why to the following activities of Henry Hangeman, the District Attorney who is prosecuting the case?

    a. Henry has put Arthur's little five-year-old daughter, Sunbeam, on the stand and has asked her if she misses her daddy.

    b. Henry has put Ben Bigeers on the stand and has asked him to state the substance of a conversation that Ben had the day after the crime was committed with Tom Timid, an eyewitness to the crime, who has not been asked to testify.

10. Comment on the following quotation: "Like the antagonism between the devil and holy water, the conflict between the lawyer and the truth is an ancient one. Among the remarks on the professional prevarication of lawyers, the following line of reasoning is typical: 'In every lawsuit there are two lawyers. One calls an object white and the other calls it black. They cannot both be speaking the truth, since their statements of facts are contradictory. Therefore one of them is sustaining a falsehood.' This reasoning leads to the conclusion that fifty per cent of the lawyers are liars. And, since the attorney who wins one case will lose another, it would seem that sooner or later every lawyer will take a case which cannot be defended honestly, and this makes liars of them all." [From Piero Calamandrei, *Eulogy of Judges*]

11. What is the function of an appellate court?

part II

The Contract

THE BUSINESS CASE

In this, and in succeeding parts, business cases based on the following hypothetical company will be used to raise and to illustrate the type of legal problem which a businessman is likely to encounter in connection with various business situations.

HYPOCASE, INC. Hypocase, Inc. is a small manufacturing company whose main office is located in the city of Berkland, in the state of Anosmia. The company's chief products are the pallets on which goods moved by fork-lift trucks are transported and stored. Most pallets are made of wood, but some are of metal or of wood reinforced with metal. Hypocase manufactures pallets of all the standard sizes, shapes, and weights and also does some special order work where pallets of unusual specifications are needed by their users. The company sells its pallets in many states in addition to Anosmia. Hypocase buys materials required in its manufacturing processes from a number of suppliers in Anosmia and other states. These materials consist largely of lumber of various types; aluminum and steel in sheets, bars, and other shapes; paints, varnishes, and other wood and metal preservatives and finishes; nails, glue, welding supplies, and other products used in fastening materials together. The company also buys machinery of several kinds and also certain packaging materials used in preparing the pallets for shipment to buyers. Other facts about Hypocase will be revealed as they become pertinent.

chapter 3

The Contract: Basic Legal Technique of Business Administration

1. THE CONTRACT IN GENERAL

A. Cases

(1)

Hattie Brown lived the last forty years of her life in a $5-a-week, cold-water, one-room flat on the 5th floor of an old building in the slum section of Berkland. She lived most frugally on money her neighbors suspected she obtained from begging, and was not above borrowing an occasional loaf of bread from a neighbor, which she never repaid. Her neighbors felt sorry for the old lady and often gave her left-over food from their own tables. It was suggested to Hattie that public relief funds were available for people in need, but she said that was "creeping socialism" and would have nothing to do with it. Hattie Brown left her flat only once or twice a week and was gone each time for only a couple of hours. None of her neighbors had any idea where she went. When Hattie died in 1960, her neighbors, some of whom were not much better off financially than Hattie appeared to be, took up a collection to provide a decent funeral. The neighbors examined Hattie's flat for letters or addresses that might reveal the existence of friends or relatives, but found nothing at all that belonged to Hattie except some very old clothes. The flat was promptly rerented.

The new tenant found a key to a safe deposit box fastened with adhesive tape to the back of a drawer. The key did not identify the bank to which it belonged, so the tenant took the key to a nearby bank and asked what he should do about it. The bank suggested he see a lawyer, which he did. An investigation revealed a safe deposit box at the Berkland National Bank in the name "Hattie T. Brown." Employees of the bank described the user of the box as an elderly, eccentric woman, and the address on the bank's lease form was Hattie Brown's. Under proper court order, the box was opened. The contents were astonishing: passbooks for five savings accounts in five different banks, totalling more than $375,000; corporate stock certificates and government bonds adding up to over $2,000,000; three paid-up insurance policies with total face values of $500,000, naming a religious charity as beneficiary; three $5 gold pieces; and a will in Hattie's own handwriting leaving everything to Paul Preston, president of Hypocase, Inc., who, the will stated, had helped Hattie across the street one day many years ago when he was a thirteen-year-old Boy Scout.

When Paul received word of this fantastic windfall, he had just finished reading a letter from his son, who was away at college. The young man had complained about having to take a business law course that devoted an entire semester to the subject of contract law; the son wondered why an entire course was given over to a subject as unimportant as this. The son's last comment was: "I wish somebody would pass a law abolishing all contracts. I'll bet they would never be missed." Paul sent his son a telegram saying: "Before abolish all contracts, consult with me."

(2)

Mr. A. M. Harrison was thrown from a street car, receiving serious head injuries that rendered him unconscious. A witness to the accident summoned Dr. F. L. Wisdom, a physician, to the assistance of the injured man. In this emergency situation, Wisdom gave Harrison medical attention and performed a difficult operation on him in an effort to save his life. The operation was not successful, and Harrison died without ever regaining consciousness. Following the death of Harrison, Dr. Wisdom sent a bill for professional services rendered the deceased to T. T. Cotnam, administrator of the estate of A. M. Harrison. Cotnam refused to pay the bill on the ground that Harrison was never conscious after his head struck the pavement and could not have assented, expressly or impliedly, to any contractual relationship with Dr. Wisdom; Cotnam said further that Wisdom's act was merciful or benevolent but could not, due to Harrison's lack of knowledge and will power, create contract obligations for Harrison or his estate.

[*Cotnam* v. *Wisdom,* 73 Ark. 601, 104 S.W. 164 (1907)]

B. Importance of the Contract

Of all the many legal arrangements that will be discussed in this book, the contract is unquestionably the most important. It is so important and has become so intimate and so normal a part of our lives that it is sometimes taken for granted. But once one stops to think about the place the contract has in our lives, it is difficult to conceive of a society that could get along without it. In even the simplest forms of society, the members must be able to rely to some extent on the acts and words of others. The rudiments of the modern contract, no doubt, developed about the same time that primitive man began living in groups or tribes instead of as isolated families or individuals, but it must be recognized that the aspect of the contract considered to be most important today, that aspect which looks to the future, did not develop to any great extent in primitive societies and came quite late in our social evolution. In the early stages of development, the concept of the contract, and of law as a whole, for that matter, was inseparable from the folkways and customs within the framework of which people spent their lives. Reliance on the words and acts of others was made possible through religion, moral or ethical customs, and through force. As the social organization became more complicated and as changes began to take place more rapidly, customs and usages tended to separate themselves into different categories. Some moved away from the realm of the mystical and made themselves amenable to change without the risk of offending the gods or basic social customs and beliefs. The contract eventually joined this secular group.

The evolution of the contract in the common law system was slow. Our ability today to rely on agreements with regard to future conduct rests on the idea that a promise given for a promise is legally binding, and this idea did not appear until the 16th century. Prior to that time, only two types of contractual liability were recognized in English law, according to Fuller.[1] A defendant who had promised to pay for goods and services became liable for the agreed price after he had received the performance, and a defendant who had made a promise under the special formality of the seal was liable on his promise. It is clear that certain voluntary arrangements were facilitated and protected long before the 16th century, but until the idea of an exchange of promises was accepted, the contract could not play the part in society that it does today.

The modern concept of contract makes it possible for people to enter into binding arrangements for the future. The importance of this objective has increased as society has become more complex, and the need for relying on the conduct of other persons has become more and more important to the operation of society. It is a rare business transaction indeed which is not either a contract itself or at least based on the contract device. Every step of each day's activity is affected in one way or another by contracts. Almost

---

[1] Lon L. Fuller, ed., *Basic Contract Law* (St. Paul, Minn.: American Casebook Series, 1947), p. 304.

everyone enters into a number of contracts every day. A ride on a bus, a streetcar, a train, or a plane involves the making of a contract, as does ordering a meal in a restaurant or the arranging for a supply of gas, electricity, or water to a home or a place of business. Every sale, every loan, every checking or savings account is a contract. A rich man, by modern terms, is not one who has many jewels or much gold stored away in his strong box, but one who is benefited by many contracts. His bank accounts, his stocks and bonds, his mortgages and promissory notes, his sales, his insurance policies, and his leases are the things that make him rich, and every one of these things is a contract. Only a very small proportion of the wealth of the world which passes from hand to hand passes in a tangible form. Wealth moves from person to person through such media as checks or notes or drafts, all of which are contracts. Were we forced to make such exchanges in bullion or in coin, commerce and finance could operate on only the most simple basis.

In addition to the importance of the contract in the sense set forth above, the contract is also important because it is basic to most of the fields of law which affect the operation of business. The law of negotiable instruments, agency, sales, suretyship, corporations, and partnerships, is largely dependent upon the concept of contract. It is extremely difficult to deal with problems in the other business law areas until the essentials of the contract are known and understood. For this reason the general format of this book is violated in order to put the law of contract apart where it can be thoroughly examined before the other legal problems are introduced.

The social impact of the contract has extended far beyond the legal realm. The contract idea, emphasizing individualism, self-determination, self-assertion, progress, and change, became the symbol of the end of the Middle Ages. "It is through contract that man attains freedom," said Sir Henry Maine. The idea of contract became deeply rooted in the moral sentiments of society, consistent with the moral philosophy that a man should lead his life as a reasonable person and accept responsibility for his own mistakes. The contract also came to express a basic political philosophy, a means of breaking out of the confines of tradition and authority, and marked the progress of mankind from slavery to freedom. Status ceased to be the prevailing influence in men's lives and was replaced by contract. In law, in politics, in economics, in all the realms of society, the concept of the freely entered into bargain and agreement made a profound impression.

These broad social views of the contract reached their peak of influence at the end of the 19th century. Although the idea of the contract is still a powerful social force, some observers suggest that it is on the decline; they forecast a gradual and continuing drift back in the direction of status as the basic social determinant. The causes of this drift are varied and controversial. Among them are factors that tend directly to limit the scope of contractual freedom: increasing density of population, the dominant role of powerful economic institutions, wide discrepancies of bargaining power, and the tendency toward a greater structuring of society as a whole. These trends, even if they actually exist, have not yet deeply affected the prevalence of the contract in the fields of law related to business.

C. The Nature of the Contract

The contract is not the piece of paper which is often referred to as the "contract" but consists of the rights and duties that are created by bringing into existence the contract relationship between the persons who are parties to it. The paper or document is just evidence of the contract and is often not necessary at all. A contract is a consensual relationship based on the willingness of the parties to be bound by its terms. Without mutual consent, express or implied, there usually can be no contract, as will be seen in detail below.

A definition, because there often is too much reliance upon its language, is an unsatisfactory tool in the law except where it is recognized as simply a starting point for further discussion. This is the use to which the following definition of a contract will be put: A *contract* is a promise or a set of promises enforceable by law. This simple definition is rather informative even without much elaboration. It indicates that the contract results from promises, discloses that not all promises are contracts, and points out that the line between those promises which are contracts and those which are not is drawn on the basis of enforceability. If a promise or set of promises is legally enforceable, there is a contract. An "agreement" is not necessarily a contract. We must distinguish between the situation where the parties have entered into an agreement and the situation where the parties have entered into an agreement that creates certain kinds of legal obligations. Not all agreements are contracts, and not all agreements creating legal obligations are contracts either. An agreement between two social golfers to meet at the club for eighteen holes on Saturday is an example of an agreement that is not a contract. Marriage and adoption are examples of agreements that impose obligations but create status, not contract; the terms of the obligations incurred are not fixed by the agreement but by law, and the parties have little or no control over them. Much of what you learn about the law of contract will have to do with the problem of determining how the contract type of agreement can be distinguished from the noncontract forms.

A promise is a declaration of intention as to the future conduct of the person who makes the promise. No businessman can operate on a moment-to-moment basis but must make plans for the next hours, weeks, and years. Whether he is hiring an office manager, purchasing a fire insurance policy, selling a quantity of merchandise, or depositing daily receipts in the bank, he is looking toward the future and relying on declarations of intention by other persons. During the course of any day, the businessman enters into many of these arrangements whereby he seeks and obtains assurances of the future conduct of others. During the same day he also participates in many similar business activities the effects of which are *not* to commit himself or others to certain future conduct. He may write to a supplier to inquire about the price and availability of materials, or interview three or four college graduates who are looking for jobs, or send a current price quotation to a prospective customer, but in these he seeks no assurances.

How is it possible for a person to be able to place sufficient reliance on the conduct of others that he may govern his own activities accordingly, and how can we distinguish between the situations where this result obtains and those where it does not? The contract is the legal device by which the binding effect is achieved, and the intentions of the parties, as manifested in their words and conduct, determine which result is to be obtained. In general, it is desirable that a binding effect be achieved only when the parties seriously intend that result. Because the intentions of human beings are not always clearly manifested by words and conduct, the law has surrounded the making of contracts with sufficient formality to give reasonable assurance that the intentions are accurately manifested, without, at the same time, destroying the usefulness of the contract device. The seal, consideration, and the other elements of the contract are basically requirements of formality inserted into the contract transaction for the purpose of maximizing the chances that the outward manifestations accurately represent the intentions of the parties, as will be seen in detail below. It is thought likely that a person who participates in the formality of the seal or gives value for the assurances of another person understands the nature of his acts and seriously intends to enter into a binding relationship.

D. Classification of Contracts and Promises

IN GENERAL.   Contracts, and the promises out of which they grow, are of many different kinds. It is well to know these kinds and classifications at this stage in the discussion in order to be able to use and understand the necessary contract terminology, and also in order to get an idea as to the immense variety of contract situations. Furthermore, the several classifications supply useful information as to some of the characteristics of both contracts and promises.

EXECUTED AND EXECUTORY.   Here we refer to the state of completion of the performance of the promises and of the contract. An *executed promise* or *executed contract* is one that has been completely performed. An *executory promise* or *executory contract* is one that has not been completely performed. A contract may still be executory although most of the promises made by its parties have been executed, and a contract may be partly executed and partly executory. Contracts usually start out being completely executory and then go through various stages of partial completion until the last promise has been performed and the contract becomes fully executed. A fully executed contract is seldom of any great legal interest or importance.

FORMAL AND SIMPLE. Custom, tradition, and long usage have created a number of contracts which derive their binding effect not only from compliance with the usual requirements for an enforceable contract but also from the form in which the contract appears. It would be impossible for a person unfamiliar with a particular formal contract to ascertain all of the terms of the contract and the nature of the various promises made by the parties to it through mere perusal of the form. Formal contracts are, of course, in writing, but the language is frequently so cryptic that it gives little clue to the uninitiated as to the real nature of that contract. Just as a scrawl has come to represent a seal and "ss." to represent "Know all men by these presents," so have a few words in some formal contracts come to represent a good deal more than meets the eye. Much of the phraseology is now stereotyped, and a whole host of legal conclusions may be arrived at as the result of the inclusion or omission of a single word. Good examples of the. formal contract are the check and the promissory note. Although the language of the check is simple and brief, the underlying contract represented by the check is a long and involved one. (See Chapter 11.) The formal contract will not be a part of the discussion of contract law. Some of the formal contracts will be considered elsewhere.

The type of contract important to the present discussion is the informal or simple contract. It derives its binding effect from the substance of the transaction and from compliance with the requirements for a binding contract. Most contracts are of this variety.

A *contract under seal* is classified in some states as a formal contract and frequently requires no consideration in order to be binding. Many states have abolished this effect of the seal and require consideration in sealed contracts as well as in other varieties.

EXPRESS AND IMPLIED. An *express contract* is one the terms of which have been set forth in words, either oral or written. One of the parties has made a definite proposal to the other party and the latter party has agreed to the terms of that proposal. For example, where A agrees to sell his car for $500 and B agrees to buy it, these terms are set forth in oral or written words.

An *implied contract* is one which is inferred from the conduct of the parties, not from their words. An implied contract is created when a person enters a restaurant, orders a meal, and consumes it. Although neither the guest nor the waiter ever uses the words of contract such as "offer," "accept," or "promise," a contract to pay the price of the meal is nonetheless entered into, and, of course, may be enforced at law. There are actually two types of implied contract, the kind we have been discussing above, called the *contract implied in fact,* and the *contract implied in law* or the *quasi-contract*. The former is a real contract in all respects. The latter type of implied contract is not a contract at all.

Contract implied in law—quasi-contract. In both the express contract and the contract implied in fact, the contract arises from the voluntary and intentional consent of the parties, which is the case with all true contracts. In a quasi-contract the binding effect is imposed by law without any pretense of requiring the consent of the parties. There are no agreements and there are no promises. The contract which results is entirely fictitious. An example of a situation where the court might impose obligations similar to those which the parties impose on themselves in the true contract would occur where *A* owed *B* five dollars and paid his debt to *B* with a $5 bill without knowing that there was another $5 bill adhering to the one *A* intended to give *B*. Were *B* not required to return the extra $5, he would be unjustly enriched at the expense of *A*. If there had been a true contract between *A* and *B* in regard to the second $5 bill, there would be no difficulty in compelling *B* to return it. But there cannot be a true contract because neither party intended to enter into such a contract. There were no promises expressed or implied in fact. Many legal solutions to the problem of compelling *B* to return the extra $5 could have been worked out, but the peculiar development of the common law system resulted in the solution we now use. There was no common law writ to cover this unusual situation, so the courts extended to it the writ used for true contracts on the fiction that contractual obligations had arisen. This was done in order to provide justice. It does not cause any great harm as long as it is realized that true contract principles are not involved and that something resembling a contract obligation is imposed for the purpose of preventing the unjust enrichment of one of the parties. Where the quasi-contractual obligation is imposed, it usually is stated in terms of the reasonable value of the benefit which has been received.

It should be noted here that the doctrine of quasi-contract is not designed to protect the careless person or the volunteer who intentionally imposes enrichment on another person in the hope of persuading the other person to pay for it. A person who paints a neighbor's fence without his request is not entitled to recover the value of the paint job from the neighbor under the doctrine of quasi-contract. There has been no "unjust" enrichment.

Void, Voidable, and Valid Contracts. A *void contract* is one having no legal effect, which the courts will refuse to enforce no matter which party brings an action, and which is really not a contract at all. Neither party will obtain any rights under the contract. Illegal contracts are generally void, as are some others. A *voidable contract* is one creating legal rights and duties which will be enforced by the courts unless the party or parties having the right to do so exercise the privilege of avoiding it, and which is a good, valid, and binding contract in all other respects. Most contracts entered into by minors are voidable at the option of the minor. A *valid contract* is one enforceable by the courts, which is not subject to being avoided by any of the parties, and to which normal consequences are attached.

E. Essentials of the Contract

Fortunately, for the purposes of study, the contract lends itself rather well to the outlining of its principles and to the breaking down of its essential

elements into topics of manageable size and complexity. The first part of the discussion will be devoted to a consideration of those elements generally assumed to be necessary in bringing into existence a valid and enforceable contract. The latter part of the discussion will be devoted largely to issues other than validity and enforceability. Some pedagogical license will be employed in order to group and to discuss materials in a form best calculated to be understood and assimilated by the reader.

The first essential of the contract is the agreement, the consent of the parties to being bound, the meeting of the minds (as outwardly manifested), or, as it is technically termed, the *mutual assent of the parties*. This requirement simply pays homage to the basic nature of a contract as a relationship between the parties established by their consenting to being bound by the terms of an arrangement they have agreed upon. The primary problems in this area are those having to do with the manner in which the assent is demonstrated and the nature of the terms assented to, but also important is the effect on this assent of such events as fraud and mistake, which may prevent the assent from being genuine in spite of the manifestations of the parties.

Even though competent parties mutually assent to the terms of an arrangement between them, there is no valid contract unless the element of consideration is present. *Consideration* is a kind of price which one party pays for the binding effect of another's promise. It is usually not money itself, although it frequently is a promise to pay money. Essentially, *consideration* is the conduct or the promise of conduct of one party given in exchange for the conduct or promise of conduct of the other party, and it is important also as evidence of the seriousness of the parties' intentions.

Another requirement applies to some contracts but not to all. Certain contracts must be in writing in order to be enforced. These contracts are discussed under the heading of "statute of frauds," the name given to the English statute of 1677 which first set forth in detail the requirement of a writing for certain types of contracts. Although this statute became a part of our common law, all states have passed their own statutes of frauds. Other elements of the contract will also be considered.

F. Problems of Proof

The reader will be saved a substantial amount of confusion and mental anguish, in the study of the material in this book, if he will heed the admonitions of this paragraph. A common error committed by almost all of those beginning the study of legal subjects is the failure to recognize the differences between problems of proof and fact on one hand, and problems of law on the other. It is not the intention of the author to convey the impression that problems of proof and of fact are not important legal problems. They are. But if the beginning student lets himself be led off on questions of how this or that fact is to be proved, he will soon find he has missed the rule or principle of law that will be applied to given sets of facts as they *are* proved. If the reader worries too much about how it can be proved that A said such and such to B

or that *B* actually wrote a particular letter, the study of the materials in this book, or any legal textbook, will be hopelessly bogged down. The reader should preface every hypothetical statement of facts with the phrase, "assuming the following can be proved, . . ." The author discusses the various rules and principles of law that come within the scope of this book by applying them to given or assumed fact situations. Occasional reference is made to proof and fact problems, but as a whole these are ignored. The establishment of facts is an area from which limitations of time, space, and objective exclude this book.

G. Uniform Commercial Code

All states but one have now adopted the new Uniform Commercial Code. The history, background, scope, and major innovations of the Code are discussed elsewhere. Material in certain chapters in this text, especially in Chapters 10, 11, and 13, has been extensively affected by the enactment of the Code, but the general law of contracts, with a few exceptions, has not been greatly altered. However, the Code has increased the number and extent of distinctions between the general law of contract and the law having to do with certain specialized types of contracts, such as sales, negotiable instruments, and many security devices. Where the law controlling these special contracts is markedly at variance with general law, such contrasts will be discussed in this chapter. Most aspects of the Uniform Code will be considered in connection with the material and chapters most affected.

2. VALIDITY AND ENFORCEABILITY—THE AGREEMENT

A. Cases

(1)

In this matter the contention of the plaintiffs is that on or about the 4th day of April, 1910, they entered into a contract with the defendant, through its agent, Rogers, to sell and deliver to it, under conditions and terms specified, "about 12 tons of 2,240 pounds each of up-river fine Para rubber," and that in January, 1911, prior to the expiration of the time agreed upon for delivery of any of the merchandise, the defendant notified the plaintiffs, in writing, that it would not accept or pay for same, or carry out any of the terms of the alleged agreement. It can be assumed that Rogers had the authority and capacity to act for and bind the defendant.

The facts established show that on April 2, 1910, which fell on a Saturday, Mr. Kelly, representing the plaintiffs, and Mr. Rogers, representing the defendant, had a telephonic communication one with the other, the subject of which was the sale and purchase of rubber of a quality or grade known as up-river fine Para rubber, and after some inquiries as to market price, etc., by Rogers and the quantity plaintiffs had for sale by Kelly, Rogers asked Kelly what he (Kelly) could do for next year—next year delivery—and Kelly replied that he could get him rubber for January-June equal monthly shipments of up-river fine Para rubber at probably $2.42 per pound, delivery to be either from Brazil or Europe. Rogers then asked Kelly if he could get him this rubber at once, and Kelly said: "No; except until I receive my cables on Monday morning."

This conference or talk may now be stated (as explanation showed that the principal markets for this product are London, Brazil, Hamburg, and New York City, and the market prices are determined on cable communications with these different places) to have had reference to market prices. Rogers then said to Kelly:

"I will take 12 tons of up-river fine Para rubber for equal monthly shipments from Brazil or Europe at $2.42 per pound."

Kelly was to let him know on Monday morning. On April 2, 1910, the same day Kelly and Rogers had their telephone communication, the plaintiffs wrote the following letter to the defendant:

New York, April 2, 1910.

Brunswick-Balke-Collender Co., Long Island City, L.I.—

Gentlemen: As per telephonic communication with your Mr. Rogers to-day this is to confirm having your offer of $2.42 per pound for twelve tons up-river fine Para rubber for shipment either from Brazil or Liverpool in equal monthly parts January-June, 1911, about which we will let you know upon our receipt of our cable reply on Monday morning. Thanking you for the offer, we remain,
    Yours very truly,

Poel & Arnold,
Per W. J. Kelly.

On April 4th, which was on the Monday referred to in the above letter, the plaintiffs forwarded to, and there was received by, the defendant the following letter:

New York, April 4, 1910.

Brunswick-Balke-Collender Co., Long Island City, L.I.—

Gentlemen: Enclosed we beg to hand you contract for twelve tons of up-river fine Para rubber as sold you to-day with our thanks for the order.
    Very truly yours,

Poel & Arnold,
Per W. J. Kelly.

There was this inclosure in the above letter:

April 4/10.

Brunswick-Balke-Collender Co., Long Island City, L.I.—

Sold to you for equal monthly shipments January-June, 1911, from Brazil
and or Liverpool about twelve (12) tons up-river fine Para rubber at two
dollars and forty-two cents ($2.42) per pound payable in U.S. gold or its
equivalent cash twenty (20) days from date of delivery here.

As to terms of credit contained therein, Kelly swore that he arranged
that with the defendant. On April 7, 1910, the plaintiffs received from the
defendant the following, which was sent on a form used by the defendant,
part of same being printed matter and part written, that constituting printed
matter being in italics:

Order No. 25409.
(This number must appear on invoices and cases.)
Purchase Dep't the Brunswick-Balke-Collender Co. of New York,
Review Ave., Fox and Marsh Sts.

Long Island City, 4/6 1910.

M Poel & Arnold, 77 Broadway, N. Y. C.: *Please deliver at once the following
and send invoices with goods:*
About 12 tons up-river fine Para rubber at 2.42 per pound.
Equal monthly shipment January-June, 1911.
Conditions upon which above order is given:
*Goods on this order must be delivered when specified. In case you cannot comply,
advise us by return mail stating earliest date of delivery you can make, and await our
further orders. The acceptance of this order which in any event you must promptly
acknowledge will be considered by us as a guarantee on your part of prompt delivery
within the specified time.*
Terms: _____   F.O.B. _____
    Respectfully yours,

The Brunswick-Balke-Collender Co. *of New York,*
Per C. R. Rogers.

No other communication passed between the parties or their representatives until January 7, 1911, upon which day the plaintiffs received from the
defendant a letter dated on that day, reading as follows, and written upon
paper bearing the letterhead of defendant company:

Executive Department.

January 7, 1911.

Messrs. Poel & Arnold, 277 Broadway—Gentlemen: We beg herewith to
advise you that within the past few weeks there has come to our attention
through a statement made to us for the first time by Mr. Rogers information
as to certain transactions had by him with you in the past and especially
as to a transaction in April last relating to 12 tons of crude rubber. Mr.

Rogers had no authority to effect any such transaction on our account nor had we any notice or knowledge of his action until he made a voluntary statement of the facts within the past few weeks. In order that you may not be put to any unnecessary inconvenience we feel bound to give you notice at the earliest opportunity after investigating the facts that we shall not recognize this transaction or any other that may have been entered into with Mr. Rogers which was without our knowledge or authority.

Yours truly,

> The Brunswick-Balke-Collender Co.
> Per Thomas P. Mills, Vice Prst.

Was there a contract? Would the Code have affected the outcome of this case?

[*Poel* v. *Brunswick-Balke-Collender Co.* 216 N. Y. 310, 110 N. E. 619 (1915)]

(2)

The action is based on a written instrument signed by defendants and reading as follows:

> $2,000. Los Angeles, Cal., July 19th, 1895. Thirty days after the completion of the double track street railway of the Los Angeles Traction Company to the intersection of Seventh and Hoover streets, for value received, I promise to pay to the order of the Los Angeles Traction Company, the sum of two thousand (2,000) dollars, negotiable and payable at Citizens' Bank, with interest at the rate of 8 per cent. per annum, payable after maturity. I further promise and agree to pay a reasonable attorney's fee if suit should be instituted for the collection of this note.

The above instrument was placed in the hands of the Citizens' Bank, together with a duly signed written escrow agreement as follows:

> To the Citizens' Bank, Los Angeles, Cal.: Herewith is handed you by the undersigned the following named notes, to be held in escrow upon the terms and conditions herein stated: You are requested to hold said notes in escrow until the completion of the line of railroad of the Los Angeles Traction Company, now being constructed in the city of Los Angeles westerly on Eighth street to the vicinity of West Lake Park; thence by a route to be selected by said company westward on Seventh street, and by one or more streets to the intersection of Hoover street with Sixth street bounding the south side of the West End University addition to Los Angeles; thence west on said Sixth street to Commonwealth avenue; thence north on Commonwealth avenue to First street; thence west on First street to Virgil avenue. Upon completion and operation of the same with electric power, you are instructed to deliver said notes to said Los Angeles Traction Company. In case a franchise for such street car line to said Hoover street is not obtained by said Traction Company within _____ months from the date hereof, then, in that event, said notes shall be returned to their respective makers upon demand, to be canceled. Said notes are made by the following named persons, and in the sums set opposite their names.

Then follow the names of the parties giving the notes, including the names of these defendants, who also signed the said agreement.

The findings show that, on the faith of the foregoing instruments and other instruments of like character executed by other parties, who, like the defendants, were the owners of property that would be made valuable by the construction of the proposed road, the plaintiff in November, 1895, less than four months from the execution of said instrument, bid and paid to the city of Los Angeles $1,505 for a franchise to construct the road over that part of the course agreed upon and within the city limits. Before the 28th of April, 1896, the plaintiff commenced work upon said railway, but said work was not performed with the intention of prosecuting the construction of said railway continuously and with diligence to completion, and the plaintiff did not commence work upon said railway with said purpose until after the 1st day of July, 1897. On July 1, 1897, defendants served upon plaintiff a written notice to the effect that they did not recognize any liability on account of the foregoing written contracts, for the reasons that the road had not been completed within the time agreed upon. Soon after the service of this notice the plaintiff actively engaged in the construction of the road, and completed it, and commenced operating the same to the intersection of Seventh and Hoover streets, as provided for in said instruments, before the expiration of the year 1897. Thereafter, and on May 17, 1898, plaintiff completed its railway to First and Virgil streets. On these facts the traction company filed an action against the defendants for breach of contract.

[*Los Angeles Traction Co.* v. *Wilshire,* 135 Cal. 654, 67 P. 1086 (1902)]

(3)

The defendants, Hiram Walker & Sons, resided at Detroit, but were in business at Walkerville, Ontario, and had a farm at Greenfield, in Wayne county, upon which were some blooded cattle supposed to be barren as breeders. The Walkers were importers and breeders of polled Angus cattle. The plaintiff, Sherwood, was a banker living at Plymouth, in Wayne county. He called upon the defendants at Walkerville for the purchase of some of their stock, but found none there that suited him. Meeting one of the defendants afterwards, he was informed that they had a few head upon their Greenfield farm. He was asked to go out and look at them, with the statement at the time that they were probably barren, and would not breed. May 5, 1886, plaintiff went out to Greenfield and saw the cattle. A few days thereafter, he called upon one of the defendants with the view of purchasing a cow, known as "Rose 2d of Aberlone." After considerable talk it was agreed that defendants would telephone Sherwood at his home in Plymouth in reference to the price. The second morning after this talk he was called up by telephone, and the terms of the sale were finally agreed upon. He was to pay five and one-half cents per pound, live weight, fifty pounds shrinkage. He was asked how he intended to take the cow home, and replied that he might ship her from King's cattle-yard. He requested defendants to confirm the sale in writing, which they did by sending him the following letter:

> Walkerville, May 15,1886.
>
> T. C. Sherwood, President, etc.—Dear Sir: We confirm sale to you of the cow Rose 2d of Aberlone, lot 56 of our catalogue, at five and a half cents per pound, less fifty pounds shrink. We inclose herewith order on Mr. Graham for the cow. You might leave check with him, or mail to us here, as you prefer.
>
> Yours truly, Hiram Walker & Sons.

The order upon Graham inclosed in the letter read as follows:

> Walkerville, May 15, 1886.
>
> George Graham: You will please deliver at King's cattle-yard to Mr. T. C. Sherwood, Plymouth, the cow Rose 2d of Aberlone, lot 56 of our catalogue. Send halter with the cow, and have her weighed.
>
> Yours truly, Hiram Walker & Sons.

On the twenty-first of the same month the plaintiff went to defendants' farm at Greenfield, and presented the order and letter to Graham, who informed him that the defendants had instructed him not to deliver the cow. Soon after, the plaintiff tendered to Hiram Walker, one of the defendants, $80, and demanded the cow. Walker refused to take the money or deliver the cow.

At the time of the alleged sale it was believed by both the plaintiff and themselves that the cow was barren and would not breed. She cost $850, and if not barren would be worth from $750 to $1,000. After the date of the letter, and the order to Graham, the defendants were informed by said Graham that the cow was with calf, and therefore they instructed him not to deliver her to plaintiff, and on the twentieth of May, 1886, telegraphed plaintiff what Graham said about the cow being with calf, and that consequently they could not sell her.

[*Sherwood* v. *Walker*, 66 Mich. 568, 33 N.W. 919 (1887)]

(4)

During the month of September, 1954, an automobile dealer ran the following advertisement in a local newspaper:

> Buy a New '54 Ford Now
> Trade Even for a '55 Ford
> Don't Wait—Buy a 1954 Ford Now; when the 1955 models come out we'll trade even for your '54. You pay only sales tax and license fee. Your '55 Ford will be the same model, same body style, accessory group, etc.
> Good Only During Period
> September 15 to 30

Johnson bought a 1954 Ford during the advertised period, paying cash for the car. Neither Johnson nor the dealer mentioned the special deal. In December, 1954, Johnson returned to the dealer's place of business and requested his 1955 car. The dealer refused to deliver a 1955 car to Johnson. The dealer called to Johnson's attention the fact that the original purchase agreement said nothing about the special deal and showed Johnson a clause in the purchase agreement which read as follows: "This is the entire agreement pertaining to this purchase." Written in pencil across the face of the purchase agreement was "No '55 deal." Johnson insists that his attention was not called to the clause in the agreement and that the penciled statement was not on the agreement when he signed it.

[*Johnson* v. *Capital City Ford Company, Inc.,* 85 So. 2nd 75 (1955)]

(5)

On Tuesday, November 7, John Parsons, president of Wood Products, Inc., received the following letter from William Perkins, the president of Grand Falls Furniture Company of Grand Falls, Anosmia:

> I have five high speed table saws which we have not been able to use in our business since we changed our product lines last year. These machines have had only six to eleven months of active use and have been in rustproof storage ever since we took them off the line, so they should be in good condition. Although I do not know much about your manufacturing processes, I have a feeling that these machines might prove very useful to you They may be inspected at my plant any time this month, but I do plan to get rid of them before the 1st of December. Please let me know right away if you are interested in the saws at my price of $7500 for all five.

Parsons was not interested in the saws, but thought his friend Paul Preston of Hypocase, Inc. might have some use for them and turned the letter over to Preston. On Wednesday, November 7, Preston wrote as follows to Grand Falls:

> My friend Parsons at Wood Products showed me your offer concerning the table saws. I have a new contract with the Navy on which I could use those machines if they are in good condition. I would like to have my plant manager look at them this week, and if they meet our requirements, we could get together Monday morning to sign the papers.

This letter was received by Perkins on Thursday. He mailed an immediate reply, saying:

> Your man can see the machines whenever it is convenient. If he comes after working hours, the watchman has instructions to let him in.

This letter was received on Friday, and the plant manager flew over to Grand Falls that afternoon and inspected the machines early in the evening and returned immediately to Berkland. The plant manager called Preston as soon as he arrived in Berkland Friday night and reported that the machines were in excellent shape. Preston sent a telegram to Grand Falls that same evening:

Will see you first thing Monday with purchase contract ready for signature.

Before the telegram was delivered to Perkins Saturday morning, he sold the machines to another buyer and sent a telegram to Preston:

Hope this will not disappoint you. Made better deal on machines this morning.

Preston received this message Saturday afternoon and tried to reach Perkins by telephone without success.

Preston arrived at the Grand Falls Furniture Company offices at 9 a.m. on Monday and tendered $7500 for the machines. Perkins rejected the payment and refused to turn over the machines. Preston feels that he has a valid contract with Grand Falls and that the contract has been breached. Perkins insists that there never was a contract between Hypocase and Grand Falls.

(6)

McKann Madison was employed by Hypocase, Inc. to manage a new advertising and public relations department recently set up by the company. This contract was to expire on December 15, 1967. Under the contract, Madison was put in complete charge of the department, which employed a number of other persons in addition to Madison. On several occasions prior to December 15, Madison approached Vance Parker, the vice-president in charge of sales and also the officer who had set up the new department and hired Madison, to inquire whether he was to be employed for another year. Each time, Parker had put Madison off by saying that the company did not yet have enough experience with the new department to be able to decide whether to retain it and Madison. In December, 1967, Madison's department was engaged in planning a substantial advertising campaign that was to go into operation after the first of the year. On December 22, after Madison's previous contract had expired, he still had received no information from Parker as to his status. Madison went to see Parker in his office and said to him that because the old contract had been lapsed for several days and because Madison believed that he ought to quit work immediately and seek other employment if Hypocase was not going to retain him for another year, he had to have an immediate answer to the question of reemployment. Parker asked Madison how the new campaign was going, and Madison replied that the people in his department were working very hard on it and that with a maximum effort, they should be ready for the deadline on January 15. Parker then said: "Go ahead, you're all right. Get the work out and don't let the future worry you." Madison went back to work, assuming that he had been rehired, and did not think about the matter again until February 1, 1968, when Parker called Madison to his office and told him that his services were no longer required. Parker remembered the conversation of December 22nd but denied that he had intended to rehire Madison.

B. In General

Many phrases are used to express the nature of the first and most important requirement for the formation of a valid contract: mutual assent, meeting of the minds, agreement, accord, consent, bargain, and others. The idea sought to be conveyed is simply that, before the contract can come into existence, the parties must have agreed to being bound by the same terms. How can it be determined whether this agreement has taken place? It is obvious that there is no contract where A offers to sell his Oldsmobile to B for $3000, and B accepts provided that A reduces the price to $2000 and delivers a Pontiac instead. This is a very simple example where the words of the parties make it clear that they have reached no agreement. But suppose that B had not replied as he did but instead had said to A: "I accept" or "I agree," while thinking to himself that he did not intend to be bound by A's terms at all? The phrase "meeting of the minds" would suggest that there was no contract in the second example either, because the minds of the parties had not actually met. "Meeting of the minds," although a colorful term, tends to mislead, because it conveys the impression, if taken literally, that it is concerned only with the actual state of the minds of the parties. The term can be used safely, however, if its limitations are well understood. The time may come, though one can hope that it does not, when we will be able to ascertain exactly what is going on in the mind of another person. Until that time, however, it is obvious that any test of contractual validity that depends solely upon knowledge of the actual state of a person's mind is impractical. Because the limits of human capacity confine our observations to the outward manifestations of what is going on in a person's mind, the law also must look to this external evidence of a person's intentions in determining whether parties have agreed to the terms of a contract.

The emphasis upon the expressions or external mainfestations of the state of a person's mind corresponds to the so-called "objective theory" of contract, where it is suggested that a valid contract is created by agreement of the outward manifestations of the parties and not by their subjective intentions. By a contrary view, the "subjective theory" of contract, it is argued that a valid contract does not come into existence unless there is an agreement of intentions, appropriately expressed. Neither view can stand wholly by itself. The first relies upon an important fact of human nature, but the second tells us that proved intentions cannot be entirely disregarded. Actual cases make it plain that a person may be held in accordance with his outward manifestations as reasonably understood by others, even though his real intentions were different. At the same time, the cases make it equally clear that the actual or proved intent of either party cannot be disregarded unless one of them has knowingly or negligently misled the other to his detriment. There are many situations, some of which will be discussed later in this chapter, where there is further evidence of the state of a person's mind than the expressions communicated to the other party. (See comments on mistakes in the transmission of the offer.)

These outward manifestations, words and conduct, may or may not convey accurately a person's intentions, but experience has taught us that these are the best evidence available and are usually reliable indications of a state of mind. Accurate or not, a person is usually held to the impressions of agreement which his outward manifestations reasonably convey to the observer. Completely apart from the law of contract, all of us know that we judge others and are judged ourselves, not on the basis of inner thoughts and intentions that are unknown to the outside world, but on the basis of word and acts, of what is actually said and done. The law, then, cannot look directly into the minds of the parties in order to ascertain their intentions, but rather must look to their words and conduct, which are the outward and observable manifestations of what is going on in their minds.

The use of the objective standard does not eliminate all problems. Many still remain. Suppose a person's conduct and written and oral words all manifest different intentions? Suppose one party misinterprets another's manifested intentions? Suppose both parties actually did agree on the same terms, but it can be shown that they would not have agreed had the true facts of the situation been known? These and many other problems will be discussed in the pages to follow.

The contract implied in fact is a good example of a contract that comes into existence as a result of outward manifestations of agreement which consist solely of conduct. A person who enters a "pay as you leave" bus or streetcar is indicating by his actions his consent to be bound to a contract obligating him to pay the fare when he reaches his destination and descends from the vehicle. No words of contract are ever spoken in this kind of situation, but the contract resulting from the conduct of the parties is none the less binding and valid. The law is justified in imputing to the minds of the parties the impressions their actions reasonably convey. A person who signs a contract without reading it is bound by the terms of that contract, in the absence of fraud, because his actions convey the impression that he agrees to the terms whatever they may be. Furthermore, if a person were permitted to avoid a contract simply on the ground that he was not aware of every term and detail, the whole contract device would be seriously weakened. The burden is put on the individual to ascertain the terms to which he is agreeing, and if he fails to learn them all by the time he manifests his assent, the risks are his, except in cases of fraud.

What has been said in regard to manifestations by conduct is even more true with regard to manifestations by words. A person who orally or in writing manifests his assent to the terms of a contract is bound by those terms in the absence of fraud or mistake.

Whether by word or by conduct, the manifestations of agreement have been worked by the law into a pattern or process by which agreements are normally arrived at. This process consists of two steps: a proposal made by one party to another, and the assent to this proposal by the party to whom it is made. The proposal is called an *offer* and the person who makes it an *offeror*. The person to whom the offer is made is called the *offeree*, and his manifestations of assent, if any, are called the *acceptance*. Mutual assent is arrived at, then, by means of offer and acceptance.

C. The Offer

THE NATURE OF THE OFFER. *In general.* Although the offer, the proposal made by the offeror to the offeree, may sound or read like "I offer to sell" or "I offer to buy" it is in legal effect a promise whereby the party making it expresses his willingness to conduct himself in a certain fashion provided that the party to whom the promise is made conducts himself in the manner requested. Thus, a warning or a demand is not an offer that is accepted by violating the warning or ignoring the demand. It should be noted also that the offer is more than just a promise. It is a conditional promise whereby the offeror promises to conduct himself in a certain way only on the condition that the offeree fulfills certain requirements. The offeror may request that the offeree promise to act in a certain way, in which case the making of the requested promise by the offeree is the acceptance of the offer. Or the offeror may request that the offeree perform some act other than making a promise, in which case the performance of the act is the acceptance.

Bilateral and unilateral contracts. Another classification of contracts becomes important at this point. A *bilateral contract* is one in which there are promises on both sides and results from an offer which requests a promise by the offeree. In effect, the offeror says, "I promise to conduct myself in a certain manner if you will promise to conduct yourself in a certain manner." When the offeree accepts the offer, he is promising to do the things requested and has brought into existence a bilateral contract. The bilateral contract, it should be noted, is completely executory at the time the acceptance by the offeree brings it into existence. An offer calling for an act instead of a promise creates, if the offer is accepted by the performance of the requested act, a unilateral contract in which there is a promise on one side and an already performed act on the other. For example, *A* offers to pay *B* $5000 if *B* runs a mile in less than four minutes. *A* is requesting, not a promise by *B*, but an act, the complete performance of which results in the acceptance of *A's* offer and the creation of a binding contract. The unilateral contract is partially executed at the time it is formed. The distinction between bilateral and unilateral contracts is rendered less significant, but not wholly removed, by Sections 2-204 and 2-206 of the Uniform Commercial Code, which blur the distinctions between offers contemplating acts by the offeree and those contemplating promises, except where the desires of the offeror are "unambiguously indicated." However, these changes apply only to contracts for the sale of goods.

While an offer is almost always a promise conditioned on an act or a promise by the offeree, it may in some cases be an act by the offeror which is given in exchange for a promise. For example, the presentation of the purchase price of a ticket at a theater box office may be analyzed as an offer, which is accepted by handing over the ticket, which in turn amounts to a promise by the theater owner to admit the ticket holder to the performance.

Requirements for a valid offer. A proposal, to constitute an offer, must be *definite and certain*. If the proposal is not definite and certain, the acceptance creates nothing that a court can enforce. A promise to pay a person a "fair share of the profits" has been held to be too vague and uncertain to constitute an offer. This requirement should not be interpreted to mean, however, that the terms of the proposal must be absolutely certain in all details. A proposal to pay the "reasonable value" of one's services, although not literally certain, is still an amount which can be ascertained from external evidence such as wages paid to others who perform the same or similar services. A proposal to sell all the raw material which a person may need or require in his business is sufficiently definite to be enforced because the purchaser, if he accepts the offer, is obligated to buy from the other party all of the material which he requires in the operation of his business. It is often said in explanation of this situation: "That is certain which can be made certain." The Code clearly adopts this view. Section 2-204(3) provides: "Even though one or more terms are left open, a contract for sale does not fail for indefiniteness if the parties have intended to make a contract and there is a reasonably certain basis for giving an appropriate remedy." Frequently a proposal which seems to some too uncertain to be an offer is held to be certain because custom or usage has supplied the certainty that would otherwise be lacking. A seemingly vague signal by a bidder at an auction may be, to the auctioneer and to others familiar with the customs of the trade, a definite and certain offer.

In order to be an offer, a proposal must be *intended as an offer*. Our earlier discussion of the "objective" and "subjective" theories of contract suggests that we must be concerned both with the intentions of the offeror and with the impressions which the offeror's outward manifestations of intention make on the offeree. It is clear that the intentions of the offeror must often be examined through the eyes of the offeree. Where, for example, an offeror knowingly or negligently leads an offeree to believe reasonably that a proposal was seriously intended as an offer, he may be held to have made a valid offer although that was not his actual intention at all.

In addition to the above requirements, the offer must be *communicated*. Obviously, unless the terms upon which the offeror proposes to bargain are made known to the person with whom he desires to bargain, no agreement can possibly be reached, but there is more to the requirement of communication than this simple truism. If *A*, while talking to *B*, mentions that he intends to offer his shotgun to *C* for $95, and if *B* later repeats *A's* statement to *C*, there is no effective communication of the offer to *C*. In order to be communicated, an offer must reach the offeree by a means selected by the offeror. If *A*, in the above example, had told *B* to go to *C* and state to him the proposal, communication would have been accomplished. The reason for the rule is simply that no offer can really exist unless the offeror has intentionally set into motion the machinery that conveys the proposal to the intended offeree. Definiteness and certainty are probably lacking also where only a rumor of a proposed offer reaches the offeree. A different result might be reached where the negligence of the offeror has permitted a seemingly properly communicated proposal to fall into the hands of an offeree, as, for example, where *A*, who writes a letter to *B* offering to sell the shotgun for $95, changes his mind before mailing the letter but leaves the addressed envelope containing the letter on his desk where his secretary finds it and mails it.

The offer may be communicated by any means whatsoever, as long as it is the means selected by the offeror for that purpose. It may be made orally, in person, by phone, or by agent. It may be by letter or telegram. It may even be by advertisement if it was intended and reasonably understood as an offer and if it is sufficiently definite and certain, as would usually be the case with an offer of a reward. It may be by posted public notice.

Mistakes in the transmission of the offer. The courts are not agreed on the rules which should be followed when mistakes are made in the transmission of the offer from the offeror to the offeree. Where the mistake is the fault of the offeror or his agent and it is not known to or obvious to the offeree, the objective approach to mutual assent would require that the offeror be held to the terms of the offer as evidenced by his outward manifestations. A contract, in other words, would come into existence when the offeree accepted, and the terms of the contract would be those manifested to the offeree. The relief available to the offeror who is subject to hardship as a result of his mistake will be considered in the portion of this chapter devoted to reality of consent.

Where the errors are made without the direct fault of the offeror, the rules vary. The better rule recognizes the fact that where the error is not a part of the offeror's manifestation of a state of mind but is caused by an external factor, there is no sound reason for using the objective standards of mutual assent. Where *A* files a telegram with the telegraph company offering to sell to *B* a particular product at $2.49 a unit, but an error of the telegraph company causes the message delivered at the other end to read "$2.29" a unit, and *B* replies that the accepts the offer, the better rule holds that there is no contract. Had *A* made the offer directly to *B* over the telephone or face to face and said "$2.29" when he intended to say $2.49," there would be no question but that a contract at $2.29 would arise on *B's* acceptance. In the example above, however, the error was not *A's* but the telegraph company's and was really no more *A's* fault than *B's*.

Two other views are followed in this country, both of which would result in a binding contract at $2.29, provided, of course, that the offer that the offeree received still manifested reasonable terms. (Had the error reduced the $2.49 figure to $0.49, the error would probably have been obvious to the offeree and under no theory could he have turned the communication into a binding contract by his acceptance.) One of these other views finds the contract binding on the theory the telegraph company is an agent of the offeror. As will be made clear in Part IV, this theory can be supported only by subjecting the law of agency to severe strain. The other view proceeds on the theory that since the offeror selected this means of communication, he should be held for the errors made by it. This is just another way of saying that the objective approach to mutual assent should be applied in this situation.

Under the better view set forth above, a more difficult problem arises in connection with the hypothetical example there used where the subject matter of the contract is shipped by *A* to *B* and resold by *B* in the course of his business before *A* discovers an error has been made. The fact that the goods cannot be retrieved by *A* does not create a contract where there was none before. But, in order to avoid the unjust enrichment of *B*, the doctrine of quasi-contract may be used here, and *B* will be obligated to *A* for the reasonable value of the goods *B* received and resold. What is a reasonable value is a question of fact, and will be determined in the light of the circumstances of each particular case.

Another facet of the problem presented by the hypothetical example is the nature and amount of the claim which *A* has against the telegraph company, but that raises issues with which we are not yet prepared to deal.

OFFER DISTINGUISHED FROM SIMILAR STATEMENTS. It has already been seen that a statement, in order to be effective as an offer which can be turned into a binding contract by acceptance, must be definite and certain, intended and reasonably understood as an offer, and communicated to the offeree. These requirements are the best tests to use in attempting to distinguish between those statements that are offers and those that may look or sound like offers but are not. Brief consideration will be given also to a few situations where custom and usage have an influence on the issue of whether an act or a statement constitutes an offer and where special problems may arise.

Offer distinguished from preliminary negotiations.   Most contracts are preceded by negotiations or a bargaining period during which each party seeks to improve his position relative to that of the other party. A seller's advertisement in a newspaper may bring an inquiry from a prospective buyer who wants to know about qualities, quantities, and specifications. The seller supplies the information. The buyer asks about possible delivery dates and whether the seller will lower his prices for large quantity purchases. The negotiations may cease without either party having made an offer, but, at some point in the negotiations, one party may set forth a definite proposal as to the obligations he is willing to incur in exchange for certain acts or promises by the other party. Once this is done, there is an offer that may be turned into a binding contract by the acceptance of the other party. Aside from problems of communication, the earmarks of an offer are its definiteness and certainty and evidence indicating it was intended as an offer and so reasonably understood.

Usually it is quite easy to distinguish an offer from the preliminary statements that seek rather to induce offers than to make them. Most advertisements, catalogs, trade circulars, published price lists, and price quotations are too indefinite about quantities, specifications, and other important terms to be considered as offers. The circumstances surrounding the making of such statements usually dispel any possibility that the statements were intended as offers or reasonably understood to be so. A seller does not generally intend his advertisement to be an offer that could be turned into a binding contract by the buyer's appearing on the store premises and accepting it or by a letter of acceptance from the buyer. The seller may have limited quantities, limited-size lots, and strict credit or cash terms, and will not want to risk having an offer turned into a binding contract that cannot be performed. The advertiser usually invites offers by the buyers, offers the seller has the power to accept or reject.

Sometimes it is said the use of the word "quote" or "quotation" is some evidence that the statements containing these words are not to be understood as offers. A test such as this is not a very valuable one, however, because the surrounding circumstances may be such as to demonstrate that an offer really was intended. The person examining the situation may miss the significance of the surrounding circumstances or of other language if he is watching for catch-words like "quote." Where, for example, "I can quote you" is followed in the same communication by "Wire immediate acceptance," the implication of no offer in the first phrase may well be overcome by the second phrase. The negotiations and communications that preceded the quotation may make it clear the quotation was, after all, intended as an offer.

It should be noted also that even an advertisement may be an offer if its terms are sufficiently definite and if it appears that the advertisement is intended as an offer. A person who states in an advertisement that he will pay one dollar for every copy of a particular issue of *Life* magazine delivered to his address before a certain time is probably intending to make an offer, and will be so reasonably understood. Reward offers are frequently made through newspaper advertisements. In *Carlill* v. *Carbolic Smoke Ball Co.*,[2] the following advertisement was held to be an effective offer:

---

[2] L. R. (1893) 1 Q.B.D. 256.

£100 reward will be paid by the Carbolic Smoke Ball Company to any person who contracts the increasing epidemic influenza, colds, or any disease caused by taking cold, after having used the ball three times daily for two weeks according to the printed directions supplied with each ball. £1000 is deposited with the Alliance Bank, Regent Street, showing our sincerity in the matter.

Although these communications usually make known only the general terms on which the advertiser may be interested in contracting and are intended to solicit offers from those reading the advertisement, the language of the advertisement and the surrounding circumstances may justify a contrary conclusion. It should be noted that the test of definiteness and certainty is made less descisive by Code Section 2-204(3), referred to above.

Statements made in jest or anger. In order for a statement to be an offer, it must be one that would lead the person to whom it is made reasonably to believe it was seriously intended as an offer. Statements made in jest, frolic, banter, anger, or excitement do not qualify as offers where the circumstances accompanying the statement make it clear to any reasonable person that no real offer was intended. If, however, the jest or excitement is not reasonably plain to the person to whom the statement is made, the statement may well be treated as an offer because a prudent person would understand it to be intended seriously.

The same type of test may be applied to the many promissory statements we make every day in regard to social engagements and other matters where no legal relations are seriously intended or understood. No real offer is intended or understood where *A* promises to meet *B* at the Press Club for lunch or offers to take *C* to the Homecoming Dance.

Baggage checks and similar documents as offers. When *A* checks a suitcase in a railroad station checkroom or leaves his automobile in a parking lot, he usually receives in exchange for his property a small piece of cardboard. This cardboard frequently bears on its surface, in addition to an identifying number or symbol, several statements in fine print outlining the responsibility of the checkroom or parking lot operator. If these statements are the terms of the offer the operator is making to *A* and which *A* accepts by leaving his property and taking the check, the depositing party is bound by the terms of such offer. It is clear that the terms are so interpreted and binding where they are specially called to the attention of the other party, but the courts are not in agreement about the effect of these terms on baggage and parking lot checks when these are not called to the attention of the other party.

Some courts hold that the fine print does not become part of the offer and of the contract unless specifically called to the attention of the party leaving the property. Other courts say it is sufficient if the face of the check refers to terms on the reverse side by the use of "over" or "see terms on reverse side." The real test, of course, is whether the party receiving the check reasonably understands it to contain the terms of the offer. The courts differ in results because they answer this question in different ways. Some courts draw what seems to be a sensible line between receipts or checks used primarily for purposes of identification and those more reasonably expected to contain the terms of bailment or storage. Baggage and parking lot checks are usually stuffed into one's pocket without any thought except that the check will be needed in order to reclaim the property, while a warehouse receipt is usually examined in detail and is usually thought to contain the terms of the bailment contract. The latter looks like a contractual, or at least a formal, instrument and is not thought of solely as a means of identification.

The Uniform Commercial Code requires that certain clauses in contractual documents be set forth in a "conspicuous" manner. Section 1-201 (10) says that a term or clause is conspicuous "when it is so written that a reasonable person against whom it is to operate ought to have noticed it." Many state and federal statutes specify the size of type to be used in certain kinds of contracts or contract clauses. Retail instalment sales contracts, insurance contracts, and wage assignments are examples of documents that often come under these provisions.

Auction sales and bids on construction work. A public notice of the intention of a person to hold an auction sale is not an offer and in no way binds that person to sell the goods advertised for sale at the auction. The notice is simply an invitation to the public to participate in the auction sale. Nor is there an offer when the auctioneer puts a particular item up for sale. The offers are made by the bidders. The acceptance is the fall of the hammer, which, by custom, generally accepts the highest bid. The auctioneer, however, may state that some lower bid is accepted or may withdraw the goods at any time before the acceptance. Even statements by the person holding the auction that he promises to sell to the highest bidder are not offers that can be accepted, and the person may accept the lowest bid or the highest bid, or reject them all.

In some states, either by custom or by statute, the rules applied to auctions advertised to be "without reserve" are somewhat different from the rules set forth in the previous paragraph. Where an auction has been so advertised, the auctioneer cannot withdraw the goods even though there has been no acceptance by the fall of the hammer. In general, the bids may still be withdrawn although the goods may not. Some courts take a countrary view. Section 2-328 of the Code accepts the former view and has modified and clarified some of the other rules with regard both to auctions with and without reserve.

Bids on construction work are offers, and, in the absence of special statute, are handled very much as bids at an auction sale. The offeree may accept the highest bid, the lowest bid, or any other bid, or may reject them all. The bidder may withdraw any time before his bid is accepted. Advertisements calling for bids are not offers but are simply invitations to make offers. Statutes in some states require public agencies receiving bids on construction work to accept the lowest bid from a responsible bidder. Under these statutes, the bid is still the offer and even the lowest bid may be rejected, but if a bid is accepted, it must be that of the lowest responsible bidder.

DURATION AND TERMINATION OF OFFERS.   The effectiveness of an offer begins when it is communicated and continues until it is terminated by any one of several methods. After termination no offer exists, and it can no longer be turned into a contract by the simple expedient of an acceptance. A contract on the same terms may eventually be entered into, but, before this can happen, a new offer is necessary. An acceptance by an offeree after the offer has expired may itself be interpreted as a new offer embodying the same terms as the terminated offer. It is sometimes said that an acceptance terminates an offer, and, speaking in the strictest sense, this is undoubtedly true. The offer is no longer an offer but has been merged into the resulting contract. Since "termination" carries connotations of destruction or ineffectiveness, it is not too wisely used in connection with the offer's becoming a part of the contract as a result of acceptance. The term is usually applied to the other methods of terminating an offer, which are: lapse of time, revocation by the offeror, rejection by the offeree, and operation of law.

Termination by lapse of time.   The offeror may specify, among the other terms of the offer, the length of time during which the offer will remain in effect. The offer terminates at the expiration of this time without any further words or conduct on the part of the offeror. The offeror may set forth the time limits in many different ways. He may name a date on which the offer expires or may provide for a period of time, such as a week or five days. In the latter case, a problem arises as to when the period of time begins to run. Because of the hardship which might otherwise be worked on the offeror, most courts hold that the time period begins to run when the offer is started on its way to the offeree by the offeror. Delays in communication that were unknown to the offeror might cause him to assume the offer had expired without being accepted; and were the time to run from the date of receipt by the offeree, the offeror might well rely upon the lapse of time and enter into a contract with someone else while the original offeree still had time to turn the offer into another binding contract. Some courts, however, take the view that the time period runs from time of receipt by the offeree. The offeror in these jurisdictions can protect himself by more detailed specification. Where the offeror requires "immediate acceptance" or "acceptance by return mail," the time period is, by implication, very brief.

Where no time limit is stipulated in the offer, it remains effective for a reasonable period of time. What is a reasonable time depends upon the circumstances of the particular case, and what is a reasonable time in one case may not be in another. An offer to sell corporate stocks or grain traded on an exchange may remain open for only a few hours at most, and, where the offer is made on the floor of an exchange, it may be effective for only a few seconds. An offer to sell a house or a business may remain open for days or weeks or even months. Many factors are useful in determining what is a reasonable time in a given case—the nature of the subject matter, whether it fluctuates rapidly in value, previous dealings between the parties, and customs or usages in the particular trade. The method of communicating the offer is significant. A telegram or a telephone call creates a presumption of a short time, while a letter would indicate a somewhat longer time. In most cases, the wiser course for the offeror to follow is not to depend on the lapse of a reasonable time for termination but to take steps to revoke the offer.

Should the offeree attempt to accept after the termination of the offer, his belated acceptance is, in legal contemplation, a new offer which the original offeror may accept or reject as he pleases. The terms of the new offer are the same as the old, but the parties have changed places.

Termination by revocation. It is important to assign the terms "revocation" and "rejection" to the proper parties. An offeror revokes: an offeree rejects. A *revocation* calls off or calls back a proposal made by the offeror. It is obvious that a person cannot call off a proposal made by someone else. At the same time a *rejection* turns down a proposal made by another person. Only the person to whom an offer is made can reject it.

The offer is simply a promise made by the offeror and is not binding on him until the offeree accepts the offer. Consequently, the offeror may withdraw his offer at any time before acceptance. Under precode law, the withdrawal could even be in violation of a promise by the offeror to keep his offer open, a position defended by the theory that the violation was not a breach of a promise the law enforces because of the lack of consideration. Business practice was often to the contrary, however, and businessmen commonly extended offers that both they and the offerees treated as irrevocable. In contracts for the sale of goods, the Code adopts the view that a merchant's written assurance that he will keep an offer open is binding for a reasonable period of time or for the period stated in the assurance but in no event for a period in excess of three months. The offeror must be a "merchant," which means almost anyone in business, and the offer must be in writing and signed by the offeror. If the assurance is on a form supplied by the offeree, it must be separately signed by the offeror. Within the conditions specified by the Code, a promise to keep an offer open is treated much as though it were an option.

Where the promise to keep an offer open actually takes the form of an option, the offer, of course, may not be withdrawn without liability. The reason is that the option itself is a contract that satisfies all of the requirements for valid contracts. For example: *A* tells *B* he will sell his house for $20,000, and if *B* will give *A* $100, *A* will promise to keep the offer to sell open for 60 days. If *B* pays the $100, there comes into existence a separate and distinct contract under which the offeror is obligated to keep the basic offer open.

This is the *option contract*. It differs from the simple promise to keep an offer open in that the option has satisfied all the requirements of a binding contract, including mutual assent and consideration. In some states the binding effect of an option contract is supplied by a seal.

The revocation of the offer, like the offer itself, must be communicated, but the requirements of communication are somewhat different. The offer, you will recall, must be communicated directly to the offeree by a means selected and intended by the offeror. Although this method may also be used for the communication of the revocation, and most frequently is, the directness and the selected means are usually not necessary. An offer to sell an automobile to B may be terminated when B discovers that the auto has been sold to someone else, even though the information did not come from the offeror or from anyone acting on his behalf. Serious objections can be raised to this point of view because of the importance which it attaches to rumors and to unsupported information.

In all but two states, California and South Dakota, the revocation is not effectively communicated until it is received by the offeree. It is usually not necessary for the telegram or letter actually to come into the possession of the offeree. It is sufficient if it is delivered to the place of business or other place where the offer may have been delivered. In California and South Dakota, a revocation sent by mail or telegram is effectively communicated when it is placed in the course of transmission. This means that dropping a letter in a mail box or filing a telegram with the telegraph company will constitute communication to the offeree, even though he may never actually receive the letter or message. The California view is not desirable. It violates one of the basic premises of contract law in that it maximizes rather than minimizes the uncertainties of the parties. Offers cannot be terminated by acts of the offeror, unknown to the offeree, without increasing the dangers of uncertainty, unfairness, and litigation. The problem of communication which is effective on dispatch will be discussed in greater detail in connection with acceptances, which are commonly thus communicated.

Offers made to the public cause a special problem of revocation. The difficulty arises because, once the notice of the offer has been made to the public, the offeror has no way of knowing what persons and how many have learned of the offer and have thus become offerees. The offeror cannot communicate directly with the offerees. The American rule in this situation was derived from the famous case of *Shuey* v. *United States*,[3] which arose out of a public reward offer published by the Secretary of War in newspapers and by other media on April 20, 1865, whereby the War Department offered to pay $25,000 for the apprehension of John H. Surratt, one of John Wilkes Booth's accomplices in the assassination of Lincoln. On November 24, 1865, the offer

---

[3] 92 U.S. 73 (1875).

was revoked, and the revocation was given substantially the same publicity as the original offer. In April, 1866, Henry B. Ste. Marie, who knew of the offer but knew nothing of the revocation, apprehended Surratt and claimed the reward. The Treasury paid him $10,000 because of the "equities in the situation." Ste. Marie sued for the remaining $15,000. The Supreme Court of the United States held that a public offer may be effectively withdrawn by giving the revocation the same general publicity that was given to the original offer, which means that the offer may be terminated without a particular offeree ever knowing of it. It has been suggested that a better rule would have been to require actual notice to all who heard about the offer unless the offer itself contained the statement that it might be withdrawn without notice. (Shuey, for those who are curious, was the executor of the estate of Ste. Marie, who had died while his suit was pending.)

Termination by rejection. One of the essential characteristics of the contract device is that the contract relationship is one into which persons enter voluntarily. An offeree, then, is free to accept or to reject the offers made to him. The offeree rejects the offer by refusing to enter into contractual relations with the offeror on the terms provided in the offer. The rejection terminates the offer, and the offeror is then free to deal with the subject matter of his offer as he sees fit. Until the offer has been revoked or rejected or terminated by some other means, the offeror cannot safely offer the subject matter to anyone else because he risks finding himself a party to two binding contracts with the facilities for performing only one. The offeror may, of course, protect himself from this eventuality by the wording of his offer or by revoking it.

Once the offeree rejects the offer, he no longer has the power to turn the offer into a binding contract by his acceptance. Any subsequent, purported acceptance will be treated as a new offer on the terms of the old, but which the original offeror now has the power to accept or reject. It should be noted that the offeree is not required to reject an offer. He may simply ignore it and let it terminate by lapse of time or by revocation.

A rejection must also be communicated. The rules of communication of the rejection are like those of the offer itself. The rejection is not effective until it is received by the offeror, and it must be received directly by a means selected and intended by the offeree. An interesting aspect of the requirement that the rejection be received in order to be effective is the fact that this rule makes it possible for a contract to result even after a rejection has been sent to the offeror. Because the rejection is not effective in terminating the offer until it is received, an acceptance sent later than the rejection, but which overtakes it and arrives first, will turn the offer into a binding contract. The arrival of the rejection will have no legal effect because the offer is no longer subject to termination, having been merged in the contract. It is important to note that although an acceptance is frequently effective on dispatch, as will be seen later, it will never be so effective where a rejection has preceded it. The acceptance will be effective only if received and only if it arrives at the offeror before the rejection. To permit the acceptance to be effective on dispatch under these circumstances would make possible a serious injustice to the offeror.

Any attempt by the offeree to change the terms of the offer or to accept the offer conditionally is the equivalent of a rejection. The attempt to change the terms of the offer by the acceptance is called a *counter-offer,* a variety of which is the *conditional acceptance.* The offeror sets forth in the offer the terms on which he is willing to be bound. If these terms are altered in any way by the offeree, the whole offer is in effect rejected because the offeree is refusing to deal on the terms contained in the original offer and is setting forth in a new offer the terms on which he will deal. Where *A* offers to sell *B* a shotgun for $95 and *B* replies that he will pay not more than $80 for the gun, *B* has rejected *A's* offer and has made one of his own. *B* may not now change his mind and accept *A's* offer. If he attempts to do so, he is simply making a new offer to *A* at $95. Where *A* makes the offer at $95 and *B* replies that he accepts the offer provided that *A* puts on a new choke, there is again a rejection because *B* has conditioned his acceptance on new terms and is, in effect, making a new offer.

It should not be assumed that every statement from the offeree to the offeror, except an unequivocal acceptance, constitutes a rejection. A counter-offer must be distinguished from a mere inquiry seeking information or the possibility of dealing on other terms. In the latter case the communication is not intended as a rejection at all. Any communication of this type should be prefaced by a statement such as, "I have your offer under consideration. . . .", so that it will be clear to the offeror that the communication is not a rejection of the offer. A communication from the offeree to the offeror such as, "This is the worst deal I ever saw. The gun is rusty and the barrel is crooked. I accept," is called a *grumbling acceptance* and is just as good as a cheerful one. An acceptance that appears to be conditional may be treated as though it were an unequivocal acceptance where the condition relates to some aspect already present in the offer. Where the offeree accepts the shotgun offer, for example, on the condition that the offeror will warrant his authority to sell it, the acceptance is not really conditional because, under the law of sales, a seller normally warrants by implication his authority to sell the goods. The condition is already present in the offer.

In connection with contracts for the sale of goods, the Code makes important changes in the rules just discussed. A timely and definite expression of acceptance or a written confirmation by the offeree operates as an acceptance, even though it states additional or different terms from those offered. Unless the offeree makes his acceptance expressly conditional on the offeror's assent to the added or different terms, the offeree is immediately bound on the offeror's terms. The additional or different terms are treated as proposals and become a part of the contract only after the offeror agrees to them. However, if both parties are "merchants," the additional terms become a part of the contract even without express consent by the offeror, unless: (1) the offer expressly limits acceptance to the offeror's own terms; (2) the additional terms materially alter the offer; (3) the offeror has already given notice of his objection to them; or (4) the offeror gives notice of his objection within a reasonable time after learning of the proposed additional terms. In other words, a counter-offer is still a rejection and terminates the offer, but the Code construes additional or different terms contained in an acceptance as proposals for additions to the contract rather than as counter-offers, unless, of course, the offeree makes his acceptance expressly conditional on the offeror's assent to the additional terms.

The Code has done much to alleviate the so-called "battle of the forms," where both parties to the negotiations for a sales contract use their own printed forms and seek to manipulate the exchange of forms in such a way as to be last and so control matters as the counter-offer accepted by performance. If the parties have exchanged writings insufficient to form a contract but have contractually bound themselves by conduct that recognizes the existence of a contract, under the Code provisions the terms of their contract consist of the terms on which both their writings agree.

Termination by operation of law. An offer is said to be terminated by operation of law when it is made legally ineffective by some event not caused by the offeror or the offeree. The prevailing American rule is that the death or insanity of either the offeror or the offeree, for example, will terminate the offer. The theory is, that in the case of the death or insanity of the offeror, mutual assent or a meeting of the minds is impossible because the offeror is no longer capable of assenting. In the case of the death or insanity of the offeree, the result is based on the rule that only the person to whom the offer is made may accept it. The result, as far as the offeree is concerned, is universally acknowledged, but some jurisdictions reason that manifestations of an offeror's assent are still present when an offeree accepts an offer without knowledge of the death or insanity of the offeror, and a binding contract is still possible. Good arguments can be made in support of either view. Do not confuse these rules, which deal with the termination of an offer, with completely different rules dealing with the effect of death or insanity on a contract that has already come into existence. An option, for example, unless it involves some sort of personal services, is not affected by the death or insanity of the offeror or the offeree. An option is not just an offer. It is also a binding contract.

The destruction of the subject matter of an offer will serve to terminate the offer. Where *A's* shotgun is destroyed by accident before the acceptance, the offer to sell is terminated. There can be no agreement in regard to a specific gun no longer in existence. Since the object of a contract must be legal, an offer that contemplated legal objectives when originally made is terminated when its objectives are made illegal by statute or otherwise. Even if acceptance has preceded the event which rendered illegal the objectives of the contract, the parties would still be discharged from the performance of the contract.

D. The Acceptance

IN GENERAL.   The second step in the accomplishment of mutual assent is *acceptance,* which is simply an indication by the offeree that he is willing to be bound by the terms of the offer. Here, as with the offer, the important consideration is not that of what is actually going on in the party's mind but the outward manifestations. The offeree may accept only by conducting himself as the offeror has requested, which means the offeree will either make the required promises or perform the required acts. Rarely will the offeree make his promises in words of promise. Frequently, he will say, "I accept," or "Go ahead," or "Okay," or he may indicate by his conduct alone that he has accepted and has made the requested promises. If the offeror has requested an act in place of a promise, the offeree accepts the offer by performing the act.

Precode law places a heavy emphasis upon the time and manner of the coming into existence of a contract through effective acceptance. The Uniform Commercial Code, applicable to contracts within its purview, imposes much looser standards. Section 2-204 states that a contract may be made in any manner sufficient to show agreement, including conduct by both parties which recognizes the existence of such a contract. Furthermore, an agreement sufficient to constitute a contract for sale may be found, even though the moment of its making is undetermined. Most contracts are subject to rather precise analysis of the time and manner of their coming into existence, but the Code properly recognizes that such determinations are not really crucial if the existence of the contract can be established in other ways. Section 2-207(3) reiterates this view in the following words: "Conduct by both parties which recognizes the existence of a contract is sufficient to establish a contract for sale although the writings of the parties do not otherwise establish a contract."

ACCEPTANCE OF AN OFFER TO FORM UNILATERAL CONTRACT.   The offer to form the unilateral contract can be accepted only by performing completely the requested act. A promise to perform the act has no legal effect whatever. Although acceptance of an offer contemplating a bilateral contract must be communicated in order to be effective, communication of acceptance in unilateral contract situations is usually not necessary unless notice to the offeror was specifically made a part of the offer or a part of the acts that constitute acceptance. A public offer of a reward, for example, is usually accepted, and a binding contract comes into existence when the acts requested are performed, even though the offeror does not know of the completion of the acts. If the offer requires notice, or if the requested acts include the return of a lost item to the offeror, no particular problems of notice arise, except that in the former case the offeror must give the offeree a reasonable time during which to communicate the notice.

The general rule is that only complete performance or tender of complete performance will constitute acceptance of an offer to form a unilateral contract. If this rule is taken literally and in connection with the rule that an offeror may withdraw his offer any time before acceptance, a source of hardship and unfairness to the offeree is revealed. The offeror would be able to revoke the offer even though the offeree had substantially performed the requested acts. For example: If A offered to pay B \$10,000 if B would design, build, and deliver to A's loading dock a machine that would accomplish a particular purpose, A might, theoretically, revoke his offer at any time before B's truck containing the machine backed against A's dock. The possible unfairness to B is obvious. If we should reverse this result and bind A to the contract as soon as B began performance, B might play around with the project for many years while A would be prevented from going elsewhere for his machine; furthermore, the result would be contrary to A's intention. Neither of these results seems fair nor desirable. No courts follow the latter view but some do apply the arbitrary former view that leaves the offeror with a club over the head of the offeree.

Courts have sought a way out of the dilemma for many years with varying degrees of success. A few courts have held that once performance begins, the situation is converted into the bilateral variety of contract in place of the unilateral contemplated by the parties. A view which resolves the conflict and protects both parties is found in the Contracts Restatement, Section 45: "If an offer for a unilateral contract is made, and part of the consideration requested in the offer is given or tendered by the offeree in response thereto, the offeror is bound by a contract, the duty of immediate performance of which is conditional on the full consideration being given or tendered within the time stated in the offer, or, if no time is stated therein, within a reasonable time." Some courts have reached similar results by implying a sort of option contract by which the offeror is bound to keep his offer open for a reasonable time once the performance is begun. An offeree will also have cause of action against the offeror where, after he has begun performance, the offeree is prevented by the offeror from completing the performance. It is clear that if the prevention occurs before performance has begun, the prevention should be interpreted as a revocation.

Contract situations within the scope of the Code are subject to different rules. Unless unambiguously indicated by the language or circumstances, the offeree may construe an offer as inviting acceptance in any reasonable manner. Thus, the offeree may treat an offer as unilateral and accept by an act, such as the shipment of the subject goods, or he may treat the offer as bilateral and accept by a promise to ship. Where the beginning of the requested performance is a reasonable method of acceptance, however, an offeror who is not notified of acceptance within a reasonable time may treat the offer as having lapsed before acceptance. Note that the beginning of performance and notice to the offeror make the contract binding on both parties, eliminating some of the uncertainty existing under the precode rules. The offeree is obligated to complete his performance, and the offeror cannot revoke the offer, which has now merged into a contract. Whether beginning performance without notice to the offeror will *itself* prevent the offeror from revoking the offer or be an acceptance of the offer is left by the Code to outside law.

ACCEPTANCE OF OFFER TO FORM BILATERAL CONTRACT. No formal procedure is required, and any conduct clearly showing the offeree's intention to be bound is sufficient. Of course, if the agreement takes the form of a written document, such formalities as signing may have to be complied with and, in spite of the presence of the necessary elements of a valid contract, some contracts are not enforceable unless they, or some note or memorandum thereof, are in writing.

Silence as acceptance. Some manifestation of assent is necessary before an offer can be said to have been accepted. Consequently, mere silence does not constitute acceptance. Even though an offeror specifies that he will interpret silence to be the acceptance of the offer, silence still cannot be acceptance because an offeror cannot impose upon the offeree the duty to speak or act in order to avoid contractual liability, and we can all be very thankful for that. If the offeree does not want to accept the offer, he is under no duty to notify the offeror to that effect. It has been said by some authorities that where the offeror states that silence will be acceptance and the offeree is silent intending his silence to be the acceptance of the offer, there is a binding contract. The situation where this view could be applied would be very unusual, and the problems of proof would create some rather interesting issues.

A merchandising device sometimes used by prospective sellers consists of sending a quantity of merchandise to the "victim" accompanied by a letter stating the price and telling the offeree to remit the price or return the goods within a specified period of time. Even this cannot impose upon the offeree the duty to reply or even to return the goods, and the offeree may completely ignore the merchandise and the offeror's instructions. But if the offeree uses the goods or treats them as his own, by destroying them or giving them away, he has manifested an acceptance of the offer and will become liable for the purchase price.

A few courts have held, in unusual situations, that a past course of dealings between offeror and offeree may impose a duty to speak, with the result that failure to speak may cause contractual liability. Note here that much more than "mere" silence is involved.

Who may accept? Only the person to whom the offer is made may accept. A public offer is made to the public as a whole, and, of course, may be accepted by any member of the public. The offeror cannot be compelled to enter into contracts with persons with whom he does not want to deal. The contract is, with rare exceptions, an entirely voluntary propostion in the eyes of the law, and a stranger, except with public offers where the offeror intends to make the offer to people he does not know, cannot step in and accept an offer made to someone else.

In general, a person must know about an offer before he can accept it. This is in keeping with our concepts of mutual assent and a meeting of the minds. A person who does not know of an offer cannot possibly supply the necessary assent to the terms. Thus, where a person returns a briefcase to its owner and does not know of the offer of a reward for the return, he cannot claim the reward when he does discover an offer has been made. In some states, exceptions are made where an offer of a reward is made by a public agency.

COMMUNICATION OF THE ACCEPTANCE. The communication of the acceptance is perhaps more important than any of the other communications that have been discussed in this chapter. The reason is clear. The effective communication of the acceptance has important legal consequences in that a binding contract is thus brought into existence. The communication of a revocation just withdraws the offer which might never have become a contract anyhow. The communication of a rejection simply prevents an offer from having any further legal consequences. It is extremely important that one knows when an acceptance is communicated because the communication of the acceptance is the creation of the contract. There are many possible situations; not all will be discussed.

Manner, time, and place specified. If an offer sets forth the method, the time, or the place of acceptance, or all of them, the acceptance is effectively communicated only when the precise requirements of the offer have been complied with. For example, if the offeror should specify that the acceptance should be sent by telegram and would not be effective unless received in the Detroit office of the offeror on or before March 10, the offeree must comply with all of the terms of the offer before there is an acceptance. A mailed acceptance, or one sent to another office of the offeror, or one received on March 11 would not create a binding contract and would, in effect, be nothing more than a counter-offer. Even if received at the proper place on time, a mailed acceptance would not be effective, because the offer specified a telegraphic acceptance.

An offeror will usually not make all of the requirements suggested above, but will frequently impose one of them. Where the offeror specifies only that the acceptance will not be effective until received by him, no contract comes into existence until the acceptance is in fact received. In this situation it is clear that the risk of loss or delay in communication is on the offeree because no binding contract is created until the acceptance is actually received. If the offeror stipulates the means of communication to be used for the acceptance, the offeree must use that means. Most courts are very strict in the application of these rules. The reason is that the offeror has the right to set forth the terms to which he is willing to be bound, and the courts will respect them.

It has been seen that where the offeror so specifies, the acceptance will not be effective until actually received. In the absence of specification in this regard, different rules are followed. If the offeror specifies the means of communication, and that means is used by the offeree for his acceptance, the acceptance is effective when placed in the course of transmission. This means that when mail is specified, the transfer of the acceptance into the hands of the Post Office Department, as by dropping the letter of acceptance into a public mailbox, is effective communication. The theory behind this rule is that dropping the letter into the mailbox, or filing a telegram of acceptance with the telegraph company, completes the requirements of the offer, and delivery to the Post Office Department, or to the telegraph company, is the virtual equivalent of delivery to the offeror. Here the risk of loss or delay in communication is on the offeror, because a binding contract comes into existence whether or not the acceptance is ever actually delivered.

No specification of time, manner, or place. The older rule holds that the offeror, in the absence of specification, impliedly authorizes the offeree to use the same means of communication employed by the offeror. The result is to make the acceptance effective on dispatch when that same method of communication is used, just as though a method had been specified and that method used. The implication is simply an authorization, however, and the offeree is not required to use the same means employed by the offeror. By this general rule, if the offeree uses a different means, the acceptance is not effectively communicated until it is actually received. The offeree has chosen to use his own method of communication and has assumed responsibility for the actual delivery and for delivery before the offer terminates by lapse of time. Where the acceptance is by a more rapid means of communication, termination by lapse of time is obviously no particular problem, but where the offeror sends the offer by a rapid means, a prompt acceptance and a short life for the offer are implied. An acceptance by mail would probably not arrive in time to be effective. The reasonable time would have expired and the offer terminated.

A rule that is becoming more widely accepted provides that where the offeror specifies no means of communication in his offer, any usual or reasonable mode may be adopted by the offeree, and the acceptance will become effective when put in the course of transmission whether or not the mode is the same as that used by the offeror. This rule does not alter the fact that if a rapid means of communication is implied from the circumstances, the offeree must use a rapid means. Otherwise, hardship would be worked on the offeror were the acceptance to become effective on dispatch, yet the means of communication be a very slow one. The Code follows this view.

In those situations where the acceptance is effectively communicated on dispatch, it is necessary that the letter or telegram be properly addressed, and, in the case of the letter, bear sufficient postage. The effectiveness on dispatch could not be very well supported were it not for the virtual certainty of delivery of a properly addressed letter placed in the United States mails. An improperly addressed letter is less likely to arrive safely, and, even if a good argument can be made for the occurrence of mutual assent on dispatch, the improperly addressed letter would seem to create more risk to the offeror than he intended to bear. Under circumstances where custom and usage make an acceptance effective on dispatch, the withdrawal of a letter of acceptance from the mails, as is permitted by postal regulations, creates special problems. Rather than abolish altogether the long-accepted practice of finding acceptances, in proper circumstances, to be binding on dispatch, most authorities appear to take the view that the withdrawal of a letter of acceptance does not alter the fact that a contract has come into existence. There is a contrary view to the effect that modern postal regulations have destroyed the justification for mailed acceptances becoming effective on dispatch.

If an acceptance is made in an unauthorized manner or arrives too late, the offeror does not have the power to waive the defect in the acceptance and treat the acceptance as complete. The faulty acceptance is a counter-offer and a rejection of the original offer. The original offeror can create a binding contract only by accepting the offer made to him by the original offeree.

The time and place at which an acceptance becomes effectively communicated are important not only because they may serve to determine whether there is a binding contract between the parties, but also because they are useful in interstate transactions, in determining which state's law is to be applied to the particular situation. Where the offeror and the offeree live in different states, the contract is usually said to be made in the state where the acceptance became effective. This is important because the law of the state where the contract was made generally governs the validity of the contract. It is not unusual for a contract to be valid in one state and invalid in another. If the contract is valid in the state where it was made, then the issues of validity cannot, ordinarily, be raised elsewhere.

E. Situations Where Consent Is Not Real

IN GENERAL. It was assumed during the discussion of offer and acceptance that the consent manifested by these two mechanical steps leading to mutual assent was not induced by mistake or fraud or threats or force. Were we to follow literally and in all circumstances the general rule that the outward manifestations of a person's state of mind are conclusive as to his consent to being bound by the terms of a contract, we would not be interested in such topics as mistake or fraud or duress. But it would obviously be unfair to hold a person to the terms of a contract to which he had assented at the point of a gun or as a result of the intentional misrepresentations of the other party.

It is less obviously unfair where a person has expressed assent as the result of a mistake. That the law should protect the victim in cases of fraud or duress or even of some mistakes is clear, but the legal analysis behind this conclusion is not always clear, nor is it uniform. It is sometimes said that a contract comes into existence in spite of the fraud or mistake, but that the fraud or mistake may give the innocent party the right to avoid the contract. The theory is that the assent is nonetheless real for having been induced by fraud or mistake, and consequently a contract is formed. Another view is that the absence of reality prevents a genuine assent or meeting of the minds, and thus no contract comes into existence. As a practical matter, a more useful approach lies somewhere in between these two extremes. It will be seen below that in some situations the event which keeps the consent from being real will also prevent the formation of any contract, while in other situations a contract comes into existence subject to the right of the party or parties so entitled to avoid the contract. In still other situations, the event may have no legal effect at all.

Some events that may have an effect upon the reality of the consent of the parties are mistake, fraud, undue influence, duress, and menace. Whether the effect is a void contract or a voidable contract or no effect at all depends upon which of these events is present and on the circumstances of the particular case. If the effect is a void contract, no court action is necessary in order to avoid the contract. Quasi-contractual principles may have to be applied in order to prevent unjust enrichment resulting from part performance. Where the effect of the lack of real consent is a voidable contract, the contract is valid but is subject to the right of one or more of the parties to avoid it.

The process by which such voidable contracts are avoided is called *rescission*. This term has a number of different meanings including simply "to abrogate, annul or cancel." As used here, however, the term carries an additional connotation, usually referred to as *restitution*, of return of consideration and restoration to *status quo ante*. Unless otherwise indicated, the term "rescission" will be used to include both ideas. Where there has been a mistake in reducing the oral agreement of the parties to written form, another remedy, called *reformation*, is used. As will be seen later in this chapter, oral testimony will usually not be received for the purpose of varying the terms of a written agreement, but where it can be shown that there was a mistake in converting the intentions of the parties into writing, the court may receive the oral testimony and reform the writing to conform with the intentions of the parties. It should be noted in this connection that the contract is not being reformed. Only the writing is changed in order that it will conform to the antecedent expressions on which the parties agreed. Reformation cannot be used to enforce terms to which the parties never agreed.

MISTAKE. *In general.* Everyone has, at one time or another, done something which he would not have done but for some erroneous belief. For example, one may drive across town to the Tower Theater to see a movie that one believed was showing but was not. Although the word "mistake" has other meanings, the meaning that is relevant to our present discussion is much like that expressed in the previous sentence. A mistake is a thought that does not conform to the facts or to the truth. Obviously, a mere thought has no legal effect, but thoughts often induce action, and action may have all sorts of legal effects. Furthermore, we are all familiar with the idea that the nature of a thought that induces action has much to do with the legal effects of that action. First degree murder and justifiable homicide have quite different legal effects for the offender, and the difference is controlled solely by the thought which induced the act of killing. We are here concerned with the legal effects, if any, of acts induced by mistaken thoughts.

Like most other humans, lawyers and judges like to classify their material for the purpose of analyzing it and drawing conclusions. It simplifies one's work if Result #1 can always (or usually) be applied to Category A and Result #2 to Category B, but differences between the categories do not always justify the differences in result. In a sense, many of the legal classifications of mistakes have been made in such a way that they do not justify all the differences in the rules that are applied to them. Different consequences are often attached, or said to be attached, to mutual mistakes, where both parties make the same mistake, than to unilateral mistakes, where only one party makes the particular mistake. Actually, there are many other factors that must be taken into consideration, and usually, the difference in consequence is better explained in terms of differences in the other factors than in terms of the difference between mutual and unilateral mistakes.

It is frequently said that there is no relief available for a unilateral mistake or for a mistake of law, but many courts do grant relief for these mistakes and with much the same analysis as is applied to mutual mistakes and mistakes of fact. It has never been satisfactorily explained why mistakes of fact and of law should be treated differently, though many courts make the distinction and apply different results.

In the small space available here, it is not possible to examine in detail the historical and theoretical background of the law having to do with mistake. There is no avoiding the fact that in many, perhaps most, courts the distinction between unilateral and mutual mistakes and between mistakes of fact and of law does have some importance. Consequently, much of the following discussion will be framed within the traditional categories. The reader may wish to speculate and to draw his own conclusions as to what the really influential factors should be in each kind of situation.

Factors important in determining the legal effects of mistakes. In order to provide the best possible basis for appraising the specific situations discussed below, it seems wise to outline briefly some of the many factors that the courts through the years have found important in deciding mistake cases. Clearly, not all of these factors will be applicable in a given case and not all of the applicable factors will be of equal importance, but in almost all situations there will be several factors of sufficient importance to justify consideration. The factors listed below are phrased as questions. The list is not by any means exhaustive.

1. Has either party, or a third person, changed his position in such a way that he cannot be returned to the *status quo*?
2. Was the mistaken party negligent?
3. Did both parties make a mistake?
4. Did one party *cause* the other party's mistake?
5. Did one party know of the other's mistake, or should he have known?
6. Was the mistake one concerning an important matter?
7. Was the risk of the mistake assumed by one of the parties?
8. What remedies are available?
9. When was the mistake discovered and the other party notified?
10. Was the mistake one concerning a matter of fact or a matter of opinion?
11. What was the result of the mistake?
12. Is the contract wholly or partly executed?

Mistakes that prevent the formation of a contract. In two types of mutual mistakes, it is generally held that the mistake prevents the formation of a contract. Where there is a mutual mistake as to the identity of the subject matter, the contract is rendered void. In the famous old case of *Raffles* v. *Wichelhaus,*[4] a buyer agreed to buy and a seller to sell the cotton arriving from Bombay on the ship *Peerless*. Neither party knew that there were two ships named *Peerless* arriving from Bombay or that the seller was thinking of one ship and the buyer of the other. When no cotton arrived on the ship the buyer was thinking about, he sued the seller for breach of contract; when the buyer refused to accept and pay for the cotton on the ship the seller was thinking about, the seller sued the buyer for breach of contract. The court held there was no contract because of the mutual mistake as to the identity of the subject matter, and the case is probably the most cited case in the literature of mistake. But is the mutual mistake as to the identity of the subject matter really the only important factor? In the first place, it is not easy to describe the precise mistake that both parties made. The court said that it was in each party's believing that the other party was describing the same ship, but this mistake is not exactly the same for both parties. Suppose the court had found that the buyer should have known that there were two ships named *Peerless*? Might the court then fairly have placed the loss on the buyer because of his negligence? Perhaps the real reason for the decision was the fact that neither party was negligent, thereby causing harm to the other, and, consequently, there was no more reason to throw the loss on one party than on the other. Even on a simple set of facts such as this, it is obvious that the mutuality of the mistake is not as good an explanation for the result as are other factors.

---

[4] 2 Hurl. & C. 906 (1864).

The second type of mutual mistake said to prevent the formation of a contract is the mutual mistake as to the existence of the subject matter. Where something essential to the contract ceases to exist before the contract is made, there is no contract. Where A and B enter into a contract whereby one is to buy and the other to sell a mountain cabin and neither party knows at the time the contract is entered into that the cabin has been destroyed by fire, there is no contract. Does this mean that if one of the parties had known about the fire but the other had not there would have been no relief for the mistaken party? Of course not. Probably few courts would say that there was a *void* contract where only one of the parties was mistaken about the existence of the cabin, but certainly recission would be available to an innocently mistaken party under normal circumstances. The difference between mutual and unilateral mistakes often does result in a difference of remedy. Be sure to note that destruction of the subject matter after the contract is entered into is an entirely different problem. It will be considered in another section of this chapter.

Mistakes that may make the contract voidable. Whether the mistake is mutual or unilateral, it usually is said that no relief is available unless the mistake was as to some material fact outside the area of the bargain. This is just a way of saying that in order to justify court intervention the mistake must be as to something important, that the mistake must be as to a matter of fact and not of opinion, and that the fact about which the mistake was made must not be a fact over which the parties were bargaining. Although the value of the subject matter is usually important, it is a matter of opinion in most cases. Furthermore, the issues having to do with value are generally at the very heart of the thing the parties are bargaining about. A buyer cannot be allowed to rescind his contract on the ground that the commodity he has purchased turned out not to be as valuable or as attractive to other buyers as he thought it would be. Because value is within the bargaining area, the risk that the value of the commodity will be different from what the parties thought it would be is assumed by the buyer and the seller. But there are probably some situations where it cannot be said that the value was within the area of the bargain or that the parties consciously assumed the risk that the value might turn out to be different from what they had contemplated. The value of an old book may depend on whether it is a first edition or of some later edition. Can it not be argued that if the parties take for granted the book is a first edition and determine the price on that basis, the buyer has assumed the risk that the value of a first edition may be less than he thought but not the risk that the book is not a first edition at all? If the parties agree on the price, however, knowing that the book may be either a first or a later edition, the whole issue of the value would seem to be within the area of the bargain and both types of risk assumed by the parties.

A court will not permit one party knowingly to take advantage of the other party's mistake. Where, for example, one party's typographical or computational error changes a bid on a construction job from $20,000 to $20.00, the obvious error on the face of the bid would prevent the party to whom the bid was submitted from enforcing the contract against the bidder. The result should be the same where the error was not obvious but where the offeree had notice of the error before he accepted. If he accepted the offer without knowledge of the mistake, some courts would refuse relief to the mistaken party, while others would permit rescission if the error was a substantial one and notice to the nonmistaken party was sufficiently timely that he could still be placed in *status quo*. Some courts have made the negligence of the mistaken party the most important factor in such cases, on the ground that the innocent party should not be denied the advantages of his contract because of a careless error made by the other party, but the change of position by the innocent party should probably be the overriding factor.

Mistake of law. Because it is used so often in deciding mistake cases, the category "mistake of law" requires a few additional words before we move on to the other subjects. A mistake of law is often described as an erroneous conclusion with regard to the legal effects of known facts or circumstances. No person is presumed to know all of the law on which his rights depend, but perhaps the popular misconception in this matter lies behind the denial of relief in many courts in cases involving mistakes of law. As mentioned above, there is probably no sound reason why mistakes of law should be distinguished from mistakes of fact, as far as the issue of determining whether to grant relief is concerned. Fortunately, in most of the cases where relief has been denied on the ground that the mistake was one of law and, thus, an inadequate reason to justify court intervention, the facts of the cases have revealed other and sounder reasons on which the same result could be based. The best advice that can be given to the reader on this confusing problem is to analyze each situation in terms of the factors listed early in this section and to avoid the use of classifications such as mistakes of "law" and of "fact" and "mutual" and "unilateral" mistakes, while recognizing that in one's own state these arbitrary classifications may, nonetheless, have considerable significance.

FRAUD. *In general.* Fraud, or intentional misrepresentation, may cause a contract to be voidable, as is usually the case, or may result in a void contract. Fraud in the inducement, that is, fraud that persuades or induces a person to enter into a contract the nature of which he knows, results in a voidable contract. Fraud in the inception or in the procurement, fraud as to the very nature of the contract into which a person enters, results in a void contract. The latter type of fraud is comparatively rare and will be referred to only briefly below. The courts have never defined fraud precisely nor even made the attempt. The reason is that the courts have always felt that were fraud to be defined in exact terms, it would not take the ingenious "bad man" very long to devise methods that would circumvent the language of the definition while still bringing about fraudulent ends by fraudulent means. Fraud is defined or described in broad, general terms with sufficient flexibility to take care of changing methods or schemes and yet sufficiently detailed to enable a court to apply the terms fairly to actual situations.

The best definition of fraud is really no more than a list of the basic elements that go to make it up. *Fraud* is the misrepresentation or concealment of a material fact, made with knowledge of its falsity, with the intent to induce the person to whom it is made to act upon it, and which is acted upon to the damage of the person so acting.

Misrepresentation of a material fact. The representation must be a statement of fact and not just a statement of opinion. The statement that a house is "worth" $20,000 is a statement of opinion because value and worth are matters of opinion. A statement that a house "cost" $20,000 is a statement of fact because it is something ascertainable without reference to opinion. Of course, a statement prefaced by the words, "It is my opinion," or, "I believe," is generally a statement of opinion and not of fact. In certain special situations misrepresentations of opinion have been held to be sufficient to establish fraud. For example, where A holds himself out as being specially qualified to give opinions on certain matters and B is so situated that he may reasonably rely on the opinion of the expert, $A's$ misrepresentation of his opinion may be fraudulent. Where A, an expert, is trying to sell a painting to B and represents to B that it is his, $A's$, opinion the painting is a Renoir when actually that is not $A's$ opinion at all, there is, in effect, a misrepresentation of a material fact, namely, $A's$ expert opinion. Similar results have been reached where opinions are stated as facts, where an opinion implies a knowledge of the facts, and where the opinion is that of a fiduciary or of another trusted person.

It should be noted that assertions that a product is the "best," or is "incomparable," "unsurpassed," or "the finest," are usually mere dealer's puffing or advertising and not relied on by reasonable men. Theoretically, it can be ascertained whether a product is the "best" or not, and consequently these gaudy statements in reference to one's own product are, in one sense, statements of fact. However, they are neither intended nor understood, as a rule, to be statements of fact.

In order to be a statement of fact, a statement must refer to the past or to the present. No statement about the future can be more than an opinion. Predictions as to the future, unless they happen to come under one of the exceptions set forth in the paragraph above in connection with opinions, cannot be statements of fact.

In addition to being statements of fact, the requirements of fraud are not met unless the fact referred to is a *material* fact. A misrepresentation of some minor, inconsequential fact in a contract transaction will not justify the rescission of a contract on fraud grounds. Where B is negotiating for a piece of land on which to raise cotton, a false statement by A, the owner, that he has grown fine cotton crops for many years on the land is a statement of a material fact. It is probably the moving influence in the contract. Where, in the same situation, A states falsely that the nearest neighbors two miles down the road are fine, congenial people, the representation is not of a material fact and possibly, not even of a fact.

While silence, in and of itself, does not satisfy the requirements of fraud, active concealment of facts material to the contract is sufficient. Where, for example, a used car dealer stuffs the gear box or differential of a car with heavy grease or sawdust in order to conceal temporarily the defective and noisy condition of the gears, his active concealment is just as fraudulent as a false statement. If the dealer had left the gears alone but had simply failed to tell the buyer about them, there would have been no fraud. There is ordinarily no duty on either a buyer or a seller to give the other relevant information about the transaction even though such information may materially affect the value of the subject matter. A duty to speak may be present because of a relation of trust and confidence between the two parties, as with an attorney and a client, or a guardian and a ward, or a trustee and a beneficiary, but does not arise where the parties are dealing at arms length. Compare this discussion with the topic of "warranties" in Chapter 10.

Knowledge of falsity.   It is not enough that the party make a false statement. He must know that it is false. The misrepresentation is not intentional where the person making it does not know it is wrong. Technically, actual knowledge of falsity is not required. If the person who makes the statement has no belief in the truth of the statement and makes it recklessly without knowing whether it is true or false, that is enough to satisfy this element of fraud. This result is proper. A person who does not know whether a statement is true or false but makes the statement simply because he thinks it will persuade the other party to act is just as fraudulent in his actions as if he knew the statement to be false.

Intent to induce the other party to act.   Even though there is a misrepresentation of a material fact, made with knowledge of its falsity, there is no fraud unless there is also an intention by the representer that a particular person or group of persons or some single person out of a defined class of persons rely upon the representation. If A makes a false statement to B intending B to rely on it, the grounds of fraud will be available to B as a defense or as the basis for rescission, but if C overhears A's false statement and relies on it, fraud is not available to C unless A intended C also to rely on it. The representer is liable only to those persons to whom the statement was made with such intent. Where a businessman supplies false information to such organizations as Dun and Bradstreet, he may find fraud used as a defense or as grounds for recission of a contract entered into with a bank or with some other person who relied on the false information obtained through Dun's.

It is obvious that the class of persons whom the businessman intended to rely on his false statements included those who subscribe to Dun's services.

Reliance. It is necessary, before fraud can be established, that the person to whom the representations were made rely on them. If the person did not rely on the false statements but conducted his own investigation and entered the contract on the basis of information obtained by himself, there are no grounds for fraud. Note, however, that the buyer of the used car in the situation discussed above may still be able to rescind on fraud grounds, even though he checked the car carefully himself, if the fact that the gears were quiet induced him not to examine the gears. The reliance must also be reasonable. Reliance on statements that no ordinary man would have relied on will probably destroy the basis for fraud. However, if all the other elements are present, unreasonable reliance may not be a major factor.

Resulting damage. Although some courts say that actual damage resulting from fraud is not necessary in order for the defrauded party to rescind the contract, what these courts are really saying is that there is almost invariably damage, and where there is no damage, the issue of fraud never comes up. For example, when *B* buys *A's* land on the strength of *A's* false statement that he has grown cotton there, *B* may rescind the contract if the land is less valuable than it would have been had the statements of *A* been true. If, however, it turns out that oil underlies the land and the land is much more valuable as oil land than as cotton land, *B* is not very likely to want to rescind. Naturally, *A* cannot seek to rescind on the basis of his own fraud. Nor would "mistake" be available to *A*, as has already been seen. Damage is ordinarily proved by evidence that the contract would have been more valuable to the innocent party had the statements been true.

Remedies of the injured party. Where the injured party's consent is induced by fraud, the contract is voidable at the option of the injured party. If the contract has been performed, the injured party must act promptly to rescind after he discovers the fraud and must return or offer to return the consideration which he received. In the cotton land example, the injured party must return or offer to return the land to the seller at the same time he demands the return of his purchase price. If the seller refuses, the legal machinery of the courts will have to be employed. If the injured party fails to act promptly, he loses his right to rescind and may only sue for damages, which will be measured by the difference between the value of the land he received and the price he paid for the land as cotton land. *B* may elect from the beginning to retain the land and sue for the damages instead of rescinding. The action for damages would be one in tort for deceit. Under the Code, neither rescission nor rejection nor return of the goods is a barrier or is deemed inconsistent with a claim for damages for fraud.

Where the contract is executory, the injured party may simply do nothing, and if the other party brings an action to enforce the contract, the injured party may use fraud as a defense. The injured party may take the initiative and sue in equity to have the contract declared void.

Fraud in the inception. The discussion thus far has been confined to those situations where the fraud simply induced a party to enter into a contract with the nature, terms, and details of which he was familiar. Fraud in the inception occurs when there is fraud as to the very nature of the contract, as where a warehouseman asks a party who is withdrawing his goods from storage to sign a receipt, but the document supplied by the warehouseman is a promissory note. The situation is not the same as that discussed earlier where a party was held to the terms of a contract he had signed without reading. Here there has been fraud in representing the contract to be one thing when actually it was another. The effect of fraud in the inception is to make the contract void. The novel, *Double Indemnity,* by James M. Cain, and the movie based on it, contain a good example of fraud in the inception. By aligning the pages in such a way as to expose only the bottom lines for signature, an insurance salesman obtained the signature of a policyholder on a double indemnity accident policy when the policyholder thought that he was signing several copies of an automobile policy renewal. Once it was discovered how the signature was obtained, the accident policy would, of course, be held void.

Stipulation against the effect of fraud. It should be obvious that one party to a contract who has been guilty of fraud in the inducement cannot remove the effects of fraud or absolve himself by any stipulation in the contract. The result is the same whether the stipulation is that no representations have been made or that any right that might be based on them is waived. The court would ignore such a stipulation and would admit evidence of fraud. The reason is simple. The fraud renders the whole contract voidable, including the stipulation. Fraud in the inception would present an even clearer case to the same end.

Where the false representations are made by an agent, and the contract contains a recital limiting the authority of the agent to make representations, the courts arrive at varying conclusions. The better view, and the one adopted by the Agency Restatement, is that such a stipulation will protect the innocent principal from a tort action for damages but will not prevent the defrauded party from rescinding the contract. Some courts hold that the principal cannot escape the effect of the fraudulent statements of the agent made within the scope of the agent's actual or apparent authority. Others hold that the third party is bound on the contract despite the fraud of the agent. A few courts have taken the view that the third party is bound except where the fraud of the agent prevented the third party from reading the contract or giving it full and free consideration.

Innocent misrepresentation. Intentional misrepresentation is fraud. *Innocent misrepresentation* occurs where a party makes false statements concerning a material fact while believing them to be true. The effect on the other party is exactly the same as though the misrepresentations had been made with knowledge of their falsity. Consequently, the remedy of recission is available to the injured party. But no action in tort for damages is possible because the element of *intentional* misrepresentation, which is necessary for the tort of fraud or deceit, is missing. Innocent misrepresentation does not include the situation where the person making the representations makes them without regard to their truth of falsity. This, we have already learned, is the equivalent of actual knowledge of falsity. Innocent misrepresentation cases do not often appear in the courts on that issue since in most of such situations, mutual mistakes can be worked out, and the cases come up on those grounds instead.

UNDUE INFLUENCE. Undue influence is most frequently charged in connection with contracts between persons in confidential relationships, such as parent and child, trustee and beneficiary, guardian and ward, or attorney and client. *Undue influence* consists of the abuse by one person of the dominion or control which he has over another person, or of the confidence which the other person places in him. It arises where one person is under the mental domination of another person or where the relation between them is such that one is justified in believing that the other will act in his best interests or for his welfare. Where the person in the inferior position has had independent advice in connection with the transaction, undue influence is not likely to be found. It is clear that the presence of undue influence prevents a real and voluntary mutual assent. One person, in effect, is acting for both. The contract is rendered voidable and may be rescinded by the party in the inferior position.

In addition to the confidential relationships, undue influence may be found under other circumstances as well. Factors other than the confidential relationship may be useful evidence in demonstrating the presence of undue influence. The financial or other distress of one of the parties may have put him at the mercy of the other party. Mental weakness, physical infirmity, or extreme youth or age may be important in proving undue influence, although not enough by themselves. Inadequate consideration may also be valuable evidence. It is important to note that where no confidential relationship exists, the burden is generally on the party seeking to avoid the contract to show that undue influence was exercised. Where the confidential relationship is present, the burden is usually on the person in the dominant position to show that he did not take advantage of his position, that the transaction was fair and equitable, and that the party in the inferior position was not prevented from using his own judgment and discretion. For all practical purposes, a contract in the latter situation is presumed voidable until the dominant party can show that undue influence was not used.

Section 497 of the Contracts Restatement states the cause and the effect of undue influence in these words:

> Where one party is under the domination of another, or by virtue of the relation between them is justified in assuming that the other party will not act in a

manner inconsistent with his welfare, a transaction induced by unfair persuasion by the latter, is induced by undue influence and is voidable.

Undue influence is a factor not only in contract situations but also in the revocation of gifts and in the contest of wills.

DURESS. *Duress* consists of a wrongful act that compels assent through fear. There may be either a *duress of person* or a *duress of goods*. The former consists of the unlawful confinement of the party himself, his wife, another member of his family, or of a close relative, or of confinement of any of these, lawful in form, but obtained fraudulently. The latter consists of the unlawful detention of the property of the party. The effect of either type of duress is to make the contract voidable at the option of the party under duress. Where duress causes a person to give an apparent assent when he does not really know the nature of the transaction, the result is the same as in cases of fraud in the inception, namely, the contract is void.

In order for there to be a duress, the act generally must be unlawful. It must be a tort or a crime. A refusal to pay money owed or a threat to breach a contract, as a means of compelling another to enter into a new agreement, is not sufficient for a duress, because the aggrieved party has his remedy at law and is not found by the courts in these situations to be under improper compulsion. An illegal attachment of goods, on the other hand, where a contract is used to obtain the release of the goods, is an unlawful act, and a duress would be present. A false criminal prosecution or imprisonment in order to induce a contract is duress.

In some jurisdictions, an unlawful act to induce a contract and a threat of an unlawful act for the same purpose are both classified as duress. In other jurisdictions, the former is duress; the latter is called *menace*. The legal effect is the same in both cases.

MENACE. Broadly speaking, *menace* is a threat to commit duress as described above. It also includes a threat of injury to the person or to the character of the party, his wife, family, or close relative. A threat of criminal prosecution or of imprisonment is a threat of injury to the character and constitutes menace. The underlying theory with both duress and menace is that a person is deprived by fear of his ability to exercise his will freely, but it is necessary that there be more than mere acts or statements causing apprehension. The fear must arise from the commission or the threat of commission of unlawful acts.

F. Interpretation and Construction of
the Contract—the Parol Evidence Rule

INTERPRETATION AND CONSTRUCTION. *In general.* Even if language could be used in such a way as to remove all possible doubts in regard to its meaning, it is not likely that it would always be so used, and problems of ascertaining the meanings of the expressions and manifestations of the parties would remain. The very nature of language, futhermore, makes it incapable of precise meanings and impressions which are the same to everyone under all circumstances. Consequently, on many occasions the courts must construe and interpret the language of a contract before the law can be correctly applied to that contract. Of course, in most contracts, language is used with sufficient care and with sufficient attention to the issue of whether all the parties have the same understanding of it, that they get by without any major problems of interpretation. Very few contracts escape without minor controversies as to meaning. Where the language of the contract is clear and not foolish, the court will follow the meaning of the contract as expressed, but if the meaning is unclear, the language of the contract must be interpreted by the court according to rather well-established rules. It is not the purpose of interpretation to change or alter or rewrite the contract. The purpose is to give effect, as nearly as possible, to the intentions of the parties when they entered into the agreement. It is obvious that what the parties say about their intentions at the time of the controversy between them is not very good evidence of what their intentions were at the time the contract was made. A basic rule of interpretation is that all contracts, with a few exceptions, should be interpreted according to the same rules.

Rules of interpretation. There is neither the space nor the need to examine all of the rules of interpretation. The important and basic rules are sufficient to resolve all but the most unusual interpretation problems. Note that some of the rules set forth below are simple, arbitrary prescriptions, easy to apply, while others require the highest measure of judgment and discretion on the part of the court.

> 1. The fundamental rule of interpretation is that the contract must be construed in such a way as to give effect to the intentions of the parties as those intentions were at the time the contract was made.
>
> 2. The intentions of the parties must be ascertained from the language which the parties used.
>
> 3. The words are to be understood in their ordinary and popular sense unless used by the parties in a technical sense, or unless a special meaning is given to them by usage or by custom.
>
> 4. Technical words are to be interpreted as usually understood by persons in the profession or business to which they relate, unless clearly used in a different sense.
>
> 5. The whole of the contract is to be taken together, so as to give effect to every part, if reasonably practicable, each clause helping to interpret the other.
>
> 6. A contract may be explained by reference to the circumstances under which it was made, and the matter to which it relates.

7. Acts of the parties and constructions placed on the contract by the parties subsequent to its making but prior to the controversy may be used in determining the meaning.

8. The construction should be one which will make the contract reasonable, operative and lawful. Interpretations making the contract valid are preferred over those which make it invalid.

9. Where general provisions are inconsistent with specific provisions, the specific provisions will control. However, words in the contract which are wholly inconsistent with the apparent main purpose of the contract are to be rejected.

10. Where inconsistent, written parts will control printed parts.

11. In cases of uncertainty not removed by the other rules, the contract will be interpreted most strongly against the party who drew up the contract or caused the uncertainty to exist. An insurance policy, for example, will be most strongly construed against the insurance company.

12. Usage or custom may be resorted to for the purpose of explaining the meaning of language and implying terms, unless there is a clear intention to the contrary.

13. Interpretation will favor a bilateral over a unilateral contract because the former gives immediate protection to both parties.

14. Obvious mistakes in drafting will not be allowed to affect the interpretation if the meaning is otherwise clear.

The Uniform Commercial Code contains elaborate provisions for the construction and interpretation of contracts within its scope. See especially those provisions having to do with sales contracts, Sections 2-301 through 2-328, discussed in Chapter 10.

THE PAROL EVIDENCE RULE. *In general.* A much misunderstood rule serves to limit the use of oral evidence to alter, vary, or add to the terms of written instruments. The rule applies to deeds, wills, and other instruments in addition to contracts, but the latter are our concern here. The theory behind the rule is a simple one. When the terms of a contract are embodied in a written instrument, it is usually fair and reasonable to presume that the parties intended to make the writing the complete expression of their agreement. To take any other view would destroy any advantage a written agreement may have over an oral one and would remove the primary reason for reducing contracts to written form. Every part of the written contract would be subject to change by the introduction of oral evidence that during the negotiation period the parties had agreed on something else.

The *parol evidence rule* is usually stated as follows: When the terms of a contract have been reduced to writing and the writing appears to be a complete contract, no oral evidence of any other agreement concerning the subject matter of the contract, made before or at the same time as the execution of the contract, is admissible to vary or add to the terms of the written contract.

If this rule were simply a rule of evidence, it would be waived by the party who failed to object to the admission of matters inadmissible under the rule. This is generally not the case, and the rule is correctly looked upon as a rule of substantive law under which the inadmissible evidence will be excluded or disregarded whether a party objects to it or not. The written instrument is, as a matter of law, the contract between the parties, and extrinsic evidence is excluded, therefore, because it is not relevant to proof of the terms of the agreement. The parol evidence rule should not be confused with the statute of frauds which requires certain contracts to be in writing in order to be enforced, while the parol evidence rule requires that if a contract is in writing, no oral evidence can be admitted to change it.

Where A and B enter into a contract whereby B is to paint A's house for a fixed price and to finish by a certain time and these terms are reduced to writing, A may not later use oral evidence to show that B had really agreed to do the job for a lower price or to finish the job earlier or to paint the house every year at the same price. The writing *is* the contract as a matter of law, and oral evidence of conflicting agreements made before the execution of the writing or at the same time will not be admitted. B does not have to plead the parol evidence rule as a defense.

Where the rule does not apply.   Like any other rule there are situations to which the parol evidence rule does not apply, and there are also exceptions to the rule. Generally speaking, the parol evidence rule operates only where the written instrument appears on its face to be complete. Where it does not so appear, parol evidence may be admitted. The parol evidence rule does not operate where the contract is invalid, and oral evidence may be admitted to show the invalidity. Set forth below are a number of exceptions to the rule and specific situations to which the rule is not applicable.

Evidence concerning validity or legal effect.   Oral evidence of mistake, fraud, duress, undue influence, or illegality is admissible even though a contract has been reduced to writing. The purpose of introducing this evidence is not to alter or contradict the terms of the writing but to show that the whole instrument is invalid or lacks legal effect. By the same token, extrinsic evidence may be used to show the lack of consideration, subject, of course, to the effect of the seal in some states. An agreement lacking in consideration is invalid and unenforceable. Even if a contract contains a recital of consideration, the recital is not binding, and oral evidence may be introduced to show the actual lack of consideration. Parol evidence is also admissible to contradict a recital of the amount or kind of executed consideration, but where the consideration consists of executory promises, parol evidence will not be admitted to alter or add to these promises. Where a contract recites the consideration of $500 when actually it was a farm tractor and a stamp collection, extrinsic evidence will be admitted to show the true consideration. But where the consideration is an unperformed promise, parol evidence will be excluded. The Code has made certain changes in the law with respect to consideration. These are discussed elsewhere in this chapter.

Where a writing appears on its face to be complete, parol evidence may still be admitted to show that the writing was not intended as a final act but was to take effect either not at all or after some condition had been performed. Where the contract was a sham and not intended to have any legal effect, oral evidence will be admitted to show the intention of the parties. Where a party is trying to introduce oral evidence to show that the effect of the contract depended on the occurrence of some condition, the evidence will be admitted to show that there was no contract at all until the condition occurred, but the evidence will not be admitted to show that one of the terms is not to take effect or to show that the obligations of the contract were to be terminated by the happening of a condition. In the latter case, a valid contract exists until the condition happens, and parol evidence would be excluded.

Evidence to prove an integration. When the parties adopt a writing as the final and complete expression of their agreement, the parol evidence rule comes into operation. This final and complete expression is called, in modern legal literature, an *integration*. It is obvious that a rather common problem would be whether or not there had been an integration. Some hold that if the face of the instruments is complete, this may be taken as conclusive proof of integration. The better view is that parol evidence is admissible to prove or disprove an integration. That the writing was not an integration may be shown by the language of the writing itself or by extrinsic evidence. The minutes of a meeting, a receipt, and an offer are examples of such evidence.

Where there is an integration, parol evidence is not admissible to alter the terms of that integration, but is admissible in order to ascertain the meaning of the instrument. In other words, parol evidence may be admitted for purposes of interpretation. This is not so where the problem of interpretation involves matters of intention. Parol evidence may be used to explain ambiguities, and, by the modern view, to show the meaning of words even though no ambiguity is asserted.

The Code adopted a more liberal view than any described in the preceding paragraph. Even a writing intended by the parties as the final expression of their agreement may be explained or supplemented by extrinsic or parol evidence, unless the court affirmatively determines that the writing was intended by the parties as a complete and exclusive statement of the terms of the agreement. Course of dealing, usage of the trade, course of performance, and even consistent additional terms may thus be admitted in evidence.

Evidence of subsequent oral agreement. The parol evidence rule does not apply to evidence of agreements entered into by the parties subsequent to the execution of the writing, and such evidence may be introduced to alter, vary, or add to the terms of a writing. It is obvious that the policy behind the rules does not apply in this situation. Parties to a contract have the right to make any changes or to cancel the contract completely if they so desire. The parol evidence rule is designed to prevent the use or oral evidence of other agreements made prior to or at the same time as the writing to change the terms of the contract expressed in the writing.

Miscellaneous. Extrinsic evidence may be admitted to show that a party to a contract acted only as an agent for an undisclosed principal who is bound by and who may enforce the contract.

3. VALIDITY AND ENFORCEABILITY— CONSIDERATION

A. Cases

(1)

William E. Story, Sr.,was the uncle of William E. Story, 2d. At the celebration of the golden wedding of his father and mother, on the 20th day of March, 1869, in the presence of the family and invited guests, William E. Story, Sr. promised his nephew that if he would refrain from drinking, using tobacco, swearing, and playing cards or billiards for money until he became 21 years of age, he would pay him the sum of $5,000. The nephew assented thereto, and fully performed the conditions inducing the promise. When the nephew arrived at the age of 21 years, and on the 31st day of January, 1875, he wrote to his uncle, informing him that he had performed his part of the agreement, and had thereby become entitled to the sum of $5,000. The uncle received the letter, and a few days later, on the 6th day of February, he wrote and mailed to his nephew the following letter:

> Buffalo, Feb. 6, 1875.
> W. E. Story, Jr.
> Dear Nephew:
>
> Your letter of the 31st ult. came to hand all right, saying that you had lived up to the promise made to me several years ago. I have no doubt but you have, for which you shall have five thousand dollars, as I promised you. I had the money in the bank the day you was twenty-one years old that I intend for you, and you shall have the money certain. Now, Willie, I do not intend to interfere with this money in any way till I think you are capable of taking care of it, and the sooner that time comes the better it will please me. I would hate very much to have you start out in some adventure that you thought all right and lose this money in one year. The first five thousand dollars that I got together cost me a heap of hard work. You would hardly believe me when I tell you that to obtain this I shoved a jack-plane many a day, butchered three or four years, then came to this city, and, after three months' perseverance, I obtained a situation in a grocery store. I opened this store early, closed late, slept in the fourth story of the building in a room 30 × 40 feet, and not a human being in the building but myself. All this

I done to live as cheap as I could to save something. I don't want you to take up with this kind of fare. I was here in the cholera season of '49 and '52, and the deaths averaged 80 to 125 daily, and plenty of small-pox. I wanted to go home, but Mr. Fisk, the gentleman I was working for, told me, if I left them, after it got healthy he probably would not want me. I stayed. All the money I have saved I know just how I got it. It did not come to me in any mysterious way, and the reason I speak of this is that money got in this way stops longer with a fellow that gets it with hard knocks than it does when he finds it. Willie, you are twenty-one, and you have many a thing to learn yet. This money you have earned much easier than I did, besides acquiring good habits at the same time, and you are quite welcome to the money. Hope you will make good use of it. I was ten long years getting this together after I was your age. Now, hoping this will be satisfactory, I stop. . . .

Truly yours,
W. E. Story

P.S. You can consider this money on interest.

The nephew received the letter, and thereafter consented that the money should remain with his uncle in accordance with the terms and conditions of the letter. The uncle died on the 29th day of January, 1887, without having paid over to his nephew any portion of the said $5,000 and interest.

Is the nephew entitled to the $5,000 and interest?

[*Hamer* v. *Sidway,* 124 N.Y. 538, 27 N.E. 256 (1891)]

(2)

On January 16, 1902, "articles of agreement" were executed by the defendant Joseph Schweizer, his wife, Ernestine, and Count Oberto Gulinelli. The agreement is in Italian. We quote from a translation the part essential to the decision of this controversy:

> Whereas, Miss Blanche Josephine Schweizer, daughter of said Mr. Joseph Schweizer and of said Mrs. Ernestine Teresa Schweizer is now affianced to and is to be married to the above said Count Oberto Giacomo Giovanni Francisco Maria Gulinelli: Now in consideration of all that is herein set forth the said Mr. Joseph Schweizer promises and expressly agrees by the present contract to pay annually to his said daughter, Blanche, during his own life and to send her, during her lifetime, the sum of two thousand five hundred dollars, or the equivalent of said sum in francs, the first payment of said amount to be made on the 20th day of January, 1902.

Later articles provided that "for the same reason heretofore set forth," Mr. Schweizer will not change the provision made in his will for the benefit of his daughter and her issue, if any. The yearly payments in the event of his death are to be continued by his wife.

On January 20, 1902, the marriage occurred. On the same day, the defendant made the first payment to his daughter. He continued the payments annually until 1912. If the father stopped making the payments, could the agreement be enforced?

[*De Cicco* v. *Schweizer,* 221 N.Y. 431, 117 N.E. 807 (1917)]

(3)

Price and McMichael entered into the following contract:

This Contract and Agreement entered into on this 25th day of February, 1929, by and between Harley T. Price, doing business as the Sooner Sand Company, party of the first part, and W. M. McMichael, party of the second part, Witnesseth:
Whereas, the party of the first part is engaged in the business of selling and shipping sand from Tulsa, Oklahoma, to various points in the United States; and, Whereas, the party of the second part is the owner of a plot of ground hereinafter described as follows, to-wit:
Lot 11, Section 11, Township 19 North,
Range 12 East, Tulsa County, and,
Whereas, the party of the second part has agreed to build a switch connecting with the Frisco Railway and having its terminal in or at said plot of ground above described; and,
Whereas, the party of the first part is desirous of buying and the party of the second part is desirous of selling various grades and qualities of sand as hereinafter set forth;
Now, therefore, in consideration of the mutual promises herein contained, the said second party agrees to furnish all of the sand of various grades and qualities which the first party can sell for shipment to various and sundry points outside of the City of Tulsa, Oklahoma, and to load all of said sand in suitable railway cars on said aforesaid switch for delivery to said Frisco Railway Company as initial carrier. Said second party agrees to furnish the quantity and quality of sand at all and various times as the first party may designate by written or oral order, and agrees to furnish and load same within a reasonable time after said verbal or written order is received.
In consideration of the mutual promises herein contained first party agrees to purchase and accept from second party all of the sand of various grades and quality which the said first party can sell, for shipment to various and sundry points outside of the City of Tulsa, Oklahoma, provided that the sand so agreed to be furnished and loaded by the said second party shall at least be equal to in quality and comparable with the sand of various grades sold by other sand companies in the City of Tulsa, Oklahoma, or vicinity. First party agrees to pay and the second party agrees to accept as payment and compensation for said sand so furnished and loaded, a sum per ton which represents sixty per cent (60%) of the current market price per ton of concrete sand at the place of destination of said shipment. It is agreed that statements are to be rendered by second party to first party every thirty days; the account is payable monthly by first party with a discount to be allowed by second party of four cents per ton for payment within ten days after shipment of any quantity of sand. . . .
This contract and agreement shall cover a period of ten years from the date

hereof, and shall be binding and effective during said period, and shall extend to the heirs, executors, administrators and assigns of both parties hereto. Dated this 25th day of February, 1929.

Sooner Sand Company,
By Harley T. Price,
Party of the first part.
W. M. McMichael,
By J. O. McMichael,
Party of the second part.

At the time the contract was executed, Price was not the owner of an established sand business. He was an experienced salesman of sand, which fact was well known to McMichael, and it was anticipated by both parties that on account of the experience, acquaintances, and connections of Price, he would be able to sell a substantial amount of sand to the mutual profit of the contracting parties. For the nine months immediately following the execution of the contract Price's average net profit per month was $516.88. In November, 1929, McMichael notified Price that he was repudiating the contract and would no longer consider himself bound thereby. He gave as his reason his belief that the contract was a mere offer and not a valid and binding contract.

[*McMichael* v. *Price,* 177 Okla. 186, 57 P. 2d 549 (1936)]

(4)

Carl Carbun, the corporate secretary of Hypocase, Inc., borrowed $5,000 from a friend, Elias Scrug, with which to pay the last instalment on his own past due income taxes. He promised to repay the money on February 17, 1969. On that date, Carl was still short of cash and unable to pay the loan. He stopped by Scrug's office late that afternoon and explained to Scrug his predicament, but Scrug was in a bad mood and did not seem willing to extend the loan for more than a few days. Just when it appeared that nothing could be worked out, Scrug suggested that he would be willing to accept Carbun's Aston-Scarab sports car in full payment of the loan. The car was worth at that time between four and five thousand dollars. Carbun agreed to this, but said that he could not deliver the car until the following Monday when his wife would return with the car from a trip to Denver. The delay was acceptable to Scrug, and the two parties made a written memorandum of their agreement. When Carbun delivered the car to Scrug on Monday, Scrug refused to accept it and demanded the immediate payment of the $5,000 loan. The reason for Scrug's change of heart may have been the bad publicity which the Aston-Scarab received as a result of two of those cars having blown up during the Le Jamb Rally the day before. Carbun insisted that Scrug take the car in payment of the loan, but Scrug said he was entitled to $5,000 in cash.

B. In General

Among non-lawyers, the least understood and most misunderstood aspect of contract law is that dealing with consideration. The problem is largely one of semantics. Most people translate consideration into price and price into money; thus, they arrive at the conclusion that consideration is just another word for money. Another cause of confusion is the fact that the requirement of consideration is, to some extent, a formality. At common law and in a few states, a seal is in effect a substitute for consideration because of the solemnity and formality incident to affixing a seal to an instrument. In the civil law countries, consideration in the common law sense is not a necessary prerequisite to a binding contract..

Consideration came into our contract law as the result of a long series of fortuitous circumstances combined with pressure from the commercial community for better enforcement of simple promises. The doctrine of consideration still bears the mark of its ancestry. Consideration was not the only possible solution to the problems which gave rise to it, and it was not itself a thoroughly satisfactory solution to these problems. Through the years, statutes and decisions have modified the doctrine considerably, and there has been an increasing realization in some quarters that the requirement of formality now satisfied by consideration can be adequately satisfied by other and simpler means. Perhaps, the anti-seal legislation has gone too far. The trend today appears to be in the direction of providing other types of simple formality by which a promisor can bind himself legally in the absence of consideration. The Uniform Written Obligations Act, for example, makes written promises enforceable without consideration if accompanied by a written statement that they are intended to be legally binding. Section 2-205 of the Uniform Commercial Code provides:

> An offer by a merchant to buy or sell goods in a signed writing which gives assurance that it will be held open needs no consideration to be irrevocable for a reasonable time or during a stated time but in no event for a time exceeding three months; but such term on a form supplied by the offeree must be separately signed by the offeror.

The Code retains the formal aspects of consideration by requiring the separate written statement and assurance that the promise is intended to be binding. The extension of these statutory changes in the doctrine of consideration to oral contracts would be difficult and inadvisable because of the lack of any convenient means of demonstrating compliance with the formalities.

The use of the seal in place of consideration did not develop as a result of the desire to find a simple substitute for consideration, as did the two statutes mentioned in the previous paragraph. The seal is one of the aspects of the formal, as compared with the simple, contract, and it developed long before the simple contract ever became conveniently enforceable and long before the concept of consideration arose. Technically, then, the seal never has been a "substitute" for consideration. It is rather a device by which a special type of contract is made binding at common law in situations where consideration has never been an issue. The use of the seal for this purpose has declined rapidly and remains in full effect in only a few states. The seal is not as satisfactory a way to supply the desirable formality as are the statutory devices set forth above. The seal lacks the express statement of intention to be bound by one's promise that is present in the other methods. Seals are still used for other purposes in all states and are not likely to vanish entirely.

Because the seal is still in use for some purposes, and in a few states for contract purposes, it is well to look briefly at the legal problems surrounding its use. As far as contract uses are concerned, it must be remembered that a contract under seal is binding only because of the formality of its execution under seal and not because the seal is consideration. A seal at common law consisted of an impression in wax affixed to the document or an impression in the document itself. The impression was originally of a coat of arms or some other heraldic device which served also to identify the parties involved. The signet ring supplied a convenient method of carrying one's seal on one's person. The seal was also frequently a substitute for a signature, necessary in feudal times because few, even of the nobility, could write. Today, however, the seal has not only lost its importance, it has also lost most of its beauty and distinction. The printed word "seal" and even a scrawl or scratch without the word "seal" have been held to be sufficient as a seal, as have been the letters "L.S." still found at the bottom of some legal documents. Since these letters are the initials of the words *locus sigilli*, meaning "the place of the seal," the courts have in effect held that the place for the seal is the seal itself. How low have the mighty fallen!

C. Nature of Consideration

The mere fact that one person has promised something to another does not create a legal duty to perform that promise or provide a remedy in the event the promise is not performed. In order to be enforceable, the promise must be accompanied by some other element or factor. This appears to be the case in all legal systems. In the common law system, this additional factor is usually called "consideration." We have already seen that in some jurisdictions the factor may still be provided by the "seal" or by some other special formality. Our task here is to examine some of the more important factors which the courts have held to constitute consideration and which, thus, make informal promises binding. Consideration is usually spoken of as *consideration for a promise,* that is, the consideration which makes a particular promise enforceable at law.

Before the discussion of consideration can go very much further, it must be pointed out that the offeror and offeree, to whom our attention was once directed, are no longer useful characters. We are not now interested in which party made the offer or in which party accepted it. Our concern has shifted to the persons who make promises and to the persons to whom promises are made. A person who makes a promise is known as a *promisor*. A person to whom a promise is made is known as a *promisee*. It should be noted that in a bilateral contract situation both parties have made promises and both have had promises made to them. The identities of the promisor and promisee depend upon which of the promises is under examination. The issue is easily solved in a law suit where one of the parties brings an action to enforce a promise made by the other party. The plaintiff, then, is the promisee and the defendant the promisor. Where *A*, for example, has promised to sell his shotgun to *B* for $95, and *B* has promised to buy it at that price, we have two promises, one by each of the parties. If *A* refuses to sell the gun and *B* brings an action against him, it is obvious that it is *A's* promise to sell which is at issue and not *B's* promise to buy. *A* is the promisor and *B* the promisee. Where the unilateral contract is involved, the promisor is easy to identify because only one party has made promises. The other party has performed an act.

Over the centuries, the courts and legal authorities have recommended a number of different factors as the *sine qua non* of consideration. It has been said that consideration for a promise is that which is bargained for and given in exchange for the promise. If any single view of consideration can be said to be dominant, then it is probably this view, but everyone recognizes that there are enforceable promises that are not really a part of any bargain. Legal detriment to the promisee and legal benefit to the promisor have also been suggested as the essence of consideration, but again there are exceptions. Furthermore, if the legal detriment or benefit is considered to be the binding effect of the contract, we have come to our conclusion by circularity of reasoning or by begging the question. It is sometimes proposed that consideration may be found in the "inducing cause" or the motivation for making the promise, but this view has its shortcomings too. These few brief comments by no means exhaust the list of factors which have (or may) be held to make a promise binding, but they do contain the more important and more frequently encountered suggestions. Probably, we should close this phase of our discussion by pointing out that it is an unusual business transaction that produces a consideration issue which could not be satisfactorily analyzed in terms of one, or a combination, of these enumerated factors. Two of these factors are examined in greater detail below.

Viewing consideration for a promise as that which is bargained for or given in exchange for the promise is a useful tool in the treatment of most problems. In a unilateral contract situation, the consideration to support the outstanding promise is usually found in the act already performed by the other party and for which the promisor expressly bargained. Where the promisor has promised to pay the promisee $500 if the promisee will deliver a certain quantity of some raw material to the promisor's loading dock, and the promisee has so delivered the material, it can easily be said that the promisor has received that which he bargained for and is bound by his promise to pay. It should be noted, however, that the promise just discussed would have been enforceable at common law long before the doctrine of consideration ever appeared, as an instance of the theory that a person ought to pay for what he has bargained for and received.

A more difficult situation to analyze is that of the bilateral contract, in connection with which it is often said that each promise is consideration for the other. Even here, however, the "bargained for" approach can be useful. In a sense, each party is bargaining for the promise of the other party, although, in another sense, each may be bargaining for what the promise affords rather than for the promise itself. Too much emphasis on the promise may lead to charges of circularity on the ground that it is really the binding effect of the promise that is sought, whereas there can be no binding effect unless there is consideration. Recognizing these shortcomings of the "bargained for" approach, it can still be a valuable analytical tool.

It is sometimes said that consideration consists of benefit to the promisor *or* detriment to the promisee. *Benefit* consists of the promisor's receiving or becoming entitled to receive performance to which he was not previously entitled. *Detriment* consists of the promisee's doing or becoming obligated to do something which he was not previously obligated to do. Thus, in the shotgun case, *A*, as promisor, became entitled to *B's* performance in buying the gun, and *B*, as promisee, became obligated to buy it, an obligation which he did not previously have. When we examine *B*, the promisor, we find that he has become entitled to *A's* performance in selling, and that *A*, now the promisee, is obligated to sell. The benefit-detriment approach may lead to amusing results when it is applied in such cases as a son-in-law's suit against the father-in-law for the failure of the father-in-law to perform his promise to pay $5,000 if the young man would marry the daughter. It should be noted that the benefit need not actually be to the promisor but may be to some third person, as when *A* promises to pay *B* $50 if *B* will promise to give *A's* nephew an atomic construction kit for Christmas. Actually, if the promisor gets what he bargains for, there is a kind of benefit to him anyhow. Note, however, that this approach is not entirely satisfactory as an explanation of consideration because both benefit and detriment appear to depend upon obligation or binding effect, when it is precisely that effect for which consideration is needed.

A promise by *A* to make a gift of $1,000 to *B* on *B's* twenty-first birthday is not usually enforceable, because there is no consideration and no public policy behind the view that promises of gifts should be enforced. (But see the discussion below of *promissory estoppel*.) *A* has bargained for nothing and has received nothing. *A's* promise brings neither benefit nor detriment. However, had *A* promised to pay the money on the condition *B* would refrain from cigarettes, whiskey, and wild, wild women until he reached the age of twenty-one, and if *B* behaved as requested, consideration probably would be found. *B* refrained from activities that he had the right to engage in, and *A* got what he bargained for. The discussion here should not be construed to mean that an executed gift, one actually carried out, would be set aside for lack of consideration.

In order to satisfy the requirements of consideration, the benefit or detriment must usually be the thing bargained for by the promisor. The mowing of *A's* lawn will not be consideration for *A's* promise to pay $5 if the act requested and bargained for by *A* was the polishing of his car. Benefit to the promisor or detriment to the promisee are completely irrelevant unless the promisor agreed to be bound in return therefor.

A contract is, in effect, an exchange of values. One party gives up something for something else which, at the time of making the contract, he desires more than the thing he is giving up. *A* gives up his right to keep his shotgun or to sell it to *C* because he assigns a higher value to *B's* promise to buy it for $95. Or, more simply, *A* wants the money more than the gun, and *B* wants the gun more than the money. The two parties have exchanged values. Need the values that have been exchanged be measured in dollars and cents? In general, the answer is no. The values we are concerned with are not monetary values but legal values. An act, a forbearance, a promise, or anything else which is bargained for in a contract situation has legal value when there is a benefit to the promisor or a detriment to the promisee. There is legal value when a party obligates himself to do something that he was not previously obligated to do even though the monetary value of the thing he is to do is nil. The crucial question may very well be: "Did the party now seeking to enforce another's promise give up something to which he was in law entitled?" If the answer is "yes," there is legal value and consideration, providing, of course, that the thing given up was the thing bargained for by the other party.

No two phrases in the law of contracts are more confusing or more subject to misuse than *adequacy of consideration* and *sufficiency of consideration*. The latter phrase is best not used at all for our purposes here. There either is consideration or there is not, and referring to consideration as sufficient introduces the confusing notion that consideration may be present yet insufficient to support a promise. *Adequacy* refers not to the existence or non-existence of legal value but to proportionate values. As a rule, the courts will not inquire into the value of *A's* consideration as compared with that of *B*. Presumably, both parties wanted what they were getting more than what they were giving, or they would not have entered into the contract. The fact that *A* agreed to exchange a $10,000 automobile for a 10¢ lead pencil cannot be attacked on the ground of the inadequacy of the consideration for *A's* promise. The 10¢ lead pencil or a promise to hand over the pencil possesses legal value and is consideration for *A's* promise to deliver the automobile, which is immensely more valuable in monetary terms. There is one situation, however, where the court will examine the adequacy of the consideration. Where *A* promises to pay *B* $10 on Monday morning and *B* promises to pay *A* $5 at the same time, it is obvious that *A* could not possibly want the $5 more than the $10 and that *A* must be motivated by something else. Were the $5 represented by a rare coin or were the larger amount to be paid to *B* six months after the $5 was paid to *A*, we could find consideration, and adequacy would be of no importance. The coin would have a value of its own in addition to face value, and it is a well-known fact that $5 presently in hand is worth more than an expectation of $5 some time in the future.

Consideration is not and was never intended to be an assurance that equal values were to be exchanged. The courts are not concerned with unequal values except as illustrated in the previous paragraph. Where the consideration on one side is grossly inadequate, however, this fact may be used as evidence that the promise which that consideration purports to support was extracted by fraud or by force. If the courts do interfere in this kind of situation, it is because of the fraud or force and not because of the inadequacy of the consideration. In the lead pencil and automobile case, it may turn out that the owner of the pencil represented to the other party that the pencil was the one used by Abraham Lincoln in writing the Gettysburg Address. The fraud will make it possible for the owner of the automobile to rescind his promise to deliver it.

D. Special Consideration Problems

COMPOSITION AGREEMENTS. A device used quite frequently in some states to enable a person deeply in debt to get started as a productive citizen again is the composition agreement, whereby the debtor pays or promises to pay a certain portion of his debts to a number of creditors in exchange for promises by the creditors to forgive the remainder of the debts due them. (See Chapter 17) If *A* has assets of $2000 and debts to *B, C,* and *D* of $1000, $1000, and $2000 respectively, he may enter into a composition agreement with the creditors where he will pay them 50¢ on the dollar and they will promise to release the balance of the debts. The creditors' promises are binding. At first glance, the situation appears to be the same as the part payment of an undisputed debt problem considered below. The binding effect of the promises may be explained in a number of different ways. Consideration may be found in the promise of the debtor not to pay more than the pro rata share to any of the creditors. Legally, the debtor may pay off creditor *D* in full and leave nothing for the others, except where this would constitute a preference under the bankruptcy laws. (See Chapter 17) The debtor, then, has given up a legal right and suffered a detriment while the creditors have incurred a benefit by becoming entitled to performance they were not previously entitled to. Consideration for the promise of creditor *B* may be found in the promises of creditors *C* and *D*. *B* probably would not have entered into the agreement had C and D not done so. All are parties to the contract, and the promise of each is consideration for the promises of the others. In some states the composition agreement is binding by statute without regard to consideration, under the theory that the enforceability of these agreements is socially desirable.

It should be noted that creditors who are not actually parties to the composition are, of course, not bound by it. The result is that the composition is a satisfactory device only when creditors representing a substantial portion of the claims against the debtor participate. Some states set up special administrative machinery to aid debtors and their creditors in working out these arrangements.

CHARITABLE SUBSCRIPTIONS. As we know already, a mere promise to make a gift is not enforceable. Since charitable subscriptions are, in general, enforceable, it must be that they involve, somehow, more than a "mere" promise. There are at least three different theories by which consideration is found in connection with charitable subscriptions. One is the same referred to in the paragraphs on compositions—the promises of one subscriber being the consideration for the promises of other subscribers. This approach is much weaker here, however, than it was when we looked at it before, because it is very doubtful if the charitable subscriber pays very much attention to the existence or non-existence of other subscribers. The "bargained for" aspects of consideration lose their significance if we so appraise the situation as to find consideration in the mutual promises. Obviously, a charitable subscription would not be binding under this theory where there was only one subscriber.

Consideration can be found easily and on normal contract grounds where the charity promises to use the subscriber's funds for a particular purpose or in a particular way. This solution would be impractical and illogical, however, were attempts made to apply it to the mass public subscriptions solicited by such charitable organizations as the Red Cross.

Section 90 of the Contracts Restatement suggests another device by which these subscriptions may be held binding: "A promise which the promisor should reasonably expect to induce action or forbearance of a definite and substantial character on the part of the promisee and which does induce such action or forbearance is binding if injustice can be avoided only by enforcement of the promise." This idea is called *promissory estoppel* and has been applied to charitable subscriptions. The doctrine of promissory estoppel is further evidence of an increasing liberalization of the formal concepts of consideration. The doctrine has also been used to prevent an offeror from revoking an offer where he has promised to keep the offer open and the offeree has relied upon the promise.

PAST CONSIDERATION. While A is away on vacation, B has painted A's fence without the request of A. When A returns, he is so pleased with the appearance of his fence that he promises to pay *B* $50 for his work. But later *A* has a change of heart and refuses to pay the $50. *B* would be foolish to take the case to court because *A's* promise is not enforceable. The painting of the fence, which appears to be the only possible consideration, occurred in the past and was not bargained for by *A*. It cannot be consideration to support *A's* promise. Because *B* was a mere volunteer, he cannot recover the reasonable value of the work on quasi-contract principles. While the result described in the example seems eminently fair and sensible, does it necessarily mean that past consideration can never support a promise? See the discussion below.

DEBTS BARRED BY THE STATUTE OF LIMITATIONS OR DISCHARGED IN BANKRUPTCY. A statute of limitations prescribes the period during which legal actions must be started. If the particular action is not begun within the prescribed period of time after the right to bring the action accrues, the right of action is barred. The purpose of these statues is to put pressure on creditors and on others who have causes of action to be reasonably diligent in pursuing those actions, and also to avoid long-delayed law suits where the parties and witnesses have died or forgotten important circumstances of the dispute. Each state has its own statutes of limitations. The periods are not uniform from state to state and the time periods vary within any given state depending upon the nature of the situation. Traditionally, and also logically, the time periods during which actions on oral contracts or on personal injuries may be brought are shorter than where rights in written contracts or real property are involved. The periods for written contracts vary from three to twenty years, on book accounts from one to eight years, and on oral accounts from two to eight years. (Some of the more serious crimes, such as murder, have no statutory period at all.) The Uniform Commercial Code provides its own statutes of limitations, but it should be noted that many states which adopted the Code elected to keep their pre-existing schedule of limitations and have not enacted that portion of the Code.

Where a debt of *A* to *B* becomes due on June 1, 1964, in a state having a three year statute of limitations for this sort of claim, *B* must begin his action to collect the unpaid debt by June 1, 1967. If he does not begin it by that time, his action is barred, and he no longer has the right to sue *A* on the debt. *B's* right to sue may be revived however by *A's* express promise to pay the debt or by his acknowledgement of the debt. *A's* promise or acknowledgement must be unqualified. In most states, the promise or acknowledgement must be in writing. In others, the writing is not necessary where the promise or acknowledgement is accompanied by part payment of interest or principal. In a few states, no writing at all is necessary. If the basic requirements of formality are met, the promise is binding, and the statutory period begins to run again.

There are numerous theories as to what explains the binding effect of such promises. The simplest situations occur where the statute states specifically that the debt may be revived by such a promise without regard to considera-tion. Where this easy solution by statutory provision is not available, the result is the same, but the explanations vary. A theory once widely accepted is that the new promise simply waives the defense which the party making the promise has as a result of the running of the statute of limitations, and the original promise which has remained binding all during the barred period may again be sued on. This view is subject to several objections. What justification is there for requiring consideration in order to create a legal obligation but not requiring it when giving up a defense to an existing obligation? Is it not really the "past" consideration that supports the new promise?

A few states have, by statute or by decision, taken the point of view that the moral obligation of the debtor to pay the debt is the consideration to support his promise. If interpreted incorrectly, this last theory is misleading and contradictory. No matter how strong moral obligation may become, we have not yet progressed to a stage of civilization where we can conveniently assign legal value to moral obligation for the purpose of satisfying the require-ment of consideration. On the other hand, this last theory may be looked upon as just a way of saying that past consideration will support a promise to do something which society feels ought to be done. Certainly, society feels one ought to pay his debts and that promises to pay debts barred by a statute of limitations should be enforced. Whatever view is accepted, the underlying idea is that some promises, though not all, should be enforced, and if the use of "past considerations" or "moral obligation" in certain situations brings about the proper result, then no great harm is done to the basic principles of con-tract law.

As will be seen in Part 5 of this book, the bankruptcy procedure discharges a debtor from all, or substantially all, of his debts. These debts may be revived by unqualified, express promises or acknowledgments in much the same way as debts barred by the statute of limitations. The reasons behind the enforce-ability of such promises or acknowledgments are precisely the same as with regard to the statute of limitations.

MODIFICATION OF AN EXISTING LEGAL OR CONTRACTUAL DUTY.　Where a person does or promises to do something he is already obligated to do, he has not suffered any detriment, and neither his act nor his promise will be consideration to support the promise of another. Where a policeman promises to arrest a burglar in exchange for the promise of the burgled home-owner to pay $250, the promise to pay is not enforceable. The policeman is obligated by law to arrest a criminal, and promising to do what he is already obligated to do will not support the home-owner's promise.

Most of the cases in this area arise in connection with pre-existing con-tractual duties. For example: A has agreed to build a house for B, and B has agreed to pay A $20,000 for it. A discovers before completion that he is not going to make as much profit as he had expected and tells B that he will cease work on the house unless B promises to pay $2500 extra. B makes the promise and A completes the house. A cannot collect the additional $2500 because *A's* performance of acts he was already obligated to perform under the contract is not consideration for *B's* promise. The practical as well as the social desirability of this rule is obvious. Where, however, A agrees to finish the house ahead of schedule or to use better materials or to do anything which he was not previously obligated to do under the contract, consideration for *B's* promise is supplied, and the promise becomes binding. Care must be used to distinguish these situations from the *novation,* which is a device by which the old contract is rescinded and a new one substituted in its place. Novations are discussed elsewhere in this chapter.

PART PAYMENT OF A DEBT AS CONSIDERATION FOR A PROMISE TO RELEASE THE ENTIRE DEBT. Where A owes B an undisputed debt of $500 currently due, a promise by B to forgive the entire debt in exchange for the payment by A of $175 is not a binding promise, and B may recover the remainder of the debt from A in spite of the promise. This is a special case of the modification of duty situation discussed above. The explanation is, of course, that there was no consideration for *B's* promise. No detriment is suffered by A because he is paying $325 less than he actually owes. No benefit accrues to B because he is getting $325 less than he has a legal claim to. The change in the legal rights which the parties bargained for here has no legal value. The above rule, although widely condemned, is generally followed; but the encouragement it may give to bad faith on the part of creditors and the fact that it is frequently contrary to business usage and understanding have caused the courts to construe it very strictly and to limit its application. The usual effect of this attitude on the part of the courts is leniency in the discovery of consideration. In such situations as part payment before maturity, part payment by a third person, part payment at a place other than the one agreed upon, giving a promissory note or some other improved form of claim, and, of course, where there is other property in addition to the money (as where A paid B $175 in cash and also gave him a stamp album or some fishing tackle), consideration for the promise is found and the promise is enforceable.

The legislatures in many states have also taken a hand in this area. Section 1524 of the California Civil Code states: "Part performance of an obligation . . . where expressly accepted by the creditor in writing, in satisfaction . . . though without any new consideration, extinguishes the obligation." An interesting problem arises under statutes of this type as to whether a check marked "paid in full" satisfies the requirements of the statute and discharges the debt if the creditor indorses and cashes the check. The general answer is that it does not. Indorsing a "paid in full" check does not constitute an "express" promise in writing to accept the amount of the check as full payment. This statutory situation should be noted as one of those where the need for consideration, though not the need for formality, is eliminated.

Where the amount of the debt is in dispute, the rules applied are different from what they are where the amount is not disputed. Where A and B have an honest dispute as to the amount of A's debt to B, any payment by A within the disputed area that is accepted by B in full payment of the debt does discharge the full amount claimed by B. For example, if in our previous illustration, A had honestly claimed that he owed only $175 while B insisted that $500 was the correct amount, a promise by B to release the rest of his claim in exchange for the payment by A of $250 would be a binding promise. Consideration is found in the fact that A has given up his legal right to go into court and prove the lesser amount and, thus, has suffered a detriment. The "paid in full" check for $250 will, if cashed by B, discharge the remainder of B's claim, because cashing the check carries with it an implied promise to accept the lesser amount there represented in satisfaction of B's claim. If the "paid in full" check is used where the debt is not in dispute, the same result does not obtain because the implied promise to release, while present in that situation, is not supported by any consideration. The payment of any sum less than the lowest amount of a disputed debt agreed to by the debtor will be treated as though there had been no dispute. If A, in the above example, paid $150 for B's promise to forgive, the remainder of the debt would not be discharged. For convenience sake, most courts will treat a payment at the minimum figure, $175 in our example, as being within the disputed area and thus supplying consideration.

The Code has made substantial changes in the rules discussed above. It has eliminated the need for consideration in modifications of contracts for the sale of personal property. An oral contract may be modified orally, but a written contract may only be modified by a written agreement or by an oral agreement fully executed by both parties. The purpose of these changes is to permit parties to make equitable modifications in the terms of sale, such as price adjustments owing to shifts in the market, without the inconvenience of having to satisfy the technical requirements of consideration. Danger of abuse of these provisions is reduced by the Code's prevailing requirement of good faith. The Code provisions are further evidence of the new public attitude opposing the enforcement of technical requirements in the face of moral and ethical considerations.

MUTUALITY OF OBLIGATION. Ordinarily, a promise is consideration for another promise if it is the thing bargained for and given in exchange for the other promise. Each promise is consideration for the other, and both parties are bound to do the things they promised to do. If one of the parties is not bound by his promise, it is plain that the presence of the promise alone is not sufficient to supply consideration. There can be no detriment to that party if he is not bound to do the thing which he promised to do or if he did not really promise to do anything. Some promises reveal, on analysis, that though the language of promise is there, the party making the promise has not really obligated himself. These promises are called *illusory* promises because they give the illusion of supplying something of legal value but actually do not. Where, for example, *A* promises to sell coal to *B*, and *B* promises to buy coal from *A* if *B* desires to, it is obvious that, in spite of *B's* language of promise, he has not really obligated himself in any way. He only promised to buy coal from *A* if he wanted to. He is in exactly the same position he was in before he made the promise. There is no consideration to support *A's* promise to sell; thus, there is no contract. There is, in effect, a continuing offer from *A* to *B* to sell coal. Words of "want" or "desire" destroy the mutuality of the obligation because the party using these words is not obligated.

Care should be used to avoid confusion with *need* or *requirements* contracts, which are binding. Had *B* in the illustration in the previous paragraph promised to buy all the coal he "needed" or "required" from *A*, there would be consideration and a binding promise. Although there is no obligation on *B* to need coal, he has given up his legal right to buy the coal from someone else if he does need it. This latter type of contract is very common in certain industries.

RECITAL OF CONSIDERATION. Consideration problems arise in situations where a written contract recites that there is consideration when actually there is not. It is obvious the party seeking to avoid the contract by showing there is no consideration is somewhat weakened in his case by the fact he has signed an instrument which states that there was consideration. On the other hand, a simple statement that there is consideration cannot actually supply consideration if we adhere to the principles set forth in the paragraphs above. In general, a recital of consideration is *prima facie* evidence of consideration but may be rebutted. This means, in effect, that if the issue is not raised the presence of consideration will be assumed; but it may still be demonstrated that consideration was not actually present. In a few special situations, such as insurance policies, a recital of consideration may be conclusive. In most of these exceptions, it is fairly easy to find other consideration present but not recited, such as a promise to pay. Some states have by statute made written instruments presumptive evidence of consideration, even without a recital, and a few states have sought to make written instruments the equivalent of instruments under seal as far as the import of consideration is concerned.

E. Discharge of Contracts

A contract is said to be *discharged* when the contractual duties arising under it have been terminated. It should be noted that "discharge" and "avoidance" are not the same thing. Where the contract is not binding upon one or more of the parties, there is no need for a discharge, as far as those parties are concerned. A party, for example, who has been induced by fraud to enter into a contract, may avoid the contract by exercising his right of rescission or by using fraud as a defense in an action to enforce the contract. Such a party is not subject to the rules governing the discharge of a contract or of a contractual obligation. In order for the rules of discharge to apply, there must usually be a valid contract that is binding in all respects. Some courts and other authorities speak of the exercise of a power of avoidance as a discharge, but such use of the term may cause some confusion. Because most of the legal problems arising in connection with discharge are related to issues of consideration, discharge is discussed here rather than in other portions of the chapter.

There are many different methods of discharging a contract, and a very substantial portion of the law of contracts is concerned with them. Performance is the most common and most usual method of discharge, but in this book it is considered separately, as the failure of conditions and some other methods are. Discussed in this section, except for brief references, are only those methods of discharge not otherwise examined. The methods of discharge fall into two broad categories: discharge by act of the parties and discharge by operation of law. Into the first group fall such methods as performance, rescission, release, accord and satisfaction, arbitration and award, and novation. Methods falling into the second category are account stated, bankruptcy, judgment, death, statute of limitations, and merger.

DISCHARGE BY ACT OF THE PARTIES. *Performance.* After all terms of the agreement have been complied with by both parties, the contract is discharged. No discharge takes place until all promises have been strictly and literally performed. It is sometimes said that substantial performance or tender of performance will bring about a discharge. Actually, a party to a contract is not discharged by either of these methods, but may become entitled to call upon the other party for his performance. Obviously, this is not the same thing as discharge. In the other direction, complete failure of performance by one party does not in itself discharge the other party, but it may give the other party the privilege of escaping from his own obligation. These and other problems of discharge by performance, such as conditions, impossibility, and breach, will be discussed in detail elsewhere.

Rescission and release. The term "rescission" may be used in several different ways. In the sense in which the term has been used in other parts of this chapter, rescission is a method of avoiding a contract that has been entered into as a result of mistake, fraud, duress, or undue influence. By rescission of an executed contract, the parties are returned as nearly as possible to the positions they occupied before the contract was entered into. By rescission of an executory contract, it is made possible, in effect, for the party who has the right to do so to avoid the performance of a promise he made in connection with the contract. As has already been pointed out, however, rescission in this sense does not really bring about a discharge.

In another sense, "rescission" is used as a substitute for "release." Where there is a mutual agreement between the parties to free each other from the obligations of a contract, a discharge takes place, and the promises to free each other from obligations are binding. In order to be effective, the promise of *A* to surrender his rights against *B* must be supported by consideration. Where there is a mutual rescission or mutual release, the promise of *A* to release *B* is supported by the promise of *B* to release *A*. Where the release is unilateral, consideration may not be present. It should be noted that the surrender of rights by one party does not have to be supported by the surrender of rights by the other party. Consideration may be supplied by other means. In this latter situation, however, the discharge is usually said to have resulted from accord and satisfaction or from some other method of discharge rather than by rescission or release.

Many states have altered by statute the above rules with regard to unilateral release. Section 1541 of the California Civil Code, for example, states that: "An obligation is extinguished by a release therefrom given to the debtor by the creditor, upon a new consideration, or in writing, with or without new consideration." The writing must show expressly an intention to discharge the obligation.

Mutual rescission may also be used where a contract has already been performed. *A* returns to *B* or promises to return to *B* the consideration which *A* received, in exchange for *B's* return or promise to return to *A* that which *B* received. Rescission in this sense should be distinguished from *cancellation* or *termination*, which simply abrogates the portion of the contract that remains unperformed and leaves prior acquired rights as they were. Rescission, when accompanied by restitution, not only terminates further liability but restores the parties to their former position. Whatever the use of "rescission," it should be remembered that in general even a contract required by the statute of frauds to be in writing may be rescinded by an oral agreement

Accord and satisfaction. An *accord* is an agreement between contracting parties whereby one of them is to do something different from what was called for by the contract and the other party is to accept, in extinction of the obligation, something different from that which he was entitled to under the contract. An accord is itself a contract. The *satisfaction* takes place when one party tenders the changed performance and the other party accepts it in satisfaction of the obligation. Where, for example, *B* owes *A* $1000 and *B* promises to give, and *A* promises to accept, an automobile in place of the money, an accord has been formed. Satisfaction will occur, and the obligation will be discharged when the car is delivered to *A* and he accepts it.

Since an accord is a contract, consideration is a necessary element. If *B* had promised to pay *A* $500 and *A* had promised to accept this in payment of the $1000 debt, there would have been no accord because of the absence of consideration, unless of course the amount of the debt had been in dispute and $500 was within the area of the dispute. In the example in the previous paragraph, consideration is supplied because *B* had promised to provide, and *A* to accept, something different and not just something less.

Accord does not discharge a contract. Discharge takes place only on satisfaction. The ramifications of this rule are that after the accord is entered into and before satisfaction, there are two contracts outstanding between the parties. If the debtor fails to perform the accord, the creditor may bring an action on either the old obligation or the new obligation created by the accord. If the creditor fails to perform the accord by refusing to accept the debtor's new performance, the debtor is still liable on the original debt but may recover damages from the creditor for the breach of the accord.

Novation. Another method by which a contract may be discharged is the *novation.* This device takes two forms; one of which is very similar to accord and satisfaction. A novation may be a substitution of one agreement for another between the same parties or may be the substitution of parties to the same agreement. Where the novation results from a substitution of parties, it should be fairly obvious that the agreement of a least three persons is necessary. The contracting party who remains with the contract must agree to a substitution of the new party and to the release of the old party. The withdrawing party must consent to withdraw and to permit another to take his place as a party to the contract. The new party must assume the contractual burdens and obligations from which the withdrawing party is being released. The new party will receive the benefits of the contract or other consideration. Once the proper consents have been supplied, the withdrawing party is discharged completely from his obligation.

If *A* buys some furniture from *B* on the instalment plan and then sells the furniture to *C* who promises to make the remaining payments to *B*, there has not yet been a novation because *B* has not consented to the substitution of *C* for *A*. *A* would still be obligated on the contract. Where the consent of *B* to the substitution of *C* is acquired, there has been a novation and *A* is discharged. The promise by *C* to pay *B*, before the novation takes place, makes *B* a third party creditor beneficiary and gives to *B*, in most states, a right to sue *C* on his promise. This type of third party beneficiary contract is called an *assumption* or an *assumption agreement* and is discussed later in the chapter.

Where the novation consists of the substitution of agreements between the same parties, the effect of the novation is to discharge immediately the old contract. The difference in the effect of an accord and of a novation is then clear. What is sometimes not clear is whether the agreement entered into is an accord or a novation. If it is the latter, the original agreement is discharged. If it is the former, the original agreement is not discharged until satisfaction. Where the second agreement plainly manifests an intention on the part of the parties to discharge the original agreement, the second contract is a novation. Where the opposite intention is manifested, the second contract is simply an accord. Whether clearly manifested or not, it is the intention of the parties which controls, and that intention may have to be determined from the surrounding circumstances. In general, the intent to release an old debtor or to discharge an old contract must be shown with reasonable clarity.

Arbitration and award. Parties to valid contracts may agree to submit a dispute about contract terms to impartial third persons for determination. The agreement to submit to arbitration may be a part of the contract itself, or ir may be entered into after the dispute arises. In either event, the parties may agree to accept the findings of the arbitrator as final. The decision and findings of the arbitrator are called the *award*, and may serve to discharge contractual obligations. If the original obligation was for a liquidated sum of money, most courts hold that the award does not substitute a new obligation but merely states what the old obligation is. On the other hand, if the original obligation was for an unliquidated sum of money, the award is generally a new obligation which is substituted for the old. The award is enforceable in court. Where the award states only what the old obligation is, the plaintiff would bring his action on the old obligation, but where the award is substituted for the old obligation, the action is brought on the award itself.

While the courts and the common law usually favor attempts on the part of persons who are engaged in controversies to settle their disputes outside of court, by compromise and by other friendly means, the courts have always looked with some suspicion on arbitration as a method of settling disputes. The use of a non-judicial tribunal may be part of the explanation for the hostility of the courts, but that use cannot explain it fully. Lawyers also opposed commercial arbitration for many years, and still do in some parts of the country, possibly because they were unfamiliar with its uses and its desirability and because arbitration was looked upon by them as a threat to their fees and livelihood. In spite of great advances in recent years in the use of arbitration and in its recognition by the courts, it still cannot be used to oust the courts completely from jurisdiction. Parties may, however, agree that arbitration will be a condition precedent to an action on the original claim.

Until the announcement of the final award, any party to an arbitration may revoke the authority of the arbitrators to continue their proceedings. This revocation may be a breach of the arbitration agreement, in which case the innocent party is entitled to damages.

DISCHARGE BY OPERATION OF LAW. *Merger.* Whenever the terms of a contract are embodied by the parties in another contract of higher legal dignity, the first contract is said to be merged into the second and thus discharged. A debt may be merged in a promissory note accepted by the creditor in full satisfaction of the debt. The debtor is no longer liable on the debt but on the note alone. Generally, where the terms of an oral contract are embodied in a written contract, the oral contract is discharged by merger into the more dignified legal obligation. The same result takes place, in states where the seal still has its common law effect, where the terms of an oral or unsealed contract are incorporated in a sealed instrument.

The act of the parties is not necessary in order for a merger to take place. Merged into a judgment on a contract are the promises the promisee enforced against the promisor. The promises are discharged by their merger into the obligation of higher legal standing.

Statutes of Limitations. As has already been discussed, a statute of limitations prescribes the periods of time during which legal actions may be brought. While most statutes result only in a barring of an action if the action is not started during the prescribed period, there are a few states in which the statutes specify that the running of the statute of limitations acts to discharge the obligation and not merely to bar an action on it.

Account Stated. There are many different "accounts" in business usage that have nothing to do in particular with the discharge of a contract, but many of these may be transformed, by the course of events, into an "account stated," which does discharge contractual obligations. Black's *Law Dictionary* defines an *account stated* as the "settlement of an account between the parties, with a balance struck in favor of one of them; an account rendered by the creditor, and by the debtor assented to as correct, either expressly, or by implication of law from failure to object." An open account or a running account or an account rendered may become an account stated by the agreement or conduct of the parties, but until it does so become, it has no effect in discharging contractual obligations.

Parties transacting business with each other, and keeping accounts of their transactions, may come to an agreement on the amount of the final balance due from one to the other. This agreement, whether express or implied, is a new and independent executory contract that discharges all of the matured debts that were merged into the account. No right of action remains on the separate debts that went into the account. The agreement may be implied from the circumstances, for example, where the creditor sends a statement to the debtor who fails to object within a reasonable time. In this case, the conduct of the parties manifests an intention to substitute the account stated for the several items on an open account. Where statements are sent periodically and the business between the parties is continued, the intention to form an account stated is usually not found. It is important to note that an account stated cannot supersede or cause the merger of a written contract or of a promissory note. The theory behind the account stated is that it is better evidence of the existence and amount of a debt than an open account, a running account, or other similar arrangements. Obviously, it is not better evidence than a debt set forth in a written instrument.

MISCELLANEOUS. There are many other situations where discharge is said to take place by operation of law. A bankruptcy proceeding generally discharges the contract debts and obligations of the bankrupt, as we will see in Part 5. The death of one of the parties or the destruction of the subject matter of a contract may discharge the contract. These matters will be discussed in the section of this chapter devoted to the performance of contracts.

The outbreak of war may discharge a contract between a citizen and an alien enemy. The intentional and material alteration of a written contract by one of the parties without the consent of the other party may serve to discharge the obligations under the contract.

4. VALIDITY AND ENFORCEABILITY—OTHER REQUIREMENTS

A. Cases

(1)

On April 15, 1929, Schoenung, a minor, nineteen years of age, purchased from Gallet an automobile for $300, for which he gave his judgment note for $250 and another automobile, which Gallet accepted in trade at a valuation of $50. At that time, Schoenung was living with his parents on a farm, which was three miles from the city where he was employed at $75 a month in an implement business. He had been working for several years, and had been permitted to keep his earnings, which he had used to provide his necessaries and to pay for two cheaper automobiles. His brother was a part owner of the business where Schoenung worked, and Schoenung usually rode in the brother's car to and from work. From April 15 to June 6, 1929, Schoenung drove the newly acquired automobile between six hundred and a thousand miles on pleasure trips and had used it occasionally in going to and from work. On several occasions he had left it at Gallet's garage for adjustments and repairs for which no charges were made. On June 6, 1929, he restored the automobile to Gallet by leaving it at Gallet's garage and he demanded the return of his note and of his former automobile. Gallet refused to accept the returned automobile and the certificate of title thereto and also refused to return Schoenung's note and the former automobile, which the defendant had sold and which had been wrecked. Later the same day Gallet removed the automobile which Schoenung had returned from the garage and parked it in the public street in front of the garage. A traffic policeman ordered Schoenung to remove it from the street, and he took it to his father's farm, where it remained. Schoenung has offered it to Gallet several times, but has always been refused. The terms of the purchase were fair and reasonable, and there was nothing wrong with the automobile when Schoenung returned it on June 6.

[*Schoenung* v. *Gallet,* 206 Wisc. 52, 238 N.W. 852 (1931)]

B. Competent Parties

In General. As pointed out in Chapter 1, the law operates by imposing duties and assigning rights. Almost without exception, the intricate rules by which society is permitted to function take effect through the mechanics of rights and duties. It is obvious, however, that rights and duties in the abstract have no significance whatever. Persons are the units to which rights are assigned and on which duties are imposed, and the word *person* is often defined in these terms. Persons may be either natural, as human beings, or artificial, as corporations, which possess in the eyes of the law much the same legal personality as a human being. All persons do not have the same rights and duties applied to them, and not all persons have full legal capacity to enter into contracts. Although all persons are presumed to have full legal capacity to contract, there are several groups which, for reasons of policy or because of some disability, do not have this full capacity. Among these groups, and with varying degrees of incapacity, are minors, sometimes called infants, insane persons, intoxicated persons, corporations, and persons deprived of their civil rights by conviction and imprisonment for crime. The effect on a contract of having a party with less than full capacity is not always the same. The effect may be to prevent the contract's ever coming into existence or may be simply to make the contract voidable at the option of one or more of the parties. Although at common law married women lack full capacity to contract, this discrimination has largely disappeared under the impact of statutes and will not be discussed here.

MINORS. *Who are minors?* In general, a person is a minor until he reaches the age of twenty-one. Most states have altered the period of minority either by lowering the age of majority for some or all purposes or by providing for increased capacity at various ages within the period of minority. Some states provide that women attain majority at the age of eighteen, while others provide that a lawfully married minor of age eighteen is an adult for purposes of making contracts. A minor who acquires adult status by marriage does not lose it, under most statutes even though the marriage be annulled or ended by divorce.

Status of Minors' Contracts. Most minors' contracts are simply voidable at the option of the minor, but there are a few types of minors' contracts that are void. The contracts that appear on this list vary somewhat from state to state, but often a minor's contract of agency is held void if the minor is the principal purporting to delegate authority to an agent; and some states treat as void a minor's contracts relating to real property or an interest therein. Theoretically, there is no real reason for the exceptions made in these cases, but historical and practical justifications are sometimes made for them. The modern view holds that minor's contracts of agency are to be treated like any other contracts which are made by minors.

It should be noted that the lack of full contractual capacity is more than just a disability. It is both a privilege and a protection in addition, and is afforded the minor out of consideration for the disadvantage he normally suffers in his dealings with adults. The fact that the minor is the equal of the adult in intelligence or in experience is of no importance in the eyes of the law. Protection is afforded to all. The purpose of this special protection is to permit the minor to deal with adults on more nearly equal terms. This has not always been the purpose. There was a time when virtually all minors' contracts were void and without any legal significance whatever. The modern view is that the minor is adequately protected by giving him the option of not performing his contracts; thus, the general rule is that a minor's contracts are voidable and not void.

Disaffirmance. The process by which a minor avoids his contracts is called *disaffirmance,* and is available only to the minor. An adult may not disaffirm or avoid a contract with a minor party simply because that party is a minor. The policy of the law in this regard is to protect the minor. The adult, presumably, can take care of himself. If the minor chooses to do so, he may enforce the contract against the adult. A minor may disaffirm a contract either before reaching majority or within a reasonable time thereafter, even if the contract has been fully executed. If a minor should die during the period when he might have disaffirmed, his personal representative may disaffirm. Disaffirmance, like offer, acceptance, and many other aspects of contract law, is evidenced by a manifestation of intention. In this case, the intention is to avoid the contract. It may be shown by express notice to the other party or by conduct of the minor which is inconsistent with an intention to recognize the existence of the contract.

It is important to remember that a minor may disaffirm contracts that are wholly executory, partially executory, or fully executed. Any other rule would so abrogate the public policy in favor of protecting minors that the protection would virtually disappear. Where a minor disaffirms a contract that has been fully or partially performed, the issue arises whether the minor must return the consideration he has received from the adult. Not all courts or state legislatures have given the same answers to the problem. If any of the rules in this connection can be said to be a majority rule or a general rule, it is that the minor must return the consideration if it is still in his possession. The adult must, of course, return the consideration received by him. This rule carries with it the implication that if the consideration in the possession of the minor has been damaged or partially dissipated or destroyed, the minor still satisfies the requirement of return of consideration by returning what is left. If the consideration has been lost or stolen, the minor need return nothing.

Some statutes and some courts have limited the right of the minor to disaffirm by requiring that the consideration or its equivalent always be returned. This would mean that a minor on disaffirming would have to pay for damage or deterioration and to substitute money where the consideration had been lost or stolen.

It is frequently argued that the legal rules with regard to minors' contracts are unfair to adults. On analysis, this argument loses most of its weight. If the minor intentionally takes advantage of the protections afforded him by purchasing a car or a bicycle, wearing it out, and then returning it and recovering his money, he would be guilty of the tort of fraud or deceit. Minors are liable for their torts. In this case, the minor would probably be denied the return of his money in full and would have to compensate for the damage and deterioration of the car or bicycle. The best protection which the adult has, however, is the fact that he can refuse to deal with anyone he suspects of being a minor. Should the minor fraudulently represent himself, by forged documents or otherwise, as being an adult, he has committed a tort and in most states the adult could recover the loss suffered as a result of the tort. A substantial number of courts would deny recovery on the tort ground under the theory that the tort is a part of the contract, and that to permit recovery in tort would destroy the minor's right to disaffirm. The majority rule seems preferable. A few states prohibit disaffirmance by the minor where he has induced the adult to enter the contract by fraud under circumstances where the adult had reasonably relied on the minor's representations. In only a few states is the fraud of the minor a bar to the use of minority as a defense in an action on the contract by the adult.

Ratification.   After reaching majority, a person may obligate himself on contracts entered into while he was a minor. This is usually referred to as *ratification.* In order for a ratification to be effective, the minor must have been in possession of accurate knowledge of the material facts of his situation. Actions that might manifest an intention to ratify may have been performed by the minor with exactly the opposite intention. The ratification cannot be partial. The minor must ratify the whole contract and not just those portions beneficial to him.

Liability of minors for necessaries.   It is often said that a minor is liable for necessaries, but stating the rule in this fashion is very misleading. A minor is not liable on his contracts for necessaries but is liable in quasi-contract for the reasonable value of necessaries actually supplied to him. The reason for the modification of the general rule that a minor is not liable is explained by the fact that a minor might be deprived of access to the necessaries of life if persons supplying these necessaries could recover nothing from the minor. Where the minor has entered into a contract for necessaries, his liability comes not from the contract but is implied in law, and the minor is not liable for the specified prices but only for the reasonable value of necessaries supplied to him.

Corollaries of this basic rule are that the minor is liable only for necessaries actually supplied to himself or to his family and actually used or consumed, and that he is liable only to the person directly supplying the necessaries. A minor is not liable for money borrowed for the purpose of purchasing necessaries, except, in some states, for the reasonable value of necessaries actually purchased with the money.

If a minor has already been supplied with reasonable quantities of necessaries by parent or guardian, nothing in addition is really a "necessary" as far as that minor is concerned. Beyond the problem of the quantity of any particular item supplied, issues also arise as to what classes and types of goods can be necessaries. Many years of judicial decisions have fairly well crystallized the area; and it can be said with certainty that food, clothing, lodging, medical attention, if in reasonable quantity, are necessaries, as is a certain amount of education. It is also clear that within these well-defined areas, quantities, qualities, and details will depend on the minor's station in life. Few courts have held that a college education is a necessary even though the station in life of the minor might seem to justify such a holding. American courts have, as a whole, confined the variations due to varying stations in life within relatively narrow bounds.

Liability of parents on minors' contracts.   Unless actually a party himself, a parent is not liable on contracts made by his minor children. Many adults will refuse to deal with minors unless the parents agree to become parties to the contract also, or where there is a clear showing that the minor is acting as an agent of his parents. A parent is responsible, however, for the support of his family, and if the parent fails to carry out this responsibility, he becomes liable for the reasonable value of necessaries supplied by third persons. Many courts have held that a parent will not be liable for necessaries furnished to a minor child who abandoned the parent without just cause.

Because a parent has a duty to support his minor children, he or she also is entitled to the custody and control of the children, to their services, and to their earnings outside the home. In the absence of a waiver by the parent, the payment of wages by an employer to the minor child does not discharge the obligation to the parent, and the parent may recover the wages from the employer if they do not reach the parent's hand from the minor. Under this rule, the burden is placed on the employer to ascertain whether the parent has waived his rights to receive the earnings of the minor child. Many states have by statute altered the rule to shift the burden to the parent.

Upon the termination of the parent's rights to custody, control, services, and earnings of a minor child, the child is said to be emancipated. The child may keep his own earnings. Emancipation may be brought about by the express consent of the parent or by such conduct as failing to support the child, permitting the child to seek his own employment and to keep his own earnings, or by other conduct indicating an intention to emancipate. It should be noted that emancipation does not serve to discharge the parent's liability to support the child, and it in no way alters the legal status of the child, except as discussed in this paragraph.

Minors' Torts.   As has already been mentioned, minors are liable for their torts or wrongs to other persons. The public policy that justifies unusual protection and privilege for minors in contract situations does not apply to tort situations because the other party has no way to protect himself. An adult may refuse to enter into a contract with a minor, but he cannot refuse to be hit on the head by a rock thrown by a minor. It would be manifestly unfair to grant the minor the same privileges with regard to his torts that he is granted with regard to his contracts. Consequently, minors have been held liable for fraud, deceit, assault, battery, negligence, and for many other torts. The liability is the same as for adults, except that minors are less subject to punitive damages.

Liability of a parent for the torts of minor children has largely disappeared in the United States. A few states still retain such liability, and most states have statutes imposing such liability in certain special situations, such as the operation of motor vehicles and vandalism.

Child actors and athletes. Some states have statutes that make child actors and athletes liable on their contracts of employment and that prevent disaffirmance of such contracts. The policy in favor of protecting minors is carried out under these statutes by replacing the right to disaffirm with supervision over the contract by the court. Section 36.1 of the California Civil Code gives the court the power to require the setting aside of up to fifty per cent of the minor's earnings for the purpose of preserving them for the benefit of the minor. This latter section no doubt resulted from the fact that many of the early Hollywood child stars earned millions before reaching the age of twenty-one only to discover that the profligacy of their parents had left them penniless.

INSANE PERSONS. The same public policy that supports the protection of minors who make contracts also operates to protect insane persons. A totally insane person is, if anything, less capable than a minor of understanding the nature of the thing he is doing, and should not be held irrevocably responsible for things he could not really have intended to be held for. A difficulty arises, however, because there are so many kinds and degrees of insanity. Some insane persons are perfectly capable of understanding the nature of a contractual act. Others have lucid intervals during which they are normal in all respects. Some insane persons have been declared so by a court and have been placed under legal guardianship. Others, possibly just as insane, have not been adjudicated insane.

As a general rule, persons who have been judicially declared insane can make only void contracts. The contractual acts of these persons are of no legal effect. Most courts treat contracts by other insane persons as being voidable. Sometimes the fairness of the contract to the insane person is taken into consideration. At other times the fact that the same party to the contract did not know of the insanity of the other party will be important, and many courts will give weight to the argument that the sane person took advantage of the insane one. In most courts, however, contracts made by a person while insane may be disaffirmed by him or his guardian or his personal representative in much the same way as contracts are disaffirmed by a minor. The same requirements for return of the consideration will apply, and an insane person may ratify, during lucid intervals or after recovery of sanity, contracts made while he was insane.

An insane person is liable for the reasonable value of necessaries actually supplied to him or to his family. The obligation is one of quasi-contract and not of contract. Insane persons are liable for their torts.

INTOXICATED PERSONS. The contracts of intoxicated persons are usually binding. Where, however, a person becomes so intoxicated that he is incapable of understanding the nature of the relationship into which he is entering, his contracts become voidable. In general, it makes no difference whether the state of intoxication was procured by the person himself or by the other party to the contract. The intoxicated person may avoid the contract when he has regained the use of his judgment and reason. Ratification may be accomplished in the same way as ratification by insane persons and minors, and the intoxicated person has a reasonable time after returning to a lucid state in which to make his election. An intoxicated person is, of course, liable for his torts.

CORPORATIONS. Corporations are discussed in detail elsewhere. It is sufficient to point out here that although corporations are usually persons in the eyes of the law, they do not possess the same, full contractual capacity normal adult human beings have. A corporation's capacity to make contracts is limited by its charter and may be narrow or broad depending upon the terms of the charter.

PERSONS DEPRIVED OF CIVIL RIGHTS. When a person is sentenced to a penitentiary after he is convicted for a crime, he generally loses most of the rights he had as a person on the outside. Most or all of these rights will be returned to him when he has completed his term. Some state statutes provide for the return of some of the rights while the prisoner is still incarcerated, usually at the option of a parole board or its equivalent. The right to make contracts is one of those rights frequently returned or retained by a prisoner. Among the rights that, as a rule, cannot be returned are the right to vote, to hold public office, to give a general power of attorney, and to hold money or property as a trustee. For certain serious crimes, the rights to vote and to hold public office are never returned, not even on completion of the term.

C. Legal Object

IN GENERAL. It should be obvious that an illegal act or purpose cannot be made legal by the use of the contract device. Murder is illegal and so is a contract to commit murder. Beyond these rather simple concepts, however, the problem is not easy to deal with. It is obvious why a contract to commit murder is illegal and why a contract for normal purposes under normal circumstances is legal, but there is a vast hinterland between these two extremes where the legality or illegality and the reasons therefor are not clear. Were "illegal" always translated as "criminal," the problem would be simple of solution. Unfortunately, for simplicity's sake, most of the illegal contracts involve no criminal act at all. The contract, nevertheless, is just as illegal, and may be just as objectionable as if it did contemplate a criminal act.

A contract may be illegal because its object is in violation of statutory or common law or because it is "against public policy." A contract that involves no violation of law may be illegal because the performance provided for may in some way be detrimental to society as a whole. This is not the type of legal concept which is readily reducible to concrete terms and examples. When we say that anything having a tendency to do harm to the general welfare is against public policy, we are setting up only the broadest and most general of standards. A fortuitous sequence of events or an imaginative interpretation could cause almost any contract to have the necessary "tendency to do harm to the general welfare." The test is much more severe. In order to satisfy it, the contract must involve some act or object the public generally feels is injurious. In other words, in order to be against public policy the contract must be of a type involving some serious and widespread injury to the general welfare. Because of the very nature of the problem, however, courts frequently observe that the question of public policy is primarily one for the legislatures, and that, in the absence of legislative mandate, the court will be very reluctant to add any new types of contracts to the list of those which are invalid on grounds of public policy. A large proportion of the area has been taken over by statute.

CONTRACTS IN VIOLATION OF COMMON LAW. There are many acts considered to be antisocial in character. On this list would have to be placed most crimes and such things as fraud, libel, slander, nuisance, and assult. Almost all crimes are established and controlled today by statute and are no longer matters exclusively of common law. The law of torts is still largely outside the statutory field, however, and is a proper subject of discussion here. Whether the wrong is civil or criminal, the fact that society has provided punishment or private redress is evidence enough that the courts should not permit any of these wrongful ends to be achieved through the use of the contract. An agreement to commit a civil wrong, such as fraud, is just as illegal as an agreement to commit some criminal wrong, such as murder. It should be noted that the list of wrongs, both criminal and civil, changes with the years, both by additions and subtractions. What may have been objectionable a hundred years ago may no longer be so, and vice versa.

CONTRACTS IN VIOLATION OF STATUTE. *Statutes requiring a license.* Contracts that seek to procure the commission of crimes are illegal, void, and unenforceable without question. The statutes have made the particular ends specifically illegal. Where a statute does not declare that an act is illegal or that an agreement to perform the act is illegal but simply imposes a penalty for doing it, questions are raised whether a contract to do it really is illegal. A good example of such a statute is one which requires a professional person to acquire a license from the state to practice his particular profession, and imposes a penalty if he fails to take out the license. These statutes do not usually say that practicing without a license is itself illegal. Most courts have classified such license statutes into two groups: those which impose the penalties and the requirements for the purpose of protecting the public, and those which impose the requirements for revenue-raising purposes. If the purpose of the statute is to raise revenue, a contract made by one who has failed to acquire the necessary license should not thereby be rendered illegal. The violation is really not of sufficient importance to justify its having an effect upon the validity of contracts made by the person committing the violation. An example is the business license most local governments require of those operating stores or shops within the jurisdiction of that government. The primary purpose of these statutes or ordinances is to raise revenue and not to protect the public. It would indeed be an extreme result were the courts to hold that shopkeepers who had not taken out their business licenses entered into invalid contracts with their suppliers and their customers.

Where the purpose is to protect the health and safety of the public, it is only logical for the courts to hold that contracts entered into by an unlicensed practitioner are void and unenforceable. The license requirement for lawyers and doctors is much more than a technicality. It is only the last step in a long series of requirements designed to assure the public that doctors and lawyers have the professional training and ability and moral character to qualify them to practice their professions on the otherwise unprotected public. An unlicensed lawyer or doctor cannot recover any fees from his clients and patients for the professional services he may have rendered. The same views have been taken with regard to unlicensed architects, engineers, real estate, insurance and stock brokers, and even masseurs.

Usury statutes. *Usury* is the taking or charging of greater amounts of interest than the statute permits. *Interest* is the price paid for the use of money, just as *rent* is the price paid for the use of real property. There was a time in the Middle Ages when all interest was thought to be usurious and an offense against God. This may be one of the reasons why interest rates are usually regulated, although rent, except in national emergencies, is not. Actually, in the kind of economic system in which we live, money is required by everyone, and, were interest rates not regulated, a lender could take advantage of the temporary but dire distress of a borrower. Housing is usually not so essential nor is there the same power on the part of the landlord for taking undue advantage of those needing housing. In periods of national emergency when the power to take undue advantage of persons needing housing arises, regulation of rents comes with it. Under circumstances in which a person will promise to pay any rent or any interest in order to get shelter or money, regulation is necessary.

In order for a transaction to be usurious, there must be a lending of money, an unqualified agreement to repay the money, and an imposition by the lender of a higher rate of interest than the law allows. Thus, where something other than money is loaned, there are no limitations on the amount which may be charged for the loan. Where there is not a loan but a sale, the usury laws do not apply, but the courts are suspicious of sales that bear the earmarks of attempts to circumvent the usury laws, an example of which is usurious loan disguised as a sale with an option to repurchase at a much higher price. The investment of money in a business is not a loan, and a promised rate of return could not be a violation of the usury laws because there is no absolute promise to repay.

Whether the rate of interest is in excess of the maximum is sometimes rather difficult to determine. Many states provide by statute for unusually high rates of interest on certain types of loans by certain types of lenders. Small loan companies, for example, may charge as much as 3 per cent per month, but the amount of money which may be loaned to any one borrower on these terms is usually limited to $500 or less. A number of loan practices have come under the scrutiny of the courts with varying results. Courts watch carrying charges with great care because they are an easy way to avoid the usury laws. In general, extra charges may be made only for the reasonable value of services actually performed. Many states have authorized the short month and short year by statute.

Through the years many subterfuges have been developed by lenders in order to avoid the usury laws, and many have been condemned by the courts: giving the borrower a check for the purported amount of the loan and requiring him to return immediately part of it in cash, requiring the borrower to date back his promissory note so that the loan comes due earlier, requiring the borrower to buy or lease some article at excessive price or rental. Many other practices have come before the courts for examination and have been held not usurious: a bona fide sale at one price for cash and at a much greater price on credit; and the voluntary prepayment clauses. In the latter situation the borrower has the option of retaining the borrowed money until it comes due or of paying it back before the due date together with the same amount of interest that would have been paid had the loan been kept for the full period. The fact the prepayment is voluntary and optional removes this arrangement from the usurious category.

The effect of usury on contracts varies sharply from state to state. In any case, the effect is determined by statute. The least strict provide only for the forfeiture of the excessive interest. Others provide for the forfeiture of two or three times the excessive interest. Some require the forfeiture of all interest, and in a few states, the usurious lender forfeits the whole loan including interest. Some states impose criminal penalties in addition to the effects on the contract. At common law only the excess interest was recoverable by the borrower, but this in itself is unusual because the common law in other circumstances will aid neither of the parties to an illegal contract. The theory, with regard to usury, apparently is that the parties are not equally guilty, and that the purpose of making usury illegal is to protect the borrower.

Sunday statutes. Although contracts entered into on Sunday were of equal validity with any other contract at common law, many states have statutes that seek to prohibit secular work or business on Sundays. The effect of these statutes on contracts made on Sunday varies from state to state. In some states such contracts are void whether they are made on Sunday or call for secular work on Sunday. If the work or business involved is necessary, the contracts are valid. Many courts reduce the coverage of the statutes by interpreting liberally what is necessary work or business. Many states which once had these statutes have now repealed them, and the statutes, as a rule, are not found in the important commercial states.

There are, of course, many other statutes having an effect upon the legality of contracts, but an exhaustive discussion or even a list would take more space and time than could be justified. Those discussed above cover a representative group of statutory situations.

CONTRACTS CONTRARY TO PUBLIC POLICY. *In general.* Many of the situations discussed below as public policy problems of illegality have actually been removed from this area in many states by legislative prohibitions. The nature of the problem is not vastly different where the prohibitions have been so enacted, and the specific issues may be discussed adequately in either connection. One of the most important types of illegal contract, the contract in restraint of trade, is discussed in detail in Part 4 and will not be referred to here.

Contracts obstructing the administration of justice. No great argument need be made in support of the rule that contracts which interfere with the proper functioning of the courts and the administration of justice are against public policy and are illegal. An agreement to suppress evidence or to conceal a witness, as well as agreements not to testify or agreements to pay a witness conditioned on the successful outcome of the case, are illegal. An agreement to refrain from criminal prosecution is itself a crime, and the agreement is obviously illegal. A provision in a contract whereby the parties agree not to take any controversies arising out of the contract to court is unenforceable. This kind of provision should not be confused with the perfectly valid agreement to submit a controversy to arbitration as a condition precedent to going to court.

An attorney's contingent fee contract, whereby his fee is based on the amount of recovery in an action at law, is valid in most states, except in divorce actions, but a contract prohibiting the client from settling the case without the attorney's consent is usually illegal.

Contracts to influence a public official. Contracts by which a public official agrees to conduct his office in a certain way or to vote in one way or another are obviously against public policy, and would tend to subject public officials to all sorts of corrupting influences if such contracts were enforceable. A contract whereby a person agrees to attempt to influence the conduct of a public official is invalid where there is any possibility that corrupting means are to be used. Contracts to exert personal influence to sway a judge's decision or to bring about favorable consideration of some proposal made to a public officer are void as against public policy, and it is usually immaterial whether illegal means are used or anticipated. In most states, it is legitimate for one to employ another to attempt to influence the vote of legislative or other officials by straightforward methods such as the presentation of facts or arguments. It is clear that such attempts may be abused, and such abuse is the explanation for the anti-lobbying statutes which have been adopted in many states and by the Congress. The purpose of these statutes is not to eliminate lobbying but to make a public record of the names of the lobbyists and the parties they represent together with information, in some states, about the fees paid for the lobbying service.

Wagering and gambling contracts. If the word "wagering" is used in its broadest sense, almost every business contract becomes a wagering contract because the parties are really speculating as to future price changes, market conditions, and the state of business in general. It is obvious that A would not usually enter into a two-year contract with B to buy the raw materials necessary in A's business at $9.50 a ton if A knew for sure that the price of the material would go lower than $9.50 during the two-year period. A is, in effect, wagering that the price will remain at or greater than $9.50 during the two-year period of the contract. A makes this speculation and many others in this single contract, and B makes several of his own. Some wagering contracts are illegal, but not the kind that was just described.

In general, *illegal wagering contracts* are those by which one of the parties promises to pay to the other something of value on the occurrence of some event which is uncertain and in which the parties have no direct interest. A puts a $5-chip on "19" in exchange for the promise of the croupier or the management to pay A 35 to 1 if the roulette wheel stops with the ball on that number. This contract satisfies all of the requirements of a valid contract except that it is unenforceable. Neither A nor the management has any interest in number 19 worth protecting. Were the complicated and expensive machinery of the law to be set in motion in order to enforce such contracts that create risks where there were none before and that serve no useful purpose as far as society is concerned, the courts would be crowded with wasteful cases, and the costs of maintaining our courts would substantially increase. Although speculations on the commodity exchanges superficially appear to be the same kind of wagering contracts as that of the roulette wheel, closer examination discloses several useful ends that these exchanges and their speculations serve. A legitimate businessman is able to reduce the amount of his speculation by the use of a device known as *hedging*. For example, a flour manufacturer will enter into a contract in June to sell wheat at $2 a bushel on October 1, intending only to settle at the difference between the contract price and the market price October 1. At the same time he will enter into a contract to buy wheat at $2 a bushel with delivery on October 1. If the market price of wheat is less than $2 on October 1, the flour manufacturer makes up on the sale contract what he lost on the purchase contract, and if the price of wheat is over $2 on October 1, he makes up on the purchase contract what he lost on the sale. The effect of the speculative contract is to assure that the manufacturer will earn his profits, if any, from the flour business and not as the result of fluctuations in the price of his raw material. The commodity exchanges are also price-determining instruments and play a valuable part in our economic system.

Insurance contracts also bear some of the earmarks of wagering, but the line between the two is an easy one to draw. An insurance contract seeks to protect a worth-while and existing interest, to shift an existing risk, and to prevent a loss. A real wagering contract creates a new risk, does not protect against loss, but only provides a gain. Were A to take out life insurance policies on the lives of total strangers, these policies would be wagering contracts because A had no interest to protect or risk to shift. He is simply wagering on the life expectancies of the parties. No insurance company would sell such policies because A does not have an "insurable interest."

Contracts involving domestic relations. Several different types of contracts in the area of domestic relations are held to be invalid because they are against public policy. A contract which seeks to restrain the marriage of any person other than a minor is illegal. The theory is that society as a whole would be injured if such contracts could be enforced. Most courts make exceptions for contracts which tend only indirectly to restrain marriage—for example, a contract which permits the use of certain property *until* marriage, and is not intended to prohibit marriage. A contract which promotes divorce is also illegal and void. Where A promises to pay B $5,000 if B will divorce her husband and marry A, the contract is unenforceable. A contract to compensate a wife for rendering domestic services incidental to the martial status is against public policy because it may encourage frauds on creditors, promote discord in the home, and degrade the wife to the status of an employee.

Limitation of and exemption from liability. Contracting parties frequently attempt, by the insertion of terms in the contract, to limit their liability for breach of contract, for torts committed against the other party, and for other acts. Sometimes the attempt is made to exempt the party altogether from liabilities of certain types. The basic principles governing both situations are the same. The treatment of these provisions varies considerably from state to state and from situation to situation, and has been extensively influenced by statute. Our efforts here will be directed at showing a few typical situations and the rules that have been applied to them.

Telegraph companies and carriers of goods may, under federal law, limit liability where rates are graduated according to declared value and where the customer-party has the opportunity of securing full protection by paying a higher rate. In many states no limitation of liability is possible except with statutory permission. In some cases such statutes impose the limitations themselves while others simply permit limitation by contract. Some statutes provide that the liability of a bailee for negligence cannot exceed the amount which he is informed by the bailor, or he has reason to believe, the property is worth. A common carrier, by a special term in its contracts, may usually limit its liability for damage to goods or baggage, due to ordinary negligence, but not for damage caused by gross negligence, intentional wrong, or fraud. Such limitations of liability are not authorized where injury to passengers is concerned.

The Contracts Restatement says that: 1. An ordinary person can only contract to exempt himself from liability for ordinary negligence, and not for gross negligence or wilful wrong. 2. An employer cannot contract to relieve himself from liability for injuries to an employee. 3. A party charged with a public interest, such as a common carrier, cannot contract to exempt itself from liability for negligence where it has received or has been promised compensation. Section 7-204(2) of the Uniform Commercial Code provides that a warehouseman may limit his liability by "(a) a term in the warehouse receipt or storage agreement limiting the amount of liability in case of loss or damage, and setting forth a specific liability per article or item, or value per pound, beyond which the warehouseman shall not be liable; provided further, however, such liability may on written request of the bailor at the time of signing such storage agreement or within a reasonable time after receipt of the warehouse receipt be increased on part or all of the goods thereunder, in which event increased rates may be charged based on such increased valuation," but no such limitation is effective with respect to the warehouseman's liability for gross negligence, wilful wrong or fraud.

The statutes of many states provide that any contracts that violate the principles set forth above are against public policy and illegal. In some cases, the whole contract will be illegal, in other cases only the offending clause.

Waiver of statutory right. Many contracts contain clauses by which one or more of the parties purports to waive rights or advantages he has been given by statute. In general, a party to a contract may waive such rights if they are intended solely for his benefit but cannot waive rights under a law established for a public reason. In the absence of statutory definition, the court is faced with the task of determining whether a particular statute is for public or for private benefit. As will be seen in Chapter 7, a tenant may waive the right he has under some statutes to repair a dwelling house at the expense of the landlord. The statute of limitations may be waived either by contract provision that any suit arising out of that contract must be brought within a shorter period, or by a contract provision whereby a party agrees not to use the statute as a defense. Some courts distinguish between a statute of limitations or time provision which merely bars an action and one which extinguishes the substantive right itself. If the latter situation the waiver is usually ineffective. Contract provisions which require that notice of claim for loss or injury must be given within a certain period of time in order to enforce liability, are upheld if the period is not so short as to be unreasonable.

On the other hand, rights under debtors' exemption statutes cannot ordinarily be waived by contract in advance. These statutes, which are in the public interest, are aimed at preserving for the debtor a dwelling, clothing for his family and himself, and the tools of his trade. While the exemption rights under such statutes cannot be waived in advance, they may be waived, expressly or impliedly, at the time of execution against the debtor. Rights or benefits under workmen's compensation and unemployment insurance laws cannot be waived. Certain protections and rights of mortgagors are not subject to waiver. Many of the family allowance and probate rights of a surviving wife are held to be public in nature and cannot be waived. Attempts of waiver in these situations are illegal and ineffective.

EFFECT OF ILLEGALITY. Illegality is usually more than just a defense the defendant may raise on his own behalf. A court may find, of its own volition, a contract to be illegal and may refuse to grant any relief or supply any remedy to the plaintiff. Illegal contracts, as a whole, are utterly void and unenforceable. The court will give aid to neither party, thus leaving the parties where the court finds them. Which party is the plaintiff is generally of no interest to the courts, nor is the fact that one of the parties gains a benefit or advantage over the other. The theory behind this arbitrary treatment is simply that the complicated and expensive machinery of justice should not be available for the enforcement of contracts whose objects are illegal or for the rescue of those who enter into such contracts. The courts will not enforce these contracts if executory and will not try to restore the parties to their former positions where the contracts are executed.

There are a few exceptions to the general rule, situations where the courts may grant some relief to one of the parties or may enforce legal portions of a contract not tainted by the illegal portions. The relief granted to the borrowing party to an usurious contract is an example of these exceptions. The explanation for not following the general rules in that particular situation is: the borrower is not equally at fault with the lender, not in *pari delicto,* and the public policy which makes such contracts illegal is primarily concerned with the protection of the borrowing party. There are other situations where the same exception will be made—where one of the parties is less guilty than the other and has not, himself, been charged with a serious moral lapse. Money loaned to pay a past gambling debt has been held recoverable, and some courts have permitted recovery of money loaned for present gambling purposes. It is often said that the explanation for the exception to the general rule is that permitting recovery by the less guilty party is more of a deterrent to illegal contracts than is the absolute refusal of the courts to grant any form of relief. Where the contract is wholly executory, this exception is not important, but where the contract is partially or wholly executed, the courts may afford relief to the less guilty party under this exception.

Another exception, called *locus poenitentiae*, is designed to encourage voluntary withdrawal from illegal contracts before they are performed. The theory is that a person who has paid consideration in order that some illegal objective be carried out should be encouraged to repent before the illegal purpose is accomplished. One way of encouraging him is to allow him to recover his consideration if he repents before the act or purpose has been carried out. Thus, if *A* places a bet on the outcome of some athletic contest, he may recover his bet if he tries honestly to withdraw from the agreement before the contest takes place. He may recover from a stakeholder or from a winning party to whom the stakeholder has paid the bet in violation of the repenting party's instructions.

A more difficult exception to assess is sometimes used in situations where a contract is partly legal and partly illegal. If the consideration for the legal promises and the consideration for the illegal promises are separate, there is no particular problem in enforcing the legal ones and refusing to enforce those that are illegal. Where, however, the legal and the illegal promises are given for same consideration, it is necessary to determine whether the illegal portions have so tainted the legal portions that they make the whole contract void. If it is possible to separate the legal parts from the illegal, and the whole has not been tainted, the courts will enforce the legal parts of the contract. For example, if *A* promised to sell *B* his business and also promised never to enter into the same business again anywhere in the world, the second promise probably is illegal and unenforceable because it is an unreasonable restraint of trade, but the presence of this unenforceable promise will not necessarily affect the enforcement of the other.

5. VALIDITY AND ENFORCEABILITY—CONTRACTS THAT MUST BE IN WRITING

A. Cases

(1)

On October 11, 1960, Gude du Buy, purchasing agent for Hypocase, Inc., heard that a lumber mill in a small town not far from Berkland was going out of business and selling its inventory of logs and finished lumber. Thinking that he might be able to get some lumber at reasonable prices under these circumstances, du Buy telephoned the offices of the lumber mill and contracted to take the entire stock of kiln-dried fir for $12,875, a price somewhat below the market price for such lumber, and agreed to send Hypocase trucks on the 14th to pick up the lumber. When the drivers went to the mill on the 14th to pick up the lumber, they were informed that all of the fir had been sold and delivered the previous day to another buyer.

(2)

In January, 1960, Hypocase, Inc. entered into a contract with the General Warehousing Corporation whereby Hypocase was to manufacture and deliver to General 54,000 reinforced hardwood pallets. This was the largest single order Hypocase had ever received. The agreement, which was reached on the telephone, provided that the pallets were to be delivered to General by June 15, 1961, at the rate of not less than 3000 pallets each month. Preston took the order himself, and as soon as he had finished the telephone conversation, he filed a telegram to General confirming in all details the agreement reached over the phone. The telegram was received by General the same day. No written communication was received from General. Hypocase hired several new employees and leased additional equipment and began immediately to step up its production to meet the General order. 5000 pallets were allocated and delivered to General the first month, but the first shipment was refused on the ground that General had obtained a better deal on pallets elsewhere. General claims that no one authorized to act for General had ever signed a written agreement with Hypocase.

B. In General

The "statute of frauds" is an historical and also shorthand method of referring to the requirement that some contracts must be in writing in order to be valid. The word "frauds" seems a bit confusing at first because it recalls the kind of fraud discussed in connection with reality of consent. While the original Statute of Frauds, passed by the English Parliament in 1677, was designed primarily to put a stop to a particular type of fraud which depended on the enforceability of certain types of oral contracts for its existence, the fraud aspects have now largely disappeared, although they are still the basic explanation for the requirement that certain contracts must be in writing to be enforced. Prior to 1677, the use of false testimony to establish the existence of valuable contracts became rather widespread. Not all types of contracts were involved in these practices or amenable to them, and consequently the original Statute of Frauds did not require all contracts to be in writing but only those sufficiently important to be attractive to abuse, or peculiarly susceptible to abuse. The English Statute of Frauds became a part of our common law, but all states have now adopted their own Statutes of Frauds, which vary somewhat from the original, but still embody the same basic requirements of the original statute.

As a general rule, oral contracts are just as enforceable as written contracts, and an oral contract, if proved, is just as effective as a written one. It is obvious, however, that written contracts have certain advantages over oral ones. The written contract is easier to prove, both as to its existence and as to its terms. If the terms of a contract are set forth in writing, they come under the application of the *parol evidence rule,* which limits the use of oral testimony to vary the written terms. Even where written contracts are not required under the statute of frauds, they are usually desirable.

Some of the terminology used in connection with the statute of frauds will be unfamiliar. A contract that must be in writing because of the statute is said to be *within the statute,* and a contract that does not have to be in writing is said to be *outside the statute.* Where a contract is of a variety required to be in writing by the statute but where this particular contract does not have to be in writing because some other condition or requirement has been met, the contract is said to have been *taken out of the statute.*

C. Requirements of the Statute of Frauds

IN GENERAL.   The original Statute of Frauds had two substantive provisions dealing with those contracts which were required to be in writing. Section 17 dealt only with contracts for the sale of personal property, while Section 4 dealt with all other contracts. Most states have retained the separate handling of the two areas in their own statutes, although there is no longer any substantial reason why this should be so, except in those few states where contracts falling under Section 4 situations are void if they are not in writing. The Uniform Commercial Code distinguishes among several different kinds of personal property and provides different requirements for each of the categories. The theory is that different characteristics and circumstances dictate different treatment under the statute of frauds.

A typical statute of frauds provides that certain contracts "are invalid, unless the same, or some note or memorandum thereof, is in writing and subscribed by the party to be charged or his agent." All of the words and phrases in the above statement are in common use, but many of them also have technical meanings or are subject to several interpretations. Consequently, some time must be spent in discussing the precise legal meanings and requirements that may be involved in the more important of these words and phrases before going on to the contracts themselves.

"INVALID."   The settled rule in most states is that this word refers only to the remedy and not to the substantial validity of the contract. In other words, the contract is unenforceable, but it is not void. The Code takes this view. In a few states the word "invalid" is interpreted to mean "void," at least with regard to those contracts coming within the terminology of the old Section 4. A proper question to ask at this time would be: What difference does it make whether a contract is void or unenforceable? At first glance, it appears as though there are no real differences. An unenforceable contract might just as well be void. Actually, however, the differences are substantial and important. Not all of them will be discussed here. If the contract is simply unenforceable but not void, the defendant will normally have to raise as a defense the fact that the contract was not in writing. If he does not raise it, the contract will be enforced. On the other hand, if the contract is void, the court will generally take cognizance of the fact that there is really no contract before it, and it is not necessary that the issue be raised by either party. The parties get no contract rights at all where the contract is void. A void contract cannot be introduced collaterally in an action which does not seek to enforce the contract, while an unenforceable contract may be so introduced. An unenforceable contract is effective for all purposes until, in an attempt to enforce it by legal action, its invalidity is urged by the defense.

"NOTE OR MEMORANDUM." The statute does not require that the entire contract should be in writing or that all or part of the original agreement should be in writing. It is sufficient if there is a note or memorandum of the agreement, even though the note or memorandum is subsequently made. The note or memorandum may be very informal, may consist of several different writings, and need not even be intended as a note or memorandum of a contract. Where *A* and *B* have entered orally into a contract that comes within the statute of frauds, a letter from *A* to *B* complaining about *B's* failure to perform may provide the necessary note or memorandum, if it contains certain basic information about the contract. In general, the parties must be identified and specified, the subject matter must be ascertainable, and the essential terms and conditions set forth. The detail with which these basic requirements must be met varies greatly from state to state, and in some states it is dealt with by statute. Specification of consideration or price is required in some states but not in others. Certainly, any unusual or special terms would have to be deducible from the written note or memorandum.

The Uniform Commercial Code abandons such terminology as "note or memorandum of the contract of sale" and substitutes "some writing sufficient to indicate that a contract for sale has been made." The purpose of the change was to get away from the requirement of the older language that the writing be a memorandum of the contract itself rather than some sort of evidence to indicate that such a contract exists. All that is required under the Code is that the writing afford a basis for believing that the oral evidence rests on a real transaction. In other respects also the Code liberalizes the requirements of pre-existing statutes of frauds, especially with reference to contracts for the sale of goods. It is not necessary that the parties be identifiable through the writing or that the essential terms and conditions be set forth. "A writing is not insufficient because it omits or incorrectly states a term agreed upon. . . ." This liberalization with regard to contracts for the sale of goods emphasizes the purpose of the writing: establishing the existence of the contract, not proving its terms. The Code requires only that the writing specify a quantity and says that the contract is not enforceable beyond the quantity so specified. Presumably, it may be left to other evidence to show that a lesser quantity was agreed upon. Note that specifications of price are not required.

"SUBSCRIBED." Technically, *subscribed* means "signed under" or "signed at the end," but the technical meaning is not used in connection with the statute of frauds. It is sufficient if the signature appears anywhere on the writing, as long as it is intended as a signature and not merely for identification. The signature may be written in ink or in pencil, may be typewritten, rubber stamped, or even printed, as long as it is apparently intended as a signature. The initials of a party have been held to be sufficient to meet the requirement.

The Code substitutes the word "signed" for the word "subscribed" and defines the new term to include "any symbol executed or adopted by a party with present intention to authenticate a writing." These changes are consistent with the better interpretations of pre-existing law.

"PARTY TO BE CHARGED." The statute of frauds requires the writing to be signed by the party to be charged or his agent. The party to be charged is the defendant in an action to enforce the contract, or, to put it another way, the party against whom the contract is sought to be enforced. The requirement is that the party to be charged must have signed. The other party may bring the action although he has not signed any contract, note, or memorandum, and may enforce the contract. In may states the authority of an agent to sign a contract that is within the statute is also within the statute, and that authority must be in writing, unless the agent signs in the presence of and at the direction of the principal.

The Code avoids the older language of "party to be charged" and uses instead "party against whom enforcement is sought," although the meaning is essentially the same. However, the Code does alter the requirement for a signing by the party to be charged where both parties are "merchants." Section 2-201(2) provides that between merchants a written confirmation of a contract sent by one party to the other, which satisfies the requirements of the statute as far as the sender is concerned, may be used against the party actually receiving it, *if* he has reason to know of its contents and does not object to it in writing within ten days. The only effect of this provision is to remove the defense of the statute of frauds. The necessity to prove the making of a prior oral contract still remains.

D. Contracts Within the Statute of Frauds

CONTRACTS NOT TO BE PERFORMED WITHIN ONE YEAR. A contract which by its very terms cannot be performed within one year from the date of making must be in writing in order to be enforced. The period commences when the agreement is made, not when performance is begun. Hence, a six-months lease, the term of which is not to begin until one year after the lease is entered into, comes within the statute and must be in writing. If by any possibility an agreement is capable of being performed within one year from the date of making, even though that possibility be very slight, the contract is outside the statute. In order to come within the statute, the contract must be impossible to perform within one year in the manner specified in the contract itself. The theory behind this requirement is simply that oral contracts are subject to the failings of the human memory, and, where the period of time necessary for performance is greater than one year, contracts should be proved by written evidence.

A two-year lease or a contract of employment for the same period cannot be performed in any time less than two years, and consequently must be in writing. A one-year lease does not come within the statute if performance is to begin on the day of making or the day following, but if performance is to begin at any time later than this, the lease comes within the statute. A life insurance contract does not come within the statute because it is performed by the payment of the proceeds to the beneficiary on the death of the insured, and obviously, this may easily take place within one year from the date of making. A troublesome problem arises where a contract cannot actually be "performed" within one year from the date of making, but the performance may be excused within one year. For example, if *A* contracts to support *B's* ten-year-old son until the child reaches the age of twenty-one, it is clear that this contract cannot be "performed" in less than eleven years, but may be excused at any time by the death of the child. Some courts hold that the possible excuse of performance within the one-year period takes such contracts out of the statute. Other courts take the opposite view. This type of situation should not be confused with the situation where an agreement is completely performed upon the happening of a contingency which may actually occur within one year. For example: a contract between *A* and *B* whereby *A* promises to take *B's* children to school "until the school bus begins to run again" is not within the statute because the school bus may begin to run again at any time.

As a matter of fairness, where the contract is unilateral, or bilateral and completely performed by one party, the remaining promise is taken out of the statute, and the party who performed may enforce the promise of the other party. The Contracts Restatement takes this view, but some courts hold to the contrary.

CONTRACTS NOT TO BE PERFORMED WITHIN THE LIFETIME OF THE PROMISOR. Statutes in some states provide that a contract which by its very terms cannot be performed within the lifetime of the promisor is within the statute of frauds and must be in writing. Where *A* promises to pay *B* $10,000 if *B* will take care of *A* for the remainder of *A's* life, some courts hold that the promise is of this type because the performance of the promise cannot take place until after *A's* death, while other courts say that performance takes place at death and is within the lifetime of the promisor. Some statutes require expressly that agreements to devise or bequeath any property or to make a provision for any person by will must be in writing.

CONTRACTS UPON CONSIDERATION OF MARRIAGE. This provision of the statute of frauds does not include mutual promises to marry, which are, as far as the statute of frauds is concerned, enforceable. Most states, however, have abolished the action of breach of promise to marry. Other contracts in consideration of marriage are within the statute of frauds and must be in writing. Where *A* promises to pay *B* $10,000 if she will marry him, *B* would be wise to get the promise in writing if the expectation of the $10,000 is her reason for going through with the marriage ceremony.

PROMISE BY EXECUTOR OR ADMINISTRATOR. Many statutes of frauds apply specifically to promises by executors or administrators to pay the debts and liabilities of the deceased out of the executors' or administrators' own property. Such promises must be in writing in order to be enforceable. It should be noted that direct undertakings by the executor or administrator, as a promise to pay a possible heir for not contesting the will, do not come within the statue because the obligations are not those of the deceased. In many states, promises to pay the debts of a deceased are included with the next category.

CONTRACTS TO MEET ANOTHER'S OBLIGATION. An additional requirement of the original Statute of Frauds and of the state statutes is that "a special promise to answer for the debt, default, or miscarriage of another" must be in writing in order to be enforced. The purpose of this requirement is to prevent over-zealous creditors from inventing guaranties by friends of debtors and from interpreting words of praise as words of surety. The requirement applies only to a promise by the surety to the creditor to pay the debt of another person. If there is no debt of the other person to the creditor, there is no guaranty, and the statute does not apply. For example, where the person whose debt is purportedly being guaranteed actually owes nothing to the creditor, there can be no guaranty of the debt of another. At best it is an original promise to pay, which does not come within the statute.

There are a number of exceptions to the requirement:

1. A promise made to the debtor himself or to a third person. In order to come within the statute, the promise must be to the creditor.

2. A promise to pay from the funds or property of the debtor. This is clearly not a promise to meet another's obligation.

3. Where the promisor directly incurs the debt and becomes an original or primary debtor himself. If the promisor, for example, requests the creditor to deliver goods to another person and to charge the goods to the promisor, there is no guaranty but only a promise by the promisor to pay a debt which is his own.

4. If the old debtor's debt is canceled and the new promise is accepted in satisfaction of the old debt. Under these circumstances, there is a novation. Since the old debt is discharged, there is no promise to stand good for another's obligation.

5. The promise of a *del credere* agent or factor guaranteeing payment of the price of goods. A *del credere* agent is a sellers' agent who guarantees the solvency and performance by the purchasers, usually in exchange for an extra commission.

It should be observed that a contract to meet the debt or obligation of another must satisfy the same basic requirement that any other contract must satisfy, including consideration. If the guaranty is just a part of the transaction by which the creditor lends money or sells on credit to the principal debtor, the consideration that supports the debtor's promise to pay will also support the promise of the guarantor to pay if the debtor does not. On the other hand, if the guaranty is a separate transaction at a later time, there must be separate consideration to support the guarantor's promise. Where *A* has already loaned money to *B* without any guaranty by *C*, a subsequent promise by *C* to pay *B's* debt if *B* does not must be supported by additional consideration in order to be binding.

SALE OR LEASE OF REAL PROPERTY OR INTEREST THEREIN.   "An agreement for the leasing for a longer period than one year, or for the sale of real property, or of an interest therein" is invalid unless the same, or some note or memorandum thereof, is in writing. The fraudulent practice probably most responsible for the passage of the original Statute of Frauds by the English Parliament was the use of false testimony to establish the existence of oral contracts for the sale or lease of land. Land is such an important commodity that the temptation to perjure one's self or to suborn perjury would be very great were it possible to establish the existence of contracts involving real property by oral evidence alone. All of the state statutes contain the provision referring real property, but vary as to the period of time at which leases come under the statute.

The statute covers the usual transactions with regard to real property: sales of land, mortgages, easements, transfers of any estate in land, except leases for a year or less, and contracts whereby a person agrees to do any of these things. It also covers the sale or contract to sell mineral rights in land and the natural products of land, called *fructus naturales*. Included here would be timber, metals, natural grass, and, in some states, fruit trees and crops even though they receive the periodic attention of men. *Fructus industriales* are planted and tended by man and are not the product of nature alone, and include all planted crops and such things as nursery stock. A contract that contemplates the immediate severance or removal of things that are *fructus naturales* is, by the majority rule, outside the statute on the theory that the contract to sever works a constructive severance, and the minerals or trees become personal property. It is important to note that leases of real property do not come within the real property clause of the statute if they are for periods of less than one year. In the original Statute of Frauds the period was three years. An oral lease for one year or less is valid, as far as this clause is concerned, but may come within the statute under the clause dealing with contracts that cannot be performed within one year from the date of making.

Partial performance of the terms of an oral contract will not ordinarily take the contract out of the statute. Part performance is important, however, in connection with the clause of the statute that deals with real property. Where the part performance is sufficient, both in kind and in quantity, to prove the existence of the contract without a writing, a court in an equitable action will ignore the statute of frauds and enforce promises affecting an interest in land. The requirements are relatively strict, as they should be, and usually there must have been substantial reliance on an oral promise to sell land. By the general rule, a buyer who takes possession of the land and pays part or all of the purchase price qualifies for specific relief compelling the seller to convey title to the land. In a few states, the buyer must make improvements on the land before he can qualify for the unusual remedy of specific performance. There are really two explanations for the exception made for these situations. To require a writing would encourage and bring about fraud because the seller could reclaim land after a grantee had substantially relied on the seller's promise to convey. Furthermore, the policy of the statute is still being complied with in these cases because additional evidence of the oral contract is supplied by the part performance.

Where the portions of a contract relating to an interest in land have been fully executed and nothing remains to be enforced by the court with reference to the land itself, the court will usually enforce the rights and duties of the parties and prevent them from using the statute of frauds as a method of accomplishing fraud. For example: a buyer who has received a deed to land cannot escape his obligation to pay for it by showing that the original contract was oral. The court does not have to enforce anything with reference to the land itself, and will enforce the oral promise to pay. In those situations that do not come within the boundaries of either of the rules of part performance discussed here, the party who parts with value in reliance on an oral promise relative to an interest in land may usually recover the value that has been conferred on the other party. The basis for recovery, however, is not the removal of the contract from the statute of frauds but the doctrine of quasi-contract, which seeks to prevent unjust enrichment.

AGENCY TO CONTRACT IN WRITING.   The statutes of frauds in many states include the *equal dignities rule.* This rule requires that the authority of the agent who is to enter into contracts that must be in writing because of the statute of frauds, must also be in writing. The dignity of the authority, in other words, must be the same as the dignity of the thing the agent is authorized to do. An agent who is expected to enter into contracts that affect an interest in real property must have written authority from his principal. Exceptions to the rule are found where the agent is acting in the presence of and at the direction of his principal, where he is an executive officer of a corporation, and where he is a partner in a partnership.

SALES OF GOODS.   The original Statute of Frauds devoted a separate section to contracts relating to the sale of goods. Section 17 states that:

> no contract for the sale of any goods, wares, or merchandise, for the price of ten pounds sterling or upwards, shall be allowed to be good, except the buyer shall accept part of the goods so sold, and actually receive the same, or give something in earnest to bind the bargain, or in part payment, or that some note or memorandum in writing of the said bargain be made and signed by the parties to be charged by such contract, or their agents thereunto lawfully authorized.

The Uniform Commercial Code contains several statute of frauds provisions: sales of goods (Section 2-201), securities (Section 8-319), security interests (Section 9-203), and sales of personal property not covered by the other sections (Section 1-206). Our primary concern at this moment is with contracts for the sale of goods and other personal property. The provision dealing with the sale of personal property other than goods is less of a departure from pre-existing law than is the former. It lifts the limit for oral transactions to $5,000 and provides that contracts for the sale of personal property in excess of that amount are unenforceable unless, first, there is some writing which indicates that a contract for sale has been made between the parties at a defined or stated price; second, unless it reasonably identifies the subject matter; and, third, unless it is signed by the party against whom enforcement is sought. This provision is designed to cover the sale of such "general intangibles" as goodwill, literary rights, rights to performance, copyrights, trademarks, and patents.

Of much broader coverage is the section dealing with contracts for the sale of goods. This provision applies to all such contracts where the price is $500 or more, and this figure is consistent with the monetary limit most often specified in pre-existing law. The Code defines the term "goods" as all things that are movable at the time they are identified to the contract, with the exception of money, investment securities, and things in action. A *thing in action,* according to Black's *Law Dictionary* is "a right to personal things of which the owner has not the possession, but merely a right of action for their possession." Stocks, bonds, promissory notes, and accounts receivable are examples of "things in action."

It is sometimes necessary to determine whether a particular agreement is a contract for sale on the one hand, or a contract for work, labor, and material on the other. The former is within the statute. The latter, as a general rule, is not, because it is not a sale. In a few jurisdictions where, in addition to performing work and labor, a party is to supply material, the transaction is held to be a sale; thus, it is within the statute. In no jurisdiction is the contract for work and labor, unless it also involves the supply of materials, held to be a sale. Thus, a contract to build a machine out of material supplied by the seller may be a sale and within the statute, but a contract to assemble a machine out of material supplied by the buyer would not be a sale and would not be within the statute. The general rule is incorporated in the Uniform Commercial Code, which states that the transaction is outside the statute of frauds if "the goods are to be specially manufactured for the buyer and are not suitable for sale to others in the ordinary course of the seller's business." However, the Code, in Section 2-201(3) (a), modifies pre-existing law by adding to the above wording the folowing: "and (if) the seller, before notice of repudiation is received and under circumstances which reasonably indicate that the goods are for the buyer, has made either a substantial beginning of their manufacture or commitments for their procurement."

The Code also provides that if a party against whom enforcement is sought admits in his pleading, testimony, or otherwise in a court that a contract was made, the contract is enforceable up to the quantity of goods admitted. Several states have omitted this provision when enacting the Uniform Commercial Code. This provision is something of a departure from precode law. The purpose behind the change was to avoid the paradoxical effect of admitting the contract in court and still treating the statute of frauds as a defense against enforcement. It is consistent with the policy of the Code aimed at using the writing to indicate that a contract *was made* rather than to prove the contract itself. The prevention of fraud is thought to be the primary objective, rather than the establishment of all the terms and provisions of the agreement. This provision is designed to prevent fraud while eliminating the use of the statute of frauds as a dilatory defense in situations where the making of the contract has been admitted.

A sales transaction may be taken out of the statute where there has been acceptance and receipt of all or part of the goods. Note that both acceptance and receipt must be present. By acceptance the buyer indicates his willingness to become the owner of the goods in pursuance of the terms of the contract. A buyer who inspects the goods to see whether they comply with the terms of the contract does not, by this act alone, accept the goods. The acceptance must be shown by other evidence. The receipt of the goods implies the taking of possession of the goods with the seller's consent, but it does not require physical delivery into the buyer's hands. It is sufficient that the parties agree that receipt has taken place, although the goods are still in the physical possession of the seller. On the other hand, the evidence may indicate that there has not been receipt by the buyer even though the goods are in his physical possession.

A sales transaction may also be taken out of the statute by part payment or by earnest. The two terms are now usually treated as meaning the same thing, but at one time *earnest* was the giving of money or something else of value to bind the bargain and to mark the assent of the parties to the agreement. In general, part payment need not be made at the time the contract is entered into but may be made subsequent thereto. Although the older statutes did not say so expressly, part payment had to be accepted by the seller in order to be effective in removing the contract from the statute of frauds. The Code now expressly makes this requirement. It should be said also that under the Code, goods received or paid for make a contract enforceable only to the extent to which goods have been paid for or received and accepted. Under most pre-existing law, receipt or payment of part of the goods or price validated the entire contract.

The provisions of the Code having to do with contracts for the sale of securities are very similar to the provisions pertaining to sales of goods.

6. PERFORMANCE—IN GENERAL

A. Cases

(1)

The parties had the following correspondence about the erection for Newbury of a concrete mill building at Monroe, N.Y.

Alexander Stewart,
Contractor and Builder

Tuxedo, N. Y., July 18th, 1911.

Newbury Mfg. Company,
Monroe, N. Y.:

Gentlemen.—With reference to the proposed work on the new foundry building I had hoped to be able to get up and see you this afternoon, but find that impossible and am, in consequence, sending you these prices, which I trust you will find satisfactory.

I will agree to do all excavation work required at sixty-five ($.65) cents per cubic yard.

I will put in the concrete work, furnishing labor and forms only, at Two and 05-100 ($2.05) Dollars per cubic yard.

I will furnish labor to put in reenforcing at Four ($4.00) Dollars per ton.

I will furnish labor only to set all window and door frames, window sash and doors, including the setting of hardware for One Hundred Twelve ($112) Dollars. As alternative I would be willing to do any or all of the above work for cost plus 10 per cent, furnishing you with first class mechanics and giving the work considerable of my personal time.

Hoping to hear favorably from you in this regard, I am,

Respectfully yours,

(signed) Alexander Stewart.

Newbury later wrote:

THE NEWBURY MFG. CO.
Steam Fittings, Grey Iron Castings,
Skylight Opening Apparatus,
Monroe, N.Y.

Telephone Connection.   Monroe, N. Y., July 22, 1911.
Alexander Stewart,
Tuxedo Park, N. Y.:

Dear Sir.—Confirming the telephone conversation of this morning we accept your bid of July the 18th to do the concrete work on our new building. We trust that you will be able to get at this the early part of next week.
Yours truly,

The Newbury Mfg. Co.,
H. A. Newbury.

Nothing was said in writing about the time or manner of payment. In July, Stewart commenced work and continued until September 29th, at which time he had progressed with the construction as far as the first floor. He then sent a bill for the work done up to that date. Newbury refused to pay the bill on the ground that no payments were due until the work was completed. Stewart discontinued the work.

[*Stewart* v. *Newbury*, 220 N. Y. 379, 115 N.E. 984 (1917)]

(2)

Williams Manufacturing Company and Standard Brass Company entered into a contract for the construction of equipment for melting brass for Standard.

The contract provided that Williams should furnish to Standard an apparatus for melting brass, erecting the same in Standard's foundry in Cambridgeport, and use crude oil as fuel, after being treated by the Strait process. Williams was to furnish one generator equipped with duplicate pumps, gauges, etc.; one six-horse-power boiler and base complete, fitted with injector, steam gauges, etc.; five burners of sufficient capacity to operate ten furnaces, and to melt twelve pounds of brass and copper, suitable for casting, for each gallon of oil burned, and to melt the same in quantities of 130 to 150 pounds every 100 minutes to each furnace, and this without expense except for the oil burned. Standard agreed to bring the oil to the generator, furnish pipes necessary to connect the boiler to the generator and the generator to the five furnaces, and to furnish fire brick necessary to build furnaces. Williams agreed further to send a competent man to set up the equipment, make connections, and instruct Standard in its proper use, "to place the above named outfit in operation for a sixty days' trial for the approval of the second party, and if the results obtained after the trial were in accordance with specifications above, and satisfactory to the second party, the second party further agrees to pay for the above named equipment the sum of $550."

In January, 1896, Kermeen, Williams' agent, went to Standard's foundry in Cambridgeport with Strait, the inventor of the process, for the purpose of setting up the equipment; that Strait set up two of the furnaces, the boiler, the generator, and the pumps, connected them with the furnaces, proceeded to make tests with the apparatus, the oil being furnished by Standard; that Strait continued at the foundry of Standard until February 21, 1896; that on or about February 21, 1896, Strait was informed by the president of Standard that he was not satisfied with the tests; that four or five days after this interview, Kermeen and Strait went to Standard's place of business and offered to put in the remaining furnaces and burners; Paine, the president of Standard, replied that the equipment was not satisfactory, was not economical, and was subject to other objections; that he did not wish Williams to put in the remaining furnaces, or continue to operate the equipment, and that Strait might as well go home and save further expense. The work had been done in accordance with the specifications of the contract and in such a way as to be satisfactory to a reasonable man.

[*Williams Mfg. Co.* v. *Standard Brass Co.*, 173 Mass. 356, 53 N.E. 862 (1899)]

(3)

In June, 1968, John Gunn, president and only stockholder of the Nu-Method Metal Strap Company, was negotiating with Paul Preston, president of Hypocase, Inc., for the sale of the entire capital stock of Nu-Method to Hypocase. Hypocase had purchased metal straps from Nu-Method for many years. Early in 1968, Gunn had told Preston at a social function that he, Gunn, felt he was getting along in years and was anxious to retire from business. He stated that because his children were not interested in the business, he was planning to sell it. Preston expressed an interest on behalf of Hypocase, but serious negotiations did not begin until later in the year. On June 20, Preston wrote Gunn as follows:

Mr. John C. Gunn
1815 Fabricant Avenue
Berkland, Anosmia
Dear Mr. Gunn:

Should the deal now under discussion for the Nu-Method Metal Strap Company go through, and after we have had the property a year, it is understood that if in my judgment the property has for any reason been worth $175,000 to our company, and we find that we can manufacture metal strapping for $20 a thousand or less, we will pay you $25,000 in cash or in the common stock of our company, as we may elect.

Yours truly,
Paul Preston, President

On June 24, 1968, the deal referred to in the letter went through in a formal agreement, which included by reference the above letter, whereby Hypocase agreed to pay Gunn $75,000 in cash and $75,000 in its common stock for the whole capital stock of Nu-Method. Gunn delivered the Nu-Method stock and Hypocase paid Gunn $75,000 and transferred to him $75,000 in common stock. However, in December, 1968, Hypocase sold the Nu-Method facilities to National Metal Products Company for $250,000, and the plant was dismantled and moved to Texas. When Gunn heard about this transaction, he immediately called Preston, accused him of breaching the contract of June 24 and demanded $25,000.

B. Performance and Failure to Perform

Most contracts are performed, and few important legal issues arise where a contract is fully and completely performed by the parties. The failure of performance, however, brings many legal issues into existence. Some of these issues will be discussed below. In between full performance and failure of performance lie a number of legal problems relating to the performance itself. The interpretation of the contract is one of these problems. It is discussed elsewhere in this chapter.

Problems arise, in the absence of specification in the contract, in regard to the time of performance. A reasonable time is normally allowed except where the performance is of a type which is capable of being done instantly, as where the performance is the payment of money. A promise to pay "when able" does not call for immediate performance, however, and the promisor is not required to pay until he is able to pay. Where no place of performance is specified, the debtor must usually seek the creditor, but custom, usage, or the language of the contract may overcome this rule. Where a contract contains an absolute promise to perform at a certain time, there is no need for a demand by the promisee, but in other situations demand is necessary before the promisor can be said to have failed to perform. The demand is often the best course of action for the promisee, whether or not it is required, because it gives the promisor an opportunity to perform without the promisee's having to incure the expense and trouble of litigation.

Tender of Performance. A *tender of performance* is a manifestation of willingness to perform which, if rejected by the other party, may amount to a discharge of the obligation. In order for the tender to be effective, the person making the tender must be ready, willing, and able to give full performance at the proper time and place, and the tender must be unconditional and in good faith. If these requirements are satisfied, the tender has the effect of placing the other party in default if he refuses to accept it. The party making the tender may rescind, may sue for damages for breach of contract, or even seek specific performance where this remedy is available. Tender of payment of a money obligation does not discharge the obligation but may stop the running of interest, discharge liens which are security for the debt, and may release sureties. A few states have statutes which provide that a money obligation is discharged by tender if the amount is immediately deposited in the name of the creditor in some bank and notice is given to the creditor.

C. Conditions

IN GENERAL. One of the most important issues arising in connection with the enforcement of contract promises is the issue of whether the promisor undertook to perform his promise absolutely or only on the happening or non-happening of some event. The event may be the performance of the other party or may be completely external to the contract. A promise that is not absolute is said to be conditional, and, probably, most contract promises are conditional in one sense or another. For example: *S* and *B* enter into a contract whereby *S* promises to deliver a quantity of steel to *B*, and *B* promises to pay $850,000. May *S* bring an action against *B* for the $850,000 in spite of the fact that *S* has not delivered the steel, or has delivered a different kind of steel from what was specified in the contract? It should be fairly obvious that *B's* promise to pay $850,000 was not intended to be an absolute promise but a promise conditioned on *S's* performance. This condition may have been set forth expressly in the contract or may have been implied by the court from the circumstances. In general, anything in a promise which modifies the absolute character of the promise, whether placed there expressly by the parties or found by implication by the court, is a condition. The happening or non-happening of a condition may have a bearing on the time of performance, the order of performance, or on whether there is to be any performance at all.

It is important that a condition be distinguished from a promise. A *condition* is a fact the happening or non-happening of which creates or extinguishes a duty on the part of the promisor. A *promise* is, as we already know, an assurance of future conduct by the promisor. If the promise is modified by a condition, the performance of the conduct assured by the promisor depends upon the occurrence of the condition. If the promise is absolute, the promisor must perform his promise when the time of performance arrives. A condition may be a promise as well as a condition, as where a party promises that a condition will happen. The best way to illustrate the situation is to compare the effect of a breach of a condition with the effect of a breach of a promise. Where *A* promises certain performance to *B* on the condition that some event takes place, and the event does not take place, *A* is excused from his performance and *B* is excused from his performance, but *B* cannot recover damages from *A* for *A's* failure to perform. If, on the other hand, *A* promises unconditionally to perform and fails to do so, *B* can recover damages from *A* for *A's* breach of promise, but *B* is not necessarily excused from his own performance. However, if *A* promises to perform on the happening of a condition and also promises that the condition will happen, the failure of the condition will excuse B from his performance and will also give B an action for damages for breach of the promise that the condition will happen.

Conditions may be classified in two different ways: 1, as express or implied conditions; or 2, as conditions precedent, subsequent, or concurrent. *Express conditions* are stated in the contract. *Conditions implied in fact* arise out of the intentions of the parties but are not set forth in words. The steel contract in the example above probably contains a condition implied in fact. A *condition implied in law* is one which the court reads into a contract, irrespective of the intent of the parties, for the purpose of preventing injustice.

CONDITIONS PRECEDENT. A *condition* is said to be *precedent* when the act or event must happen before the duty of the promisor to perform arises. For example: where A promises to pay $25,000 on the condition B performs his promise to build A a house in conformance with *A's* specifications, *A's* obligation to pay does not arise until *B's* performance has been completed. Should B bring an action against A for the $25,000, B would have to prove his own performance and the happening of the condition precedent before he could recover.

Time is frequently an express or implied condition precedent. Where S agrees to deliver goods to B by June 1st, there is usually an implied condition precedent to the effect B is excused from his obligations under the contract if S does not deliver the goods within a reasonable time after June 1st. A delay of a few days would not be of sufficient importance as a general rule, to justify attributing to that delay the status of a condition the occurrence of which relieves the other party from his performance. It is clear that what is a reasonable time for these purposes will vary with the type of goods and the nature and language of the contract. Parties who wish to make it clear that time is important and wish to reduce the length of time that would otherwise be considered resonable may include an express condition in the contract, usually by the use of the phrase "time is of the essence." It is sometimes said that an express or implied term of a contract is of sufficient importance to be classed as a condition if the failure to perform it changes the essential character of the agreement. A five-year delay in delivery of goods would meet the test; a five-day delay ordinarily would not.

Performance to satisfaction. A common variety of condition precedent is created by a contract providing that performance must be satisfactory to the promisor or to some third person. In some circumstances, the determination of whether the requirement and condition of satisfaction have been fulfilled is extremely important. Where the parties agree that it is a third person who must be satisfied, the determination by that person that the performance is or is not satisfactory is conclusive if there is no fraud, mistake, collusion, or arbitrary refusal. Most major building contracts provide that the builder, before becoming entitled to payments under the contract, must furnish the certificate of a designated architect to the effect the work conforms to the plans and specifications. In many other contract situations, where the party receiving performance lacks sufficient technical knowledge to enable him to judge for himself the sufficiency of the other party's performance, the approval of a qualified third person is required. As long as that person acts in good faith, his conclusions are final, but where there has been fraud or some other evidence of bad faith, the issue arises whether the performing party may bring suit to recover on the contract without presenting the certificate or other proof of a third person's satisfaction. In some cases, the courts will dispense with the requirement entirely, especially where the defendant has been a party to a bad faith refusal. In other cases, the court will require a statement by another expert that the performance is satisfactory. This would seem to be desirable in those cases where the defendant is entirely innocent of any wrongdoing. In most situations of this kind the performance can be compared with external standards, and the satisfaction required is not so much one of personal whim or fancy but of technical conformance with specifications.

Where the performance is to be the satisfaction of the promisor himself, two different types of situation must be recognized: those involving mechanical utility or operative fitness, and those where the test is the taste or fancy or judgment of the promisor. In the latter case, the promisor is the sole judge of his satisfaction, and no external standard can be applied. If the promisor states in good faith that he is not satisfied, there is no possible way of determining the reasonableness of his attitude.

In most of the cases where the contract involves mechanical utility, the promisor is not the sole judge of his satisfaction. In this type of contract, it is sufficient if the performance would be satisfactory to a reasonable person. An external standard is available in these situations, and will usually be applied by the courts. However, if the personal satisfaction of the promisor is clearly and unequivocally set forth in the contract, the language of the contract will be followed even though mechanical utility is the only issue.

CONDITIONS SUBSEQUENT. A *condition subsequent* is an event the occurrence or nonoccurrence of which terminates an obligation that has already been incurred. A promisor is *not* liable until a condition precedent occurs, but he *is* liable until a condition subsequent occurs; then, he is relieved of liability. Conditions subsequent are not common in contract law. They generally are frowned upon by the courts and are interpreted as conditions precedent where that is at all possible. Some authorities claim that there really is no such thing as a condition subsequent as far as contracts are concerned. It is probably more accurate to say that the distinction between conditions precedent and subsequent is not of much importance except possibly with regard to procedural issues such as burden of proof.

CONDITIONS CONCURRENT. *Conditions concurrent* are mutual conditions that are to be performed at the same time. The ordinary sale of real property is an example. Where *S* agrees to convey land to *B* on a certain day and *B* agrees to accept the deed and to pay the purchase price on that day, the performance of these acts on the given days is presumably concurrent. Actually, in order for one of the parties to put the other in default, he must show that he performed or tendered performance. This sounds very much like a condition precedent. The only really important difference between the two is that the condition precedent must happen or be performed before the duty arises, while a mere tender or offer of performance of a concurrent condition will cause the duty of the other party to arise.

DEPENDENT AND INDEPENDENT PROMISES. In almost all contracts, the question of the order of performance arises to a greater or lesser degree. Where a promise by one party is full consideration for the promise of the other party, and the promises are to be performed or can be performed at the same time and place, the promises are usually held to be mutually dependent and the performances of the promises to be conditions concurrent, except where there are clear indications to the contrary. In some states, promises contained in leases are held to be independent although they conform to the above rule. Promises conditioned on other events or happenings do not come under this rule, such as some insurance contracts where the promise to pay premiums and the promise to insure against losses are consideration for each other, but the promise to pay premiums is absolute while the performance of the other promise is conditioned on the occurrence of a particular event. It is obvious here that concurrent conditions could not be implied. Where promises are to be performed at different times, they are usually regarded as independent unless it appears that the performance of one promise was to be a condition to the performance of the other.

When one promise requires time for performance and the other does not, the former is generally looked upon as independent and the latter as dependent. Where one party promises to pay for real property in instalments and the other party promises to convey title on the payment of the last instalment, the promises to pay the instalments are independent, except for the promise to pay the last instalment, which is mutually dependent with the promise to convey.

SUFFICIENCY OF PERFORMANCE. Another important problem, which frequently arises, is: How much performance is required by the party whose promise of performance is a condition to the obligation of the other party? Must he perform completely or may he call upon the other party for his performance after the first party has performed substantially but not completely? At common law, complete performance was necessary, and at best the performing party could recover only the reasonable value of the work done if his performance was less than complete. The modern rule is different and requires only substantial performance with damage compensation available to the party who has received less than full performance. For example, where *A* has promised to pay *B* $150,000 when *B* completes a building, and *B* has completed all of the work except the replacement of $75 worth of defective roofing tiles, *B* may recover the $150,000 from *A* less the cost of replacing the tiles. Had *B* left off the whole roof or built a five-story building instead of a six-story building, the performance would not have been substantial, and the condition would not have been performed. In the latter case, *B* would have been able to recover from *A*, on quasi-contract principles, only the value of the building to *A*, and this might be a great deal less than the contract price or the market value, especially where major expenditures would be required in order to conform the building to specifications. What is substantial performance is a question of fact for the jury, but, in general, the defects must be easily remedied or compensated for, and the breach must not be intentional.

7. PERFORMANCE—REMEDIES FOR FAILURE TO PERFORM

A. Cases

(1)

Clark delivered a number of paintings to Marsiglia to be cleaned and repaired, at a certain fixed price for each. After Marsiglia began work on the paintings, Clark decided not to have the work done and told Marsiglia to stop his performance of the contract. Marsiglia ignored the order and finished cleaning and repairing the paintings. Marsiglia has now sued Clark for the full contract price.

[*Clark* v. *Marsiglia,* 1 Denio 317, 43 Am. Dec. 670 (1845)]

(2)

Newsome was planning on sending rafts of timber down the river during high water in February, 1902. He sent the following telegram to a whiskey dealer: "Send by express four gallons of corn. Mints Siding. Rush. Raft Hands. (signed) T. J. Newsome." When he sent the message, he told the Western Union operator that he was sending rafts to Wilmington and that the raft hands who were to take the rafts downstream would not make the trip without an adequate supply of whiskey. The telegraph company garbled the signature on the message and delivered a telegram signed "T. J. Sessions." Because of the error, the whiskey dealer was unable to send the whiskey. The raft hands refused to take the rafts down the river. By the time whiskey was obtained, the high water had passed, and it was too late to send the raft down-stream. Newsome sued Western Union for damages, including the loss suffered as a result of a decline in the market value of the timber and the wages paid to the raft hands while they were waiting to go down the river.

[*Newsome* v. *Western Union Telegraph Company,* 153 N.C. 153, 69 S.E. 10 (1910)]

(3)

On June 21, 1947, Campbell Soup Company, a New Jersey corporation, entered into a written contract with George B. Wentz and Harry T. Wentz, who are Pennsylvania farmers, for delivery by the Wentzes to Campbell of all the Chantenay red cored carrots to be grown on fifteen acres of the Wentz farm during the 1947 season. Where the contract was entered into does not appear. The contract provides, however, for delivery of the carrots at the Campbell plant in Camden, New Jersey. The prices specified in the contract ranged from $23 to $30 per ton according to the time of delivery. The contract price for January, 1948 was $30 a ton.

The Wentzes harvested approximately 100 tons of carrots from the fifteen acres covered by the contract. Early in January, 1948, they told a Campbell representative that they would not deliver their carrots at the contract price. The market price at that time was at least $90 per ton and Chantenay red cored carrots were virtually unobtainable. The Wentzes then sold approximately 62 tons of their carrots to Lojeski, a neighboring farmer. Lojeski resold about 58 tons on the open market, approximately half to Campbell and the balance to other purchasers.

On January 9, 1948, Campbell, suspecting that Lojeski was selling it "contract carrots," refused to purchase any more, and instituted suits against the Wentz brothers and Lojeski to enjoin further sale of the contract carrots to others, and to compel specific performance of the contract.

The contract entered into by the parties was a printed form furnished by Campbell containing blanks for name of grower, quantity, and price. The form was drafted by Campbell with Campbell's interest in mind. Paragraph 2 provided for the manner of delivery. The carrots were to have their stalks cut off and be delivered in clean sanitary bags or other containers approved by Campbell. This paragraph concludes with a statement that Campbell's determination of conformance with specifications should be conclusive.

The next paragraph allows Campbell to refuse carrots in excess of twelve tons to the acre. The next contains a covenant by the grower that he will not sell any carrots to anyone else except those rejected by Campbell nor will he permit anyone else to grow carrots on his land. Paragraph 10 provides liquidated damages to the extent of $50 per acre for any breach by the grower. There is no provision for liquidated or any other damages for breach of contract by Campbell.

Paragraph 9 reads as follows: "Grower shall not be obligated to deliver any Carrots which he is unable to harvest or deliver, nor shall Campbell be obligated to receive or pay for any Carrots which it is unable to inspect, grade, receive, handle, use or pack at or ship in processed form from its plants in Camden (1) because of any circumstances beyond the control of Grower or Campbell, as the case may be, or (2) because of any labor disturbance, work stoppage, slowdown, or strike involving any of Campbell's employees. Campbell shall not be liable for any delay in receiving Carrots due to any of the above contingencies. During periods when Campbell is unable to receive Grower's Carrots, Grower may with Campbell's written consent, dispose of his Carrots elsewhere. Grower may not, however, sell or otherwise dispose of any Carrots which he is unable to deliver to Campbell." The Wentz brothers argue that Campbell should not obtain equitable relief.

[*Campbell Soup Co.* v. *Wentz,* 172 F. 2d 80 (1948)]

(4)

In August, 1967, Hypocase, Inc. entered into a contract with Barton Bilder, a building contractor, to construct an addition to the company's main factory building in Berkland. The contract called for completion of the project on or before April 15, 1968. Because Hypocase had ordered new machinery to be delivered in mid-April, 1968, and had taken on substantial additional orders for its pallets, based on its expected increase in production capacity in 1968, the company insisted that the following clause be included in the contract with Bilder, to which Bilder agreed: "If Barton Bilder should fail to complete the addition by April 15, 1968, he shall pay to Hypocase, Inc., the sum of $50 a day for each and every day thereafter the said work shall remain incomplete." Bilder began the construction promptly but carried on the work at a very slow pace. By April 1, 1968, the work was only a little more than half finished, and at that time Bilder ceased work entirely. By the end of April, Hypocase had been successful in persuading another building contractor to undertake the completion of the project, at a considerably higher cost, and the building was finally completed on September 1st. Hypocase had to cancel many orders and also lost some good customers who were angered by the cancellations. The new machinery arrived on time and had to be stored at a public warehouse until September. Hypocase estimates its total loss as a result of the delay to be in the neighborhood of $50,000. Bilder insists that the maximum for which he could be liable is the $50 a day specified in the contract.

B. In General

A contract is a promise or a set of promises enforceable at law. Another way to say a promise is enforceable is to say that on the breach of the promise, the other party has a remedy. As has already been discussed in Chapter 2, there are a number of different types of remedies available to a person aggrieved, a number of different ways in which a promise may be enforced. It is this quality of enforceability that makes the contract a useful legal device and separates it from the host of promises and agreements made every day which have no binding effect. In order to attain the desired end of enforceability, the agreement must satisfy the many requirements discussed in detail in the first portion of this chapter.

Although there are many sanctions that aid in making contracts enforceable, including that of social pressures, the primary concern of this discussion is with the type of sanction imposed by the courts. This judicial sanction or remedy may take the form of *damages,* which is a substitutional remedy involving the substitution of money for performance. Or the remedy may be a specific one where the defendant is compelled to do the thing he promised to do or to stop doing the thing he promised not to do. There are remedies, such as *rescission* and *restitution,* which seek to return the parties to the positions they were in at the time the contract was entered into. There is a remedy, *declaratory judgment,* which attempts to resolve disagreements between parties before a breach takes place and damage inures. The most common of all these remedies is damages. The primary purpose of damages as a remedy is to compensate the innocent party for the harm he has suffered as a result of the breach of contract and not to punish the person who has failed to perform his promises. In tort actions, however, one of the important purposes of awarding damages to an innocent party is to punish the guilty party for his wrong. The punishment type of damages is usually called *punitive damages,* but its use is rare in contract actions. The remedies of injunction and declaratory judgment were discussed in Chapter 2. Specific performance is discussed below.

C. Damages

MEASURE OF DAMAGES.   It is not enough that damages be explained as a method of compensating an innocent party to a contract for the harm suffered as a result of the other party's breach. In order to make this clear in an actual situation it is necessary to inquire how the damages are to be measured. It is obvious that if damages were measured in terms of out-of-pocket losses, the amount would be quite different from what it would be if damages were measured in terms of the loss of an expectancy. Actually, both methods are used in connection with contract actions, but the latter is the usual *contract measure of damages.* Were the out-of-pocket method, the *tort measure of damages,* used in all contract actions, the innocent parties would as a rule recover only small amounts from the other party, and there would be little deterrent to breaches of contract. The sensible and proper remedy is to give to the plaintiff the benefit of the bargain he made with the defendant, in so far as this can be accomplished by substituting money for performance. To put it another way, the contract measure of damages seeks to place the innocent party in the position he would have been in had the guilty party performed as he promised to do. Where *S* agrees to sell tomatoes to *B* for $2 a case but fails to do so, and *B* must buy tomatoes from another seller at $3 a case, both measures of damages achieve the same result. The out-of-pocket loss is $1 a case, and, by awarding him $1 a case damages, *B* is put into the position he would have been in had the contract been performed. There may be situations where there is no out-of-pocket loss at all but where the innocent party is deprived of an expectancy, for example, where *B* fails to perform his promise to buy the tomatoes at $2 and *S* must sell the tomatoes in a depressed market for $1. Where the contract measure seeks to give the innocent party his expectancy, the tort measure seeks only to restore the party to the position he was in before he suffered an out-of-pocket loss. In either case, the amount of the damages to be awarded to the innocent party is a question of fact for the jury. It sometimes happens that in spite of a breach of contract by one party, the innocent party suffers no loss either out-of-pocket or in expectancy. In this case there is no need to award the innocent party damages as compensation because no loss has been suffered, but the innocent party may recover some nominal amount simply in recognition of the fact the contract was breached. His "winning" the case in this fashion usually results in the imposition of the court costs upon the breaching party.

It should be noted that a breach of contract by one party cannot be used by the innocent party to put himself in a better position than he would have been in had the contract been performed. Where the tomato buyer refuses to perform, the seller cannot sell the tomatoes elsewhere and then recover the full contract price from the defaulting buyer.

DAMAGES REASONABLY CONTEMPLATED.   The damages awarded in any case must be such as would be reasonably contemplated by the parties. If special circumstances cause some unusual injury, damages are not recoverable therefor unless the offending party knew or should have known the circumstances at the time the contract was breached. Where a trucking company negligently or intentionally delayed the shipment of a broken drive-shaft to a place of repair, it could not be held liable for the total loss of profits resulting from the shut-down of an entire mill during the period of the delay, unless the trucking company had notice that unusual damage might flow from the late delivery of a piece of metal shaft. Where *A* sends a telegraphic acceptance to an offer of a million dollar contract, he cannot hold the telegraph company for the loss of the contract resulting from the misdelivery of the telegram, unless the telegraph company had notice from the language of the telegram or otherwise that unusual damages might flow from a breach. With such notice the telegraph company would have given the message special handling to assure its proper delivery. (Note that a telegraph company will ordinarily seek to limit its liability for its breaches by stating in the terms of its contract with the sender a maximum liability it will bear without having been given special notice. The effect of these limitations of liability has already been discussed.)

DUTY TO MITIGATE DAMAGES. A party injured by a breach of contract is required to do everything reasonably possible to minimize his own loss and thus reduce the damages for which the party guilty of a breach has become liable. This is not a real, enforceable duty but simply a limitation on the extent of the injured party's recovery. The innocent party generally cannot recover damages for harm he could have prevented by the expenditure of reasonable efforts and expense. Where *A* refuses to supply water to *B*, an orchard owner, except at a price in excess of the contract price, *B* cannot recover from *A* the loss he suffered as a result of his trees dying because he refused to take any water at all. *B* should take the water, pay the higher price, and sue for the difference between that price and the contract price. An employee discharged without cause before his employment contract has expired has an action against the employer for breach of contract, but he must do everything reasonably possible to mitigate the damages by seeking other employment. In general, the wrongfully discharged employee does not have to seek or accept employment in any fields other than those in which he is accustomed to working or outside the locality where he lives. The employee is entitled to the difference between the salary he would have earned with his original employer and the salary he did earn with another. If he earns as much or more with the other employment, the discharged employee has a right only to nominal damages.

LIQUIDATED DAMAGES AND PENALTY CLAUSES. Clauses in contracts providing for the payment of penalties for nonperformance are usually void and unenforceable because they amount to a forfeiture of money or property without regard to the damage which may actually flow from a breach of contract. Where *S* has agreed to sell and *B* to buy one case of tomatoes and their contract provides that a party shall pay a penalty of $100 should he fail to perform the contract, it is obvious that, except in the most unusual of circumstances, the $100 penalty has no reasonable relation to any damage which might possibly result from a breach, and is intended, not to compensate for loss, but to force the performance of the contract. The courts have always frowned upon such penalties and forfeitures, and many states have statutes expressly prohibiting their use.

Provisions in contracts stipulating damages are valid, however, where they meet two tests: (1) accurate estimates of damages, at the time the contract is made, must have been very difficult or impossible. (2) The damages specified must bear some reasonable relation to the damages that might actually result from a breach of the contract. If these two tests are met, the damage stipulating clause is usually referred to as a *liquidated damages clause* instead of a *penalty clause*. It should be noted that using the label "liquidated damages" on a damages provision in a contract is not enough by itself to satisfy the tests, nor is the use of "penalty" necessarily fatal, although the latter word may be an indication that the parties intended the provision to secure the performance rather than to compensate for loss.

The two tests may, at first glance, seem contradictory because one test requires that the ascertainment of damages must be difficult or impossible while the other necessitates a reasonable relation between the stipulated damages and those that might actually flow from a breach. A good example of the actual consistency of the tests is a building construction contract where, no matter what kind of building is involved, it is usually very difficult to make accurate estimates of the damages which might result to the owner if the builder is late in completing the structure. Bear in mind, of course, that the estimates we are concerned with are those made at the time the contract is entered into. The fact that damages turn out to be easily ascertained at the time of action is immaterial. Although the damages may be difficult to estimate accurately, this does not mean that it is impossible to tell whether the specified damages bear any reasonable relation to damages which may actually result. Specified damages of $10,000 a day for delay in the completion of a $25,000 building would be clearly unreasonable in relation to any actual damage which might result. Liquidated damages of $10 or $50 a day, on the other hand, do bear a reasonable relation to likely damages, as may even higher amounts.

What was largely a matter of case law in most states has been made the subject of specific provision in the Uniform Commercial Code. Section 2-718 provides that contract terms fixing unreasonably large liquidated damages are void as penalties. It should be noted that an unreasonably small liquidated damage amount may be subject to question under the Code provision on unconscionable contracts or clauses. In order to be valid under the Code, a liquidated damage clause must be "reasonable in the light of the anticipated or actual harm caused by the breach, the difficulties of proof of loss, and the inconvenience or nonfeasibility of otherwise obtaining an adequate remedy."

In further support of the strong public policy against penalties and forfeitures, the Code provides that a buyer, who is himself in breach of contract, may obtain from a seller who has rescinded the contract because of the buyer's breach the return of any amount by which the buyer's payments exceed either of the following: (1) the amount to which the seller is entitled under a liquidated damage clause; or (2) if there is no such clause, twenty per cent of the value of the total performance on which the buyer is obligated under the contract or five hundred dollars, whichever is smaller. The buyer's rights to restitution under this provision are subject to limitation to the extent the seller establishes either a right to damages other than through a liquidated damage clause or the value of any benefit received by the buyer under the contract.

D. Specific Performance

Damages is a legal remedy, one which had its origins in the common law. Specific performance is one of the many unusual and ingenious remedies developed by the courts of equity. It is said that, as a general rule, neither specific performance nor any other equitable remedy is available unless the remedy at law is inadequate, that is, that damages awarded to the innocent party will not do justice to him. As the name itself implies, specific performance is not a subsitutional remedy but a specific one where the promisor is required to do the thing which he promised to do. It is an unusual remedy, and will not be granted by the court execpt where the circumstances themselves are unusual, which in most cases means that the injured party cannot be adequately compensated by damages.

The situation in which the courts have most commonly granted the unusual remedy of specific performance is the enforcement of contracts for the purchase and sale of real property. Although frequently explained in terms of inadequacy of the remedy at law, this explanation is not always statisfactory—for example, where the purchaser of real property is compelled to accept performance by the seller and pay the price. Here damages would be a perfectly good remedy for the injured seller. It must be pointed out, however, that not all courts will grant specific performance against a defaulting purchaser. Those which do often reason that if the purchaser can get specific performance against a defaulting seller, it would be unjust or inequitable to deny this remedy to the seller as against a defaulting purchaser. The purchaser's specific remedy against the seller is more easily justified in terms of the inadequacy of the legal remedy because real property is a unique commodity, no two parcels being exactly alike, and money damages to a purchaser who has failed to obtain the seller's performance would often be an unfair measure of the loss the purchaser has suffered.

The characteristic of uniqueness is the test generally applied in cases involving specific performance of promises with regard to personal property. Most personal property is not unique in the sense here required, and consequently specific performance is not available as a remedy. Personal property may be unique, however. The uniqueness of Rembrandt's "Man in the Golden Helmet," of which there is only one in the world, cannot be disputed. A family heirloom may be unique. Patents and trademarks and copyrights are unique because they represent temporary or semi-permanent monopolies. Shares of stock may be unique if they are not obtainable anywhere except from the party who promised to sell them or if they represent a controlling interest in a corporation. In all of these situations, the remedy of specific performance has been granted by the courts. Section 2-716 of the Uniform Commercial Code provides that "specific performance may be decreed where the goods are unique or in other proper circumstances." Specific performance cannot be used to compel one person, under a contract of employment, to work for another. Not only is the remedy at law likely to be adequate but also such compulsion is a violation of the Constitutional provision against involuntary servitude.

E. Hard Bargains and Unconscionable Contracts

Refusal by the courts to enforce contracts is not a "remedy" in the strict sense of the word, but the discussion of this subject belongs, logically, in the same company as the enforcement of contracts and remedies for failure to perform, especially the equitable remedy of specific performance. It is important to remember that equity's historical origins have surrounded the granting of its remedies with an atmosphere entirely different from that which pervades the common law. Many of the dogmas of equity, which often have rather quaint names, are taken very seriously by a court engaged in administering equitable remedies. A court of equity, for example, requires that persons who seek equitable relief must come to court with "clean hands." This means much more than the fact that a court will not enforce a contract obtained by fraud or force. A court of equity will not grant specific performance where the defendant has not received an adequate consideration, where the contract is unjust or unreasonable, where there have been unfair practices, where the contract is uncertain, and on many other grounds. Even in those states where the effect of the seal in supplanting consideration has not been abolished, as far as actions at common law are concerned, a court of equity may ignore the seal and deny relief on the ground that there is no consideration or that there is inadequate consideration.

Courts of equity have long refused to enforce certain contracts, or portions of contracts, obtained as a result of the vastly superior bargaining power or strategical position of one of the parties. Hard bargains, or now more commonly, "unconscionable contracts," thus driven may often not be enforced against the party in the subordinate position. The test is not easy to describe with any degree of certainty. Generally, however, if the contract is so one-sided or so oppressive, against the background of the particular trade or circumstances, that one could not in good conscience view it as the result of genuine bargaining, it will be found unconscionable. Unfortunately, courts are much more likely to refuse enforcement of such contracts when sitting in equity than when sitting as courts of law. Ancient distinctions based upon different historical origins still serve to keep law and equity apart.

However, there are signs that the treatment of unconscionable contracts is approaching similarity on the two sides of the court. Many courts will refuse enforcement of such contracts even when the remedy sought is legal and not equitable. Perhaps the most important recent development in this regard has occurred as a result of the adoption of the Uniform Commercial Code, which states in Section 2-301(1):

> If the court as a matter of law finds the contract or any clause of the contract to have been unconscionable at the time it was made the court may refuse to enforce the contract, or it may enforce the remainder of the contract without

the unconscionable clause, or it may so limit the application of any unconscionable clause as to avoid any unconscionable result.

This language is important because it is broad and flexible, and because it
applies equally to legal and equitable proceedings.

F. Anticipatory Breach

Most contracts are breached at or after the time for performance has arrived.
Is it possible for a contract to be breached before the time of performance?
In January, A and B enter into a contract whereby A will employ B in June to
take a tour-party to Europe, and B will appear in New York by June 10th
in order to begin performance. No performance is required of either party
until June 10th. If B notifies A in March that he will not appear in June and
does not intend to go through with the contract, A is in a serious dilemma
if B's notice to A does not constitute a breach. If there has been no breach, the
contract is still in effect. If A hires C to take the tour-party, he runs the risk
that B will change his mind and show up on June 10th to perform. If A uses
B, C will sue for breach of contract. If A uses C, B will sue for breach of contract. Or if A does not hire anyone to take B's place but waits to see if B will
appear, A runs the risk that B will not appear and that the tour-party cannot be
escorted to Europe, in which case, the members of the party may sue A for
breach of contract. Because of this kind of dilemma there has arisen the doctrine
of *anticipatory breach,* or *anticipatory repudiation,* which permits A to treat any
such communication as S's as a breach of contract although no actual breach
can take place until failure of performance at or after the time performance
is due. An implied repudiation may take place where one party puts it out of
his power to perform, for example, where S sells to C property that S had
already contracted to sell to B.

The doctrine of anticipatory breach permits the party who has been directly
informed by the other that there will be no performance at the time performance
becomes due, or where there has been implied repudiation, to take the other
party at his word and to treat the contract as though it had already been breached.
The innocent party may bring an action for damages immediately or may wait
and sue after the actual breach. The information must come to the innocent
party directly. Information obtained by rumor is not sufficient. The party
who repudiated the contract may withdraw his repudiation any time before the
other party materially relies on it. This means that B, in the example in the
previous paragraph, may effectively retract his notification of nonperformance
any time before A hires C to take B's place, before A brings an action against
B for breach of contract, or before A relies in some other material fashion.
In effect then, the innocent party has a choice, under the doctrine, of treating
the contract as having been presently breached or of waiting until there is an
actual breach at or after the time of performance. He may resort to any available

remedy for breach of contract, even though he has notified the repudiating party that he will await the latter's performance and has urged retraction.

The Code contains several provisions having to do with anticipatory breach, but there are few variations from the precode law described above. The Code provides that the innocent party, after learning of the repudiation, may await performance for a "commercially reasonable time" before any duty arises to mitigate or avoid resulting damages. Pre-existing law usually permitted him to wait until time for performance.

The doctrine of anticipatory breach does not apply to a promise to pay a money debt. Even though a debtor notifies his creditor directly that he will not pay the debt when due, the creditor must wait until maturity in order to sue for breach of contract. The theory of the exception is that there is no need for the creditor to bring an action before the due date or to take steps to protect himself from loss. The creditor is placed in no dilemma, and may safely wait until the actual time of performance to take action on a breach.

Although volumes could be written on the subject of anticipatory breach and related problems, it is not necessary here to examine all, or even many, of them in order to convey a reasonably accurate impression of the nature of the issue and of the usual methods of approach. However, one additional problem should be considered. Suppose that after the contract is entered into, events, which the promisor had no reason to foresee and of which he was not the cause, made his performance impossible, but that these events did not occur until after the promisor had already repudiated the contract and committed an anticipatory breach. The general view is that the duty of the promisor is discharged by the events making performance impossible, unless they occurred after the time when performance was due. Other aspects of "impossible" performance are considered in the next section.

8. PERFORMANCE—EXCUSES FOR FAILURE TO PERFORM

A. Cases

(1)

Hanford and the Connecticut Fair Association entered into a contract whereby Hanford was to promote and manage a baby show at Charter Oak Park in Hartford on September 6, 7, and 8, 1916. The contract provided that Hanford was to supply 120 prizes and certain printed matter for advertising the show, and to do certain other things in connection with the show. The Association agreed to furnish a room in which to hold the show and to pay Hanford $600. During August and early September, 1916, the disease of infantile paralysis was epidemic in the city of Hartford, and throughout the state of Connecticut, which disease attacked children, especially babies and young children, in large numbers. The disease proved fatal in a large proportion of the cases and permanently crippled many of those afflicted with it. The Association notified Hanford about the middle of August that it wished to cancel the contract on the ground that the disease was so widespread and so serious as to make assemblies of children highly dangerous to the health of the community. Hanford argued that the Association could not avoid its promises on this ground, but the Association refused to perform, and Hanford has filed an action claiming danages for breach of contract.

[*Hanford* v. *Connecticut Fair Ass'n., Inc.,* 92 Conn. 621, 103 A. 838 (1918)]

(2)

On August 4, 1941, Lloyd leased to Murphy for a five-year term beginning September 15, 1941, certain premises located at the corner of Almont Drive and Wilshire Boulevard in the city of Beverly Hills, Los Angeles County, "for the sole purpose of conducting thereon the business of displaying and selling new automobiles (including the servicing and repairing thereof and of selling the petroleum products of a major oil company) and for no other purpose whatsoever without the written consent of the lessor" except "to make an occasional sale of a used automobile." Murphy agreed not to sublease or assign without Lloyd's written consent. On January 1, 1942, the federal government ordered that the sale of new automobiles be discontinued. It modified this order on January 8, 1942, to permit sales to those engaged in military activities, and on January 20, 1942, it established a system of priorities restricting sales to persons having preferential ratings of A-1-j or higher. On March 10, 1942, Murphy explained the effect of these restrictions on his business to Lloyd, who orally waived the restrictions in the lease as to use and subleasing and offered to reduce the rent if Murphy should be unable to operate profitably. Nevertheless Murphy vacated the premises on March 15, 1942, giving oral notice of repudiation of the lease to Lloyd, which was followed by a written notice on March 24, 1942. Lloyd affirmed in writing on March 26th the oral waiver and, failing to persuade Murphy to perform his obligations, rented the property to other tenants pursuant to his powers under the lease in order to mitigate damages. The leased premises were located on one of the main traffic arteries of Los Angeles Country; they were equipped with gasoline pumps and in general adapted for the maintenance of an automobile service station; they contained a one-story storeroom adapted to many commercial purposes; Lloyd had waived the restrictions in the lease and granted Murphy the right to use the premises for any legitimate purpose and to sublease to any responsible party; Murphy continues to carry on the business of selling and servicing automobiles at two other places. It was estimated that 90 per cent of Murphy's gross volume of business was new car sales and 10 per cent gasoline sales. Lloyd sued Murphy for unpaid rent.

[*Lloyd* v. *Murphy,* 25 Cal. 2d 48, 153 P. 2d 47 (1944)]

(3)

Hypocase, Inc. entered into a contract with the Berkland Lumber Company for a large quantity of a certain type of lumber used in making pallets. Berkland did not produce this particular lumber itself nor did it keep any large quantities on hand. When Berkland received a large order for this type of lumber, it immediately placed an order with its supplier, the Short-Cheim Lumber, Inc., of Seattle, Washington. Short-Cheim agreed to provide the necessary quantity. This type of lumber had long been in short supply, due primarily to the international situation and to the great need of the armed services for this material. As a matter of fact, long before the Hypocase contract with Berkland Lumber was made, the Federal Emergency Production Board had assigned priorities to the users of this lumber and made it possible for high priority users to requisition the material even though this interfered with existing contracts of users lower on the priority list. One of the Regulations of the FEPB stated, however: "No person shall be held liable for damages or penalties for any default under any contract or order which shall result directly or indirectly from compliance with any rule, regulation or order of the Federal Emergency Production Board."

Shortly after the above contracts were entered into, the U.S. Space Service requisitioned the entire output of the Short-Cheim mills, as a result of which Short-Cheim could not perform its contract with Berkland Lumber Company. Berkland also failed to perform the contract with Hypocase. The latter contract contained no clause referring to possible difficulties in providing Hypocase with the lumber. Hypocase has demanded delivery of the lumber but without success. Hypocase is now planning to file an action against Berkland for breach of contract, and feels that the FEPB provision quoted above does not apply to Berkland but only to Short-Cheim.

B. Excuses for Failure to Perform a Contract

In General. In a very real sense, the discussion of excuses for failure to perform a contract is closely related to the earlier discussion of the discharge of contracts. Some texts and treatises include this material with the discussion of the many different ways in which contract duties and obligations may be discharged. There is nothing wrong with this approach. There are also several other places in the broad law of contract where this material could properly be treated. For several reasons, the author has chosen to discuss this material within the framework of failures to perform. In the first place, most of the law having to do with impossibility, for example, has developed as a result of the failures of parties to perform their contracts. The atmosphere surrounding the cases has been, for the most part, that of the failure of performance by one party followed by an action for breach of contract by the other party and the attempt by the party who failed to perform to raise a successful defense to that action. In the second place, most of the traditional "methods of discharge" result from the acts of the parties themselves, for example, accord and satisfaction, novation, and account stated. The most important excuse to be discussed below has nothing whatever to do with the acts of the parties. In the third place, the emphasis here is on the word "excuse," or perhaps "defense," and the discussion is oriented in that direction, in sharp contrast to the earlier handling of "discharge," where the orientation was that of consideration and the binding or contractual effects of certain acts or promises. In both situations, however, an important issue is the termination of contractual duties and obligations.

It should be noted that the failure of one party to perform may very well be an excuse for the failure of the other party to start or complete his performance, but this excuse has been considered in connection with the discussion of express and implied conditions. The failure of an external condition may also be an excuse for failing to perform a contract promise. These topics will not be reconsidered here, except indirectly.

Not every failure of performance gives the other party a right of action against the party who does not perform. The general rule that there is a remedy for the innocent party whenever there is a breach of contract, regardless of how minor the breach, does not apply where the failure to perform is excused. An excuse for failure to perform is not the equivalent of performance. It is only a defense to an action for breach of contract brought by the other party. A party who fails to perform and has for the failure a valid excuse is normally not entitled to enforce the promises of the other party. It has already been seen in the section on the statute of frauds that an excuse for nonperformance is not a substitute for actual performance to the extent that it can remove the contract from the requirement of the statute of frauds applying to contracts which by their very terms cannot be performed within one year.

PREVENTION.   Where one of the parties to a contract prevents or hinders the performance of the other party, the other party is usually excused for his failure to perform. In every contract there is an implied promise and condition that neither party will interfere with the other's performance. When a party breaches this condition, he relieves the other party of his obligation to perform and subjects himself to a suit for damages resulting from the breach of condition. For example, O and B enter a contract whereby B is to build for O a house on O's land and O is to pay a certain price. If O prevents B from bringing the necessary materials and workmen onto the land, O has breached the implied condition not to interfere and has discharged B from his obligation to perform.

WAIVER.   A party to a contract may conduct himself in such a way as to indicate that he does not intend to hold the other party strictly to the terms of a contract. Where *A* has the right to accelerate the payment of an instalment debt if *B* fails to make his payments promptly, *A* waives the requirement of prompt payment where he accepts a late payment from *B*. This waiver does not apply to future defaults. Since there is no consideration in this kind of waiver, it may be withdrawn any time before the other materially relies upon it.

THE EFFECT OR UNANTICIPATED RISKS AND HARDSHIPS.   Historically, two terms have been used in connection with the effects of extraordinary circumstances occurring after a contract is entered into: "impossibility" and "frustration of purpose." Although both refer to the issues created by unanticipated risks, they are usually treated separately as though they really dealt with different types of problems. The reason is historical. For many years after executory promises were recognized and enforced at common law, failure of performance by one promisor was not excused on the ground that performance had become impossible. The theory was that the promisor assumed all risks of unforeseen occurrences unless there was in the contract an express condition to the contrary. While some flexibility resulted from interpreting the promise before enforcing it, most interpretations were strict and literal. "Impossibility," in a very literal sense, appeared first on the scene as a kind of implied condition in mitigation of the harsh rules then in use. As the doctrine of excuse for failure to perform expanded through the years, the atmosphere of actual or physical impossibility was retained by the courts in order to maintain consistency with the original exception. Even today, a starting point for a discussion of this whole area of the law is often the statement that in order for impossibility to serve as an excuse for nonperformance, the performance must have become impossible "in the very nature of things," that is, literal impossibility; the discussion then goes on to the exceptions or modifications of this basic idea. In order to avoid the connection with actual impossibility, other terms were sometimes used to describe particular expansions of the doctrine of legal excuse. One such term was "frustration," used to describe a situation where performance was by no means impossible but where the very purpose of the contract has been frustrated by unanticipated events. In the discussion below, special attention will be given to the kind of situation usually referred to under the heading "frustration," but this treatment should be looked upon as simply an example of how the law deals with the basic issues raised by the occurrence of unforeseen events.

A substantive distinction that should be made, however, is based on two different kinds of facts that may lead a party to believe that he has a legal excuse for failure to perform. Where *A* and *B* enter into a contract whereby *A* promises to climb a certain tall flag pole and *B* promises to pay him $100, *A* is not excused from his performance on the ground it is impossible for *him* to climb the pole. But if a high wind dashes the pole to the earth and shatters it into many pieces, *A* would have a vaild defense of impossibility because, under these circumstances, it is impossible, not only for *A*, but for anyone, to climb the pole. In order to discharge the duty of the promisor, supervening events that deprive hims of the ability to perform must also be such that they deprive other persons of the ability to perform. This distinction is often referred to in terms of "objective" and "subjective" impossibility.

Change in the law. An excuse for failure to perform may be afforded a promisor where the performance is still physically possible but where that performance has become illegal. A change in the law after a contract is made may make performance illegal although still physically possible, but the effect will usually be the same as though performance were physically impossible. It is certainly proper to say that it has become impossible to perform "legally."

Death or incapacity. Most contracts are not terminated by the death, insanity, or illness of one of the parties, nor is performance excused. The contract must still be performed by the representatives of the deceased or incompetent party or by the agents of the ill party. Where, however, the contract involves personal services of some sort, the death, insantiy or illness of one of the parties may discharge the contract and supply a defense to an action to enforce the contract. It is obvious that where *A* agrees to work for *B* but dies before the terms of employment is completed, *B* should not be able to bring an action against *A's* estate for damages resulting from *A's* failure to perform the contract. The impossibility of performance due to *A's* death is a good defense to the action. In a contract for personal services, the illness of the party who was to render the services excuses him from liability for his breach. If the absence of the employee is a material breach, the employer is also freed from his obligation to perform, and he may terminate the contract without liability. Where the illness is temporary and no subsitute for the employee is needed, or, if needed, is available on a temporary basis, the breach by the employee is not material, and the employer is not free to terminate the contract. These situations should not be confused with the effect of death or insanity of offeror or offeree.

Destruction of subject matter. The destruction of a specific thing that is to be transferred under a contract will usually operate to excuse the party who was to have transferred it, unless the destruction resulted from the intentional or negligent act of that party. Where only a part of the specific thing has been destroyed, the buyer can choose to avoid the contract entirely, or he can take what there is and pay fct it on a *pro rata* basis, where that is possible, or pay the full contract price, where the amount of a proportional payment cannot be established. A line is drawn by the courts between those situations where the specific subject matter has been destroyed and those where the source from which a party expects to supply the subject matter is destroyed. Originally, the courts afforded no relief where the source of performance was destroyed unless that source was expressly mentioned in the contract as part of the performance.

A promise to manufacture and sell 1000 pairs of shoes was not excused, under this strict view, where the factory in which the promisor intended to manufacture the shoes was destroyed. A promise to manufacture the shoes in a particular factory would be excused if the factory were destroyed. There is an increasing trend in the courts toward *implying* an agreement that goods are to be manufactured in a particular factory which the parties reasonably understand is to be the source of the subject matter of the contract. Many contracts contain specific provisions dealing with the effect of destruction or of other events such as strikes, insurrection, and war, which affect the ability of the parties to perform.

A basic rule of impossibility is that the risk of impossibility of performance, where reasonably foreseeable by the promisor when the contract was made, rests on the promisor. The theory is a simple and a sensible one. If a promisor makes an unqualifed promise to perform in a certain way when circumstances at the time of entering the contract would make the risk of inability to perform foreseeable to a reasonable man, it will be taken for granted he assumed that risk. The normal conduct of a person who foresees the risk of occurrence of a certain event and who intends to avoid the risk would be to provide in the contract for his excuse should the particular event occur. Where the event is not reasonably foreseeable, the occurrence of the event will usually supply the party who fails to perform with an excuse for nonperformance. Under ordinary circumstances, both parties contemplate the continued existence of the subject matter of a contract and do not foresee any great risk of impossibility of performance due to destruction. Under the more modern view, the same is true of the source or means of performance.

Frustration of purpose. An unusual group of legal controversies arose in England as the result of the postponement of the coronation of Edward VII. A number of persons had leased for one or two days apartments and rooms, and even windows, along the procession route for the sole purpose of viewing the coronation procession. When the coronation was postponed, the very purpose of these contracts was destroyed, and many of the short-term tenants sought the return of rent which had been paid or resisted efforts to collect unpaid rent. The English courts did not deal uniformly with these cases. From these and similar cases, however, has come the view that such frustration may be handled in very much the same manner as impossibility. Where there has been no performance by either party, there is no great difficulty encountered in relieving a promisor of his promise on the grounds of the frustration. But where there has been part performance or reliance, the rules in regard to restitution and other relief are not as clear, primarily because of the problem of apportioning losses among the parties. The English Parliament enacted a Frustrated Contracts Act in 1943 which purported to solve some of the problems and injustices, but the Act appears to have created some injustices of its own. Under American law, relief has been afforded for contract frustration, and no great trouble has arisen in connection with apportionment of losses among the parties. The foreseeability of the frustrating event is important, and should be considered in these cases on the same grounds discussed in the preceding paragraph.

Unexpected hardship. Mere unforeseen difficulty or expense does not constitute impossibility, and is ordinarily no excuse for the failure to perform a contract. Were either of these an excuse, a very large proportion of all contracts would go unperformed, and the efficient and careful businessman would be penalized by the inefficient and the careless. The fact that a particular job is more difficult than a party thought it would be, or that the profits as a result of its performance will be less than anticipated, is not a ground for rescission or discharge and is not an excuse for nonperformance. Many business contracts do, of course, contain express provisions releasing a party from his obligation to perform if certain events take place.

Impracticability. In an effort to avoid some of the stultifying effects of the strict requirements of the precode law of impossibility, the Uniform Commercial Code has provided somewhat more flexible principles for the sales contracts coming within its scope. The theory behind the changes is simply that the unusual historic developments of the law of impossibility, discussed above, has resulted in widely divergent rules in the several states and in rules that do not accurately reflect actual trade practices and intentions, especially in the broad and important area of sales. The Code emphasizes the changes and the actual commercial practices on which they are based by employing different language and terminology than is usually found in this area of the law.

Performance by a seller may be excused in whole or in part where it is "made impracticable by the occurrence of a contingency the nonoccurrence of which was a basic assumption on which the contract was made." The substitution of "impracticable" for "impossible" is the logical conclusion of a trend that has been underway for a century or more. In some states, the substitution simply recognizes a change that was already approaching the Code terminology through the avenue of case law.

In most jurisdictions the term "basic assumption" is not really new. It is similar to the language that has for many years been found in cases involving frustration and impossibility. While the Code does not define the term, it is reasonably clear that failure of an agreed source of supply, beyond the seller's control, and a farmer-seller's crop failure, beyond his control, would be among the contingencies included. Performance will not be excused, however, where the seller has assumed, either expressly or as a result of trade practice, the obligation to perform in spite of the nonoccurrence of contingencies affecting a basic assumption. The seller must, under these provisions of the Code, notify the buyer seasonably that there will be delay or nonperformance.

Some of the most interesting changes brought about by the Code occur in situations where the contingency affects only part of the capacity of the seller to perform. While existing law on partial impossibility often excused performance to the extent of the disability, the Code goes further in requiring the seller to allocate his production and deliveries in any fair and reasonable manner among his customers, including regular customers who are not then under contract. The seller must notify the buyers of the estimated quotas to be made available to them. Where the deficiency substantially impairs the value of the whole contract, the buyer need not take his available quota and may elect to terminate the contract. If the buyer takes no action for a reasonable time, not exceeding thirty days, after receiving notification from the seller, the contract lapses.

Under the Code, a seller is also excused, first, when strict performance is made impracticable by compliance in good faith with any applicable foreign or domestic governmental regulation or order whether or not the order later proves to be invalid; and second, where goods identified and agreed upon at the time the contract was made suffer loss or deterioration without the fault of either party. In the former case, the rules of allocation discussed above are relevant where applicable. In the latter case, total loss avoids the contract; if the loss is partial, the buyer may accept the goods with due allowance in the price for the deterioration or deficiency.

The Code contains special provisions dealing with situations where facilities or the manner of transportation or delivery become commercially impracticable without the fault of either party. In these circumstances, any available and commercially reasonable substitute must be tendered and accepted. Substituted performance is also made available where the means or manner of payment fails because of some domestic or foreign governmental regulation.

Conclusion. From the above discussion of "impossibility." it should be clear that the term is quite misleading. As a practical matter, there are many situations where a party may be excused where his performance is a long way from being impossible. On the other hand, a party may be held to have assumed even the risk of literal impossibility, for example, where a person makes an unequivocal promise to perform in circumstances where the risk of literal impossiblity is foreseeable. In the latter situation, we have in effect an insurance contract. It is important also to note that different rules are sometimes applied: 1, where a party is seeking an excuse from his own promise; 2, where a party is seeking an excuse simply from some act he would normally have to perform before he could enforce the contract against the other party; 3, where the party is seeking escape from all liability; and 4, where the party is seeking to have his liability reduced or made less onerous by the excusing circumstances.

It should be remembered that where impossibility existed at the time the contract was made, as where the flag pole in an earlier example had already been destroyed, no binding contract arises, but this results from the application of the principles of mutual assent and not from the doctrines we have just been discussing.

9. THE CONTRACT AND THIRD PARTIES.

A. Cases

(1)

On December 30, 1909, William A. Barton entered into a written contract with the San Francisco Gas & Electric Company to furnish the labor and material and do the brick and terra cotta work on a certain building to be constructed for the company, which agreed to pay him therefor the sum of $2,940. The contract expressly provided that no assignment of it should be made by Barton nor any portion of the work sublet by him to any subcontractor without the written consent of the company and that Barton should personally supervise and direct the work contracted for. On February 12, 1910, Barton entered into the following contract with his brother Frank I. Barton:

> This agreement made this twelfth day of February, 1910, between Frank I. Barton, party of the first part, and William A. Barton, party of the second part, both of the city and county of San Francisco, witnesseth: That the party of the first part does hereby agree for and in consideration of $2,940, to furnish all labor and material required to do all the brick work and set all terra cotta, for building of the addition of the central station 'C' of the San Francisco Gas & Electric Company, east of Fourth street, all in accordance with the plans and specifications furnished by D. H. Burnham & Co., architects, and included in the contract entered into by the said W. A. Barton and the said San Francisco Gas & Electric Company. In consideration of this agreement the said W. A. Barton will pay or cause to be paid to the said Frank I. Barton the above-mentioned sum when it becomes due from the said San Francisco Gas & Electric Company.

Under this contract the work was commenced by Frank I. Barton, although it was personally supervised by William A. Barton. On March 19, 1910, the company paid to William A. Barton $1,350 pursuant to the terms of its contract with him, which left a balance to become due under the contract of $1,590. On March 23, 1910, William A. Barton assigned to Henry T. Johns, a personal creditor of long standing, "all the money coming to me from the San Francisco Gas & Electric Company on the completion of my contract with them." On April 2, Johns notified the company of the assignment. On April 7, Frank I. Barton notified the company in writing that he was the subcontractor for the work, that he had received from his brother $1,350, the first payment thereon, and that another payment would be due in a few days, as the work would then be finished, and notified the company to withhold the money due on its contract with William A. Barton for Frank I. Batron. This notice was accompanied by a copy of the contract between William A. and Frank I. Barton. The company was never asked for its consent to this contract nor did it know of such contract until the notice on April 7. The work was completed and accepted by the company on April 14, 1910. Both Johns and Frank I. Barton are demanding the balance due from the company.

[Based on: *Butler* v. *San Francisco Gas & Electric Co.,* 168 Cal. 32, 141 P. 818 (1914)]

(2)

Erickson is an accountant and tax counselor. He performed services in his professional capacity for the Grande Ronde Lumber Company in connection with income taxes assessed prior to January 1, 1929. Before he was paid for his services, the board of directors of the Stoddard Company adopted a resolution which authorized the officers of the corporation to purchase all of the property and assets of the Grande Ronde Company for a consideration of 3600 shares of capital stock of the Stoddard Company, and, in addition, to assume "all the liabilities of the said The Grande Ronde Lumber Company, except the liability for income tax incurred prior to January 1st, 1929." The offer was transmitted to the Grande Ronde Company in a letter dated March 11, 1929, which, besides mentioning the 3600 shares, added: "It is understood that in addition to the stock to be delivered to you that we are to assume all of the indebtedness of the Grande Ronde Lubber Company, except liability for income tax incurred or accrued prior to January 1st, 1929." On the same day the stockholders of the Grande Ronde Company accepted the offer, and the transaction was shortly concluded. Erickson is seeking to recover from Stoddard the compensation for his services.

[*Erickson* v. *Grande Ronde Lumber Co.,* 162 Ore. 556, 92 P. 2d 170 (1939)]

(3)

A contract was entered into between the city of Duluth and Jens O. Rhude and his partners whereby the latter obligated themselves to do certain work on sewer construction. Because the contract contemplated excavation in solid rock and the consequent use of heavy charges of explosives, the effect of which might cause damage in the vicinity of the work, the contract contained a clause making Rhude and his partners "liable for any damages done to the work or other structure or public or private property and injuries sustained by persons" in the operations. Property belonging to Henry E. La Mourea was damaged by the blasting operations. La Mourea seeks to recover his damages from Rhude and his partners on the basis of their contract with the city of Duluth.

[*La Mourea* v. *Rhude,* 209 Minn. 53, 295 N.W. 304 (1940)]

(4)

Hypocase, Inc. in need of additional office space and not desiring to build facilities for this purpose on its own premises, leased a portion of a building in downtown Berkland owned by George Ohner. At the time the lease was made, the entire building was equipped with a sprinkler system. Hypocase made it known to Ohner that is would be keeping many valuable records on the leased premises and was as much concerned about leaks in the sprinkler system as about fire. Ohner then entered into a contract with the Anosmia Signal Company whereby the latter agreed to install and maintain on the sprinkler system an automatic central station signaling device which would immediately signal any leakage of water into the portion of the building leased by Hypocase. During the weekend of May 28 to 30, 1960, a large leak occurred in the sprinkler system in the premises leased by Hypocase and continued until discovered on the morning of May 31. Considerable damage was done to files, records and furnishings. The alarm system failed to operate. Hypocase has filed suit against Anosmia Signal Company.

(5)

Under the contract between Hypocase, Inc. and Barton Bilder (see Case 4, page 151), Hypocase was to pay the contract price for the addition to its factory in three instalments: the first $10,000 when the foundations and subflooring were completed; the second $50,000, when the construction was completed; the third $50,000, 35 days after completion. The first instlment was paid on November 5, 1967, on the completion of the foundations and subflooring. Neither of the other instalments has been paid. Bilder is heavily in debt to the Anosmia National Bank. When pressed in early December for the payment of a loan then due, Bilder executed a written instrument assigning to the bank "all money due or to become due to me under the contract with Hypocase, Inc." In March, 1968, Bilder assigned $25,000 of the second instalment to the Berkland Lumber Company in order to obtain the necessary materials with which to continue the Hypocase job. Berkland immediately notified Hypocase of the assignment. When the construction was finally finished on September 1, a vice-president of the bank called Paul Perston and asked for the $50,000 instalment due on completion of the work. This was the first notice to Hypocase of the assignment to the bank. Preston, of course, refused and explained to the bank officer that Bilder had stopped performance in April and that another building contractor had finished the job. The bank officer said that he was sorry to hear that Bilder had caused Hypocase so much trouble, but that problem was between Hypocase and Bilder and had nothing to do with the bank's claim. The same day, Berkland Lumber demanded payment of its $25,000 assignment, which Preston also refused. Thirty-five days after completion, the bank demanded the last instalment. Both the bank and Berkland have continued their demands for payment and are now threatening suit.

B. In General

As a rule, persons who are not actually parties to a contract receive no rights and incur no obligations thereunder. This result is in keeping with the basic nature of a contract as a voluntary, personal, private relation between or among the persons who entered into it. Nobody can be compelled to enter a contract nor can a person who is not a party to an existing contract compel those who are parties to admit him as a party. Parties who are willing to enter into contractual relations may do so, if they possess the legal capacity, but the essential characteristics of the contract are lost where an attempt is made to bring an unwilling person into a contractual relationship with another person. This freedom of contract is one of the fundamental legal aspects of our economic system. Much of the law of contract which has been discussed and described so far in this chapter would have to be changed completely were the voluntary basis for the contract device abolished. The law has a way of expressing the idea that a person must, in general, be a party to a contract in order to get rights and incur duties under that contract. It is said there must be *privity of contract* between persons before one person may enforce the rights and duties of a contract against the other. When two parties have actually entered into a contract with each other, there is no question that they are in privity and may enforce the contract against each other. A person who is not a party to the contract is usually not in privity with those who are parties and may not enforce the contract against them.

There are a few exceptions to these rules. Practically speaking, they are not exceptions at all, but are modifications resulting from the fact that the rules discussed above occasionally come into conflict with other, and sometimes equally important, rules and principles. One of these exceptions, the *assignment,* results from a conflict between the rule just discussed, that a person has a right to select the persons with whom he will contract, and the rule that a person who owns rights or property may dispose of them as he pleases as long as he does not unduly interfere with the rights of others. Out of these conflicting principles has come the rule that one party to a contract may assign his rights under the contract without the consent of the other party, when such transfer of contract rights does not disturb the essentials of the existing contractual relationship between the two parties. The Code is very explicit in saying that contract rights may be assigned where they do not "materially change the duty of the other party, or increase materially the burden or risk imposed on him by his contract, or impair materially his chance of obtaining return performance." The other important exception to the rule is the *third party beneficiary contract,* which is entered into by *A* and *B* for the express purpose of benefiting *C,* who is not actually a party to the contract. It is obvious that little modification is required in the concept of privity where the very purpose of the contract is to confer benefit on a third person. In both of these exceptions, however, the third person is, in effect, in privity of contract because of the unusual nature of the situation.

C. Assignment

NATURE OF AN ASSIGNMENT. The term *assignment* is one which may be applied to the transfer of the ownership of any kind of right or property from one person to another. In the sense in which we use it here, however, it refers to the transfer of a contract right to a third person who is not a party to the contract. An ordinary sale, which involves just the seller and buyer, could qualify as an assignment under the broader definition, but it is not an assignment under the technical meaning of "assignment" used here. The "assignment" we are concerned with involves three parties, not just two. Two of these are actually parties to the contract while the third is not. These parties have legal names. Where *A* has promised to pay *B* $1,000 in exchange for *B's* building *A* a garage and *B* transfers his rights to the $1,000 to *C*, *A* becomes an *obligor, B* an *assignor* (and *obligee*), and *C* an *assignee*. An *assignment,* then, is the transfer of rights against an obligor by an assignor (or obligee) to an assignee. Note that the assignment does not transfer the $1,000, but, instead, transfers a right to the $1,000.

Under precode law, no particular formality was necessary for assignments, except where the statute of frauds required them to be in writing. The Code has substantially altered this situation, however. It is now more accurate to say that in order to be enforceable the assignment of most contract rights or accounts must be in writing, must be signed by the assignor, and must describe the obligation being assigned. Assignments which do not come under this rule would still be subject to Section 1-206(1) of the Code, discussed above in connection with the statute of frauds, requiring that sales of personal property beyond a value of $5,000 be in writing. The Code defines *account* as the right to receive payment for goods already delivered or services already performed, and it defines *contract right* as the contingent right to receive payment when performance later takes place. These matters are discussed in greater detail in Chapter 13.

A promise to assign rights is not enforceable unless it is supported by consideration and satisfies the other requirements of a valid contract. The assignment may be a gift, because it is without consideration, but it may not be revoked once the assignment is executed. Most assignments result from the acts of the parties, but assignments may also take place by operation of law, as where the executor or administrator of a decedent's estate succeeds to the contract rights of the decedent.

WHAT MAY BE ASSIGNED. Only rights may be assigned. The concept of ownership does not exist with regard to a duty. A person is not said to own a duty. Consequently, contractual duties cannot be assigned, although they may be delegated with effects quite different from assignment. The most common assignments are those of money rights, but rights to other types of performance are also assignable. As a matter of fact, almost all contract rights can be assigned. It is easier, for purposes of discussion, to consider the rights that cannot be assigned than it is to attempt to list all the rights that can be assigned.

WHAT CANNOT BE ASSIGNED. A contract may expressly provide that rights arising under it may not be assigned. An assignment in violation of the provision is usually voidable, not void. Leases, which are treated as contracts, frequently contain such prohibitions against assignment, but the lessor must take active steps to regain the premises where the right to occupy them has been assigned by the tenant in violation of such a provision. Otherwise, the assignment will be effective. Future rights under a contract not yet made cannot be assigned, and such an assignment usually continues to be ineffective even when the contract is made and the rights created. Future rights under a presently existing contract may be assigned. The requirement is simply that there must be a contract in existence on which the assignment may operate. It is not necessary that the rights be already in existence. Certain types of rights, either by reason of a specific statute or at common law, cannot be assigned. Examples are the rights to alimony, rights to damages for personal injuries, some claims against the United States Government, and, in some states, claims that will be enforced in special courts such as small claims courts. Public officials are usually prohibited from assigning their future wages and salaries.

Where the contract calls for the skill, credit, or other personal quality of the parties, the rights to the benefits of these qualities cannot be assigned. B's right to work for A cannot be assigned to C, even where the work is of the most routine and unskilled sort. B's right to his wages can be assigned. A's right to B's services ordinarily cannot be assigned to someone else. Where B has obtained a line of credit from A, B cannot assign his right to credit to C. The extension of credit is on a personal basis and depends upon B's character and qualifications, not C's.

Owing to the unusual economic pressures of the depression of the 1930's and the abuses by creditors in obtaining assignments of wages, most states during that period enacted special statutes to cope with the problem by limiting a wage earner's right to assign his wages.

EFFECT OF ASSIGNMENT.   The assignee, after assignment, is the owner of the rights previously owned by the assignor. He may, in most states, enforce these rights in his own name and in his own right, but many states and the common law require the suit to be brought in the name of the assignor. After a proper assignment, the assignor has disposed of his rights. As has already been noted, he cannot thus dispose of his duties. A party to a contract cannot escape his obligations by a mere assignment. Unless the other party to the contract releases him in some way, a party obligated on a contract remains obligated in spite of his attempts to assign or delegate. Where the duties are not personal in nature, they may be delegated to a third person, as is the case with the delegation by a general contractor to a subcontractor on a building contract. The general contractor does not escape liability by the delegation, and he will be held responsible if the subcontractor fails to perform or performs improperly. The delegation, for obvious reasons, cannot be accomplished without the express or implied consent of the person to whom the duties are being delegated.

An important aspect of an assignment is the fact that the assignee gets no more of a right than the assignor had to give. It is sometimes said that the assignee simply *stands in the shoes of the assignor*. This means that any defense the obligor had against the assignor, he also has against the assignee. If the obligor was induced to enter the contract through the fraud of the assignor, the rights of rescission and the defense of fraud are available against the assignee as well as against the assignor. Note in Part 4 the contrasts between the ordinary assignment and the negotiation of a negotiable instrument, in connection with which the assignee may actually get greater rights than the assignor had to give. An assignee who suffers a loss because of a defense the obligor has used against him may recover the loss from the assignor.

REQUIREMENT OF NOTICE. When an obligor without notice of an assignment pays his debt to the assignor, the obligor is protected from any action by the assignee. This result places a responsibility upon the assignee, if he is to protect himself fully, to give immediate notice of the assignment to the obligor. Of course, the assignee has an action against the assignor should the assignor accept payment from the obligor, but this action may or may not be as good as one against the obligor. An obligor who pays the assignor with knowledge of the assignment is still liable to the assignee.

SUCCESSIVE ASSIGNMENTS OF THE SAME RIGHT. Occasionally, an assignor will assign the same contract right to more than one person. Where, for example, B, assigns his right to the $1,000 rising out of the garage contract, discussed above, to C on June 1, then to D on June 5, and then to E on June 10, B has in effect sold the same property to three different people. Unfortunately, the courts have not agreed on the solution that should be applied in this situation. Some took the view that the assignor had nothing to assign after the first assignment to C. Consequently, D and E would get no rights at all, except against B. This view set a trap for the obligor who paid D or E without knowing of C, who had the only rights. C could recover the amount of the assignment from A in spite of the fact A had already paid D or E in good faith.

Another view, followed by many courts, was to give priority to the first assignee to notify the obligor of his assignment. This view avoided the trap and was well justified on practical grounds. In either case, actions were available to the losing assignees against the assignor.

Under the Code, a third approach was taken to the same problem and will prevail in those states adopting the Code. In order to protect himself against third persons, the assignee must file with an appropriate public officer a statement pertaining to the assignment. Notification of the obligor is no substitute for filing, and it will serve only to prevent the obligor from discharging his obligation by paying the assignor. It will not give the assignee priority over an innocent later assignee who files a statement. These statements, called "financing statements," are discussed in greater detail in Chapter 13.

PARTIAL ASSIGNMENTS. Where an assignor assigns part of his rights to each of several assignees, the situation is substantially the same as where all the rights have been assigned to one assignee. There is nothing illegal or unethical about assigning $300 from a $1,000 claim to *C*, $300 to *D*, and $400 to *E*. Each is entitled to receive the amount of his assignment from the obligor. Generally, however, partial assignees are required to join in an action against the obligor in order to avoid a multiplicity of suits. This requirement is based on the fundamental principle that contract rights may be assigned only where the assignment does not interfere unduly with the rights of the obligor.

WARRANTIES OF ASSIGNOR. In general, an assignor makes certain implied warranties or promises to the assignee in connection with an assignment, unless he expressly stipulates to the contrary. He warrants that he is the owner of the right or that he has the power to assign it, that the right is valid, and that there are no defenses available to the obligor except those about which the assignor has given the assignee notice. The assignor does not, by the mere act of assignment, warrant the collectibility of the obligation from the obligor.

ASSIGNMENTS UNDER THE CODE. Provisions of the Uniform Commercial Code make some changes in the general conclusions set forth in the paragraphs above, although the variations from the law of a few specific states are not substantive. The policy of the Code is to enhance the assignability of rights arising under certain kinds of contracts. In keeping with this policy, the Code provides that the assignment of certain contract rights cannot be prohibited even by the agreement of the parties. Among these rights are a right to a sum due or to become due, a right to damages for breach of a whole contract, and any right arising out of the assignor's performance of his entire obligation, such as the right to receive goods after payment is completed. [These provisions are contained in Sections 2-210(2) and 9-318(4).] The theory is that these rights are no longer executory and in no way raise questions of delegation of duties.

Furthermore, the Code provides that routine contractual prohibitions against assignment of "the contract" are to be construed as barring only the delegation of the assignor's performance, unless circumstances indicate the contrary. No assignment is authorized by the Code, however, where it would materially affect the other party.

The parties are free to prohibit delegation of performance. Unless they do so, the Code says expressly, a party may perform through a delegate unless the other party has a substantial interest in having his original promisor perform or control performance. An assignment in general terms, e.g. "the contract" or "all my rights under the contract," is both an assignment of right and a delegation of performance, unless the language or the circumstances indicate the contrary. When such an assignment is accepted by the assignee, it constitutes a promise by him to perform the duties called for in the contract, and this promise is enforceable by either the assignor or the other party to the original contract.

Obviously, the assignor is not released from his duties to the other party to the contract by this arrangement between himself and the assignee. Generally, these Code provisions recognize both assignment of rights and delegation of performance as normal and permissible incidents of most contracts.

Section 9-318(2) contains a provision that is considerably at variance with precode contract law. This section permits the original parties to the contract to modify their contract even after assignment and notification, as long as they act in good faith and with reasonable commercial standards. The assignment may provide, however, that modification or substitution is a breach by the assignor. The justification for this change in pre-existing law is said to be the prevalence today of large-scale procurement, especially by the government, where the necessity for cutting back or modifying existing contracts may affect thousands of subcontracts lying on many levels below the prime contract.

D. Third Party Beneficiary Contracts

IN GENERAL. Contracts are sometimes made for the express purpose of benefiting a third person not a party to the contract. Such third persons are called *third party beneficiaries*. The best known example of a contract for the benefit of a third person is the life insurance contract, where the insured and the insurance company enter into a contract for the express benefit of some third person. The beneficiaries of these third party contracts fall into two types— *donee beneficiaries* and *creditor beneficiaries*. Where, for example, *A* and *B* enter into a contract under which *B*, in exchange for consideration supplied by *A*, promises to do something for the benefit of *C*, it is clear that *C* is a third party beneficiary. If *A* is indebted to *C* or owes some legal duty to *C*, which *B* promises to discharge, then *C* is a creditor beneficiary. If, on the other hand, *A* is not indebted to *C*, the performance by *B* amounts to a gift to *C*, and *C* is a donee beneficiary. In neither situation is *C* a party to the contract, nor has he supplied any consideration for *B*'s promise to *A*. It is not necessary, in order to have a third party creditor beneficiary contract, that the beneficiary be a real creditor. It is sufficient if *A* intends to satisfy a supposed obligation to *C*. Nor is it necessary for any beneficiary contract that the beneficiary know of the contract when it is made.

In all states the beneficiary of an insurance contract may sue the promisor (*B*), but the courts are divided in regard to all other types of third party beneficiary contracts. The problem, of course, is privity of contract. In most states privity is found, and the beneficiary may sue the promisor on his promise to do something of benefit for the beneficiary.

INDIRECT BENEFICIARIES. Unless the contract is made expressly for the direct benefit of the beneficiary, he may not maintain a suit even in those states where suits are normally allowed. Where *A*, *B*, and *C*, merchants, entered into a contract whereby all agreed to keep their places of business closed on Sunday and provided that violators were to pay $100 to the *X Orphanage* for each violation, it was held that *X* could not maintain a suit against a violator because the contract was not for the express benefit of X but for the benefit of the parties to the contract. Some very interesting cases have developed over the issue of whether inhabitants of a town are direct or incidental beneficiaries of contracts between the town government and, for example, a water company or a gas company. There have been decisions in both directions. It is not necessary that a person be the exclusive beneficiary in order to maintain an action on the contract.

RIGHTS AND LIABILITIES OF BENEFICIARIES AND PARTIES. A creditor beneficiary really has two claims: one against the promisor on his promise to do something of benefit for the beneficiary, and one against the promisee on the debt or other legal obligation existing between them. Obviously, he cannot recover full satisfaction from both. A donee beneficiary, on the other hand, may only bring an action against the promisor. There is no ground for an action against the promisee. On the failure of the promisor to perform, the promisee may bring an action to enforce the promise and may recover nominal damages in addition to those recovered by the beneficiary. The promisor, in failing to perform, has in effect breached the contract with regard to both promisee and beneficiary. It is clear that the beneficiary has no duties but only rights.

RESCISSION BY THE ORIGINAL PARTIES. Different rules have been applied to the attempts by the original parties to the contract to rescind the contract so as to destroy the beneficiary's rights. In all states the parties are prevented from rescinding a life insurance contract without the consent of the beneficiary unless the right to do so was reserved in the insurance contract. Most life insurance contracts contain a clause permitting a change of beneficiary without the consent of the beneficiary. For other beneficiary contracts the situation is confused. The Contracts Restatement takes the view that creditor beneficiary contracts may be rescinded or varied any time before the beneficiary brings suit on the contract or materially changes his position in reliance on the contract. Apparently, the theory behind this rule is that the creditor can still pursue his old claim against the promisee. The Restatement would not permit the rescission or variation of donee beneficiary contracts except where the right to do so has been reserved by the parties. The donee beneficiary, obviously, loses all his rights if the contract is rescinded. Some courts take the approach that if the beneficiary has knowledge of the contract and has assented to it, the contract cannot be rescinded.

PROBLEMS

1. Explain the part that the contract plays in our modern commercial society.

2. Give examples of each of the following types of contracts: executed, executory, formal, simple, express, implied in fact, implied in law, bilateral, unilateral, void, voidable.

3. How does one differentiate between agreements and promises which are contracts and those which are not contracts?

4. Does the law employ an objective or a subjective standard in determining whether parties have agreed to the terms of an alleged contract? Explain.

5. How can it be determined whether a communication from one party to another is an offer?

6. Selir sent a telegram to Biar offering to sell him 1,000 cases of mangoes at $3.48 a case. Due to an error in transmission, the telegram read "$3.08" when it was delivered to Biar, who filed an immediate reply with the telegraph company saying: "I accept your offer to sell 1,000 cases mangoes." The mangoes were delivered to Biar in due course and were resold by him a few days after he received them. When Selir presented his bill for $3,480, Biar refused to pay that amount, and Selir learned for the first time of the error. What are the rights of the parties?

7. On April 5, 1952, N. E. Yanki in Provincetown, Massachusetts, wrote to Wes Cost Saler in Seattle as follows: "If you will deliver your 100 foot, clipper-rigged schooner, Flying Saucer, to Provincetown by October 1, 1953, I will pay you $350,000 cash for it." As soon as Saler had read the letter, he hired a crew and set sail for Provincetown. Due to many mishaps enroute, Saler did not arrive in Cape Cod waters until August, 1953. As Saler rounded the Provincetown breakwater on August 22, 1953, he received a blinker message from Yanki saying: "Sorry to disappoint you, but I have decided to buy a motor vessel. Good luck on your return trip to Seattle." What are the rights of the parties?

8. On October 1, Selir wrote to Biar as follows: "I offer to sell you my 10,000 shares of stock in the Creamed Chicken Corporation for $200,000; terms: $50,000 on acceptance, $50,000 six months thereafter, balance one year after date of acceptance. For $150 I will keep this offer open until November 1st." On October 3, Biar replied: "Your offer of October 1st is very interesting. Would you take $175,000 cash for your stock?"

On October 5, Selir replied: "No!"

On October 7, Biar wrote Selir: "I will accept your offer to give me until November 1st to consider the matter further. Enclosed find money order for $150."

On October 9, Selir wrote Biar: "I have changed my mind. The stock is not for sale."

On October 15, Biar wrote Selir: "I want to buy the stock. I will pay $50,000 now, $50,000 in six months, and the balance as soon as I sell my old warehouse. Send stock certificates by registered mail."

On October 17, Selir wrote Biar: "I do not want to sell."

On October 25, Biar wrote to Selir: "I accept your original offer. Bank draft for $50,000 is enclosed. I will pay $50,000 in six months and balance in one year."

On October 30, 1953, Selir wrote Biar: "See my letter of October 9th. Stock is not for sale."

Was there ever a binding contract? If so, when? Explain.

9. Under what circumstances is relief available for unilateral mistakes of fact?

10. Selir contracted to sell to Biar ten shares of stock in the Lethur Lung Corporation at a price not to be less than the book value of the shares. The books of the corporation showed the book value to be $157 per share. Accordingly, Biar paid Selir $1,570 and received the certificates. Unknown to both parties an employee had embezzled a considerable amount of the corporation's funds and had falsified the books to cover up. The actual book value at the time of the sale was $60. The employee

was not bonded and is now insolvent. When Biar discovered the true state of affairs, he attempted to rescind the contract. What are the rights of the parties?

11. Werm Hohl is a dealer in antique furniture and is considered to be one of the country's leading experts on antique furniture. Bill Biar, a customer, purchased four chairs from Hohl in reliance on the following statement made by Hohl: "It is my opinion that these chairs are genuine Duncan Fie, made by the master just prior to his death in 1854." The price was $12,000. Biar has just discovered that the chairs were fakes manufactured in 1954 and were known by Hohl to be fakes at the time of the sale. What are Biar's rights against Hohl?

12. Give examples of situations where one or more of the rules of contract interpretation would have to be applied.

13. X and Y entered into a written contract by the terms of which X employed Y for a period of one year at a salary of $100 a week. X now claims that the parties agreed orally at the time they made their written contract that Y was to kick back to X the sum of $15 a week. Will X be allowed to prove this oral agreement? Explain.

14. Consideration is often defined as "benefit to the promisor or detriment to the promisee." What are "benefit" and "detriment?"

15. Carlus, while operating his automobile in a negligent fashion, ran over and injured Victum. While Victum was still in the hospital, Carlus came to see him, admitted his responsibility and said that if Victum would promise not to sue, Carlus would promise to give Victum $5,000 when Victum got out of the hospital. Victum agreed.

a. Assume that Victum has been discharged from the hospital and that Carlus has refused to pay. What are Victum's rights?

b. Assume instead that Victum was discharged from the hospital but has threatened to sue Carlus for $75,000 unless Carlus promises to give Victum $15,000. Carlus has made the promise. Carlus later paid Victum $5,000, but Victum is now suing for the additional $10,000. What are Victum's rights?

16. You have just subscribed $500 to the fund-raising campaign of the Children's Home Society of Lower Montclair. Should you fail to pay your subscription, on what theories might the Home base an action against you?

17. Comment on the following quotation:

"Probably the doctrine of consideration has some utility. Just as oral gifts are invalid without delivery, so promises not under seal are invalid unless there is an exchange given for them. The aims in both cases are to make more certain that the transaction was seriously intended and to make more difficult the fabrication of a gift or a contract. Justice Holmes long ago said: 'Consideration is as much a form as a seal.' This notion should be constantly kept in mind. The question should be: Has there been something given for this promise which shows us that it was seriously meant and which convinces us of its genuineness? If such a test were applied, many of the nice problems of consideration, interesting as intellectual entertainment but unhappily serious to disappointed litigants, would disappear."

18. Compare novation and "accord and satisfaction" as methods of discharging a contract.

19. Describe the following methods of discharging a contract: release, merger, account stated.

20. What persons have limited capacity to enter into contracts?

21. What are the rights of Mosco, a minor, and Abdul, an adult, after the following series of events has taken place?

a. June 2—Mosco, age 17, opened a charge account in his own name at Abdul's general store and purchased a sport coat for $50, a bicycle tire for $5.50, and a small canned ham, a loaf of bread and some other groceries. The groceries were consumed by Mosco and two friends the same day.

b. June 15—Mosco was deserted by his parents, who, until this time, had been supporting him.

c. June 17—Mosco purchased at Abdul's store a pair of shoes, five T-bone steaks and a hunting knife, charging all to his account.

d. July 7—Mosco has his 18th birthday.

e. July 20—Abdul was told by a lawyer friend that minor's contracts are not binding and can be avoided by the minor. Abdul sought out Mosco in front of the local high school that evening and offered him a new shotgun if Mosco would sign an agreement not to disaffirm the contracts with Abdul. Mosco accepted the gun and signed the agreement.

22. Compare the following types of contracts with regard to their legality: insurance contracts, wagering or gambling contracts, speculative contracts such as are used in hedging operations.

23. What effect does illegality have on a contract?

24. Explain the following terms: *pari delicto* and *locus poenitentiae*.

25. Give examples of contracts which are illegal because they are: in violation of common law, in violation of statute, or contrary to public policy.

26. What is the statute of frauds and what is its purpose?

27. Compare the statute of frauds in your state with the one described in the text. Does "invalid" mean the same? Do the same types of contracts come under both statutes?

28. On January 3rd, Selir called Biar on the telephone and offered to sell him Selir's prize Dalmatian hunting dog "George" for $550, the dog to be delivered to Biar after the next field trials. Biar accepted the offer then and there. After he hung up, Biar wrote and mailed a letter to Selir confirming the details of the agreement. If Selir refuses to deliver the dog to Biar after the field trials, what rights will Biar have against Selir? Would these rights be the same as those of Selir against Biar should Biar refuse to perform the contract?

29. Distinguish a condition from a promise.

30. Bilder entered into a contract with Oner whereby Bilder was to construct, in accordance with architect's plans and specifications, a summer house for Oner at Fallen Leaf Lake. The contract price was $32,000. For an additional $2,500, Bilder agreed to erect in front of the house a suitable monument in honor of those who have drowned while water skiing on the lake. The work on both house and monument was to be done to the satisfaction of Oner. Both have been completed, but Oner refuses to pay for either on the ground that he is not satisfied. What are the rights of Bilder?

31. Explain the contract measure of damages and compare it with the tort measure of damages.

32. *X* and *Y* entered into a contract whereby *X* was to build for *Y* a small bridge across a ravine on *Y's* farm. The contract price was $3,000. When the bridge was approximately two-thirds finished, *Y* told *X* that he did not want the bridge

finished and ordered X to stop work. X finished the bridge in spite of Y's order and is now suing for the contract price. What are the rights of X against Y? To how much is X entitled?

33. Koler and Smeltur entered into an oral contract in March, 1967, whereby Koler was to sell and deliver and Smeltur was to buy 100 tons of coal a month for two years beginning on November 1, 1967. In August, 1967, a fire in the mine from which Koler had contemplated getting the coal he was to deliver to Smeltur closed the mine permanently. A few days after the fire, Koler wrote to Smeltur to notify him that Koler would be unable to perform the contract. Smeltur replied by mail that Koler was still bound on the contract and would have to perform or pay damages for breach of contract. Smeltur made no other arrangements for a supply of coal. Koler delivered no coal on November 1st nor at any other time thereafter. Smeltur's factory remained closed until November, 1968, when Smeltur decided to purchase coal elsewhere. Also in November, 1968, Smeltur sued Koler for breach of contract, claiming as his damages the losses he suffered as a result of the factory having been closed for a year. What are the rights of the parties in this action?

34. Under what circumstances is the unusual remedy of specific performance available in contract cases?

35. Explain the doctrine of anticipatory breach.

36. Under what circumstances may a party to a contract be excused for his failure to perform that contract?

37. Selir agreed to sell to Biar 150 quarts of milk every day for one year, and Biar agreed to come to Selir's premises and obtain the milk. In the middle of the year, by order of the Commissioner of Public Health, all of Selir's cattle and all products of his farm were quarantined, and Selir was not allowed to leave the premises. Shortly thereafter, all of Selir's cattle were destroyed by order of said Commissioner. Selir furnished no milk to Biar during the remainder of the year. Biar has brought a breach of contract action against Selir. Who will win and why?

38. Bilder and Oner entered into two contracts whereby Bilder was to erect a new factory building on Oner's property and to repair an old factory building which already stood on another part of the same property. The contract price of the new building was $185,000 and of the repair job $37,000. The new building contract contains a clause stating that Oner is not obligated for the price until Bilder obtains a certificate of approval from John Haybank, an architect. A week before the new building and the repair job were completed, both the old and the new building were completely destroyed by fire through no fault of either Bilder or Oner, and Haybank was trapped in one of the buildings and burned to death. What are the rights of Oner and Bilder?

39. Is the tendency of the courts toward stricter or more lenient use of impossibility as an excuse for failure to perform a contract? Explain and give examples.

40. The Wedder Waterworks Company entered into a contract with the City of Cornfield whereby the Company agreed to supply "the city and inhabitants with water suitable for all domestic, sanitary, and fire purposes and for individual use" and to keep water of a specified pressure in all of the fire mains at all times. Ralph Resadunt, who lives in Cornfield, has filed a suit for damages against the Company because the inability of the Cornfield Fire Department to get sufficient water pressure at the hydrant in front of Ralph's house resulted in the complete destruction of that house by fire. The pressure was far below the standard specified in the contract. What rights has Ralph?

41. What contract rights are not assignable?

42. On January 2nd, Albert and Benje entered into a contract whereby, in exchange for consideration, Benje was to pay to Albert's adult daughter, Carla, $500 on January 22nd, which day is Carla's birthday. Carla learned of the contract on January 5th and, for valuable consideration, transferred her rights under the contract as follows: on January 6th, transferred her rights to the $500 to Dexter; on January 8th, transferred her rights in the $500 to Ella; on January 10th, transferred her rights in $200 to Frank and her rights in the remaining $300 to George; on January 12th, Carla again purported to transfer her rights in the entire $500 to Helen. George notified Benje of the transfer on January 10th; Frank gave notice on January 12th; Ella gave notice on January 14, and Helen filed a financing statement in the appropriate public office on January 17. Dexter gave no notice at all. On the morning of January 22, Dexter, Ella, Frank, George, and Helen all appeared at Benje's place of business demanding the money. What are the rights of the parties against Benje when he refuses to pay them? (See Chapter 13 for further details of the law.)

43. Do the original parties to a third party beneficiary contract have the power to rescind the contract so as to destroy the rights of the beneficiary? Explain.

part III

Organizing
a Business

THE NATURE OF THE LEGAL PROBLEMS
IN THIS PART

With the background supplied in Parts I and II, the reader should be able to proceed rapidly to the legal problems and issues involved in the various stages of development and operation through which a business firm moves. Some knowledge has been gained of the sources and nature of law, our legal system, of the important aspects of legal procedure, and of the methods by which our legal rights and duties are enforced. The law of contract, which is the fundamental field of business law, must be understood in considerable detail before the other fields and areas of business law can be discussed with any measure of satisfaction. The contract is basic to most of the remaining material in the book, and the importance of the contract device at all stages of business operation cannot be overemphasized.

The particular legal problems encountered when a business is organized are not of as wide a variety as those met in the actual operation of business. These problems are concerned with selecting the form of organization by which the business will be conducted, the procedure of organization, the financing of the new business, and with some legal issues that become important in relation to the selection and acquisition of a site and the acquisition of property with which the business will operate. The selection of the form of organization is largely a matter of examining the legal and other characteristics of the various forms in the light of those attributes necessary or desirable for the proper operation of the particular business. A knowledge of the procedure of organization is less important for forms such as the corporation than it is for those forms which may be brought into existence without expert or technical advice. Corporations are rarely organized without such technical aid. The financing of a new business is, of course, one of the most important problems to be considered. Both corporate and noncorporate financing problems will be examined. Certain aspects of the law of property, both real and personal, will be discussed in Part III in connection with the acquisition of the property in, on, and with which the business will be conducted.

Simuco Toyland, a partnership.   Al Able, Bob Baker, Cal Charles, Don Danton, and Earl Eaton are partners in SIMUCO TOYLAND, a partnership operating a retail toy store in Berkland, Anosmia. They sell a wide variety of toys and bicycles in many price ranges and also operate a bicycle repair shop. The store and repair shop are located at 701 Main Street, at the corner of Central Avenue. The partners have been in business together for several years. There are other toy stores in Berkland, but SIMUCO has an excellent location in the downtown section and is generally considered to have the widest choice of toys and to be the most likely to have the new toys and games just coming onto the market. The firm buys its toys and bicycles from manufacturers and dealers in all parts of the world. Though not as seasonal as it once was, the retail toy business reaches a very high level just before Christmas and is relatively constant during the rest of the year. The bicycle business follows a similar pattern, but less extreme, and the repair shop is busiest during the summer months.

The partnership agreement does not differentiate among the partners, as far as duties and responsibilities are concerned, but four of the partners have each come to assume primary responsibilities for some phase of the operation. Able does most of the toy buying; Baker is looked to as a sort of store manager; Charles takes care of the accounting and financial aspects of the business; Danton buys bicycles and runs the repair shop; Eaton has no particular responsibilities but, among the partners, is probably the best known to the townspeople and the best liked by the customers of the store.

The state of Anosmia has adopted the Uniform Partnership Act.

chapter 4

Forms of

Organization

1. IN GENERAL

A. Factors Important in Selecting a Particular Form

Those who organize small businesses actually have a choice of the form of business organization. Except for those few situations discussed in the next section where there are statutory restrictions that either make a particular form mandatory or prohibit it, the organizers of small businesses must make a decision as to the best possible form in which to operate the business. There is a popular belief that the corporate form is always best if the business organizers can afford to use it, but a decision based on this belief will lead only to danger and disillusionment. For very large business enterprises, the corporate form is usually the only satisfactory form to use, but where the small business is concerned, it must be realized that forms other than the corporate may supply the characteristics necessary or desirable and may have definite advantages over the corporate form. No two business concerns are ever exactly alike or have identical requirements. Even where the type of business and the locality are the same, the likes and dislikes, motives, objectives, personalities, and methods of the individuals will be different, and the form of business organization which best suits their needs may very likely be different too. The decision as to which form to use is one of the first important decisions that an organizer of a business must make, and the decision will vary with the facts and circumstances of each particular venture. We will examine here some of the more important factors that must be taken into consideration in making this decision.

AMOUNT OF CAPITAL AND CREDIT REQUIRED. If the organizers themselves will supply all of the capital requirements, no form of business organization has any particular advantage over the others in the light of this factor. While some states impose minimum capital requirements on corporations and occasionally on joint stock companies and business trusts, the minimum requirements are usually so low that they create no serious difficulty. There are no such limitations on sole-proprietorships, general or limited partnerships, nor, as a rule, on the other forms either.

The necessity for obtaining outside captial or credit presents an entirely different problem. Outsiders look upon the different forms of organizations with varying degrees of enthusiasm. A sole-proprietorship or a general partnership is not attractive to outside investors unless they desire to join in the management of the venture, and neither one will be a satisfactory way of raising funds where the organizers do not want any outside interference in the operation of their business. The power of a sole-proprietorship or partnership to obtain credit is measured by the resources and financial standing of the individual proprietor or partners.

The limited partnership is more tempting to the investor who does not want to participate in the management, and it also limits his liability to the amount of his investment. However, he is in a weaker position in regard to the protection of his investment than he would be if he actually participated. The prospective lender of funds will measure the attractiveness of the limited partnership by the resources of the general partners, both in assets and in skill.

The corporate form normally has more appeal to the outsider, and it is certainly the device best suited to raising very large amounts of capital. As anyone who has participated in the promotion of a corporation knows, however, the corporate form alone gives no assurance it will attract outside capital. While the business trust and the joint stock company are probably more favored by outsiders than the sole-proprietorship or the partnership is, these forms are undoubtedly less popluar than the corporation, and the lack of familiarity with them puts them at a distinct disadvantage.

LIABILITY. As a general rule, corporate shareholders, limited partners, and the beneficiaries of the business trust are not subject to the unlimited personal liability that is characteristic of the sole-proprietor, general partners, and the members of joint stock companies. The decision as to the form of organization is made somewhat easier where the issue of personal liability is of primary importance to the organizers, because the possibilities are quickly narrowed. It should be understood, however, that limited liability, in any sort of absolute sense, is nonexistent, and even the corporate shareholder may be subject to liability greater than his investment or his commitments to invest.

EXPENSE OF ORGANIZATION. Except where the organizers have very limited funds, the costs of organization are usually not of major importance in making the decision as to form. Where they are important, though, it is clear that the corporation is at a disadvantage, as are the joint stock company or the business trust in those states where these forms are classified as corporations for organizational purposes.

MANAGEMENT AND CONTROL. Sharp contrasts among the various forms begin to arise in this area. The sole proprietor has no particular procedures or formalities to contend with; he makes his own decisions, and is relatively free from interference by governmental authorities. At the other extreme is the corporation, even the small one, whose operation is surrounded by all kinds of formalities and regulations having to do with everything from bookkeeping to the voting procedure at a directors meeting. The partnership falls near the sole-proprietorship end of the scale; the joint stock company and the business trust fall nearer to the corporation end.

The differences among the forms are obvious too where the organizers have strong feelings one way or the other about their personal participation in the management.

TRANSFERABILITY OF INTEREST. If the easy transferability of the ownership interest, and hence the liquidity of the investment, is important to the organizers, then the corporation, the joint stock company, and the business trust have distinct advantages. Partnership interests are relatively difficult to dispose of. The sole-proprietor's interest is transferred only by the sale of the entire business. Because the transfer of a corporate stock interest often carries with it voting power and an indirect voice in the management, easy transferability may be obtained at the expense of admitting outsiders. In this respect, the joint stock company and the business trust have an advantage over the corporation in that both easy transferability and self-perpetuating management may be provided for. Note that "easy transferability" is a relative term. It is easier to transfer stock in a corporation than it is to transfer a partnership interest, but the ownership of stock does not guarantee the existence of a willing buyer.

LEGAL ENTITY. As with most of the issues outlined in this section, the real significance of this factor will be much better appreciated and understood after we have examined in later portions of the book the characteristics and operation of the various organizational foms. It is sufficient at this point to say that the ability to hold property, transact business, sue, and be sued in a firm name is usually to be desired. This attribute is possessed by the corporation and to a somewhat lesser degree by the business trust and the joint stock company. Statutes in some states award one or more of these rights to the partnership form.

CONTINUITY OF EXISTENCE. The partnership and the sole-proprietorship are at a severe disadvantage in this area because the death or withdrawal of a participant usually terminates the business or, at best, creates serious problems of distribution and settlement among the interested parties. The other forms, including the limited partnership, are much more stable in this regard, and, as a rule, the death, incapacity, or withdrawal of a participant has no direct effect on the life of the organization except in so far as the loss of the personal skills or services of the individual may have their own effects.

RELATIVE ABILITY OF ORGANIZERS. Where the organizers can only provide funds and not much experience or management ability, there is no doubt that the sole-proprietorship and the general partnership are unsuitable business forms. The hiring of professional managers would be necessary, and one of the forms which lends itself to this possibility will have to be utilized.

TAX CONSIDERATIONS. A factor extremely important in making the decision on form of organization and which grows in importance each year is the comparative tax cost of operation among the various forms. Expert advice should be obtained in this connection.

BLENDING THE FORMS OF BUSINESS ORGANIZATION. The discussion to this point has created the impression that partnerships are partnerships, and corporations are corporations, and never the twain shall meet. This is not an accurate picture. Some corporate advantages may be blended into the partnership form, and some partnership characteristics may be approximated in the corporation. It is not possible to obtain all the best of both worlds, but it is an attractive goal, none the less, and, in some situations, an approachable one. Only careful planning and drafting and expert advice can achieve the optimum blend for any given situation. Consequently, the discussion here will be confined to a few general principles to serve as guideposts.

Limited liability in the partnership. Although the value of the limited liability of shareholders is often exaggerated, it is still an important advantage of the corporate form, an advantage which partners would sometimes like to enjoy. There are ways in which some amount of limited liability may be achieved within the framework of the partnership. Insurance, for example, can give protection to partners from many types of risk: public liability, tort claims, and workmen's compensation claims. Obviously, insurance cannot provide protection from ordinary business losses.

Extensive protection from all sorts of risks may be obtained for associates who do not plan to participate actively in the business. This kind of "inactive partner" may, instead of making a capital contribution, simply lend money or property to the firm and receive interest on the loan in the form of a share in the profits. He will not, of course, thus become a partner. As will be seen later in this chapter, the receipt of a share in the profits is evidence that the recipient is a partner, but this is not true where the profits are received as interest on a loan, even though the amount of interest is made to vary with the profits. As a creditor, this person is protected from personal liability and will participate with other creditors in the assest of the firm in the event of business failure. In this respect, such a person has an advantage over a limited partner, whose claims are subordinated to the claims of outside creditors. Furthermore, the right of a limited partner to participate in the business is severely circumscribed, while the creditor may participate to some extent "in order to protect his loan." The general partners are not protected by either the creditor or limited partner techniques, and their position, in the former technique, may actually be worsened owing to their potential liability on the loan.

Some partners have heeded the advice contained in the old observation that one "cannot get blood out of a turnip," and have simply removed their personal estates from the reach of the firm creditors. This method is more attractive in some states than in others. A partner may convey his estate to his wife, for example, and leave himself with nothing significant that the firm creditors might reach. This technique, however, has certain risks. The wife may die and the property revest in the husband. Furthermore, such transfers may be subject to attack under fraudulent conveyance acts. See further discussion of fraudulent conveyances in Chapter 17.

Continuity of existence in the partnership. One of the serious disadvantages of the partnership form is its instability in the face of a partner's death or withdrawal. The corporation, in contrast, is a very stable form of organization and has a continuity of existence that is appealing to partners too. However, the stability of the corporation is accompanied by the easy transferability of its ownership interest, a characteristic which the partners may wish to avoid. The problem of withdrawing members may be minimized by a agreeing to a fixed term in the partnership contract, by imposing certain penalties on a partner's untimely withdrawal, and by providing for the purchase of a withdrawing partner's interest at a price favorable to the remaining partners. The Uniform Partnership Act also provides that the remaining partners may retain a wrongfully withdrawing partner's capital in the business until the agreed upon period comes to an end. Ways and means of dealing with the problems created by the death of a partner are discussed in detail in Chapter 15.

Restricted transfer of interest in the corporation. Corporate associates, especially in small corporations, are often anxious to restrict the free transferability of shares. Limited liability and continuity are usually nice to have, but becoming associated with strangers or outsiders as a result of stock transfers is not always pleasant or desirable. Restrictions may be achieved in a number of ways. In the first place, however, schemes involving general prohibitions against transfer have invariably been held invalid by the courts where not expressly proscribed in the incorporation statutes. Transfers permitted only with the consent of the directors or other shareholders have usually been held invalid also, but the 1967 Amendments to the Delaware Corporation Law considerably extend the scope of permissible transfer limitations of this sort. Actually, such restrictions are usually more than the associates need for their protection and would often be undesirable even if upheld by court or authorized by statute. Reasonable restrictions are valid without argument, however, and a provision that before a shareholder may sell or transfer his shares, or upon his death, the corporation or the other shareholders must be given the opportunity to purchase the shares at some fixed or formula price are very common. The Uniform Commercial Code and most incorporation statutes specifically require that restrictions on transfer be conspicuously noted on the certificate to be effective against persons without actual knowledge of them. The mechanics for effectuating some restrictions and the obvious problems of valuation of the shares may cause considerable difficulty, but may also be worth the trouble.

B. Statutory Restrictions

Most states have statutes restricting the use of the various forms of business organization either by requiring that a certain form be used for a particular type of business or by prohibiting the use of certain forms for the conduct of specified types of business. A common requirement is that the banking business be carried on by means of the corporate device. Most states have statutes expressly prohibiting the use of the corporate device for the practice of law or medicine or other licensed professions. The purpose of the prohibition is usually described in terms of the preservation of the close personal relations which are an essential part of the proper conduct of some of the professions or a means of encouraging greater care and skill in professional practice. The details vary considerably from state to state, although the statutes are similar in approach and outline, and reference should be made to the law of your state for the requirements of local law. Statutes in many states today authorize professional corporations where essential safeguards are provided and a certain degree of judicial supervision is maintained.

2. THE SOLE-PROPRIETORSHIP

Little need be said here about the legal aspects of organizing a sole-proprietorship because there are few legal problems peculiar to this form of business organization. The more formal types of organization create special legal problems simply because a particular organizational device is used. Local law should be consulted, but, in general, the organizational problems of sole-proprietorships, as far as the law is concerned, consist of no more than compliance with business license or sales tax laws.

3. THE PARTNERSHIP

A. Cases

(1)

Earl Eaton, one of the SIMUCO partners, was injured in the store one day while unpacking crates of unassembled Vibretta bicycles. The crates were reinforced with strands of heavy wire which were wrapped around the crates and placed under considerable tension. When Eaton cut one of the strands, it recoiled and struck him in the left eye, seriously impairing the vision in that eye. In addition to his share of the profits, Eaton also received a small, but regular, salary from the firm. Eaton is now claiming compensation for his injury under the workmen's compensation law of Anosmia. The relevant portion of that law reads as follows:

> Liability shall, without regard to negligence, exist against an employer for any injury sustained by his employees arising out of and in the course of the employment where, at the time of the injury, the employee is performing service growing out of and incidental to his employment and is acting within the course of his employment and where the injury is proximately caused by the employment, either with or without negligence.

Should Eaton be able to recover?

(2)

It has just been discovered by the other partners that Cal Charles, one of the SIMUCO partners, has been misappropriating partnership funds. The amount is so large and the circumstances so flagrant that the partners have consulted with the District Attorney with regard to preferring criminal charges against Charles. "Theft" is defined in the Anosmia Penal Code as the "felonious taking of the personal property of another," and "embezzlement" is defined in the same code as the "fraudulent appropriation of property by a person to whom it has been entrusted by another." Can Charles be charged with theft or embezzlement?

(3)

A well-known international banking firm, a partnership, was in serious financial condition during the deflationary period following World War I. A member of the firm negotiated a loan of $2,500,000 in securities, to be used as working capital. The lenders were to have the right to attend all meetings of the firm, to inspect the books of the firm and to veto any speculative ventures with which they did not agree. The management of the firm was to be left with Hall, one of the original partners. As compensation for this so-called loan, the lenders were to have a share of the profits of the business. One part of the agreement between the lenders and the firm read as follows:

> The parties of the first part shall not be interested in the profits as such. Their interest in profits shall be construed merely as a measure of compensation for loaning said active securities to said firm and granting permission to the firm to hypothecate the same and for services to be rendered. The parties of the first part shall not be responsible for any losses that may be made by the said firm. The parties of the first part shall not in any way be deemed or treated or held as partners in said firm. No one of the parties of the first part shall be under any partnership liability or obligation. It is not the intention of any of the parties of the first part to assume any of the liabilities of the said firm.

As further security to the lenders, the members of the firm assigned to them all the members' interests in the firm. Creditors of the firm are now seeking to recover from the lenders on the theory that they are partners.

[*Martin* v. *Peyton,* 246 N.Y. 213, 158 N.E. 77 (1927)]

B. History of the Partnership Form

In those fields of law intimately related to commerce and trade, legal rules and principles have developed not so much through the evolutionary processes of the common law as through a fusion or combination of principles that had their roots in the civil law, in equity, and in the Law Merchant, as well as in the common law. This is particularly true of the law of partnership. Some of the important concepts underlying the partnership device can be traced to origins apart from and older than the common law, and the effects of the merger of these concepts with the common law are apparent throughout the field.

The common law courts in medieval England did not provide the merchants with machinery adequate to handle the legal affairs in which the merchants were involved. The result was that the legal affairs of the merchants were dealt with in special courts. These merchants' courts were unusual in several ways. Since most of the trade in England was carried on at fairs and markets which were temporary in character, lasting only a few days or weeks at a time, and since the merchants moved from one fair to another, the courts were also temporary and itinerant. The merchants came not only from England but from all over the western world and were unfamiliar with common law methods and, principles which had little to do with commercial matters anyhow. The courts which these medieval merchants set up and operated and to which they went for justice in commercial matters applied a sort of international commercial law which was made up largely of the customs of the merchants and was called the *Law Merchant.* Many of the rules and principles of the Law Merchant originated in Roman Law.

Two forms of partnership were already well known in Europe by the thirteenth century, the *Societas* and the *Commenda,* the general partnership and the limited partnership, both inherited from Roman Law. These two devices were slow in working their way into the common law. The limited parnership never did get in all of the way, and in the United States today that device requires statutory authority for existence. After the common law courts began to entertain commercial cases in substantial numbers, these courts also began to develop their own rules and principles with regard to commercial problems, including those of partnerhip, borrowing from the Law Merchant and from the Roman Law. The courts of equity were also developing principles in this area. The result was great confusion and much uncertainty, especially in the United States, where we had a multitude of jurisdictions to compound the difficulty.

The only satisfactory solution appeared to be statutory restatement. The best solution in the United States was the Uniform Partnership Act, which not only restated the law of partnership but also encouraged a number of states to adopt the same Uniform Act. Today, almost all states, including most of the important commercial states, have adopted this statute. The Uniform Partnership Act does not cover all aspects of partnership law, nor does it resolve all of the controversies. Some of these areas will be referred to later.

C. Characteristics of the Partnership Form

IN GENERAL. The partnership is a device of intermediate complexity lying somewhere between the corporation and the sole-proprietorship but probably having more characteristics in common with the latter. It is a distinct organizational form and raises distinct legal problems. The partnership form has advantages over the sole-proprietorship and also over the corporation, but, at the same time, it has characteristics which place it at a disadvantage.

DEFINITION AND ESSENTIAL ELEMENTS. Section 6 of the Uniform Partnership Act defines a partnership as "an association of two or more persons to carry on as co-owners a business for profit." This definition sets forth most of the essentials of the partnership form. Although each of the words or phrases in this definition has a meaning in ordinary usage, it has a technical meaning too. In order to apply the definition to a particular business to determine whether that business is a partnership, it is necessary to understand the technical meanings of the words and phrases and to know the answers to some of the problems arising in connection with these meanings.

An *association,* as far as a partnership is concerned, is a group of persons who have joined together voluntarily and intentionally to accomplish a certain object. No person may be forced into being a partner without his consent or without his intent to become a partner. This does not mean that a person, in order to become a partner, must know that the relationship into which he is entering is one of partnership. It is sufficient that the person intend to enter into a relationship which possesses the characteristics of a partnership and satisfies its requirements.

Calling a particular relationship a "partnership," although it may be persuasive evidence that the relationship is a partnership, is not conclusive. The relationship must still possess the elements of a partnership, and the simple intention of the parties to form a partnership, which is evidenced by the reference to the relationship as such, is not enough. At the same time, failing to call a relationship a partnership, calling it something else, or even expressly stating it is not a partnership, is not conclusive evidence the relationship is not a partnership. If the relationship into which the parties intend to enter satisfies the requirements of a partnership, that relationship is a partnership.

Another aspect of "association," which is important here, is that it implies a close personal relation, so close and so personal that no person can become a member of the partnership association without the consent of all the other associates. This veto power, called technically *delectus personae,* may be waived by an associate, but it is usually not waived. The close personal relationship that exists among partners and the ramifications of the close personal relationship are probably the most important factors that distinguish a partnership from a corporation.

An "association" is brought into existence by an agreement or contract among the associates, but this agreement may be very informal and may be proved by nothing more than the acts and declarations of the parties. It is not often, however, that a business association of the partnership variety is brought into existence by these informal means. The agreement is usually set forth in a document called the *articles of partnership* or *contract of partnership,* or simply *partnership agreement.* The formal method has many obvious advantages, although it is not really necessary. It supplies certainty and provides an easily proved means by which the partners may modify or vary the terms and characteristics of their relationship, the elements of which would otherwise be implied by law simply because the partnership realtion had come into existence. The formal agreements usually contain clauses dealing with such matters as the sharing of profits and losses, the distribution of powers and duties among the partners, and the procedure to be followed on the death or withdrawal of a partner. The agreement is an important part of the law of partnership. We will see more of it later.

The phrase "two or more persons" is a good example of a phrase containing ordinary words in everyday use but which still presents technical legal problems. "Two or more" should be subject to no ambiguity, but the word "persons" raises several legal issues. It should be noted that in this connection "persons" includes not only individual human beings but also corporations, other partnerships, and other associations. Partnerships whose membership comprises a human, a corporation, and another partnership are not by any means unknown. The word "person" has various meanings in the law, as we shall see, but here it is used very loosely.

We are already acquainted with the fact that not all persons, even human ones, possess full legal capacity to enter into contracts or agreements. Inasmuch as the partnership contract is essentially the same as any other contract as far as the necessary elements of contract are concerned, the partnership contract may encounter problems of the limited capacity of its parties. Minors' contracts of partnership are voidable by the minor with the usual incidents, varying somewhat from state to state, which were discussed in Chapter 3. Some new problems are raised, however, when a minor is a partner. The minor partner is not only a party to the contract of partnership but also, directly or indirectly, a party to the contracts the partnership has made with outsiders. In those cases, it is quite likely that the outsider dealt with an adult employee or partner and had no notice or warning that one or more of the partners was a minor with the power of disaffirmance. In connection with the partnership, the public policy aimed at protecting minors in general and the policy of protecting third persons from booby traps meet head on. The legal result is a compromise. The minor may repudiate and escape his personal liability to outsiders, but he must leave his investment in the business until the outsiders' claims have been satisfied. In some states the same result is reached where the claims are those of the minor's co-partner.

A corporation lacks full legal capacity to contract, and, in most states, it may not become a partner without a specific grant of authority by statute or by the articles of incorporation. Married women lacked full capacity to contract and to become partners under the common law, but today legislation in most states has removed these bars, although some states still prohibit a married woman from becoming a partner with her husband.

"To carry on a business" is a relatively easy phrase with which to deal. Section 2 of the Uniform Partnership Act states that "business" includes every trade, occupation, or profession. It is important to note, though, that unless the associates intend to carry on some trade, occupation, or profession, they do not have a partnership. A single transaction or a series of unrelated transactions does not constitute a business, nor does the pooling of the profits from the separate businesses of the individual associates satisfy the requirements for a partnership. Joint or common ownership of property, even where there is profit sharing, is not enough by itself to establish the existence of a partnership.

"For profit" calls attention to the fact that unless the purpose of the association is to make profits directly from the business activities of the association, the partnership label cannot be applied. This limitation prevents religious, charitable, and fraternal associations from being classified or treated as partnerships. The purpose must be to earn profits immediately from the business being carried on. Thus, an agreement to form a partnership, or to carry on a business for profit, at some time in the future will not bring a partnership into existence immediately. It is, of course, not necessary that a profit actually be made. The intent or purpose is sufficient.

The last phrase, "as co-owners," is an important and difficult one. Even though all other tests have been satisfied, an association is still not a partnership unless the associates are co-owners of the business in which they are engaged.

The most useful test for co-ownership is the sharing of profits, but this test, alone, is not conclusive. The sharing of losses, the sharing of the ownership of the capital, and the sharing of management may be important also, but the sharing of profits is probably the only essential one of the group. Section 7 of the Uniform Partnership Act gives this sharing test the dignity of being *prima facie* evidence. This means that if profits are shared, the existence of a partnership will be assumed unless clear proof is made to the contrary. The profit sharing evidence is not a *prima facie* test when the profits are received: 1, as payment on a debt by instalments or otherwise; 2, as wages of an employee or rent to a land-lord; 3, as an annuity to a widow or representative of a deceased partner; 4, as interest on a loan even though the amount of the payment varies with the profits of the business; 5, or as consideration for the sale of goodwill of a business or other property by instalments or otherwise. These situations are simply those where the amount of profit is a measure by which an independent obligation will be discharged and where there is no separate right to share in the profits as such.

Apart from the requirements of the definition, there is at least one other requirement which goes to the important issue of the existence of the partner-ship. That requirement is that the object of the business must be a legal one and also that it be legal for these particular partners to carry on the business. By the general rule, if these tests are not met at the time the partnership should come into existence, the partnership does not come into existence, and, by the same token, if either of these tests fails of performance after the partnership comes into existence, the partnership ends automatically. The classic illustration is the "Highwaymen's Case." A group of enterprising young Englishmen formed a partnership to carry on the business of highway robbery. Because one of the "partners" was not receiving his share of the profits, he asked a court for justice through the equitable proceeding known as an "accounting." The petition was refused on the grounds there was no partnership but justice was not ignored; the parties were hanged and the attorneys for the plaintiff were fined.

This rather arbitrary rule, applied where the purpose of a business or its method of conduct is illegal, frequently works a hardship on the wrong people, though usually not as serious as hanging or fining. An outsider entirely innocent of any wrongful act or even knowledge of the illegal object of the business may be injured if he is prevented from bringing a claim against "partners" other than the one with whom he originally dealt. It would seem here that the "partners" are being protected at the expense of an innocent party. It is the view of many experts in the field that partnership rights and remedies should not be denied to innocent third parties who may be injured by the present rule.

Other problems in this area which, though relevant, normally have no direct bearing on the existence of the partnership will be discussed below in connection with the procedure for organizing a partnership.

PARTNERSHIP AS A LEGAL PERSON.   A *legal person* is an entity recognized by law as capable of being a subject of legal rights and duties as a separate and distinct unit. A legal person can own property, commit wrongs, sue and be sued, acquire property, dispose of property, and make contracts all in his own name. The legal person must be an entity separate and distinct from other entities. A human being is such an entity. A business firm, in order to qualify, must be separate and distinct from the human persons who make up the firm. The corporation possesses this characteristic; others like the sole proprietorship do not; still others, of which the partnership is the best example, have it for some purposes, but not for all.

The situation with regard to partnerships is very much confused and has been so for a long time. The Uniform Partnership Act removed some of the confusion in connection with the buying, holding, and selling of property by a partnership, but it took no clear stand on most other problems where the question of legal entity is important. One reason for the confusion is that businessmen have always looked upon the partnership as a firm, a separate entity to which the partners owe certain duties and against which the partners have certain rights, and not as a group of individuals with rights and duties among themselves. Meanwhile, the common law has always looked upon the partnership as simply a group of individuals and has refused to attribute any personality to the firm. The courts have been influenced in recent years first by one view and then the other. Legislatures have stepped in from time to time with solutions to particular problems. However, the basic question still remains.

It must be said in fairness that, outside of those areas which have been dealt with by statute, it does not usually make very much difference which view is taken. The results are much the same whether or not the partnership is looked upon as an entity. Those areas where it does make a difference will be discussed in connection with the operation of a business by means of the partnership form. It should be pointed out, however, that the trend is probably in the direction of extending the doctrine of legal separateness to the partnership. There are decisions holding that the partnership is so much a legal person that even a partnership made up entirely of minors may not disaffirm its contracts.

4. THE CORPORATION

A. Cases

(1)

In January, 1930, the Old South Engraving Company, a corporation, entered into a contract with the International Photo Engravers' Union of North America which regulated generally the conditions of employment and prices to be paid to employees. In this contract, Old South also agreed to "employ none but members of the International Photo Engravers' Union of North America, or applicants for positions holding permit from the Boston Photo Engravers' Union No. 3, I.P.E.U." Later the same year, the Company was dissolved and a new corporation, bearing the same name, was organized to replace it. The new corporation was identical in all respects to the old. The purpose of the change was to escape the "union shop" provisions of the contract with the Photo Engravers' Union. As soon as the corporate change had been made, the Company dismissed its union employees and hired nonunion men to take their places. The Union then sought to enjoin the Company and its officers from violation of the contract entered into in January. The old company was no longer in existence at the time of the suit, and the new company argued that it was an entity distinct from the old and not bound by the terms of a contract to which it was not a party.

[*Berry* v. *Old South Engraving Co.*, 283 Mass. 441, 186 N.E. 601 (1933)]

B. Importance of the Corporate Form

Adam Smith, in 1776, wrote: "The pretence that corporations are necessary to the better government of the trade, is without foundation."[1] So many changes, both in fact and in attitude, have taken place during the two hundred years since those words were set down that the corporation may now be described as the "characteristic institution of our age."[2] When Adam Smith wrote, the corporate form of organization had only just passed the midpoint of a century-long period of suspended development, public disfavor, and sub rosa activity, during which it remained aloof from the mainstreams of economic, political, and social evolution. Although England had provided the corporation with the environment, nourishment, and conceptual roots that permitted its flowering during the sixteenth and seventeenth centuries, leadership in the development and improvement of the corporate form was stifled in England during the eighteenth century and shifted to the New World, where it remained.

In part, the dark age of the corporation in England was brought on by the Bubble Act of 1720,[3] an incredibly gross and inept parliamentary reaction to a period of wild stock speculation and other abuses of the corporate form. Among the worst offenders at this time was the South Sea Company (chartered in 1711), which not only foisted unsound shares on the public but manipulated and speculated in its own shares. Taking advantage of the strong public reaction against the booms and busts, this Company persuaded its friends in Parliament to enact a statute which, while purporting to control the abuses, actually served to block new corporate ventures and channel funds into the South Sea Company and others like it. Poor draftsmanship also played a role in making the Bubble Act a serious barrier to corporate forms of organization for almost a century. The Bubble Act, without doubt, had its effects in the American colonies, but it

---

[1] Adam Smith, *The Wealth of Nations* (New York: Modern Library, Inc., 1937), p. 129.

[2] Dow Votaw, "The Politics of a Changing Corporate Society," *California Management Review*, III, No. 3 (Spring, 1961), 109.

[3] 6 Geo. I, Chap. 18 (1720).

seems likely that the effects were submerged by deeper and stronger currents running in other directions. After 1776, of course, the colonies were released from the stultifying consequences of this confusing statute, and the development of the corporate form resumed its measured pace in a new environment.

Today, in the United States, a comment like Adam Smith's could only be made in jest. The corporation is now more accurately portrayed as "the dominating institution of modern American society,"[4] one of the only two systems that has emerged as a vehicle of modern industrial economics,[5] or "our most important economic institution."[6] William T. Gossett, vice-president and general counsel of the Ford Motor Company, has said:

> The modern stock corporation is a social and economic institution that touches every aspect of our lives; in many ways it is an institutionalized expression of our way of life. During the past 50 years, industry in corporate form has moved from the periphery to the very center of our social and economic existence. Indeed, it is not inaccurate to say that we live in a corporate society.[7]

In a very real sense, the great corporation *is* our way of life.

So thoroughly has the corporation permeated our society and our civilization that its importance and its role are often not perceived. Just as we rarely give a thought to the supply of electricity that heats and cools our homes, operates our home laundries, cooks our meals, illuminates our evening newspaper, and even opens and closes our garage doors, so do we infrequently, if at all, appreciate the many and intimate ways in which the corporation affects our lives. The corporation influences us and our way of life more broadly, more deeply, and more subtly than does a house full of electrical appliances. In far more ways are our habits, attitudes, values, and decisions influenced by the great corporation than by almost any other institution in our society.

Most of us work for corporations; most of the goods and services we buy with our earnings are bought from corporations; many of the basic economic decisions of our society are made by corporations. Corporate policies concerning prices, wages, dividends, and capital investment may stimulate or slow the entire economy. A corporate decision on the location of a plant may create a new city or destroy an old one. In short, the corporate system is a repository of power, the biggest non-governmental power center in our society.

Does this conclusion suggest that every corporation is a center of great power simply be   se it is a corporation? Of course not, although it should be

---

[4] Abram Chayes, *Introduction* to John P. Davis, *Corporations* (New York: Capricorn Books, 1961), p. i.

[5] A. A. Berle, Jr., *Foreword* to Edward S. Mason, ed., *The Corporation in Modern Society* (Cambridge, Mass.: Harvard University Press, 1960), p. ix.

[6] Edward S. Mason, *Introduction* to *The Corporation in Modern Society*, p. 1.

[7] William T. Gossett, *Corporate Citizenship* (Lexington, Va.: Washington and Lee University Press, 1957), p. 157.

noted that corporations with little power and influence may grow into corporations that have great power. Statistical evidence to support this view of the overwhelming economic importance of the corporation, and of the large corporation in particular, is well known, but for the sake of clarity it may be wise to review some of that evidence here.

If any additional evidence is needed to show the great size and importance of the large corporations, the following may be helpful: in terms of the size of annual revenue in 1958, the federal government stood first, but the next eight places were occupied by corporations. The State of California was tenth. Corporations filled the next six places ahead of the State of New York and New York City in seventeenth and eighteenth places respectively. Then came ten more corporations before the Commonwealth of Pennsylvania in twenty-ninth place. Of the first 55 places, only nine were governments.

The corporation is more than just a legal pattern. It is not the corporate form as such that wields vast power and has so great an impact on our society. Rather, it is the giant business enterprise organized in the corporate form. It is General

TABLE 1

Comparative Importance of Forms of Organization, 1963 (and 1954)
Manufacturing Establishments

	ESTABLISHMENTS			VALUE ADDED BY MANUFACTURE (IN MILLIONS)		
	number	*per cent of total*	*(1954)*	*amount*	*per cent of total*	*(1954)*
Corporations	176,190	58	52	$184,100	96	94
Partnerships	27,677	9	17	2,726	1	4
Sole Proprietorships ..	99,174	32	31	3,916	2	2
Others	3,576	1	—	1,361	1	—
Total	306,617	100	100	$192,103	100	100

Source: *U.S. Department of Commerce, Bureau of the Census, Census of Manufactures:*
1963, Vol. I, p. 3–2; 1954, Vol. I, p. 204–1.

TABLE 2

Comparative Importance of Forms of Organization, 1963 (and 1954)
Retail Establishments

	ESTABLISHMENTS			TOTAL SALES (IN MILLIONS)		
	number	*per cent of total*	*(1954)*	*amount*	*per cent of total*	*(1954)*
Corporations	359,409	21	14	$151,093	62	49
Partnerships	210,694	12	16	23,873	10	17
Sole Proprietorships..	1,124,583	66	70	65,737	27	34
Others	13,245	1	—	3,498	1	—
Total	1,707,931	100	100	$244,201	100	100

Source: *U.S. Department of Commerce, Bureau of the Census, U.S. Census of Business:*
1963, Vol. I, p. 5–1; 1954, Vol. I, p. 5–2.

TABLE 3
Comparative Importance of Forms of Organization, 1963 (and 1954)
Wholesale Establishments

	ESTABLISHMENTS			TOTAL SALES (IN MILLIONS)		
	number	*per cent of total*	*(1954)*	*amount*	*per cent of total*	*(1954)*
Corporations	197,481	64	50	$298,662	83	72
Partnerships	27,961	9	16	20,392	6	11
Sole Proprietorships ..	73,355	24	28	23,553	7	10
Others	9,380	3	6	15,778	4	7
Total	308,177	100	100	$358,386	100	100

Source: *U.S. Department of Commerce, Bureau of the Census, U.S. Census of Business:* 1963, Vol. IV, p. 7–1; 1954, Vol. III, p. 7–2.

TABLE 4
Concentration of Industrial Corporations, 1964 (and 1960)

number of corporations	*sales (in millions)*	*per cent of total*	*(1960)*	*assets (in millions)*	*per cent of total*	*(1960)*
100*	$172.6	36	35	$150.3	44	43
200	214.8	45	44	183.6	54	52
500	266.5	56	54	224.7	66	63
199,448**	478.1**	100	100	342.9**	100	100

* Data are for 100, 200, and 500 largest industrial corporations, with at least 50 per cent of revenues from manufacturing or mining. Excludes certain large corporations which did not report sales.
Source: *Fortune,* New York, N.Y.; annual supplement, *The Fortune Directory,* as reported in 1964 (1963) *Statistical Abstract of the U.S.*
** Total figures for manufacturing and mining corporations.
Source: Internal Revenue Service, as reported in 1964 (1963) *Statistical Abstract of the U.S.*

Motors or Standard Oil or A.T. & T. or Lockheed. May we then pass over the small corporation and concentrate our attention only on the large ones? The answer is no, for several reasons. The corporate form of organization is useful in all kinds of industry and in all sizes of enterprise. Furthermore, the incorporation statutes do not distinguish between large and small corporations. Consequently, most of what will be said in this book about the law of corporations will be, at least in theory, as applicable to the one as to the other. Again, what is today a small corporation may tomorrow become large. One of the most interesting questions about the corporation is why that particular form is capable of adapting itself so readily to large and small enterprises alike and to tremendous rates of growth. It should not be concluded that the role of small business is not important. Just as the small trees and shrubs and trailing vines play a significant role in the ecology of the giant redwood forests, so do small organizations play a role in our economy, although that economy is dominated in appearance and in effect by the giant firms.

In addition to being the major economic institution in our society, the corporation has also become one of our leading political and social institutions. Perhaps, in the long run, the latter roles will prove to be even more important than the former. Through the services they provide, the products they produce, the consumer demands they satisfy (and also help to create), and the public relations techniques they employ, large corporations have a profound influence on the American standard of living, culture, and way of life. Through their wage, salary, employment, and promotion policies, they affect our political and social conduct and loyalties. The great corporations also help to shape our goals and values. Their conduct at home and abroad may influence national policies; their influence may mold legislation. Large corporations are important centers of research, social as well as scientific, and have performed an important function in the advance of technology. They are growing sources of support for educational institutions of all kinds and are the biggest market for the educated products of these institutions.

There is good evidence that the large corporation is changing our political behavior and political institutions and altering social customs and organizations as well. It would be strange if this were not the case. To say that the dominant institution in American society had little or no influence on society would be a contradiction in terms. It is obvious, then, that we can no longer think of the corporation in strictly economic or legal terms and that we must give due consideration to its political and social manifestations. The economic importance of the corporation is familiar and reasonably well understood, but it is impossible in the 1960's to examine the legal aspects of corporations without noting some of their political and social aspects at the same time. In reality, this is just another way of saying that no major institution in society can be understood properly and accurately without placing it in its own setting and devoting time to a study of its total environment.

Knowledge of the legal, economic, political, and social environment is a necessary prerequisite to an understanding of any institution. Many of the successes and most of the failures that the United States has enjoyed in our foreign economic aid programs, for example, can be attributed to the appreciation, or lack of appreciation, of the environment in which the aid was administered. We have all too often assumed—or attempted to impose—conditions of our own environment in connection with peoples to whom our environment is totally foreign or even anathema. It is just as important that we refrain from appraisals or alterations of domestic institutions until we are informed about their cultural and historical setting and the premises on which they are built.

In spite of its obvious importance and great influence, the corporation's social and political roles in society have been ignored until very recently, even by those segments of the academic community that one might expect to take a strong interest in this sort of phenomena. The political scientists have hardly noticed the corporation. Historians have usually attended to it only to note scandal or economic collapse, but a few have done yeoman service in tracing portions of its evolution. Sociologists have done a little better in recent years, but they sometimes leave their audience with the impression that the corporation, and commerce in general, are some sort of carcinoma on the body politic. Economists and lawyers have the best records, although each group has been concerned primarily with those aspects of the corporate anatomy that are of direct and immediate interest to its own specialty.

There are good indications today, however, that a field of "political economy" is returning to respectability and is making it possible to look at the whole corporate system rather than at just one or two of its many expressions. The results of the long period of closely confined specialization or total neglect are a relatively high level of economic and legal appreciation of the modern corporation, subject to the limits of specialization, on one hand, and an embryonic social and political awareness on the other. A. A. Berle[8] and Peter Drucker[9] were among the first to search for a modern interdisciplinary concept of the corporation, and their work still figures prominently in the field. Others have joined them during the last decade, and many heretofore unexplored avenues are being opened to view.

C. History of the Corporate Form

There is neither the space nor the need here to trace in detail the origins of the modern corporation. In a very real sense, the modern corporation is an aggregate of characteristics and of legal, political, and cultural concepts that have been evolving over many centuries. This form of organization is the product of such basic ideas as freedom, freedom of association, contract, and property. Some modern corporate characteristics can be traced back to medieval cities, universities, and ecclesiastical groups. Among the ancestors of the corporation were the partnership, which finds its own origins in Roman Law, the medieval guilds, and the societies of merchant adventurers which dominated English export trade for centuries. Each of these ancient antecedents contributed something to the corporate form of organization: the idea of voluntary association of individuals for commercial objectives, legal personality, common funds for common purposes, administrative structure, and many other attributes.

Closer in time and more influential in detail were the great English trading companies of the sixteenth and seventeenth centuries, created by royal charter

---

[8] A. A. Berle, Jr., *The Twentieth Century Capitalist Revolution* (New York: Harcourt, Brace & World, Inc., 1954); and *Power Without Property* (New York: Harcourt, Brace and World, Inc., 1959).

[9] Peter Drucker, *Concept of the Corporation* (New York: The John Day Company, Inc., 1946).

and by Acts of Parliament, granting corporate existence, trading rights, and even privileges of exploration and colonization beyond English shores. Much of the colonization of the New World was carried out under the auspices of these organizations. Attributes such as permanent capital, joint stock, limited liability, perpetual existence, and easily transferable ownership interests originated in or were influenced by the *chartered joint stock companies,* as these early corporate forms were called. The first of these great companies was the Russia Company, chartered in 1555 by Mary Tudor. Among others that followed were the East India Company in 1600, the Africa Company in 1619, the Hudson's Bay Company in 1670, the Bank of England in 1674, and the South Sea Company in 1711.

In the latter part of the seventeenth century, there also appeared in England the *unchartered joint stock company.* Under pressure from the commercial community, the common law lawyers created out of the contract and the trust a form of organization that possessed most of the attributes of the chartered companies but did not require the participation of Crown or Parliament; these companies avoided the high costs and appeals for special favors which were inherent in the chartering procedure.

Abuses in connection with both forms of joint stock company during the early years of the eighteenth century led to the enactment by Parliament in 1720 of the infamous "Bubble Act," which slowed the evolution of corporate forms in England for over a century. The mainstream of development shifted to America during that century and never returned.

The next important step in the history of the corporate form was the general incorporation law. After separation from England, corporations in the United States continued to be chartered by the various state legislatures. Public opposition to the special privileges implicit in this sort of procedure led in 1811 to the enactment in New York of the first statute which extended to all who complied with the law the advantages of the corporate form. No longer was it necessary to bribe or cajole legislators in order to gain access to corporate characteristics. Those characteristics became available to all.

Although one might have expected a great expansion in the use of the corporate form immediately following the appearance of the general incorporation acts, no such rapid expansion took place until after the middle of the century. The needs of the American economy had not yet reached the point where they required the corporation for their satisfaction. The Civil War, the development of nationwide markets, the growth in the optimum scale of industry, and the need for vast sums of capital which these changes entailed finally brought the corporation into its own as the dominant form of business organization.

D. Nature of Corporations

IN GENERAL.   Before we can proceed safely to a discussion of the history, law, or modern role of the corporation, an effort must be made to delineate our field and to define the scope of our study. In its simplest terms, this endeavor necessarily involves a search for the answer to either of two fundamental questions. The answer to either will suffice, because the answers to both questions are the same. The questions are: what is a corporation and what is the nature of "corporateness"? It is possible to combine the two questions in one, as follows: what distinguishes the corporation from other forms of organization?

One might expect a quick, easy, and detailed definition that would enable any reasonably intelligent person conveniently to differentiate between corporations and other forms. But it is by no means easy to define a corporation or to explain the nature of corporateness. Some authors are very frank about it: "It seems clear enough that there is no rigid stone wall erected between associations, self-organized outside the corporation statutes, and corporations. For many purposes they may be treated as one and the same."[10] It can be argued that this statement is too conservative in its scope; not only *may* corporations and other forms be treated as though they were one and the same, but they actually are so treated.

Yet lawyers and judges and others do speak and write of corporations and partnerships and business trusts and joint stock companies and other associations as though they were distinct and separable. The explanation for this paradox lies deeply buried in the history and culture of our society. For our purposes here, we can say that the same social, political, and economic pressures of society created other forms of organization besides the corporation. Where the same pressures are felt and the same ends sought, the resulting institutions are almost certain to have many of the same characteristics. Perhaps our problem will be simplified if we focus our attention at first on the characteristics of corporateness rather than on a particular form that bears the title "corporation." If we recognize that several forms of organization possess some, or many, of the elements of corporateness and that corporations do not necessarily possess them all, we can proceed to our task.

There is another factor that blurs the line between corporations and other forms of business organization. Usually, though not invariably, for tax or regulatory purposes, state and federal statutes treat, or make it possible to treat, other forms of organization as though they were corporations and treat corporations as though they were other forms. Under federal law today, it is possible for a corporation to be treated as a partnership for income tax purposes and for a partnership to be treated as a corporation.[11] Under many state laws, business trusts are treated as though they were corporations for many purposes.[12] Generally speaking, these metamorphic statutes do not affect the large-scale

---

[10] E. Merrick Dodd and Ralph J. Baker, *Cases and Materials on Corporations,* 2nd ed. (Brooklyn, N.Y.: Foundation Press, 1940), p. 37.

[11] *Internal Revenue Code,* Sections 1361(R) and 1372(S).

[12] See, for example, *Revenue Laws of California,* 23038.

corporation in any direct way, but they do tend to blur our understanding of the concept of corporateness and certainly affect the organizer's choice of organizational form.

CORPORATENESS. As a practical matter, most organizations today which possess the important characteristics of corporateness are corporations by whatever definition we employ. They were organized under special statutes enacted by state legislatures for the express purpose of making possible the creation of corporations, but this fact does not reveal the nature and meaning of corporateness. Other forms commanding the important elements of corporateness, without bearing the label of "corporation," are no longer common. The business trust and the common law joint stock company, for example, have almost vanished from the scene. The particular form we call "corporation" proved to be better able, under modern conditions, to take advantage of the characteristics of corporateness and has won out in what was once a vigorous competition.

While we appear to have solved a practical problem, we have not, on an intellectual level, answered the question about the nature of corporateness itself. Historically speaking, two basic theories concerning the nature of corporateness have dominated the field: the *concession theory* and the *inherence theory*. The first holds that the characteristics of corporateness can be obtained only by grant to the incorporators from the state. The second sees in any group of men the inherent right to form organizations possessing corporate characteristics without having to ask the indulgence of the state. The fact that many organizations possessing characteristics of corporateness are not brought into existence by direct state action is made consistent with the first theory by arguing that their creation and continued existence are the result of implied consent by the state.

The concession theory is the generally accepted view in common law and Roman Law, whereas the inherence theory arose from German legal principles. In fact, if not in theory, American law has long been moving toward the inherence view. The role of the state in the incorporation procedure is so passive as to be almost functionless, because among other things, incorporation statutes customarily permit the formation of corporations "for any lawful purpose."[13] Furthermore, the inherence theory appears to be more nearly consistent with American traditions of freedom and, in particular, of free association. Because the granting and controlling role of the state is largely without substance today, the trend toward acceptance of the inherence view is probably desirable but has implications of its own with regard to the social responsibilities of such "voluntary" organizations.

Characteristics of corporateness. Whether inherent or a matter of govern-

---

[13] See, for example, *California Corporations Code*, Section 300; *General Corporation Law of Delaware*, Section 102 (a) (3) ("any lawful act or activity").

mental concession, most of the characteristics of corporateness may be easily agreed upon. It should be obvious that possession of a long list of corporate characteristics does not make an organization a corporation, and that the absence of several characteristics does not prove that no corporation exists. A list of corporate characteristics would certainly include the following: an organized body, common fund, permanent capital, joint stock ownership, easily transferable ownership interest, limited liability, perpetual succession, concentration of management, capacity to sue and to be sued in a common name, protection of the common property from claims based on a member's separate debts, legal personality, and a standardized method of organization.[14] Note that some of the characteristics listed appear to be elements necessary before a state of corporateness can be achieved, whereas others appear to be the results of having achieved that state.

It should also be observed that partnerships and most other forms of business organization possess many of these characteristics, and that the limited partnership and the business trust possess almost all of them. Were many of the great economic institutions of our day organized in these other forms, our task in explaining the meaning of corporateness would be much more difficult. However, as a matter of actual fact, our greatest economic institutions are organized, almost without exception, in the legal form which we know as a corporation. Although much of what will be said in the pages to come will have application to other forms of organization as well, this discussion is concerned primarily with those private business institutions that are organized as corporations in a technical, legal sense. That means that they have been organized pursuant to the terms of one of the statutes called *incorporation acts*.

Triumph of the corporate form. It may fairly be asked at this point why a particular form with the characteristics of corporateness apparently has triumphed over all others and has become the dominant nongovernmental institution in our society. There is no single answer to this question, but rather a combination of answers. Unquestionably, some mixtures of corporate characteristics proved more useful than others, especially in the conduct of large-scale enterprises. This factor would account for the unsuitability of general and limited partnerships and the common law joint stock company. The standardized method of organization, uniform statutory treatment, and the more or less uniform aggregations of characteristics of the corporation gave to it a position of stability and security that the others could not duplicate. An issue litigated with regard to one corporation under a general incorporation act, for example, might well be looked upon as settled with respect to another corporation formed under the same act. Other forms, lacking standardized procedures, might not enjoy such security from further litigation.

---

[14] For another method of classifying corporate characteristics, see John P. Davis, *Corporations* (New York: Capricorn Books, 1961), pp. 13–34.

A series of judicial decisions helped further to standardize and crystallize characteristics of the corporation. The *Dartmouth College Case*[15] brought corporate charters within the contract clause of the Constitution, and the Supreme Court later extended the due process provisions of the Fourteenth Amendment to the corporate "person,"[16] thus providing considerable protection against subsequent attempts by the state to exercise sovereignty. The concept of the corporation as a legal person, separate and distinct from the human beings who make up the organization, was widely accepted at an early stage of the corporation's development. It provided a valuable practical tool as well as a conceptual one, but it also caused much confusion and generated countless pages of scholarly expletive.

Competition among the states for the business of incorporating led to grants to corporations of rights, powers, flexibility, and various advantages that the other forms of organization did not enjoy. In other circumstances or with another sequence of historical events, the corporation might not have become the dominant form of business organization. As a matter of fact, it is still only in the large-scale enterprise that the corporate form has achieved complete dominance. In small-scale operations, other forms are often more numerous, more important, and more desirable, from the point of view of the associates.

THE "MODERN" CORPORATION. Although the corporation can be distinguished from other forms of organization for the purposes of our discussion here, and the fact of its domination can be explained, our basic concept of the corporation is not as easily agreed upon. The problem is not only that of the concession versus the inherence theory, but also whether either of these theories provides a satisfactory conceptual framework for a study of the "modern" corporation.

One of the most quoted definitions of the corporation and one of the clearest expressions of the concession theory was Chief Justice Marshall's statement in the *Dartmouth College Case*:

> A corporation is an artificial being, invisible, intangible, and existing only in contemplation of the law. Being the mere creature of law, it possesses only those properties which the charter of its creation confers upon it, either expressly or incidental to its very existence.[17]

The following quotation is often recommended as a clear statement of the inherence view:

> Their [corporations'] effectiveness depends upon the social bonds that unite their members and upon the need of human nature for a group-life such as

---

[15] Dartmouth College v. Woodward, 4 Wheaton 518 (1819).

[16] San Mateo County v. Southern Pacific R. R., 116 U.S. 138 (1885); Santa Clara County v. Southern Pacific R. R., 118 U.S. 394 (1886).

[17] 4 Wheaton at 636.

they afford. The state cannot make them; it cannot always destroy them. It may recognize them, but in so doing it merely recognizes something which exists as a fact and which is in no sense produced by recognition.[18]

Is either of these theories satisfactory when applied to the General Motors Corporation? Is General Motors either a "creature" of the State of Delaware or a good example of a voluntary association of free men seeking a group-life?

It is probably sufficient for our needs that the term "corporation" be understood to refer to private profit, business organizations formed in compliance with a state incorporation act and operating under a charter or articles of incorporation drafted and filed under the terms of such act. These organizations will usually possess all the characteristics of corporateness previously listed. The fact that organizations formed outside the incorporation acts may possess all or substantially all the same characteristics should not disturb us.

ELEMENTS COMMON TO ALL CORPORATIONS. The drive toward corporateness in the sixteenth and seventeenth centuries is largely inexplicable today except in terms of prestige or protection flowing from manifestations of royal favor. The advantages of the corporate form of organization in our time are neither difficult to discover nor formidable to explain, but one should not jump to the conclusion that corporate characteristics are always necessarily superior to attributes that may be possessed by other forms of organization. Let us devote a few moments to the elements possessed by all corporations, to a greater or lesser degree, which constitute at the same time the attractions and disadvantages of the corporate form. Most of these elements were discussed in another connection at the beginning of this chapter.

Legal personality. There is much confusion over the term "legal person" when applied to the corporation. It should be clearly understood that the use of such terminology is merely a convenience and a manner of speaking. It is a fiction, an intentional assumption of a thing as a fact for purposes of analysis or orderly reasoning, an invention to serve some specific end or object. Most of us refer to ships and airplanes as "she," not because we believe that such vehicles are really persons but because their intentional personification makes it easier for us to think about them and to deal with them. The "government" would be extremely difficult to talk or write about, to be irate at, or even to form a conception of, if we did not personify it for these purposes. When we call a corporation a legal person, we are just using a convenient and colorful way of saying that a corporation is a distinct legal unit with status and capacity of its own, a legal instrument for carrying on some business or other type of activity.

The corporation may take, hold, and transfer property in its own name; it can make contracts with its own members; it is not directly affected by the death, withdrawal, or disagreement of its members; it can sue and be sued in its

---

[18] Hugo Krabbe, *The Modern Idea of the State,* trans. and introduction by George H. Sabine and Walter J. Shepard (New York: Appleton-Century Crofts, 1922), p. xliii.

own name; and it is entitled to the protection of the due process and equal protection clauses of the Fourteenth Amendment to the Constitution, protection to which it is entitled because the corporation is a "person" under the language of that amendment. A corporation is not a "citizen," however, under Article IV, Section 2, of the Constitution, which says that "the citizens of each state shall be entitled to all privileges and immunities of citizens in the several states." This means that although a natural person may go freely from state to state doing business in each state on the same terms as citizens of that state, the corporation does not have this right.

It is obvious that there are certain advantages that accrue to the organizers or associates in having a fictional legal person acting on their behalf and serving as a kind of shield against adversity. In some situations, the corporate device is used to conceal the identities of the human beings involved. The valuable protection of limited liability (discussed separately below) is consistent with the concept of the corporation as a separate person which incurs its own debts and obligations. But the courts will not permit a legal fiction to be used to accomplish a fraud or bring about an unjust result. Under such circumstances, the court will disregard the corporate entity, "pierce the corporate veil," and assess liability or impose obligation as though there were no legal personality.

Limited liability.   Although limited liability can be obtained without legal personality, and legal personality exist without limited liability, the two attributes clearly have a close connection. As a matter of fact, most of the important characteristics of corporateness are related directly or indirectly to the concept of legal personality. The limited liability of the corporate shareholder is one of the greatest sources of popular appeal for the corporate form of organization. See the detailed discussion in Chapter 9.

Transferability of ownership interest.   Associates or participants in other forms of organization are not barred from transferring their interests, but for several reasons the shareholder has a distinct advantage over the others. Normally, the shareholder has in his possession a piece of paper, the stock certificate, which represents his ownership interests in the corporation and also provides the means (indorsement and delivery of the certificate) by which his interest can be transferred. Organized exchanges provide a market and a pricing mechanism for the transfer of shares. A partner's ownership interest, in contrast, is not represented by a written instrument, has no access to organized markets, and is extremely difficult to evaluate.

It must not be forgotten, however, that not all corporations desire to list their shares on exchanges or can do so even if they desire, owing to rules of the exchanges, which set certain minimum standards of quality and quantity. There is no guarantee that the owner of shares can find a buyer for his shares or that he can obtain his desired price. In many small corporations, the transferability of shares is severely limited by the terms of the share contract or by the conditions of original issue set down by some state regulatory authority. Easy transferability of corporate shares may, in these cases, be a delusion, and the shareholder may be even worse off in this respect than the partner.

Concentration of management. The corporate form makes it possible to concentrate management in the hands of a few, although share ownership may be in the hands of many. The services of skilled and experienced managers may be obtained for the corporation even though these managers may be unable or unwilling to contribute significant amounts of capital.

Continuity of existence. Implicit in the concept of legal personality is a continuity of existence for the corporation wholly unrelated to the lives and vagaries of the human beings who make it up. The death of a partner dissolves the partnership automatically. The death of a shareholder, officer, or director, or even the deaths of all the shareholders, officers, and directors, would have no direct effect on the life of the corporation. Blackstone's metaphor is a very descriptive one: a corporation is "a person that never dies; in a like manner as the River Thames is still the same river, though the parts which compose it are changing every instant."[19]

E. Disadvantages of Corporate Form

IN GENERAL. Compared with the partnership and most other forms, the corporation is costly to organize. For a large enterprise, these costs would be relatively unimportant, but in bringing a small organization into existence, the costs of incorporation may be a factor worth considering and will add up to several hundred dollars, at the very least. The question of tax advantages in the various forms of organization is one that cannot be considered here. It is enough to say that expert advice should be obtained before making a decision based on tax considerations.

Corporations are singled out for special regulations of all sorts. There are special tax laws for corporations; mergers, consolidations, and reorganizations are the subject of special state and federal legislation; the issuance of corporate shares of stock is regulated by both state and federal governments. The use of the corporate form carries with it certain formalities that must be observed by the associates: minutes and records that must be kept, douments that must be filed periodically, and procedures that must be followed. The corporate device cannot be used casually or altered informally. Associates who intend to behave casually toward their organizational form should probably avoid the corporation.

OFFSETTING CORPORATE DISADVANTAGES. Expert advice and careful drafting of corporate instruments may make it possible to reduce or offset some of the disadvantages inherent in the corporate form. As has already been pointed out, for example, the corporate form raises some obstacles in the path of the organizers of a small enterprise who wish to maintain personal management and

---

[19] 1 Blackstone, *Commentaries,* 468.

control, owing to the easy transferability of shares and to the fact that the transferee succeeds to the rights possessed by the transferor. Corporate associates, consequently, are often anxious to restrict the free transferability of shares. Such restrictions may take any one of a number of forms. It should be noted, however, that general prohibitions against transfer and transfers permitted only with the consent of the directors or other shareholders have almost invariably been held invalid by the courts. Reasonable restrictions are valid. It is often provided in appropriate corporate documents that a shareholder, before sale or transfer to outsiders, must give first option to the corporation or to the other shareholders, frequently at some fixed or formula price. In this fashion, one of the advantages of the partnership form may be blended, at least in part, into the corporation.

Partners may distribute the management and control of their business in any way they please. If a partner's wishes are ignored, he can withdraw and dissolve the firm. The managerial authority of the corporation, however, is vested in the board of directors, not in the shareholders. The shareholders participate in the selection of the board, of course, but it is the number of shares, not the number of shareholders, that is counted. Various means exist for protecting the managerial rights of shareholders in small corporations and for balancing the membership of the board among the shareholders in order to make the operation of the corporation more like that of the partnership. The following, and combinations thereof, are methods by which these ends may be brought about: the use of nonvoting stock; equal division of the voting stock among the associates; cumulative voting; pre-emptive rights; classification of shares; voting trusts and pooling agreements; agreements among the associates to elect each other as directors. The use of these techniques does not create the exact advantages of the partnership, because the board of directors takes action by majority vote, and this procedure usually cannot be altered. Attempts to require unanimous shareholder or board approval before action can be taken, thus giving each shareholder or director veto power, have been struck down by the courts, whether such provisions appeared in separate agreements among the parties or in the corporation's bylaws or charter.

F. Types of Corporations

The corporate mechanism is used not only to carry on business for private profit, but also for many other purposes. Many cities are municipal corporations; churches and other religious organizations often conduct their affairs through the corporate device; there are educational, scientific, and charitable corporations of many kinds. Most corporations issue stock, but non-stock corporations may be used for some purposes. Almost all corporations conform to the same basic pattern, and much can be learned about public corporations by examining private corporations. All corporations mentioned above are important in their own fields. Our discussion, however, will be confined to the private, profit, stock corporation because it is the most important use, as far as business law is concerned, to which the corporate device is put.

The corporation employed to conduct business for private profit differs in certain respects from varieties of the form used to carry on governmental, religious, charitable, social, educational, and other nonprofit activities. The traditional classification of "public" as compared with "private" corporations is no longer very useful, as almost any large private, profit corporation serves important public needs, plays a variety of political and social roles, and can accurately be described as being quasi-public in character, although legally it is a private corporation.

The corporate mechanism is widely used to carry on certain kinds of governmental activity, ranging from the government of cities by municipal corporations to commercial activities like those conducted by the Federal Deposit Insurance Corporation and the Tennessee Valley Authority. The government corporation has been used very little in the United States for the conduct of strictly business activities, but abroad, where circumstances and needs may be different, the government corporation often plays a major role in the total economy.

In many states, the law provides for the formation of nonprofit corporations by private parties for charitable, educational, social, recreational, religious, cemetery, cooperative, and other purposes. Golf and country clubs, neighborhood recreational associations, and fraternal societies are often incorporated. Such organizations receive special tax treatment but are prohibited, of course, from making profits that may accrue to individual members. A special type of corporation, known as the *corporation sole,* is available in some states for holding title to ecclesiastical property.

Although almost all private, profit corporations issue shares of stock, many nonprofit associations are organized as membership, or nonstock corporations. Such organizations usually issue membership certificates but cannot issue shares that entitle the holder to dividends.

Each of the many kinds of corporations differs from the others in diverse ways. Each has its own set of legal rules and principles and its own published literature. Further information about them can be obtained by consulting specialized library collections.

G. Foreign Corporations

Another classification of corporations, which has not previously been mentioned, but which is, nonetheless, important, is that of domestic corporations as compared with foreign corporations. The word *foreign* used here does not necessarily mean Bolivian corporations or French corporations, but it does mean corporations operating in any state except the state where they were organized. A corporation is domestic in the state where it was organized, but it is foreign in all others. The significance of this classification lies in the fact that corporations, although they are persons for many constitutional purposes, are not "citizens" under Article IV, Section 2 of the Federal Constitution and do not have the right to do business in every state.

Theoretically, a state could keep out foreign corporations entirely. As a practical matter, it would be a very unusual situation where a state would want to do this. What most states do is to admit foreign corporations for the purpose of doing business, but they impose certain conditions on this privilege. Commonly, these conditions include a requirement that the corporation must file a copy of its charter with some state officer. And, possibly, copies must also be filed in counties where the corporation does business, owns real property, or has its principal office. The purpose of this requirement is to make information regarding the corporation available to persons in that state. A prospective customer or creditor may learn, among other things, something about the capital structure of the corporation, its corporate purposes, or the location of its home office.

Some states require the filing of separate documents setting forth the location of the home office and the location of the principal office in the state. Many states also require the foreign corporation to designate an agent within the state for the service of process. Of course, the purpose of this is to make it easier for residents of that state to sue the corporation in regard to business done within the state. Thus, a local court may acquire jurisdiction over the corporation. Because the designated agent may leave the state, many states also require corporations to consent in advance to service of process on some state officer as an agent of the corporation. The state officer must take reasonable steps to notify the corporation of the suit brought against it in the particular state, but, even if the corporation does not appear to defend, jurisdiction is acquired, and a valid judgment may be obtained.

A state will usually insist also that the foreign corporation do business under a name that is not the same as the name of a corporation already doing business in that state, or not so similar as to cause confusion. This requirement is frequently the explanation for the fact that a corporation, well known under a particular name in one state, may be doing business under a different name in another state.

It is important to remember that a state, under the Federal Constitution, must refrain from interfering unduly with interstate commerce, because the federal government holds almost exclusive sway over this field. This means that the state which imposes conditions upon foreign corporations has no right to impose them unless the corporation is "doing business" within the boundaries of the state. The state may regulate intrastate commerce, and thus has the power to impose conditions on the foreign corporation doing business there. Where the state imposes conditions on corporations that do not do business within its borders, the courts have held that it has unduly interfered with interstate commerce. An important issue, then, is: When is a corporation "doing business" in a particular state?

The phrase "doing business" is important in a number of different legal situations largely as a result of our federal system, which assigns certain powers to the federal government while reserving others to the states. Its meaning is not the same in all of these situations. An oversimplified but still useful explanation, as far as our problem here is concerned, is that a corporation *does business* within a state when it engages in a regular business consisting of repeated and successive transactions within that state. An interesting illustration is a mail order company that solicits business in many states. If a contract between a customer and the company comes into existence in the customer's home state, a court would very likely hold that a transaction had taken place in that state, and, if there were more such transactions, the court would hold that the company was "doing business" in that state. On the other hand, if the contract comes into existence in the home state of the company (as is usually the case in these situations), the transaction would take place there, and the company would not be "doing business" in the customer's state.

The power of the state to impose conditions on foreign corporations, though broad, is not unlimited. Once a corporation is admitted to a state, it may not be discriminated against in comparison with domestic corporations. The reason is simple: Although a corporation is not a "citizen" under Article IV, Section 2, it is still a "person" under the Fourteenth Amendment and is entitled to the benefits of the "due process" and "equal protection" clauses. But a corporation may be required, as a condition of its entry into a state, to consent to certain discriminations after it is admitted. However, where a state required foreign corporations to waive their rights to take cases involving local business into the federal courts, the United States Supreme Court held that this was an unconstitutional use of the state's power.

A question which must be answered here in regard to foreign corporations is: What happens when a foreign corporation ignores the local requirements and proceeds to do business anyhow? The answer is simple: Not much. The penalties vary from state to state, but they commonly include fines and a provision that the corporation may not sue on any intrastate business until it does comply with the law. Of course, the corporation may be sued. Because the requirements, as a whole, are routine and non-restrictive in nature, the motives for violation are missing; consequently, stiff penalties are unnecessary.

5. OTHER FORMS OF ORGANIZATION

A. In General

The other forms of organization are not as important as the partnership and the corporation; therefore, less time will be spent in considering their characteristics and attributes. Furthermore, much that has been said about the partnership and the corporation is true also of the other forms, and only the distinguishing characteristics will be discussed in detail here.

B. The Limited Partnership

Essentially, the limited partnership is very much like the general partnership, but it has a few important contrasting characteristics. Because the limited partnership, like the corporation, is a creature of statute, it cannot exist without a statute. Almost all states have limited partnership statutes of one kind or another, but most states have adopted a Uniform Limited Partnership Act, a companion piece to the Uniform Partnership Act. The limited partnership form is not as common or as popular as it once was, owing largely to the increasing ease of incorporation and increasing familiarity with the corporate form. However, as was pointed out above, the corporation is barred from some fields by statute. In these fields the limited partnership is a convenient device for obtaining limited liability for at least some of the members.

The limited partnership has two kinds of partners—*general partners* and *special* or *limited partners*. The former are almost idential with the partners in the general partnership, but the special or limited partners are a different type. The Limited partner, as his name implies, has liability limited to the amount of his investment. Unlike the corporate shareholder, however, the limited partner may not participate in the business at all. If he does, he runs the risk of losing his limited liability and of becoming a general partner. Under the Uniform Limited Partnership Act, the limited partner may lose his limited liability if his name is used as part of the name of the business, unless his name was used before he became a limited partner or his name is the same as that of a general partner.

The limited partnership is a somewhat more stable form of organization than the general partnership because the act, death or bankruptcy of a limited partner does not ordinarily dissolve the firm. The limited partner's ownership interest is probably no more easily transferred than that of the general partner, but he may deal with his firm and even lend money to it in much the same manner as an outsider would.

C. The Business Trust

Another instrument offering the attraction of limited liability to some of its associates is the business trust. This form, however, is much better suited to large scale operations than is the limited partnership, but in the area of large scale operations the corporation is usually a more satisfactory device. As incorporation has become easier and the corporate form better understood, the business trust has faded into minor importance.

There are two types of associates in the business trust, the *trustee* and the *beneficiary*. The former holds title to the property and manages the business. The latter puts up the capital and receives in exchange a transferable share entitling the holder to participate in the profits. The beneficiary has limited liability, but he may lose it if he participates in the management or if ultimate control of the trustee is in his hands. The trustee has unlimited liability, in spite of the fact that the agreement between trustee and beneficiary, which brings the trust into existence, usually contains a clause to the contrary. Such clauses are not binding on outsiders who deal with the firm unless the outsider agrees to be bound.

The business trust is a stable device, as compared with the partnership, limited or general, but it lacks many of the advantages of the corporation. There was a time when the great advantages which the trust had over the corporation were its relative freedom from regulation and from special taxes. However, today, the trust is classed as a corporation for most tax and regulatory purposes, and the advantages are gone.

D. The Joint Stock Company

This is the same form as the unchartered joint stock company which was one of the ancestors of the modern corporation. It still survives today, in spite of the fact that its dynamic offspring now dominates the field in which the joint stock company was once so important. Aside from the transferable shares and concentration of management, the joint stock company might well be classified as a partnership. Although these particular characteristics may give it preference over the partnership in some situations, the corporation usually provides a better form where these attributes are important. The joint stock company faded from the scene as the use of the corporation expanded.

E. The Joint Venture

A device still common and popular within its own narrowly defined area is the joint venture or joint adventure. Again, this form is much like a partnership, but it differs in its extreme informality, its limited scope and duration, and the fact that it may be used where the actual carrying on of a business or the profit objective is not present. Because the joint venture is so much like a partnership, in most states it is subject to many of the principles of partnership law.

Although a partnership is usually organized to remain in business for a definite or indefinite period of time, the joint venture is ordinarily formed for a single undertaking, and it is not intended to continue in existence beyond the accomplishment of that undertaking. Situations where the joint venture has been used are: management of a prize-fighter, production or writing of a play, survey of oil fields, speculation in real estate, and construction of a building. The rights and duties of the associates are much the same as among partners, but some states have, by statute, limited in one way or another the power of the individual member to bind the others by his acts. The legal entity concept is almost completely absent in the joint venture.

Under the Uniform Partnership Act, profit must be the objective of the particular activities in which a partnership is engaged. If this test is not met, there is no partnership. A joint venture may, and frequently does, exist where profit or even the conduct of a business as such is not the immediate objective—for example, writing a play or surveying an oil field.

PROBLEMS

1. What factors need to be considered in selecting a form of business organization? Explain why each factor is important.

2. Apply the factors from Problem 1 to the various hypothetical business situations which can be created by combining in different ways the characteristics which follow. Size: large, medium, small. Organizers: all experienced businessmen, some experienced, none experienced, few, many, old, young, want to participate in management, do not want to participate, plan to remain with business, temporary interest only. Liability: all want limited, some want limited, do not care. Capital source: organizers provide all, some, or none. Capital requirements: great, medium, small. Duration of business: long term, short term, fixed term, indefinite.

3. How does the Uniform Partnership Act define a partnership? Explain each of the important terms used in the definition. Is an organization which fits the definition necessarily a partnership?

4. Under what circumstances may a person who is sharing the profits of partnership not be a partner?

5. Why has the corporate form of business organization been so popular in the United States, and why has it played such a predominant role in the economic development of the United States?

6. What are the important characteristics which distinguish the corporation from other forms of organization?

7. Is it true that the legal entity nature of a corporation may be disregarded under certain circumstances? Explain.

8. What are the disadvantages of the corporate form when compared with the partnership form of business organization?

9. What is the significance of Article IV, Section 2, of the Federal Constitution with regard to the use of the corporate form of organization?

10. Describe the limited partnership, the business trust, the joint stock company, and the joint venture.

chapter 5

The Procedure of

Organization

1. IN GENERAL

Once the decision on the form of organization has been made—a decision based on the nature of the business, the number and character of the organizers, the attributes which the organizers expect of a form of business organization, and on many other factors—the next legal problems arise in connection with the procedure of organization. If the sole-proprietorship is the device selected to carry on the business, the legal problems of procedure are minor, and they will not be discussed here. The non-procedural problems of getting a sole-proprietorship started will be discussed in other portions of the book. The partnership and the corporation present unique problems of procedure, which will be examined in some detail. The miscellaneous forms will be discussed only where their problems are important or substantially different.

Corporations are seldom organized without the technical advice and help a lawyer can provide. Actually, it is very unwise in most cases to attempt to organize a corporation without good legal advice. The procedure is formal and technical, and it is sometimes confusing to the layman. In many states, the failure to comply completely and correctly with the statutory requirements may produce

219

serious results for those who participate in the organization. Because legal advice is ordinarily sought in connection with the organization of a corporation, even a small one, it is probably less important for the layman to know the details of corporate procedure than it is for him to know the legal problems of procedure that face the organizer of a partnership. However, the procedure by which a corporation is organized has important ramifications at later stages of a corporation's life, and much of the information that a layman should have about corporations cannot really be understood or appreciated without the background knowledge of the formation procedure. For this reason, the procedure whereby corporations are brought into existence is given a thorough discussion below.

2. THE PARTNERSHIP

A. Cases

(1)

Heinrich Hibner, a wealthy retired toy manufacturer, moved to Berkland several years ago in order to enjoy the mild Anosmia climate. Shortly after his arrival, he struck up an acquaintance with one of the SIMUCO partners and has since come to know all of them quite well. He spends a great deal of time around the store examining toys, talking to the customers and chatting with any of the partners who happen to be on the premises. The partners have learned a lot from him about the toy business and, on several occasions, have taken Hibner's advice on specific purchases of toys. As a matter of fact, the partners, among themselves, have often referred to Hibner, jokingly, as their "senior partner." Hibner has attended occasional toy shows and trade fairs with one or more of the partners, and his contacts and advice on these trips have proved to be very useful to the firm. Hibner has enjoyed his relationship with the store and with the partners and has often referred to them when in the company of his old business associates and friends, as "his store" and "his partners," often in the presence of the partners themselves. Recognizing the prestige and value the name "Hibner" enjoyed in the industry, and not wanting to embarrass the old man, the partners have never made it clear that Hibner was not really a partner. As a result, the general impression among the dealers and manufacturers from whom SIMUCO buys its toys is that Hibner is a partner. This fact is known to the partners. Al Able and Hibner recently attended a toy manufacturers' show in New York, where Able placed most of his orders for the toys SIMUCO will need during the next Christmas season. Able saw little of Hibner at the show but did ask his advice on two or three orders about which Able felt uncertain. After Able returned home, order confirmations from manufacturers revealed to him and to the other partners that Hibner had placed several large orders on behalf of SIMUCO for toys that the firm did not want and could not use. When questioned about it, Hibner said that he thought he was doing the firm a favor. The partners notified the manufacturers immediately that Hibner was not authorized to place the orders and that SIMUCO would not honor them. With one exception, the manufacturers replied that they would go to court, if necessary, to enforce the contracts.

B. In General

The partnership is a common law device, and, as such, can exist without any statutory grant of authority from the state. If this were not so, most states would have special statutes granting authority to organize partnerships. Undoubtedly, these statutes would go further than a grant of authority, and would prescribe in some detail the procedure by which the device was to be brought into existence. This is the case with the limited partnership statutes. All states do have statutes on their books dealing with general partnerships—if not the Uniform Partnership Act, then another—but these statutes do not purport to grant authority to organize. This would be unnecessary and ineffectual. What these statutes do is to set forth a codification or a restatement of the rules and principles that control the use of the partnership form. Few, if any, of these partnership statutes deal with problems of organization procedure. The result is that the procedure by which partnerships are created is informal and unstandardized. No documents have to be drawn up. No papers have to be signed or filed. No particular words have to be spoken. No formalities need be gone through. None of these things is essential to the creation of the legal form known as the partnership. This is not to say that none of these things is done; actually, most of them are done. The point is that the performance of these acts is not a prerequisite to the existence of a partnership. All that is needed is an agreement by the parties to associate themselves for the purpose of carrying on a business for profit as co-owners, plus the actual starting of the business that has been agreed upon. As a practical matter, the agreement may be written or oral, or it may even be implied from the conduct of the parties who are carrying on the business. Most businessmen who form partnerships use a formal written agreement signed by those who are participating. Although this procedure is usually preferable, it is not necessary.

C. The Partnership Agreement

ORAL OR WRITTEN. As far as the law is concerned, an oral contract, with a few exceptions, is just as good as a written one, but from the standpoint of convenience and security, written contracts will be preferred most of the time. So it is also with the partnership contract. The oral agreement is much more subject to the human weaknesses of forgetfulness or misunderstanding or bad faith than the written agreement is. A partner's memory, like anyone else's, is subject to lapses and mistakes, and these may happen where the life of the firm may be at issue. For these reasons, most partnership contracts are in writing. Much work and thought goes into many of them, and expert legal advice is often obtained when these agreements are drafted.

EFFECT OF THE STATUTE OF FRAUDS.   Although partnership agreements, as such, do not need to be in writing, certain clauses that are sometimes desirable in partnership agreements do come under the statute of frauds and must be in writing in order to be enforced. The clauses that fall into this category vary somewhat from state to state. Only one clause really deserves to be on the list, and that is the clause whereby the partners fix the duration of the firm at longer than one year by agreeing to stay in business together for that time. This is clearly "a contract which by its very terms is incapable of performance within one year from the date of making"; consequently, it comes under the statute of frauds. But if this clause is not in writing, a "partnership at will" instead of for a fixed term has been created. This means that any partner may withdraw at any time without breaching the partnership contract. Other matters are sometimes said to come under the statute, but only in very unusual circumstances will any of these conclusions stand up under analysis. In any event, the failure to have all or any part of the agreement in writing will not affect the coming into existence of a partnership.

WHAT THE AGREEMENT CONTAINS.   It is obvious that what should go into a partnership agreement will vary with each situation. A list of general recommendations can be drawn up, however, and some general principles arrived at. A partnership agreement may perform either or both of two functions. It may seek simply to get the business started by setting forth its purpose, the amount and form of capital to be contributed, and, possibly, the method of sharing the profits. Or it may try to anticipate future problems and to provide the machinery by which these anticipated problems may be solved if and when they arise. Or the agreement may do both.

Many routine, though important, clauses should appear in the agreement. The name of the business is first among these, and it may be, in some cases, of primary importance. The name should not conflict with any other name already in use in the field. Many states have statutes requiring the registration or filing of so-called "fictitious names" that do not disclose the names of the persons conducting the business. This is a simple and inexpensive requirement with which to comply, and in many states a firm complies as a routine part of organization, whether the name of the firm is really fictitious or not. The statutes usually demand no more than a statement of the firm name together with the names and addresses of the persons under it. The purpose is to make a public record of the individual members of firms for the benefit of those who deal with the firm. Failure to comply is not severely punished, but it usually prevents suits by the firm on firm business until there has been compliance.

The agreement should contain the full names and addresses of the partners, a reasonably accurate description of the business, and provisions for possible future expansion into other fields and lines. The location of the principal office ought to be set forth. A duration clause may also be useful where the withdrawal of a partner might do serious harm to the other partners or to the firm.

There should be clauses setting forth the contributions in money or property that each of the partners will make and stating the time for turning the contributions over to the firm. The valuations of any property contributions should be agreed upon. If any property is simply being loaned or if a partner will be entitled to get his property back in kind on dissolution, this should be clearly stated. It should be made plain if a partner may make additional contributions, if a partner may withdraw part of his contribution, if a partner is to receive interest on his contribution or a salary, if a partner may withdraw profits before the end of an accounting period, and if partners are to have expense accounts. It may be necessary to deal with the problem of retaining profits in the business.

An important clause is the profit sharing clause. Will the profits be shared equally, in proportion to capital contribution, or in some other ratio? In the absence of any agreement, profits are shared equally. How are losses to be shared? In the absence of a contrary provision, losses are shared in the same way that profits are. Certain acccounting questions probably should be answered. What is meant by "profits?" What accounts are to be established for the partners? Accrual or cash basis? What accounting period?

In some situations it may be desirable to divide up and assign management responsibility among the partners. In the absence of a clause, all share equally. Are the partners to devote full time to the business? To what extent may they engage in other activities? Are any acts to be placed beyond the authority of the individual partner? And will the acts require consent of some or all of the other partners?

How are disputes to be settled? Many partnership contracts contain an arbitration clause whereby an outsider is given dispute-settling powers. Are new partners to be admitted? If so, by whom? In absence of a contrary provision, every partner must consent to the admission of a new partner. Need provision be made for the expulsion of a partner?

One of the most important clauses any agreement can contain is a clause dealing with procedures on the death, withdrawal, disability, or bankruptcy of a partner. Many a partnership investment has been lost because the partners failed to look ahead to dissolution. Technically, as will be discussed in greater detail in Part V, the death, withdrawal, disability, or bankruptcy of a partner causes an automatic dissolution of the firm. The effects of dissolution may be offset to a great degree by a little foresightedness when the agreement is drafted. The importance of a dissolution clause cannot be over-emphasized, because too many of them are recklessly drawn or not drawn at all, with the result that what is at best a traumatic experience for the business becomes a fatal one.

It is probably wise to point out at this time that a partnership agreement, even if written, may be amended at any time by the unanimous consent of the partners, and it is not necessary that the amendments be in writing except where affected by the statute of frauds.

PARTNERSHIP BY ESTOPPEL. Some characteristics of the partnership relation may be created other than by a partnership contract among the parties. If a person permits himself to be held out as a partner or holds himself out as a partner to third persons who rely on this holding out, the person being held out may be treated by the courts very much as though he were a partner. This end is brought about by the *doctrine of estoppel*. The doctrine appears in many areas of the law. It is designed to prevent a person from denying the truth of an intentional or careless statement or act that has led another reasonably to rely upon it. As far as partnerships are concerned, a court may, under the doctrine of estoppel, make a person who was held out as a partner liable for partnership obligations as though he had been a partner, or make partners liable for the acts of a non-partner who was held out as a real partner. The common law in this regard has been crystallized in Section 16 of the Uniform Partnership Act.

The first element necessary to establish grounds for imposing the doctrine of estoppel is the holding out. This holding out may be done either by the particular person being held out or by others who are associated with the business. It may be done in various ways: by the person's name forming a part of the firm name, by his name appearing on signs, letter-heads, advertisements, or lists of partners, or simply by his being referred to as a partner. It is obvious, however, that even the clearest holding out by the partners accompanied by the most extensive and most reasonable reliance by third persons will not make the person being held out liable as a partner unless he has in some way consented to the holding out. Nor may a person holding himself out make the real partners liable for his acts unless they have consented, expressly or impliedly, to the holding out. A crucial issue here is: What steps must be taken, in order to avoid liability, by a person who knows he is being held out as a partner or by partners who know someone is holding himself out as their partner? The answer, unfortunately, varies from state to state. It is a disputed question whether the necessary consent can be inferred from knowledge of the holding out plus failure to do anything about it. There are cases holding squarely that a duty arises and that affirmative steps must be taken to contradict alleged partnership relations. The better view, probably, is that there is no duty to deny false representations of partnership, to the making of which one is not a party. The draftsmen of the statute make it clear that the Uniform Partnership Act was designed to impose liability only where there is consent in fact to the representations.

In addition to holding out and to consent, another necessary element is the reasonable reliance by the third person on the holding out. If the third person does not rely on the holding out, there would be no reason to impose the estoppel, inasmuch as the holding out was not responsible for an injustice to the third person. A clear example of this would be the situation where the third person did not know of the holding out at the time he entered into a contract with the partnership. Note, however, that where the holding out has been done in a public manner, by advertising or by the firm name, a presumption that a third person relied on it may be created.

A special situation results where less than all of the partners participate in or consent to the holding out of another person as their partner. Under the Uniform Partnership Act, the liability that may be created is not a partnership liability but is only the joint liability of the person being held out and of those partners who participated in or consented to it. The dissenting partner is not liable, nor is partnership property. Where all the partners consent or participate in the holding out, the liability is a partnership liability, and all partners and the firm property are subject to the obligation.

As among the partners and the person being held out, the doctrine of estoppel does not apply. The reason is plain. These persons know the true state of affairs and are not misled. Consequently, there is no basis for an estoppel. The relations between the real partners and the person being held out must be governed by the terms of their actual agreement.

3. THE CORPORATION

A. Cases

(1)

Davis and three other men agreed to form a corporation and divide the stock equally among themselves. The purpose of the corporation was to buy, gin, and sell cotton. Articles of incorporation were drawn up in June and signed by the associates but were not filed until December 22. Between June and December, the associates looked upon themselves as a corporation and actually began business as a corporation, conducting their operations under the name of Coweta Cotton and Milling Company. Prior to December 22, they purchased from Harrill $4,700 worth of goods on credit, and, after December 22, purchased about $500 more on credit from Harrill, none of which debt has been paid. On December 22, the associates filed the articles of incorporation in one of the two places required by the relevant incorporation law but did not file a copy in the local political subdivision where their place of business was located. No stock was ever issued. When Harrill demanded payment of his claim for $5,200, the Coweta Company had no assets of any significant value. Harrill has filed suit against the four associates as partners.

[*Harrill* v. *Davis,* 168 Fed. 187 (8th Cir. 1909)]

(2)

Wells, Carruth and Jones undertook to form a corporation for the purpose of manufacturing wooden spokes and handles. The name of the corporation was to be Ficklen Spoke and Handle Company. Before the corporation came into existence, a contract was entered into by the three promoters with the Fay and Egan Company for the purchase of certain machinery. The actual contract was signed "Ficklen Spoke and Handle Company, by L. M. Wells, R. K. Carruth, J. Jones." The machinery was shipped and received by the promoters, who issued a promissory note to Fay and Egan for the amount of the purchase. The note, with the approval of Wells and Jones, was signed "Ficklen Spoke and Handle Company, per R. K. Carruth, Sec. & Treas." At a later time, articles of incorporation were filed and other necessary steps for incorporation were completed. The corporation made certain payments on the note, which payments Fay and Egan accepted. The payments finally stopped, however, before the note was fully paid, and Fay and Egan attempted to collect the balance from the corporation. This attempt was unsuccessful, and the Fay and Egan Company is now suing Wells, Carruth and Jones as individuals. Are they liable?

[*Wells* v. *Fay and Egan Co.,* 143 Ga. 732, 85 S.E. 873 (1915)]

B. Preliminary Decision : Where To Incorporate

In General.   The corporation depends upon statutes both for its permission to exist and for the procedure by which it will come into existence. Because of this fact the corporation stands in sharp contrast to the partnership, which requires a statute for neither permission nor procedure. Probably more important, however, is the fact that the extent of the statutory permission and the details of the procedure vary somewhat from state to state. Depending upon the circumstances of the particular incorporation, some corporation laws are more attractive to incorporators than other laws. Thus, some states such as Delaware have attracted incorporations far out of proportion to the number of corporations actually doing substantial business there. The State of Delaware had, for many years, a corporation law that offered to incorporators certain privileges, advantages, and facilities of internal corporate organization which could not be obtained elsewhere. During the 1920's when Delaware's liberal and attractive corporation law had been on the books for many years, some states such as California still had laws that imposed unlimited proportional liability on shareholders, prohibited the use of par and no-par shares at the same time, and contained many other antiquated and unattractive provisions. It was no accident that made Delaware the "incorporators' state."

Today, however, the differences in corporation laws among the major commercial states are not great, and incorporation is usually preferred in the state where the major share of the business will be done unless some peculiar attribute of another state's law is necessary or important. Where a corporation will do a nation-wide business or operate in many states, the choice of sites must still be made, and the factors, in addition to those already discussed, on which this choice should be made are worth considering.

FACTORS. The cost of incorporation may be important in some situations, but the variations among the states in this connection are usually offset by the variations in the cost of qualifying as a foreign corporation. Not just a few corporations have found the cost of incorporating in one state largely wasted when they have had to pay substantial fees to qualify as foreign corporations in the state where they planned to transact most of their business.

Another factor, the importance of which is frequently exaggerated, is that of taxes, especially state income taxes. Some states try to attract incorporators by advertising the absence of, or the low rates of, local corporate income taxes. What the advertisements do not point out is that the state where the corporation does business may still tax the income of that corporation received from business transacted within that state and that the absence of income tax in the state of incorporation may be of no real significance.

Among the other advantages various state statutes may offer are: no regulation of the issuance of securities, more liberal sources of corporate dividends, and no restrictions on place of directors' and shareholders' meetings. In spite of these attractions elsewhere, domestic incorporation may still be preferable for the local corporation.

C. The Charter

STEPS PRIOR TO THE DRAFTING OF THE CHARTER. Although the procedure of incorporation varies in detail from state to state, the pattern is much the same everywhere. Certain important steps must be taken before the incorporators can draw up a charter. Some of these steps will be discussed later in this chapter in connection with the promoter's duties and functions. Included among the preliminary steps are: 1, the discovery of a business opportunity; 2, the investigation of the business opportunity; 3, the making of promotional and financial arrangements; 4, the taking of preliminary options for property and for material supply; 5, the solicitation of pre-incorporation stock subscripitons under the terms of local or federal regulatory statutes; 6, and the reservation of a corporate name.

Competent legal advice should be sought before any of these preliminary steps is undertaken by the organizers. The whole incorporation procedure and, indeed, the life of the corporation itself may be jeopardized by wrong moves at this stage. While the organizers are taking these first steps, they are probably also working out the details of the charter, the drafting of which is the next step in the incorporation procedure.

Different names are given to the charter in different states. It is variously known as a *charter,* the *articles of incorporation,* and a *certificate of incorporation.* Whatever the name, the document is basic to the formation of a corporation. If an analogy were drawn between a corporation and a government, the charter would correspond to the constitution; the corporate by-laws, to the statutes enacted by the legislature. The charter is sometimes looked upon as sort of a franchise or a grant of authority by the state, as a contract between the state and the organizers or the corporation, or as a contract between the state and the shareholders. None of these views withstands analysis very well, but it probably does not make much difference. The charter, together with the relevant state laws, is the constitution of the corporation. It may be properly regarded as at least part of the contract between the corporation and the shareholder.

WHAT SHOULD BE IN THE CHARTER. Generally speaking, charters are *required* to have certain clauses and are *permitted* to have others. Some state laws specify only that certain issues must be dealt with in the charter; others specify in addition the manner in which the issues are to be handled. Only an examination of local law will disclose the details. The usual statute will require or permit all or most of the clauses discussed below.

Corporate name. First in order is the corporate name. Though routine, the selection of the name is important, and serious thought should be given to it. The name should not conflict with any other name already in use in the state. It should, ordinarily, be easy to pronounce and spell, and it may be desirable, or even required, in some situations, that the name describe the nature of the business. Some, but not all, states require the name to include the standard abbreviations such as *Ltd., Inc., Corp.,* or *Co.,* or the words for which these abbreviations stand. The incorporators should give serious thought to the ramifications of the use of one or more of their own names in the name of the corporation. Among other things, the incorporator who so permits his name to be used may lose the right to use his own name for business purposes, even though his connections with the corporation may be severed.

Many states permit the reservation of a proposed corporate name for a limited period before the charter is filed. The prior reservation gives the state officer with whom the reservation is made an opportunity to determine whether there is a conflict with any other name in use, and if there is, time to notify the incorporators before the charter is filed.

Purpose clause. One of the most important clauses in a corporate charter is the *purpose clause*. This sets forth the purposes, objects, or the general nature of the business. State laws vary in regard to the detail with which this information must be stated, but the better modern statutes permit corporations to be formed for "any lawful purpose" or combination of lawful purposes, and they impose no particular requirements about detail except that a purpose clause authorizing a corporation "to carry on any business not contrary to law" would probably not be sufficiently specific under most of the statutes, although it is now expressly authorized under the new 1967 Delaware Corporation Law. Many corporate charters go to extremes in the opposite direction with much useless elaboration and repetition.

In addition to the statutory limitations, the corporate purpose clause must be confined within certain practical limits. Too broad a purpose clause may discourage investors who probably want to know the nature of the business into which they are putting their capital. On the other hand, too narrow or too detailed a purpose clause may unduly restrict the corporation's functions at some time in the future, and it may necessitate a later charter amendment.

The importance of the purpose clause lies in the fact that, in the eyes of the law, it is the primary source of the management's authority to do all those things reasonably incident to carrying out the purposes of the business. Acts outside this authorized area are said to be *ultra vires*. The purpose clause may be used also to set forth negatively the activities and powers from which the management is to be excluded.

Capital structure.   Most corporation laws require in the charter a more or less detailed statement of the proposed corporation's capital structure, including the authorized number of shares, the rights, preferences, privileges and restrictions on the various classes and series of shares, whether the shares have a par value, and the voting rights of the shares. This provision limits the corporation's power to alter the capital structure without a charter amendment.

Miscellaneous provisions.   Other provisions appearing in the charter have to do with the location of the principal office, the number of directors, the names and addresses of the first directors and requirements regarding the directors being shareholders, duration of the corporation, existence of the preemptive right, powers of directors to assess the shares, statement that the corporation may become a partner in a partnership, and optional provisions dealing with a host of special matters that may be important to some corporations but not to all.

EXECUTION, ACKNOWLEDGMENT, AND FILING OF THE CHARTER.   After the charter has been drafted, the incorporators or directors, depending upon state law, must personally sign the charter. It is also necessary, in most cases, that each of the signatures be personally acknowledged before a notary public or some other officer authorized to take acknowledgments. The next step consists of turning over the charter to some state officer, usually the Secretary of State, and of paying the required fees and franchise taxes. In some states the state officer examines the charter, and, if it complies with the law, files it. In other states the officer issues some sort of certificate stating that the charter has been received and that the corporation is authorized to do business in that state. Many statutes require copies of the charter to be filed with county clerks of counties where the corporation does business or owns real property.

It is sometimes important to know at what stage in this procedure of organization the corporation comes into existence. The first moment of corporate life is not the same in all states, but it is usually rather closely associated with the turning over of the charter to a state officer. If no approval by the state officer is required, the corporation may spring to life when the papers are handed over and the fees are paid. If approval is required, the filing of the charter by the state officer after approval will likely be the moment of birth. If certificates are issued by the state officer, this may signify the happy event. Some statutes specify the time at which the corporation springs into existence. Only a close examination of case and statutory law in a particular locality can answer this question.

AMENDING THE CHARTER. Amendments to the charter are, ordinarily, rather easy to accomplish before the shares of stock have been issued. The approval of a majority, or some larger proportion, of the incorporators, together with the filing of evidence in the proper state offices, are the usual requirements. Where shares have been issued, however, an amendment to the charter customarily requires the approval of the shareholders as well as the directors of the corporation. The shareholders' approval must usually be indicated at a properly convened shareholders' meeting at which a quorum of the shares is present. As a rule, a majority vote is all that is necessary, but in certain special situations much larger proportions may be required. On some issues, shares that do not ordinarily have a vote are allowed to participate. Sometimes the approval of some particular class or series of shares is necessary. There are in some states issues on which a unanimous shareholder vote is a prerequisite to amendment.

D. The By-Laws

The filing of the charter is not the last step in the procedure of corporate formation. Many important steps still remain. In those states where the directors are not named in the charter, it is necessary to hold an organization meeting of the incorporators for the purpose of electing directors and adopting by-laws. If the first directors are named in the charter, there must be a first meeting of the directors to elect officers and to adopt by-laws. Other important activities take place at these "first" meetings, but they will be discussed after a brief glance at the by-laws.

The *by-laws* are the rules for the internal management of the corporation. They are subordinate to, and must be consistent with, the charter of the corporation and the laws of the state. Although ultimate power to make by-laws rests with the shareholders, in most states the directors also have the power, either expressly, by statute, or by the charter. Where there is a conflict between the by-laws enacted by the directors and those passed by the shareholders, the shareholers' by-laws will normally prevail.

By-laws usually deal with matters such as: the duties and compensation of corporate officers; the qualifications for membership on the board of directors; executive and other directors' committees; the date and place of the annual shareholders' meeting; procedures on voting and proxies; records and reports; methods of calling and conducting directors' and shareholders' meetings; provisions for audits; other matters related to the conduct of corporate affairs.

In addition to the adoption of the by-laws, the last steps in corporate organization include: 1, authorizing the issue of shares and taking of subscriptions; 2, adopting a corporate seal and stock certificate; 3, adoption of promoters' contracts; 4, establishing the location of regular directors' meetings; 5, authorizing an application for permit to take subscriptions and issue shares; and 6, compliance with the state and federal statutes regulating the issuance of securities.

Minutes of the directors' meeting must be prepared, and corporate books and records must be opened.

E. Defectively Formed Corporations

IN GENERAL. A partnership is created solely by the agreement of the parties and by the commencement of business. There are no formalities to be complied with. The situation is much different with regard to corporations. The unusual privileges granted to the corporate device, such as the limited liability and the corporate entity, are granted only when there has been substantial compliance with the conditions and provisions set forth in a general incorporation law. The primary questions raised here are: What is the status of the corporation whose incorporators have not complied fully with the statutory requirements for organization? Does it possess any or all of the corporate characteristics? If not, what are the rights, duties, and liabilities of the directors, officers, shareholders, and outsiders who have dealt with the organization? A myriad of subsidiary questions is also raised if there is a defect in compliance with the statutes. The answers to any of these questions depend, to a large extent, on the nature and extent of the defect and on the manner in which the questions arise.

In considering problems of this kind, the courts usually, though not invariably, classify the provisions of the law as mandatory or directory. A *mandatory provision* is one that must be followed substantially, while a *directory provision* refers to non-obligatory instructions that are more a matter of convenience than of substance. The courts have held, for example, that the provision in a state incorporation law that requires filing of the charter with the Secretary of State is a mandatory provision, while, at the same time, they hold that the provision that requires filing of copies of the charter with the clerks of certain counties is a directory provision. A failure to comply with directory provisions is much less serious than a failure to comply with a mandatory one.

Depending upon the seriousness and the type of defect, the organization may be: a *de jure* corporation, which is the same as a corporation without defects in compliance; a *de facto* corporation, which is treated almost the same as a corporation without defects but is subject to attack by the state because of the defects; or a *seriously defective* corporation, which is really no corporation at all.

DE JURE CORPORATIONS. If there has been substantial compliance with the mandatory provisions of the statute, the corporation is a corporation for all purposes even though there has been no compliance with directory provisions. In other words, if the defects are immaterial and not as to matters of substance, the corporation is just as much a corporation as though there had been no defects at all. It is a corporation both in law (*de jure*) and in fact (*de facto*). It is safe even from attack by the state. This result is sensible. Where a corporation omitted its corporate seal from the charter when the document was filed, though the statute required the seal, the court said that the seal was not the essence of the thing to be done and no one could be injured by its omission.

DE FACTO CORPORATIONS. If compliance with the mandatory provisions of the incorporation laws has been complete or substantial, the business organization resulting is a corporation, both in law and in fact, for all purposes. However, where the organizers have not complied with the law to an extent sufficient to create a *de jure* corporation, the resulting organization may be a corporation for many purposes, a corporation for some purposes, or no corporation at all. The last possibility is not common where shares or the equivalent have been sold to innocent parties. The *de facto* corporation is a corporation for almost all purposes. The characteristics of the normal corporation are present, and, in all respects but one, the *de facto* corporation is treated the same as a *de jure* corporation even though the mandatory provisions of the statute have not been substantially complied with. The one important difference is simply that the *de facto* corporation is subject to attack by the state, but even the state may attack the corporate existence only in a special action brought for that purpose.

In theory, no state will hand out lightly or without good reason corporate characteristics and attributes to an organization that has not followed substantially the requirements of the law. The legal theory or policy underlying this *de facto* doctrine is one that seeks to confine the right to object to the existence of a corporation to those whose interests are prejudiced by the defects in organization and to those situations where the defects in organization affect the merits of the case. The courts, through the years, have translated this broad, general policy into more specific tests which an organization must meet in order to qualify as a *de facto* corporation. The basic test is: Was there an attempt in good faith to form a corporation under a valid corporation law followed by the transaction of business by the organization as though it were a corporation?

The test of the good faith attempt to organize a corporation is met in those situations where the organizers tried honestly and straightforwardly to create a corporation and to comply with the law. Some compliance is probably necessary also. It does not take very much compliance, but the "good faith" part of this test would be extremely difficult to satisfy if there had been no compliance at all. The situation must be such that the incorporators could reasonably believe they had succeeded in bringing a corporation into existence. It would be, for example, an unusual situation where the incorporators had knowingly failed to turn over the charter to some state officer, yet still believed in good faith that they had incorporated. The courts look on the "good faith" portion of this test with an especially jaundiced eye where the incorporators are trying to avoid personal liability by showing *de facto* status.

It is generally stated that *de facto* status may not be achieved where the statute under which the corporation purports to have come into existence was unconstitutional. Although there is sound ground for an argument in the opposite direction, this view is almost universally followed. It apparently makes little difference whether or not the statute had been declared unconstitutional at the time of the purported incorporation. An important factor to note, however, both here and in connection with any failure to achieve *de facto* status, is that an estoppel may arise under certain conditions, and it may bring about results similar to that of *de facto* status, especially where the liability of the corporation or of an outsider is at issue.

The good faith attempt to organize under a valid law is, by itself, insufficient to create a *de facto* corporation. The purported corporation must actually have behaved as a corporation, and it must have used some of its corporate powers. Recent cases leave a clear impression that only a very little user of corporate power is necessary and that acts such as electing officers and directors, taking subscriptions for shares of stock, issuing shares of stock, or adopting by-laws may be sufficient evidence of corporate user. However, the majority view probably requires "substantial user." The theory behind this is that where the organization has not carried on any appreciable business, there is no harm done by refusing to recognize *de facto* status. Even the stricter view does not require actual dealings on a corporate basis between the parties involved.

As long as the basic public policy mentioned above is carried out, the courts are quite lenient with corporations that have failed to comply strictly with the incorporation laws, but, where there are doubts in this connection, these doubts are usually resolved against the corporation. All problems considered, the issues of fairness to the various parties are the really important issues here just as they are with the seriously defective corporation where the doctrine of estoppel is sought to be applied. The two doctrines should not be confused, however, because corporate existence under the *de facto* doctrine is real, but "corporation by estoppel" is just another way of saying that where certain circumstances justify it an organization clearly not a corporation may be treated for some purposes as though it were a corporation.

SERIOUSLY DEFECTIVE CORPORATIONS. Where neither *de facto* nor *de jure* status can be attained, the resulting organization is not a corporation at all, except within the narrow area of an estoppel. The problems that arise here are different from those that appear in connection with the *de jure* or the *de facto* corporations where the organizations are corporations for all or virtually all purposes. The seriously defective corporation is not a corporation, and it does not possess the characteristics of a corporation. It is most frequently treated as a partnership. This naturally raises the issues of the liability of share-holders and associates.

If the seriously defective corporation really is a partnership, the unlimited liability of the normal partnership would apply to these partners. But who are the partners—the organizers? The shareholders? Both? We do not encounter much difficulty, either theoretically or morally, if we hold the organizers liable as partners. They are the ones whose omissions have prevented the formation of a corporation and whose acts have brought some sort of organization into existence. When it comes to the shareholder, however, the issue is not so easily or conveniently solved, except where all of the shareholders have participated in the organization or in the conduct of the business. If some of the shareholders are innocent of any knowledge of the acts or omissions which precluded corporate existence, we run into difficulties both with regard to theory and with regard to fairness. A shareholder who intended to invest in a corporation would usually lack the intent necessary to make him a partner, and it would seem unfair to hold liable as a partner a person who had no knowledge that might reasonably have led him to believe that he might be subjected to unlimited liability. Most court decisions appear to follow the more or less obvious results suggested here.

CORPORATIONS BY ESTOPPEL.   As already intimated, some of the effects of corporate existence may be brought about by the estoppel doctrine even where the purported corporation is so seriously defective that it is no corporation at all. Where the *de facto* corporation *is* a corporation and possesses all the characteristics of the normal corporation, except for its vulnerability to attack by the state, the "*corporation* by estoppel," like the *partnership* by estoppel, is a misnomer. There are elements of estoppel in the *de facto* doctrine. In some courts there has been confusion about the line between the two concepts, but, essentially, the estoppel doctrine appears only in those situations where *de jure* or *de facto* status is not possible because of the serious nature of the defects and the absence of a good faith attempt to organize a corporation. The estoppel operates only in regard to the particular transaction or group of transactions with respect to which the estoppel itself arose. Estoppel is almost always a matter of preventing a party or parties from denying corporate existence in order to escape liability; the estoppel has no further effect. No corporate taxes may be imposed under the estoppel doctrine. Those familiar with the nature of true estoppel will find that the elements usually necessary there are frequently missing in the estoppel doctrine with regard to corporations. The effect is the same, but the foundation on which the estoppel is based is often different, as we will see below.

Depending upon the circumstances, the purported corporation or third persons who have contracted with it may be estopped to deny its corporate existence. A necessary element to the estoppel, however, is the holding out of the organization as a corporation, either expressly or impliedly, or treating it or dealing with it as though it were a corporation. The mere fact of contracting with the organization is not enough to support the estoppel doctrine because the organization may have been dealt with as something other than a corporation. Where the conduct of the organizers, associates, or third persons is as consistent with some other form of organization as it is with the corporate form, there can be no estoppel. The organization must have been looked upon, treated, and contracted with as a corporation. The courts have held that the use of such words as "company" creates at least a *prima facie* estoppel as would other terminology that customarily conveys the impression of incorporation rather than some other business form.

As noted previously, the estoppel may be invoked either against the alleged corporation and those associated with it or against third persons who have dealt with the organization. Elements of equity and fairness are important in the estoppel situations, and, as a general rule, the estoppel issue arises only where some party is attempting to escape liability for himself by denying corporate existence. However, it is important to note, that the doctrine of corporation by estoppel is not a device designed to protect the shareholder or organizer from the unlimited liability of a partner.

F. Promoters

THE FUNCTION OF PROMOTERS. Corporations do not create themselves. Nor do states or courts or governments take the initiative in bringing private corporations into existence. This very important task is accomplished by the promoter. It is surprising that so few people realize how much non-legal effort goes into the creation of a corporation and how important is the job of the promoter who performs most of these non-legal services for the corporation which will, some day, come into existence. A promoter is a sort of pre-incorporation developer and manager. He may also be a risk-taker and a speculator in the true sense of these words. He is also an entrepreneur, but of a peculiar type, who develops a business opportunity and then sells it to the corporation which the promoter, himself, has created. The technical, and especially the legal, part of this process is very small, in relation to the whole, and the promoter's part is correspondingly large.

A book could be devoted to the things the promoter does and to the ways in which these things should be done. In this brief reference to promoters made here, there is space for not much more than an outline of his many functions and a short description of each. The promoter, it should be noted first, is not just the fellow who appears to sign the articles of incorporation or to become one of the first directors. The promoter has frequently been on the scene for months or even years before this ceremony takes place. The promoter's first task is to discover and to investigate a business opportunity that may be anything from the exploitation of a new oil field to the manufacture and sale of the latest gadget. The investigation may show that the opportunity is either too remote or too expensive. He checks on the amount of capital needed, on the market potential, on costs, on the scope of the business, and on a host of other important items. He makes estimates of all kinds in a an effort to determine whether the particular opportunity is worth going ahead with.

If the promoter comes to the conclusion that a real opportunity exists, he must then formulate in more detail the business and financial plans that will become the framework of the enterprise he is starting. Once this is done, he must undertake to arrange for the necessary land, buildings, and materials the corporation will need in order to carry on the business. These things usually cannot wait until the corporation comes into existence. The promoter may have to enter into contracts or options to assure the availability of material, labor, and premises in which to utilize them. He may even have to purchase the necessary items outright in order to secure them for the corporation.

The promoter must also make arrangements for the financing of the business and for the floating of securities. These functions would include obtaining permission from state commissioners of corporations, filing statements with the Securities and Exchange Commission, preparing advertising, hiring agents, and negotiating with underwriters and investment bankers.

The promoter's reward. After these preliminary tasks are finished, the promoter brings the corporation into existence. At this stage, the promoter encounters the aspect of the process usually most important to him—devising some means by which he may get his own reward out of his efforts. His reward may take the form of cash, stock, stock warrants, a job, or almost anything else of value. The promoter is not like other sellers, however, because he is in the rather unusual position of being able to negotiate for the sale of a business opportunity that he has developed to a corporation that he has created. This position is advantageous to him, and it is sometimes abused. The promoter may place unreasonable valuations on the property he has acquired for the purpose of reselling to the corporation; he may place excessive values on his own services; he may, in other words, take advantage of the situation in which he finds himself, a situation characterized by the fact that the promoter may not be dealing at arms length with a person of equal bargaining power and that the promoter has in his possession information important to the transaction but unavailable to others except through him.

Situations where one person has advantages of unusual position or trust are not uncommon, and the law has devised methods of protecting those who cannot protect themselves. One of these methods is the creation of something called the *fiduciary relation*. The protection afforded by the fiduciary relation lies in the fact that the party with the advantage is subjected to certain duties and obligations which would not be present were he dealing at arms length. One of these duties is that of full disclosure. This requires the party under the duty to give full and true information concerning the transaction into which he is entering. As far as the promoter is concerned, this would mean a duty to tell the truth about the costs of property now being resold to the corporation and about other relevant matters. The fiduciary relation exists between the promoters, on one hand, and the corporation and its shareholders, on the other.

Obviously, imposing the duty of disclosure does not solve all the problems of the promoter because there still exists the question of the party or parties to whom the disclosure may be made. In general, the promoter may discharge his duty of disclosure to an independent board of directors or to all existing shareholders. Where the board of directors consists of promoters or is under the promoters' control, disclosure to that board would be the equivalent of disclosing to one's self and would not discharge the fiduciary duty. Disclosure to all existing shareholders would then become necessary. Where the promoters are both the board of directors and the shareholders, there is no need to impose a fiduciary duty, except for one situation, because all interested parties are the same. The one situation where the duty may still arise, even where promoters are the directors and own all of the shares, is that which occurs when a future issue of shares to the public is contemplated at the time of the sale of the business to the corporation. In this situation, there may be a duty to disclose to these potential shareholders information relevant to the sale and to the valuation of the property.

Of great importance in all problems of fiduciary duty and obligations is the question of what remedies are available to innocent or injured parties where fiduciary duties have been breached. As a general rule, the innocent party, whether it be the corporation or the shareholders, may compel the promoter to pay over to the corporation the secret profits made in the transaction or may rescind the transaction. Individual shareholders normally may rescind the share contracts or recover damages for individual frauds by the promoters. There is a difference of opinion about whether the corporation may sue where the corporation was composed entirely of promoters at the time of the transfer, and sales were later made to new shareholders.

PROMOTERS' CONTRACTS. *Liability of corporation.* From the standpoint of the promoter, one of the most important legal problems faced by him is that of his liability on contracts made by him on behalf of the corporation before the corporation comes into existence. Likewise, one of the most important legal problems the corporation faces in its early life is that of its liability on the contracts made for it by the promoters before the corporation came into existence. The second question is more easily solved. Except in one or two states, where statutes somewhat alter the general rule, the promoters are not agents of the corporation, and the corporation is not bound automatically to the contracts made for it by the promoters but may expressly or impliedly adopt those contracts as its own after incorporation. The general rule and better rule is supported by the view that the right of the corporation to decide, after it comes into existence, which obligations it wants to assume is much fairer and much less subject to abuse than is the other rule that gives the corporation little or no choice.

The process by which the corporation becomes a party to the promoter's contracts is called *adoption*. Adoption may consist of a formal vote of the shareholders or directors or may be implied from the conduct of the corporation and those representing it. Examples of such conduct would be: accepting the benefits of the contract, performing the contract, suing to enforce the contract, and other conduct manifesting an intention to become a party to the contract. The effect of adoption is to make the corporation a party to the contract, just as though it had been a party from the beginning. Some courts explain the same result through other theories such as ratification, acceptance of a continuing offer, or novation.

An interesting problem occasionally arising in connection with incorporations is that of the corporation's liability for promoters' preliminary expenses and organization services. A majority of the courts follow the view that the corporation is not liable unless there is an express promise by the corporation to pay the expenses. Sometimes the liability is imposed by the charter. It has been held in some states that a promise to pay the reasonable value of necessary services and expenses will be implied, but this rule seems contrary to the general policy of giving the corporation the option of rejecting obligations incurred before incorporation.

Liability of promoter. The liability of the promoters on their contracts made before incorporation is a separate problem entirely from the one already discussed. The promoters are personally liable on the contracts made by them before incorporation, and the adoption of the contracts by the corporation does not, by itself, relieve the promoter of liability. A promoter is usually anxious to reduce his liability in this connection to the minimum. A number of devices are available by which this may be accomplished, but these substitutes for the ordinary contract have weaknesses of their own. One device commonly used is the option. This relieves the promoter of liability but has at least one weakness: that some parties are not willing to give options. Another method is simply to obtain offers, but this method suffers the serious weakness of being revocable at any time before acceptance; thus, it lacks the binding effect which the promoter is most anxious to obtain for his prospective corporation. The promoter is not personally liable on a contract purporting to look only to the future corporation, but consideration may be a problem in these cases unless the promoter undertakes to form a corporation and to use his efforts in getting the corporation to adopt the contract, in which case the promoter is liable for his failure to carry out these undertakings.

Where the promoter is bound by a pre-incorporation contract and the corporation later adopts this contract, the effect is to obligate the corporation on the contract but not to discharge the promoter from liability. This result occurs because of the principle of contract law that one party may not free himself of liability under a contract by substituting another person, unless the other party to the contract consents to the substitution. The consent of the other party may be expressed or implied from conduct. An agreement between the promoter and the other party that the contract will be taken over entirely by the corporation when it comes into existence may be sufficient to manifest such consent.

4. OTHER FORMS OF ORGANIZATION

A. In General

No detailed discussion is necessary for the procedure of organizing the various forms other than the partnership and the corporation. An individual may form a business as a sole-proprietorship without any expense or formalities of organization at all. The limited partnership, because of its contrasts and of its occasional tendency to be confused with the general partnership, will be discussed separately. Although statutory formalities usually do not apply to joint stock companies and business trusts, the general trend is toward classifying either or both of these devices as corporations and toward requiring of them some of the organizational formalities of the corporation. The joint stock company is usually created by written articles, and the transferable shares are required to be in some sort of writing. The business trust is created by a written declaration of trust, and this document is usually publicly recorded, but, except as previously indicated, no particular statutory approval or procedure is required. Reference should always be made to local law before any of these devices is formed. Expert legal advice is frequently necessary.

B. The Limited Partnership

The limited partnership is very much like the corporation, and very unlike the general partnership, in respect to statutory control of organization. The limited partnership, like the corporation, cannot be brought into existence without statutory authority; consequently, the procedure of formation is usually prescribed more or less specifically. Under the Uniform Limited Partnership Act, the partners must draft a certificate setting forth information such as: the name of the firm; the nature of the business; the name and address of each partner with an indication as to whether he is a general or a limited partner; the duration of the partnership; the amount of cash and the description and valuation of other property to be contributed by the limited partners; the share of the profits for each limited partner; the right of the limited partner to assign his interest; the right to admit additional limited partners; the right of the remaining general partners to continue the business on the death of a general partner; and other matters. The statute makes mandatory the consideration of these matters in the certificate. The document, when drafted, must be signed and sworn to by all the partners and then filed with the county clerks or other officers of those counties where the firm does business.

The problem of the defectively organized firm is not as important with the limited partnership as it is with the corporation, for a number of reasons. The entity concept is not present, and most of the unusual attributes of the corporation are missing in the limited partnership. The public policy that supports the strict rules in regard to corporations, because of the possible widespread effect upon the public, is not present in the same degree with the limited partnership, which as a rule does not solicit the public for capital. The Uniform Limited Partnership Act states simply that a limited partnership is formed if there has been substantial compliance in good faith with the requirements in regard to the certificate and its filing. The only real effect of the failure to comply substantially would be to deprive the limited partners of their limited liability. Furthermore, the person who believes that he is a limited partner and does not participate in the business as anything but a limited partner retains the protection of limited liability, even where there has been no substantial compliance, as long as he acts promptly to renounce his interest in the profits when he discovers the omissions. The liability of the general partners is no different whether they are members of a general partnership, a limited partnership, or a limited partnership that has complied insufficiently with the statute.

PROBLEMS

1. Why may it be more important for the layman to know about the details of organizing a partnership than about the details of organizing a corporation?

2. What is the function of the partnership agreement? Must it be in writing? What important subjects should be dealt with in the agreement? Is the use of the partnership agreement the only way in which the attributes of the partnership relation may be created?

3. What factors should be considered in determining the state in which a corporation should be organized?

4. Trace the formal steps required for incorporation.

5. What does a corporate charter usually contain? What is it usually required to contain? Why are certain clauses required?

6. What are the by-laws? Who enacts the by-laws?

7. What are the possible effects when a group of incorporators fails to comply in complete detail with the requirements of the statutes governing incorporation?

8. You have been asked by some other businessmen to join them in investigating and possibly promoting as a business opportunity a device invented by Professor Snarf that would simplify note-taking in college lecture courses. The businessmen plan to organize a corporation to manufacture and sell the device if the market seems favorable. Trace from the discovery of the invention to the actual manufacture and

sale of the device by the corporation the steps that you and the others would take. What duties, risks, and liabilities might you and the others incur during the process?

9. Basil Seal was one of the organizers of the Azania Uranium Corporation. Before the corporation came into existence, Basil entered into several contracts to purchase mining machinery and equipment in the name of the prospective corporation. The corporation has now come into existence. Is it bound automatically on the contracts made for it by Basil? If not, how may it become a party to these contracts?

10. Distinguish the limited partnership from the general partnership.

chapter 6

Financing the
New Business

1. IN GENERAL

Problems of financing a business are too often ignored in courses and books on the law of business organization. The legal devices by which these problems are solved are, of course, familiar ones, but the understanding of and familiarity with these devices in the abstract are not of very much use unless the actual transactions in which the devices are important are familiar too. The purpose of this section and of the whole book is to consider legal rules in the framework of business situations. In the sole-proprietorship or in a partnership where the proprietor or the partners have sufficient financial resources to get the business started and keep it going, the problems of financing are not very serious. But where the proprietor or partners do not have adequate resources or where a somewhat more sophisticated form like the corporation is being put into use, the financing problems are important.

No business operates without any capital, but it is obvious that the amount of capital required depends both upon the size of the business and upon the kind of business. Even the small corner grocery requires capital for the purpose of buying or leasing a store building, acquiring a stock, or paying clerks' salaries. The capital may be supplied by the proprietor out of his own resources, or it may be supplied by several proprietors, as in a partnership, or is may be borrowed from a bank or other lending agency. In a corporation, the *preliminary capital,* that capital to be used in getting the business started, is usually supplied through a sale of ownership interests to a number of people, each of whom may supply a relatively small amount.

"Capital" should not be an abstract concept. The *capital of a business* is the aggregate of the money and other property that the business uses in its operations. Although capital is usually expressed in terms of monetary values, land, buildings, and goods are just as much a part of capital as money is. It is also true that capital includes such intangible things as negotiable instruments, patents, and accounts receivable. The capital of a business is used in the production of other values, part of which usually comes back into the business as increases in its capital. In addition to this broad, general, and non-technical meaning of capital, the word has many technical meanings. Some of these will be discussed as they become important.

Many methods are used to raise capital. Most of these methods are equally applicable to all business forms, but others are peculiar to a particular form. The only classifying that will be done in this chapter will be to divide the discussion of capital-raising into those problems appropriate to business forms in general, but especially to non-incorporated business, and those more or less peculiar to the corporation. It should be borne in mind that the discussion here in connection with raising the first capital is also generally applicable to increasing the capital after the business is in operation. Many of the legal devices by which capital-raising is facilitated and by which the supplier of capital is secured are discussed in Part IV, Chapter 13, in connection with the operation of a business. Only the general principles of the raising of initial capital for non-corporate enterprise are discussed in this chapter.

2. FINANCING NON-INCORPORATED BUSINESSES

SCOPE OF THE DISCUSSION. Frequently, the separation of one topic of discussion from another is accomplished by the careful selection of the topic headings. There is, for example, little difficulty in drawing a line between "corporations" and "partnerships," or between "real property" and "agency." No particular problems are encountered when an attempt is made to define the scope of a discussion of "negotiable instruments" or of "torts." When the technical legal headings are not used, however, it sometimes becomes a problem of major significance to define the area within which the discussion is to take place. This is certainly true of "financing a business," where, unless properly circumscribed, the trails lead off hopelessly and endlessly into almost all of the fields of law. Because of this an attempt is made here, at the beginning of the treatment of the financing of non-incorporated business, to describe the scope of the discussion.

It has already been pointed out that what is applicable to the financing of the new business is usually also applicable to the financing of an already established business and that what is applicable to the financing of the non-incorporated business is, with the exception of stock financing, generally applicable to the financing of corporations as well. Thus, the following discussion, although presented within the framework of financing non-incorporated new business, is still relevant to corporate enterprise and to established organizations.

NATURE OF THE FINANCING PROBLEM.   Where the proprietor of a business has sufficient personal resources to finance the organization and operation of his business, the financing problem is of a relatively minor nature. Financing has a bearing, of course, upon the form of organization to be employed, on the extent to which others are to participate in the business operations, and on many other aspects of the broad problem of business administration, but these issues are considered elsewhere, if they merit consideration at all. Where, on the other hand, the proprietor must seek funds from sources other than his own, the question of how he most favorably can obtain these funds is indeed a perplexing problem. The businessman must weigh the attractiveness of his proposition to the person who will provide the funds against the needs and interests of the business and its proprietor. The scheme most attractive to the creditor, for example, may make it impossible for the proprietor to conduct the business.

Alternatives.   Several broad alternatives for financing a business present themselves to the businessman. If the problem consists in getting the business started, the alternatives are two: persuading others to invest their capital, and incurring debt. The first alternative is discussed in other parts of the book, and is not our concern here. If the problem is that of increasing the capital of an established business, the businessman's alternatives are three: obtaining investment capital, incurring debt, and using the earnings of the business. The last alternative does not essentially raise legal issues. Our present discussion will be largely confined to the alternative of incurring debt obligations.

It will be remembered from the discussion in Chapter 4, relating to the selection of the form of organization, that both debt and investment financing have their advantages and disadvantages to the particular firm, depending upon the circumstances. Investment financing usually carries with it a share in the management and in the profits of the business. These may be distasteful to the proprietor who desires to retain full control and who also desires the fruits of his efforts. Debt financing, on the other hand, imposes on the business fixed obligations that must be satisfied.

Effect of size of business.   Although not primarily a legal problem, it is worthwhile to call attention at this point to certain operational and organizational characteristics that tend to cause the financing decisions of small business to be somewhat different from those of large business. Many of these characteristics have been referred to, directly and indirectly, before; others are new. At any rate it is desirable to have these characteristics freshly in mind when a discussion of business financing is begun. Small businesses tend to rely more heavily on retained earnings and on short-term debt than large firms do and less heavily on investment capital and long-term debt. Small businesses generally require more working capital than fixed capital. Sales and earnings fluctuate more rapidly than with large firms. Sales and earnings figures for small firms are not widely publicized. Proprietors are reluctant to share ownership and control, so they naturally prefer debt capital to investment capital.

The factors listed in the preceding paragraph are interesting and important in many different ways. Although a small business typically prefers, and usually utilizes, debt financing, its inability to satisfy the lender's highest standards of credit-worthiness often results in the small business having to accept disadvantageous credit terms, to be subjected to inconvenient security restrictions, and to pay a higher price for the borrowed funds. Lack of evidence may affect the borrowing capacity of the small firm.

Credit-worthiness of the debtor. One of the most important aspects of raising debt capital is the attempt to reduce the prospective creditor's apparent risks to a minimum by persuading him that the debtor will be willing and able to pay the obligation when it comes due. The creditor, obviously, is apt to be more interested in the ability of the debtor to pay than he is in the debtor's willingness. Probably most bankrupts are only too willing to pay, but lack the ability to do so. Even though the debtor has the ability to pay, however, the creditor is still interested in the willingness to pay as a criterion for making the loan. The reason is that the creditor always prefers the obligation to be paid off promptly and voluntarily in order to avoid the expense, time, and strain involved in the use of formal methods of enforcement.

There are many ways in which the debtor may supply evidence and assurances of his ability to pay when the obligation comes due. He may supply the prospective creditor with financial information about his business and its conduct. The creditor may seek further assurance by requiring that the debtor's finanical statements be verified by an independent examination of the books and records. If the creditor is satisfied with the ability and willingness of the debtor to repay, he may lend the funds on the simple promise of the debtor to return them when due, but if the creditor is not completely satisfied, he may require some additional assurance that may be provided by a secured transaction. (See Chapter 13.)

SOURCES OF DEBT CAPITAL. Before consideration is given to other problems, a brief glance at the sources of debt capital is necessary. Four sources of debt capital are referred to here: private lenders, governmental lending agencies, banks, and other business sources.

Private lenders. A considerable quantity of financing is probably accomplished by loans from private persons. Although many of the documents and security devices used in connection with a private loan, such as the mortgage, are matters of public record, there is no practical way to determine the total amount of such loans or which security devices predominate. In general however, the factors of interest to our discussion would be much the same in connection with a private loan as they would be in connection with banks or other business sources. The standards of credit-worthiness are, however, possibly somewhat lower.

Governmental lending agencies. A number of different federal agencies have been available through the years as sources of business capital. The Federal Reserve Banks rarely make the loans they are authorized to make under the Federal Reserve Act for the purpose of establishing businesses unable to secure capital elsewhere. The Small Business Administration is the one active, non-specialized federal lending agency. The purpose of the lending authority of the SBA is to provide funds to businesses that can aid in the defense program or that are necessary to maintain a well-balanced national economy but cannot obtain capital on reasonable terms elsewhere. The statute which describes the lending power of the SBA requires an applicant to furnish the names of other lending institutions to which he has applied for loans and proof of their refusal. An SBA loan to a single borrower is usually limited in amount.

The Small Business Investment Company Act of 1958 was designed to fill a gap in small business financing by providing equity capital and long-term loans for growth and development purposes, the idea being that previously there was no institutional source to which small business could turn to meet its capital needs. A small business investment company is a privately owned corporation operating under the supervision of the Small Business Administration. These companies may be organized by individuals or as subsidiaries of existing corporations. Many banks have organized them as subsidiaries. The investment companies are authorized to purchase convertible debentures from small business concerns and to make long-term loans to small businesses. The investment companies themselves are entitled to loans from the Small Business Administration and to certain tax benefits.

Commercial banks. Lending is a bank's business. Consequently, the bank is one of the most important sources of debt capital. There are certain limitations upon a bank's power to make loans. Of these, some are imposed by law; some, by the bank's policies with regard to the kind and amount of loan it will make or to whom. A bank's officers will try to adopt a lending policy that will enable the bank to make the proper amount of sound and profitable loans under the general policies of the bank and the general conditions of the area in which it does business. Banks may make loans to individuals, business firms, and farmers without any security other than the ability and willingness of the borrower to repay the loan. The decision to make such a loan is based on the financial condition of the borrower as evidenced by his financial statements and by his past credit performance. Such loans are normally for short periods of time, usually for not more than a year. The bank is concerned with the borrower's ability to meet his other current obligations as well as to repay the bank loan.

A bank may make a loan secured by real estate or by other property. This means that the bank has some sort of claim against the particular property that is superior to, or prior to, the claims of other creditors. A borrower under such a loan arrangement will have to demonstrate his own financial condition, and the bank will also appraise the property being used as security to determine whether its value is likely to be sufficient to cover the loan if the borrower should fail to make repayment.

Unusual circumstances may require unusual types of loans, such as flooring loans, property modernization loans, industrial equipment loans, commercial vehicle loans, trucking concern loans, factoring, and many other types. In all of these cases, the unusual requirements of borrowers have created unusual types of financing arrangements and unusual security methods.

Other business loan sources. In addition to the above sources, finance companies, industrial banks, small loan companies, accounts receivable and factoring companies, insurance companies, and others are sources from which a businessman may obtain debt capital. In general, the nature of the arrangement and of the security required by these sources is the same as with the commercial bank.

In order to avoid confusion at a later time, it should be noted here that a considerable portion of business financing is accomplished without the actual lending or transfer of funds by the creditor to the debtor. A person who sells goods to a buyer may actually finance the purchase of the goods by keeping the goods until they have been paid for. This is a protection for the seller because he has an *unpaid seller's lien* against the goods and runs little risk. The arrangement is convenient for the buyer because he knows that he can get possession of the goods as soon as he has the money to pay for them. Many of the legal devices to be discussed in detail in Chapter 13 are used in situations where there is no actual lending of money by creditor to debtor.

REQUIREMENTS OF THE PARTIES DETERMINE TYPE OF ARRANGEMENT. A creditor who is satisfied with the debtor's financial statements and with the debtor's simple promise to pay will lend money without any further assurances if the loan is for a short period of time. A businessman who desires funds for a substantial period of time, or in large amounts, or whose financial statements are not satisfactory, as would certainly be the case where the capital was needed to get a business started, would probably not be able to secure funds on his promise alone. He would have to supply the lender with additional assurances that the loan would be repaid. These additional assurances may take many different forms ranging from obtaining the promise of another person to pay the debt to the actual transfer of property into the hands of the creditor so that the creditor may conveniently sell it to recover his loan if the debtor defaults.

A seller may retain possession or control over goods until they have been paid for by the buyer and may extend his control to situations where the goods have passed from the seller's hands into the hands of a carrier or an independent warehouseman. This is done by taking a bill of lading or warehouse receipt in the sellers's own name so that the goods can be delivered only on his order, or by taking the bill or receipt in the name of the debtor but retaining possession of it, or by sending the bill or receipt to an agent of the seller with instructions to deliver it to the buyer only when he has paid the price. (See Chapters 12 and 13 for a discussion of the nature and the use of bills of lading and warehouse receipts.)

The method suggested here is frequently not at all satisfactory to a buyer who needs to have possession of the goods and the right to sell them before he is obligated to pay their price. A number of methods are available by which this end may be accomplished while still providing security for the seller-creditor. The buyer-debtor may deliver possession of some other property, such as stocks or bonds, to the seller as security for an obligation to pay for goods the seller has delivered to the buyer. Or the buyer may deposit the stocks or bonds with a bank as security for a loan used to pay the seller of goods. The debtor may execute a mortgage on his home or on his business property as security for a loan used to buy goods.

The foregoing paragraphs set forth a few examples of the many forms of financing and security arrangements with special emphasis on the adaptation of the device to the needs and requirements of the parties involved. The specific methods by which the desired ends are brought about are discussed in Chapter 13.

3. FINANCING THE CORPORATION

A. Cases

(1)

Morgan, a grain dealer in San Francisco, conceived the idea of forming a corporation to take over the grain business then conducted by several operators on the Pacific Coast. With this object in mind, he consulted Collins, a grain operator in Oregon, and Sibley and Anderson, American managers for Wills & Sons of London, and proposed that Wills & Sons, Sibley, Anderson, Collins, and himself take stock in the proposed corporation. The idea was looked upon with favor by Wills & Sons, and they directed their American managers to proceed to New York to discuss the matter with one of their directors and Morgan. A conference was held in New York, attended by Morgan, Sibley, Anderson, and a director of Wills & Sons, and as a result of this conference, Morgan wired Collins concerning the matter. In response to this telegram, Collins wired Morgan, agreeing to take $25,000 in stock in the proposed corporation, to be payable in instalments. Upon receipt of the message from Collins, Wills & Sons agreed to subscribe for 1260 shares, Anderson and Sibley for 10 shares each, and Morgan for 625 shares, at the par value of $100. Sibley and Morgan then returned to San Francisco, stopping off in Chicago on their way. While in Chicago, they obtained two further subscriptions for 50 and for 25 shares. After the return to San Francisco, Collins met Morgan and Sibley in that city and informed them that he was withdrawing his subscription, except for the amount of $5000. The Morgan Grain Company was organized shortly thereafter under the laws of the state of Delaware, and Morgan became president of the company. Morgan reported to the board of directors that he had obtained subscriptions to stock as described above. The subscriptions were accepted by the board, and the board voted to ask for a 20 per cent payment on the subscriptions immediately. All the subscribers, including Collins, paid this call, and certificates were issued for the fully paid shares. When the next call was made, Collins refused to pay it, and suit was filed against Collins.

[*Collins* v. *Morgan Grain Co., Inc.,* 16 F. 2d 253 (1927)]

(2)

At the present time, the state of Anosmia has no statutory regulation of the issuance of corporate securities. Widespread abuses among some dishonest brokers and dealers and a rash of unsound and even fraudulent promotions have created considerable clamor from certain sections of the public for some statutory solution to the problem. Being almost the last state to adopt such legislation, Anosmia is in a good position to benefit from the experience of the other states and the federal government with various types of securities regulation. The Governor has appointed a commission to study the problem and make recommendations. The commission is holding hearings this week in your city and has invited certain interested parties, including you, to appear before the commission. What would you say?

(3)

With the approval of all the partners, SIMUCO Toyland loaned $5000 to Pure Riske, a small toy manufacturer whose line of toys was very popular with SIMUCO's customers. The loan was not secured. Before his debt to SIMUCO was due, Riske sold his business, paid off all his creditors, except SIMUCO, and invested the balance in the stock of Hypocase, Inc. Aside from this stock, Riske has no assets of any value. He has refused to pay his debt to SIMUCO. How can Riske's shares of stock be seized in order that SIMUCO can realize something on its claim against him?

B. In General

Although a corporation may raise capital by the use of other devices, especially after it has been in operation for a time, the usual method of financing the beginning corporation is through the sale of shares of stock. Because of the importance to the corporation of the other methods of capital-raising when the corporation has come into operation, some of these methods will be discussed along with the shares of stock. Others which are equally applicable to all forms of organization are discussed in Part IV. It should be noted that financing through the sale of stock is *owner* or *equity financing;* the use of the other devices is *creditor* or *debt financing,* where a claim against the corporation is created in someone outside the corporation.

C. Capital Stock—Owner Financing

IN GENERAL.   It is well to point out at the beginning that the phrase "capital stock" is one of the most abused, confused, and misunderstood terms in the law of corporations. Some modern corporation statutes avoid the use of the term, substituting for it terms with more definite meanings. It will be used in this book only as a means of differentiating one capital-raising device from another. When more specific applications are necessary, other terms will be employed.

A *share of stock* is the interest that the shareholder has in the corporation, and it is usually evidenced by a formal written instrument called the *stock certificate* or *share certificate*. It has been described as a profit-sharing contract whereby the corporation acquires capital while giving in exchange a proportional right to participate in the earnings of the corporation and a very limited right to participate in the management. The terms of this contract are seldom found all in one place but are made up of relevant laws of the state of incorporation, the corporation's charter, and the terminology of the share certificate. This fractional interest in the corporation, this proportional right to share in the profits, is the thing the corporation sells in order to raise capital.

Technically, the certificate is not the share of stock itself but is only evidence of the share. The certificate may, and usually does, contain the more important terms of the share contract in addition to a statement about the number of shares that the particular shareholder owns. It is the certificate, however, that makes this type of ownership interest easily transferable.

A person obtains an ownership interest in the corporation and becomes a shareholder either by subscription contract with the corporation or with its promoters, or by acquiring the shares of another shareholder. The latter method, except where the shares obtained are shares the corporation has already issued but has reacquired, is not a method of raising corporate capital. The subscription agreements may be entered into either before or after incorporation. Many legal problems arise in connection with these agreements.

Pre-incorporation subscriptions have caused much judicial confusion, most of it as the result of the fact that no corporation is in existence at the time of the subscription. A majority of the courts regard these pre-incorporation subscriptions as no more than continuing offers by the prospective shareholder, offers that may be revoked any time before the corporation is formed. Some courts, which follow this view, also require express or implied acceptance by the corporation after it comes into existence. The continuing offer approach is unrealistic because it fails to recognize the intent of the parties and business needs. Except in rare situations, both the subscriber and the promoter intend the subscription agreement to be binding immediately, and it is obvious that this binding effect is very important to the financing of corporations. Some courts reach the conclusion that the subscription is a contract among the subscribers, but this becomes unrealistic, too, where the subscribers are complete strangers, and do not intend to contract with each other. The desirable result of making subscriptions binding and irrevocable as soon as they are made can now be best achieved by statute. The Uniform Business Corporations Act makes these pre-incorporation subscription agreements irrevocable for six months from the date of signing unless expressly provided to the contrary in writing.

There is also confusion in regard to post-incorporation subscriptions, largely as a result of an unhealthy and unnecessary line drawn by some courts between a subscription agreement and an executory contract for the sale of shares. The better view is that a contract for the original issue of shares should always be considered a subscription without regard to the payment of the price or the delivery of the certificate. The effect of a present subscription when the corporation is in existence is to make the subscriber a shareholder and to make him liable to pay the subscription price for the shares, subject to the terms and conditions of the agreement. Treating the subscription as a contract for the sale of shares raises problems of passage of title, dependent, independent and concurrent conditions, and effect of bankruptcy or insolvency of the corporation on the promise of the shareholder to pay for the shares.

TYPES OF SHARES. Corporation statutes generally permit a corporation to issue two or more classes of stock that differ among themselves in regard to dividend rights, voting rights, and rights on dissolution of the corporation. The most usual classification is that of common stock and preferred stock. In addition to these two basic classes there may be different series of stock within each class. Preferred shares are especially subject to this sub-classifying. Shares may also be classified as par and no-par or issued and unissued. In most states, the variety of classes of shares and share contracts that a corporation may employ at any given time has no real legal limit as long as certain basic rules are observed. Among these minimum standards are the following: at least one class or series of shares must have voting rights; the distinction between outside creditors and owners must always be maintained; all shares of the same class or series must have the same rights and preferences.

The ideal capital structure would probably be a structure that had only one class of common shares. This structure would be uncomplicated by different rights and preferences among the shareholders and would be free of the fixed claims of outside creditors. *Common stock* is that class of stock that has no special rights of preferences over any other class of stock. The common stockholders represent the corporate ownership interest in its purest form. They usually have the right to elect the board of directors and to participate in other aspects of the shareholders' meetings. The holder of common shares usually stands to profit most if the corporation is successful, but he stands to lose most if the corporation fails. The preferred shareholder generally has preference over the common shareholder in regard to dividends and in regard to assets on liquidation, but the dividend preference is usually limited in amount or in percentage, and the preferred share does not have the voting right except in special situations. The common stock represents a residual interest which includes most of those rights and privileges not specifically assigned elsewhere.

As a rule, the terms of a preferred share contract are limited only by a few basic principles and by the imagination of the person drafting them. The preferred share may be *cumulative,* which means that if the preferred share dividend is not paid in any given year, the passed dividend, together with the current preferred dividend, must be paid before anything may be paid to the common shareholders. Where the shares are *non-cumulative,* passed dividends are lost and only the current preferred dividend need be paid before common share dividends are paid. Sometimes the preferred dividend is cumulative only if the corporation earned enough that year to pay it. There are preferred share contracts that *require* the corporation to pay a preferred dividend if the dividend is earned. The amount of the preferred dividend is usually expressed in dollars, as "$2.25 preferred," or in percentages, as "$2\frac{1}{4}\%$ preferred." The former designation describes a preferred share that is entitled to a $2.25 dividend preference each year and a preferred share that probably has no par value. The latter describes a share that has a preference, but this time the preferred share has a par value against which the percentage could be applied. If the par value were 100, the preference would be the same as for the $2.25 preferred.

A preferred share may also be *participating.* This means that the preferred share participates with the common shares in dividends in excess of the preference. In the examples used in the previous paragraph, the $2.25 preferred is entitled to its $2.25 preference but also to share with the common in any other amounts available for dividends. Usually, but not always, the common shares are entitled to an amount equal to the amount of the preferred share preference before the preferred begins to participate, and in most preferred share contracts, the participation is limited to a fixed amount or percentage.

Corporate shares may also be classified as par or no-par shares. The par value of a share of stock is a very misleading concept. It is popularly believed that a par value share is worth the par value, or that there are assets of the par amount to back up the share. Neither of these statements is true. There may at one time or another be some relationship between the par value and the market value of the share or the assets, but this relationship is rare even at the time the corporation originally issues shares. Although some statutes have imposed restrictions on the issue of par shares at less than par, it is still possible that the par value does not even bear a clear relation to the price received by the corporation for the shares when they were first issued. The par value may serve some purpose in setting forth the amount of corporate assets that the shareholder may be entitled to upon liquidation of the corporation, but this is not a very valuable purpose because it is no guarantee that there are any assets, and the same result can be accomplished with a no-par share simply by inserting a liquidation figure in the contract. The confusion caused by par shares led, many years ago, to statutory authorization of shares that have no par value at all, that are, consequently, much more flexible when it comes to setting prices, and that are much less confusing. Nominal par shares, shares where the par value is very small, are also used to accomplish much the same result as no-par shares. There are, of course, other factors to be considered before electing to use either par or no-par shares.

ISSUE OF SHARES. *In general.* The *issue* of shares is the transaction by which a person becomes the owner of shares and by which share contracts are created. The issue of shares has nothing in particular to do with the delivery of a share certificate, but a shareholder who does not have his share certificate may be deprived of some of his rights as a shareholder until the certificate is delivered.

Valuation of shares. Some attention should be paid at the beginning of this discussion to the problem of determining the issue price or valuation of shares. In general, the price is set by the directors in the light of current market conditions. The directors may perform this function by setting a par value. This value is really nothing more than an indication of the minimum subscription or issue price, and it is not a "value" by any stretch of the imagination. Ordinarily, the directors fix the issue price of no-par shares, but under a few statutes, the incorporators or even the shareholders fix the price. The issue price of shares may be fixed in terms of property or services instead of dollars. In establishing the price of new shares, the directors are under a fiduciary duty not to dilute the value of outstanding shares by fixing the price at an inadequate or unfair level.

Distribution of shares. The promoters of a new corporation or the management of a going concern, with the aid of agents and salesmen, may distribute the shares to the public directly. This process is employed by most small corporations and by some large ones too. Another method of distribution, usually unavailable to small concerns because of its expense, is the underwriting by investment bankers. In connection with the distribution of large issues of stock, however, the underwriting process performs many valuable services, such as the supplying of information and advice, giving the corporation access to the best dealers and customers, assuming the risk of an unsuccessful sale, and many others. Depending upon the underwriting agreement, the underwriters may actually purchase all of the shares and then resell them to the public, or they may simply agree to buy at a fixed price the shares that the corporation cannot sell. The arrangements between the underwriters and the corporation take a number of different forms.

Stated capital.   Another aspect of the problem of share issuance, and an extremely important aspect, is that of the "stated" or "legal capital" of the corporation. This is one of the areas where the phrases "capital" and "capital stock" were once used with great confusion owing to the many possible meanings of these terms. The question is, essentially: What are the significant balance sheet entries to be made in connection with the issue of shares? Because a corporation may not have issued any or all of the shares it was authorized to issue by its charter, it is obvious that the "authorized capital" or "authorized capital stock" is not very significant information from the balance sheet point of view. The "issued capital stock" would seem to be much more useful information, but even here it may not be clear whether it is the sale price or the par value or some other figure that should go into the stock accounts. Most modern corporation statutes have minimized the problem by avoiding the phrases "capital" or "capital stock" and by substituting in their place, for these purposes, a new and closely defined term, "stated capital." Many of the statutes define stated capital in such detail that the confusion and uncertainty are largely eliminated.

Technically, *stated capital* is an amount that measures the margin of net assets or value that is to be retained in the business as against withdrawals in favor of the shareholders. It is a sort of buffer or safeguard for the corporation's creditors against the possibility of the corporation's assets being reduced to the point where the creditors' claims might be endangered. Stated capital has sometimes been described as the substitute in the corporate form of organization for the unlimited liability of the partners in the partnership form. The practical problems to which our attention is directed here are those of the relation between issued shares and stated capital, and the precise meaning of stated capital in given situations. The first problem is easily solved. Stated capital has only an historical relation to issued shares and is not descriptive of shares, authorized or issued, or of assets or liabilities. It rises from the consideration received for the issue of shares and from the transfers from surplus.

The answer to the second problem and a better understanding of stated capital can be obtained from specific examples. Where par value shares are issued at par, the stated capital is the aggregate par value (the number of shares issued times the par value). Where par value shares are sold at less than par, the stated capital is the amount actually received. In most states, shares may not be issued at less than par unless special permission is obtained or special procedures are gone through. If par value shares are issued at more than par, stated capital is the aggregate par value; the excess goes into paid-in surplus. Where no-par shares are issued, the directors usually have the discretion to apportion the proceeds between stated capital and paid-in surplus, another advantage of the no-par share. In some states this discretion is lost where the no-par shares carry a liquidation preference. Transfers may be made from surplus to stated capital by means of stock dividends and other devices. Stated capital may also be reduced by transfers from stated capital to surplus, but many statutes impose rather severe restrictions upon this reduction of stated capital, frequently requiring the approval of the shareholders.

REGULATION OF THE ISSUE OF SHARES. *In general.* Frauds, abuses, and sharp practices in connection with the financing of corporations have led to the enactment of both state and federal legislation designed to protect investors. Among the practices the statutes have been concerned with are: the fraudulent promotion of unsound enterprises having no reasonable chances of success; the charging of exorbitant commissions by organizers and underwriters; the unsound quality of many of the securities issued, as, for example, large blocks of watered stock that dilute the shares sold to the public; the dishonest practices of brokers, dealers, and salesmen; the failure of the common law to control the situation. The earliest of these statutes, called *blue sky laws* when enacted by a state legislature, was passed by the Kansas legislature in 1911. Since that time almost all the other states have passed securities acts of their own. (It should be noted that the word "security" has several different meanings.)

State regulation. The state statutes fall roughly into four categories: fraud laws, disclosure laws, laws for the registration or licensing of brokers and dealers, and registration or permit laws. The *fraud laws* usually provide for investigation and prosecution by the Attorney General, but they supply no administrative machinery for the supervision of the issue of securities. The fraud laws have not proved satisfactory. Their chief weakness lies in the fact that they seek to punish or redress rather than to prevent. In spite of their weaknesses, however, the statutes are in use in important commercial states such as New York, New Jersey, and Delaware.

The *disclosure laws* regulate advertising and other information supplied to prospective subscribers, and these laws sometimes require the filing of detailed information with an administrative body. These laws require the telling of the truth which, when properly enforced, may be a powerful restraint. The federal securities laws are largely disclosure laws. Acting on the theory that honest men will not handle fraudulent or unsound securities, many states *license* or *register dealers, brokers,* and *salesmen.* Some of these states do a very thorough job of weeding out dishonest operators, but most of the laws are drawn in such a way that little is accomplished toward correcting the difficulties set forth in the paragraph above. Frequently, this type of law is combined with one or more of the others.

The fourth type of state securities act provides for the supervision of the securities either by requiring *registration* or by requiring a *permit* before the security can be issued. There are many varieties of this type of statute, and they range from the very strict to those that have no real effect at all. This approach is almost always combined with the licensing of dealers and brokers, and frequently with the other two types also. The statute that requires a permit before the security may be issued has the greatest potential strength of any of the statutes, because the permit is a prerequisite to issuance and because shares issued without a permit are often expressly made void by the statute. Some statutes require a corporation commissioner or other state officer to investigate all applicants for permits and to find affirmatively that the issue is "fair, just and equitable" before issuing a permit. Often the state officer may issue a permit only upon certain conditions that are designed for the additional protection of both investor and company.

The effect of such permit statutes has been said to be beneficial to corporate financing "in checking the overenthusiasm and greed of the promoter, decreasing the amount of securities to be issued, improving the type of securities, increasing the assets behind them and making more conservative and reasonable the plans of operation."[1] On the other hand, overzealous enforcement and rigid or arbitrary interpretations of statutory language may unnecessarily delay the issue of shares, increase the costs of issue, and discourage desirable new promotions. The Uniform Corporate Securities Act does not employ the permit approach and falls considerably short of the degree of regulation presently provided in many state statutes. Because of the great divergence in method and approach of the blue sky laws, a heavy burden is imposed upon the promoter whose corporation will issue shares in more than one state. Greater uniformity would be advantageous, but sharply differing points of view in the various states make uniformity extremely difficult to achieve.

Federal regulation. The Congress did not pass any significant statutes in the securities field until 1933, and these were enacted largely as a result of the stock market crash of 1929, the ensuing depression, and the lax financial and ethical standards that preceded the crash and the depression. Since the passage of the Securities Act in 1933, a number of federal statutes in this area have been passed. Basically, these statutes are disclosure acts, but in many special situations the courts or administrative bodies—usually the Securities and Exchange Commission—are given extensive additional powers. The power to compel dis-

---

[1] Henry W. Ballantine, *Corporations,* rev. ed. (Chicago: Callaghan & Company, Inc., 1946), p. 867.

closure is the power to compel the telling of the truth, and, once the truth is told, the regulatory power generally ceases, and the shares may be issued. The shareholder who reads and understands the truth may thus protect himself, but the shareholder who does not bother to read or who does not have the background to understand what he is reading may not be any better off than he would have been without disclosure.

Exemptions. The federal statutes and most state statutes exempt from the operation of the securities regulation certain types of transactions and certain classes of securities. Some statutes exempt issues below a particular monetary amount, issues by well-established corporations, or securities listed on the national stock exchanges. Most statutes exempt securities issued by public agencies, banks, utilities, or insurance companies, all of which are generally subject to other regulation. The federal laws, for constitutional reasons, exempt securities sold only to persons residing within the state where the issuer is incorporated and doing business. Reference should be made to one's local law for details.

THE TRANSFER OF SHARES. Although it does not fit squarely within the topic of organizing a business, the transfer of shares is so closely related to the nature and use of shares of stock as to make it almost mandatory that the subject be discussed in close proximity to the material already examined. It is conceded that the easy transferability of corporate shares is one of the most attractive aspects of the corporate form, but, although the transfer is usually quite easy, it is not devoid of legal problems. Some of these problems are important enough to be worthy of discussion.

The share of stock, as we already know, is not a tangible thing; it cannot be felt or seen any more than an interest in a partnership can be felt or seen. The share of stock, however, unlike the partnership interest, is usually evidenced by a piece of paper called the share certificate or stock certificate. Furthermore, the share itself, even though it is intangible, is property. It is capable of ownership and of being bought and sold just like any other property.

The share certificate makes the share of stock relatively easy to transfer, because under our law the share may be transferred by transferring the certificate. This is accomplished by indorsing the certificate and delivering it to the transferee or his agent. It has not always been so. The transfer of a share of stock was once considered to be an assignment which could only be completed when the issuer had been notified and had entered the transfer on his books as a sort of act of novation. Thus, *S*, a shareholder in *X* Inc., assigned his share certificate to *B*, a buyer, by signing the certificate and delivering it to *B*. The transfer was thought to be complete when *B* surrendered the certificate to *X*, and *X* entered *B*'s name on the share register of the corporation, issued a new certificate in *B*'s name, and canceled the old certificate.

Although some of the terminology and formality of stock transfers convey the impression that these concepts of transfer still persist, both as a practical and as a legal matter, these concepts were abandoned many years ago. At one time, all states had adopted the Uniform Stock Transfer Act, which stated expressly that the "only" manner in which shares could be transferred was by indorsement and delivery of the share certificate. That statute has now been clarified, somewhat amended, and merged into the Uniform Commercial Code.

Many corporation laws and corporate charters contain the statement that a transfer of shares shall not be effective at all until the transfer is recorded on the corporation's books. The purpose of this requirement was to make it possible for the corporation to protect itself from liability by keeping currently informed about the identity of its shareholders in order that the corporation may accord to the proper persons the right to receive dividends, the right to vote, the right to receive notices of shareholders' meetings, and the right to share in the corporation's assets upon dissolution. The Uniform Stock Transfer Act and the Code superseded these strict provisions, but the objectives of these provisions are still achieved. Under the Code, the corporation is protected if the transferee does not make "due presentment" of the security for registration, and the corporation grants the shareholder's rights to the registered owner. The phrase "due presentment" is used by the Code in order to require something more than mere notice. This rule has no effect upon the rights of the transferee against the transferor. Even though a corporation pays a dividend to a transferor who is still a registered owner, the transferee has a right to that dividend as against the transferor but not as against the corporation, unless there has been due presentment of the security for registration.

The Code makes even clearer what was reasonably clear before, namely that transfer is complete when the security is indorsed and delivered. When the issuer cancels an old security and issues a new one, he is simply performing a ministerial act, recording or registering a transfer which takes place elsewhere.

In this connection, the purpose of both the Uniform Stock Transfer Act and the Code was to endow certain "investment securities" with the attributes of negotiability in order that they might be freely dealt in. The Code, however, is much broader in its scope and in its endowment of the attributes of negotiability. The Stock Transfer Act was confined largely to ordinary stock certificates, while the Code extends its impact to a much wider category of securities. The Act made the certificate negotiable in the sense that a bona fide purchaser for value without notice could not be defeated by a prior claim of ownership, but it did not afford such purchaser any protection whatever against the defenses that might be raised by the issuer. The Code endows investment securities with negotiability in its full sense. (For a much fuller discussion of "negotiability," see Chapter 11.)

It should be noted that under the Code, mere delivery without indorsement is enough to complete the transfer, as against the transferor, and also gives the purchaser a specifically enforceable right to have the necessary indorsement supplied. However, the purchaser cannot become a bona fide purchaser, as against parties other than the transferor, until the indorsement is supplied. The indorsement does not operate retroactively. Under the Uniform Stock Transfer Act, the transfer was not complete, even as between the transferor and the purchaser, until indorsement.

The effects of the transfer of a share of stock are to pass the ownership or title in the share to the transferee, to cause the transferee to become the shareholder in place of the transferor, to entitle the transferee to dividends declared after the transfer, and to entitle the transferee to vote the stock if it carries voting rights. These things are only what the transferor himself would normally have. Under the Code, the transferee may get more than the transferor had to give. This is accomplished by attributing to the share certificate the characteristics of a negotiable instrument, giving a transferee without notice protection against certain defects or infirmities in the instruments or in the title of the transferor. The negotiable character of the share certificate makes it possible, for example, for a transferee to get good title to the share even from a person who had stolen or found a properly indorsed share certificate but who did not himself have title.

Another important question arising in connection with transfers of shares of stock is whether the transferee is liable for any portion of the price of the stock that may have been left unpaid by the transferor. Although the details of the answer to this question in the past varied from state to state, the Uniform Commerical Code now provides that the transferee is not liable for the unpaid portion of the price unless the rights of the issuer are "noted conspicuously" on the security.

Many of the detailed problems that appear in connection with the transfer of shares are solved by custom, tradition, and business practice, as for example, the "ex div" symbol used in stock market quotations to mean "without dividends."

The Code makes an interesting and important change in the earlier rule that a *share* of stock may be attached by a creditor of a shareholder without actual seizure or surrender of the *certificate*. The common law result was possible because of the rule, already mentioned, that the certificate is not the share of stock but is only evidence of it, and because the share of stock was said to be located at the situs of the corporation. Under the common law approach, difficulties arose because the certificate remained free and could be transferred to a purchaser who had no notice of the attachment, and because the creditor might find on attachment that the certificate had just previously been transferred. The possible conflicts between transferees and attaching creditors are obvious. Section 8-317 of the Code states that

> No attachment or levy upon a security or any share or other interest evidenced thereby which is outstanding shall be valid until the security is actually seized by the officer making the attachment or levy; but a security which has been surrendered to the issuer may be attached or levied upon at the source.

The old conflict is now avoided inasmuch as it is impossible for the shareholder to transfer the certificate after it has been seized.

D. Bonds, Notes, and Debentures—Creditor Financing

IN GENERAL. It is often stated that the ideal financial structure for a corporation would be the simplest one, namely—one class of common stock. Not many corporations could have such a financial structure. Most corporations are financed, not only by the issue of ownership interests, shares of stock, but also by creditor or debt financing. It should be noted now, if it has not been noted already, that the corporation is not a debtor, in the ordinary sense of the word, to the stockholders, because they are theoretically the owners of the business. The stockholders have purchased an interest in the business, but have not thus become creditors of the corporation, and they have no fixed or certain claims against it. With debt financing, however, the corporation incurs fixed and certain obligations that must be paid when they become due. Although the particular devices of credit and security used may have unusual names, the corporation that employs debt financing is really doing no differently than the individual who borrows money from a bank. Because this book is not intended to encompass the field of "corporation finance," the pros and cons of the various methods and combinations of corporate financing methods are not examined except in a very general way.

The usual borrowing devices are the bond, the note, and the debenture. These are, generally, negotiable instruments, and all are really just varieties of the promissory note. The *bond,* in corporate usage, is a long term promissory note usually secured by a mortgage or deed of trust on corporate property. The "secured" aspect of the bond makes it possible for the creditors to recover their funds out of the sale of the property put up as security if the corporation should default on the payment of the bonds. A *debenture* may be explained as a long term note or as an unsecured bond. As a practical matter, there are many secured debentures, though usually not by mortgages. The term "debenture" is often used interchangeably with both "note" and "bond." The important thing to recognize here is that the terms of the contract between the corporation and its lenders vary greatly from situation to situation.

The corporation's capital structure should be carefully and thoughtfully planned. The decisions as to methods and details will be based on many considerations ranging from taxes to the marketability of debt financing instruments. But this aspect of the problem is in the field of corporate finance and outside the scope of this book. It should be pointed out here, however, that the great disadvantage to which creditor financing is subject, when compared with owner financing, is the fact that it imposes upon the corporation fixed charges and interest burdens that cannot be avoided, as a rule, even during periods of severe financial stress. The corporation can pass its dividends, but it cannot pass the interest payments on its debt or the repayment of the principal if it wants to remain in business. This is not to say that debt financing should always be avoided. It has some advantages of its own, and many situations exist where the creditor financing is preferable to owner financing.

E. The Sale and Lease-Back

A financing arrangement that has received a great deal of attention during recent years is the "sale and lease-back." As the name implies, the *sale and lease-back* scheme involves the sale of land and buildings by a business firm to an investor, accompanied by a simultaneous leasing back of the property under a long term contract. The device has been used quite frequently by charitable and educational institutions, as investors, and by chain and department stores and others, as vendor-lessees. Insurance companies, other private investors, and business firms other than those in the retail field have also made extensive use of the arrangement. The selective use of the sale and lease-back can provide certain tax advantages to the vendor-lessee, especially where he is willing to treat the transaction as a genuine sale and lease and not to try to retain complete dominion over the property and the right to repurchase at the end of the lease period at a price far below what arm's-length bargaining would produce. The device provides investment opportunities for insurance companies and tax-exempt institutions, but it may be a booby-trap in situations where the attractiveness of the investment is based only on the fact that the rental payments are not treated as income to the investor.

Certain non-tax advantages may also accrue to the vendor-lessee from the use of the sale and lease-back arrangement. The vendor may be able to obtain more funds and greater aggregate capital, and he may very well improve the appearance of the balance sheet by reducing the fixed liabilities and preferred share claims and restrictions. These advantages come only at a price, however, and the prospective vendor-lessee should consider that price. Most of the duties of ownership remain with the lessee under these arrangements. The interest cost of this type of financing is characteristically high. The title to the property is lost by the vendor-lessee where it could be retained under conventional financing plans. A vendor-lessee who employs the sale and lease-back device for the purpose of reducing the dangers of insolvency due to the fixed charges of debt financing is likely to find that the fixed rental charges under the lease are no more benevolent.

PROBLEMS

1. What are the means of financing and the sources of capital for a new non-incorporated business? What factors will be important in determining which means and sources are to be employed in a particular situation?

2. What additional means and sources are available to the the new incorporated business?

3. Are pre-incorporation stock subscriptions binding? Explain.

4. What are the essential differences between common stock and preferred stock?

5. Describe the basic types of preferred share contract.

6. You are a preferred shareholder in the Liberal Dividend Corporation. The company has available for dividends the sum of $36,000, all of which will be paid out as dividends this month. The company has both common (1,000 shares) and preferred (1,000 shares $5 preferred) stock. The company paid no dividends during the three years immediately preceding this year. Would you rather have your preferred shares be cumulative, non-participating preferred or participating, non-cumulative preferred? Explain.

7. How is the price on a new issue of shares set, and by whom? How is a new issue of shares distributed by the issuing corporation?

8. What is the stated capital in each of the following situations?

   a. 10,000 shares of $50 par stock sold at $43\frac{1}{2}$.

   b. 5,000 shares of no-par stock sold at 21.

   c. 5,000 shares of $1 par stock sold at 107.

   d. 10,000 shares of $100 par stock sold at par.

   e. 10,000 shares of $100 par 5% cumulative, participating preferred stock sold at 101.

   f. Stock dividend of $100,000. (Before dividend, accounts were as follows: Capital Stock . . . . $50,000, Surplus . . . . $150,000.)

9. What are the blue sky laws? What problems led to their enactment? How do these laws go about dealing with the problems they were enacted to solve? How successful have they been?

10. Describe briefly the nature of federal securities regulation.

11. How are ownership interests in a corporation transferred? Compare with the transfer of partnership interests. What changes does the Uniform Commercial Code make in the common law?

12. Compare owner financing of a corporation with creditor financing.

13. What is a "sale and lease-back" and what advantages are claimed for it?

chapter 7

Property

1. ACQUISITION OF A SITE

A. Cases

(1)

Paul Preston, president of Hypocase, Inc., obtained the approval of the board of directors to buy a piece of land in the mountains near Berkland and develop thereon a rest and recreation center for employees of Hypocase and their families. Paul examined many parcels of land. One particular parcel, consisting of 150 acres belonging to Hy Graid, seemed much superior to the others and he purchased it for the company. Before the deal was closed, however, Paul asked the legal department of Hypocase to look into the matter to see if everything was all right. The general counsel reported to Preston that there was some confusion as to the real ownership of the property. Probate records in the County Court showed that Graid had acquired his rights from his father. The County Clerk's records showed a deed from one Grant Smith to Graid's father in 1948 but no explanation of where Smith acquired any rights in the land. The last recorded transaction prior to the transfer from Smith to Graid was one from John H. Willett to Elmer Gantry in 1919. The general counsel also reported that there was no evidence that the property had ever been occupied, fenced, or used for any purpose whatsoever. In spite of the uncertainty in the ownership, Preston decided to buy the land from Graid anyhow. The price was low, and the property was exactly what Preston had in mind for the recreation center. Hypocase, due largely to Preston's personal interest in the matter, proceeded to develop the property very rapidly. Approximately one-half the land was fenced; a recreation and dining hall, several bunkhouses and small cottages, a swimming pool, two tennis courts, and a small stable were erected on the land. Hiking and bridle trails were cut through the woods and onto a high, rocky bluff that occupied one portion of the property. Some of the timber was cut and sold, and rocks from the bluff were used in some of the construction work. A permanent caretaker was employed and a small house erected on the property for his use. For three months in the summer and on weekends for the rest of the year, other help was employed for cooking, cleaning, and other purposes. The first group of employees used the center in June, 1960, and from that time on, the place was used regularly and frequently by officers and employees of the company. Hypocase, Inc. paid the taxes on the property each year when they came due. In October, 1966, Hypocase received notice that an action had been filed in the local court by one Laust Gantry, the grandson of Elmer, to confirm the title to the property in him and to eject Hypocase from the premises. An investigation revealed that the Gantrys had never conveyed the property to anyone and that Grant Smith had never had any rights in the property at all. Should Hypocase fight the suit?

(2)

During a period of very heavy orders, Hypocase, Inc. leased on a temporary basis for 8 months an empty warehouse in Berkland from L. L. Lord, its owner, and set up a manufacturing operation there. Before the premises could be used, however, it was necessary to install certain machinery and equipment for making pallets, to enlarge and improve the ventilating system in the building, and to install new electrical wiring and lighting fixtures. All of these things were done by Hypocase, not by the owner of the property. The machinery was bolted to the floor; the new ventilating equipment was housed in a small room specially enclosed for the purpose; holes were cut in some interior walls to accommodate the ducts for the ventilating system; the lighting fixtures were securely fastened to the ceilings, and the new wiring was attached to the walls and ceilings by means of large insulated staples. Orders had dropped off near the end of the lease period, and Hypocase notified Lord of its intention to vacate the premises. However, when Hypocase began to remove its machinery, ventilating equipment, wiring, lighting fixtures, and other materials, the work was stopped by a temporary court order obtained by Lord on the ground that Hypocase had no right to remove these things which had been attached to Lord's property. Will Hypocase be permitted to remove the machinery and materials it installed in Lord's warehouse?

(3)

Akers owned a parcel of land which he called lot 1, the east 30 feet of which consisted of a dirt road or driveway running the length of the land to a public highway. Adjoining this road on the east were two lots, 2 and 3, facing onto a side street, both also owned by Akers. Lots 2 and 3 had dwelling houses located on them facing onto a side street but with rear walks and entrances leading to the private road. Both sides of the road were lined with fences, access to the road being through gates in the fences. In 1930, Akers sold lot 1 to Babbit by a simple grant deed that contained no mention of easements. In 1931, Akers sold lot 2 to Carter and lot 3 to Dalton. Carter immediately obtained from Babbit a deed conveying the right of passage for men and vehicles along the private road to Carter's lot. From 1931 to 1955, both Carter and Dalton used this road as a rear entrance to their houses for their families and guests and as a passageway for men and vehicles. In 1955, the houses of both Carter and Dalton were destroyed by fire. Babbit immediately tore down the fence on his side of the private road, plowed up the road, and planted it with trees and bushes. In 1958, Carter and Dalton sold their lots, which had been empty since the fire, to Hypocase, Inc., whose factory was just across the public highway from Babbit's lot 1. Hypocase plans to build an employees' cafeteria covering both lots 2 and 3. Hypocase is anxious to determine its rights along the east 30 feet of Babbit's lot as a walkway for employees on their way from the plant to the cafeteria.

(4)

During the same period of peak orders which caused Hypocase to lease the warehouse from L. L. Lord, it also leased some additional office space from George Ohner. In order to get the kind of facilities it needed, the company had to sign a lease for two years. The lease contained a clause whereby Hypocase agreed not to "assign this lease or any interest therein" without the written consent of Ohner. After occupying the premises for 8 months, the need for the extra office space terminated. There being a strong possibility that Hypocase would need the premises again in about 6 months, the company leased the offices for a 6 month period to Safe Insurance Group, which was constructing its own office building in Berkland and expected to be able to move to its permanent quarters at about the time its lease with Hypocase expired. No consent was obtained from Ohner for this arrangement with Safe, but Ohner accepted 4 rent checks from Safe without any questions being raised. Safe's own offices were completed much earlier than expected, and Safe asked Hypocase for permission to terminate its lease after 4 months, to which Hypocase agreed. The premises were immediately leased by Hypocase for 2 months to Anosmian Eye, a firm of private detectives. This lease provided that rent checks were to be sent to Hypocase. Ohner refused to accept Hypocase's next payment of rent and gave Hypocase notice of termination of the lease on the ground that Hypocase had not obtained the written permission of Ohner for either the Safe or the Anosmian Eye leases. What are the rights of Hypocase?

B. In General

At some stage before the business is actually put into operation, the sole proprietor, the partnership, or the corporation must select and acquire a site on which to conduct its activities. This site may be nothing more than a small rented office necessary only for the keeping of records and the installation of a telephone. The actual location of this office may be of minor importance if customers are not expected to come there and if contacts are made on the outside or by telephone. If this is the nature of the site required, the legal problems involved are those having to do with leases and the relation between landlord and tenant. On the other hand, the conduct of the business may require: large areas of land; substantial quantities of floor space; and strategic location in order to make maximum use of markets, the shopping habits of prospective customers, access to rail, water, or highway transportation, and availability of labor supply. The facilities may be purchased or leased. Land may be acquired and the buildings erected upon it, or the land and buildings may be acquired ready for use. Zoning ordinances may limit the type of structure and the use to which certain land may be put.

The economic and other non-legal factors involved in selecting and acquiring a site are outside the scope of this book, but the importance of these factors cannot be overemphasized. No proper evaluation of the economic factors is possible, however, without a thorough understanding of the legal factors. The legal factors with which this discussion will be concerned are those relative to the purchase and to the lease of real property. No effort will be made to trace the origins of the principles of real property, except to say that the origins of real property law are so intimately related to the origins of the common law itself that it is impossible to separate the two. Rising as it did under the feudal system in England following the Norman Conquest, the common law has always been closely linked to land and other real property. For many generations the primary, if not the sole, preoccupation of the common law was with land and with the relation of persons to land. The sharp differences in the common law between treatment of real property and of personal property are largely explained by the unusual importance of real property in the English feudal system from which the common law grew. Until comparatively recent times, personal property was not an important form of wealth, and it was, and to some extent still is, given a subordinate position in the law.

The concept of "property" has always been an important one in our legal system and in our society. Much of our law in regard to property comes from the English origins of the common law, as has been pointed out above, but in the United States property has an unusual position because of the special treatment that is accorded to it by the Federal Constitution. The Fifth Amendment states, among other things, that "No person shall be . . . deprived of life, liberty, or property, without due process of law; nor shall private property be taken for public use, without just compensation." This statement is a protection against the activities of the federal government. The Fourteenth Amendment extends similar protection to persons against the activities of the state governments. "No State shall . . . deprive any person of life, liberty, or property, without due process of law." Notice that the draftsmen of the Constitution gave to property a status second only to life and liberty.

Property is not an easy concept to define. The most difficult task in any definition of property is to put over the point that, strictly speaking, the tangible things we so frequently speak of as property are not really important aspects of property at all. Houses and automobiles are property, but they would be almost valueless were it not for the more important aspects of property—the legal rights and duties one has with regard to property. The primary characteristic of owning an automobile, for example, consists of the owner's right to use it, to sell it, to dispose of it by will, and to protect it against the invasions of others. *Property* is really a group of rights entitling the owner to possess and use something to the exclusion of others. This description of property applies with equal force to both real and personal property.

The line between real and personal property is usually drawn with regard to the movable or immovable nature of the property referred to. Land and things permanently attached or related to land are immovable; thus, they are real property. Land, itself, consists not only of the right to use the surface but also of the right to remove minerals from beneath the surface and to use the airspace above the surface. Personal property consists, in general, of all other property. Because of the basic differences between movable and immovable property, it is not surprising to find that the law with regard to the two types of property is somewhat different, but many of the legal differences are such that they cannot be explained solely by the difference in the nature of the property, and resort must be made to the feudal origins of our legal system for explanation. It should be remembered that the classification of real and personal property does not correspond exactly to the classification of movable and immovable property, but the precise delineations between real and personal property are not crucial to our discussion here.

A term used very frequently in connection with property of all kinds is *title,* which, for the purposes of the present discussion, may be used synonymously with "ownership." Technically, considerable hair-splitting is done over the term, but that should not influence our use of it.

C. Purchase of Real Property

THE CONTRACT OF SALE AND THE OPTION. The purchase of real property is generally a much more involved and complicated procedure than is the purchase of personal property. The feudal origins of real property law have surrounded the transfer of such property from one person to another with formalities and requirements not found in connection with the sale of personal property. Before any property is actually purchased, however, the person desiring to buy must select the particular property that he wants. In order to do this, economic factors must be considered, together with such legal problems as the uses to which the particular property may be put and the limitations and restrictions that may have been imposed upon the method, manner, or use. Zoning ordinances, for example, may exclude certain commercial enterprises from all areas except those especially zoned for that purpose. An ideally situated piece of land in an area zoned "residential" will not be of much use to a person who desires to operate thereon an abattoir. Zoning ordinances, generally speaking, cannot be retroactive in effect. They cannot require the removal of existing but non-conforming uses, but this is no solace to the person who owns a piece of land upon which he wants to start a nonconforming use.

The use of particular property may be restricted by covenants, servitudes, and limitations set forth in prior deeds to the property, for example, where S transfers title to property to B "so long as the property shall not be used for commercial purposes" or "so long as no structure over two stories in height shall be erected on the premises," or where B *promises* that the property shall not be used for commercial purposes or that no structure over two stories shall be erected thereon. These limitations may be binding on owners who follow B even though a successive owner knows nothing of the restriction. Sometimes the effect of a violation is to cause an automatic return of the title to the property to S, the original grantor. The use of the property may be considerably reduced by a right-of-way owned by a power company for the erection of a high voltage power line across the center of the property. The purchaser of real property should be aware of these problems. A thorough search of the title and the records for the purpose of determining the existence of such restrictions, among other things, is a desirable prerequisite to the purchase of real property. Furthermore, the search may disclose whether the seller actually owns the property and has the right to sell it. In many states, title insurance companies provide searches and insurance to protect purchasers of real property.

A person seeking to acquire a site for his business may have several different sites under consideration while the information in regard to the sites is being collected and analyzed for the purpose of aiding in the selection of the best one. This person runs the risk that a desirable site may be sold to someone else while the collection and analysis are going on. In these circumstances the option contract is a useful device for giving the prospective buyer time to investigate while still protecting him from a loss of the property. The option was discussed in Chapter 3. Of course, it is useful only where the prospective seller is willing to enter into such an arrangement.

Another preliminary to actual transfer of ownership of real property from one person to another is the *contract of sale,* which results when the buyer accepts the seller's offer to sell or the seller accepts the buyer's offer to buy. The contract of sale, as a distinct step in the procedure, is not required. There is nothing to prevent the buyer's handing over the price in exchange for a deed to the property, but in most cases it would be foolish for him to do so. In the contract of sale the buyer agrees to buy and the seller to sell upon certain terms and conditions, and it also provides that a period of time will elapse before the transaction will be consummated, time during which the buyer raises the funds and investigates the seller's title, mortgages are paid off, insurance policies transferred, deeds are drawn, and many other activities take place. In many states, after the contract of sale is entered into, the transaction is turned over to a third person, called an *escrow holder,* who receives the deed from the seller and the price from the buyer and turns them over to the opposite parties when the terms and conditions of the contract have been met. The drafting of the contract is an important step in the whole procedure because it sets forth the conditions under which the parties become obligated to go through with the deal.

Under the statute of frauds, contracts for the sale of real property must be in writing. The contract must contain a description of the property sufficiently definite to make it possible to identify the property with reasonable certainty. The contract must be signed by the parties or by their agents. It is important to note that the contract for the sale of real property is one of the situations where the unusual equitable remedy of specific performance is available, and the court may compel the actual performance of the contract.

DEEDS. *Definition and types.* Although the deed is not the only method of transferring title to real property from one person to another, it is the most important method. Other methods will be examined briefly later. A *deed* is defined as a document or instrument used to transfer the ownership of real property from one person to another. There are three basic types of deeds—the quitclaim deed, the grant or "bargain and sale" deed, and the warranty deed. The *quitclaim deed* purports to convey only the rights, title, and interest that the grantor has at the time of the conveyance. There are no warranties of title. (A warranty is a promise or guaranty by the grantor in regard to some aspect of the transfer.) If the grantor had nothing, the grantee gets nothing, and he cannot complain, fraud being absent. The *grant deed,* or *"bargain and sale" deed,* is the typical deed used in most states. This type of deed carries with it two implied warranties by the grantor: 1, that previous to the time of the execution of the deed, the grantor has not conveyed the same estate, or any right, title, or interest therein, to any person other than the grantee; 2, that such estate is at the time of the execution of the deed free from encumbrances done, made, or suffered by the grantor, or any person claiming under him. Note that these warranties relate to the grantor's activities only, and do not apply to the acts of others. In the *warranty deed*, the grantor agrees to defend the premises even against the lawful claims of third persons. The practice of obtaining title insurance has decreased the importance of the implied warranties of the grant deed and of the warranties of the warranty deed.

In addition to the three types of deed mentioned in the paragraph above, there are a number of other varieties, most of whose names are descriptive of their uses—the trust deed, the reconveyance deed, the sheriff's deed, the gift deed, and the tax deed. The designations and usages of deeds vary from state to state, and it is wise not to assume any particular characteristics for a deed by its name alone.

Requirements of a deed. Although details vary somewhat from state to state, the matters essential to a valid deed are approximately the same throughout the country.

1. Grantor. Every deed must have a grantor, who is, of course, the party who conveys the property. A grantor must have legal capacity. In general, anyone who has the legal capacity to contract may make a deed. In some states, the deeds of minors, or minors under eighteen years of age, are void. In most states, a deed by a married woman may be made in the same manner and with the same effect as if she were unmarried. Where the property is held in co-ownership, or is community property, or is subject to marital claims, the signature of the co-owner or of the spouse may be necessary for a valid deed. Even if a person signs a deed, the instrument is not considered to be that person's deed unless his name also appears in the body of the instrument. The fact that the name used by the grantor is not his true name does not invalidate the deed, but if title is taken in one name and transferred in another name, the grantor must set forth in the deed the name in which he received the title to the property. Failure to do so does not affect the validity of the deed between the grantor and grantee, but it would destroy constructive notice to subsequent encumbrancers or purchasers. (See discussion of Recording, below.) The vote of the directors of a corporation is sometimes necessary to authorize the sale of real property belonging to the corporation. Where the agent of the person holding the title to property signs the deed on behalf of his principal, it is important that the signature be as follows: "True Owner, By Henry Hart, Agent," or "XYZ Corporation, by Henry Hart, President," and not: "Henry Hart, Agent for True Owner," or "Henry Hart, President of XYZ Corporation." Special additional details and requirements in regard to the grantor appear in all states, but few of them affect the actual validity of the deed.

2. Grantee. It is obvious that a deed can have no effect at all unless there is a grantee. Legal capacity is not necessary for a proper grantee; minors may be grantees, but the grantee must be a legal person. Thus, a grant to a dead person is a nullity as is the deed to an ordinary unincorporated association, in

the absence of a special statute like the Uniform Partnership Act. Corporations are legal persons and are proper grantees. It is not necessary that the name of the grantee appear in the granting clause if the name appears elsewhere and is clearly intended to designate him as grantee.

3. Writing and Subscription. An estate in real property can be transferred only by operation of law, as by inheritance, or by an instrument in writing subscribed by the party transferring the property or by an agent authorized in writing. The grantee does not sign the deed. The deed should describe the property with reasonable certainty, but the description need not employ any of the usual methods of describing real property. In case of ambiguity in the description, natural objects or monuments referred to will prevail over courses, distances, lines, and angles. In some states, the signature of the grantor must be accompanied by a seal, but this formality has been abolished in many states as a deed requirement.

4. Delivery. Another essential of a valid deed is its delivery. A deed does not take effect until it is delivered. It is important to note that delivery does not require actual, physical delivery to the grantee. Delivery depends upon the *intention* that title shall pass irrevocably even where possession and enjoyment may be indefinitely postponed. Delivery may be actual or constructive. Delivery is actual when physical delivery to the grantee has taken place; it is constructive where by agreement of the parties it is understood to be delivered and the grantee is entitled to immediate physical delivery, or where it is delivered by the grantor to a third person for the benefit of the grantee with intent on the part of the grantor to give up all control. A presumption of non-delivery arises when the deed is found in the possession of the grantor; a presumption of delivery arises when the deed is found in the possession of the grantee. A deed cannot be delivered to the grantee conditionally. Depending upon the circumstances, attempted conditional delivery to the grantee is either absolute and free and clear of the condition or else is completely void. If the grantor wishes to transfer property only after some condition is performed, he should deliver the deed to some third person. This is one of the purposes of an escrow where the deed is delivered to the escrow holder for further delivery to the grantee if the grantee performs the condition of paying the price.

5. Acceptance. Actually a part of the requirement of delivery is the acceptance of the deed by the grantee. This is, like delivery, a matter of intention. Increased use of presumptions of acceptance has, in many states, virtually dispensed with the requirement except where the rights of third persons have intervened.

There are other deed requirements that are essential only in a few states. Some elements are usually present because they are a matter of form or offer certain advantages, although they are not necessary to the validity of the deed. Consideration falls into this mixed category. It is not necessary for a valid deed, although a deed does possess some characteristics of a contract. Some states require a recital of consideration. Lack of consideration may be evidence of fraud or duress. Acknowledgement is another non-essential of a deed, but which, nonetheless, is usually present because it is a prerequisite to recordation and permits introduction of the deed into evidence without further proof. An *acknowledgement* is the act of a person who has executed an instrument declaring before a competent officer, such as a notary public, that it is his instrument. Where there are several grantors, each must acknowledge. Witnesses to the execution of deeds are not required, except in a few states.

Recording. The recording of deeds is not an essential matter, but it does serve several useful purposes, and it is done in most states almost as a matter of course. Recording furnishes a safe and convenient method of preserving evidence of ownership, gives publicity to real property transactions, and gives a buyer some protection in a situation where the seller has previously transferred the property to someone else. Most of the state recording laws provide either that unrecorded conveyances are void as against subsequent purchasers without notice or that the prior unrecorded conveyance is void only in respect to subsequent conveyances without notice which are themselves recorded. Generally, any instrument or judgement that affects the title to, or possession of, real property may be recorded. Deeds, of course, fall into this broad category of recordable instruments. Contracts and options for the sale of real property may also be recorded. A document not properly executed and acknowledged normally will not be accepted for recording, and if such a document is recorded, it does not achieve the intended results of recording.

Proper recordation of an instrument imparts constructive notice of the contents of the instrument and of the transaction it represents. *Constructive notice* means that all persons who subsequently deal with the property are treated as though they had actual notice of everything that would have been revealed by an examination of the instrument that has been recorded. If the instrument is not recorded, a subsequent purchaser or creditor may prevail over the prior purchaser or creditor who failed to record. For example: In 1960, *S* conveyed property to *B* who failed to record the deed. In 1964, *S* conveyed the same property to *C*. If *C* did not know of the prior conveyance to *B*, *C* would prevail over *B* and would be entitled to the property. In some states, *C* must himself record before he becomes entitled to his priority. Had *B* recorded his deed, it would be assumed that *C* knew of the prior transaction whether or not he had inspected the record. In order for a subsequent purchaser to be entitled to the protection of the recording laws and to be allowed to prevail over a prior purchaser who failed to record, the subsequent purchaser must have given value for the property. A person who receives the deed to the property as a gift is not protected, nor, by the majority rule, is a person who receives a deed in payment of a pre-existing debt. All states protect subsequent purchasers for value. Most states protect subsequent mortgagees. The statutes of many states contain protection for creditors who have converted their claims into liens or charges on the land by levy or by attachment. In some states, the fact that a deed is unrecorded affords protection to a subsequent purchaser or other person entitled to protection whether or not he has notice by other means. But by the better and prevailing rule, a purchaser who has notice of a prior unrecorded interest in the property is subject to the prior interest; thus, he is not protected by the recording laws. Knowledge of facts such as the possession of the property by someone other than the grantor, which would lead a reasonable person to investigate the grantor's title, is, usually sufficient evidence that the purchaser had notice.

OTHER METHODS OF ACQUIRING TITLE. *Adverse possession.* The deed is not the only method by which title to real property may be acquired. Other methods are—adverse possession, dedication, accretion, by will, by intestate succession, and by eminent domain. *Adverse possession* is a means of acquiring title to property by continued possession over a period of time. Title thus acquired is an absolute title, and it is a new title not based on the old title of the original owner, as would be the case where the title was acquired by deed. Title by adverse possession is the result of a policy of the law to the effect that confusion and uncertainty about the rights of persons in real property should be removed, as far as possible, by compelling them to exercise diligence in the declaration and protection of their rights. Where a person occupies and improves land over a long period of time, claiming it as his own, he may actually acquire title to that land through the doctrine of adverse possession, even against the claims of the person who originally owned the property. Of course, the original owner will not be deprived of his ownership except where he failed to be reasonably diligent in claiming and enforcing that ownership.

The requirements for acquiring title by adverse possession are as follows (these requirements are not discussed in detail because adverse possession is not a common method by which a beginning business acquires a site for its activities): 1. The adverse possessor must actually occupy the premises and must do it openly and notoriously. The occupation must be such as to constitute reasonable notice to the owner. 2. The possession of the premises by the adverse possessor must be hostile and adverse to the rights of the owner. A person who occupies the premises with the permission of the owner is not an adverse possessor. 3. The possession must be accompanied by a claim of right in the property or a claim of ownership based on an instrument, judgment, or decree which purports to convey the land to the adverse possessor but is, for some reason, defective. The claim of ownership based on a defective instrument is called *color of title*. The *claim of right* is usually inferred from the conduct of the adverse possessor toward the land—as, for example, improving it, enclosing it, or erecting structures on it. Such extensive occupation and possession are usually not necessary where there is color of title. 4. The possession by the adverse possessor must be continuous and uninterrupted for the period specified in the statutes. The statutory period varies from five to twenty years, depending upon the state. In the states that have short periods, the payment of the taxes assessed against the property is often required before the adverse possessor can get title. Some states have two periods, a short one for situations where taxes are paid or where the adverse possessor holds under color of title, and a longer period where neither of these factors is present.

Dedication and accretion. *Dedication* is the gift of land or an interest in land to the public for a public use, as the dedication to the county or city of streets in a new subdivision. *Accretion* or *alluvion* is the gradual addition to land bordering streams or bodies of water of particles deposited in imperceptible degrees; *reliction* is the addition to land caused by the gradual recession of water from land.

Inheritance. Title to real property may also be acquired by will or by operation of the rules of intestate succession. A *will* is an instrument by which a qualified person legally and intentionally directs the disposition of his property at his death. Wills are said to be *ambulatory,* which means that they are ineffective during the person's life and are capable of dealing with the disposition of the testator's property only at the person's death. The person who makes a will is called a *testator.* In most states, any person eighteen years of age or over who is of sound mind may make a will. Under the common law, the making and execution of wills, the interpretation of language in wills, and the effect of wills are surrounded by special legal formalities, many of which have now been considerably altered by statute in the various states. Wills which fail to comply with the technical requirements are usually of no force or effect. In most states, the title to real property disposed of by will passes to the designated person immediately upon the death of the testator, subject only to the management and administration of the estate by the executor who is named in the will and who is empowered to carry out the provisions of the will.

Intestate succession refers to the disposition of a person's property when he dies without leaving a will. A person who dies without a will is called an *intestate,* and the court will appoint, usually from among the intestate's near relatives, an *administrator* to settle the estate and distribute the property. There is considerable variation among the states as to the rules of distribution, and the laws of one's own state should be inspected for the details. Court action is required in connection with most estates regardless of size. These proceedings are usually called *probate proceedings,* although technically the word *probate* refers only to the proving of a will.

Eminent domain. Another method of acquiring title to property is *eminent domain.* This refers to the taking of private property for public use, in exchange for which the owner receives just compensation. The power of eminent domain can be exercised by the federal government and its agencies, by the state and its subdivisions and agencies, by public utilities, and by various others such as higher educational institutions. The details vary from state to state. In general, however, in order to justify a taking by eminent domain it must appear that the taking is for a public use and that the taking is necessary for that use. The required compensation is stated in different ways, but it is usually the *market value* or the "highest price property would bring in a free and objective market." One aspect of eminent domain condemnations which many people do not seem to understand is that only the real property is being condemned and not the use to which the property is being put. For example, when property on which a profitable business is being conducted is condemned in eminent domain proceedings, the condemning authority must pay only the value of the real property taken; he does not have to pay the value of the business. Of course, the value of the property is affected by the value of the business that is capable of being conducted on the premises. Many states expressly permit compensation for *damage* resulting from governmental action as well as for an actual taking, and much the same end is reached in other states and in the federal courts by a liberal interpretation of the word "taking."

ESTATES IN REAL PROPERTY. *Definition and classification.* An *estate* is an interest in real property. Estates vary with respect to the size of the interest, common or sole ownership, present or future interest, absolute or conditional interest, and in many other ways. With respect to size, quantity, or duration, estates are classified either as *freehold* or *non-freehold estates.* The latter variety consists of different types of leasehold estates. These types will be discussed below in connection with the lease of real property. This classification is a survival of the feudal system where freehold estates carried with them the obligation of feudal dues and services but the less-than-freehold estates did not. The freehold estates were entitled to greater protection and were of much greater dignity than the non-freeholds. The discussion below is necessarily brief because most of the categories and sub-categories of estates in land have lost the importance they once had. We shall examine the field only in outline form, except for those problems and estates which are still likely to be of interest or importance to a person seeking a site for the conduct of his business.

FREEHOLD ESTATES. The freehold estates are the fee simple absolute, the fee simple defeasible, the fee tail, and the life estate. All but the last are referred to as *estates of inheritance* because they are capable of passing from one person to another by will or by intestacy. The *fee simple absolute* is the greatest of all the estates because it represents complete ownership of the property. The owner of such an estate is entitled to the entire property with unconditional power of use and disposition during his life, and these same rights descend to his heirs and legal representatives upon his death intestate or to his devisees if he dies testate. The *fee tail* or *estate tail* is an estate that has virtually disappeared from use in the United States as a result of statutes specifically abolishing it. The fee tail limited the right to succeed to a fee to certain classes of heirs. If there were no such persons, the property reverted to the original grantor. Estates not otherwise identifiable are presumed to be fee simple absolute.

A *fee simple defeasible* results from the language in the conveyance that causes the estate to terminate upon the occurrence of a stated event. For example: *A* conveys to *B* in fee "so long as the property shall be used for church purposes." If the property ceases to be used for church purposes, it reverts to *A* or to *A's* heirs or successors. Such conveyances are not very common.

A *life estate* is an interest in land that continues as long as the life by which it is measured. The life is usually that of a person to whom the life estate is granted, but the life may be that of some other person. A life estate may be granted to someone else or may be reserved in the grantor himself. Examples are: *A* may grant to *B* for *B's* life; or *A* may grant to *B* for the life of *C;* or *A* may grant to *B* in fee, subject to a life estate in *A.* Life estates are either conventional life estates or legal life estates. The conventional life estate, which is illustrated in the above examples, is created intentionally by the deed or will of the party concerned. A *legal life estate* is created by operation of law. The most important legal life estates are the marital estates of "dower" and "curtesy." *Dower* is the life estate a wife has in the real property of her husband after his death; *curtesy* is the life estate a husband has in the real property of his wife after her death. The common law marital estates have been considerably modified by state statute, and they are abolished in states that have the community property system.

It is obvious from the very nature of the life estate that the owner has somewhat lesser rights than the owner of a fee simple. It is interesting to note at this point, incidentally, that the owner of an estate is called a *tenant* even where he has a fee simple absolute. The explanation is found again in the feudal system where everyone held his land as a tenant of someone higher up the feudal scale. The life tenant has the same right of possession that the owner in fee simple has except that the life tenant's right is subject to the privilege of the *remainderman* to interfere to protect any of his own rights. The remainderman is the person entitled to the property when the life tenant's estate expires. The life tenant is entitled to the produce and profits of the land. Where a third person causes injury to the property, the life tenant can recover damages only for the harm to his life interest, but the remainderman may also recover damages for the harm to his interest. The life tenant must pay taxes and other current charges and a fair proportion of the assessments that benefit the whole property. The life tenant is under a duty not to injure the property so as to depreciate substantially its market value. Thus, the life tenant cannot cut timber or pump out the oil or dig out the minerals unless the property was already being used for those purposes when the life tenant came into possession. Of course, the grant itself may alter any of the above general rules.

Future estates. Another classification of estates is made in terms of the time at which the possession of the property may be enjoyed. Thus, estates may be *present* or *future estates.* The former entitles the owner to the immediate possession of the property; the latter entitles the owner to possession of the property only at some future time. When A grants to B for life and then to C in fee, B has a present estate because he is entitled to immediate possession, but C has a future estate because he will not be entitled to possession until the death of B at some future time. The two basic types of future estates are the "reversion" and the "remainder." A *reversion* is the residue of an estate left in the grantor or his successors by the operation of law, commencing in possession on termination of the estate that was granted. For example, where A grants a life estate to B, the residue of A's fee simple remains in A and his successors as a reversion, and A or a successor will be entitled to possess the property again on B's death. Whenever a grantor grants a smaller estate than he has, there is a reversion in the grantor for the portion that was not granted.

A *remainder* is a future interest created in favor of a person other than the grantor to give the remainderman the right to possession upon the termination of some precedent estate. Where A grants to B for life and then to C in fee, C has a remainder that will take effect in possession only on the termination of B's life estate. Probably no area of the law is still as thoroughly surrounded by feudal rules and doctrines as is that area concerned with remainders. It is far outside the scope of this book to examine in detail the principles and sometimes incredible intricacies of the law with respect to remainders.

Remainders are subject to a number of different classifications, but the basic classification is that of remainders that are "vested," and those that are not. A *remainder is vested* when, at the time of the grant, a person or group of persons is in existence who can take possession on the termination of the prior estate. Where there is no such person, the remainder is said to be *contingent*. There seems to be a natural tendency among human beings to attempt to impose their ideas upon future generations. If left unrestrained, this tendency, generations ago, would have tied up most property for all time. The common law, very early, developed a strong policy against this tendency when carried beyond a certain point. This policy is set forth in the so-called *rule against perpetuities*. This rule provides that no interest in land is good unless it must become vested, if at all, within a certain period of time. The common law period, modified in some states by statute, is twenty-one years after some designated life in being at the time the interest was created. This means that a contingent remainder must be such that, if it is going to vest at all, it must vest within that period. Otherwise the remainder is invalid. Present interests, reversions, and vested remainders do not come within the rule because they are, by definition, already vested when they come into existence.

COMMON OWNERSHIP. The discussion until now has assumed, for the sake of simplicity, that a single person owned or held title to an estate in real property. An estate in real property may be owned by several persons. Such ownership may be of joint interests, of interest in common, of community interests of husband and wife, or of partnership interests. Partnership interests are considered elsewhere. The others will be discussed below.

Joint tenancy.   A joint interest, usually called a *joint tenancy*, is an interest owned by two or more persons in equal shares and created by a single will or grant. In general, a joint tenancy can be created only where the will or grant expressly states that a joint tenancy is intended. At common law no express statement of intention to create a joint tenancy was necessary, and in many states the express statement is not required where the grantees are husband and wife. The chief characteristic of the joint tenancy is *survivorship*. This means that on the death of one joint tenant his interest goes to the survivor or survivors; and, on the death of the last survivor, the whole goes to that person's heirs or to those named in his will. For example, where *A, B,* and *C* are joint tenants, *A's* interest goes, on his death, to *B* and *C*; on the death of *B,* *B's* interest goes to *C*; and on *C's* death, all goes to *C's* heirs. The common law theory of joint tenancy is that the title of each tenant extends to the whole estate. Thus, when one dies, the entire estate survives to the others.

The use of the joint tenancy has been much abused in some states, usually because it's use may avoid the necessity of probate proceedings when one of the joint tenants dies. Although probate is generally avoided by this device, other procedures are usually necessary in order to establish the death of the joint tenant and confirm the title in the survivor or survivors. The disadvantages, in many situations, far outweigh the advantages of joint tenancy. A joint tenant loses his right to dispose of the property by will, and there may be serious tax consequences. Property, especially real property, should never be put into joint tenancy without carefully weighing the reasons for doing so against the dangers and disadvantages.

At common law, corporations could not hold property as joint tenants because they usually had perpetual life and were almost certain to survive. In many states, however, corporations may hold property as joint tenants. The modern law is not as favorable toward survivorship as the common law once was. Many states have purported to abolish survivorship; thus, for all practical purposes, joint tenancy as well.

A joint tenancy may be terminated in many ways. Where there are only two joint tenants, the conveyance of his interest by one of the tenants to a third person destroys the joint tenancy. The other joint tenant and the third person hold as tenants in common. Where there are three or more joint tenants, a conveyance by one joint tenant to a third person causes the third person to become a tenant in common, but as among themselves, the other joint tenants remain joint tenants. A joint tenant cannot dispose of his interest by will because "survivorship" is said to operate before the will does; thus, nothing is left of which the will may dispose. A judgment creditor of a joint tenant may sever the joint tenancy of the debtor and become a tenant in common with the other joint tenants by levy of execution and purchase at a sheriff's sale. A joint tenancy may be terminated by *agreement,* for example, where one tenant transfers his interest to the other or where the agreement is simply to eliminate survivorship. Another method of termination is by *partition*—a proceeding in equity which actually divides up the property among the tenants. If the property cannot be divided without prejudice to the owners, the court may order a sale and will then divide the proceeds.

Tenancy in common. A *tenancy in common* lacks the characteristic of survivorship. When an interest is created in favor of several persons and those persons are not partners or husband and wife, they are presumed, in most states, to be tenants in common. On the death of one tenant in common, his interest passes to his heirs who also become tenants in common. Whereas the title of a joint tenant is said to extend to the whole estate, the tenant in common has only a fractional, but undivided, interest in the whole. It is necessary only that each tenant in common be entitled with the others to the undivided possession of the property. Generally speaking, a tenancy in common can be terminated only by the consent of the parties or by partition proceedings. A conveyance by one tenant to a third person does not terminate the tenancy in common but simply substitutes one tenant for another.

Except for survivorship, the property rights of joint tenants and tenants in common are substantially the same. Each tenant is entitled to share in the possession of the entire property, and no tenant can exclude the others from any part of it. One tenant who pays taxes or other charges against the property is entitled to contribution from the others. A single tenant can bring or defend an action for enforcement or protection of rights in the property, but he can only recover for damages to his proportionate interest. One tenant cannot, ordinarily, bind the others by an agreement relating to the property.

Marital interests. At common law, the conveyance by a third person to husband and wife creates what is called a *tenancy by the entireties.* This is very much like the joint tenancy except for restrictions on its termination while the marriage exists. This tenancy was based on the notion that husband and wife were one person. Because this notion no longer receives much support, the tenancy by the entireties has been considerably modified by statute in most states, and it has been completely abolished in many states.

Another variety of co-ownership exists in some states[1] as a substitute for the common law property rights of dower and curtesy. This type of co-ownership, called *community property,* is derived from the civil law. Community property is based on the idea that both husband and wife contribute to acquisitions of property during the marriage and both should have a present interest in such property. The common law evolved dower and curtesy as methods of giving each spouse some economic security in the property of the other, but

---

[1] Arizona, California, Idaho, Louisiana, Nevada, New Mexico, Oklahoma, Texas, and Washington.

dower and curtesy recognize no present interest in the parties, are effective only on the death of one spouse, and apply only to real property. Community property comes into existence during the marriage, recognizes present interests, and applies to all forms of property. Essentially, community property consists of all property acquired during marriage except for property acquired by gift, devise, bequest, or descent and the income from property which is not community property. Property acquired before marriage is not community property. The husband, generally, has power of control over community property, but in most states where the system is in use, the wife's rights are reasonably well protected. On the death of either spouse, the other is entitled to at least one-half of the community property, and, in some states, to all in the absence of testamentary disposition of one-half by the deceased spouse. Upon divorce the community property is usually divided equally between husband and wife, except that in some states the innocent party is entitled to more than one-half if the grounds for divorce are of certain types, such as adultery or extreme cruelty. Statutory changes in the civil law rules of community property have resulted in extensive divergence among the several community property states.

Residents of community property states had certain tax advantages over residents of non-community property states until 1948. Prior to 1948, pressures brought to bear on the legislatures of several non-community property states resulted in some of these adopting the community property system by statute. Some of these states adopted the system without any realization of the ramifications of the move, except from the tax point of view, but a tremendous amount of confusion and difficulty was avoided when these states repealed their community property statutes following the 1948 amendments to the Internal Revenue Code, which gave certain community property tax advantages to the residents of all states.

FIXTURES.   The definition of real property set forth at the beginning of this chapter paid no particular attention to the peculiar problem that arises when a thing, originally personal property, is fastened or affixed to real property in such a way as to cast doubt on whether it remains personal property. The solution to this problem is important to the farm tenant who makes improvements on rented property, to the person who rents a house and installs carpeting or venetian blinds, to the storekeeper who installs showcases, signs, and other equipment on rented premises, to the owner of the real property in all these cases, and to purchasers and mortgagees of both personal and real property. When personal property has been so affixed to real property that it becomes real property itself, it is called a *fixture*. The basic test of whether such affixation has taken place is the intention of the parties. If the parties intend to make the personal property a part of the realty, the personal property becomes a fixture. Where the intention to affix or not to affix is manifested expressly, no particular problems arise. In the ordinary situation, however, the intention of the parties is ascertained from their conduct, from the manner of annexation, from the relation of the parties, and from the adaptability of the personal property to use with real property. All of these factors aid in determining the intention of the parties.

Where the personal property becomes a fixture, it is a part of the real property, and, as such, it may be a part of a mortgagee's security, it may pass to the buyer of the real property, and it usually cannot be removed by a tenant on termination of his lease. It is extremely important, then, to be able to determine whether certain property is or is not a fixture. In general, an intention to affix to the real property is presumed where the personal property is attached to the land by roots (except for annual crops), imbedded in the land (walls or foundations), permanently resting upon the land (buildings), or permanently attached to one of the above things by cement, plaster, nails, bolts, or screws (doors, windows, screens, linoleum, light sockets, and window shades). A contrary intention, however, may be manifested in some other way.

The adaptation of the personal property to use with real property is also a factor that must be considered in determining intention. If an article is attached to, or placed on, land to promote the purpose for which the land is used, the intention is more likely to be that of making the article a fixture than it would be when the article is incompatible. Where the article is installed by the owner of the premises, the doubts will normally be resolved in favor of affixation, but where the article is installed by a tenant, the doubts will be resolved against affixation on the theory that a tenant is less likely to intend an affixation to real property than the owner of the real property is.

A special application of the presumption in favor of a tenant is used where personal property is added to real property by a tenant for the purpose of trade, manufacture, ornament, or domestic use, unless the personal property is so affixed that it becomes an integral part of the premises. Such additions, which are called *trade fixtures,* remain personal property. The term "trade fixtures" is confusing because these things are really not fixtures at all because the intention to make them so is lacking.

In the absence of the express consent of the owner of the real property, personal property cannot be removed from the real property if the removal will cause material injury to the real property. There are probably not many situations to which this rule can be applied, because, in general, personal property affixed in such a way that it makes removal injurious to the real property would be a fixture. Agreements between lessor and lessee or between buyer and seller that articles affixed to realty are to remain personal property are binding as between those parties but not as to third persons without notice of the agreement. Thus, things which would ordinarily be fixtures would be part of a mortgagee's lien where the mortgagee did not know of an agreement between mortgagor and tenant whereby the property affixed to the realty was to retain its personal character.

A special type of problem arises where the personal property is itself subject to a security interest. Prior to the adoption of the Uniform Commercial Code, persons with security interests in fixtures often did not have much protection against purchasers or mortgagees of the real property, owing in large part to the lack of uniform provisions in most states for the filing or recording of security interests in personal property and to the inconsistency with which such filing or recording, when feasible, was made to affect purchasers or encumbrancers of the realty. The Code now gives uniform treatment and substantial protection to parties with security interests in personal property which has become affixed to real property. The details are set forth in Chapter 13.

It should be obvious that the above discussion calls attention to only a few of the possible priority problems which the affixation of personal property to real property can raise.

RIGHTS OF ADJOINING LANDOWNERS. *Encroachments.* In many types of situations, rights and duties arise with regard to adjoining landowners. Only two of those situations will be discussed here; those, only briefly. The first of these problems is that of *encroachments,* where, for example, buildings or other structures or the limbs or roots of trees extend from the land of one owner onto the land of the adjoining owner. Where a building overlaps or encroaches upon adjoining land, there is a continuing trespass or nuisance which gives the encroached-upon owner a right of action for damages or for an injunction. Where, however, the encroachment is slight and the cost of removal is great, the court will deny injunctive relief and award only damages. It should be noted that in many states an encroachment for a long period of time may ripen into ownership under the doctrine of adverse possession. Where the encroachment is above the surface of the ground, as by eaves or balcony, the lapse of time may create an easement. (See discussion of Rights in the Land of Another, below.) When one is buying a piece of property, the possibility of encroachments should be considered, and, depending upon the circumstances, a survey should be ordered. Trees whose branches overhang or whose roots enter the land of the adjoining owner constitute a nuisance to the extent that they encroach. The owner of the adjoining property may abate the nuisance by cutting off the offending branches or roots, or may bring an action for damages. If the trunk of the tree is partly on the land of one owner and partly on the land of the other, the tree is the property of both as tenants in common, and neither may injure or destroy it without the consent of the other.

Right of support. Another important problem of adjoining landowners is the right of support, which each landowner has with reference to the use of the land of the other. At common law, the owner of land had a right to have his land in its natural state supported by the adjoining land. The owner of the adjoining land could not excavate his own land in such a way as to remove support from the other land. The excavating owner was absolutely liable for collapse or other damage to the land regardless of the degree of care he used in the excavation. The right to support was looked upon as a property right and not as just another manifestation of a general right to be free from the harm caused by the negligent acts of others. The excavator had to provide a substitute support at his peril. This protection extended only to the land in its natural state, and the excavating owner was not liable for damage caused to buildings or other structures unless he was negligent. If the land in its natural state would have collapsed even without the buildings on it, the excavating owner was liable for damage to the buildings also. Many states have modified these common law rules, and reference should be made to the law of one's own state for the details of the right to support. Most of the modifications have removed the absolute liability, but have imposed a duty of notice to the adjoining landowner of pending excavations so that he will be provided with an opportunity to protect his own land.

RIGHTS IN THE LAND OF ANOTHER. *Easements.* It is possible for a person to have rights not only in his own land but also in the land of another. Examples of such rights are easements and covenants running with the land. Only the first of these will be examined in any detail. An *easement* is an interest in the land of another which entitles the owner of the easement to a limited use or enjoyment of the other's land. An easement is an interest in real property. It may be a perpetual right in fee or of a lesser duration. An easement may be either affirmative, allowing the doing of acts, or negative, preventing the doing of acts.

Easements are of two basic types: *appurtenant* and *in gross*. An easement is *appurtenant* when it is in some way attached to the land of the owner of the easement, for example, where *A*, the owner of Blackacre, has an easement to drive his automobile to the highway over the adjoining land, Whiteacre, belonging to *B*. Blackacre is said to be the *dominant tenement,* the land to which the benefits of the easement attach. Whiteacre is the *servient tenement,* the land on which the burden of the easement is imposed. An easement is *in gross* when it is not attached to any particular land as a dominant tenement but belongs to a person individually. Thus, a person may own the right to fish in a certain pond or hunt on a certain tract, or a power company may own the right to erect its lines across many parcels of land without owning any particular piece of land to which the benefits of this easement attach. The difficulty involved in identifying the successors to an easement in gross has led, in some states, to a prohibition of the transfer of such easements.

An easement may be created by an express grant or reservation, by an implied grant or reservation, and by prescription. An owner of land may sell or convey a right in his land to another person or he may sell land and reserve for himself some right in the land. Thus, *A* may convey to *B*, the owner of Whiteacre, a right-of-way across *A's* land, Blackacre, or *A* may sell Blackacre and reserve a right-of way across it to adjoining land that he owns. In the absence of contrary provision in the grant, the owner of the easement has the duty to keep it in repair.

A transfer of real property also transfers all easements attached thereto, either as burdens or benefits, and it may create easements by implication from the circumstances. Thus, a transfer of real property creates in favor of that property an easement to use other real property of the transferring party in the same manner and to the same extent as such property was obviously and permanently used by that party. For example: *A* owns a piece of land on one part of which he has built a house. From another part of the land where there is a spring, *A* has built a pipeline to the house. *A* later sells the piece of land on which the house is built and retains for himself the piece containing the spring. The purchaser of the land gets an implied easement to use the pipeline and the spring water because that was the obvious and permanent use that *A* made of the land when he owned all of it. Had *A*, in the above example, sold the spring portion of the land and retained the house, the buyer would, in some states, have to assume the burden of the pipeline and the use of the spring because *A* would have an implied reservation of easement. The easement, however, is not implied either as a grant or as a reservation unless it is apparent and continuous. There must be something either visible or something in the nature of a permanent artificial structure.

In the United States, there is no implied grant of easement for light and air, except between landlord and tenant where the premises might be untenantable without it. In England, such easements are implied much like any other.

A special type of implied easement, called the *way of necessity,* arises when a grantor conveys land shut off from access to a road by the grantor's remaining land. The grantee has a right-of-way across the grantor's remaining land to reach the road. The way is strictly one of necessity, however, and will not arise where there is other access to the road no matter how inconvenient. A way of necessity will usually not arise where a grantor cuts *himself* off from the road, but in some states an implied reservation may occur.

An easement may also be created by prescription, a device very much like adverse possession. *Prescription* does not give title to property but creates a right to use the property in the manner in which it had been used for the statutory period. The requirements for prescription are similar to those for adverse possession. If these requirements are met, the person using the land of another acquires an easement just as good as one acquired by express or implied grant. It is important to note that the extent of the easement is governed by the extent of the use during the statutory period. An easement gained through long use as a foot path is not an easement for the passage of trucks and automobiles.

Easements are property rights and, as such, are transferable and descendible, subject to the limitations imposed in some states on easements in gross. The owner of an easement appurtenant cannot separate the easement from the dominant tenement, however, without destroying the easement. The easement passes with the dominant tenement or not at all.

An easement terminates if one person becomes the owner of both the dominant and the servient tenements or becomes the owner of an easement in gross and also the land subject to the easement. A person cannot have an easement in his own property. The owner of an easement may release or surrender his easement to the owner of the servient tenement, as by a quitclaim deed. An easement acquired by prescription may be terminated by mere nonuser for the statutory period, but an easement acquired by either express or implied grant cannot be lost in this fashion. Any easement may be lost by abandonment or by intentional relinquishment, either of which is evidenced by the conduct of the owner of the easement, such as building a fence or planting trees across the entrance to a right-of-way or by building another drive to the street across his own property and abandoning the use of the easement. An easement may be terminated by the involuntary destruction of the servient tenement, as where there is an easement to use the stairs on an adjoining building and the building is accidentally destroyed by fire.

Covenants. Another type of right a person may have in the land of another is the covenant running with the land. A covenant is a promise. Here we are concerned with promises concerning land. When a covenant runs with the land, a successor of the person to whom the promise was made may enforce it against the person who made it or against his successor. The essentials of a running covenant are: an intention that the covenant run, a requirement that the covenant touches or concerns land, and privity of estate between the original parties. The last is the most troublesome requirement, and it is dealt with differently in different states. The *requirement of privity* is simply a requirement that the original parties have had mutual or successive interests in the same property. In most states, this test is met by the landlord-tenant relationship, the mortgagor-mortgagee relationship, and by the seller-buyer relationship. Thus, where a seller of land covenants to maintain a supply of water to the land from his neighboring land, not only may the buyer enforce the covenant against the seller, but the successor to the buyer may maintain it against the seller or the seller's successor. If it is a true running covenant, no notice to the successors of either the buyer or the seller is necessary in order to make the covenant enforceable. In a few states, the buyer-seller relationship does not supply privity, and a covenent between these parties will not run. The area has been invaded by statute in many states with varying results.

When a covenant does not run with the land because some essential requirement is absent or when a covenant does run but the damage remedy is inadequate, a court of equity will sometimes enforce the covenant between successors of the original parties by an injunction against a breach of the covenant. However, this relief will be denied where the successor against whom the covenant is sought to be enforced had no actual or constructive notice of the covenant at the time of the transfer to him. Relief will also be denied in equity where the enforcement would work a hardship or an unfairness, where there has been a general disregard for the restrictions, where the restrictions appear in some deeds in the tract but not in others, and where conditions in the surrounding territory have changed so that it is impossible to achieve the benefits originally sought by the making of the restrictions. It is unconstitutional for a court to enforce racial covenants either in law or in equity.

D. Lease of Real Property

In General.   As mentioned above, a classification of estates in land with regard to duration is divided into two groups—freehold and non-freehold estates. The former has already been discussed. The latter, the leasehold estate, is the topic of discussion here. A sole proprietor, a partnership, or a corporation may not desire to purchase a site on which to conduct its business, or it may be unable to do so either because of the capital required or because the usable sites have already been acquired by others and are available only for lease. Furthermore, many firms that once owned their sites have sold them to investors and leased them back for use under a scheme known as *sale and lease-back,* which may provide certain tax and other advantages. Many business firms lease some of their sites and buy others or lease temporary space for special purposes. Most businessmen, business firms, and individuals encounter the lease and the landlord-tenant relationship at one time or another; consequently, an understanding of the essential nature of the relation and the rights, duties, and obligations which go with it is important to almost everyone.

A person entering into a lease, as either a lessor or lessee, is confronted with an unusual situation some of the aspects of which are based on the law of real property, others on the law of personal property, and still others on the law of contract. Sometimes it is difficult to separate and identify the principles with which one must deal. Essentially, a leasehold estate is a *chattel real,* a form of personal property having something to do with real property, governed largely by the rules relating to personal property. An assignment of a lease, for example, is for most purposes considered to be a sale of personal property and not a transfer of real property. A lease may be looked upon both as a contract and as a conveyance of real property.

Types of tenancy. The less-than-freehold estates are of many different types, all closely related. The *estate for years,* in spite of its name, is any estate for a definite period regardless of the length of that period. Technically, an estate for one day is just as much an "estate for years" as is an estate for 999 years. Another type of non-freehold estate, the *tenancy at will,* is created by the express or implied agreement of the parties, but it has no fixed or definite term, and may be terminated at the will of either party. A common form of tenancy at will is the *periodic tenancy.* This tenancy is created by the parties to continue for successive periods of the same length unless terminated by notice at the end of one such period. Tenancies from year to year, month to month, and week to week are examples of periodic tenancies. An original tenancy at will may be construed as a periodic tenancy upon the payment of rent at fixed intervals. Another variety of non-freehold estate is the *tenancy at sufferance*. This type arises when the tenant goes into possession lawfully but holds the property afterwards without any title at all, for example, where a tenant holds over after the expiration of his term. It should be noted, however, that a tenant holding over is not necessarily a tenant at sufferance. If his occupation is wrongful, the landlord may elect to treat him as a trespasser. If the landlord treats him as a tenant, as he may by accepting rent, the tenant holding over may become a tenant at sufferance, a tenant at will, or a periodic tenant, depending upon the circumstances. It is a common practice in some states for the landlord to provide in a lease that a tenant holding over shall become a tenant from month to month at a specified rental. This device is especially useful in areas where there is a sharp seasonal variation in rental values, as would be the case in a summer or winter resort.

Care should be taken to distinguish between the landlord-tenant relationship and the relationship between hotelkeeper and guest. The latter is not a variety of landlord-tenant relation, and it is governed by considerably different rules and principles, in many states largely by statute. A guest merely has the *use* of a portion of the hotelkeeper's premises, but a tenant has an exclusive right to possession. A tenant may maintain such legal actions as trespass and ejectment against third persons invading the premises. A guest cannot. Our concern here is with the landlord-tenant relation.

Attornment. In feudal times, when a lord's interest in land was transferred to another person, the tenants of the first lord went through a ceremony known as *attornment,* whereby the tenant agreed to become the tenant of the new lord and the feudal dues and services were transferred to the new lord. In this sense, of course, attornment has no modern significance. A landlord, however, may sell his property to a third person while a lease is outstanding, and the recognition of the new landlord by the tenant does have some importance. In the absence of contrary provision in the lease, the transfer does not affect the lease, but a tenant who pays rent to the first landlord prior to notice of the transfer is protected from claims for rent by the new landlord. After notice of a transfer, a tenant who pays rent to the old landlord is liable to the new landlord for rent, and a tenant who attorns to a person who does not have title to the property is still liable to the old landlord or to the one who does have title. Furthermore, a tenant who denies his landlord's title and attorns to one without title becomes a trespasser and may be ousted. In many states a tenant caught between the conflicting claims of persons alleged to be his landlord may interplead the competing landlords so as to free himself from possible liability for paying the wrong one.

Leases. A *lease* is an instrument creating the relation of landlord and tenant.

It has a double nature—as a conveyance of an estate in land and as a contract between the landlord and the tenant. Two sets of rights grow out of the landlord-tenant relation—those based on privity of estate and those based on privity of contract. The modern tendency is to construe the lease and determine its obligations in accordance with the rules for the interpretation of contracts, but the real property ramifications are not thus entirely avoided.

No particular form or terminology is necessary to create a lease. It is sufficient in most states if the words show an intention to lease, the names of the parties, and a description of the premises. The important terms, such as rent and the period of the lease, should be included but are not essential. It is wise to note here that most tenancies may be implied from the conduct of the parties and need not be expressed. Some statutes of frauds require all leases for periods of more than one year to be in writing. The requirement varies from state to state, especially with regard to the time period that brings the lease under the statute. In some states, leases are surrounded by formality requirements similar to those applicable to deeds.

In order to be effective as a conveyance of an interest in real property, the lease does not have to be signed by the tenant, but it must, of course, be signed by the landlord. Delivery of the lease to the tenant and his acceptance are sufficient to create the landlord-tenant relation. The tenant's acceptance may be indicated by taking posession or paying rent. Upon acceptance, both the landlord and the tenant become bound under the lease, but, generally, the tenant who has not signed is not bound by any special promises in the lease such as a promise to repair or pay taxes. It is the almost universal practice, however, for the lessee also to sign the lease.

Many states have statutes setting maximum periods for which leases may be created. A lease for more than 99 years, for example, is in some states invalid, and a substantial number of states impose different maximum terms for different types of land or land use. In California, agricultural land may be leased for no more than 15 years, and the property of a minor or incompetent for only 10 years, but town and city land may be leased for 99 years.

RIGHTS, DUTIES, AND LIABILITIES OF THE PARTIES. As with most legal relationships, rights and duties and liabilities accrue to the parties simply because the landlord-tenant relationship exists. Usually, these rights and obligations may be modified or eliminated by agreement of the parties, but in the absence of change by agreement, they come into existence at the same time the relation does. The tenant owes certain duties to the landlord; the landlord, to the tenant. Both parties have certain rights, and on both various types of liability are imposed. Not all of these can be examined in this book, but an attempt is made to outline and examine briefly the important areas.

Estoppel to deny landlord's title. It would be manifestly unfair to permit a tenant, who has gained possession of premises with the consent of the landlord, to question the title of the landlord. Possession gives the tenant certain advantages over the landlord, and the courts will not permit a tenant to assert an ownership inconsistent with his landlord's ownership unless the tenant first surrenders the premises. The theory is simply that the tenant has been entrusted with possession by the landlord and cannot justly dispute the validity of the landlord's title until possession is restored to the landlord. Exceptions are made where the tenant was induced to enter into the lease by the landlord's fraud, where the landlord puts his title in issue, as where he sues to recover the premises, and in a few other situations.

Rent. The consideration for the use of property is *rent,* and the obligation to pay rent arises from a lease or from mere occupancy with consent but without any express agreement. Obviously, in most situations, the rent is of primary importance to both parties, and it is rarely omitted from the lease. In the absence of contrary usage or lease provision, rent is payable at the termination of the successive periods of the holding, but leases almost universally make the rent payable in advance of the periods. Rent may be payable in money, in crops, or in other goods and services. In general, the person who holds title to the property when the rent becomes due is entitled to the rent although the rent may have accrued during a period when this person did not hold title. Rent, in other words, is not apportionable, although some recent cases have apportioned it.

Eviction. The landlord must ordinarily put the tenant into possession of the premises at the beginning of the term, and in every lease there is an implied covenant by the landlord for quiet possession and enjoyment by the tenant during the term. This covenant by the landlord is against his own acts and not against the acts of strangers. An eviction by the landlord is a breach of this covenant.

Eviction may be actual or constructive. Eviction is *actual* when the tenant is actually deprived of possession by the landlord. Actual eviction may be total or only partial. An actual ouster, however, is not necessary; *constructive eviction* takes place where any disturbance of the tenant's possession renders the premises unfit or unsuitable for occupancy, in whole or in substantial part, for the purpose for which they were leased, or where threats of expulsion or attempts to lease to others interfere with the enjoyment of the premises. Constructive eviction may also take place where the landlord enters the premises and makes extensive and unwarranted alterations or where the landlord insults, assaults, or in other ways harasses the tenant.

Where there is either actual or constructive eviction, the tenant may abandon the premises and pay no more rent. Generally speaking, the tenant must surrender possession. He cannot stay on in possession while he refuses to pay rent. On the theory that a landlord should not be allowed to apportion his wrong, however, a tenant who is the victim of partial eviction may usually remain and refuse to pay rent. Where the eviction is accompanied by force and threats, the tenant may recover damages in an action for forcible entry.

Warranty of fitness for use. In the absence of express agreement, there is ordinarily no warranty by the landlord that the premises are fit for a particular or intended use, even though the landlord knows of the use. The theory is that the tenant has the opportunity to inspect and to determine for himself whether the premises are suitable for the use to which he intends to put them. Where, however, the premises are to be built or altered subsequent to the lease, there is an implied warranty by the landlord that they will be suitable for the intended use. In many states, where the property is a dwelling, a statutory duty is imposed upon the landlord to have the premises fit for human occupation.

Repairs. There is normally no duty on the landlord to make repairs to the premises or to keep them fit for the tenant's use. The tenant takes the estate as he finds it, and the duty to keep the premises in safe condition and fit for his uses falls upon him. In many states, however, a statutory duty is imposed upon the landlord, not only to have premises intended for dwelling purposes fit for that use at the beginning of the term, but also to keep them fit for human habitation during the term and to repair such dilapidations, not caused by the tenant's negligence, as may render the premises untenantable. There is a common law warranty to this effect in a few states. Generally, the landlord cannot be forced to perform his duty, and his failure to repair in these circumstances gives the tenant the right to take certain steps on his own behalf. The tenant may give the landlord notice to repair, and the failure of the landlord within a reasonable time to do so permits the tenant to spend some limited amount, usually one month's rent, on repairs, or the tenant may abandon the premises and be discharged from payment of rent and other conditions. The notice is essential, and the tenant's rights under such statutes may be waived by a provision in the lease.

As far as his duty to the landlord is concerned, the tenant is normally required only to use ordinary care in maintaining the premises, but the tenant, by a covenant in the lease, may obligate himself to repair or to surrender the premises in good condition. A simple covenant to repair does not require a tenant to rebuild premises totally destroyed without his fault.

Liability of landlord for injuries. In general, a landlord is not liable to the tenant, his family, or his guests for injuries resulting from defects in the rented property. As has already been seen, the landlord does not owe any duty to keep the premises in safe condition after the transfer of possession, even though he might have discovered the defects through the exercise of reasonable diligence. The person who occupies the premises is liable, to some extent, to guests, visitors, and strangers, but this liability will be discussed later. It is interesting to note that the landlord is not even liable for injuries resulting from the landlord's failure to repair dilapidations of a dwelling house, where the tenant stays on instead of abandoning.

There are some exceptions to the general rule that no liability rests on the landlord: 1. A special promise of the landlord to repair, in the lease, or elsewhere if supported by consideration, may make him liable to the tenant or to the tenant's guests for injuries resulting from his negligent failure to repair. In most states, the landlord is not liable if the tenant knew of the dangerous condition. 2. If the landlord voluntarily undertakes to repair a defect and his work is negligently done or so incomplete that it gives the premises a deceptive appearance of safety, he may be liable to the tenant or to guests for injuries resulting therefrom. The mere promise of the landlord to repair, if unsupported by consideration, imposes no liability. 3. Where the landlord has actual knowledge of defects not known to the tenant nor apparent and the landlord fails to disclose them to the tenant, he is liable both to the tenant and to guests who may be injured by the defects. The landlord's liability is for his failure to disclose and not for his failure to repair; thus, disclosure to the tenant discharges the landlord from liability, and only the tenant would be liable for injuries to guests. Some courts do not require actual knowledge by the landlord. Others impose a sort of duty to inspect for such defects. 4. Where the landlord lets building space to several tenants and retains control over portions of the premises such as the halls, stairways, and roofs, he is liable to tenants and guests who may be injured as a result of the landlord's negligent failure to keep these parts in safe condition. The landlord cannot relieve himself of this obligation by delegating the duties of maintenance to an independent contractor, nor can he escape liability to third persons by an agreement with the tenants. 5. Where the landlord leases premises such as theaters or auditoriums with knowledge that many members of the public will be admitted to the premises, he may be liable to such persons for injuries resulting from unsafe conditions that existed when possession was transferred and about which the landlord knew or should have known.

The law in regard to the liability of the occupier of premises divides persons coming on the premises into two groups: *licensees,* such as social guests, and *business visitors,* which group includes all those who come onto the premises for non-personal reasons. In general, the duty of the occupier toward the former group is to warn them of known hidden defects. The duty toward the latter is more extensive, and it includes the duty to warn them of known dangers and of those dangers which reasonable diligence would have disclosed.

Covenant not to lease to competitor. Often a landlord will promise not to lease part of the same premises or neighboring premises to a competitor of the tenant. This promise is sometimes implied from the circumstances. Such covenants are valid as long as they are not part of a scheme to achieve monopoly and do not unreasonably restrain trade.

PERCENTAGE LEASES. Although most leases provide for what is called a *flat rental,* which means that the amount of the rent is fixed and is paid at an unvarying rate throughout the term of the lease, there are other methods of determining the rent, some of which have substantial advantages over the customary method. *Graded rental,* which is sometimes employed, especially in long term leases, provides for a rent starting at a low figure and gradually increasing during the term of the lease. Where the premises are leased for business purposes, the rigidity of both of these systems of rent payment may prove disadvantageous to both the landlord and the tenant. The fixed rental may become unduly burdensome to the tenant because of the inadequate return he derives from his business and from the use of the premises, or the rental may become completely inadequate to the landlord owing to the increase in the value of the property or the great economic value gained by the tenant from the use of the premises. Because of the inequities that may develop in such situations, there has come into rather common use a lease that bases the rental, at least in part, on the lessee's sales or profits. This lease is generally called the *percentage lease*.

Many different types of percentage leases exist—some in much more common use than others—but all fall into three basic categories. They may provide for a percentage of sales, a share of gross income, or for a share of net profits. It should be obvious in all of these situations that the precise definition of the key words is crucial to the satisfactory operation of the lease. Some percentage leases give the landlord a straight percentage or share with no guaranty on the amount of rent. This type of lease may be unsatisfactory to the landlord if the tenant's sales, income, or profits do not measure up to expectations, and it may be unsatisfactory to the tenant if no maximum is imposed on the landlord's participation. Many such leases impose a minimum fixed rental with a percentage or share rental added. Some leases impose both a minimum and a maximum. Where a straight percentage or share lease is used, the landlord should be protected by a clause permitting him to cancel the lease after a reasonable period of time if the tenant's business is unsatisfactory. The tenant is usually accorded the same privilege. Of course, detailed explanation of the circumstances permitting cancellation of the lease will be necessary in most situations.

A lease providing for rent or additional rent measured by the tenant's sales, income, or profit does not alter the landlord-tenant relation except in regard to the method of paying rent. The lease should be clearly and explicitly drawn so that any possibility of the arrangement's being construed as a partnership or a joint venture will be avoided.

As will be seen immediately below, the tenant's interest in an ordinary lease may be freely assigned or the premises sublet without the consent of the landlord, except where there is a statute or agreement to the contrary. The percentage lease, however, is generally not assignable nor may the premises be sublet. The reason is clear. The rent to the landlord depends upon the success of the tenant's business, which in turn depends upon the personal skill, character, reputation, and responsibility of the tenant. Such a lease is, in essence, a personal contract, and it cannot be assigned without the landlord's consent. Many percentage leases contain a clause to the effect that the lease shall inure to the benefit of "the respective parties, and to their personal representatives, successors and assigns," but such clauses have been held to apply as far as assignment is concerned, only to assignees by operation of law. Consequently, a change in the general rule with regard to the nonassignability of percentage leases requires a clear and explicit statement in the lease.

ASSIGNMENT AND SUBLEASE.   In the absence of an agreement to the contrary, a tenant may assign or sublease his interest in the property. An *assignment* is a transfer of the entire remaining leasehold, and in effect the assignee purchases the leasehold interest. The assignee becomes a tenant of the landlord, and he becomes liable for the payment of rent because the landlord and the new tenant are in privity of estate because the latter holds of the former. Generally speaking, the assignee has the same rights and remedies against the landlord as the assignor had, and the landlord has the same rights and remedies against the new tenant as he had against the old tenant. A *sublease* is a transfer of less than the leasehold with a sort of reversion in the sublessor. The sublessee does not hold of the landlord but of the original tenant.

Effect of assignment.   Where there is no express covenant by the original tenant to pay rent, the implied obligation to pay rent that arises from the landlord-tenant relation and the occupation of the premises by the tenant comes to an end when the landlord consents to the assignment, as by accepting rent from the assignee. Where the lease contains an express promise of the original tenant to pay rent, he does not escape liability for the payment of rent by an assignment and consent by the landlord, and he is liable as a surety should the assignee fail to perform. The explanation for this latter rule is that the landlord's release of the original tenant's contractual obligation to pay rent is ineffective without new consideration. Note the important difference in result between those situations where the obligation to pay rent arises out of the privity of estate and where it arises out of privity of contract.

Where the assignee expressly assumes the obligations of the lease, the assumption agreement between assignee and assignor is for the benefit of the landlord, and the landlord may sue as a third party beneficiary to enforce the terms of the lease against the assuming assignee. The assumption creates privity of contract between the landlord and the assignee to accompany the privity of estate which results from the assignee's occupation of the premises with the landlord's consent. Where the assignee does not assume the obligations of the lease, he is still liable for all the obligations incident to the landlord-tenant relationship and is therefore liable for rent, but he is not liable on the special covenants or promises of the lease unless they happen to be such as would run with the land.

Effect of sublease.   Because the sublease is a transfer of less than the leasehold, most jurisdictions hold that there cannot be a valid sublease of the entire remaining term and that such a transaction purporting to be a sublease is actually an assignment. In some states, however, there may be a sublease of the entire remaining term. A real sublease is subordinate to the main lease, and the sublessee is charged with knowledge of the terms of the main lease. This does not mean that he is bound by its terms but that he cannot complain if some use of the premises or other condition terminates the main lease and brings an end to the interest of the sublessee. A forfeiture of the original tenant's interest will oust the sublessee except where the original tenant voluntarily surrenders his interest.

The sublessee who does not expressly assume the obligations of the main lease is in neither privity of contract nor privity of estate with the landlord. Covenants in the lease cannot be enforced against him, and the landlord has no action against him for the rent. The landlord looks to the original tenant for rent and for the performance of covenants. Where the sublessee expressly assumes the obligations of the main lease, privity of contract is created, and the landlord may sue as a third party beneficiary. But the original tenant is not discharged from his obligations.

Condition or covenant against assignment. Many leases contain conditions or covenants against assignment without the consent of the landlord. An assignment in violation of such a clause is not void but only voidable, and the landlord can waive the breach by accepting rent. The leasehold does pass to the assignee, subject to forfeiture by the landlord. The landlord, in order to bring about a forfeiture of the lease, must do more than give the assignee notice that the assignment is invalid. He must declare a forfeiture and demand surrender of possession. If he does not do this, the assignee may become a tenant in spite of the landlord's refusal to accept his rent payment.

Covenants against assignment are always construed very strictly by the courts because forfeiture is involved. For example, a covenant against assignment does not cover a sublease or even an assignment by operation of law, which takes place on the death of a tenant. Death of a tenant does not ordinarily terminate the lease, and the tenant's interest passes to his heirs and legatees in spite of a covenant against assignment.

A case decided in England in 1578[2] stood for the proposition that a condition against assignment either operates always or not at all. This means that if a landlord once waives the condition by consenting to an assignment, the condition is permanently destroyed. Most modern courts that have considered the problem have taken a different view, but some courts still apply the rule of this case.

TERMINATION OF TENANCY. Unless there is a contrary provision in the lease, a tenancy is not terminated by the death, insanity, or bankruptcy of either party. The expiration of the term, as well as surrender, abandonment, or forfeiture, will terminate the tenancy. Although the word "surrender" seems to have primarily unilateral connotations, it is a bilateral proposition when

---

[2] Dumpor's Case, 76 Eng. Rep. R. 1110 (1578).

applied to a tenant giving up an estate. It really is an agreement, either express or implied, whereby the tenant offers to give up his estate and the landlord accepts. When the surrender becomes effective, the tenant is freed from his obligation to pay rent. It is the landlord's acceptance that separates the surrender from the mere abandonment by the tenant. Ordinarily, mere abandonment does not terminate the tenancy. The landlord's acceptance is required. But in a few situations, as where the landlord has breached a condition, the abandonment will release the tenant from the obligation to pay rent and will, in effect, terminate the tenancy. Forfeiture by the landlord corresponds to abandonment by the tenant. Where a tenant breaches a condition, the landlord has a right to declare a forfeiture. Forfeiture differs from eviction in that the former is done with cause and with right, but the latter is done without cause and gives the tenant, as we have seen, the right to abandon and terminate the lease.

An important problem that exists with regard to abandonment and forfeiture is whether the failure of performance by the landlord or by the tenant is a breach of condition entitling the other to bring the tenancy to an end or just a breach of a promise entitling the innocent party to damages. For historical reasons, the majority rule makes most landlord's promises conditional on the performance of the tenant's promises and covenants, but leaves most tenant's promises independent of the landlord's performance. Thus, a tenant's breach gives the landlord the right to declare a forfeiture, but a landlord's breach only gives the tenant a right of action for damages. The modern trend is to treat all mutual promises as conditional or dependent; thus, it eliminates the double standard for landlords and tenants.

The landlord's acceptance of a tenant's offer of surrender may be express or implied. Where a tenant simply abandons the premises, the abandonment usually constitutes an offer of surrender which the landlord accepts by retaking unqualified possession of the premises. In many states, either because the landlord has a duty to mitigate damages or because he is simply given the privilege of doing so, the landlord may retake possession and relet the premises on the tenant's account. This does not constitute surrender and a discharge of the tenant's rent obligation; it is a qualified retaking, done on the tenant's behalf. The landlord must, ordinarily, give notice to the tenant of the landlord's intention to relet for the tenant's benefit. If the landlord does not give such notice, his repossession is deemed inconsistent with the continuation of the tenant's estate and will result in a surrender. Where the landlord elects to relet on the tenant's behalf, he must usually wait until the end of the term to sue the tenant for damages because only then can the damages be determined. The statute of limitations does not begin to run until the end of the term.

Where the landlord elects to leave the premises vacant and simply recover rent from the tenant, he cannot wait until the end of the term to sue because the statute of limitations begins to run as each rent instalment comes due. Periodic suits will be necessary. The doctrine of anticipatory breach does not apply to contracts to pay sums of money; thus, the landlord cannot recover future rent instalments or the entire balance in advance.

Termination by notice.   If neither party has been guilty of a breach or other act justifying termination by the other and there has been no surrender, the tenancy will continue until it expires. The tenancy for years will continue until the term has come to an end. Tenancies at will and periodic tenancies are terminated by proper notice given either by the landlord or by the tenant. The notice of termination is the normal and necessary means by which these tenancies are brought to an end. In most states, the notice must precede the termination by some reasonable or specified period of time. Thus, an ordinary tenancy at will is terminated by not less than thirty days' notice. In some states, the tenancy may be terminated at any time. Periodic tenancies are commonly terminated by notice given at least as long before the termination as the period on which the tenancy is based. A tenant at sufferance is usually not entitled to any notice.

Possessory actions by landlord.   Where a landlord seeks to regain possession of premises as against a defaulting tenant or a tenant holding over after expiration of a lease, the landlord may institute court proceedings to oust the tenant. In many states, some of the older common law actions available to the landlord have been abolished, modified, or simply supplanted by statute. For example, a common law action known as *distress,* whereby a landlord could seize the personal property of the tenant as security for unpaid rent and even sell the property, has been widely abolished or modified to alleviate its harshness. Many states have *unlawful detainer* statutes that give the court discretion to award triple damages to a landlord whose tenant has held over. Means are also provided for returning actual possession to the landlord, sometimes even before trial of the issues.

E. Zoning Ordinances

A problem that cannot be ignored by anyone who is buying, building, or leasing premises for the conduct of a business or for any other purpose is that of planning or, as it is more commonly called, *zoning. Zoning* is the regulation by districts of the height, bulk, and use of buildings, the use of land, and the density of population. All cities of any size and many counties regulate the uses to which certain property may be put and the kind of structure that may be erected or maintained. Zoning ordinances were not known to the common law. The pros and cons of planning the development of land use in order to assure minimum standards of public health and safety have been topics of vigorous discussion for several generations, but only in the last forty years have public authorities been given the power to impose the restrictions necessary to carry out such planning. The first comprehensive zoning ordinance was enacted in 1916 in New York City. Since that time the use of zoning ordinances has spread very rapidly, especially after constitutional doubts had been resolved by the courts.

Zoning ordinances are exercises of police power by the state or its political subdivisions and agencies, and, as such, they must meet the requirements for the proper exercise of police power. The zoning cases have established the principle that private property rights are relative rather than absolute and that the rights of the owners of private property are subject to regulation for the benefit of the community at large. Under this general principle, the exercise of police power through the zoning ordinance may prohibit future uses of private property and limit existing and established uses. The basic tests of validity are met if the regulations have a reasonable relation to the public welfare and if there is no oppressive, unwarranted, or unreasonable interference with property rights. The wisdom of the regulations is not a matter for the court to determine, but is left to the discretion of the legislative body establishing the regulations. The traditional view has been that police power, and thus zoning ordinances, cannot be exercised for purely aesthetic purposes but must be justified on grounds of public safety, health, or order. But some of the zoning cases indicate a tendency to recognize aesthetic values as well.

The primary limitation on the zoning power is the requirement that it must operate prospectively. If it operates to prohibit present and established uses that are not nuisances, it amounts to a taking of property without due process of law. In many states, this view is carried to the point where there cannot even be an interference with existing or established uses, but other states have permitted ordinances providing for the gradual elimination of non-conforming uses through the prohibition of maintenance, repairs, expansion, and other activities that might prolong indefinitely the non-conforming use.

Every person who is buying or leasing property or buying land on which to erect a building should discover what the legal limitations are with regard to the use of the property and to the height, bulk, and use of buildings erected or to be erected thereon. It should be remembered that zoning and building ordinances are not fixed and immutable for all time. When a buyer acquires a parcel of vacant land that is at the time of the purchase zoned for the use to which the buyer wishes to put the property, he must take into consideration the fact that if the land is not put promptly to the intended use, the zoning laws may be changed so that the intended use will be prohibited.

It should be noted that zoning does not necessarily have anything to do with the maintenance or abatement of nuisances. The common law covers that area reasonably well. A *nuisance* exists when the unreasonable, unwarrantable, or unlawful use by a person of his own property produces material annoyance, inconvenience, discomfort, or harm to other persons or to the public. Nuisances may be stopped by court order or, in some cases, by private abatement by the person or persons injured. It is obvious that the tort law of nuisance does not provide a satisfactory means of planning or zoning the use of land and buildings for the purpose of furthering the health and safety of the public at large. Reliance on the law of nuisance for such purposes would result, at best, in a haphazard elimination of only those existing uses which caused harm or discomfort. Zoning goes much further because it is not confined by the test of harm or discomfort or existing use.

2. PERSONAL PROPERTY

A. Case

(1)

During the night of July 15, thieves entered the lumber storage yard adjacent to the Hypocase factory and removed a large quantity of hardwood boards valued at about $10,000. This lumber was sold by the thieves to the Berkland Box Company, which did not know that the lumber had been stolen. It was a common practice in Anosmia for individual truckers to bring in loads of hardwood lumber from the northern part of the state and offer it for sale to building contractors, lumber yards, and manufacturers. Berkland Box had turned more than half of the lumber into crates and boxes, valued at $25,000, when the thieves were caught and it was learned what disposition they had made of Hypocase's lumber. What right does Hypocase now have in this lumber?

B. In General

In addition to acquiring a site, a person who is organizing a business and beginning its operation must also make arrangements for acquiring his stock in trade, or the raw materials with which he will work, and for the other property that will enable him to conduct a business enterprise. In other words, the beginning entrepreneur must consider not only the acquisition of real property or the use of real property but also the acquisition and use of personal property. He must know something about the legal principles relating to personal property as well as those principles applying to real property. Unlike the law of real property, which has remained through the centuries a more or less integrated body of law, the law of personal property has been standardized and specialized to deal with the requirements of particular aspects of business, and, as a result, it has come to be broken up into a number of separate and almost independent bodies of law. The law of sales, the law of insurance, the law of negotiable instruments, the law of bailments, the law relating to security transactions in personal property, and the law of patents and copyrights are examples of the fragmentation that has taken place in the broad field of personal property. These portions of the law of personal property are dealt with elsewhere in this book in connection with those phases of commerce to which they are most closely related. Discussed here are those aspects of personal property law not considered elsewhere.

In general, personal property is everything capable of ownership, except those things that are real property. As has been already explained, the origins of our common law in the feudal system have caused a greater difference between the laws of real and personal property than could be accounted for by the basic differences between the two types of property. Real property, generally speaking, is immovable; personal property, movable. This basic difference in character would naturally be expected to cause some differences in the law relating to the two types of property. Personal property includes tangible objects that are, themselves, capable of being transferred from person to person, such as a watch, an automobile, or a suit of clothes, and intangible things or rights that are not capable of physical possession or transfer, such as stocks, patents, copyrights, and promissory notes. The intangible forms of personal property are often referred to as *choses in action*. They are not tangible property themselves but usually give their owners the right eventually to enjoy possession of tangible property such as money or goods.

C. Acquiring Title to Personal Property

In General. There are many different ways of acquiring title to personal property. Some of them, such as purchase and sale, will be discussed elsewhere. Our concern here will be with the acquisition of ownership in personal property by accession, confusion, gift, satisfaction of judgment, finding, original possession, and adverse possession.

By Accession. A principle borrowed from civil law is that by which the owner of personal property becomes also the owner of all that his property produces, by the birth of a calf to a cow, for example, and of all that is added or united permanently to the property either naturally or artificially. This principle is called *accession*. Generally speaking, the person who contributes the greater part of the material in the finished product is the owner of the whole. The natural increase in property causes no particular trouble. Most problems arise where property belonging to one person is added to or united with property belonging to another person.

When the owner of materials delivers them to another for the purpose of processing or improving them, the ownership of the materials does not change even though the form of the materials may be altered completely. When the owner of personal property delivers it to another for repairs, the repairman does not become the owner of the property even though he performs services with regard to it or adds parts or other materials. The ownership of the parts and added materials passes automatically to the owner of the property being repaired, but the repairman may have a claim or lien against the whole property to secure payment of his charges. Where, however, a manufacturer engages to produce for a buyer an article out of the manufacturer's own materials, the ownership of the materials and of the produced article remains in the manufacturer until the acts required for transferring title to the buyer have taken place. (See Chapter 10 on the distribution of goods.) If the manufacturer or repairman adds more of his own materials than there is of the other party's materials, the ownership of the whole will usually be in the manufacturer or repairman until title passes in accordance with the law of sales.

More difficult problems arise where one party joins some of his own property to the property of another person without the consent of the other person, or where one party so completely changes the form of another party's property that it loses its previous identity. The solutions to the problems thus raised depend upon several different factors: the intention of the party who does the adding or altering; what constitutes a change of identity; the increase in value resulting from the change or alteration; and whether the article can be converted into its original form. For example: Without *A's* consent, *B* uses *A's* lumber and builds a table. The table, upon completion, is worth ten times as much as the lumber. The court is faced with the problem of protecting *A's* ownership of the lumber while not punishing *B* too harshly for his wrongful conduct. A sharp distinction is drawn in the law between the situations where *B*, knowing that he has no right to do so, wilfully uses *A's* property and where *B* honestly believes that the lumber is his own.

Most courts hold the view that where the wrongdoing is wilful, the wrongdoer acquires no ownership in the property even though he has changed the identity and has greatly increased the value. The owner of the lumber is entitled to recover his lumber in its vastly improved form, and owes no obligation to the improver.

Where the party has acted in good faith, believing that the lumber was his own, most judicial opinion holds that the owner is no longer entitled to recover his property but may recover the value of the property in its original form. However, most courts are quite strict in requiring that the value be substantially increased by the work and the identity of the property be substantially changed. It should be noted that some courts follow the harsh rule that the original owner of the materials is entitled to recover the improved article even from an improver who had no wrongful intent.

The owner of the materials may recover the improved article not only from the wilful wrongdoer but also from innocent parties who purchased the improved article from the wrongdoer. Where an innocent purchaser buys materials from someone who has stolen them or otherwise acquired them wrongfully and the purchaser improves the materials, the original owner usually loses his ability to recover the material in its changed form, but he may recover the value of the material in its original form.

BY CONFUSION. Where the personal property of more than one owner is mixed together in such a fashion that the property of one owner is indistinguishable from that of the other, a *confusion of goods* is said to exist. Property that is of a sort where one unit cannot be distinguished from another is known as *fungible property*. It is obvious that there is no particular problem where the goods of the various owners can be readily separated. Each is entitled to his own goods although one of the owners intentionally caused the intermingling. The one causing the mixture is normally responsible for making the separation, and he acts at his own peril in so doing.

Where the goods are mixed without the consent of the owners and are of substantially the same quality and value, each owner is entitled to his proportionate share of the whole mass. Each owner becomes a tenant in common of the whole mass, and each has an undivided interest in the whole to the extent of his contribution to the mass. Where the goods are of different quality and value, an owner who wrongfully mixes his goods with those of another person loses all of his property in the goods. Where the goods are mixed accidentally, the owners are made tenants in common of the whole mass. No other solution seems possible even though the mixing of the goods may actually depress the value of the whole mass, as the case might be with commingled grains or liquids. If the mixing destroys or depresses the value of the whole mass, it would seem that the party who caused the mixture, even though innocently, should lose his interest in the goods.

In some situations, the best example of which is the grain elevator, the parties actually consent to the mixture of their property. The parties become tenants in common of the mass, and each owns an undivided interest in it. Each owner bears the risks of loss or damage in proportion to his interest in the mass. If one half is destroyed, each owner suffers the loss of one half of his interest. In the case of grain elevators and similar consensual mixings, the separation of the mass is usually accomplished by weight or count and not by a proportion of the mass.

By Gift. *In general.* A *gift* is the voluntary transfer of the ownership in personal property from one person to another without consideration. It is the absence of consideration that makes promises of gifts unenforceable. In order to be valid, a gift must actually be performed or executed. Thus, where *A* promises to make a gift to *B*, *A* is not bound by his promise. But where *A* actually makes the gift, he cannot recover the thing he has given.

Gifts inter vivos. Gifts are usually classified into three categories: gifts *inter vivos,* gifts *causa mortis,* and testamentary gifts. The first type of gift, *inter vivos,* which is made during the lifetimes of the parties, takes effect immediately on the delivery of the property. Delivery of the property is absolutely necessary for a valid gift, and the importance of delivery in this connection is equalled only by the importance of delivery to the effectiveness of a deed of real property. Here, as with the deed, actual physical delivery to the donee is not required. Physical delivery may be made to a third person with instructions to give it to the donee, but such delivery is not effective if the third person is an agent of the donor, because, in the hands of an agent, the property has not really left the possession of the principal. In some situations, no physical delivery of the property is required, for example, where the property is incapable, because of its size or location, of immediate physical delivery. In this case symbolic or constructive delivery is made. For example: Where A delivers to B the key to $A's$ safety deposit box and an authorization to open the box, this symbolic delivery may be an effective delivery of the contents of the box.

Delivery, alone, is not enough for a gift. The other essential requirement is an intention on the part of the donor to make a gift. It is clear that A may deliver property to B for many purposes other than that of making a gift. When the delivery is accompanied by an intention or conduct manifesting an intention to make a present gift, the ownership of the property passes to the donee, and the donor has no further claim on the property.

Gifts causa mortis. Although a gift *causa mortis* is essentially a gift among living persons, it is made in contemplation of the death of the donor and is subject to somewhat different rules than the gift *inter vivos.* The principal difference between the two types of gifts is that the gift *causa mortis* is conditioned on the death of the donor from a present illness or an impending disaster. If the donor does not satisfy the expectations and does not die, he is entitled to recover his property.

Testamentary gifts. The third type of gift is accomplished by a transfer of the ownership of property effective only on the donor's death. A qualified person has the power to dispose of his property by will. The transfer has no effect until the testator dies, at which time the title to the personal property disposed of by the will goes, depending upon the law of the particular state, to the person for whom it is intended, known as the *legatee,* or to the executor or administrator during the administration of the estate and then to the legatee. Where the decedent dies without leaving a will, his personal property descends to those persons specified in the intestate succession laws of the particular state.

By Satisfaction of Judgment. Where a party takes property belonging to another and refuses to return it, the owner has a choice of remedies. He may bring an action to recover his property, or he may treat the wrongful party's act as a conversion and recover the reasonable value of the property. *Conversion* is a tortious interference with a person's right to immediate possession of his property. Although the conversion itself does not affect the title to the property, the owner may, by bringing an action for conversion, getting a judgment for the value of the property, and executing the judgment, put the title in the converter. The title does not pass to the defendant when the suit is filed, although it was once rather commonly held by the courts that the recovery of judgment passed title to the converter on the theory that a person should not at the same time have the ownership in goods and also a judgment for the value of the goods. Most courts today hold that the owner does not lose his title in the property until the judgment has been satisfied.

By Finding. A very interesting, and important, little corner of the law is that having to do with the ownership of lost or abandoned property and with the rights of the finder of such property. Property that has been voluntarily given up or abandoned by its owner without any intention to reclaim it is *unowned property,* and it is subject to acquisition by the first person who accomplishes its possession. Possession may be accomplished by reducing the article to physical control or by owning the land on which the article was abandoned. Ordinarily, the first finder gets the ownership, but under the rules of some states, if the article is on the ground, the first claim goes to the owner of the ground.

Property is said to be *lost* when, by accident, negligence, or otherwise, it is found at some place other than that chosen by the owner. Lost property, unlike abandoned property, is still owned by its true owner. The finder has rights superior to those of everyone except the true owner. The finder may keep the property until the owner has been discovered. Except where found upon the ground, the owner of the premises on which lost property is found has no right to its possession. The finder is obligated to hold the property for the true owner and to exercise slight care for the property's preservation. Statutory provisions in many states alter the above rules, and some states require the finder to take certain steps to discover the true owner.

Mislaid personal property is property placed in a particular location by the owner but then forgotten by him. The mislaying of the property does not affect its ownership. The presumption is that he will, sooner or later, remember where he left the property and return for it. Consequently, the owner of the premises upon which the property is found is entitled, in priority to the finder, to the possession of such property. Again, statutes in many states alter or add to these general rules. Rather arbitrary lines are sometimes drawn between mislaid property and lost property. A handbag left by a customer on a store counter is often said to be mislaid while still on the counter, but it is lost if accidentally pushed to the floor by another customer.

BY ORIGINAL POSSESSION.   Like abandoned property, which has no owner, personal property that is in its native state and has not yet been reduced to exclusive possession by anyone belongs to the first person so reducing it to possession. Wild animals and fish in their native habitat are owned by no one, but when captured, dead or alive, they become the property of the person capturing them. A majority rule finds an exception where the animal or fish is captured by a trespasser on private property. The captured animal or fish belongs to the owner of the property. Should the animal escape and return to its wild state, it is again without ownership. The states and the federal government both regulate the killing and capture of wild animals, birds, and fish, and the common law has been somewhat modified by these statutes.

BY ADVERSE POSSESSION.   As with real property, title may be acquired in personal property by long continued use and possession. The statutory periods required are usually much shorter than those needed to acquire title to real property, but the theory and the general requirements are very much the same. The use must be continuous, uninterrupted, hostile to the true owner, and under a claim of right, for the statutory period. The problems of proof are somewhat different owing to the difference in the basic natures of real and personal property.

PROBLEMS

1. What are the differences between real property and personal property?

2. Is the option contract of any use to a person seeking to acquire a site for the conduct of his business?

3. What is the function of the contract of sale in a real estate transaction?

4. Describe the three basic types of deeds. Under what circumstances will each be used?

5. List and describe the matters essential to a valid deed.

6. What is the purpose of the recording laws? What may be recorded? How do the recording laws operate?

7. Name three methods of acquiring title to real property, other than the deed, and describe each briefly.

8. Outline the various estates in real property and comment on the characteristics of each. Compare the reversion and the remainder.

9. What have the following in common: tenancy in common, joint tenancy, partnership, community property, tenancy by the entireties? Compare tenancy in common with joint tenancy.

10. List and describe four types of marital property interests.

11. What is a fixture?

12. What relief is available to a landowner whose neighbor has built a shed that extends several feet onto the landowner's property?

13. Al has a right-of-way from his land over Ben's land to the highway. Answer the following questions with regard to the right-of-way:

    a. What is the name given to Al's rights in Ben's land?

    b. In what ways might Al's rights have been acquired?

    c. Could Al have a right-of-way over Ben's land if Al did not own the adjoining land?

    d. What name is given to Al's land? What name is given to Ben's land?

    e. Who must maintain the right-of-way and keep it in repair?

    f. Will Al lose his right-of-way if Ben sells his land to Carl?

    g. In what ways may the right-of-way be terminated?

14. Lots 1, 2, 3, and 4 are adjoining lots fronting on Main Street. Lot 1 is owned by *A*, who erected thereon a two-story building which has long been unoccupied and in a state of disrepair. Lots 2 and 3 are owned by *B* and are unimproved. Lot 4, owned by *C*, is also unimproved. One summer *B* decided to erect a tall building on lot 2. Without notifying either *A* or *C* of his intentions, *B* proceeded to excavate lot 2 to a uniform depth of 10 feet. The excavation was made in a careful manner. Because of the firmness of the soil and because he intended to have the foundation completely installed before the fall rains, *B* reasonably believed that it was unnecessary to shore up the sides of the excavation. Shortly after the excavation was completed, an unusually severe summer rain storm occurred and softened the soil. As a result

of the softening, part of lot 1 slid into the excavation causing *A's* building to settle and crack in many places, and a slide occurred on lot 3 and extended several feet into lot 4. Neither *A* nor *C* knew of the excavation until all of the above events had taken place. Discuss the liability of *B* in a state where the common law rules apply.

15. Explain the following terms: escrow, constructive notice, claim of right, color of title, ambulatory, testator, probate, fee simple defeasible, covenant running with the land, attornment, rule in Dumpor's Case.

16. What do the following have in common: tenancy at will, periodic tenancy, tenancy for years, tenancy at sufferance?

17. Is a landlord liable to a tenant for injuries resulting from defects in the property? If so, under what circumstances?

18. *L* is building a suburban shopping center, the space in which he expects to lease to retail stores. Describe the various types of rental arrangements he may use. Describe the circumstances under which each of these arrangements may have certain advantages over the others.

19. *L* and *T* entered into a 5-year lease of certain store premises owned by *L*. The written lease contained a covenant against assignment. After 1 year, *T* entered into an arrangement with *S* whereby *S* was to have the use of the premises. Compare the rights of *L, S,* and *T* where the arrangement with *S* is a sublease with their rights where it is an assignment.

20. Is it true that if a person owns a piece of property he may conduct himself as he pleases on that property? Explain.

21. Outside the provisions of the lease itself, how may a leasehold be terminated?

22. In what ways may title to personal property be acquired?

23. *A* deposited 10,000 bushels of wheat in a grain elevator filling it to its capacity of 100,000 bushels. Shortly afterwards the elevator was damaged by a fire that destroyed all of the wheat except 10,000 bushels, which *A* can prove are largely the bushels which he deposited. What rights does *A* have in the remaining wheat?

24. What should be the policy of a department store with regard to lost and misplaced property found on the premises by customers or employees and turned in to the office?

25. Why are transfers of title to personal property surrounded by so much less formality than are transfers of real property?

part IV

Operating
a Business

THE NATURE OF THE LEGAL PROBLEMS
IN THIS PART

It is difficult, of course, to draw a sharp line between the organization and the operation of a business enterprise. It is virtually impossible in most businesses to point to a time at which the organizing function has been completed and the operating function has just begun. Nor is it possible to distinguish clearly between those bodies of law concerned with the organization of a business and those concerned with the operation. The phases of the business and the bodies of law applicable to them blend and overlap and merge in a way that makes it impossible to draw clear lines of distinction. Actually, the drawing of sharp lines is not necessary, even in a book that purports to do so for the purposes of discussion. But the examination of legal problems in the light of the business situations in which those problems actually arise is necessary. If different business situations create similar legal problems, it is so much the better for the understanding of the law. Contract problems, for example, arise in all phases of commerce and in almost all types of business situations. Because it is necessary to understand the contract and because the contract device is so important throughout the whole field of business law, the law of contract was singled out for discussion before any particular business situation was presented. This has not been done with other bodies of law. Most of them are applicable to more than one type of business situation and to more than one phase of commerce. Some bodies of law are more applicable to one type of situation or one phase of commerce than to others. Thus, although sales problems can and do arise at all stages of a business, the law of sales is most important to the operating phase. Because financing problems arise both in organizing and in operating a business, they are discussed in both connections. What is learned with reference to one stage, however, need not be forgotten in connection with another.

Some bodies or fields of law cannot be assigned to one stage or situation and cannot be dealt with satisfactorily unless their effects on several different phases and situations are noted. Thus, the legal aspects of the forms of business organization are discussed at all stages of the enterprise.

In Part IV, legal problems rising out of employment relationships, the distribution of goods, the use of instruments of credit and security, and the regulation of business by government are discussed. Considerable attention is also given to the special types of legal problems that arise during the conduct of a business simply because a particular form of business organization is used. It will be apparent that in the study of all of these areas an understanding of the contract is a prerequisite.

No attempt is made to appall the reader with the number and variety of legal octopi lurking at every turn to enmesh the unwary businessman or student. Nor is it the author's intention to persuade the reader of the hopelessness of his situation unless he rushes out and hires the best counsel to keep him out of the clutches of these legal monsters. The basic objective is to set forth the legal problems of administering a business in such a way that those problems will be readily and easily recognizable to the businessman or the student. This end is sought to be accomplished by presenting the problems in the context and against the background of typical business transactions out of which they are likely to arise. Emphasis is put on this objective as an introduction to Part IV because it is in the actual operation of a business that legal problems are apt to be least obvious and least frequently subject to expert supervision, and the manager least on guard against them.

chapter 8

Employment Relationships

1. IN GENERAL

Few aspects of the operation of a business create more legal difficulties than that aspect having to do with employment relationships. Two different groups of problems arise here. The first has to do with the essential legal characteristics of the relationship between employer and employee; the second is concerned with those problems that arise, and the legal principles that come to bear, when the employees organize into groups for the purpose of dealing with their employer. The first group of problems and principles is usually referred to as *agency*; the second group generally comes under the heading of *labor relations*. Considerable time will be devoted to the principles of agency law, and time, though less in amount, will be spent in an examination of the important aspects of the law specifically concerned with labor relations. Agency and, to a lesser extent, labor relations are small specialized corners of the broader field of contracts. The law of contracts is basic to both, and neither can be effectively dealt with until contract law is well understood. The importance of agency and labor relations to a consideration of the legal problems of business cannot be overemphasized. Next to the ordinary contract itself, the businessman probably has more contact with these closely related fields of the law than with any other. It is difficult to imagine a business, or, for that matter, an individual, who does not either make use of these fields of the law or come into contact with them when used by others.

The law of agency is largely a matter of common law, and it has been interfered with very little by statute. The law of labor relations, on the other hand, is now almost entirely controlled by statute, both state and federal. This is not to say that there are not statutes in the agency field or that non-statutory law is of no importance in the field of labor relations. Some states have codified their law of agency or modified the common law in certain special situations, and the common law frequently becomes important in connection with labor relations.

Although the field of labor relations is primarily concerned with problems arising from the organization of employees into groups for certain purposes, the field also includes things such as workmen's compensation and employers' liability, social security statutes, and statutory enactments dealing with wages and hours. These and other aspects will be dealt with briefly below.

2. THE LAW OF AGENCY

A. Nature and Usefulness of the Agency Device

(1)

CASE. Hiltel Holton owns a resort hotel in Humble Bay, a small seacoast town in Anosmia. The hotel is open only during the summer months, but is a profitable operation, due to a large and loyal clientele that returns to the hotel year after year. One of the most attractive features of the hotel is a wide porch that completely encircles the hotel and provides lovely views out over the ocean or toward the wooded hills that surround Humble Bay. The hotel has furnished the porch with tables, comfortable chairs, shuffleboard, table tennis, and other recreational facilities, and the porch has come to be the social and recreational center for guests of the hotel. During the last summer season, however, the use of the porch was considerably curtailed by the appearance of many pigeons in the eaves overhanging the porch. Many of the guests told Holton that they would not come to the hotel again unless something was done about the pigeons. Holton and his employees made numerous attempts during the summer to rid the hotel of pigeons but without success. When the season was over, Holton made a trip to Berkland to talk to Frank Peake, the owner of a roofing business, who Holton had been informed was an expert in ridding buildings of infestations of pigeons. As a result of these and subsequent conversations, Holton and Peake entered into a contract whereby Peake agreed to de-pigeon Holton's hotel. Work was begun in April of the following year.

In the course of his work, it became necessary for Peake and his workmen to erect a scaffold around the hotel reaching up to the eaves. The scaffold on the street side of the hotel was negligently put together. As a result of the faulty construction, one of Peake's employees accidentally dislodged a plank from the scaffold, and the plank struck and seriously injured Mary Melton, a passerby using the public sidewalk in front of the hotel. Mary has brought an action against Holton alleging that Holton is liable for the injuries resulting from the negligent acts of his agents.

[See *Hexamer* v. *Webb*, 101 N.Y. 377, 4 N.E. 755 (1886)]

IN GENERAL.   Only a hermit barricaded in the remotest reaches of the high Sierra and completely self-reliant as regards all the necessities of life can avoid contact with the agency device. A person who buys a loaf of bread from a grocery clerk or who takes advantage of the service provided by a streetcar or bus line has dealt with an agent. A person who deposits money in a bank or withdraws it has been in contact with an agency. Both the person for whom another works and the person working are parties to an agency relation. A person who employs another to sell his goods for him has created an agency relation. A corporation can exist and operate only through human agencies. Partnerships and joint stock companies are, in many ways, just special applications of the agency form.

All of these things are true because the agency is the primary device employed in our modern society for the purpose of enabling a single person to project his own ideas and activities beyond the reach of his own voice and conduct. Were each person's activities limited to the things he could do personally, business enterprise and our economic and social organization could not have progressed much beyond the simple village or home industry. No seller could contact prospective buyers except personally. No buyer could buy except from a seller who actually owned the goods he was selling. No corporations would exist because they could not operate if they did come into existence. There would be no partnerships because, if each partner could act only for himself, there would be no advantages to the partnership form of organization. A society in which no person could act for or on behalf of another person would indeed be a simple society. The agency device provides the means by which one person may act for or represent another.

Agency may be defined in a somewhat more technical fashion than was done in the previous paragraphs, and it may be defined more narrowly. Actually nothing is gained by so defining except to call attention to the fact that *agency* is a legal relation whereby one person, called the *agent,* acts for or on behalf of another person, called the *principal.* Some authorities distinguish between the relation of principal and agent, on one hand, and the relation between master and servant, on the other. The distinction is often extremely difficult to make, and there is usually little need for making it. The modern use of the term "agency" includes the relation of master and servant. The general principles and rules of agency law apply with very few exceptions. It has been suggested that, essentially, a servant sells his services measured by time, while an agent who is not a servant sells his ability to produce results. There is no particular reason why this difference should be used to justify sharp distinctions between the two relations. If use of the distinction is made, it is usually for the purpose of indicating that the master-servant relation is a variety of agency where the discretion of the agent is very limited, where the agent's activities are more or less routine or mechanical in nature, where the agent is under the detailed direction and control of the principal, and where the agent is not conducting contract transactions for his principal. Unless otherwise indicated, the discussion of agency in this chapter will be equally applicable to the master-servant relation.

THE BUSINESS PROBLEM.   Before we go on to the detailed discussion of the law of agency, let us first consider briefly the nature of the business problems that give rise to agency issues. The basic problem has already been described: How can one person extend the scope of his activities beyond the reach of his own voice and conduct? The subsidiary problems arise when the agency device is selected as the solution to the basic problem. How may the agency be brought into existence? How far may a person's activities be extended by the use of this device? What is the responsibility of the person employing the device for the acts of the person so employed? What duties and responsibilities do the principal and the agent owe to each other? Let us look at some examples.

X owns and operates a small wholesale grocery. When the business was begun, X knew that he alone could not contact the retail grocery stores that would be his customers, do the purchasing from the manufacturers and packagers who would be his suppliers, load and unload trucks and railroad cars and maintain the warehouse, drive the delivery trucks, and keep the books and records. In other words, X knew that if he was going to operate his business at all, he would have to employ other persons. He hired a salesman, two warehousemen, three truck drivers, a bookkeeper, and a stenographer. The hiring was accomplished and the agency relations brought into existence by means of contracts with the employees involved. There was nothing elaborate about any of these contracts. The individuals agreed to work for X, and he promised them compensation for their services. X wonders how much authority to give his salesman. Should he permit the salesman to enter into contracts with the retailers? If so, will X be liable for a breach of contract if he cannot deliver certain goods the salesman has contracted to sell? If X does not give the salesman such authority, will the retailers be willing to place orders? On inquiring around, X learns that the retailers in his area insist on being able to make contracts with the salesmen rather than placing orders with the salesmen and then having to wait for the wholesalers' acceptances. Competing wholesalers give their salesmen such authority. X decides to do the same. In order to reduce the risk of contracts that X cannot perform, he requires his salesman to report to the office the first thing each morning before beginning his calls to receive the latest information on prices and available stocks. X knows that this is no insurance against contracts made by the salesman that X cannot perform, but X has checked the salesman's references and experience, and feels that he can rely on his judgment. The salesman is using his own automobile to call on the retailers, but X has agreed to pay him mileage for such use. X wonders if he might be liable should the salesman operate the car in a negligent fashion and injure other persons or property.

The duties of the warehousemen are described to them by X. These duties consist of loading and unloading trucks and freightcars, moving and stacking goods in the warehouse, and maintaining the warehouse records. X, who is concerned about his duty to provide safety shoes and other such equipment to the warehousemen, wonders about his responsibility for injuries the warehousemen and other employees may suffer while engaged in their work. Because some of the unloading of goods into the warehouse will have to be done across a public sidewalk, X takes precautions against the possible injury of passersby and instructs the warehousemen to use extreme care in moving goods across the sidewalk. X is still concerned about the extent of his liability should the carelessness of one of his workmen cause an injury to another person.

X is especially worried about his liability for injuries his truck drivers may cause while operating his trucks. Two of the large trucks will be left in the warehouse at night and over weekends and holidays, but X has agreed to let one of the drivers use the small truck for driving to and from work. The driver, who has supplementary duties as janitor, will be driving to and from work at hours when no public transportation is available. X has instructed the driver that the truck is to be used only for deliveries during regular working hours and for the driver's transportation to and from his home.

X plans to do his own purchasing and ordering for a few months, but then he plans to hire someone for the job while X shifts his attention to the sales end of the business. X wonders what sort of authority to give to the purchasing man. Should the purchasing agent be instructed to buy in specified quantities or at not more than specified prices or to bid at distress sales at not more than a specified amount? Would X be bound on contracts entered into by the agent that exceed these limits? If such a contract were made and X were held liable, would he have any claim against his purchasing agent?

During the few weeks in which the firm has been operating, a number of orders have been telephoned into the office by retailers, received by the bookkeeper or the stenographer, and performed by X and his employees in the normal course of business. Furthermore, the bookkeeper has, on several occasions, obtained orders on his own initiative and without X's knowledge or permission. Each time this has happened, X has told the bookkeeper that it would be wise for him to stick to his bookkeeping, but the orders have been filled in the normal way. X wonders if he might be liable on an order solicited by the bookkeeper or received by the stenographer or the bookkeeper, if it were one that X did not or could not perform. Would discharging the bookkeeper necessarily free X of all possible liability resulting from the bookkeeper's actions? X wonders also if he is liable for errors made by the bookkeeper in the records or in income tax and other tax returns.

These problems, and many others suggested by the facts, are primarily problems of agency. They are legal problems that most businessmen must face, either as the principal or as a third party dealing with an agent. Many of them can be avoided by an appreciation of their existence, by an understanding of their legal nature, and by a little forehandedness. Some of the problems are of a particularly insidious nature because they can be drifted into very easily and almost without warning. It is hoped that the discussion below will make the danger areas recognizable, as well as suggest the proper courses of action for avoiding the dangers or for dealing with them when they arise.

INDEPENDENT CONTRACTORS.   The relation between an "independent contractor" and the person with whom he has contracted is sometimes included in the agency area. Unless the term "agency" is defined so broadly that it loses all meaning, this inclusion is not proper. The agent agrees to achieve a certain result for his principal, as the independent contractor does for the other party to the contract, but the principal retains control over the manner in which the result agreed to by the agent is to be attained. The person who deals with an independent contractor does not retain a general right to control the manner in which the agreed-upon result is to be achieved. The independent contractor, furthermore, is employed only to accomplish a certain result and is not empowered to deal with third persons on behalf of, or in the place of, the person with whom he contracted. Usually, it is easy to distinguish between an agent and an independent contractor. A building contractor who has agreed to build a house to certain specifications is not an agent, ordinarily, because the prospective owner of the house cannot control the manner in which the result is to be achieved, because the contractor is not empowered to enter into contractual relations on behalf of the owner, and because neither party intended to enter into an agency relation. A traveling salesman, on the other hand, although he is remote from his employer, is under the direction and control of the employer, who tells him where and what and how to sell the employer's products. In addition, the very purpose of the salesman's job is to enter into business relations with third persons on behalf of his principal. There are always borderline situations where the distinction is hard to make, and these situations can only be dealt with by applying in the most reasonable manner possible the guides and tests set forth above together with the aids described in the next paragraph.

In general, it is not the *exercise* of control over the agent but the *right* to control which is determinative. A certain amount of freedom may be inherent in certain types of employment, but this is not necessarily inconsistent with an agency relation. The fact that a person is engaged in an occupation separate and distinct from that of the other party may be evidence that the person is an independent contractor and not an agent, but there are many who have distinct callings yet are employees and agents of corporations and business firms. A person who furnishes his own tools and equipment is more likely to be an independent contractor than an agent, but this fact is not conclusive. The custom of the trade or community may also have a bearing on the decision as to whether or not a person is an agent.

Unlike the line between the relations of master-servant and principal-agent, where the difference is seldom important, the line in regard to independent contractors is a significant one in several situations. As will be seen later, a principal is personally liable for the tortious acts of his agent committed while the agent was acting within the scope of the agent's employment, under the doctrine of *respondeat superior,* but the person who employs an independent contractor is, generally speaking, not liable for the torts of the contractor, however committed. An independent contractor cannot receive compensation under workmen's compensation laws, and he does not come under the provisions of unemployment insurance acts and similar statutes. A person utilizing the services of an independent contractor does not have to withhold federal income taxes from the contractor's compensation, as he would have to do for most agents and employees under the definitions of the Internal Revenue Code.

Note that the term *agent,* denoting an actor, doer, force, or power that does things, is not confined to the law but is also found in use in such phrases as chemical agents and reagents, catalytic agents, therapeutic agents and many others.

TYPES OF AGENTS. Agents can be classified only in the broadest of terms because there are almost as many different types of agency as there are persons creating such legal relationships. One classification, which has no particular significance except to call attention to the very wide scope of agency, is that of *general agents* and *special agents.* The latter represents his principal in special, narrowly defined ways such as selling a particular piece of property. The general agent, as his title implies, represents his principal generally—for example, managing the principal's business or taking care of all of the principal's financial affairs. Basically, the legal rules and doctrines applied to both types are the same.

Some agents have distinct titles that serve to identify the nature of the function they perform. A *broker,* for example, is a special agent whose primary function is to act as a sort of go-between for two parties—a buyer and a seller. Sometimes the authority of this type of agent is so special that he has only the power to bring the buyer and seller together, as is usually the case with real estate agents or brokers. The broker rarely has possession of his principal's property. A *factor,* on the other hand, is an agent employed by the principal to sell goods actually consigned or delivered to him for that purpose. Where a factor, also known as a *commission merchant,* guarantees to the principal to pay the price of all goods sold by him even if the buyer defaults, he is known as a *del credere* agent. *Consignment,* also, is a variety of agency. It is frequently used as a device by which a seller may retain control of his goods until they have actually been delivered into the hands of the buyer, and by which the seller may retain control over the price at which the goods will be resold. Because the use of the device tends to increase the consignor's inventories, it is not suitable to trades in which the keeping of large inventories in the hands of many consignees would be unnecessarily expensive or burdensome. The Fair Trade Laws, in some states, provide another means by which resale prices may be controlled, and the consignment device is now less popular for that purpose. (See Chapter 14.)

PURPOSES FOR WHICH AGENCY MAY BE CREATED. We have already defined the agency as a legal relation in which one person acts for, or on behalf of, another. By altering this definition slightly, light is thrown on another aspect of the agency device. *Agency* is the relationship whereby the principal empowers the agent to do what the principal could legally have done himself. Or, to put it still differently, anything that a person may legally do himself, he can delegate to an agent to do for him. There are a few exceptions to the rule stated in this fashion, such as voting, marriage, and making a will, but this is the general test of the purposes for which an agency may be created. Anything that a person cannot legally do himself is not capable of being delegated to an agent.

B. Creation of the Agency

(1)

CASE. Hypocase, Inc., employed A. L. Norton as its district sales manager in Chicago, the best market in the country for pallets. The job called for supervision of 7 to 10 salesmen and a small office force of 3 or 4. The district manager had considerable authority, including complete authority to hire and fire salesmen and office employees in his district. Norton received a salary plus a percentage of the total sales made through the Chicago office. Norton entered into a contract with Art Kale whereby Kale was to be Norton's successor as district manager in Chicago and was to receive the same salary and percentage of sales that Norton had been receiving. Kale resigned another position to take the Hypocase job. When Vance Parker, vice-president in charge of sales, heard of the change that had been made in Chicago, he telephoned Kale and told him that Norton had no right to employ Kale as district manager and that Hypocase owed Kale nothing for his services in Chicago. Kale has brought suit against Hypocase for salary, percentage of sales made while he was acting as manager and damages for breach of contract.

(2)

CASE. During a toy dealers convention in Los Angeles, Don Danton, one of the partners of SIMUCO Toyland, learned that a small bicycle manufacturer in Detroit was going out of business and planning to put his inventory of 650 bicycles up for sale the next week in lots of 50. Danton was interested in buying 50 bicycles, but did not want to go all the way to Detroit. When he expressed these feelings to Chuck Ryder, a toy dealer acquaintance from St. Louis, Ryder said that he was going to Detroit anyway and would be glad to do Danton a favor and bid in one lot of bicycles for him. Danton expressed his appreciation to Ryder and said: "I won't have to go to Detroit then. Bid up to $35 each. I'll return the favor some day." Ryder went to Detroit, bid in 3 lots of bicycles for himself at $27.50 a bicycle but bought none for Danton. Do Danton and SIMUCO have any rights against Ryder?

IN GENERAL. Although three parties, principal, agent, and a third person, are required before an agent may enter into business transactions for his principal, only two parties, principal and agent, are necessary to create the agency relation. In most situations, the agency is created by means of a contract between these two parties, but the agency may also be created by other means.

WHO MAY BE AN AGENT. Whatever method is used to create an agency, the legal capacity of the two parties comes into issue. Any person who has the legal capacity to act for himself may also act for others. As a matter of fact, full legal capacity is not required of an agent. A minor may be an agent, as may an alien or even an insane person. The basic reason is simple: the agent acts not in his own capacity but for the principal in the principal's capacity. The contract that the agent makes for his principal runs not between agent and third person but between principal and third person. Even if a minor agent, for example, disaffirms his contract with the principal, the contract between the third person and principal is not affected. The courts say that an agent must possess some capacity to act as an agent, but it is not clear how much. It would probably be proper to say that a person who has the capacity to understand the nature of the transaction into which he is entering has the capacity to be an agent. Actually, serious problems of an agent's capacity seldom arise.

WHO MAY BE A PRINCIPAL. The problem of the capacity of the principal is not as easily solved. Of course, a person with full legal capacity may be a principal. At the same time, a person who has no capacity to contract for himself cannot enter into contracts through an agent. In between lies an area in which the courts do not agree. The problem of the minor as a principal is a good enough example of the difference of opinion. A minor does not have full legal capacity to enter into contracts, but most minor's contracts are voidable, not void. This means that a minor may enter into contracts that are valid and binding except for the right of the minor to disaffirm them. It would seem that this same general idea would be applied to the minor's contracts of agency. Many early decisions, however, took the view that a minor's contracts of agency were utterly void when the minor was seeking to be the principal in the relationship. The reasons given were: the third person, because he did not confront the principal face-to-face, had no notice or warning that he was really dealing with a person of limited capacity; and the disaffirmance by the minor of the contract of agency also acts to disaffirm all contracts made by the agent on the minor's behalf. Many courts still follow this view. The modern view holds that minors' contracts of agency are to be treated as any other minors' contracts. Because the contract executed by the agent for a minor is the contract of the minor, it may be disaffirmed, under this view, in the same fashion as if the minor had negotiated the contract personally.

A corporation may of course be a principal, as a partnership may. A married woman, in almost all states, may be a principal. An unincorporated club or association, other than a partnership or stock company, cannot be a principal, but the members may delegate authority to an officer or to another member as an agent of the joint principals so delegating. Note that where a court appoints a guardian for the person or property of a minor, no agency relation is created between minor and guardian. Whatever the circumstances or the rule to be followed, a principal with limited capacity cannot do things through an agency that he could not do directly.

SUB-AGENTS AND DELEGATION OF AUTHORITY BY AN AGENT.   An agent may not, as a general rule, delegate his authority to someone else without express permission of the principal. If he does purport to do so, the persons to whom he delegates authority become his own agents and not the agents of the principal. The principal is not liable for their wages or salaries or for their acts, and the principal may have a claim against his own agent for any damages the principal may suffer by reason of the agent's unauthorized conduct. The reason for these rules is sound. The principal selects an agent on the basis of his personal qualifications and puts trust and confidence in the agent's judgment and discretion. If an agent delegates his authority to someone else, the relationship of trust and confidence based on personal knowledge is broken. The agency would not be a very popular device under these circumstances. An exception to the rule is frequently recognized where the duties delegated by the agent are purely mechanical or ministerial in character and no exercise of discretion is needed by the person to whom the duties are delegated. This person becomes the agent of the agent and has no claim against the principal for compensation, but the principal's own agent has not violated his duties by the delegation. The salesman for the grocery wholesaler discussed above could probably employ a boy to carry his sample case without violating the salesman's duties to his principal, but the salesman would clearly be violating his responsibilities if he attempted to transfer to another person his authority to enter into contracts on behalf of his principal. In neither situation would the grocery wholesaler be liable for any compensation to the persons employed by the salesman, nor would he be liable on contracts made by these people. He might be damaged, however, in his relations with his customers by the acts of the sub-salesman.

The authority of the agent to delegate to another may be found in the express grant of the principal or may be implied from the nature of the circumstances. In either case, the person to whom the authority is delegated becomes the agent of the principal and not of the agent, and as such he is entitled to the same rights and is obligated by the same duties as if the principal himself had done the delegating. No particular problems, except of interpretation, exist where a principal gives his agent express authority to delegate to another. Such authority in the agent may be implied from custom; from the nature of the agent's duties, e.g., a person given the general authority to manage a store or a business; or from necessity, as where the particular acts required cannot be performed by the agent. Where, however, the agent attempts to delegate the exercise of discretion, skill, or trust without express or implied authority from the principal, the delegation is improper.

METHODS OF CREATION. *By contract.* An agency relation is usually created by a contract. The principal and agent enter into a contract of agency just as they would enter into any other contract, and the usual requirements for a valid contract must be met. Many different names are given to the contract of agency: employment contract and power of attorney, to mention just two. No particular formalities are required for the agency contract, and it is just as valid in oral form as it is in writing, with an exception that will be noted later. The contract may be very explicit in its terms—delegating, describing, and detailing the agent's rights, powers, duties, and authority with great particularity. Or it may be very general—outlining in very broad terms the nature of the agent's duties and authorities. Where a general agency is created by a contract, the parties must depend upon the custom and usage of the trade, the duties and powers of agents in similar positions, and the duties and authorities implied from the nature of the contract.

The contract basis for most agencies serves to emphasize the voluntary nature of the agency relation. A person cannot make himself the agent of another person except in accordance with the desires of that other person, nor may one person compel another person to be his agent. There can be no agency without the express or implied consent of both parties.

The exception to the general rule that the contract of agency need not be in writing is called the *equal dignities rule,* which was discussed in connection with the statute of frauds in Chapter 3. It is based on the idea that the dignity of the agent's authority should be the same as the dignity of the thing the agent is authorized to do. If the agent is being authorized to enter into contracts that must be in writing because of the statute of frauds, then many states follow the rule that the authority of the agent must be in writing also. In states where the seal still has a contract effect, a similar rule is applied with regard to the authority of the agent to enter into sealed contracts. Exceptions to the equal dignities rule are set forth in Chapter 3.

The creation of the agency relation does not depend on compensation for the agent or even on an agreement to compensate the agent. Many agents act gratuitously without affecting the authority of the agent to represent his principal. If there is no consideration for the prospective agent's promise to be the agent of the principal in the future, there is, of course, no binding force to the promise. When the agent actually undertakes to transact business for the principal, however, the agency relation arises. For example: *P* asks *A*, who is going to the city anyway, if *A* will take some of *P*'s chickens to the city the next day and sell them at the best price he can get. *A* agrees to do so. At this stage there is no contract, because there is probably no consideration for *A*'s promise to take the chickens, as well as no agency. *P* could recover nothing from *A* should *A* fail to take the chickens to the city the next day. Where *A* appears and takes the chickens from *P*, an agency does come into existence, and *A* is obligated to take the chickens to the city, to exercise his discretion in getting the best price for them, and is further obligated to pay over the proceeds to *P*. The explanation in this case seems to be that a contract of agency came into existence when *P* turned the chickens over to *A*. The consideration for *A*'s express or implied promise was the reliance of *P* on the promise, under the doctrine of promissory estoppel. The chickens had been entrusted to *A* in reliance on *A*'s promise, and to say that there was no obligation on *A* to perform his promise would be to fly in the face of fairness and to contradict the intention of the parties. Some authors explain the result by saying that it is one of the peculiarities of agency that the binding effect may occur without a contract.

By estoppel. Perhaps the following paragraphs can be more easily understood if we add to our tools of analysis the recognition of a possible difference between an agency-like liability and an agency relation itself. Some take the view that only by contract can a genuine agency relation be created, but that agency-like liability can be brought about in other ways. It should be noted that some of the ways in which agency-like liability may be created can also be used to create additional authority where an agency relation already exists. These ways will be discussed in greater detail in the latter connection.

The principal may create the impression or appearance of an agency where none really exists. Where the principal does so and a third person reasonably relies on the conduct as manifesting the existence of an agency, the principal may be estopped to deny that there is an agency. An *estoppel,* as has been pointed out before, is a bar raised by the law. It precludes a person from denying a certain fact that his previous conduct has led others to rely on because they believe it to be true. Estoppel does not really create an agency relation, but it may bring about agency-like liability.

By ratification. Where a person acts for another without authority, and the other later confirms the act by word or by conduct, the act is said to be *ratified.*

The effect is to supply authority for the act, to impose agency-like liability, and to make it binding on the person ratifying. The details and requirements for ratification will be considered below in connection with the creation of additional authority.

By operation of law. Although the voluntary acts of the parties may serve as the basis for all the other methods of creating an agency or agency-like liability, not by the remotest stretch of the imagination can these acts be found underlying the agency or agency liability created by *operation of law*. In a few situations, the law may raise an agency result, even where it is directly contrary to the intentions of the parties, and even over their objections. Some authors confuse this creation of an agency by operation of law with the extension by emergency of actual authority already existing. This aspect of the problem will be discussed below in connection with actual authority. In some states, however, the agency itself may be created by operation of law, for example, where a husband fails to support wife or children and the wife or child becomes entitled to purchase necessaries as the agent for the husband. In many states, this result is not explained as an agency device at all but as the application of the common law rule imposing liability on the husband or father who fails to support his family.

C. Operation of the Agency:
Principal or Employer

(1)

CASE. The Admiral Oriental Line had been employed by the Atlantic Gulf & Oriental Company as ship's agents in the Philippines and had fitted out the steamship "Elkton" on a voyage out of Pulupandan, on which she was lost with all hands in a typhoon. The ship had been entrusted to the AGO Company by its owners. The owners of the cargo lost on the "Elkton" sued Admiral for their losses, a suit which Admiral won but at considerable expense to itself. Admiral now seeks to recover these expenses from AGO.

[*Admiral Oriental Line* v. *Atlantic Gulf & Oriental S. S. Co., Inc.,* 86 F.2d 201 (1936)]

(2)

CASE. The Metropolitan Club, an incorporated organization, owns a large clubhouse in the downtown section. A portion of its building was rented to a restaurant company doing business under the name of "Cafe des Arts." A salesman for Hopper, McGaw & Co., a restaurant supply firm, obtained an order from the assistant manager of the restaurant company, who told the salesman to charge the goods to the club. The salesman did so under the mistaken belief that the club owned and operated the restaurant. For a period of six months, goods were ordered by employees of the restaurant in the name of the club. Bills for these goods were mailed monthly by Hopper to the club, where they were opened by the bookkeeper, whose duty it was to open and sort all mail and deliver bills to the offices for approval of payment. The restaurant bills, however, were simply turned over by the club's bookkeeper to the bookkeeper for the restaurant. All of the bills indicated that the orders had been placed in the name of the club, and several indicated that restaurant employees had receipted for the goods on behalf of the club. The restaurant paid the bills for the first two months and went out of business at the end of the six month period. Hopper is now suing the club for the unpaid bills.

[*Metropolitan Club* v. *Hopper, McGaw & Co.,* 153 Md. 666, 139 A. 554 (1927)]

(3)

CASE.   Because of his good taste in music, Reel Gruvy, a junior clerk in the purchasing office at Hypocase, Inc., had been authorized by du Buy, the purchasing agent, to buy phonograph records for the public address system which broadcast music during the employees' lunch hour. Gruvy had purchased records on a number of occasions at Berkland Music Store and charged them to Hypocase. The bills were submitted and paid in the ordinary course of business. In October, Gruvy purchased 4 new records from Berkland Music Store, charging them to Hypocase as usual, and also purchased a new record player for $159.50, charging that also to Hypocase. When du Buy found out about the record player, he severely reprimanded Gruvy and told him he had no authority to buy anything except records. A new record player was needed, however, and du Buy approved the payment to the music store when the bill came in at the end of the month. In December, Gruvy purchased some records and a remote control attachment from Berkland Music Store, charging the purchases to Hypocase, and purchased a new amplifier and 5 records from Bridge-to-Music, Inc., charging these purchases also to Hypocase. Is Hypocase liable for these December purchases by Gruvy?

(4)

CASE.   Gude du Buy, the purchasing agent for Hypocase, Inc., entered into a contract with Knute Schur to purchase for $5,000 several used woodworking machines which du Buy thought belonged to Schur. Actually, the machines belonged to Umberto Post who had authorized Schur to sell the machines for him. In spite of the prior contract with Hypocase, Schur found another buyer willing to pay $6,000 for the machines and sold and delivered them to him. Hypocase had sued Schur for breach of contract and actually obtained a judgment against him before it was discovered that Schur was only acting for Post. It is unlikely that Hypocase will collect anything from Schur, who became a voluntary bankrupt shortly after the Hypocase judgment against him. Can Hypocase pursue Post?

(5)

CASE. One morning, in early December, shortly before the store had opened for business, Earl Eaton, one of the partners in SIMUCO Toyland, sent Rod Hotspur, a young man who worked part time for SIMUCO, to the airport to pick up a shipment of Swiss music boxes that had been ordered by SIMUCO and had arrived the evening before. Eaton told Rod to take the store's pick-up truck on the errand and to return immediately, as Eaton wanted to get the music boxes unpacked and on display in the store before he had to devote all of his time to the rush of Christmas shoppers. Rod drove to the airport, a distance of about 10 miles, and picked up the crate of music boxes but, instead of returning directly to the store, Rod drove to his own home, about two miles away from the most direct route to downtown Berkland where the store was located, to pick up his lunch, which he had forgotten that morning when he left for work. After he picked up the lunch, he started back to the store. On the way, however, he engaged in a race with another truck and, while trying to pass the other truck at high speed, he collided headon with an automobile driven by an elderly woman, Liti Gant, seriously injuring her. Rod was cut and bruised but was otherwise unhurt. He told the investigating officer that the accident was all his fault. Miss Gant has filed suit against SIMUCO Toyland and all of the partners for $75,000.

IN GENERAL. The best way to examine the operation of the agency device is to approach it from the point of view of each of the three important parties: the principal, the agent, and the third person with whom the agent deals. Seen through their eyes, the duties, rights and liabilities that the agency relation creates will be more vivid and more accurate. Furthermore, the reader who is interested in the problem from one particular point of view can concentrate on that point of view to the temporary exclusion of the others. Some duplication will necessarily occur because what is a right in one of the parties is likely to be a duty in another.

Each of the relevant parties is interested in his rights, and in his duties and liabilities to the other parties. All of these areas will be considered. The principal or employer is particularly concerned with the power of the agent, by his acts, to create liability for the principal, either in contract or in tort. Much of the discussion about the principal will be devoted to this topic.

DUTIES TO THE AGENT. Although the most important duties run in the opposite direction, from the agent to the principal, the principal does owe to his agent certain duties, an understanding of which is very useful in getting a clear picture of the true nature of the agency relation. Some of these duties arise simply because a contract exists between the two parties, but others are present because of the agency relation.

Duty not to breach the contract. This duty is not peculiar to the contract of agency, and no detailed discussion of it is required. However, there is a belief in some circles that the principal may discharge the agent with impunity even though there is a contract between them. This, of course, is not true. If the contract calls for the employment of the agent for a fixed period of time or until the completion of a particular task, a discharge by the principal before that time is up or before the task is completed is a breach of contract unless the agent's own conduct is such as to excuse the principal from further performance of his own promises. These conclusions should not be interpreted to mean that the principal *cannot* discharge the agent. What they do mean is that the principal cannot discharge the agent *with impunity,* if the discharge is a breach of the contract of agency. With the exception of the "agency coupled with an interest," which is discussed later, the principal may discharge the agent whenever he pleases, but not necessarily without liability. The principal may also incur liability if he fails to perform other portions of the contract that have nothing to do with the discharge.

Duty to compensate the agent. Except where the agreement or the conduct of the parties indicates that the agent is acting gratuitously, the principal has a duty to pay the agent for his services. Of course, in most agency situations, the compensation is provided for in the contract of agency, and the promise to pay the agent is the consideration to support the agent's promise to perform certain services for the principal. Where provision for compensation is not made in the contract, the principal is not relieved of his obligation to compensate the agent but is obligated to pay the agent the reasonable value of his services. Such reasonable value is a question of fact to be determined by the jury.

A special situation exists in connection with the employment of certain types of agents, such as real estate agents and brokers, where the principal may employ several agents at the same time. For example: *A* lists his house for sale with several different real estate agents. Ordinarily, the agent who produces the buyer is the one who becomes entitled to the compensation; or, if the owner sells the house himself, no agent becomes entitled to compensation. Some of these agency contracts, however, will specify that the agent with whom the house is listed is entitled to the compensation no matter who sells the house. This kind of contract creates what is called an *exclusive agency*. The purpose of such an agreement is usually to confine the owner to the employment of only one agent. If the owner does employ another agent and that agent produces the buyer, both agents become entitled to the commission. Ordinarily, in the absence of an express provision to the contrary, the owner may sell the house himself without having to pay the "exclusive agent" a commission, but many contracts contain this contrary provision. Contracts with real estate agents should be examined in detail to determine which kind of contract is being entered into.

Depending upon the agreement and custom in the trade, an agent's compensation may consist of a wage or salary, a commission, a fee, a share in the profits, or a combination of these. Where the agency is created to accomplish some limited purpose, the compensation is usually in the form of a commission or a fee.

In the event of a wrongful discharge of an agent or employee, the party discharged does not have the privilege of standing by idly for the remainder of the contract period and of collecting the full contract compensation as damages for the principal's breach. Although this has not always been the rule, the contract duty to mitigate damages is now generally applied to the innocent party in this situation. The imposition of this duty requires the agent to seek other employment in the same locality and in the same line of work. (See Chapter 3.) Where he is wrongfully discharged, the agent may choose from among several remedies. He may wait until the expiration of the contract period and sue for his damages, less what he earned in mitigation thereof. He may treat the contract as rescinded and sue for the reasonable value of services rendered. In some states, the wrongfully discharged agent may sue at once for prospective damages during the remainder of the contract period. Many states do not permit this last choice on the ground that it is too speculative.

Duty to reimburse the agent. The principal has a duty to reimburse the agent for all sums spent by the agent in the principal's behalf while acting within the scope of his authority. Thus, an agent is entitled to be reimbursed for travel and similar expenses that are paid by the agent in reasonable and necessary amounts in connection with the performance of his duties. The terms of the contract may alter the duties of the principal under this rule. An agent who expends money while acting outside the scope of his duties or authority is not entitled to reimbursement. A real estate agent, in the absence of contrary provision in the contract, is not entitled to reimbursement for money expended on advertising or on other expenses incurred in attempting to find a buyer.

Duty to exonerate the agent. In addition to the principal's duty to repay the agent sums the agent has already expended on behalf of the principal, a duty also arises to step in and pay losses or liabilities the agent has incurred while acting as directed by the principal. The transaction must have been legal, or at least not known to the agent to be otherwise. *Exoneration* or *indemnity* carries with it a connotation of paying off a liability before the agent must pay it; but *reimbursement* means the repayment of sums already expended. Where *P* negligently directed *A* to cut timber on certain land that *P* neither owned nor had the right to invade, *P* was compelled to exonerate *A* for the liability in trespass incurred by *A* to the owner of the land. Had *A* himself known or had reason to know that the act was wrongful, his right to exoneration would probably not have arisen.

Statutory duties. Statutes, both state and federal, impose on employers duties such as the maintenance of safe and healthful working conditions, payment of minimum wages, and the recognition of properly qualified unions as representatives of the employees. These problems will be discussed in greater detail in Section 3 of this chapter.

Agent's lien.   Where a principal becomes indebted to an agent on a valid claim based on any of the duties set forth above, the agent has a lien on the principal's property that is in the agent's possession. This lien consists of the agent's right to retain possession of the principal's property until the principal's indebtedness is paid. The agent's lien is not, as a rule, a very extensive one. The lien consists only of a right to retain the property but not to sell it, and it is usually limited to claims arising in connection with that particular property. The details vary somewhat from state to state. (See Chapter 13 for a discussion of liens.)

LIABILITY OF THE PRINCIPAL ON CONTRACTS.   The principal's liability on contracts made for him by the agent with third persons depends primarily upon the power of the agent to make his principal liable. Thus, the relationship between the principal and the third person and the liability of the principal to that third person can be approached only through a discussion of the agent's powers. It is often said that the agent represents his principal for all purposes within the scope of the agent's actual or apparent authority. The statement is true, but it leaves much to be desired in outlining the total area that must be considered here. It is somewhat more illuminating to say that the agent's power to bind the principal in contract may be found in at least three different places: in the agent's actual authority, in apparent authority or estoppel, and in ratification. Brief comment will be made below about a possible fourth source of the agent's power to bind his principal in contract.

Actual authority—express or implied.   In the ordinary agency situation, much of the agent's authority to act for his principal is conferred upon the agent expressly by the terms of the agency contract. Additional authority is conferred upon the agent by implication or inference from the terms of the contract. If the terms are so clear that no implication or inference is necessary, the authority is said to be *express actual authority*. If the terms are more general in nature and implication or inference is required, the authority thus resulting is called *implied actual authority*. Note that both are "actual" authority. The link binding the express and implied actual authority together and separating them from "apparent" or "ostensible" authority is the fact that actual authority, whether express or implied, is intentionally conferred on the agent by the principal. A principal who gives his agent "authority to manage my business" would usually intend, though he does not say so expressly, that the agent would have whatever authority is reasonably necessary to carry out the task assigned, and this implied authority is just as real as if it had been set forth expressly. Implied authority may result from a previous course of dealings between the same parties, or it may be based on the customs and usages of the particular trade or type of agency. The law implies, in the absence of a contrary showing, that the principal intended the agent to have the authority to do everything necessary, proper, or usual in the ordinary course of the transactions that are the object of the agency.

If there is no conduct of the principal that might create apparent authority or an estoppel, and if there is no ratification, the agent can bind his principal only within the scope of his actual authority. Therefore, the burden is upon the third person to ascertain the extent of the agent's actual authority. This may be done by examining any documents of authority the agent may have in his possession or by inquiring of the principal. The agent's own representations are, of course, valueless for this purpose. The burden on the third person to determine the actual authority of the agent does not require a long interrogation of the principal. The point is simply that the third person cannot complain if he fails to get a contract with the principal because of the agent's lack of actual authority. The third person must decide for himself, on the basis of his investigation, whether the agent does or does not possess particular authority. The fact that he did investigate does not assure the third person of getting a binding contract with the principal. If the contract has been ratified or if apparent authority is present, a binding contract results not from the agent's actual authority but from other sources, and of course the duty of the third person to ascertain the actual authority no longer has any bearing on the problem. The principal's conduct may actually have lulled the third person into foregoing any investigation of actual authority.

The degree to which a principal will make the authority of his agent specific varies from situation to situation. Only very rarely will a principal be able to set forth an agent's authority in sufficient detail that nothing is left to be determined from custom, usage, or implication from the terms of the agency contract. Because the authority of some types of agents is so clearly established by the customs or usages of their trade, it is not necessary for a principal to be specific at all. Probably in most situations the principals will describe the agent's authority in general terms leaving the details to be supplied by the rule that an agent has that authority reasonably necessary to carry out the purposes of his employment. In the absence of a contrary showing, it must be assumed that the principal intends his agents to have that authority. If the principal desires to limit the authority in some way, or to give the agent authority that would not be needed for his normal duties, or to make clear authority that might otherwise be in doubt, the principal should set forth his intentions specifically. Where the agent is being given the authority to bind the principal to contractual relations with third persons, it is particularly important that the principal be familiar with the authority agents of the same type have under similar circumstances. The principal will not be heard to complain where the agent has exercised authority possessed by similar agents but which this principal did not intend his agent to have, unless the principal has specifically limited his agent's authority and this limitation was known or should have been known to the third person with whom the agent dealt. The drafting of agency contracts is a task to which careful thought should be given even where the contract will finally appear in the broadest and most general of terms.

An additional type of actual authority is one which is implied as a result of an emergency. If an emergency exists, an agent may even violate his express instructions if it is clearly in the interest of the principal to do so. No emergency exists, however, unless there is insufficient time for the agent to communicate with his principal. An emergency, when it does exist, is not a *carte blanche* to the agent to violate his instructions freely. The emergency gives the agent no greater authority than is necessary to meet the emergency. The driver who has been instructed never to take passengers in his principal's delivery truck may, if circumstances permit, do so in order to take to a hospital a third person injured by the agent's negligence. This act is in the principal's interest because he is liable for the negligent acts of his agent committed while the agent is acting within the scope of the employment, and the damage may be increased if the driver delays in getting the injured third person to the hospital. But the agent would not have the authority in this situation to contract with a doctor on behalf of the principal to pay $1000 for services rendered to the injured man.

Apparent authority. Let us assume that, unnoticed by any employee or officer of the *X Bank, A,* an impostor, has slipped into one of the empty teller's cages and has spent several hours accepting deposits from customers of the bank. When *A* feels that he has accumulated sufficient cash, he quietly departs. The persons who made deposits at *A's* window are somewhat perturbed when those deposits do not appear on their monthly bank statements, and they demand that the *X Bank* credit their accounts for the amounts deposited with *A.* One does not have to be a lawyer to see that the bank will have to do so, but what is the legal explanation? It is obvious that there is no "actual authority" of any kind. *A* was not an agent of the bank for any purpose; there are no grounds for implying an intention on the part of the bank's management that *A* should have authority to accept deposits. What has been illustrated here is a kind of *apparent authority.*

The basic idea with apparent authority, sometimes called *ostensible authority,* is simply that the principal by his intentional or careless conduct has caused or allowed a third person to believe that another person has authority as an agent of the principal when actually that person does not have such authority. As pointed out previously, either the power of a non-agent to bind the principal, as in the bank example, or additional authorization to a person already an agent, may be created by apparent authority. There are no important differences between the two situations. However, one should be careful not to confuse apparent authority with implied authority, which is a form of actual authority intentionally given to the agent by the principal. It may be helpful to conceptualize implied authority as what the principal manifests to the agent and apparent authority as what the principal manifests to the third person.

An essential element of apparent authority is, of course, some conduct by the principal. If there is no conduct of the principal on which the third person may rely, no problem of apparent authority exists. This does not mean that the conduct of the principal must be affirmative. Negative conduct or inaction, as was the situation in the bank case, is sufficient for apparent authority. The bank carelessly allowed an impostor to occupy the teller's cage. Conduct of the agent, no matter how strong or unequivocal it may be, cannot establish the basis for apparent authority. The third person is not justified in relying solely on the conduct or representations of the agent. The conduct of the principal must be such that it would lead a reasonable person, in good faith, to believe that the agent had authority. If A, the impostor, had presented himself at the front door or office of one of the bank's customers and had represented that he had authority from the bank to accept deposits, it is clear that the gullible depositor would have had no claim against the bank.

In order for apparent authority issues to arise, even more than conduct of the principal is necessary. The conduct must be known to the third person, and the third person must reasonably rely on that conduct. Generally, it is also required that the third person be injured before he may take advantage of the doctrine of apparent authority, but the authorities disagree on this point.

Although the underlying idea is essentially a simple one, there is a great deal of confusion in the law in connection with apparent authority. Many courts treat it as being nothing more than an application of the doctrine of estoppel. Under this view, apparent authority serves only to estop a principal to deny the authority of the so-called agent where the principal's conduct has led a third person to believe that the agent had authority; and the issue can arise only where the third person seeks to enforce a claim against the principal. Another group of courts looks upon apparent authority as genuine authority and not as an estoppel at all. These courts do not estop the principal to deny the existence of the authority; they say that there *is* authority. The practical difference between the two views is that, in the former view, apparent authority becomes an issue only in actions by the third person against the principal, but in the latter view, the principal may also enforce claims against the third person just as he could have done if the agent had possessed actual authority. In the former situation there is no contract between the third person and the principal, while in the latter there is a contract that may be enforced by either party.

A special problem arises in situations where a principal has entrusted an agent with possession of his, the principal's, property. The problem is whether the entrusting of the property alone is enough to create in the agent apparent authority to sell the property. The Agency Restatement takes the view that the entrustment alone is not enough. The agent must also be entrusted with some evidence of ownership, such as a bill of lading or a certificate of title, or there must be separate grounds on which to base an apparent authority to sell, as where some goods are turned over to an auctioneer or to a professional selling agent.

The discussion above should also make it clear that secret limitations imposed by a principal upon the authority of his agent will not be binding on a third person where custom, usage, or prior course of dealing is inconsistent with these limitations.

Authority of the agent in special situations. In some particular types of situations, long usage and many court decisions have crystallized the law to the extent that it can be said with certainty just what implied and apparent authority will result from a given set of circumstances. For example: Although the implied authority which goes along with the authority to manage a business is quite extensive, there are certain things which the agent does not usually have the authority to do except where expressly authorized. Among these are the power to borrow money; the power to sell or mortgage the premises in which the business is carried on; the power to engage in a new or different business; the power to issue negotiable instruments in the principal's name, except for checks in payment of ordinary business debts; and the power to dispose of all or part of the business. The authority of an agent to borrow money, incidentally, is an authority rarely implied, and, then, only under the most unusual of circumstances.

An agent's authority to sell land usually includes only the authority to find a purchaser; it does not include the authority to make a contract for the sale of land. The latter authority must be granted expressly. In any case, the contract of agency to sell land or to make a contract to sell land must be in writing and is, therefore, available for the inspection of the third person.

In many situations, the rights of a party may hinge in whole or in part on notice or lack of notice to that party of certain facts. Special problems are raised with regard to the effect which notice to the agent has on the principal's rights. The general rule is that notice to the agent is notice to the principal. This means that the principal will be held to have had notice even though his agent never actually informed the principal. Of course, the notice, in order to bring about this result, must have been related to the subject matter of the agency and received or acquired by the agent while he was acting within the scope of his authority. Thus, notice to a department store clerk of a pending legal action against the store is not notice to the store. Notice to an agent before he became an agent is generally not notice to the principal.

Ratification. When a principal confirms a prior act of an agent performed without authority, he is said to ratify that act. Where an agent who is authorized only to contract to sell the heavy industrial equipment that his principal manufactures purports to enter into a contract to sell small domestic appliances that his principal also manufactures, no binding contract exists between the buyer and the principal because there is no authority in the agent. However, if the principal undertakes to perform the contract, or indicates in some other way his intention to do so, he has ratified his agent's prior unauthorized act and has made it binding on himself. The ratification may be express or implied from the conduct of the principal. If the ratification is express, it is not necessary that it be made to the third person, who expected all along to get a binding contract and who should not be unduly surprised to learn that he has succeeded. The express ratification may be made to the agent, or, in the case of a corporation, it may simply be entered in the minutes of the directors' or shareholders' meeting. Implied ratification may result from the performance of the contract by the principal, from the principal's acceptance of the benefits of the contract, or from the principal's suing on the contract. Mere silence by the principal after learning of the agent's unauthorized act will not normally constitute ratification, but silence, when combined with other facts and circumstances, may result in ratification.

Requirements for ratification. Although probably a truism of little value, it is a fact that ratification will not become an issue in a situation where there is authority, actual or otherwise, but in some cases the proof of ratification might be easier than the proof of apparent authority.

The principal must have been competent to enter into the contract at the time it was made by the agent. If not competent at that time, the principal cannot later ratify. In those states where a minor cannot be a principal, a contract, made without authority by an agent for a minor principal, cannot be ratified by that principal even when he reaches majority. Where a person purporting to act for a corporation enters into a contract on behalf of the corporation before it comes into existence, the corporation cannot ratify the contract after it is organized. The corporation may become a party to the contract, however, by an entirely different process known as *adoption*. Of course, the principal must be competent also at the time he purports to ratify.

The principal must confirm the entire transaction. He cannot ratify those portions that benefit him and refuse to ratify those that impose a burden upon him. If the principal does not ratify the whole act, he does not ratify it at all.

In general, the principal cannot ratify a contract unless the agent *intended* to act for that particular principal and unless he also *purported* to act for him. In some courts, however, it is not necessary that the third person understand that the agent is acting for any particular principal or for any principal at all. It is the universal rule that if A intends and purports to act for P, D cannot ratify a contract made by A with T.

A ratification is not effective to bind the principal unless at the time of ratification the principal was in possession of all of the facts material to the unauthorized transaction. A principal who ratifies without full information may rescind the contract, except where he ratifies with careless or intentional disregard for the facts. If a principal rescinds, he must, of course, return any consideration he received unless he is unable to do so through no fault of his own.

Effect of ratification. When a principal effectively ratifies an unauthorized contract made on his behalf by an agent, the defect of lack of authority is cured, and the contract becomes effective *as of the time it was made,* not as of the time of the ratification. This phenomenon is known as *relation back*. The ratification makes the contract in all respects what it would have been had the authority existed at the time the contract was made. It is said that relation back is necessary in order to supply authority at the time and place it was needed. Authority supplied on July 1st to make a contract on June 1st would be ineffective except through the doctrine of relation back. However, the relation back will not be allowed to interfere with another person's rights acquired after the unauthorized transaction and before the purported ratification. Where an agent without authority contracts to sell his principal's property to T, and the principal, without knowledge of that contract, sells the property to D, subsequent ratification by the principal cannot deprive D of his rights in the property and the ratification would be ineffective. Some courts have held that ratification will not be allowed to defeat the claims of creditors who have levied on the property after the contract was made and before the purported ratification.

Position of the third person. There are at least three different views applied to the status of the third person who has become a party to an unauthorized contract. The best of these views holds that the third person may withdraw from the contract any time before ratification, and that after ratification the third person is bound as though the authority had been present from the beginning. Another view takes the stand that not only is the third person not bound before ratification but he is not bound even after ratification unless he "accepts" the ratification. This view is difficult to defend, and, if followed, would, for all practical purposes, cause the concept of ratification to disappear. Another view, sometimes called the *English view,* takes the approach that the principal should have a reasonable time after being informed of the unauthorized contract during which to make up his mind whether or not to ratify, and that the third person is bound during this reasonable time. Between the making of an unauthorized contract and the expiration of a reasonable time, the third person is bound, but the principal is not. This view gives the principal more of an advantage than can be justified under the circumstances. The first view is the fairest of the three.

As mentioned earlier in this chapter, ratification may supply authority where no agency at all existed, or it may simply add authority where there was already an agency relation. No substantial differences exist between the two situations, and no distinction is made between the two in the above discussion.

In addition to taking heed of the matters discussed above, especially in regard to getting full information before attempting to ratify, the principal must take into account the effect his ratification may have on future events. The problem is this: A principal who ratifies the unauthorized acts of his agent without making known to the third parties that the acts of the agent were unauthorized and that the principal is simply ratifying acts which would not otherwise be binding on the principal runs the risk of creating apparent authority to bind the principal. Without such notification, the third person may be found by the court to have been justified in believing that the agent had authority to bind his principal to these contracts that the principal had always performed without comment.

Power theory. In order to explain a number of situations in which principals have been held liable even though an agent acted without actual or apparent authority, a theory has developed that bases the principal's liability on a *power* arising from the agency relationship.[1] Section 172 of the Agency Restatement sets forth one of the possibilities under this theory:

> Unless otherwise agreed, a disclosed or partially disclosed principal who author-izes a general agent in the regular course of his employment to issue documents representing chattels or choses in action if an event happens or a specified fact exists, the happening or existence of which is peculiarly within the knowledge of the agent, is subject to liability to purchasers of such documents who have no notice that the agent improperly issued them.

In the now famous case of *Gleason* v. *Seaboard Air Line Ry. Co.,*[2] an agent was employed by the defendant railway company to carry out the rather simple task of notifying consignees of goods shipped on the railroad that their goods had arrived at the particular terminal in which the agent worked. The necessary information, routine though it was, was peculiarly within the knowledge of this agent. By forging and negotiating a bill of lading and by falsely notifying the consignee that goods under this bill had arrived, the agent caused the consignee to lose $10,000. The consignee brought an action against the railway company. The Supreme Court held for the plaintiff on the ground that the principal had put into the hands of the agent the power to accomplish this unfortunate result while still apparently acting within the scope of his authority. While the agent's motives were wrong and some of his acts fraudulent, it was the simple authority he possessed to notify consignees that made possible the harm to the plaintiff. The consignee was entitled to rely on the accuracy of the notice of arrival received from the defendant's agent. Although the Gleason case was itself a tort action, the Restatement has carried over the power theory expressed in that case to contract situations as well.

It is only fair to point out that not all courts follow the power theory or the views of the Restatement and the Supreme Court.

DISCLOSED, PARTIALLY DISCLOSED, AND UNDISCLOSED PRINCIPALS. In addition to the authority of the agent, the status of the principal himself is also an important factor in determining the nature and extent of the principal's liability on contracts made for him by his agent. The status with which we are concerned here is the disclosure of the identity and existence of the principal to the third person. A principal is said to be *fully disclosed* when the third person knows not only that there is a principal but also knows the identity of that principal. A

---

[1] Restatement, Agency, Section 140.
[2] 278 U.S. 349 (1929).

principal is *partially disclosed* when the third person knows that he exists but does not know his identity. A principal is *undisclosed* when the third person does not even know that there is a principal or that he is dealing with an agent; the third person believes that he is dealing with the principal party. It should be obvious that apparent authority dwindles in importance where the principal is only partially disclosed, and it virtually disappears where the principal is undisclosed. And, as mentioned above, most courts do not permit an undisclosed principal to ratify an unauthorized contract made on his behalf by the agent. The reason for that rule is the usual requirement for ratification—to the effect that only the person for whom the agent purported to act can ratify the contract made by the agent. If the principal is undisclosed, the agent could not have purported to act for him.

Contracts of disclosed principal. Little need be added here to what has already been said in the last several pages concerning the liability of a disclosed principal on contracts made for him by his agent. The principal is liable on all contracts made for him by the agent while the agent is acting within the scope of his actual or apparent authority or where the contract is later ratified by the principal. Of course, the third person is also bound by such contracts.

Contracts of partially disclosed principal. The rules applied to the partially disclosed principal are almost identical with those applied to the fully disclosed principal. The principal is liable on contracts made for him by an agent acting within the scope of the actual or apparent authority. Ratification is possible only in those states where effective ratification does not depend on the agent's purporting to act for a named principal. The third person in these partially disclosed principal situations knows an agency exists, but he does not know the identity of the principal who is the other party to the contract to which the third person is now bound. Because the third person entered into the contract voluntarily without requiring the disclosure of the identity of the other party at interest, the courts will not listen to his complaints that he has become liable in contract to someone whose identity he did not know at the time the contract was made.

Where the contract arranged by the agent is a negotiable instrument, a rule of negotiable instruments law, which holds liable on negotiable instruments only those persons whose names appear thereon, frees the principal from liability. Obviously, if the principal's name appears on the instrument, he is a fully, not a partially, disclosed principal. Most courts also prevent the principal from enforcing such an instrument, but some recent cases have permitted the enforcement by the principal. In any event, there may be liability for the principal on the underlying obligation even where there is no liability on the negotiable instrument itself. This discussion of the negotiable instrument applies with equal force to the situation where the principal is undisclosed. Sealed instruments, in states where the seal still has a contract effect, are subject to much the same rules.

The use of either the partially disclosed or the undisclosed principal device need not raise issues of unfairness or sharp dealing. There are many perfectly legitimate reasons why a principal may want to keep his identity or his existence a secret. Furthermore, the courts will not permit the use of the devices in order to accomplish a fraud or an unfairness. Knowledge of the identity of a principal may enhance the consideration to the point where a contract is impossible, as might be the case where one of the large insurance companies is acquiring land on which to build a group of apartment buildings or offices. Where a party is dealing with an agent known to be such but does not know and cannot ascertain the identity of the principal, the party is under no obligation to enter into a contract. If the principal's identity is of sufficient importance to him, he will refuse to enter into contractual relations until he finds out who the principal is.

Contracts of undisclosed principal. In this situation, the agent enters into a contract without disclosing to the third person that he is acting in a representative capacity or that he is not the principal party at interest. In general, the principal may enforce such contracts, and he is bound by them in spite of the fact that this means the third person has become a party to a contractual relation he neither sought nor anticipated. This result also seems to run counter to the basic principle of contract law—that contractual relations are voluntary and rise out of the agreement of the parties. The result is, nonetheless, well established, and is not without reason. In only a few situations will the imposition of the rule be harmful to the third person, and these situations are exceptions to the rule, as will be seen below. The third person has recourse against the agent, which recourse was sought and intended by the third person, but he also has recourse against the principal. Consequently, the third person is compensated for his being liable to a person whose contract he had not sought by being given recourse against a person whose liability he had not contemplated. Furthermore, the general rule about undisclosed principals offers a great convenience to principals who wish to remain unknown during the negotiation of a contract. Frequently, the disclosure of the principal party will complicate the negotiations, or, because of the affluence of the principal, will unnecessarily increase the consideration.

There are several specific exceptions to the general rule that an undisclosed principal may claim the benefits of contracts made for him by his agent.

1. The first of these occurs where the contract is a negotiable instrument or a sealed instrument and has already been referred to in connection with partially disclosed principals.

2. The second, and more important, exception occurs where the third person, either expressly or impliedly, makes it clear that he intends to deal with the agent and with the agent alone. The explanation for the exception is that the third person is entitled to rely on the representations of the agent about the identity of the other party to the contract and is deceived when the agent does not disclose the fact that there is another party. The third person may rescind in such a situation. Where the third person does not state expressly that he will

not be bound to anyone except the agent, the surrounding circumstances may justify an implication of that intention, as is generally the case where the contract is of a personal nature. If the skill, credit, character, discretion, or other personal quality of the agent is involved in the contract, the principal acquires no right enforceable against the third person. If a person is interested in further protection against undisclosed principals, he can always ask the parties with whom he deals whether or not they are acting in a representative capacity. If an agent for an undisclosed principal answers falsely, the misrepresented fact is usually considered to be of sufficient materiality to lay the groundwork for fraud and later rescission when the principal is discovered. If the agent answers truthfully, the party is under no duty to proceed further with the negotiations.

3. Another exception occurs where the third person had already settled with the agent when he discovered that there was a principal. Settling with the agent *after* discovering the principal will not be a defense to a suit on the contract by the principal.

Generally speaking, the third person has available against the principal all the claims and defenses that the third person would have had against the agent. Thus, where the agent was in debt to the third person at the time the contract was made, the amount of this debt may be set off against the principal's claim just as it would have been against the agent's claim. This rule does not apply where the principal is fully or partially disclosed.

Note that the parol evidence rule does not apply to evidence introduced to show that the agent who signed a written contract was simply acting for the principal. The third person may show that the principal was the real party at interest and seek recourse against him. Note also that the requirement of the statute of frauds that the contract, or some note or memorandum thereof, must be signed by the party to be charged does not apply here. Most statutes of frauds contain the phrase "party to be charged *or his agent*."

Election by the third person. Where there is an undisclosed principal, the third person has a choice of holding the agent or the principal. Obviously, the third person cannot recover from both, and he must, at some stage, elect between them. Two distinct situations present themselves: First, where the third person is pursuing legal action against the agent without knowledge of the principal, at what stage is he barred from bringing an action against the principal when his existence is discovered? Second, assuming that the third person knows of the principal, at what stage must he make an election whether to hold the principal or the agent? The first situaion is more easily dealt with. The only absolute bar is satisfaction of the third person's claim by the agent. Thus, where a third person gets a judgment against the agent and the judgment is only partially satisfied when the principal is discovered, the third person is not barred from suing the principal. If the discovery is made after complete satisfaction, the third person is barred from bringing an action against the principal.

The courts do not agree on the solution to the second situation suggested above. Some hold that there is no bar under any circumstances until satisfaction, even though the third person knew of the principal at earlier stages. Others take the view that if the third person knew of the principal at the time he brought the suit, filing an action against either the principal or the agent is a bar to a suit against the other. A third view is that no election need be made until judgment. If the principal is known at time of judgment, the third person must elect, and the election is final once there is a judgment against either principal or agent. In some states, the third person may join principal and agent in the same suit, but he must usually elect between them before judgment.

LIABILITY OF PRINCIPAL IN TORT. There is probably no rule in the law of agency which seems more correct in general, but for which it is so hard to find an entirely satisfactory explanation, than the rule of *respondeat superior,* by which the principal is made liable for his agent's torts. The old common law explanations were: first, that the principal and agent were really one, and second, that what one does through another he does himself. Neither of these makes very much practical sense in connection with torts. Another explanation, which has some basis, is that a person who expects to derive advantage from an act done for him by another must answer for injury caused by the other's act. The lack of care by the principal in selecting his agent cannot be an explanation because lack of care is the principal's own wrong, for which he is responsible anyway, and because the principal is held liable under *respondeat superior* where there has been no lack of care on his part. Another theory sometimes advanced is that the principal, having selected the agency as a method of extending his own activities, must assume the risk of injury caused to third persons during the operation of that agency. This explanation is a widely accepted one, and is reasonably satisfactory. It becomes more satisfactory, however, when used in conjunction with the view that the public as a whole is best served by imposing liability upon the principal as well as upon the agent. The latter view is based on several ideas: 1, the principal is better able to spread the risk, as by insurance or by an increase in price; 2, the principal will exercise more control over the agent if the principal is liable for the agent's tortious acts; 3, the principal will be more inclined to introduce safety devices, training courses, and other steps calculated to gain safe operation of the principal's instrumentalities. It should be noted that the principal's liability does not relieve the agent of liability for his own torts. Furthermore, if the principal is held liable for the agent's wrong, the principal has a claim against the agent for the agent's violation of his duty to be careful. (See later discussion of agent's duties.)

Whatever the explanation for the rule, the rule is nonetheless well established that a principal is liable to third persons for harm caused to them by the torts of the agent acting within the scope of his employment. Of course, the principal is liable for torts that he authorizes or directs the agent to commit or that the principal later ratifies, but these torts, after all, are the torts of the principal as well as of the agent, and there is nothing unusual about a person being liable for his own torts. Our concern here is with those problems arising when the agent commits torts without the authority, knowledge, direction, or consent of the principal. A thorough discussion of these problems would have to assume considerable knowledge of the law of torts. Consequently, our treatment is confined to the agency aspects of the problems and all but basic tort concepts are ignored.

Some authorities insist that the liability of a master for the torts of his servant is different from the liability of a principal for the torts of his agent. What these authorities perceive as a difference in rules governing liability in the two situations is usually only a manifestation of the fact that principals are much more likely to be held liable for the torts of agents who are under their close personal control or supervision or who use the principal's instrumentalities. The difference has more to do with the scope of employment than it does with any basic difference in the relationship or in the law. The discussion here will use the broader terms of principal and agent.

Although much of the discussion below is of peculiar relevance to the principal employing agents who drive trucks or other vehicles, the discussion also applies to agencies where the automobile tort is of no importance. An agent, too, may be guilty of torts other than negligence. Assault, battery, and deceit are also torts an agent may commit, for which a principal may become liable. It should be recognized here that the principal has much less control over the legal problems of an agent's torts than he does over many of the other problems of agency that have been raised in the paragraphs above. Of course, a principal can use care in the selection of his agents and may attempt to minimize his tort liability by carefully training and instructing the agents and by using mechanical safety devices, where possible, to reduce the human element. Detailed study may also be devoted to the cost and coverage of insurance protection against the tort risks. But although a principal can make a provision in the agency contract for most of the legal problems we have been discussing, this kind of foresight is not of much use with tort liability, except as suggested in this paragraph.

Scope of employment. A principal is not liable for every tort his agent commits. With few exceptions, the principal is liable only when the tort was committed while the agent was acting within the scope of the activity he was employed to carry out. Thus, a principal is not liable for the injury done to a third person by the agent's negligent operation of his own vehicle on his own time. While the agent is going about the principal's business the negligent operation of the principal's vehicle would create liability for the principal if injury is caused to a third person. In both situations, the agent would himself be liable. Obviously, it is very difficult to define with any degree of accuracy the phrase "scope of employment." Whether a particular act is within the scope of an agent's employment is a question of fact. Sometimes the fact is easy to determine;

at other times, it is difficult. There are factors, however, considerably helpful in making the determination, and these can be examined.

The first thing to note is the significance of the fact that the word "scope" is used. *Webster's Dictionary* defines *scope* as "the range in which an activity displays itself." The word is not used by accident in connection with the agent's employment. The purpose is to indicate that the employment within which the agent may make his principal liable in tort is not the "straight and narrow" or the closely defined limits of the agent's employment but a "range" or "area" surrounding the "straight and narrow." The fact that an agent was, at the time of the commission of a tort, violating the instructions of his principal does not necessarily absolve the principal of liability. Many factors must be considered in determining the extent of the range within which the agent's tortious acts may impose liability on his principal.

Among these factors to be considered are: 1. How much deviation from the "straight and narrow" has there been? Absolute figures, in miles or hours, do not provide much of value unless they are compared with the total length of the trip or with the time required to complete a particular activity. A fifty foot deviation in a five hundred mile trip, where for example, a truck driver pulls off the highway to buy a pack of cigarettes, is not very much of a deviation, and it would probably still be within the scope of employment. A fifty foot deviation where there was to be no trip at all might be a substantial deviation, for example, where a clerk in a store leaves the premises and crosses the street.

2. Which direction was the agent going at the time of the tort? Was he on his way back to the "straight and narrow" or away from it?

3. What was the agent's intention at the time the tort took place? Was he intending to carry on his principal's business, or was he intending to do something for himself?

4. Did the tort occur on the principal's premises, or while the agent was using the principal's instrumentalities? Different weight is given this factor in different courts. Some authorities say that if the agent is not carrying on the principal's business, the fact that he is on the principal's premises or using his instrumentalities is not significant. Others take the view that the principal is liable for the torts of the agent whenever the agent is on the principal's premises or uses the principal's instrumentalities, such as automobiles or trucks, *and* the principal can control *and* knows, or has reason to know, of the necessity for controlling the agent.

In a few states, including California, New York, and Michigan, the unusual mobility of the automobile and its substantial capacity for harm have been recognized in statutes that impose upon motor vehicle owners liability for the tortious harm caused by the vehicle, regardless of who was driving it at the time harm was caused. Exceptions are made where persons, such as thieves, drive the vehicle without the express or implied consent of the owner, and the amount of liability of the owner is limited to maximum figures set forth in the statute, except where the owner himself was operating the vehicle. A few states follow what is called the *family purpose doctrine*. This imposes liability on the owner of a motor vehicle where harm results from its negligent operation by members of the family. The doctrine is based on an implied agency, which is of course completely unintended in most cases. Better results are obtained through the statutory approach. Statutes are becoming increasingly important in regard to automobile torts.

5. Was the deviation from the "straight and narrow" expected by the principal? Where the deviation by the agent is intended or expected by the principal, such deviation may still be within the scope of the employment. Where a bill collector or a private detective sends one of his operatives to collect a bill or to gather evidence, he may reasonably expect the agent to use harsh or aggressive methods in order to carry out his employment. Debtors injured in fights with collectors have been allowed to recover from the principal on the theory that such occurrences are within the scope of the agent's employment because the principal may reasonably expect language and acts by the agent that will lead to altercations.

Some principals feel that they can escape liability for the torts of their agents by instructing the agents to be careful and not to commit torts. If this view were accepted by the courts, the average citizen might be a little reluctant to leave the safety and protection of his own home. A principal may contract with a third person to absolve the principal of some liability for harm that may result from his own acts or the acts of his agents. The rules vary somewhat as to the extent to which liability may thus be limited. In general, an ordinary person can contract to exempt himself from liability only for ordinary negligence but not from gross negligence or wilful wrong; an employer cannot contract to relieve himself from liability for injuries to an employee; a party charged with a duty of public service, such as a common carrier, cannot contract to exempt itself from liability for negligence where it has received or has been promised compensation. Before entering into contracts that contain limited liability clauses it is wise to check the local law in this regard. This admonition is directed as much at those who write such clauses into contracts as at those who are asked to enter into contracts containing them. Where the defendant is being sued as a principal for the acts of his agent, the limitations of liability, even though otherwise valid, will not always apply. (See the more detailed discussion of contractual limitations of liability in Chapter 3.)

The principal is ordinarily not liable for the intentional wrongs of his agent, but if taken too literally, this rule may be grossly misleading. It is based on the theory that when an agent commits a wilful or malicious wrong, he is acting for himself and not for his principal. Obviously, this is not always true. The agent may be seeking to further his principal's interests through the wilful wrong. If this is the case, the principal should be held liable, and most courts would so hold. For example: A bus driver, who is being prevented from maintaining his time schedule by the driver of another vehicle who refuses to let the bus over-take, forces the other vehicle off the road or assaults the driver of that vehicle at the next highway stop. The bus driver may be furthering his principal's interests in maintaining the schedule; thus, he may make the principal liable for his, the agent's, intentional wrong.

A principal is not liable, ordinarily, for his agent's crimes. Liability for most crimes requires criminal intent as a necessary element, and a principal, unless actually directing or participating in the commission of a crime, would lack the necessary intent. A few exceptions are found in connection with statutory crimes, such as the sale of liquor to a minor or the possession of illegal drugs, where the public interest in preventing the crimes is so strong or the problems of enforcement so great that a person may be subjected to the statutory penalty without criminal intent or even knowledge of the crime.

LIABILITY FOR TORTS OF INDEPENDENT CONTRACTOR. Because an independent contractor is not an agent, the person who employs an independent contractor is not liable for the contractor's torts committed in the performance of his work. There are a few exceptions to the general rule. In most of the cases alleged to demonstrate exceptions to the rule, however, the liability of the employer of the independent contractor is or could have been based on the employer's own negligence. Some of the exceptions are:

1. Where the tort resulted from the contractor's incompetence and the employer was found to have been negligent in selecting the contractor.

2. Where the injury resulted in whole or in part from the negligence of the employer.

3. Where the tort resulted from the maintenance by the contractor of a public nuisance on the employer's premises, as, for example, an unguarded or unlighted excavation.

4. Where the work to be done by the contractor is extra-hazardous or inherently dangerous, as, for example, the use or storage of blasting materials in a populous locality.

There appears to be a trend, however, toward the extension of liability for the acts of independent contractors to some situations where fault on the side of the employing party is difficult or impossible to establish.

D. Operation of the Agency: The Agent

(1)

CASE. Bill Stryker is one of Gude du Buy's assistants in the purchasing department of Hypocase, Inc. Stryker has recently been made responsible for the purchase of all non-manufacturing supplies and equipment. He had discovered that with his new job go many invitations to lunch and dinner offered by representatives of suppliers trying to get the Hypocase business. On several occasions he has been asked to bring his wife along for the evening and has done so. Stryker looked on these invitations as nothing more than simple business courtesies, which most of them were. One day, however, the representative of a large supplier with whom Hypocase had long done business offered to split his commissions with Stryker on any purchases made from that supplier by Hypocase. Stryker resisted at first but finally agreed after he persuaded himself that he would not let his share of the commissions influence his decisions; if the prices and products from this company were not competitive, he would buy from somebody else. Stryker felt that he had been objective in making his purchases but he also enjoyed the extra money the arrangement brought in. He was somewhat shocked when du Buy called him into the office one day, told Stryker that his dishonesty had been found out, and fired him then and there. The purchasing agent also informed Stryker that Hypocase was planning to file suit against Stryker for the $1,750 in commissions that he received from the supplier's representative.

(2)

CASE. Fuhl Hardy, the Los Angeles district sales manager for Hypocase, Inc., had never been authorized, nor had any of the other district managers, to enter into contracts on behalf of Hypocase for the design and installation of materials handling and storage systems. The nature of this activity was so specialized and so technical in character that all such contracts were negotiated by representatives from the home office in Berkland. It was not an important part of Hypocase's business, but it was reasonably profitable and also helped develop new customers for pallets. The Los Angeles manager did negotiate and sign on behalf of Hypocase a contract with the International Cargo Terminals Corporation to design and install an entirely new cargo handling and storage system for International. When the contract was forwarded to the home office, the vice-president in charge of this part of the company's business notified International that Fuhl Hardy had no authority to make such a contract, and that Hypocase had a three-year backlog of such jobs and could not do anything for International within the time limits specified in the contract. It was also pointed out to International that the contract price would not even cover the costs of a preliminary investigation of International's problems. International has now filed suit against Hypocase, Inc. for breach of contract and against Hardy for breach of his warranty of authority and also for breach of contract.

IN GENERAL. An agent is interested in several aspects of the operation of the agency: his duties to his principal, his liabilities to the third person, and, of course, his authority. Because the third aspect has been dealt with in detail in connection with the discussion of the agency from the principal's point of view, it will not be repeated here except where it becomes relevant to the other aspects.

Like the principal, the agent has a duty not to breach the contract. The agent may refuse to perform the contract, however, but he subjects himself to possible liability if he does. Because a court will not compel an agent to return to his principal's employ, specific performance is not available as a remedy to the principal when the agent quits the employment in violation of the contract. To enforce employment contracts specifically would be to violate the constitutional prohibition against involuntary servitude and a long-established common law policy. An agent may be prevented from supplying his services to others. This may have the indirect effect of bringing the agent back to work for the principal, but even that sort of injunction is awarded by a court with some reluctance, especially where it might seriously handicap the ability of the agent to earn a living. A court, under certain circumstances, may order an employer to reinstate employees who have been wrongfully discharged.

Specific duties imposed upon the agent by the contract of agency are not our field of interest here. The agency relation is a fiduciary relation, and this type of relation carries with it certain duties and obligations that exist in the absence of any contrary provision in the contract. These duties are our concern. A *fiduciary relation* is one founded on trust or confidence reposed by one person in the integrity and fidelity of another. The parties to such a relation cannot deal with each other at arm's length or as strangers. They owe each other unusual duties not present in the ordinary contract situation. The agency relation is only one among many fiduciary relations. The relation among partners is fiduciary, as is that between trustee and beneficiary, guardian and ward, attorney and client, and parent and child. Usually, one party owes greater duties than the other.

DUTIES TO PRINCIPAL. The duties of the agent to the principal fall into two broad categories: those having to do with the agent's loyalty to the principal, and those having to do with the manner in which the agent shall perform his services for the principal. Both groups are in addition to the duties imposed on the agent by the contract.

Duties of loyalty. Speaking generally, the agent has a duty of good faith and loyalty to his principal in all matters connected with the agency and under this duty must act solely for the benefit of the principal in all such matters. This broad, general duty may be broken down into a number of subsidiary duties.

The first of these subsidiary duties is the duty not to compete with the principal. An agent who engages in the same business as his principal, on his own account and in competition with the principal, is clearly violating his basic duty to act only in the interest of his principal. If an agent does so compete, the principal may recover from the agent profits made by him as a result of the competition, and the principal may, normally, rescind the contract of agency. Of course, if the agent competes with the knowledge and consent of the principal, there is no liability. The agent also has the duty not to act as an agent of a competitor of the principal.

The agent has a duty not to sell or buy from himself in his representative capacity without the consent of the principal. Where an agent sells his principal's property to himself or buys his own property on behalf of the principal, it is usually immaterial that the price and terms were fair or that the principal was not actually injured. The principal, on discovering the facts, may have the transaction set aside and may recover any compensation paid to the agent. The reason for the rule is obvious: The principal is not being represented in this transaction by an agent who will act solely in the principal's interest.

The agent is under a duty not to make a profit from the agency except in the form of the agreed compensation. If the agent gets a better deal than the principal was expecting, the agent is not entitled to keep the saving or the profit for himself. The problem of the agent's accepting bonuses, rebates, gifts, and other payments from the third persons with whom he deals is taken up in the chapter on competitive practices. It is sufficient to point out here that the acceptance of such awards casts doubt on whether the agent was acting solely in his principal's interest. The duty of the agent not to disclose confidential information, the duty to disclose to the principal discoveries and inventions made while in the principal's employ, and other related matters are discussed in Chapter 14.

The agent has a duty not to act as agent for both the principal and the third party. The agent of a seller, for example, is expected to obtain the highest possible price, but the agent of a buyer is expected to get the goods at the lowest possible price. The two objectives cannot be reconciled. Both parties may, of course, consent to such dual representation by the agent, but neither can give effective consent unless he was in possession of full information on the arrangement at the time the consent was given. If the agent so acts without consent, either of the parties may rescind the contract the agent made for them. An important exception to the prohibition against acting for both parties is found where the agent is a mere middleman whose duties are simply to find a buyer or seller and not to negotiate the terms or enter into a contract on behalf of the parties. The ordinary real estate agent is an example of such a middleman.

An agent has a duty to devote full time to his principal. This means that the agent shall put in the full time expected of him. If he is expected to put in an eight hour day, he should devote that time to his principal and use the remainder of the day for his own projects or the projects of others. A traveling salesman, for example, who travels for a wholesale drug firm should not spend part of the time devoted to customer contacts in trying to induce the customers to buy the salesman's own line of comic books or trade novelties. If the agent violates this duty, the principal may recover from the agent the profits made as a result of the agent's own activities on the principal's time.

The agent is under a duty to account to the principal for funds and other property coming into the hands of the agent in the course of the agency. This is required whether the funds or property are on their way out to third persons or on their way in to the principal from third persons. The agent should keep reasonably accurate accounts of all transactions between himself and the principal and between himself and third persons. A closely related duty is that of not mixing the principal's funds with the agent's own funds. If the agent does mix the funds and the whole of the funds is lost through the failure of a bank or otherwise, the agent may be liable to the principal for the full amount of the principal's funds thus commingled and lost. If the agent had deposited the funds separately and had used reasonable care in the selection of a bank, he would not be liable for the principal's loss. The principal may, of course, authorize the deposit in the agent's own account or other commingling.

Duties connected with service. An agent has a duty to obey the instructions of the principal, and he is liable to the principal for any damages resulting from his disobedience. Even a gratuitous agent has a duty to obey instructions once he has entered on the performance of his acts. Naturally, an agent does not have to obey instructions outside the scope of his employment, for example, where the hosiery salesman is instructed to mow the principal's lawn or wax his car. A closely related duty is the duty of the agent not to exceed his authority.

An agent has a duty to exercise care and skill in carrying out the purpose of the agency. The degree of care and skill is that which a reasonable man would exercise under the same circumstances. If an agent professes to have certain skills, he is held liable when he fails to exercise those skills whether he really had them or not. The agent does not have to perform according to the highest degree of professional skill, but only to that degree which an ordinary person possessing this agent's real or purported background would exercise. The principal may recover damages for the injury resulting from a breach of this duty. The agent must also conduct himself in a way such as not to bring discredit upon his principal or the business or not to alienate the principal's personal or business relations.

Another duty of the agent is to keep his principal fully informed of material facts that may affect the subject matter of the agency. If the agent fails to keep his principal informed, he will be liable for injury resulting to the principal.

LIABILITY TO THE THIRD PERSON. The agent may incur liability to the third person either in contract, in tort, or for breach of an agent's warranty. Because everyone is liable for his own torts, no more need be said here about the agent's tort liability but that he is liable to the third person for torts committed while acting inside or outside the scope of his authority. The fact that the principal may become liable for the agent's tort has no effect on the agent's own liability to a third person. If the tort against the third person should happen to be one directed by the principal and committed by the agent without knowledge of the wrong, the agent has a right against his principal to be exonerated.

Liability in contract. Where the principal is fully disclosed, the agent is usually not liable on the contract at all. The purpose and result of an agent's activities are the creation of contractual relations between the principal and the third person. The agent is not a party to the transaction, and he is ordinarily under no liability to either the principal or the third person if one or the other should fail to perform. If the agent acts without authority, the principal is not liable on the contract nor, in the ordinary situation, is the agent. Because the contract purports to be with the principal, not the agent, the third person cannot look to the agent for satisfaction of the contract where the contract with the principal fails. Under some circumstances, however, the agent may become liable on the contract even where the principal is fully disclosed. Where the agent expressly or impliedly, with the consent of the others, makes himself a party to the contract, he incurs liability, as any other party would. The defective execution of a written contract may result in the agent's personal liability on the contract, as where the agent signs only his own name. The rule with regard to negotiable instruments is even more strict, and a signature such as "A, Agent" results in personal liability for the agent unless the principal is disclosed either in the signature or in the body of the instrument. On an ordinary contract the signature "A, Agent" will usually relieve the agent of personal liability if the identity of the principal is known to the third person, whether by disclosure in the contract or not. The safest way for an agent to sign is to place the name of the principal first and to follow it with the name of the agent and his designation as such: for example—"Peter Piper, by (or per) Simple Simon, Agent," or "Welsh Rarebit Company, by Charles Cheez, President." A signature like "Simple Simon for Peter Piper" is sometimes held not to be the equivalent of the proper form set forth in the previous sentence. It purports to be the signature of Simple Simon, not of Peter Piper.

The rules with respect to the liability of agents on contracts made for partially disclosed principals vary somewhat from state to state. Many courts do not hold the agent liable, but, in general, the agent is liable unless from the evidence an intent on the third person's part to hold only the principal is shown. Some courts, which take a more arbitrary view, hold the agent liable on the contract unless the principal is fully disclosed. The reason for the rules seems clear. The third person does not know the identity of the principal, and, unless there is evidence to the contrary, it will be assumed that the third person intends to look to someone else in addition to the ghostly principal. These rules appear to apply also where the agent acts without authority.

The liability of an agent acting for an undisclosed principal is obvious. As a matter of fact, a much better case can be made for the liability of the agent than for the liability of the principal. The third person's rights against the agent are exactly what the third person thought he was getting. The claim against the principal is thrown in as sort of a bonus. Because the agent is the only party of whom the third person is aware, no rule other than the liability of the agent on the contract would be possible.

Agent's warranties. In addition to the liability of the agent on the contract in certain circumstances, the agent may also incur liability on his implied warranties. The two warranties commonly found in connection with an agent's activities are the *agent's warranty of authority* and the *agent's warranty of the principal's capacity*. It should be clear that neither of these warranties can arise where the agent does not purport to act in a representative capacity. Another obvious point is that if an agent expressly warrants or guarantees his authority or his principal's capacity, the agent will be liable to the third person for breach of the warranty if the third person fails to get a binding contract with the principal owing to the lack of authority on the agent's part or lack of capacity on the principal's part.

An express statement of the warranty is not necessary, however, and when an agent deals with a third person as the purported agent of the principal, the agent impliedly warrants to the third person that he has the authority to do so. If the agent does not have the authority that he impliedly warrants he has, the third person will not get a contract good against the principal, and he may suffer a loss as a result. Because the loss is due to the agent's breach of his warranty of authority, the agent is personally liable to the third person for the loss thus suffered. The agent's good faith and honest belief that he had authority are immaterial to his liability, for such is the nature of a warranty. Note that the liability is not on the contract itself; instead it is for a breach of an implied warranty. The contract measure of damages generally consists in giving the innocent party the benefit of his bargain, but in breach of warranty actions he will only recover his out-of-pocket loss. Where the agent knows that he does not have authority but negotiates the contract anyway, he is generally said to be guilty of the tort of deceit, in which case he may be held liable for exemplary as well as compensatory damages. The tort of deceit is committed whether the agent, knowing that he has no authority, remains silent or fraudulently states that he has authority. In a few states, the agent who knows he does not have authority is held liable on the contract itself; the result is that the third person has a choice of actions.

An agent who is not sure of his authority or who wants to avoid the possible liability for breach of warranty may state expressly that he does not warrant his authority, or he may fully inform the third person of the facts concerning the agent's authority. In the latter case, the third person, if he enters into the contract, is relying on his own decision about the authority of the agent and not on an implied warranty.

In some states, an agent also impliedly warrants that his principal has the legal capacity to contract, and the agent will be liable to the third person if this is not the case. In most states, however, there is no liability on the agent except where an express warranty of capacity exists or where the principal's incapacity is fraudulently concealed. An agent is generally liable on the contract where he purports to act for a nonexistent or fictitious principal.

Restitution. Under certain circumstances, money or property delivered to the agent by a third person may be recovered by the third person from the agent. Where an innocent agent receives money or property on the principal's behalf and the third person delivered it to the agent by mistake or in reliance on the principal's fraud, the agent is usually under a quasi-contractual obligation to return the money or property to the third person. The agent is not obligated, however, where, before learning the facts, he delivered the money or property to the principal or to a creditor of, or bona fide purchaser from, the principal. This rule does not affect the principal's own liability. An agent who delivers the money or property to his principal or to others after learning the facts is still liable to the third person. Where the agent, by his own fraud or wrongful act, obtains money or other property for the principal, he is personally liable to the third person whether or not the money or property has been paid to the principal.

E. Operation of the Agency: The Third Person

Little now remains to be added to the discussion of the operation of the agency. Most of the rights, duties, and liabilities of the third person have already been discussed in connection with their counterparts—the principal and agent. The third person has no claim against the principal unless the agent has authority, actual or apparent, to make the contract or unless the principal later ratifies. If the third person fails to get a contract with the principal, he may still have claims against the agent, on the contract, for a breach of the agent's warranty of authority, or in tort. The third person may have contract claims or tort claims against both the principal and the agent, but he cannot, of course, receive full satisfaction from both parties unless the basis for the claims is different.

The third person has a duty to ascertain the extent of the agent's actual authority except where the apparent authority created by the principal's conduct removes the necessity. The third person can never rely on the representations of the agent alone as to the agent's authority. If the contract of agency is in writing and is available to the third person for inspection, he is bound by those provisions contained therein relative to the agent's authority, whether the third person actually inspects the document or not. When dealing for the first time with a particular agent, a third person should always inquire about the agent's authority and credentials unless the apparent authority created by the agent's presence on the principal's premises or other factors make such inquiry unnecessary. A bank depositor does not have to inquire about the authority of a teller in the teller's cage because he is entitled to rely on the belief that the person would not be in the cage except with the consent of the principal and unless clothed with the usual authority of bank tellers.

Where the principal is disclosed and the agent has not been made a party to the contract, the third person is not liable to the agent. Where the agent is a party to the contract, either because the principal is undisclosed or for some other reason, the agent is liable to the third person, and by the same token the third person is liable to the agent; but the agent's right to sue is subject to the principal's control and supervision, and if both parties bring suits against the third person, the principal's right to sue will prevail. The control and supervision of the principal will apply, of course, only where the principal also has rights under the contract negotiated by the agent. Even where the agent is not himself a party to the contract, he may be authorized to bring an action on the contract for the principal.

Third persons, obviously, are liable for their own torts. A third person's fraud in connection with the contract will make him liable to the principal but usually not to the agent. The third person would be liable to the agent if the negligent operation of the third person's vehicle had caused injury to the agent, but this would be true without any consideration of the law of agency.

F. Termination of the Agency

(1)

CASE. When Bill Stryker (see Case 1, page 341) was fired from his job as assistant purchasing agent with Hypocase, Inc., the company gave no notice of his discharge to the many suppliers with whom he had dealt. After the discharge, Stryker, using Hypocase purchase order forms he had taken with him, entered into a number of contracts, personally and by mail, with suppliers with whom he had been in contact when he was employed by Hypocase. Over a period of about 7 days, he submitted orders totalling more than $10,000, all in the name of Hypocase, Inc. Some of these orders were discovered by du Buy when confirmations were received in his office, but others did not come to light until the goods were actually delivered to the Hypocase receiving dock. All of the suppliers involved have been notified that Stryker had already been fired when the contracts were made, but most of them are insisting that the contracts be performed because they believed Stryker still to be acting for Hypocase when he made the contracts.

IN GENERAL. As a rule, an agency may be terminated at any time by either the principal or the agent. An agency is a voluntary relation, and either party may withdraw from it whenever he pleases. A principal cannot, ordinarily, be compelled to continue an agent in his employ, nor may an agent be compelled to work for the principal. This does not imply that either party may terminate the agency at any time without liability. The parties have the power to terminate, but they may be violating or breaching the contract by doing so; thus they would be subjected to liability for the injury caused by the breach. However, the ability of the principal to terminate at will does not exist in the agency coupled with an interest, discussed below.

Agencies may be terminated either by operation of law or by the act of the parties.

TERMINATION BY OPERATION OF LAW. The death or incapacity of either the principal or the agent automatically terminates the agency. The agency relation is a personal one, and the principal is under no obligation to accept a deceased agent's personal representative as a substitute for the agent. Because the agent acts for, and on behalf of, his principal, it is obvious that the death of the principal terminates the authority of the agent, who has no greater capacity to act than has his principal. The termination takes place regardless of the state of performance of the contract at the time. By the general rule, the bankruptcy of either the principal or the agent will terminate the agency except where the bankruptcy has no effect upon the agency or its purpose.

The destruction of the subject matter of the agency will terminate it, as will the becoming illegal of the purpose of the agency. A state of war between the principal's country and the agent's country will also bring an end to the agency by operation of law.

TERMINATION BY ACT OF THE PARTIES. The most common causes of the termination of an agency are the revocation of the agency by the principal and the renunciation of the agency by the agent. Other methods of terminating by act of the parties are: mutual agreement, accomplishment of the purpose for which the agency was created, the expiration of the time for which the agency was created, and the lapse of a reasonable time if no time is specified. As between the principal and agent, the termination of the agency by revocation or by renunciation is not effective until notice actually reaches the other party. The effectiveness of an agency termination, as regards third persons, is discussed below.

IRREVOCABLE AGENCIES. It should be noted that statements in a contract of agency to the effect that the agency is "irrevocable," whether for an indefinite period or for a fixed term, do not bring about that result. Actually, the language of the contract is of very little importance in determining the existence of a truly irrevocable agency. Only in two types of situation does the irrevocable agency arise. Both of these situations are usually referred to as agencies or powers *coupled with an interest.* Where the agency is created for the purpose of protecting some title, right, or interest in the agent, or created to secure for the agent's benefit some performance by the principal, the agency is said to be *irrevocable.* This means that the principal cannot revoke the agency without the consent of the agent. The death or incapacity of the parties will not ordinarily cause a termination.

Where the ordinary agency is created for the primary benefit of the principal, the irrevocable agency is created for the primary benefit of the agent. The interest or title or duty that the irrevocable agency secures or protects must be the subject matter of the agency. The agent's interest in his wages or commissions or in a share of the profits is only incidental to the subject matter of the agency and is not sufficient to create an agency coupled with interest. Another contrast between the ordinary agency and the irrevocable agency is that in the ordinary agency the agent's interest does not arise until the performance of the agency begins, but in the irrevocable agency the agent's interest has already arisen when the agency is created.

Two simple illustrations may serve to enhance the understanding of this unusual type of agency. It should be pointed out that once the situations have moved away from the simple examples set forth below, the cases in this field become difficult to analyze and hard to distinguish.

First illustration: Where P mortgages land to A as security for money loaned to him by A, the mortgage has a disadvantage, from A's point of view, because A, in the event of P's default, must go through the slow and sometimes complicated process of foreclosure. In order to avoid this problem, a special type of mortgage, called the *power of sale mortgage,* was created. This mortgage is also an agency contract because the mortgagee, A, is made the agent of the mortgagor, P, with authority to sell the mortgaged land in the event of a default. This means that A can sell the land himself, without going through foreclosure, and he may sign a deed "P, by A, Agent." This is not an ordinary agency because the primary purpose is to protect or to improve the agent's mortgage security. No particular benefit accrues to the principal. P cannot revoke this agency without A's consent, and the death or incapacity of either party has no effect upon it. The agency may be exercised by or against the successors of the parties.

Second illustration: Where P borrows money from A and gives A a promissory note, a default by P simply gives A the right to bring an action against P for the nonpayment of the note. This requires the normal court trial and procedure. A type of note, called the *judgment note,* was developed to save A some of this trouble. The note is also an agency contract whereby the lender, A, is made the agent of the borrower, P, with authority to confess judgment on P's behalf and, thus, to avoid the necessity for a trial. When a debtor confesses judgment, he confesses that he owes a stipulated sum. Judgment is then entered against him without the institution of other legal proceedings. In the judgment note, the creditor, in order to secure the debtor's performance, is made the agent of the debtor to confess judgment.

In some courts, the insanity, death, or bankruptcy of the principal will terminate the irrevocable agency where it is created for the purpose of securing performance of the payment of a debt, but the modern trend is to hold both types of irrevocable agency irrevocable by any means, except agreement of the parties, until they have accomplished the purpose for which they were created. There is little ground for distinguishing between the agency created to secure a performance and the agency created to protect an interest.

NOTICE OF TERMINATION.   It is obvious that the revocation of the agent's authority by the principal terminates the actual authority of the agent to act for the principal, but it is equally obvious that such revocation, by itself, will not have any effect upon apparent authority that may exist. Consequently, the principal should take reasonable steps to inform third persons of the termination of the agency. The same steps should be taken whenever the termination results from the acts of the parties. On the theory that such events as death, bankruptcy, and illegality are matters of public knowledge, the principal is excused from giving notice to third persons when the termination of the agency is caused by operation of law. In some courts, however, the agent's authority may survive the principal's death unless the third person has actual notice of the agency's termination.

If the principal fails to give the proper notice where it is required, the result is that the agent continues to have apparent authority to bind his principal in contract. As regards third persons who have dealt with the principal through the agent before termination, the apparent authority of the agent can be destroyed only by *actual* notice to those third persons. For those third persons who knew of the agency before termination but have never dealt with the principal through the agent it is sufficient notice to advertise the termination in a newspaper of general circulation in the community where the agency was conducted. Actual knowledge of the termination is not necessary as far as this second group of third persons is concerned. As a practical matter, notice is rarely advertised for the benefit of the second group.

3. LABOR RELATIONS

A. In General

The law of agency does not by any means include all of the law applicable to the relation between an employer and his employees. Much more is involved in the administration of a labor force and in the conduct of industrial relations than the simple application of the rules of agency and contract that have already been examined. Because the legal aspects of industrial relations now cover such a large area by themselves, thorough consideration of them is far beyond our scope. The best that can be done is to outline and to consider briefly the more important nonagency aspects of the relation between an employer and his employees. The purpose will be to acquaint businessmen, prospective businessmen, and other laymen with the nature and scope of the legal problems in that area.

The law of industrial relations developed very slowly until the field was entered by extensive statutory enactment during and after the 1930's, a period in which common law concepts and principles proved to be totally inadequate to deal with the pressures created by war, industrial expansion, and a severe economic depression. A large proportion of the so-called "labor law" is now governed by statute. No real understanding of the law of this area is possible any longer except within the framework of the statutes. As is always the case with the growth and development of the law in a new area, the statutes are being changed and will continue to be changed for many years. Some of the principles appear to have crystallized, and will change only with sharply changing conditions, but many of the principles and rules of labor law are still fluid and will change with use and experience.

The few pages devoted to labor law are divided about equally between the contract of employment, which includes a brief glance at the common law and a consideration of modern legislation affecting both the terms and conditions of employment and collective bargaining, and the employer's liability for injuries to his employees. Neither portion is comprehensive, but both portions seek to present the basic principles and problems.

This section dealing with labor relations is set forth in the conventional textbook manner. The justification for the abandonment of the basic concept of the presentation is that we are faced here with the need to outline briefly a wide range of common law and statutory rules with which a businessman will likely meet and we do not have the space to devote to placing each problem in its own particular frame of reference. The general frame of reference is the same as in the earlier portions of the chapter: the rights, duties, and responsibilities rising out of the employment relationship. It is hoped that this outline method of presentation for a few pages will serve to supply background information that will be useful in examining and dealing with those problems that grow out of the employment aspects of business enterprise.

B. The Contract of Employment

THE COMMON LAW AND EARLY STATUTES. Those aspects of the employment contract governed by the general law of contract will not be reviewed here, but brief attention will be given to those aspects of contract law that are peculiar to the contract of employment or that have particular importance in that connection. As a whole, the common law courts treated employment contracts much as any other type of contract. This policy, in itself, had important ramifications. For example, on the theory that there is the same equality of bargaining power between employer and individual employee that there is between ordinary contracting parties, the courts under the common law enforced contracts of employment without regard to the unfairness and harshness they imposed upon the employee, unless of course there was fraud or duress. Although this view may have been justified at some stages of our economic development, increasing industrialization, increasing size of the firm, and increasing dependence by large segments of the population on wages from factory employment removed long ago any individual equality of bargaining that may once have existed.

As the employees turned to joint efforts for dealing with their employers, further common law problems arose. Many employers stipulated in the contract of employment that a condition of employment was the employee's promise not to join a union. This *yellow-dog contract* and similar contracts were upheld by the courts as exercises of the fundamental right of freedom of contract. Statutes making it illegal for an employer to use such contracts or to discriminate in other ways against members of unions were held unconstitutional. In early American law it was held that combinations of employees to raise wages were criminal conspiracies; thus, they were punishable as crimes. This doctrine did not receive universal support, and it had disappeared by the end of the nineteenth century. But another doctrine, that of civil conspiracy, had arisen to take its place. Under the latter doctrine, a combination to do a lawful act by unlawful means or an unlawful act by lawful means was a tort; thus, it was enjoinable. The result was that a motive that could not make the act of an individual tortious could, nonetheless, make the otherwise lawful act of a group unlawful. Then, the injunction entered upon the scene as a major method of settling labor disputes. In addition, the doctrine that it was unlawful to induce the breach of a contract unless there was justification was applied to labor disputes, and it seriously hampered effective joint activity by employees.

The Sherman Act, passed in 1890, prohibited combinations or conspiracies in restraint of trade. Violations were crimes and were enjoinable; they subjected the violators to triple damage liability to persons injured by the violations. The Sherman Act was held to apply to some union activities. In 1914, the Clayton Act became law. It contained a statement that

> no restraining order or injunction shall be granted . . . in any case between an employer and employees . . . involving, or growing out of, a dispute concerning terms or conditions of employment, unless necessary to prevent irreparable injury to property, or to a property right, of the party making the application, for which injury there is no adequate remedy at law . . .

The Clayton Act provided further that no injunction should issue prohibiting any person or persons, singly or in concert, from leaving work, from persuading others by peaceful means to do so, or from paying strike benefits; nor were these acts to be considered or held to be violations of any law of the United States. There was also in the Clayton Act a statement that the labor of a human being is not a commodity or an article of commerce.

It was argued that the Clayton Act was intended to take labor union activity out from under the Sherman Act, but the courts took a much narrower view. It was held that the Clayton Act applied only to disputes between employers and employees and that it did not cover boycotts, picketing, or dogged persuasion. A state statute similar in language to the Clayton Act was held unconstitutional by the Supreme Court in 1921 on the ground that it violated the equal protection clause of the Fourteenth Amendment of the Constitution, because the statute prohibited the use of injunctions only in labor disputes. The equal protection clause requires the equal treatment of persons equally situated. This decision made it clear that the inability to recognize any differences between the employer-employee relationship and other relationships was still common in 1921. While the statutes were being interpreted into ineffectiveness or declared unconstitutional, courts were issuing injunctions, framed in the broadest kind of language, against every conceivable sort of organized employee activity. The typical injunction during this period was issued *ex parte*. This means that it was done on the application of only one party without any adversary procedure.

Because of governmental experience gained in collective bargaining while operating the railroads during World War I, Congress set up in 1920, and strengthened in 1926, a Railroad Labor Board as a means for the peaceful settlement of labor controversies in the railroad industry. Under the 1926 Act, it was held that employees were free to organize and choose their representatives without interference from the company and that these rights were enforceable. The Act was further strengthened in 1934.

Beginning in 1931, state and federal legislation recognized the need to free labor unions in general from the restrictive decisions against their activity and to protect employees from employer interference with their right to bargain collectively and to choose their own representatives. Congress enacted the Norris-LaGuardia Act in 1932; that Act severely limited the injunctive power of the federal courts and explicitly placed peaceful picketing and striking outside the scope of injunctions in labor disputes. The Act was not very successful. In 1935, the National Labor Relations Act, granting employees the right to organize free of employer interference and to bargain collectively, was passed. The period of government-protected freedom of employees to organize and to bargain collectively and the principle of non-intervention by the courts in labor disputes had begun.

At common law, the terms and conditions of employment were left almost exclusively to the agreement of the parties. Under circumstances of unequal bargaining power, this left the employee at a great disadvantage, especially with regard to wages and hours of work and to the employment of women and children. Collective efforts were blocked by common law principles and adverse judicial interpretations of corrective statutes. The courts generally conceded the constitutionality of laws that regulated the hours of work of certain classes of persons, such as women and children, or of persons working in certain industries, such as mining, provided that the laws were reasonable in the light of the object sought to be attained. The courts have accorded similar treatment to state laws prohibiting child labor. Because many states did not have such laws, Congress, in 1916, enacted a statute prohibiting the interstate transportation of goods manufactured in whole or in part by persons under sixteen, but that statute was declared unconstitutional by the Supreme Court as was a statute a few years later that imposed a special tax on industries employing child labor.

Few states have enacted minimum wage laws. Prior to 1937, those enacted were declared unconstitutional when they came before the Supreme Court. In 1937, the Supreme Court reversed its stand on minimum wage laws. In 1938, Congress passed the Fair Labor Standards Act, which dealt with wages, hours, and child labor. The Act has been held constitutional in all respects; thus, the Supreme Court's previous stand on federal child labor laws was reversed.

Many states have passed statutes regulating the method and the time of wage payments. These statutes seek to eliminate payments in coupons or scrip and the practice in some industries and areas of paying the employees at such infrequent intervals that most were forced to live on credit. They have been upheld, in general, where there was no singling out of special classes of employers. The lack of uniform treatment is demonstrated by the fact that the imposition of some of the statutes on corporations alone has been held by different courts to be both an unreasonable and a reasonable singling out of that particular class of business firm.

CONCERTED ACTIVITIES UNDER MODERN LEGISLATION. As might well have been expected in the light of the history of labor relations prior to 1935, the National Labor Relations Act, or NLRA, swung far in the opposite direction, and, in some ways, it was unnecessarily weighted in favor of labor. This fact, coupled with certain improper union practices carried on under the protection of the Act, led to a retreat from the position taken by the NLRA. In 1939, some states began to enact legislation to limit the type of union or concerted employee activity that was deemed to be legitimate, but not until 1947 was the reaction evident on the federal level. In that year, Congress enacted the Labor-Management Relations Act better known as the Taft-Hartley Act. That Act amended the NLRA and added certain provisions not contained in the older law. A section was added that condemned certain union practices as unfair labor practices, and the Norris-LaGuardia Act was modified to permit injunctions, on the application of the National Labor Relations Board, to stop such practices. The National Labor Relations Board, the NLRB, set up by the NLRA to administer many of the provisions of that Act, was retained in the Taft-Hartley Act. The new statutes also authorized the issuance of an injunction upon the application of the United States Attorney General to enjoin for a period of eighty days a threatened strike or lockout in a major industry if the national health or safety would be harmed by such strike or lockout.

The new Act gives injured parties the right to bring actions against unions in connection with certain unfair labor practices and permits suits by or against the union in its collective name. Unions are required to furnish detailed information about their organization and financial condition and the union officers are required to sign affidavits that they are not Communists. Government employees are barred from striking. The Act also restricts the use of funds by unions for political activities and regulates the creation and control of welfare funds. One can rest assured that these are not the last changes that will be made in the law of labor relations. The Taft-Hartley Act had as its primary purpose the equalizing of the legal responsibilities of employers and unions. The difficulty is that there is little agreement about what is "equal" and considerable disagreement about whether there should be equality in the first place. The basic right to organize and to bargain collectively has not been seriously affected. The Act, of course, applies to all employment except that which is strictly intrastate in character and which does not have even an indirect connection with interstate or foreign commerce.

Negotiating collective bargaining agreements. Certain obligations are imposed upon the parties with regard to collective bargaining. The employer's duties are the same as those imposed under the NLRA. The duties are new in regard to the labor organizations, however, because they were under no duty to bargain as far as the old law was concerned. Some of the duties imposed are as follows:

1. The duty to meet. Both the union and the employer are required to meet if either one desires to bargain. The employer does not have to bargain unless the union represents a majority of the employees and meets certain other qualifications. Once a majority union asks the employer to bargain, the employer is bound to arrange suitable meeting times.

2. The duty to treat with the representatives. An employer who goes over the heads of the majority union representatives and bargains or attempts to bargain directly with the employees is guilty of an unfair labor practice. The employer must refrain from raising or lowering wages or otherwise making decisions about matters within the scope of the collective bargaining process without consulting the representatives of the majority union.

3. Duty to confer in good faith. The parties are not required to reach an agreement, but once the parties meet and sit down to negotiate their contract, they must confer in good faith. This does not require them to make counter-proposals. A refusal to bargain occurs where either employer or union insists that the other give up any rights guaranteed by the Act.

4. The duty to sign a written agreement. This is only necessary where one of the parties requests it.

An employer is not required to recognize a labor organization or its representatives before certification by the NLRB, but he may do so if he wishes. If the employer refuses to bargain prior to Board certification, any employee, or group of employees, or organization acting on their behalf, may file a petition before the Board asking to be certified as the bargaining representative. The employer may file a petition asking that the bargaining representative be determined. If the Board finds that certain requirements, such as the filing of financial statements and anti-Communist affidavits, have been met, an election is held, and the labor organization receiving a majority of the votes cast is certified as the bargaining representative. It is possible, of course, that no organization will receive a majority; thus, none will be certified.

An important aspect of the collective bargaining process is the determination of just what issues must be submitted to the negotiations. The following have been held to be within the bargaining area: wages, hours, vacations, holidays, merit increases, sick leave, union security, seniority, pensions, group health and accident insurance plans, apprentices, job classifications, promotions, discipline, discharge, homework, sub-contracting, grievance machinery, no-strike clauses, no-lockout clauses, duration of contract, and renewal. The determination of what is within the collective bargaining area is important because issues that are within *must* be submitted to negotiation.

Stalemates that occur in the bargaining process are not, by themselves, evidence of a failure to bargain. They come into existence when neither side will move from a position it has taken. Unless mediation, conciliation, or arbitration can break the stalemate, strikes or lockouts may result. Mediation and conciliation consist of the participation of a third party in the negotiations, but the third party does not make the decision. In arbitration, the impartial third person actually makes the decision, and the parties are bound by it.

Carrying out collective bargaining contracts. It is important to note here that collective bargaining contracts take precedence over individual contracts between employer and employee, and such individual contracts do not excuse the employer from entering into a collective bargaining contract. Any other rule would make collective bargaining agreements virtually impossible to achieve. Almost all collective bargaining contracts contain clauses that set up machinery for the handling of the grievances of individual employees; thus, the lack of an individually negotiated contract does not prevent an individual employee from discussing and settling his own problems. The grievance machinery typically provides for handling employee grievances by union and management representatives from the lowest to the highest levels, and it often provides for going on to arbitration from the highest level if an agreement cannot be reached there. The Act also requires that an employee should be allowed to contact the employer without going through the grievance procedure, but there is some question whether a clause in the collective bargaining contract can take away this privilege.

Once the contract has been entered into, no duty is imposed on either party to bargain over modifications except at times provided in the agreement itself, but there undoubtedly is a duty, although the statutory language is not clear, to bargain over disputed interpretations of clauses in the contract.

The rights of the parties to obtain judicial enforcement of collective bargaining contracts is not entirely settled. Were these contracts treated for all purposes as ordinary contracts, the answer would be obvious. It can be said, however, that employers and unions can sue each other for breach of a collective bargaining contract, and such suits have been sustained for specific performance, injunction, and damages, although suits for damages are rare. Individual employees have been allowed to sue an employer, and vice versa, but these suits are uncommon. The Act permits money damage suits for breach of contracts between employers and unions without regard to the amount in controversy or the citizenship of the parties. It has been learned that the lawsuit is not a very satisfactory device for settling disputes between parties who will have to continue to work and get along together.

A few states make the breach of a collective bargaining contract an unfair labor practice. Neither the NLRA nor the Taft-Hartley Act makes the breach of contract an unfair labor practice, but the activities that constitute a breach may themselves be unfair labor practices. If so, action by the NLRB is possible.

One of the most common and most useful methods of settling labor disputes, whether they arise during the negotiation of a contract or after a contract has been entered into, is arbitration. Because general legal principles of arbitration are discussed in the chapter on contracts, they will not be repeated here. The use of arbitration in labor disputes varies widely, and the varieties are further added to by local statute. In at least one state, Pennsylvania, arbitration agreements are specifically enforceable in the sense that either party can set the arbitration machinery in motion over the objections of the other party, as long as there is, of course, a dispute.

Unfair labor practices. There is no intent on the part of the author to set forth here an exhaustive discussion, or even outline, of unfair labor practices. The sole purpose of these paragraphs is to list and discuss briefly the general categories of unfair labor practices with regard to both employer and union. The Act describes five unfair labor practices by employers: 1. Interference, restraint, and coercion of employees in the exercise of their rights to organize and bargain collectively and of other rights under the Act. The list of activities included in the prohibition would include: yellow-dog contracts, blacklists, espionage, threats of discharge, discrimination against union members, and anti-union propaganda. 2. Domination of unions. This prohibition is designed to keep unions free from employer control and financial support. 3. Discrimination in hiring or in tenure, terms, or conditions of employment for the purpose of encouraging or discouraging membership in a union. These restrictions are not designed to limit the employer's rights to reward deserving employees and discharge incompetent, disloyal, or disobedient employees. 4. Discrimination against an employee because he has filed charges or given testimony under the Act. 5. Refusal to bargain collectively.

The Taft-Hartley Act also sets forth certain activities by unions that are unfair labor practices:

1. Restraint or coercion of employees in the exercise of their rights. Just as the employer is prohibited from restraining or coercing the employees in the exercise of their rights, so the union is prohibited from these activities. The Act also makes it an unfair labor practice for a union to restrain or coerce an employer in the selection of his bargaining representatives. This prohibition against restraints and coercion is not designed to stop strikes or peaceful picketing, but it appears to have been enacted for the primary purpose of preventing threats and violence.

2. Causing or attempting to cause an employer to discriminate against an employee with respect to whom membership in the union has been denied or terminated on any ground other than his failure to pay the dues or fees uniformly required as a condition for membership. The purpose of this clause is to protect union shop employees who have antagonized the union. The union could arbitrarily throw the employee out of the union, and this, under a union shop contract, would also result in the loss of the employee's job.

3. Refusal to bargain collectively.

4. Illegal strikes and boycotts.

5. Excessive or discriminating initiation fees under union shop contracts.

6. Featherbedding. It is an unfair labor practice for a union "to cause or attempt to cause an employer to pay or deliver any money or other thing of value, in the nature of an exaction, for services that are not performed or not to be performed."[3]

The new Act provides several methods of preventing unfair labor practices. Among them are: a proceeding before the NLRB which results in a negative or affirmative order by the Board, and a proceeding brought by the Board in a Federal District Court for a temporary injunction restraining the commission of unfair practices while the Board is hearing the charges.

Strikes, picketing, and related activities. Not all aspects of concerted activities under modern legislation can be examined here, but no discussion in this area can be terminated without at least a brief consideration of strikes, picketing, and other devices used by unions to enforce their demands on the employer. In general, union activity against employers takes two forms: refusal to work, together with the publicizing of the dispute or the encouraging of others not to work for or deal with the employer. The refusal to work may be a strike, for example, where the employees refuse to work for the employer with whom the union has the dispute, or a boycott, for example, where the employees refuse to work for an employer who deals with another employer with whom the union has a dispute. The publicizing of the dispute and encouragement of others to participate may be done either by picketing or by boycott, depending upon whether individuals patrolling a place of business are stationed at the place of business of the employer with whom the union has a dispute or at the place of business of his customers or suppliers.

The basic judicial attitude toward strikes is that they are legal or illegal depending on the objectives the strike seeks to achieve, apart, of course, from the legality of other activities that may accompany a strike. If the purposes of a strike are justified, the strike is legal. If the purposes are not justified, the strike is illegal. The courts decide what is justified and what is not. Strikes to raise wages, decrease hours, or improve working conditions are usually held to be legal, but the legality of strikes to enforce or compel a closed shop is upheld in some states but not in others. In general, what is true of strikes in this regard is true of boycotts.

The injunction is the quickest and simplest way of ending a strike or a boycott. Most of the law dealing with the legality and illegality of a strike or a boycott has been developed in connection with the use of the injunction. The Norris-LaGuardia Act has had considerable effect on the objectives considered to be legal in a strike, and, in general, it has prohibited injunctions in labor disputes except where violence is involved. The concept of "labor dispute," as set forth in this Act, was very broad, but it was limited to controversies concerning terms

---

[3] Labor-Management Relations Act of 1947, Section 8 (b)(6).

and conditions of employment and similar issues. A dispute among businessmen does not involve a "labor dispute."[4] A controversy between an individual and a union about the right of the individual to belong to the union is not a "labor dispute,"[5] nor is a sympathetic strike by stagehands to compel an employer to use musicians instead of transcriptions in the performance of operas a "labor dispute."[6] The Act also uses very broad language when it comes to enumerating the parties who could participate or be interested in a "labor dispute" so as to come under the anti-injunction provisions of the Act. It is not necessary, under the Act, that the disputants stand in the relation of employer-employee or that they have any more than an indirect interest in the dispute. Thus, boycotts involving the refusal to work on unfair goods or to work for an employer who uses unfair goods come within the Act. Even strikes by minority unions where majority unions had already been certified by the National Labor Relations Board were held to be within the Norris-LaGuardia Act and entitled to its protection.

The Taft-Hartley Act imposes some limitations upon the right to strike and narrows the application of the Norris-LaGuardia Act. As has already been seen, because certain labor practices are said to be unfair when carried on by unions, an injunction-like relief is available in some of these cases. Strikes by one union where another has already been certified as the bargaining representative are unfair labor practices. Jurisdictional strikes are prohibited and are made unfair labor practices. Almost all types of boycotts carried out by unions to induce one employer to stop dealing with another or to induce the public to stop dealing with an employer who buys the products of an unfair employer are prohibited by the Taft-Hartley Act. The Act forbids strikes or boycotts to force a self-employed person to join a union, and it makes illegal the sitdown strike and slowdown.

Little law exists on the constitutional aspects of the right to strike, but there is considerable law with relation to picketing, which has been identified in some cases by the Supreme Court with the right of free speech. Furthermore, strikes and picketing are closely associated. Although either may occur without the other, that is usually not the case. Prior to 1940, picketing was dealt with by the courts in much the same fashion as strikes, but, after 1940, the Supreme Court held that peaceful picketing was merely the exercise of the right of free speech; thus, the Court afforded to it additional protection. Statutes forbidding all picketing are unconstitutional, but statutes limiting picketing in various ways and degrees have been upheld. Most of the law with regard to picketing is local, and reference should be made to state statutes and decisions. Violence, threats, and intimidation are enjoinable even under the Norris-LaGuardia Act,

---

[4] *Columbia River Packers Ass'n Inc.* v. *Hinton,* 315 U.S. 143 (1942).

[5] *Dorrington* v. *Manning,* 135 Pa. Super. 194 (1939).

[6] *Opera On Tour, Inc.* v. *Weber,* 285 N.Y. 348 (1941).

but full court hearings are required for anything more than a five day restraining order. Picketing, when accompanied by violence, by threats of violence or loss of jobs, or by intimidation, and mass picketing are unfair labor practices under the Taft-Hartley Act, as is peaceful picketing in connection with one of the prohibited strikes. The injunctions issued under the Norris-LaGuardia Act do not necessarily avoid the constitutional problems.

As has been pointed out above, the Taft-Hartley Act provides that if, in the opinion of the President of the United States, a threatened or actual strike or lockout affecting an entire industry or a substantial part is likely to imperil the national health or safety, he may direct the Attorney General to seek an injunction against the strike. This procedure is accompanied by the reports of a board of inquiry and by a vote of the employees on whether they desire to accept the "final offer" made by the employer.

In 1959, Congress enacted the Labor-Management Reporting and Disclosure Act,[7] which seeks to strengthen internal union democracy and also deals with certain conduct of union officials and employers.

TERMS AND CONDITIONS UNDER MODERN LEGISLATION. Another major category in the field of labor law is that relating to governmental regulation of employment standards affecting the individual employee without regard to his affiliation with organized labor. Whereas much state legislation exists in this area, our concern here will be almost exclusively with the federal Fair Labor Standards Act of 1938.[8] This Act deals only with minimum wages, hours of employment, and child labor. The Act does not regulate interstate commerce, but it prohibits the shipment in interstate commerce of goods produced under substandard labor conditions.

The original Fair Labor Standards Act, the FLSA, was adopted in an atmosphere of severe and prolonged economic depression, widespread unemployment, low pay scales, and the dependence by many wage-earners on public relief. Although these conditions were replaced, soon after the passage of the Act, by the inflationary pressures, expanding production, and general economic prosperity that accompanied and followed World War II, it is a widely accepted view that the Act still has its usefulness as a stabilizing factor, as an encouragement for reducing excessive working hours and spreading employment, and as a bar to the labor of children.

Provisions of the Act. The basic requirements of the Act are few and simple. Section 6 of the Act, as amended, provide: "Every employer shall pay to each of his employees who is engaged in commerce or in the production of goods for commerce wages at the following rates: (1) not less than $1.60 an hour." Section 7 states, subject to a few exceptions, that "no employer shall employ any of his employees who is engaged in commerce or in the production of goods

---

[7] 29 U.S.C.A. 401 *et seq.*
[8] 29 U.S.C.A. 201 *et seq.*

for commerce for a workweek longer than forty hours, unless such employee receives compensation for his employment in excess of the hours above specified at a rate not less than one and one-half times the regular rate at which he is employed." Section 12 deals with child labor as follows: "No producer, manufacturer, or dealer shall ship or deliver for shipment in commerce any goods produced in an establishment situated in the United States in or about which within thirty days prior to the removal of such goods therefrom any oppressive child labor has been employed." Thus, the Act affects wages, hours, and child labor.

Much controversy has centered around the Act, as would be expected of any such broad and novel plan affecting a large portion of the American economic scene. Most of the conflicts have arisen as a result of differences of interpretation of the statutory language and of the failure of the statute to define with sufficient particularity many of its important words and phrases. Some of the problems have been resolved by court decision, and many by amendments, but some uncertainties still remain.

Although the coverage of the Act is broad, many classes of employees are exempted from one or more of its provisions; such exclusions include, for example, any employee employed in a bona fide executive, administrative, or professional capacity or in the capacity of outside salesman; any employee engaged in any retail or service establishment, the greater part of whose selling or services is in intrastate commerce; seamen; any employee employed in the catching or harvesting of fish; certain persons employed in agriculture; employees of railroads; and any children employed as performers in the motion picture or theatrical industry.

The phrase "regular rate" in Section 7 was one of the most troublesome phrases in the whole Act; consequently, it is subjected to extensive definition and description in the 1949 amendments to the FLSA. It is now more or less clearly defined to include all remuneration for employment except: sums paid as gifts; payments made for occasional periods when no work is performed, as vacation or sick pay; discretionary bonuses; contributions by employer to old-age, retirement, and insurance plans; overtime; premium payments for work outside the normal hours or for weekend, day-off or holiday work where the premium rate is not less than one and one-half times the rate for work during regular hours. The regular rate of any employee is normally determined by dividing his total compensation for a workweek by the total number of hours actually worked by him during that week, excluding any payment properly credited as overtime premiums.

"Oppressive child labor" is defined in the Act as the employment of any child under sixteen years of age, other than by parent or guardian, or the employment of any person between the ages of sixteen and eighteen years of age in any occupation that the Secretary of Labor shall find and declare to be particularly hazardous for the employment of children or detrimental to their health or well-being. The Secretary may determine that the employment of persons between fourteen and sixteen years does not constitute "oppressive child labor" if such employment is confined to periods that will not interfere with their schooling and if there are no conditions in the employment that may interfere with their health and well-being.

To administer and enforce the Act, a Wage and Hour Division of the United States Department of Labor was established. At the head of the Division is the Administrator, who is appointed by the President with the consent of the Senate. In 1942, the Division was assigned the task of administering the Walsh-Healey Act.[9] That Act provides that anyone selling more than $10,000 worth of material to the federal government must conform to federal employment standards. Because the Division had to administer this additional Act, it was renamed the Wage and Hour and Public Contracts Division. In addition to ordinary administrative functions, the Administrator and his Division have the general responsibility for securing compliance with the Act. In order to carry out this duty, the Administrator and the Division have the power to investigate and inspect, to encourage voluntary settlements and to negotiate consent decrees, to seek injunctions, to bring suit for back-pay for employees, and to refer cases to the Department of Justice for criminal action. Conviction in a criminal action may subject the convicted person to fines of not more than $10,000 or to imprisonment of not more than six months or both. First offenders are subject only to fines. The penalties imposed are for each offense; thus, the aggregate fine may substantially exceed $10,000.

The constitutionality of the FLSA has been well tested and consistently upheld, thereby overruling some of the earlier decisions in regard to the lack of federal power to regulate child labor. The Act has been challenged on a wide and imaginative list of grounds, but all challenges have been knocked down by the courts. The wage-hour standards do not violate the "due process" and "equal protection" clauses of the Fifth and Fourteenth Amendments. The Act does not violate the Tenth Amendment's reservation to the states of non-delegated power. The FLSA does not violate the "freedom of the press" guaranty of the First Amendment, and it does not authorize "unreasonable searches and seizures" in violation of the Fourth Amendment.

A variety of other legislation affecting wages, hours, child labor, and other conditions of employment exists. The FLSA states specifically that the Act shall not affect any higher standards imposed by other statutes, either state or federal. A number of federal statutes, such as the Walsh-Healey and Davis-Bacon Acts, regulate labor standards for those who contract with the government. Specific industry controls are imposed by statutes such as the Motor Carrier Act, the Interstate Commerce Act, the Civil Aeronautics Act of 1938, the Merchant Marine 8-Hour Law, and the Sugar Act of 1948. Many state laws prescribe maximum hours, minimum wages, and time and methods of

---

[9] 41 U.S.C.A. 35.

wage payments; regulate female and child labor; impose safety regulations; and deal with such matters as discrimination in employment, workmen's compensation, and unemployment insurance. Also note that wage-hour problems and other problems of terms and conditions of employment cannot be considered realistically without reference to those branches of labor law relating to concerted labor activities, collective bargaining, and union-management relations.

Fair employment practices. Increasing recognition in recent years of the plight of minority racial groups in this country has produced a large quantity of legislation aimed at preventing discrimination in the hiring and treatment of employees. Fair Employment Practices Acts have appeared in many states and are primarily concerned with discriminatory practices in hiring, firing, and conditions of employment on grounds of race, creed, color, or national origin. The statutes vary considerably in detail. Some provide for strict enforcement, while others are largely voluntary in character. Attempts to enact federal statutes against discriminatory practices have finally been successful and take a number of different forms, including strict provisions applying to those who enter into contracts with the government. The Civil Rights Act of 1964[10] is probably the most important piece of federal legislation in this area, and this act declares it to be an unlawful employment practice for an employer

> to fail or refuse to hire or to discharge any individual, or otherwise to discriminate against any individual with respect to his compensation, terms, conditions, or privileges of employment, because of such individual's race, color, religion, sex, or national origin; or to limit, segregate, or classify his employees in any way which would deprive or tend to deprive any individual of employment opportunities or otherwise adversely affect his status as an employee, because of such individual's race, color, religion, sex, or national origin.

C. Liability of Employer for Injuries to Employees

AT COMMON LAW. No doubt existed at common law that the employer was liable for injuries caused to his employees by the employer's negligence. For two reasons, however, this statement is very misleading and gives a completely false picture of the situation. In the first place, the burden of litigation was upon the injured employee, who had to assume the financial and evidentiary task of proving his employer's negligence. In the second place, even though negligence could be shown, the employer had at his command three common law defenses that virtually eliminated any real liability on his part for injuries to his employees. The statutory history in this area of labor law is largely a matter of attempts to reduce or abolish the social and economic costs these harsh rules imposed. The three defenses merit some discussion.

The first of the employer's defenses was a common law doctrine known as

---

[10] 42 U.S.C.A. 2000e-2.

the *assumption of risk,* whereby a person who accepts employment in a business assumes all the ordinary hazards of the business and the risks of defects in the equipment that were sufficiently obvious for the person to notice and recognize. The employer was liable for injury caused by secret or hidden defects. Whether a particular risk was an ordinary risk of the business and sufficiently obvious to the person accepting employment were questions of fact. It was frequently said in support of this doctrine that when an employee accepts particular employment, he has impliedly agreed to accept the ordinary risks of that employment. If the emphasis is on the word "agreed," the justification is meaningless because most employees probably never gave a thought to the risks of the business, and they certainly never "agreed" to accept them. If the emphasis is on the word "impliedly," the justification is just another way of saying that the courts placed the risk on the employee without paying any attention to his consent.

The second defense was the famous *fellow-servant rule,* which absolved the employer of liability for an employee's injuries where the injury was caused by a fellow employee. The theory apparently was that the person accepting employment not only assumed the ordinary risks of the business but also assumed the risks of injury arising out of the negligent acts of his fellow employees. Had the injured employee been instead just a third person, the employer would have been liable for the injury under the doctrine of *respondeat superior.* Why the courts made an exception to the much older principle when the injured person was also an employee is not entirely clear, but their motives appear to have been good. It often was said that such a rule would secure higher standards of care and skill among the employees. In the simple, small-scale, and unmechanized industry that existed at the time the rule was first enunciated, higher standards might very well have been the result of the rule, but the advent of large-scale, complicated, and mechanized industry turned the rule into a horrible and unfair anachronism when it was strictly applied by the courts.

The third defense was the doctrine of *contributory negligence,* which deprived the employee of any recovery if he had in any way contributed to the injury by his own conduct. The result frequently was that an employee who knew of a dangerous condition had the choice of quitting his job or running the risk of injury knowing that he could not recover.

If these three obstacles were overcome, the employee still faced the long legal process during which he and his family had no income and after which he might find the recovery eaten up by legal fees and expenses. Nor were all employers pleased with these rules, because a successful suit left the employer at the mercy of the jury's whim.

In spite of these obstacles for the employee, the employer did have to bear some risks at common law, and he did have certain common law duties toward his employees, though these were usually shifted to the employees who knew that the duties and risk-bearing responsibilities were being ignored. Employers had duties to furnish a safe place to work, to furnish safe tools and equipment, to furnish competent fellow-servants, and to establish reasonable rules for the operation of the business. In all of these situations, however, the duty was simply to exercise reasonable care in circumstances where the standards of care were often very low.

EMPLOYERS' LIABILITY ACTS.   The harshness and unfairness of the common law rules became more and more obvious as the industrial system expanded and powerful machinery came into greater use. Legislation, both state and federal, stepped into the picture to remedy the situation. The first such legislation, usually called *Employers' Liability Acts,* approached the problem by changing or abolishing the defenses of assumption of risk, the fellow-servant rule, and contributory negligence. Although these statutes were an improvement over the previous situation, they still required proof of the employer's negligence as a prerequisite to recovery and still placed the burden of litigation on the injured employee who was frequently in no position to sustain it. This type of legislation supplied only a temporary palliative, and it became completely inadequate as industry continued to mechanize. A new type of legislation then made its appearance.

WORKMEN'S COMPENSATION LAWS.   Where the common law had based liability on the employer's negligence, the new legislation moved the basis of liability away from the employer's fault and made it depend largely upon whether the injury in a given case was a risk of the industry. The theory that supports the legislation is exactly the reverse of the theory upon which the common law rules were founded. Instead of placing on the employee the risks of the industry, the legislative theory puts the risk on the industry itself, and on the employer. The California Workmen's Compensation Act, for example, provides that

> liability for the compensation provided by this division, in lieu of any other liability whatsoever to any person . . . , shall, without regard to negligence, exist against an employer for any injury sustained by his employees arising out of and in the course of the employment and for the death of any employee if the injury proximately causes death, in those cases where the following conditions of compensation concur: (a) Where, at the time of the injury, both the employer and the employee are subject to the compensation provisions of this division. (b) Where, at the time of the injury, the employee is performing service growing out of and incidental to his employment and is acting within the course of his employment. (c) Where the injury is proximately caused by the employment, either with or without negligence. (d) Where the injury is not caused by the intoxication of the injured employee. (e) Where the injury is not intentionally self-inflicted.

Compulsory and elective compensation.   The states have enacted two different types of compensation laws: *compulsory* and *elective*. The *compulsory laws* require every employer who comes under the provisions of the law to compensate employees for injuries incurred in the course of employment whether or not the parties concerned have consented. The elective laws appear, at first glance, to give the parties concerned a choice whether they will come under the legislation or be governed by the common law. Actually, little choice remains under most of the statutes because the alternatives provided are set up in such a fashion that statutory compensation is usually the more attractive to both employers and employees. For example: In some states, where the employer elects to come under the statute and the employee does not, the employee may use his common law remedy, but he is also subject to the common law defenses on the part of the employer. In some states, the compensation statutes are compulsory only in certain industries deemed to be unusually hazardous, but in other states, all occupations are included. Farm and domestic labor are often excluded from provisions of the compensation laws.

Insurance and security.   At common law, the risk that the employer or the industry would be unable to sustain the liability imposed in employees' suits for injuries was on the employees. The financial ability of the employer and of the industry was the only assurance that employees could collect their judgments. In a large-scale disaster, either to a single employer or to an industry, the employees could not collect their judgments; thus, they had to bear the losses themselves. Because most compensation acts recognize this possibility, they take steps to assure payment of the claims of injured employees. Some statutes only require that the employer demonstrate financial ability to carry all the risks himself. Some create a state insurance fund to which employers contribute and from which employees' claims are paid. Others permit the employer to secure insurance through private insurance companies or to set up cooperative insurance schemes among several employers in the same class or industry. Many statutes afford the employer a choice of method, but they usually require some sort of approval by a state administrative officer. Whatever the method, the burden of the losses is spread over a much larger segment of the society than was the case when the single employee or employer bore all of the risks and losses himself.

Amount of compensation.   Unlike the scale of compensation at common law where the amount depended upon the whim of the jury, the compensation statutes establish fixed schedules of payment based on the previous earning capacity of the deceased or injured employee, the nature and extent of his injury, and whether the disability is total or partial, permanent or temporary. A typical statute, for example, provides that in the case of total, temporary disability, "the disability payment is sixty-five per cent of the average weekly earnings during the period of such disability, consideration being given to the ability of the injured employee to compete in an open labor market." Where there is a partial temporary disability, "the disability payment is sixty-five per cent of the weekly loss in wages during the period of such disability." It also provides that the disability period for a temporary disability shall not extend beyond 240 weeks from the date of the injury. Permanent injuries are dealt with similarly. The statute sets up a rather strict schedule:

If the injury causes permanent disability, the percentage of disability to total disability shall be determined and the disability payment computed and allowed according to the following schedule:

percentage of permanent disability incurred	number of weeks for which 65% of average weekly earnings allowed	percentage of average weekly earnings allowed for remainder of life after 240 weeks
1	4	0
10	40	0
20	80	0
30	120	0
40	160	0
50	200	0
60	240	0
70	240	10
80	240	20
90	240	30
100	240	40

Ordinarily, disability or death benefit payments are made in instalments, but where it is necessary or desirable, as where the employer is disposing of all of his assets or is a nonresident of the state, many states permit the payment of lump sums at once. Most statutes, in order to prevent malingering, prohibit compensation for disabilities for short periods such as seven, ten, or fourteen days. Some of the statutes provide for payments covering the initial period if the aggregate period of disability extends beyond the intitial period, but other statutes make no provision at all for payments during the first few days of disability.

Administration of compensation acts. The methods of administration vary somewhat from state to state, but, in general, contested claims are heard by a commission or board from which appeals can be taken to the courts. Although some of these commissions or boards function as courts, their procedure is usually very informal, and the technical rules of evidence do not apply. In some states, contested claims are heard directly by the courts.

One of the great disadvantages of the common law remedies, from the standpoint of the injured employee, was the expense involved in obtaining the services of a lawyer. The lawyers representing an injured employee usually based their fees on a percentage of the recovery, with the result that the net amount reaching the employee was frequently as much as a third less than the amount recovered. However, this difficulty has been largely removed by the compensation laws. In most situations, the injured employee does not require the services of a lawyer, and in those situations where a lawyer is necessary or desirable, his fees are usually subject to the approval of the administrative board or commission.

Although most statutes require written notice by the employee to the employer as a necessary step in the establishment of a claim, in practice the requirement is frequently excused on the ground that the employer or his agent knew of the injury or that the employer was not misled or prejudiced by the failure to give the notice. Also note that an employee's advance agreement to waive his right to compensation is utterly without binding effect upon him, and he may claim compensation for an injury in spite of his contrary agreement. The reason for this provision is obvious.

Compensable injuries. The statutes provide compensation for injuries due to "accidents arising out of and in the course of employment." This simple language raises three problems to be solved or three tests to be met: 1. There must be an accident. 2. The accident must arise out of the employment. 3. The accident must arise in the course of the employment.

An *accident* is an unexpected, unusual, or undesigned occurrence, and, in compensation cases, has been held by the courts to include many things not ordinarily understood to be accidents. For example: a disease, such as silicosis, arising out of contact with foreign materials associated with the employment; pneumonia following a severe bodily injury incurred in the course of the employment; the murder, in the course of a robbery, of an employee engaged in his usual duty of paying other employees.

The second test requires that the injury have some causal connection with the employment. Thus, an injury that cannot be fairly traced to the employment as a contributing proximate cause and that comes from a hazard to which the employee would be equally exposed apart from his employment would be excluded from compensation. The above, of course, is very easy to say, but not so easy to apply in some cases. Consider the following: 1. An employee is killed by falling walls resulting from an earthquake. 2. An employee dies of a heart attack. 3. While standing on a railroad platform waiting for his train, an employee employed to travel on his employer's business is killed by a stray bullet fired by a police officer at a fleeing criminal. 4. An employee working outdoors dies from sunstroke. 5. An employee is injured as the result of an altercation between other employees. 6. An employee's negligence causes him injury.

There is no compensation for injuries caused solely by an "act of God," even though the employee was working at the time at his regular employment, but, as in 1, above, where an earthquake caused a *defective* wall to fall, the court held that the act of God could be disregarded as a cause of the injury. The death of an employee from a heart attack has been held to arise out of the employment if the attack was precipitated by some exertion or strain in the employee's work. In example 3, the court held that the injury was compensable although the general rule is that where an employee is required to be on the street or in public places when on his employer's business, injuries occurring there are compensable only when the injury is caused by some instrumentality incidental to the use of the street or public place. Sunstrokes and other results from climatic exposures are normally compensable only where the employee is specially exposed in a manner different from the rest of the community, or where he is exposed without prior acclimatization. The rule commonly applied to injuries resulting from altercations is that the participants have no claim for injury but that innocent employees do have proper claims for injuries resulting therefrom. The rule is based on the theory that some horseplay and the like is to be expected whether the employer permits it or not. As regards the employee's own fault, as in 6 above, it can only be said that generally the employee's fault is relevant in only a few situations: where the injury is self-inflicted or arises from intoxication, where the employee unreasonably refuses to submit to medical treatment, and where the injury is caused by serious and wilful misconduct by the employee.

The third test, that the injury must arise in the course of the employment, is best described as a requirement that the employee must have been engaged, at the time of the injury, in the work he was hired to perform. The test is clearly met when the employee is on the employer's premises, performing acts within the scope of his duties, and doing so in accordance with the employer's directions. An employee is, ordinarily, not in the course of his employment where his particular activity at the time of the injury was not related to the employment, where his acts were outside the scope of his duties, where he performs the specialized work of another employee, or where he is not on the employer's premises. A difficult problem arises when an employee disobeys instructions given him by his employer to guide him in his work. Compensation is usually allowed where the employee was doing his work but in a manner different from that prescribed by the employer, but where an employee does something that he should not do at all, compensation is usually refused. Consider the following problems: 1. An employee is injured while getting a drink of water or while he is in the washroom. 2. An employee is injured while on his way to or from work. 3. An employee in a railroad yard is injured while waiting for the next boxcar to be moved into place so that he can unload it. 4. An employee is injured while attempting to rescue guests of the employer from danger. 5. An employee is injured while removing the cap from a bottle of a soft drink provided by the employer.

1 and 5 above are generally included in the rule that injuries occurring during an employee's lunch hour or while he is engaged in an act of a personal nature on his employer's premises are compensable except where the acts are unnecessary or are unduly extended. A *going and coming* rule has evolved in connection with situations like 2 above. As a general rule, an employee is not in the course of his employment when he is on his way to or from work. There are several exceptions to the rule, however, such as where the employee is on his way to perform or where he is returning from the performance of a special errand for his employer, unless the employee deviates substantially for purposes of his own. (It is interesting to speculate on the difference between the measure of deviation used in this connection and the measure of deviation necessary to remove the acts of an agent from the scope of his employment in connection

with the principal's liability for the torts of his agent.) Other exceptions to the "going and coming" rule are found where the employee's work is such that he is required to live on the employer's premises, where he is paid for his coming and going time, and where the employee has come into close proximity to the place where his work will be done, as where the employee is walking through other buildings on his way to the one in which he is to work. Injuries taking place during waiting periods, as in 3, are compensable because they are usually a necessary part of the work. The act in 4, above, was not a part of the required duties of the employee, but was held to be in the course of employment because it was normal, proper, and reasonably to be expected.

D. Miscellaneous Statutes Affecting
Labor Relations

SOCIAL SECURITY LEGISLATION. The common law recognized no duty on an employer's part to make any provision for employees who might be unemployed and unable to find work or for employees who have reached an age at which they can no longer be productive workers. The risks of unemployment and of old age were borne by the employee alone until he and his family had descended to the level at which public or private charity might provide some support. In 1935, Congress enacted the Social Security Act, which contained a comprehensive program of unemployment insurance, old age pensions, aid to the physically handicapped, and many other benefits. Most of the features of the Act are designed to be carried out in cooperation with the states.

The unemployment insurance portions of the Act encouraged states to adopt unemployment insurance plans of their own, in conformity with the federal insurance plan. All of the states have now adopted them. The unemployment insurance plans provide that the employers and, in some states, the employees, shall make payments, in the nature of a tax, to a fund that is deposited partially in the U. S. Treasury and partially with the individual states. The tax is a percentage of the wages paid or earned, as the case may be. The fund is distributed to those who, in times of economic distress, are unable to secure employment. The details have been worked out by the different states and vary considerably with regard to time for which payments are to be made, amount of payment, waiting periods, and methods of administration. The federal statute exempts employers who have less than eight employees, but many of the states have omitted such limitations, and provide for much broader coverage. The tax does not apply to amounts in excess of $6,600 paid by an employer to any employee during any one calendar year.

Another feature of the social security legislation involves the old age benefits provided. The tax is imposed in the same way as the unemployment tax, but it is paid by both the employer and the employee on amounts up to and including $7,800 for any one calendar year. The funds, however, are administered exclusively by the federal government and are distributed to those employees no longer in regular employment who have reached the age of sixty-five. The number of persons employed by any particular employer is of no significance in regard to the payment of the old age benefit tax.

Certain classes of employment are exempt from certain provisions of the Social Security Act. Full-time agricultural labor and domestic workers are exempt from the unemployment insurance tax, but they are not exempt from the old age benefit tax. Services performed in the employ of the United States Government or of any state are subject to the old age benefit tax, unless covered by a retirement system, but these services are not subject to the unemployment insurance tax. There are other special classes of exemptions. The tendency, however, has been in the direction of extending the coverage of the Act, especially with regard to old age benefits, and even classes of self-employed persons are now covered by the Act.

The Social Security Act also authorizes a federal-state arrangement by which the federal government provides grants-in-aid, matched by the state, for allowances to aged outside the old age benefit program, to the blind, and to dependent children.

PROBLEMS

1. What function does the agency perform in our modern economic society?

2. How does one differentiate between an independent contractor and an agent?

3. Explain the following terms: general agent, special agent, broker, factor, *del credere* agent.

4. Who may be an agent? Who may be a principal?

5. What is the nature of the relationship between a principal and a person to whom an agent has delegated some of his authority?

6. Describe briefly four methods of creating an agency relation or agency-like liability.

7. Describe briefly the duties of a principal to his agent. What is an "agent's lien?"

8. In what ways may an agent bind his principal in contract? Give examples of each.

9. Describe briefly the contract liability of each of the following kinds of principals for the acts of their agent: fully disclosed principal, partially disclosed principal, undisclosed principal.

10. Under what circumstances might a principal not want his identity or existence known to persons with whom his agent is dealing?

11. What rational explanation can be made for the doctrine of *respondeat superior*?

12. What factors are important in determining whether an agent is acting within the "scope of his employment"?

13. Describe briefly five duties that an agent owes to his principal.

14. List the ways in which an agent may become liable to a third person with whom he has dealt on behalf of his principal.

15. What is the nature of the "agent's warranty of authority"?

16. What precautions should a person who is dealing with a known agent take in order to assure his getting a binding arrangement with the principal? Explain.

17. Under what circumstances may an agency become irrevocable?

18. May a principal avoid any liability for future acts of his agent simply by notifying the agent that he is fired? Explain.

19. George told his friend Henry that he was going to a land auction the next day to bid on a particular piece of land. Henry said that he was going to the auction himself to bid on another piece of land and would be only too happy to save George a trip by bidding for George on the land in which George was interested. George authorized Henry to bid up to $10,000. Henry changed his mind about going to the auction and did not appear to bid on any of the land. Henry did not tell George that he was not going to the auction. The land that George wanted was sold for $6,500. Is Henry liable to George?

20. Albert was a salesman for Paul, a manufacturer of widgets. While Albert was away on a selling trip, the factory burned down, and Paul was killed in an automobile accident three days later. What is the liability of Paul's estate and of Albert in each of the following situations, assuming that Albert knew nothing of the destruction of the factory or of Paul's death at the time the contracts were made?

    a. Contracts entered into by Albert before the factory burned.

    b. Contracts entered into by Albert after the factory burned but before Paul's death.

    c. Contracts entered into by Albert after Paul's death.

21. Calvin Callus is the owner of the Liverspot Department Store. Calvin employs, among others, these four persons: Cannonball Swenson, who drives the delivery truck; Sam Broom, who is the janitor; Bill Bargan, who is a buyer; and Lucky Smith, who is in charge of advertising and sales promotion.

    a. Cannonball has Calvin's express permission to use the store's truck for the purpose of transporting himself to and from work, and Cannonball keeps the truck in his own garage. While on his way home from work one day, Cannonball engaged in a race with a friend who was driving another truck; the two men had done the same thing many times before. Due to Cannonball's excessive speed and inadequate control of the truck, Eva Evans, age 3, was struck and seriously injured. What is the liability of Calvin?

    b. Sam was accustomed to sweeping off the walk in front of the store each morning before the store opened. One morning while Sam was sweeping the walk, George Spender, a regular customer of the store, left $75 with Sam to be applied to George's account with the store. Sam accepted the money but dropped his broom as soon as George was out of sight and was never heard from again. Can Calvin still collect this $75 from George? Would it make any difference if Sam had accepted money from customers in the past but had always given it to the cashier when the store opened?

    c. Calvin discharged Bill, but Bill, who was off on a buying trip when he received notice of his discharge, went on with his trip for several days. During this time, Bill entered into the following contracts on behalf of the store: bought $1,000 worth of goods on credit from the X Company, an old supplier; bought $500 worth of goods from the Y Company, a firm with which he had never dealt before. When the goods were delivered to the store, Calvin refused to accept the goods or to pay for them. What are the rights of X and Y against Calvin?

d. While vacationing in Chicago, Lucky contracted in his own name to buy $1,000 worth of basketware that he thought would sell well in the Liverspot Store. After he returned to work, he told Calvin what he had done, and Calvin replied that although Lucky had no authority to make such a contract for Calvin, it looked like a good deal and that he, Calvin, would ratify the contract. When the baskets were delivered, neither Lucky nor Calvin would accept or pay for them. What are the rights of the seller against Lucky and Calvin?

22. *S* entered into a contract with *B* whereby *S* was to sell and *B* to buy a large phonograph for $1,500; at the time the contract was entered into *S* owed *B* $500. *B* assumed that *S* owned the machine; actually the owner was *O*. The contract provided for immediate delivery of the machine with payment of the price in cash in 30 days. At the end of 30 days, *O* demanded $1,500 from *B* who refused to pay more than $1,000. *O* has brought an action against *B*. What are the rights of the parties?

23. *A*, acting on behalf of *P*, obtained *T*'s signature on a contract containing a clause stating that *A* was not authorized to make any representations with regard to the subject matter of the contract and that if any false statements were made by *A*, *T* waived any rights he might otherwise have had to rescind the contract. *A* did make several false statements on which *T* relied. What are the rights of *P* and *T*?

24. Albert and Tom made a written contract whereby Albert was to sell and Tom to buy a horse named Seacrumpet for $10,000. Tom assumed that Seacrumpet was owned by Albert, but actually the horse was owned by Paul, an undisclosed principal.

a. If Albert was authorized by Paul to sell the horse, what are Tom's rights against Albert and Paul if the horse is not delivered as required in the contract?

b. Same facts as (a), except that Tom has already brought suit against Albert when he discovers that Albert was simply an agent acting for Paul. Can Tom now recover from Paul?

25. Willy borrowed $1,000 from the Greenfield Insurance Company. Shortly before the debt became due, Willy realized that he could not pay and went to the offices of Greenfield to see if he could work out some sort of compromise or extension. He told the clerk at the reception desk what he wanted and was instructed to see Mr. Price; Willy explained to Price what it was he wanted, and was told by Price to see Mr. Swacker. Swacker agreed to accept a piece of real estate and $250 in bonds in full satisfaction of the debt. The insurance company rejected both the deed to the property and the bonds when Willy tendered them on the date the debt was due. The company argues and is prepared to prove that Swacker was not authorized to make this sort of agreement. What are the rights of Willy and Greenfield?

26. Describe the changes that have taken place during the last two hundred years in the attitude of the law toward contracts of employment and toward concerted activities by employees.

27. What important changes did the Labor-Management Relations Act make in the National Labor Relations Act?

28. What duties are imposed on unions and on management with regard to negotiating collective bargaining agreements?

29. What issues *must* be submitted to negotiation?

30. What is an "unfair labor practice"? By employers? By unions?

31. Is picketing legal?

32. What is the Fair Labor Standards Act? What are the meanings of the following terms as used in that act: regular rate, oppressive child labor?

33. Was the employer liable at common law for injuries to his employees?

34. What defenses were available at common law to an employer against whom an employee made a claim for injuries?

35. What is the modern law with regard to industrial injuries and accidents?

36. Describe the requirements which must be met under modern laws in order to qualify an injury for compensation.

37. What statutes are there in your state affecting employment and labor relations?

chapter 9

Legal Problems Peculiar to Particular Forms of Organization

1. IN GENERAL

The only business forms that will be discussed in detail in this section will be the partnership and the corporation. As has already been pointed out, major legal problems do not grow out of the use of the sole-proprietorship form. The problems of the sole-proprietor are the same ones that any business or individual faces, and these need not be discussed with special reference to the sole-proprietorship form. The limited partnership, the joint stock company, and the business trust do create special problems simply because these particular forms of business organization are employed, but these forms are not in sufficient use to justify extended examination. The partnership and the corporation are the most common and the most important forms of organization participated in by two or more persons.

2. THE PARTNERSHIP

A. In General

Three classes of problems arise in connection with the operation of a business by means of the partnership device. The first class of problems concerns partnership property. Because a partnership is not a legal entity, questions arise as to the title and ownership of the property which the partnership uses in carrying on its business, as to the rights of the individual partners in the property, as to the means of distinguishing partnership property from separate property of the partners, and as to the rights of the creditors, both partnership and separate, in this partnership property.

In the second class of problems, the question of the rights and duties and obligations of the partners among themselves is raised. Obviously, this kind of problem is not present in the sole-proprietorship, but in the partnership, with its close personal relations among its members, the problem is present in a much more critical form than in any of the other methods of business organization.

The third class of problems concerns the powers and liabilities of the partners with regard to third persons, as, for example, the power of the individual partner, through his dealings with third persons, to bind his fellow partners and the firm.

B. Partnership Property

(1)

Case. SIMUCO Toyland owned a pick-up truck which was used primarily for the purpose of carrying shipments of toys and bicycles from the railroad station and airport to the store and, occasionally, for making deliveries. Because he had a certain knack with machinery and did some of the routine maintenance on the truck himself, and because there was no garage or other facility for keeping the truck at the store overnight, Don Danton drove the truck to and from work and kept the truck in his garage at home. Sometimes Danton used the truck to haul garden cuttings and trash from his home to the city dump, and two or three times each year used the truck for hunting and camping trips in the mountains near Berkland. The other partners knew about Danton's use of the truck for non-partnership purposes but did not object. Danton did take good care of the truck, and none of the other partners had empty garage space where the truck could be kept. One Friday, about two weeks before Easter, Bob Baker told Danton that he (Baker) would like to have the use of the truck over the weekend in order to pick up two shipments of Easter toys and stuffed animals that were due to arrive by rail late Saturday afternoon. Baker explained that he planned to pick up the goods on his way home

Saturday evening and would work all day at the store on Sunday unpacking, pricing and putting the toys out on the shelves so as to be ready for the opening of business on Monday. Danton said he was taking the truck to Anosmia Pines on Sunday to get a load of wood for his fireplace and could not let Baker have the truck. Danton suggested that Baker use his own car or rent a truck from an automotive rental agency. Who has the prior right to use the truck?

WHAT IS PARTNERSHIP PROPERTY? The issue of what constitutes partnership property is sometimes difficult to resolve. There are a number of places, however, where one may look for evidence, and the Uniform Partnership Act supplies some presumptions that may be useful in certain situations. The necessity for determining what is and what is not partnership property occurs frequently.

Basically, what is or is not partnership property is governed by the agreement among the partners. Therefore, the partnership contract, if it is in writing, would be a good place to start the search for information. If one of the partners is simply lending some of his property for the partnership's use, it is very likely that his own self-interest has resulted in a statement in the contract that certain property is the separate property of that partner. If the partnership agreement is not in writing, the problem is more difficult.

The mere use by the partnership of particular property is not enough to establish that property as partnership property, but the conduct of the partners toward it, the purpose for which it is used, and the way in which it is used are important. If the property is listed as a partnership asset or if the title to property is transferred to the firm, in those states where the firm may hold title, a reasonable conclusion would be that the property is partnership property. Agreement to the contrary would usually be controlling, but in the absence of such agreement, partnership property would seem to be the proper category. Section 8 of the Uniform Partnership Act supplies two presumptions that aid in resolving those situations where the intention of the parties cannot otherwise be ascertained:

1. All property originally brought into the partnership stock or subsequently acquired by purchase or otherwise on account of the partnership is partnership property.

2. Unless the contrary intention appears, property acquired with partnership funds is partnership property.

A proper question to ask at this point would be: What difference does it make whether property is partnership property or the separate property of the individual partner? The answer to the question is clear. A partner may take his separate property with him when he withdraws from the firm or when the firm winds up its business. Property contributed by a partner, if it becomes partnership property, is not returned to the partner in kind but in cash. Creditors of the individual partner may reach his separate property directly even though it is in use by the firm, but they cannot, under the Uniform Act, directly reach the partnership property, even that portion of it that was contributed by the debtor partner. On dissolution, creditors of the individual partner have priority over partnership creditors in the separate property of that partner, but partnership creditors have priority in partnership property. These reasons, it should be observed, may be important not only to the partners themselves but also to persons who deal with a partnership. If the most valuable portion of the property used by a partnership in its business is the separate property of one of the partners, a prospective creditor may want to think twice before becoming a firm creditor, especially where the particular partner has substantial debts of his own.

WHAT CAN BE PARTNERSHIP PROPERTY? Anything capable of being separate property is, in general, capable of being partnership property. Real estate, whether or not held in the name of the firm, may be partnership property. Both tangible and intangible personal property may be partnership property. Insurance policies, seats on stock exchanges, patents, copyrights, and inventions may all be partnership property. The firm name and goodwill may also be partnership property. The name of a firm, used to identify a business or a group of individuals, is frequently one of a firm's most valuable assets. A firm name is property; it is capable of being owned and of being bought, sold, or exchanged.

It is a well-known fact that any successfully operating business has a value sometimes far in excess of the value of its physical property and tangible assets. In other words, if the business were sold, it would bring a price greater than the total of the values of the property employed in the business. This excess is known as *goodwill,* or sometimes, *going concern value.* Goodwill does not result from store buildings, machinery, and raw materials, by themselves, because they do not operate a business or make it successful; it comes from the favor with which customers and the public look upon the products and the method of conducting the business. These views give to a going business a value that cannot be measured in terms of ordinary property values. Goodwill is property; it is capable of being owned and of becoming partnership property. In better accounting practices, a business should not put goodwill into its books and onto its balance sheet unless the firm has actually paid something for goodwill. The purchaser of an already going business will show goodwill, or its equivalent, on his opening books because he will, undoubtedly, have paid for the business something more than the value of its operating assets. A business that has started from scratch and has not changed hands will not usually show goodwill on its books.

Under some circumstances, however, a partnership may show goodwill on its balance sheet even though the business has not actually been sold. A partner who withdraws from the firm without violating the agreement is entitled to receive from the firm not only his capital and his share of the undistributed profits but also his share of the goodwill he has helped to create. In order to determine the amount of the retiring partner's share, the members of the firm may estimate the price at which the going business might be sold, subtract from that figure the value of the book assets, and divide the resulting goodwill value by the number of partners or apply to it the profit-sharing ratio or some other formula. This final amount will be paid to the outgoing partner as his share of the goodwill. Because the continuing partnership is, in effect, buying a certain amount of goodwill from the retiring partner, the amount paid to him may properly appear on the firm's books.

Obviously, the firm name and goodwill are rather closely related. As a matter of fact, in many states, in the absence of a showing of contrary intention by the parties, the purchaser of the goodwill of a business gets, along with other goodwill, the firm name and even trade marks and trade names used in the conduct of the business. In some jurisdictions, the purchaser of goodwill does not get the right to use the firm name. This problem has another facet: Does the seller have a right to start a business similar to the one just sold, to use the old firm name, or to advertise that this new business is a continuation of the old? In a very few jurisdictions, the sale of a going business carries with it an implied promise not to compete with the business sold. Most courts go no further than to say that the seller cannot, in the absence of contrary agreement, use the old firm name, advertise that he is carrying on the same business, or actively solicit the old customers. The seller may not be allowed to use even his own name if its use might convey the impression that the old business was being continued by him. There are sound reasons for these rules. The buyer of goodwill has bought something more than the stock of goods, the showcases, and the office typewriter. He has purchased the reputation of the firm, the favorable attitudes of its customers and of the public, and has bought the right to receive the benefits of these things. If the seller goes back into business purporting to be continuing the old operation, the buyer may lose a large portion of what he has paid for. Were this allowed to happen, the result would really be no different from that which would occur should the seller also take the stock of goods and the showcases with him. (For a detailed discussion of these problems, see Chapter 14.)

PARTNERSHIP CAPITAL. A term that should be carefully distinguished from partnership property is *partnership capital*. The phrase "partnership property" refers to the particular items of property, such as the store building or the stock of goods, that belong to the firm. These items appear on the left side of the firm's balance sheet. "Partnership capital" has no reference to particular property at all. It is simply a monetary figure made up of the totals of the permanent investments made by the partners in the business and would usually appear on the right side of the balance sheet as the capital accounts of the partners. Except possibly at the very first moment of the partnership's existence, the capital and the property are not the same even in monetary amount. The partnership property changes with every partnership transaction, but the partnership capital only changes when the partners add to or subtract from their permanent investments, under the terms of the partnership agreement. The foregoing discussion is based on the legal point of view. Accountants sometimes use the phrase "partnership capital" in a somewhat different sense.

TITLE TO PARTNERSHIP PROPERTY. Even under the common law, no particular problems arose in connection with a partnership's buying and selling and holding title to personal property. However, this cannot be said of real property. The modern ramifications of the feudal origins of our common law system are apparent today in this area as well as in many others. In the eyes of the law, personal property and commercial enterprise were given subordinate positions. The concept of "title" and the restrictions surrounding that concept never developed to the same extent in the common law system with respect to personal property as they did with real property. Under the common law, only legal persons could take title to real property; thus, the partnership was disqualified. Personal property, being unimportant to the feudal system and slighted by the common law, never really came under such a restriction, and partnerships had, as a rule, bought, sold, and held personal property in their own names without any particular issues being raised.

In those states that have not modified the common law to permit partnerships to handle real property in the partnership name the title to the property must be held in the name of one or more of the partners. A deed purporting to convey real property to the firm alone is a nullity. Under the common law, if a deed purports to convey real property to the firm and to one or more partners, the title vests in the named partners as trustees for the firm. However, the Uniform Partnership Act provides, in Section 8: "Any estate in real property may be acquired in the partnership name." This statement, in effect, recognizes the partnership as a legal person for the purpose of holding title to real property. Logically, the Uniform Act goes on in the same section to say that if title is taken by the firm in its own name, the title so acquired may be conveyed only in the partnership name. This means that a partnership deed in such a case should be signed: "The X Company, by A, B, and C, Partners." Title may still be held in the names of the partners, but in most situations, the other method is preferable.

The improvements worked by permitting the partnership to hold title in its own name are substantial, but the discussion of most of them is postponed until Part V.

RIGHTS AND POWERS OF THE PARTNERS WITH RESPECT TO SPECIFIC PARTNERSHIP PROPERTY. If viewed broadly, the rights and powers of the partners with respect to the property of the firm fall into three distinct categories, only one of which is discussed in detail in this section. These categories are: the rights of the partners in specific partnership property, the partner's "interest" in the partnership, and the partner's right to participate in the management of the business. The third of these categories is a rather indirect, though important, right with respect to partnership property, and will be discussed in another connection. The second category refers to the thing the partner really owns, namely: his rights to share in the profits, to have his capital returned on dissolution, and to share in any surplus. This group of rights corresponds to the "share" that represents the stockholder's interest in the corporation. The partner does not "own" partnership property because that property, by definition, is owned by the firm, but he does own his "interest." This category will be discussed only incidentally here. The category discussed in this section is the first one: the rights of the partner in specific partnership property. These are the rights of the partner with regard to the store building, the stock of goods, the office furniture, and other specific property belonging to the firm.

Tenancy in partnership. The rights with respect to specific partnership property are enjoyed by all of the partners. Situations where more than one person has rights at the same time in the same property are not at all unusual in the law. Through the years, various devices and methods of dealing with the problems thus created have evolved, and in the past some of these methods have been used for the purpose of adjudicating partnership controversies. One of these older common law devices, whose chief distinguishing characteristic is "survivorship," is the *joint tenancy*. In joint tenancy the interest possessed by one of the joint tenants passes on his death, not to his heirs and devisees, but to the surviving joint tenants. Another of these devices is the *tenancy in common,* which resembles the joint tenancy, but does not have the characteristic of survivorship, Neither of these devices proved very satisfactory to describe the nature of the rights partners have in specific partnership property. The draftsmen of the Uniform Partnership Act sought a better way of explaining these partnership rights, a way that avoided some inconvenient aspects of the older devices and that was consistent with a sort of modified entity theory of the partnership. Section 25 of the Uniform Act sets forth the starting point of their solution: "A partner is a co-owner with his partners of specific partnership property holding as a tenant in partnership." The use of the unique phrase, "tenant in partnership," avoids confusion with the older devices. The draftsmen then went ahead in the same section to set forth some of the elements or characteristics of this new type of tenancy.

The first of these incidents is the right of each partner to possess and to use specific partnership property for partnership purposes, subject to the partnership agreement and the Uniform Act itself. This right is necessary if the partnership is to operate at all, but by agreement, the right may be limited to certain of the partners. If one or more partners wrongfully excludes another partner from the exercise of this right, the remedy is found not in the usual possessory actions at law but in an accounting for profits derived from the property, as a part of a dissolution and winding up proceeding. During the partnership's existence, actions between and among the partners cannot usually be maintained for claims arising out of partnership affairs.

A partner's rights in specific partnership property are not assignable or transferable except in connection with the assignments of all partners. A partner's rights in partnership property were assignable at common law, but they were still subject to some privileges in the other partners. A partner's "interest" is, of course, assignable. It is property that he owns.

A partner's rights in specific partnership property are not subject to attachment or execution, except upon a partnership claim. The separate creditors of the individual partner cannot reach specific partnership property under the Uniform Act. The opposite was true at common law, and it was not unusual for a partnership to be put out of operation by the attachment of a partner's share of partnership property by one of the partner's own separate creditors. It is rather difficult to attach one-third of a building or of a stock of goods without interfering with the use of the other two-thirds. Under the Uniform Partnership Act, the specific property is owned by the firm, and the partners have only non-attachable rights in that property, at least while the firm is in operation. (See Part V.)

The charging order.   Although the separate creditors of a partner may not reach partnership property, except on winding up—and then only after partnership creditors are satisfied—these creditors may reach the partner's "interest." The partner's rights to profits and to a return of capital are reached by means of a device known as the *charging order.* This device is simply a matter of the court's charging the "interest" of the partner with an unsatisfied judgment. In connection with the order, the court may appoint a receiver to receive and to pay to the creditor the partner's share of the profits until the debt is paid, or the court may order the sale of the partner's entire "interest," in which case the debt is paid out of the proceeds, and the excess, if any, goes to the partner. The sale of the interest, by itself, does not cause a dissolution of the firm nor does the purchaser become a partner. The debtor partner remains a partner with the usual rights and powers, except for those incident to his "interest," and the purchaser acquires the right to receive the debtor partner's share of the profits, the return of his capital on winding up, and his share of any surplus. The purchaser also acquires the right to ask the court, under certain circumstances, to dissolve the partnership. The purpose of this step would be to acquire the partner's capital and share of surplus. (These dissolution problems are discussed in Part V.)

Homestead and exemption laws.   Specific partnership property may be reached by the partnership creditors, and the partners cannot claim any rights under the homestead or exemption laws. The partners' rights in specific partnership property are not such that they entitle the partners to the protection of these laws.

Rights in specific property on death of partner.   When a partner dies, his rights in specific partnership property vest in the surviving partner or partners, except where the deceased was the last surviving partner, in which case his rights vest in his legal representative. This means that when a partner dies, his rights in specific property pass to the other partners and not to the deceased partner's own heirs or devisees. The common law result was uncertain and confused. The partner usually had title to some partnership real property, and, upon his death, this title passed to his heirs or devisees. The other partners had certain rights with regard to this property, but the enforcement of the rights was sometimes difficult and expensive. Under the Uniform Act, a partner's rights in specific partnership property are not subject to dower, curtesy, or allowances to widows, heirs, or next of kin. A contrary rule existed at common law.

Insurable interest.   A partner's rights in partnership property are such that he has an insurable interest in the property and may actually take out fire or other indemnity insurance on specific partnership property. Of course, the firm may carry and pay for its own indemnity insurance on partnership property, and the proceeds are payable to the firm even though by the terms of the policy they are made payable to a partner. Property purchased with partnership funds, it will be recalled, is partnership property.

POWER OF PARTNER TO SELL PARTNERSHIP PROPERTY.   Each individual partner, unless the partnership agreement is to the contrary, has the power to sell partnership property, either real or personal, if the property is held for the purpose of sale. Any other rule would destroy a large part of the usefulness of the partnership form. As we will see in greater detail in a later section, the limitation of the partner's authority in this area by ageement is not binding on third persons unless they know of the limitation. Along with the power to sell the property, the partner also has the power to execute those documents necessary to bring about a transfer of title and the power to make the customary warranties in respect to the property. Where real estate is held for the purpose of sale, for example, an individual partner has the power to sign the deed on behalf of the firm and the other partners.

A third person dealing with an individual member of a partnership may normally feel perfectly safe in buying property through that partner if the third person has no notice of any limitation on the partner's authority and if the property is of the type usually held for the purpose of sale. If the property is such that one would not expect it to be held for the purpose of sale, such as office furniture or real estate where the firm is not in the business of selling either kind of property, the third person should look further for authority than the word of the individual partner. The transaction may be voidable by the other partners.

The power of the individual partner to sell real estate can be assumed by the third person only where the partnership is in the business of selling real estate. In all other situations, the third person would be unwise to purchase real property on a single partner's word that he had authority to sell. If title to the real property is in the name of the firm, as is quite likely in those states that have adopted the Uniform Partnership Act, a single partner has the power to execute a deed to that property by signing the firm's name. If the individual partner had the power to sell that property, the third person gets good title to it, but if the partner did not have the power to sell, the other partners may have the conveyance set aside. No undue sympathy should be afforded the third person in the latter situation because the title is presumably recorded in the firm's name. Thus, the third person has constructive notice of that fact, and he should also have known that a single partner does not ordinarily have the power to sell real property belonging to the partnership. If this third person conveys to another party, however, the second purchaser may get good title to the property unless he had notice of the defect in the prior transaction. The reason for this result is that the title is in the name of the first purchaser and the deed is signed by him. If there is no notice to the second purchaser of an infirmity due to an unauthorized partnership sale, the second purchaser is not required to investigate all prior sales to determine whether or not partners had sold improperly any partnership property.

If the title is not held in the firm name, but in the names of one or more partners, a deed signed by those partners in whose names the title is held will pass good title to a purchaser who does not know that the title was held for the partnership. There is nothing in the record title to give the purchaser any warning that the property being sold is really partnership property. Good title will, of course, pass to the buyer where the partners signing the deed and holding title to the property were authorized to sell by the other partners.

Power of a Partner to Mortgage or Pledge Partnership Property. One might reasonably expect to find the same result in connection with mortgaging or pledging firm property as was found in connection with the sale of such property. The rules are different, however, largely because the approach to the problem is from a different direction. As we will see later, an individual partner usually has the power to borrow money for the partnership. The power to borrow money would be an empty power if the partner did not also have the power to give the ordinary types of security. Where a pledge or mortgage is a usual type of security, the partner, because of his power to borrow, has the power to pledge or mortgage partnership property. The power to pledge or mortgage is subject to the broad limitation on the partner's general powers which prevents him from doing any act which would destroy the business or make its conduct impossible. Thus, a mortgage that would give the mortgagee power on default to foreclose all or virtually all of the firm's assets would be outside the single partner's power because such foreclosure would destroy the partnership's business.

C. Rights and Duties of the Partners
Among Themselves

(1)

CASE. Although the old truck was still in good working order, the partners in the firm of SIMUCO Toyland had been talking for some time about buying a new one. They felt that a newer and more rakish model bearing the name of the firm and perhaps a clever drawing of a toy or a child might be good advertising for their business. Several of the partners, on different occasions, had inquired about the price of newer models and had even obtained estimates of the cash or trade-in value of the old truck. The highest figure that had been memtioned by any dealer or prospective purchaser of the old truck was $750. A friend of Don Danton's, knowing the truck had received good care and was in excellent condition, offered Danton $850 for the vehicle. Danton accepted the offer, received cash for the truck and delivered both the truck and the certificate of title to the buyer. Danton signed the certificate: "SIMUCO Toyland, by Don Danton, partner." Danton then turned over $750 to the firm and retained $100 for himself on the ground that he had taken care of the truck and was primarily responsible for its good condition and, furthermore, had found the buyer who was willing to pay $850. Is Danton entitled to keep the $100?

IN GENERAL. Where a partnership has a written partnership agreement, some of the details of the relations among the partners will be set forth therein. Areas covered by the agreement do not concern us here, but where the agreement fails to provide for a given situation, a knowledge of the legal rule to be applied to that situation becomes important. The rules and principles discussed below are those used when the partnership agreement is silent.

It is worthwhile to repeat at this point the crucial fact of partnership life that the partnership relation is a close, personal, fiduciary relation wholly unlike the relation among corporate shareholders. The relation between and among the partners is really the most important aspect of the partnership form of organization. A sound knowledge and understanding of this relation is the key to an understanding of partnership law, and these attributes make the other aspects of the field fall properly into place.

Considerable space is devoted in some textbooks to a description of the various types of partners. Most of these types are without real significance. Those that have significance, such as general partners, special or limited partners, ostensible partners, or partners by estoppel, have been discussed in this book in connection with relevant material. Among the classifications that are frequently encountered in other books and articles but that have little legal significance are the following:

1. *Dormant partners.* These partners are merely passive in the firm; they do not take an active part in the management. They may be known to third persons as partners, or they may be unknown.

2. *Silent partners.* Same as dormant partners.

3. *Secret partners.* Their connection with the firm is actually or purportedly kept secret from the world. (This type, as well as the two above, with a few special exceptions, is treated just as any other partner under the terms of the Uniform Partnership Act.)

4. *Nominal partners.* Those persons whose names appear in connection with the business but who are not actually partners. They may be partners by estoppel.

5. *Sub-partners.* Those persons who, by contractual arrangement, are entitled to share in the profits received by a real partner but are not partners themselves.

SHARING OF PROFITS AND LOSSES. A partner is always interested in that portion of partnership law related to the sharing of profits and losses. His interest is justified because the basic purpose of the business and the chief risk of the business come together here. The rules are essentially quite simple. The partners may agree upon any kind of profit or loss sharing arrangement that happens to meet their fancies. They may share profits and losses in the same way, or, differently. The partners may share equally, or in accordance with capital contributions or in any other proportion they may desire. If a method of sharing profits is specified, but nothing is said about losses, then losses are shared in the same manner as profits. If the partnership agreement is silent on the sharing of profits and losses, both are shared equally without regard to the amounts of the partners' capital contributions.

Note that the duty of a partner to share losses is not confined to operating losses alone. Capital losses are included also. The following, for example, illustrates a loss sharing problem: *A*, *B*, and *C* made capital contributions of $9,000, $4,000, and $2,000, respectively, creating a firm capital of $15,000. They share profits equally. The firm has been dissolved; all outside creditors have been paid: and $6,000 remains to be divided among the partners. Because only $6,000 remains of an original capital of $15,000, there has been a capital loss of $9,000 which, if shared equally, would mean a $3,000 loss for each partner. In order to reduce *A*'s loss to $3,000, he will have to get $6,000 out of the business. In order to reduce *B*'s loss to $3,000, he will have to receive $1,000, and *C* will have to put in $1,000 to bring him up to the $3,000 level. *C*'s $1,000 and the $6,000 available out of the firm's assets after creditors are paid make a total of $7,000, of which $6,000 will go to *A* and $1,000 to *B*. The capital losses of the partners are thus equalized. A more detailed problem of this type will be found in Part V in connection with the discussion of dissolution.

The partnership agreement may provide for the time of distributing profits. It may also supply rules for the retention of all or part of the profits in the business. In the absence of a provision in the agreement, both issues are determined by a majority of the partners. It is well to remember, however, that a partner's share of profits retained in the business is still taxable as income to the individual partner. The Internal Revenue Code does not tax partnerships as such, because they are not legal entities, but it does tax the profits of the individual partners. The profits are taxable to the partner whether they are distributed or not. A partnership files an income tax return for information in connection with the returns of the partners; it is not a basis for any tax to be paid by the firm.

RIGHT TO RETURN OF CONTRIBUTIONS. Each partner has a right, on dissolution, to be repaid his contributions to the partnership whether they were by way of capital or advances. Occasionally a partner will be entitled, by the agreement, to the return of capital in an amount different from that actually contributed. Usually, the amount is the same, subject of course to loss sharing. A partner who has made advances to the firm is entitled to the return of the amount advanced before any of the partners receive their capital contributions. If the firm's assets are insufficient to repay the advances, the deficiency is charged against all the partners in the same way as other losses are.

RIGHT TO INDEMNITY. A partner who has spent money out of his own pocket or reasonably incurred personal liability in the ordinary and proper conduct of the partnership business or for the protection of the business or property is entitled to be indemnified by the partnership. If the partner has already spent his own money, the partnership must repay him. If the partner has simply incurred liability, the partnership must step in and pay the obligation.

RIGHT TO PARTICIPATE IN MANAGEMENT. All partners have the right to participate in the management of the business, and no partner may be excluded from participation without his consent. Even where profit sharing or capital contributions are unequal, the partners presumably have equal rights in management. Frequently in the large partnerships, the partnership agreement will provide for the concentration of management in a few partners.

RIGHT TO INTEREST. In the absence of a contrary provision in the partnership agreement, a partner is not entitled to interest on his capital contributions. The right to share in profits takes the place of any right to interest. The partner is entitled to interest on his loans and advances, and he becomes entitled to interest on the contributed capital from the date when the repayment of the capital should be made to him. Profits retained in the business, in the absence of custom, usage, or agreement to the contrary, are not in the nature of loans or advances; they are usually considered to be additions to permanent capital. The partner is entitled to no interest on such amounts.

RIGHT TO COMPENSATION FOR SERVICES. No partner, unless the partnership agreement provides for it, is entitled to remuneration for acting as a partner. The profits, again, are the partner's reward. Where some of the partners are inactive, provision for extra compensation to the active partners is sometimes made, but this problem may be handled just as satisfactorily in most cases by adjusting the shares in the profits. Where a partner renders unusual services to his partnership under circumstances indicating an intention to pay and to receive extra compensation, the partner so rendering services may become entitled to the fair value of those services.

At common law the partners who had to participate in the winding up of the partnership were usually not entitled to compensation for their services. This activity was treated as being one of the risks incident to the partnership form. However, a partner doing something more than just liquidating and distributing the property might, at common law, become entitled to extra compensation. The Uniform Partnership Act, which goes somewhat beyond this common law rule, provides, in Section 18, that "a surviving partner is entitled to reasonable compensation for his services in winding up the partnership affairs."

RIGHT TO INFORMATION AND RIGHT TO INSPECT THE BOOKS.　Section 20 of the Uniform Act provides that "partners shall render on demand true and full information of all things affecting the partnership to any partner or to the legal representative of any deceased partner or partner under a legal disability." In addition to the partner's duty to give information on demand, he may, in certain circumstanaces, also be under a duty of voluntary disclosure. Even during the negotiating period before the partnership's formation, there may be a duty of disclosure of material facts relating to such things as the cost at which certain partnership property will be acquired by one of the prospective partners or the nature of the partner's interest in the property. When one partner sells his interest to another partner both partners are under a duty to disclose important facts having a bearing on value. Facts to which all partners have equal access do not give rise to duties of disclosure. The partnership contract may restrict certain partners in the information to which they may have access.

Section 19 of the Uniform Act requires that the partnership books be kept at the principal place of business, subject to a contrary provision in the contract, and that all partners at all times shall have access to the books, and may inspect and copy them. As a rule one of the partners may not remove the books from their place of keeping without the consent of the other partners. Nor may a partner inspect or copy the books except for purposes reasonably related to his interests as a partner. A partner seeking to inspect the books for the purpose of getting information for a competitor could rightfully be prevented from such inspection.

MAJORITY RULE.　A majority of the partners have the authority to decide matters within the scope of the business, but the majority cannot override the minority in performing acts outside the scope of the business. Any difference of opinion arising about ordinary matters connected with the partnership's business may be decided by a majority of the partners, but no act that is in violation of any agreement among the partners may be done rightfully without the consent of all of the partners. These rules are subject to change in the partnership contract.

Where the issue of whether a particular act contemplated by the majority is within the scope of the business is honestly disputed, the majority may normally decide that the act is within the scope and then go ahead with the act. But, where the act is clearly outside the scope, the majority do not have the power either to decide that it is within the scope or to perform the act if a minority objects. Where the partners are evenly divided about whether an act that is within the scope of the business should be carried out at all, court decisions are somewhat confused. One view is that transactions within the scope of the business cannot be limited except by a majority, but half of the partners does not consitute a majority. The effect of this view is to make both groups of partners equally capable of acting for the firm, even where third persons know of the even disagreement. This could easily lead to disastrous duplication. A better rule, from the practical point of view, is to limit the authority of either group to those situations where the third persons dealt with are ignorant of the even division of the partners.

The Uniform Partnership Act, in a departure from its usual policy of stating only general policies, has listed in Section 9 a number of acts that a majority of the partners, and thus individual partners also, do not have the authority to do unless authorized by the other partners:

1. Assign the partnership property in trust for creditors or on the assignee's promise to pay the debts of the partnership.

2. Dispose of the good will of the business.

3. Do any other act which would make it impossible to carry on the ordinary business of the partnership.

4. Confess a judgment.

5. Submit a partnership claim or liability to arbitration or reference.

The theory behind the prohibition in the statute is that, although the partners are agents of the firm and of the other partners, they are agents for the purpose of carrying on the business and not for the purpose of destroying it. The same policy presumably applies to petitions for involuntary bankruptcy by less than all the partners. The other prohibitions in Section 9, which are based on similar policies, are largely self-explanatory.

FIDUCIARY RELATION AMONG THE PARTNERS.   To some extent, the rights and duties already discussed are simply the ramifications of a fiduciary relation among the partners. However, there are certain duties that are traditionally a part of the fiduciary relation wherever it may be found. It is with the discussion of these duties that we are concenred here. One of the best statements of these fiduciary duties as applied to the partnership is that of Mr. Justice Howell Edmonds Jackson:

> The general principles on which the court proceeded admit of no question, it being well settled that one partner cannot, directly or indirectly, use partnership assets for his own benefit; that he cannot in conducting the business of a partnership, take any profit clandestinely for himself; that he cannot carry on the business of the partnership for his private advantage; that he cannot carry on another business in competition or rivalry with that of the firm, thereby depriving it of the benefit of his time, skill, and fidelity, without being accountable to his copartners for any profit that may accrue to him therefrom; that he cannot be permitted to secure for himself that which it is his duty to obtain, if at all, for the firm of which he is a member; nor can he avail himself of knowledge or information which may be properly regarded as the property of the partnership, in the sense that it is available or useful to the firm for any purpose within the scope of the partnership business.[1]

Section 21 of the Uniform Act says that

> Every partner must account to the partnership for any benefit, and hold as trustee for it any profits, derived by him without the consent of the other partners from any transaction connected with the formation, conduct or liquidation of the partnership or from any use by him of its property.

This view, and that of Mr. Justice Jackson, taken separately or together, make it plain that the partners cannot conduct themselves toward each other or toward the firm as though they were strangers. The obligations and duties created by the partnership relation itself, without regard to the agreement, render the partners fiduciaries as to each other and as to the firm.

A partner has a duty not to compete with his firm, but this duty does not prevent him from taking employment of a nature different from the partnership business as long as it does not interfere with the services needed of him by the partnership. The partnership agreement or the consent of the other partners may result in a waiver or a modification of the fiduciary duties.

An important aspect of the fiduciary relation, whether with regard to the partnership or to some other situation, is that of the degree of care or skill with which the person under a fiduciary duty is expected to carry out his activities. A paid agent, for example, is under a duty to his principal to act with standard care and with the skill standard in the locality for the kind of work that he is employed to perform, and in addition, to exercise any special skill he has. A partner is not expected to conform to these rather strict requirements of care and skill. The partner's duty is to render to the partnership faithful performance of his services on behalf of the firm and his fellow partners. He is not liable to the partnership, except indirectly, for the losses flowing from his

---

[1] *Latta* v. *Kilbourn,* 150 U.S. 524 (1893).

bad judgment in the operation of the business. A partner is expected to perform only to the best of his own ability, and his performance cannot be compared, for purposes of assessing liability, with the performance of other partners in similar situations or with any standard for the particular kind of work.

PARTNER'S RIGHT TO AN ACCOUNT. Because the partnership is not a legal person, certain theoretical, practical, and procedural difficulties arise in connection with the enforcement of the partner's rights, duties, and obligations during the operation of the firm as a going business. Ordinarily, the courts will not entertain suits by the partners in reference to partnership affairs except in connection with the dissolution and winding up of the business. There is, however, no policy against entertaining suits among or between partners if the subject matter is not directly related to their partnership rights and duties. Where partnership affairs are directly involved, the courts are reluctant to substitute legal opinion for the judgment of the partners in connection with the operation of the business. If the issues involved are simply those of establishing the rights of the partners in connection with the winding up of the business, law suits are not being substituted for the partners' business judgment. There are some exceptions to these rules, even with regard to breaches of fiduciary duties, but in general, partners' claims are litigated as part of the winding up process.

The device by which the claims and obligations of the partners among themselves are usually settled is the equitable procedure known as an *accounting*. The device is rarely found except as one of the events related to the dissolution of a partnership. Section 22 of the Uniform Partnership Act gives any partner a right to a formal accounting of partnership affairs where he has been wrongfully excluded from the business or from possession of its property, where there has been a breach of fiduciary duty by one or more of the other partners, whenever circumstances render it just and reasonable, and whenever the right exists under the agreement. The accounting establishes what is due to one partner from another. The usefulness of the device in connection with the final settlement of partnership affairs is obvious. It is not necessary that every partnership dissolution and winding up be accompanied by a formal accounting. Where no real dispute exists among the partners, the accounting may be informal, and it can be conducted by the partners themselves. In effect, the winding up and settlement of partnership affairs constitute an accounting.

D. Powers and Liabilities of Partners in Relation to Third Persons

(1)

CASE. SIMUCO Toyland, a large toystore in Berkland, Anosmia, extends credit to its customers and carries rather substantial amounts in accounts receivable. One summer, a slack season in the toy business, when three of the five partners were on vacation and a fourth was ill, Cal Charles sold a large portion of the firm's accounts receivable to an accounts receivable factor for $5,000, considerably less than the face value. The firm had never sold or assigned its receivables before, and, because the firm was adequately financed, the subject of accounts receivable financing had never been discussed by the partners. Charles then contracted, on behalf of the firm, to buy $2,500 worth of shelves, showcases, and office furniture and 100 shares of the common stock of the Dipsey Toy Company, a toy manufacturer, at $25 a share. The other partners returned to work before either of these contracts had been performed. They refused to accept or pay for any of the things which Charles had contracted to purchase and demanded the return of the receivables. What are the rights of the parties?

(2)

CASE. Earl Eaton, one of the partners in the firm of SIMUCO Toyland, drove the firm's truck to the railroad station to pick up a shipment of toys. On the way back to the store, Eaton's negligent operation of the vehicle caused him to strike and seriously injure a pedestrian, his wife, Ellen Eaton. It is the settled law of Anosmia that a wife may not maintain an action against her husband, nor a husband against his wife, for personal injuries caused by negligent or wilful conduct. It is also the settled law of the state of Anosmia that all members of a partnership are jointly and severally liable for torts committed in the course of the partnership business by a partner or by an employee. Will Mrs. Eaton be able to recover from the members of this partnership?

[See *Caplan* v. *Caplan,* 268 N.Y. 445, 198 N.E. 23 (1935)]

IN GENERAL. The ability of the individual partner to act for and bind his fellow partners and the firm is one of the important advantages of the partnership form over the sole-proprietorship form. Were it necessary for each partner to participate in each transaction, the partnership device would be so cumbersome that no business enterprise would ever bother to use it. It is an advantage, however, only as long as the partners trust each other's judgment. Once this element of trust and confidence disappears, the partnership form of business organization ceases to be either satisfactory or attractive. Attempts by the partners to circumscribe the authority of individual partners are not binding on third persons unless these persons have actual knowledge, and these attempts cannot be effective, even among the partners, unless the partner whose authority is limited has consented. The consent may be obtained when the original partnership agreement is entered into. That is the best time to obtain it because it may be difficult to get such consent once the firm has begun its operations. The ordinary agency device offers the sole-proprietor an opportunity to extend the scope of his activities, but it lacks the capital-raising attributes and many other attractions of the partnership.

In order to describe the nature of the authority and power that the individual partner has to bind his fellows and the firm, partnership law falls back upon the principles of agency. At common law, where the partnership was not a legal entity for any significant purpose, the individual partner was said to be the agent of his fellow partners in carrying on activities within the scope of the business. This approach led to some confusion inasmuch as a partner was simultaneously both principal and agent. The Uniform Partnership Act provides a much better means of analysis by making the individual partner "an agent of the partnership for the purpose of its business,"[2] and adds another item to the list of situations where the partnership is looked upon as an entity. Agency law governs almost exclusively under the Uniform Act, subject to the observation that apparent or ostensible authority is relatively much more important with regard to the partnership than it is with regard to the ordinary agency.

Section 9 makes it plain that the only situation where a partner apparently carrying on the normal business of his firm does not bind it occurs where that partner lacks authority in fact, and the lack of authority is known to the third person with whom the partner deals. For example: Where a partnership has instructed its bank that no check drawn on partnership funds shall be valid unless it is signed by at least two partners and the bank pays a check signed by only one partner, the bank may be compelled to restore the funds to the partnership account provided the bank knew of the lack of authority on the part of a single partner. Of course, the bank cannot be compelled to restore the funds if the benefit of the wrongfully paid funds was enjoyed by the firm. Section 9 sets forth no real change in the law of agency. It simply recognizes an unusual agency situation where the doctrine of apparent authority has peculiar significance. Actual authority, both express and implied, is present also in most partnership situations, but it has little effect on the ability of the individual partner to bind his firm, except where the authority is outside the scope of the normal business or where usual authority has been denied a partner and the third person with whom he deals knows of the denial.

USUAL POWERS. Whether certain specific acts are within the scope of the normal business depends to a large extent on the nature of the particular business. It is impractical to classify all the possible acts of a partner, but there are some acts that are common enough or important enough to demand attention, especially where some doubt may exist as to whether these acts are partnership acts. First, a group of acts generally held to be within the normal business

---

[2] Section 9(1).

will be considered. Then, we will consider a group of acts, though borderline, that are usually held to be outside the scope of the partnership business.

Power to borrow money.   In an ordinary agency relation the power of the agent to borrow money on behalf of his principal is seldom implied, and it must usually be an express power. In the partnership, however, a different result is found. The reason for the difference is clear. The ordinary partnership might well be handicapped in the conduct of its business if the consent of all the partners were necessary before the firm could borrow money. The courts have not found the implied or apparent authority of the individual partner to borrow money in all types of partnership, however, and have, in this connection, classified partnerships into *trading* and *non-trading* firms. If a court finds that a particular firm is a trading partnership, engaged primarily in the business of buying and selling commodities, the court will rule as a matter of law that the power to borrow money is possessed by the individual partner. If a firm is a non-trading partnership, not engaged in buying and selling commodities—for example, a law firm—the power of the individual partner to borrow money for the firm will not be found to exist as a matter of law. Of course, even in the non-trading partnership the power to borrow money may be found to exist in fact. Much the same rules apply where the power in question is the power to issue negotiable instruments on behalf of the firm.

Power to hire and fire.   Another possibly borderline power, which is usually held to be within the scope of the normal business, is the power to hire and fire employees. A partner has the power to hire a reasonable number of employees and to make reasonable arrangements for their compensation. A partner may also discharge an employee. The individual partner may not abuse these powers. This is another one of the areas where the partners' inability to co-operate effectively in the management of the business may easily destroy the firm.

Miscellaneous powers.   A partner may purchase property on behalf of the firm as long as the property purchased is reasonably incident to the business, and the partner may sell partnership property if it is held for the purpose of sale. A partner has the power to institute law suits for the collection of claims due the partnership. A partner has the power to accept delivery of goods or instruments on behalf of the firm and to accept payment of partnership claims and to receive performance of other obligations owed to the partnership.

ACTS NOT APPARENTLY FOR CARRYING ON THE BUSINESS.   The corollary of the basic rule that a partner binds his firm so long as he is apparently carrying on the normal business, is that an act of a partner that is not apparently for the carrying on of the business of the partnership in the usual way does not bind the partnership unless, of course, the act is authorized by the other partners. A few examples of such acts will be useful in getting a clearer picture of the authority of the individual partner. The reader's attention is called to the fact that included among these examples, by implication, are those acts that Section

9 of the Uniform Partnership Act specifically forbids except with the consent of all the partners. These unauthorized acts were discussed above in connection with the powers of the majority.

Other examples of acts not apparently within the scope of the normal business are: the giving away of partnership property, other gratuitous undertakings, and assuming, in the name of the firm, the debt of a third person. It is conceivable, of course, that some gratuitous undertakings would be within the scope of the business, such as reasonable amounts to recognized charities, free samples in connection with an advertising campaign, and free services or goods where customary in the trade or area. As far as assuming the debts of another is concerned, the nature of the business may justify the implication of the power. There may be actual authority either as a result of past dealings or expressly, and the act of the partner may be ratified by the other partners. In the latter situation, the general rules of agency with regard to ratification will normally apply.

Notice and Admissions. Another ramification of the application of agency principles to the partnership is the fact that each of the partners has the authority to receive notice on behalf of the firm, where the notice concerns partnership business. "What the agent knows within the scope of his authority, the principal knows" is translated here into "What the partner knows within the scope of the business, the partnership and other partners also know." Ordinarily no need exists, when notice is given to a partnership, to notify more than one of the partners, provided that the notice has something to do with the partnership business. An individual partner may not take advantage of this rule, however, in order to perpetrate a fraud on his fellow partners.

Admissions made by a person outside the courtroom may sometimes be used as evidence against that person in the courtroom. Such an admission by a partner with regard to partnership affairs may be used against a firm. An example might be an admission of fault by a partner involved in an automobile accident while he was driving a partnership vehicle on partnership business. A partner speaking only for himself would not bind the firm.

Nature of Partners' Liability: Contract. Even though the partnership is treated as a legal entity for many purposes, the liabilities of the firm are ultimately the liabilities of the partners. Where two or more persons become liable together, their liability may be either joint or joint and several. Where the liability is *joint*, an action against those liable must name all of them who are living. Omitting to name all of them and to take reasonable steps to serve process on all may result in the dismissal of the action. Persons liable jointly are liable only together; they are not liable separately. A procedural difficulty more than a substantive one is raised here. If a person jointly liable is named and reasonable steps are taken to serve process, his failure to appear or the failure to get jurisdiction over him is not necessarily fatal to the chances of getting a judgment against those who do appear and over whom proper jurisdiction has been acquired. In suits against large partnerships or against partnerships whose partners' names are not publicly available, the procedural difficulties may indeed be serious. Another characteristic of joint liability is that in most states the release by a creditor of one of the joint obligors releases them all. A few states have changed this result by statute.

Where the liability is *joint and several,* each person is liable separately as well as jointly, and it is not necessary to join all in the suit, but it may be wise, as a practical matter, to join as many as possible. In most states the release of one of a group of joint and several obligors only releases that one, but in some states all are released. While a judgment against all known joint obligors who are served with summons will generally be a bar to a suit against any others, a judgment against one joint and several obligor does not release the others nor serve as a bar to a suit against them until the judgment is satisfied.

Section 15 of the Uniform Partnership Act provides that the partners are jointly liable on all contract obligations of the firm; thus, what has just been said above in reference to joint liability will apply to partners in contract situations. In most states, the partnership, not being an entity, cannot be sued in its own name. This means that where contract liability of the firm is involved, suit must be brought against all of the partners, subject to the rules and principles of joint liability. Many states have, by statute, made it possible to sue partnerships and other unincorporated associations in their own names. Under these statutes, service of process on at least one of the partners or members is required, and the judgment obtained is good only against firm property and against the separate property of those partners or members served with process.

NATURE OF PARTNERS' LIABILITY: TORT.   The tort liability of partners is joint and several whether the tort is committed by a partner or by a servant or other agent of the partnership. In keeping with agency principles, a partner is liable for the torts of a fellow partner only when they are committed while the latter partner is acting within the scope of the normal business. A partnership and its partners are liable for the torts of employees only when the employee is acting within the scope of his employment. As far as establishing the tort liability of the firm and partners is concerned, agency principles apply to the partnership situation, and the question of whether the partner or other agent was acting within the scope of the business is usually the most important one.

SET-OFF.   When A sues B for $10,000, and B counterclaims for $7,000, and both claims are upheld in court, the usual procedure is for A to get a judgment for the net amout of $3,000. This is a somewhat oversimplified description of a process called *set-off*. B is allowed to set off against A's claim a claim B has against A. Obviously, B cannot set off against A's claim a claim which C has against A, unless C's claim is B's claim also. Set-off requires mutuality of parties in the claims involved. Because of the nature of the partnership device and the fact that the partners are liable for partnership obligations, some interesting set-off situations arise with regard to partnership law suits. Set-off is allowed in partnership situations *except* in the following cases:

1. When a partnership sues a third person on a partnership demand, the third person cannot set off the debt of an individual partner.

2. When a partner sues a third person on a separate demand, the third person cannot set off a debt of the partnership.

3. When a third person sues a partnership, the defending partners cannot set off a demand of a partner against the third person.

4. When a third person sues a partner, the partner cannot set off a demand of the partnership.

In all of these situations, the mutuality of parties is lacking because the debts and demands of the partner are held not to be the same as the debts and demands of the partnership.

3. THE CORPORATION

A. In General

Just as it is important for those who are partners and are operating a business by means of the partnership form of organization to know something about the legal problems that arise in connection with the use of the partnership form, so it is important for the directors, officers, shareholders, and employees of corporations to know some of the legal aspects of the operation of a business with the corporate device. The two areas are not really susceptible of analysis in the same way. The partners are both owners and operators, and they have a close personal relationship among themselves, but the ownership and the operating responsibilities in the corporation are often spread very widely among several groups and large numbers of individuals. The close personal relation is absent from most corporations. It is not necessary to devote a portion of the discussion to "corporation property," as was done with respect to "partnership property," because the corporation is a legal person, separate and distinct from the human beings who make it up; thus, it holds title to its property in its own name just as a human person does. Confusion about property is unlikely. However, two areas are important to investigate. In the first of these areas we will be concerned with three topics: the persons and groups of persons who act for a corporation; the rights, duties, and liabilities of these persons with regard to each other and to the corporation; and how these persons act for the corporation. The second area is concerned with the powers of the corporation itself and with what the corporation may or may not do.

Although a corporation is a legal person, it is obvious that a corporation cannot act for itself but must have its affairs conducted through individual human beings and groups of human beings. These individuals and groups—the shareholders, the directors, and the officers—will be considered first.

B. The Shareholders—Their Rights and Powers

(1)

CASE. Cochran owned 4,900 shares of the common stock of the Penn-Beaver Oil Company, a Delaware corporation. In order to determine the value of his shares, it was necessary for Cochran to examine the books of the corporation. He made repeated demands to see the books. He made these demands on the president and on the resident agent in Delaware, at the principal offices of the company in Philadelphia and at the principal offices in Delaware, but all demands were refused. The corporation relies on a provision in its articles of incorporation authorizing the directors

> to determine from time to time whether and, if allowed, under what conditions and regulations the accounts and books of the corporation shall be open to the inspection of the stockholders, and the stockholders' rights in this respect are and shall be restricted or limited accordingly, and no stockholder shall have any right to inspect any account or book or document of the corporation, except as conferred by statute or authorized by the board of directors, or by a resolution of the stockholders.

The corporation also calls attention to a by-law providing that "stockholders may, in the discretion of the board, inspect the books of the company at such reasonable times as the board of directors may by resolution designate." Both of these provisions, in the eyes of the company, are authorized by a clause in the General Incorporation Law of Delaware which permits the corporation to adopt provisions "creating, defining, limiting and regulating" the powers of shareholders. Cochran argues that the statutory provision does not permit the corporation to deny absolutely the right of a stockholder to inspect books and records, and has asked the court to compel the corporation to permit him to inspect the books and records. What should be the outcome of this request?

[*State ex rel. Cochran* v. *Penn-Beaver Oil Co.,* 34 Del. 81, 143 Atl. 257 (1926)]

(2)

CASE. Describe in detail the source, kind, amount, and recipients of the dividends which the directors of Hypocase, Inc. might declare on the basis of the following balance sheet. Assume that the relevant corporation law is the same as the law of your state.

**Hypocase, Inc. Consolidated Balance Sheet,
December 31, 1968**

Current Assets	$1,500,000	Current Liabilities	$ 350,000
Plant and Equipment ..	2,000,000	Long-term Liabilities ..	500,000
Patents...............	200,000	Capital Stock	
Other Assets	150,000	Preferred Stock–5% ..	
	$3,850,000	Cumulative $50 par	400,000
		Common Stock–$5 par	1,600,000
		Surplus	
		Earned...........	100,000
		Reduction	100,000
		Paid-in	300,000
		Revaluation	500,000
			$3,850,000

(3)

CASE.   The courts of Anosmia have always recognized the importance of shareholders' representative suits as a method of calling outsiders or directors and other insiders to account for their wrongful acts with regard to the corporation. However, during the last few years, the courts of Anosmia have been clogged with unfounded actions filed by litigious shareholders whose purposes appear to be simply harassment, notoriety, or out-of-court settlements by defendants anxious to have the suits dropped. Many corporations, especially those whose officers and directors have been plagued by these time-consuming and expensive actions, have brought pressure on the Anosmian legislature to do something about the problem.

Assume that you are a member of the Anosmian legislature and that you have just been appointed to an interim committee on corporation problems. This committee has been charged with the responsibility of drafting legislation aimed at eliminating the abuses of the representative suit. What would you recommend?

IN GENERAL.   The shareholder is a peculiar specimen. He is reputed to own the corporation, but he is frequently ignored by the directors, officers, and employees of the corporation. He puts up much of the capital with which the corporation operates, but he does not have very much to say about what will be done with his capital. He puts up the capital with the expectation of getting some return on it in the form of a share of the profits, but the directors often decide that there are better uses to which the profits can be put. He has the right to elect the directors and to vote on some other important matters, but, in order to exercise his right to vote, he may have to travel a thousand miles or else take the word of the directors themselves that they have done a good job or that a particular proposal is a good or bad one. He usually has the right to inspect the corporation's books, but he has discovered that having the right and actually inspecting the books are two entirely different things.

The directors and officers are also puzzled by the shareholder. He says he owns the corporation, but he seldom takes any interest in it. The shareholder voluntarily puts up the capital, but he frequently acts as though the corporation stole it from him. He complains about what a poor job the directors are doing, but he does not bother to cast his vote in the election of directors. He gives discretion to the directors in the management of the business; then, he complains because the directors exercise it. He has a contract with the corporation, but he rarely bothers to find out what it says. The shareholder used to be a widow or an orphan, but now seems to be an insurance company or a pension trustee.

Whoever he is or whatever he is or however he behaves, the shareholder has certain rather well-defined rights. A person who owns a share certificate is not necessarily the person entitled to exercise these rights as against his corporation. The corporation is not clairvoyant. It cannot tell who owns its widely scattered shares unless somebody takes the trouble to inform the corporation, and it cannot send a dividend check or a notice of shareholders' meeting to a shareholder it knows nothing about. The result is that, as against the corporation, only a special category of shareholder is entitled to exercise a shareholder's rights. This special category is made up of those shareholders whose names appear on the corporation's books, the *shareholders of record*. A person who buys shares from another shareholder should let the corporation know about the transfer so that the buyer's name may be placed on the corporation's records. A corporation will send out its dividend checks to those shareholders whose names appear on the record as of a certain date, and, although a shareholder whose name does not appear on the books may be entitled to the dividend as against the person to whom it was sent, he ordinarily has no rights against the corporation. In most of the problems discussed below it will be the "shareholder of record" who is referred to, even though he is called simply "shareholder."

THE RIGHT TO VOTE. Although the rule was somewhat different many years ago, a shareholder in a modern corporation has as many votes as he has shares that carry with them the voting right. Not all shares carry the right to vote. Some have no vote at all; others get to vote only on special issues; still others get to vote only when the corporation is in financial difficulty. The voting rights with regard to a particular share can be determined only by an examination of the share contract. Most state laws require, specifically, that at least one class or series of shares have the voting right. A corporation without any voting shares would be an anomaly.

The only way in which a shareholder, as such, may act on behalf of his corporation is to exercise his right to vote at a properly convened shareholders' meeting at which a quorum is present. The shareholder has little control over what it is he will vote on. He is usually restricted to electing the board of directors, adopting by-laws and amendments to the articles of incorporation, and authorizing, ratifying, or directing certain important acts by directors or officers. The shareholder rarely has an opportunity to vote on matters of a routine business nature. The directors, who are elected by the shareholders, are charged with the responsibility for the management of business.

What is a properly convened meeting and what is a quorum varies somewhat from state to state. In general, state law requires a corporation to hold regular annual meetings for the election of directors and requires some sort of notice to the shareholders. Special meetings for special purposes are permitted, and these meetings may be called by the board of directors, certain officers, or by the shareholders representing a certain minimum portion of the shares or voting power. Where special meetings are called and where business other than routine business will be considered at regular meetings, notice to the shareholders is especially important, and it is usually required. A shareholders' meeting can transact no business, except to adjourn, unless a quorum is present. Technically, a quorum is simply the presence of enough shares to make the meeting valid. At common law, and still in a few states, a quorum of any size group is two, but most states now require the presence of either one-third of the shares or of a majority of the shares entitled to vote at the meeting. Proxies are, of course, counted in determining the presence of a quorum. Otherwise, most large corporations would find it impossible to hold a valid meeting.

The method of casting and counting shareholders' votes is much more important with regard to the election of directors than it is with regard to other matters on which shareholders vote. Under the ordinary system of voting for directors, where each shareholder has as many votes as he has shares and casts all of his votes for his candidate for each of the vacancies, an organized group of shareholders representing a majority of the shares will elect all of the members of the board of directors even though the majority is of but one share. Minority groups will not be represented at all. It has been argued that better management would result and that minorities would be more interested and more active if provision could be made for minority representation on the board of directors. The method by which this objective is usually sought is called *cumulative voting.* This method of voting makes it possible for organized minorities to acquire representation on the board in roughly the same proportion which the number of minority shares bears to the total shares. A few states require the use of cumulative voting; many permit it expressly; others say nothing about it one way or the other. Studies of the effects of cumulative voting have been inconclusive. This fact, in itself, indicates that no revolutionary improvements have resulted from its use.[3]

The cumulative system is based on two principles: The shareholder has as many votes as he has shares multiplied by the number of directors to be elected; the shareholder may distribute his votes among the candidates in any way he pleases. In order to make the system work, all vacancies on the board

---

[3] Charles M. Williams, *Cumulative Voting for Directors;* a George F. Baker Foundation Publication (Cambridge: Harvard University Graduate School of Business Administration, 1951).

of directors must be voted on at the same time. If directors are voted for singly, cumulative voting will not work at all. If only portions of the board of directors come up for election at a given time, the effects of the system are much reduced. Cumulative voting may prove to be a trap for the greedy majority that tries to elect more than its due proportion to the board of directors in the face of an organized minority.

Proxies. A *proxy* is the authority given by a shareholder to another person to vote his shares at a shareholders' meeting. As has already been hinted, the proxy is not just a convenience, it is also a necessity in the large corporation if any reasonable portion of the shares is to be represented at a shareholders' meeting. The proxy is not as important to the small, closely held corporation where all or virtually all of the shareholders will appear at the meetings. In some states the proxy right may be modified or abolished by a provision in the by-laws or charter, but other states limit the effect the by-laws or charter may have on this right.

The proxy is a special form of agency whereby the shareholder, as principal, delegates authority to another person, as agent. The usual attributes of agency law apply, subject to occasional modification in the corporation laws. The proxy form of agency, unless coupled with an interest, is revocable. The delegation of authority may be general, and the proxy holder may have the authority to vote the shares in any manner he pleases, or the power may be limited in such a way that the proxy holder is required to vote the shares as directed by the principal. Some statutes require both proxy and revocation to be in writing in order to be effective. Some statutes limit the duration of the proxy.

Although the proxy device is useful, convenient, and sometimes necessary it can be abused and has been employed, both intentionally and unintentionally, as a method of perpetuating a particular management in office. The method is simple. When notices of shareholders' meetings for the election of directors are sent out, the management usually sends along with the notice a proxy form to solicit the shareholders' signatures. The proxy holders designated on the proxy form are selected by the management, and they can be counted on to vote the proxies as the management wants them voted. Where there is no active solicitation of proxies by groups other than the management, the shareholders who cannot attend the meeting are presented with the alternatives of not voting the shares at all or of turning the voting right over to the existing management. Until recent years, when regulation of proxy solicitation has entered the picture, the management proxies usually made no provision for telling the proxy holder how the shareholder wanted the shares voted. Consequently, the shareholder could not control the way his own shares would be voted, unless, of course, he could afford to go to the meeting himself or to send someone of his own selection in his place. Even where opposition proxy groups exist, the management has a tremendous advantage because the corporation pays for the management proxies and for the postage, an advantage that even the best financed opposition committee may find it difficult to overcome.

Furthermore, normal shareholder apathy plays into the hands of management interested in perpetuating itself.

Abuse of the proxy system has also been used as a method of securing adoption of undesirable by-laws and amendments to the charter. The shareholder will send in a general proxy power giving the management authority to vote the shares as it pleases, or else the statement of the proposal that accompanies the proxy may be so vague or misleading as to persuade the shareholder to vote in the way favored by the management.

Regulation of proxies.   Under the Securities Exchange Act of 1934, it was declared unlawful to solicit any proxy from the holder of any security listed on any national securities exchange except under the rules laid down by the Securities and Exchange Commission. Although this legislation does not apply to all corporations, it has had a salutary effect on proxy solicitations in general. The rules laid down by the Commission have covered a wide area, but they have been aimed, as a whole, at the difficulties and abuses just mentioned. The proxy rules require that the security holder be provided with sufficient information on candidates, issues, and proposals to enable him to know what it is that he is authorizing the proxy holder to vote on. The shareholder must also be given the opportunity to tell the proxy holder how to vote. The proxy material must be filed with the Commission before the beginning of the solicitation in order that the Commission may examine the material to see whether it complies with the regulations.

The rules of the Commission also provide that if the shareholder (or a group of shareholders) desires to solicit his own proxies, he may require the management to mail the proxies supplied by him to the same shareholders solicited by the management. The soliciting shareholder must pay any additional costs of mailing, and, of course, he must pay for the printing of his own proxy forms. The rules also make it possible for a shareholder who desires to present his own proposals to have them included on the agenda for the shareholders' meeting and submitted to the shareholders along with the other proposals on the proxy statement.

The increased protection and additional rights supplied to the shareholder under these Securities and Exchange Commission rules have encouraged the shareholder's activity and participation in shareholders' meetings and have resulted in somewhat more democratic procedures in the meetings and in the events preceding the meetings. Shareholders' meetings have been moved to more convenient places, and are held at more convenient times. Although the management still enjoys a favorably strategic position, the apathetic shareholder must now take a portion of the blame when management is unjustifiably perpetuated in office through the use of the proxy.

Methods of voting control.   As long as the voting rights of the shares are in the hands of the shareholders, at least a possible means remains by which the shareholder may exercise restraint or control over the management. A number of devices exist, however, by which the voting power and the ownership may be separated and by which a small group may acquire and retain control over the management. The voting trust is one of these devices. It is, in effect, an irrevocable proxy, and its primary purpose is to overcome the revocable characteristic of the ordinary proxy. Under the voting trust arrangement, the shareholder transfers his shares to a trustee who gives to the shareholder in exchange a trust certificate, which, for practical purposes, returns to the shareholder all of his rights as a shareholder except the right to vote. Although a few courts have condemned the voting trust as illegal, the device has been upheld in most jurisdictions where its motives and purposes were found to be proper.

Other devices for obtaining voting control are: voting agreements among the shareholders, classification of common shares and assignment of voting rights to a small class of "management stock," holding companies, staggered elections of directors so that only a small portion of the board comes up for election in any one year, and management contracts whereby the management is hired by the corporation for a fixed period of time under a contract. It should be remembered that concentration of voting control of a corporation often has legitimate objects, and it should not be condemned *per se*.

RIGHT TO INSPECT THE RECORDS. A right that may, under certain circumstances, be a very valuable one to the shareholder is the right to inspect the corporation's records. At common law the shareholder has the right to inspect the books and records for purposes reasonably incident to his rights as a shareholder. The inspection may be carried out personally or by an agent, and copies may be made. The right to inspect the books by an agent is an essential element in the right to inspect. Without it the right to inspect would be a sham because few shareholders possess the technical knowledge necessary in order to know what to look for and where and how to recognize important information when it is found.

What is a proper purpose is, in general, easy to determine. A shareholder may inspect the books, 1, to establish the value of the shares; 2, to ascertain the financial condition of the company; 3, to determine whether there has been mismanagement; 4, to obtain a list of the other shareholders in preparation for a shareholders' meeting; and 5, for other purposes incident to his rights as a shareholder. It is obvious that the right to inspect should not exist where the purpose is to obtain information for a competitor or to get customer lists or business secrets for the shareholder's own use.

The right to inspect is subject to abuse, and the corporation should be protected from these abuses. Many states seek to accomplish this end by the use of statutes that require that the demanding shareholder be the record holder of a certain minimum number or proportion of the shares, or that he have been a shareholder of record for a certain period of time, or that the shareholder have the burden of proving a legitimate purpose. Some statutes permit alteration of the right of inspection in the charter or by-laws. Many require written demand and limit the inspection to reasonable times. Some use has been made of severe charter limitations that give the directors discretion whether to allow inspection. These extreme provisions have, as a whole, been declared void, but they are still in use because of the advantage they give the corporation when facing the usual shareholder who does not know that the restrictions on his rights are invalid. Some corporations will refuse the right to inspect on the assumption that most shareholders will not argue about it. A corporation that has any doubts about the purposes for which a shareholder demands to see the books should refuse to permit the inspection; thus, it will force the shareholder to go to court for his relief and give the corporation time to investigate more thoroughly the purpose. Except where altered by statute, the burden is usually on the corporation to show wrongful purpose rather than on the shareholder to show wrongful refusal by the officers or directors.

Some states provide for inspection or investigation of corporate affairs by the court on the petition of a fixed portion of the shareholders.

RIGHT TO AN ANNUAL REPORT AND FINANCIAL STATEMENT. The right to inspect the corporation's books is an expensive and impractical method of getting current corporate financial information for the shareholder. Where there is no annual report to the shareholders, however, no other method of obtaining the information is available except under some statutes that require interim reports when demanded by a certain portion of the shareholders. A few states now require annual reports to shareholders, and reports are required of some corporations under such federal statutes as the Securities and Exchange Act and the Public Utility Holding Company Act. A brief glance at some of the corporate financial reports is all that is necessary to make it clear that merely requiring a report is not enough to assure a supply of necessary information to the shareholder. Some, of course, are relatively complete and supply the shareholder with the needed information, but many of them cost the corporation large sums of money and tell the shareholder nothing.

PRE-EMPTIVE RIGHTS. In order to protect his proportionate interest in the corporation, a shareholder at common law has the right to purchase a pro rata share of every offering of stock by the corporation. For example, where a shareholder owns 1000 shares out of a total of 10,000 shares issued by the corporation, he is entitled to purchase one-tenth of any new issue of shares before they are offered to the public. Of course, the shareholder is not *required* to buy the shares. He usually receives from the corporation a stock purchase warrant entitling him to his proper number of shares at a price fixed below the prevailing market price for the purpose of giving the warrant, itself, some value. The warrants are transferable, so the shareholder who does not want to exercise his pre-emptive right may sell the warrant for an amount within the difference between the prevailing market price of the shares and the offering price specified on the warrant.

Many of the issues arising under the pre-emptive right are in a state of confusion. It is uncertain, for instance, how far the holder of shares in one class has a pre-emptive right to new issues in another class. Pre-emptive rights are not now as important as they once were, however, because many modern corporation statutes permit provisions in the charter to limit or deny the pre-emptive right, and some corporation statutes abolish the pre-emptive right except where specifically retained by the corporation's charter.

RIGHT TO A CERTIFICATE.   A shareholder has a right to have his owner-ship of shares evidenced by a stock certificate. In many states, although the corporation *may* issue certificates for shares that are only partly paid for, the shareholder has no *right* to a certificate until the shares are fully paid. A share-holder also has the right to have his name and address entered on the corpora-tion's records in order that he may receive dividends, notices of shareholders' meetings, and annual reports and financial statements. Once the shareholder's name appears on the corporate books, the certificate is important to him primarily as a method of transferring his shares to someone else. He may have a new one issued to him if the old one is lost or destroyed, subject to his protect-ing the corporation against possible loss resulting from the reappearance of a lost or stolen certificate in the hands of a bona fide purchaser.

RIGHT TO DIVIDENDS.   To many shareholders, the right to dividends, which is the right to share in the profits, is the most important right they pos-sess. It is paradoxical that the right to dividends is one of the most impalpable of the shareholder's rights. The share of stock is essentially a profit sharing contract contemplating a return to the shareholder in the form of dividends. The dividends are not little Christmas presents distributed through the kindness and charitable motives of the directors; they are the fruits of investment just as rent and interest are the fruits of other forms of investment. An implied obligation rests with the management to exercise good faith and reasonable business discretion in distributing the profits to the shareholders. Yet, the violation of this implied obligation is the only possible ground for the actual enforcement of a shareholder's right to a dividend.

This result is proper. The directors are the judges of the financial and business situation, and they are in the best position to know what that situa-tion is and to decide whether it justifies the declaration and payment of divi-dends. The courts cannot be substituted for the directors in this important function. It is only where the directors act so unreasonably in refusing to declare dividends that their conduct amounts to an abuse of their discretion that the shareholder has any chance of enforcing a right to a dividend. Proof of the reluctance of the courts to assume the normal prerogatives of the directors is found in the paucity of cases in which a shareholder has successfully compelled a dividend by his corporation. In the most famous of these successful cases, the directors had refused to declare a dividend where the corporation had a surplus of $112,000,000, a net income of $60,000,000, and $54,000,000 in cash. The court, which compelled a $20,000,000 dividend, stated that a business corpora-tion is carried on primarily for the profit of its shareholders.[4] Abuse of discre-

---

[4] *Dodge* v. *Ford Motor Co.,* 204 Mich. 459 (1919).

tion by the directors, it must be pointed out, may also be found in too many dividends distributed as well as in too few.

Where a dividend has already been declared the shareholder usually gets a vested right. This right, which is a debt of the corporation, stands on the same level as debts to outside creditors. The directors cannot revoke the dividend, and the shareholder may sue to enforce its payment. A line is usually drawn, however, between cash and property dividends on one hand and stock dividends on the other. The former are not revocable when once declared, but the stock dividend, in most jurisdictions, may be revoked. The reason for the difference lies in the fact that a stock dividend, which consists of a transfer from surplus to stated capital, does not give the shareholder anything he did not have before. Even the Bureau of Internal Revenue recognizes this result and finds no "income" to the shareholder who receives a dividend in the same stock he already holds. Where the dividend is of another class of stock, "income" is found, but the result is probably no different, as far as revocation by the directors is concerned, from that which occurs when the dividend is in the same stock. A "psychological dividend" has been noted in connection with stock dividends of the same stock in that the market price does not always fall in proportion to the amount of the dividend, but this has not affected the conclusions set forth above. Generally, the binding effect of a cash or property dividend declaration does not occur until some sort of announcement by the board of directors is made, and even a declaration of a cash or property dividend may be revoked where the declaration or payment is illegal or unauthorized.

Sources of dividends. In order to prevent the corporate directors from distributing so much of the corporation's assets to the shareholders in the form of dividends that the rights of both creditors and shareholders would be impaired, limitations are imposed upon shareholders' distributions. Corporations are required to establish and to maintain a margin of asset values in excess of the claims of outside creditors. This margin, in general, is measured by the stated capital, and it is, as was pointed out in Part III, a sort of substitute for the unlimited personal liability to which the owners of other forms of organization are subjected. It is, in effect, the price paid for the limited liability afforded to shareholders. In addition to protecting creditors and shareholders from improvident distribution of assets, the dividend limitations also restrict the corporation's ability to increase the market value or saleability of its shares by false impressions of its financial prosperity. Dividends paid from an unauthorized source are generally illegal, and they may create liability on both directors and on shareholders who receive them.

The statutes are not uniform in the way they try to achieve dividend limitations. Some are very broad and general, but others are quite specific. Some prohibit "impairment of capital"; others require dividends to be paid out of surplus. Some limit dividends from certain sources to particular classes of shares. The combinations and permutations of provisions in the statutes are many. One of the best of the modern corporation laws can be used as an illustration. It permits any type of dividend to any class of share to be paid out of *earned surplus*. *Earned surplus* is simply an accumulation of net profits. (Dividends from earned surplus are permissible in all states.) Cash, property, and stock dividends may be distributed out of paid-in or reduction surplus to preferred shares, but only stock dividends may be paid to common shares from these sources. *Paid-in surplus* results from the issue and sale of stock at more than its par or stated value. *Reduction surplus* is created by formal corporate action reducing the par value or stated value of stock already outstanding. This statute requires notice to the shareholder when his dividends derive from sources other than earned surplus or profits. The purpose is, of course, to avoid any misconceptions about earnings or the prosperity of the company. In most states, by statute or by judicial decision, dividends are not payable out of revaluation surplus. *Revaluation* surplus results from the revaluing of fixed assets. This type of surplus is not a proper source of dividends because it is purely arbitrary in existence and amount, is nothing more than a book entry, and represents no real increment in the corporation's assets. If the appreciation has actually been realized through sale of the property, then a dividend would be proper because the surplus is more in the nature of an earned surplus and does represent an addition to the assets.

The laws of several states permit corporations to pay dividends on the basis of net profits for a preceding accounting period. This means that a corporation with no surplus at all may pay a dividend out of the net profit, on a profit and loss statement, before that profit is closed into and eaten up by a balance sheet deficit. The accounting period must be the one immediately preceding the declaration of the dividends, and may not be longer than one year nor shorter than six months. The purposes of these limitations are to prevent abuse of the privilege by corporations in seasonal industries and to prohibit unusually long accounting periods that are used to pick up the profits of years far in the past. Normally, where the corporation has a deficit, it would not be good financial policy to pay dividends out of net profits. A good policy would be to use the profits for the purpose of reducing the deficit. There are situations, however, where dividends at a reduced rate or dividends to preferred shares may be justified in spite of the deficit. The directors must exercise their discretion and use good business judgment when they decide to pay dividends from annual net profits. A statutory limit is imposed in some states to the effect that no dividends may be paid from this source if the net assets are less than the aggregate amount of stock having liquidation preferences. Dividends may be paid to the shares with such liquidation preferences.

Another limitation, imposed both by statute and decision and applying to cash and property dividends from all sources, prohibits the declaration of dividends where there is reasonable ground for believing that such would cause the corporation's debts and liabilities to exceed its assets or make it impossible for the corporation to meet its debts and obligations as they mature.

Special provision is frequently made in the statutes for the so-called *wasting asset* corporations. These corporations are engaged in the exploitation of mines, mineral deposits, and other assets that are irreplaceably depleted. The special treatment of these corporations usually consists of permitting the distribution of profits without taking into consideration the amount of the depletion. Generally, provision must be made for creditors and for protecting the liquidation preferences of preferred shares, but these requirements are so uncertain as to be of doubtful use. Notice to shareholders that no allowance is being made for depletion frequently is required.

SHAREHOLDERS' REPRESENTATIVE SUITS. The fact that a corporation is a legal entity poses some problems as to shareholders' rights and remedies where there has been fraud or mismanagement by the directors or wrongful acts by third persons affecting the corporation. Clearly, if the director has been fraudulent in his direct dealings with the shareholder, or a third person has injured the shareholder directly, the shareholder has his own separate law suit against the director or third person for the wrong that has been done him. Where, however, the acts of the director or third person affect the corporation directly and the shareholder only indirectly by impairing the value of his shares, the shareholder does not usually have a personal right of action. This does not mean that the shareholder has no remedy at all. The corporation has a right of action, and, where the management wrongfully fails or refuses to utilize the corporation's right of action, the shareholder may sue on behalf of the corporation. A suit by a shareholder under these circumstances is called a *shareholder's representative* or *derivative suit*. Occasionally, a personal right of action also arises where a separate duty to the shareholder is violated or where the representative suit does not provide sufficient relief.

The theory behind the representative suit is that an injury to the corporation is an injury to the shareholders as a group and that if the directors fail to enforce the right of action, a shareholder may step in to pursue or defend an action the directors should have handled. Usually, any recovery the shareholder may succeed in obtaining in his suit will go to the corporation and not to the shareholder. If the shareholder wins the action, the costs will be borne by the corporation. The shareholder is frequently limited in his right to bring a representative suit, but the degree of limitation varies from state to state. In general, the shareholder must first demand that the directors pursue or defend an action, but even this demand may not be necessary where it would be useless, as would be the case where the prospective defendants were the directors themselves. In some states an additional demand must be made on other shareholders to join in the suit, or the shareholder may be required to have held his shares at the time of the alleged wrongful acts or to post security for the costs of the action or both. The risk of losing the suit and of having to bear the costs himself are usually enough to deter the shareholder. The corporation is brought into the suit as a party defendant although the corporation is actually a sort of plaintiff.

Until recent years, shareholders' representative suits were used quite often by shareholders whose motives were not to benefit the corporation or to redress a wrong to it but to gain something for themselves. These suits are generally called *strike suits*. The sole purpose may be to blackmail the directors into paying off the suing shareholder so that he will drop the suit. The alleged wrong may be substantial, trivial, or even non-existent, but this is not important to the strike-suer who is interested only in his nuisance value. Although many states require court approval of the settlement or compromise of this type of suit, no thoroughly satisfactory method exists for preventing all possibility of a strike suit without taking away from the shareholder one of his few effective remedies for stopping abuses of power by the managers of the business.

C. The Shareholders—Their Liabilities

CASE. In 1958, the Anosmian Manufacturing Company issued 1,000 shares of its $100 par value capital stock to Roger Rabin in exchange for a patent assigned to the Company by Roger. One year later, the Company became insolvent and ceased its manufacturing operations. Just prior to the cessation of operations, several large creditors of the Company obtained judgments against the company, but the judgments were returned unsatisfied. These creditors have now filed an action against Rabin, alleging that the patent was grossly overvalued and not worth even a small fraction of the $100,000 value at which it had been placed on the company's books, and have demanded that Rabin pay them the difference between the actual value and $100,000. Some of the creditors were already creditors when the stock was issued to Rabin; others did not become creditors until afterwards. Rabin, of course, is resisting the suit. What are the rights of the parties? Assume that this is the first time this issue has been before the courts of Anosmia and that there is no applicable legislation.

IN GENERAL. It would be a dangerous oversimplification to say that a shareholder is never liable for more than the amount of his investment. This is not to say that the shareholder's liability is not limited. In comparison with the partner, the liability of the shareholder is very much limited, and it would be misleading to describe the situation in any other way. The point is this: Although a shareholder's liability is limited, and generally limited to his capital investment, the shareholder may become liable to the corporation or even to creditors of the corporation for additional amounts if special circumstances are present. A person who purchases a share and pays in full a reasonable price imposed by the directors does not normally have to worry about the imposition of further liability. He may well lose what he has invested, but neither the corporation nor its creditors can look to the shareholder for more.

LIABILITY TO THE CORPORATION. *Partly paid shares.* Generally speaking there are three types of situation where a shareholder may become liable to the corporation for amounts in addition to those he has already invested in the business. The first of these is liability for partly paid shares. Subscribers and persons to whom shares are issued are liable for the full consideration which was agreed on. (Shares, as it will be recalled, may be issued in some states whether or not they have been paid for in full.) If a purchaser of shares does not pay the full price of the shares at the time of purchase but agrees either to pay on demand of the corporation, at some definite time in the future, or to pay in regular instalments, the purchaser of the shares becomes a debtor of the corporation in the amount of the unpaid balance. This person's liability to the corporation on partly paid shares is an asset of the corporation, much like an an account receivable, and will appear on the corporation's balance sheet as *subscriptions payable* or *unpaid subscriptions* or *partly paid shares*. Thus, the shareholder is liable for an amount in excess of that amount he has actually invested, but not, it must be noted, in excess of what he promised to invest.

Assessments. Another form of shareholder liability to the corporation, which is not as common as it once was, owing to legislation in many of the states where it was once prevalent, may rise out of the power of the directors to assess the shares for additional amounts even though the shares are fully paid. Some states once permitted more or less unrestricted assessments, and the power was sometimes badly abused, but the power to assess is now strictly limited. The liability may be only against the shares, in which case the shareholder has the option of paying the assessment or losing his shares; thus, he may limit his liability to the amount of his investment. Under some statutes, there may be a personal claim against the shareholder. One modern corporation statute prohibits assessment for fully paid shares except where the charter specifically provides for it, and requires the shareholders' unanimous consent to amend the charter in order to permit the directors to impose *personal* liability by assessments. In this statute, a provision in the original charter making possible personal liability for assessments is not binding on the shareholder unless the share certificate itself contains a statement of this liability. The power to assess without creating personal liability is dealt with somewhat more leniently.

Illegal dividends. A shareholder who receives an unlawful or unauthorized dividend with knowledge of the facts is usually liable to the corporation for the amount of the dividend, but in some states the obligation to return the dividend depends upon the bad faith of the shareholder or the insolvency of the corporation. The shareholder is usually not required to return the illegal divided where he acted in good faith and had no notice or knowledge of the facts and where the corporation was solvent. Even a shareholder acting in good faith without notice will have to return a dividend paid while the corporation was insolvent. It should be noted that in some states the shareholder may be liable to creditors of the corporation, as well as to the corporation itself, for illegal or unauthorized dividends.

LIABILITY TO CREDITORS OF THE CORPORATION. *Statutory liability.* The average shareholder is probably more interested in his possible liability to the corporation's creditors than he is in his liability to the corporation. Actually, in comparing the liability of the shareholder with that of the partner, it is the liability to outside creditors that establishes the ground for comparison. It was once rather common practice for a corporation statute to impose a sort of proportional unlimited liability on shareholders in corporations. Other statutes imposed on shareholders an obligation to contribute, in addition to the amount invested, an amount equal to it in order to pay the debts of the corporation. The latter, the so-called *double liability*, has been retained in a few states with reference to special types of corporations, such as banks or building and loan companies. Neither of these forms of personal shareholder liability on fully paid shares proved satisfactory, and both caused a great deal of unnecessary litigation, in addition to discouraging incorporation in the states that imposed such liability. Legislative policy has made a complete reversal in this area, and statutory liability has almost vanished from the scene.

Partly paid shares. Other grounds remain, however, on which shareholders' liability to creditors of the corporation may be based. One of these grounds is also the basis for liability to the corporation. The liability of the shareholder on partly paid shares is an asset of the corporation, and as an asset it may be reached by the creditors of the corporation just as the ordinary assets may be reached by them. The capital that the shareholders invest or promise to invest is the foundation for the corporation's credit and financial responsibility, as has already been outlined in some detail. It is not surprising that the creditors insist that any of these subscriptions remaining unpaid should be paid in order to satisfy creditors' claims that would otherwise remain unsatisfied. The details by which the right of the creditors is worked out vary from state to state. In general, the shareholder is not liable directly to the creditors on the basis of his unpaid subscriptions unless such liability is imposed by statute. Many states impose liability on the shareholder only to the extent that the amount of his unpaid subscription is necessary to pay his proportionate share of the creditors' claims, but others take the view that the shareholder may be compelled to pay the full amount of his unpaid subscription. It is important to note that the corporation's creditors cannot pursue the shareholders personally on the basis of unpaid subscriptions until the legal remedies against the corporation itself have been exhausted, as by the return of a judgment unsatisfied.

Watered stock. The third and last basis of shareholder liability to corporation creditors, to be discussed here, is liability on watered stock. The stock of a corporation is said to be *watered* when it purports to be fully paid although actually it was acquired either for less than a full consideration or for property or services grossly overvalued. The origin of the term "watered stock" is not entirely clear, but it was supposedly borrowed from the cattle industry where it was once common practice to permit thirsty cattle to have their fill of water just before they were weighed for purposes of determining the sale price. A person with imagination can carry the analogy between the two situations a good deal further than the dishonesty involved. It is often reported that some of the swashbuckling financiers of the late nineteenth century employed in their dealings with corporate stock much of the experience they had obtained in their dealings with four-footed stock. Whatever the origin of the term, the meaning is relatively clear. The term is frequently used, and will be used here, to cover three different situations: 1, *bonus shares,* which are simply given away but put onto the books of the corporation as though full consideration had been received; 2, *discount shares,* which are issued at less than full consideration but which are put on the books as though full consideration were received; 3, *shares issued for over-valued property or services.* In the last case, shares are issued in exchange for property or services that are placed on the corporate books at excessive values for the purpose of conveying an impression that consideration equal to the par or market value of the shares was received by the corporation.

The reasons for watering stock are many and varied, but among them are the following: 1, the corporation cannot sell its stock at par; 2, the incorporators or directors may desire the assets and the capital of the corporation to appear larger than they really are; 3, rates in some regulated industries may be based on investment, 4, it is sometimes used as a method of raising quick cash, as where bonus shares are given to a friend of the corporation, who donates the shares back to the corporation, which can then sell the shares as treasury shares at any price that can be got for them; 5, promoters may use watered stock in order to increase their profits.

Again the seriousness of the situation is explained by the fact that the paid-in capital is the basis for the credit and financial responsibility of the corporation. Creditors and others who deal with the corporation look to the capital as a partial protection against loss. Obviously, the creditors should be entitled to some sort of relief where the capital is misrepresented, as it certainly is with watered stock. Within this simple framework, two different theories of shareholder liability on watered stock have appeared and, in recent years, have virtually merged. The first of these theories was the *trust fund* theory. This theory is based on an implied promise by the shareholder to the corporation to pay the par value of the shares. The proceeds and the promises were held in trust by the corporation for the benefit of its creditors, who could reach these promises in much the same way as they could reach unpaid subscriptions. Evidently, under this theory, as simply stated here, all creditors could take advantage of the rights thus created whether the creditors became such before or after the watering. Confusion between this theory and the other led to some rather inconsistent conclusions and a general discrediting of the trust fund theory.

The second theory is the *fraud* or *holding out* theory. This theory, which represents the prevailing view, is based on a hypothetical tort against the creditors. The reasoning is that watered stock is a misrepresentation on which creditors rely to their harm. It is clear that creditors whose claims antedate the watering are excluded from the protection of the theory because they did not rely on the misrepresentation. The weakness of this theory lies in the fact that in order to make the shareholders liable, the theory must make them at least partially guilty of the fraud, when actually the public subscriber is more likely to be a victim himself. The courts, of course, have been aware of this paradox. The result has been an extreme reluctance to rule against the shareholders in watered stock suits by creditors, except where the shareholders actually participated in the watering.

Theoretical difficulties are encountered not only with regard to the basis of the liability but also with regard to methods of valuing consideration for shares. Again two theories have appeared. The first is the so-called *true value* theory. This theory, which has never gained much support, clearly represents a minority view. The *true value* approach holds that stock is watered unless the true value of the consideration is the value at which the consideration is put onto the books of the corporation. It was soon realized that a true value approach was impractical if viewed at all objectively, and that view has been largely abandoned. Almost every sale of stock for a consideration other than money would be subject to question and to litigation under this view.

The other valuation approach is the *good faith* theory. This theory, though vague and intangible, is more practical and operates more conveniently. Valuation of property or services made by the directors in good faith is conclusive. A few states impose liability where the valuation is made without reasonable investigation or the use of reasonable care. This theory does not by any means solve all of the problems of valuation. "Good faith" itself may be a difficult concept to deal with, and the use of future earning capacity and prospective value as a basis for valuation of property to be exchanged for shares is a problem which has been viewed differently by different courts. Some of the blue sky laws and the federal securites acts impose controls upon the valuation of the consideration for shares and supply administrative regulation of such valuation. The administrative machinery seems to offer a much better means of protecting the creditor, the shareholder, and the corporation. The scarcity of creditors' watered stock suits against shareholders in recent years is some evidence of the success of the administrative methods of alleviating the watered stock problem.

Some attempts, other than setting up machinery for administrative supervision, have been made through legislation to restrain stock watering. A statutory obligation to pay the par value of shares, for example, would seem to create a corporate asset reachable by creditors when the consideration is less than par. This sort of legislation is a statutory return to something like the original trust fund theory. It has not been widely used and has met with some adverse decisions in the courts. It runs into trouble immediately where no-par shares are used.

Miscellaneous liability.   In addition to the types of liability already described, there are a number of other forms that shareholder liability may take under special circumstances. Statutes in some states, for example, impose upon shareholders of insolvent corporations personal liability for debts due laborers, servants, and other classes of labor. The theory underlying this liability is that there is an implied agreement made by the stockholder with his corporation and its creditors that he will pay these *labor debts.* In smaller corporations, the shareholders may have to assume personal liability in order for the corporation to be able *to obtain credit.* There is nothing magical about the corporate form that would soften the heart of a bank loan officer when he feels that the corporation's assets and prospects are inadequate to justify a loan. The personal credit of the shareholders may be necessary in order to tip the scales. *Disregard of the corporate entity* and *defective formation* of the corporation may impose liability on shareholders. There are other forms of shareholder liability, mostly statutory, that are not mentioned here. For a complete list, the law of one's own state and certain federal legislation should be examined with care.

D. The Directors

(1)

Case.   Eldur Stadtmun, Chairman of the Board of Hypocase, Inc., owns a piece of land adjoining the company's present manufacturing plant. Stadtmun acquired the land many years before Hypocase was organized, and Hypocase acquired its present site before Stadtmun joined the company. It has become necessary for the company to expand its facilities. Several members of the board feel that, instead of expanding the present plant in Berkland, the company should acquire additional facilities in the Northeast or Midwest. Another group of directors feel that it would be more economical to keep the manufacturing operation in one location. These directors favor the acquisition of the Stadtmun property and the erection of the new manufacturing plant there. Stadtmun is willing to sell the land to Hypocase but is afraid that the split in the board may lead to hard feelings and perhaps to charges that he used his position as Chairman to make a profit for himself. How should Stadtmun conduct himself in connection with this situation?

(2)

Case.   After a long period of negotiation, Paul Preston, the President of Hypocase, Inc., obtained a large contract from the Air Force for the design and construction of a movable rocket pad. The deal was consummated in Washington, D.C., late on a Friday afternoon, and Preston phoned the good news back to Berkland where a directors' meeting was then in progress. Preston said the he was flying home the next day and would bring with him a copy of the contract and full details of the arrangement with the Air Force. The directors decided to make no public announcement of the contract until Preston returned.

Wheeler N. Deler, one of the directors, spent Friday evening and most of Saturday buying up all the shares of Hypocase stock he could. He called personally on several shareholders living in and around Berkland and purchased shares from several of these people, paying slightly more than the price at which Hypocase stock had recently been selling. (Hypocase stock was not listed on a stock exchange.) Deler also bought some shares through his stockbroker. The directors met at 9 o'clock on Monday morning to hear Preston's report and then issued a statement to the press outlining in very general terms the nature of the Air Force contract. Within a few hours after the news was made public, brokers were being flooded with inquiries about the stock, and the price had risen by many dollars. Does Wheeler N. Deler have anything to worry about?

IN GENERAL. A corporation, although it is a legal person, is not a human person and cannot act for itself. Its only means of action are through individual human beings and groups of human beings. It was learned during the discussion of the shareholders that this group acts for the corporation only within the narrowly defined limits of the shareholders' meeting, which usually has jurisdiction only to consider such basic matters as the election of the members of the board of directors and alterations in the corporation's charter. The shareholders have very little to say about the day-to-day and month-to-month operation of the corporation's business. The ultimate business responsibility rests upon the directors. Just how much of this responsibility is delegated to the officers and other employees of the corporation varies from one corporation to another. Some boards of directors retain a large portion of the management responsibility, even down to the making of minor decisions; other boards keep for themselves only the basic policy-making functions and ultimate control over important financial problems. The gradations between these two extremes are many.

In terms of legal categories and relationships, the director and the board of directors are very difficult to classify. They are literally "neither fish nor fowl" if one is looking for a convenient legal niche in which to insert them. The directors are not, themselves, agents of the corporation because they normally do not act independently but only as members of the group. Paradoxes are encountered if it is said that the board is an agent of the corporation, unless we alter the law of agency to permit the agent to control the principal. The directors and the board cannot be properly classified as trustees because they do not hold title to any of the corporation's property; thus, the essential trust *corpus* or *res* is absent. Directors are fiduciaries, however, just as agents and trustees are, and this aspect of the directors' function will be examined in some detail below. It is best not to try to categorize the directors except to put them into a category all their own.

QUALIFICATIONS OF DIRECTORS. The legal qualifications of directors are usually few and unimportant. The business qualifications are important, but they are outside the scope of this book. At common law no qualifications are required at all for directors. Many states have imposed qualification standards by statute, but the trend in the modern statutes is away from such limitations. The requirements, where there are any, are usually that the director be a shareholder, a resident of the state of incorporation, twenty-one years of age, and not an alien. The problems implicit in the latter two requirements would seem to be taken care of by general law. The requirement that a director be a shareholder is so easily avoided as to make the requirement useless, and the requirement that a director be a resident of the state of incorporation hardly makes any sense when shareholders, property, and business may be scattered over many states.

Many statutes require that the board consist of a minimum of three directors; maximum limits are usually not set. Some statutes require only a portion of the board to be residents of the state of incorporation or to be shareholders; others impose the requirement of residence on the incorporators instead of on the directors.

ELECTION AND REMOVAL OF DIRECTORS.   Because the election of directors has been discussed elsewhere, it will only be referred to indirectly here. Although directors are usually elected for a one-year term, state statutes commonly provide that they shall hold office until their successors are elected, and some corporation laws provide for terms of longer than one year and also for the division of directors into groups with only one group coming up for election at a given shareholders' meeting. The procedure of staggering provides for more continuity, especially with large boards, but lack of continuity has never really been a serious problem among boards of directors. With the staggering, it becomes more difficult for the shareholders to exercise control over the directors and to "throw the rascals out," where the shareholders think their directors are rascals. Vacancies due to death or resignation during the course of a director's term may usually be filled by the remaining members of the board, but the shareholders, if they can muster a large enough portion of the voting shares to call a shareholders' meeting, may as a rule fill the vacancy and even replace the directors' choice.

In most states a director may be removed by his fellow directors where he has been judicially declared insane or where he has been convicted of a felony. Generally speaking, a director may be removed by a court on the petition of some fixed portion of the outstanding shares, where the petition sets forth grounds for removal, such as fraud or gross abuse of authority. In a few states, the draftsmen of the corporation laws and the legislatures have been impressed by the argument that the shareholders should be the ultimate masters of the corporation and that the control over the directors should be somewhat more direct. Some statutes provide that a director or the entire board may be removed by a majority of the outstanding shares entitled to vote at an election of directors. In order to protect the minority directors and shareholders under a cumulative voting system, however, cumulative voting also applies to removal, except that a majority may remove an *entire* board. The removal formula for cumulative voting is: no director shall be removed if the number of shares voted against the resolution for his removal exceeds the quotient arrived at when the total number of outstanding shares entitled to vote is divided by one plus the authorized number of directors. Thus, the effect of cumulative voting is not destroyed.

It is well known that an arrangement whereby the discretion of an individual director or of a board of directors is subordinated to the dictates of a shareholder or a group of shareholders is against public policy and invalid. Legislation providing for removal by the majority of the shares has sometimes been confused with this type of abdication agreement by the directors. It takes little reflection to realize that the removal legislation is simply a device whereby a majority of the voting shares have the power to remove directors whose policies and discretion are not approved; it is not an abdication of directors' responsibility.

COMPENSATION OF DIRECTORS. It sometimes comes as a shock to those unacquainted with corporation law to learn that directors, as such, are not entitled to compensation. Customarily, the corporation's by-laws provide for the payment of the directors' expenses incurred in attending board meetings and for the payment of a small amount in addition, as a sort of honorarium. In recent years some corporations, in order to obtain expert advice and counsel which could not otherwise be obtained, have contracted to pay one or more directors somewhat more substantial sums for their services, but as a rule the preliminary statement still holds true. The reason for this rule is usually based on two things: first, on custom, and second, on the directors' fiduciary relation to the corporation. No legal policy exists against an agreement entered into before the director begins his sevrices providing for a salary or other compensation, but there is no implication of a contract to pay the director the reasonable value of his services simply because he performs the services he is expected to perform as a director. An exception probably occurs in the situation where the director performs extraordinary services at the request of the board and with the understanding that he is to be compensated for the services. An officer who is also a director may be precluded from being paid the reasonable value of his services except where there has been a prior agreement, and the prohibition has even been extended to executive officers of corporations where those officers were not also directors. There is no question that non-executive officers and other employees are entitled to the reasonable value of their services performed for the corporation in the absence of specific prior agreement. Fixing the directors' compensation may be done in the by-laws, by a shareholders' vote or resolution, or by contract, and it is not uncommon for the shareholders to delegate the task to the directors themselves.

DIRECTORS' MEETINGS. The directors, as a general rule, do not have the authority as individuals to act for the corporation. They act as a group. Of course, if a director is also an officer, he may act for the corporation as an individual but only in his capacity as an officer. Under normal circumstances, the directors have the authority to act, even as a group, only at a properly convened directors' meeting. Where the directors act separately in approving a proposal or signing a deed, their action is usually ineffective. Directors may not vote by proxy at a directors' meeting, and a majority of a quorum present is the usual method by which acts and business are accomplished. The very purpose of the board of directors is to discuss, debate, and consider problems and policies. This cannot be done very effectively except at a meeting of the board.

It is only fair to point out that in many corporations the "meeting of the board" is little more than a "rubber stamp" session where the members of the board vote "aye" on acts that have already been performed. The growing use of committees of the board, to which the board delegates most of its own power, decreases further the importance of the board meeting. Many boards of directors are large or unwieldy or consist of men who cannot devote very much time to the business of any particular corporation. In these situations, the board may appoint from among its members small committees to take the actions the whole board might otherwise have to take. Generally, however, the dividend and by-law powers cannot be delegated to a committee. Much of the authority and responsibility may be delegated to the officers. A distinction between "inside" and "outside" boards of directors is important to note in this connection. An *inside* board is one made up largely or entirely of persons who are also officers of the corporation. An *outside* board is made up largely of persons from outside the corporation. There is usually at least one member of the board who is also an officer, so a completely outside board is not common. Most of the larger corporations have boards with several outside members.

POWERS AND DUTIES OF DIRECTORS. The board of directors is the supreme authority in matters pertaining to the management of regular and ordinary business affairs. The board's authority does not extend to fundamental changes in the organization or in the business. These areas are controlled by the shareholders. Except for this ultimate or basic control over fundamental matters, the board of directors is the repository of all the authority possessed by the corporation. Customarily, a large portion of this authority is delegated to the officers and employees of the corporation. Before this delegation can take place, however, the directors have to exercise their authority to select the chief executives and senior officers of the corporation. The authority to select the officers is normally not delegated, nor is the power to declare and pay dividends. The directors usually retain the authority to determine basic pricing, labor, financial, and product policies, but sometimes even these are delegated. No matter how hard a board of directors may try, however, it cannot delegate or abdicate the ultimate management responsibility. The board of directors cannot, for example. turn over complete management responsibility to a group of creditors or to management consultants, or even to a group of shareholders or to the officers of the corporation. But the lines of demarcation may be rather difficult to draw.

A list of specific powers of the board of directors under various statutory provisions would serve no particular purpose. The statutory enumerations, much as the enumerations in the corporation's charter, are usually nothing but redundant expressions of powers the directors would have without specific grant.

Fiduciary duties of directors: to the corporation. It is clear that directors are fiduciaries as regards their corporations, but the actual effects of this relation are uncertain. Were a director a trustee or an agent, it would be relatively simple to outline the scope and extent of his fiduciary duties and obligations, and some courts take this way out. But a director is neither a trustee nor an agent. The nature of his fiduciary duties must be examined on its own facts. The director is in a peculiarly advantageous position to exploit the corporation and the shareholders who have turned over the management of their investments to the directors. Because of this position, the director may not deal with his corporation at arm's length. The chief difficulty arises because the courts and legislatures do not agree on how rigid, how strict, or how extensive the director's duties should be.

Generally, the primary duty of the director is to the corporation and not to the shareholder. The statutes that face up to the problem seem to agree on this much. Some provide that "directors and officers shall exercise their powers in good faith, and with a view to the interests of the corporation." Just what these or any other statutes mean when applied to specific cases is difficult to ascertain. The essence of the fiduciary duty, wherever it is found, is the resolving of all doubts in favor of the person toward whom the duty is owed in those situations where the interests of that person and the self-interest of the person under the duty do or may conflict. This means that a director cannot make any secret personal profit from his activities as a director and must account to the corporation for it if he does. A director who secures for his corporation a contract that profits him personally has violated his fiduciary duty to the corporation unless he has made full disclosure of his interest. A director must be extremely careful about using inside information in order to make profits for himself or others. The fiduciary duty would seem to prohibit a director from accepting clandestine favors or commercial bribes from those interested in dealing with or obtaining concessions from the corporation. The courts, in these situations, are usually not very interested in whether the director was influenced by the bribe or favor but are concerned with the fact that a director has obtained a profit for himself from someone who may be seeking favorable relations with the corporation.

A closely related fiduciary duty is the *duty of full disclosure,* which requires a director to tell the corporation, through the other members of the board of directors, of any interest he may have in any transaction being considered by the corporation. The director may not compete with his corporation, but this prohibition usually will not prohibit a director from being a director of two competing corporations where no bad faith or fraud is present. The difficulty inherent in trying to represent both corporations properly and in trying not to let what a director knows about one influence his action with regard to another, however, makes such an interlocking directorate undesirable. Some statutes prohibit it, and most courts scrutinize closely transactions between corporations with common directors. The relation between the director and his corporation is very much like that of a guardian toward a minor ward. Neither the guardian nor the director may treat the persons toward whom he owes responsibilities as though those persons had the full capacity, independence, and information that are assumed when parties are dealing at arm's length. A ward trusts and relies on the guardian to act in the ward's best interest. So it is, figuratively speaking, with a corporation and its directors.

A special problem arises when the director enters into contracts with his own corporation. Such contracts might be prohibited by statute, but this would prevent a corporation from getting aid, financial and otherwise, from its directors and would make it difficult for the corporation to acquire from a director certain property that might be useful or necessary to its business. A blanket prohibition would be unwise, but the imposition of duties on the director when he is engaged in such transactions is the height of reasonableness. The fiduciary duties would certainly require full disclosure of all the circumstances surrounding the transaction, including the profit the director would make as a result of it. Because of the natural dangers here, some states have surrounded the director-corporation contract with a number of unnecessary restrictions, such as forbidding the director to be present at the meeting where his contract comes up for vote. The preferable way to handle these situations is to make the director's contract voidable where the contract is not just and reasonable. It is not the mechanics the director has gone through that should determine the status of his contract with the corporation as much as it is the question of how just and reasonable the transaction is to the corporation. In some states the director may even vote for his own proposition as long as his vote is not necessary for approval.

One of the most important problems in this area and one that has caused a substantial amount of litigation has to do with the acquisition by a director for himself of an opportunity encountered because he was a director, and that would have been of benefit to the corporation. Where, for example, a director of a grocery chain acquires for himself an interest in a grocery corporation he knows his own corporation has been seeking to acquire, he has violated his fiduciary duties and will be compelled to turn over the new interest to the corporation of which he was a director. A director cannot use his position of trust and confidence and the information he acquires in this position to take for himself opportunities that would be of value to his corporation. The remedy is a suit in equity by the corporation or by shareholders' representative suit.

Fiduciary duties of the directors: to the shareholders. As has already been made clear, the directors owe their primary duties to the corporation. Although the shareholders are the indirect beneficiaries of the fiduciary duty running from the directors to the corporation, the shareholders may only enforce these duties on behalf of the corporation in a shareholders' representative suit. The director owes no direct duty of careful management to the shareholder. An area remains, however, where the question of fiduciary relation between the directors and the shareholders does arise, and that is where the director and the shareholder enter into transactions with each other. Although other transactions occasionally raise the issue, the transactions most frequently concerned are those involving shares of stock. Were the director dealing with his corporation, he would owe it the duty of full disclosure, but where the transaction takes place with a shareholder, the nature of the director's duty is in doubt.

For example: *A* is the director of a mining corporation that has fallen on difficult days. The veins in the company's properties are largely exhausted. No profits have been made for years, and no dividends paid. The market value of the shares is about 10¢, if buyers can be found. One of the company's exploratory parties has reported to the board of directors a very rich strike, which, when the news is made public, will substantially increase the value of the shares. As soon as *A* hears the news, he contacts a number of shareholders and offers to buy their shares at 11¢ a share, an offer the discouraged shareholders accept. A few days later, news of the strike becomes widely known and the market price of the shares rises quickly to $5.50 a share. The shareholders who sold their shares to *A* are somewhat disturbed, to say the least, when they hear about the strike and discover that *A* knew of the strike when he offered to buy the shares. If there is a fiduciary duty between director and shareholders, the shareholders in this example should be able to recover from *A* either the shares or the profit he made out of them. If, on the other hand, director and shareholder deal at arm's length, there is no duty on the part of *A* to tell the shareholders what he knows about the strike. The conclusions of the courts on these points vary.

Where a director and shareholder are dealing with each other, three different rules have been followed with regard to the existence of a fiduciary duty between them.

The so-called *majority rule* takes the view that there is no fiduciary duty at all and that the directors may deal with the shareholders at arm's length without disclosing relevant facts surrounding the transactions. As long as the director does not actually misrepresent the facts, the shareholder has no grounds for recovery.

A second view, known as the *special facts doctrine,* is a modification of the "majority rule." The approach here is that while a director does not ordinarily owe any fiduciary duty of disclosure to the shareholder with whom he deals, a duty of disclosure arises where special facts are present. In general, special facts are found to exist where the director has come into possession of information simply because he is a director, and where the information is such that the shareholder has no means of acquiring it for himself except from the director. The "special facts doctrine" would seem to cover the hypothetical situation set forth above. It has been held to apply to situations such as prospective mergers that will increase the value of shares, unusual dividends declared but not announced, agreements with third parties to buy stock at a high price, and the prospective sale of the business or the entire assets.

A third view, usually referred to as the *minority rule,* finds the same fiduciary duty existing in regard to transactions between director and shareholder as is found between the director and his corporation. Most authorities, and a growing number of courts, have rejected the "majority rule" and have adopted the third view. Whether the "minority rule" or the "special facts doctrine" is followed, problems are encountered where the director purchases his shares, not directly from the shareholder, but on the open market. It is very doubtful, as a practical matter, if the director's responsibility can be extended to situations where the director's transactions are carried on behind the protecting screen of the stock market. Little legislation has entered this field except for the Securities Exchange Act, which seeks to prevent the use of inside information for speculative purposes by requiring the filing of information concerning stock transfers and acquisitions by directors and officers and by providing that any profits realized on these transfers within six months are recoverable by the corporation.

Where there has been a breach of a fiduciary duty to the shareholder by the director, the remedy is of course the shareholder's own suit against the director. Because there has been no breach of duty to the corporation, the shareholder's representative suit would be improper and useless.

LIABILITY OF DIRECTORS.   It is most important to note that the directors of a corporation are not liable to the corporation, to the shareholders, or to anyone else for errors of judgment or for innocent mistakes. The directors do not guarantee a successful corporation. This is not to say that director's mistakes or bad judgment will not affect the corporation. Obviously, the skill, ability, energy, experience, and good business judgment of the directors may be some of the most important factors in a corporation's success, but the director is not required by law to have these traits. He is required only to be loyal to his corporation, to be honest and truthful in his dealings with the corporation or on its behalf, and to use in his corporate activities that degree of care one would expect of a reasonably prudent man in the same circumstances. Only a failure to appreciate the real nature of the corporate device could lead one to say that the shareholders have only themselves to blame if a director is stupid or incompetent, but the fact does remain that the shareholders elect the directors and, if organized, can exercise some control over the selection of the candidates, at least in a small or medium-sized corporation. Acquiring good directors is important to the corporation, and all parties concerned should take seriously the problem of selecting these directors.

Although the requirements imposed upon directors are not particularly strict, there are a number of different ways in which a director may incur liability as a result of his activities in his corporate capacity. Some of these have already been discussed, as in connection with the director's fiduciary duties to the corporation and, under some circumstances, his fiduciary duties to shareholders. Directors are liable for losses caused to the corporation as a result of the directors' negligent or intentional mismanagement. This area of responsibility would cover the negligent selection of employees and would make the director liable for losses caused by such negligently selected employees. Directors are normally not liable for the negligent or wilful acts of carefully selected employees, but the rule may be different for officers, as will be seen later. However, a certain amount of supervision is expected of the director, and he may be held liable for the employees' acts or defalcations that he knew or should have known about. In most corporations the directors exercise no routine management supervision except possibly with regard to the executive officers. The directors are entitled to rely, in most cases, on the reports of the company's condition submitted to them by the executive officers.

Directors and officers are restricted by the charter provisions defining the scope of the authorized business and are liable to the corporation for any losses suffered by knowingly departing from the specified purposes. By the better rule the directors and officers are not liable for losses that may result when they exceed corporate authority unless they acted negligently or in bad faith.

The directors are liable for the unauthorized payment of dividends, as where improper sources are used or the corporation is insolvent, and for the withdrawal or distribution of assets among the shareholders, except on dissolution or on having made adequate provision for the creditors. They may become liable for authorizing the purchase by the corporation of its own shares and for any loss sustained as a result of their assenting to a loan of corporate funds to another director or officer.

Inasmuch as the directors ordinarily act as a board and not as individuals, certain technical questions arise in connection with the transactions discussed above where a director was not present at the meeting when an unlawful action was taken, or was present but voted against the action. Directors who do assent to the action taken are jointly and severally liable, and, generally, a director who was present at the meeting is presumed to have assented. In order to escape liability, a director present at the meeting must see to it that his dissent is entered in the corporate records. This may usually be done at the meeting itself or immediately afterwards. A director who attempts to record a dissent only when the liability itself becomes apparent will generally be unsuccessful in avoiding the liability. In any of these situations, however, a director who acts in good faith in reliance on financial and other reports of the other directors or officers that he has no reason to doubt will not be liable. An absent director is normally not liable for the actions taken at any particular directors' meeting, but an habitually absent director may become liable for his failure to exercise a reasonable amount of supervision. For example: Where a director failed to attend a single board meeting during a five and one-half-year period, he was held liable for the losses resulting from the officers' unsupervised acts that could have been discovered by a routine examination of the books and records normally examined by the directors.

Civil liability for damages is not the only type of liability that may be imposed upon a director. Many statutes provide for criminal prosecution, fines, and imprisonment where directors make false reports or authorize illegal distributions of dividends or unlawful issues of shares.

E. The Officers

QUALIFICATION, APPOINTMENT, AND REMOVAL. The officers of a corporation are its employees and, as individuals, its agents. The higher officers, usually known as *executive officers,* are, as a general rule, selected by the board of directors, and may be employed under contract or, more commonly, at the will of the board. Many corporations operate with "inside" boards, where the officers also compose the board of directors. However, officers, as a rule, need not be directors or shareholders unless the articles or by-laws require it. Many state laws require each corporation to have certain specified officers, such as president, vice-president, secretary, and treasurer, but allow additional officers if the by-laws so provide, and permit one person to hold two or more offices. It is frequently forbidden that the offices of president and secretary be held by the same person. The reason for this prohibition is that the secretary is a sort of authenticating officer who keeps the corporate seal, vouches for the accuracy of records and minutes, and performs many other acts that may later be used as evidence. It is considered unwise to permit the chief executive officer to authenticate his own acts.

POWERS AND AUTHORITY OF OFFICERS. The officers are merely agents of the corporation and are subject to the control of the board of directors. Their powers are derived from: by-laws, resolutions by the board of directors, or by implication through acquiescence in a course of dealing. Authority to bind the corporation is usually not conferred on the officers, with the possible exception of the president, simply by virtue of the offices they hold. In other words, the vice-president has no particular authority simply because the door to his office is labelled "vice-president." The law of agency applies to the officers of the corporation and helps to solve problems arising in connection with their ability to bind the corporation by their acts. The "equal dignities rule," however, is usually not followed with regard to the executive officers of corporations. Ratification and the doctrines of estoppel and of apparent authority are of particular importance in analyzing the authority of corporate officers.

DUTIES AND LIABILITIES OF OFFICERS. The duties of the corporate officer are very much the same as those of the director. He is expected to be honest and to use reasonable care and skill in carrying out his activities on behalf of his corporation, and it is clear, of course, that his primary duty, even more so than the director, is to the corporation and not to the shareholders. He is liable for wilful or negligent mismanagement and may be the target of a suit by the corporation or of a shareholders' representative suit. One difference that does exist between the responsibility of the officer and that of the director is the much greater responsibility an officer has for the fraud or neglect of subordinates. The reason is obvious. Because the officer is presumably on the scene as a full time employee, he is expected, as part of his routine day-to-day duties, to supervise the activities of his subordinates. The directors, on the other hand, usually meet infrequently, and even at their meetings must rely to a great extent for their information about the conduct of the business on the executive officers' reports. In the famous case of *Bates* v. *Dresser*,[5] the defalcations of a bank's bookkeeper were charged to the officers of the corporation because they were negligent in relying unquestioningly on the bookkeeper's honesty. The directors, with one exception, were exempted from liability on the ground that they were justified in relying on the officers' reports of the bank's financial condition. The exception was a director who failed to take warning from the knowledge he had of the eighteen-dollar-a-week bookkeeper's high standard of living.

Note that it is a rather common practice today for a corporation to obtain the consent of its shareholders in regard to certain limitations of the liability of company officers and directors. Just how effective such limitations may be is not clear. Obviously, an attempt to discharge directors and officers from all liability, including that for their own fraudulent or negligent acts, would run counter to public policy and would be unlikely of approval by the shareholders or the courts. Some corporation laws permit a corporation to idemnify its directors or officers against expenses incurred in defending an action brought against the director or officer by reason of his being or having been such director or officer, except in actions where he is found to be liable for negligence or misconduct in the performance of his duties.

---

[5] 251 U.S. 524 (1920).

F. Corporate Powers

(1)

CASE. The corporation law of Anosmia provides that a shareholder who votes against a proposed merger that is approved by the required number of shareholders is entitled to be paid the fair market value of his shares by the corporation. There is no such provision for the shareholder who votes against the purchase by his corporation of another corporation's assets.

Alder Glen, Inc., and Last Corporation are both Anosmian corporations. Under a proposed "reorganization" plan, Alder Glen was to acquire all the assets of Last in exchange for shares of Alder Glen stock which would be distributed directly to the Last shareholders. Additionally, Alder Glen was to assume all of Last's liabilities, and the name of the surviving corporation was to be Last Alder Corporation. The directors of both corporations were to become directors of Last Alder. Under the plan, the majority of the Alder Glen stock would go to the Last shareholders, and the book value of Alder Glen stock would be reduced from $38 to $21. The directors of Alder Glen insist that this plan provides only for the purchase of assets and as such does not require more than majority approval of the existing Alder Glen shares nor give dissenting sharehodlers any rights of appraisal or sale of their shares to Alder Glen. Harris, a dissenting minority shareholder in Alder Glen, argues that the "reorganization" is not a sale of assets at all but a merger and, as such, requires two-thirds approval of the shares and entitles the dissenting shareholders to the purchase of their shares by Alder Glen at the fair market price.

[See *Farris* v. *Glen Alden Corp.*, 393 Pa. 427 (1958)]

(2)

CASE. In the spring of 1960, Paul Preston, the president of Hypocase, Inc., was approached by Ben S. Need, the chairman of the board of Need Terminals Corporation, a large public warehousing firm in Berkland and also a very good customer of Hypocase. Need told Preston that Terminals wanted to borrow $100,000 from Hypocase to get the company through a period of financial stringency brought on by a major expansion program that severely depleted the company's working capital. Need said that the Chicago, Berkland and Tulsa Railroad Corporation would guarantee the loan. C., B. and T. was Terminals' largest customer. Preston, with the approval of his board of directors, made the loan to Need Terminals, as Hypocase was authorized by its charter to do, and C., B. and T. guaranteed the loan. Within six months, Need Terminals had become hopelessly insolvent, and Hypocase was unable to collect its loan. Demand was made on C., B. and T. for payment, but the demand was refused on the ground that C., B. and T. was not authorized in its charter to make such a guaranty and, thus, was acting outside its legal authority when it did so. Can Hypocase recover the $100,000 from C., B. and T.?

IN GENERAL. The powers and the authority of the directors, officers, and shareholders of a corporation have already been discussed in detail. Inasmuch as the corporation is not human, it cannot act for itself; consequently, the human agencies through whom it does act and the powers and authorities of these agencies are important topics for consideration. There comes a time, however, when it is realized that even the most thorough knowledge of the corporation's human agencies leaves some gaps in what it is necessary to know in order to understand adequately the corporate form of business organization. It becomes important then to look upon the corporation as the legal person it is and to consider the powers this non-human, fictional person possesses on its own account. By *powers* is meant the legal ability or capacity to carry out the purposes for which the corporation was organized.

Were corporations still created by special acts of the various state legislatures, it would not be misleading to say that the source of a corporation's power is the state. Although this is still true when speaking in absolute terms, since the corporation depends upon a corporation law for its ability to come into existence, what creates corporations today under general incorporation laws is the formal agreement of the incorporators, who set forth in this agreement the purposes and objects of the business they authorize the directors to carry on. The statutory limitations on corporate powers are so broad and general, as a rule, as to supply little information about the scope of corporate power in any given situation. Even if we look upon the corporate charter as a contract between the corporation and the state, we must still recognize that the contract is drawn by the incorporators, and its terms, within broad limits, are the sole responsibility of the incorporators. Realistically speaking, then, the source of corporate powers is not the state but the charter.

The corporation's powers, found largely in the purpose clause of the charter, may be either express or implied. Many purpose clauses state the objects of the business in general terms and then go on to detailed descriptions of the powers the incorporators intend the corporation to have, frequently going to ridiculously redundant and itemized extremes. If the powers are express, legal problems arise only with regard to the interpretation of the language of the charter or in connection with powers not permitted by the statute or otherwise illegal. A danger of undue detail in a corporatate purpose clause is that the list of powers may tend to become exclusive, and questions may be raised as to whether a corporation really has certain powers omitted from the list when these same powers might be freely implied had the purpose clause been stated more broadly. It is dangerous to omit any necesssry power once the draftsman starts extensive itemization.

INCIDENTAL POWERS. The corporation has, by implication, the power and authority to do those things that are necessary to carry out its purposes.

The management has the implied authority to enter into all contracts and other transactions that may be reasonably incident to the purposes of the business. Consequently, it is not necessary to list in the charter those powers clearly implied from the stated purposes of the business. Unusual powers should, of course, be listed, as well as those powers a statute may deny to the corporation in the absence of express provision in the charter. Some statutes cause confusion by unnecessarily listing corporate powers one would expect a corporation to possess anyhow.

A few of these incidental or implied powers are worth separate discussion. A corporation, because it is a legal person, has the power to buy, sell, and hold both real and personal property in its own name, but only as long as the particular situation is incident to the purposes of the business. A grocery corporation would, ordinarily, have the power to buy real estate for the purpose of conducting its grocery business but not for speculative purposes, unless the charter so provided. Many states have enacted legislation expressly granting the power to buy, sell, and hold property, but because they do not limit this power to the purposes of the business, the question of whether the statute was a grant of power to buy, sell, and hold real property "under any circumstances" is thus raised. A special type of personal property that has caused some controversy in regard to corporate power is stock in other corporations, the ownership of which has usually been justified where reasonably incident to the owner's corporate purposes. The practice, which is widespread even where not reasonably incident, is frequently authorized by statute or by charter provision. Corporations may borrow money and issue bonds or incur other forms of indebtedness and may secure the payment by the usual types of security. Neither statutory nor charter provision seems necessary to the existence of this power.

STATUTORY LIMITATIONS AND RESTRICTIONS.   Most corporation statutes prohibit corporations from becoming partners in partnerships and from entering the licensed professions. Charter provision may authorize the former. The latter prohibition is usually absolute. The reasons for the partnership limitation are the possible abdication of management responsibility and the delegation to the other partners of power to bind the corporation. The corporation is excluded from the licensed professions because of the public policy in favor of close personal relations and responsibilities in this field. Statutes in many states today authorize professional corporations where essential safeguards are provided and a certain degree of judicial supervision is maintained. The 1967 amendments to the Delaware Corporation Law give a corporation power to become a partner even without charter authorization.

The power of a corporation to purchase its own shares is also limited by statute in many states. The abuse of this power by the directors can injure the corporation, its creditors, and its shareholders. A typical statute permits the corporation to purchase its own shares out of earned or reduction surplus but prohibits purchase from other sources except for certain purposes, such as performing repurchase agreements with employees, redeeming shares subject to redemption, eliminating fractional shares, or paying dissenting shareholders for their shares on merger or consolidation. Shares purchased by the corporation that issued them are called *treasury shares,* and they may be held by the corporation, retired, returned to authorized but unissued status, or resold. Some of the statutes limiting such purchases deprive the shares of voting rights while in the hands of the corporation and prohibit their treatment as assets for dividend purposes. Many accounting problems arise in connection with treasury shares, as brief reflection on the possible journal entries will reveal.

MERGER AND CONSOLIDATION. A group of corporations may, for the purpose of pooling their resources or products, improving their management or financial condition, taking advantage of large scale operation, or meeting market and industry changes, merge or consolidate into one corporation. Although the statutes generally deal with merger and consolidation similarly, *merger* is a process by which one or more corporations may be absorbed or merged into another existing or surviving corporation, while *consolidation* involves the combination of two or more corporations to form a new or consolidated corporation. The assets of all the original corporations go to the surviving or new corporation as do the debts and obligations, which become the liabilities of the surviving or new corporation. The shareholders of the disappearing corporations usually receive in exchange for the shares of their own corporations the shares of the corporation that remains or is newly created.

The procedural requirements for merger or consolidation vary from state to state, but, in general, both require a resolution of the board of directors of each corporation involved and the approval of the shareholders of each corporation. Some statutes require the two-thirds approval of each class of shares in each corporation, whereas other statutes are less strict. Mergers and consolidations across state lines are possible by the simple expedient of each corporation's complying with the law of its own state.

Shareholders who vote against a proposal for merger or consolidation, which is nonetheless approved by the required majority of shares, do not have to ride along with the impending change and be forced to take their chances on what it may do to the value of their shares. Dissenting shareholders may demand that the corporation buy their shares at the fair market value. Even where shares of the corporation are listed on an exchange, the determination of their fair market value may still raise serious difficulties with regard to the effect which the impending merger or consolidation has had. Clearly, the dissenting shareholder should not suffer a loss of value or receive the benefits of an increase in value resulting from expectations of the merger or consolidation. Many statutes so expressly provide, but the actual determination of the appropriate value may still be difficult.

SALE OF ENTIRE ASSETS. Many of the same results obtained by merger or consolidation may be achieved through the device of purchasing the assets of other corporations. Without regard to the solvency of the corporation or the condition of its business, statutes permit a corporation to sell, lease, transfer, exchange, or otherwise dispose of all or substantially all of its property and assets. This device may be more attractive in some circumstances than the merger or the consolidation, because the requirements are more easily met. Generally, all that is required is a resolution by the board of directors and the approval of a majority of the voting shares. When this device is used, no corporations disappear, dissenting shareholders have no claims, and each corporation continues its corporate existence with only the form of its assets altered. The selling corporation now has in place of its former operating assets a quantity of cash or of the shares of the purchasing corporation. On dissolution these will be distributed among the creditors and the shareholders. The Model Business Corporation Act and the corporation laws of many states require much the same procedure for the sale of assets as they do for merger or consolidation. It should be noted here that although the sale of the assets does not bring to an end the corporate entity nor in itself dissolve the corporation, such a sale of all or substantially all of the assets frequently does give the directors, shareholders, or courts the power to dissolve the corporation. (See Part V.)

Where the requirements for the sale of entire assets are less stringent than for mergers or consolidations, especially where dissenting shareholders do not have the right to demand the corporation's purchase of their shares, there is some temptation to try to conceal a *de facto* merger as a sale of assets. Courts have occasionally found such attempts to be mergers and have imposed upon them the requirements of mergers. The statutory tendency appears to be toward imposing many of the same requirements on sales of entire assets as are usually imposed on mergers.

ULTRA VIRES ACTS. There was a time when the fact that a corporation had been acting outside its express or implied powers could be used as a defense against liability, both by the corporation and by third persons who had dealt with the corporation within the excluded area. These acts were said to be *ultra vires,* beyond the power of the corporation. Most modern corporation statutes abolish this use of the *ultra vires* doctrine where third persons are involved. This doctrine is still available however, not as a defense, but as grounds for the following: 1, an injunction proceeding brought by a shareholder against the corporation to restrain the further commission of *ultra vires* acts; 2, a suit by the corporation, acting directly or through representatives, such as trustees or shareholders, against the officers or directors of the corporation; and 3, a proceeding by the Attorney General of the state of incorporation to dissolve the corporation or to enjoin it from the further transaction of unauthorized business.

PROBLEMS

1. Under what circumstances would it make a difference whether particular property used in a partnership business was partnership property or the separate property of one of the partners?

2. *A, B, C,* and *D*, who have been carrying on businesses as sole proprietors, have decided to merge all of their businesses into a general partnership. Their contributions to the firm were as follows:

   A: cash $ 5,000, other assets $12,000.
   B: cash $ 2,000, other assets $25,000, debts $19,000.
   C: cash $ 3,000, other assets $ 5,000.
   D: cash $15,000, other assets $ 7,000, debts $ 6,000.

B also loaned $10,000 in cash to the firm.

At the end of the first year of business, before any payments had been made to partners, the firm had: cash $22,000, other assets $68,000, and debts $17,000.

 a. What was the amount of the partnership capital: At the beginning? At the end of the first year?

 b. What was the amount of the partnership property: At the beginning? At the end of the first year?

3. What changes did the Uniform Partnership Act make in the common law rules with respect to holding title to partnership property?

4. What rights do the individual partners have in specific partnership property?

5. A partner ordinarily does not have the power to sell partnership property not held for the purpose of sale. Does he have the power to mortgage or pledge partnership property which he could not sell? Explain.

6. What are the rules of partnership law with respect to the sharing of profits and losses by the partners?

7. The relationship among partners is essentially a fiduciary relation. What does this mean specifically in terms of the duties of the partners to each other?

8. Are partners entitled to interest on their invested capital or to compensation for services they perform for the firm? Explain.

9. What methods are available for enforcing the rights and duties of the partners among themselves?

10. Describe briefly the power of the individual partner to bind his fellow partners and the firm on contracts with third persons. May a third person bring a partnership contract action simply by naming and serving one of the partners? Explain.

11. What is the significance of the terms "shareholder of record" and "registered owner"?

12. Assume that you own 4,600 of the 9,000 outstanding voting shares in the *ABC* Corporation. The company has a seven man board of directors; all positions on the board are to be filled at a shareholders' meeting. How would you vote your shares under the ordinary system of voting? Under a system of cumulative voting?

13. What is a shareholder's proxy? How is it used? How may it be abused? What is the general nature of federal legislation and regulation aimed at reducing abuses of the proxy system?

14. What are the methods by which the voting power of shares and the ownership may be separated? How do these methods work? What is their purpose? Are they legal?

15. Is the right of a shareholder to inspect the books and records of his corporation uniformly recognized and dealt with in all states? Explain.

16. Assume that you are a shareholder in the Soap Flats Uranium Corporation and that you have received no dividends for several years. The annual reports show that the corporation is in serious financial condition. During the last year or two, however, the salaries of the officers have increased substantially, and the directors and officers have been living higher, wider, and more handsomely than ever before. You are convinced that fraud and mismanagement on the part of the officers and directors are to blame for the poor financial condition of the company. What steps might you or a group of shareholders take toward finding out more about the situation and trying to remedy it?

17. You are already a shareholder in the Wooden Nickel Company, a corporation. You have just read in the financial section of your daily paper that your company has offered a new issue of shares to the public and that the response has been very good. This is the first that you have heard of such an issue. Have your rights as an existing shareholder been invaded in any way? Explain.

18. What is the nature of the shareholder's right to dividends? From what sources may a corporation declare and pay dividends?

19. It is frequently stated that a shareholder's liability is limited to the amount of his actual investment. Is this statement accurate? Explain.

20. What name is given to stock which purports to be fully paid but was actually issued for something less than full consideration? What are the various techniques by which this may be accomplished? What are the motives behind such activity?

21. What is the function of a board of directors? Is it true that directors may act only as a body and cannot act individually for their corporation? Explain.

22. Calvin Carlus, a director of the Hasty Pudding Corporation, performed the following acts:

    a. sold to his corporation a quantity of machinery which he had purchased at a war surplus sale in 1950.

    b. voted, along with the other directors, to declare a dividend.

    c. bought 1,000 shares of Hasty Pudding stock directly from another shareholder.

    d. bought 1,000 shares of Hasty Pudding stock on the open market.

What liability may Calvin have incurred as a director as the result of these activities? Explain.

23. Compare the duties and liabilities of corporate officers with the duties and liabilities of directors.

24. What is the source of a corporation's authority? How can corporate directors and officers determine the area within which their corporation has been authorized to act? What is the present status of the doctrine of *ultra vires*?

25. May a corporation purchase its own shares? Under what circumstances? What dangers may be involved in the practice? What reasons can there be for a corporation to purchase its own shares? Are the shares in the hands of the corporation entitled to the same rights and privileges as they were entitled to in the hands of a shareholder?

26. You are Assistant to the President of the Kitchen Gadget Corporation. The President has asked you to submit to him a memorandum concerning the various ways in which the resources of your company and those of the Household Gadget Company, a Delaware corporation, could be combined. What would you put into the memo? Explain.

chapter 10

Distribution
of Goods

1. IN GENERAL

A. Scope of Discussion

IN GENERAL. Not every person, or even every businessman, encounters the legal problems of distribution from
the standpoint of a distributor, but everyone comes into
contact, in one way or another, with the law surrounding
the distribution of goods. Because much of the law relevant
to the vital economic function of distribution has been
discussed already, the reader should have a workable
knowledge of the following: the basic contract device,
by which most distribution is accomplished; some of the
methods by which distribution is financed; and the concepts of title and ownership of personal property. Other
aspects of distribution will be discussed in the chapters
immediately following. The reader will later examine
methods by which capital is distributed and transferred
and will become familiar with such legal devices as bailments which are also important in the broader area of
distribution. In Chapter 14, the reader will be exposed to
those aspects of distribution primarily concerned with the
competitive practices of those engaged in the distributive
activity. The present chapter will be devoted to the basic

437

legal problem of transferring ownership in personal property from one person to another, a field of the law usually referred to as *the law of sales*.

The law of sales has a relatively narrow focus, as far as the whole function of distribution is concerned, but it should be clear from the very nature of the situation that, without the transfer of ownership in property from one person to another, there would be no distribution, except on an exceedingly cumbersome basis. Actually, the transfer of property from one person to another embodies a much wider variety of legal problems than is at first apparent. In addition to the transfer problem itself there are the important collateral problems rising out of the terms of the transfer and in connection with the rights and remedies of the parties to a sales transaction; it must be remembered that sales transactions are contract transactions and fall heir to the legal problems of contract as well as to their own special problems. The discussion below will concern itself with the more important groups of legal issues relevant to the sales transactions: formation of sales contracts, with special attention paid to warranties; performance; breaches and other breakdowns of the bargain; and remedies of the parties.

THE BUSINESS PROBLEM.   Before we go on to the detailed discussion of the law of sales, let us pause for a moment to consider somewhat more realistically the nature of the business problem we will be concerned with in the next few pages. If we can set the scene properly, the law of sales, which can become quite technical, should appear as the natural outgrowth of the business situations we describe rather than as a group of abstract legal principles. Consider the following situations:

1. Assume that X owns and operates a small furniture factory in Ohio. He buys his hardwoods and veneers, paints and varnishes, hardware, and other materials used in furniture-making from suppliers all over the country and sells his products through independent retail furniture stores. In order to finish a new line of expensive furniture that he was manufacturing, X purchased from Y 500 gallons of high quality varnish. Unknown to either X or Y, a quantity of a very strong caustic substance was present in the batch of varnish from which X's 500 gallons came. X had inspected the varnish carefully before ordering it and had inspected it again before he paid for it, but it never occurred to him to test it for caustic substances. When the varnish was used, it caused many thousands of dollars of damage to the furniture and seriously burned several of X's skilled craftsmen. Assume that the presence of the caustic did not result from Y's negligence or from the negligence of any of his employees. X now seeks to recover from Y the cost of the varnish, the damage to the furniture, and the loss X has suffered due to the hospitalization of his best workmen. The workmen also seek to recover from Y for their own injuries. Is Y liable to X and to X's workmen? Illustrated above and in the next paragraph are some problems of warranty.

2. X sold a shipment of flexible steel lawn furniture to a dealer in Oregon. Through no fault of X, and unknown to X, the steel tubing was defective.

Several people to whom the Oregon dealer had sold furniture were badly injured when the steel tubing broke while the furniture was occupied. Is X liable to the injured persons? Is the dealer liable to the ones injured? Would either X or the dealer be liable to the guest of a purchaser of the furniture?

3. While on one of his buying trips, X entered into a contract to buy from Z a certain lot of hardwood X had carefully inspected and had asked Z to ship to X's factory. Later the same day the wood was destroyed by fire through no fault of Z. Who will bear the loss?

4. An Illinois dealer ordered a quantity of furniture to be manufactured by X. The furniture had been completed, crated, and loaded onto a railroad car alongside X's loading dock when a runaway switch engine struck the car and destroyed it and the furniture. Does the loss fall on X or on the dealer?

5. A large quantity of furniture ordered by a dealer in Florida was still in transit to the dealer when X learned that the dealer was insolvent. Can X get back his furniture or must he stand by and let it be delivered and then simply become one of the dealer's general creditors who will receive only a portion of their claims against the dealer? An unusual remedy of the law of sales is probably available to X in this case. Suppose the goods had been delivered to the dealer when X learned of the insolvency?

6. If furniture has been delivered to a dealer who has failed to pay the price at the time agreed upon, what steps may X take with regard to the furniture or the recovery of the price?

7. X ordered varnish from Y for delivery on April 10. It is now May 1 and the varnish has not yet arrived. What remedies are available to X?

All of the questions raised above are within the purview of the law of sales. Several of the situations described are somewhat extreme, but they illustrate the nature of the legal issue involved probably more clearly than would milder forms of the same situations. It should be obvious from the above examples that there are a great many more problems raised by a sale than the simple issues of what is sold and how much it costs. A careful reading of the pages that follow should make it possible for the reader to answer the questions asked above, and, more important, make it possible for the reader to deal much more readily with these and other sales problems that may arise. The reader should try to visualize each portion of the discussion as an actual business problem in which he plays a part either as a buyer or a seller. In this way other issues not raised specifically in the discussion will be recognized and considered, and the reader's knowledge will be increased.

Before one has read very far into the law of sales, it becomes obvious that most of the rules and principles governing this area of the law are designed for the primary purpose of aiding, simplifying, and facilitating the sales transaction and are not simply the result of random experience by hundreds of courts with thousands of cases over dozens of generations of commercial practice. In many situations it will be realized that the applicable rules are expressed in such a way as to remove terms and conditions from the bargaining process between the parties involved. This is done in order to make the sales transaction as simple, certain, and safe as possible. The parties are usually left free to set forth their own intentions, but in the absence of such a showing, the law stands ready to fill the gaps. This result is not the product of historical accident. Both the Uniform Commercial Code and the Uniform Sales Act had as their original purposes the simplification and clarification of the law of sales and the facilitation of continued expansion of commercial practices through custom, usage, established procedure, and the agreement of the parties.

B. The Uniform Commercial Code

SOURCES OF SALES LAW. One of the first areas in which the National Conference of Commissioners on Uniform State Laws, many years ago, sought to achieve uniformity among the states was the law of sales. The mixed ancestry of existing legal principles regarding sales when combined with the federal system in the United States had by the end of the nineteenth century resulted in seriously divergent laws of sales in the various states and had produced major barriers to trade and commerce. The Uniform Sales Act, promulgated in 1906, was the first effective effort in this country to make the law of sales more nearly uniform. It was adopted by the large majority of the states, but, for reasons discussed in Chapters 1 and 3, real uniformity was not achieved, even among the states adopting the Uniform Act. The Uniform Sales Act has now been replaced by the Uniform Commercial Code in all but one state. The Code makes certain important changes in the rules set forth in the older statute. Broadly, these changes are as follows:

1. The emphasis placed by the Uniform Sales Act and other precode sales law on the location of title to property when resolving questions having to do with risk of loss, priority of creditors, and other matters has been abandoned by the Code. These determinations are made by separate rules independent of the location of title. The motive behind this change is simply that important events in the practical affairs of businessmen should not be governed by the location of an intangible which cannot be established by ordinary evidence.

2. The Uniform Sales Act and most precode law permitted most matters having to do with the formation and performance of the sales contract to be governed by principles and rules of contract law, and, generally speaking, these rules and principles were not covered by statute. The new Code introduces many of these contractual concepts into the statutory law of sales and makes certain changes in these concepts as well. The purpose is to make the law of sales a more or less unitary whole and to minimize the need to go outside the Code for the answers to questions having to do with problems arising in connection with sales contracts.

3. The Code, in some situations, distinguishes rather sharply between professional merchants, on the one hand, and casual sellers and buyers, on the other, and applies different rules and concepts to the professionals—especially to transactions *between* professional merchants. Precode law recognized some of the important differences between professionals and others, but only in a very limited way.

4. The statute of frauds provisions of the Uniform Sales Act have been considerably modified in certain respects by the Code.

5. The requirement of pre-existing law that offers, in order to be binding, must be supported by consideration has been, to a large extent, removed by the Code.

It will be noted that the second, fourth, and fifth above are largely matters of contract law and have been discussed in detail in the chapter of this book devoted to that subject. Only casual consideration will be given to those issues here.

SCOPE OF THE CODE. Article 2 of the Uniform Commercial Code is devoted to the law of sales, and it applies, in the terms of the statute itself, to "transactions in goods," except for transactions intended to operate *only* as security transactions, such as conditional sales or mortgages. Apparently, however, Article 2 would regulate the usual sales aspects of even these excepted transactions.

Section 2-105 defines *goods* as all things that are movable at the time of identification to the contract for sale, except the money in which the price is to be paid, investment securities, and things in action. Transactions in investment securities and things in action, including negotiable instruments, are subject to treatment by other portions of the Code. They are discussed elsewhere in this book. The term "goods" also includes growing crops, the unborn young of animals, timber to be cut, minerals to be removed, and certain other property to be severed from real property. *Transaction,* as the term is used in Article 2, gives the statute essentially the same scope as would the term *sale.*

C. Definitions

"SALE" AND RELATED TERMINOLOGY. The Code defines *sale* as the passing of title from seller to buyer for a price. *Present sale* means a sale that is accomplished simply by the making of a contract. Where a sale is not accomplished by making a contract, the result is what is known as a *contract to sell.* The Code uses the term *contract for sale* to encompass *both* the present sale and the contract to sell. The reason for this usage is that under the Code the rights of the parties do not vary according to whether the contract is one or the other, unless expressly so provided.

Because concepts of title and ownership still have considerable importance in the law of property, apart from the law of sales, and because the term "sale" has a long history of usage as the passing of title, the draftsmen of the Code were not free to alter the traditional meaning of sale. In order, however, to remove the precode importance of the passage of title as a determining factor in certain important areas of sales law, the term "transaction" was substituted.

In order to be subject to a present sale, and before any interest in goods can pass, the goods must be both existing and identified. If the goods are not both existing and identified, they can only be the subject of a contract to sell and are said to be *future goods*. There may be a sale of a part interest in existing identified goods. The identification of goods really has two dimensions: distinguishing particular goods from other similar goods, and, more important, identifying particular goods to the contract between the parties. The latter is the more significant aspect in connection with sales transactions.

IDENTIFICATION OF GOODS. The identification of existing goods to the contract can be made at any time and in any manner explicitly agreed to by the parties. In the absence of such agreement, the time and manner of identification are provided by the statute. If the goods are existing and identified, in the first sense referred to above, they are identified to the contract when it is made. If the contract is for the sale of future goods, identification usually occurs when goods are shipped, marked, or otherwise designated by the seller as the goods to which the contract refers, but identification may also be made by the buyer. If the contract is for the sale of unborn young of animals or future crops, identification takes place when the young are conceived or when the crops are planted or otherwise become growing crops.

Identification of goods to the contract has several important effects. The buyer obtains a special property in the goods, including an insurable interest; this is so *even though* the goods do not conform to the contract, and the buyer, as a result, has an option to return or reject them. The fact that the buyer has an insurable interest does not necessarily mean that he holds title or bears the risk of loss, as will be seen in detail below. In addition, a buyer who has paid all of the purchase price, or part of the price and has tendered the balance, may recover the goods from the seller in the event the seller becomes insolvent within ten days after receiving the price or the first instalment. However, if the identification of the goods is by the buyer, he has the right to recover the goods only if they conform to the contract for sale. The purpose of these provisions is to make it possible for the buyer, if he really wants the goods, to obtain them in priority over the seller's creditors. On the other hand, where the identification is by the buyer, he should not thus be able to obtain goods which may be superior to those provided for in the contract.

The seller retains an insurable interest in the goods as long as he holds title or any security interest in them, and, where identification is by the seller alone, he may substitute other goods for those identified until his default, insolvency, or notification to the buyer that the identification is final.

Goods which are not in strict compliance with the contract are said to be *nonconforming*. Ordinarily, the seller must tender to the buyer goods that are in strict compliance before the buyer has an obligation to accept them, but, as has been seen, the Code makes it possible for the buyer, under certain circumstances, to accept nonconforming goods if he wishes to do so. Furthermore, the Code permits a seller to *cure* a nonconforming tender if the time for his performance has not expired, if the seller notifies the buyer of his intention to cure, and if, within the appropriate time, he does make a conforming delivery.

It is clear that the purpose of all of these provisions is to substitute clarity and certainty for uncertainty and to reduce the opportunities for litigation.

FUNGIBLE GOODS. As is discussed elsewhere in this book, *fungible goods* are those whose individual units are sufficiently similar to each other that they are sold by weight, measure, or number rather than by identifiable unit. Raw cement, grains, and liquids are examples. An undivided share or proportion of an identified bulk of such goods is subject to a present sale although the total quantity of the bulk is not determined. The buyer becomes an owner in common with the seller of his proportionate share in the whole or to the extent of the agreed quantity or measure.

SALES TRANSACTION DISTINGUISHED FROM OTHER TRANSACTIONS. The sales transaction is usually clearly differentiated from the bailment, but in some special circumstances, as a sale with option to return and a bailment with option to buy, some confusion may exist. The best test is whether there is a binding promise by the person to whom the possession of the goods is transferred to pay for the goods. If there is such a promise, the transaction is a sale. If there is no such promise, the transaction is a bailment. A *bailment* is simply a contract whereby the possession of the goods is transferred by the owner with provision for the return of possession at a later time.

A sales transaction may be confused with a pledge. A *pledge* is the deposit of personal property as security for the performance of some obligation by the person making the deposit. The distinguishing test of the above paragraph may be used here also, but the further test of whether there was an existing obligation to be secured may be an easier one to apply.

Some agency relations, such as the consignment, may resemble sales transactions. In a *consignment,* goods are turned over by the owner to an agent for the purpose of having the goods sold by the agent, ownership passing to the ultimate buyer when the agent sells the goods. If a person buys goods from another to sell as his own, there is a sale. If the goods are taken as the property of the other person for the purpose of sale, the transaction is that of consignment.

2. FORMATION AND CONSTRUCTION OF THE SALES CONTRACT

A. Cases

(1)

On December 2, Mrs. Keenan bought from Cherry & Webb, a clothing store, a French Coney coat for $99. Coney is a kind of rabbit skin. The saleswoman represented the coat as "a good coat," said that it would "wear very well," and told Mrs. Keenan that she "would not be sorry if she bought it." Mrs. Keenan knew nothing about the quality of fur coats and took the saleswoman's word for it. She tried on many fur coats in the store before selecting

Operating a Business

this one. Having but a few dollars with her, and the occasion being a special sale for three days, Mrs. Keenan was permitted to make the purchase at the reduced price and leave a few dollars as a deposit. She returned the next day for the coat and paid the balance of the purchase price.

However, before Mrs. Keenan paid the balance and took the coat, she told the saleswoman that she had seen elsewhere another Coney coat for only $69 and would like her deposit back as she planned to buy the other coat. Her request for the return of her deposit was refused by the saleswoman who assured Mrs. Keenan that the other coat was third quality, and that her coat was first quality, and that Cherry & Webb "stood behind" their goods. Mrs. Keenan took the coat. The first time she wore the coat it developed a ten inch split from the shoulder down the back. The split was along a seam and developed because the stitches sewing the pelts together had cut through one of the skins. Inspection by one having no knowledge of furs would not have revealed the defect. On several occasions, the store attempted to sew up the split, but without success. The store refused to take back the coat and return Mrs. Keenan's money and also refused to replace the coat. Mrs. Keenan sued for damages for breach of warranty. Who will win?

[*Keenan* v. *Cherry & Webb,* 47 R.I. 125 (1925)]

(2)

On the night of November 28, thieves broke into the SIMUCO Toyland store and removed five large crates of toys that had not yet been unpacked. The thieves sold the toys to Frank Flier, who operated a small "surplus" store in Berkland and who often bought distress goods and other merchandise outside the normal channels of trade. Flier did not know or suspect that the goods were stolen. One of the thieves was a man with whom Flier had had legitimate business dealings in the past, and this man told Flier that the toys had been purchased at a distress sale in another city. Flier sold all of the toys to the Childfair Toy Store in Berkland where they were discovered by the police and returned to SIMUCO. (See Chapter 7.) Does Childfair have any rights against Flier?

(3)

The Wire Products Company of Anosmia sent a sample of a new baling and binding wire to Hypocase, Inc., for inspection, in an effort to get the Hypocase business. Hypocase used such wire for building pallets and also in packing them for shipment. After examining the wire, Gude du Buy, the purchasing agent for Hypocase, placed a $5,000 order with Wire Products. The order referred only to the type of wire and to its minimum tensile strength. When the wire was received and an attempt was made to put it into use, it was discovered that the wire was not of uniform diameter and did not thread easily through the baling machines. Some of the wire was put to use in a process where it did not have to be threaded through a machine and appeared to be satisfactory for that process. However, customers began to complain that pallets purchased from Hypocase and made with this wire were not holding up under use. Investigation revealed that a new protective coating put on the wire by its manufacturer contained a corrosive material that destroyed the strength of the wire in a relatively short period of time. Hypocase has been unable to get satisfaction from Wire Products and has filed an action for breach of warranty alleging as defects both the lack of uniformity and the deterioration of the wire. What are the rights of the parties?

(4)

Miss Chysky was employed as a waitress in a restaurant owned and operated by Abraham, for which services she was paid a salary and furnished board and lodging. On the 4th of May, she received from her employer, as part of her lunch, a piece of cake which had been baked by Drake Bros. Co., Inc., and sold by Drake to Abraham. While Miss Chysky was eating the cake, a nail, baked into the cake in such a way that it could not be discovered by inspection, penetrated the roof of her mouth, which became so infected that it was necessary to remove three of Miss Chysky's teeth. Is the Drake Bros. Co. liable to Miss Chysky?

[*Chysky* v. *Drake Bros. Co., Inc.,* 235 N.Y. 468 (1923)]

B. In General.

Unlike the situation under precode law, where it could be said with accuracy that the general principles of contract law apply to the sales contract as fully and as readily as they do to other simple contracts, the Code introduces many contractual concepts into the statutory law of sales, often in considerably altered form. While broad principles of mutual assent, consideration, competent parties, and legal object are still relevant, generally speaking, to sales contracts, there are now some exceptions and many alterations of detail. Offers, for example, may be binding under the Code even though there is no consideration, and the Code makes several important changes in the requirements of the statute of frauds, as we have seen. Many of the changes were made in order to enhance further the simple, practical, routine nature of most sales contracts. Others were made for the purpose of giving recognition to actual commercial practice and of modernizing outmoded rules and principles.

ORDERS FOR PROMPT OR CURRENT SHIPMENT. Differences between preexisting contract law and the Code treatment of offer and acceptance have been described elsewhere. In general, Code rules are much more lenient and much less inclined to give recognition to traditional standards or ceremonies, especially where these events are not really crucial to the coming into existence of a contract. In keeping with its policy of permitting acceptance by any reasonable mode, including performance, the Code states expressly that an offer to *buy* goods for prompt or current shipment shall be construed as inviting acceptance by a prompt promise *or* by prompt or current shipment of the goods, unless the offeror has unambiguously provided to the contrary. Ordinarily, the seller would be wise to send a notice of acceptance, but the notice is not necessary to an acceptance.

Where, under precode law, shipment of the goods could constitute acceptance of an offer, shipment of nonconforming goods was not an acceptance. The Code has reversed this doctrine. If the order is for prompt or current shipment, a shipment of nonconforming goods *is* an acceptance and, it will be noted, a breach at the same time. If the seller has goods he thinks will be satisfactory but still wishes to avoid uncertainty, he may notify the buyer that the shipment is offered only as an accommodation to the buyer, in which case the shipment will not constitute acceptance. The buyer can remove his risk by unambiguously requesting a promise as acceptance. Because goods are said to be nonconforming when a different quantity is shipped, as well as when different goods are shipped, a seller furnishing a different quantity in response to an order for prompt or current shipment should always notify the buyer that the shipment is an accommodation. Of course, the buyer may specify that the goods must be in strict compliance with the terms of the order.

INCOMPLETE TERMS.   It is basic policy of the Code to move away from the invalidation or failure of sales contracts on grounds of uncertainty or indefiniteness. Such a policy was no stranger to precode law, but the Code provisions are more far-reaching and state the policy and implement it more clearly and consistently. Under the Code, a contract for the sale of goods may be made in any manner sufficient to show agreement between the parties, including subsequent conduct that manifests recognition of the existence of a contract. It is of no relevance to the existence of a contract that the actual moment of its making is undetermined. A contract for sale will nevertheless be enforced even though one or more essential terms have been left open, if two conditions can be met: *if the parties intended to make a contract, and if there is a reasonably certain basis for giving an appropriate remedy.* Certainty in the description of each party's duties is no longer necessary. Obviously, however, the more terms the parties leave open the less likely it is that they will be found to have intended to create a binding agreement.

Where the terms are not expressed in the agreement, it becomes necessary to look for them elsewhere. The Code establishes an order of priority in which outside sources must be looked to for terms not expressed in the contract:

1. Repeated occasions for performance by either party acquiesced in by the other party.

2. The course of dealing of the parties among themselves before entering into the contract.

3. Usages of the prevailing or appropriate trade of which the parties are or should be aware.

4. Specific Code provisions designed to fill certain terms left open by the parties, such as price, quantity, delivery, and payment. (See Sections 2-305 to 2-311.)

Each of these sources may be displaced only by an express contractual term or by a source of higher priority. The result of this Code policy is to make enforceable many agreements which would not have been enforceable under prior law. Specific examples of the Code treatment of certain open terms will be discussed below.

C. Warranties–Promises and Representations of the Seller with Regard to the Sale

IN GENERAL. If the only aspects of a sales transaction that were of interest or importance to the buyer and seller were those aspects dealing solely with the passage of ownership from one to the other, the law of sales would be considerably simplified, but, at the same time, the sales transaction would not be a very useful legal device. A buyer, for example, would be reluctant to buy from a seller who did not, expressly or impliedly, promise that the goods were the seller's to sell, that the goods were the ones purchased by the buyer, and that they measured up to certain standards of quality. To a large extent, these problems can be taken care of by the parties themselves, during their negotiations, but it has been realized for centuries that commerce and the distributive activity are considerably facilitated and speeded up if some of the more common terms of a sales transaction are present automatically, without the parties actually having to stop to negotiate about them. If the parties want to change these terms, they may do so. In the absence of such changes, certain terms are always present. The theory is that certain terms are almost invariably present anyhow and that certain others are desirable in order that one party will not have an unfair advantage over the other.

One group of these terms consists of *warranties*. These are promises or representations by the seller concerning some aspect of the sale, and they resemble the "conditions" discussed in the chapter on contracts. A warranty may be express or implied. It is express when the seller makes the warranty in express words or the Code classifies it as "express." It is implied when it does not appear in so many words but is made a part of the transaction by custom, statute, or court. The fact that the seller uses or does not use the word "warranty" is of minor importance. The use of the word does not make a statement a warranty; many actual warranties do not contain the word; and many warranties are implied, without the use of any words at all. Although a warranty usually arises at the same time as the sales transaction occurs, it may come into existence at a later time. Note that if a warranty does arise after the sales contract has been entered into, the Code has removed the older contract requirement that it be supported by separate consideration.

If a warranty is treated as a promise, a breach of warranty entitles the innocent party to damages for the breach. If a warranty is treated as a condition, a breach entitles the innocent party to rescind. Most warranties, as will be realized more fully during the discussion, are treated as both promises and conditions entitling the innocent buyer to a choice of remedies.

Warranties and fraudulent representations. Warranties bear more than a superficial resemblance to fraudulent representations, but the basic differences between the nature and the effect of the two events require the drawing of careful distinctions. A warranty is a part of the sales contract, coming into existence when the contract is entered into or made a part of the contract at a later time. A fraudulent representation is not a part of the contract but is antecedent to it, and it is used as an inducement to enter into the contract. For example, where a contract contains a clause stipulating that no representations have been made adding to or modifying its terms, this clause is a bar to the introduction of evidence of certain warranties but not to the introduction of evidence of false representations, which render that clause, as well as the whole contract, voidable. As will be recalled from the chapter on contracts, one of the necessary elements of a fraudulent representation is knowledge of the falsity of the statement by the person who makes it. Knowledge of falsity is neither necessary nor relevant to the establishment of a warranty. Furthermore, many warranties arise without any conscious statement at all by the seller.

EXPRESS PROMISES AND REPRESENTATIONS.   In a very real sense, the law of warranty has to do with the determination of what it is that the seller has in essence agreed to sell. It is obvious that statements of fact about the goods, descriptions of the goods, and samples or models of the goods are directly related to the question of what it is that is being sold, and, as such, they create express warranties that the goods will conform to these representations. The Code deals with these statements, descriptions, samples, and models exactly as it would deal with any other part of negotiations which end in a contract. If any of these factors is made part of the basis of the bargain, no specific intention to make a warranty is necessary and no specific words or forms need be used. Under the Uniform Sales Act, the buyer had to show reliance on these affirmations in order to make them a part of the agreement, but the Code recognizes that in actual practice such expressions of fact by the seller about the goods during the negotiations are regarded as part of the description of what is being sold; thus the Code shifts the burden of proof to the seller if he wishes to take these affirmations, once made, out of the agreement.

Although older case law classified descriptions, samples, and models as express warranties, the Uniform Sales Act moved them over into the realm of implied warranties. The Code puts them back. The primary reason for doing so was to bring the law into conformity with the essence of the bargain. The change also has the effect of making warranties that rise out of descriptions, samples, and models difficult to disclaim. (See discussion of disclaimers below.)

The Code does not remove the distinction between a representation and an opinion. Statements as to the "worth" or "value" of goods, or other statements of the seller's opinion, do not ordinarily create warranties. When a seller "puffs" his goods by using such statements as "the finest on the market," "incomparable," or "best," common experience tells us that these expressions cannot usually be seen as entering into the bargain. However, the basic question remains the same: What statements of the seller have in the particular circumstances and in objective judgment entered into the basis of the bargain? As indicated above, *all* affirmations by the seller do so unless good reason is shown to the contrary. It would appear, therefore, that "puffing" is more likely to create a warranty under the Code than under previous law.

If a seller wishes to minimize the creation of express warranties, he may, during the drafting and negotiating, avoid unnecessary description and make it clear that any samples or models are intended only to "suggest," not to "describe," that which is being sold. It should also be noted that the seller may make express warranties even after the transaction is closed without additional consideration, so he cannot afford to abandon all caution simply because a contract is made. This result is brought about by a general provision of the Code, Section 2-209(1), referred to in the chapter on contracts, which provides that agreements modifying contracts for sale need no consideration to be binding.

In many states, case law supports the view that advertising warranties are express warranties running in favor of anyone reading and relying on the advertisements. Although the Code appears to require that the seller, as distinguished from the manufacturer, make a representation to the buyer, the Official Comments on the Code suggests that there was no intention to disturb lines of case law which have recognized that warranties need not be confined to sales contracts or to the direct parties to such contracts. Actually, language in the Uniform Sales Act, similar to that of the Code, was so interpreted by the courts.

Does the fact that a buyer has actually inspected the goods destroy the effect of an express warranty? Certainly express warranties will not cover defects actually known to the buyer at the time the contract was made. Beyond this situation, the results are not clear, and the Code is not explicit. The degree of reliance on the inspection and on the warranty, the experience of the buyer, and the obviousness of the defect must all be taken into account. It must be remembered that warranties are part and parcel of the contract and are not mere inducements. Custom and usage in a trade, for example, cannot be used to negate an express warranty, on the ground that the custom or usage would be inconsistent with the express terms of the contract. The effect of inspection on implied warranties will be discussed below.

IMPLIED PROMISES AND REPRESENTATIONS. *Caveat emptor.* A great deal of confusion exists among non-lawyers, and even among lawyers, as to the meaning of the phrase *caveat emptor*. Almost everyone can translate it, "let the buyer beware," and even pronounce it, but beyond that the phrase has been given an uncertain treatment. Without taking time to examine all of the things *caveat emptor* has been held to mean, let it simply be said here that the phrase expresses, in a shorthand fashion, the common law rule that the buyer assumes the risk of getting goods of the quality and in the condition he desires if he is furnished by the seller with goods that substantially correspond to the description of the goods that were the subject matter of the contract. It is clear from this brief statement that the principle of *caveat emptor* is not an unqualified shifting of responsibility to the buyer: the seller must supply goods that correspond substantially to the goods described in the contract. As a practical matter, the doctrine has changed considerably through the years, both by court decision and by statute, and is really just another way of expressing the thoughts set forth at the beginning of this discussion of warranties. The terms of the sales contract are the product of the negotiations between the parties, and the buyer does not have to buy if he is not satisfied with his opportunity to inspect the goods or with the promises and representations that he can persuade the seller to make. In the interest of improving and simplifying sales transactions and of furthering justice, modifications have been made, from time to time, in the general rule, and more qualifications have been placed on the doctrine of *caveat emptor*.

Nature of implied warranties. Added to and clarified by statute, but still essentially common law principles, are the modifications and qualifications to the doctrine of *caveat emptor,* which are known as *implied warranties*. Courts and legislatures have come to the conclusion that commerce and justice are furthered if certain warranties are always made a part of a sales contract, unless the parties indicate a contrary intention. These warranties are just as much a part of the sales contract as are express warranties, even though the implied warranties do not actually appear in the contract. Implied warranties may usually be excluded from the contract by a provision to that effect. Many sales contracts will contain both express and implied warranties. Unlike express warranties, however, implied warranties are destroyed by contrary custom, usage of trade, course of dealing, or course of performance. The nature and effect of disclaimers will be discussed below.

Effect of inspection. The relevance to implied warranties of the inspection of the goods by the buyer is described in Section 2-316(3)(b). When the buyer before entering into the contract has examined the goods or the sample or model as fully as he desired or has refused to examine the goods, there is no implied warranty with respect to defects which an examination ought, under the circumstances, to have revealed to him. This language makes several changes in precode law. It is not sufficient, in order to bring the transaction within the phrase "refused to examine," that the goods were available for inspection. There must be a *demand* by the seller that the buyer examine the goods fully. This demand puts the buyer on notice that the risk of defects which inspection ought to reveal now falls on him.

Inspection of the goods by the buyer does not exclude all defects, even where there are no express warranties. The skill of the particular buyer and the normal method of inspecting the particular goods under the circumstances are the determining factors. Failure to notice obvious defects will not excuse the buyer, but an examination under circumstances which do not permit testing will not exclude defects which could be ascertained only by such testing. Professional buyers will be held to standards of professionals in their field, while nonprofessionals will be held to have assumed the risk only for such defects as a layman might be expected to observe.

Warranty of merchantability. Although it is explicitly recognized that a course of dealing or usage of trade may create implied warranties, specific attention is given in the Code to only two implied warranties: merchantability and fitness for particular purpose. These two have been known, historically, as the "implied warranties of quality." They are the most common and the most important. The other implied warranties will not be discussed here. The Official Comments on the Code suggest as an example of another kind of implied warranty the obligation of a seller to provide pedigree papers to evidence conformity of a pedigreed dog or blooded bull to the contract. Unless excluded by agreement, implied warranties form a part of every sales contract.

A warranty that the goods shall be "merchantable" is implied in a contract for the sale of those goods if the seller is a merchant dealing in goods of that kind. The Code spells out in considerable detail the meaning of the key word "merchantable." To be merchantable, the goods must pass without objection in the trade as the goods described in the contract; the goods, in the case of fungible goods, must be of fair average quality within the description; they must be fit for the *ordinary* purposes for which such goods are used (to be distinguished from fitness for *particular* purpose, discussed below); they must be, within the variations permitted by the agreement, of the same kind, quality, and quantity within each unit and among all units involved; they must be adequately contained, packaged, and labeled as the agreement may require; and they must conform to the promises or affirmations of fact made on the container or label, if any. This list of attributes is not intended by the Code to be exhaustive, and the way is left open for other possible attributes of merchantability. Note that this warranty does not apply to the casual seller who does not ordinarily deal in goods of the kind involved in the transaction. No reliance on the warranty is required of the buyer.

The Code states expressly that serving of food or drink for value, whether it is to be consumed on the premises or elsewhere, is a "sale" within the meaning of the statute. This provision brings an end to an old controversy over whether the serving of food was a sale or a service. If the latter, it was not subject to the warranty of merchantability. The area of the law concerned with liability for personal injuries resulting from defects in food, drink, and other products is increasingly pulling away from its sales and warranty orientation and moving into a field of its own known as "products liability," which is oriented to a large extent around concepts of tort. These matters are discussed in greater detail at the end of this section.

Warranty of fitness for particular purpose. A seller may know or have reason to know a particular purpose for which goods are required by the buyer. If so, and if the seller also knows or has reason to know that the buyer is relying on the seller's skill or judgment in selecting or furnishing suitable goods, there is, unless disclaimed, an implied warranty that the goods shall be fit for that particular purpose. The seller may know of the purpose or reliance because the buyer has so informed him, or he may have reason to know from the circumstances. Of course, the buyer must actually be relying on the seller, and his reliance must be reasonable. Thus, if a buyer tells a seller that he wants a waterproof fabric that will stand up under the heavy wear of chemicals packaging and that he will rely on the seller's judgment in selecting the fabric, and if the seller furnishes a fabric, there is an implied warranty on the part of the seller that the fabric he supplies will be fit for that purpose. If the fabric turns out not to be fit for that use, the warranty has been breached. No warranty will arise where a buyer supplies the seller with a sample or plans and at specifications.

Under the Uniform Sales Act, the warranty of fitness for particular purpose was not applicable where the goods were sold under their patent or trade name. The theory was that a buyer, under such circumstances, was not relying on the seller's skill or judgment. Unfortunately, some courts interpreted this language to mean that if the goods simply possessed a patent or trade name, the warranty of fitness was destroyed, even though the buyer had not specified or insisted on a particular brand. The Code removes the requirement, which has the effect of making the existence of a patent or trade name only one of the facts to be considered when the question of whether the buyer actually relied on the seller arises. In many states this was the result that the courts had arrived at in any event.

It should be clear from the discussion that both the warranty of merchantability and the warranty of fitness for particular purpose may exist in connection with the same goods in the same transaction. In the fabric example above, the former warranty would cover several attributes of the goods in addition to their fitness for the buyer's particular purpose.

WARRANTY OF TITLE. The warranty of title is neither express nor implied, under the Code, but it occurs in a special category along with the warranty against infringement. The purpose in so classifying it is to protect it from broad disclaimers (like "as is") without requiring that it be express. Sellers warrant that the title conveyed to the buyer shall be good, its transfer rightful, and that the goods shall be delivered free from any security interest or other

lien or encumbrance of which the buyer at the time of contracting has no knowledge. Because it is apparent to the buyer that sales by sheriffs, executors, and
other persons similarly situated are far out of ordinary commercial channels,
no personal obligation is imposed on such persons, who usually purport to sell
only an unknown or limited right.

The warranty is made whether the seller is in possession of the goods at
the time of the contract or not, and it is irrelevant that the seller did not have
good title at the time of the sale, if he has it at the time of delivery. The
Uniform Sales Act described a related, though separate, warranty of quiet possession, which warranted that the buyer would not be disturbed in his possession of the goods. The Code abolishes this warranty on the ground that
disturbance of possession is only one of many ways in which the breach of the
warranty of title may be established. Note that the breach takes place at the
time of delivery, not the time of disturbance; this rule has important effects
on the running of the statute of limitations.

Many sellers act, not for themselves, but for others, selling in a representative capacity. These sellers, like agents and auctioneers, do not warrant that
they personally have the title but do warrant that they have the right to sell
by reason of their representative capacity.

WARRANTY AGAINST INFRINGEMENT.   This warranty applies only to sellers
who are merchants regularly dealing in goods of a particular kind. Such sellers
warrant that the goods will be delivered free of any rightful claims by third
persons growing out of infringements of patents or trade-marks. It is not
necessary that the buyer be actually interfered with by the party claiming
infringement. The buyer's remedy becomes available immediately upon receipt
of the notice of infringement. The warranty does not apply, however, where
the buyer orders goods to be assembled or manufactured by the seller in
accordance with specifications supplied by the buyer. In this situation, the
buyer is obligated to indemnify the seller for any loss he may suffer as a result
of the infringement.

EXCLUSIONS AND DISCLAIMERS.   *Express warranties.*   The effect of inspection of the goods by the buyer has already been discussed. It remains to be
seen what effects are had by other exclusions and disclaimers. Section 2-316(1)
of the Code seeks to protect buyers from clauses in sales contracts which
purport to exclude "all warranties, express or implied" and from unexpected
and unbargained for language of disclaimer. The basic problem is simply that
both the warranties and the disclaimers are express parts of the contract and
may be in conflict. The Code takes the view that words of warranty and words
of disclaimer should be construed, wherever reasonable, as consistent with
each other, and where such construction is unreasonable, the Code finds that
words of disclaimer or limitation are inoperable to the extent that they are
inconsistent with the warranty.

There is one situation under the Code, however, where the disclaimer may prevail over an express warranty with which it is in conflict: where the warranty is subject to exclusion by the parol evidence rule. Although the Code considerably liberalizes the parol evidence rule with regard to sales contracts, a written agreement found by the court to have been intended by the parties as a complete and exclusive statement of the terms cannot be contradicted, explained, or supplemented by evidence of any prior agreement or of a contemporaneous oral agreement. Where the writing is not intended as a complete and exclusive statement, a writing may be explained or supplemented by evidence of consistent additional terms or, in any event, by course of dealing, usage of the trade, or course of performance. Unless, then, the writing contains a clause stating that it is the complete statement of the terms, a written disclaimer will not be effective even against oral express warranties.

Implied warranties. The disclaimer of implied warranties raises issues very different from those raised in connection with express warranties. Implied warranties arise as a matter of law, not as a result of the seller's words, and they are not in any way affected by the parol evidence rule. The Code sets forth the rules governing the disclaimer of implied warranties in considerable detail. The warranty of merchantability may be disclaimed orally or in writing, but the language must mention "merchantability" and, if in writing, must be conspicuous. In order to disclaim the warranty of fitness, the exclusion must be in writing and conspicuous even if the rest of the terms of the contract are not in writing.

Section 2-316(3) describes three exceptions to the above rules:

1. Unless the circumstances indicate otherwise, all implied warranties are excluded by expressions like "as is," "with all faults," or other language which in common understanding calls the buyer's attention to the exclusion of warranties and makes plain that there is no implied warranty.

2. An implied warranty may be excluded or modified by course of dealing, course of performance, or usage of trade.

3. Under certain circumstances, inspection of the goods by the buyer or refusal to inspect may exclude implied warranties.

Title and infringement warranties. Catch-phrase disclaimers like "as is" do not exclude the warranties of title or infringement. Specific language can disclaim the warranty of title, by express provision of the Code, but it would probably be wise for the seller to include in this language a statement that the buyer is assuming the risk of defects in the title. While the Code does not give specific attention to disclaimers of the warranty against infringement, it does preface the description of the warranty with the phrase "unless otherwise agreed." This would suggest that courts will recognize provisions in the contract by which the seller disclaims such warranties.

CONFLICTS AMONG WARRANTIES. Warranties, whether express or implied, may conflict with each other. The basic rule of construction under the Code is that they shall be construed as consistent except where such construction is unreasonable, in which case the intention of the parties shall determine which is dominant. Among the rules in Section 2-317 to be used in ascertaining the intentions of the parties is one that states: "Express warranties displace inconsistent implied warranties other than an implied warranty of fitness for a particular purpose."

SUMMARY. Knowing what the reader now does about warranties, how will his conduct in sales transactions be affected? As a buyer, he does not have to ask the seller to guarantee his right to sell; he is protected if the goods he has ordered by sample or description do not conform substantially to the sample he examined or to the description he supplied to the seller; he does not have to ask the seller to promise that goods ordered for some special purpose will be fit for that purpose; and he is afforded a remedy if goods he has purchased do not prove to be suitable for the uses to which such goods are normally put. Although he does not have to bargain about any of these things, he still is on his guard for attempts by the seller to reduce the scope or eliminate some of the seller's responsibilities with regard to the quality of the goods or the status of the seller's title. He knows that the parties may alter the terms of the implied promises by the seller but only by their express agreement.

Our buyer also knows that his rights under the warranties are good against the seller and that if he is injured as a result of defects in the goods he has purchased, he may have rights on negligence, warranty, or even strict tort grounds against the manufacturer. He may be equally well protected against damage to his property as a result of these defects in purchased goods. The buyer knows that he does not lose the protection of the warranties by simply failing to inspect the goods, even if he had the opportunity to inspect; he must refuse to inspect after the seller has demanded that he do so; if he does refuse under such circumstances, defects which reasonable inspection ought to have revealed will be excluded from his protection. If he does inspect, he should do so carefully, because he will be held to reasonable standards of inspection for one of his skill in accordance with normal methods of inspecting these goods.

As a seller, the reader knows that certain promises with respect to the goods are present even without his express statements, unless he has clearly and conspicuously disclaimed them. His descriptions of the goods and his samples and models may well become warranties. Broad disclaimers will not affect his express warranties, except in some cases where the parol evidence rule applies, and they may not even exclude all the implied warranties. Warranties of title and infringement are not implied warranties and are not excluded except by explicit disclaimer. Our seller will probably use greater care in the manufacture and inspection of his goods, or, if he is a retailer, will use greater care in the selection of products he chooses to sell. These and many other effects are brought about by the law with regard to warranties.

D. Products Liability

In General. The legal responsibility of manufacturers and sellers to compensate buyers and users for losses suffered because of defects in the goods manufactured or sold has been a matter of interest for centuries to courts, legislatures, and society, as well as to the parties involved. We have just examined a few of the many aspects of the problem in connection with the law of warranties. It is also intimately related to the law of contracts, the law of property, and, in particular, to the law of torts. Indeed, it is only partly a matter of law. The protection of the consumer and the maximization of his welfare are matters of economics. Causation and the assignment of social burdens are largely matters of philosophy or ideology. There is no question but that politics have played a role in some of the issues.

There are several reasons for including a brief discussion of products liability here, in a chapter on sales and adjacent to a section on warranty. Sales are involved in almost all situations where issues of products liability arise; modern law is, to a large extent, still concerned with products liability in connection with warranties, although there is a pronounced drift in the direction of torts. (Earlier editions of this book contained at this point a discussion of warranties in connection with sales of food and drugs.) The area of products liability is one of the most rapidly developing in the law and has been very prominent in the news for the last decade. The subject is a large and growing one and new case law is appearing every day, but we will make no attempt here to be exhaustive and detailed and will only suggest what is happening generally in this area of the law. Some history is necessary for proper perspective, and no discussion of a topic in the midst of rapid development can be comprehensive without some prognostication.

Remedies available to buyers, as well as to sellers, where sales relationships break down for one reason and another, are discussed in detail in the last section of this chapter. The treatment is oriented around failures to perform obligations imposed on the parties by the contract and around the rights that these failures produce in the other party. Recovery of the price and of the goods is considered, as well as various alternatives for avoiding the obligations of the contract where one of the parties has failed in some way. Damages for breach of contract or warranty will also be an issue. Unlike litigation rising out of most sales transactions, however, products liability is primarily concerned with personal injuries, to a much lesser extent with damage to property, and only in a most peripheral sense with loss of value or expectancy. Furthermore, and of paramount importance, much of the law of products liability today is concerned with parties who have no contractual relationship with each other at all, although sales contracts are almost certain to have been involved at one or more stages of the physical transfer of the goods from a manufacturer, for example, to an injured ultimate user. In a real sense, the major strands of the law of products liability consist of the ways in which the primary interested parties have ceased to be the contracting parties themselves and have become persons who are contractually remote from each other.

HISTORY. There was a time when not even a buyer who was injured by a defect in goods sold to him by another could have recovered from the seller. The doctrine of *caveat emptor,* discussed above, originated in the medieval Christian belief that commerce was outside the law and outside the mainstream of human existence. There was little legal protection for buyers, under any circumstances, and they were required to rely on their own skill and skepticism in their dealings with sellers. If a buyer were poisoned by defective food that he had purchased, he had no rights to recover damages from the seller, although in some countries the state prescribed minimum levels of quality for certain foodstuffs and might punish a seller who sold goods that were below those standards. These harsh rules regarding the buyer's rights were feasible and workable during the medieval era owing to the simple state of technology and the close personal nature of trade.

The commercial revolution in the fifteenth century and the Renaissance tended to make commerce and profits respectable and brought them into the mainstream of life. The Industrial Revolution destroyed the conditions of technical simplicity and close personal relationships and substituted the impersonal market, technical complexity, distribution of goods far beyond the neighborhood, a high degree of specialization, a division of labor, and many other changes that effectively ended the ability of the buyer to protect himself. The law began to change also. It avoided the no longer tolerable aspects of *caveat emptor,* not by finding a new doctrine, but by discovering exceptions to the old one, exceptions based to a large extent on other and more basic principles of law which, theretofore, had not been applied to relationships between sellers and buyers. Chief among these other principles was one which holds that everyone must use reasonable care to minimize the risk of injury to others. The exceptions to the doctrine of *caveat emptor* followed three different paths: fraud, warranty, and negligence.

For centuries, the primary, if not the only concern of the law was with the rights of the buyer against the seller. Thus, if a buyer were harmed by a defect in the food or other product which he had purchased from the seller, he could pursue the seller on the basis of one or more of several appropriate theories. Of course, a claim based on fraud required the proof of fraud (see discussion of the elements of fraud in the chapter on contracts). A claim based on negligence required proof that the seller's conduct fell below that standard established by law for the protection of others against unreasonable risk of harm (see discussion of negligence in Chapter 2) and usually necessitated the buyer's showing that the seller had a duty to conform to the standard, that he failed to conform, that the failure was the cause of the buyer's injury, and that the buyer was actually injured. While these theories might have application under special circumstances, it is obvious that they could not really play much of a role in disputes involving buyers and sellers, especially where the latter was simply a retailer.

The buyer's rights against a seller (retailer) are now usually stated in terms of warranty. Sellers do not always make express warranties and cannot always be induced to make them. The law slowly, however, imposed implied warranties on sellers, in keeping with common business practice and consistent with changing public views of commerce, and made them enforceable by contract action. While warranties began as a tort idea, akin to deceit (failure of the seller to perform his duty not to misrepresent the goods) and still retain some of their tort characteristics, they came in time to be largely matters of contract. The courts imposed them on sellers even where the goods were manufactured or processed by somebody else. A buyer, then, could recover from a retailer damages for harm done to the buyer as a result of a defect in the goods sold, even if there were no fraud or negligence on the part of the retailer. (Although he does not manufacture the goods himself, a retailer may be negligent in these situations in a number of ways, including being careless in inspecting or handling the goods.)

It should be clear that the availability of remedies by the buyer against the seller leaves many problems unsolved. The retailer-seller, for example, may be judgment proof (i.e., he has no assets with which to pay a judgment). In most cases the goods probably contained the defect when they left the hands of the manufacturer. If the buyer recovers from the seller on grounds of breach of warranty, the loss thus suffered by the seller may be recovered by him from the wholesaler or other intermediary and his loss, in turn, from the manufacturer. If it appears a bit foolish to the layman to require two or more lawsuits in order to impose liability on the one most nearly responsible, the manufacturer, the law cannot really make a very convincing argument in response. Furthermore, the person injured may not be the buyer at all but a member of his family, a guest or a friend; under older views, this person probably could not recover from anybody.

The explanations for these paradoxes lie in the fact that the law, for a variety of reasons, came to regard both warranty and negligence in these actions as contractual matters. The major implication of this view was that parties who were not in contractual relationship with each other were not so situated that warranty or negligence actions based on injuries resulting from defects in goods were available to them. The result was the multiplicy of actions necessary in order to shift the responsibility for the buyer's injury from seller to wholesaler to manufacturer, where it ultimately belonged, while precluding the guest or friend from recovery because he had entered into contractual relations with nobody. The buyer could sue the retailer because there was a contract between them; the retailer could sue the wholesaler because there was a contract between them; and the wholesaler could sue the manufacturer with whom he had entered into a sales contract. This requirement is known as the doctrine of "privity of contract." It is obvious that in some connections it makes very good sense, at least as a starting point for analysis, but in the products liability cases it led to harshness, unfairness, unnecessary time and expense, and often foolish results. The reasons why the law came to regard both negligence and warranty in these cases as essentially contractual in character and to ignore origins and overtones of tort are complex and, in some aspects, obscure, but they are not unrelated to the strongly held view of a century or so ago that to make manufacturers liable to consumers, their friends, and other remote persons, would discourage industry.

No sooner had the privity doctrine become firmly established, however, than the process of making exceptions began. That process continues today, but there is now, in some jurisdictions, a strong tendency to start from entirely different premises, as will be seen. Almost by the time the rule was established, it was out of phase with the Industrial Revolution and rapid changes in society and public policy. In keeping with the basic principles of the common law system, the rule began to change as the reasons for it changed and as the social, political, and economic environment changed also.

CHANGES ON THE NEGLIGENCE SIDE. During the nineteenth century, most of the changes took place in connection with the liability of manufacturers to remote persons such as consumers, their guests, families, and employees, and others who had no contractual relations with the manufacturers. At the beginning of the nineteenth century, manufacturers were not liable for injuries resulting from negligently caused defects in their products, except to those who had bought the products directly from the manufacturer. Thus, the manufacturer of a stagecoach was not liable to a coachman who was lamed for life by an accident resulting from a defect in a wheel caused by the manufacturer's negligence. By the middle of the century, exceptions to the requirement of privity began to appear, and, by the second decade of the twentieth century, the requirement itself almost vanished. A manufacturer became liable for the injury caused to almost anyone by defects in goods resulting from his negligence.

The injured user or consumer still had to prove negligence, however, and this was often an extremely difficult task, especially where the particular manufacturing process was highly technical or the facts surrounding the process peculiarly within the knowledge of the manufacturer. A doctrine used for many years in other fields of negligence law rose to mitigate the proof problems of plaintiffs in product liability cases. In some situations, it can sensibly and reasonably be said that a particular event could not have taken place except through the defendant's negligence and that there is no reason why the fact of negligence should be proved separately. This was known as the doctrine of *res ipsa loquitur* ("the thing speaks for itself"). The injury could, under some circumstances, be evidence of the defect and the defect, in turn, evidence of the negligence, thus establishing a rule of almost *per se* negligence.

By the time these developments took place, however, negligence was no longer the main battleground of products liability cases. Negligence grounds could be used only against those who were negligent. Thus, where the manufacturer could not, for whatever reason (out of the jurisdiction of the court or judgment proof), be reached, the buyer could fall back on the retailer using warranty grounds, but these grounds were not available to family, friends, guests, employees, and donees, for the same old reason: privity. Furthermore, *res ipsa* was not always available in negligence cases, and the proof of negligence might be expensive, cumbersome, or impossible under the circumstances. For many reasons, some good and some bad, the battle had shifted to warranty and to the attempts to remove privity of contract as a requirement in those cases.

Side by side with these more material changes were some important changes in public attitude. Increasingly, there has come to be accepted the view that human life, health, and safety are best promoted and that maximum protection against dangerous defects is best encouraged by imposing liability as simply and directly as possible on the manufacturer who has produced the product; that packaging, advertising, and placing goods on the market are a sort of "implied" express warranty that the goods are suitable and safe for use; and that there was already strict warranty liability on the manufacturer, in a sense, except that it had to proceed through a multiplicity of suits (buyer-retailer-wholesaler-manufacturer) in order to reach him.

CHANGES ON THE WARRANTY SIDE. The deterioration of the privity requirement in warranty cases first appeared in situations involving food. As far as the law is concerned, there was no particular reason to distinguish between food and other products, but there were practical reasons why the ice broke here first. Special responsibilities have been imposed on manufacturers, processors, and sellers of food and drink since the thirteenth century; and there was violent public agitation in the early years of the twentieth century as a result of a number of well publicized scandals against defective food and drugs. The first food and drug legislation was enacted during this period. At any rate, the courts began to impose liability in food and drug cases on warranty grounds without privity about 1913 and in non-food cases in the early 1950's.

The courts did not make this important change simply by abolishing the requirement of privity. They have still not done that and probably will not do so completely in the foreseeable future. What the courts have done is to seek, ingeniously, for grounds on which to justify exceptions to the requirement; a member of the family, for example, might be said to be a third party beneficiary of the contract between the buyer and the seller and, consequently, in a sort of privity of contract with the seller. One author has documented twenty-nine different ways in which the courts have sought to overcome the privity barrier. Section 2-318 of the Uniform Commercial Code extends the benefits of express or implied warranties beyond the buyer to "any natural person who is in the family or household of the buyer or who is a guest in his home," further limiting the scope of the privity doctrine.

The weakening of the privity requirement in food and drug cases has been going on for more than half a century and now offers little that is new or different. One of the two important trends now taking place is the extension of the leniency with regard to privity to all kinds of products, and this trend will, no doubt, continue. The other, and more important, trend is away from both negligence and warranty as a legal basis on which to impose product liability.

STRICT LIABILITY IN TORT. Over the last two or three decades, there has been a noticeable shift among the state courts toward imposing product liability without regard for the language of negligence and warranty. From a strictly legal point of view, this approach has several very important advantages. It avoids the necessity for approaching every product liability case as though it were an unusual situation whose uniqueness may or may not qualify it to be an exception to some older rule or principle. For a century and a half, the law of products liability has been built up as a family of special cases entitled to abnormal treatment under principles of negligence and warranty. A good argument can be made for the fact that these two principles should never have been moved over into the contract area in the first place, at least not to the extent where they came under the doctrine of privity. A second reason for the shift is that it permits direct confrontation with the question of where the responsibility for injuries resulting from product defects should fall: on the injured party or on the manufacturer who, even without fault in the ordinary sense, sent the product out into society.

Many courts are now answering the question in words like these: "A manufacturer is strictly liable in tort when an article he places on the market, knowing that it is to be used without inspection for defects, proves to have a defect that causes injury to a human being." Although the kind of liability described here is strict, it is certainly not absolute. The plaintiff must still prove that the article was not in a reasonably safe condition when it left the manufacturer's control. It does not have to be perfectly safe or foolproof. Perhaps, it would be better to phrase the basic question as one of whether a reasonably prudent man would put the product on the market if he knew of the dangers in it.

Many factors must be taken into consideration and weighed one against the other before a conclusion can be reached in a given situation. Among these factors would be: the usefulness of the product, the availability of safer substitutes, the likelihood of injury and the probable consequences, obviousness of the danger, the common knowledge of the danger and normal public expectations, avoidability of injury by care in use, and the ability to eliminate the danger without impairing the use of the article or pricing it out of reach. The answers can be found in this list to many special problems: penicillin (many people are intensely allergic), pasteur treatment for rabies (some people die from the treatment), pork infested with trichinae (a nematode worm destroyed by proper cooking), cigarettes, blood plasma, and many others.

The newer approach to product liability cases does not solve all problems —including the relevance of the plaintiff's own fault, the effect of disclaimers and warnings, whether the liability should extend to damage to property and to loss of value or expectancy, and the liability of manufacturers for defects in unfinished products turned over to a dealer or retailer for completion— but many are on the way toward solution.

SUMMARY.   It is likely that the social, technological, and economic trends which have produced such profound changes in our law of products liability will accelerate in the future. Automation, mechanization, packaging, and wider distribution of products will leave the consumer with even less opportunity to protect himself than he enjoys now. The drift toward strict liability in tort and away from emphasis on liability in negligence or warranty will continue. It seems highly unlikely at this time, however, that the manufacturer will become an insurer of the absolute safety of his products, at least within the foreseeable future. He will be liable only where he puts on the market a product which is not reasonably safe and where the plaintiff is injured as a result of an anticipated use of it.

3. PERFORMANCE OBLIGATIONS
OF THE PARTIES

A. In General

Under the Code, the obligation of the seller is "to transfer and deliver" and that of the buyer is "to accept and pay" in accordance with the contract. A seller's lien on the goods may delay the delivery, and credit terms may postpone the time at which the price must be paid, but inherent in every sales transaction is the ultimate obligation on the seller to deliver the goods and on the buyer to pay for them. Simple as all of this may seem, there has been an incredible amount of litigation concerning the nature and extent of these universal duties. The Code has attempted to minimize the confusion, uncertainty, and litigation and to eliminate the bad law that has grown up around the obligations of delivery and payment.

The parties may provide in the contract for the time, place, and manner in which the seller is to deliver and in which the buyer is to pay. In the absence of such provisions in the contract, the obligations of the parties in these and in other important respects are set forth in the Code. Even where the parties do make provision for these matters, the Code seeks to clarify and simplify by supplying rules of interpretation and construction, based largely on commercial practice and the presumed intentions of the parties. Explicit recognition is given to the fact that in many sales transactions the performance of these basic obligations by either buyer or seller may be dependent upon the cooperation of the other party, and the Code broadly excuses either one where the other's cooperation is necessary but is not "seasonably forthcoming." For example: the Code provides that, unless otherwise agreed, specifications relating to the assortment of goods are at the buyer's option and specifications or arrangements relating to shipment are at the seller's option; where such specification is necessary to the delivery or payment and is not seasonably forthcoming, the other party is excused from the resulting delay in his own performance and may, under certain conditions, treat the failure to specify or cooperate as a breach of the obligation to deliver or accept the goods.

It is interesting to note that where the price is made payable, in whole or in part, in goods, each party is treated by the Code as though he were the seller of the goods which he is to transfer.

B. Performance by the Seller

DELIVERY OF THE GOODS. *In general.* *Delivery* is a matter of possession. A seller delivers by transferring to the buyer actual, physical possession of goods strictly conforming to the contract. Because a seller cannot force his goods on the buyer, his performance obligations cannot accurately be described as "delivery." All that the Code requires is that the seller make a *tender of delivery.* Tender is accomplished by the seller's putting and holding conforming goods at the buyer's disposition and giving the buyer any notification reasonably necessary to enable him to take delivery. The time, place, and manner of delivery are determined by the agreement and, in the absence of specification in the agreement, by the Code. The term "delivery" will be used below to include "tender," unless distinction is necessary for clarity.

Place and time of delivery. The parties may make any provision for the place and time of delivery that they wish, but many sales contracts contain no express agreement on this matter. Long before the appearance of the Code, the common law and the Uniform Sales Act had established guiding presumptions, based on notions of business practice, to determine the intentions of the parties in the absence of agreement. These presumptions fell into two major categories: those dealing with contracts in which delivery by carrier was not called for or authorized and those dealing with contracts in which delivery by carrier was required or authorized. The Code retains these distinctions and many of the older principles.

Both the Uniform Sales Act and the Code adopted a common law view that, in the absence of contrary provision in the contract, the proper place for delivery is the seller's place of business or, if he has none, his residence. It is further presumed that if the parties knew at the time the contract was entered into that identified goods were located at some other place, that place is the proper place for delivery. These presumptions have persisted because they have worked well and because they conform to the usual intentions of the parties. However, they can be varied by usage of trade, course of dealing, surrounding circumstances, and course of performance, as well as by agreement of the parties. If not provided for in the contract, the time of delivery is a reasonable time.

Where the goods to be delivered are in the possession of a third party, such as a warehouseman or other bailee, special problems arise as to how the delivery is to be effected. The problems arise because there are really two separate issues involved: the delivery necessary to satisfy the seller's obligation to the buyer and the delivery necessary to protect the buyer from the bailee and other third persons. The Code adopts older rules to the effect that such delivery to the buyer can be made in any one of three ways: by tender of a negotiable document of title for the goods (as a warehouse receipt), by obtaining acknowledgement by the bailee of the buyer's right to possession of the goods, or by tender of a non-negotiable document (as the seller's written order to the bailee to deliver the goods to the buyer) unless the buyer seasonably objects. All three ways permit the seller to discharge his obligations while, at the same time, protecting the buyer from third parties. The third method accomplishes the protection of the buyer through a specific Code provision which holds the risk of loss of the goods, or of any failure of the bailee to obey directions, in the seller until the buyer has had a reasonable time to present the document, and which states that the refusal of the bailee to honor the document or obey the directions defeats the tender of delivery.

Tender of delivery by the seller must be at a reasonable time, and he must hold the goods available for a period reasonably long enough to enable the buyer to take possession, but the buyer must furnish facilities suitable to receive the goods. When delivery by means of documents is intended, delivery of the documents through ordinary banking channels is sufficient.

Because of much confusion in the precode law where delivery by carrier was required or authorized, the Code specifies in detail the obligations of the seller in these situations. A distinction must be made between contracts where the seller obligates himself to deliver the goods at a particular destination, a *destination contract,* and contracts where the seller is required or authorized to ship the goods to the buyer but is not required to deliver them to a particular destination, a *shipment contract.* The Code eliminates much of the uncertainty prevalent under the Uniform Sales Act by establishing a presumption that a contract is one of shipment unless there is an express agreement or a clear commercial understanding to the contrary. Not even a term requiring the seller to pay the costs of transportation to the buyer will, by itself, make the agreement a destination contract. Under the Uniform Sales Act, these matters were all closely intertwined with issues of risk of loss and passage of title, but, as will be seen in the next section, the Code has separated these topics in the interest of greater clarity, simplicity, and commercial flexibility.

Because a destination contract really alters only the place at which "delivery" is to occur, the seller's obligations differ only slightly from what they are in the ordinary, non-carrier situation. As discussed above, the seller in such case tenders delivery by putting and holding conforming goods at the buyer's disposition at the particular destination and giving the buyer any notification reasonably necessary to enable him to take delivery. In addition, the seller must, in appropriate cases, tender documents of title and any other documents specified in the contract.

Section 2-504 of the Code sets forth the seller's obligations in shipment contracts. In the absence of contrary agreement, his obligations are:

1. to put the goods in possession of the carrier and make such contract for their transportation as may be reasonable under the circumstances;

2. to obtain and promptly deliver or tender in proper form any document necessary to enable the buyer to acquire possession of the goods or required by agreement or usage;

3. to notify the buyer promptly of the shipment.

Should the seller fail to make a proper contract for transportation or to notify the buyer, the buyer may reject the goods, but only if material delay or loss ensues. Under some circumstances, the buyer would be wise to insist that the agreement state that failure to give prompt notice is a ground for rejection. Attention is called at this point to the effect of the conditioning of performance on the "cooperation" of the other party. (See the discussion above.) In addition, commercial understanding and general requirements of good faith require the seller to make all reasonable arrangements to protect the goods in transit and to enable the buyer to recover from the carrier in the event of loss, for example, by avoiding contracts with the carrier that value the goods below their true value.

There are in use a number of commercial shipping terms which make possible considerably abbreviated sales contracts. The Code defines the legal consequences of the more commonly employed terms, a few of which are sufficiently important to justify brief discussion here. The most frequently used symbol is *F.O.B.* (which means "free on board"). Owing to the failure of precode law to define this and other symbols accurately and to take notice of different types of usage for the same symbol, there has been much confusion, uncertainty, and unfairness in the application of the law. The Code has greatly improved the situation.

When the F.O.B. term simply names the place of shipment (as "F.O.B. San Francisco"), the seller must bear the expense and risk of putting the goods into the possession of the carrier. Where the place named is the destination (as "F.O.B. New York," in a shipment from San Francisco to New York), the seller must at his own expense and risk transport the goods to that place.

It will be noted that the first example is a shipment contract and the latter example a destination contract. In addition to the obligations imposed on the seller under this paragraph are the usual obligations described in preceding paragraphs. F.O.B. terms sometimes use such phraseology as "F.O.B. car, San Francisco" or "F.O.B. vessel, New York," in the above example. The Code defines these terms to mean that the seller must in addition to his other obligations, at his own expense and risk, load the goods on board the freight car or ship. If "vessel" is used, the buyer must name the vessel.

Another common symbol is *F.A.S.* (which means "free alongside"). The implications of its use are that the seller must, at his own expense and risk, deliver the goods alongside the vessel in the manner usual in the named port or on a dock designated and provided by the buyer and obtain and tender a receipt for the goods in exchange for which the carrier is obligated to issue a bill of lading. Note that "F.O.B. New York" would deliver the goods, free of expense to the buyer, to the railroad or truck terminal in New York; "F.A.S. New York" would deliver alongside the vessel; and "F.O.B. vessel, New York" would deliver on board the vessel.

The buyer clearly has obligations also under these arrangements, and his failure to name the vessel or dock, for example, may excuse the seller, owing to the lack of the buyer's cooperation.

The term *C.I.F.* (sometimes *C.F.&I.*) means that the price includes in a lump sum the cost of the goods, of the insurance, and of the freight to the named destination. The term *C.F.* (sometimes *C.&F.*) means that the price includes the cost of the goods and the freight to the named destination. These terms require, unless otherwise agreed, that the seller at his own expense and risk put the goods into the possession of a carrier at a port for shipment, bear the expense of loading the goods on the carrier, obtain negotiable bills of lading covering the entire voyage, prepay or provide for the freight charges, secure the insurance (except C.F. and C.&F.), invoice the goods, procure any other documents necessary for the shipment, and forward all papers to the buyer with any indorsements necessary.

There are many variations on the use of the terms discussed above and many other mercantile symbols not mentioned at all. The few that have been examined are illustrative of the way in which the Code deals with all the matters in this category. Further details can be obtained from Sections 2-319 to 2-325 of the Uniform Commercial Code.

Single or instalment delivery. Unless the contract or the circumstances entitle the seller to make, or the buyer to demand, delivery in lots, the seller must usually tender delivery of all the goods at once. The "circumstances" are limited to situations in which it is not commercially feasible to deliver or receive goods in single lots, as where, in a contract for the shipment of twelve carloads of sand, only three carloads are ever available at one time or the buyer's storage space can only accommodate three carloads at once. If delivery is properly made in lots, the price, if it is apportionable, may be demanded for each lot.

CURE BY THE SELLER. Implicit in what has been said above about the obligations of the seller in connection with delivery is the conclusion that certain remedies are available to the buyer in the event the seller does not strictly and completely perform his duties. The remedies of the buyer will be discussed in detail later in this chapter. It is important at this point, however, to call attention to a basic policy of the Code, which, although related to failures of complete performance by either buyer or seller, is more concerned with avoiding unnecessary and insubstantial breaches wherever possible. Section 2-508 empowers the seller to *cure* breaches in certain circumstances by substituting a proper delivery of the goods. Where, for example, the buyer has rejected a tender or delivery because it was nonconforming, and the time for the seller's performance has not yet expired, the seller may seasonably notify the buyer of his intention to cure and may then, within the contract time, make a conforming delivery. The buyer cannot summarily treat the nonconforming tender or delivery as a breach or an anticipatory breach.

If the nonconformity arises from a particular defect which is ascertainable by reasonable inspection, the buyer may not reject the goods or use the nonconformity as a basis for showing the seller's breach without seasonably notifying the seller of the defect in order that the seller may cure. If the seller tenders the buyer a known nonconforming delivery of goods which the seller had reasonable grounds to believe would be acceptable with or without money allowance, and the buyer nonetheless rejects, the seller is permitted to cure the defect within "a further reasonable time" after he has seasonably notified the buyer of his intention to do so.

The purpose of the policy manifested in these rules is to discourage surprise rejections for minor nonconformities and to encourage the performance of sales contracts in accordance with the original intentions of the parties.

C. Performance by the Buyer

PAYMENT OF THE PRICE. *In general.* The price of goods is usually specified in the contract and may be payable in money, goods, or any other thing of value the parties agree upon. However, the contract may be wholly silent on matters of price or may provide that the price will be determined by later agreement between the parties or by a third party. The price can be tied to a market price at a future time and specific place, to a specified competitor's price, or to a published price list or index. The price can even be made unilaterally determinable by the buyer or seller, provided that he acts in good faith.

Where the contract is wholly silent on price, where the parties fail to agree, or where a third party fails to set a price, the price is then a reasonable price at the time of delivery. Where any other price-setting method fails, other than owing to a party's fault, the price is a reasonable price. Except where the price is left to be fixed by agreement of the parties, a failure to fix the price in some other way, owing to the fault of one party, gives the other party the option of fixing a reasonable price himself or as treating the contract as canceled. In the latter case, he retains all of his remedies for breach of contract. The parties may have agreed to be bound on the contract only if the price is determined by some specified method. If the price is not determined by this method, the contract fails, and the parties are not bound. However, part performance may have occurred. The Code, under these circumstances, requires the buyer to return any goods he may have received or, if he cannot do so, pay their reasonable value at the time of delivery; the seller must return any portion of the price that may have been paid on account.

The buyer's basic obligation is to accept the goods tendered by the seller and to pay for them in accordance with the agreement between them. Of course, this obligation is conditioned on the seller's tender of delivery being in accordance with the contract, as we have seen above. It is obvious that acceptance and payment are two distinct actions on the part of the buyer and will be so discussed.

Acceptance and inspection. Unless provided otherwise in the contract, the buyer has a right to inspect the goods before acceptance or payment. The right extends to inspection in any reasonable manner at any reasonable time or place. Under ordinary circumstances, inspection is an integral part of the process of determining whether the buyer must accept and pay for the goods. The parties may fix the place and method of inspection. If inspection at the place or in the manner specified should become impossible, the buyer does not lose his right of reasonable inspection at a reasonable time and place, unless inspection at the specified place and in the agreed upon manner was clearly intended as an indispensable condition to the performance of the contract.

The buyer must bear the expense of inspection, but may recover it from the seller if the goods do not conform and are rejected. If goods are shipped to the buyer, inspection may be made after their arrival. The fact that title has passed to the buyer or that he has obtained an insurable interest in the goods does not in any way impair his right to inspect before accepting the goods.

Although the buyer does not ordinarily have to pay the price prior to his inspection of the goods, he may be forced to do so if the sale is C.O.D., C.I.F., or if delivery is authorized and made by way of documents of title. If nonconformity of the goods appears without inspection, however, the buyer is excused from making payment. The fact that the buyer may be forced, under some circumstances, to make payment before he has an opportunity to inspect does not alter his right to inspection before acceptance. The buyer's payment for the goods does not constitute acceptance. An exception to the documentary sale, where the buyer must make payment before inspecting the goods, is found in what is called a shipment "under reservation." In this type of documentary sale, the seller obtains a bill of lading for the goods and attaches thereto a sight draft. Section 2-310(b) gives the buyer the right to inspect the goods before accepting the draft. The bill of lading in such cases is usually marked "hold until arrival; inspection allowed." (The documents referred to here are discussed in the chapters on commercial paper and secured transactions.)

Section 2-606, which controls the acceptance of goods, states that acceptance occurs when the buyer, after a reasonable opportunity to inspect the goods, signifies to the seller that the goods are conforming or that he will take or retain the goods in spite of their nonconformity; or when he fails to make an effective rejection after a reasonable opportunity to inspect; or when he behaves toward the goods as though they were his own. The buyer may accept all of the goods, reject all of the goods, or, if the goods fail to conform to the contract in any respect, accept individual commercial units and reject the rest. A *commercial unit* would be a single television set, or vehicle, or box of apples. The buyer may also retain a part of the goods for use as evidence in the event of litigation concerning the quality or condition of the goods.

Payment. Unless otherwise agreed, payment is due at the time and place at which the buyer is to receive the goods, even though the place of shipment is the place of delivery, and the buyer's tender of payment is a condition to the seller's duty to complete delivery. The buyer must pay the contract price for any goods accepted. While sales contracts usually state the price in dollar terms, the manner of payment is rarely mentioned. Unless there is agreement to the contrary, the seller may demand cash if he allows the buyer a reasonable time in which to obtain it. If there is no such demand, tender of payment is accomplished if it is made in any manner which is acceptable in the ordinary course of business. Thus, payment by check would be sufficient tender but, because such payment is usually conditional, would be defeated as effective payment by dishonor of the check.

If goods are delivered on credit, payment is due when the stated credit period has expired. Where the contract fails to state when a specified credit period begins to run, the Code provides that the period begins to run from whichever of the following is the latest: the time of shipment, the date of the invoice, or the date of dispatch of the invoice.

Rejection of nonconforming goods. As discussed above, if the goods or seller's tender of delivery fail to conform to the contract, unless otherwise agreed, the buyer is empowered to accept or to reject the whole or to accept any commercial unit or units he wishes and reject the rest. The rejection must be within a reasonable time after delivery or tender of the goods, and the seller must be seasonably notified. The buyer must inform the seller of any particular defect ascertainable by reasonable inspection. Where the seller could have cured, the buyer's failure to inform the seller defeats his reliance on the unstated defects to justify the rejection or to establish the seller's breach. If the transaction is between "merchants," the seller can require a written statement of all defects on which the buyer proposes to rely. The buyer may reject any nonconforming instalment of an instalment contract if the nonconformity substantially impairs the value of the instalment and cannot be cured by the seller.

A buyer cannot reject goods that he has already accepted, but he may revoke his acceptance if he can show that he did not know of the nonconformity or that he reasonably assumed that it would be cured.

After proper rejection by the buyer, he has no further obligations with regard to the goods rejected, and his exercise of ownership over them is wrongful as against the seller. However, the buyer does have a duty to hold the goods with reasonable care for sufficient time to permit the seller to remove them. If the buyer is a merchant, he is required to follow any reasonable instructions received from the seller with respect to the goods or, in the absence of instructions, to reship the goods to the seller, or he may make reasonable efforts to sell them for the seller's benefit if they are perishable or threaten to decline rapidly in value. If the buyer sells the goods in this manner, he is entitled to reimbursement for reasonable expenses incurred in caring for the goods and selling them. (See the discussion of the buyer's security interest in rejected goods at end of chapter section on buyer's remedies.)

D. Special Types of Contracts

OUTPUT AND REQUIREMENTS CONTRACTS. In many sales contracts, the quantity involved is measured by the output of the seller or by the requirements of the buyer. The Code limits the effects of such contract terms to actual outputs or requirements that occur in good faith. Even where there is good faith, the Code specifies that no quantity unreasonably disproportionate to any stated estimate or otherwise comparable to prior output or requirement may be tendered or demanded. Output and requirements contracts are not to be confused with the "desire" contracts discussed in Chapter 3, where a buyer or seller agrees only to take or deliver that amount which he desires or wants. "Desire" contracts, it will be remembered, are illusory and void.

EXCLUSIVE DEALING CONTRACTS. Where a buyer agrees to distribute only the seller's products or a seller promises not to deal with any other buyer in a prescribed territory, there is what is called under the Code an *exclusive dealing contract*. In the absence of other agreement by the parties, the Code implies in such contracts an obligation by the seller to use his best efforts to supply the goods and by the buyer to use his best efforts to promote their sale. While this was the case law of some states prior to adoption of the Code, it is now set forth expressly in Section 2-306(2). Because exclusive dealing contracts may be used to restrain trade or lessen competition, some of them are in violation of the antitrust laws. For this reason, the effect of the Code provision is limited to "lawful" agreements. (For further information on the legality under the antitrust laws of exclusive dealing contracts, see Chapter 14.)

4. RISK OF LOSS AND PASSAGE OF TITLE

A. Cases

(1)

On December 15, Gude Du Buy, purchasing agent for Hypocase, Inc., entered into a contract with Alex Carpon for the purchase of some lumber. The portion of the contract relevant to this case is set forth below.

> I hereby agree to sell 100,000 board feet of fir planks (or what I have in storage at the P. Church Lumber Yard) to Hypocase, Inc., at the rate of $21.45 per thousand; to be delivered when said Hypocase, Inc. may call for it. I agree to hold the lumber free of storage costs until the 1st of January. The lumber is to be measured at the yard, unless Hypocase, Inc. shall agree to take the quantity that appears on Church's books. Hypocase agrees to pay the full price within 5 days after delivery.

The contract was signed by Carpon and du Buy for Hypocase, Inc. On the 14th of January, the entire Church Lumber Yard, including Carpon's fir planks, was accidentally destroyed by fire. Carpon has demanded the price of the lumber, which Church has said amounted to 140,000 board feet, and 14 days storage charges. What are the rights of Carpon and Hypocase?

[See *Olyphant* v. *Baker,* 5 Denio, 379 (Supreme Court of New York, 1848)]

(2)

Hypocase, Inc. entered into a contract to purchase 10 milling machines from the Northwestern Machine Tool Co. of Chicago, at a price of $2,500 each. The machines had originally been manufactured for another buyer who had become insolvent. A representative of Hypocase had inspected the 10 machines in Chicago and had found them satisfactory for use in building pallets and had entered into the contract on the spot. The contract provided that the machines were to be thoroughly oiled and greased and bolted into heavy wooden packing crates before shipment. The machines had been oiled and greased but had not yet been crated when an accidental explosion in the Northwestern plant destroyed them all. Northwestern had demanded $25,000 from Hypocase, Inc. in payment for the machines. What are the rights of the parties?

(3)

Earl Eaton, one of the partners of SIMUCO Toyland, waited on John Blair in the store on June 20. Blair was interested in one of the large plastic swimming pools that SIMUCO had for sale but appeared reluctant to buy it because he was not sure his children would be interested in it. After some discussion of this point, Eaton finally said: "Take it home and use it for a couple of weeks, and if the kids don't like it, you can return it." Blair selected a $500 pool, paid a $50 deposit, and asked Eaton to deliver the pool on the 22nd. The pool was delivered on the 22nd to Blair's yard, where it was set up and put into use the next day. On July 8, a child in a tree located in a neighboring yard used the pool as a target for his new bow, and fired many arrows into the plastic material completely destroying the pool. Blair has refused to pay SIMUCO the $450 balance due on the pool. What are the rights of Blair and SIMUCO?

(4)

In 1968, Paul Preston entered into a contract with the Adams Boatyard in Newport, Anosmia, whereby Adams was to design and construct for Preston a large racing sloop at a price of $50,000. Preston approved a design, and construction was begun. Preston had occasion to be in Newport every month or two during the following year and usually stopped by the yard to see how his boat was progressing. When Preston was in Newport in August, 1969, he visited the yard and found the boat almost completed. Even the name he had selected for the boat, "Good Grief," had been painted on the stern. Adams told Preston, however, that the boat would not be ready for him until the next week. Although the boat was finished, Adams wanted a few more days to give it a thorough inspection before turning it over to the buyer. Adams completed his inspection on Monday, but late that night a sudden and unprecedented storm drove the boat under its pier and left it a total wreck. Adams has demanded payment from Preston on the ground that the boat was completed and ready for delivery to Preston when it was wrecked and, thus, the title and risk of loss had passed to Preston. What are the rights of the parties?

B. In General

No segment of the law of sales has been more extensively altered by the Code than that having to do with passage of title, risk of loss, and related matters. Most sales litigation under the common law and the Uniform Sales Act involved the problem of "passage of title," but that will not be so under the Code. The explanation lies in the fact that the courts at common law and the draftsmen of the Uniform Act, with admirable intentions, sought to solve as many sales problems as possible simply by locating the ownership of the goods. Thus, such questions as the following were answered simply by trying to find out whether the seller or the buyer happened to have the title to the goods at the appropriate time: who bears the loss when the goods are destroyed before the sales transaction is complete? who has an insurable interest in the goods? in case of a failure of performance by the buyer, can the seller sue for the price of the goods or only for breach of contract? if a third person injures the goods, who is permitted to sue him? what are the rights of the parties in special situations like the "sale or return" and "sale on approval"? Many other important legal questions were made to turn on a determination of who was the owner of the goods at the particular moment.

While the goals may have been admirable, the actual operation of the system was not. The time at which the transfer of the title in the goods from the seller to the buyer was completed was said to depend entirely on the intention of the parties, which suggests that the passage of title was meant to be a contractual issue. In actual practice, however, the parties rarely expressed any intentions on the matter, and the courts were forced to resort to certain presumptions, many of which were carried over into the Uniform Sales Act. Although the objective continued to be stated as that of ascertaining the intentions of the parties, the emphasis came more and more to be placed on the property aspects rather than the contractual aspects of the transaction, with the result that what the parties *did* became of more importance than what they were obligated to do under the contract. The result was confusion, uncertainty, and conflict, and many of the narrow questions, such as risk of loss, were being resolved in terms of issues which were largely irrelevant to the questions sought to be answered.

The Code abandons the passage-of-title-approach in favor of specific provisions with respect to the rights and duties of the buyer and the seller and an issue by issue handling of the separate questions whose answers used to be found in the location of title. Thus, risk of loss, insurable interest, and the right to price or damages are dealt with individually and without reference to the passage of title. The "title" concept is not entirely abandoned in the Code, however, because it must still be employed where there are no specific provisions dealing with particular issues at hand. All of the important or frequently encountered issues are the subject of specific provisions in the Code, with the result that while the title concept still has some significance, that significance is not very great.

C. Risk of Loss

In General. The Code permits the parties to make their own agreements with regard to the risk of loss. They may place it all on one party or share it between them on an equal or unequal basis or even link it to the title. While buyers and sellers should give some attention to the problem of risk of loss, the fact is that they almost never do. Consequently, the specific provisions of the Code come frequently into play in sales situations and should be thoroughly understood by all those engaged in buying and selling goods. The Code distinguishes between risk of loss problems where there has been no breach of contract and those arising in situations where there has been a breach. In both situations, the goals of the Code provisions are to relate the issues to contractual matters rather than to property matters based on arbitrary locations of title.

RISK OF LOSS WITHOUT A BREACH. With the possible exception of the simple cash, over-the-counter sale, probably no sales transaction is wholly free from the risk that the goods may be destroyed during the period between the making of the contract and its complete performance by both parties. Clearly, the risks of such loss must fall on the seller before the contract is made and on the buyer after complete performance has taken place, but in between may be a substantial period of time, the coming into existence of some goods, the acquisition or segregation of others, the movement of the goods from one place to another through the hands of several intermediaries, and a number of other events of greater or lesser import. How do the parties know who bears the risks at any particular point of time or stage of the transaction? They may settle this question by their own agreement or they may rely, as most buyers and sellers do, upon the provisions of the Code.

In most sales transactions where there has been no breach of the sales contract, the risk of loss passes to the buyer on his actual receipt of the goods, if the seller is a "merchant," or on tender of delivery, if he is not. This rule is found in Section 2-509 and recognizes the general principle that the risk ought to be with the party who has possession of the goods, in the absence of a breach of contract, on the theory that one in possession of the goods is more likely to have insurance and is in a better position to prevent a loss to them. A distinction is made between merchant and non-merchant sellers on the ground that professionals are more likely to insure and to protect the goods and should be held to a somewhat higher standard. It will be recalled that tender of delivery means the seller puts and holds conforming goods at the disposition of the buyer and gives him reasonable notice so that he may take possession. Neither the reservation of a security interest in the goods by the seller nor the fixing of a place or method of inspection has any effect on the location of the risk of loss.

Where the contract requires or authorizes the seller to ship the goods by carrier, but not to deliver them to a particular place, the risk of loss passes to the buyer when the goods are *duly* delivered to the carrier. It will be recalled from our earlier discussion of "shipment contracts" that delivery to the carrier by the seller includes making a proper contract for transportation, obtaining the necessary documents and delivering them to the buyer, and notifying the buyer promptly of the shipment. Consequently, the risk of loss passes to the buyer only when these duties have been completed. Just what the contract requires or authorizes is often determined by the use of the mercantile shipping terms (like F.O.B. and C.I.F.) discussed in the previous section.

If the sales contract is of the "destination" variety and does require the seller to deliver to a particular destination, the risk of loss passes to the buyer when the goods are at the particular destination and are there duly tendered so as to enable the buyer to take delivery. The goods are "duly tendered" when the seller puts and holds conforming goods at the buyer's disposition, gives the buyer notice, and provides necessary documents where appropriate.

Where the goods are held by a bailee and are to be delivered without being moved, the risk of loss passes to the buyer *on* his receipt of a negotiable document of title covering the goods; or *on* acknowledgment by the bailee of the buyer's right to possession; or *after* the buyer's receipt of a non-negotiable document of title or other written direction to deliver. Note that risk does not pass "on receipt" of a non-negotiable document of title but "after receipt," which means that the risk remains with the seller until the buyer has had a reasonable time in which to present the documents to the bailee and obtain his acknowledgement of the buyer's rights in the goods. This action by the bailee is called *attornment*. If the buyer makes no effort to obtain the bailee's acknowledgment, the risk of loss passes to him anyhow after a reasonable length of time; if the bailee later fails to attorn, the risk passes back to the seller.

RISK OF LOSS WHEN THERE HAS BEEN A BREACH. Generally speaking, the Code in Section 2-510, attempts to shift the risk of loss to the party who has breached the contract. Although this rule appears at first glance to be a sharp departure from precode law, closer inspection of actual results reveals very little difference. The Uniform Sales Act used a different reasoning but usually ended up placing the title in the breaching party. One aspect of the Code treatment is new, however, and should be examined carefully. The new element is the attention given to insurance coverage enjoyed by the nonbreaching party.

That the risk remains in the seller until cure or acceptance when he tenders or delivers goods that fail to conform to the contract is consistent with precode law. However, where the buyer has accepted the goods, either because he had no way of knowing of a latent defect or because he knew of a defect but believed that the seller would cure any nonconformity, and then revokes his acceptance, he shifts the risk of loss back to the seller only to the extent of any deficiency in his effective insurance coverage. Actually, the Code says that the buyer in these circumstances may treat the uncovered risk of loss "as having rested on the seller from the beginning." Where the buyer repudiates the contract or otherwise breaches it after the seller has identified conforming goods to the contract and before the risk has passed, the seller may, to the extent of any deficiency in his effective insurance coverage, treat the risk of loss as resting on the buyer for a "commercially reasonable time."

D. Insurable Interest

Closely related to risk of loss discussed above and to the passage of title under precode law is the nature and extent of the insurable interest which the buyer and the seller have in goods constituting the subject matter of their sales contract. In precode law, it was generally held that an insurable interest did not accrue to the buyer until title had passed to him. The Code could have taken a similar approach and tied insurable interest to the risk of loss, but it did not. Broader principles of insurance law hold that any person who has an interest in property such that its destruction would cause him a direct monetary loss has an insurable interest therein. Section 2-501 of the Code is concerned with the manner of identifying goods to the contract so that an insurable interest will accrue. The Code recognizes that the buyer should have an insurable interest at an early stage in the sales transaction and establishes rules giving the buyer such an interest when the goods are identified as the goods to which the contract refers.

Because identification of the goods to the contract is significant only in giving the buyer an insurable interest, the requirements for "identification" are minimal and are met even when the goods are nonconforming and the buyer has an option to return or reject them. Identification can be made at any time and in any manner agreed to by the parties. In the absence of such agreement, identification to the contract occurs when the contract is made if it is for the sale of goods already in existence and identified. (Recall the two senses in which the Code uses "identify.") It occurs when the goods are shipped, marked, or otherwise designated by the seller as goods to which the contract refers if the contract is for the sale of future goods. If the contract is for the sale of the unborn young of animals to be born within twelve months after the contract is made, identification takes place when the young are conceived. The identification of crops takes place when the crops are planted, or otherwise become growing crops, provided it is a contract to sell crops to be harvested within one year or the next harvest season after contracting, whichever is longer.

The insurable interest of the seller is even more simply dealt with. The seller retains an insurable interest in the goods so long as title or any security interest remains in him. Under the Code, as we have seen, the seller retains the title to the goods, in the absence of explicit agreement to the contrary, until he completes his performance with reference to the physical delivery of the goods. Where the identification is made by the seller alone, he may substitute other goods for those identified until default, insolvency, or notification of the buyer that the identification is final. These sentences are just another way of saying that the seller has an insurable interest in the goods as long as he bears all or part of the risk of loss and as long as he has a security interest in the goods. An insurable interest always accompanies a risk of loss, as we know, and it is also present where the seller has rights in the goods for purposes of security.

E. Right to Sue Third Persons

In most states, only the "owner" of goods is permitted to sue third persons for injuries to the goods. The Code extends the principle behind this view by providing that after the goods have been identified to the contract, a right of action against the third party is in either party to the contract who has title to or a security interest or an insurable interest in the goods. If the goods have been destroyed, there is also a right of action in the party who either bore the risk of loss under the contract or who has, since the injury, assumed that risk. As a practical matter, it is hard to imagine any situation in which it would not be possible for both the seller and the buyer to sue a third party for injury to goods which had been identified as the subject matter of the contract. Before identification, standing to sue would seem to be exclusively that of the seller, and, after acceptance by the buyer and expiration of his right to revoke his acceptance, an exclusive right to sue would probably accrue to the buyer.

F. Special Situations

In General. Two types of sales contracts, of long standing use in mercantile practice, are unusual in the sense that they give buyers the right to return goods to the seller even though the goods conform to the contract. Much confusion existed under the Uniform Sales Act with regard to these contracts not because the Act had failed to describe or define them accurately, but because the courts had difficulty in placing particular contracts in one group or the other. The legal effects of a contract's being classified in one group rather than the other were substantial. Furthermore, these contracts were sometimes confused with consignments and other agency arrangements. The draftsmen of the Uniform Commercial Code appear to have resolved the problem and dispelled the confusion. They have done so by looking beyond the old statutory language to general business understanding and common mercantile practice. Where the language of the Uniform Sales Act was primarily concerned with establishing the location of title at all times, the Code provides specific answers to questions of risk of loss, creditors' rights, and other narrow issues.

Sale on Approval. Most consumers are not aware that the ease with which they can usually return goods which do not suit their fancies to the department store or other seller from whom the goods were purchased is the result of a special type of sales contract known as the *sale on approval*. The business understanding behind this contract is simply that an ultimate consumer is often unwilling to buy unless he has the opportunity to try out the goods and to return them if they do not meet his needs or suit his fancy. A buyer, for example, purchases a new chair for her living room but wants to be able to return it to the seller if her husband does not find it comfortable or if it does not match the decor of the room. Such transactions are entered into by the thousands every day and are usually consummated, by return or approval, without incident, but certain legal issues do sometimes arise. If the goods should be destroyed while in the hands of the buyer, through no fault of his, on whom does the loss fall? Do the buyer's creditors have a claim against the goods?

The Code answers these and other questions in Section 2-326 and 2-327. Unlike the ordinary sales contract, neither risk of loss nor title passes to the buyer until he accepts (approves) the goods. The use of the goods does not constitute acceptance as long as it is consistent with the purpose of the trial. Acceptance is accomplished by notifying the seller to that effect, by use inconsistent with the trial (as by having the chair refinished), or by failing to notify the seller seasonably of the decision to return the goods. After due notification of the election to return, the return is at the seller's risk and expense. Acceptance of any part of the goods is acceptance of the whole, provided that they all conform to the contract, but it should be noted that taking home several chairs in order to select the one wanted would not come under this rule; there is considered to be in this situation a separate contract for each chair. Any conduct by the buyer which is consistent only with his viewing the goods as his own would constitute acceptance. Thus, the buyer's selling or mortgaging the goods would be acceptance and would pass the risk of loss to him. Goods held on approval by the buyer are not subject to the claims of his creditors until his acceptance.

SALE OR RETURN.   Unlike the sale on approval, where the buyer is almost invariably the ultimate consumer and the purpose of the special arrangement is to provide an opportunity for testing, the buyer in a *sale or return* situation is almost invariably buying the goods for resale and is concerned not with whether he will approve the goods but with whether, if he does not sell them, they can be returned to the original seller. In the meantime, the title and the risk of loss pass to the buyer. If the goods are not resold, the buyer may return them all, or any commercial unit, to the seller as long as he acts seasonably and the goods are still in substantially their original condition. The return is at the buyer's risk and expense. Actual return of the goods is required before the title and risk of loss are revested in the seller.

Very important in this kind of sales transaction is the fact that the buyer's creditors may reach the goods while they are in his possession. In order to eliminate the precode confusion between "or return" sales and sales on consignment or on "memorandum," the Code states in Section 2-326 that all contracts for goods delivered to a person for resale will be treated as sale or return contracts, as far as creditors of that person are concerned, unless it is established that the person conducting the reselling business is generally known by his creditors to be substantially engaged in selling the goods of others. Sellers who deliver goods on consignment or memorandum may wish to protect their rights in the goods by giving public notice of their rights through compliance with the appropriate state statute. (See discussion in Chapter 13.)

G. Passage of Title

Although the Code has considerably diminished the importance of the concept of title in sales transactions, it has not entirely eliminated its relevance in the law of sales. Instead of looking for the solution to all kinds of problems by starting with the location of the title, as was the procedure under the Uniform Sales Act, the Code requires an approach through each specific narrow issue, as we have seen. Matters external to the law of sales may be much concerned with the title to goods, however, so it was necessary for the Code to set forth general rules on the subject. The application of some tax and criminal laws, for example, may depend upon the location of title at a given time, and the courts may deem a public regulation of this kind to incorporate the defined terms of private law set forth in the Code. Section 2-401 sets forth these general principles.

There are two limitations upon the freedom of the parties to arrange by their own explicit agreement for the passage of title to existing goods. Title cannot pass before the identification of the goods to the contract, and a "reservation of title" by the seller is limited in effect to the reservation of a security interest only. In the absence of explicit agreement between the parties, title passes at the time and place at which the seller completes his performance with reference to the physical delivery of the goods. As has been discussed in detail above, what constitutes completion of performance by the seller with regard to the physical delivery of the goods varies with the terms of the contract.

The rules as to the passage of title can be summarized as follows. If the contract requires or authorizes the seller to send the goods to the buyer, title passes at the time and place of shipment. If the contract requires delivery at destination, title passes to the buyer on tender of the goods at that destination. Where delivery is to be made without movement of the goods, title passes at the time and place of delivery of documents of title required under the contract, or, if no documents are required and the goods are already identified at the time of contracting, the title passes at the time of contracting. A refusal by the buyer to receive or retain the goods, whether or not justified, as well as a justified revocation of acceptance, revests the title in the seller. The Code points out that this revesting occurs "by operation of law" and is not a "sale."

In some situations it becomes an issue as to how much title or interest a seller transfers to his buyer. Section 2-403 of the Code says that a "purchaser of goods acquires all title which his transferor had or had power to transfer except that a purchaser of a limited interest acquires rights only to the extent of the interest purchased." Generally speaking, a person can transfer no greater interest in goods than he owns or has the rights to transfer, but in several situations, primarily concerned with the protection of buyers who have purchased goods in good faith, the Code and noncode law have modified this rule. Examples are the agency doctrines of apparent authority and estoppel discussed in an earlier chapter. Sections 2-402 and 2-403 list other modifications of the rule. These can be summarized briefly.

A buyer purchased a refrigerator under circumstances where the seller had the right to rescind the contract and retake the equipment, because the buyer paid for the machine with a worthless check, but the buyer sold and delivered the refrigerator to an innocent purchaser for value before the seller had an opportunity to exercise his rights. Under the Code, the innocent purchaser gets a good title to the machine, and the seller's rights are cut off. On the other hand, a thief would not cut off the owner's rights by a sale of the refrigerator to an innocent purchaser for value.

The Code also adopts the view that where an owner entrusts his goods to a merchant who deals in goods of that kind, the merchant has power to transfer all the rights of the owner to a buyer in the ordinary course of business, even though the goods were not entrusted for the purpose of sale. The entrustment alone is all that is necessary to empower the merchant to pass good title. An example provided by the Official Comments is illuminating: If an owner leaves his watch for repair with a jeweler who is also in the business of selling watches, a sale by the jeweler to a buyer in the ordinary course of business would pass good title to the buyer. Of course, the owner would have an action against the jeweler. The policy behind this rule is the commercial desirability of increasing the marketability of goods.

We will close with one more example of the operation of those sections of the Code having to do with the quality or quantity of the title passed. Because sellers will sometimes retain in their possession goods which have been sold, for the purpose of enhancing the appearance of their assets and deceiving their creditors, the laws of many states now make such retention fraudulent with regard to the creditors and subject the goods to creditors' claims. If the seller no longer owns the goods after their sale, yet his creditors can gain an interest in the goods, we have another example of a greater interest being found in the creditors than the seller himself had. The Code states that a creditor of the seller may treat such a sale as void if, as against him, the retention of possession is fraudulent, but the Code adds that it is not fraudulent for a merchant seller to retain possession of the goods in good faith for a commercially reasonable time. The buyer is, thus, protected for a reasonable period of time if the sale was in good faith, in the current course of business and not in satisfaction of preexisting debt.

H. Bulk Sales

Closely related to the issues of creditors' claims against sellers and buyers, discussed briefly above, is the problem raised by the sale of an entire business or stock of goods. Where all or most of a merchant's stock in trade is sold in one transaction, however, many of the rules and principles governing the law of sales, especially in connection with creditors' rights, lose their meaning and efficacy. The problems are no longer essentially those of sales but have joined a family of problems whose orientation is closer to that of insolvency or the protection of creditors. For this reason, bulk sales under Article 6 of the

Uniform Commercial Code, as well as other matters associated with sales but more closely akin to fields of law other than sales, are dealt with elsewhere in this book. (See Chapter 17.)

5. BREAKDOWN OF THE BARGAIN AND REMEDIES OF THE PARTIES

A. Cases

(1)

See Case 1, page 471. Assume that the lumber had not been destroyed but, instead, that Carpon ordered Church to refuse to deliver the lumber to Hypocase. (Carpon had received a better offer for the lumber.) What remedies are available to Hypocase against Carpon?

(2)

See Case 4, page 472. Assume that the "Good Grief" had not been destroyed and that Preston came with a crew to sail the boat to Preston's own mooring some distance down the coast. The contract between Preston and Adams called for periodic payments during the construction of the boat and the balance on delivery. All the periodic payments had been made, but Preston refused to pay the balance until he had sailed the boat in the Acapulco race and given it a full trial. Adams refused to let Preston take the boat until the payment had been made. What other remedies are available to Adams?

(3)

Hypocase, Inc. entered into a contract with Credut Weeks whereby Hypocase was to manufacture and sell and Weeks to buy 500 hardwood pallets. One-third of the price was paid with the signing of the contract, and the balance was made payable ten days after delivery by rail to Weeks in Dallas, Texas. The pallets were manufactured, prepared for shipment, and turned over to the Texas and Southwest Railroad for delivery to Texas. After the pallets had left Berkland, but before they arrived in Dallas, Hypocase learned that Weeks had defaulted on a large bank loan and on several other current obligations. What course of action should Hypocase now follow?

B. In General

SCOPE OF THE DISCUSSION. The basic policy of the Uniform Commercial Code is to encourage the making and the normal performance of sales contracts, but no amount of legislative or judical encouragement, or even the good intentions of the parties, can assure the performance of all contracts in the ordinary course of affairs. Events may considerably alter the circumstances that prevailed when a contract was made: one of the parties may become insolvent; unforeseen circumstances may make performance infeasible; warranties may be breached; or one of the parties may simply fail to perform, perform properly, or perform completely his part of the bargain. Because many bargains are certain to break down for one reason or another, the Code, and the precode law before it, devote a great deal of attention to the rights of an aggrieved party where a sales contract is breached, repudiated, or in some other fashion not performed. Some of these matters are already familiar as a result of earlier discussions in the chapter on contracts or in this chapter, and many of the remedies available to the parties are not peculiar to the law of sales. Much time is wasted, however, if the reader is compelled to recall or research all the previously examined law that might have an application to the failure of performance of sales contracts. There will be an attempt here to refer, at least, to the more important matters to which the reader has been exposed as well as to describe the new issues which the breakdown of sales bargains brings before us.

Before examining the more formal remedies of seller and buyer, we shall take a brief look at excuses for failure to perform, where, of course, the aggrieved party cannot hold the other party liable for the failure. We shall also consider repudiations of contracts under various circumstances and review very briefly the problem of forced breaches and of their cure and alleviation under the Code. At that point it will be possible to move on to the actual remedies of the parties in a number of different business situations.

In sharp contrast with the Uniform Sales Act, where the dominant factor in assigning remedies to the parties was the passage of title to the goods, the Code builds its important conclusions with regard to remedies on the concept of acceptance of the goods by the buyer. The Code is perfectly consistent in this respect with its policy of making the outcome of important practical issues hinge on real business-oriented events rather than upon abstract legal concepts like "title." Because "acceptance" and its counterpart "rejection" play central roles in the allocation of remedies under the Code, the reader would do well to review the earlier discussion in this chapter of the elements necessary to the proper accomplishment of these two acts.

EXCUSES FOR FAILURE TO PERFORM. Both general contract law and the Code tell us that the destruction, substantial deterioration, or unavailability of the subject matter of a contract excuses the promisor from his obligations under the contract unless the casualty was his fault or he had promised to be responsible for the continued existence, good condition, or availability of the subject matter. Under the Code, if the loss is partial or the goods deteriorated, the buyer has a choice of *avoiding* the contract or accepting the goods with due allowance from the contract price for the deterioration or the deficiency in quantity. In neither case does the buyer have any further rights against the seller. It should be obvious that the principles set forth here do not apply where the casualty occurs after the risk of loss has passed to the buyer, or where the goods are not identified when the contract is made. The reader's attention is invited to the detailed discussion of "unanticipated risks and hardships" in the chapter on contracts.

Several sections of the Code deal with the problems that may result from the failure of certain presupposed conditions underlying the contract. Section 2-614, for example, provides that when agreed berthing, loading, or unloading facilities fail or an agreed type of carrier becomes unavailable or the agreed manner of delivery becomes commercially impracticable, then a substitute performance must be tendered and accepted if a commercially reasonable substitute is available, assuming, of course, that the failure was the fault of neither party. Similar provisions apply to a buyer who is unable to tender the agreed means or manner of payment because of a domestic or foreign governmental regulation.

A broader issue is considered in Section 2-615. Here the seller is expressly excused from the delivery of goods where his performance has been made impracticable "by the occurrence of a contingency the non-occurrence of which was a basic assumption on which the contract was made or by compliance in good faith with any applicable foreign or domestic governmental regulation." The seller may, however, have assumed a greater obligation, and his excuse may be destroyed if he does not notify the buyer seasonably of the delay, non-delivery, or partial delivery. Section 2-616 protects a buyer who has received notice from the seller of partial excuse; this is made necessary by the requirement under Section 2-615 that the seller, where the contingency affects only part of his capacity to perform, must perform to the extent possible, including allocating production and deliveries among his customers. A buyer who has received such notice may terminate the contract as to any particular delivery or terminate the whole contract where the value of the whole contract has been impaired.

REPUDIATION OF THE CONTRACT. *In general.* The noncode law of anticipatory breach of repudiation is discussed in detail in the chapter on contracts. It will be recalled that the aggrieved party can suspend his own performance or sue for breach of contract when the other party to the agreement makes it reasonably clear that he cannot or will not perform. While the Code does not alter the basic doctrine, it does vary from noncode law in recognizing three distinct situations where general law usually sees only one. The difference revolves around the problem of the positiveness or certainty of repudiation. Many courts recognize no distinctions among situations involving a mere decline in the ability of a party to perform, the breach of part of an instalment contract, and an outright declaration of an intention to repudiate. The draftsmen of the Code felt that the law of sales required distinctions among these situations and so provided.

Decline in ability to perform: right to assurance. Buyers and sellers are often as much concerned, if not more so, by an apparent decline in the ability of the other party to perform as by an outright failure of performance. Section 2-609 actually "imposes an obligation on each party that the other's expectation of receiving due performance will not be impaired," and provides three means to protect the aggrieved party where reasonable grounds for insecurity arise. Where, for example, a buyer falls behind in his account with the seller, even though the items have to do with separate and legally distinct contracts, he may impair the seller's expectation of future performance. The seller may demand adequate assurance of due performance by the buyer; he may, if commercially reasonable, suspend any part of his own performance for which he has not received the agreed return until he receives adequate assurance; he may treat the contract as broken if the other party fails to provide adequate assurance of performance within a reasonable time after receipt of a justified demand for it. What is "reasonable uncertainty" and "adequate assurance" is determined by commercial standards under the particular circumstances. In the example above, adequate assurance may consist of a verbal statement by the buyer, or a credit statement from the buyer's bank, or even more forceful assurances, depending upon the reputation and record of performance of the buyer and other circumstances. Acceptance by a party of improper delivery or payment does not impair his right to demand assurance of future performance.

Breach of instalment contract. Historically, the courts have regarded a material breach of an instalment contract (one which requires or authorizes the delivery of goods in separate lots to be separately accepted and paid for) either as justifying the aggrieved party in treating the whole contract as being broken, which is the prevailing view, or as permitting a breach of a single instalment to be treated as a total breach only if the breach shows an intention to repudiate the contract. The Code resolves the conflict by placing instalment breaches wholly outside the rules of anticipatory repudiation.

Under Section 2-612, the buyer is given the right to reject nonconforming instalments only if the nonconformity substantially impairs the value of that instalment and cannot be cured or if the nonconformity is a defect in the documents. (The definition of "instalment contract" should be carefully noted; in a non-instalment contract, the buyer may reject goods which "fail in any respect to conform to the contract.") A nonconforming instalment delivery may not only substantially impair the value of the instalment, but it may also substantially impair the value of the whole contract, permitting the aggrieved party to treat the whole contract as being breached. The significance of the Code's removal of instalment breaches from the doctrine of anticipatory breach is that the test as to whether the nonconformity in a single instalment justifies canceling the entire contract rests on a determination whether the nonconformity substantially impairs the value of the entire contract and not on whether it indicates an intention to repudiate the rest of the contract.

The discussion of Section 2-612 does not compel the conclusion that instalment breaches are never related to the rules of adequate assurance, considered above, or to anticipatory repudiation of the whole contract. A breach of an instalment contract might not substantially impair the value of the whole contract but might still be reasonable grounds for insecurity. If so, the aggrieved party could demand adequate assurance of performance. Furthermore, an overt communication unequivocally showing an intention to repudiate the entire contract may be manifested in a breach of an instalment contract, and the aggrieved party could treat the whole contract as repudiated.

In spite of a nonconformity with respect to one or more instalments which substantially impairs the value of the entire contract, the aggrieved party reinstates the contract if he accepts a nonconforming instalment without seasonably notifying the other party of cancellation, if he brings an action with respect only to past instalments, or if he demands performance as to future instalments.

Anticipatory repudiation. All that remains after the discussion of instalment contracts and the decline in the ability to perform, with regard to anticipatory repudiation, is the overt communication of intention or an action rendering a party's performance impossible or showing his clear intention not to make it. Under Section 2-610, the aggrieved party may await performance by the repudiating party for a commercially reasonable period of time, or negotiate for retraction, or resort to any available remedy for breach, and, in any case, suspend his own performance. Until the aggrieved party indicates that he considers the repudiation final, the repudiating party may retract his repudiation. Retraction is effective as long as it clearly indicates to the aggrieved party that the repudiating party intends to perform, but it must be accompanied by adequate assurances of performance under Section 2-609. With regard to overt repudiations of performance, the Code has retained in almost all respects the precode law. See the discussion in the chapter on contracts.

FORCED BREACHES: CURE. The policy and provisions of the Code with regard to forced breaches and the procedures of cure have been discussed in earlier sections of this chapter in connection with the "performance obligations of the parties." It is enough to remind the reader at this point that the Code prevents both parties from forcing breaches on the other, as where, for example, a seller demands cash of the buyer at a time when cash cannot be obtained within the time for performance or a buyer makes surprise rejections at a time when the seller cannot cure within the time of performance. Opportunity for cure is provided in these situations as well as where the time for performance has not expired.

CANCELLATION AND RESCISSION. The right of a party to cancel or avoid a contract is, of course, an important remedy in many sales situations. Most of the situations where it becomes important or relevant have already been discussed elsewhere in this chapter. Cancellation is one of the remedies available to the buyer when the seller fails to make delivery or repudiates or the buyer rightfully rejects or justifiably revokes acceptance. Cancellation is available to the seller when the buyer wrongfully rejects or revokes acceptance, or fails to make a payment due on or before delivery, or repudiates with respect to a part or the whole of a contract. However, the Code makes it very clear that cancellations and rescissions of contracts, unless the contrary intention definitely appears, do not renounce or discharge any claim or right to damages for breach of contract. This ends the unreasonable precode rule that a party may not both "rescind" or "cancel" and recover damages.

C. Remedies of the Buyer

In General.   As we have seen, rejection and acceptance are intimately related to questions of the remedies available to the parties in sales situations, and rejection is, in a real sense, a remedy itself, available to the buyer when the goods do not conform to the terms of the contract. Because these subjects are also integral parts of the discusssion of matters connected with the performance of sales contracts, however, they have been examined in that light and will not be reconsidered here except as they become important factors in the determination of remedy issues. The remedies of buyer and seller will be examined separately. The buyer's remedies are divided into several subgroups depending on whether the remedy is related to damages or to the goods themselves.

Buyer's Right to Damages.   *Cover.*   Section 2-712 of the Code recognizes explicitly the need for some aggrieved buyers, when a seller has failed to deliver conforming goods, to obtain goods for their own use or for resale and gives such buyers greater protection than did precode law. A buyer, under such circumstances, is permitted to procure goods in substitution for those due from the seller. This procedure is known as *covering.* Under the Uniform Sales Act, the buyer's damages were measured by the difference between the contract price and the market price prevailing at the time the seller's goods should have been delivered. The Code allows the buyer to recover from the seller, subject only to his duty to be reasonable and act in good faith, the difference between the contract price and the actual price paid for substitute goods, plus any incidental or consequential damages sustained (as through delay), less any expenses saved by reason of the seller's breach.

Damages for nondelivery.   The buyer is not *required* to cover, and his failure to do so does not bar him from his other remedies. Instead, the buyer may elect to recover damages for the nondelivery of the goods or for repudiation. The measure of his recovery under the Code is the difference between the contract price and the price current *at the time the buyer learned of the breach,* together with consequential damages, but less any expense saved as a result of the breach. This changes the precode law, which based the recovery on the difference between the contract price and the market price of the goods at the time they should have been delivered. If the Code had retained the precode rule and made the noncovering buyer compute his damages with reference to the time of performance rather than the time of breach, the buyer would have been forced to speculate on the wisdom of covering. Consequently, considerations of cover are used as the basis for the recovery of damages for nondelivery. The place at which the current price is calculated is the place at which the buyer would have covered had he made that election. If the prevailing price is not reasonably available at the relevant time or place, an alternative method of determining the market price is set forth in Section 2-723(2).

Damages where nonconforming goods are accepted. A buyer who accepts goods may, as we have seen, revoke his acceptance under proper circumstances. If he does so, his remedies are the same as though he had originally rejected the goods. In many cases, however, the buyer cannot revoke his acceptance although he could have rejected originally. This result would accrue where the buyer could not meet the tests of Section 2-608, including a showing that the nonconformity substantially impaired the value of the goods. The buyer, of course, can still recover damages for the nonconformity usually measured at the time and place of acceptance by the difference between the value of the goods accepted and the value they would have had if they had conformed to the contract. The buyer must have given notice within a reasonable time after he discovered or should have discovered the breach. This claim may consist of or include a claim for breach of warranty. Where special circumstances show proximate damages of another amount, the measure described above does not apply. Injuries resulting to persons or to property may be included.

Counterclaim or recoupment. Where a buyer accepts goods under circumstances where he has no right to revoke, he has no absolute defense to the seller's action for the price. If he has not barred all recourse by lack of proper notice, his redress against the seller is a counterclaim for damages or a recoupment from the price. The latter remedy is spelled out in Section 2-717. A buyer, on notifying the seller of his intentions, may deduct all or any part of the damages resulting from any breach from any part of the price still due. There is no reason why this notice should not be included with the notice referred to in the paragraph above.

Incidental and consequential damages. Most of the damage provisions of the Code permit, in proper cases, the recovery of incidental or consequential damages. Section 2-715 describes the circumstances under which recovery of these damages is proper. All incidental damages resulting from the seller's breach may be recovered, including "expenses reasonably incurred in inspection, receipt, transportation and care and custody of goods rightfully rejected, any commercially reasonable charges, expenses or commissions in connection with effecting cover and any other reasonable expense incident to the delay or other breach." *Incidental damages* are those expenses and charges directly related to the breach. *Consequential damages* have to do with less direct effects of the breach, such as loss of a profitable resale or injury to person or property.

The Code permits recovery for consequential damages which the seller at the time of contracting had reason to foresee as a result of his breach, unless the buyer could have prevented the loss by cover or otherwise. Under precode law, there was little agreement as to whether injuries to persons or property resulting from defective goods were too remote to justify the imposition of consequential damages on the seller. The Code allows consequential damages for such injury if it proximately results from a breach of warranty.

BUYER'S RIGHTS AGAINST THE GOODS. *Rights on seller's insolvency.* Under precode law, the seller could usually recover goods sold to an insolvent buyer, but the buyer could not recover goods from the insolvent seller. The old emphasis on the location of title was the primary explanation for the paradoxical result. Section 2-502 of the Code gives the buyer the right to reach the goods on the insolvency of the seller if the buyer has an insurable interest in the goods (see earlier discussion of "insurable interest") and if the insolvency occurred within ten days of the payment for the goods. If the goods have not been fully paid for, the insolvency must have occurred within ten days after the first instalment payment, and the buyer must make and keep good a tender of the balance due. Whether there is an insurable interest depends primarily on the identification of the goods with the contract. The buyer, as well as the seller, can identify the goods to the contract even though they are nonconforming, but identification by the buyer is limited to conforming goods only, if such identification is in connection with his attempts to reach the goods on the insolvency of the seller. The reason is that a contrary rule would permit the buyer to enrich himself at the expense of the seller's creditors by identifying to the contract goods greatly superior in quality or quantity to those called for in the contract.

Reclaiming the goods themselves on the insolvency of the seller does not preclude the buyer from recovering damages. Although he would be just another creditor of the insolvent seller as far as the damages are concerned, he may recover something and should, consequently, give the appropriate notice to the seller that the goods or their delivery are nonconforming.

Specific performance or replevin. Our discussion of the specific performance remedy in the chapter on contracts pointed out that the traditional view of the remedy requires the subject matter of the contract to be unique. Where personal property is concerned, the traditional view excludes almost everything except works of art and property that possesses some historical or sentimental value. The Uniform Sales Act attempted, with limited success, to extend the availability of specific performance. The Code is much more explicit and, presumably, will prove much more successful in its attempts to expand the buyer's remedy. The goods do not even have to be specific or ascertained. Section 2-716 simply states that "specific performance may be decreed where the goods are unique or in other proper circumstances." The Official Comments make it clear that the word "unique" is not confined to the traditional list of heirlooms and works of art, and it mentions specifically certain modern examples of unique goods, including output and requirements contracts involving a particular or peculiarly available source or market. Goods which the buyer could "cover" would seem to be excluded from the category of "unique."

However, the Code does not confine the remedy to "unique" goods. It may be granted in "other proper circumstances." Apparently, the remedy of specific performance can be granted even where the goods are not unique, if damages are an inadequate remedy for the buyer and would not put him in as good a position as if the seller had performed. Note that the specific performance remedy does not preclude damages or other relief.

Where the conditions for specific performance cannot be met, replevin may be available to the buyer. *Replevin* is an action for the possession of goods. Under precode law, the buyer could not replevy goods unless the title had passed to him, another example of the improper results flowing from the precode "title" thinking. The real issues had nothing to do with title to the goods but with whether the buyer could obtain substitute goods. If he could obtain substitutes, he obviously did not need the replevin remedy. He could use "cover." If he could not obtain substitutes, then he should be entitled to the goods identified to the contract. The Code adopts this practical view and gives the buyer a right of replevin for goods identified to the contract, if, after reasonable effort, he is unable to effect cover for such goods, or the circumstances indicate that such effort will be useless, or if the goods have been shipped under reservation and satisfaction of the security interest in them has been made or tendered. The right of replevin is in addition to the buyer's right to recover identified goods on the insolvency of the seller.

Security interest in the goods.   When a buyer rightfully rejects or justifiably revokes his acceptance of the goods, he has a security interest in the goods in his possession or control to the extent of any payments made on their price plus any reasonable expenses incurred in their inspection, receipt, transportation, care, and custody. He may also retain and resell such goods in the same way and under the same provisions as an aggrieved seller. The buyer may retain out of the proceeds of resale the amount he paid on the price and his other expenses, but he must remit the surplus to the seller. (See the detailed discussion below of the rights of the aggrieved seller.)

D. Remedies of the Seller

IN GENERAL.   Where the discussion of the remedies of the buyer seems best understood if divided into the right of the buyer to damages and his rights with regard to the goods themselves, the remedies of the seller are best organized around the situations which give rise to them. Obviously, the seller has most frequent occasion to pursue his remedies where the buyer wrongfully rejects the goods, repudiates the contract, or fails to make a payment due;

the first group of remedies discussed below will be those arising in these situations. Where the buyer has already accepted the goods or they have been destroyed after the risk of loss has passed to him, the seller's remedies are reduced to his right to the price of the goods. As with the buyer on the seller's insolvency, a special group of remedies is available to the seller on the insolvency of the buyer. It will be seen, as the seller's remedies unfold, that many of them are really counterparts of certain buyer's remedies and are designed to afford the same sort of protection to the seller that is afforded to the buyer. The seller's rights to withhold goods from delivery to a breaching buyer, for example, are the equivalent of the buyer's right to reject nonconforming goods.

SELLER'S REMEDIES WHERE THE BUYER WRONGFULLY REJECTS, REPUDIATES THE CONTRACT, OR FAILS TO MAKE A PAYMENT DUE ON OR BEFORE DELIVERY. *In general.* Section 2-703 of the Code enumerates the remedies available to the seller before the buyer has received or accepted the goods. Wrongful revocation of acceptance is treated as being the same as wrongful rejection, consistent with the Code's handling of these matters throughout. It is clear that failure to make a payment due *after* delivery would be a situation substantially different from the one being considered here. The section states that, with respect to the whole undelivered balance of the goods, the aggrieved seller may withhold the goods, stop delivery by any carrier or other bailee, identify conforming goods to the contract, take steps to salvage unfinished goods, resell the goods and recover damages, recover damages for nonacceptance (or, in special circumstances, recover the price), or cancel. Each of this wide variety of alternatives will be discussed below.

Right to withhold the goods. It is obvious that a seller should not be obliged to deliver goods to a buyer who has already breached the contract by wrongful rejection, by repudiation, or by failure to make a payment due on or before delivery. A seller in these circumstances may withhold the goods from the buyer. His election so to do, as with the buyer's situation in rightfully rejecting goods, does not bar the seller from the damage remedy or other appropriate relief.

Stoppage in transit. At common law and under the Uniform Sales Act, the seller could exercise his right to stop goods that were already en route to the buyer only on the insolvency of the buyer, only when the goods were in the hands of a carrier, and only if the "seller" was an "unpaid *seller*," and not a bank or other party with a security interest in the goods. The precode law was also a bit weak in terms of protecting the carrier in whose possession the goods were when stopped. Clearly the basic principle is a valuable one. It would make no commercial sense for the seller to be forced to stand by helplessly while his goods continued to wend their way into the hands of a breaching buyer or of an insolvent buyer or his creditors. The Code appears to have corrected the defects in the earlier law.

Section 2-705 extends the rights of the seller to stop in transit by including within the rule goods in the hands of bailees other than carriers, such as warehousemen, and by expanding the remedy to cover the buyer's breach of contract and his fraud, in addition to his insolvency. One of the complaints made by carriers under precode rules of stoppage was the practical difficulty of stopping shipments of less than carload or planeload lots. The Code took these complaints into account in connection with stoppage on grounds of the buyer's breach or fraud and now limits the right to "carload, truckload, planeload or larger shipments of express or freight," but retained the older view where the buyer has become insolvent. At least one aspect of stoppage in transit is left uncertain by the Code. Under precode law, a seller could not stop goods which were on their way, not to the buyer, but to the buyer's customer. While the Code does define the coverage of the right very broadly, it does not clearly or expressly alter this older rule, which may still be the law.

Much of the uncertainty surrounding stoppage in transit in the past has had to do with the point at which the right to stop the goods terminates. The Code is very specific: goods may be stopped until receipt of the goods by the buyer or his representative, or until a bailee other than the carrier acknowledges to the buyer that the goods are held for him, or until a carrier, such as a warehouseman, acknowledges to the buyer that it holds the goods for him, or until documents of title covering the goods have been negotiated to the buyer, or until reshipment. "Reshipment" occurs where a buyer reships the goods to a third person without taking actual possession of them. It is not the same as mere redirection.

How stoppage is actually accomplished is another matter spelled out in considerable detail by the Code. The seller must notify the bailee in such a way as to make it possible for him, with the exercise of reasonable diligence, to stop the goods. After the bailee receives the notice, he must hold and deliver the goods in accordance with the directions of the seller, but the seller is liable to the bailee for any charges or damages that may ensue. If a negotiable document of title has been issued, the bailee is not obligated to obey the stoppage order until the document of title is surrendered, for obvious reasons.

Section 2-707 provides that a "person in the position of a seller" may exercise the right to stop goods in transit. The purpose of this section is to give essentially the same sort of protection that the seller has with regard to stopping goods to other persons who have paid for or become responsible to pay for goods or who otherwise hold as against the buyer "a security interest or other right in goods similar to that of a seller." A bank, for example, which has financed the sale would have rights in the goods similar to that of the seller and could utilize the power to stop goods in transit.

Unless the right to stop has terminated, as discussed above, a carrier (or other bailee) must always recognize a notification to stop received from the consignor, i.e., the person who made the contract with the carrier for the shipment of the goods, but, if the bailee has issued a non-negotiable bill of lading, he does not have to obey a stop order coming from a financing party or anyone other than the consignor. Even if the carrier obeys an improper notification from the consignor, he is immune, under Section 7-303, from liability to the buyer. This result is contrary to precode law but appears to be a justified change on the ground that the carrier is in no position to determine whether the seller is entitled to stop the goods in transit. Obviously, the seller is not immunized, and the buyer has available a full panoply of remedies against him. Actually, a carrier would not be obligated to obey an improper order to stop goods in transit, but the point is that under the Code, he does not have to worry about an issue which he has little opportunity to resolve. The bailee's reactions to notifications to stop can be more or less automatic. He knows whether he has issued a non-negotiable bill of lading or a negotiable document of title or has acknowledged to the buyer, as discussed above, and he can obey or refuse as obvious circumstances dictate.

After the seller has effectively stopped the goods in transit, his rights are exactly the same as though he had never made any delivery at all.

Seller's right to damages: resale. A seller who has withheld goods because of a breach by the buyer or has stopped goods in transit because of the buyer's breach, fraud, or insolvency is still entitled to damages. Section 2-706 authorizes the seller to resell the goods, or the undelivered balance, and to recover the difference between the resale price and the contract price, together with incidental damages, less any saving enjoyed in consequence of the buyer's breach. The resale must be made in good faith and in a commercially reasonable manner if the seller is to recover damages in addition to the proceeds of the resale. The purpose of the resale is to establish the measure of damages; if the seller does not act reasonably, the resale is worthless as a measure of damages and the seller is thrown back on his right to damages for nonacceptance or repudiation (discussed below), where the measure of damages is based on the market price. If the resale provisions of the Code are complied with, the resale sets the *absolute* measure of the damages and is not just evidence of the damages. It will be noted that this remedy is the equivalent of the buyer's rights to "cover."

Whether or not the title has passed to the buyer, the seller may resell goods which he is withholding and recover any deficiency and retain any profit made on the resale. Were he not allowed to retain the profits, the Code would be saying that the buyer owned the goods. As we know, the Code has rejected the concept of passage of title as having material relevance under its provisions.

The resale may be made at a public or private sale and may be as a unit or in parcels and in any method, manner, time, place, or terms, as long as they are commercially reasonable. The resale must be reasonably identified as referring to the broken contract. Where the resale is by private sale, the seller must give the buyer reasonable notification of his intention to resell.

Where the resale is by public sale (auction), the Code imposes special restrictions upon the seller. Where he does not comply with them, the only penalty appears to be his being deprived of the right to use the resale as an absolute measure of damages. Among the requirements for public sale are reasonable notice to the buyer of the seller's intention to resell, together with the time and place of resale, except where the goods are perishable and subject to rapid decline in value. The resale must be at a usual place or market for public sales, if one is reasonably available, or, if not, in another place where buyers might be reasonably expected to attend. If not to be in view at the sale, the goods must be available for reasonable inspection by prospective bidders, and the notification must state when and where. The seller may bid and buy at public sales. Unless there is a recognized market for the public sale of futures, goods subject to public sale must be identified. The reason for this rule is that futures would not bring a very good price under circumstances in which they are not usually sold. The detailed requirements for public sales are probably subject to the controlling test of commercial reasonableness. Under any conditions, a good faith buyer at the resale, whether public or private, takes the goods free of any rights of the original buyer.

Seller's right to damages: nonacceptance or repudiation. Just as the aggrieved buyer is not required to cover, the aggrieved seller is not required to resell. His reason for reselling would be his desire to obtain an absolute measure of damage, but, with goods of fixed or standard price, for example, that may be no particular advantage. Under Section 2-708, the seller may elect to measure the damages for the buyer's nonacceptance by using the market price at the time and place of tender. The Code describes this measure, as we have now come to expect, as the difference between the market price and the unpaid contract price, together with incidental damages, but less any expense saved as a consequence of the breach. It must be remembered that the market price is only evidence and does not provide an absolute measure of damages. There may be several relevant markets, or problems surrounding the availability of a price at a particular time, and other issues. These have been discussed in connection with the buyer's remedies.

Section 2-708 contains an unusual recognition of the realities of commercial practice by merchants. The section states that if the measure of damages based on the market price is "inadequate to put the seller in as good a position as performance would have done then the measure of damages is the profit (including reasonable overhead) which the seller would have made from full performance by the buyer, together with incidental damages." At first glance, this provision appears incongruous. How can a seller be entitled to damages where the market price equals or exceeds the contract price, providing that incidental damages are taken into account? Won't he just sell his television set to another buyer at the same or even a higher price? The answer lies in the difference between a nondealer and a dealer who has an unlimited supply of the particular goods available for sale. When a buyer of a television set repudiates his contract, and a dealer sells the set to another buyer at the same price, it is not really a matter of the seller's replacing one buyer with another, because he would have had the second buyer anyhow, but a matter of having lost a sale.

Seller's right to the price. The right to the price is the seller's primary remedy where the buyer has already accepted the goods or where the goods are destroyed after the risk of loss has passed, but it is also available, under special circumstances, where the buyer has wrongfully rejected or repudiated the contract. If a seller is unable, after a reasonable effort, to resell goods which he has withheld from a breaching buyer, he may recover the contract price from the buyer. This right of the seller will be recognized as the equivalent of the right of the buyer to specific performance, a right which he loses if he can cover. If the seller cannot resell at a reasonable price or if the circumstances indicate that such effort would be worthless, the seller may recover the price. If the seller does sue for the price, he must hold the goods for the buyer. Obviously the seller cannot have both the price and the goods. If resale becomes possible before the seller has collected his judgment, he may resell the goods, but the proceeds must be credited to the buyer.

Seller's right to identify goods to the contract. From the general law of contract comes the duty of the innocent party to a breached contract to mitigate damages as much as he can through his reasonable efforts. Under precode law, courts applied the mitigation rule in such a way to prevent manufacturers from recovering an increase in loss resulting from their continuance of performance after buyer's repudiation of the contract. Again the Code modifies a rule in the interests of practicality and commercial reality. The risks of increasing the loss are often much greater where the manufacturer does not complete performance than when he does. There may be no market for the partially completed goods, and the buyer may be financially unable to respond in damages. In these circumstances, the seller may prefer to finish the goods in order to have marketable goods on hand should the buyer become insolvent. Precode law left the seller in a serious dilemma.

Section 2-704 brings an end to the dilemma and permits the seller to identify to the contract conforming goods not already identified, if at the time he learned of the breach the goods were in his possession or control, and the seller can treat as the subject of resale goods which have demonstrably been intended for the particular contract even though those goods are unfinished. The burden is on the breaching buyer to show the commercial unreasonableness of the seller's action. This change in the law gives the seller a practical remedy once denied and makes more useful his remedies for damages or price. A seller who has completed 400 of the 500 pairs of shoes called for in his contract with a breaching buyer may identify the 400 pairs to the contract and resell the finished shoes and the raw material or, where the goods could not be resold, sue for the price. In addition, however, he has the alternative under the Code of finishing the shoes, identifying 500 pairs to the contract, and re-selling the lot, or suing for damages for nonacceptance, or suing for the price under Section 2-709 if resale is not practical. (See discussion below.)

Incidental damages. The basic principles covering the right of the seller to incidental damages are the same as those discussed above in connection with the buyer.

SELLER'S REMEDIES WHERE THE BUYER HAS ACCEPTED OR THE GOODS HAVE BEEN DESTROYED AFTER THE RISK OF LOSS HAS PASSED. *Seller's right to the price.* In our previous discussion, based on situations where the buyer had not accepted the goods, we saw that the primary remedy available to the seller is that of damages. An action for the price was available only where resale was not feasible under the provisions of the Code. Where the buyer has accepted, however, or where the goods are destroyed after the risk of loss has passed to the buyer, the considerations to be taken into account are very differ-ent, and the action for the price becomes the dominant remedy. Section 2-709 allows the seller to recover the price of "goods accepted or of conforming goods lost or damaged within a commercially reasonable time after risk of their loss has passed to the buyer," together with incidental damages. Note that the buyer may have accepted nonconforming goods and would not, by this action, have barred his right to recover damages. He could still by counterclaim or recoupment offset the seller's claim for the price. You will also recall at this point that where the tender or delivery of goods fails to conform to the con-tract, the risk of loss remains on the seller until cure or acceptance. Thus, Section 2-709 does not permit the seller to recover the price of destroyed goods unless they were conforming.

SELLER'S REMEDIES ON DISCOVERY OF BUYER'S INSOLVENCY. *Right to refuse or stop delivery.* Good sense tells us that a seller should not be com-pelled to deliver goods to an insolvent buyer or to stand by and let them be delivered if the insolvency is discovered after the goods have been consigned to a bailee. We have already discussed in detail the right of the seller to stop goods in transit. He may also refuse delivery except for cash, including pay-ment for all goods previously delivered under the contract. A buyer's insolvency is not a breach of contract, and the seller's right to refuse delivery or stop delivery on the ground of insolvency is merely a right to suspend performance owing to insecurity and to demand adequate assurances. If the assurances are forthcoming, the seller cannot resell or otherwise divert the goods. If they are not forthcoming, the seller may treat the contract as breached and proceed as in connection with his rights to withhold or stop in transit.

Right to reclaim the goods. Obviously, a seller cannot refuse to deliver or stop in transit goods which have already been delivered to an insolvent buyer, and his action for the price may be useless. What the seller needs in these circumstances is some sort of right to reclaim the goods, and Section 2-702(2) of the Code gives him just that, though under considerable restriction. The Code provision is based on well established common law rules that a seller may reclaim goods where a buyer has obtained them on credit after fraudulently misrepresenting his solvency. On the theory that goods obtained by buyers within a short time of insolvency are obtained under a misrepresentation as to the buyer's financial condition, the Code states that a seller may reclaim goods received by the buyer on credit within ten days of insolvency. The demand for reclamation must be made by the seller within ten days after the buyer received the goods, but actual repossession can be accomplished at a later time. If innocent or fraudulent misrepresentation of solvency has been made to the particular seller in writing within three months before delivery, the ten day limitation does not apply.

The potential conflict between this provision of the Code and the Bankruptcy Act, on the ground that the section may give the seller an unjustified preference in bankruptcy, can probably be avoided if the courts view realistically the connection between the proof of delivery within ten days and the inference that such delivery was induced by a fraudulent representation of solvency. The seller cannot reclaim goods that have been resold to a buyer in the ordinary course of business or to other good faith purchasers. However, because the right of the seller to reclaim goods does, in a sense, constitute preferential treatment as against the buyer's other creditors, the Code provides that reclamation bars all of the seller's other remedies with regard to the goods involved.

E. Miscellaneous Remedies

LIQUIDATION OR LIMITATION OF DAMAGES. The Code has adopted the basic principles of general contract law with regard to the legal and practical effects of the liquidation or limitation of damages by agreement of the parties. Liquidated damages are enforceable only "at an amount which is reasonable in the light of the anticipated or actual harm caused by the breach, the difficulties of proof of loss, and the inconvenience or nonfeasibility of otherwise obtaining an adequate remedy." Section 2-718 also states expressly that excessive liquidated damages are void as penalties. It would also appear that a clause fixing the damages at an unreasonably small amount would be unenforceable. (See discussion in Chapter 3.)

RESTITUTION. Where the seller justifiably withholds delivery of goods because of the buyer's breach, Section 2-718 provides that the buyer is entitled to the restitution of any amount by which the sum of his payments *exceeds* the amount to which the seller is entitled by virtue of terms liquidating the damages or, in the absence of such terms, twenty per cent of the value of the total performance for which the buyer is obligated under the contract, or $500, whichever is smaller. The purpose of this provision is to prevent unreasonable forfeitures of deposits or down payments. The buyer's right to restitution can be offset to the extent that the seller establishes a right to recover damages in excess of the liquidated damages and the amount or value of any benefits received by the buyer by reason of the contract.

Other contractual modifications of remedies. Aside from the matters discussed in the previous two paragraphs, the Code leaves the parties free to shape their own remedies, subject to the restraints of unconscionability under Section 2-302.

PROBLEMS

1. Distinguish between a present sale and a contract to sell. What is a contract *for* sale?

2. Distinguish between a sale with option to return and a bailment with option to buy. Distinguish between a sale and a consignment.

3. Explain the following terms: existing goods, future goods, identification of goods, nonconforming goods, order for prompt or current shipment.

4. List and explain each of the important ways in which the Uniform Commercial Code alters general principles of contract law as they apply to the sales contract.

5. Selir has sold certain goods to Biar, neither party knowing at the time of the sale that the goods had been badly damaged by fire. What are the rights of Selir and Biar?

6. Distinguish between warranties and fraudulent representations.

7. Explain the term *caveat emptor*.

8. Mrs. Jones bought from Gifford's Department Store a Lion Rose lipstick manufactured by John of the Palace. The lipstick was delivered to Mrs. Jones in the same metal container in which it had been purchased from John of the Palace by the department store. Mrs. Jones had asked the saleslady for a "good brand of lipstick." The saleslady recommended this brand and stated that it was guaranteed under the pure food and drug laws. Mrs. Jones found that the lipstick did not stick to her lips but that it was extremely difficult to remove from tableware, glasses, and her teeth. After using the lipstick for a short period of time, Mrs. Jones began to have stomach trouble; her face became swollen and her eyes red. Her doctor made an analysis of the lipstick and found that it contained a harmful chemical matter. Mrs. Jones recovered quickly after the doctor's treatment and after she stopped using the lipstick. What are the rights of Mrs. Jones against Gifford's and against John of the Palace?

9. Selir, whose regular business was operating a warehouse, bought a thousand bales of reclaimed wool at a bankrupt sale. He advertised this wool for sale and sent samples around to those buyers of wool he thought might be interested. Biar, after inspecting the sample, wrote to Selir that he would buy 100 bales if the wool would be suitable for making clothing. Selir shipped 100 bales to Biar who paid for the wool. What warranties might become important issues in connection with this sale? Explain.

10. Compare implied warranties and express warranties with regard to the effect of inspection of the goods by the buyer. Describe the effect of disclaimers on warranties.

11. Explain why the location of the title to goods is not an important issue in sales transactions under the Code.

12. Distinguish between a destination contract and a shipment contract. What are the seller's obligations in each?

13. Explain the following commercial shipping terms and their relevance to the law of sales: F.O.B., C.O.D., C.I.F., C. & F., F.A.S.

14. Explain the term "cure" and describe the situations in which it may become an important matter for seller or buyer.

15. How does a buyer "accept" goods? Does he always have the right to inspect goods before accepting them? Explain. If a buyer has already accepted goods, may he change his mind and reject them?

16. Saler and Yawl entered into an oral contract whereby Saler was to buy (and Yawl to sell) a certain cabin cruiser owned by Yawl for $7500 to be paid on delivery of the cruiser. The contract included a promise on the part of Yawl to make certain alterations on the boat before it was delivered to Saler. These alterations included some structural changes which were peculiar to Saler's personal needs and were ordered especially by him. These alterations were completed on January 10; the boat was completely destroyed by fire on the night of January 11; Saler had not been notified that his boat was ready for delivery. Yawl is now suing Saler for the price of the boat. What are the rights of the parties? Did both of them have insurable interests? Explain.

17. With regard to the risk of loss, does the Code distinguish between situations where there has been no breach of contract and those where there has been a breach? Explain. Does the insurance coverage of either party play any role in the determination of who bears the risk of loss?

18. How and why did the Code change precode law with regard to the insurable interests of buyer and seller?

19. Selir delivered a television set to Uncerten under a "sale or return" arrangement whereby Uncerten had 30 days in which to return the set if he did not want it. Dealer delivered a refrigerator to Uncerten under a "sale on approval" arrangement. Producer delivered a quantity of gold watches to Uncerten on consignment. All of these items were in Uncerten's home on May 31, when a tornado destroyed the house and all of its contents. What are Selir's, Dealer's, and Producer's rights against Uncerten?

20. Although the Code has considerably diminished the importance of "passage of title" as a concept relevant to sales situations, it has not entirely eliminated the concept. Why not?

21. Describe briefly the remedies available to the buyer where there has been a breach of the seller's express or implied warranties. What circumstances will be considered by the buyer in making his choice of remedy?

22. Compare the traditional availability of the unusual remedy of specific performance with the availability of that remedy under the Uniform Commercial Code.

23. What protection does the Code afford to a buyer or a seller who believes that the ability of the other party to perform his promises and obligations has declined since the contract was made?

24. How does Code law vary from general contract law with regard to anticipatory breach or repudiation of a contract?

25. Explain in detail the significance of "cover." To what remedy of the seller does it correspond? Explain.

26. Outline and describe briefly the buyer's rights to damages and his rights against the goods themselves. If a buyer reclaims the goods themselves from an insolvent seller, does he still have a right to damages? Explain.

27. Describe a situation in which a seller might elect to use each one of the following remedies: withhold the goods, stop in transit, collect damages, resell the goods, sue for the price, identify incomplete goods to the contract, reclaim the goods.

28. List and describe briefly the special remedies available to the other party under the Uniform Commercial Code where the buyer or seller has become insolvent.

chapter 11

Commercial Paper: Transferring Funds and Facilitating Credit

1. IN GENERAL

A. Importance and Use of Commercial Paper

The term "commercial paper" encompasses several, but not all, of the many varieties of "negotiable instruments." The use of the former term in place of the latter is necessary in this chapter because of certain distinctions made in the Uniform Commercial Code among different types of negotiable instruments. Negotiable instruments which are classified by the Code as commercial paper are the object of our attention at this point. Some of the others will be discussed in other chapters.

The use of commercial paper and many other negotiable instruments is so routine and so commonplace that probably only a very small proportion of the persons who employ them have any real idea about their exact nature or about the legal principles that make them possible. This result is not entirely unfortunate nor is it accidental. The negotiable instrument is a special application of the contract device, but if it were treated like any other contract, it could not perform the function for which it was created. Its function is one of facilitating, speeding up, and encouraging certain aspects of commerce, and it has developed in such a way that it achieves this end without doing away with the essential character-istics of the contract. The elements of the contract and the steps leading to its formation are combined and blended and formalized in the negotiable instru-ment until they lose their separate identities and merge into the brief but formal procedures and language that bring this unusual device into existence.

If the average person who pays his monthly bills by check found it neces-sary to bargain for separate contracts with the bank for each check and to explain to each payee what must be done in order to turn each piece of paper into cash or a bank deposit, this particular type of negotiable instrument would rarely be used. Checks and most other negotiable instruments do not disclose on their faces the terms and the nature of the legal relationship they represent. Most people learn how to use a check at an early age, but few ever learn very much about the terms of the check contract. One of the great attributes of the device is, however, that one does not need to know the terms of the check contract in order to use it. This does not mean, necessarily, that it is not important to know something about the terms of the negotiable instruments contract. The routine simplicity with which most negotiable instruments are created, handled, and paid lulls many businessmen and others into a sense of familiarity and security with regard to such dealings that only a loss can dispel. Consequently, every person should have some knowledge of the basic principles involved, with particular attention paid to some of the elementary precautions that may be taken to avoid losses that may arise through the misuse of nego-tiable instruments.

The fact that the formalized language and procedures of the negotiable instrument have speeded up and simplified common commercial transactions, such as the transfer of funds from one person to another, is not the most important fact in regard to the device. Of greater importance is the concept of negotiability that makes the free and confident transfer of negotiable paper from hand to hand possible. If ordinary contract principles applied, each person about to come into possession of a negotiable instrument would want to examine in some detail the circumstances surrounding the original contract before he would accept the instrument. The concept of negotiability is all that keeps the transfer of a negotiable instrument from being a simple assignment in which the assignee is subject to all of the defenses that would have been good against the assignor. Before we examine the concept of negotiability and the law of negotiable instruments, let us set the business scene and consider the business function that negotiable instruments and commercial paper in particular, perform so unobtrusively.

Assume that X owns and operates a small ceramics factory in New York. Although small, the factory turns out very high quality work, and its products are sold all over the United States. Special clays and glazes are purchased from suppliers in many states. X's sales are made to retailers and wholesalers only.

Although production remains more or less constant throughout the year, sales are seasonal, with the peak in August and September when buyers stock up for the Christmas trade. The result is that X's costs do not vary much from month to month, but the receipts are heavily concentrated in the fourth quarter. X is frequently compelled to seek bank loans during the summer in order to meet his payroll and cover the accounts with his suppliers. Let us see how X comes into contact with negotiable instruments and examine briefly the convenience they afford to him.

X pays his employees by check. Both X and his employees find this method convenient. It is never necessary for X to keep large amounts of cash on hand because X's funds are deposited in a bank that has agreed to pay out the funds as checks signed by X order it to do. With little cash on the premises, X need maintain no very elaborate security measures, his burglary insurance rates and the rates on fidelity bonds for office employees are low. Furthermore, the making out of the checks and the canceled checks themselves supply a constant record of payments to employees, and X has accounting machines that take full advantage of the fact. Most of the employees are highly skilled artisans who are accustomed to handling substantial weekly paychecks, and a large portion of the workmen maintain bank accounts and either deposit their checks by mail or have X do it for them.

X pays most of his other obligations by check. Some of X's creditors are at a considerable distance from X, and the check makes possible safe payment by mail. All of the customers with whom X has dealt for any period of time pay for merchandise by check. These checks are stamped with the "for deposit only" indorsement by one of X's employees and are routinely sent to X's bank to be credited to his account. X's bank then sends the check (usually through special banking channels organized for the purpose) to the customer's bank for payment. The immense convenience of the negotiable instrument becomes obvious when X's simple transaction with a customer is multiplied by the billions of such transactions taking place every year. One can only imagine the confusion and effort involved in attempting to make these transfers in cash or even by instruments representing cash if there were no concept of negotiability.

When X ships merchandise of any substantial amount to a new buyer or to one whose credit is weak, X will frequently make use of another type of negotiable instrument that gives X the security he might not otherwise have. This instrument is drawn by X and orders the customer or the customer's bank to pay the amount specified, either on sight or at some specified time. This type of instrument is usually accompanied by a bill of lading, which the customer must have before he can obtain the goods from the carrier but which he cannot have until he has paid or agreed to pay as ordered by the negotiable instrument drawn by X. This instrument is known as a *draft* or a *bill of exchange*. It affords X a measure of security, and, also may be used as a credit-creating device by which X may receive prompt payment for the goods although the customer is not obligated to pay until some time in the future. This latter purpose is accomplished when X sells to his bank the instrument the customer has agreed to pay at some later time.

If X has a good credit rating with his bank, he may be able to borrow substantial sums from the bank with no more security than his own signature affixed to another type of negotiable instrument known as the *promissory note*. The note represents the contract by which X agrees to repay the loan, but it is more than an ordinary contract. The bank is willing to lend money to X on the strength of this note because it is negotiable. If the bank needs funds, it can sell X's note to another bank, something which X's bank would probably have difficulty in doing were the note a simple contract. If X does not pay the note when it comes due, X's bank, or anyone else into whose hands the note has come legitimately, will find that the legal steps required for recovering the amount of the note from X, or from other persons who may have held the instrument, are considerably simplified by the fact that the note is a negotiable instrument.

The above discussion is not by any standards complete; many other ways remain in which X might use or be affected by negotiable instruments.

B. Scope of Discussion

IN GENERAL. Nobody knows when negotiable instruments were first used. They were well established in Europe during the Middle Ages, and there is some evidence to suggest that the idea of negotiability goes back much farther in history even that that. The Law Merchant was the avenue by which the use of negotiable instruments came into the common law. Owing to its utter dependence upon uniformity, simplicity, and routine for effective use, the law of negotiable instruments was particularly vulnerable to the problems caused by the multiplicity of sovereign jurisdictions in the United States. By the end of the nineteenth century, the laws of the various states were widely divergent, and commerce was being seriously inconvenienced. The first of the great uniform statutes drafted by the National Conference of Commissioners on Uniform State Laws was the Uniform Negotiable Instruments Act. In 1897, Colorado, Connecticut, Florida, and New York became the first states to adopt the Act. Unfortunately, it was 1933 before all American jurisdictions had accepted it.

THE UNIFORM COMMERCIAL CODE. The legal experience of the Uniform Negotiable Instruments Law was not unlike that of the Uniform Sales Act, discussed earlier. Over the period of fifty years following the first adoptions, interpretations of the Uniform Law varied substantially from one state to another, and many states had actually adopted versions of the Law which were at variance with the original. The version adopted in Arizona, for example, had variations in more than fifty sections. The Negotiable Instruments Law, consequently, did not achieve uniformity. Furthermore, methods of doing business had changed considerably in a half century, causing many sections of the Uniform Law to become obsolete. For two additional reasons, the Code did not simply incorporate the older statute. First, the integrative concept behind the Code required many changes for the sole purpose of bringing language and terminology into conformance with the rest of the Code, and second, the material contained in the old statute was badly in need of reorganization. In spite of many changes and improvements of wording and substantial condensation, Article 3 makes the least departure from precode law of all the Articles of the Uniform Commercial Code.

The change in terminology from "negotiable instruments" to "commercial paper" was made necessary by the fact that, while the old statute purported to deal with all negotiable instruments, the Code expressly excludes from coverage under Article 3 investment securities and documents of title, which are dealt with separately under other articles. Essentially, what is left under Article 3 is that kind of negotiable instrument known as commercial paper, which includes checks, drafts (bills of exchange), promissory notes, and certificates of deposit. Actually, separate uniform statutes had come into existence to give specific coverage to documents of title, but the language of the Negotiable Instruments Law remained all-encompassing. Money is expressly excluded from the Code, but this is in conformity with older law.

The most important change of classification was made in connection with investment securities. The serious confusion and uncertainty of precode law have been eliminated by treating investment securities under their own part of the Code, Article 8. Because some investment securities are really forms of promissory notes, it was necessary for the Code to provide tests by which the appropriate article could be determined. Instruments come under the article on commercial paper, Article 3, when they take a particular form, a matter to be discussed in detail below. Instruments qualify for coverage under Article 8 if they are commonly dealt in upon security exchanges or commonly recognized as a medium for investment. It will be noted that the Article 3 test is one of form and the test of Article 8 is functional. Because it is possible for a single instrument to satisfy both tests, the Code provides that in cases of overlap Article 8 will apply.

In comparing Article 3 with the older law, it has been said that the Code just puts "old wine in new bottles." With certain exceptions, as we shall see, the statement is descriptive of the actual situation. The Code treatment is much more intense and specific than precode law, but the rules spelled out are largely those that had evolved under a half century of experience with the Uniform Law. There was no need to change the form of the basic types of commercial paper; check or draft or note forms in use before the adoption of the Code, with very rare exceptions in a few states, are being and will continue to be used under the Code. Brief attention will be devoted at the end of this chapter to an area of the law which is largely new in statutory form, although some of it was covered by the Uniform Negotiable Instruments Law and other statutes. This area has to do with bank collections and deposits, essentially the bank collection process. Special treatment in the Code (Article 4) was made necessary by the fantastic growth in the volume of checks and other instruments processed through the banking system. Here, perhaps more than in any other area covered by the Code, changes of business practice in the last few decades have dictated uniform rules and more efficient procedures.

C. Types of Commercial Paper

In General.   Although there are many varieties of commercial paper, all fall into a very few major families. As a matter of fact, commercial paper is often classified into just two groups: bills of exchange (three-party paper) and promissory notes (two-party paper). A *bill of exchange* is an order by one person to a second person to pay money to a third person. A *promissory note* is a promise by one person to pay money to another. Note that one is an "order" and the other is a "promise." While this classification is useful in a conceptual sense and has the advantage of being simple, it is not the one used by the Code. The differences are not great, but it is of particular importance to be familiar with Code usages and terminology.

The Code refers to bills of exchange as "drafts" and places in a category by itself a particular and very important kind of draft, the check. Promissory notes constitute a third category under the Code, and a special kind of promissory paper, called certificates of deposit, a fourth. Each of these four types of commercial paper, together with a few major subcategories, will be discussed below. Local usage and terminology vary to some extent, and many types of commercial paper carry special titles, but all belong to one of the four categories mentioned in the Code.

Drafts.   A *draft*, stated simply, is an order by the *drawer* to a second party called the *drawee* instructing him to pay money to a third party called the *payee*. When a draft is on its face drawn or payable outside the United States, it is said to be an *international draft;* if it is both drawn and payable in the United States or its territories, it is called a *domestic draft*. A draft payable at sight is known as a *sight draft*, and a draft payable at some time in the future a *time draft*. A time draft may be made payable at a certain time after the date of the instrument or at a certain time after sight. If it is the latter, the drawee does not have to pay the instrument until the specified period of time has passed after the payee has presented the instrument. The requirements of presentment will be discussed later.

A common and very useful type of draft is the *trade acceptance,* which is a favorite instrument of professional buyers and sellers. It differs from the ordinary draft in that the drawer and the payee are the same person. A seller, as drawer, draws the trade acceptance on the buyer, as drawee, payable to the seller at some future time, for the sale price of the goods. The seller then sends the draft to the buyer who "accepts" it by writing "accepted," together with the date and the buyer's name, across the face of the instrument. After acceptance, the drawee is called the *acceptor.* The acceptance may contain further factual information about the transaction out of which the instrument arises, such as the number and date of the invoice for the goods. The buyer then returns the instrument to the seller, who may retain it and collect the amount of the draft when payable or sell it to a bank or deposit it as collateral for a loan. The attractive characteristics of the trade acceptance are that once the buyer has accepted, he can no longer dispute the debt against any person who may hold the instrument and that the holder may collect from the drawer or the acceptor or indorsers if there is a default. This latter characteristic makes the acceptance readily saleable and makes it easier for the seller to obtain a loan than would be the case with the assignment of an open account; this characteristic also makes it possible for the seller to get his money immediately and still extend credit to his buyer.

Another type of draft is the *banker's acceptance,* which is even more easily marketable than the trade acceptance. Instead of being drawn on the buyer, as is the case with the trade acceptance, it is drawn on the buyer's bank. Obviously, the buyer must make arrangements with his bank to accept the draft before he purchases the goods. The bank will usually require him to deposit collateral with the bank or keep enough money on deposit to pay the draft when it is due. Professional buyers usually have continuing arrangements with their banks to accept drafts, in order to avoid the necessity for separate arrangements in connection with each one. When the draft is presented to the bank for acceptance, the procedure is the same as when a trade acceptance is presented to the buyer. Although a loan may be involved in the buyer's arrangement with his bank, the acceptance of the draft by the bank is not itself a loan or a commitment to make a loan. The bank is simply making its own credit available to the buyer. As with the ordinary trade acceptance, the seller can sell the banker's acceptance to his own bank or to someone else and get his money immediately, and the buyer is given the opportunity to buy on credit. Because the banker's acceptance carries the credit of the bank, instead of just the credit of the buyer, it is looked on with greater respect than the ordinary trade acceptance by those who may later come into possession of it.

CHECKS. Although the Code classifies checks separately from drafts, and for good reason, the check is itself a draft, but a very special kind. Checks are always drawn on banks and are always payable on demand. Unlike the trade acceptance, for example, the check is not designed for circulation but for immediate payment. Checks may circulate before being presented for payment, as we shall see, but their primary function is not a credit function but to provide a convenient, routine means for making payment. Checks are almost always written on standard, printed forms provided by the drawer's bank. They are excellent examples of the "formal contract" discussed in the chapter on contracts, where the binding effect is the result, not of the substance of the agreement between the parties, but of the form in which the instrument is written. Checks contain very few words, but those words manifest a contractual arrangement whose details can be extremely complex. Measured by the amount of funds thus transferred from one person to another, the check is by far the most important of all the forms of commercial paper. Neither a check nor another draft operates in itself as an assignment of any funds in the hands of the drawee available for its payment. The holder of an instrument has no cause of action against a drawee who refuses to accept or pay, unless the drawee has accepted or certified. Assignments of funds in the hands of drawees may be accomplished under ordinary contract principles but not by means of checks or drafts alone.

In addition to the ordinary check, with the appearance and use of which almost everybody is familiar, there are several special types of checks. A *cashier's check* is a check issued by the cashier of a bank ordering the bank itself to pay a certain sum of money. The bank is both the drawer and the drawee of the instrument. Cashier's checks are often used where a buyer, for example, is not personally known to a seller or, for some other reason, his personal check is not acceptable. The buyer may ask his bank to issue a cashier's check, payable to the seller, which, because it carries the bank's credit and not the buyer's, is likely to be more acceptable. The bank, of course, will transfer funds from the buyer's account and charge a small fee for the service of issuing the check. A *bank draft* is also useful in situations like those described in connection with the discussion of the cashier's check. A bank draft is a check drawn by one bank on another bank where the drawer bank has funds on deposit. A buyer in one city can obtain a draft from his own bank drawn on a bank in the seller's city and made payable to the payee-seller. Again, the particular form of the check is attractive because the credit of the bank is usually more acceptable than the credit of the individual.

The *traveler's check* is a special adaptation of the check form for the purpose of providing travelers with ready access to funds while traveling, without the risks and inconvenience of carrying large quantities of cash or several varieties of foreign currency. The traveler's check is much like the cashier's check in that the bank or other financial institution that issues it is both drawer and drawee. The user of the checks is like the buyer of goods who employs a cashier's check in order to pay for them. He is not the payee; instead, he simply delivers the instrument to the payee. Traveler's checks use the double signature method of identifying those who have purchased the checks and are entitled to use them. The first signature is put on the checks when they are purchased, and the second in the presence of the payee who is accepting the checks in payment for goods or in exchange for local currency. Some of the best known traveler's checks are issued by such organizations as American Express, which, while not primarily engaged in the banking business, engage in certain banking functions.

Certified checks are not special types of checks but are ordinary checks which have been subjected to special procedures. They will be discussed below in connection with "certification of checks."

PROMISSORY NOTES. A *promissory note* is simply a promise by a *maker* to pay another person, the *payee*, a specified sum of money. The promise may be to pay on demand or in instalments or at some stated time in the future. There are many different kinds of promissory notes. Some are commercial paper and come under the provisions of Article 3 of the Code; some are investment securities under Article 8; some do not come under the Code at all and may be treated as simple contracts. The distinction between commercial paper and investment securities has already been discussed.

It should be obvious that a simple promissory note carries only the promise of the maker, and its value is limited by his ability to perform his promise. Many business situations require something more in the way of security than the mere promise of the maker. Consequently, many promissory notes are supported by the promises of other persons ("comakers" or "cosigners"), by contracts making certain property available as security on the note, by contracts providing for certain kinds of remedies in case the maker defaults, and by other collateral matters. These supplementary factors may affect the classification of the promissory note, the applicable article in the Code, the negotiability of the instrument, and whether it comes under the Code at all. At this point we are concerned primarily with the classification of promissory notes. Other matters will be discussed as they become relevant.

A *mortgage note* is one secured by interests in property. Where the maker gives the payee a security interest in personal property, the note is called a *chattel mortgage note*. Where the interest is in real property, the note is a *real estate mortgage note*. The usual provision in such transactions is to the effect that the mortgage can be foreclosed if the note is not paid. If the note satisfies the requirements of Article 3, it is not affected by the security transaction.

When a note is given in exchange for merchandise, it may be secured by a conditional sales contract which provides that the title to the goods shall remain in the payee-seller until the note is paid. Such notes are called *conditional sale notes*. The note and the sales contract may be parts of the same instrument or may be separate, and the note may or may not come under Article 3. Conditional sales contracts as security devices will be discussed elsewhere in this book.

Promissory notes may be secured by the maker's actually putting into the payee's possession such personal property as stock certificates, other notes, bonds, and goods. Notes secured in this fashion are called *collateral notes*. Some of the standard forms contain space for descriptions of the collateral and provisions giving the holder the right to sell the property in the event of a default.

As was discussed in the portion of the book devoted to "agency," a *judgment note* makes the payee the maker's agent for the purpose of taking judgment against the maker without the formality of a trial if the note is not paid when due. The agency aspects of these notes are unenforceable in many states.

Bonds are long-term promissory notes issued under seal by public and private corporations and are usually intended to be investment securities. They are very formal documents carrying on their faces much language having to do with the nature of the security and the kinds of remedies available on default. Under the old Negotiable Instruments Law, this extra language often impaired their negotiability. The Code restores their negotiability where appropriate but classifies them as investment securities under Article 8.

CERTIFICATES OF DEPOSIT. The *certificate of deposit* is a promissory note but is classified separately under the Code, just as checks get separate treatment in spite of the fact that they are a type of draft. Certificates are issued by banks to a depositor, both as a receipt for the deposit and as a promise to repay the amount of the deposit. They should not be confused with the ordinary deposit slip, which is only a receipt, contains no promises, and lacks words of negotiability. Certificates of deposit are not as well known nor as often used as the other three types of commercial paper.

D. Contract Matters

The reader is by this time thoroughly familiar with the rules and principles of contract law. He is accustomed to examining contract situations in the light of the factors necessary for the creation of valid and binding contractual relations between parties. To be sure, the reader has already witnessed a few departures from contract principles in certain specialized areas of contract, like the law of sales, but even in those specialized areas the flow of basic contract elements was little changed, and in almost all cases the parties were free to make their own bargains under their own rules if they were explicit about it. The same cannot be said about the law having to do with negotiable instruments, especially commercial paper. The commercial roles which "negotiable" documents are designed to play dictate certain important deviations from the contract principles we have become used to, and they preclude broad freedom of the parties to make their own bargains. Were this not so, the concept of negotiability would have only limited scope and usefulness. Examples will be seen often during the ensuing discussion, but a few of the more important departures from contract principles will be mentioned here.

The primary goal of "negotiability" is exactly what the term itself suggests: to encourage and facilitate the use and transfer of certain types of instruments through the channels of commerce. Were the holders of negotiable instruments required, for example, to prove consideration in the original bargain before they could establish their causes of action, they would be much less willing to accept such instruments. A negotiable instrument is *presumed* to have been issued for consideration, and a holder may pursue his claim without any reference to consideration whatever. Similarly, our earlier discussion of the law of contract revealed that certain contract rights may be transferred from one person to another, but the assignee takes the rights subject to all the defenses that could have been set up against the assignor were he the one trying to enforce the rights. Assignees must, necessarily, concern themselves with the possibility of such defenses and always run the risk that defenses unknown to them at the time of the assignment may arise to bar their claims against the obligor. The more remote the assignment becomes from the original transaction the less likely the assignee will be to pay anything of value for the rights. The holder of a negotiable instrument usually takes free and clear of most defenses that might have been raised against an original party to the transaction. This is what "negotiability" is all about, and it is to that subject that we now turn.

2. ELEMENTS OF NEGOTIABILITY

A. In General

CONCEPT OF NEGOTIABILITY. The meaning of the terms "negotiable" and "negotiability" suggested above is both accurate and useful from a broad conceptual point of view. It tells us that certain types of paper have the ability to pass from person to person in almost the same way that money does. These pieces of paper are not money, but they are treated almost as though they were. A person who rightfully holds a piece of this paper may transfer it to someone else in payment for goods or in exchange for currency or bank deposits, or he may present it for payment when due to the person who made it or to whom it is directed. In doing so, he does not have to worry about the circumstances of its original launching into the channels of commerce. These circumstances have become more or less irrelevant. As with money, however, the holder may have to concern himself with whether certain signatures on the instrument are counterfeit (forged). Even if the person primarily responsible for paying the instrument when due is insolvent and unable to pay, the holder may be able to pursue other persons whose names appear on the instrument. So useful, convenient, and important are these unusual instruments that only a small fraction of one per cent of all the transfers of money and credit in the United States take place by any other means. All of these things are the result of the law surrounding the unique characteristics of negotiability.

A glowing description of the unusual attributes of negotiable instruments does not lead us necessarily to conclude that non-negotiable instruments are void or valueless. On the contrary, they may have great value. Most of the contracts discussed in the chapters on contracts and on sales were non-negotiable. When we say that a contractual instrument is non-negotiable, all we are indicating is that the rights and duties of the parties are determined by the law of contracts and not by the specialized law of negotiable instruments. The non-negotiable instrument may be perfectly valid and enforceable, but whether it is or not is determined by ordinary contract principles, and holders of the instrument will usually not obtain any greater rights than those possessed by the transferors or the original parties.

NEGOTIATION. The term "negotiable" describes a condition or characteristic of certain instruments. It is not to be confused with "negotiation," which is an act or a procedure in connection with a negotiable instrument. We are about to examine the elements or requisites that must be satisfied before an instrument may be said to possess the characteristics of "negotiability." At a later time, we will consider the nature and effect of "negotiation."

B. Formal Requisites of Negotiability

IN GENERAL. In case our discussion of the classification of negotiable instruments may not have been entirely clear, let it be said at this point that the classification or label which an instrument bears generally has no effect upon whether it is negotiable or not. Negotiability, as far as commercial paper is concerned, is achieved by satisfying the requirements set forth in Section 3-104 of the Uniform Commercial Code. There are some minor differences in the requirements for other types of negotiable instruments under other articles of the Code. It should be noted also that negotiability is strictly a matter of form. Unlike ordinary contracts, negotiable instruments must be in certain form, must sometimes use specific words, must contain certain promises or orders, and must, to a much greater extent than other kinds of contracts, be definite, specific, and certain. Consequently, it is important that the requirements for negotiability be learned accurately and in detail.

The Code states that any writing, in order to be a negotiable instrument under Article 3, must be signed by the maker or drawer, contain an unconditional promise or order to pay a certain sum in money, be payable on demand or at a definite time, and be payable to order or to bearer. Each word and phrase in the preceding sentence is necessary and important, and each will be examined in detail below. The Code makes it very clear that "no other promise, order, obligation or power given by the maker or drawer" can be included in the instrument without destroying its negotiable character, except as authorized by the Code itself. We shall have occasion to examine this restriction in detail.

WRITING AND SIGNATURE. An instrument, to be negotiable, must be in writing and signed by the maker if it is a promissory note or by the drawer if it is a check or draft. Perhaps it is redundant to point out that a negotiable instrument must be in writing; the word "instrument" would clearly require that there be a basic written document involved. At any rate, there is no such thing as an oral negotiable instrument. The Code does not require any particular kind of writing. The instrument may be printed, typewritten, set forth in longhand, or in any other way intentionally reduced to tangible form. It may be placed on any kind of material. It may be written in ink, pencil, blood, or anything else that makes a visible mark or impression.

The signature may be in almost any conceivable form. It may be printed or stamped; it may be a mark or a symbol; it may be a fictitious name or even the name of some other person. All that is required is that the "signature" be executed and adopted by a party with the present intention to authenticate the writing. Unusual signatures should be avoided, however, because of the problems of proof. The more one must rely on extrinsic or oral evidence to prove a signature, the greater the risk that it will not be proved. Because of the risks of forgery or alteration, the use of pencils should be discouraged for either the body of the instrument or the signature. The signature may appear anywhere on the instrument, but the traditional lower right hand corner is to be preferred. Printed, perforated, or impressed signatures placed on instruments by automatic accounting machinery are in wide use and do not effect negotiability.

PROMISE AND ORDER.   A promissory note must contain a *promise*. It is not actually necessary that the word "promise" be used, as long as the words that are used clearly manifest a promise or undertaking. The quaint I.O.U. form, celebrated in song and story, is not a negotiable instrument. It does not contain words of promise; it only acknowledges the existence of a debt and does not promise to pay it. The promise must be found in the words used, not in the fact that there is a debt. If the words of promise are missing, the instrument may still manifest a binding engagement but not a negotiable one. Unless there are very good reasons not to do so, the word "promise" should be used.

A draft or check must contain an *order* to pay. The drawer is ordering the drawee to pay the payee, and the words to that effect must be unmistakable. The words must demonstrate something more than an authorization or a request; there must be a clear *direction* to the drawee to pay. Note that the word "order" in a check or draft is not the order to pay; it is simply a direction to the drawee to pay the payee or someone else whom the payee may order to be paid. The traditional phrase on drafts and checks is "pay to the order of." "Pay" is the order of the drawer. While other phraseology will suffice, the traditional language is preferable unless there are compelling reasons to the contrary. The word "order" in a check or draft will be discussed in connection with the last requirement of negotiability.

UNCONDITIONAL PROMISE OR ORDER.   *In general.*   It is obvious that instruments intended to circulate almost as though they were money could not perform that role if their payment were contingent upon the happening of some event, other than the passage of time. Were we compelled to make our payments and transfer our funds by means of currency only, economic conditions in the developed world today would quickly be reduced to something less than primitive. For these reasons, there is a strong public policy in favor of negotiable instruments as substitutes for money. The greatest barrier to their money role would be the presence of conditional promises or orders. Consequently, the law not only requires that the promises and orders be unconditional, but it also construes doubtful language as being unconditional, wherever that is possible. The role of negotiable instruments in representing the future payment of money, as well as the present payment, would be equally defeated by conditional language.

The goals of the old Uniform Law were identical with those of the Code in this regard, but, unfortunately, the language used to express and to implement them was loose and general. The old language left too much to the discretion of the courts, and many decisions wholly inconsistent with the concept of negotiability were the result. The Code corrects this defect by setting forth the requisite of unconditional promises and orders in the clearest possible terms. The details are found in Section 3-105.

Reference to other agreements.   The problem of conditional language will always come up where the instrument contains words other than those of promise or order. Under precode law, one of the most troublesome problems had to do with references to other contracts or documents. Some courts went so far as to say that mere informational references contained in the instrument could impair its negotiability. The Code makes it clear that the negotiability of an instrument is not affected by the mere reference in the instrument to some other contract or document, and it enumerates the situations where the reference is considered to be informational in character and not such as to make the promise or order conditional. Under precode law, the disclosure in the instrument of an executory promise given in exchange for the instrument, as an unperformed promise to deliver goods at some future time, might impair the negotiability of the instrument. Some courts interpreted this situation as an implied condition that the promise to deliver the goods had to be performed before liability arose on the promise to pay. The Code took the opposite view, on the ground that such recitals only call attention to the possibility of a defense which one of the original parties might have against the other. All negotiable instruments imply the possibility of a defense, and many could thus be made non-negotiable under the precode view. The Code states that implied or constructive conditions of this sort do not affect the negotiability of the instrument.

The Code makes a sharp distinction between words of the instrument which make the promise or order *subject to* the terms of another contract and words which simply *refer to* the consideration or to the transaction which gave rise to the instrument. Language such as "as per contract" would not render the promise or order conditional. A draft may have been drawn under a letter of credit, but reference to this fact does not impair negotiability. Reference to the security given for payment of the note is looked upon by the Code as simply conveying to the holder the information that the promise to pay is secured by something more than the general credit of the maker. Notes given in payment for property purchased on the instalment plan often state that title to the property does not pass to the maker until all payments have been made, but such provisions should not, and do not under the Code, render the note non-negotiable.

Obviously, if a holder or prospective holder of an instrument has to make reference to some other contract or document in order to discover whether the promise or order is or is not conditional, the promise or order *is* conditional, and the instrument non-negotiable. But a note that is "subject to" the terms of a mortgage is very different from a note which states simply that it is secured by a mortgage. The distinctions drawn by the Code are roughly along these lines. To put it another way, an instrument is not negotiable unless the holder can ascertain all of its essential terms from its face.

Particular fund doctrine. Another area in which problems arose under pre-code law had to do with references to particular funds from which instruments may or must be paid. The Code continues the basic distinction established by precode law between references to particular funds for bookkeeping purposes and references made for the purpose of conditioning payment upon the existence of such funds. In the first case, the negotiability of the instrument would not be affected, but, in the latter case, the promise or order is obviously conditional. "Bookkeeper: charge this note to cash on deposit in bank" would not render a note non-negotiable, but "charge this to my share of profits" or "pay out of proceeds of sale" would defeat negotiability on the grounds that the facts could not be determined from the face of the instrument.

The Code does change and clarify two types of "particular fund" problems. First, an instrument issued by a government or by an agency of government is not rendered non-negotiable simply because payment is restricted to a particular fund. Restrictions to particular funds are common practice among governmental agencies. To hold such instruments to be non-negotiable would deprive many government units of access to short-term credit. Second, an instrument issued by or on behalf of a partnership, unincorporated association, trust, or estate may be negotiable although the instrument is limited to payment out of the "firm's" assets. The theory behind the older, contrary rule was that individual members of these associations were also liable and that limiting payment to the assets of the firm made those assets a "particular fund," as compared with the total funds available. The Code observes that notes issued by corporations are automatically limited to funds of the corporation, because the shareholders have no personal liability, and the Code affords unincorporated associations similar treatment with regard to the negotiability of instruments issued by them.

CERTAINTY OF THE SUM. Just as the convenience and certainty of money would be destroyed if it were not possible to ascertain its value by examining its face, the negotiability of an instrument is defeated if the amount due at maturity is not certain or cannot be determined from the face of the instrument. The Code, apparently, makes no important changes in precode law in this connection. If the principal sum to be paid at maturity is certain, the negotiability of the instrument is not affected by the fact that it is to be paid with stated interest, by stated instalments, with a stated discount, or with costs of collection or an attorney's fee in case of default. The obligation to pay the costs of collection or an attorney's fee is looked upon as part of the security contract, separate and distinct from the primary undertaking to pay money. Some instruments provide for a higher rate of interest after default, but the Code states specifically that such provisions do not affect negotiability. The basic principle followed throughout the Code is that a sum that becomes uncertain after maturity does not destroy negotiability, as long as the sum at maturity is certain.

Rules of general law may provide certainty where it appears to be lacking on the face of the instrument. Negotiability is not affected, for example, where the face of the instrument fails to specify a rate of interest, for the reason that, in the absence of such specification, the "legal" or "judgment" rate prevails. Instruments made payable in a stated sum of foreign currency are not rendered non-negotiable by the fact that the exchange rate in dollars may change before maturity. The theory is that the purchasing power of all money, domestic as well as foreign, is constantly varying, and anyone who exchanges property for the promise of money must necessarily run the risk that the future value of the property will be different from the future value of the money. Strangely enough, the Code is silent with regard to the effect which promises to pay taxes assessed against an instrument may have on negotiability. This omission leaves the result to precode law, where many courts, in spite of the absence of any substantive differences between taxes and other matters discussed above, held that promises to pay taxes rendered an instrument non-negotiable.

THE SUM TO BE PAYABLE IN MONEY. Although problems raising the question of the meaning of "money" do not often appear, the failure of the old Uniform Law to define money did cause some confusion and difficulty, especially with regard to instruments payable in foreign money or in money that was not legal tender. The Code removes confusion by establishing governmental sanction as the test of money. Money, says the Code, is a "medium of exchange authorized or adopted by a domestic or foreign government as a part of its currency." An instrument is payable in money if the medium of exchange in which it is payable is money at the time the instrument is made. Under this definition of money, an instrument made payable in some foreign currency is still negotiable even though the parties have no contact with or interest in the country whose currency it is. Although residents of a particular locality might customarily treat stones or pemmican or cigarettes as a medium of exhange, the lack of governmental sanction would defeat the negotiability of instruments made payable in those items.

Unless otherwise agreed, instruments made payable in foreign currency may be satisfied by payment of that number of dollars which the stated foreign currency will purchase at the buying sight rate for that currency on the day on which the instrument is payable or, if payable on demand, on the day of demand. The place at which the exchange rate is to be determined is, apparently, the place of payment. We have already seen that fluctuations in the rate of exchange for foreign currencies do not affect negotiability. Note that the instrument may provide that payment *must* be made in the foreign currency. Instruments made payable just in "currency" or "current funds" are, under the Code, payable in money and negotiable.

TIME OF PAYMENT. The instrument, to be negotiable, must be payable on demand or at a definite time. The reason is obvious. The holder of the instrument must be able to determine when he may legally demand payment, and those liable on the instrument must know when their liability accrues. Any other view would destroy much of the value of negotiable instruments. Interest and discount rates could not be fixed, credit risks could not be measured, and the starting of the statute of limitations could not be established. Although the nature and rationale of the requirement seem simple enough, it is not always easy to determine whether an instrument is payable on demand or at a definite time. In addition to the usual tightening and clarification of precode statutory language, the Code makes several changes in the older rules.

An instrument is payable on demand when it so states in those words, or is made payable "at sight" or "on presentation," or when the instrument contains no mention of the time of payment. A check, as we know, is designed to facilitate immediate payment. It contains no mention of the time of payment and is, thus, payable on demand. Instruments which are due or past due are demand paper also; the Code has removed some confusing language in this connection contained in the old Uniform Law.

The Code uses the language "definite time" in place of the old terminology "determinable future time," but this does not change the substance of the requirement, except as noted below. In defining "definite time," however, the Code does make some changes in the old law. The most important of these is a reversal of a conclusion reached by many courts under precode law with regard to the effect on negotiability of "acceleration clauses" contained in the instrument. Such clauses may make an instrument payable before the arrival of the fixed date of maturity. This result is sometimes achieved by using the traditional language "on or before," but more elaborate provisions are common. Some instruments containing these clauses were deprived of their negotiability by courts acting under precode law, but the same courts did not consider demand instruments to be non-negotiable in spite of the fact they contain automatic acceleration rights for both parties. The draftsmen of the Code make it clear that they do not consider acceleration matters to be relevant to concepts of negotiability. The result is that, under the Code, the certainty of time of payment is not affected by acceleration clauses, whether operable at the option of one or more parties, or automatically, or even conditionally.

A particular kind of acceleration clause has been especially troublesome for the courts through the years. This is the so-called "insecurity clause," which permits the holder to accelerate "if he deems the note insecure." The purpose of such clauses is clear, but the courts were concerned about the self-serving holder who might try to accelerate by the simple statement that he feels insecure. The problem is real, but the Code recognizes pragmatically, that it is a matter of good faith, not negotiability, and deals with the problem by giving a green light to all acceleration clauses and by mitigating abuses through special provisions related to good faith.

The liberal stand by the Code in connection with acceleration clauses was not adopted with regard to instruments made payable upon the happening of a particular event. The old Uniform Law specifically stated that such clauses did not affect the certainty of the time of payment for purposes of negotiability. Thus, persons who wished to borrow money on their inheritance, for example, could issue a negotiable promissory note "payable six months after the death of my Aunt Jane." Clearly, the time of payment of such notes was not in any sense certain. The Code takes the opposite view from precode law and provides that an instrument which "by its terms is otherwise payable only upon an act or event uncertain as to time of occurrence is not payable at a definite time even though the act or event has occurred." The ingenious will note that an acceleration clause can be used to render post-obituary notes negotiable under the Code!

Some instruments contain clauses which extend, rather than accelerate, the time of payment. An instrument payable on July 1, 1969, for example, may permit a party to extend the time of payment to July 1, 1970. As with acceleration clauses, many decisions under precode law held that extension clauses defeated the negotiability of the instrument. Section 3-109 of the Code reverses those holdings. An instrument is still payable at a definite time if it is payable "at a definite time subject to extension at the option of the holder, or to extension to a further definite time at the option of the maker or acceptor or automatically upon or after a specified act or event." Authorization of clauses permitting a holder to extend indefinitely the time of payment would appear to be unnecessary, on the ground that any holder, by simple inaction, can extend the time of payment. What he has, of course, is the right to keep the interest charges running by failing to present the instrument at maturity, but he has that right even without the extension clause. Consequently, it has no bearing on negotiability.

The situation with regard to extensions by others than the holder is, of course, very different. If the maker of a promissory note is given the option of extending the time of payment indefinitely, his promise to pay is illusory, there is no certainty of the time of payment, and the instrument is clearly non-negotiable. It may also be void. Where the maker's right to extend is limited to a further definite time, however, the extension clause has no more effect on negotiability than an acceleration clause. Where the time of payment is automatically extended on the occurrence of an act or event, it is sufficient to satisfy the requirements of negotiability if the extension is limited to a definite time.

Instruments made payable "thirty days after date" or "thirty days after sight" are payable at a definite time and negotiable. The Code makes it clear that the negotiability of an instrument is not affected by the fact that it is undated, antedated, or postdated. Where an instrument is postdated or ante-dated, the time when it is payable is determined by the stated date if the instrument is payable on demand or at a fixed period after the stated date. When an undated instrument is made payable at some fixed period after date, it is not negotiable, because it is not payable at a definite time. It is, however, treated as an incomplete instrument, and the date may be inserted later. An instrument simply undated is treated as a demand instrument.

WORDS OF NEGOTIABILITY: PAYABLE TO ORDER OR BEARER. Even if all the other requirements of negotiability are met, the instrument is not negotiable unless it demonstrates on its face the intention of the maker or drawer to create a negotiable instrument. This intention is shown by the words of negotiability: "order" or "bearer." The Code does not require the use of these exact words, but it would be extremely unwise to use anything else. The courts are not in agreement as to what words may be substituted. Theoretically, any words which clearly indicated an intention to make the instrument negotiable would be sufficient. The Code makes one partial exception to the requirement of words of negotiability in providing that an instrument satisfying all the other requirements of negotiability may be treated for most purposes as though it were negotiable. This minor exception is present in the Code only for the purpose of recognizing certain commercial and banking practices. In a sense, it is not an exception at all, because the instrument is not a "negotiable" instrument in the full meaning of the word.

The words that surround "order" or "bearer" are not particularly important. An instrument made payable "to the order of X" is essentially the same as one made payable "to X or order." The same result applies to instruments made payable "to bearer," "to the order of bearer" or "to X or bearer." Other phraseology and special problems will be discussed below. The required words must be used in such a way that the clear import of the language is that the maker or drawer of the instrument contemplates the possibility that the instrument will be transferred to other persons beyond the original payee. The reader should also become aware at this point that "order" and "bearer" are not interchangeable. They produce different legal and practical results, and create "order paper" or "bearer paper," depending on which word of negotiability is used and how.

Order paper. When an instrument is made payable to the order of a specified person, *order paper* is created. It differs from bearer paper in one very important respect: it is negotiated by indorsement and delivery, while bearer paper is negotiated by delivery alone. The full import of this difference will not be understood until we have come to later sections of this chapter. The payee must be named or indicated with reasonable certainty. The reason is plain. An instrument could not be negotiated by indorsement if no payee were named. The significance of the phrase "with reasonable certainty" lies in the issues which would otherwise be raised if the payee's name were misspelled or a corporate name set forth in a fashion slightly different from its charter name. Small variations of this sort will not prevent the instrument from being order paper.

Section 3-110 of the Code enumerates to whom order paper may be made payable. While the usual negotiable instrument is made payable to a payee who is not the maker, drawer, or drawee, the Code and precode law provide that the instrument may be made payable to the order of the maker himself, or the drawer or the drawee. We have already noted that the trade acceptance is an example of an instrument made payable to the drawer as payee. An instrument may be made payable to two or more payees, together or in the alternative. If together, both must indorse; if in the alternative, either may negotiate by indorsing.

Several unsettled issues under precode law with regard to payees have been clarified by specific language of the Code. An instrument may be made payable to the order of an estate, trust, or fund, an office or an officer by his title, to a partnership or an unincorporated association, as long as the payee can be identified. If an instrument is so made payable, it is payable to the order of a representative of the estate, trust, or fund, to the incumbent officer or his successors, or to any person authorized to indorse or transfer on behalf of a partnership or other unincorporated association. Precode law often made such instruments bearer paper in spite of the use of "order" language. Instruments made payable both to order and to bearer caused trouble under precode law but are now expressly dealt with under the Code. Doubts are resolved in favor of order paper unless the bearer words are handwritten or typewritten. Explanation is found in the significance attached to inserting the name of the payee or to writing in especially the "bearer" language.

Bearer paper. The requirement of a named or identifiable payee is not repeated with bearer paper. An instrument is payable to bearer when by its terms it is payable to "bearer" or "order of bearer," to a specified person "or bearer," or to "cash" or the "order of cash," or "any other indication which does not purport to designate a specific payee." (Section 3-111.) The payee need not be named in bearer paper because such paper may be negotiated by delivery; indorsement is not necessary. The Code continues the older law with little change, except for the resolution of several uncertainties. An instrument made payable to "order of bearer," for example, is bearer paper under the Code, on the theory that "bearer" is the dominant and controlling word. The Code omits an older provision that an instrument is bearer paper when made payable to the order of a nonexistent or fictitious person; such paper under the Code is order paper and requires an indorsement for negotiation. Even though an imposter has been designated as payee or an instrument is made payable to a person who is not intended to have any interest in it, indorsement is still necessary.

A source of controversy for many years was a provision of the old Uniform Law that an instrument on which the only or last indorsement was "blank" (see discussion of indorsements below) was bearer paper and a related rule that an instrument which is bearer paper on its face remains bearer paper in spite of "special" indorsements that may appear thereon. The Code changes both of these rules. Any negotiable instrument which is specially indorsed becomes payable to order, and order paper indorsed in blank becomes bearer paper, but is restored to order status by special indorsement. Under precode law, instruments in order form but with the name of the payee omitted were bearer paper; under the Code, they are simply incomplete order instruments.

As noted above, an instrument is bearer paper when it does not purport to designate a specific payee. What this means is that if there is no payee named who could indorse the instrument, it is payable to bearer. "Cash" does not designate a payee who can indorse, nor does the name of a ledger item or account like "bills payable."

IDENTIFICATION OF DRAWEE. Not specifically set forth as a requirement for negotiability, but nonetheless implicit in the nature of negotiability, is the need to identify with reasonable certainty the drawee on a draft. (Notes do not have drawees.) The reason for the requirement is obvious. The payee or holder must know whom it is he is to call upon for acceptance or payment, or the instrument is worthless. There is no rule that the address of the drawee must appear on the instrument, but the facts of a particular case may necessitate its inclusion in order to identify the drawee.

C. Factors Related to but Not Affecting Negotiability

IN GENERAL. No amount of legislation can ever foresee all the variations which human errors and ingenuity can produce in even the most routine activities. The draftsmen of the Uniform Commercial Code have done an amazingly good job of providing for some of the more important variations which one might expect in connection with the creation and transfer of negotiable instruments. Many of these variations are related to negotiability and to the drafting of negotiable instruments. Only a few will be mentioned here. As the reader must already be aware, the economic role played by negotiable instruments requires them to be brief, standardized, and readily understood. Therefore, additions, omissions, variations, and ambiguities loom much larger in these highly formal contracts than they do in the ordinary contracts to which we have become accustomed. For this reason, the Code tries to anticipate the more likely and the more serious variations and to provide rules for resolving them. We have already examined the rules covering undated, antedated, and postdated instruments and many other examples of variant terms and omissions which may affect negotiability. We turn our attention now to those which do not affect negotiability but which may raise problems of conduct, interpretation, and construction.

Terms and Omissions Not Affecting Negotiability. The Code sets aside a specific section (3-112) for the purpose of dealing with terms and omissions which have or might raise issues of negotiability, but which the Code specifically states will not affect negotiability. Among them are the following: omissions of statements of consideration or of the place where the instrument is drawn or payable; a term purporting to waive the benefit of any law intended for the advantage or protection of any obligor (as a waiver of the statute of limitations); a term in a draft providing that the payee by indorsing or cashing it acknowledges full satisfaction of an obligation of the drawer; a promise to maintain or protect collateral, to give additional collateral, or to furnish financial information. Another section of the Code states that the negotiability of an instrument is not affected by the instrument's being under seal.

Incomplete Instruments. Special problems are raised where necessary elements have been omitted from an instrument whose contents at the time of its signing clearly show that it was intended to be a negotiable instrument. Such instruments are referred to as "incomplete" and are not enforceable until they are complete. When completed in accordance with authority given, the instrument is effective as completed. If the completion is unauthorized, the applicable rules are those having to do with material alteration and will be discussed elsewhere in this chapter. A signed check with the space for the date, the payee, or the amount left blank would be an example of an incomplete instrument. If the drawer authorizes the payee or a holder to fill in the blank spaces, the completion is *with* authorization. Common sense would dictate the issuance of incomplete instruments only when absolutely necessary. The risks are great, and the burden of proving completion without authorization is on the person so asserting. If it does become necessary to issue an incomplete instrument, the authority for completion should be set forth in writing at the time of signing.

Ambiguous terms and rules of construction. In spite of their standardized forms and common usage, negotiable instruments are still subject to the threat of ambiguity, and ambiguity, where it arises, can destroy the very purpose of the instrument. Any document which circulates as money must be clear, definite, and unambiguous, and it must mean the same thing to everyone into whose hands it may come. The Code contains special provisions designed to eliminate as much ambiguity as is humanly possible. Section 3-118 contains the basic rules of construction, but others are found throughout the statute. These rules are:

(a) Where there is doubt whether the instrument is a draft or a note, the holder may treat it as either. A draft drawn on the drawer is effective as a note.

(b) Handwritten terms control typewritten and printed terms, and typewritten control printed.

(c) Words control figures except that if the words are ambiguous, figures control.

(d) Unless otherwise specified, a provision for interest means interest at the judgment rate at the place of payment from the date of the instrument, or, if it is undated, from the date of issue.

(e) Unless the instrument otherwise specifies, two or more persons who sign as maker, acceptor or drawer or indorser and as a part of the same transaction are jointly and severally liable even though the instrument contains such words as " I promise to pay."

(f) Unless otherwise specified, consent to extension authorizes a single extension for not longer than the original period. A consent to extension, expressed in the instrument, is binding on secondary parties and accommodation makers. A holder may not exercise his option to extend an instrument over the objection of a maker or acceptor or other party who tenders full payment when the instrument is due.

The meaning of these rules seems clear. However, a word of explanation about the last one is not out of place. This rule is not inconsistent with our earlier discussion of indefinite extensions at the option of the holder. It refers to agreements to extend made in advance for the purpose of binding secondary parties so that they will not be released when an extension is made. The clause usually reads like this: "The makers and indorsers of this note agree that it may be extended without notice to them." Because the purpose of such a clause is to hold secondary parties after an extension and not to protect the holder's right to keep interest running, the maker has the right to discharge the obligation by tendering full payment when the unextended instrument is due.

MISCELLANEOUS PROVISIONS. *Instruments payable to two or more persons.* As we have seen, an instrument may be made payable to two or more payees, either together or in the alternative. Where made payable in the alternative, any one of the payees may indorse and deliver; where made payable to the order of "X and Y," both must indorse, or one may authorize the other to indorse on his behalf. Payment to one will not discharge the obligation to the other. In both cases, problems arise when one of the payees dies. If the right of survivorship is intended, it should be spelled out. Otherwise, the personal representative of the deceased payee will, in the case of alternative payees, probably succeed to the rights and, in the case of joint payees, certainly succeed to the rights. An Official Comment in the Code states that joint payees are treated as tenants in common unless there is express language to the contrary. If an instrument is made payable "to X and/or Y," it is payable to X or to Y, or to X and Y together, and it may be negotiated, enforced, or discharged by any one payee or by both payees.

Instruments payable with words of description.   An instrument which is made payable to a named person with the addition of words describing him, as "John Jones, Agent of Bill Smith" or "Tom Brown, Treasurer of XYZ Corp.," is payable to the principal, but the agent or officer may act as if he were the holder. It is the commercial understanding in such cases that the real payee is the principal and that the name of the agent or officer is inserted only for the convenience of enabling him to demand and collect payment. Where a person is described as "John Jones, Trustee of Smith Trust" or "Tom Brown, Administrator of the Estate of Joe Green," the instrument is payable to the individual named and may be negotiated, discharged, or enforced by him, subject, of course, to his fiduciary duties. Any other words of description, such as "John Jones, Attorney," or "Tom Brown, Administrator," are without effect, and the instrument is payable unconditionally to the named payee. The significance of these rules is that subsequent holders of an instrument that reveals the fiduciary capacity of the named payee and the identity of the principal are put on notice of that fiduciary capacity and may be deprived of the full rights of holders if they know of breaches of the fiduciary duty.

Other writings affecting the instrument.   We have already seen that the Code takes the view that separate agreements do not affect the negotiability of an instrument even when they are all a part of the same transaction. As between the original parties, all the writings executed as part of the same transaction are read together as a single agreement, and the parties are bound by them. Third persons, on the other hand, who are not parties to the agreements are not affected by them and may still be holders in due course. If third persons have knowledge of any defenses arising out of the separate agreements, they may not become holders in due course. (See discussion below of "holders in due course.") When instruments are made "subject to" or otherwise conditioned upon other agreements, negotiability is defeated because the promise or order is conditional.

Instruments "payable through" and "payable at" a bank.   Many negotiable instruments, especially in connection with pension and payroll checks and dividends, are made "payable through" a particular bank. Questions arise about the role or function of the bank. The Code holds that an instrument which states that it is "payable through" a bank designates that bank as a collecting bank to make presentment of the instrument but does not of itself authorize the bank to pay the instrument. The bank is not the drawee and its role is the very limited one of handling the item for collection.

Where the instrument is made "payable at" a particular bank, a different situation arises. Actually, the Code recognizes two views of banking practice and permits each state to adopt the version of the Code which is consistent with practice in that state. The first view represents the practice in New York and surrounding states, which is to the effect that a note or acceptance made payable "at" a bank is the equivalent of a draft drawn on the bank, and the bank must make payment out of the account of the maker or acceptor without consulting him. In the western and southern states, the view is that such an instrument simply designates the place of payment, and the bank's only duty is to notify the maker or acceptor that the instrument has been presented and to ask for instructions. The reader should check the law of his own state on this matter.

3. TRANSFER AND NEGOTIATION

A. In General

The fact that an instrument satisfies all of the requirements discussed above is of no legal significance until the instrument is properly transferred from the original payee to some other person. The transaction that may activate for the first time the unusual characteristics of negotiability is that transfer. Having examined the formal requirements of the instrument itself, we must now turn our attention to what constitutes the proper transfer of the instrument so as to call into operation the principles of negotiability.

A negotiable instrument takes its first step into the channels of commerce by *issuance,* which consists of the delivery of a properly drawn instrument into the possession of the first holder, usually the payee. *Delivery* merely means the transfer of possession from one person to another. A note or check, as we have seen, is usually delivered directly from the maker or drawer to the payee, while a trade acceptance or banker's acceptance passes through the hands of the drawee (acceptor) on its way into the possession of the payee, usually the drawer himself. The original delivery to the first holder is comparable with matters of form, as far as calling into operation the characteristics of negotiability is concerned. It has been likened to "cocking" a gun. It is the following step that has unusual significance. If properly carried out, the transfer of the instrument by the payee may create unusual rights and duties in the parties.

Transfer is a broad legal term which describes the act by which the owner of property delivers it to another person with the intention of passing his rights in it to the other person. Negotiable instruments may be transferred by negotiation or assignment. *Negotiation* is the transfer of an instrument in such form that the transferee becomes a holder. A *holder* is a person who is in possession of an instrument which, by its terms, is issued, drawn, or indorsed to him or to his order, or to bearer, or in blank. We have already seen that a payee in possession of an instrument is a holder. A transfer which is not a negotiation is an *assignment*. The significance of the distinction between negotiation and assignment lies in the fact that only a holder can become a "holder in due course," and it is to the latter that the important characteristics of negotiability accrue. (The holder in due course will be discussed in the next section of this chapter.) After negotiation, the transferee is eligible to become a holder in due course. The assignee is not, but this is not to say that the assignee has no rights or power. He has all the rights which the transferor had; he may have the right to compel the transferor to negotiate the instrument in order to make the assignee a holder; and he may have other rights as well.

NEGOTIATION. Bearer paper, as we know, is negotiated by delivery, and order paper by indorsement *and* delivery. If an instrument is payable to bearer, even a thief or a finder may negotiate it simply by delivering it to another person. Order paper is not as easily disposed of; the matter of delivery, while essential, is still simple, but the requirement of indorsement has many aspects and many dimensions. There are numerous kinds of indorsements. Indorsements control the way in which further transfers of the instrument are made; they may be used to alter the rights and liabilities of the parties, may turn order paper into bearer paper, and even destroy the further negotiability of the instrument.

An indorsement is usually made on the back of the instrument, but it may actually be any place on the instrument or even on a separate, though firmly attached, paper called an *allonge*. There may be risks attached to indorsing outside the usual place on the back. A person who indorses on the face of a note, for example, may be held as the maker if his role as indorser is not clear. The indorsement must be for the entire amount of the instrument or for its unpaid balance. If it is for less than the full face amount or balance, the indorsement acts only as a partial assignment and not as a negotiation; the rights of the parties will be determined by the general law of contract. Under precode law, words added to the standard words of indorsement often were held to have destroyed the effect of an indorsement and to have accomplished instead an assignment. The Code rejects this view on the ground that such language is rarely intended to have that result, and it provides that words of assignment, waiver, condition, guaranty, limitation, disclaimer of liability, and the like accompanying an indorsement do not affect its character as an indorsement. An indorsement with such words still serves to negotiate the instrument but may affect events and rights after negotiation.

Where a payee's name has been misspelled or an instrument has been made payable to a person under a name other than his own, he may indorse in the misspelled or other name or his own or both. However, a person paying or giving value for the instrument may require signatures in both names. Order paper may be transferred without an indorsement, through oversight or otherwise. The transferee is not an indorsee or holder, but only an assignee. However, he has the right to the indorsement of the transferor, and negotiation takes place when he obtains that indorsement.

B. Negotiation by Indorsement

In General. The Uniform Commercial Code makes few substantive changes in the earlier law, but clarifies and considerably reorganizes the statutory material dealing with indorsements. Unfortunate language in the old Uniform Law created the impression that there were only five kinds of indorsements and that these were mutually exclusive. Actually, every indorsement must convey four kinds of information, and, in each kind of information, there are two alternatives. An indorsement must tell us: 1, how subsequent negotiations are to be made (blank and special indorsements); 2, the type of interest being transferred (restrictive and nonrestrictive indorsements); 3, the liability of the indorser (qualified and unqualified indorsements); and 4, whether there are limitations on the holder and the obligor with respect to payment (conditional and unconditional indorsements). Consequently, every indorsement must be blank or special, restrictive or nonrestrictive, qualified or unqualified, and conditional or unconditional. Each type of indorsement is discussed below.

Blank Indorsement. An indorsement is *blank* when the indorser writes only his signature on the instrument. No indorsee is indicated. Such an indorsement converts order paper into bearer paper and tells us that it may be further negotiated by delivery alone. Bearer paper indorsed in blank is not altered as far as the method of further negotiation is concerned. Note that a blank indorsement, because it contains nothing except the indorser's signature, is necessarily nonrestrictive, unqualified, and unconditional as well as blank.

It will be recalled from our earlier discussion that order paper, converted into bearer paper by blank indorsement, may be reconverted into order paper by special indorsement, and paper originally made payable to bearer may be similarly converted into order paper. The last indorsement controls. These Code rules are modifications in precode law. The Code also permits the holder of an instrument indorsed in blank to protect himself against the risk that a thief or finder might present the instrument to a maker or drawee who pays it in good faith. The holder does this by writing over the blank indorsement words which convert it into a special indorsement. If Tom Brown is the holder of an instrument indorsed simply "John Jones," he may write in over the signature the words "Pay to Tom Brown" and thus, convert the paper into order paper requiring his signature for further negotiation.

Special Indorsement. Section 3-204 of the Code describes a special indorsement as one which specifies the person to whom, or to whose order, the indorsement makes the instrument payable. "Pay to Tom Brown" and "Pay to the order of Tom Brown," followed by the signature of the indorser, have exactly the same effect. Words of negotiability, required to make an instrument negotiable in the first place, are not necessary in the indorsement. The effect of a special indorsement, of course, is to require the indorsement of the indorsee for further negotiation.

RESTRICTIVE AND NONRESTRICTIVE INDORSEMENTS. *In general.* A restrictive indorsement controls the type of interest being transferred and restricts or limits the indorsee's rights in some way. The most common restrictive indorsement is the indorsement "for collection" or "for deposit." Other types of restrictive indorsement listed in the Code are those purporting to prohibit further transfer of the instrument ("Pay Tom Brown only"), those stating that they are for the benefit or use of or in trust for the indorser or other persons ("Pay Tom Brown in trust for John Jones"), and conditional indorsements (see discussion below). In contrast with precode law, the Code provides expressly that restrictive indorsements do not prevent further transfer or negotiation of the instrument. As a matter of fact, an indorsement "Pay Tom Brown only" has no restrictive effect at all.

Under precode law, a restrictive indorsement stopped further negotiation and prevented any person thereafter from becoming a holder in due course. The theory was that such indorsements were not made for the purpose of transferring title to transferee but to make the transferee an agent or trustee. While this is usually the case, it is not always so, and some transferees for value were deprived of rights that would otherwise have been theirs. The Code permits further negotiation and even permits a restrictive indorsee to be a holder in due course, if he otherwise complies with the statutory requirements for that status. Under most circumstances, banks can simply ignore restrictive indorsements, under Section 3-206(2), unless the indorsement is that of the immediate transferor. The purpose of this provision is to free banks involved in the collection process from the need to examine and interpret all restrictive indorsements in the vast number of items handled every day. Clearly, this policy does not apply to situations where the restrictive indorsement was placed on the instrument by the person who transferred the instrument to the bank. The restrictive indorsement still has an effect outside the collection system.

While a restrictive indorsement does not prevent further negotiation, it does, except as indicated above, affect the type of interest being transferred. Generally, this means that persons who take an instrument restrictively indorsed must respect the indorsement and act consistently with it. A transferee of such an instrument must pay or apply any value given by him in a manner consistent with the language of the indorsement, but, to the extent that he does so, he becomes a holder in due course. Where the indorsement is a trust indorsement ("Pay Tom Brown in trust for John Jones"), the duty to act consistently is confined to the first taker. If the instrument is delivered to Tom Brown, he is a trustee and owes a fiduciary duty to John Jones, but if he sells the instrument to Smith, Smith does not have to concern himself with the indorsement or with a possible breach of duty by Brown. The reason is that trustees usually have the power to sell trust assets of this kind. Of course, if Smith has actual notice that Brown has breached his duty to Jones, Smith would not be a holder in due course.

Conditional and unconditional indorsements. Under the Code, conditional indorsements are treated as a type of restrictive indorsement. Under precode law, such indorsements did not affect the negotiability of the instrument, and the Code retains this view. Conditional indorsements tell us of limitations on the holder or obligor with respect to payment, because they provide for payment on the occurrence of some condition. An example of a conditional indorsement would be: "Pay to the order of Tom Brown on the completion of the Main Street Bridge." It will be remembered that an instrument so made payable on its face would not be negotiable in the first place, but conditional indorsements do not affect the negotiability of the instrument. As we know, this does not mean that transferees, except as described above, can ignore the condition. The transferee must pay or apply any value given by him consistently with the indorsement. Fortunately, conditional indorsements are not very often used, and a person may well hesitate before accepting an instrument bearing such an indorsement.

QUALIFIED AND UNQUALIFIED INDORSEMENTS. Because the issue of qualified and unqualified indorsements has to do with the nature and extent of the indorser's liability, the subject will be examined in greater detail in that connection. It is enough to say at this point that when an indorser uses such words as "without recourse," he is qualifying his liability as an indorser. Without the words of qualification, the indorser guarantees payment of the instrument under certain circumstances. The use of the words relieves him of this liability. While qualified indorsements have a certain appeal to indorsers, it should be noted that words of qualification may depress the value of the instrument and make it difficult to negotiate, simply because a prospective transferee of the instrument may desire the assurances of payment by the indorser. Outside this practical issue, a qualified indorsement does not affect the negotiability of an instrument.

IRREGULAR INDORSEMENTS. Section 3-402 of the Uniform Commercial Code states specifically that unless the instrument indicates clearly that a signature is made in some other capacity, it is an indorsement.

C. Rescission and Re-aquisition

RESCISSION. The lack of full contractual capacity by such persons as minors and corporations has a bearing on the negotiation of instruments.

Both the Code and precode law have recognized that the application of ordinary contractual principles would seriously impede the use of negotiable instruments. The older law and the Code provide that the indorsement of an instrument by a minor or by a corporation is still effective to transfer the instrument, although the minor or corporation lacks capacity and may incur no liability. However, the public policy behind the protection of minors and of corporations whose officers exceed corporate powers must be recognized also. Minors and corporations, under proper circumstances, may still avoid or rescind their indorsements, except against a subsequent holder in due course. The Code extends the concept to negotiations obtained by fraud, mistake, or duress, and to negotiations which are part of an illegal transaction or made in breach of duty. The taker of an instrument which has been negotiated is a holder until the instrument has been recovered from his possession, and a person who negotiates an instrument gives up all his rights until he recovers it. Thus, a minor or other person entitled to rescind must recover the instrument by appropriate legal procedures, but the holder in due course takes free of rescission or any other remedy. (See discussion later in this chapter on "real defenses.")

Re-acquisition. Sometimes commercial paper comes back into the hands of a party who earlier held it. This party is known as a *re-acquirer*. It is not necessary that the instrument be "negotiated" back to this prior party. The re-acquirer may cancel any indorsement which is not necessary to his title and reissue or further negotiate the instrument. Persons whose indorsements have been canceled are discharged from liability even as against holders in due course. If the re-acquirer reissues or negotiates without canceling any of the intervening indorsements, those indorsers are discharged as against the re-acquirer and all holders not in due course. The basic reason for these rules is the view that a party, by re-acquiring an instrument, should not be able to make liable to him parties to whom he was once liable as a result of his earlier negotiation or issue of the instrument.

4. HOLDERS IN DUE COURSE

A. In General

We have already seen that a holder is a person who is in possession of an instrument which is issued, drawn, or indorsed to him or to his order, or to bearer, or in blank. A holder may be no better off than the assignee of any simple contract right, subject to all the defenses that the maker, drawer, or other parties prior to him may have had against the payee. Or he may be a *holder in due course,* who is free from these personal defenses, and whose rights against the obligated parties are greater than those possessed by the person who transferred the instrument to him. An ordinary holder may transfer or negotiate an instrument, as we know, and may even discharge it or enforce its payment, but he may also discover that his rights against the maker of a note, for example, are cut off by the defense of the maker who claims that he was induced to issue the note by the fraud of the payee or that there was a failure of consideration in the original transaction. The holder in due course is not affected by these and other personal defenses. The special position of the holder in due course has already been illustrated frequently in this chapter, especially in the section on "transfer and negotiation."

A holder does not become a holder in due course simply by acquiring an instrument. The Code lays down certain specific requirements that must be met before a holder can achieve this special status. Section 3-302 sets forth these requirements as follows: a holder in due course is a holder who takes the instrument 1, for value, 2, in good faith, and 3, without notice that it is overdue or has been dishonored or of any defense against or claim to it on the part of any person. Each one of these requirements will be examined in detail below. The discussion of the rights of a holder in due course will be postponed until the requirements are thoroughly explained and understood.

PAYEE AS HOLDER IN DUE COURSE.   Uncertain language in the old Uniform Law led some courts to conclude that payees could not be holders in due course. Because payees are usually parties to the original transaction, they would ordinarily have notice of defenses against the instrument, but this is not always the case. The Code makes it clear that a payee may be a holder in due course if he can meet the requirements for the status.

B. Requirement for a Holder in Due Course

THE REQUIREMENT OF VALUE.   Because we have already examined the requirement that a holder in due course must first be a "holder," we can move on to the next requirement, that a holder must take the instrument for *value* before he can qualify as a holder in due course. It should be noted, however, that a holder who takes the instrument from a person who is himself a holder in due course obtains the same rights as a holder in due course and need not take the instrument for value. In a sense, this value requirement is unusual. It says that a donee, a person to whom the instrument has been transferred as a gift, cannot be a holder in due course. In most other countries, the donee is given the same protection as the purchaser. The explanation for this paradox of Anglo-American law is not entirely clear, but certainly the historical development of the doctrine of consideration plays a role in it. Cultural differences are undoubtedly also factors. Distaste for those who get something for nothing is much more strongly felt among Anglo-Saxons than it is in civil law countries. The draftsmen of the Uniform Commercial Code were no more immune than the rest of us from these cultural attitudes and continued the requirement.

Although the terms "value" and "consideration" have much in common, there are important differences, and the two terms must be distinguished. The first distinction is that, while a mere promise is consideration under ordinary contract principles, it is not "value" in the eyes of the Code requirement. A holder takes an instrument for value to the extent that the agreed consideration has been performed. If X indorses a $500 note to Y in exchange for Y's promise to deliver certain goods, Y has not taken the note for value. If Y delivers one-half the goods, he is a holder for value to the extent of $250. In the bank collection process, the issue may be raised as to the exact time at which a bank has given value to its customer for an item left with it for collection, and various approaches have been taken to this problem in the common law, but the Code takes no stand on the matter. Generally, crediting the account of a customer is not, by itself, giving value.

The second distinction works in the opposite direction. Antecedent debts cannot be consideration to support an ordinary contract promise, but they are "value" under the Code. If Y takes a $500 note from X in settlement or as security for an antecedent debt, Y has given "value" and may qualify as a holder in due course. It makes no difference whether the debt was due or not when Y took the instrument.

Nothing that has been said above should lead one to the conclusion that the holder must give full face value for the instrument. Some negotiable instruments do not command their full face values on the market. There is usually a discount for interest, or risk, or other factors. Of course, excessive discounts may be evidence of bad faith.

The Code spells out in some detail (Section 3-303) what "taking for value" is and establishes rules which are essentially the same as under precode law. Some issues are clarified, however, and one matter which the old Uniform Law did not deal with at all is spelled out in the Code. Section 3-303(c) states that a holder takes an instrument for value when he gives a negotiable instrument in exchange for it or makes some other irrevocable commitment. The reason is that a negotiable instrument, while only an executory promise, may come into the hands of a holder in due course. If it does, the person who gave it cannot refuse to pay and is treated by the Code, from the time he issues the instrument, as though he had already paid.

THE REQUIREMENTS OF GOOD FAITH AND TAKING WITHOUT NOTICE. *In general.* Although separately stated in the Code, as they were under precode law, the requirements of good faith and taking without notice are really just a general and a specific way of describing the same basic requirement: in order to qualify for the unusual status of a holder in due course, a holder must take the instrument without knowledge of defenses or claims against it. *Good faith* is the broad, encompassing way of stating this rule. It signifies honesty and honest intentions. Mere suspicion is generally not enough to destroy good faith, nor is negligence. If the holder is honest, it usually does not matter how stupid or gullible he may be. The Code requires the holder to be honest and that he take the instrument believing it to be valid and genuine. However, in an area of law as dependent upon certainty as the law of negotiable instruments, the situation could not be left to such broad terms as "good faith." Consequently, the Code spells out several of the more important issues in detail. Section 3-302, as we have seen, requires the holder to take without notice that the instrument is overdue or has been dishonored or notice of any defense or claim against it. Section 3-304 enlarges upon these major areas and resolves certain precode problems. The more important issues will be considered below.

The key word is "notice." A person is said to have notice of a fact when he has actual knowledge of it, or has received a notice or notification of it, or, from all the facts and circumstances known to him at the time in question, he has reason to know that it exists.

Notice of defense or claim. The old Uniform Law included in the definition of a holder in due course the requirement that the instrument be "complete and regular on its face," meaning that obvious erasures, alterations, or blank spaces on an instrument prevented a purchaser from becoming a holder in due course. The Code removed this specific provision and made it a part of the good faith requirement, with the result that the purchaser of an incomplete or irregular instrument may still become a holder in due course if he bought it in good faith. Section 3-304(1) states, in this connection, that the purchaser has notice of a claim or defense only if the instrument is so incomplete, or bears such visible evidence of forgery or alteration, or is otherwise so irregular, as to call into question its validity, terms, or ownership, or to create an ambiguity as to the party who is to pay. Under this provision, minor erasures, easily explicable changes of date (January 2, 1969, to January 2, 1970), and blanks left as to unnecessary matters need not even arouse suspicion.

A purchaser has notice of a defense against the instrument if he has notice that the obligation of any party is voidable, in whole or in part, or that all the parties have been discharged. This provision of the Code, like most of the others in Section 3-304, simply codifies law that developed under the old Uniform statute. A note, for example, would come under this provision if it were obtained by the payee through fraud, and if the purchaser of this note from the payee had notice of this fact at the time of transfer to him.

When a purchaser buys an instrument from a known fiduciary, he may still qualify as a holder in due course unless he has knowledge that the fiduciary negotiated the instrument in payment of or as security for his own debt or was otherwise in breach of his fiduciary duty. The purchaser may safely assume that the fiduciary acted properly, unless the circumstances set forth in this paragraph are present.

Notice that an instrument is overdue. In order to become a holder in due course, a holder must take an instrument without notice that it is overdue. This was a common law rule and was continued by the old Uniform Law and the Code. Although the rule originated as a matter of good faith, it has come to have an independent status of its own. The Code sets forth the rule in such a way as to avoid problems arising under precode law with regard to demand paper and paper whose due date has been accelerated. The logic behind the rule rests on the assumption that instruments are paid at maturity and, if they are not, there must be something wrong. The holder is put on notice by the mere fact that he acquired the instrument after maturity.

Section 3-304(3) provides that the purchaser has notice that an instrument is overdue if he has reason to know "(a) that any part of the principal amount is overdue or that there is an uncured default in payment of another instrument of the same series; or (b) that acceleration of the instrument has been made; or (c) that he is taking a demand instrument after demand has been made or more than a reasonable length of time after its issue." The Code states that a reasonable time for a check drawn and payable within the United States is presumed to be thirty days. Under these provisions, a purchaser may still take as holder in due course an instrument which has in fact been accelerated or on which demand has been made, as long as he is ignorant of the demand or acceleration. For instruments other than checks, what is an unreasonable time after issue is determined by the nature of the instrument, custom, and usage of the trade, and all other relevant facts and circumstances. The thirty day period specified by the Code for checks is merely a presumption and may be rebutted by other evidence.

The Code provision having to do with defaults in the payment of another instrument "in the same series" refers to the fact that negotiable instruments are often issued in a series with different dates of maturity. Notice to a purchaser that there has been a default in the payment of an instrument in the series with an earlier date of maturity than the instrument that he has purchased will prevent him from qualifying as a holder in due course. The same result is provided for instruments whose payments are to be made in instalments.

Knowledge of facts not constituting notice. Much of the uncertainty under the old Uniform Law with regard to what facts the knowledge of which will constitute notice to the purchaser has been eliminated in the Code by specific provision. Section 3-304(4) lists a number of the situations which were subject to inconsistent treatment under precode law and states that they do not, by themselves, give notice of a defense or claim. For example, knowledge that an instrument is antedated or postdated does not prevent a holder from qualifying to take in due course. The same result holds where the purchaser has knowledge that the person negotiating the instrument is or was a fiduciary, as we have seen, that there has been a default in the payment of interest on the instrument, or that the instrument was issued or negotiated in return for an executory promise. In the latter case, of course, negotiation to the purchaser in return for an executory promise would prevent him from becoming a holder for value. Knowledge that an incomplete instrument has been completed after issue does not give notice of a defense or claim unless the purchaser has notice that it was completed improperly. The Code also makes it clear that the filing or recording of a document does not of itself constitute notice. Section 3-304 concludes with a statement that no notice is effective unless it is received "at such time and in such manner as to give a reasonable opportunity to act on it."

SUMMARY. If a holder meets all of the above requirements, he qualifies as a holder in due course and is given special treatment and special protection under the law governing commercial paper. The personal defenses of the maker or drawer may not be asserted against him. The holder in due course occupies a very special status under the law, because the policy of the law is to encourage easy and convenient negotiability by protecting innocent persons who purchase or take negotiable instruments in the regular course of their activities.

C. Other Holders

HOLDERS FROM A HOLDER IN DUE COURSE. A holder in due course might find his exalted status an empty honor indeed were he unable to transfer the instrument further. This result could arise where a defense of which the holder in due course had no knowledge when he took the instrument comes later to be widely known in the community. Our holder might find it very difficult to transfer the instrument to anyone else. Because of this problem, precode law and the Code have provided that holders from holders in due course have all the rights of the former, unless, of course, that subsequent holder was himself a party to the fraud or illegality which is the defense at issue. One further limitation is imposed on this important rule in that a prior holder cannot improve his position by negotiating to a holder in due course and then re-acquiring the instrument. If he employs this technique, he ends up with exactly the same rights he had the first time he held the instrument. Note that a holder from a holder in due course does not have to be a holder for value or meet any of the other requirements for the holder in due course. These rules, it is clear, are perfectly consistent with the general theory of assignment. The transferor passes along to the transferee such rights as he has, including such special rights as accrue to a holder in due course.

SUCCESSORS IN INTEREST. Many holders come into possession of negotiable instruments under unusual circumstances that indicate that they are merely successors in interest to the prior holder and can acquire no more than he had. Examples would be purchases at judicial sales and other acquisitions through legal process, an executor's coming into possession of instruments as part of an estate, or purchases as part of a bulk transaction not in the regular course of the transferor's business. Of course, if the prior holder was a holder in due course or a holder from a holder in due course, our unusual holder would have the rights of a holder in due course, but in other situations would only succeed to the rights possessed by the prior holder.

D Rights of a Holder in Due Course

IN GENERAL. It has taken a long time to reach the point where the advantages of qualifying as a holder in due course can be described in detail. Section 3-305 of the Uniform Commercial Code describes the rights clearly and briefly. In the first place, the holder in due course takes the instrument free of *all* claims to it on the part of any person. This requires little discussion or elaboration. It means that the holder in due course takes the instrument free not only of all claims of legal title but also of all liens, equities, or claims of any other kind. The second major category of rights has to do with defenses which might be set up by one or more parties to the instrument. The Code provides that the holder in due course takes the instrument free of "all defenses of any party to the instrument with whom the holder has not dealt except. . . . " The distinction between those defenses from which the holder in due course is protected and those following the word "except" are the subject to which we now move. The explanation for limiting the protection of the holder in due course to defenses of parties with whom he has not dealt is obvious.

Defenses to actions on negotiable instruments are divided into two categories: real and personal. Real defenses are available even against holders in due course. Personal defenses are cut off by the qualification of a holder in due course. The former are sometimes referred to as absolute defenses. Generally speaking, personal defenses are the usual contract defenses and the ones most likely to occur in ordinary business transactions. The real defenses refer to more serious situations and are usually associated with circumstances which deprive the instrument of legal efficacy at its very inception. In these situations, the policy of permitting the defense to be asserted overrides the general policy in favor of protecting the holder in due course and encouraging negotiability. Fraud in the inducement is an example of a personal defense, and forgery an example of a real defense. The holder in due course takes the instrument free of the fraud defense, but not from the defense of forgery.

Real defenses are indeed available against holders in due course, but, under some circumstances, they are not as absolute or unconditional as they may appear. The doctrine of estoppel (discussed elsewhere in this book), may prevent a party from asserting a real defense. It has been held that a drawer should be estopped to set up the real defense of material alteration where the negligent manner in which the instrument was drawn facilitated the alteration. Although there has been some disagreement with this view through the years, the Code (Section 3-406) expressly adopts it. The result is that a person who, by his negligence, substantially contributes to a material alteration or to the making of an unauthorized signature is precluded from asserting his defense against a holder in due course. The Code goes even further and estops the use of the defense against a drawee or other payor who pays the instrument in good faith and in conformance with reasonable commercial standards.

PERSONAL DEFENSES. *In general.* Because the Code, in effect, lists the real defenses and protects the holders in due course from all others, it is not necessary for us here to enumerate all the personal defenses. A brief glance at some of the more important examples of personal defenses, however, and at the changes made in precode law is in order. Fraud in the inducement and lack or failure of consideration are personal defenses with which we are already familiar from our earlier discussion of contracts. They are not available against a holder in due course. It should be remembered, however, that the law we are concerned with here is designed to protect the holder in due course, for reasons we have examined, and not to deprive a party of his rights against one who has defrauded him or failed to perform his promises. If, for example, a maker or drawer was induced to issue the instrument by the fraud of the payee, he may still pursue his claim against the payee as long as he does not involve a holder in due course to whom the payee or other subsequent holder may have negotiated the instrument. By the same token, original parties to the contract who have some dispute over lack or failure of consideration are welcome to litigate this issue in a separate proceeding not involving the holder in due course.

Nondelivery of instruments. Under precode law, the nondelivery of a completed instrument was only a personal defense, while the nondelivery of an incomplete instrument was a real defense. An example of the first situation would occur where the maker or drawer completed the instrument but left it on his desk where a thief found it and negotiated it. Obviously, the thief could not enforce the instrument against the maker or drawer, but a holder in due course could. An example of the second situation would involve a maker or drawer who signed the instrument but did not complete the rest of it. Under precode law, a thief who found, completed, and negotiated this instrument would not deprive the maker or drawer of his defense even against a holder in due course. This latter rule presented somewhat of a paradox, on the ground that neither nondelivery nor unauthorized completion of an incomplete instrument created a real defense. Why the combination should result in such a defense was not easy to figure out. The Code reverses the rule and makes lack of delivery and/or unauthorized completion a personal defense only. It will be recalled that an incomplete instrument, if delivered, may be completed by a person with that authority. If the instrument is completed in an unauthorized fashion, a holder in due course may enforce payment in accordance with the manner in which the instrument is actually completed.

Payment before maturity. In some cases, the maker or other person obligated to pay the instrument may pay it before maturity without insisting on surrender of the instrument. Although the payor should always insist that the instrument be surrendered, whether paid before, at, or after maturity, the risks of not doing so are much greater where the instrument is paid before maturity. If paid at or after maturity, the instrument is overdue on its face, and a holder cannot qualify as a holder in due course. The defense of payment is only a personal defense. A payor who pays before maturity will also have to pay a holder in due course who presents the instrument for payment at maturity. The rule is harsh but eminently sensible.

Discharge.   Later in this chapter, we will discuss in detail the matter of discharge. At this point it is enough to say that the discharge of a party is ineffective as against a holder in due course, unless he had notice when he took the instrument; discharge is, therefore, a personal defense. A holder who has notice that *all* parties have been discharged cannot qualify as a holder in due course, but notice that less than all have been discharged does not prevent his becoming a holder in due course. Those of whose discharge he had notice could use the defense of discharge against him, but the other parties could not.

REAL DEFENSES.   *In general.*   The holder in due course is, perhaps, more interested in the defenses which can be used against him than those which cannot. While there are many kinds of real defenses, their actual occurrence is relatively rare. The Code reorganizes and regroups much of the statutory material having to do with real defenses, without major changes in the law, but our discussion here will conform largely to the traditional defenses, for the sake of clarity and of convenience in organizing the material. In most cases, the reader is not interested in the exact language of the Code or in the precise location of the Code treatment. Thus, the real defenses will receive their primary discussion here, rather than in connection with the liabilities of the parties. Reference will again be made to some of them in later portions of this chapter.

Fraud in the inception.   We are familiar with the nature of fraud in the inception, and the distinction between it and fraud in the inducement, from the chapter on contracts. In keeping with the basic characteristics of real defenses, fraud in the inception goes to the very existence of the instrument itself. Where the language of a negotiable instrument is written over a signature placed on a piece of paper for some other purpose (a celebrity's autograph), or where a person signs an instrument under such circumstances that he does not realize that he is signing a negotiable instrument ("Please sign this receipt"), the fraud or misrepresentation goes to the intention of the party and to the creation of the instrument. Not even a holder in due course is protected against this defense. The policy of protecting him is far outweighed by the policy against holding people to promises or engagements that they never intended. As we have seen, however, the negligence of the party may estop his use of the defense against a holder in due course.

Forgery.   No great amount of time need be devoted to explaining why forgery is a real defense. A person should not be held to the terms of an instrument when his name was placed thereon by someone else and without his authority. The Code somewhat revises the language of the old Uniform

Law and makes a few changes in detail. Any unauthorized signature is said to be wholly inoperative as the signature of the person whose name is signed unless he ratifies it or is barred from denying it. The term "unauthorized signature" includes forgeries and the signatures of agents who exceed their authority. Although an unauthorized signature will not operate as the signature of the person whose name is signed, it will operate as the signature of the unauthorized signer in favor of any person who in good faith pays the instrument or takes it for value. As a practical matter, it is not very often that the liability of a forger could be enforced, but an agent who exceeds his authority may find himself liable for the full value of the instrument.

It is worth noting that no title to an instrument would pass through a forged indorsement. A person holding an instrument under a forged indorsement would be met by the real defense of lack of title, based upon the fact that the indorsement was a forgery. This conclusion would be true, however, only in those cases where the indorsement was necessary for the negotiation of the instrument, and would not apply to bearer instruments.

Clearly, a bank that honors a check bearing the forged signature of the drawer will have to replace the funds in the drawer's account, although the negligence of the drawer may be a factor in such cases. The bank is also liable if it cashes a check bearing the forged indorsement of the payee. Cases involving imposters, while related to matters of forgery, are handled differently under the Code and will be discussed in the next section of this chapter.

Incapacity. As we have seen, valid and binding contracts require competent parties, and not even commercial paper is entirely immune from this requirement. The Code distinguishes between infancy and other forms of incapacity. It provides that the defense of infancy may be asserted even against a holder in due course. The conflict between two policies, that of protecting infants and that of protecting holders in due course, is resolved in favor of protecting infants against those who may take advantage of them, although this may mean a loss to an innocent purchaser. The Code does not try to determine when infancy is to be available as a defense but leaves this wholly to the law of the local jurisdiction. The reader should review at this point the discussion of "competent parties" in the chapter on contracts. It makes no difference under the Code whether the effect of state law is to render infants' contracts void or simply voidable. In either case, infancy is available as a defense.

Mental incompetence, *ultra vires* acts of corporations, guardianship, and other kinds of incapacity are handled in a slightly different way by the Code. Although state law still controls, Code Section 3-305(2)(b) provides that the defense can be used against a holder in due course only where the effect of local law is to render the obligation entirely null and void. Where the effect is simply to render the obligation voidable, the defense is cut off.

Duress or illegality. The Code includes duress and illegality among the real defenses but leaves the details to state law. Again, however, the Code provides that the defense is available against a holder in due course only where the effect of local law is to render the obligation entirely void. Where the effect is only a voidable obligation, the defense is cut off. Not only are there degrees of duress and many varieties of illegality, but contracts involving these elements are treated differently from state to state. The law of one's own jurisdiction should be checked for details.

Material alteration. Any alteration is material if it changes the obligation of any party in any respect. Examples are: changes in the number or relations of the parties; completing an incomplete instrument otherwise than as authorized; changing the instrument after it is signed, either by adding to it or by removing any part of it. The most common type of alteration is found where the amount payable is raised to a greater sum than that originally stated in the instrument. An alteration is a real defense only to the extent of the alteration, and a holder in due course can enforce the instrument according to its original tenor. This result obtains whatever the nature of the alteration. When an incomplete instrument has been completed, a holder in due course may enforce it as completed, even if completed improperly. A holder who is not a holder in due course can enforce the completed instrument only to the extent of the authority given.

Although a holder in due course can enforce a materially altered instrument according to its original tenor, a holder who is not a holder in due course cannot enforce it even to that extent, because the party whose contract is changed is discharged from his obligation. However, it should be noted that a material alteration does not discharge any party unless its purpose was fraudulent and it was made by an actual holder of an instrument. A "meddling stranger" does not affect the rights of a holder, and there is no discharge where the alteration is made in the belief that it is authorized or made for some benevolent purpose. If not made by a holder and not fraudulent, the alteration does not affect the right of even the ordinary holder to enforce the instrument according to its original tenor. Thus, a material alteration is not even a personal defense under these circumstances, except as to the extent of the alteration.

The reader is again reminded that the negligence of a party may estop him to assert his defense of material alteration, as where the maker of a note or drawer of a check leaves large open spaces between numbers or words, which can easily be filled in to create larger amounts.

Discharge in insolvency proceedings. A person who has issued or otherwise become liable on a negotiable instrument may later be discharged in bankruptcy. The Code makes clear that the defense of discharge in bankruptcy is not cut off by the instrument's coming into the possession of a holder in due course. The Code uses language that goes beyond bankruptcy and includes all "insolvency proceedings" intended to liquidate or rehabilitate the estate of the person involved.

SUMMARY. The discussion above of real and personal defenses is not and is not intended to be a full discussion of these defenses or even to include all the possible defenses that might arise under these categories. All that is intended is that the discussion be enough to give the reader an understanding of the general nature of real and personal defenses and of the rights of a holder in due course. Those who wish greater detail should consult one of the exhaustive treatises on the subject of commercial paper.

RIGHTS OF ONE NOT A HOLDER IN DUE COURSE.   In a sense, the rights of a holder who is not a holder in due course are simply the other side of the coin that we have just examined. As a matter of fact, much space has already been devoted to the one who does not hold in due course. Because the Code devotes a special section to a summary of the rights of one not a holder in due course, however, it seems wise to comment briefly on a few of the matters raised in that section (Section 3-306). The Code states that unless a person has the rights of a holder in due course, he takes the instrument subject to

> (a) all valid claims to it on the part of any person; and (b) all defenses of any party which would be available in an action on a simple contract; and (c) the defenses of want or failure of consideration, non-performance of any condition precedent, non-delivery, or delivery for a special purpose; and (d) the defense that he or a person through whom he holds the instrument acquired it by theft, or that payment or satisfaction to such holder would be inconsistent with the terms of a restrictive indorsement.

Most of the issues raised in this section of the Code have already been discussed in connection with the personal defenses or elsewhere, but the effect of theft requires additional comment.

It is obvious that a person who acquired the instrument through his own theft could not be a holder in due course and would be subject to the defense of lack of title to the instrument if he tried to enforce it. In addition, however, it should be noted that the holder who is not a holder in due course is still subject to the defense, even though he was not the thief, if a person through whom he holds the instrument acquired it by theft. The purpose of the rule is clear. A proved thief should not be able to recover on the instrument nor should he be aided indirectly by permitting his transferee to recover unless, of course, the transferee is a holder in due course.

BURDEN OF PROOF.   Although it is a policy of this book not to devote much attention to technical issues of legal procedure, a small deviation from that policy at this point appears to be justified in the interests of clarity and understanding. There is a general presumption under the Code that a signature is genuine or authorized, except where the action is to enforce the obligation of a person who has died or become incompetent. Unless a defense is shown to exist, the holder need not establish that he is a holder in due course. The burden of establishing defenses is always on the defendant. If he has established a defense, the holder then has the burden of proving that he is a holder in due course or holds the instrument through a holder in due course.

5. LIABILITIES OF THE PARTIES

A. In General

The reader will recall the discussion in the chapter on contracts of the formal contract, where the words which appear on an actual document may reveal little or nothing of the terms of the contract involved. Custom, usage, and legal practice through the years have so formalized and simplified the language of some of these contracts that only an expert can describe all of their terms and provisions. A promissory note does reveal in part the obligation of one party, the maker, but discloses nothing of the nature of the commitment of payee or indorsers. Checks and other bills of exchange order someone other than the drawer to pay and reveal nothing about the obligations of any of the parties. As we know, however, promissory notes and bills of exchange have been in common use for centuries, and the basic contractual engagements of those who use these instruments have been, as a whole, well understood. One of the purposes of negotiable instruments, of course, is to minimize the need for extensive bargaining over specific terms and to encourage easy, routine procedures that do not require intimate knowledge on the part of those involved. This is not to say that persons who become parties to negotiable instruments need not bother their heads about the legal rules; in one sense, because the instruments themselves reveal very little, it may be even more important that the parties know something of the law. But it is to say that these instruments usually pass easily, frequently, and almost automatically through commercial channels whether the parties appreciate all the details of their undertakings or not.

It is already clear from earlier discussions that the obligations of the parties to negotiable instruments are not all the same. Although there are many different ways in which the parties could be classified with regard to their liability, the most useful way is based upon whether a party is absolutely liable or liable only after other events and conditions have occurred. The first category describes primary parties, who are absolutely liable, and the second category describes secondary parties, who are liable only on the occurrence of certain conditions precedent: presentment, notice of dishonor, and, where required, protest. These conditions will be discussed in the next section. Makers and acceptors are the primary parties, and drawers and indorsers are the secondary parties.

The Code states expressly that no person is liable on an instrument unless his signature appears thereon. Thus, a principal whose agent signs the instrument without indicating the name of the principal is not liable on the instrument although he may be liable, of course, on the original obligation for which the instrument was given. A person who negotiates a bearer instrument by delivery alone is not liable on the instrument. The Code also states that unless a signature is made in some other capacity, it is considered to be an indorsement. The indication that the signature is made in some other capacity must be clear without reference to anything but the instrument. Long usage has established that a signature in the lower right hand corner of an instrument indicates an intention to sign as a maker of a note or a drawer of a draft, but, in the absence of similar clear indication of intention, the signer will be treated as an indorser.

The question of the liability of an agent who signs for his principal is discussed in the chapter on agency. In order to avoid confusion and to make commercial practice more uniform, the Code deals specifically with the liability of authorized representatives in Section 3-403. A signature in the name of the principal only does not bind the agent, unless he was unauthorized. The liability of the unauthorized agent who signs his principal's name is an exception to the rule that only those whose signatures appear can be liable on the instrument. If the agent signs only his own name, he is personally liable and cannot introduce parol evidence to show his representative capacity. If the agent signs his own name, but the signature also discloses either the person represented or the representative capacity of the signing agent, as between the immediate parties, the agent may introduce parol evidence to prove the signature in his representative capacity. Uncertainty can easily be avoided by using the standard form "Tom Brown, by John Doe, Agent." Similar rules apply to signatures by corporate officers. Again, the standard form avoids trouble: "XYZ Corporation, by Bill Smith, President."

Under Code provisions, an unauthorized signature is wholly inoperative as the signature of the person whose name is signed, unless he ratifies it or is estopped to deny it. The unauthorized signer is personally liable, however, to anyone who in good faith pays the instrument or takes it for value. A forgery is an "unauthorized signature" under the Code. These matters have been discussed in detail above.

B. Primary Parties

MAKER. It seems obvious that the maker of a promissory note is the party primarily liable on the instrument. The basic, and only explicit, promise connected with the instrument is his promise to pay a certain sum on demand or at a definite time. Each party who takes the instrument, from the payee to the holder who presents it for payment, intends to look first to the maker, who has promised unconditionally to pay the instrument. The Code states that the liability of the maker is to pay the instrument according to its tenor at the time he signed it or, if it is issued as an incomplete instrument, as properly completed. In addition to promising to pay the instrument, the maker admits the existence of the payee and the capacity of the payee at the time of making the instrument to indorse. What this means is that the maker states that the payee is a person in existence who has legal capacity to make an indorsement which will pass title to the instrument to subsequent holders and bind the indorser to his liability as such. The maker cannot avoid liability by showing that the payee was a fictitious person or one lacking capacity to indorse.

ACCEPTOR. *In general.*   The liability of an acceptor is essentially the same as that of the maker. It should be noted, however, that a draft has no primary party until the drawee accepts the instrument, and, if the drawee does not accept, there is never a primary party. Once the instrument is accepted, the drawee becomes an acceptor and is obligated to pay the instrument according to its tenor at the time of acceptance. The acceptor makes the same admissions with regard to the existence and capacity of the payee that the maker does. He also admits the existence of the drawer, the genuineness of the drawer's signature, and the drawer's capacity and authority to draw the instrument. Thus, an acceptor of a draft, or check, on which the signature of the drawer has been forged will still be required to pay the instrument. A draft may be accepted although it has not been signed by the drawer, or is otherwise incomplete, or is overdue, or has been discharged. The drawee does not have to accept; if he does so, he is liable in spite of the deficiencies mentioned in the previous sentence.

It need not be emphasized that the question of when a drawee becomes an acceptor is an important one. Under the Code, an acceptance is not effective as such unless it is actually written on the draft. It may be by the signature alone and anywhere on the instrument, but the better practice is to write "accepted" across the face of the instrument followed by the signature of the drawee-acceptor. The acceptance is not complete until the instrument has been delivered to the person who presented it or that person has been notified of the acceptance. These rules eliminate a very confused and illogical situation under the old Uniform Law where acceptances could be accomplished on separate instruments or even by the conduct of the drawee. The drawee may still incur contract or tort liability as a result of engagements on other documents or of his conduct, but he does not become an acceptor unless he accepts by an appropriate writing on the instrument itself.

Where the drawee in his purported acceptance in any way alters the draft as presented, the holder may refuse the acceptance and treat the draft as dishonored. The drawee is a debtor who is obligated to obey in full the order of the drawer. By refusing to accept or by qualifying his acceptance he may be breaching his contract with the drawer. If the holder chooses to take the varied or altered acceptance, the drawer and the indorsers are usually discharged from their liability unless they consent to the new terms. Fortunately, acceptances varying the draft are not common.

Certification of checks.   It is usually not anticipated or intended that checks will be accepted, but when a bank does accept a check in order that it may go on to further circulation, such acceptance is called a *certification*. Because a check is not intended in most cases to be accepted or certified by the bank, the refusal of the bank to do so does not constitute a dishonor. Of course, the opposite is true of the ordinary draft. All of what has been said above with regard to drafts is equally applicable under the Code to certifications. The bank becomes the primary party, and its liability is the same as that of an acceptor. The bank admits the genuineness of the drawer's signature, that the drawer's account contains enough funds to pay the check, and that the money will not be withdrawn. Actually, the certification itself acts as an appropriation of funds in the drawer's account to the extent needed to pay the check, and these funds are usually set aside for the purpose of paying the check when it is finally presented.

When the drawer himself has the check certified before issuing it, his act provides additional security but does not alter his own liability. On the other hand, if the holder of the instrument procures certification from the bank, he indicates that he is looking to the bank as the only party liable on the instrument; the drawer and all prior indorsers are released from liability.

C. Secondary Parties

IN GENERAL. Most commercial paper is drawn, issued, negotiated, presented for payment, and paid without ever raising any issues having to do with secondary parties. Most makers and acceptors pay their instruments when due, as was their intention when they assumed the role of primary parties. Were this not the usual result, commercial paper would not be in common use. Two matters should be noted, however, in connection with negotiable instruments and with their progress through the channels of commerce. First, not all makers and acceptors do or can pay their instruments when they become due, and, if they do not pay, recourse must be had, if at all, against other parties. Second, the availability of recourse against other parties, in the abnormal situation when the primary parties do not perform their engagements, is one of the characteristics of negotiable instruments that make it possible for such documents to circulate with almost the same general acceptability as money. In most cases, then, the liability of the secondary parties becomes important only when the primary parties have failed to keep their promises.

The liability imposed upon the secondary parties is actually of two sorts, the drawer being subject to one sort, the qualified indorser to the other, and the unqualified indorser to both. The first kind of liability is the *contract liability* of the drawer and the unqualified indorser; this kind of liability is avoided by the qualified indorser. Although all liability of secondary parties is, in a sense, conditioned on the failure of the primary parties, contract liability is often described as "conditional" liability, in reference to certain formal conditions precedent which must occur before this kind of liability may be imposed. These formal conditions are presentment, notice of dishonor, and, where required, protest; they will be discussed in detail in the next section of this chapter. Contract liability results when a person affixes his name to a negotiable instrument and becomes a party to the many contractual engagements involved therein. In addition to its role as written evidence of a number of contracts, however, the negotiable instrument is also a kind of property and is subject to sale. As we know, certain implied warranties attach to the sale of chattels. For the same reasons and in much the same way, certain implied warranties are involved in the sale of a negotiable instrument. This *warranty liability* is the other kind of liability imposed on the secondary parties. Because the drawer is not "selling" the instrument he creates, he is not subject to these warranties. Because an indorser is a "seller," even though he indorses "without recourse," he *is* subject to them.

DRAWER.   The drawer is a secondary party and, as such, does not engage unconditionally to pay the instrument. His obligation is to pay the instrument only if it is dishonored on presentment and he receives notice of the dishonor. He can avoid even this obligation if he signs "without recourse," but drawers rarely do so, for the reason that such a signature would usually seriously impair the acceptability of the instrument. The fact that a drawer normally signs an instrument in the same location used by the maker of a promissory note is wholly irrelevant as far as his liability is concerned. In addition to his basic contract liability, the drawer makes the same two admissions with regard to the payee that are made by the maker and acceptor: that the payee exists and has the capacity to indorse the instrument. For obvious reasons, indorsers do not make these admissions.

INDORSER'S CONTRACT LIABILITY.   Like the drawer, the unqualified indorser promises to pay the instrument according to its tenor at the time of his indorsement, if it is dishonored and he has received any necessary notice. Where words of qualification are used, the indorser is relieved of this liability. The Code, incidentally, does not use the terms "qualified" and "unqualified," but these terms are useful ways of describing two distinct kinds of indorsements, and the Code rules with regard to them are the same as in precode law. The indorser's contract liability rises out of the fact that a negotiable instrument is written evidence of a group of contracts to which a number of persons, including the indorser, have agreed to become parties. If negotiable instruments were simple contracts, the terms of the contracts would be set forth in the agreement. Being formal contracts, however, the terms of negotiable instruments do not themselves usually appear in the writing nor are they a conscious part of the transactions between the parties.

INDORSER'S WARRANTY LIABILITY.   In addition to his contract liability, the indorser, as a seller of property, incurs certain implied warranty liability. The Uniform Commercial Code distinguishes between two different kinds of indorsers' warranties: warranties on transfer and warranties on presentment. The former are given by one who transfers the instrument, while the presentment warranties are made *by* a party who receives payment or obtains acceptance of an instrument *to* a party who pays or accepts. It will be recalled that no person is subject to contract liability on an instrument unless his signature appears thereon. This requirement of a signature does not apply to warranty liability. The explanation for the difference in treatment is simply that a person will not be held to the terms of a negotiable instruments contract which he has not signed, but may be held to warranty liability, which rises, not out of the terms of the contract, but out of public policy and duties imposed by law.

Although there is usually considerable overlap, warranty liability does not exactly coincide with contract liability growing out of an indorsement. One obvious difference, already noted, is that a qualified indorser escapes the contract liability but is still subject to certain warranty liabilities. Furthermore, damages for breach of warranty may be less than damages for breach of the contract itself, and, as will be seen below, the liability in warranty may run to a smaller group of parties than does the contract liability.

Transfer warranties. Only a person who transfers an instrument and receives consideration is subject to the warranty liability. If he transfers by delivery only, his warranty runs only to his immediate transferee; if he transfers by indorsement, his obligation runs to any subsequent holder who takes the instrument in good faith. The requirement of good faith prevents a holder who had knowledge of defects when he bought the instrument from benefiting from the warranty. Precode law was very confused on this point, and some courts held that the warranties ran only to holders in due course.

The Code lists and describes in detail the warranties that are given by a transferor. The same warranties, with one exception, apply whether the transfer is by delivery or indorsement and whether the indorsement is qualified or unqualified. These transfer warranties, set forth in Section 3-417(2), are as follows: The transferor warrants that

> (a) he has good title to the instrument or is authorized to obtain payment or acceptance on behalf of one who has a good title and the transfer is otherwise rightful; and (b) all signatures are genuine or authorized; and (c) the instrument has not been materially altered; and (d) no defense of any party is good against him; and (e) he has no knowledge of any insolvency proceedings instituted with respect to the maker or acceptor or the drawer of an unaccepted instrument.

The one exception to the uniform application of these warranties to all transferors is (d) above. The Code states that a qualified indorser limits his obligation to a warranty that he "has no knowledge" of such a defense. The theory is that the "without recourse" indorsement should, in addition to disclaiming general contract liability, warn the transferee that he cannot expect anything but minimum warranties. Note that the Code imposes full warranty liability under subsection (d) even on transferors by delivery. There is some doubt whether this result is proper, on the ground that the mere transferor has usually, and for good reason, been treated the same as the qualified indorser. The explanation for the Code rule is not clear.

The Code states that a selling agent or broker who does not disclose his representative capacity gives all of the warranties listed above. If he does make disclosure that he is acting only as a representative, his warranty includes simply his good faith and authority. This result is consistent with an agent's usual warranty of authority discussed in the chapter on agency.

Presentment warranties.   The usual situation in which warranties on presentment become relevant occurs where a payor or acceptor pays an instrument on which a signature later turns out to be forged or where a material alteration has taken place. A drawee bank which pays a check on which the drawer's signature has been forged, for example, cannot charge the payment to the drawer's account and will be most anxious to shift its loss to the party who receives the payment or to some other party. The Code provides that any person who obtains payment or acceptance and any prior transferor warrants to the payor or acceptor that 1, he has a good title to the instrument or is authorized to obtain payment or acceptance on behalf of one who has a good title; and 2, he has no knowledge that the signature of the maker or drawer is unauthorized; and 3, the instrument has not been materially altered. Note that our bank example is covered by 2. The bank cannot charge back against the party receiving payment or any prior transferor unless that party had knowledge of the forgery at the time he presented or transferred. If the forgery had been of an indorsement instead of the drawer's signature, the bank could have recovered from the person receiving payment or any prior transferor without any knowledge on their part of the forgery. The justification for the distinction between forgery of the signature of the drawer and forgery of an indorsement is that the drawee is in a position to verify the drawer's signature by comparison with others in his possession, but usually has no means or opportunity to verify an indorsement. The remedy of the payor or acceptor, where available, is to recover on the breach of warranty.

The reader should recall at this point that no title passes by a forged indorsement, and a person who is in possession of such an instrument has no right to keep money paid to him. His lack of knowledge of the forgery is irrelevant. The party whose name was forged may recover from the party receiving payment or from the payor. The party who paid or accepted may recover the payment or avoid the acceptance.

A moment of reflection reveals that there are certain situations where the rules discussed above with regard to the presentment warranties should not apply. A holder in due course acting in good faith, for example, should not be held to warrant to a maker that he has no knowledge that the maker's own signature is unauthorized, or to a drawer with respect to the drawer's own signature. By the same token, a holder in due course should not be held to warrant to an acceptor that he has no knowledge that the drawer's signature is unauthorized, if the holder took the draft after acceptance or if he obtained the acceptance without knowledge that the drawer's signature was forged. The Code provides specifically for these exceptions.

A person who pays a materially altered instrument can recover the amount in excess of the original tenor of the instrument, and an acceptor can avoid his acceptance. Again, however, the warranty that the instrument has not been materially altered is not imposed on a holder in due course in favor of a maker or drawer. The reason is obvious: These parties are presumed to know what the terms of the instrument were when they issued it. The Code also provides that a holder in due course does not make this warranty to an acceptor with respect to an alteration made prior to acceptance if the holder took the instrument after acceptance, or to an acceptor with respect to an alteration made after acceptance. The reason for these latter rules is that the holder relied in good faith on the acceptance of an instrument materially altered before acceptance. In the case of alteration after acceptance, the acceptor could have checked his prior records before making payment.

Disclaimer of warranties. Both transfer warranties and presentment warranties may be disclaimed by agreement between the immediate parties. The Code contains no specific language on this point, but the Official Comment approves this view, apparently rejecting a contrary view that warranties imposed by law cannot be disclaimed.

ORDER OF INDORSER'S LIABILITY. Unless they otherwise agree, indorsers are liable to one another in the order in which they indorse, which is presumed to be the order in which their signatures appear on the instrument.

D. Anomalous Parties

IN GENERAL. Most parties to whose liability the law of commercial paper is relevant fall into one of the categories discussed above: makers, acceptors, drawers, and indorsers. Occasionally, however, a person will place his name on an instrument or authorize the placing of his name thereon, not as an original party or as a holder or transferee holding title to the instrument, but as one who is lending his name and credit to another person. Such a person is known as an *accommodation party*. On other occasions, a real party to the instrument, like a maker or indorser, will add to his signature language which may make his capacity ambiguous or appear to alter the nature of his liability. A common example is an indorser who adds to his signature the words "payment guaranteed" or "collection guaranteed." The indorser, in this case, is known as a *guarantor*. There are other kinds of ambiguous signatures and anomalous parties, but only these two merit discussion here.

An accommodation party makes it possible for another person to obtain credit under circumstances where he might not otherwise be able to do so or may enhance the value of the instrument and facilitate its further negotiation.

A person who signs as a guarantor usually does so in order to strengthen the value of the instrument by adding his own guaranty to that of the primary parties. Precode law was confused and unclear on some aspects of the liability of these anomalous parties, and the courts produced some paradoxical decisions. The Code substantially improves the clarity of the rules and removes the troublesome paradoxes.

ACCOMMODATION PARTY.   Section 3-415 of the Code defines an accommodation party as one who "signs the instrument in any capacity for the purpose of lending his name to another party" to the instrument. He is, in effect, promising to assume the liability or pay the debt of another person. A person who makes this kind of promise is called a *surety*. (The law of suretyship is discussed in Chapter 13.) When a surety signs a negotiable instrument, the law of suretyship comes into contact with the law of negotiable instruments. The two are not always consistent. The rights and defenses of a surety, for example, may be different from the rights and defenses of parties to negotiable instruments. This problem was a major source of difficulty under precode law. The Code spells out in considerable detail the rules governing accommodation parties. The more important elements are discussed below.

The Code recognizes the suretyship character of accommodation signatures and concedes the availability of certain suretyship defenses. The nature of the obligation of an accommodation party is determined by the capacity in which he signs. An accommodation maker or acceptor, therefore, is liable on the instrument in the same fashion as a primary party and must pay it even though the person presenting the instrument has not first proceeded against the party being accommodated. If X "cosigns" a note as an accommodation for the real maker, X must pay the person who presents the instrument when due. On the other hand, an accommodation party who signs as an indorser is liable only after the usual conditions precedent: presentment, notice of dishonor, and protest. If an accommodation party pays an instrument, he possesses his suretyship rights against the party accommodated, including exoneration, reimbursement, contribution, and subrogation. An accommodation party is not liable to the party accommodated.

The accommodation party may introduce oral evidence to show his accommodation status and the availability of defenses resulting from that status except against a holder in due course without notice of the accommodation. An important example of such a defense would be the discharge of the accommodation party if the time of payment is extended without his consent. The Code states specifically that any indorsement which shows that it is not in the chain of title is notice of its accommodation character. Eliminated by the Code is a requirement of the old Uniform Law that a person cannot be an accommodation party if he received value for his signing.

GUARANTOR.   A party to a negotiable instrument may add to his signature certain words of guaranty. If the sole maker or acceptor uses phrases such as "payment guaranteed," his liability is not affected in any way. The reason is that he is just stating what is already the case. Where one of several makers or acceptors uses words of guaranty, the Code creates a presumption that his signature is for the accommodation of the others. It is difficult to imagine any other explanation. Words of guaranty are used most often by indorsers of promissory notes, and, in that connection, their use has an important effect: the indorser becomes liable as a co-maker. He promises that he will pay the instrument when due, according to its tenor, and without the holder's having first presented the instrument to the maker. Occurrence of the conditions precedent is not necessary.

Although the liability of the guarantor is the same as that of co-maker, he is still considered by the Code to be an indorser. The reason for this is to make it possible for the transferee from the guarantor to become a holder in due course. If the guarantor is held not to have intended to indorse, his transferee cannot be a holder or a holder in due course.

An indorser who adds "collection guaranteed" or equivalent words to his signature makes a different sort of engagement than the indorser who guarantees payment. He still waives presentment and the other conditions precedent, but the holder must first proceed against the maker or acceptor and reduce his claim to judgment. If the judgment is returned unsatisfied, meaning that the primary party has no property from which the judgment can be paid, the holder may then collect from the guarantor. If, however, the maker or acceptor is insolvent, or it is otherwise apparent that it is useless to proceed against him, the holder is excused from the requirement of reducing his claim to judgment. Words of guaranty which are neither expressly of "collection" nor of "payment" are said by the Code to guarantee payment.

E. Conversion

Under the old Uniform Law, a drawee to whom a draft was delivered for acceptance who refused to return the draft was deemed to have accepted it. As we have seen, the Code rejected this unrealistic approach to the problem. Similar problems arise where any party refuses to pay or return an instrument presented to him for payment. In both situations, the Code treats the refusal of the drawee or other party as a conversion of the instrument and also treats the payment of an instrument which contains a forged indorsement as a conversion of property belonging to the person whose signature was forged. A *conversion* is simply an unauthorized exercise of ownership rights over the property of another person. In general law, the person whose property is converted has an action in tort for damages resulting from the conversion, and the same is true of negotiable instruments. The action is not on the instrument but for damages. The measure of liability is presumed to be the face amount of the instrument, but evidence is admissible to show that, owing to insolvency or other reasons, the obligation is worth less than the face amount. In the case of the drawee, however, the liability is absolute.

F. Imposters

A group of situations, related in some degree to forgery, conversion, and fraud, issues elsewhere discussed, have been singled out for special treatment by the Code in order to eliminate the effects of a confusing history under precode law. A maker or drawer, for example, intends an instrument to be payable to a certain named payee, but an imposter represents himself to be that named payee and has the instrument issued to himself; or an employee who is authorized to sign his employer's name on checks or to draw checks for his employer's signature makes the checks payable to real or fictitious persons whose names the employee himself plans to indorse in order to cash the checks. Ordinary civil and criminal liability is of importance in these cases but is of no particular interest to the law of negotiable instruments. Our primary concern is with the question of whether the imposter's indorsement or the indorsement of the dishonest employee is effective to negotiate the instrument or, to put the same question in another way, of who is to bear the loss.

The Code answers the question by making the indorsements effective to pass title and, thus, imposes the loss on the maker or drawer. Precode law came to the same result but by a different train of reasoning. The Code removes an unfounded precode distinction between two kinds of imposters. Under the Code, three basic situations are described. The first is where an imposter, by the use of the mails, face-to-face, or otherwise, induces the maker or drawer to issue an instrument to him or to his confederate in the name of the payee. The second describes a situation where a person signing as or on behalf of a maker or drawer intends the payee to have no interest in the instrument. This situation covers the employee who is authorized to sign for his employer and who names payees whom he does not intend to have an interest in the instrument. The third Code situation is where an agent or employee of the maker or drawer supplies him with the name of a payee not intending that payee to have an interest. Here the employee is not authorized to sign the instruments for his employer, but he is permitted to draw the instruments and name the payees.

All three situations are treated alike under the Code. The indorsements are effective, and the maker or drawer must bear the loss. The reason for resolving the doubts in this direction is simply that the maker or drawer is in a better position than some subsequent holder or a drawee to protect against this dishonest behavior or to insure against potential losses resulting therefrom. In short, impersonations and padded payrolls provide only a personal defense for maker or drawer.

6. CONDITIONS PRECEDENT: PRESENTMENT, NOTICE OF DISHONOR, AND PROTEST

A. In General

The contract liability of secondary parties, as we have seen, usually depends upon the occurrence of certain conditions precedent: presentment, notice of dishonor, and, occasionally, a formal type of notice called "protest." Actually, dishonor is a necessary condition precedent also, but the requirement of notice of dishonor obviously embraces the dishonor itself. Unless a secondary party has waived the conditions precedent, a subject to which we will turn at the end of this section, he is not liable on the instrument until the conditions have been performed. Primary parties, of course, are unconditionally liable, protected only by the possibility of real or personal defenses. It must be remembered, however, that the failure of the conditions precedent does not wholly relieve the secondary party of liability, because his warranty liability, in the case of an indorser, is not affected by the conditions, and because he may be liable, in some cases, on the underlying obligation itself.

In stressing the fact that a secondary party is not liable until the conditions precedent have been performed, there is no intention to suggest a preoccupation on the part of the law with the rights of secondary parties. Our topic would be just as accurately described if we were to say that a holder cannot collect on the instrument from a secondary party until he has duly presented the instrument to the maker or acceptor for payment, had it refused, and given proper notice of the refusal to the secondary party, unless these conditions are waived or excused. In addition, it must be said that the failure of a holder to present an instrument properly to the maker or acceptor for payment may actually discharge the secondary parties and cut off the holder's recourse to them if the primary party does not pay the instrument.

The Code does not materially alter the rules applicable to the conditions precedent, but it does simplify and clarify them. In keeping with the basic policy of the Code, the rules are essentially uncomplicated and clear.

B. Presentment

IN GENERAL. The concept of presentment is not a particularly difficult one. It contemplates that the instrument will be exhibited at the proper time, in the proper manner, and at the proper place to the person who is supposed to pay it or accept it. In order to encourage and preserve the easy, routine use of negotiable instruments in commercial channels, it is necessary that the basic procedures associated with those instruments be performed properly, uniformly, and in a timely fashion. The whole system would collapse if parties could present instruments or not, as they pleased, or ignore the due dates and other terms of the contracts. Secondary parties would be very reluctant to accept even conditional liability in such an uncertain environment. Consequently, the rules with regard to presentment, and the other conditions precedent, are strict but easy to comply with.

Circumstances require a distinction between presentment for acceptance and presentment for payment. Presentment for acceptance has no relevance for promissory notes, but is usually required with drafts. Drawees are not bound as primary parties on drafts until they have accepted; thus holders will usually seek acceptance at the earliest possible moment in order to enhance the salability of the instrument during its term. Presentment for payment applies to both notes and drafts and is necessary in order to charge secondary parties.

PRESENTMENT FOR ACCEPTANCE.   Some drafts must be presented for acceptance; some may be; and some cannot be. A draft *must* be presented for acceptance in any of the following situations: 1, where presentment is necessary to fix the maturity of the instrument, as in the case of an instrument made payable "thirty days after sight;" an instrument so worded would be payable thirty days after the holder presented it to the drawee; 2, where the instrument expressly provides that it shall be presented for acceptance; and 3, where the instrument is made payable elsewhere than at the residence or place of business of the drawee. The reason for requiring presentment for acceptance in the last instance is that the drawee has no way of knowing that he is supposed to pay at a different place until he has seen the draft. The convenience of a party is often the explanation for making an instrument payable elsewhere than at the drawee's residence or place of business.

In all other situations, drafts *may* be presented for acceptance, if they are payable at a stated date. Thus, a holder may present an instrument for acceptance at any time before its date of maturity, but he is not required to do so. Reasons for presenting are clear, but it should be noted that if a holder does present a time draft for acceptance, and acceptance is refused, he must treat the instrument as dishonored, which means that he cannot safely negotiate it further. The holder, however, has an immediate right to proceed against the drawer and the indorsers and does not have to present the draft for payment, but he must, of course, satisfy the other conditions precedent. Demand drafts (payable "on demand" or "at sight") *cannot* be presented for acceptance, or, to put it more accurately, the holder of such a draft does not have the right to present it for acceptance. A demand draft entitles the holder to immediate payment, and the parties do not contemplate that it will ever be presented for acceptance.

PRESENTMENT FOR PAYMENT.   Promissory notes, accepted drafts, and time drafts which the holder has elected not to present for acceptance must be presented for payment in order to charge the secondary parties. If due presentment is not made, the secondary parties are discharged. However, the Code extends a precode rule—previously applicable only to drawers of checks

—to *all* drawers, to acceptors of drafts payable at a bank, and to makers of notes payable at a bank. The earlier rule provided that while the drawer of a draft was completely discharged by the failure of a holder to make timely presentment (see discussion below of "time of presentment"), the drawer of a check was discharged only to the extent of the injury he suffered as a result of the failure. A holder of a check, for example, delays in presenting the check to the bank for payment; during the delay, the bank fails; if the drawer recovers forty cents on each dollar of his account, he is discharged from his liability on the untimely-presented check only as to the sixty cents on the dollar which he lost as a result of the delay.

Section 3-501 of the Code extends this rule to the other parties mentioned above. Indorsers are still discharged as before. Where makers and acceptors, being primary parties, were not discharged at all under precode law by delay in presentment, the Code now discharges such parties to the extent of the loss caused by delay, *if* their instruments were made payable at a bank. Note that this change in the law gives the liability of primary parties, under some circumstances, part of the attributes of secondary liability, namely, a condition precedent of due presentment. There is some controversy among the experts over the justification for the new Code rules. In commercial parlance, instruments made payable at a bank are called "bank-domiciled" instruments.

The effect of the changes discussed in the previous paragraph is somewhat mitigated by the requirement that the party claiming the discharge is discharged only if he maintained with the drawee or bank sufficient funds to cover the instrument, and if the drawee or bank became insolvent during the delay, and if the party makes a written assignment to the holder of the instrument of his rights against the drawee or bank in respect of such funds.

How Presentment Is Made. Modifying in some respects the precode law, the Code provides that any demand upon a party to pay is a presentment no matter where or how made. It is not even necessary that the instrument itself be exhibited, but the party required to pay may insist upon it. Presentment may be made by mail, through a clearing house, or even by telephone. The place is usually immaterial. The one exception to the rule that presentment can be made at any place occurs where a draft is accepted or a note is made payable at a bank. Presentment must be made at such bank. Where an instrument is made payable at a specified place, presentment may still be made at any place, but the party to whom presentment is made may require that presentment be made at the specified place. If no place is specified, the instrument may be presented at the residence or place of business of the party who is to accept or pay it. If neither the party expected to accept or pay nor anyone authorized to act for him is present or accessible at such place, presentment is excused. Although the Code is very liberal with regard to the mode and place of presentment, the party to whom presentment is made is protected against being imposed on by a holder who presents at an odd or inconvenient place or does not exhibit the instrument. The party to whom presentment is made may without dishonor require that the instrument be exhibited, that reasonable identification or authorization of the person making presentment of either bearer or order paper be proffered, and that the instrument be produced at a place specified in the instrument or, if there be none specified, at any place reasonable in the circumstances. Failure of the holder to comply with any of these requirements invalidates the presentment, but the holder has a reasonable time during which to comply. With rare exceptions, however, presentment is made at the primary party's place of business.

The Code also states to whom presentment is to be made. Where there are two or more makers, acceptors, drawees, or other payors, presentment may be made to any one of these. Precode law required presentment to each one, but this rule appeared to be inconsistent with the usual expectation of holders that any primary party will pay or accept. Presentment may be made to any person who has authority to make or refuse the acceptance or payment.

TIME OF PRESENTMENT.   The basic rules having to do with the time of presentment are very simple and very obvious. Unless the instrument sets forth a different time, an instrument payable at a stated date or a fixed period after a stated date must be presented for *acceptance* on or before the date it is payable. Instruments payable at a stated date must be presented for *payment* on the stated date. Other rules are somewhat more involved. Instruments payable after sight must either be presented for acceptance or negotiated within a reasonable time after the date of the instrument or the date of issue, whichever is later. Accelerated instruments must be presented for payment within a reasonable time after acceleration, which is sensible, but the rule does not apply to a holder in due course who does not have notice of the acceleration at the time he takes the instrument. With respect to the liability of any secondary party, presentment for acceptance or for payment of any demand instrument must be made within a reasonable time after such party becomes liable thereon. This rule applies equally to notes and drafts and is designed to prevent demand paper from being negotiated indefinitely.

Because a "reasonable time" is the standard of measurement in all the rules mentioned in the preceding paragraph, the Code lays down the principles by which "reasonable time" is to be determined. The nature of the instrument, usages of banking or trade, and the facts of the case are the controlling factors in all situations except those of the uncertified check. The Code lays down specific presumptions in connection with the presentment for payment or the initiation of collection of that instrument. With respect to the liability of the drawer, a reasonable time is presumed to be thirty days after the date of the check or the date of its issue, whichever is later. It will be recalled that this is the same period during which a purchaser of a check may still become a holder in due course. With respect to the liability of an indorser of an uncertified check, the Code specifies a period of seven days after his indorsement. Note that the liability of drawer and the liability of indorser are measured from different times, so it is possible that the drawer's liability may expire before that of the indorser.

The Code takes into account the fact that banks and businesses are closed on certain days each week and on holidays and provides that any presentment which is due on a day which is not a full business day for either the presenting party or the party to accept or pay becomes due on the next day which is a full business day for both parties. Presentment must be made at a reasonable hour and, if at a bank, during regular banking hours. If made by mail, presentment is effective when the mail is received.

C. Dishonor, Notice of Dishonor, and Protest

IN GENERAL.   Although dishonor is itself one of the conditions precedent to the liability of secondary parties, it is usually discussed in connection with the notice of dishonor. Section 3-507 of the Code states that an instrument is dishonored when proper presentment is made and payment or acceptance is refused or when presentment is excused and the instrument is not accepted or paid. The return of an instrument for lack of a proper indorsement is not a dishonor.

The question of how much time a party to whom an instrument is presented has to accept or pay it often becomes an issue. Code Section 3-506 supplies simpler and more sensible rules than those in use under precode law. Acceptance may be deferred without dishonor until the close of the next business day following presentment, and the holder may, in a good faith effort to obtain acceptance and without either dishonor of the instrument or discharge of secondary parties, allow postponement of acceptance for an additional business day. With certain exceptions, including an earlier time agreed to by the party to pay, "payment of an instrument may be deferred without dishonor pending reasonable examination to determine whether it is properly payable, but payment must be made in any event before the close of the next business day following the day of presentment." Even the choice of words in the Code manifests a dual concern for the protection of secondary parties and for the avoidance of unnecessary and precipitous dishonors.

Some drafts and indorsements on drafts expressly allow a stated time for re-presentment in the event of a dishonor of the draft by nonacceptance, if a time draft, or by nonpayment, if a sight draft. Ordinarily, a dishonor gives the holder an immediate right of recourse against secondary parties, subject to necessary notice or protest, but re-presentment provisions *permit* the holder to present the instrument again if it is dishonored the first time. The first dishonor is waived, in effect, without discharging secondary parties who are bound by the provision for re-presentment.

NOTICE OF DISHONOR.   When an instrument is dishonored, the holder must give prompt notice thereof to secondary parties. The purpose of the notice is obvious. It tells secondary parties that the maker, drawee, or acceptor has failed to pay or accept and informs the secondary parties that they will be required to make payment on the instrument. Section 3-508 states that notice of dishonor may be given *to* any person who may be liable on the instrument *by* or on behalf of the holder or any party who has himself received notice, or any other party who can be compelled to pay the instrument. This section considerably broadens a precode rule that limited the secondary parties who could give notice to those who had a right of reimbursement against the notified party.

The notice may be given in any reasonable manner, including oral as well as written, as long as it is in terms which identify the instrument and state that it has been dishonored. A misdescription of the instrument which does not mislead the party notified is still effective as a notice of dishonor. The instrument itself is sometimes used as the notice and is effective as such if it contains a stamp, ticket, or writing which states that the instrument has been refused acceptance or payment. Except for banks, notice must be given before midnight of the third business day following dishonor or receipt of notice of dishonor. Banks must give notice before midnight of the next banking day following dishonor or receipt of notice. Written notice is effective when sent, although it is not received.

Notice of dishonor operates for the benefit of all parties who have rights on the instrument against the party notified. It is not necessary that everybody notify everybody. One notice is enough to charge the party notified, without regard to who gave notice or who seeks recourse against that party. Notice is sufficient if it is sent to the last known address of a deceased or incompetent person, and notice given to one partner is notice to all the partners. A holder who has presented an instrument and had it dishonored may notify only the indorser from whom he purchased the instrument, who will notify the next prior indorser, and so on. Normally, a holder will notify all the secondary parties he can reach conveniently.

Proper notice of dishonor, following presentment and dishonor, charges with liability on the instrument those secondary parties who were given notice. With the exception of drafts drawn or payable outside the United States, nothing more is necessary.

PROTEST.   The old Uniform Law required the formal act of "protest" where a draft was drawn in one state and payable in another, but the Code has eliminated that requirement. Only where the draft is drawn or payable outside the United States is protest necessary. Unlike notice of dishonor, protest is highly formal: "a certificate of dishonor made under the hand and seal of a United States consul" or other official authorized to certify dishonor by the law of the place where the dishonor occurs. Protest is a separate and distinct condition precedent and does not remove the necessity for notice of dishonor.

The purpose of protest, essentially, is to provide evidence of dishonor. While required in connection with international drafts, the protest *may* be used with any instrument. Under the Code, however, there is no particular reason to do so, as the proof of dishonor and notice of dishonor are greatly simplified in comparison with precode law. The Code, in Section 3-509, sets forth the requirements for proper protest.

D. Waiver, Excuse, and Delay

The Code takes cognizance of the fact that performance of one or more of the conditions precedent is sometimes made impossible or useless by the circumstances of the case. Consistent with its policy of simplifying and facilitating the use of commercial paper, the Code, in Section 3-511, spells out these circumstances. Distinction is made between situations where failure to comply with the requirements is excused only while the causes of failure are still in operation and those situations where the failure is entirely excused.

Delay in presentment, notice of dishonor, or protest, for example, is excused when the party is without notice that one or more of those acts is due, as where there has been an acceleration without a holder's knowledge. Delay caused by other circumstances beyond a holder's control will also be excused. These excuses are only temporary in nature, however, and the holder must act diligently after the cause of delay ceases to operate. He would, in the acceleration example, be expected to make prompt presentment when he learned of the acceleration.

If the secondary party to be charged has waived the conditions precedent, either expressly or by implication, they are entirely excused, and it makes no difference whether the waiver occurred before or after the performance of the conditions became due. The conditions are for the protection of the secondary parties, and such parties cannot be heard to complain if they are injured or inconvenienced by their own waivers. Where a waiver is written in the body of the instrument, it is binding upon all parties. If it is written above the signature of an indorser, it binds him alone.

Conditions precedent are also excused entirely where the party to be charged has himself dishonored the instrument or, for any other reason, could not really expect or have any right to require that the instrument be accepted or paid. The same result obtains where a holder, after reasonable diligence, was unable to make presentment or protest or give notice. If a holder reasonably believes that payment is an impossibility because the primary party is dead or in insolvency proceedings, presentment is excused; he may proceed against the secondary parties immediately, leaving it to them to file claim against the estate of the deceased or insolvent party. If a holder has presented an instrument for acceptance and the instrument is dishonored, it is not necessary that he make a later presentment for payment, and notice of dishonor and protest for nonpayment are excused, unless the instrument has, in the meantime, been accepted. If it has been determined that a primary party will not pay an instrument other than for lack of proper presentment, presentment is excused. It will be recalled that an indorser who adds words of guaranty to his indorsement waives the conditions precedent, in effect, and becomes liable as a co-maker.

7. DISCHARGE

A. In General

Discharge of a party or a contract or an instrument is simply a way of saying that a party is released from his obligations or that a contract or instrument no longer has any binding effect, as where it has been completely performed. Frequent use has been made of the term in this chapter and in the chapter on contracts. Because of some confusion under precode law with regard to the nature and effect of discharge in connection with negotiable instruments, the Code devotes several sections to clarification and review of the subject.

Probably the most important context in which the term is used is that of a defense by a party to a negotiable instrument who has been released from his obligation. Where there has been an unexcused delay in presentment or notice of dishonor, for example, an indorser is discharged and may so defend himself if a holder pursues him for payment. Discharge, as is obvious from earlier discussions, is only a personal defense and is cut off by a holder in due course. It is not often necessary to make this point, however, because the very nature of most acts of discharge prevents a subsequent holder from becoming a holder in due course. Payment discharges the parties, and the payor normally acquires and destroys the instrument. Even if he does not, time paper would be past due on its face, and a holder could not become a holder in due course. The same is not true of demand paper, however, and such paper could come into the hands of a holder in due course even after payment, and this would cut off the defense. Similarly, a canceled instrument is usually plainly so marked on its face, but it may not be, and could come into the hands of a holder without notice of the cancellation.

The purpose of our brief discussion of discharge here is not to review all the causes of discharge but only to examine some of the more important or more troublesome situations not already examined, where discharge may become an issue. Sections 3-601 to 3-606 of the Code contain the new language on the subject. The Code takes the view that one should not speak of the discharge of the instrument itself, because it is only a piece of paper, and that the term should be used only in reference to a party or parties to the instrument. The Code distinguishes between discharges of a single party and discharges of all the parties. Our discussion will recognize the distinction but will be organized around the methods of discharge.

B. Methods of Discharge

PAYMENT OR SATISFACTION.   There is no need to emphasize that a party is discharged from liability on an instrument to the extent of his payment or satisfaction to the holder, and the discussion of most situations can be terminated with that. Suppose, however, that the payor knows that a third party has a claim on the instrument; can he safely pay the presenting holder or must he wait until the adverse claim is settled? Precode law provided no satisfactory answer. The Code resolves the problem by providing that the payor can safely pay the holder if he acts in good faith and if he pays a restrictively indorsed instrument in a manner consistent with the indorsement. The adverse claimant is protected by his right to stop the payment by court action or to supply the payor with indemnity against double liability. In either event, the payor is safe in refusing to pay the holder.

TENDER OF PAYMENT.   Occasionally, a holder will fail to present an instrument for payment at or after the date of maturity and may refuse payment when tendered by the payor. Among the motives for such behavior may be that of prolonging the interest payments. Under the Code, however, tender of full payment discharges all subsequent liability for interest, costs, and attorney's fees, and the holder's refusal wholly discharges any party who may have a right of recourse against the party making the tender. The question of what constitutes effective tender is also provided for in the Code by a statement that the maker or acceptor of an instrument payable other than on demand who is able and ready to pay at every place specified in the instrument when it is due has made the equivalent of tender.

CANCELLATION AND RENUNCIATION.   The holder of an instrument may discharge any party, even without consideration, in any manner apparent on the face of the instrument or in the indorsement. He may intentionally cancel the instrument or a party's signature by destruction, mutilation, or striking out. He may discharge a party by renouncing his own rights either by a signed and delivered writing or by surrender of the instrument to the party to be discharged. Without surrender of the instrument, neither cancellation nor renunciation affects the title to the instrument.

IMPAIRMENT OF RECOURSE OR COLLATERAL.   As is well known, negotiable instruments are often intimately involved with matters of suretyship, and the discharge of parties to negotiable instruments raises special problems where sureties are concerned. For good reasons, the Code bows in favor of suretyship law in most of these cases, and the rules set forth here are largely derived from that source. Some of the basic principles are:

> 1. The release of the principal debtor by a creditor discharges the surety. Otherwise, the creditor could recover from the surety, who, in turn, could recover from the principal debtor, which would make the release meaningless.

2. A surrender by the creditor of property furnished as security by the principal debtor discharges the surety.

3. A binding agreement between the creditor and the principal debtor to extend the time of payment discharges the surety.

A creditor may release the principal debtor but expressly reserve his rights against the surety; if so, his release of the principal debtor really amounts to no more than an agreement not to sue him; the surety can still recover from the principal debtor.

When these principles are carried over to negotiable instruments, we find that the holder is, in effect, the creditor; the maker or acceptor is the principal debtor; and the secondary parties are the sureties, as are accommodation makers or acceptors. Thus, if a holder releases a maker or acceptor, he releases the secondary parties as well. Where an accommodation maker or acceptor is not known by the holder to be such, the release of the real maker or acceptor does not release the accommodation party. A holder may release the primary party or extend the time of payment and expressly reserve his rights against the secondary parties, provided that they are notified of the reservation. The effect of so doing is to preserve the holder's rights against the surety as of the time the instrument was originally due; the surety may pay the holder and pursue the released party. Of course, sureties are bound by releases and extensions of time to which they consent.

MISCELLANEOUS DISCHARGES. Discussed at an earlier point was the rule that the re-acquisition of an instrument by a prior party discharges all intervening parties to whom he was once liable, but further negotiation to a holder in due course revives the liability of the intervening parties. However, re-acquirers often strike the names of intervening indorsers, discharging them by cancellation, and their liability would not be revived by further negotiation.

The Code provides that any party is discharged from his liability to any other party on an instrument by any act or agreement with such party which would discharge a simple contract for the payment of money. Consequently, rescission, novation, accord and satisfaction may be effective as between immediate parties.

Although the certification of a check by a bank is an acceptance on the part of the bank, the Code affords special treatment to certifications in several different connections. One of them is that certification discharges the drawer and all indorsers prior to the holder who obtained certification. After certification, a drawer may not stop payment on the check. Unless otherwise agreed with the drawer, a bank is not obligated to certify his checks.

There are many other methods of discharge under the Uniform Commercial Code. Those omitted from our discussion in this chapter are not of sufficient importance to justify comment here or are of such a technical nature as to be of little interest to the reader.

8. BANK DEPOSITS AND COLLECTIONS

A. In General

The very nature of a bank thrusts it into a major role with regard to commercial paper. We have already seen some special rules and exceptions to rules designed to take into account the role of banks. The old Uniform Negotiable Instruments Law contained little that had specific application to banks and bank collections. Some states had adopted their own statutes on the subject, while others enacted a statute prepared by the American Bankers Association, but not until the Uniform Commercial Code appeared was there any widely approved uniform treatment of this important aspect of commercial law. The fantastic growth in recent years of the volume of checks and other instruments passing through the bank collection process made uniform legislation of the highest priority. The Code devotes its Article 4 to the subject of bank deposits and collections.

The subject is highly technical in many of its aspects, and the Code contains great quantities of detail in which the ordinary person would have no interest. Set forth here is only a brief summary of some of the more important aspects of Article 4. The Code does not change substantially the precode law, but it does clarify many confusing areas and resolve most of the discrepancies existing among the various states and among legal principles evolving out of court decisions, legislation, and commercial practice. In addition, the Code takes great care to provide for variations from Code provisions contained in agreements between the bank and its depositor and among banks involved in the collection process.

In order to improve the understanding by the reader of the matters to be discussed, let us outline a typical bank transaction. Because the check is the negotiable instrument most familiar to most people, and because a bank is always the drawee of a check, let us use an ordinary, routine check situation as our example. Denton, who lives in Greenville, makes out a check for $150 and sends it to Parsons, whose place of business is in Ashmont, in payment for some merchandise which he has purchased from Parsons. Denton has a commercial checking account with the *W* Bank of Greenville and has been provided with a book of blank checks by the bank. The checks name *W* Bank as the drawee. As a customer of *W* Bank, Denton has already entered into a contract with the bank whereby the bank, in exchange for his deposit of funds with it, agrees to honor checks made out by Denton as long as there are funds on deposit to cover them. This particular check names Parsons as the payee and is signed by Denton. When Parsons receives the check, he deposits it in his own account at the *X* Bank of Ashmont. *W* Bank is known as the "payor bank," and *X* Bank as the "depositary bank"; Parsons is the "customer" and the "depositor." The depositary bank usually credits the account of the depositor at the time of the deposit.

W and *X* Banks do not have accounts with each other, so *X* Bank forwards the check to *Y* Bank in Capital City, which in turn forwards the check to *Z* Bank, a larger bank in the same city. *Y* and *Z* are known as "intermediary banks," and *X, Y,* and *Z* are called "collecting banks." *Z* Bank, the "presenting bank," presents the check to the payor bank, *W*, which honors it, charges Denton's account, and, eventually, returns the canceled check to Denton with his monthly statement. Each of the collecting banks has credited the account of the prior bank, or simply remitted the funds, and the payor bank credits the account of the presenting bank or remits $150 to it. If the payor bank and the presenting bank belong to the same "clearing house," the amount of the check is simply added to the presenting bank's balance in the clearing house, which is an association of banks set up for the purpose of facilitating the clearing of such commercial items as our check.

Until the payor bank honors the check, the transactions described above are referred to as "provisional settlements," for the reason that it is not known until the check is honored whether it is good. If the check is dishonored, all the provisional settlements are revoked, including the credit to Parson's account. The time in which a check must be presented has been discussed above. The Code contains specific provisions governing the days and hours during which presentments can properly be made to banks. Missing indorsements of items deposited with a bank by its customer for collection may be supplied by the bank without the necessity of returning the item to the customer.

Much of Article 4 will be omitted in the discussion below. Only matters having to do with the collection of items and the relationship between the payor bank and its customer will be considered. Even these will be reduced to important essentials.

B. Collection of Items: Depositary and Collecting Banks

Unless a contrary intent clearly appears, the status of a collecting bank, until settlement becomes final, is that of agent or subagent of the owner of the instrument, and it makes no difference whether the owner is the depositor (Parsons, in our example) or the depositary bank or some other bank. Under precode law, a lot of time was wasted in trying to establish whether a collecting bank was the owner of an instrument or merely an agent for collection. The Code minimizes the importance of status and ownership, but provides guidelines for making their determination in situations not specifically covered by the Code. The presumption of agency applies regardless of the form or even lack of indorsement and whether or not the provisional credits can be withdrawn or actually are withdrawn. The effect of all this is that the depositor remains the owner of the check until it is paid by the payor bank, and he bears the risk of loss in the event of nonpayment of the check or the insolvency of one of the collecting banks before final settlement.

A bank which has received an item for collection has a duty to use ordinary care in its collection operations. The bank must present the check or forward it for presentment, send notice of dishonor or nonpayment, return the check after learning that it has not been paid, and remit for the check when it receives final payment. The Code provides specifically the time during which these collecting operations must be performed; normally, a bank must present or forward, send notice or remit, or initiate other necessary action by midnight of the banking day following the day on which the item, notice, or payment was received. If the bank fails to use ordinary care, the depositor can recover damages, limited, unless the bank acted in bad faith, by the amount of the depositor's loss. The Code provides for extensions of the normal time periods in certain circumstances, including emergencies, but the burden is usually on the bank to establish the facts underlying the exception.

Under the Code, each customer (Parsons) and each collecting bank who obtains payment or acceptance of an instrument, and each customer and collecting bank who transfers the instrument, makes certain warranties to the payor bank which pays or accepts, or to his transferee or subsequent collecting bank in the case of a transfer. These warranties are essentially the same as the presentment and transfer warranties discussed earlier.

Because the depositor is the owner of the instrument and the depositary and intermediary banks are his agents for the collection of the instrument, the issue sometimes arises as to whether a bank has such an interest in the instrument or in its proceeds that the bank can hold the item against the depositor or his creditors to the extent that the bank has advanced funds on the instrument or that withdrawals have been made against the credit. The Code answers in the affirmative and states that the interest (called a "security interest") continues until the bank receives final settlement. Closely related is the question of whether a collecting bank can be a holder in due course. The security interest constitutes value, so if a bank satisfies the other requirements of a holder in due course, it can qualify and may be able to enforce an instrument which its depositor could not. It will be recalled that intermediary banks and payor banks which are not depositary banks are not affected by restrictive indorsements except those of the immediate transferor. Notice of claim or defense is not established by such indorsement.

Where a check is dishonored, the presenting bank revokes its provisional settlement and charges the instrument back to the next preceding collecting bank, which does the same thing, until the depositary bank charges back against the customer's account. At each step, the instrument must be returned or notice given within the midnight deadline. The right of a depositary bank to charge back against its customer is not affected by withdrawals made by the customer against the provisional credit. An item is finally paid by the payor bank when the bank has paid the instrument in cash, or settled without having a right to revoke, or settled with a right to revoke and failed to revoke in the time and manner permitted. The Code contains elaborate provisions on the subject of a depositor's right to withdraw credits given by the depositary bank for an instrument, but withdrawals may be allowed by the bank without compliance with these provisions.

C. Collection of Items: Payor Banks

Obvious from the circumstances is the difference between the situation of the payor bank and that of the collecting banks. A collecting bank simply handles an instrument for collection, but a payor bank is expected to pay the instrument as drawn or accepted. When an instrument is presented to a payor bank for payment over the counter, the bank has until the close of business on the day of presentment to pay or dishonor. The midnight deadline does not apply. If the instrument is presented by mail or through the clearing house, as is the case with most instruments, the bank has until midnight of the next following business day to initiate payment or dishonor. Normally, it must make provisional settlement on the day the item is received, but the bank has until midnight the following day to decide whether the instrument is good. During this time, the bank may pay the item, revoke the settlement and return the item, or, if this is not possible, send notice of dishonor or nonpayment. The same principles apply where the drawer and the depositor have accounts in the same bank.

If a bank fails to take action within the time limits described in the previous paragraph, it may be held accountable to the depositor of the check, although the check is not paid and the drawer did not have sufficient funds to cover it. This liability is imposed if the bank retains the check presented, other than over the counter, beyond midnight of the day of receipt without making provisional settlement for it, or does not pay, return, or send notice within the midnight deadline of the next following business day, or does not pay or dishonor an over the counter presentment on the day of presentment. If the payor bank is also the depositary bank, it is not held to the requirement of provisional settlement on the day of presentment. (Under the Code, reference to the "midnight deadline" means midnight of the next following business day, unless otherwise indicated.)

Before or during the processing of a check presented to a payor bank, the bank may receive information concerning the check. The information may consist of notice or knowledge that the drawer is in bankruptcy or that his creditors have attached his account or that the drawer has stopped payment on the check. If the information is received before the check becomes involved in the bank's processes, the bank simply refuses payment and takes what other action is necessary under the circumstances, but if the check is already in process, the answer is not always that easy. When is the information effective to place the bank under a duty to refuse to pay the check? If the bank answers this question incorrectly, it may find itself liable to its customer, to the attaching creditor, or to a trustee in bankruptcy.

The Code provides specific rules to cover these and similar situations. If the notice or information is received after the bank has done any of the following things, it is too late to prevent payment by the bank: accepted or certified the instrument, paid the instrument in cash, settled the item without reserving or having the right to revoke the settlement, completed the posting of the item to the customer's account or otherwise evidenced by examination of the account and other action its decision to pay the item, or become liable for the instrument owing to its failure to settle or return the item on time. The theory behind all of these events is that notice has come too late for the bank reasonably to take action on it. There is no priority among checks by the same drawer presented to the bank on the same day. The checks and other items may be accepted, paid, certified, or charged to the account of the customer in any order convenient to the bank, a rule of obvious importance when there are insufficient funds in the account to cover all the items.

D. Relationship Between Payor Bank and Its Customer

The relationship between the payor bank and its customer is a contractual relationship, but the terms of the contract are rarely set forth in one place where interested parties may examine them. So routine, so well understood, and so efficient are most contacts between a bank and a particular customer that most of us do not give much thought to the terms of the underlying contract. Probably most bank customers, for example, write hundreds of checks each year for year after year without ever having occasion to think about the rights and duties of bank and customer. Certainly one of the major explanations for this phenomenon is the clarity, uniformity, and simplicity of most of the applicable terms. But years of trouble-free relationship with one's bank should not lull one into the belief that disturbances never occur or that knowledge by the customer of some of the basic characteristics of the relationship is wholly unnecessary.

One of the most common questions that arises between a bank and its customer is that of when a bank may charge a customer's account. The Code answers the question by stating that a bank *may* charge against its customer's account any item which is otherwise properly payable from that account, *even though the charge creates an overdraft.* In the event of an overdraft, of course, the bank has a right to a refund of the amount of the overdraft. It will be remembered that a holder in due course may enforce a materially altered instrument according to its original tenor and an incomplete instrument as completed.

The Code extends the same protection to the drawee who pays such an instrument in good faith by permitting the bank to charge the account of its customer.

A frequent source of irritation between a bank and its customer rises out of the bank's wrongful or mistaken dishonor of a check or other instrument issued by the customer. The Code makes the bank liable to its customer for all damages proximately caused by the wrongful dishonor, including, if supported by the facts, damages resulting from the arrest and prosecution of the customer. If the dishonor is the result of a mistake, as distinct from willful or malicious dishonor, damages are limited to those actually proved.

A customer has the right to stop the payment of any instrument payable for or drawn against his account, but the bank may disregard the order unless it is in writing, is signed by the customer or his agent, describes the instrument with certainty, and is received by the bank in such time and manner as to afford the bank a resonable opportunity to take action. If a check has been certified, the customer cannot stop payment. Unless renewed in writing, the bank may disregard a written stop order six months after receipt. Many states have adopted a version of the Code which makes oral stop orders binding on a bank for fourteen calendar days; oral orders may be confirmed in writing during that period. If a bank pays a check the payment of which has been properly stopped, it is liable to the customer for resulting damages, but the burden is on the customer to prove the fact of the wrongful payment and the amount of the loss. The loss is limited to the amount of the instrument unless the bank is guilty of negligence.

A bank is under no obligation to pay a check, other than a certified check, which is presented more than six months after its date, but it may do so and charge the customer's account. Certified checks are considered to be the primary undertaking of the *bank* and are not subject to this rule.

The Code contains a long, detailed section dealing with the rules surrounding the death or incompetence of a customer. Only a brief summary is necessary here. In the chapter on agency, it was pointed out that the death or incompetency of a person usually terminates the authority of others to act on his behalf. If applied without modification to banks, this rule would work a severe hardship. Very sensibly, the Code provides that the death or incompetency of a customer does not revoke the authority of the bank to pay his checks until the bank knows of the event and has a reasonable opportunity to act. In addition, another provision authorizes the bank to pay or certify a decedent's checks for ten days after his death unless the bank has received notice of a type specifically set forth in the Code. There is some variation among the states on the details. The purpose of the ten day exception is to permit holders to cash checks for a short period without having to file claims in probate.

Attention so far has been devoted primarily to the duties of a bank with regard to its customer. The customer also owes duties to the bank. Among them is a duty to notify the bank promptly of any forgeries or alterations discovered in the canceled checks returned by the bank to the customer. He is also obligated to report promptly any irregularities he discovers in his account. Although a bank has no right to pay forged checks or materially altered checks, beyond their original tenor, a customer who fails to notify the bank of a forgery or alteration may be liable for any loss the bank suffers as a result of his failure promptly to give notice, for example, where the bank might have been able to reach the forger if it had had notice in time. Section 4-406 contains many other details related to the customer's duty to discover and report unauthorized signatures and alterations.

Under certain circumstances, a bank may be subrogated to the rights of other parties to the instrument in order to prevent unjust enrichment to a party or a loss to the bank. Where, for example, a bank wrongfully makes payment in spite of a stop order and is sued by the drawer, the bank can assert the defense that the check was in the hands of a holder in due course, and the drawer would have been liable to that holder whether the stop order was obeyed or not. Similar provisions are made for subrogating the bank to the rights of a payee or other holder against the drawer or maker, or to the rights of a drawer or maker against the payee or other holder, in order to prevent unjust enrichment or a loss to the bank. Where a bank has wrongfully paid in spite of a stop order, but the drawer has been defrauded by the payee, for example, the bank may pursue the fraudulent payee after it has reimbursed the drawer.

9. ILLUSTRATIVE CASES

Case No. 1

Consider the following instrument:

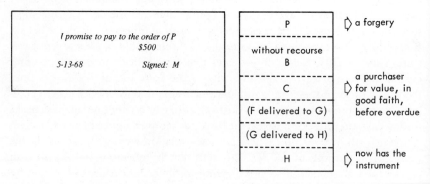

FACTS. Assume that *P's* indorsement is a forgery and that the nature of the subsequent indorsements and the status of the parties are as indicated above. *H* properly presented the instrument for payment, but the instrument is dishonored because *M* does not have the necessary cash to pay it. *H* fails properly to notify any of the parties of the dishonor.

Discussion of Case 1

Requirements of form. The instrument should first be examined to ascertain whether it is in proper form. Always assuming that the letters represent the names of actual parties, the basic requirements of form should be checked against the instrument. It is evident that the instrument is in writing, is signed, and contains an unconditional promise to pay a sum certain in money. In fact, the words "I promise" are used to denote the promise, and the amount payable is specifically indicated to be $500. Because no time for payment is stated, the instrument is automatically payable on demand; consequently, it meets the requirement that it be payable on demand or at a definite future time. Note also that the instrument is payable to the "order" of *P*, the named payee. Therefore, the instrument contains words of negotiability, i. e., the instrument is payable either to a named person or to somebody ordered by him to receive payment. The words of negotiability have been used in such a manner as to indicate that the maker anticipates that the instrument will be transferred from one person to another. This instrument happens to bear a date, but as we have seen, no date is necessary.

Effect of forgery. Passing now to the rights of the various parties, we note that the instrument is in the hands of *H*, that he properly presented the instrument for payment, and that the instrument was dishonored. The facts indicate that the maker, *M*, apparently would have paid the instrument had he had the necessary cash to do so. However, the crucial point in this problem is to note that the instrument has never been properly negotiated by *P*, the named payee. A proper indorsement is required in order for the instrument to be negotiated to subsequent persons. *P* has not indorsed this instrument; in fact, his indorsement is a forgery. It is a cardinal principle of negotiable instruments law that no title to an instrument will pass through a forged indorsement, where that indorsement is necessary for the negotiation of the instrument. Because the paper is order paper to start with, the indorsement of *P* is necessary for a proper negotiation. Consequently, the true owner of the instrument is still *P*, the named payee, and no title has passed to any of the other persons into whose possession the instrument has passed.

H is interested in proceeding against someone and in being reimbursed for the instrument on which he has been unable to obtain payment. Let us consider the rights of *H* against each of the parties to the instrument to see whether or not these parties are liable to him.

Liability of maker. The maker of the instrument, *M*, is the primary party and is unconditionally liable on the instrument. Although he apparently has no defenses on the instrument, he still is not liable to *H* because the maker is not liable to anyone who does not have title to the instrument. The maker is presumably liable to *P*, the named payee, who is the true owner of the instrument. Since *P* was the original party to the contract with *M*, the instrument in the hands of *P* is nothing more than an ordinary contractual claim, and *P* is subject to any defenses that the maker might have. However, no defense, either real or personal, is apparent in this case.

Liability of G, transferor by delivery.   *G* is a transferor by delivery. As such he has no conditional (contract) liability, inasmuch as he did not indorse the instrument. A transferor by delivery, however, has warranty liability. One of the warranties made by *G* was that he had title to the instrument. This warranty, in the nature of a representation, is not true, because as we have seen, no title passed through the forged indorsement of *P*. It is immaterial for this purpose whether or not *G* knew he had no title. Presumably he did not know. Nevertheless, he is liable to *H* on his warranty of title. The liability of a transferor by delivery runs only to his immediate transferee. In this case *G's* immediate transferee is *H*. *H*, therefore, may proceed against *G* and demand that *G* reimburse him for the loss occasioned by *H's* inability to collect the instrument from *M*.

Liability of F, transferor by delivery.   *F* is also a transferor by delivery. As such he has warranty liability. We have seen that no title has passed through the forged indorsement of *P*. In this case, *F* would not be liable to *H*, because the liability of a transferor by delivery runs only to his immediate transferee, and *F's* immediate transferee is *G*, not *H*.

Liability of C, unqualified indorser.   *C* is an unqualified indorser. As such he has incurred two distinct types of liability on the instrument. First, he has incurred conditional liability, or as it is sometimes described, he has guaranteed payment of the instrument by making an indorser's contract. This liability is not absolute but is conditioned upon the happening of the conditions precedent of due presentment, dishonor, and notice of dishonor. The facts of the problem recite that the instrument was properly presented for payment. It was dishonored; thus, two conditions precedent are satisfied. Because the facts indicate, however, that *H* failed to notify properly any of the parties, *H* will not be able to proceed against *C* to enforce *C's* conditional liability. In this problem, the question of *C's* conditional liability is unimportant, for the reason that *C* is liable on a warranty to *H*. Like the other indorsers and transferors of the instrument, *C* has warranted that he had title to the instrument. *C's* liability as an indorser runs to all subsequent persons. Consequently, *H* can proceed against *C*.

Liability of B, qualified indorser.   *B* is a qualified indorser, having indorsed "without recourse." The words "without recourse" expressly relieve *B* of any conditional liability, i.e., by using the words "without recourse" he has indicated that he declines to guarantee payment of the instrument upon due presentment, dishonor, and notice of dishonor. Nevertheless, as a qualified indorser, B does undertake to warrant certain things. He warrants that he had title to the instrument. The liability of any indorser runs to all subsequent holders, so B is liable to H on his warranty of title.

Liability of forger. The forger who actually indorsed *P's* name on the instrument would undoubtedly be liable also on the instrument as an indorser, because the indorsement is actually *his* indorsement. At the very least, the forger would have been a transferor of the instrument and, as such, he would have warranted his title and would be liable to H on this warranty. The forger may also be liable on other principles of law outside the field of negotiable instruments. In most cases, as a practical matter, the forger is not available or is unable to respond to civil liability even if he is available.

P, the named payee of the instrument, whose indorsement was forged thereon, is in no way liable to H. He has a real defense of forgery. Because the indorsement is not his indorsement in fact, P can avoid all liability to H. Actually, P is the true owner of the instrument and may recover possession of the instrument from H, who has wrongful possession thereof.

H may proceed against any party liable. We have noted that all of the parties, except M and P, are liable to H on the instrument. Although F is not directly liable to H, he would be liable to G if H proceeded against G, and if G in turn proceeded against F. H can proceed against any party he wishes. Ordinarily, H would proceed against G, his immediate transferee, because G is the person who negotiated the instrument to H. However, H could skip G and proceed directly against C or B, if he chose to do so. If, for example, H proceeded directly against B, all the parties subsequent to B would be discharged and relieved of all liability on the instrument.

Ultimate loss. In the logical course of events, whether directly or through the various other parties subsequent to B, the instrument will undoubtedly work its way into the hands of B. B, who is the party who dealt with the forger, will doubtless bear the ultimate loss, being left merely with his claim against the forger himself. While it makes no particular difference to the solution of this problem, it might be pointed out that C meets all the requirements for a holder in due course, except that he is not a "holder" of the instrument. He is not a holder, by definition, because a holder of the instrument is either the bearer of bearer paper or the indorsee or payee in possession of order paper. Since the instrument is order paper and has not been properly indorsed, C (or B) does not meet our definition of a holder; consequently, he could not be a holder in due course, even though he meets all of the other requirements and is essentially a bona fide purchaser. Note, as a practical matter, that P may also suffer a loss if he gave value to M, and the latter is insolvent and has no assets from which a judgment could be satisfied.

Case No. 2

Consider the following check:

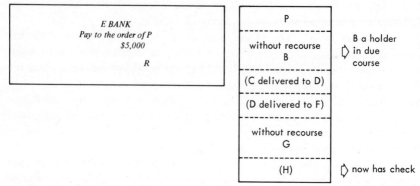

FACTS.   R issued the instrument to P in payment for a shipment of goods which were never delivered. The instrument was negotiated as appears above. R ordered E Bank to refuse payment, and the bank dishonored the instrument upon due presentment by H. H properly notified B of the dishonor. No other notices of dishonor were given.

Discussion of Case 2

Discussion of facts.   In this case, we have an ordinary check which was delivered by the drawer to the payee in a routine business transaction in payment for a shipment of goods. The facts indicate that these goods were never delivered. The instrument is now in the hands of H, and he has been unable to secure payment from the drawee bank, which was ordered by R to stop payment. Let us now consider the rights of H against the various parties to the instrument.

Liability of drawee bank.   The drawee bank is not liable to H. A drawee of a draft, including the drawee bank on a check, is not liable to holders of the instrument unless the instrument has been accepted (or, in the case of a check, certified) by the drawee. Since a check, or draft, does not automatically operate as an assignment of funds from the drawer to the named payee, it follows that the holder does not have the rights of an assignee against the bank even though the bank may be obligated to the drawer. Consequently, the bank is fully justified and, in fact, bound to honor the stop payment order of the drawer, its depositor, and has suffered no liability because it complied with such stop payment order.

Liability of drawer.   The drawer, R, is liable to H in this case. In order to arrive at this conclusion, a careful analysis of the liability of the drawer of a check is necessary. The drawer of a check is not a primary party under the Uniform Commercial Code. The drawer of a check, as well as the drawer of any type of draft, is only conditionally liable. He guarantees payment of the instrument, providing that it is duly presented, dishonored, and notice of the dishonor is received. In addition to incurring this conditional liability, the drawer admits the existence of and legal capacity of the payee, which is not an issue in this problem. Therefore, our first inquiry should be whether or not the drawer can be held on his conditional liability. The facts recite that the instrument was properly presented, so there appears to be "due presentment." In the case of the drawer of a check, the instrument must have been presented within a reasonable time after issue, presumed to be thirty days. We note that the instrument was dishonored, which is the second condition precedent, but the facts recite that no notice of dishonor was given to the drawer. However, no notice of dishonor was necessary as far as this drawer was concerned because the drawer himself caused the dishonor by ordering the drawee bank to stop payment of the instrument. We conclude then, that the drawer is liable on his conditional liability unless he has a defense he can assert against *H*. It might also be noted that even if the drawer had been discharged from his conditional liability, he would still be liable on the instrument, because, in the case of the drawer of a check, he is relieved of liability only to the extent that the delay in making due presentment or meeting the conditions precedent has caused him a loss. As was indicated previously, the only important type of case the courts have recognized as causing loss to the drawer is a case of bank failure, which is not involved in this problem. The drawer would therefore be liable, even if the conditions precedent were not met.

As a matter of ordinary contract law, the drawer has incurred liability on this instrument incident to a contract, but the goods for which the liability was incurred were never delivered. Therefore, the drawer has the defense of failure of consideration. This defense, which is only a personal defense, may not be asserted against a holder in due course or a holder from a holder in due course. Therefore, it is important to ascertain whether or not *H* has the rights of a holder in due course. The facts do not indicate whether or not *H* in his own right meets the requirements for a holder in due course. We do not have to inquire about these facts, however, because *H* has derived his title from *B*, and *B* is a holder in due course, presumably meeting all of the requiremements that are prerequisite to such status. As against *H*, the drawer, *R*, may not assert his personal defense of failure of consideration. In this respect the problem points up the fundamental feature of negotiability. Here we see that the law of commercial paper has departed from ordinary contract law and that *H* has obtained greater rights against the person obligated on the instrument than the original party to the transaction had. The drawer is liable to *H*. The idea is that the drawer ought to pay an innocent holder of a negotiable instrument, and, if the drawer does have claims as a matter of contract law against the payee, he is at liberty to pursue these claims in a separate action.

While we have seen that the drawer is liable to *H*, he was probably well advised, as a practical matter, to stop payment. It is true that *H* may proceed against the drawer and enforce the drawer's liability. However, it is more probable that the holder will proceed against other parties to the instrument, and that the instrument will, as a matter of routine, work its way back into the hands of *P,* the original payee. If that is the case, the instrument in the hands of *P* cannot be enforced against the drawer, and the burden of proceeding against the drawer is thereby forced upon *P.*

Liability of G, qualified indorser. By indorsing "without recourse," *G* has avoided conditional liability on the instrument. We have seen, nevertheless, that a qualified indorser does have warranty liability. The issue squarely presented in this case is whether *G* has violated any of the warranties. Under the statutory language of the Code, a qualified indorser warrants merely that he has no knowledge of a defense. Since the facts do not indicate that *G* had any knowledge of the defense of the drawer, he apparently would not be liable to the holder.

Liability of C and D, transferors by delivery. *C* and *D,* as transferors by delivery, have only warranty liability. However, regardless of whether *C* and *D* may be liable on a warranty, it is perfectly clear that they are not liable to *H.* This follows because of the principle that the liability of a transferor by delivery runs only to his immediate transferee and does not run to subsequent holders of the instrument. Consequently, *C,* if liable at all, is liable only to *D*; *D,* only to *F.*

Liability of B, qualified indorser. *B* is a qualified indorser and in the same position as *G,* and the discussion about the liability of *G* also applies to *B.* Note that *B's* liability as an indorser would run to *H.*

Liability of P, unqualified indorser. *P* is an unqualified indorser and, by indorsing in such a manner, has incurred both conditional and warranty liability. About *P's* conditional liability, we can note that *P* was not notified of the dishonor in this case. Consequently, he is discharged and released from his conditional liability on the instrument. However, *P,* as an unqualified indorser, does warrant that no defense of any party is good against him. In other words, *P* has warranted that the instrument represents a valid and enforceable claim against the drawer. We have seen that as a matter of contract law it does not represent such a valid and enforceable claim. It is immaterial in this case that the instrument is in the hands of a person who *can* enforce it against the drawer because of the special treatment accorded a holder in due course under the Code. This concept in regard to the broad nature of the warranties made by the unqualified indorser is consistent with the liability that *P* would have incurred as an assignor of an ordinary contract right. Although not guaranteeing collectibility, such an assignor would nevertheless have warranted that the claim is a valid claim against the person obligated. Consequently, we can conclude that *P* would be liable to *H* on his warranty.

Selection of person against whom to proceed. It appears from the above analysis that *H* will be able to proceed against any of a number of persons on the instrument. Again, he is most likely to proceed against the person from whom he obtained the instrument. Unless *H* elects to proceed against the drawer, the instrument should work its way back into the hands of P; and in the hands of P, the drawer's defense of failure of consideration will be a good defense and will defeat or reduce P's rights to receive payment.

Case No. 3

Consider the following check:

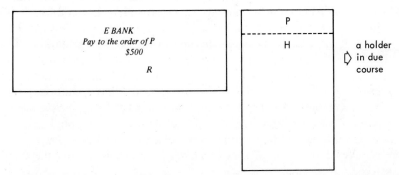

FACTS.   Assume that the above instrument was indorsed as indicated and negotiated to H, a holder in due course. H took the instrument to E Bank and received payment over the counter. H wrote his name in blank on the back of the check before receiving payment. R's signature was a forgery with P the forger. Shortly after H left the premises, the bank discovered the forgery and gave immediate notice to H and asked for return of the sum paid.

Discussion of Case 3

Discussion of facts.   As is readily apparent from the facts of this case, P has committed a fraud through the simple expedient of forging the drawer's signature to a check and of negotiating that check to H, a holder in due course. We can assume that P, who has also named himself as the payee of the instrument, has now departed for places unknown and has left the bank, the drawer, and the holder behind to fight among themselves about who shall bear the loss.

Right of bank to charge drawer's account.   The drawee bank, having paid the instrument to H, is now faced with the choice of attempting to secure a refund of the money paid to H or of proceeding against the drawer. In either case, the drawee bank is going to be unsuccessful. It should be perfectly clear that the drawee bank has no right to charge the account of the named drawer. The drawer's signature was forged on the instrument. The real drawer in no way ordered the bank to pay any money. Consequently, the bank has no right to charge the account of the drawer, and, if the account has been so charged, the bank must restore the credit.

Right of bank against innocent holder.   The next question, whether the bank may proceed against the holder to whom the money was paid, is perhaps a more interesting one. As a common principle of law, when money is paid under a mistake of fact (a mutual mistake in this case because both parties believed that the instrument was a genuine instrument), the money can be recovered and the parties can be restored to their original positions. In this special situation, however, where the drawee bank or other drawee has paid out money on an instrument bearing the forged signature of the drawer, the rule is not applied; thus, the drawee is denied recovery as against the innocent holder to whom the money was paid. This doctrine is known as the rule of *Price* v. *Neal.*[1] Although this rule may have no sound theoretical basis, the doctrine is well established, has been incorporated into the Code, and has worked well in practice. By the application of the doctrine of *Price* v. *Neal,* the loss caused by the fraud of *P* falls on the drawee bank. A bank is not likely to suffer large losses of this nature. A bank will not ordinarily pay out a large sum of money without checking the signature of the drawer and the general status of his account. The fact remains, however, that the result is somewhat anomalous. Because the holder did deal with the forger, he would ordinarily bear the loss. It should be carefully noted that the doctrine of *Price* v. *Neal* applies only to this type of a case, where the instrument bears the forged signature of the drawer.

Liability of H as indorser. It is to be recalled that *H* wrote his name on the back of the instrument before he presented it to the drawee bank for payment. Why is it that *H* is not liable to the bank as an unqualified indorser? An indorsement is made incident to a negotiation of the instrument. In this case the instrument had not been negotiated to the drawee bank, but merely surrendered to the drawee bank for payment. A surrender for payment is not a negotiation; consequently, *H* has incurred no liability to the bank as an indorser. The bank is not a holder of the instrument, but a special party in its own right—namely, the drawee.

Case No. 4

FACTS. Assume that the following instrument, which appears to be an ordinary payroll check, was issued by *T*, the treasurer of *R* Corporation, who was duly authorized by the corporation to issue such instruments. Assume further that *T*, the treasurer, had decided to embezzle money from the corporation through the simple expedient of "padding" the payroll. As treasurer, he was charged with the responsibility of issuing payroll checks. When he issued this particular check, he named as the payee of the instrument a former employee of the corporation who had left his job some months before. The

---

[1] 3 Burrow's 1354 (1762).

```
┌─────────────────────────────────────┐   ┌──────────────────────┐
│              E BANK                  │   │      John Jones      │
│      Pay to the order of John Jones  │   │   - - - - - - - - -  │
│              $347.90                 │   │          H           │
│                                      │   │                      │
│      Payroll        R Corporation    │   │                      │
│      Check          by T, Treasurer  │   │                      │
└─────────────────────────────────────┘   │                      │
                                           │                      │
                                           │                      │
                                           │                      │
                                           └──────────────────────┘
```

former employee's name was inserted as the payee on the check that is payable to his order. Assume further that after signing the above instrument on behalf of the corporation, the treasurer took the instrument, indorsed the name, "John Jones," on the back and negotiated it to *H*, a bona fide purchaser. Assume that *H* presented the instrument to the drawee bank for payment and that the drawee bank paid the instrument routinely and debited the corporation's account therefor. Assume further that upon audit, the embezzlement scheme of the treasurer is discovered, and that the treasurer hastily leaves for South America. The corporation now demands that the drawee bank restore the credit to the corporate account, claiming that the bank had paid out money on an instrument bearing the forged signature of the payee, and, because the paper was order paper, no title passed to *H* through the forged indorsement. Who must bear the loss in this case—the drawee bank? the corporation? or the innocent holder?

Discussion of Case 4

Loss on corporation. Under the Code, the loss in this case must be borne by the corporation. The theory is that the corporation (or other drawer) is in a better position to control the dishonest behavior of its agents and employees than an innocent holder. This result is consistent with prior law, which arrived at the same conclusion by other reasoning.

PROBLEMS

1. What are the uses and advantages of a trade acceptance?

2. What are the rights of a transferee of unindorsed order paper where there was no prior holder in due course? Under what circumstances may he become a holder in due course?

3. What is the nature of the liability of the maker of a promissory note? Contrast it with the liability of the drawer of a check.

4. Illustrate and explain the following types of indorsements: restrictive, blank, special, qualified.

5. What are the basic requirements of form that the Uniform Commercial Code prescribes for negotiable instruments?

6. Assume that you are manager of a grocery store. A stranger offers you a bank draft drawn by the *X* Bank on the *Y* Bank and made payable to the order of *P*. The draft is dated the previous day and bears the blank indorsement "*P*" on the back. The stranger says that his name is *B*; he also has indorsed the instrument in blank. You give value for the instrument, and take it in good faith before it is overdue. Under these circumstances, can you accept the instrument with reasonable safety? Explain.

7. What is an "accommodation indorser"?

8. What fundamental idea tends to distinguish a negotiable instrument from an instrument that is not negotiable?

9. What are the rights of the drawee bank against the drawer-depositor of a check where it is discovered after payment that:

a. the signature of the drawer was a forgery, or that

b. the signature of the payee was a forgery.

In the same two situations, what are the rights of the drawee bank against the person to whom money was paid on a check?

10. Does it make any difference in the liability of the parties to a check whether a certification is secured by the drawer or by a holder? Explain.

11. By impersonating *P*, *T* obtained a $500 negotiable instrument from *R*; the instrument was made payable to the order of *P*. *T* wrote *P's* name on the back of the instrument and negotiated it to *H*, a holder in due course. *R* stopped payment, and *H* is now suing *R* on the instrument. What are the rights of *H* and *R*?

12. *R* drew a check for $500 payable to the order of *P*, who immediately presented the instrument to the drawee bank and requested payment. The officers of the bank refused to cash the check because *P* would not indorse it. *P* is now suing the bank. What are the rights of *P, R,* and the bank?

13. What warranties are made by a person who indorses a negotiable instrument in blank? Compare these warranties with those made by the other types of indorsers.

14. Explain the following terms: payor bank, depositary bank, collecting bank, intermediary bank, presenting bank, clearing house.

15. As a check moves through the various stages of the collection process, how can it be determined who owns the instrument?

16. What is the significance of the term "provisional settlement"?

17. How long does a bank have to decide whether it will pay a check that has been presented for payment?

18. What are the rights of a depositor when his bank fails to obey his order to stop payment on a check? Explain. What duties does a bank's depositor (customer) owe to the bank?

chapter 12

Bailments:
Storage and Carriage
of Goods,
Documents of Title

1. IN GENERAL

A. The Nature and
Use of the Bailment

By the time the reader has arrived at the subject of bailments, he is well aware of the fact that all of us establish legal relationships with other persons through a wide variety of mechanisms, devices, and instrumentalities. The contract is the most important and the broadest in scope of these devices, but a discussion of the general principles of the contract alone would leave the reader relatively unenlightened. Some of the other devices are themselves contracts in all respects. Others may be basically contracts but with non-contract overtones, origins, or applications. Still others may not be contracts at all. However closely these devices conform to contract patterns, though, their special uses and unique problems justify some separate consideration. Many of these devices, such as the sale, the agency, and commercial paper, have already been considered. A variety of financial mechanisms will be discussed in the next chapter. Among those not examined elsewhere is the bailment, one of the oldest, simplest, and most common of all legal devices.

579

Possibly to a greater extent than in any other field of law, the principles and procedures of commercial law have grown out of the practices and requirements of those who were most concerned with that field of law. Mention has already been given to the fact that for many generations the common law was too preoccupied with land and the feudal system to take much notice of the problems of merchants. The result was that the merchants were left to devise their own rules of conduct, and, very sensibly, they devised rules and laid down principles that were useful to them in carrying out their commercial activities. Many of the legal devices with which we are familiar today in the commercial fields were developed simply to explain and regulate that which the merchants were already doing or to supply the merchants with legal instrumentalities for the purpose of facilitating their activities. As commercial transactions took place over greater and greater distances and as the transfer of currency and bullion became increasingly inconvenient the negotiable instrument evolved. To a greater or lesser degree, the partnership, the corporation, the agency, many varieties of financial devices, and the bailment grew and developed in answer to particular commercial needs. The law of bailments consists largely of rules governing the rights and duties of the parties in those situations where one person delivers his personal property to another person for some special purpose and with the expectation that the property shall be returned when that purpose has been realized. After a moment's reflection on the large number of daily transactions where such transfers of personal property are involved, it becomes obvious that such bailment transactions are useful and the rules governing them are important.

Every businessman who has stored goods in a warehouse, or shipped or received goods by means of any public or private form of transportation, or rented machinery, or sent out a piece of equipment for repair, or delivered stocks, bonds, or other valuable property into the custody of a creditor as security for a debt has come into contact with the bailment device. Every person who has left clothing at a laundry to be washed, or checked a hat, or sent a wristwatch to the jeweler for repair, or borrowed a lawnmower from his next-door neighbor has been a party to a bailment relation. Most persons entering into one of the bailment relations described here do so without knowing the precise legal nature of the device they have encountered. Yet, if queried, these persons could probably give a reasonably accurate description of their basic rights and duties under the particular bailment. The person who has turned his goods over to another person is entitled, sooner or later, to get them back The person entrusted with the goods should be careful of the property while it is in his possession and should not employ the property for his own use unless that is necessary in order to carry out his duties toward the property or unless it is permitted by the nature of the bailment or the agreement of the parties. An understanding of the law of contract would disclose the basic characteristics of most bailments, but the considerable variation in the nature and type of bailment, the noncontract elements present in many bailments, and the civil law origins of much of the law of bailment would destroy a large part of the value of logical reasoning and analogy starting from contract premises. It is necessary, then, to devote some amount of time to the bailment device itself.

Although there is some disagreement on the details, it is generally accepted that a *bailment* is the relation created by the transfer of the possession of personal property, by actual or constructive delivery or otherwise, by one person called the *bailor* to another person called the *bailee* for some specific purpose, the accomplishment of which requires the bailee to return the property to the bailor or dispose of it at the direction of the bailor. Several points should be noted about the bailment thus defined. There are two parties: the bailor and the bailee. The subject matter must be personal property. The bailee has possession of the property; he does not have its ownership. It is not necessary that the bailor actually own the property, either, in order for there to be a valid bailment. All that is required, generally speaking, is a right to possession in the bailor. Thus, the bailee may himself bail the goods and become a bailor as regards a second bailee. An absolute duty rests with the bailee either to return the property to the bailor or to dispose of it as the bailor directs.

Delivery of the property may be *actual* or *constructive,* i.e., the bailor may actually deliver the property into the hands of the bailee or, having purchased goods from the bailee, the bailor may leave the goods in the bailee's hands without any actual delivery having taken place. Although the origin of the word "bailment," in the French *"bailler,"* meaning to deliver, would seem to indicate that delivery was an absolute requirement, that is not actually the case. A bailment may be raised by operation of law even where there is no delivery in either an actual or constructive sense, as when a person finds and takes into his possession lost property. The original owner of the property still owns it while it is in the possession of the finder, and the finder has a duty to return it to the person who owns it. Note here also that this bailment comes into existence without the consent of the parties.

Ordinarily, however, delivery and consent of the parties are required for an effective bailment. As we saw in Chapter 7, acceptance is required for an effective delivery. A customer in a store or restaurant, for example, does not generally create a bailment relation when he just hangs his coat and hat on a hook or drapes them over a chair or table while he eats or shops. There has been no delivery to or consent by the proprietor, and the customer retains possession of his property. If the customer hands his coat and hat to an attendant or a clerk, a bailment is created, as is probably also the case where the customer, in the presence of the clerk, deposits his hat on a showcase or table while he tries on a new one.

Considerable hairsplitting is done among the authorities about whether a bailment is really a contractual relation or not. Reasonable arguments can be made on both sides of the issue, but little is to be gained by so doing. Actually, it is less confusing to look upon the bailment as a contractual relation than it is to deny that such is the case. Almost all bailments result from a contract, express or implied in fact, and the terms of the agreement between the parties are of paramount importance in most bailments. The fact that a bailment is gratuitous does not necessarily destroy the possibility of a contract. It must be remembered, however, that not all of the ramifications of a bailment and not all of the rights and responsibilities involved will be expressed in the bailment contract. It is these unexpressed aspects of the bailment relation with which we are primarily concerned here.

B. The Bailment Distinguished from Other Transactions

IN GENERAL. The bailment is not the only legal transaction that deals with personal property. Some of the other transactions are of such a character that they are not likely to be confused with the bailment, but a few of them may require a moment of reflection before the differences become clear. It is important to be able to make the distinctions because the effects of entering into a bailment relation may be quite unlike the effects of entering into other transactions that bear a superficial similarity to the bailment.

SALE. The very purpose of the sale is to transfer the ownership of goods from one person to another. Inherent in the bailment is the retention of ownership by the bailor even though possession of the goods has been transferred to the bailee. It is sometimes said that a transaction is a *bailment* if the identical goods must be returned in the same or in an altered form and a *sale* if the party to whom they were transferred may return money or something else of value in exchange for them. In a bailment, the transfer of possession is essential; in a sale, the transfer of ownership is essential and may be accomplished without a transfer of possession. However, the Uniform Commercial Code requires only that a bailee "acknowledge possession" of goods, which means that actual possession by the bailee is not necessary. If he acknowledges possession, he is bound by the obligations of bailees. It should be noted that in the performance of many sales contracts, there may be several bailments involved, especially those of carriers and warehousemen.

The context in which it often becomes necessary to distinguish between a sale and a bailment is the destruction of the goods and the question of who bears the loss. With a bailment, the loss usually falls on the bailor, unless the terms of the bailment contract provide otherwise or the destruction was caused by the bailee. We have seen that the risk of loss in sales situations, under the Code, is determined, not by the ownership of the goods, but in accordance with principles set forth in the statute, largely unrelated to ownership.

Although the distinctions between sales and bailments are usually rather easy to make, there are situations where they may be difficult. Transactions where a seller expressly retains ownership of goods for security reasons may be particularly troublesome. However, even these arrangements usually make it clear that the buyer is primarily obligated to pay for the goods, not to return them. The Code further minimizes the dangers of confusion and uncertainty as we have seen. The modern practice of handling large quantities of cases, containers, and bales with pallets and fork-trucks raises an interesting bailment problem in that the goods are often delivered on the pallet with the understanding that the pallet is to be returned. Consequently, there may be a sale of the goods and a bailment of the platform on which the goods rest. If both goods and pallet are destroyed, the loss of the goods may fall on the buyer and the loss of the pallet on the seller-bailor.

If the goods transferred are to be exchanged for other goods, the transaction is not a bailment but a sale or barter, because there is a transfer of ownership. Where the goods transferred will simply be returned in another form, the transaction is a bailment because the ownership does not pass to the person who has possession of the goods. This latter rule has been followed with regard to contracts to manufacture wheat into flour, to saw logs into boards, and to manufacture leather into shoes.

GIFTS.   As has been learned elsewhere, the delivery of both possession and title is required for an effective gift, but in an actual case it may be difficult to determine what the intentions of the parties were with regard to the transfer of title.

MORTGAGES.   Transfer of possession is neither required for an effective mortgage nor common in practice. Traditionally, a mortgage of personal property transfers the title to the property to the mortgagee as security for the performance of the obligation. In a bailment, possession passes to the bailee but title does not.

BANK DEPOSITS.   The ordinary bank deposit is not a bailment because the bank is not obligated to return the same money, checks, or other items, and the title to the funds passes to the bank The relationship between bank and general depositor may be described for most purposes as that of debtor and creditor, but even this requires some straining to make it fit all situations. When property is deposited with a bank with the understanding that the identical property deposited is to be returned to the depositor, the relationship, called a *special deposit,* is a bailment. Banks that provide safe deposit boxes for the safekeeping of papers and other valuables are bailees of the property deposited in the boxes.

TRUSTS.   A *trust* is a legal device by which property is held by one person for the benefit of another. Because it may include real as well as personal property, it differs from a bailment, and the trustee must have both title and possession in order for there to be an effective trust. The person who has possession of the property in a bailment does not have the title.

MISCELLANEOUS. Some interesting problems present themselves in connection with the care and safekeeping of automobiles, problems which were not even dreamed of when the law of bailment arose. An automobile that is turned over to a garage for storage or is put into the hands of a parking lot attendant who parks the car, keeps the keys, and redelivers the car to the owner on his return is obviously the subject of a bailment. Where, however, the automobile owner simply pays a fee for the privilege of leaving his car in a particular space and the owner locks the car and takes the keys with him, the owner of the lot on which the car is parked is leasing the space and not taking custody or possession of the car. The relationship is that of lessor and lessee. The control or degree of control over the automobile is the chief test for determining which arrangements are bailments and which are not.

C. Formation of the Bailment Relation

As has already been mentioned, the bailment relation is one of the most simple of all legal relations. In keeping with its essential simplicity is the lack of formality required for its formation. It is probably most accurate and least misleading to say that a bailment relation is a contractual relation and results from an express or implied contract between the parties. A warning is issued, however, that although contractual relations carry with them connotations of consent by the parties to liabilities and obligations imposed on them by the contract, a person may find the duties and liabilities of a bailee imposed on him without his intention to incur such obligations. Thus, the finder of lost property may have certain responsibilities for the safekeeping of the property until it is delivered to its proper owner. These duties and responsibilities are imposed by law without regard to the bailee's actual intention. The parallel in the law of contract can be found, of course, in the contract implied in law or quasi-contract.

It should be noted that the *mere* possession by one person of another person's property does not make the possessor a bailee. A thief has possession of another's goods but is clearly not a bailee. A person who is a bailee may transform himself into a convertor. A *convertor* is one who has committed the civil wrong of conversion, by appropriating the bailed goods to his own use. (See discussion of conversion in Chapter 7.) However, a person who takes possession of another's goods without any present intention to appropriate the goods to his own use would seem to satisfy the basic requirements for a bailment.

D. The Business Problem

The firm that is in the business of storing or carrying goods for others or of letting property for hire does not have to be told that the elements of the relation between it and its customers are important, and such a firm is usually acutely aware of its rights, duties, and liabilities with regard to those who hire its services or property. The same is true of most other professional bailees and bailors. While this chapter does have application to the professional bailee and bailor, the principal orientation of the chapter is toward illuminating the law of bailments for the casual bailor and bailee. In keeping with the basic premise of this book, the author seeks to discuss the important fields of commercial law within the framework of the business problem or activity the businessman is most likely to encounter and with the legal aspects of which he is least likely to be familiar. The discussion, then, is centered largely around the concern the casual bailor may have for the safe return or proper disposition of his goods, for his rights against the bailee, and for the extent of the bailee's power over the bailor's goods, and around the duties of the casual bailee with regard to the property of others that may come into his possession. It should be pointed out here that the person whose business is primarily that of repairing or improving the personal property of others ought properly to be considered a casual bailee, inasmuch as his attention is likely to be focused on the details of his repairing or improving function rather than on his rights and duties as a bailee. It will be noticed here, as elsewhere, that the discussion of one party's rights is generally also the discussion of another party's duties.

This chapter is so organized that the reader may acquire an understanding of bailments in general together with some information on particular types of bailments with which the average businessman is fairly certain to come in contact. The last portion of the chapter is devoted to a discussion of the special documents accompanying such bailments as those for carriage and for storage.

2. TYPES AND CLASSIFICATIONS OF BAILMENTS

A. In General

There are two types of modern classifications of bailments: one that is concerned with whether the bailment is public or private in character; the other, with the existence of compensation. Both will be considered briefly here, but the chief classification used in this chapter will relate simply to those particular bailment transactions that are of major importance in the operation of a business.

Some bailees hold themselves out to serve the public generally to the extent that the bailee has facilities available. These bailments of a public character are called *special bailments*. Innkeepers and common carriers are examples of special bailees. In contrast with the special bailment is the *private* or *ordinary bailment*. This bailment occurs where the bailee does not hold himself out to the public generally to the limit of his facilities. The rights and duties of the parties are somewhat different in the two types of bailment. Examples of both types are discussed below.

The most useful modern classification of bailments groups private or ordinary bailments under three headings: bailment for the sole benefit of the bailor, bailments for the sole benefit of the bailee, and bailments for the mutual benefit of the bailor and the bailee. The first two headings are sometimes referred to as *gratuitous bailments* and the last category as *mutual-benefit bailments* or *bailments for hire*. Special bailments are usually excluded completely from this classification. Bailments for the sole benefit of the bailor include both gratuitous custody and gratuitous services; as where the bailee agrees to store, repair, or transport the property without compensation. Bailments for the sole benefit of the bailee usually include only the gratuitous lending of property to the bailee for his use, as where *A* lends his lawn mower to his neighbor. As compared with the third type of bailment and the special bailments, these two types are of minor importance in the field of business law. The mutual-benefit bailments include not only all of the bailments where compensation is paid, but also pledges, where the bailor transfers possession of goods to the bailee as security for an obligation owed by the bailor to the bailee. (Pledges are discussed in Chapter 13.) It will be noted below that the gratuitous or non-gratuitous nature of a bailment is an important element to be considered in determining the amount of care with which the bailee must protect the goods.

B. Warehousing

Warehousing is the business of storing the goods of others for compensation, and a *warehouseman* is one lawfully engaged in that business. The relation between the warehouseman and the person handing over goods to be stored is that of bailee and bailor. Note that warehousing is a "business" and does not include the casual bailee even though he may store the goods of another for compensation. A warehouse may be private or public depending upon how the business is operated, upon the kind of goods stored, and, in many states, upon warehousemen's statutes. In general, warehousemen who store grain, cotton, and some foodstuffs are public warehousemen and are subject to public regulation, which requires that the warehouseman's facilities be available to all without discrimination, fixes rates, and provides for public inspection. In some states this is not the case.

C. Safe Deposit Companies

Property deposited in a safe deposit box is bailed to the bank or other organization operating a safe deposit vault. Although this is true in most states, there are a few states where the transaction is not a bailment at all, on the ground that the safe deposit company does not have possession of the contents of the box inasmuch as it does not have access to the interior of the safe deposit box. The key belonging to the renter of the box and the key kept by the safe deposit company are *both* necessary in order to open the box. Although the company does not have access to the interior of the box, there is no question that the company has possession of the safe deposit boxes themselves and has exclusive control over the vault in which the boxes are kept. Consequently, the majority rule that the relationship between the depositor and the company is one of bailment is the convenient and sensible rule. In some states, the operation of a safe deposit vault is controlled in considerable detail by statute, and the precise nature of the transaction may not be important in those states.

D. Innkeepers

Two types of "special" bailment will be discussed in this section: innkeepers and carriers. Although *inn* is the technical common law term used in connection with public houses where all travelers will be admitted and will receive accommodations in exchange for the payment of compensation, the term "inn" is synonymous with "hotel," as the latter term is used in the United States. A *hotelkeeper* holds himself out, within the limits of his facilities, to furnish lodging or lodging and meals to transients for compensation. Because lodging-houses and boarding-houses are not hotels, they do not fall within the category being discussed here. Lodging-houses and boarding-houses do not offer their facilities to all persons and usually do not cater to transients.

The hotelkeeper is, generally speaking, the bailee of property brought into his hotel by the guests, because he has possession and control of that property during the guests' stay. While the guest in his room is in possession and control of his own property, unless it has been specifically delivered to the hotelkeeper for safekeeping, a bailment is usually said to exist nonetheless. The argument is made that the hotelkeeper is in actual control of the hotel and, to a limited extent, in some sort of control of the guests' property as well. The reason for the extension of the bailment relation to this doubtful situation is probably historical in origin. The early English inns were often located in remote areas where the countryside was infested with thieves and robbers. It probably seemed wise to the courts at the time to put the responsibility for protecting the guests' property on the innkeeper so as to discourage his collusion with thieves. As a practical matter today, the hotelkeeper is not the bailee of property kept in the exclusive possession of the guest. As we will see below, the hotelkeeper's responsibility may be greater in some situations than in others, and has been considerably altered by statute.

E. Carriers

Carriers are classified as *common carriers* and *private carriers*. The latter engages by special contract to carry goods or persons from one place to another for compensation but only for such others as the carrier himself decides to accommodate. The private carrier does not hold out his services to all comers. He is an *ordinary bailee*. The *common carrier,* on the other hand, holds himself out for hire to transport persons or property for all comers and to the full extent of his facilities. Examples of common carriers are: airlines, railroads, bus lines, ferries, steamboat companies, taxi companies, and trucking companies.

Although a person who delivers goods to a common carrier is technically a bailor and the carrier a bailee, the terms bailor and bailee are usually not employed in this connection. The shipper is called the *consignor;* the carrier, the *carrier;* and the person to whom the goods are to be shipped the *consignee.* The common carrier is not required to accept for transportation goods that he cannot handle, goods that cannot be shipped legally, goods that have not been properly prepared for shipment, goods injurious to public health, or dangerous goods, such as some explosives.

The law of common carriers, in addition to the pure bailment aspects, is sufficiently important to justify separate treatment below.

3. RIGHTS, DUTIES, AND LIABILITIES OF THE PARTIES

A. Cases

(1)

A machine used by Hypocase, Inc. in the manufacture of pallets broke down one morning shortly after it was put into operation. The plant repair crew did not have the facilities to repair the machine. With the approval of the production manager, the machine was loaded onto a truck and taken to the Acme Machine Shop in Berkland, Anosmia, for repairs, which a representative of Acme estimated would take two days. Acme's shop was located in a part of Berkland which was devoted primarily to industrial activity. The front of the shop faced onto a street that was very lightly traveled at night, and the back of the shop opened on a deserted railroad siding and was not visible from the street. Acme and several other small firms in the neighborhood jointly employed a night watchman who made regular visits to the front and back entrances of Acme during each night. The watchman was accustomed to eating a light lunch between 1:00 and 2:00 A.M. and making himself a cup of coffee on a hot-plate available in one of the other shops. During the first night the Hypocase machine was in the Acme shop, and while the watchman was eating his lunch, thieves entered the Acme shop through the back doors, whose locks the thieves broke, and stole the Hypocase machine. When Acme refused to pay for the stolen machine, Hypocase sued Acme for damages. What are the rights of the parties?

[See *Fox Chevrolet Sales* v. *Middleton,* 203 Md. 158, 99 A. 2d 731 (1953)]

(2)

See Case 1 above. Assume that the Hypocase machine was not stolen but that the repairs were completed and Hypocase had been notified that the machine was ready to be picked up. A truck similar in color to the Hypocase trucks but bearing no company name or other markings appeared at the Acme shop, and the driver said he had come for the Hypocase machine. Acme employees helped load the machine on the truck, which drove away. Shortly thereafter, a Hypocase truck came to Acme, and it was then discovered that the first truck had not been from Hypocase at all. The machine has not been recovered. What are the rights of Hypocase against Acme?

(3)

Harold Harmon, one of the senior men in the Hypocase sales organization, attended a warehousemen's convention in Anosmia City. His purpose was to demonstrate the use of pallets and fork-lift merchandise handling in a warehousing operation and, perhaps, to negotiate some sales contracts with representatives of warehouses. He took along some model equipment and several layouts and other displays, which he kept in his room at the Barbizon-Holton Hotel. He also had in his hotel room an antique brooch which the wife of the president of Hypocase had asked him to have appraised while he was in Anosmia City. One evening, while Harmon was attending one of the sessions of the convention, his room was robbed, and all the display material, which was worth about $2,500, the brooch, and all of Harmon's personal possessions were removed from the room. What is the liability of the hotel for these stolen articles?

B. In General

The bailor of property has the right to have the contract of bailment performed according to its terms and to have the property either returned to him or disposed of in compliance with his directions. This kind of right, of course, is a part of any contractual relation and is essential to any bailment, and it does not require much more elucidation here than has already been supplied elsewhere. A large portion of the law peculiar to bailments, on the other hand, is devoted to the duties and liabilities of the bailee. The bailee's rights to possess and use the bailed property will be discussed elsewhere.

In all bailments the bailee is required to exercise some degree of skill, care, and diligence in the safekeeping of the property that has come into his hands under the bailment. The ordinary bailee is not an insurer in this respect. In other words, if he has been exercising the proper degree of care required of him, he is not liable for the loss, damage, or destruction of the goods in his custody. The liabilities and duties of the bailee depend, to a large extent, upon the nature of the bailment and upon the circumstances surrounding it. Special bailees, as will be seen below, may be virtual insurers of the safety of the goods. Statutes have intervened in many areas.

The traditional approach to the degrees of care required of bailees classifies care into three degrees: *slight, ordinary,* and *extreme.* Where the bailment is for the exclusive benefit of the bailor, the bailee is required only to use slight care and is liable only for gross negligence. The theory is that the bailee receives no benefit out of the relation; consequently, he should not have to exercise much care with regard to the property in his possession. Where the bailment is for the sole benefit of the bailee, because the bailor receives no benefit from the transaction, the bailee is required to use extreme care and is liable for slight negligence.

In a bailment for mutual benefit, where both parties are benefited, the bailee must exercise ordinary care and is liable for ordinary negligence.

Although these traditional degrees of care serve some useful modern purpose in calling attention to the basic differences among the three types of ordinary bailment, many courts refuse to recognize degrees of care and of negligence. The basic legal principle of negligence is that a person is negligent when his conduct falls below that expected of a reasonably prudent person in the same circumstances. Under this approach to negligence, it is difficult to understand why degrees of care or of negligence are necessary in the three bailment situations. Courts frequently and properly say, therefore, that the liability of the bailee is established by that care which should be observed by men of prudence in keeping property of like value under like circumstances. This approach provides, automatically, for differences in the type of bailment, in the value of the property, and in other circumstances. Obviously, the care to be exercised toward a 60-point diamond engagement ring will be somewhat less, in absolute terms, than the care which should be exercised in the safekeeping of the Hope Diamond or the Kohinoor, but both quantities of care can be described as "reasonable care *under the circumstances*." The same phrase can be used to describe the different amounts of care required where the bailment is for the sole benefit of the bailor and where the bailment is for the sole benefit of the bailee. The type of bailment is simply one of the "*circumstances*."

Inasmuch as the amount of care and the kind of protection a bailee owes to property in his custody vary with the type of bailment, it is important to be able to differentiate among the types of bailment. The usual problem is not to distinguish the bailment for the sole benefit of the bailor from the bailment for the sole benefit of the bailee but to distinguish these two gratuitous bailments from the bailment for mutual benefit. There are several important characteristics of the latter type. A mutual benefit bailment is almost always accompanied by an express contract resulting from a period of bargaining over the terms of that contract. Were it possible always to demonstrate benefit actually flowing from the bailment to both of the parties, the test would be simple. Frequently, it is not possible to demonstrate such benefit. The real test should not be whether the parties both actually receive benefits but whether they bargained for or expected benefits. This test obviates the confusion that might otherwise result when both parties to a gratuitous bailment actually receive benefits.

COMPENSATION AND EXPENSES.   It should be obvious that in all bailments for mutual benefit the bailor or the bailee, as the case may be, is under a duty to pay the other the agreed compensation. A more difficult question is that pertaining to expenses incurred in connection with the safekeeping or the use of the bailed property. The general rule is that the bailee must pay the ordinary expenses, but the bailor is obligated to pay the extraordinary expenses. *Ordinary expenses* are those which are only incidental to the bailment itself, as where a rented automobile requires gasoline, oil, or possibly the repair of a punctured tire. *Extraordinary expenses* are those which are unusual and not reasonably to be expected, as where the generator on the rented automobile burns out. A bailee who pays extraordinary expenses is normally entitled to be reimbursed by the bailor. The above rules are held to apply to bailments for the sole benefit of the bailee but not to bailments for the sole benefit of the bailor. In the latter case, the bailee is entitled to reimbursement from the bailor for all expenses reasonably incurred by him in connection with the goods.

DUTY OF BAILEE TO RETURN PROPERTY. As has been mentioned previously, one of the characteristics of the bailment relation is the duty of the bailee to return the bailed goods to the bailor or to dispose of them in accordance with the bailor's directions. The property need not be returned in its original form if the terms of the bailment provide otherwise. Many bailments require the bailee to make certain changes in the goods before return, as where the bailee is to manufacture wheat into flour. A few special situations exist where the storage or handling procedure for the goods involved makes it impossible for the bailee to return the identical goods he received but where the fungible nature of the goods makes it possible for the bailee to return goods of precisely the same nature and quantity. An example, of course, is the grain elevator. There, the grain delivered to the elevator by the bailor is irretrievably mixed with the grain of other bailors. The bailor becomes entitled to a quantity of grain equal to that which he delivered, but because the grain is fungible, the delivery of any grain of the same quantity is the equivalent of the delivery of the same grain, and the transaction is still a bailment. Presumably, the operator of the grain elevator mixes only those grains of the same grade and quality. (See the discussion on this point in Chapter 7.)

If the bailee has performed toward the bailed property the care required of him, the loss or destruction of the property frees him from the duty to return it to the bailor or to dispose of it under the terms of the bailment. If the bailee has failed to meet the standard of care and the property is lost as a result, he is liable to the bailor for the loss.

One aspect of the duty of the bailee to return the bailed goods which may be particularly troublesome is his duty to return them to the proper person. Usually, this is the bailor, but it may also be someone whom the bailor has designated, or it may be neither of these, as where the bailor had no rights in the goods and the proper person for redelivery is the true owner. Delivery of the property to the wrong person renders the bailee absolutely liable no matter how much care he exercised. If, however, the bailee delivers to a person in compliance with a court order or delivers to the true owner, he is not liable to the bailor. The same result is generally true where the goods are taken from the bailee under proper legal process. Where the bailee delivers the goods to a person claiming to be the true owner, he does so at his own risk. In circumstances where both the bailor and some person claiming to be the true owner demand delivery of the goods, the bailee may do well to utilize some sort of interpleader procedure, if it is available, in order to free himself of the dilemma in regard to the person to whom delivery should be made.

BAILEE AS INSURER OF THE SAFETY OF THE GOODS.   There are a few situations where the bailee becomes absolutely liable for loss or damage to the goods in spite of his having exercised the proper degree of care. One of these situations has been discussed above: delivery to the wrong person. Other situations of this nature arise where the bailee agrees, expressly or impliedly, either to assume this sort of responsibility or to obtain a policy of insurance to cover the goods but fails to do so. Liability in the latter case arises only when the loss was caused by the peril that the insurance was to indemnify against. Absolute liability may also arise where the bailee varies from the terms of the bailment, as by using the goods when he has no right to do so, by using the goods for a purpose not permitted in the bailment contract, and by moving the place of storage without the bailor's consent.

The departure by the bailee from the terms of the bailment or his delivery to the wrong person amounts to a conversion of the goods. Where a bailee sells the goods, or gives them away, or otherwise transfers them to a third person in violation of the bailment, the bailor has a choice of recovering the goods from the third person or holding the bailee liable for their value. Inasmuch as the bailee did not have title to the goods or the right to pass title to a third person, the third person acquires no ownership in the goods even though he purchased or otherwise acquired the goods in complete good faith. Note that the bailee has a sort of special property in the goods giving him rights in regard to the property, and these rights are good against the whole world, except the bailor or true owner. Some of these rights may even be good against these parties, as a bailee's lien or rights to possession and use created for a fixed time by the contract.

LIMITATIONS OF LIABILITY.   Ordinarily bailees may limit or reduce or even avoid the liability imposed on them by law, but they may do so only by special contract with the bailor. This is only partially possible in bailments of a public nature. Contract problems in this area, especially with regard to the use of baggage checks and ticket stubs as notification to the bailor of the limiting terms of the contract, are discussed in Chapter 3. Limitations of liability are discussed elsewhere in this and other chapters.

C. Warehousing

A warehouseman is an ordinary bailee and, as such, is not the insurer of the goods entrusted to his care unless he makes himself such by the terms of the contract or by his conduct in violation of the agreement. He is required to exercise reasonable care under the circumstances and is liable only if his standard of conduct falls below that level. By the older view, he would be required to exercise ordinary care, as compared with slight or extreme care, and would be liable only for ordinary negligence.

A warehouseman, although an ordinary bailee, is in a business affected with a public interest. As we have already seen, he is subject to certain special types of regulation. The old Uniform Warehouse Receipts Act provided that the contractual terms in warehouse receipts could not impair the warehouseman's obligation to exercise ordinary care with regard to the good in his possession. A controversy arose as to whether this provision was violated by terms which limited the bailee's liability to stated amounts. The Code eliminates the controversy by setting forth the conditions under which liability may be so limited, including a requirement that the warehouseman accept higher limits of liability at the request of the bailor and at higher rates where lawful. No limitation of liability is effective with respect to the warehousman's liability for conversion of the bailor's goods to his own use. Higher standards of liability may be imposed by the states and by the Federal Government.

The liability of the warehouseman ends when he yields control over the goods in his custody to a person entitled to receive them. If he delivers them to the wrong person, the warehouseman is guilty of conversion.

D. Safe Deposit Companies

In most jurisdictions the safe deposit company is the bailee of property deposited in the safe deposit boxes. The care with which the bailee must protect that property is what one would expect. Although it is the standard of care for other bailments for mutual benefit, it is obvious that in this situation the circumstances would require care of a much higher order than in most other mutual-benefit bailments. It has been held that the renter of a safe deposit box could recover from a bank the loss suffered by him when the bank permitted the finder of the key lost by the renter to enter the box and remove the contents. What would have been reasonable care for an ordinary warehouseman would not be sufficient for a safe deposit company. Note, however, in the case above, the difficult burden of proof the renter of the box might have in establishing its contents.

E. Innkeepers

IN GENERAL.   The duties of an innkeeper are of a public nature, and this type of bailment is properly classified as a public bailment. The innkeeper must accept as guests all reputable persons able to pay, provided there is room to accommodate them. This duty is imposed not by contract but by law. It is just as much the duty of the hotelkeeper to accept the guest's goods and belongings as it is to accept the guest himself. The hotelkeeper is not an insurer of the guest's safety, but he must exercise reasonable care for the safety and comfort of the guest.

LIABILITY FOR GUEST'S PROPERTY. When it comes to the property of the hotel guest, the liability of the hotelkeeper is exceptional. He is generally liable as an insurer of the safety of the guest's property except where the loss or damage is caused by an act of God, by the act of a public enemy, by the act of a public authority, by the very nature of the property, or by the fault of the guest himself. The historical explanation for this extensive liability was discussed briefly above. Many modifications have been made in the common law rule by court decision and especially by statute. In a few states, the hotelkeeper is treated as an ordinary bailee. In other states, the hotelkeeper cannot be held liable where the loss was caused by circumstances beyond his control (the rule of superior force). In still other states, the liability of the hotelkeeper is limited to a certain fixed amount unless the loss was caused by his own or his employee's negligence. A hotelkeeper may limit his liability, except for negligence, fraud, or intentional harm, by special contract with the guest.

Almost all states have statutes permitting the hotelkeeper to keep a safe or vault or strong box on the premises for the protection of money, jewelry, and other valuables of the guests. If the hotelkeeper does provide such a service and gives proper notice to the guests by posting information in appropriate places, he limits his liability to guests who have retained their property to losses resulting from the negligence of the hotelkeeper or his employees. If goods are deposited with the hotelkeeper, his liability is usually limited to a specific amount, without regard to the actual value of the property, unless the loss was caused by the hotelkeeper's negligence or that of his employees, in which case the hotelkeeper is liable in full. These statutes usually do not protect the innkeeper if the guest has not had time to read the notice and deposit his valuables or where the valuables would have been returned to the guest, preparatory to his departure, at the time they were stolen. The special liability of the hotelkeeper ceases after the guest has paid his bill and has left the hotel, except that if baggage is left in the hotel, the guest has a short time under the protection of the special liability during which he may return to pick it up. If the hotelkeeper agrees to deliver the guest's baggage to an airport or to some other place, the special liability lasts until such delivery.

Although the hotelkeeper's liability extends to virtually all of the property brought into the hotel by the guest, including the property of other persons rightfully in the possession of the guest, it does not extend to property brought into the hotel for the purpose of sale or demonstration there. The hotelkeeper's liability in that case is only that of an ordinary bailee. The hotelkeeper is not an insurer of the safety of the property of persons staying in the hotel as boarders and not as guests.

4. POSSESSION AND USE OF PROPERTY

A. Case

(1)

A delivery truck belonging to SIMUCO Toyland was taken to the Berkland Garage for some minor repairs. When Don Danton, one of the partners, went to the garage to get the truck, he refused to pay the bill for the repairs because he thought it was excessive. At first, Cam Schaaf, the proprietor of the garage was not going to let Danton have the truck without paying the bill, but finally let Danton take the truck when Danton said he had to have the truck to pick up some merchandise at the railroad station before the freight office closed at 5 p.m. Nothing more was said or done about the bill for the repairs. Several months later, the truck was again at the Berkland Garage for minor repairs. Earl Eaton, another of the partners, stopped by to get the truck, but Schaaf would not let him have it until he paid the old, as well as the new, repair bill. Eaton was willing to pay the bill for the current repairs but refused to pay for the old ones. What are the rights of the parties?

B. In General

Many of the aspects of the right to possession and use have already been discussed, but some important problems still remain. Upon the creation of the bailment relation, the bailee has a right to *immediate* possession, but the bailor is left with a right of *ultimate* possession. The bailee's right to immediate possession is protected against the whole world, including the bailor, unless the terms of the contract permit the bailor to regain possession at will. If the property is to be used by the bailee, the agreement will usually specify some period during which he is entitled to such use, and the bailor cannot regain possession until that period has expired. Where the bailment is simply for storage, the bailor may usually regain possession whenever he pleases. Where some third person interferes with the bailee's possession of the property, and the bailee is entitled to exclusive, though temporary, possession, the bailee alone may maintain actions against the third person to recover possession of the goods. Where the bailor has a right to possession at will, he also may maintain such an action. Of course, the bailor may maintain the possessory action where the bailee has wrongfully surrendered possession to a third person.

The use of the property that is permitted the bailee is determined by the agreement and by the nature of the bailment. If the bailment is for the sole benefit of the bailor, the bailee has no right to use the goods in the absence of permission by the bailor. A bailment for the sole benefit of the bailee is probably a bailment for use anyway, and the bailee is permitted to use the property within the scope of the bailment. Whether a bailee uses goods he has no right to use or uses goods in a way in which he has no right to use them, he becomes absolutely liable for any harm the goods may suffer as a result of the use. Many uses are justified by the nature of the property itself, and the bailee may even have a duty to use the property in order to maintain it, as, for example exercising a dog or a horse. A warehouseman, a hotelkeeper, or a safe deposit company has no right to use the property placed in his custody, except within the scope of the discussion above.

C. Bailee's Special Rights in Bailed Property : Liens

IN GENERAL. It is a widely known legal fact that frequently when one person performs services upon the goods of another person, the person performing the services has a right to keep possession of the other's property until the charges for performing the services have been paid. Furthermore, if the charges are not paid, the property may sometimes be sold to satisfy the charges. The legal device by which one party is given these unusual powers over the property of another is called a *lien*. The lien is usually defined as a qualified legal right which one person may have in the property of another to secure the performance of some obligation owed by the latter party to the former. A lien may be *possessory* or *non-possessory* depending upon whether the person with the right to a lien must have possession of the property in order for the lien to be effective. There may be lien rights in either real or personal property. (The lien is discussed in greater detail in Chapter 13.)

Liens arise quite commonly in bailment situations. Of course such liens apply only to personal property. With the exception of a few special situations, the lien rights that the various types of bailee may acquire are possessory liens, indicating that the lien does not exist where the bailee does not have possession of the subject property and is lost when the bailee relinquishes possession of the property. Some of the more important lien situations in connection with bailments are discussed below.

Both by common law and by statute a warehouseman has a lien for storage charges on the property left with him. Although common law liens do not usually permit the sale of the goods, the statutory warehouseman's liens do permit such sale. The Uniform Commercial Code provides for either a private or a public sale following notification of parties interested in the goods, provided that the goods were stored by a merchant in the course of his business. Otherwise, the sale must be public and then take place only after somewhat more severe notification requirements have been met.

When the *lienor,* the person who has the lien, voluntarily releases the goods subject to the lien, the lien is destroyed and is normally not even revived if the goods should come back into the possession of the lienor. Special statutes in some states revive liens for automobile storage even though the automobile was voluntarily released by the lienor. Where the property is forcibly removed from the possession of the lienor, either by the lienee or by a third person, the lienor maintains his interest, as he does where the release is voluntary but obtained by fraud. It is important to note, however, that when the property leaves the possession of the bailee, voluntarily or otherwise, innocent third persons may acquire rights that will conflict with those of the bailee. Usually these rights take precedence over the bailee's lien rights, except where the property was removed without the bailee's consent. Some statutes permit a bailee to release the property and maintain his lien by filing notice in some public office.

When property already subject to a mortgage or a conditional sales contract becomes subject also to a bailee's lien, a problem of priority arises. Should the lienor's rights prevail over those of the prior mortgagee or conditional seller? Normally the priority of legal interests is determined by the order of their creation. Although subsequent legal interests sometimes prevail over prior interests because the holders of the prior interests have created or permitted situations likely to deceive holders of subsequent interests who acquire the subsequent interests in good faith and for value, the requirements of public recordation in the case of secured transactions almost universally assure that the holders of the subsequent interests can ascertain in advance the existence of the antecedent interests. Thus, with the general exception of the hotelkeeper, the interest of the prior mortgagee or conditional seller prevails over that of the lienor. In some states, artisans' liens may prevail even over recorded earlier security interests. An artisan is one who is skilled in some mechanical art or craft, as an automobile mechanic or an appliance repairman. The Code takes this view but permits contrary state law to prevail.

It is interesting to note that a lien is not terminated by the running of the statute of limitations against the claim secured by the lien, nor by the discharge of the claim in bankruptcy.

A lien may be either a *general* or a *special lien*. Most bailee's liens are *special lines*. This means that the bailee may retain possession of personal property only to secure his claims arising out of the same transaction. A garagekeeper who has made repairs to one car belonging to *A*, for example, has a lien against that particular car for the amount due on the repairs, but he would have no lien on that car for the prior storage charges on another car or a lien against another car for the repairs made on this one. A *general lien* is one which secures not only the particular claim rising out of the bailment but also a general balance of accounts rising out of prior but similar dealings between the same parties.

5. COMMON CARRIERS

A. Cases

(1)

Hypocase, Inc. delivered a large number of pallets to the Eastern Pacific Railroad for further delivery to a buyer in San Francisco. The pallets were promptly loaded onto freight cars and dispatched to San Francisco, where they arrived after a normal lapse of time. The consignee was not notified of the arrival, and ten days later the entire shipment, while still stored on railroad company premises, was destroyed by a fire which started in a nearby manufacturing plant. What is the liability of Eastern Pacific?

(2)

Hypocase, Inc. shipped a carload of pallets to its Philadelphia warehouse. The pallets were turned over to the Eastern Pacific Railraod in Berkland but, because Eastern Pacific does not serve Pennsylvania, the pallets were transferred to the Keyboard Shoreline Railway in Chicago for delivery to Philadelphia. While in the possession of Keyboard, the pallets were totally destroyed without any fault on the part of Keyboard. The shipment was valued at approximately $10,000. The Eastern Pacific contract entered into by Hypocase for the shipment of the goods contained a clause, as do all Eastern Pacific contracts, limiting the liability of Eastern Pacific to a maximum of $1,000 unless the shipper paid a special rate. Hypocase did not pay the special rate. What are the rights of Hypocase against Eastern Pacific and Keyboard?

(3)

Bob Baker, one of the partners in SIMUCO Toyland, went to the Berkland airport to board a plane for St. Louis, where he was going to visit a new toy factory that had been soliciting the SIMUCO business. Baker checked in at the Amalgamated Airline ticket counter and walked around inside the terminal for a few minutes waiting for his plane to be called. When the plane was called, Baker went to the proper gate and had just handed his ticket to the gate attendant for inspection when a service vehicle owned by another airline and standing near the passenger gate suddenly caught fire and exploded, seriously injuring Baker and several other waiting passengers. What is the liability of Amalgamated Airline for Baker's injuries?

B. In General

All businessmen, either as consignors or as consignees, come occasionally into contact with the special type of bailee known as the common carrier, and most businessmen have frequent contact with this bailee. A large proportion of the people dealing with carriers have an incomplete understanding of the rights and duties attaching to such transactions, with the result that unnecessary trouble and inconvenience are caused to all parties concerned. The discussion below is for the primary edification of such businessmen and of the students of their problems. As with negotiable instruments, the fact that the vast majority of the contracts for carriage are entered into and performed without a ripple of disturbance lulls most people into complacency. It is hoped that the ensuing discussion will protect rather than destroy this peaceful state of mind.

As it has been pointed out before, a private carrier is an ordinary bailee and is subject to the general rules discussed above. The common carrier, on the other hand, is a public or a special bailee and is subject to special rules and regulations under the law. Not only must a common carrier serve all those who apply, but he is also liable as an insurer of the property delivered to him for transportation. Statutes have invaded this area to a considerable extent. The law discussed below is only a general statement of the law without any attempt to differentiate between those principles which are of common law origin and those which stem from statutes. Although common carriers of persons are not bailees of the persons they carry, but are of course bailees of the passengers' baggage, we will briefly consider anyway the duties and responsibilities of the carriers of persons.

C. Common Carriers of Goods

LIABILITY OF THE CARRIER.   When goods have been delivered to a common carrier for immediate shipment, the special bailment of the common carrier comes into existence, and imposed on the carrier is the unusual liability of an insurer. Where the goods are delivered to the carrier but not for immediate shipment, an ordinary bailment is created instead of the special bailment of the common carrier. The special bailment of the common carrier begins when goods are accepted for immediate shipment, or, if the goods were accepted for future shipment, at the time the goods were to be shipped. The special relationship ends when delivery is made in accordance with the terms of the contract between consignor and carrier. This contract may provide for actual delivery to the consignee, in which case the special bailment relationship does not end until the goods have been delivered to the proper person at the proper place within a reasonable time. Rail and water carriers, unless they have expressly contracted to do so, are not required to deliver to the consignee; in which case delivery normally takes place at the freight house, dock, or depot. The unusual liability of the carrier continues until the consignee has had a reasonable time to remove the goods. By the better and prevailing view, notice to the consignee by the carrier is necessary, but there is a minority view to the contrary.

Unlike rail and water carriers, express companies are required to deliver the goods to the consignee. In either case, the carrier is liable as an insurer for the delivery of the goods to the proper person, except where he delivers the goods under a court order or to a person with a title superior to that of the consignee. A carrier who accepts C. O. D. shipments becomes in effect the agent of the consignor to collect the price from the consignee and turn it over to the consignor. The carrier is liable for any loss if he fails to collect the price. As it has been mentioned elsewhere, the consignee of C.O.D. shipments is not entitled to examine the goods before paying for them, unless the consignor has agreed to such examination.

Unique problems may arise in situations where goods are transferred from one carrier to another in the process of transportation from origin to destination. The carrier receiving the goods is called the *initial carrier;* the others, *connecting carriers.* The initial carrier is liable to the consignor for loss or damage to the goods suffered while in the hands of a connecting carrier. The reason for the rule is simple. The initial carrier is in a much better position than the consignor to determine which carrier was liable for the loss or damage. After the initial carrier has paid the consignor for the loss, he is entitled to recover the amount of the payment from the connecting carrier in whose possession the goods were when the loss occurred.

EXCEPTIONS TO THE INSURER'S LIABILITY. It will be recalled that the carrier's liability as an insurer of the safety of the goods imposes upon the carrier an absolute liability without regard to care or negligence. The origins of the rule were probably much the same as the origins of the innkeeper's absolute liability: to prevent collusion between carriers and the highway robbers and thieves who were prevalent during earlier times in England. Furthermore, the consignor would be in a very difficult position if he had to prove negligence on the part of a carrier or its agents. As it was previously pointed out, however, there are certain exceptions to the general rule.

Loss caused by act of God. An *act of God* is an event of nature that could not reasonably have been foreseen by the carrier. Catastrophes, such as earthquakes, hurricanes, tornadoes, lightning, and extraordinary rains or snowstorms are generally classified as acts of God. The act of God must be the sole cause of the damage or of the delay, but if there has been an intervention by some human agency, the carrier is still liable. A difference of opinion exists where a delay is caused by the carrier itself, and a loss, which would not have occurred but for the delay, is caused by an act of God. The better rule seems to be that the carrier's delay did not create the risk of loss by an act of God; thus, the carrier is not liable. There is opinion to the contrary, especially where the delay by the carrier is for an unreasonable length of time.

Loss caused by a public enemy. In spite of the popular use of the term "public enemy" to refer to gangsters and robbers, the legal meaning does not include these persons. Nor does it include mobs or rioters. A public enemy, in the sense the term is used legally, includes only revolutionaries and the hostile military forces of countries with whom the United States is at war.

Loss caused by act or fault of consignor. Where the person shipping the goods fails to pack or prepare them properly for shipment, and the loss is caused by such improper preparation, the carrier is not liable except where he knew of the improper preparations and failed either to correct the defect or to refuse to accept the goods for shipment. If the goods are described and loaded by the consignor, the carrier may, by inserting in the contract the words "shipper's load and count," indicate that the goods were loaded by the shipper and the description made by him. If such statement is true, the carrier is not liable for damages caused by the improper loading, by the non-receipt, or by the misdescription of the goods described in the contract.

Loss caused by the inherent nature of the goods. A common carrier is not liable for the natural deterioration of perishable goods unless he knew the nature of the goods and failed to take reasonable precautions to preserve them. The carrier is, of course, under a duty to provide adequate facilities for the shipment of perishable goods of which the carrier is aware.

Loss caused by act of public authority. If goods, while in the possession of the carrier, are seized under order of court or by any other legal process, the carrier is not liable for such loss. This exception is as applicable to the destruction by a public health authority of property infected with a disease as it is to seizure by a sheriff under an attachment.

CONTRACTUAL LIMITATIONS ON THE CARRIER'S LIABILITY. Inasmuch as the contractual limitation of liability has been discussed elsewhere, only brief reference will be made to that particular issue here. A common carrier may reasonably limit his liability by contract with the consignor provided that four conditions are met:

1. The person shipping the goods had reasonable notice of the limitation and agreed to that limitation.

2. There was reasonable consideration given to the shipper by the carrier in exchange for the shipper's agreement to limit the carrier's liability. The consideration usually takes the form of reduced rates.

3. The shipper must have had the opportunity to hold the carrier to full liability by paying a higher rate.

4. The limitation itself must be reasonable.

If any of these factors is missing from the situation, the limitation is void.

A common carrier may, by complying with the above requirements, avoid liability for loss caused by fire, theft, delay in transport, breakage, shrinkage, mobs, riots, and other events short of the carrier's own negligence. In a manner similar to that in which a precode controversy over the limitations of a warehouseman's liability for his own negligence was eliminated, the Code deals with the problem of limitations of a carrier's liability for his own negligence. Such limitations are effective where the carrier's rates are based on the stated value of the goods and where the shipper has an opportunity to declare a higher value. The Code provisions apply both to the carrier's liability as an insurer and to his liability based on negligence. As with the warehouseman, the carrier cannot limit his liability for conversion of the shipper's goods to his own use.

CARRIER'S LIEN. The carrier has a common law lien for his charges on goods delivered to him for transportation. The Code extends the carrier's lien to include the power to sell the goods in satisfaction of the carrier's claim. The carrier's lien varies only in minor details from the bailee's liens discussed in general above.

D. Common Carriers of Persons

IN GENERAL. The common carrier of persons engages to accept for transportation all reputable persons able to pay, except where the facilities of the carrier cannot accommodate those requesting transportation. Wrongful refusal by the carrier to accept a person as a passenger makes the carrier liable to that person for damages. Included among the common carriers of persons are those operating buses, railroads, airlines, taxicabs, subways, streetcars, and steamships.

LIABILITY WITH REGARD TO PASSENGERS. Obviously, the most important duty of the common carrier of persons is to carry the persons safely to their destinations. However, the carrier is not the insurer of the passenger's safety. The carrier's duty is to exercise the highest degree of care consistent with the practical operation of the carrier's facilities, or, to put it another way, the carrier is liable for injuries resulting from the slightest negligence on the part of the carrier.

In addition to the duty of care, the carrier also has the following duties: 1, to make reasonable rules and regulations for the transportation of passengers; 2, to avoid unreasonable delays; and 3, to give the passenger a reasonable opportunity to board the conveyance and to depart from it. The issue as to what a "passenger" is sometimes arises. In general, a *passenger* is one who has put himself within the confines of the carrier's facilities with the carrier's permission. Such a description has been held to include a person waiting on a railroad station platform to board a train.

LIABILITY WITH REGARD TO BAGGAGE. The carrier's liability with regard to the passenger's baggage is the same as that of a common carrier of goods. This absolute liability of the insurer comes into operation when the passenger delivers his baggage to the carrier a reasonable time before the departure of the conveyance and ends when the passenger has had a reasonable time to remove his baggage after arrival at the passenger's destination. The carrier holds baggage delivered or left in his possession outside these times as an ordinary bailee. The rules in connection with the contractual limitation of carrier's liability are substantially the same as with the common carrier of goods.

Some special problems do arise in regard to the determination of what property constitutes baggage A carrier may be able to escape liability as an insurer, or all liability, by showing that particular goods claimed to have been lost or damaged were not baggage. In general, *baggage* consists of those articles the passenger carries with him in reasonable quantity and value for the convenience or necessity of the passenger during his journey or after his arrival at his destination. The articles must normally be for the passenger's personal use. Salesmen's samples, merchandise, household goods, and valuable stocks and bonds, jewelry or money in unreasonable amount or of exceptional value are not baggage. It should be noted that the insurer's liability of the carrier extends only to the baggage that has been *delivered* to the carrier. Consequently, the carrier is not the insurer of hand baggage kept in the passenger's own possession or on his person. Toward this baggage the carrier has only the duty of ordinary care. Nor is the carrier an insurer of baggage checked in his parcel room. This transaction is an ordinary bailment.

6. TERMINATION OF THE BAILMENT RELATION

The bailment relation may be terminated either by act of the parties or by performance of the acts or services for which the bailment was created. In the latter situation, it should be noted that the bailee is not necessarily released from his duties as a bailee when he completes the services with respect to which he contracted with the bailor. Where a bailee, for example, finishes the repairs that he agreed to perform on the bailed property, he still has the duty to redeliver the goods to the bailor or to some other person as directed by the bailor. The bailee is liable for the misdelivery of bailed goods whether or not he used due care.

A bailment relation may be terminated by the joint act of the parties, as where the bailee voluntarily returns the bailed goods to the bailor with the bailor's consent. Normally, that which is created by an agreement can be terminated by an agreement between the parties involved. Where the bailment is for the sole benefit of the bailor, he may terminate the bailment at will. The bailee has no interest in the property and cannot complain if the bailor terminates the bailment relation.

In a bailment for mutual benefit, which arises out of contract, the duration of the bailment is usually specified in the contract. Premature termination by either party is possible but subjects the terminating party to liability for breach of contract. Where the bailor delivers property to the bailee for the bailee's use and for hire, the bailee has a special property interest in the goods which prevents the bailor from prematurely terminating the relation by his own act. The result is the same where the bailment is gratuitous and the bailor has given the bailee the use of the property for a fixed time. Where the time is indefinite, the bailor may terminate at will without liability.

Note that the bailee may terminate the bailment even though it is created under contract. He may redeliver the property to the bailor or may simply refuse to retain possession of the property. There is no legal machinery by which the bailee can be compelled to retain possession of bailed goods or to perform services with regard to them. Of course, the bailee's termination of the bailment may amount to a breach of contract for which the bailor is entitled to damages. A bailee may terminate a bailment that is for his sole benefit without any risk of liability, but where the bailment is for the sole benefit of the bailor, the bailee may be liable to the bailor for such damage as the bailor may have suffered as a result of the premature termination. There is usually no obligation under the common law to perform gratuitous undertakings, but when a bailee begins performance by taking possession of the goods of another person, he must exercise reasonable care in the undertaking. The premature return of the goods or abandonment of the undertaking may be a violation of this duty.

7. DOCUMENTS USED IN BAILMENT SITUATIONS

A. In General

In most bailments, the documents involved, if any, are just ordinary simple contracts, but in connection with some of the bailments of a public nature, especially those for transportation or storage, special documents are used. When they receive bailed goods for transportation or storage, common carriers and warehousemen issue to the bailor written instruments which may serve a number of different purposes. As a rule, the instrument is a receipt for the goods delivered to the bailee, represents title or ownership of the goods delivered, and contains the terms of the contract under which the goods are received by the bailee. The instrument issued by a common carrier is called a *bill of lading*. That issued by a warehouseman is called a *warehouse receipt*. Both are frequently referred to as *documents of title* because they are physical manifestations or symbols of the ownership of the goods. Although many of the legal problems rising out of the issue of these documents are ordinary contract problems, there are some legal questions peculiar to instruments of this type. These latter questions are discussed briefly below.

The real significance of the document of title is that it represents and is equivalent to the ownership of the property described therein. What this means, as a practical matter, is that the holder of the document may own the goods without the necessity of actual or physical control over the goods themselves. By the mere transfer of the piece of paper, the ownership in a very large quantity of goods may be passed from one person to another. The convenience of this legal device in a wide variety of transactions is obvious. Goods may be sold without the need for physical transfer of possession of the goods, and, probably more important, goods may be pledged or mortgaged without pledgees or mortgagees having to take custody of the goods themselves. Other financial transactions are also facilitated by the documents of title. The important areas of inquiry are the method of transfer of the documents and the rights of the transferee. Baggage and parking checks and the like are not documents of title.

The law in this area is largely a matter of statute. Prior to the adoption of the Uniform Commercial Code, the major applicable statutes were the Uniform Bills of Lading Act, the Uniform Warehouse Receipts Act, and the Federal Bills of Lading Act. The first two have been replaced by Article 7 of the Uniform Commercial Code. The Federal Act still controls bills of lading issued for interstate and foreign commerce.

The fact that documents of title are, at the same time, receipts for goods bailed, contracts for storage or shipment, and evidence of the ownership of goods makes them extremely useful instruments in the channels of trade. Used in connection with commercial paper, especially drafts, they can help to obtain a seller's money for him immediately or assure him of continued control over those goods, even while they are in the hands of a carrier or a warehouseman or until a buyer has paid for them. By way of illustration and in order to complete the description of normal business practice begun in the chapter on commercial paper, let us consider the shipment of a quantity of swimsuits from a seller in California to a buyer in Chicago. Either because he wishes to retain control over the goods as security or because he wants to obtain money from the sale at the time of shipment, the seller obtains from the carrier a bill of lading issued to the seller's own order, which makes him both the consignor and the consignee. The buyer appears on the bill only as the person to be notified. The seller will draw a draft on the buyer, with himself as payee, attach the draft to the bill of lading, and take or send the documents to his own bank. If the seller has properly indorsed the draft and the bill, the bank will discount the draft and deposit the proceeds in the seller's account. The seller now has his money without having to wait for the buyer to pay. The bank sends the documents to its correspondent in Chicago, who presents the draft to the buyer for payment. When the buyer pays the draft, he is given possession of the bill of lading. When the swimsuits arrive in Chicago, the carrier notifies the buyer, who surrenders the bill and gets possession of his goods.

Had the credit rating of the buyer been high, the seller could have obtained a straight bill of lading, when he delivered the goods to the carrier, with the buyer named as consignee; he could thus have simply forwarded the bill to the buyer, who could then obtain the goods without even giving up the bill.

Both negotiable and non-negotiable documents of title can be used as security for loans. The owner of goods deposits them in a warehouse and then delivers the warehouse receipt to the lender as collateral on the loan. This use of the documents will be discussed in greater detail in the next chapter.

B. Negotiable and Non-Negotiable Documents

Documents of title are, as a whole, formal contracts whose effect is derived from the presence of certain formality and certain language. A negotiable bill of lading, or *order bill*, is one in which the goods are consigned "to the order of" the person specified in the bill. The phrase "to the order of" or its equivalent must appear on the instrument. A non-negotiable bill of lading, or *straight bill*, states that the goods will be delivered to the person who deposited the goods or to some other specified person. A non-negotiable bill must have the words "non" or "not negotiable" printed plainly across its face. If not, a person unaware of its non-negotiable nature may be able to treat it as a negotiable bill. If a bill contains the phrase "to the order of," it cannot be made non-negotiable by writing or printing on it a statement that the bill is not negotiable. A negotiable warehouse receipt states that the goods will be delivered "to the order of" or "to the bearer." "Bearer" rarely appears in bills of lading. A non-negotiable receipt makes the goods deliverable to the depositor or to some other specified person.

As one might expect, different rights and duties accrue to the holders of negotiable bills and receipts than accrue to holders of the non-negotiable variety. When a negotiable document of title has been issued, a bailee is under a positive duty to deliver the goods only upon surrender of the document. In the case of a non-negotiable bill or receipt, the bailee may deliver the goods upon the authority of a separate written instrument and without surrender of the document. So much significance is attached to the difference between the two kinds of documents that federal regulations now require them to be printed on different colors of paper: order bills on yellow and straight bills on white.

Section 7-502 of the Code provides that a holder to whom a negotiable document of title has been duly negotiated acquires thereby:

(a) title to the document;

(b) title to the goods;

(c) all rights accruing under the law of agency or estoppel, including rights to goods delivered to the bailee after the document was issued; and

(d) the direct obligation of the issuer to hold or deliver the goods according to the terms of the document free of any defense or claim by him except those arising under the terms of the document . . . .

As was learned in Chapter 11, the chief characteristic of a negotiable instrument is the ability of its transferor to give to the transferee even greater rights than the transferor himself had. Except for defenses similar to those discussed in Chapter 11, the transferee of a negotiable bill of lading or warehouse receipt has a claim against the carrier or warehouseman which is free of any defenses the carrier or warehouseman might have had against other parties to the transaction. The holder of a bill of lading or warehouse receipt is subject, however, to the carrier's or warehouseman's lien for transportation or storage charges.

The transferee of a non-negotiable document of title is, for most purposes, merely the assignee of the transferor's contract rights and, as such, is subject to all of the defenses by the carrier or warehouseman which would have been good against the transferor. If the transferor of the instrument, for example, obtains the goods from the carrier after having made a previous transfer of the instrument, the carrier is not liable to the transferee unless the carrier had notice of the prior transfer. This result is possible because the non-negotiable bill or receipt tells the carrier simply to deliver the goods to a named person, and this the carrier can do without the presentation of the document itself. Unless the transferee has previously given notice of the transfer to the carrier, the rights of the transferee against the carrier may be destroyed by seizure of the goods by the transferor's creditors. Furthermore, if the transferor sells the goods to a purchaser after the transfer of the instrument, and notice of the sale of the goods is given to the carrier before notice of the transfer, the transferee may lose his rights against the carrier. In all of these cases, however, the transferee may give himself reasonable protection by prompt notice, and does, of course, have rights against the transferor. These problems are avoided where a negotiable bill is issued because the carrier will not deliver the goods except on surrender of the bill. If he should deliver without surrender, the holder of the negotiable instrument may recover from the carrier. The discussion above applies with equal force to warehouse receipts.

C. Negotiation of Documents

The non-negotiable document is transferred by simple assignment. No writing or indorsement is necessary, though it may be present. The transfer of negotiable documents is accomplished by negotiation. Where the document is in the "order" form, it is negotiated by the indorsement of the transferor and delivery to the transferee. If it is in the "bearer" form, the document may be negotiated by delivery alone. As with commercial paper, an order bill or receipt indorsed to a specified person can be further negotiated only by the indorsement of that person, but where a bill is indorsed in blank or to bearer, it becomes a bearer document and further negotiation may be by delivery alone. A finder or a thief of a bearer document may negotiate by mere delivery and may give to an innocent purchaser the same rights the purchaser would have received from the true owner. However, negotiation under Code rules is not effective unless made in the regular course of business or financing, and it cannot be made in settlement of a money obligation. Thus, a finder or thief might find it difficult to create circumstances establishing a "regular course of business." A few states omitted this requirement when they adopted the Code.

Once a document of title becomes a bearer document, it cannot be reconverted into an order document requiring indorsement for the negotiation thereof. In this respect, the Code provision for negotiable documents of title is contrary to its rule for commercial paper. It is important to remember that negotiable documents of title are not really "negotiable instruments" in the sense that promissory notes, drafts, and checks are. They are not designed to pass through the channels of trade almost as though they were money. On the other hand, trade and commerce are facilitated by giving them many of the characteristics of commercial paper, at least as far as that is necessary in order to make them effective symbols of the ownership of personal property.

The indorser or transferor of a negotiable document of title does not guarantee payment or performance and cannot be held liable by anyone if the bailee fails to deliver the goods to the holder of the document. However, he does make certain warranties with regard to the genuineness of the document, his lack of knowledge of any fact that would impair its validity or worth, and his rightful negotiation or transfer of the instrument—but these warranties run only to his immediate transferee. Discounting banks do not make these warranties, but they do warrant their good faith and authority.

PROBLEMS

1. What is a bailment? Give examples.

2. What property may be the subject of a bailment? Is it necessary that the bailor actually own the property in order for there to be a valid bailment?

3. Distinguish a bailment from the following: sale, gift, mortgage, trust, bank deposit.

4. *A* drives his automobile into a parking lot, parks it, and leaves it. Has *A* entered into a bailment relation? Explain.

5. Bailments are of many different varieties. How are they classified?

6. Describe briefly the bailment aspects of the following: warehousing, safe deposit box, hotelkeeper, carrier.

7. Describe the care that *A* should exercise toward *B*'s automobile in each of the following situations:

    a. *A* borrows *B*'s automobile to use while *A's* is being repaired.

    b. *A* rents *B's* automobile at $5 a day.

    c. *B* stores his automobile in *A's* garage while *B* spends the summer in Europe.

Who will have to pay for gas, oil, routine maintenance, and the repair of the speedometer in each of the above situations? On whom would fall the loss resulting from accidental destruction of the automobile by fire in each of the above situations?

8. In 7(c) above, *C* claims that the automobile is his, not *B's*, and demands possession. What should *A* do? Explain.

9. Under what circumstances could a bailee become the insurer of the safety of bailed goods?

10. *A* pledged a diamond ring to *B* as security for a $1000 loan. *B*, in turn, pledged the ring to *C* as security for a loan to *B*. What are the rights of *A, B,* and *C*?

11. What courses of action are open to a pledgee whose pledgor has defaulted?

12. Describe the liability of an innkeeper for the property of his guests.

13. Does a bailee have the right to use bailed property? Explain. Does he ever have the *duty* to use it?

14. Oner placed his freezer in Handy's shop for repairs. Handy expended labor and materials on the freezer and presented Oner with a bill for $65. Oner said that he would send Handy a check the first of the month, and Handy permitted Oner to take the freezer. Two days later, Oner placed his refrigerator in Handy's shop for

repairs. Handy expended labor and materials and presented a bill for $35. Oner offered to pay but Handy refused to let him remove the refrigerator until the charges for the freezer repairs had been paid also. This Oner refused to do. Late that night, Oner broke into the shop and removed his refrigerator. The next day he sold it to Paul, who knew of the claim by Handy. What are Handy's rights?

15. Explain the terms common carrier and private carrier.

16. How does the bailment relation of the common carrier differ from the ordinary bailment?

17. Explain the following statement: The initial carrier is liable to the consignor for loss or damage to the goods suffered while in the hands of the connecting carrier.

18. Under what circumstances may the common carrier not be liable as the insurer of the safety of goods being carried? Can he limit his liability by contract? Explain.

19. As a result of an accident on the X Railroad, P, a passenger, was seriously injured and his baggage destroyed. What is the liability of X to P?

20. List and describe briefly the ways in which a bailment may be terminated.

21. What function is performed by such documents of title as the bill of lading and the warehouse receipt?

22. What are the differences in wording between an order bill and a straight bill?

23. A delivered goods to a common carrier and received a bill of lading drawn in his favor. A endorsed the bill of lading and delivered it to B, a bona fide purchaser for value. What are B's rights where the bill is an order bill? Where the bill is a straight bill?

chapter 13

Financing the Going Business and Securing Credit

1. IN GENERAL

Our discussion in this chapter will be focused on those legal techniques that have evolved for the purpose of facilitating the raising of capital and the extension and securing of credit. Closely related and sometimes almost indistinguishable from the techniques themselves are the rights and remedies of the creditors who have provided the capital or afforded the credit. A businessman may be concerned with the methods by which the necessary money for starting or operating his business will be provided and with the details of the financial arrangements he may encounter in his search for capital, credit, and financing. What is of interest to the businessman-borrower or debtor is equally applicable to the businessman-lender or creditor. The businessman who seeks financing for his own activities may find at the same time that he is being called upon to help with the financing of someone else's business. A wholesaler, for example, may seek aid in financing his own purchases from a manufacturer, and be called upon by his customers for credit or other financial aid in connection with his sales to them.

Much of the material related to these universal needs of businessmen and other buyers and sellers is discussed elsewhere in this book. Some of the most important financial instruments—drafts, promissory notes, and checks—have been examined in detail in the chapter on commercial paper. The rights of creditors on the default of a debtor and the special problems of insolvency are dealt with in the final chapter. Issues primarily associated with raising capital for a new business are considered in detail in Chapter 6. Our basic concern in this chapter is with going business and with various types of security interest in real and personal property. Although the subject matter is approached largely from the point of view of the person engaged in business, much of what is said has broad application also to the ordinary consumer who seeks aid in making his purchases and to the person who seeks to raise money, for whatever purpose, by giving his property as security or by obtaining access to the credit reputation of others.

The list of financial arrangements discussed below is by no means exhaustive, but it does contain the more important and more frequently used methods by which financing is accomplished and credit secured. Actually, the list is much more nearly exhaustive since the well-nigh universal enactment of the Uniform Commercial Code than it was before, because the Code has brought a very large proportion of all the devices in use in this area under the aegis of its broad Article 9: Secured Transactions. Our first look, however, will be at the lien, not because it is itself an important financial arrangement, but because the lien concept plays a valuable role in most of the legal techniques of finance and secured credit. After the lien, we shall move to a discussion of Article 9, which encompasses most of the field of our concern. The chapter concludes with a treatment of the real estate mortgage and of suretyship and guaranty.

2. LIENS

A. Case

(1)

When SIMUCO Toyland purchased its present store building in 1966, the firm borrowed $17,500 from William Watson and gave Watson a mortgage on the property as security for the repayment of the loan. The mortgage was never recorded. Through regular payments of interest and principal, the unpaid balance had been reduced to slightly less than $12,000 by June, 1970. Early in 1960, the partners decided to remodel the store building and engaged the services of an architect and Hiram Bild, a building contractor. Work was begun in April and completed by the end of May. On the 27th of June, SIMUCO paid the last instalment of the amount due to Hiram Bild under the contract for the remodeling. On July 1, the partners found out that Bild had not paid the Berkland Lumber Company for materials valued at $5,000 used by Bild in the SIMUCO job and that Berkland Lumber had filed a lien against the store building. What are the rights of SIMUCO, Watson, Berkland Lumber, and Bild?

B. In General

USE OF THE TERM. There has been frequent occasion throughout this book to use the term "lien." Easy understanding of the term is complicated by the fact it is used in a number of different ways. In the broad sense, the term embraces or is intimately related to almost all security devices affecting both real and personal property. In a narrow sense, it may apply only to personal property in one's possession. Modern usage suggests that when *lien* is employed without qualifying adjectives or possessive nouns, it simply refers to a qualified right or power a creditor has over the property of another person as security for the performance of an obligation. Although most of the security devices embody liens or rights in the nature of a lien, there is a good deal more to the security devices than this type of right. Consequently, while the understanding of the lien is important, it is only a small part of the understanding of most security devices. Much of the discussion here is very general and largely historical in character and is designed primarily to provide the reader with the background necessary for understanding the other material in this chapter.

Certain special types of liens, such as the artisan's lien and the hotelkeeper's lien, have been referred to elsewhere. The mechanic's lien will be discussed below, after a brief look at liens in a broader sense.

TYPES OF LIENS. The original liens, now called *common law liens,* gave to a creditor the right to retain in his possession specific personal property of a debtor as security for some debt or obligation owed by the debtor to the creditor. These liens applied only to personal property. (See Chapter 7 for detailed distinctions between real and personal property.) The common law lien was also a *possessory lien.* This meant that the existence of the lien depended upon the actual possession of the property by the creditor. Note that the lien right simply gave to the creditor the right to retain possession of the debtor's property and not to sell it in satisfaction of the obligation. The common law liens were the artisan's or repairman's lien, the innkeeper's lien, the warehouseman's lien, the carrier's lien, and mercantile liens, such as the attorney's. Some of these are discussed also in Chapter 12 in connection with the use of the bailment relationship.

The principle of the lien has been extended far beyond the original common law concept, and liens of the strictly common law type are very rare today. Liens now extend to real property as well as to personal; some liens do not require possession of the property by the creditor; the right of sale by the creditor now attaches to most liens; liens are now found in areas and situations where the common law lien could not have applied. Historically, the extension of the lien has come about through statutory enactment and through the recognition in courts of equity of liens which did not exist at common law.

As can be gathered from the above discussion, liens may be classified as *common law, equitable,* and *statutory* or as *possessory* and *non-possessory.* The former classification will be referred to in the following paragraphs as paragraph headings indicating the origin of the liens under discussion. Liens may be classified also as *general* or *specific.* A *specific lien* is the right of a creditor to retain possession of the specific property in regard to which services have been performed or in regard to which a specific obligation arose. With a specific lien there would be no lien on one piece of property for services performed on another. A *general lien,* on the other hand, is the right of the creditor to retain property, not merely for obligations arising out of the particular property, but for debts due him on a general account with the debtor. The law favors specific liens. Consequently, general liens only come into existence as the result of express agreement, mercantile custom, or statute.

C. Common Law Liens

Common carriers, warehousemen, and innkeepers have liens on property on which they perform services. The lien is usually possessory, and the lienor ordinarily has the power to sell the property after complying with certain statutory requirements. Improvers of property, such as repairmen, also have a lien on the property they improve to secure the payment of their charges. These liens are also possessory and are destroyed, as a general rule, when possession of the property is surrendered. These and other common law liens are discussed in detail in Chapter 12.

D. Equitable Liens

The equitable lien differs in several respects from the old common law lien as it was before its scope and details were modified by statute. Equitable liens may arise with regard to either real or personal property. They are not possessory liens and are not founded on a right to retain possession. They are instead an interest in or a "charge" on the property. An equitable lien is enforceable only by a procedure in equity. An equitable lien will arise, for example, where one party is to receive compensation for services out of a particular fund which has yet to come into existence, as where *A* agrees to market timber for *B* and is to be paid from the proceeds of the sales. *A* will have an equitable lien on the proceeds whether or not they are in his possession.

E. Statutory Liens

It is now somewhat difficult to segregate the statutory liens from the others for the simple reason that statutes have extended, modified, and affected virtually all liens, in addition to creating new ones. The breakdown of our discussion is based on the origin of the particular liens. On this ground statutory liens may be distinguished from the other types. Statutes have created a number of new liens with regard to personal property, such as the landlord's lien and the finder's lien, but the most important statutory liens are those that apply to real property. In this latter category are the mechanic's lien and the betterment liens. The *betterment liens,* which are found in some states, but not all, create a lien upon land in favor of a person who places permanent improvements on the land in good faith and under the mistaken belief that he is the owner.

MECHANIC'S LIEN. The mechanic's lien is purely statutory and is non-possessory in nature. It is probably the most important of the statutory liens. It exists in favor of persons who have performed work or services or furnished materials for the improvement of real property. Thus, contractors, suppliers, and workmen who have participated in the building of a house have a lien against the property for their unpaid claims. The lien attaches to the land as well as to the building. Obviously, the lien cannot arise unless the work was done at the express or implied request of the property owner.

In order to establish their liens, lienors must file a notice of lien within a certain specified period of time, usually from sixty to one hundred twenty days after completion of the work, and then they must bring action to enforce the lien within another specified period, varying from ninety days to two years, depending upon the jurisdiction. Liens are generally enforced by a procedure similar to the foreclosure of real estate mortgages, which will be discussed later in this chapter. In some states, if the lienor is a subcontractor, workman, materialman, or any other person except the general contractor, the lien is good even though the owner has paid part or all of the contract price to the general contractor. In other states, the lien is good only to the extent of what is owing by the owner to the general contractor. Notice of the filing of the lien is usually required to be served on the owner or on his agent.

The mechanic's lien is not superior to prior liens on the property unless a prior lien is unrecorded and the lienor under the mechanic's lien had no actual notice of its existence. It is frequently stated that the priority of earlier liens extends only to the value of the property in its unimproved state and that mechanic's liens do have priority to the extent that an improvement has been made, if this is capable of being determined. It is important to note that the priority of the mechanic's lien, in any event, dates not from the completion of the work but from the commencement of the work. Thus, a prospective creditor of the owner looking to the property as security should examine the situation with care if improvements appear to have been begun on that property.

Any businessman or other person contemplating having improvements made on his real property should investigate the mechanic's lien laws of his own state. In some states, the lien law makes it possible for a claimant to tie up an owner's property over a disputed claim of a very small amount. On occasion the threat of filing a lien is used as a method of getting the owner to pay a claim he honestly disputes. If a lien is filed, the owner may be handicapped if he tries to use his property as security in other transactions. In those states where the owner may be compelled to pay twice—for example, where he pays the general contractor who fails to pay the subcontractors, material suppliers, and workmen—it is usually a good practice for the owner to require some sort of proof from the contractor that the others have been paid. The contractor's bond, if worded properly, may also be used to protect the owner against the claims of subcontractors and others.

F. Extinguishment of Liens

Where the lien is based on possession, the voluntary surrender of possession by the lienor to the owner destroys the lien. If the owner acquires possession of the property by fraud or force, the lien is not lost, except that a sale by the owner to a bona fide purchaser while the owner is in actual possession of the goods terminates the lien. An attempt by the lienor to sell or mortgage or lease the goods in his possession terminates the lien, and the same is true where the lienor claims some other interest, such as ownership interest, in the goods in place of the lien interest. Full payment of the obligation terminates the lien.

An equitable lien is extinguished either by the express release of the owner of the lien or by conduct implying a release or waiver of the lien. Statutory liens are extinguished in the manner prescribed in the statutes creating them. The lienor may release or waive his lien rights, thus terminating the lien. Failure to file notice of some liens terminates them or prevents their ever coming into existence. Conduct of the lienor may be such as to justify the inference that he has released the lien. Payment of the debt extinguishes a statutory lien.

A question arising with regard to most liens is whether the acceptance by the lienor of other security extinguishes the lien on the original property. It was once the view of the courts that the lien was terminated under such circumstances, but the modern view is that the intention of the parties should govern and that there is no reason to infer a release of the lien just because a lienor accepts additional security.

G. Enforcement of Liens

The common law lien, as unaffected by statute, gave the lienor no right of enforcement except the right to retain the property until paid. Of course, the lienor could sue the owner of the goods on the unpaid obligation, recover a judgment, and then execute the judgment against the goods in his possession, but he had no authority to sell the goods in the absence of express agreement. In most states, a lienor under even the common law liens is given the right to sell the goods in satisfaction of his claim, provided that the statutory requirements of notice and type of sale are complied with. Agreement between the parties may still alter the statutory or common law rules relative to the enforcement of liens.

3. SECURED TRANSACTIONS

A. Cases

(1)

On February 15, Sam Selir sold a color television set to Bill Biar for $750 payable in instalments, retaining a security interest in the set to secure the payments. Selir immediately perfected his interest by filing. In June, Biar removed the set from his home and installed it in a cocktail lounge which he owned and operated. In September, an inebriated customer threw a glass through the face of the set, shattering the picture tube and doing other damage. Biar took the set to Roger Repar, a television repairman, and incurred $150 in repair bills. While the set was still in Repar's shop, Biar became bankrupt. By the time of his bankruptcy, Biar had reduced his unpaid balance with Selir to $250. What are the rights of Selir, Repar, and Biar's unsecured creditors in the television set?

(2)

SIMUCO Toyland borrowed $5,000 from Anosmia National Bank and gave a security interest in its bicycle inventory as security for the loan. The security agreement expressly provided that the lien of the bank would carry over to the proceeds of sales of the bicycles. The bank immediately perfected by filing a financing statement. Shortly thereafter, SIMUCO sold eleven bicycles to Bobby Biar for his eleven children. The total price was $900. SIMUCO obtained from Biar a writing manifesting an obligation for the unpaid balance of $700 and a security interest by SIMUCO in the eleven bicycles. SIMUCO perfected by filing. SIMUCO then borrowed $250 from Len Lendur and gave possession of Biar's writing as collateral on the loan. In the event of SIMUCO's default on its obligations to the bank and to Lendur, what would be the rights of those two parties in the proceeds of the sale to Biar, in the bicycles, and in Biar's writing?

(3)

Hypocase, Inc. regularly finances its current operations by selling its accounts receivable to Anosmia Factors with no right of recourse against the seller. On several occasions since the State of Anosmia adopted the Uniform Commercial Code, minor disputes between Hypocase and Anosmia Factors have raised the question of the law applicable to accounts receivable financing. Representatives of Hypocase insist that an outright sale of receivables is just a sale of personal property where the creation of a security interest is not intended and, as such, is not subject to Article 9 of the Code. The representatives of Factors contend that Article 9 covers the transaction whether or not a security interest is intended or created. Who is right? Explain.

B. In General

It has been said that the policy and rules of Article 9 of the Uniform Commercial Code are probably of greater importance than those of any other article in the Code. The reason behind this statement is not that the subject of secured transactions is more important than any other treated in the Code, but that the improvements over the precode situation are greater and affect a broader area of commercial law than do the other articles, and that they create, in effect, a new and integrated branch of law. This one article of the Code brings about the repeal of at least five prior Uniform Acts and replaces all precode security devices associated with personal property. Where previous editions of this book had to devote whole sections to such security devices as conditional sales, chattel mortgages, trust receipts, pledges, equipment trusts, field warehousing, accounts receivable financing, and factor's liens, this edition need only discuss the one Code category into which all of these devices have now been placed: secured transactions.

Precode law with regard to transactions intended to create a security interest in personal property was an unbelievable hodgepodge of separate techniques, devices, and instruments coupled with an almost total lack of uniformity among the states. Although all of the relevant transactions had as their aim the creation of security interests in personal property, no two dealt with such matters as notice, recording, priorities, and rights and duties of the parties in the same way. Perhaps to a greater extent than in any other field of commercial law, legal rules and principles were at variance with the intentions and practices of merchants and served more to hinder and confuse, than to facilitate and clarify, the conduct of trade. Precode law was not designed to bring about clarity. Precode law was, rather, a combination of history, accident, the failure of the law to adjust to changing circumstances, and the survival of ancient dogma far beyond its period of usefulness. For a variety of historical reasons, for example, the law had a deep prejudice against financing secured by interests in personal property. This prejudice persisted for generations beyond the end of the history which gave it birth. The Code recognizes the important role which secured financing plays in our economy, brings the law into phase with sound business practice, and achieves substantial uniformity.

In bringing about these improvements, the Code abolishes the distinctions among the precode transactions and devices and integrates the whole panoply into one coherent field. There is no longer any need to learn the distinctive details of each of the old techniques. There is need only to learn the Code rules and principles applicable to "secured transactions." Before we can actually begin our examination of these rules and principles, however, we must describe with certainty the area which the Code has pre-empted. Much thought and careful drafting by the authors of the Code have made this task relatively easy.

Aim and Scope of Article 9.   Consistent with the basic policy of the Uniform Commercial Code, Article 9 seeks to provide rules under which commercial transactions can be conducted with simplicity and candor and with legal safety and certainty. The Official Comments explain that the purpose of Article 9 is "to bring all consensual security interests in personal property and fixtures" under one category, "as well as sales of accounts, contract rights and chattel paper." The principal test of whether a transaction comes under the Article, except for sales of accounts, contract rights and chattel paper, is whether "the transaction is intended to have effect as security." The aim of the Code in providing a simple and unified structure is furthered by the establishment of a single-lien theory, the details of which vary, not with the form of the transaction, but with the functional use to be served. All of the old forms and names are terminated and replaced by the descriptive term *security interest,* which simply means an interest in personal property which secures payment or performance of an obligation. Security interests are either *possessory* or *non-possessory* with regard to the property involved, and the rules applicable to all security interests are the same, except where the relationship between the parties, the effects of the transaction, and other substantive matters dictate different treatment.

Where a transaction is a matter of agreement between the parties and involves personal property which the parties intend as security, Article 9 applies. The form of the transaction is of no importance. A landlord's lien for rent cannot qualify, for example, because it is not consensual but grows out of the status of landlord and tenant. The liens of carriers, warehousemen, and artisans do not qualify because there is no intention to create a security interest. The Code specifically excludes from its coverage a few transactions which, under the basic test, would often qualify. This is done for a number of reasons, including pre-emption by federal law and the fact that some of these transactions are not really commercial in nature. Among the exclusions as set forth in Section 9–104 are: transfer of a claim for wages of an employee; equipment trusts covering railway rolling stock; sale of accounts, contract rights, or chattel paper as part of the sale of a business or the assignment of these items for collection only; a transfer of an interest or claim to or under a policy of insurance; a right represented by a judgment; tort claims; deposit or savings accounts maintained with a bank, credit union, or like organization. The list set forth here is not complete; the Code should be examined for details.

DEFINITIONS. The terminology of Article 9 is not particularly technical and is much less technical than precode law, but there are several basic definitions and identifications of parties which should be clearly understood in advance of discussion. An illustration will help to fix the definitions and identifications in the reader's mind. Jones, a small manufacturer, borrows $5,000 from the Bank of Anosmia and uses some of the equipment in his plant as security for the loan. In doing so, Jones, the *debtor*, and the Bank of Anosmia, the *secured party,* have entered into a *security agreement* whereby the secured party has obtained a *security interest* in the equipment, the *collateral*. Notice that the form of the transaction is not even mentioned. Under precode law, it would have been necessary, first of all, to identify, out of many possibilities, the particular security device employed and to define and identify the terms and parties relevant to that device and probably to no other. The terms in our simple example hardly need further elucidation and are applicable to all secured transactions under Article 9.

The *debtor* is the person who owes payment or performance of the secured obligation, whether or not he has rights in the collateral; the term includes the seller of accounts, contract rights, or chattel paper. Where the debtor and the owner of the collateral are not the same person, the term applies to the owner in connection with matters dealing with the collateral and to the obligor in connection with the obligation. The *secured party* is a lender, seller, or other person in whose favor there is a security interest; the term includes a person to whom accounts, contract rights, or chattel paper have been sold. The *security agreement* is an agreement which creates or provides for a security interest. A *security interest,* as we have seen, is the interest in personal property which secures the payment or performance of an obligation. *Collateral* means the property subject to a security interest and includes accounts, contract rights, and chattel paper. What kind of property may constitute collateral will be discussed in greater detail below.

C. Creation of the Security Interest

FORMAL REQUIREMENTS. Security interests are created by agreement between the parties. Unless the collateral is in the possession of the secured party, the security agreement must be in writing in order to be enforceable and must be signed by the debtor and contain a description of the collateral. While the signature of the secured party is not required, it is usually advisable to have it, and both signatures are necessary for filing as a means of public notice, as will be discussed below. All that Article 9 requires of a description is that it make possible the identification of the thing described. The requirement is satisfied if information in the agreement enables one to ascertain what the collateral is in fact. Descriptions should not be needlessly detailed, but, on the other hand, care should be exercised not to describe more or less than is actually intended as security.

The formal requirements specified in the Code are indeed minimal, but most security agreements will and should contain additional provisions. For obvious reasons, it is usually wise to include the nature and amount of the indebtedness, the terms of payment, and the interest and finance charges. Terms and provisions describing the debtor's duties in respect to maintenance and care of the collateral are often desirable. Inventory or accounts receivable financing will usually dictate the inclusion of terms dealing with such matters as taxes, furnishing of financial statements, and the disposition of the proceeds of sale or collections of receivables. If the secured party is to have the right to possess the collateral prior to default or when he feels himself insecure, the agreement must so provide. Particular circumstances may suggest many other kinds of provisions.

One of the optional provisions most frequently found in security agreements pertains to the treatment of property acquired after the agreement was entered into and to future advances of funds by the secured party. If property acquired after the agreement is intended to be added to the collateral, the agreement must spell it out. The Code is very liberal with regard to the treatment of after acquired property in commercial situations, primarily in recognition of the importance of simple continuing arrangements with manufacturers and merchants. Limitations are imposed on after acquired property clauses, however, especially in farmer or consumer types of financing, and usually confine the effectiveness of such clauses to limited time periods. In connection with consumer goods, the clauses are ineffective for goods acquired more than ten days after the loan; for crops, the period is one year.

Some security agreements provide that collateral may secure future loans and advances as well as present ones. Precode law often drew sharp distinctions between advances which the secured party was obligated to make and those which he could make if he wished. The primary problem had to do with the priority of the secured party's interest in competition with third persons who obtained claims against the collateral after the original agreement was entered into. The Code sweeps away most of the confusion by providing that if the security agreement contains a clause for a present security as collateral for future advances which the secured party may or may not make at his option, the secured party has an effective security interest with priority dating to the time of the agreement, if the advance is actually made at a later date. If there is no future advance clause in the agreement, the secured party gets no priority even if he does make later advances, except, of course, from the actual date of the advance.

ATTACHMENT OF THE SECURITY INTEREST. It is unfortunate, perhaps, that the term "attach" is used by the Code in connection with security interests, because it has other meanings and usages from which confusion may arise. Its use in Article 9 makes the term almost synonymous with the "creation" of the security interest. *Attachment* is intended to convey the idea that something more than the mere description of a security interest in the agreement is necessary before that interest comes into existence. In other words, something more is needed before the rights which attach to a security interest are created. The Code spells out the requirements for attachment as: 1, the making of the security agreement; 2, the giving of value by the secured party; and 3, the debtors having acquired rights in the collateral to which the security interest can be applied. Attachment should not be confused with "perfection," to be discussed later, where the secured party has rights in collateral as those rights come into contact with third persons. Attachment, to put it still another way, refers to the rights of the secured party in collateral as between himself and the debtor. Perfection refers to rights as between the secured party and third persons.

The security interest attaches as soon as all three requirements listed above have occurred. The making of the agreement has already been discussed. The requirement of value, generally speaking, is met by finding any consideration sufficient to support a simple contract, but is also satisfied when the secured party acquires his rights as security for, or in total or partial satisfaction of, a pre-existing claim. Obviously, a binding commitment to extend credit also constitutes value, whether the credit is actually extended or not. The third requirement recognizes the fact that the debtor may not himself have any rights in the collateral at the time the agreement is entered into and that no security interest could be created in the secured party until the debtor obtains rights in the property. A merchant may borrow money from a bank in order to finance the purchase of goods and may agree to the creation of a security interest in those goods while the goods are still in the hands of the seller and before the merchant has any rights in them.

The Code describes in certain specific cases the time when the debtor obtains rights in collateral. He has no rights in crops until the crops are planted or otherwise become growing crops. A debtor has no rights in the young of livestock until they are conceived, in fish until they are caught, in oil, gas, or minerals until they are extracted, in timber until it is cut, in a contract right until the contract has been made, or in an account receivable until the account comes into existence.

We have already seen that a security interest in consumer goods under an after acquired property clause does not attach to goods acquired by the debtor more than ten days after the secured party has given value, or to crops planted more than a year after advancing value. By their agreement, the debtor and the secured party may postpone the attachment of a security interest, as may be desirable where the debtor has arrangements with more than one secured party.

D. Collateral

In General.   Although the basic policy of the Code is to treat all secured transactions as nearly alike as is possible under the circumstances, it is clear that the rules and mechanics governing different kinds of collateral cannot be exactly the same. A stove or dishwasher purchased on instalments by a consumer cannot be treated in precisely the same fashion as an account receivable sold by a businessman. The Code devotes considerable space to classifying the many types of collateral into a number of major categories and builds its rules on these categories. In addition, the Code distinguishes between commercial parties on one hand and farmers and consumers on the other. Within these broad categories of collateral and character of parties, uniformity of treatment is sought.

Essentially, three categories of collateral are described: tangible and intangible personal property and documentary collateral. The latter represents a kind of combination of tangible and intangible property in that the document is tangible, while the promises set forth in it are intangible. The general law of property usually classifies documentary property as intangible, but for purposes of collateral under the Code, it becomes desirable to recognize the physical aspects of its nature as well as its basically intangible character.

TANGIBLE PERSONAL PROPERTY. *In general.* In the Code, tangible personal property is called "goods." At this point, the second basis used in the Code for the categorization of collateral, the character of the buyer or borrower, makes its appearance in the four classifications of goods: consumer goods, equipment, farm products, and inventory. It is clear from these classes that the physical characteristics of the property are of little relevance. Notice should be taken of the fact that the same property may, at different times and under different circumstances, occupy different categories. A stove may be inventory in the hands of the seller, may become consumer goods in the hands of the buyer, and may return to inventory or even become equipment if the buyer sells the used machine to a dealer or to a small restaurant owner for use in his business. The same property cannot be in two different categories at the same time, however. If the debtor-owner holds the stove for sale, it must be inventory; if he holds it for personal household use, it is consumer goods. In the first example, the secured party has a security interest in inventory, in the second, in consumer goods. Problems arise where the debtor-owner uses the property in two or more ways, because the property can only be in one category at once. Determination of the categories is important in resolving the rights of persons who buy goods from debtors, in establishing the priority of claims, in fixing the rights of the parties after default, and in other circumstances. These matters will be discussed later.

Consumer goods. The Code, in Section 9–109, states that goods are *consumer goods* if they are used or bought for use primarily for personal, family, or household purposes. A debtor who acquires a stove for personal use may later transfer it to his business, but the change in the primary use does not alter the classification as long as the property remains in the hands of the same owner. Once the primary use is established by declaration or by the physical facts, the property remains in that classification even though the primary use may change. The reader should take note of the fact that statutes other than the Code may be applicable to secured transactions involving consumer goods. Small loan acts, retail instalment selling statutes, and "truth in selling" acts are examples.

Equipment. Goods are *equipment* if they are used or bought for use primarily in business, including farming or a profession, or for use by a debtor who is a nonprofit organization or a government agency, or if the goods are not included in the definitions of inventory, farm products, or consumer goods.

The term is so defined in order that any secured transaction involving equipment will be a commercial transaction and not a consumer one. Businessmen are presumed to know what they are doing when they enter into secured transactions and are presumed to be able to take care of themselves. Consequently, commercial transactions are treated differently from consumer transactions under the Code, and commercial parties are given considerable leeway in agreeing to waivers of their rights, claims, or defenses. Remedies of secured parties are also broader with respect to commercial transactions.

If the primary use of property is determined to be in one category, it makes no difference that secondary uses are in other categories. A bar owner who uses a television set primarily to entertain his customers does not alter the category of the set if he takes it home occasionally to entertain himself and his family. Classifying goods as equipment may encounter other issues also, some of which will require examination of the law outside the Code. Affixing equipment to real property raises the question of whether "fixtures" have been created. The Code provides that the real property law of the particular jurisdiction shall control on this matter. If the goods are found to be fixtures, the rules governing removal and repossession by the secured party will be substantially different from when the goods are personal property. (See discussion of "fixtures" in Chapter 7.)

Farm products. Farmers, like consumers, receive special treatment under the Code. Goods are *farm products* if they are crops or livestock used or produced in farming operations or if they are products of crops or livestock in their unmanufactured state and in the possession of a debtor engaged in farming operations. If goods are farm products, they can be neither inventory nor equipment. A farmer's tractor is equipment, but his crops and produce are farm products. Note that the debtor must be a farmer before the goods can be farm products. If the farmer has sold his crops to a dairy or a mill for processing and resale, the goods are inventory of the dairy or mill. If the farmer processes his own products, they cease to be farm products and become inventory—an exception to the rule that the category does not change once the primary use is established. What constitutes a manufacturing process is not clear from the Code, but the term would probably not include such activities as straining honey or pasteurizing milk, on the ground that these are intimately related to the farming activity itself.

Inventory. The last category of tangible personal property listed in Section 9–109 is, like equipment, essentially a commercial category. Goods are *inventory* when they are held for sale or lease. This includes raw materials, work in process or materials used or consumed in business, and goods to be furnished under contracts of service. The basic test is whether the goods are held for immediate or ultimate sale in the ordinary course of business. Inventory and equipment are mutually exclusive categories; goods cannot be classified in both. The requirement that inventory be held for sale in the ordinary course of business avoids confusion where used or obsolete equipment is held for sale; it cannot be classed as inventory.

Secured transactions involving inventory usually contemplate that the debtor will resell the inventory and that the buyer will take the goods free and clear of the interest of the secured party. The same is clearly not the case with the financing of equipment. Consequently, the distinction between inventory and equipment is of basic importance to the parties. The essential difference between inventory and equipment results in one of the important changes brought about in precode law by the Code. Security interests in inventory have always been handicapped by the fact that inventory is meant to be sold and, consequently, does not present a very stable basis for security interests aimed at specific property. Precode law found great difficulty in solving this problem and never really accomplished a satisfactory solution. The Code rules concerning after acquired property and a sort of floating lien that follows the proceeds resulting from the disposition of inventory provide a sensible solution and considerable legal safety.

INTANGIBLE PERSONAL PROPERTY. *In general.* The Code establishes three categories of intangible personal property: accounts, contract rights, and general intangibles. Section 9–106 defines all three of these terms. *Account* refers to any right to payment for goods sold or leased or for services rendered which is not evidenced by an instrument or chattel paper. *Contract right* means any right to payment under a contract not yet earned by performance and not evidenced by an instrument or chattel paper. *General intangibles* means any personal property other than goods, accounts, contract rights, chattel paper, documents, and instruments. This language makes it clear that the classification of intangible personal property excludes those intangible rights which are also evidenced by written documents such as negotiable instruments, documents of title, and chattel paper. These types of property will be discussed separately. The reader should at this point refresh his memory with regard to the specific exclusions from coverage of Article 9 discussed above.

Accounts. The definitions of the Code make clear the intention of the draftsmen to include in the term "account" only accounts receivable which have been created by an obligation already performed, in contrast with a "contract right" which is not yet earned by performance. A contract right, when earned by performance, may become an account. Accounts are created upon the sale or delivery of goods or the performance of services on open credit terms and are usually evidenced only by a seller's invoice and the book entries of the parties. The accounts receivable on the books of the seller are a form of property which the seller can use as collateral in financing his business operations. The use of accounts in financing transactions is probably more extensive than the use of any other type of property.

Accounts may either be sold or simply assigned as collateral security. Article 9 governs the transaction in either case. When accounts are simply assigned as collateral for a loan, the debtor on the account usually gets no notice of the transaction, but when purchased outright, the account debtor generally receives notice that his account has been purchased and that he should make payment to the account buyer (called a "factor") only. Probably the most important difference between the assignment and the sale of accounts is that, in the latter case, the buyer of the account usually assumes the risk that the account debtor will not pay, except, of course, where the reason for nonpayment is something other than the financial inability to do so. The sale arrangement provides the owner of the account with a form of credit insurance, the premium for which is the charge made by the factor.

In some situations, accounts are sold outright with no right of recourse by the buyer against the seller. Because the Code was intended to embrace the whole field of receivables financing, sales of this kind are included within the Code coverage although this form of transaction is clearly not made with the intention to create a security interest in personal property. The same broad coverage is given to contract rights. Outright sales are not the only situations involving accounts and contract rights where the parties do not intend to create security interests in personal property, but all come under the Code nonetheless. The only exceptions are the sales of accounts or contract rights as part of the sale of a business or where they are assigned only for the purpose of collection. The reason for these exceptions is that the draftsmen of the Code did not view these situations as having anything to do with commercial financing transactions.

Contract rights. Because contract rights are treated almost identically with accounts under the Code, there is no need here for detailed discussion. Contract rights are rights to payment which have not yet been earned by performance and are not evidenced by an instrument (such as a promissory note) or by chattel paper. A building contractor who has a contract to construct an office building may actually use his rights under that contract as security for a loan, although no work has yet been done. If instalment payments become due as work is completed, these rights are earned and become accounts receivable.

General intangibles. The category of general intangibles is a residual category encompassing intangible personal property which is neither an account nor a contract right and is not evidenced by chattel paper, documents, or instruments. Examples of the types of property contemplated by the draftsmen of the Code as coming within this category are literary rights, goodwill, rights to performance, copyrights, trademarks, and patents. Federal law is important in connection with some of these kinds of property and must be examined before the coverage and treatment by the Code can be accurately determined. The use of these rights as collateral in secured transactions is not at present extensive, but the trend appears to be toward greater use. As said in the Official Comments, this provision of the Code looks more to the future than to the present.

DOCUMENTARY COLLATERAL. *In general.* The last major category of collateral involves property which, in some respects, resembles tangible personal property and, in other respects, is similar to intangible personal property. This kind of collateral consists, essentially, of promises and rights that are evidenced by formal writings, instruments, or documents. Examples are: documents of title; negotiable instruments; negotiable securities, such as stock certificates; and chattel paper, such as instalment sales contracts and chattel mortgages. Other articles of the Code, as we have seen, regulate the rights and duties of parties to such formal writings but do not concern their use in giving security for considerations separate and distinct from those related to the issuance of the instruments or documents. The rights of makers, payees, and holders of promissory notes, for example, are determined by Article 3 of the Code, but, when the holder of a note pledges it to his own creditor as collateral security, Article 9 will control the rights of these two parties and of the holder's other creditors. Similar comments could be made of documents of title and stock certificates.

Chattel paper is the only type of formal writing at issue here which does not have its own article in the Code. Consequently, *all* the rules relating to chattel paper are found in Article 9. This result causes no problems, however, because the very issuance of chattel paper is itself a secured transaction.

Instruments. The definition of *instrument* under Article 9 is somewhat broader than "negotiable instrument" under Article 3. It includes "investment securities" as defined under Article 8 and also any other writing which evidences a right to the payment of money and is of a type which is transferred in the ordinary course of business by delivery with any necessary indorsement. Instruments which are themselves security agreements or leases of specific property are specifically excluded from the term "instrument" under the Code, although they might otherwise qualify.

Because instruments and documents are designed for easy transferability and create unusual rights for bona fide purchasers, they present special problems when used as security. In order to solve these problems it is usually contemplated that the secured party will have possession of the collateral. Security interests involving most other types of personal property will be nonpossessory in character. A precode and common law security device based upon possession by the secured party was the *pledge,* essentially a bailment used as a security device, and the Code has retained most of the rules applicable to pledges in setting up the provisions relating to instruments and documents.

Documents. Under the Code, *document* means "document of title," but this latter term is not confined to the usual bill of lading and warehouse receipt. To be a document of title, a document must only purport to be issued by, or addressed to, a bailee and purport to cover goods in the bailee's possession which are either identified or portions of an identified fungible mass. This approach to the definition leaves the way open for the invention of new documents of title not presently in use or even contemplated. The draftsmen had in mind the increasing rapidity with which goods are being transported and the likelihood of wide commercial acceptance of documents transmitted by telegram, teletype, or radio. One might also anticipate the eventual use of documents transmitted by electronic or photographic processes or recreated at great distances by other means.

Chattel paper. *Chattel paper* is defined in the Code as "a writing or writings which evidence both a monetary obligation and a security interest in or lease of specific goods." By definition, then, chattel paper is usually itself a security agreement. What this means is that a basic sales transaction, for example, may make the goods themselves collateral to secure the payment of the purchase price, and the secured party in this transaction may transfer the chattel paper as collateral for his own obligation in another transaction. Under precode law, the original transaction would have been a "conditional sales contract" or a "chattel mortgage," both now included in the Code term "secured transaction." A buyer who wished to purchase a new dishwasher but did not have the full purchase price might have signed a security agreement with the seller whereby the buyer got possession of the appliance while the seller retained a security interest in it to protect the payment of the purchase price. This would be a secured transaction involving consumer goods. If the seller of the appliance now wished to obtain a bank loan to finance his business operation, he might deliver possession of the chattel paper from the first transaction to the bank under a second security agreement creating a security interest in the paper with the bank as the secured party. This would be a secured transaction involving the documentary collateral known as chattel paper.

It should be noted that much more complicated uses of chattel paper as collateral may result where the dishwasher involved in the example above had originally been held by the seller subject to a security interest in his inventory. Three secured transactions may be applicable in these circumstances: the seller and the first secured party, with inventory as collateral; the buyer and the seller as secured party, with the dishwasher (consumer goods) as collateral; and the seller and a second secured party, with the chattel paper as collateral. Rules governing the conflicting claims that might result from these and other transactions will be discussed briefly below.

E. Perfection of the Security Interest

In General. As we have seen, the perfection of the security interest is necessary in order to protect a secured party when other creditors of the debtor become involved, or when the collateral has been transferred to, or become encumbered by, other persons. When a security interest has been perfected, the secured party, generally speaking, will be permitted to realize on the collateral even after the debtor's bankruptcy or the legal attachment of the collateral by another creditor. If not perfected, the security interest is subordinate to the claims of persons who become lien creditors without knowledge of the security interest and before it is perfected, to transferees in bulk or other buyers to the extent that such persons give value and receive delivery of the collateral without knowledge of the security interest and before it is perfected, and to transferees of accounts, contract rights, or general intangibles to the extent that they give value without knowledge of the security interest and before it is perfected.

The method of perfection of the collateral is determined by the classification of the collateral. The Code describes three methods of perfection. In most cases involving a commercial transaction, perfection is accomplished by the filing of financing statements in the appropriate office. In some cases, perfection is accomplished by possession of the collateral. In others, perfection is brought about by attachment alone.

PERFECTION BY POSSESSION. Were possession the only method of perfection, the most valuable secured transactions would not be feasible. There are a few types of collateral, however, in which security interests can be perfected *only* by possession, such as negotiable instruments. In the case of documents of title and chattel paper, a limited type of perfection can be obtained by filing, but the only safe method, legally and practically, is by possession. Possession may become desirable in connection with usually nonpossessory secured transactions where something has gone wrong or the secured party has reason to feel that his chances of recovering on the obligation have been impaired.

It must be remembered that the rights of a holder in due course of commercial paper are not affected by secured transactions that may take place with regard to the instrument, and the holder in due course will prevail over the secured party even where the nature of the transaction required the secured party to permit the debtor to retain possession for some limited purpose, and the debtor transferred it to the holder in due course. The Code makes clear its preference for the principles of negotiability over the needs of secured transactions. A secured party in possession of a negotiable instrument or document may find it necessary to surrender possession to the debtor to enable the debtor to pay off the loan or to obtain, load, ship, or even sell the goods involved. If the secured party does so, he runs the risk of losing his security by an improper transfer. Short of transfer to a holder in due course or his equivalent, however, the Code gives the secured party considerable protection where release to the debtor becomes a practical necessity. Section 9–304 provides that the perfected security interest in negotiable instruments and documents may continue without the secured party being in possession for a maximum period of twenty-one days, where the secured party permits the debtor to have possession for some limited purpose.

Although possession is the easiest, most effective, and most obvious method of perfection, it has little practical importance outside the area of documentary collateral. It will be recalled that where collateral is in the possession of the secured party, no writing is necesssry for an effective security agreement.

PERFECTION BY FILING. With the exception of some of those special situations discussed above, where perfection was accomplished by possession, all secured transactions of the commercial type involve security interests which are perfected by filing a financing statement. Section 9–402 describes the formal requirements of a financing statement as follows: The statement is legally sufficient if "it is signed by the debtor and the secured party, gives an address of the secured party from which information concerning the security interest may be obtained, gives a mailing address of the debtor and contains a statement indicating the types, or describing the items of collateral." Note that both parties must sign the financing statement. Descriptions of collateral are not meant to be detailed. It is enough if the description makes possible the identification of the collateral or the location of the real estate to which fixtures may be attached or on which crops may be grown. No authentications are required by way of affidavits, acknowledgements, or witnesses.

The purpose of filing, of course, is to give notice of security interests in personal property. The theory of the Code is that the filing need only provide a means by which interested parties can discover the existence of security interests in particular property and the identities of the debtor and secured party. If the filing provides this much information, the complete state of affairs can be learned by inquiry from the parties themselves. With that in mind, the draftsmen were able to keep the requirements for filing at a minimum.

The parties may file the security agreement as the financing statement, providing both parties have signed. But they do not have to place all the details of their transaction on the public record if they do not desire to do so. The financing statement need not contain any information about the debt or obligation secured by the collateral. If the statement does not disclose any maturity date, or if it shows that the obligation matures on demand, the filing is effective for five years from the date of filing unless, within that period, it is renewed by the filing of a *continuation statement.* If the financing statement shows a maturity date of five years or less, the filing is effective until the maturity date and for a further period of sixty days. A continuation statement may be filed in order to extend this period. If a filing lapses, the security interest becomes unperfected. A continuation statement need be signed only by the secured party and may be filed within six months before and sixty days after a stated maturity date or within six months before the expiration of five years from the date of original filing if the financing statement contained no maturity date. The statement must refer to the original statement by file number and must state that the original statement is still in effect. Further continuation statements may be filed in the same manner. Each continuation statement extends the effectiveness of the original statement for an additional five-year period. Financing statements may be amended from time to time, and a secured party may assign his rights under a financing statement by proper procedures.

In order to protect debtors from detrimental filings where there are no longer any outstanding obligations or commitments to make advances, debtors may demand from the secured party a statement that he no longer claims a security interest under the financing statement. If the secured party does not send such a *termination statement* within ten days after proper demand, he becomes liable to the debtor for a one-hundred-dollar penalty, as well as for actual damages suffered by the debtor.

Because of the many local preferences and variations in filing and recording techniques, the Code makes few mandatory prescriptions in this connection. Section 9–401 was left open for local provisions within the scope of several alternatives and should be inspected by the reader in his own state. Many states have special filing procedures for security interests in motor vehicles. Where the collateral consists of goods which are, or will become, fixtures, the Code provides that filing must be in the office where mortgages on real estate are filed.

PERFECTION BY ATTACHMENT. Attachment alone is enough for perfection in a few noncommercial situations. Article 9 recognizes two such situations as exceptions to the general rule of perfection by filing or possession. The first is a nonpossessory purchase money security interest in farm equipment which is neither a fixture nor a motor vehicle required to be licensed and which has a purchase price of $2,500 or less. The second is the nonpossessory purchase money security interest in consumer goods, regardless of its purchase price, if the collateral is neither a fixture nor a motor vehicle required to be licensed. A security interest is a purchase money security interest to the extent that it is taken or retained to secure all or part of the price of the collateral.

Even without filing, the secured party is protected against all claimants with respect to the collateral in these purchase money situations except another consumer who purchases the collateral from the debtor without knowledge of the security interest. A financing statement may be filed in these cases to give the secured party additional protection. Certain other benefits flow to the secured party in purchase money transactions that are not enjoyed by secured parties in other types of transactions, including protection during a ten-day grace period between giving of value and filing.

PROCEEDS. Earlier reference was made to some of the unusual provisions of the Code in connection with the proceeds of the sale of collateral in which the secured party has a security interest. Whether a debtor sells collateral in the ordinary course of business or not, the secured party has a continuing security interest in the proceeds of the sale. The Code defines *proceeds* to include whatever is received when collateral or proceeds of collateral are sold, exchanged, collected, or otherwise disposed of. This broad definition includes accounts receivable created when collateral is sold by the debtor and other non-cash proceeds as well as money and checks. The security interest in proceeds is created by operation of law and does not require the agreement of the parties. It is created whether or not the original security interest in the collateral survives its sale or other disposition, and whether or not the debtor was authorized by the security agreement to sell the collateral.

The matter of the perfection of security interests in proceeds is clearly described in the Code. If the security interest in the original collateral was perfected at the time of the sale or disposition, the security interest in the proceeds is perfected as well, at least for a limited time. If the financing statement for the original collateral shows that the secured party makes claim to the proceeds, the security interest in the proceeds continues without further action by the secured party. However, if the original statement does not show the claim of the secured party, or if the original security interest was perfected by other than filing, the security interest in the proceeds continues for only ten days after the sale or disposition. If, during that period, the secured party files a statement covering the proceeds or actually takes possession of the proceeds, the interest continues thereafter.

In the event of the debtor's involvement in any proceeding intended to liquidate his assets or rehabilitate his financial affairs, a secured party whose security interest in proceeds is perfected is entitled to reclaim identifiable non-cash proceeds and identifiable cash proceeds not mingled with other money or deposited in a bank account prior to the insolvency proceedings. If the cash proceeds cannot be identified, the secured party has a perfected security interest in all cash and bank accounts of the debtor to the extent of the cash proceeds actually received by the debtor within ten days before the beginning of the insolvency proceedings, less the cash proceeds paid by the debtor to the secured party during the ten day period.

PRIORITIES AND CONFLICTING CLAIMS. The perfected security interest is the greatest protection possible, with respect to the collateral, for the secured party to obtain. When such an interest comes into conflict with the rights of third persons, such as buyers from the debtor or the creditors of the debtor, the secured party will usually prevail. In some situations, however, this usual approach to problems of conflict will not suffice, and further rules and principles are necessary in order to resolve conflicts and determine priorities. It is to these problems that we now shift our attention. We have already seen that unperfected security interests do not usually prevail over the claims of third persons except where the third person acquired his lien or purchased the collateral with knowledge of the security interest. Even this exception does not apply to inventory or chattel paper, for reasons we have examined elsewhere.

Under many different circumstances, two or more persons may claim an interest in the same collateral. Some of these situations have already been discussed, as in connection with proceeds and negotiable instruments, but several others deserve brief comment at this time. If two parties claim a security interest in the same property, and both have perfected by filing, the first filing prevails even if that secured party knew of an earlier interest when he acquired his. If neither has perfected by filing, the order of perfection controls without regard for when the security interest attached. If neither interest is perfected, the order of attachment controls. Under the Code, a continuously perfected security interest is always treated as if perfected by filing if it was originally so perfected, and always treated as if perfected otherwise than by filing if it was originally so perfected.

Under certain conditions, the Code gives priority to purchase money security interests over other security interests. A purchase money security interest in collateral other than inventory has priority over a conflicting security interest in the same collateral if the purchase money interest is perfected at the time the debtor receives possession of the collateral or within ten days thereafter. A purchase money security interest in inventory has priority over a conflicting security interest in the same collateral if the purchase money security interest is perfected at the time the debtor receives possession of the collateral and the purchase money secured party, prior to the delivery of the collateral to the debtor, gives notice of the purchase money financing to the holder of any other security interest known to him or to any holder of a security interest who has filed a financing statement covering the same items or types of inventory. One effect of these Code provisions is to give priority to purchase money security interests in inventory over a prior security interest claimed under an after acquired property clause. The preference manifested for purchase money security interests was well supported by precode law and is founded on a policy of encouraging inventory financing techniques and protecting such secured parties from fraudulent debtors who seek advances from the secured party even after giving security interests in new inventory to another secured party.

While leaving to local real property law the rules governing the question of when personal property is or becomes a fixture, Article 9 does set forth rules concerning conflicts among parties having interests in real estate and persons claiming security interests in fixtures. Some states omitted the Code section dealing with this matter and elected to rely on precode law. The Code makes clear that its provisions do not apply to goods actually incorporated into a structure, such as lumber, bricks, cement, and the like. Heating systems, sinks and other plumbing fixtures, and window shades, for example, are usually affixed to but not incorporated in a structure and come under the Code provisions. Several separate situations are dealt with in the Code.

A security interest which both attaches and is perfected before the goods become fixtures takes priority over the claims of all persons who have an interest in the real estate. A security interest which attaches to goods before they become fixtures, but which is *not* perfected, still has priority over a prior real estate encumbrance; but it is subordinate to the claims of a subsequent purchaser or mortgagee for value of any interest in the real estate, and to the claims of a creditor with a lien on the real estate subsequently obtained by judicial proceedings. It is also subordinate to the claims of a prior purchaser or mortgagee whose encumbrance is recorded, to the extent that he makes subsequent advances, provided that the purchase or mortgage is made, the lien by judicial proceedings is obtained, and the subsequent advance is made or contracted for without knowledge of the security interest and before it is perfected. Where the security interest attaches after the goods have become fixtures, the rights of the secured party, with respect to persons with subsequent interests, are the same as where the security interest attaches before the goods become fixtures. However, previous real estate claims take priority unless the holder of the real estate interest disclaims, in writing, any interest in the goods as fixtures or consents, in writing, to the security interest. The reason for the differences in treatment of pre- and post-affixation security interests is the view of the Code draftsmen that in pre-affixation situations, the fixtures are really additions to the value of the real estate, while the security interest in existing fixtures works as a kind of reduction in the value contemplated by the real estate interest holder.

If the secured party with a security interest in fixtures has priority over all the persons with interests in the real estate, he may, on default, remove his collateral from the real estate, but he must reimburse any interested party, other than the debtor, for the cost of repair of any physical injury resulting from the removal. As we have seen, filing of security interests in fixtures must be in the place where interests in real estate are filed or recorded, and the financing statement must contain a description of the real estate.

In addition to the special problems occurring when personal property is affixed to real property are the problems that arise when personal property is installed in or affixed to other personal property, as when a new motor is installed in an old car. Where the security interest in the goods attaches before they are affixed to the other property, and where the goods do not lose their original identity, the security interest in the goods affixed prevails over the claims of all persons except a subsequent purchaser for value of an interest in the whole, and other situations such as those discussed above in connection with security interests attaching to goods before they become fixtures. Security interests attaching after installation or affixation are dealt with in much the same way as in the counterpart situation involving fixtures. Similarly also, the party with priority may remove his collateral on default.

Manufacturing operations may result in the mingling of many components and raw materials where the separate identities are lost in the mass. Generally, the holders of security interests in the different components and raw materials share in the new product or in the proceeds of its sale, in proportion to the cost of their collateral used in its manufacture. Obviously, there can be no right in a secured party to remove his collateral from the whole if the identity has been lost.

Statutory and common law liens often come into conflict with security interests, and assignment of priorities becomes necessary. The Code gives priority to the statutory and common law liens over perfected security interests, even though the liens may be second in time, as long as the lienholder retains possession of the goods. Thus, the warehouseman, the carrier, the artisan, and the others who are protected by these liens prevail over secured parties unless the statute or an agreement provides to the contrary. The theory is that the repairs or services of the lienholder have enhanced the value of the collateral.

Many other conflicting interests in the same collateral can, and do, arise, but all of the more common and more important examples have been discussed here. Further details can be obtained from the Code or from one of the exhaustive treatises on the subject of secured transactions.

F. Rights and Duties of the Parties

In General. The only matters yet to be discussed in connection with secured transactions are those having to do with the rights and duties of the immediate parties to the security agreement and, in particular, with their handling of the collateral. Procedure on default is covered in the paragraphs following this discussion.

As with most parts of the Code, the immediate parties to security agreements have considerable leeway in setting forth the terms of their own contracts. Only occasionally does the Code prescribe or proscribe specific provisions in the security agreement. The Code may require certain provisions, forbid others, or simply supply rules to be followed when the parties fail to set forth their own terms. All three approaches are found in the Code sections dealing with the rights and duties of the immediate parties. We will devote our attention to issues having to do with the possession of the collateral.

Collateral in Possession of Secured Party. *Right to possession.* The nature of the transaction and the terms of the agreement will determine whether the collateral will be possessed by the secured party or by the debtor. Brief attention was given in our earlier discussion to certain types of collateral which will almost certainly be intended to come into the possession of the secured party, such as negotiable instruments and documents, and to other collateral where possession by the secured party would destroy the very purpose of the financing arrangement, such as inventory. Where the transaction is in the nature of a pledge, the secured party is meant to have possession, and Section 9-207 of the Code sets forth the duties of the secured party under these circumstances.

Duties of the secured party. The Code provisions are largely a codification of precode rules having to do with the duties of pledgees toward property in their possession. The secured party must use reasonable care in the custody and preservation of collateral in his possession. This duty may not be disclaimed, but the standards of care may be determined in the agreement as long as they are reasonable. For obvious reasons, instruments and chattel paper are given special treatment in the Code, and the secured party must use reasonable care in observing due dates, making presentment, giving notice, and taking other steps necessary to preserve the rights of prior parties to the instrument or chattel paper. These obligations may be shifted to the debtor even though he does not have physical possession of the collateral.

Unless otherwise agreed, when collateral is in the secured party's possession, reasonable expenses incurred in the custody, preservation, use, or operation of the collateral, including the cost of insurance and payment of taxes, are chargeable to the debtor and are secured by the collateral. The risk of accidental loss or damage is on the debtor to the extent of any deficiency in insurance coverage. The secured party may hold as additional security any increase or profits received from the collateral, but money so received must be remitted to the debtor or applied in reduction of the obligation. The secured party must keep the collateral identifiable but may commingle fungible collateral. He may repledge the collateral as long as the terms do not impair the debtor's right to redeem it. The secured party is liable for any loss caused by his failure to meet any of these obligations, but he does not thereby lose his security interest. The secured party may use or operate the collateral, for the purpose of preserving it or its value, or in the manner and to the extent provided for in the security agreement.

Although very similar, the duties of the secured party discussed here are not the same as the duties of a secured party who has come into possession of the collateral as a result of exercising a remedy on default.

COLLATERAL IN POSSESSION OF DEBTOR. Much more so than in connection with the duties of the secured party, the Code leaves the duties of the debtor in possession of property to the terms of the security agreement. Section 9–205 does make it very clear, however, that "a security interest is not invalid or fraudulent against creditors by reason of liberty in the debtor to use, commingle or dispose of all or part of the collateral." The duties of the debtor will vary with the circumstances and may range all the way from simple acknowledgement of a security interest in the creditor, to a strict accounting for use and disposition of collateral. A debtor may be required to obtain permission from the secured party before selling any part of the collateral and to turn over the proceeds of sale in the identical form received by the debtor. On the other hand, the debtor may have no duties in respect to the collateral as long as he continues to pay stated instalments.

The approach which the Code has taken to this matter emphasizes the importance with which the draftsmen viewed the need for ease and convenience in the use of inventory, accounts receivable, and similar types of financing. The parties are in the best position to recognize the requirements of their transaction and to fix the terms of the agreements related to it. Because the Code does not provide all the answers, it is particularly important that the parties draft or examine security agreements with great care.

G. Default

IN GENERAL.　Had businessmen themselves drafted the provisions of the Code related to default, the remedies could not be more in tune with commercial practice and expectations. The practical basis for the Code rules is the recognition of the fact that it is the rights of the secured party in the collateral that distinguishes the "secured" party from the general creditor or unsecured lender. Security in the collateral, in other words, is what the game is all about, and commercial reasonableness is the basic rule of the game. Except for situations involving consumer goods, where other aspects of public policy come to the fore, the Code approaches foreclosure and liquidation of the collateral almost as though the goods were to be sold or disposed of in the ordinary course of business. The major remedies which carry out this policy are discussed below. They are found in Sections 9–501 to 9–507.

RIGHT TO POSSESSION.　The preceding paragraph makes it obvious that the secured party's most important remedy on default of the debtor is his right to take possession of the collateral, unless, of course, he is already in possession as a result of a pledge type of security transaction. The right to possess the collateral on default is inherent in every secured transaction involving tangible collateral. The security agreement, however, may provide to the contrary, but usually does not. The secured party may take possession without any judicial process as long as he can do so without breaching the peace. He may obtain judicial process, if he wishes, to aid him in taking possession. The Code has encouraged each state to spell out in its statutes or rules of court just what kinds of judicial process are available in these situations, especially where concepts of title are associated with a particular legal process. It will be recalled that the location of title is of no relevance under the provisions of Article 9.

The Code gives further protection to secured parties in situations where it is not practicable to assemble collateral or remove it from the debtor's premises and permits secured parties to prevent the debtor's use of the collateral and even to sell the collateral while still on the debtor's premises. The security agreement often provides that the secured party may require the debtor to assemble the collateral and make it available at a designated place.

COLLECTION RIGHTS.　Some kinds of collateral are not capable of being taken into physical possession. The Code makes special arrangements for accounts receivable, contract rights, general intangibles, chattel paper, and instruments whereby the secured party, following default, is authorized to notify account debtors and obligors to make payment to the secured party. The secured party may also take control of any proceeds of such collateral in the hands of the debtor, but must do so in a commercially reasonable manner. The secured party is entitled to receive from the debtor any deficiencies in his collections and must turn over to the debtor any surplus, except where the original transaction was an outright sale of the accounts receivable or the like.

RIGHT TO DISPOSE OF COLLATERAL. After default, the secured party may dispose of the collateral by sale or lease or in any other manner calculated to produce the greatest benefits for all parties concerned, but all aspects of the disposition must be commercially reasonable. Disposition may be through public or private proceedings and may be made through one or more contracts; collateral may be sold as a unit or in parcels and at any time or place and on any reasonable terms.

Unless the collateral is perishable, or is likely to decline rapidly in value, or is of a type customarily sold on a recognized market, the secured party must give reasonable notification of the time and place of any public sale to the debtor and, except in the case of consumer goods, to any other person who has a security interest in the goods and who has filed a financing statement or is otherwise known by the secured party to have a security interest. If there is to be a private sale, the same persons are entitled to notice, but the notice need only state the date after which disposition will take place. The purchaser of goods thus disposed of takes free or all rights and interests, even though the secured party fails to comply with the Code or other applicable law, as long as the purchaser acts in good faith, has no knowledge of any defect in the proceedings, and is not in collusion with the secured party, other bidders, or the person conducting the sale. The secured party himself may buy at a public sale or a sale in a recognized market for such goods.

Under Section 9–504, the proceeds of disposition are applied, first, to the reasonable expenses incurred in connection with taking possession and selling, second, to the satisfaction of the obligation, and third, to the satisfaction of indebtedness secured by any subordinate security interest in the collateral if written notice is received before the proceeds are distributed. The secured party must then account to the debtor for any surplus, and the debtor is liable for deficiencies.

DISPOSITION OF CONSUMER GOODS. The harshness of some precode laws in connection with the disposition of consumer goods purchased by debtors under conditional sales contracts has been alleviated by the Code, which provides, in Section 9–505(1):

> If the debtor has paid sixty per cent of the cash price in the case of a purchase money security interest in consumer goods or sixty per cent of the loan in the case of another security interest in consumer goods, and has not signed *after* default a statement renouncing or modifying his rights under this Part a secured party who has taken possession of collateral must dispose of it under Section 9-504 and if he fails to do so within ninety days after he takes possession the debtor at his option may recover in conversion or under Section 9-507(1) on secured party's liability. [See discussion of Section 9-507 below.]

Note that the debtor may waive his rights under this section if he does so *after default*.

ACCEPTANCE OF COLLATERAL IN DISCHARGE OF OBLIGATION. In situations not coming under Section 9–505(1) above, a secured party in possession of collateral may, after default, propose to retain the collateral in satisfaction of the obligation. The proposal must be made in writing and sent to the debtor and, except in the case of consumer goods, to any other secured party who has a security interest in the collateral and who has filed a financing statement or is otherwise known to the secured party in possession to have an interest. If the debtor or other person entitled to receive notification objects, in writing, within thirty days from receipt of the notification, the secured party must dispose of the collateral under Section 9–504. In the absence of objection, the secured party may retain the collateral in satisfaction of the obligation and free of any further duty to account for its disposition.

DEBTOR'S RIGHT OF REDEMPTION. The debtor or any secured party may redeem collateral at any time before the secured party in possession has disposed of it or entered into a contract for its disposition by tendering full satisfaction of the obligation, together with expenses reasonably incurred by the secured party in taking, holding, and selling the collateral.

SECURED PARTY'S LIABILITY FOR FAILURE TO COMPLY. Section 9–507 states that if it is established that the secured party is not proceeding in accordance with the provisions of the Code relating to default, disposition may be ordered or restrained by a court. If the disposition has already taken place, the debtor, or any other person entitled to notification or whose security interest has been made known to the secured party prior to disposition, has a right to recover from the secured party any loss caused by failure to comply. If the collateral is consumer goods, the debtor has a right to recover, in any event, an amount not less than the credit service charge plus 10 per cent of the principal amount of the debt or the time price differential plus 10 per cent of the cash price. The purpose of these provisions is further to restrain unfair treatment of consumers by instalment sellers. Unfortunately, some states omitted them from adopted versions of the Code.

4. REAL MORTGAGES

A. Cases

(1)

Vance Parker, a vice president of Hypocase, Inc., purchased a small farm near Berkland, Anosmia, with the idea of someday building a modern house thereon and providing a pleasant place to which to retire when he reached the mandatory retirement age at Hypocase. He paid $58,000 cash for the property. In 1967, two years after he bought the farm, Parker wanted to raise some money with which to buy stock in the Ionic Propulsion Company and mortgaged the farm to Lon Lendur as security on a loan of $15,000, payable in 1970. Lendur did not record his mortgage. In 1968, Parker sold the farm to Cain Groer, who knew nothing about the mortgage. A few days later, Lendur sold the mortgage to Tom Purcinter, who recorded the mortgage. If the mortgage is not paid when due, what are the rights of Purcinter against Parker and Groer? (Assume the law of your own state.)

(2)

Mark S. Hart, who owned a large clothing store in Berkland, mortgaged his store building to Lon Lendur for $10,000 "and such further amount as Hart may desire up to a total of $25,000." The mortgage was recorded. Shortly thereafter, Hart established a line of credit, giving a second mortgage on the property as security, at the Berkland National Bank, and began to borrow sums from the bank, eventually increasing his indebtedness to the bank to $32,000. During the same period of time, Hart increased his debt to Lendur to $25,000. The building is worth approximately $35,000. Hart has defaulted on both loans. What are the rights of Lendur and Berkland National Bank?

B. In General

The mortgage is one of the most widely used of all the security devices. It is used extensively both to finance the purchase of property and to raise capital. By means of the mortgage, either real or personal property can be employed as security for the performance of some obligation. If the property used as security is real property, the mortgage is known as a *real mortgage*. Prior to the adoption of the Uniform Commercial Code, a mortgage of personal property was called a *chattel mortgage*. As we have seen, the chattel mortgage was one of the security interests in personal property brought under the broad scope of Article 9, and the term is no longer of great importance, although it is still in some use. Our concern here will be with real mortgages.

Because the mortgage provides a very high order of security, it is attractive to prospective creditors. It is also attractive to the debtor because he ordinarily retains possession and use of the mortgaged property. There are disadvantages, as well as advantages, to both parties, and neither party should adopt the mortgage technique until he has considered its rather extensive ramifications. The person who lends money and takes a mortgage as security is called the *mortgagee*. The person who borrows money and gives a mortgage is called the *mortgagor*.

It should be realized here, if not before, that the type of security device to be employed depends, to a large extent, on the bargaining strength of the parties involved. A prospective borrower who is in desperate financial condition is in no position to quibble about the type of security a prospective creditor requires. On the other hand, a large and financially secure business organization often will have prospective creditors bidding against each other for the privilege of making the loan. In between these two extremes fall most credit transactions, with varying degrees of bargaining power in the hands of prospective debtors and creditors. Bargaining power is of course not the only factor. Custom and usage also are important, as are the amount involved, the term of the loan, the reputation of the debtor, and many other considerations. Where the circumstances require a high degree of security for the creditor and the use of the property by the debtor, the mortgage is one of the most satisfactory devices to employ.

C. Nature and Effect of the Mortgage

The earliest mortgages were not nearly so much security devices as they were outright conveyances of property to the creditor with the understanding that the debtor could get back the ownership when he paid his debt. The mortgage was actually a deed subject to the condition that it became void if the debtor settled his obligation when it came due. The original mortgage was a very harsh credit device because the courts interpreted it to be a genuine conveyance of title. When the debt was not paid on time, the debtor lost any right to recover the property and the creditor gained the right to immediate possession. To avoid these cruel results, the courts of equity invented what is called the *equity of redemption,* discussed in greater detail below, which gave the mortgagor additional, but still limited, time during which he could pay the debt in full and obtain the return of his property. This additional period was originally set by the court in each particular case, but it is now fixed by statute. Another important modification worked in the common law mortgage by the courts of equity was to recognize the transaction for what it really was, namely, a *security device.* The courts of equity afforded the mortgagee only a lien on the property and left the ownership and the right to use and possession in the mortgagor. Most states today follow the equitable or *lien theory,* but there are still some which stay with the common law or *title theory.* Even in the latter states, however, the harsh results of the old common law mortgage are not present, and the equity of redemption and other characteristics of the lien theory are recognized.

It is not surprising to learn that creditors did not appreciate the intervention of the courts of equity in mortgage situations; they soon began to resort to all kinds of gimmicks and sleight-of-hand in an effort to avoid the equitable doctrines. Most of these mortgage substitutes lost their usefulness rather quickly, however, as the courts of equity adopted a rule, which is still followed today, that any transaction in the nature of a mortgage will be treated as a mortgage, carrying with it the equity of redemption and other equitable modifications of the harsh common law device. Moreover, the courts will admit parol evidence to establish the true nature of a transaction, in spite of the general rule to the contrary. (See Chapter 3.) Even an ordinary deed may be shown to be a mortgage by the use of parol evidence.

Types of Mortgage. In addition to the real mortgage and the chattel mortgage already mentioned, there are other classifications and kinds of mortgages that should be examined briefly. The *purchase money mortgage* is a mortgage given in part or full payment of the purchase price of real property. It may be given to the seller of the property or to a third person. A *building and loan mortgage* is the name often given to an instalment mortgage to secure the funds used in erecting a building. The money is paid by the lender in instalments as the building reaches certain stages of completion. A *first mortgage* is one which is first in a series of mortgages or is a first lien on the property. A *second mortgage* is one which is second in a series of mortgages against the same property. The term may also be used in connection with a mortgage which is first in a line of mortgages but is second to some other type of lien.

In many states a transaction known as the *deed of trust* is used as a substitute for the mortgage. The device purports to transfer legal title to the property from the borrower to a third person who holds the title for the benefit of the lender. In most of the states where the deed of trust is used it is treated as a mortgage under the rule, discussed above, that a transaction in the nature of a mortgage will be treated as a mortgage. But in a few states, notably California, the deed of trust has been held to be a separate and distinct device conveying legal title to the trustee, in spite of the fact that the California courts have followed the lien theory of mortgages.

It is sometimes convenient to have a continuous mortgage on the same property to secure a series of loans, rather than to have a series of mortgages. Thus, a debtor and a creditor engaged in a series of loan and payment transactions, usually for working capital purposes, will find it desirable to execute one mortgage to secure present and future loans. Such mortgages are commonly referred to as *mortgages for future advances*. As payments are made by the debtor and additional funds borrowed, there is no need to execute separate mortgage instruments.

D. Creation of the Mortgage Relation

REQUIREMENT OF MORTGAGE OBLIGATION. Since a mortgage is a security device, it is essential for its creation that there be some sort of obligation for which the mortgage is given as security. Many courts confine the required obligation to those for the payment of money, but no sound reason exists why other sorts of obligations should not also be available for mortgage purposes. The mortgage for future advances is a perfectly valid type of mortgage, yet the obligation may not even exist at the time the mortgage relation is created. Although some courts require the obligation to be described with particularity in the mortgage instrument, the usual rule is that a general description is sufficient even though an interested party is compelled to look and inquire elsewhere for the details of terms and amount. Furthermore, as it has been pointed out, a conveyance of property may be shown by parol evidence to have been nothing more than security for a debt, and parol evidence is admitted, not only to show that there is a debt, but also for the purpose of showing the details of the transaction. Though not usually required, a detailed description in the instrument is a good practice, because it may be important in establishing priority over other liens, as in the mortgage for future advances. The priority problem is discussed at the end of the section on mortgages.

PROPERTY THAT MAY BE MORTGAGED.   Generally speaking, any real property or interest in real property may be the subject of a mortgage. It is not necessary that the mortgagor be the sole or outright owner of the mortgaged property. Any interest capable of being conveyed is capable of being mortgaged. Thus, lease interests, life estates, joint interests, remainders, other future interests, and even the uncertain dower interest of a wife may be mortgaged. (For details on these property interests, see Chapter 7.)

It will be recalled from Chapter 7 that, although crops may be mortgaged, there may be an issue whether the proper mortgage is a real or a chattel mortgage. Growing crops are generally considered to be real property and severed crops personal property, but the statutes of many states alter this status for mortgage purposes. Fixtures create a similar problem.

One of the presently and historically important controversies in the area of what property may be mortgaged is that having to do with property that has not been acquired at the time of the mortgage. The original rule was that such property could not be the subject of a mortgage, and this view was consistent with the concept of a mortgage as a present transfer of title or ownership. Today, however, equity will recognize an equitable lien on the property when it is acquired and that lien will be good against all third persons except bona fide purchasers without notice of the mortgage, but the mortgage must purport to apply to after acquired property.

FORMALITY IN CREATION.   A mortgage, in addition to being a conveyance of an interest in property, is a contract. If it involves real property, it must be in writing because of the statute of frauds. Probably in most states the actual form of the mortgage makes the instrument appear as though the lien theory had never come into existence, but the actual form is of minor importance in establishing the transaction as a mortgage and in bringing into being the attributes of a mortgage. A more sensible form is in use in some states, and, instead of purporting to convey title to property, the mortgagor is said to "mortgage" the property. The mortgagor is usually required to acknowledge the instrument before some public officer, such as a notary. The acknowledgment consists of a statement by the mortgagor that the instrument is his. (See Chapter 7 for further discussion of the acknowledgement.)

A mortgage usually contains the names of the parties, the consideration, a description of the subject matter and of the obligation on which the mortgage is based, and the signature of the mortgagor. In the older forms there is also a clause providing that the mortgage becomes void if the debt is paid on time. Sometimes the rights and duties of the parties are set forth in the mortgage in substantial detail. The rights and duties, however, are so clearly established by the mortgage relation itself that, unless some change is being made in the rights which operate automatically, there is no need to enumerate. Witnesses to the mortgagor's signature are required in some states. A few states still require the medieval ritual of a seal. After the mortgage contract is properly executed, it must be delivered to the mortgagee and accepted by him before it becomes effective.

RECORDING.   Although not necessary to the essential validity of a mortgage, the recording of the instrument with the proper public officer is a desirable and usually routine part of the mortgage transaction. Recording is for the protection of the mortgagee and of third persons who may at a later date be considering the purchase of the mortgaged property or the extension of credit on that property as security. If not recorded, the mortgage may be ineffective against a third person who buys the property or takes another mortgage on it without knowledge of the original mortgage. The extent of the protection and the effect of failure to record vary somewhat from state to state. Reference should be made to one's own law for details. The recording laws are discussed at considerable length in Chapter 7. Acknowledgment is usually required before an instrument may be recorded.

Even without recording, the mortgage is effective as between the mortgagor and the mortgagee. Recording is not necessary where the mortgaged property is in the possession of the mortgagee. The reason is obvious.

COLLATERAL INSTRUMENTS.   The mortgage itself is only a part of the total transaction. The remainder of the transaction consists of the obligation on which the mortgage is based. Thus, most mortgages are accompanied by a contract, note, or bond signed by the mortgagor. The collateral instrument establishes the personal liability of the mortgagor. Without the personal liability of the mortgagor, the mortgagee would not be able to recover any deficiency from the mortgagor if foreclosure of the mortgage failed to satisfy the obligation.

E. Rights and Duties of the Parties

POSSESSION AND USE.   Under the proper view of the mortgage, the mortgagor is entitled to the possession and enjoyment of the mortgaged property. In the states following the lien theory, the right to possession and enjoyment continues after default and until the mortgage is foreclosed. In the title theory states, the mortgagee is entitled to take possession immediately after default. As a matter of fact, it is frequently stated in connection with the title theory that the mortgagee is entitled to take possession immediately on the execution of the mortgage unless there is agreement to the contrary. The contrary agreement is almost always a part of the mortgage, because the ability of the mortgagor to retain possession is one of the chief advantages in the use of the mortgage. If the mortgagee does take possession, he must account to the mortgagor for all rents and profits flowing from the property during his possession. Even in the lien states, the mortgagee may stipulate in the mortgage contract that he is entitled to take possession if the mortgagor abuses or wastes the property. In general, the parties may agree on almost any modifications they desire, except the waiver of the mortgagor's equity of redemption.

In the lien states, the mortgagor is still the owner of the property, and he may deal with it as the owner. He may sell, lease, dispose of by will, or give away the property, subject only to the mortgage. The mortgagor's creditors can reach the property. Practically speaking, it is the mortgagor's equity of redemption that he would be dealing with in any of these cases. If a piece of property has a value of $10,000 and a mortgage on it for $2,500, the mortgagor may deal with his $7,500 equity.

RENTS AND PROFITS. The mortgagor in possession is entitled to the rents and profits flowing from the property. Furthermore, he is under no obligation to make any sort of accounting for them to the mortgagee. If the mortgagee is in possession, he must account for rents and profits and may not abandon possession without consent of the mortgagor. He must remain in possession until redemption or foreclosure. The mortgagee is entitled to set off against the rents and profits he holds for the mortgagor his own expenses for taxes, insurance, and repairs in reasonable amounts. He is not entitled to set off the value of permanent improvements he has made unless the mortgagor has agreed.

CARE OF THE PROPERTY. Even though the mortgagor has the right to possession and use of the mortgaged property almost as though it were not mortgaged, he is required to avoid such acts of waste as would tend to impair the security. Some states hold that any waste satisfies this test, but others take the view that the only waste the mortgagee can prevent is that which would reduce the value of the property to the point where it would be of doubtful sufficiency to cover the mortgagee's claim.

The mortgagee in possession may continue the ordinary use of the property, but he must exercise the same degree of care in the use that a reasonably prudent owner would exercise under the circumstances. The mortgagee is liable to the mortgagor for waste. He is under a duty to make ordinary repairs.

TRANSFER OF MORTGAGOR'S OR MORTGAGEE'S INTEREST. The interests of both the mortgagor and the mortgagee can be transferred. The rights of the persons to whom the interests are transferred will depend, to a large extent, on the agreement between the transferor and the transferee as limited by the rules designed to protect the original party to the mortgage who was not a party to the transfer.

The mortgagor may sell his interest in the property. If he does so, the purchaser is not personally liable for the mortgage debt, but the property is still subject to foreclosure to satisfy the debt. The purchaser from the mortgagor, however, may agree to be personally liable for the debt; in which case the mortgagee, as third party creditor beneficiary, may hold the transferee personally and directly liable on the debt and may still hold the original mortgagor on his promise to pay. Just what language is necessary to make the transferee thus personally liable is not clear. An express promise to that effect would cause no difficulty, but where the transferee takes the property "subject to the mortgage," there may be questions about the real nature of his agreement. Generally, the quoted words alone are not enough to make him liable, but his subsequent actions may justify the conclusion that personal liability was the intention. It should be remembered that the mortgagor cannot escape his own liability by transferring his interests to another person, in the absence of agreement by the mortgagee. Note also that if the mortgage is not recorded, the purchaser from the mortgagor may get the property free and clear of the mortgage. On the mortgagor's death, his interest in the property passes by his will or by the law of intestate succession. In either event, the property remains subject to the mortgage.

The mortgagee owns the mortgage, and he may transfer it to others. Because under the common law the mortgage amounts to a conveyance, a transfer of a mortgagee's interest would amount to a further conveyance. This would mean, as far as real property mortgages are concerned, that the transfer by the mortgagee would be effective only if done by means of a formal written instrument of conveyance. In many states, both lien and title, the mortgage interest may be transferred by a mere assignment of the debt, whether formal or not. This view is consistent with the lien theory, which makes the mortgage essentially a security transaction rather than a conveyance of property. An assignment of the basic debt carries with it the security.

The assignee of the mortgagee's interest should see to it that the assignment is recorded. If the assignment is not recorded, the assignee runs the risk that other parties may subsequently deal with the mortgage without knowledge of the assignment and thus get rights superior to his own. The recording of the assignment is not notice to the mortgagor, however, and the mortgagor may discharge his debt and cut off the rights of the assignee by paying the original mortgagee, as long as he does so without knowledge of the assignment. The assignee, consequently, should notify the mortgagor of the assignment.

The rights and duties of the parties to a deed of trust are much the same as those discussed above.

F. Discharge and Redemption

One of the essential characteristics of the mortgage is the ability of the mortgagor to pay his debt and thus remove the mortgagee's lien from the property or, in the title states, to recover the title to his property. The debt must, of course, be paid in full with interest. A very common misbelief exists to the effect that a debtor has the right to pay off his debt any time he pleases before the due date. Generally speaking, a debtor does not have the right to pay before the due date unless the terms of the loan provide for it or the creditor consents. This holds true of a mortgage debt where the mortgagor has no right to discharge the debt and remove the mortgagee's interest in the property, except by making full payment at the due date.

At common law, payment of the mortgage debt at the due date automatically returned the title in the property to the mortgagor, and no reconveyance of title was necessary. As it has already been pointed out, however, payment or offer of payment after the due date did not have such an effect, and only the the equitable right of redemption after the due date made it possible for the mortgagor to get his property back at all. Some states still follow this view, subject of course to a right of redemption, and an actual reconveyance is necessary in order to return the title to the mortgagor. In the lien theory states, payment of the full obligation any time before foreclosure removes the mortgagee's lien without the necessity of any reconveyance. It should be noted that the tender of payment has the same effect, but it does not, of course, discharge the debt itself. The creditor may still bring an action on the debt, but he has lost the security of his lien on the debtor's property. Where a creditor does refuse a proper tender of payment, he loses not only his lien but also his right to any further interest, and he must bear the costs of the action brought on the debt itself.

Although formal reconveyance is unnecessary in most states, it is a good idea, as a practical matter, for the mortgagor to secure a written statement from the mortgagee that the mortgage debt has been discharged and the lien removed from the property. This document should be recorded with the mortgage to show that the mortgagor's property is free and clear of the mortgage claim.

STATUTORY RIGHT OF REDEMPTION. The equitable right of redemption, discussed above, permitted the mortgagor in default to redeem his property by paying his debt within a period of time fixed by the court of equity. Because under the common law title theory the title became fixed in the mortgagee after the mortgagor's default, the mortgagor had to petition the court of equity for a decree setting the time during which the mortgage debt had to be paid and stating that on the expiration of that time the mortgagor's right to redeem was foreclosed. The periods of time set by the courts were usually quite long. Under this procedure, the foreclosure of the mortgage did not take place until the equity of redemption had expired. The mortgagor had a right, until foreclosure, to redeem.

Today, the right of redemption is controlled almost exclusively by statute. Instead of cutting off the right of redemption at the foreclosure, the statutes give the mortgagor the right to redeem even after a foreclosure sale, but the period of redemption after the sale is usually quite short—six months to one year. It has probably been noticed already that there is some variation in the use of the term "foreclosure"; at one time it referred simply to the expiration of the equity of redemption and the fixing of the title to the property in the mortgagee. Now the term is used interchangeably with the "foreclosure sale" and with other steps necessary under the lien theory in order to deprive the mortgagor of his title. *Foreclosure* is sometimes used to indicate not only that the sale has taken place but that the statutory period of redemption after the sale has also expired.

It must be remembered that the mortgagor is not the only one who may redeem. The holder of a second or subsequent mortgage may also redeem as may an heir or a person to whom the mortgagor left the property by will. The equity of redemption may be assigned, and the assignee may redeem. A judgment creditor who has perfected a lien on the property may exercise the right of redemption. If the right is exercised before foreclosure sale, the redeeming party must pay the mortgagee the principal obligation, interest due thereon, and expenses incurred by the mortgagee, including costs resulting from the mortgagor's default and from the anticipated foreclosure sale. Where the right is exercised after the sale, the redeeming party must pay to the purchaser of the property at the sale, or to the proper public official, the price at which the property was sold. When this has been done, a document is issued to the mortgagor giving notice that the property has been redeemed. This document should, of course, be recorded. The effect of redemption after sale is to cancel the sale and restore the title to the mortgagor or his successor, still subject of course to the liens that were on the property at the time of the sale.

STATUTE OF LIMITATIONS. A conflict exists among the decisions in regard to the right of a creditor to foreclosure on mortgage security where the statute of limitations has run on the mortgage debt. Some courts permit such foreclosure, but in most of the lien theory states the barring of the principal debt by the statute of limitations also extinguishes the mortgage lien. In these latter states, the revival of the principal debt by new promise or by acknowledgment will not revive the mortgage lien.

One of the reasons that the deed of trust is used to the almost complete exclusion of the real mortgage in a few states is that in those states a general rule has been established that the statute of limitations never runs on a deed of trust even though it does run on the principal obligation. For further discussion of deeds of trust see the next subsection on foreclosure.

G. Foreclosure

IN GENERAL. Under the old common law theory of the mortgage, the mortgagee had title to the property from the time the mortgage was entered into. His title was limited only by the right of the mortgagor to pay the obligation promptly on its due date and thus recover the title. If, however, the mortgagor failed to pay on the due date, the title became absolute in the hands of the mortgagee. When the equity of redemption was established and it became possible for the mortgagor to get back his title even after default, the mortgagee was deprived of a simple and convenient means of realizing on the mortgage security. To take the place of the lost right, the court of equity gave to the mortgagee the right to bring a proceeding to foreclose or terminate the mortgagor's equity of redemption. This proceeding culminated in a decree by the court that ordered the mortgagor to pay his obligation by a certain time or lose irretrievably his rights in the property. Today the mortgagee has a choice of foreclosure remedies which he can utilize in enforcing his mortgage security. In addition to these remedies, the mortgagee may also bring an action on the principal debt.

The mortgage instrument will usually describe in detail what constitutes a default by the mortgagor. It may be a failure to pay principal, interest, or taxes on the property or to perform any other obligation created in the mortgage contract. Frequently, the contract provides that a default on an instalment of the debt causes the entire debt to become due. The mortgage is enforceable after the mortgagor has defaulted, whatever that default may consist of. The enforcement of the mortgage is carried out by foreclosure proceedings. These proceedings may be brought by the mortgagee at any time during the period provided by statute. In many states, the period applied is simply the period used in connection with other actions involving real property, whereas in others there is a special period for mortgage foreclosures. Characteristically, however, the periods for foreclosures are shorter than the twenty-year period selected by the courts of equity when the equity of redemption and the corresponding right of foreclosure first arose.

Four types of foreclosure are in use in this country: strict foreclosure, foreclosure by judicial sale, power of sale, and foreclosure by entry. The first three are generally available; the last is available only in a few states. These four types will be considered very briefly below, as will some of the problems arising out of certain uses of the deed of trust.

STRICT FORECLOSURE. The strict foreclosure was the first type used by the English courts after the rights of redemption and of foreclosure came into existence. As mentioned above, when a mortgagor asked a court for the right to redeem his property in spite of his default, the mortgagee usually appeared in court also to ask the court to set a date by which time the mortgagor must pay or lose his rights forever. The court would issue a decree that ordered the mortgagor to pay his debt by a certain date and that stated that if he did not do so, his interest in the property would forever be foreclosed. On the failure to pay by the designated time, the mortgagee got an unconditional title to the property. The defects in this type of foreclosure are that it made no changes in the harsh common law rules of mortgages except to postpone the unfortunate day. The mortgagee got property which might be far more valuable than the amount of the debt. The mortgagor did not get the excess. Although still available in many states, strict foreclosure is not the usual method employed, except in one or two states. Where it is available, the courts will not permit its use except where the value of the property does not exceed the debt, where the mortgagor is insolvent, or where the defendant does not appear to defend the action. Even in these situations, however, the court must be convinced that strict foreclosure is not unfair or unjust. Strict foreclosure does have the general advantage of saving the expense of a judicial sale. Such foreclosures are expressly prohibited in some states.

FORECLOSURE BY JUDICIAL SALE. The most common method of foreclosure is by suit and judicial sale. The mortgagee obtains a decree from the court ordering that the property be sold by an officer of the court, usually the sheriff, that the debt be paid out of the proceeds, and that the excess, if any, go to the mortgagor. Notice of the sale must be given to the public and to interested parties. The sale itself is conducted as a public auction, and the mortgagee may bid. He obviously has an advantage over the other bidders in that he is actually bidding only the excess over his claim and will have to put up funds only in that amount. All liens and claims inferior to the mortgage lien are extinguishable by the sale, except to the extent they have the right in any surplus remaining after the mortgage debt is paid. The sale must usually be confirmed by the court. Courts, during the depression years of the 1930's, often refused to confirm because the sale price was inadequate.

One of the characteristics of the judicial sale method of foreclosure is that the court may grant a *deficiency judgment* against the mortgagor if the proceeds of the sale are insufficient to cover the debt. Many states have special procedures for deficiency judgments.

Statutes in almost all states, as pointed out above, give the mortgagor a further six months to one-year period of redemption even after the judicial sale. This extended period of redemption often has the effect of depressing the sale price inasmuch as a buyer will probably not want to wait six months or a year before his title becomes absolute; consequently, he will bid less than he would have otherwise.

POWER OF SALE. Foreclosure by judicial sale is frequently a lengthy and expensive proceeding. In order to avoid these disavantages of the judicial sale type of foreclosure, mortgagees began inserting into mortgage contracts provisions by which the mortgagor consented to sale of the property by the mortgagee without the court order and the complicated judicial sale. The actual machinery by which this was accomplished was the creation of an agency whereby the mortgagor as principal delegated authority to the mortgagee as agent to sell the property. This was a special type of irrevocable agency called an *agency coupled with an interest* or *power coupled with an interest*. This type of agency was discussed in Chapter 8.

The net result of a power of sale mortgage is that the mortgagee may himself sell the property and give a deed to the buyer on the default of the mortgagor, retaining the amount of the debt and costs and paying the excess to the mortgagor. In some states, statutes require the sale to be a public auction, but in many states it may be either public or private. Because of the unusual nature of the power given to the mortgagee, the courts examine such foreclosures with great care and insist on strict compliance with statutory regulations and limitations and with the terms and conditions of the mortgage. Any variation from strict compliance by the mortgagee may result in the court's setting aside the sale. The mortgagor's right to redeem even after sale applies after these sales as well as after judicial sales. Should the sale raise insufficient funds to pay the debt, the mortgagee may, by an appropriate action, secure a deficiency judgment against the mortgagor. The mortgagee is not permitted to bid or buy at a public sale nor to buy at a private sale. To do so would be to violate his duties as an agent of the mortgagor. The use of the deed of trust avoids this problem because the trustee, and not the creditor-mortgagee, sells the property.

FORECLOSURE BY ENTRY. In a few states, the mortgagee is permitted to enter and take possession of the mortgaged property after default by the mortgagor. If the mortgagee remains in undisputed possession of the premises for the period specified in the statute, usually one to three years, he gets an absolute title.

FORECLOSURE OF DEEDS OF TRUST. The use of the deed of trust varies somewhat from state to state, as was pointed out above. Some states treat these devices exactly as though they were mortgages; whereas others recognize differences, some of them substantial. In some states the deed of trust may be foreclosed as though it were a mortgage, but the creditor also has a choice of foreclosing by a sort of power of sale proceeding where there is no right of redemption after the sale but where the creditor is not entitled to a deficiency judgment. The decision as to which device should be employed will depend upon the circumstances of the particular case and especially upon the value of the property as compared with the amount of the debt.

PRIORITY PROBLEMS WITH MORTGAGES FOR FUTURE ADVANCES. Mortgages given to secure existing debts and also future advances are valid and quite common. The special problem this type of mortgage creates is that raised by the rights of subsequent mortgagees, creditors, and purchasers. Where, for example, *A* mortgages a piece of property to *B* to secure a $5,000 loan presently made and also to secure such other sums as *B* may advance to *A* from time to time, the issue arises as to the priority of *B*'s security on later advances when *C* has, in the meantime, advanced $2,500 to *A* and has taken a second mortgage as security. The general rule is that if *B* is *obligated* to make advances on *A's* demand, he is protected against subsequent creditors and purchasers even though he knew about them at the time he made advances. Furthermore, even if *B* is not so obligated, he is still protected as to advances made optionally if, at the time he made them, he did not *actually* know of intervening claimants. If he knew about the rights of third persons at the time he made advances, *B* is not protected. Another issue arising, however, is whether the recording of the second mortgage is sufficient notice to *B* to deprive him of his protection when he makes optional advances. The better answer seems to be that it is not.

5. SURETYSHIP AND GUARANTY

A. Cases

(1)

The president of the Anosmian Service Company, a small Anosmian corporation, negotiated a loan on behalf of his company with Lon Lendur. The loan contract was submitted to the shareholders at a shareholders' meeting on Tuesday. The shareholders not only approved the loan contract but also unanimously adopted a motion whereby the shareholders individually guaranteed the repayment of the loan to Lendur. When the loan was not repaid, Lendur sued the shareholders on their guaranty. The shareholders argue that there was no consideration to support their promises. What are the rights of the parties?

[See *McMillan* v. *Dozier,* 257 Ala. 435, 59 So. 2d 563 (1952)]

(2)

Earl Eaton personally guaranteed a loan by Lon Lendur to Ned Cash on June 1, 1965. The loan was payable on June 1, 1966. Cash did not pay the loan. On May 15, 1969, Eaton paid it. The statute of limitations on such contracts in the state of Anosmia is 3 years. Eaton now seeks to recover from Cash. After making frequent demands on Cash for several months, Eaton has decided to file suit. Would it be wiser for Eaton to exercise his right to indemnity or his right to subrogation?

B. In General

NATURE OF SURETYSHIP. All the methods of financing a business and providing security that have been discussed above involved the use of property or rights in property as the security. The creditor obtained possession of property, or the right to possess property, or had a lien on certain property, or had the right to retake property on the debtor's default, and so on. In suretyship we find security in the promise or undertaking of a person other than the debtor. Property is not here directly involved as security, although it may be a part of the transaction, and the thing that the creditor looks upon as supplying him with protection beyond the word of the debtor is the word or promise of someone else. *Suretyship* is a risk-shifting device whereby a creditor shifts part or all of his risk of the debtor's non-performance to another person. For example: *A* desires to borrow money, or buy goods on credit, from *B* who demands some assurance that the money will be repaid or the goods paid for. *C* agrees that, if *B* lends the money or sells the goods to *A* and *A* does not make payment, *C* will make such payment. If *B* now sells the goods or lends the money to *A*, *B's* risk of non-performance is shifted to *C*. Actually, *B* may now look to two people for the payment of the obligation. In this example, *C* is called a *surety; A* is called the *debtor* or *principal debtor; B,* the *creditor.* Note that suretyship is both a risk-shifting device to the creditor and a credit device to the debtor.

DEFINITIONS. Simply defined, suretyship arises whenever one person promises to answer or to stand good for the debt or default of another. There are many different kinds and types of suretyship, but all have this characteristic in common. The suretyship may take the form of a *strict suretyship,* where the surety makes himself liable on the same debt the debtor owes the creditor, or it may involve simply the promise of the surety to pay the debt if the debtor does not. It may also take the form of an indorsement on a negotiable instrument. (See Chapter 11.) All of these situations are forms of suretyship.

A great deal of confusion exists as to the proper use of the terms "suretyship" and "guaranty." Historically, the two were quite different, and the terms were not used interchangeably, but today not only are the terms used interchangeably but also a few states have statutes abolishing any different legal meaning that might have existed between the two. It must be noted, however, that the interchangeable use of the terms does not abolish the fact that there are two essentially different types of suretyship relation. The first, which has always been called *suretyship,* rises out of an original promise by the surety to pay the debt. The surety is primarily liable on the debt right along with the principal debtor. The second type, which was once called *guaranty,* rises out of a promise by the surety or guarantor to pay the debt if the principal debtor does not. The distinction is particularly important in connection with the statute of frauds, which requires that a special promise to answer for the debt or default of another must be in writing. The guaranty type of promise is a promise to answer for the debt of another and it must be in writing. The strict suretyship promise has always been looked upon by the courts as the surety's own debt and not that of another; thus, it does not have be in writing. In some states, both types come under the statute of frauds.

Other distinctions between the "surety" and the "guarantor" types of suretyship are worth noting. Because the surety is liable on the original debt, along with the principal debtor, the creditor does not even have to make a demand on the debtor before pursuing the surety. In the case of the guarantor, however, the creditor not only must make a demand on the debtor but also must give notice of the default to the guarantor. If the guarantor has guaranteed "collection," in contrast with "payment," the creditor must press his claim against the debtor through an unsatisfied judgment, or show that such action would be fruitless, before he may pursue the guarantor. The contract of the surety is usually made at the same time as the promise of the debtor and is supported by the same consideration. The contract of the guarantor, on the other hand, is usually made separately and supported by different consideration.

In the Uniform Commercial Code, the term "surety" is defined to include "guarantor." However, problems of suretyship are treated only collaterally in the Code, and the law of suretyship is not materially affected thereby. There was prior discussion of this matter in the chapter on commercial paper.

FORMATION OF CONTRACT. Whatever particular type of suretyship is involved, the relation arises out of contract, and this contract, like any other, must meet all of the usual contract requirements, including mutual assent, consideration, and competent parties. It should be noted, however, that special problems of interpretation and intent are likely to arise in suretyship situations. For example, statements made by one person in recommending another for credit may be taken as mere commendations or as an offer to stand good for the other person's debts. Persons writing such letters should be very careful in the choice of language if they want to avoid the possibility that their letters will be taken as offers to become sureties. Like any other offer, however, the offer to become a surety may be revoked any time before acceptance. This is true even of a continuing offer to guarantee the debts of another. The surety cannot escape liability for those advances which have already been made in reliance on his offer, but he may revoke the offer as to the future. Acceptance of an offer to become a surety may take place as a result of an exchange of promises or on the actual extension of credit to the principal debtor. The only purpose in reviewing here matters that were discussed in greater detail in the chapter on contracts is to call attention to some of the unusual problems which are created by the very nature of the suretyship transaction. A special *caveat* is issued in regard to problems of consideration, especially where the suretyship involves a debt or obligation already in existence at the time the contract of suretyship is entered into, as where a bank that has already loaned the debtor $10,000 asks for additional security, and the debtor supplies a surety. The old debt cannot be consideration for the surety's promise. New consideration is necessary.

C. Defenses of the Surety

IN GENERAL. One of the most important aspects of the law of suretyship has to do with the defenses which a surety may raise in an action by the creditor against the surety on his promise. The creditor has the right to proceed against the surety only when the surety's promise becomes enforceable under the terms of the contract. If the promise was of strict suretyship, the creditor may proceed against the surety as soon as the debt becomes due, but if the promise is in the nature of a guaranty, where the surety promises to pay if the debtor does not, the creditor cannot proceed against the surety until the debtor has defaulted. When the creditor does bring his action against the surety under the terms of the contract, the surety still may have one or more of a large number of defenses which he may interpose. Some of these defenses are available only to the surety, whereas others are primarily defenses of the principal debtor and are available to the surety through him. In addition, certain acts of the creditor may discharge the surety.

DEFENSES OF THE DEBTOR.   With the exception of a few defenses which may be entirely personal to the debtor, the debtor's defenses against the creditor are also available to the surety. Lack or failure of consideration and illegality are possible defenses for a debtor and would be available to the surety as well. Fraud and duress raise special problems because debtors have a choice of rescinding or affirming contracts entered into as a result of either. The courts do not agree, but most take the view that if the debtor elects to rescind, the surety may use the defense, but if the debtor affirms the contract, the surety is still bound. The incapacity of the debtor, as by infancy, is usually not a defense available to the surety, probably on the ground that the incapacity of the debtor may have been the reason the creditor required a surety in the first place. However, if a minor disaffirms his contract and returns all or part of the consideration to the creditor, the surety is discharged to the extent the consideration is returned.

SURETY'S OWN DEFENSES.   A creditor may induce a surety to enter a contract by fraud or duress. Obviously, such conduct would provide the surety with a defense against any action by the creditor. The failure of the creditor to disclose material facts to the surety is also a defense, but there is considerable variation from state to state on details. In every case, an employer would be under a duty to disclose a record of prior defalcations by an employee for whom the employer was seeking a surety. Lack or failure of separate consideration, where necessary, would clearly be a defense available to the surety.

ACTS OF THE CREDITOR.   Among the more common defenses employed by sureties are those based on certain conduct by the creditor. They include the release of the principal debtor without the consent of the surety. A partial release operates to discharge the surety to the extent of the release. The effect of releasing the debtor but reserving rights against the surety was discussed in the chapter on commercial paper. A creditor who releases property held as security for a debt also releases the surety to the extent of the value of the property released, except where the release does not work a material injury on the surety as where property retained is more than enough to cover the obligation. In some states, a creditor must use reasonable care in preserving and protecting security in his possession, and a surety will be released to the extent the security is dissipated. There is a contrary view based on the idea that the surety may always pay the debt and proceed against the debtor or utilize his right of subrogation.

Without the consent of the surety, material alterations in the contract between the debtor and the creditor will usually discharge the surety, but the law is not entirely consistent. Some recent cases distinguish between compensated sureties and gratuitous sureties in this connection, and they require the former to show injury in order to be released. One of the defenses most often arising in surety litigation is the extension of time of payment by the creditor without the consent of the surety. In a contract sense, many extensions are not binding anyway, owing to lack of consideration, and would not release a surety. Even where the extension is binding, however, there are many exceptions to the rule releasing the surety. Among them are situations where the creditor reserves his rights against the surety, where the surety is fully indemnified through property in his possession or on which he has a lien, and where the creditor was not aware of the suretyship relation. A valid tender of payment by either the debtor or the surety will, if refused, discharge the surety. The refusal will not, of course, release the debtor.

D. Remedies of the Surety

IN GENERAL. It should be clear from the very nature of the suretyship arrangement that the surety has remedies against the debtor when the surety's obligation becomes enforceable. One of these remedies is available before the surety has performed his obligation. Three remedies are available after part or full performance by the surety.

EXONERATION. The surety will sometimes find himself in the position of having to make an unnecessary, burdensome, and costly payment. The creditor, it may be assumed, is within his rights in demanding payment of the surety, but the hardships involved in the situation entitle the surety to the equitable relief of exoneration. Exoneration takes several different forms. The surety may bring an action to compel the debtor to pay his debt. This course of action will be taken by the surety where the debtor appears to be able to pay the debt, but has failed to do so, and there is danger that the debtor's assets may be dissipated or lost. The action by the surety would not stop the creditor from proceeding against the surety, but the surety could post a bond as security for the creditor's claim against him and ask the court to stay the creditor's action until the surety's suit against the debtor is completed.

Another type of exoneration may result from an action by the surety against the creditor to compel the creditor to proceed against security in his possession before he makes a claim against the surety. This type of exoneration, like the first, is available only when the payment by the surety would be unnecessary or unusually burdensome.

A third variety of exoneration involves an action by the surety against co-sureties to get contributions before the surety pays the creditor. Ordinarily, the surety may not ask or get contribution from co-sureties until he has paid the creditor, but where the full payment by a particular surety would work a serious hardship on him, the courts may require the contribution by the co-sureties before payment. A stay of a creditor's action against the surety may also be obtained in connection with this type of exoneration, as it may with the others.

SUBROGATION. A surety who pays the principal debtor's debt has a right to be put in the place of the creditor as regards the creditor's rights, remedies, and security against the debtor. After the surety pays, he is entitled to recover from the debtor to the same extent and in the same manner that the creditor could have recovered. If the creditor held some of the debtor's property as security for the debt, the surety is entitled to sell that property and apply the proceeds on his claim against the debtor. A prerequisite to the surety's right to subrogation is the full payment of the creditor's claim. If the creditor is left even partially unsatisfied, he is entitled to the security. It is not necessary that the surety himself have paid the full amount of the debt, as long as the creditor is paid in full. The debtor may have made a partial payment and the surety paid only the balance. Although the surety becomes entitled to the security, his rights exist only to the extent of the payment he actually made. The surety may surrender his right of subrogation if he states that he does not intend to use it, and he may lose his right by the running of the statute of limitations.

REIMBURSEMENT OR INDEMNITY. In addition to the rights of exoneration and of subrogation, the surety has a direct right to be repaid or indemnified by the principal debtor in the amount of the payment which the surety paid the creditor. If the surety pays the creditor unnecessarily, the right of indemnity or reimbursement does not come into existence, and the surety cannot exercise the right against the debtor. Examples would occur where the alleged debtor owed no debt to the creditor or where his debt has turned out to be invalid. Furthermore, no right of indemnity exists where the surety was not legally obligated to pay the creditor. This does not mean that the surety must wait for the creditor to sue him, but it would cover the situation where the contract of suretyship was not binding on the surety.

It should be noted that the surety's right to indemnity is his own personal right and is not the right of the creditor, as is the case of subrogation. This fact becomes important in connection with the statute of limitations. If the statute has run on the debtor's debt to the creditor, the surety gains nothing by subrogation, unless there is security in the creditor's hands. The reason is that the creditor would be barred from an action against the debtor and, on subrogation, the surety succeeds only to the rights which the creditor has. With the right to indemnity, however, the situation is different. The statute of limitations does not even begin to run until the surety has paid the matured debt.

CONTRIBUTION. A co-surety who has paid the principal debtor's debt is entitled to contribution from the other sureties. Many suretyship transactions involve the promises of more than one surety to answer for the debt of the principal debtor. In seeking payment, the creditor, it must be remembered, does not have to join all of the sureties, in the absence of contrary agreement, but may demand payment of only one. The one of whom the demand is made is obligated to pay the debt, but he may avoid undue hardship by the exercise of the right of exoneration as discussed above. When a surety has paid a valid and enforceable obligation, his rights against his fellow sureties for contribution arise.

The right to contribution depends not so much on contract as it does on principles of equity. Sureties standing in the same relation to the creditor are entitled to enjoy equally the benefits of the relation and are obligated to bear equally the burdens. Thus the right of contribution means a right to have all of the sureties share equally in the payment of the debt. Thus, if surety *A* is one of five sureties on a debt of $20,000 and he pays the debt in full, he is entitled to $4,000 from each of the other sureties. The problem sometimes arises as to the method of calculation of the shares where one or more of the sureties is insolvent or unreachably out of the jurisdiction. On equity principles, it would seem that the payment should be shared equally among the solvent sureties in the jurisdiction rather than equally among all of the sureties. The latter view puts an unjust burden on the particular surety who happened to be the object of the creditor's claim. Most courts follow the equitable view. The release by the creditor of one surety or an extension of time to one surety does not release the others except to the extent that the released surety would have been obligated to contribute. In the example above, the release of one surety would not alter the obligation of each of the remaining sureties to contribute $4,000, but it would release them from the obligation to contribute the released surety's share.

PROBLEMS

1. Explain the following terms: lien, common law lien, possessory lien, equitable lien, statutory lien, general lien, special lien, mechanics' lien.

2. List and describe the common law liens.

3. How do the equitable liens differ from the common law liens?

4. How may liens be extinguished? How are liens enforced?

5. Why has Article 9 been described as the most important article in the Uniform Commercial Code?

6. Explain the following terms: security agreement, security interest, secured party, collateral, attachment, perfection.

7. List and explain briefly the formal requirements for the creation of a security interest. What additional provisions will usually appear in a security agreement?

8. What are the Code requirements for the attachment of a security interest?

9. List and describe briefly the three categories of collateral established by Article 9.

10. The Code classifies goods into four groups. What are they, and what is the significance of each? What are the factors to be considered in determining to which classification a particular article belongs? Under what circumstances may particular goods be classified in more than one category at the same time or change from one category to another?

11. Distinguish between accounts and contract rights. What is a general intangible?

12. Explain the following terms: documentary collateral, instrument, document, chattel paper. How may a bill of lading or a warehouse receipt be used as collateral for a loan?

13. Explain the circumstances under which the various kinds of perfection must be, may be, or cannot be used. Which is the most important method of perfecting a security interest? How does it work? May the holder of a perfected security interest ever have priority against general creditors in bankruptcy? Explain.

14. Describe the priority rules applied to purchase money security interests.

15. How does Article 9 resolve the conflicts between parties having interests in real estate and parties having security interests in fixtures?

16. *S* has a security interest in a new Ford motor sold to *B*; *B* installs the motor in an old car in which *C* has a security interest and then sells the car to *D*. Discuss the rights of *S, C,* and *D*.

17. What duties does the Code impose upon secured parties in possession of collateral? Contrast these duties with those of the debtor in possession.

18. *D*, a debtor, has defaulted on an obligation owed to *S*, a secured party. The collateral is in the possession of *D*. Describe the various steps that may be taken by *S* in order to realize on the collateral. Suppose *D* has sold the collateral and deposited the proceeds in his bank account?

19. List and describe briefly the ways in which the Code affords special treatment to consumer goods with respect to the creation of security interests and the disposition of the goods on default.

20. Does the secured party run any risks if he disposes of collateral other than in compliance with Code provisions?

21. Explain the following terms: real mortgage, equity of redemption, lien theory, title theory, purchase money mortgage, first mortgate, deed of trust, mortgage for future advances, foreclosure, deficiency judgment.

22. What property may be mortgaged? What requirements must be met in order to create a valid mortgage? Is it necessary that a valid mortgage be labeled a mortgage?

23. What effect does a mortgage have on the mortgagor's rights with regard to the use of his own property?

24. Compare the mortgage with the deed of trust.

25. List and compare the various types of foreclosure.

26. Trace the steps which a mortgagee would follow in an attempt to realize on the security after the mortgagor has defaulted.

27. *A* borrowed $15,000 from *B*, giving *B* as security a mortgage on Blackacre. Because it was possible that *A* might require additional funds at a later time, the mortgage was drawn as a mortgage for future advances. *B* recorded the mortgage.

A then borrowed $5,000 from *C*, giving *C* as security a mortgage on Blackacre. *C* did not actually know of the prior mortgage to *B*. *C* recorded his mortgage. *B*, being unaware of *C's* claim, loaned an additional $5,000 to *A*. Since the last loan, *A* has become insolvent. His only asset is Blackacre, which is worth approximately $17,500. What are the rights of *B* and *C*?

28. Explain the following terms: exoneration, subrogation, reimbursement, indemnity, contribution, suretyship, guaranty.

29. List and describe briefly some of the defenses of a surety.

30. *A* borrowed $6,000 from *B* secured by the agreement of three co-sureties, *C*, *D*, and *E*, to pay if *A* defaults. *A* has defaulted, but *B* has not been very diligent in attempting to collect from the sureties. However, *B* demanded payment from *C* just a few days before the statute of limitations had run on the debt, and *C* paid the full $6,000. What are the rights of *C* against *A, D*, and *E*?

chapter 14

Competitive Practices

1. INTRODUCTION—THE COMPETITIVE SYSTEM

A. In General

Probably none of the legal aspects of business affects the average businessman so intimately or so extensively as those aspects related to his competitive practices and activities. It is a rare business indeed that sets its prices, selects its customers and suppliers, picks a name, selects a form of organization, builds its stores or factories, pays its wages, manufactures its products, designs its labels, and advertises its wares without coming into contact with those fields of the law regulating and controlling the conduct of economic affairs in our society. A mere list of the ways in which trade is regulated by statute or by common law would be of book length without any descriptions or explanations. It is not necessary, however, to list or to consider them all in order to get a relatively clear picture of the general problem and of the more important areas within it. This chapter will be devoted largely to those aspects of the regulation of trade which are concerned with competition, its preservation, its protection, and its restriction. Other aspects of regulation, such as zoning, safety and sanitary requirements, wages and hours, and the regulation of the financing and formation of the various business forms will not be discussed in this chapter. Many of these types of regulation, which are not concerned with competitive practices, are discussed elsewhere in the book.

The competitive practices that have been subjected to public regulation, either by statute or by the common law, have changed considerably through the years. Most of the changes have been in the direction of extending the list of practices that have been brought under the control of society. Very few have been dropped from the list in the last century. As our economic society has become more complicated and as the effects of economic behavior and business practices have become more widespread and more direct, the need for public regulation of business practices has become greater. When business units were characteristically small, the effects of the activities and practices of these units were usually quite local in scope. But as the size of the business unit has increased, so have its influence and the effects of its activities. The policies and practices of a single large corporation or of a small group of large corporations may produce significant changes in the general price level, in the standard of living, in economic activity, and in government. They may even affect the policies and economic conditions of foreign countries.

It should be noted that as the effects of business practices on the public have become more pronounced so has the businessman acquired a greater sense of public responsibility. The law has not had to fill a complete vacuum but only to erect protective barriers in those spots where the sense of responsibility left something to be desired or where the dangers to the public were especially great. It should be noted also that the word "public" is not here confined to the consuming public but is intended to extend to society as a whole, including the business segment of society, which is as much, or even more, affected by the practices and policies of its members as are the other segments of society. It will be seen below that much of the regulatory legislation and many of the common law rules are designed more to protect one business from another than they are to protect the consuming public. It is obvious that if everybody is protected from everybody else with regard to all activities, there is no room left for the competition which is the desirable end the basic policy of regulation is alleged to preserve and to protect.

(In 1953 the Attorney General of the United States established a National Committee to Study the Antitrust Laws and appointed to this committee a group of lawyers, economists and others who were specialists in antitrust and related fields. After two years of intensive study, the Committee submitted its report to the Attorney General.[1] The report, hereafter referred to as the Attorney General's Report, contains much valuable material in the form of

---

[1] Report of the Attorney General's National Committee to Study the Antitrust Laws (1955).

analysis, conclusions and recommendations. It will be mentioned occasionally during the discussion that follows.)

.B Development of the Competitive System

Competition has not always been a characteristic of our economic society nor has it always been a desirable element. While competition was recognized and casually analyzed by some observers during the Middle Ages and even before, it was so atypical of those times that rarely was it thought to be desirable, and usually it was condemned and suppressed. Competition was not generally recognized as either characteristic or desirable until the Industrial Revolution and the eighteenth century. In the year 1410, the English Court of Common Pleas was faced with a case involving two schoolmasters of Gloucester who complained of having been injured by a third schoolmaster who had started a school in the same town and had initiated a little price cutting in order to get students.[2] The schoolmasters were refused relief, but not before the several judges who sat on the case had made it clear that this was a very odd situation and that they did not know exactly what to do with it. A few of the judges thought relief should be allowed because they just could not imagine a situation where this sort of competitive activity could properly take place. The society in which they lived was characterized by almost complete monopoly in economic affairs. The markets, the guilds, the fairs, and the merchant towns did not compete with each other and were not permitted to do so. Each had an exclusive franchise for some particular function in some particular area, and nobody was allowed to invade the franchise. Some of the judges saw procedural difficulties in allowing relief to the plaintiffs, but only one or two analyzed the issue in terms of competition, without, of course, using that word.

Despite the fact that monopoly was typical of the times and was thoroughly protected, some of the earliest traces of the common law policy against monopoly are found in the statutes designed primarily to protect the market monopolies. There were statutes that prohibited sales outside the market. Obviously, the market privilege would be worthless to the owner of the privilege if sales were made outside and if he could not collect the fees for the right to buy and sell goods in the market. Along with these statutes, however, were others that prohibited corners or monopolies within the market itself. If was a crime for one person to buy goods in a market for the purpose of reselling in the same market. Although the underlying purpose of this sort of statute was probably to protect the market's reputation, there was also an element of trying to protect buyers who would have to pay unfair prices if one seller got a monopoly or corner on the supply of some item. Where foodstuffs were involved, the regulation was more severe, and buying for the purpose of

---

[2] The Schoolmaster Case—Anonymous, Y. B. Hen. IV, f. 47, pl. 21 (1410).

reselling was almost completely prohibited. There had always been a strong common law policy against fixing or boosting the prices of food products, and the feeling against monopolies in such products was a natural result of the policy. These prohibited activities carried such names as *forestalling, engrossing,* and *regrating.*

The merchant and craft guilds, which were powerful economic agencies until the seventeenth century, were also based on monopoly concepts. Except for some regulation by the Crown of quality and quantity standards, of excessive tolls and fees, and of the wages and treatment of apprentices, the guilds were little sovereign states. The internal disorganization of the guilds and external economic changes caused the weakening of both the market system and the guild system and their eventual destruction. The natural progression from apprentice to journeyman to master craftsman, which kept the underlings loyal to the guild system, broke down in the seventeenth century, and journeymen began to compete with the guilds in such large numbers that little could be done about it. A national merchant class was arising in England during this period, and commerce was becoming more and more national in scope. The local monopolies of guild and market could not long survive.

Another significant development was taking place in the seventeenth century as a result of the struggle for power between parliament and the Tudor Kings and Queens. The Crown, in search of revenue, had increased the practice of selling monopoly privileges to private persons for substantial fees. There was great popular opposition to this practice, especially from the guilds, many of which lost some of their own privileges and prerogatives as a result of the grants from the Crown. These practices were alleged to be in violation of the statutes against forestalling, regrating, and engrossing, which were supposed to discourage monopoly by private persons. Queen Elizabeth avoided an open battle with parliament by abolishing all crown monopolies by royal proclamation in 1601. The next year the decision by the King's Bench in the case of *Darcy* v. *Allein,* the Case of Monopolies,[3] established the supremacy of the common law over royal prerogative in this matter. James I, however, did not accept this view, and he began once more to sell monopolies. The result was the Statute of Monopolies[4] in 1624, which stated that such monopolies "or any other monopolies" shall be utterly void. At first glance this statute would seem to reduce the later need for anti-monopoly legislation in the United States where the Statute of Monopolies is a part of our common law. The statute is really not as broad as it seems. It was concerned primarily with grants of monopoly by the Crown, something with which we were not much concerned in 1890 when the Sherman Anti-Trust Act was passed, and was not at all interested in monopolies resulting from

---

[3] 11 Coke 84-b (K.B. 1602).
[4] 21 Jac. I, c. 3, 1623–4.

the agreement of several persons. Furthermore, the statute had in mind the absolute or 100 per cent monopoly, which is a minor problem in our modern economic society. The Statute of Monopolies did establish one clear common law policy against monopoly, and, by excluding letters patent from its terms, laid the foundation for our patent system, which grants a limited monopoly as a reward for invention. Here was a policy *against* monopoly but, as yet, no policy *for* competition.

Competition was not generally recognized as an automatic regulator of business until the Industrial Revolution, during the period of which economic organization and theory shifted from those of thorough and complete monopoly and regulation to the doctrine of *laissez faire*. The word "revolution" has been subjected to much criticism in this connection, but if the connotations of sudden change and upheaval are deemphasized, it is a very descriptive term. Chief credit for the Industrial Revolution usually goes to inventors, such as James Watt. Actually, the philosophical and intellectual contributions of the period were just as important. The growth of enlightened self-interest, the desire for greater liberty, and the development of a consistent body of economic thought were the framework within which the inventions reorganized economic society. It is difficult to imagine an industrial revolution without Adam Smith, Ricardo, Malthus, Young, and Jeremy Bentham. During the period, economic organization improved, and new devices for the conduct of economic affairs came into prominence. Banking and exchange improved and increased, and trade expanded all over the world. Competition had emerged as something desirable and as the chief characteristic of economic activity. Any other view of competition would have been inconsistent with the doctrine of *lassez faire*, the natural way, and freedom. It was not realized for many years that competition may tend to be self-destructive and that some regulation may be needed in order to protect competition from those who exercise it unfairly or with monopoly as their object. It has been well said that competition, after all, is a condition and not a strategy.

C. Legal Characteristics of Competition

(1)

CASE. The Standard Oil Company was a wholesale dealer in oil in the city of Des Moines, Iowa. In the year 1893, the Crystal Oil Company, a local corporation, entered the retail trade in oil in the city, selling its goods from tank wagons hauled about the streets, and delivering oil to its customers at their homes. Its business grew from year to year until, in 1898, it employed from four to eight wagons, covering the entire city. Crystal supplied its customers with green cards which could be placed in a window to notify the wagon driver that the customer needed oil. From 1893 to 1898, Crystal Oil purchased its supplies of oil from Standard, but, in 1898, for some reason, it began to make purchases from other wholesale dealers. Trouble at once ensued. Standard, which up to that time had not been in the retail trade, proceeded to equip itself with tank wagons and drivers equal in number to those of the Crystal Company, and began the active solicitation of retail customers. Standard instructed its drivers to "give special attention to the Crystal Company's green cards" and to keep quiet about the real ownership of the new tank wagons, which were unmarked. Standard's drivers occasionally impersonated Crystal drivers and often carried away the green cards. At the end of several months, Crystal gave up the fight and retired from business at a considerable loss. When Crystal had been eliminated, the manager in charge of the Standard operation called his drivers to a meeting at his home and told them: "The fight is over and we have bought them out." Standard then withdrew from the retail oil business. What are the rights of Crystal against Standard?

[*Dunshee* v. *Standard Oil Company,* 152 Iowa 618, 132 N.W. 371 (1911)]

IN GENERAL. Competition, having been traced from its humble origins to its emergence as the chief characteristic of our economic society, is now the hub around which the remainder of this chapter will revolve. In order that the most be obtained from the succeeding discussion, it is important that the reader have some knowledge of competition from the economic point of view and also an understanding of the legal aspects and characteristics of competition. Some economic knowledge of competition will be assumed, but a few words will be said about the legal aspects without which competition would largely lose its importance. These legal aspects, it will be noted, are discussed in terms of *rights*, which, as was pointed out in Part I, is just a shorthand way of saying that particular interests, powers or privileges are recognized and protected by the law.

RIGHT TO COMPETE. A person has a legal right to compete with others engaged in the same business. Were it not for this right to compete, the whole concept of competition would have to be eliminated because where there is no right to compete, there can be no competition. The right is not unqualified, however, and a person may be legally restrained from competing where his sole or primary purpose in competing is to injure another person. Where a person engages in a business or an occupation in good faith and for the purpose of promoting his own interests and improving his own position, loss of business or harm caused to another person is not actionable, and the exercise of the right to compete cannot be enjoined. In the case of *Tuttle* v. *Buck*,[5] however, it was held that the right to compete did not protect a banker in a small town in Minnesota who supported a barbering business for the sole purpose

---

[5] 107 Minn. 145, 119 N.W. 946 (1909).

of driving out another who was regularly engaged in the business of barbering, and where the banker intended to retire from the barbering business as soon as his object had been achieved. Where the motives are mixed, some good and some bad, the right to compete is usually protected even where the bad motives are of major importance. In *Beardsley* v. *Kilmer,*[6] a patent medicine manufacturer was held to be properly exercising his right to compete where he started up a newspaper and forced out of business another newspaper that had made derogatory remarks about the medicine and its manufacturer. The new paper remained in operation for two years after the other was gone, was by general agreement a better paper, and was finally sold to another newspaper publisher at a profit. The right to compete, however, does not include the right to compete in any manner a person may desire, as we shall see in detail below.

RIGHT TO ENGAGE IN BUSINESS. Another legal cornerstone of competition is the right to engage in business. In chronological order, this right should come before the right to compete. The latter right could not exist were there no right to engage in business in the first place. Our concern here is with the legal right to engage in business and not with the economic problem of freedom of entry, which may be severely reduced or eliminated by the character of the market and the status of those already in it. A person may have a legal right to engage in a business but, as a practical matter, may not have the freedom to enter because of the huge investment required, the lack of marketing outlets, or other reasons. Nor is the right to engage in business an unrestricted right even from the legal point of view. Public utilities, commercial transportation, and occupations such as law and medicine often may not be engaged in without prior permission from a governmental agency.

RIGHT TO SELECT OWN CUSTOMERS. An important but not unrestricted right is the right of a person in business to select his own customers. Public utilities and railroads, because of the public service character of their calling, have only a very limited right to pick their customers. Although other types of business may refuse to deal with certain persons under ordinary circumstances, they cannot enter into arrangements with others whereby they all agree not to deal with prospective customers or suppliers. These refusals to deal are known as *boycotts,* and will be discussed later. Statutes in some states and federal law prohibit certain types of business from refusing to deal where the reasons for refusal are such non-business grounds as race, color, sex, or religion.

INDIVIDUAL PRICE DETERMINATION. Buyers and sellers ordinarily have the right to set the prices at which they will do business, but this right is somewhat more circumscribed today than are the others mentioned above. In time of national emergency, the federal government may set limits on the prices of certain commodities or services that are under particular stress from the

---

[6] 236 N.Y. 80, 140 N.E. 203 (1923).

emergency. The *fair trade laws* permit manufacturers and others to set the prices at which goods will be resold to dealers or to the public, and these prices are binding even on those who did not agree to them. *Loss leader acts* in many states prohibit sales "below cost," again limiting the right of a person to set his own prices. The prices of certain vital commodities, such as milk, are frequently regulated by a public agency. The same is true of prices charged by public utilities, commercial transportation companies, and others.

FREEDOM OF CONTRACT. The most important of all commercial law techniques is the contract, and the voluntary nature of this technique is an important element of competition. Most business activity contemplates contracts, consists of contracts, or results from contracts. The absence of the right to enter contracts freely or to refrain from entering them would make nonsense out of most of the other legal characteristics of competition. The right to compete would be made worthless if the holder of that right did not also have the right to contract freely. The right to contract is not unrestricted, as will be seen below. A person is not free to enter into a contract that is illegal or furthers an illegal purpose. Even though a person purports to enter into such a contract, he does not achieve the usual legal results attendant on a valid contract.

2. MONOPOLY AND RESTRAINT OF TRADE

A. In General

The variety of competitive practices which could be discussed is almost limitless, and the time and space involved in such a discussion would be more than either the readers or the author would care to invest. Fortunately, however, most of the competitive practices group themselves rather conveniently into categories which can be examined without untoward reference to specific and detailed situations. Furthermore, some of the practices and problems are so much more important than the others that cutting the list down to manageable size is not difficult. The areas that will be considered here include: 1, monopoly and restraint of trade; 2, certain price practices, such as discrimination, sales below cost, and resale price maintenance; and 3, a group of miscellaneous business practices, such as exclusive dealing and tying, false and misleading advertising, and interference with another's trade relations. At the end of this chapter there is a brief discussion of patents and of the relationship between patents and antitrust policy.

In all of the areas mentioned, the common law and legislation are both important, and both will be referred to. The common law is relatively more important in connection with the discussion of monopoly and restraint of trade than with the discussion of some of the other areas, because the statutes in that area are phrased largely in common law terms and are, consequently, more closely related to their common law antecedents. In many of the other areas, the common law has been substantially superseded by the statutory language.

B. At Common Law

(1)

CASE. J. D. Boone sold to M. E. Everett the grocery business which Boone owned and operated in Macon, Georgia. One portion of the contract of sale contained the following clause: "This is to certify that I will not operate any business that will conflict in the least with the business sold to and operated by M. E. Everett for the next three years without his consent." A few weeks after the sale, Boone began to operate a grocery business on the same street and only a block and a half away from the business he had just sold to Everett. Can Everett enjoin the continuation of Boone's new business?

[*Everett* v. *Boone,* 157 Ga. 372, 121 S.E. 240 (1923)]

(2)

CASE. On September 1, 1947, Lynch, an accountant of considerable experience and reputation, joined a new firm of accountants organized by Bailey. The new firm had offices in most of the large metropolitan areas of the United States. Lynch took with him when he joined the firm the clients that he had acquired during his many years of practicing accountancy in New York City. The partnership agreement contained a clause providing that if a partner should withdraw voluntarily from the firm he would not for four years thereafter either individually, as a member of a partnership, or as an employee, practice accountancy within 100 miles of any city in which the firm or any associated partnership was located at the time of the withdrawal. On October 10, 1947, Bailey notified Lynch that he was to move to Hartford, Connecticut, to take charge of a new office there. Lynch objected on the grounds that it was not in the best interests of the firm and that he had his residence and his family in New York and had practiced accountancy there all of his adult life. Bailey told Lynch that if he did not go to Hartford, it would seriously impair his participation in the business and that his share would probably be reduced by the management committee. Lynch then informed Bailey, on October 30, 1947, that he would withdraw from the firm as of January 31, 1948. In spite of assurances by Lynch that he would not infringe on any of the firm's clients, he and Bailey were unable to work out any system by which Lynch would be able to practice accountancy without the firm claiming violation of the clause in the partnership agreement. Lynch brought suit asking for a declaratory judgment holding the restrictive clause in the agreement invalid.

[*Lynch* v. *Bailey,* 275 App. Div. 527, 90 N.Y.S. 2d 359 (1948)]

In General. Common law policies in regard to certain competitive practices had developed long before American statutory law entered the picture late in the nineteenth century. A common law basis for regulation had been established in at least three areas before statutory regulation became important. These areas were: 1, contracts in restraint of trade; 2, combinations or conspiracies in restraint of trade; and 3, unfair competition. The latter two have been almost completely supplanted by statute in the United States, and will be discussed in this chapter largely in connection with the statutes. The first area has not been untouched by statutes, but in large portions of it statutes have never been greatly important. The portions that are as a whole unaffected by statute will be discussed here; the remainder, in connection with statutory regulation.

The statutory regulation and, to a more limited extent, the common law regulation were the result of the growing realization after the eighteenth century that completely unrestrained competition bore the seeds of its own destruction and was a paradise for the unscrupulous. Common law policies, many of which had developed centuries earlier without any reference to competition, were adapted to the task of regulating and protecting competition, some within the tort field and some in contract law. The common law policy with regard to contracts in restraint of trade was one of these adaptations.

Origins of the Common Law Policy. When the famous Dyer's Case[7] of 1415 is read today, one is somewhat startled by the vehemence with which the judge spoke of a contract between two parties whereby one of them agreed not to practice his dyer's trade in a certain town for six months. One of the judges said: "Per Dieu, if the plaintiff were here, he should go to prison till he paid a fine to the king." It is fairly obvious that in 1415 the court was not *that* concerned with a reduction of competition. The explanation for the court's strong feeling is found in the fact that the Black Death, which swept England in 1348 and 1349, destroyed one half of the population and created great shortages in the supply of labor. Parliament enacted and re-enacted several statutes during the next century designed to force every able-bodied person to work, to compel laborers to remain at work in their ordinary place of residence, and to regulate wages and prices. The penalties were fines and imprisonment. It is easy to see why an agreement to refrain from one's craft was against the policy of the common law at this time. Furthermore, the guild economy at the time made it likely that if a man agreed not to practice the trade in which he was apprenticed, he might not be able to make a living at any other. The common law policy sought to keep men from bargaining away their means of livelihood. The phrase "contracts in restraint of trade" has a much wider meaning today than that of a contract or covenant creating a voluntary restraint on the right of an individual to practice his trade or profession, but it should be noted that the narrower meaning has not been

---

[7] 2 Hen. V, 5 pl. 26 (1415).

abolished and still exists almost untouched by statute, but not unchanged by time, since the days of the Dyer's Case. A knowledge of the rules in regard to these voluntary restrictions on a person's right to engage in trade, although now a minor part of "restraint of trade," is important because these rules supplied the framework into which most of the broader meanings and applications were fitted.

As will become only too obvious during the course of reading the next few pages, the phrase *restraint of trade* is not one which lends itself readily to a brief definition. It is possible, however, to describe with reasonable accuracy the nature of the situation to which the phrase ordinarily applies. Where, by agreement or otherwise, a person is prevented from entering into or continuing a business, access to a market by either buyers or sellers is restricted, the amount of goods offered for sale or the amount of goods bought is interfered with, competitors divide up a market among themselves so as to reduce or eliminate competition, prices or terms of sale are removed from the free operation of the economic laws, or the public is deprived of the benefits or advantages of competition, trade is said to be restrained. Not all such restraints are illegal or against the best interests of the public. The development of our law of trade regulation has been characterized to a great extent by the multitude of approaches and solutions to the problem of which restraints of trade should be prohibited and which should not. This précis of "restraint of trade" is considerably enlarged upon below.

MODERN RULES.   Although originally most contracts not to carry on a business or occupation were void, the three centuries following the Dyer's Case saw the law change to the extent that in 1711 the Court of King's Bench could set forth rules, almost indistinguishable from those followed today, to the effect that such restraints of trade are valid if they are reasonable.[8] Reasonableness was not the only criterion then nor is it now, but it is the most important. A sharp line is sometimes drawn between those contracts in restraint of trade that are related to another transaction that is valid and those that are not so related. The former are said to be valid and enforceable if reasonable, whereas the latter are usually held to be invalid. For example: An agreement not to compete is much more likely to be held valid if it is ancillary to the sale of a business than if it is a completely independent agreement. It is not unusual nor is it unreasonable for the purchaser of the goodwill of a business to require the seller to agree not to reenter the same business in the same neighborhood for a reasonable period of time, but an independent promise not to engage in business is suspect. Actually, some varieties of non-ancillary agreements have been held valid, but there is neither the time nor the need to examine these possibilities here.

The basic test of reasonableness is often referred to as the *rule of reason,*

---

[8] *Mitchell* v. *Reynolds,* 1 P. Williams 181, 24 Eng. Rep. 347 (K.B. 1711).

under which title it becomes of special interest in discussions of the Sherman Act, as will be seen later. In general, a contract in restraint of trade is valid if the restraint is reasonable, and the restraint is reasonable unless it falls into one of the following categories: 1, is greater than is required for the protection of the person for whose benefit the restraint is imposed; or 2, imposes undue hardship upon the person restricted; or 3, tends to create, or has for its purpose the creation of, a monopoly; or 4, seeks to control prices or to limit production artificially; or 5, unreasonably restricts the alienation or use of anything that is a subject of property; or 6, is based on a promise to refrain from competition and is not ancillary either to a contract for the transfer of goodwill or other subject of property or to an existing employment or contract of employment. Were *B*, the purchaser of the goodwill of a small grocery business in San Francisco, to extract from *S*, the seller, a promise not to engage in the grocery business anywhere in the State of California for a period of fifty years, the promise would clearly be invalid on several of the grounds mentioned above. It is far more than is needed to protect *B*. The competitive area for a small grocery store is, at most, a few miles, and no conceivable loss could be suffered by *B* as a result of *S's* setting up another grocery business in Los Angeles, 450 miles away. Furthermore, such a promise may work undue hardship on *S*, whose only real means of obtaining his livelihood may be the grocery trade. Were the business involved the manufacture and sale of automobiles or munitions or petroleum products, a statewide restraint might well be held reasonable as might a nationwide or even a worldwide restraint.[9]

Where the restraint imposed by the parties is unreasonable, an important problem arises—a problem which, unfortunately, has not been dealt with uniformly by the courts. Is the whole restraint invalid and unenforceable or will the court enforce as much of the restraint as it considers to be reasonable? The courts have provided several different answers. Some of the older decisions take the view that such restraints are completely invalid and unenforceable under all circumstances. The restraint in the grocery case would, under this view, be no restraint at all, regardless of how it was stated, and *S* could start a new grocery business next door to the old one or across the street.

Most of the other views recognize a difference, as far as result is concerned, between divisible and indivisible restraints. Where the seller of a business in California agrees not to compete in California, Oregon, and Washington, and the inclusion of Washington is unreasonable because the seller has never done, or contemplated doing, any business there, the court may, by simply striking out "Washington," enforce a reasonable restraint that the parties have themselves written into the contract. This sort of restraint is said to be *divisible*. It is, in effect, as though the parties had entered into separate agreements for each of the three states mentioned. The agreement in regard to Washington

---

[9] See *Nordenfelt* v. *Maxim Nordenfelt Guns & Ammunition Co.,* Ltd., [1894] App. Cas. 535.

is unreasonable and unenforceable but the other agreements are reasonable and valid. Were the restraint in the same case phrased as "the Pacific coast states," there is no divisibility, and the whole restraint would be unreasonable. In spite of the lack of divisibility, however, there are a few courts that will enforce what the court finds to be reasonable. Others will enforce nothing. The chief objection to enforcing what the court considers to be reasonable in an indivisible restraint is that such acts on the part of the court amount to the court's rewriting the contract and putting into it terms the parties themselves did not include. Some courts take the view that where the restraint is divisible, the reasonable portions will be enforced and the unreasonable stricken. There is, of course, some difference of opinion as to what is divisible and what is not.

Time limits are not examined by the courts with the same degree of severity as are the limits of space; hence, permanent restraints are not necessarily invalid. The chief test is the necessity of the particular restraint to the protection of the party to get the benefit, but the courts are usually liberal in the application of the test. Where time is unspecified, the contract is usually held to be unlimited as to time, and the reasonableness is determined on that basis. Where the business involved is one of the learned professions, many courts apply somewhat stricter rules in regard to time on the grounds of undue hardship for the person who is to abstain from the practice of his profession at a time when his doing so would not materially benefit the other party.

There has been some litigation involving the reasonableness of restraints covering areas where the business sold did not actually operate at the time the sale took place. Most of the decisions seem to take the view that where expansion into those areas was contemplated for the reasonably near future, the restraints covering those areas are reasonable. Much the same results have obtained for related or contemplated products and product lines.

Restraints in contracts of employment. While the rules applied to restraints contained in contracts of employment are essentially the same as those already discussed in reference to the sale of a business, the courts recognize the disparity of bargaining power that frequently exists between employees and employers, and take note of the lapse of time between the making of the agreement and its becoming effective on the severance of employment relations. The result is that the courts examine with more care the employer's need for the restraint and the effect of the restraint on the departing employee, and deal rather strictly with the reasonableness of geographical and time limitations. Many employers feel that these agreements with employees are especially important to the protection of the employer's business where trade and business secrets or customers' lists are involved. It should be noted, however, that the common law provides a certain amount of protection in situations such as these even where there is no agreement. This protection will be discussed briefly in Section 4c of this chapter. In several states, covenants by the employee not to carry on a similar business or to solicit old customers are controlled by statute, and in a few states are declared void.

Statutory law on contracts not to compete. Some states have attempted to codify the common law rules in this area and have met with varying degrees of success. The Business and Professions Code of California, for example, states that "every contract by which anyone is restrained from engaging in a lawful profession, trade or business of any kind is to that extent void" except that "any person who sells the goodwill of a business may agree with the buyer to refrain from carrying on a similar business within a specified county or counties, city or cities, or a part thereof, in which the business so sold has been carried on, so long as the buyer, or any person deriving title to the goodwill from him, carries on a like business therein." This type of statute encourages divisible restraints and obviates, to some extent, the uncertainties with respect to time limitations, but, unfortunately, creates some problems of its own.

C. Sherman Antitrust Act

(1)

CASE. Several years ago, most of the members of the pallet industry, including Hypocase, Inc., joined together to form an association for the "purpose of encouraging cooperation among its members, exchanging information on sales, prices, production and trade practices, substituting cooperative competition for cutthroat competition, keeping prices at reasonably stable and normal levels, and for improving the human relations among the members." Paul Preston, president of Hypocase, who was not president when Hypocase joined the pallet association, has recently become interested in the legality of certain association activities under the antitrust laws. Preston has read the opinion of the Supreme Court in the *American Column and Lumber Co.* case, where the court found the association involved in that case to be in violation of the Sherman Act. Preston was somewhat startled to discover that whoever drafted the charter for the pallet association had simply copied the purpose clause quoted above from the charter of the association condemned in *American Column and Lumber*. The directors of the pallet association, of which Preston is one, are meeting next week, and Preston wants to present at that meeting a statement on the activities in which he feels the association may safely engage. He plans also to propose an amendment to the purpose clause in the charter. He has asked you as his assistant to prepare a tentative report and also an amended purpose clause.

IN GENTRAL. The phrase *antitrust* no longer has any specific meaning, but is used broadly to refer to the legislative attempts to cope with the practices of private enterprise that restrict competition. The phrase originated in the nineteenth century when it was popular to describe some of the predatory industries or firms as the *oil trust* or the *sugar trust*. Actually, some of these were common law trusts and some were controlled through the voting trust device, but the word "trust" soon lost these connotations. Nor does *monopoly* have a strict and easily defined meaning. The term denotes the existence of a measure of unified control over the supply of a definite commodity in a particular market and is not often used in its 100 per cent, absolute sense. Elements of monopoly appear in virtually all markets and in all industries. The legal, and economic, problem is to determine whether in any given situation the degree of monopoly power or control has reached forbidden levels.

After the Civil War, the industrialization of this country proceeded very rapidly, accompanied by the growth of large-scale industry, predatory practices of young and aggressive industrial leaders, wide-spread financial abuses, and the difficulties of reconstruction. The inadequacy of the common law to deal with these problems led to a vigorous public demand for reform. The primary common law sanction was to make unenforceable the contracts or arrangements that violated the policy of the law. Where there is no move to enforce, this sanction loses its effectiveness. Devices and methods of restraining trade did not always conform to the common law framework. Attempts by the states to deal with the "trust" problem were doomed to defeat because of the national character and the shifting or uncertain domicil of the great trusts. Aside from the negligible effect of the Interstate Commerce Act of 1887, the Sherman Act,[10] signed into law by President Harrison on July 2, 1890, was the first national attempt at a solution to the problem. The Act added civil and criminal penalties to the common law and provided for the initiation of actions by the government as well as by private parties.

The language of the statute was broad and general and employed many terms already well known in the common law. The two substantive sections state simply: "Every contract, combination in the form of trust or otherwise, or conspiracy, in restraint of trade or commerce among the several States, or with foreign nations, is hereby declared to be illegal" (Section 1) and "Every person who shall monopolize, or attempt to monopolize, or combine or conspire with any other person or persons, to monopolize any part of the trade or commerce among the several States, or with foreign nations, shall be deemed guilty of a misdemeanor" (Section 2). The Act applies only to practices arising in connection with interstate and foreign commerce.

Public policy toward monopoly and competition has taken two forms in the United States. The first is the policy of preserving competition by preventing or eliminating monopoly and other restraints on competition. This is the basic antitrust policy and is best exemplified, in its statutory form, by the Sherman Act. Another policy seeks to prevent or restrict competition

---

[10] 15 U.S.C.A. 1-7.

in areas where it is believed that unregulated competition is unworkable. The two policies are not necessarily inconsistent, but specific applications of the second often appear to be more concerned with protecting competitors from competition than with alleviating situations where competition has been found to be unworkable. Statutes and other aspects of this second type of policy will be considered in later portions of this chapter.

Even within the framework of the first antitrust policy, however, different legislative approaches may be employed. The Sherman Act approach was essentially to seek the dissolution of already existing monopolies and other prohibited restraints on competition and to frustrate significant or intentional efforts to achieve monopoly or other prohibited restraints. That the Act went about as far as it could go in the direction it took is attested to by the fact that it has been substantively amended only once since its original enactment in 1890. That amendment, the Miller-Tydings Act, reduced, rather than increased, the extent of the Sherman Act's coverage. In 1914 Congress employed another approach under the basic policy by attempting, in the Clayton[11] and Federal Trade Commission[12] Acts, to restrict specific business practices that were thought to lead to undue restraints on competition or to give their users undue competitive advantages.

All statutes pose problems of interpretation for the courts to resolve, but statutes with language as broad in scope as that of the Sherman Act pose special problems having to do with the context in which the broad language will be examined. Chief Justice Hughes commented that the Sherman Act "has a generality and adaptability comparable to that found to be desirable in constitutional provisions. It does not go into detailed definitions which might either work injury to legitimate enterprise or through particularization defeat its purpose by providing loopholes for escape. The restrictions the act imposes are not mechanical or artificial. Its general phrases, interpreted to attain its fundamental objects, set up the essential standard of reasonableness."[13] Between 1890 and 1933, when Hughes made the statement, the Supreme Court had established the context in which the language of the Sherman Act must be interpreted. The most important link in the process of determining the proper context consisted of the opinions in the *Standard Oil* and *American Tobacco*[14] cases in the year 1911. Here the Court said that the Act must be examined in the light of antecedent common law and that the key phrases "monopolization" and "restraint of trade" take their basic meanings from that common law. These opinions also made it clear, however, that it was no narrow construction of the pre-existing law that was intended as a guide but

---

[11] 15 U.S.C.A. 12 *et seq.*

[12] 15 U.S.C.A. 41 *et seq.*

[13] *Appalachian Coals, Inc.* v. *United States,* 288 U.S. 344, 359–360 (1933).

[14] *Standard Oil Company of New Jersey* v. *United States,* 221 U.S. 1 (1911); *United States* v. *American Tobacco Co.,* 221 U.S. 106 (1911).

instead a broad and practical conception of that law based upon a flexible public policy aimed at all undue limitations on competition.

Probably the most important effect of the determination that the Act should be construed in a common law context was the establishment of the "rule of reason" as the primary rule of construction in all Sherman Act cases. This result came about because the Court, in analyzing the common law with regard to monopoly and restraints of trade, reached the conclusion that the basic common law policy was to prohibit only those activities or conditions that were *unreasonably* restrictive. (See the above discussion of the origin of this common law policy.) The word "every" in Section 1 caused momentary difficulties in reaching this conclusion but was made compatible by an inter- pretation that there was no restraint in the eyes of the common law unless it was unreasonable. The *rule of reason* requires the courts to determine whether the conduct being reviewed under the Sherman Act constitutes an undue restraint on competition. The *Standard Oil* and *American Tobacco* decisions were once hotly debated, especially with regard to the analysis of the antecedent common law, but these controversies have long since disappeared. Whether the Court was right or wrong has lost all but its philosophical interest in the face of a rule of construction that has proved itself to be a practical and sensible inter- pretive tool.

Another important lesson to be learned from these two decisions is that some activities may be found illegal under the Sherman Act without separate proof of unreasonable restraint. This conclusive presumption of illegality is usually referred to as the *per se* or "illegal *per se*" doctrine. It is founded on the idea that some conduct, such as price fixing among competitors, necessarily has the effect of unreasonably restraining competition. The doctrine will be referred to in the discussion to follow.

Remedies under the federal antitrust laws.   Before proceeding to a discussion of the federal statutes, it is well to have in mind a general picture of certain of the more important remedies available under the antitrust laws. The laws provide for two classes of action: those available to the government, and those available to private parties. The government has a choice of four remedial procedures.

1. Criminal prosecution. Violations of Sections 1, 2, and 3 of the Sherman Act are misdemeanors, minor grades of crime, and are punishable by fines and imprisonment. Fines have been imposed frequently, but most of them after pleas of *nolo contendere,* by which the defendant admits his guilt. Rarely has imprisonment been imposed. The dramatic episode of the "electric cases" in 1960–62 resulted in fines and imprisonment for many officers and employees of the offending companies.[15] Almost all of the defendants, both corporate

---

[15] See John Fuller, *The Gentlemen Conspirators* (New York: Grove Press, 1962); John Herling, *The Great Price Conspiracy* (Washington: Robert B. Luce, Inc., 1962); Clarence C. Walton and Frederick W. Cleveland, Jr., *Corporations on Trial: The Electric Cases* (Belmont, California: Wadsworth Publishing Company, Inc., 1964); and Richard Austin Smith's articles in *Fortune* (April and May, 1961).

and individual, pleaded guilty to the criminal charges or *nolo contendere,* and the civil actions culminated in a large number of consent decrees. Some of the thousands of private treble damage actions against the corporate offenders have still not been settled. (See discussion below of consent decrees and treble damage actions.)

2. Injunctions and other equitable relief. Section 4 of the Sherman Act authorizes the district courts "to prevent and restrain violations" of the Act. This authorization has been interpreted to include not only injunctions but also temporary injunctions and decrees of dissolution, divestiture, and divorcement.

3. Concurrent injunctive and criminal proceedings. The Sherman Act authorizes the use of both remedies, and cases frequently arise where effective protection of the public requires both criminal prosecution and an injunction.

4. Libel actions. Section 6 of the Sherman Act authorizes seizure and forfeiture to the United States of property that is in the course of interstate or foreign commerce and that is owned under any contract, combination, or conspiracy made illegal by the Act. This remedy has been used only three times since 1890, and all of these were cases that never went to trial.

5. In recent decades, the federal government has become the single largest consumer in the American economy and, as such, has sometimes suffered injury as a result of conduct by private parties in violation of the antitrust laws. In 1955 the Congress authorized the United States to recover damages from offending parties. The authorized damages are only those actually suffered, however, and not treble damages as provided under the Sherman Act for private parties injured by violations of the antitrust laws.

It has become reasonably obvious through the years that criminal prosecutions under the Sherman Act are usually ineffective as a means of restoring competition in markets where violations of the Act have restrained or destroyed it. In recent years, the Department of Justice has been resorting more and more to civil suits in equity where the remedies of divestiture, divorcement, and dissolution are available. *Divestiture* refers to situations where the defendants are ordered by the court to divest themselves of property or other assets, such as controlling stock interests in other companies. *Divorcement* is a special application of divestiture in situations where violations grow out of closely integrated ownership and control. *Dissolution* usually refers to situations that involve the dissolving of illegal combinations or associations. Actually, the Department of Justice and the courts have used the terms interchangeably. Whatever the term used, the purpose is to restore competition by breaking up those combinations or other activities that have restrained or destroyed competition. Because these remedies are drastic, they are used with reluctance by the courts. The details of the orders are extremely difficult to frame, and there is seldom any assurance that competition will be restored or even improved by compliance with the court's order. In most cases, the most effective relief is attained by the simultaneous use of several different types of remedy.

Many antitrust actions terminate in what is called a *consent decree,* by which the parties agree on certain facts relative to the case and on future conduct. A defendant, under a consent decree, may agree to stop doing something alleged to be in violation of the law or may agree to take certain affirmative steps to remove restraints on competition. The consent decree provides advantages to parties on both sides: 1, by avoiding expensive and drawn out litigation; 2, by making possible quicker relief; and 3, by avoiding a trial where the outcome is reasonably certain. The consent decree does not become binding until both parties have agreed to it and the court has approved.

A private person who is injured by a violation of the antitrust laws is entitled to bring an action against the guilty party for treble damages. This was the limit of his relief under the Sherman Act, but Section 16 of the Clayton Act entitles a private person to injunctive relief against loss by violations of any of the antitrust laws. Section 5 of the Clayton Act provides that "a final judgment or decree hereafter rendered in any criminal prosecution or in any suit or proceeding in equity brought by or on behalf of the United States under the anti-trust laws to the effect that a defendant has violated said laws shall be *prima facie* evidence against such defendant in any suit or proceeding" brought by any private person. The fact that a consent decree, not being a "final judgment or decree," is not admissible against the defendant in a suit by a private party is another reason why a defendant might agree to the entry of a consent decree.

APPLICATION OF THE ACT. There are many ways of organizing Sherman Act cases and material for discussion. Each method has certain advantages, depending upon the objective or orientation of the discussion. A common and particularly effective method for teaching purposes organizes the material according to three general types of problems to which the statute has been applied: 1, the industrial combination or merger, known as a close-knit combination, where there is an actual unification of resources and control and a disappearance of separate corporate identities; 2, the restraint of competition through collusive agreements among competitors, the loose-knit combination, where distinct entities remain in existence but govern some aspects of their conduct in accordance with the terms of the collusive agreement; and 3, activities which do not violate Section 1 but which may constitute "monopolization" under Section 2. There is a great deal of overlap between Sections 1 and 2 of the Sherman Act. Until recent years, there have been many competent observers who felt that Section 2 did not really describe a distinct offense, but courts now appear to recognize some violations of Section 2 that are not also violations of Section 1. Each of the three types of problems will be discussed in detail below.

The simple explanations in the paragraph above may lead one to the erroneous conclusion that the three categories selected as a basis for our discussion are coextensive with the Sherman Act and are easily distinguished one from the other. Without untoward stretching, the categories do not include all of the Sherman Act, and it is not very often that an actual situation falls neatly and cooperatively into just one category. This fact should not frustrate our discussion, however, any more than a patient's having both a broken leg and pneumonia should frustrate a doctor's diagnosis and treatment of these afflictions. No exhaustive consideration of the Sherman Act is possible in the few pages allocated to that subject here, and arbitrary division and selection of topics is necessary in order to present the material. Thus, the application of the Sherman Act to close-knit combinations can be examined in some of its aspects without a confusing mixture of other problems.

CLOSE-KNIT COMBINATIONS. Section 1 of the Act uses the term "combination" without supplying a list of forms or methods of combination that Congress may have had in mind. Seventy years of litigation have made it plain, however, that courts see the emphasis in the Act as being on the effect of the "combination" and not on its form. Pools, trusts, holding companies, common sales agencies, mergers, consolidations and many other forms of combination have been condemned where they resulted in unreasonable restraints on competition.

Although the meaning of "combination" has been sufficiently well established that it is no longer of major importance in applying the Act, the same certainly cannot be said for the statutory measures of violation as expressed primarily in the "rule of reason." Although the *Standard Oil* decision was of paramount importance in fixing the context for interpreting the Sherman Act, the facts and holding in that case were not very useful guides for the future. It was, perhaps, too easy a fact situation, involving, as it did, a high degree of monopoly power obtained and preserved through illegal or predatory means. If this was not a violation of the Act, what was? *Standard Oil* left most of the important issues unanswered. For example, can there be a violation where the illegal or predatory practices are missing or minimal? In the Terminal Association[16] case the Supreme Court answered this question in the affirmative where an unusual geographical conformation made potential competition impossible. In the same year, the Court gave another affirmative answer where competition was not only possible but actual, and where the combining companies were not in direct competition with each other. In the latter situation, the unification of the Southern Pacific and Union Pacific railroads,[17] the Court talked of violations in terms of the *power* to stifle competition rather than in terms of any actual effects. While the sweeping language of that decision has been widely quoted, it has not been widely followed. As a matter of fact, the legality of mere power to stifle competition is still something of an issue today and will be examined again in our discussion of Section 2 of the Sherman Act and Section 7 of the Clayton Act. In *United States* v. *United States Steel Corporation*,[18]

---

[16] *United States* v. *Terminal R.R. Association of St. Louis*, 236 U.S. 194 (1915).

[17] *United States* v. *Union Pacific Railroad Co.*, 226 U.S. 61 (1912).

[18] 251 U.S. 417 (1920).

the Court was confronted with a holding company which had been organized to acquire the stock of twelve operating companies for the avowed purpose of achieving a monopoly in the steel industry, and which had probably obtained control of more than 70 per cent of it. The portion controlled had dropped to 50 per cent at the time of suit, however, and the defendant had, in the Court's view, abandoned its illegal purpose to monopolize. The majority of the Court, in a 4 to 3 decision, gave great weight to the fact that the Steel Company had got together with its competitors at the famous Gary dinners to fix prices, a social practice discontinued by the time of the suit, and the Court interpreted this conduct as evidence of weakness and failure to achieve monopoly power. Having established that competition was not restrained and that the illegal intent had been abandoned, there was nothing left to the case except the element of sheer size. In this connection, the Court remarked that mere size is not an offense nor is the mere existence of unexerted power, making it clear in the latter phrase that the sweeping language of the *Union Pacific* case could not be taken at face value.

The issue of "size" has received a great deal of attention from commentators of all kinds, but its relevance in Sherman Act cases is probably best described in Justice Cardozo's words from *United States* v. *Swift and Company*[19]: "Mere size, . . . is not an offense against the Sherman Act unless magnified to the point at which it amounts to a monopoly, . . . but size carries with it an opportunity for abuse that is not to be ignored when the opportunity is proved to have been utilized in the past."

Vertical integration. Prior to 1940, judicial consideration of close-knit combinations was largely directed at horizontal combinations where competition between the combining entities was immediately eliminated. Little attention was given to the vertical form of combination, where the combining companies had not been competitors. There appeared to be no reason, however, why vertical integration should be treated any differently from most other conduct or conditions coming within the purview of the Sherman Act; its validity should be governed by the "rule of reason." The cases condemned its use in order to obtain or extend horizontal monopoly power or unreasonable restraint of trade or when accompanied by illegal combination or conspiracy. Unfortunately, lack of agreement among economists with regard to workable concepts of vertical integration and some misleading language by the Supreme Court on a procedural issue in the first *Yellow Cab*[20] case led some observers to the conclusion that vertical integration had been condemned *per se*. The Court devoted much time to this question in the *Columbia Steel*[21] case. The Government insisted that it was illegal *per se* for a steel producer to acquire even a small steel fabricating company on the ground that this naturally foreclosed the producer's competitors from the market they might once have had

---

[19] 286 U.S. 106 (1932).

[20] *United States* v. *Yellow Cab Co.,* 332 U.S. 218 (1947).

[21] *United States* v. *Columbia Steel Co.,* 334 U.S. 495 (1948).

in sales to the fabricating company. The "rule of reason" was applied in this case to the advantage of the defendant, and the Court said that "vertical integration, as such without more, cannot be held violative of the Sherman Act."[22] That vertical integration is none the less a relevant issue under the Sherman Act cannot be denied, especially where used by a firm that already has a considerable amount of economic power on one or more horizontal levels. Vertical integration can foreclose competitors both from markets and from sources of supply and can give its user important leverage at various levels of competition. If these effects amount to unreasonable restraints on competition, violation may be found. (See discussion below under Clayton Act, Section 7.)

Importance of "intent" under the Sherman Act.　Is a specific intent to achieve a prohibited restraint of trade a necessary element of the Sherman Act violation? In general, such intent is not necessary, but a more thorough answer to the question requires the recognition of four distinct situations: 1, no specific intent to restrain trade and no trade restrained; 2, specific intent to restrain trade and a prohibited restraint achieved; 3, specific intent to restrain trade but no restraint achieved; 4, no specific intent to restrain trade but a prohibited restraint achieved. It is obvious that there can be no violation of the Act in the first situation, and it is equally obvious that there is a violation in the second situation. The issue is not as clear in the other two. It would seem, in general, that the Act should come to bear on the third situation where there is specific intent without achievement, as long as there is some sort of overt conduct. To hold otherwise would compel the Sherman Act to be held in abeyance while specific attempts were made to achieve illegal restraints, and this would permit action only when the illegal end had been reached. Section 2 does include "attempts to monopolize." The remaining situation, prohibited restraint without specific intent, raises the issue of whether it is necessary to a violation that the alleged offender specifically intend the illegal result of his acts. A person usually is presumed to know the logical and natural result of his acts, and will be held responsible for the result although he did not specifically intend the result but did intend to do the acts that brought about the result. A person who pulls the trigger of a gun known to be loaded and pointed at the victim may be guilty of murder even though he did not intend to kill. A logical and natural result of the act which the person did intend, the pulling of the trigger, is the death or serious injury of the person at whom the gun was pointed. The Supreme Court has held that no specific intent should be necessary for a violation of the Act where illegal restraint did result logically and naturally from acts, not themselves illegal, which were intended.[23] Another aspect of the fourth situation will be discussed below in connection with Section 2.

LOOSE-KNIT COMBINATIONS.　The line between loose-knit and close-knit

---

[22] *United States* v. *Columbia Steel Co.,* 525.

[23] *United States* v. *Patten,* 226 U.S. 525 (1913); *United States* v. *Masonite Corp.,* 316 U.S. 265 (1942).

combinations is not always an easy one to draw. As a rule, the latter involve the merging or blending of the management, control, or facilities so that the separate identities of the participants tend to disappear, whereas in the former, unity of action or of policy is achieved by agreement among participants who maintain at least nominally separate identities. Attempts to restrain trade by various forms of agreement among independent enterprises have come before the courts continuously since the first days of the Sherman Act. The forms of agreement and control are many and varied, but most of the important decisions have been concerned with some type of trade association. Originally, the type of association most frequently before the courts was one whose very purpose was to affect and to control the conduct of a particular trade or industry and whose members often came from all levels of competition in that trade or industry. Because so many of these associations and their activities were condemned by the courts, their use has died out. The newer types of association are much looser in form and much less comprehensive in object. Usually they perform services that the individual member could not perform for himself, and the most common function is to collect and distribute to their members information on the market and on developments in the industry in order to permit intelligent adjustment of price and production policies. Within this broad description may be contained countless variations of activity ranging all the way from overt price fixing to conduct which is strongly *promotive* of competition. It should be noted also that in recent years many combination and conspiracy cases have involved neither associations nor even agreements in any formal sense. More will be said about this litigation below.

Illegal per se doctrine. Mentioned earlier in the discussion was the development of the doctrine that certain types of conduct or the existence of certain market conditions have been declared to be in violation of the Sherman Act without regard for their reasonableness. Most of these illegal *per se* activities have had to do with agreements among competitors. Included in the list of activities that have been declared to be *per se* violations are market allocation or market splitting, production or output control, price fixing agreements, and agreements among firms not to deal with certain customers or suppliers. The reasoning of the courts in reaching these decisions is probably best demonstrated by *United States* v. *Trenton Potteries Co.*,[24] where competitors formed a trade association and agreed to fix prices. The chief issue in the case was whether the "rule of reason" required a determination of whether the prices actually fixed were reasonable or not. The court held that agreements to fix prices are not necessarily reasonable merely because the prices themselves are reasonable. The power, said the court, to fix a reasonable price is also the power to fix an unreasonable price, and what is a reasonable price one day may not be the next. The Court concluded that price-fixing agreements are illegal or unreasonable in themselves and no determination of reasonableness

---

[24] 273 U.S. 392 (1927).

is necessary or possible. The decision in this case was extended in *United States v. Socony Vacuum Oil Co.,*[25] where the court held that agreements to raise, lower or stabilize prices were all equally objectionable under the Sherman Act. The license of a patented device on condition that unpatented materials be used also is sometimes said to be another example of an activity which is illegal *per se*.

Association activities. Most trade associations and trade association activities are legal. Some horizontal agreements in certain specified industries or sectors of the economy have been exempted from the antitrust laws: labor unions, agricultural cooperatives, certain agricultural marketing agreements, export associations of domestic firms seeking to sell in foreign markets, and railroads if their agreements are approved by the Interstate Commerce Commission. Our problem here is to discuss briefly the prohibited association activities in the nonexempt areas of our economy. It should be noted first, however, why it is that trade associations present special antitrust problems and why the antitrust laws confront the associations with certain risks. Perhaps most important is the fact that these organizations consist, by definition, of competitors, thus making suspect almost any cooperative activity. Second, many of the useful association activities have to do with areas closely related to competition, such as prices, production, customer relations, channels of distribution and other particularly sensitive functions. Furthermore, the pressure for potentially illegal activity is greatest when the competitive situation is hardest and the effects of the activity are likely to be most attractive. Risks of antitrust litigation are especially great for associations whose members conduct themselves in such a way as to suggest collusion when actually there may have been none. A uniform price structure, for example, may be very difficult to explain in terms of legitimate competition even where there has been no collusive action. For all of these reasons, antitrust litigation involving trade associations is very extensive. A realistic view of trade associations recognizes areas in which businessmen may legally cooperate to the benefit of the public, the industries involved and antitrust enforcement. The scope of these legitimate areas is outlined in the following paragraphs.

Statistical reporting is one of the most common and most useful trade association activities. Generally speaking, such activities are legal where the data supplied to the association or exchanged among the members is information with respect to past prices and production and other historical conduct and where no effort is made to induce or compel members to adhere to certain price, production or other policies adversely affecting competition. Where, however, information in regard to future prices, production and other conduct is exchanged, the association has wandered into dangerous territory where the slightest evidence of a purpose to induce higher prices or reduce production is enough to constitute a violation. If the information exchanged, even though

---

[25] 310 U.S. 150 (1940).

historical in nature, is too detailed, or if members of the association are permitted direct or indirect access to one another's accounts and records, violation is likely to be found. Competition under these circumstances would be unlikely. As the Supreme Court has said:

> Genuine competitors do not make daily, weekly and monthly reports of the minutest details of their business to their rivals, as the defendants did; they do not contract, as was done here, to submit their books to the discretionary audit and their stocks to the discretionary inspection of their rivals for the purpose of successfully competing with them; and they do not submit the details of their business to the analysis of an expert, jointly employed, and obtain from him a 'harmonized' estimate of the market as it is and as, in his specially and confidentially informed judgment, it promises to be.[26]

Many other trade association activities have been considered by the courts. None of them has been found illegal in itself, but any may become illegal when used to achieve an object prohibited by the antitrust laws. Among those activities that have been examined are:

1. Product standardization, which has been found legal except where used to bring about an unnatural uniformity of product for the real purpose of obtaining uniformity in price.

2. Joint research and patenting, both probably legal unless used to accomplish an illegal end. Joint research has never been directly questioned in the courts.

3. Uniform cost accounting procedures or use of average-cost calculations; the former is not an important antitrust issue although it might be used in such a way as to raise antitrust questions; the latter has been before the courts and the Federal Trade Commission and has been generally upheld except where used illegally to fix prices.

4. Credit reporting; the use of the data is again the test, and such reporting is legal unless used collusively for some illegal end.

5. Disparagement of competitive trades or industries; in the famous *Eastern Railroad Conference* case, an association of truckers sued an association of railroads alleging a conspiracy to drive truckers out of business by disparaging the trucking industry. Although a District Court had found for the plaintiffs, the Supreme Court held that the activities at issue were outside the Sherman Act.[27] A combination of sensitive activities by a trade association is much more likely to lead to antitrust problems than is any one activity.

Recent developments. Overt agreements not to compete have been out of fashion for several years. Very rarely does an antitrust plaintiff have the benefit of express agreements whereby the defendants sought to restrain competition. The problem of proving a conspiracy in the absence of overt agreement is not

---

[26] *American Column & Lumber Co.* v. *United States,* 257 U.S. 377 (1921).
[27] *Eastern Railroad Presidents' Conference* v. *Noerr Motor Freight,* Inc., 365 U.S. 127 (1961).

an easy one. Because of this problem, there has come into use an implied conspiracy doctrine whereby a conspiracy in violation of the antitrust laws may be inferred from circumstantial evidence. Some development along this line seemed necessary because extreme caution by collusive competitors could eliminate, or prevent coming into existence, any direct evidence of the agreement; yet the anti-competitive effects would still be present. However, it is obvious that great caution must be used in the employment of this doctrine if unfair and inconsistent results are to be avoided. One manifestation of this doctrine, known as "conscious parallelism," has been stated to infer conspiracy where businessmen adopted the same business practice, each being aware that the others had adopted it also. In its extreme form, this approach would seem to find conspiracy in the uniformity of conduct alone. The Supreme Court rejected this view in these words: "Circumstantial evidence of consciously parallel behavior may have made heavy inroads into the traditional judicial attitude toward conspiracy; but 'conscious parallelism' has not yet read conspiracy out of the Sherman Act entirely."[28] The doctrine of conscious parallelism is not completely at rest, however, and it can be looked to for further judicial comment in the future.

Trade associations and their members have two new causes for worry in the attempts to make mere membership in a trade association sufficient circumstantial evidence to justify a finding of guilt on the part of all members of the association and in the use of class suits in antitrust actions to make possible an order or decree running against all members of the association or "class" although only a few members were named as defendants and evidence was introduced only as to those few. There is no wide acceptance of either technique, but their support from any direction at all adds to the hazards of trade association membership and activity.

Monopoly and Monopolization under Section 2. For the first fifty years of the Sherman Act, the "monopolizing" clause, Section 2, was treated in most cases as though it were a mere appendage of Section 1 without any real significance of its own. The courts often mentioned it and occasionally even discussed it but never really discovered a set of facts that raised Section 2 issues without also raising issues under Section 1. The result was, until the 1940's, that little was known about the meaning of the word "monopolize" or precisely how it could be distinguished from the phrase "restraint of trade." *Obiter dicta* made some contributions along this line, but not until 1945 did a set of facts present itself which could be considered alone under Section 2. In the *Alcoa*[29] case, Judge Learned Hand analyzed the offense called "monopolizing" with considerable care and found that the defendant was guilty of that offense without also being in violation of Section 1. Other decisions have

---

[28] *Theatre Enterprises, Inc.* v. *Paramount Film Distributing Corp.* 346 U.S. 537, 541 (1954).
[29] *United States* v. *Aluminum Co. of America,* 148 F. (2d) 416 (1945).

followed Hand's lead, a lead which, in all fairness, was suggested in the *Standard Oil* case in 1911.

"Monopolize" equals monopoly power plus "deliberateness." The Sherman Act, as we know, must be interpreted in the context of the antecedent common law. We have already seen such interpretations of the phrase "restraint of trade." The noun "monopoly" describes a condition or a static situation and was so used and understood at common law, but Congress used the verb "monopolize." Judge Hand, from these and other premises, reasoned that the Sherman Act offense of monopolizing consists of "monopoly" plus some other element that gives meaning to the fact that Congress used the verb and not the noun. Essentially, the common law used "monopoly" in the economic sense, in which context "monopoly power" is perhaps a better and more descriptive term. Used in this way, the term "monopoly power" means the power to fix prices or exclude competition, and Hand's formula takes on more meaning. Before we can look at the "plus factor" necessary in order to make monopoly power a Section 2 offense, we must consider briefly the measures and tests of monopoly power.

The relevant market. Most Sherman Act offenses, whether of the restraint of trade or of the Section 2 variety, take on real meaning only within a market concept. "Monopoly" and, in most cases, "restraints of trade" are simply market terminology. What is said here with regard to relevant markets in connection with Section 2 offenses is also of importance in the determination of Section 1 offenses. The one general store at Four Corners, Texifor101, probably has a considerable degree of monopoly power, within the context of the Four Corners market, but obviously has no such power in a statewide or nationwide market or in the dry goods or grocery markets as a whole. Consequently, the determination of the relevant market must precede any conclusions on monopoly power. Does the person charged with the offense have the power to fix prices or exclude competition in the market which is relevant to his operations?

Markets may be defined in a number of different ways: geographically, in terms of customers, according to products or product lines, even in terms of the uses to which a product or a service will be put, or in combinations of these methods, and in many other ways as well. Courts are increasingly recognizing that the choice of relevant market is, to a large extent, an economic problem which is best handled with the aid of economic analysis. In *Alcoa*, three different markets were called to the attention of the court. These ranged from virgin aluminum ingot, where the Aluminum Company's share was in excess of 90 per cent, through two other definitions of the market based on various patterns of inclusion and exclusion of "secondary" (re-used) and fabricated aluminum, where the Company had market percentages of 64 and 33. The court concluded that the ingot market was the relevant market, not because Alcoa's share was largest, but because Alcoa was, at the time of the case, the sole domestic producer of virgin aluminum, and because the other two markets, necessarily, had to use metal originally produced by Alcoa. Other aspects of market determination will be commented on below in connection with particular cases.

How much power for "monopoly power"? Once the relevant market has been established, the problem still remains as to how much power is necessary in order to constitute monopoly power. The answer to this difficult question is usually sought first in the market shares themselves. Judge Hand, in *Alcoa,* said that 90 per cent was enough, that 64 per cent was doubtful, and that 33 per cent was not enough. The Supreme Court has properly qualified this rather definitive statement by saying that arbitrary sets of percentage figures cannot be prescribed. Certainly, the effects of certain percentages of control will depend on other factors in the market, except, perhaps, in the very highest ranges. Thirty-three per cent may not be monopoly power in a market where, for example, a competitor has 60 per cent, but it may very well constitute sufficient power in a market where the largest competitor has less than 1 per cent. Market structure may not be the only important factor, and the courts also examine actual behavior in the market and scrutinize how prices are set and other decisions made. Note here that the courts are talking again about "power" to control prices or exclude competition and not about actual raising of prices or proof that competitors have been excluded. But this is only the "monopoly power" part of "monopolizing" and is probably not by itself an offense.

"Deliberateness," the plus factor. Hand's reasoning does not foreclose the use of factors other than deliberateness in his formula. Illegal acquisition of the power or illegal use, for example, or the specific intent to use the power would be satisfactory substitutes, but these factors, in most cases, would seem to involve violations of Section 1 as well as Section 2 and are not here our concern. "Deliberateness" means deliberately obtaining or maintaining or extending monopoly power of the kind and degree described in the previous paragraph. It differs from the much more exacting requirement of specific intent which would be important where the offense charged is an attempt to monopolize. The method used to obtain or maintain monopoly power may be restraint of trade illegal under Section 1, but it may not amount to that at all.

The *United Shoe Machinery*[30] and *Alcoa* cases are illustrations of the "plus factor" where no Section 1 offense was involved. In *United Shoe,* where the degree of monopoly power was comparable with that of *Alcoa,* the court found that the company's policy of leasing, but never selling, its shoe machines to shoe manufacturers together with certain terms of the leasing contract, resulted in the exclusion of competition. The refusal to sell blocked any second hand market; ten year lease periods kept lessees from using competitors' equipment; "full capacity clauses" prevented lessees from storing United Shoe equipment

---

[30] *United States* v. *United Shoe Machinery Corp.,* 110 F. Supp 295 (1953).

and using that of a competitor; penalty charges for premature lease termination were much heavier where a competitor's equipment was to be substituted. These and many other provisions and practices almost completely blocked the avenues by which competitors might enter the industry. None of these practices was illegal in itself, and some of them, if used in a competitive market situation, would actually have strengthened or maintained competition. But, said the court, when used by a company with the degree of monopoly power possessed by United Shoe, they served little purpose other than that of excluding competition, a result which was, of course, well known to the company. In other words, United Shoe Machinery Corporation deliberately employed distribution and leasing policies that minimized the possibility that competition might successfully enter the industry.

The "plus factor" in the *Alcoa* case is much more subtle. The court found that because Alcoa was the only domestic producer of virgin aluminum ingot and possessed a very high degree of monopoly power it could exclude or discourage competition by embracing for itself every competitive opportunity that arose or seemed likely to arise, whether it was a source of bauxite or a new use for aluminum. Possibly, the element of "deliberateness" will take on more shape and greater substance as the years go by, but at the present time, *United Shoe* and *Alcoa* are the best guides to its significance.

Remedies. In both cases the government asked for dissolution of the defendants, and in both cases the courts refused. In *United Shoe,* the court deemed it impossible to separate the company into competitive pieces because almost the entire operation of the company was carried on under one roof. By the time *Alcoa* reached the remedy stage, World War II made it unwise to attempt any basic reorganization of one of the important war industries. Furthermore, with the help of the government, two competitive aluminum producers had entered the scene. The court held the remedy issue open for five years to see what might happen in the aluminum industry after the war. In 1950, a District Court found the situation still inconclusive and retained jurisdiction for five more years, but, in 1957, the government's petition to extend the period of judicial supervision was denied.[31] Competition in the aluminum industry now appears to be healthy and vigorous, although Alcoa's share of primary production is in the neighborhood of fifty per cent.

Attempts, combinations and conspiracies to monopolize. The other offenses specified in Section 2 also have come in for some judicial attention. If monopoly power has been obtained through a combination or conspiracy, there is probably no need to show any more. The intent or purpose to use that power is found in the proof of combination or conspiracy.[32] As has been mentioned

---

[31] *United States* v. *Aluminum Co. of America,* 91 F. Supp. 333 (S.D.N.Y. 1950), and *United States* v. *Aluminum Co. of America,* 153 F. Supp. 132 (S.D.N.Y. 1957).

[32] *American Tobacco Co.* v. *United States,* 328 U.S. 781 (1946).

before, the attempt to monopolize requires proof of a specific intent to accomplish an illegal result.

SUMMARY OF THE SHERMAN ACT.   The Sherman Act became law under the pressure of gross and flagrant abuses of economic power during the late years of the last century and may not be the most effective tool for bringing about results that are now considered to be desirable. Although the Act has been likened to a constitution in the flexibility of its language, this approach to statutory interpretation has many unpleasant ramifications and is not a satisfactory way to accommodate an old statute to substantially changed conditions. This is not to say that the Sherman Act has no further usefulness. It is still the cornerstone of national antitrust policy, and properly so, but sensible procedure would probably suggest that the solution to new problems may be more happily approached through new legislation oriented more specifically to the problem. There is a growing realization that monopoly and competition are essentially economic and social problems whose solutions, as matters of public policy, should be determined in the light of economic and social factors rather than in the dim glow of common law rules developed long ago under entirely different circumstances. This change of policy is much easier to state, however, than it is to accomplish, and the difficulties involved in equitable utilization of economic and social factors may override the theoretical advantages of such a change.

D. Clayton Act : Sections 7, 8, 10.

(1)

CASE.   Late in 1960, the board of directors of Hypocase, Inc. appointed a special committee of its own members to study certain proposed acquisitions of other companies and to report back to the board in one year with recommendations. At the conclusion of its study, the committee recommended the following acquisitions:

1. Happy Vale Lumber Mill. The committee argued that Hypocase could save considerable sums each year by milling its own lumber and ceasing its purchases of lumber from mills and other suppliers. Happy Vale produced the types of lumber required by Hypocase and, as a matter of fact, had long supplied most of the lumber which Hypocase had been purchasing from the Berkland Lumber Company, a lumber dealer and the source of most of Hypocase's supply.

2. Denver Pallet Company. Hypocase had never done much business in the mountain states, largely because Denver had underbid Hypocase in almost all situations where the two companies had competed for customers. Denver was efficient and well managed, but the majority stockholder was advanced in years and anxious to find a buyer for his shares.

3. Granite City Warehouse Corporation. Hypocase competed with several

other pallet companies for the business of Granite City. Hypocase supplied, on the average, about one-third of the pallet needs of Granite City. The committee pointed out in its report that this warehouse company was located in a rapidly growing industrial area and predicted that within five years this company would be one of the largest users of pallets in the northern part of the country.

4. Berkland Box, Inc. The committee recommended that Hypocase diversify its activities by acquiring this manufacturer of cardboard and fiberboard boxes and cartons. Many of Hypocase's present customers for pallets also purchased these other products and probably would be a good market for the output of the box company.

The board of directors looks favorably on all four of these proposals but wants the committee to submit a detailed opinion on the legality of these acquisitions under the amended Section 7 of the Clayton Act. As assistant to the president of Hypocase, you have been asked to prepare for the committee a memorandum outlining the problem areas and issues raised by these proposals and suggesting the kind of data that should be collected before any conclusions on their legality can be reached.

IN GENERAL. Although the Clayton Act was primarily concerned with other problems, it did devote three sections to some of the combination and restraint issues which have been considered in connection with the Sherman Act. In these sections, the Clayton Act sought to deal with some forms of combination and aspects of restraints on competition with which the Sherman Act seemed inadequate to cope. There is some overlapping here, as there is with all of the antitrust statutes. Section 7 is concerned with stock and asset acquisitions and with holding companies, all of which may also be within the scope of the Sherman Act, but the Clayton Act was designed to clarify and strengthen the antitrust policy with regard to these problems. After lying virtually dormant for many years, Section 7 has now become one of the most active and important phases of the national antitrust policy. The reasons for this will be discussed below. Sections 8 and 10 deal with interlocking directorates and related activities to which the Sherman Act was not readily applicable.

MERGERS: STOCK AND ASSET ACQUISITIONS. Originally, Section 7 read in part as follows: "No corporation engaged in commerce shall acquire, directly or indirectly, the whole or any part of the stock . . . of another corporation . . . where the effect of such acquisition may be to substantially lessen competition between the corporation whose stock is so acquired and the corporation making the acquisition, or to restrain such commerce in any section or community, or tend to create a monopoly of any line of commerce." Another clause in Section 7 dealt similarly with the holding company device. It is obvious that as long as stock is not acquired there is no possible violation of the above language. In many situations, the acquisition of assets accomplished the same results as an acquisition of stock but without the legal risks.

Consequently, Section 7 was little litigated between 1914 and 1950, when Congress amended the section to correct this defect.

The relevant portions of the amended Section 7 read as follows: "No corporation engaged in commerce shall acquire, directly or indirectly, the whole or any part of the stock . . . and no corporation . . . shall acquire the whole or any part of the assets of another corporation . . ., where in any line of commerce in any section of the country, the effect of such acquisition may be substantially to lessen competition, or to tend to create a monopoly." In addition to correcting the asset defect and eliminating the split infinitive, Congress made another major change in the language of the statute, a change whose effect is both to broaden and to narrow the application of the old language. The narrowing occurs in the application to horizontal acquisitions. The old Section 7 test was the probable substantial lessening of competition between the acquired and the acquiring corporations, language which would seem to apply to any horizontal acquisition, while amended Section 7 uses a test consisting of a lessening in a whole line of commerce in a whole section of the country. Actually, the old language was much too broad, and Congress probably did not intend to ban all horizontal mergers. In order to avoid such a result, the courts applied a kind of "rule of reason" in Section 7, although the ties of that section to the common law were at best remote and probably Congress had sought to avoid them.

A more important effect of the changed language was a much wider application of the section to vertical and conglomerate acquisitions. The emphasis was shifted from the effects on competition between the companies involved to the effects on competition in any line of commerce. The old language did contain the phrase "or tend to create a monopoly," which certainly would apply to effects other than those on the companies involved, but this test is more tenuous and perhaps more difficult to establish than the "substantial lessening" test, and it was not used by the courts until after 1950, when the Supreme Court employed the phrase in the *du Pont-General Motors*[33] case.

"May be substantially to lessen competition." Because this basic Clayton Act test has had a longer and more thorough history of interpretation in connection with other sections of the Act, additional attention will be given to it in later portions of this chapter. "May be" usually has been said to mean "reasonable probability," rather than "possibility." The Sherman Act test of unreasonable restraint was replaced in the Clayton Act by "substantially lessen," but the effect of this change is not entirely clear. There is little doubt that Congress intended a less difficult burden of proof for the plaintiff, but here agreement ends. Some feel that the Clayton Act sets up an only slightly less confining "rule of reason," but others take the view that Congress created an almost *per se* violation, requiring only that the amount of commerce affected be "substantial" in either absolute or relative terms. The courts and the Federal

---

[33] *United States* v. *E. I. du Pont de Nemours & Co.*, 353 U.S. 586 (1957).

Trade Commission appear to be settling down somewhere in between these two extremes, but not without considerable vacillation. Some conclusions can be drawn from the decisions and from the statute, however. The Clayton Act is concerned with probabilities of, or tendencies toward, anticompetitive effects and not with *actual* anticompetitive effects. Intent is not important in Clayton Act situations, and no predatory or unethical practices are needed for a violation. It is not necessary to show monopoly power. All of these conclusions are consistent with the obvious Congressional policy of trying to attack the problem of economic concentration in its incipiency rather than after its accomplishment.

Decisions under the amended Section 7. The new Section 7 has now had twenty years of judicial and administrative scrutiny, yet it cannot be said that all, or even many, of the major questions of enforcement and interpretation have been settled. It must be remembered, however, that twenty years is not an unusually long period of time in which to clarify some of the basic issues of our economic system. The *Standard Oil* decision followed the enactment of the Sherman Act by twenty-one years, and it might be said that the courts are farther ahead now with the interpretation of the amended Section 7 than they were at the *Standard Oil* stage of the Sherman Act's career. To a much greater degree than with the Sherman Act, perhaps, the development of Section 7 is being held up by deep uncertainty in our country as a whole as to how some fundamental social, political, and economic issues should be resolved. This uncertainty manifested itself in the very language of the statute and plays a major role in the courts and agencies charged with the task of enforcing and interpreting the law.

An "American schizophrenia" has had an effect upon antitrust legislation, enforcement, and interpretation for two generations and still has a profound impact upon many facets of antitrust policy. Americans, with almost equal devotion, appear to admire bigness and fear it, respect smallness and doubt its efficiency. Some segments of society, including some influential small businesses, believe that "smallness" is a goal in itself and that it should be protected and encouraged at all costs. Others call attention to the efficiency of large-scale operations and to the degree to which our economy now relies upon large corporate units. The result is that no clear public policy has been established. Congress reflects this uncertainty when it drafts or enacts antitrust legislation. No statute makes it clear that Congress abhors bigness and prefers smallness, or the other way around, or even suggests that the policy is one of balance. In turn, the courts reflect the lack of strong public feeling and of clear legislative direction. Peter Finley Dunne, through his inimitable Mr. Dooley, describes the American schizophrenia by making a parody of Theodore Roosevelt's alleged attitude toward the "trusts:" "The trusts are hideous monsters, built up by the enlightened enterprise of the men that have done so much to advance progress in our beloved country. On the one hand I would stamp them underfoot; on the other hand, not so fast."

A series of cases involving horizontal mergers followed a more or less predictable pattern and came to some sort of culmination in the *Brown Shoe*[34] and *Philadelphia Bank*[35] cases. While certain elements of these two decisions, and of others in the series, were and still are controversial, the courts did not drift very far from long accepted approaches to market definition and to the assessment of competitive effects. The cases were decided in the essentially traditional atmosphere of market shares of the acquired and acquiring companies, the economic size and strength of the acquiring company, trends in the industry with respect to concentration, ease of entry by new companies, and the cumulative effects of a series of mergers. The legality of both horizontal and vertical aspects of the mergers was tested in terms of the amount of competition thus eliminated. Although there might well be disagreement over the amount of competition which the court determined to be "substantial," there is no real disagreement over the factors taken into account in reaching the decisions. These cases suggest that very small market shares may subject a merger to attack where a history of mergers or a trend may pose a threat of industry-wide concentration, but these conclusions are clearly in the mainstream of antitrust policy.

The same cannot be said of another series of cases having to do with conglomerate and product extension mergers. Where vertical and horizontal mergers may have obvious anticompetitive effects in absorbing or foreclosing competition, the conglomerate merger has no direct effect on competition at all. In order to bring such mergers under the new Section 7, it was necessary to approach the situations in an untraditional way. This the Federal Trade Commission has done by developing a number of concepts revolving around the idea that extra market power may be derived from absolute size and diversification. Where no competition was either absorbed or foreclosed, and the merger involved only the substitution of one company for another in the relevant market, the forbidden effects on competition prescribed by the statute may become highly conjectural.

The Commission has pursued this approach on the basis of one or more of several specific theories, each of which is founded on the assumption that the acquiring firm is very large and the market in which the acquisition is made is usually characterized by small units. These theories include the following:

1. The acquired firm may be operated at a lower cost as part of a large enterprise, tending to drive its smaller competitors out of business.

2. A large, diversified firm may charge abnormally low prices for its newly acquired product line, supported by profits from other lines.

3. The mere entry of the large firm into the new market may have adverse effects on competitive behavior in that market owing to the fear by the smaller

---

[34] *Brown Shoe Co.* v. *United States,* 370 U.S. 300 (1961).
[35] *United States* v. *Philadelphia National Bank,* 374 U.S. 321 (1963).

firms of retaliation by the large firm should they compete too vigorously and to the reluctance of new firms to enter the market because of the presence of the giant.

4. Potential competition is lessened where the large acquiring firm would have entered the industry anyhow by internal expansion of its own facilities or where, even if it would not have entered, it was enough of a threat to existing firms to exert a competitive influence on their pricing and other decisions.

5. Companies that buy in the new market and who wish to sell to the large conglomerate may, in order to obtain reciprocity, shift their purchases to the newly acquired firm.

The courts have not yet had good opportunities to consider all of these theories. The following comments can be made, however. Evidence of economies, as in the first theory, should certainly not be a factor dictating a finding of unlawfulness of a merger under Section 7, nor should they be a defense where other grounds for unlawfulness are present, although they might be used to offset some adverse effects, e.g., the adverse effects on competition described in the third theory. The second theory appears to be based on a myth. Actual studies show that such predatory pricing is highly unlikely. Even large firms do not often indulge in acquisitions for the purpose of losing money. Where the purpose is to achieve market control by driving competitors out of business, the activity would seem to be covered adequately by other statutes, including the Sherman Act.

The third, fourth, and fifth theories would seem to have some substance under special circumstances; under theory 4, for example, where the new market is a tight oligopoly, and the entry of the acquiring firm from internal expansion appears to have been certain. Under theory 5, there may be some substance where the reciprocity involves a large percentage of the new market. Under normal circumstances, adverse effects on competition, at the level prohibited by the statute, would appear to be marginal and highly speculative. Certainly, where the anticompetitive effects of conglomerate mergers are clear and strong, such mergers should be prohibited, and size may be an important factor. To forbid conglomerate mergers, however, where the effects are very tenuous at best may have some serious, unfortunate, and unexpected impacts upon the economy as a whole. The market for capital assets, for example, could be dangerously impaired.

Many of the attacks by the Federal Trade Commission on conglomerate mergers raise questions of basic economic, political, and social values. Where statutory guidance is not clear, it may be inappropriate for the Commission and courts to push too far ahead without further illumination from Congress. The leading conglomerate merger case at the moment is *Federal Trade Commission* v. *Procter & Gamble Company*,[36] actually a product extension merger,

---

[36] 386 U.S. 568 (1967).

where the Supreme Court affirmed an order by the Commission to Procter & Gamble to divest itself of the Clorox Chemical Company. The Court apparently approved several of the Commission's theories, especially theories 3 and 4, and determined the findings of anticompetitive effects to be supported by the evidence. Needless to say, the case has caused much comment and criticism. This decision did not approve, or even involve, some of the more extreme Commission views but has begun what may be a long process of appraisal and reconciliation. Time will provide more answers.

Interestingly enough, one of the most publicized, and perhaps eventually most important, cases under Section 7 since 1950, the *du Pont-General Motors*[37] decision, was decided under the old language, not the new. This case involved acquisitions by du Pont of General Motors common stock during the period 1917 to 1920. The Supreme Court found a violation of the old Section 7. The case is interesting for a number of reasons. Perhaps first among these is that the Court apparently has made Section 7 a method of picking up for challenge acquisitions which may not have had any discernible anticompetitive effects at the time the acquisitions were made, but where, as a result of later developments in the company, industry, or market, actual or potential anticompetitive effects appeared. If followed, such a view could make every acquisition, however harmless at the time, subject to challenge many years later when changed conditions bring about or make more probable the prohibited effects. It would seem that problems of this sort might better be dealt within a Sherman Act context. This decision applied the old Section 7 to a vertical integration situation by using the "or tend to create a monopoly" phrase.

Summary of Section 7. The amended Section 7 has become one of the most active portions of the antitrust laws. Both the Federal Trade Commission and the Department of Justice have been aggressive in their use of the new language. There are many people who feel, however, that Section 7 is still not a satisfactory antimerger weapon. Some take this point of view because they feel the statute does not go far enough; others are concerned because the unclear language of the section is encouraging the Federal Trade Commission, the Department of Justice, and the courts to move much too far into the realm of social, political, and economic value judgments, an area thought better to be left to Congress. There are many who firmly believe that further concentration of assets in the bands of large conglomerate firms is a very bad thing indeed and should be prohibited even where there are no anticompetitive consequences. Unfortunately, the statute itself is the end product of this divergence of public opinion. The fact remains, however, that the test set forth in Section 7 is one measured in terms of harm to competition, and the statute does not give the

---

[37] *United States* v. *E. I. du Pont de Nemours & Co.,* 353 U.S. 586 (1957). The amended section could not apply because the acquisitions had been completed thirty years before the new language became law. See also *United States* v. *E. I. du Pont de Nemours & Co.,* 366 U.S. 316 (1961).

courts or the Commission a mandate to proceed against mergers involving large conglomerates, in the absence of harmful effects on competition. It appears likely that Section 7 will continue to be battleground for conflicting social, economic, and political views.

There have been a number of bills in Congress designed to strengthen, extend, clarify, and alter antimerger policy. Some of them aim at requiring premerger notification to the Attorney General or the Federal Trade Commission in order to minimize the problems of post-merger divestments as well as to discourage or delay impending mergers. It is fairly likely that something along these lines will be enacted in the near future. The volume of proposed antitrust legislation has been building up for several years. A large share of these proposals has been aimed at protecting certain firms and groups from effective competition. So far, Congress has shown admirable, though not universal, resistance to the attempts to secure exemption from competition.

INTERLOCKING DIRECTORATES.   The draftsmen of Section 8 felt that the antitrust laws were being avoided by the substitution of interlocking directorates for outright combinations of competitors by merger or by agreement. The theory was that where two or more competing corporations have common directors, competition may be eliminated without any overt merger or agreement. The Section reads in part: ". . . no person at the same time shall be a director of any two or more corporations, any one of which has capital, surplus, and undivided profits aggregating more than $1,000,000, . . . if such corporations are or shall have been theretofore, . . . competitors, so that the elimination of competition by agreement between them would constitute a violation of any of the anti-trust laws." Little attention has been paid to Section 8 because of the difficulty of enforcement and because there are many other devices that are not prohibited by the statute and that make good substitutes for the interlocking directorate. Interlocks of officers, of officers and director, or of major shareholders and director, and vertical interlocks and communities of interest, as where competing corporations have directors in the same bank or other financial institution, are not specifically prohibited; yet they seem to be subject to the same objections as the interlocking directorate. Whether or not there is a serious problem in this area is an issue that has not been settled. A Federal Trade Commission Report of 1950 would lead one to conclude that the problem is both serious and extensive, but there is evidence and expert opinion to the contrary, and some of the conclusions of the Commission are subject to question in the light of the Commission's own evidence. It is interesting to note, however, that Section 10 of the Clayton Act prohibits dealings between common carriers and any other firms where there are interlocking directors, officers, substantial interests, or combinations of these. This extensive prohibition is aimed at vertical interlocks with suppliers or customers, but applies only where common carriers are involved.

Sections 8 and 10 of the Clayton Act have never been of major importance in the antitrust field and do not now appear likely to achieve any greater importance in the near future.[38] A 1965 survey of 74 of the largest corporations by a Congressional committee revealed 182 persons with multiple directorships, although not all of the interlocks would have been in violation of Section 8.[39] Perhaps lackadaisical enforcement accounts in part for the fact that the section is almost completely ignored.

3. PRICING PRACTICES

A. Price Discrimination

(1)

CASE. What are the implications of the situation described in the news story from the Wall Street Journal:

A battle for California's baby food market is moving nearer a showdown in the courts. It's a battle with wide implications for consumer goods industries throughout the U.S.

Involved are the three biggest baby food producers: Gerber Products Co., Beech-Nut Life Savers, Inc., and H. J. Heinz Co. Pretrial depositions are being taken now; a trial date is yet to be set.

Beech-Nut touched off the fight last fall when it cut the prices of its baby food in California. Gerber and Heinz, among other things, charge Beech-Nut flouted the Federal antitrust law's ban on territorial price discrimination, because it made no similar reduction east of the Mississippi.

The Basic Issue

Ramifications of the court fight could extend beyond the tender field of baby foods, a field where retail sales currently are running at a rate of some $280 million a year. The basic issue is this: Can packaging alone add enough value to a product so that it can and should command a premium price over similar but differently-packed items on the market?

Under the antitrust law, a company can cut prices in one area without cutting them in others if it can prove the cuts are necessary to meet competition. Until last fall, baby food packed in glass had been priced higher in California than that sold in tins; Beech-Nut's price cut on its glass-packed products removed the historic differential. Beech-Nut claims the cut was made to meet the competition of Gerber, which sells its baby food in tins in California.

Gerber, however, disputes this claim, contending Beech-Nut's glass jars make its baby food a premium product, not directly competitive with Gerber's tins. Soon after the Beech-Nut price cut, Gerber slashed its prices, restoring the historic tin-glass price differential. Beech-Nut then cut again, and this time Gerber

---

[38] But see *United States* v. *Sears, Roebuck & Co.,* 111 F. Supp. 614 (S.D.N.Y. 1953).

[39] Staff of Antitrust Subcommittee, House Committee on the Judiciary, 89th Cong., 1st Sess., *Interlocks in Corporate Management.* See Ephraim Jacobs, "Interlocks," 29 A.B.A. Antitrust Section Rep. 204 (1965).

countered with its law suit. Heinz filed a similar suit, and Beech-Nut tossed some counterclaims into the legal fray.

Some side issues entered into the dispute too. For instance, Beech-Nut charged that Gerber's salesmen 'remodel and rearrange retailers' baby-food departments . . . and in so doing whenever possible physically limit the space accorded by the retailer to competitors' products and in particular those of (Beech-Nut) and rearrange competitive products in a mixed-up fashion so that prospective purchasers cannot find what they want.'

Beech-Nut further charged that Gerber's salesmen reshuffle Beech-Nut displays so that 'items having a rapid turnover are placed behind slower-moving items on lower shelves or even in the retailers' storerooms.' Another alleged practice of the busy salesmen was that they tampered with the jars of their competitors' baby food 'so as to partially open jars to destroy their usefulness and to spill over and spoil the appearance of Beech-Nut's baby foods display in retail stores.'

Gerber, in turn, charged that Beech-Nut 'secretly purchased from certain retail dealers in California their entire stock of (Gerber's) baby food for the deliberate purpose of preventing the public from purchasing such products and requiring the purchase of (Beech-Nut's) products instead.' Similar complaints about offers to buy up its products were made by H. J. Heinz Co.

Market Share Dwindles

Before the court, Beech-Nut declared it made its price cut in California because its survival there was at stake. It explained that in 1956 its share of the California market began to decline from a high of 6.6% and by last July had dwindled to 4.3%. It said large chains, wholesalers and cooperatives had started to discontinue its line and others threatened to do so. It decided, therefore, that it could recapture its market only by reducing prices of its glass-packed items to the level of baby food in tins. H. J. Heinz, which also packs its baby items in glass and has about 16% of the California market, followed Beech-Nut's action and dropped its prices too.

Gerber, which last July had about 73% of the California market, charged Beech-Nut with an attempt to destroy competition and monopolize the market in the West Coast state. It asked for injunctive relief.

Federal Judge Edward Weinfeld, before whom this plan was presented, noted that 'despite higher prices for glass-packed baby food many consumers prefer to buy it because of a belief (right or wrong) that its contents are better preserved and of greater nutritional value—that, in effect, it is a premium product which commands a higher price in competition with tin.' He added that the substance of Gerber's position is that 'marketwise the products are not comparable and that Beech-Nut's reduction was not meeting (Gerber's) price but undercutting it.'

Gerber also contended that it costs more to package and distribute in glass than in tin. Heinz said that using glass instead of tin is about 15% more expensive.

Core of the Controversy

Observing that since 'neither party makes any substantial claim that the food content of its product is superior to or more costly than the others,' Judge Weinfeld concluded that 'the hard core of the controversy revolves about the packaging of their respective products—tin against glass containers.'

Beech-Nut argued that it's true some customers prefer glass to tin at any price, just as some others prefer tin to glass at any price. But it contended that most prefer glass to tin only when the two are sold at the same price. As evidence that the vast majority will not pay a premium for glass, the company cited its own decline on the California market.

Specifically, Gerber charges Beech-Nut with violation of Section 2(a) of the Robinson-Patman Act on the basis that its price decrease in California without a similar reduction east of the Mississippi is territorial price discrimination. It also charges Beech-Nut with various other violations of the same act and with false advertising and with an attempt to monopolize. Heinz also charged Beech-Nut with violation of Section 2(a).

The first price cut by Beech-Nut was made last September 4 when wholesale prices of its strained baby food were reduced to 96 cents per dozen from $1.11 and its junior foods to $1.16\frac{1}{2}$ per dozen from $1.59 on maximum shipments; strained baby food is for infants and junior for babies from about nine months to 15 months of age. Heinz made similar reductions. On October 11 Gerber brought down prices of its strained baby food to 86 cents per dozen from 96 cents and its junior baby food to 95\frac{1}{2} cents per dozen from $1.16\frac{1}{2}$. On the same day Beech-Nut again dropped its prices to the Gerber level and Heinz followed suit.

East and West

Gerber and Heinz assert that the cuts in California have put Beech-Nut's quotations in that state about 23% lower on its strained foods and about 40% lower on its junior foods than its prices east of the Mississippi.

Gerber recently announced, however, that effective May 26 it will return its prices to the level where they were before the reduction last fall. Presumably, Beech-Nut and Heinz also will move their quotations up a notch, wiping out the second cut but not the first one they made last fall.

Gerber, Beech-Nut and Heinz are the three major producers of baby foods, accounting for 47%, 21% and 16.5%, respectively, of total national sales. Among the others are: Duffy-Mott Co., Libby, McNeill & Libby, Mead Johnson & Co., Swift & Co., Armour & Co. and Geo. A. Hormel & Co.

Beech-Nut has taken the first round in the battle. The plea for the temporary injunction that would force it to restore the price differential between tin and glass-packed products was denied by the court. The Gerber and Heinz suits against Beech-Nut have been consolidated. The amounts being sought in damages by the disputants are: $45 million by Beech-Nut, $17 million by Gerber, and $9 million by Heinz.

(2)

CASE. Paul Preston, president of Hypocase, Inc., has just received a telephone call from a Hypocase salesman in Chicago. The salesman reported that one of Hypocase's best customers is going to give his business to the Midwest Pallet Company unless Hypocase can meet the Midwest price. The price offered by Midwest is somewhat below the prices quoted by Hypocase to any of its customers. Preston told the salesman that a decision on the matter would be made later in the day. Shortly after the conversation with the salesman was completed, Gude du Buy, the purchasing agent for Hypocase, stopped by Preston's office to tell him that du Buy was taking the five o'clock plane to New York for the purpose, among other things, of closing a deal that would be very favorable to Hypocase. Most pallet manufacturers purchase the steel straps and bands needed for their products from the Atlantic Strap and Band Corp. in New York, although there are a few other suppliers. Hypocase has had Atlantic under considerable pressure for some time to increase the discount on steel straps and bands. Hypocase is not the largest pallet manufacturer in the country, but it is located in a rapidly growing industrial area, and its business is much sought after by suppliers. Du Buy has just heard from the sales manager of Atlantic that the larger discount will be offered to Hypocase if orders are placed at least three months in advance and are in amounts of not less than $25,000. Preston told du Buy that he wanted a while to think it over but would let du Buy know his decision before he left for the airport. Preston has asked various members of his staff to work on these two problems. He has asked you to outline for him any issues with regard to the Robinson-Patman Act that might be involved in the decisions.

IN GENERAL. By 1914 it had become apparent to Congress that pure "antitrust" legislation, such as the Sherman Act, could not check corporate expansion and concentration or prevent monopoly, and another approach to the problem was attempted. This new approach had the two objectives, pointed out before, of offsetting the concentration already established by taking away its advantages, and of checking further concentration by eliminating the business practices that had become identified with the development of concentration and monopoly. Both of these objectives required the regulation of business practices and methods of competition, and, because it could not be told in advance which firms were likely to become monopolies, the regulation had to be directed at all business regardless of size. Constitutional barriers prohibited classifications of business that might be deemed arbitrary. The principal federal statutes utilizing this new approach are the Clayton Act, the Robinson-Patman Act of 1936, which was an amendment to Section 2 of the Clayton Act, and the Federal Trade Commission Act of 1914.

The very nature of the new approach and of the statutes embodying it necessitated a change in the enforcement procedure. The regulation of business practices in general and the direction of the regulation at all trade made the Sherman Act methods of enforcement inadequate to handle either the volume or the type of problem involved. Initiative may still be taken by the Attorney General in both civil and criminal actions, although the latter has not been used under the newer statutes, and private suits for injunction or damages are still available as methods of enforcing these statutes, but the primary means of enforcement is the cease and desist order by the Federal Trade Commission. Such an order, which is an administrative counterpart of the judicial injunction, simply orders the person involved to stop his violations

of the law. When the Commission has reason to believe that a person is violating or has violated the law, it issues and serves on that person a complaint
setting forth the charges and containing the notice of a hearing to be held
on the matter. The person charged with the violation may appear at the
hearing and show cause why a cease and desist order should not be entered.
If the order is entered, the party involved may apply to a Court of Appeals
for a review of the order, and the Commission may apply to such court for
enforcement of the order. A very large proportion of the proceedings under
these statutes is finalized in the Commission and never reaches the courts.

The Federal Trade Commission Act, as amended by the Wheeler-Lea Act
of 1938, makes unlawful "unfair methods of competition" and "unfair or
deceptive acts or practices." Some of the methods and practices that have been
affected by the Act will be discussed later in this chapter. The Clayton Act
contains four important substantive Sections: 2, 3, 7, and 8, dealing with
a wide variety of situations and practices. Sections 7 and 8 have already been
examined. Section 3, concerning exclusive dealing and tying arrangements,
will be discussed later. Section 2, one of the most active sections in the statute,
deals with price discrimination, a business practice thought by Congress to be
influential in the development of concentration and in the creation of monopoly. Far-reaching changes were made in Section 2 by the Robinson-Patman
Act of 1936, and the discussion will be concerned primarily with the amended
section. The interpretations and shortcomings of the old language are important background for the new, however, and a brief consideration will be given
to them. Unlike the Sherman Act, which is a concise statute containing only
two short substantive provisions and a few enforcement provisions, the Clayton
Act is a lengthy declaration of principles containing many substantive provisions and numerous enforcement clauses.

Section 2 Before the Robinson-patman Act. In order to understand
the reasons why the provisions of the old Section 2 were found to be in need
of amendment in 1936, it is necessary to consider the change in the economic
scene between 1914 and 1936 and to examine the alleged defects in the older
wording of the statute. In 1914 the only type of price discrimination with
which Congress was concerned was the locality or area discrimination, by
which a large manufacturer or distributor kept his prices high in localities
where he had no competition but lowered them in communities where there
was competition. Often the purpose of the lower price in competitive areas
was not to "meet" the competition but to drive it out of business. The level
of competition primarily affected by these practices was the competition with
the discriminating seller and not the competition among the seller's customers
who paid different prices for the goods.

This concern with seller's competition was reflected in the language of
the statute itself, which prohibited discrimination in price between different
purchasers of commodities "where the effect of such discrimination may be

to substantially lessen competition or tend to create a monopoly in any line of commerce." Congress apparently intended "line of commerce" to mean "line of goods" and not "levels of competition." It was very doubtful whether the injury to an individual purchaser who was discriminated against by a seller could satisfy the test of "substantial lessening of competition," and the interpretations by the courts were, as a whole, to the effect that only the seller's level of competition was involved in the statutory language. The Supreme Court held, in 1929, that other levels of competition were included,[40] but the difficulties in meeting the test still remained. The growth of the chain stores and their tremendous buying power during the 1920's and early 1930's changed the type of price discrimination in common use and shifted much of the initiative from the seller to the powerful buyer who sought the preferential price for the purpose of affecting competition on his own level of competition.

The original language of Section 2 also contained a proviso that left serious weaknesses in the coverage and application of the Section: "Provided, That nothing herein contained shall prevent discrimination in price between purchasers of commodities on account of differences in the grade, quality, or quantity of the commodity sold, or that makes only due allowance for difference in the cost of selling or transportation, or discrimination in price in the same or different communities made in good faith to meet competition." The proviso supplied a justification for price differences where there were differences in the quantity sold but imposed no limit on the amount of discrimination which would be permitted for a difference in quantity. For all practical purposes, any difference in quantity would justify any discrimination in price. The *good faith to meet competition* phrase was interpreted to permit all discriminatory price differences to "meet" competition and thus to authorize oppressive retaliation. An additional weakness seen in the old section was the fact that indirect methods of discrimination, such as bogus or preferential discounts, brokerage fees and allowances, and allowances for advertising and services, were not adequately covered by the statute. Most of the defects were not of major importance until the initiative and motive for discrimination shifted from seller to the large buyer. The effects of the shift were aggravated by the Great Depression, and it was felt generally that the Clayton Act was inadequate to protect the independent merchant from the competition of the chains.

With their survival in the competitive struggle threatened, independent wholesalers and retailers were particularly interested in stopping pricing practices they regarded as unfairly advantageous to large-scale buyers and distributors. The political power of the independent businessman was shown to be no less strong here than in the fight to legalize resale price maintenance. An extensive investigation of chain stores by the Federal Trade Commission also led to conclusions which were favorable to independent wholesalers and

---

[40] *Van Camp & Sons* v. *American Can Co.,* 278 U.S. 245 (1929).

retailers and gave support to the movement to tighten the Clayton Act. The Commission arrived at the conclusion, as a result of its investigation, that not all of the ability of the chains to sell at lower prices was due to greater efficiency, quantity buying, and lower profit margins. Some of the explanation was found in the forced and coercive concessions the powerful chains could exact from their suppliers. All of these events combined to set the stage for the drafting and passing of the Robinson-Patman Act, often referred to as the *chain store bill*.

ROBINSON-PATMAN ACT. The amendments to Section 2 of the Clayton Act made most of the changes suggested by the defects that were discussed above. The section was somewhat reorganized with new Section 2(a) corresponding to old Section 2, and Sections 2(b) to 2(f) being added. Section 2(a) now makes it clear that the Act is intended to apply to all levels of competition by making discrimination in price unlawful "where the effect of such discrimination may be substantially to lessen competition or tend to create a monopoly in any line of commerce, or to injure, destroy, or prevent competition with any person who either grants or knowingly receives the benefit of such discrimination, or with customers of either of them." The new section retains the justifications for differences in grade, quality, and quantity, but authorizes differentials "which make only due allowance for differences in the cost of manufacture, sale, or delivery resulting from the differing methods or quantities in which such commodities are to such purchasers sold or delivered," and thus eliminates the unlimited differentials in price which were once available where there were differences in quantity. Section 2(a) takes casual notice of the loophole which the old language provided for indirect discriminations by making it unlawful for any person engaged in commerce, "directly or indirectly," to discriminate in price. Further notice is taken of this problem in 2(c), (d), and (e).

On the surface, the cost justification provision of the statute would seem to be of very great importance if the law is not to discourage efficiency, and Congress seemed to put considerable weight on this right to justify price differences. However, the cost justifications have proven to be of little consequence in Robinson-Patman Act proceedings. Several explanations have been offered for this unusual result:

1. Limitations of cost accounting make it extremely difficult or impossible and very expensive at best to maintain records that will permit the kind of segregation and allocation of costs that the statute appears to require for the cost defense. The Attorney General's Report suggested that the failure of the Federal Trade Commission to adopt realistic standards recognizing the shortcomings of accounting measurements was the primary reason for the fact that the cost defense had become largely illusory in practice.

2. The language of the statute discourages sellers from making price concessions unless the cost savings they are to produce are certain and immediate. A seller who reasonably expects cost savings to result may be disappointed

and, if so, will be in violation of the law. Some cost savings are not immediately realized, but this is little consolation to the seller who must defend against a challenge by the Commission. Certainly, there are grounds to support these explanations, but substantial improvement can be looked for only in terms of modified statutory language. Consideration may also have to be given to the fact that "efficiency" cannot always be equated with "competition." Protecting one may injure the other. (See discussion of "quantity limit" provision below.)

The wording of the "good faith to meet competition" proviso was changed to "good faith to meet the equally low price of a competitor," in order to avoid the oppressive retaliation found to be authorized by the old language. A more important change in this justification, however, was its removal from the original position alongside the other justifications for price discrimination and its relocation in Section 2(b). This section is a procedural provision which says that when proof has been made that there has been discrimination, the burden of showing justification shifts to the person charged with a violation, provided, however, "that nothing herein contained shall prevent a seller rebutting the prima facie case thus made by showing that his lower price" was made in good faith to meet an equally low price of a competitor. It seems sensible to shift the burden of showing a justification to the person who is in possession of the evidence, if any, which might support a justification, but Section 2(b) is not that easily dispensed with. The most troublesome problem was how much proof the Commission or a private party had to make before the burden shifted. It was contended for some time that it was only necessary to show a substantial difference in price plus the existence of competition. If the person charged with a violation could then show one of the justifications from Section 2(a), he had an absolute defense, but if his justification was that of "good faith to meet competition," it was not a defense but only a further procedural step that shifted the burden back to the plaintiff or Commission, who could still establish a violation by showing the likelihood of injurious effects on competition. After many years of controversy, the Supreme Court held in 1951 that Section 2(b) requires the plaintiff or Commission to show not only the price difference but also the injurious effects on competition before the burden shifts.[41] This decision also had the effect of making the "good faith" proviso an absolute defense as it had been in the old Section 2. Many problems with regard to Section 2(b) and the "good faith" proviso still remain unsolved.

One recent issue to come before the courts under Section 2(b) is whether a seller may offer a lower price for the purpose of obtaining new customers as well as to retain an old customer. The Federal Trade Commission ruled that the "good faith" defense could be used only to retain old customers, but the courts reversed this ruling and held that price discriminations otherwise

---

[41] *Standard Oil Co.* v. *Federal Trade Commission,* 340 U.S. 231 (1951).

prohibited under Section 2(a) can be defended by showing that a price discrimination in favor of a new customer was made in good faith to meet the equally low price of a competitor.[42] There are a number of restrictions on the use of the defense, however, including the requirement that the seller cannot claim his defense if he knows or should have known that the competitor's lower price he met was itself unlawful under the Robinson-Patman Act. Furthermore, the Federal Trade Commission insists that the seller's price discrimination must be limited to meeting the price of a specific individual competitor offered to specific individual customers, but the courts have somewhat mitigated the severity of this view.[43]

Two new matters were added to Section 2(a). The Commission was given authority to fix and establish quantity limits "where it finds that available purchasers in greater quantities are so few as to render differentials on account thereof unjustly discriminatory or promotive of monopoly in any line of commerce." The purpose is to permit the Commission to prohibit quantity discounts on purchases in quantities so large as to be available only to a very few large purchasers, even though otherwise justified by differences in cost. Underlying this provision is the assumption that the cost savings resulting from efficiencies of operation should not be passed on to the ultimate consumer where such economies can be used as an instrument of monopoly. This unusual power has been used by the Commission only once, but the order putting it into effect was set aside by the courts on the ground that the Commission's findings of fact did not support it.[44] The other new matter was to exclude from the coverage of the statute price changes made from time to time in response to changing conditions in the market, such as deterioration or obsolescence of perishable or seasonal goods, distress sales under court process, or sales in good faith on discontinuance of business. This clause removes the doubt that once surrounded differences in price where sales were made at different times under different conditions.

Sections 2(c), (d), and (e) deal with the indirect methods of discrimination which the old Section 2 did not specifically include. Section 2(c) prohibits paying or accepting commissions, brokerage, or other allowance or discount in lieu thereof, "except for services rendered." Although badly and ambiguously worded, this section has been the most active section of the Robinson-Patman Act and has left fewer questions of interpretation unanswered than any other section. Unlike the rest of Section 2, Section 2(c) does not require proof of "discrimination," as such, or unequal treatment, and only one purchaser need be concerned. It is important to note that the courts have uniformly held that Section 2(c) is wholly independent of Section 2(a). Consequently, no proof

---

[42] *Sunshine Biscuits, Inc.* v. *Federal Trade Commission,* 306 F. 2d 48 (7th Cir. 1962).

[43] *Forster Mfg. Co.* v. *Federal Trade Commission,* 335 F. 2d 47 (1st Cir. 1964).

[44] *Federal Trade Commission* v. *B. F. Goodrich Co.,* 134 F. Supp. 39 (D.C. Dist. Col. 1955); 242 F. 2d 31 (Dist. Col. Cir. 1957).

of any possible injury or effect on competition is needed for a violation. Paying or receiving the brokerage is what is prohibited, and 2(c) creates, in effect, a *per se* offense. Because the economic test does not apply to Section 2(c), many persons charged with violations of that section have attempted, some successfully, to show that their conduct was really an "indirect discrimination" under Section 2(a) and, thus, not a violation without proof being made of the effects on competition. Also, under 2(a), the person charged would have available the justifications and defenses. The phrase "except for services rendered" has been virtually deprived of meaning by the courts. Although the major objective of Section 2(c) was to prohibit bogus or unjustified payments, Congress also made it clear that it sought to prohibit the large buyer from compelling his suppliers to pay him, or brokers or agents under his control, brokerage fees and allowances such as would have been paid to an independent broker who was performing services for the seller. Obviously, a broker acting under the orders of the buyer cannot really be acting for the seller. Consequently, the courts have interpreted the "services rendered" phrase to read "except for services rendered by an independent broker."

Sections 2(d) and (e) are concerned with discrimination in the furnishing of merchandising services and facilities to competing customers and with discriminatory payments and allowances to such customers in consideration for services and facilities actually or purportedly supplied by them. The statute does not prohibit such payments and services but requires that they be offered to all customers on proportionately equal terms. Where a large buyer, for example, is paid for his special advertising displays or promotions on behalf of a supplier, the same opportunity must be afforded the buyer's competitors on a proportionate basis. Or where a supplier furnishes a buyer with special advertising services, displays or material, the same must be made available to the buyer's competitors who are also the supplier's customers.

The Commission was not very active in the enforcement of Sections 2(d) and (e) until 1955, but since that time the Commission's activity has been greatly increased. Some cases have reached the courts, and many questions of interpretation and construction have been settled. It is plain that these sections, like Section 2(c), are separate offenses largely independent of the tests and defenses of Section 2(a). The conduct which comes under 2(d) and (e) is prohibited as an unfair trade practice without regard to its effect on competition. If a seller offers advertising allowances or merchandising payments or services to one customer, he must inform all of the competing customers that the allowance is available to them as well. Whether the customers are competitors is largely a geographical matter, but other factors enter the picture also. The general meaning of "proportionately equal terms" is clear, but the application of the phrase to actual cases raises many difficult problems of interpretation and construction.

The Attorney General's Report has condemned the inequality and unfairness that result when the same conduct may be a *per se* violation under Sections 2(c), (d), or (e), or no violation at all as an indirect discrimination under 2(a). Because of this and other disparities, the Report recommends the reconciliation of these subsections with the rest of Section 2.

Section 2(f) provides that "it shall be unlawful for any person engaged in commerce, . . . knowingly to induce or receive a discrimination in price which is prohibited by" Section 2(a). The purpose of this section is obviously to impose on the buyer the same responsibility that is imposed on the seller. This section simply recognizes the fact that while the discrimination is granted by the seller, it is frequently induced by the buyer. Section 2(f) does not apply to 2(c), 2(d), and 2(e) because 2(c) is not concerned with "discriminations" and 2(d) and (e) are not concerned with "discriminations in price." If Section 2(b) imposes the same burden of proof on the buyer that it does on the seller to show justification for the seller's price discrimination, the buyer is placed in the rather uncomfortable position of having to use in his defense evidence that is in the exclusive possession of another. In 1953, however, the Supreme Court held that a defendant buyer cannot be required to prove that discriminatory prices he received were justified by the seller's cost differentials.[45] The Court commented that the determination of the seller's costs is an extremely intricate process, and that the necessary data are ordinarily obtainable by the seller himself only after a detailed study of his business. The Court reasoned that the buyer was in no position to produce evidence about the seller's costs, which it would be required to do if it had the burden of proof Section 2(b) imposes upon the seller. But note that the Commission or the plaintiff, under this decision, has the burden of showing that the discrimination in favor of the buyer charged with a violation was *not* justified under any of the provisions of Sections 2(a) or (b). Court interpretations of the word "knowingly" indicate that the Commission or the plaintiff must show that the buyer knew or was put on notice that the price he paid was substantially lower than the seller's price to other purchasers and that the lower price was not justified by any of the defenses available to the seller. There has been little use by the Commission or by private parties of the terms of Section 2(f).

Functional discounts. Functional discounts represent an inexact acceptance by manufacturers of the distributive services performed by marketing middlemen. When a wholesaler assumes the burden of servicing small accounts, of warehousing and of other functions that a manufacturer might also perform, the manufacturer may give recognition to this fact through price concessions. Early drafts of the bills that came to be the Robinson-Patman Act sought to describe certain uses of this type of discount which should come within the purview of the statute, but the final draft contained no specific mention of this problem. That does not mean that functional discounts have received no atten-

---

[45] *Automatic Canteen Company of America* v. *Federal Trade Commission*, 346 U.S. 61 (1953).

tion under the terms of the Act. Problems have arisen with regard to two situations involving suppliers who sell both to wholesalers and to retailers: where the wholesaler passes on to his retailer customers some of the functional price concession he obtained from the supplier, and where the wholesaler also does a retail business. In either case, the retailer who buys direct from the supplier may complain that his competitors, the wholesaler himself or his customers, are being favored with a lower price. Several approaches have been taken to these problems, none being entirely satisfactory. Certainly, no subterfuges should be tolerated, but, at the same time, it seems unwise to impose on the supplier the legal responsibility of policing the prices at which his functional customers resell the goods.[46]

The Robinson-Patman Act leaves much to be desired. It has come under severe attack from several different quarters. An influential wing of the legal profession takes the stand that the Robinson-Patman Act should be repealed on the ground that it (1) discourages competition and encourages price fixing; (2) runs diametrically contrary to the basic policy of our antitrust laws as expressed in the Sherman Act; and (3) fosters a soft, painless competition where nobody gets hurt and the inefficient and efficient alike remain in business. It is also argued that the Act, by legislating on prices, is concerning itself with the end product rather than with the causes, which are the existing firm and market structures. There is some foundation for these charges, but there is also room for the argument that not all of the Act has either these results or these objectives and that portions of the Act, certainly, are consistent with basic policy and are useful in the furtherance of that policy.[47]

WHAT IS PRICE DISCRIMINATION? The discussion so far has largely ignored one of the fundamental problems of Section 2 which has existed without resolution since 1914. The problem is not so much that of the meaning of the terms "price," "discrimination," and "price discrimination" as it is one of *measuring* discriminations in price. Since the Act does not define "price," the ordinary trade meaning must be used, and the history and the language of the statute make it reasonably clear that this meaning was intended. The ordinary legal meaning of *"price"* is *the amount actually paid or agreed to be paid by the buyer to the seller for the goods purchased.* The price of goods must always be looked upon as a delivered price because the delivery, either actual or constructive, is required before there can be a sale. But be sure to remember that delivery does not necessarily take place at the buyer's place of business. Goods may be delivered at the seller's place of business or at any other place,

---

[46] *Federal Trade Commission* v. *Rubberoid Co.,* 343 U.S. 470 (1952); *Standard Oil Co.* v. *Federal Trade Commission,* 340 U.S. 231 (1951); Standard Oil Co., 41 F.T.C. 263 (1945), *modified,* 43 F.T.C. 56 (1946), *modified and aff'd,* 173 F. 2d 210 (7th Cir. 1949).

[47] Thorough appraisals of the Act can be found in Corwin D. Edwards, *The Price Discrimination Law* (Washington: Brookings Institution, 1959), and Frederick M. Rowe, *Price Discrimination Under the Robinson-Patman Act* (Boston: Little, Brown & Co., 1963).

but wherever the place of delivery, the amount the buyer pays for the goods delivered is the price. Where goods are delivered at the seller's place of business and title passes at that time but the seller transports the goods to the buyer at the seller's expense, such transportation would be a service rendered to the buyer and the cost would have to be deducted in order to ascertain the price. The buyer, in other words, has paid for something more than the "goods delivered."

"Discrimination" was not used in the Act with its unjust or unfair connotations but with a simple connotation of difference in treatment. This conclusion is dictated because the Act sets up its own tests of what differences in price are unjust or unfair. Thus, difference in price treatment is a discrimination within the terms of the Act, and if it has the prohibited effect, it is illegal unless it can be justified. But defining "discrimination" in terms of unequal price treatment does not solve the problem of what price treatment is unequal. It is the measure of the inequality, then, that is the problem requiring solution and not the meaning of the words used. Until this problem is solved, it cannot be seen whether there is a discrimination in price so as to bring the statute into operation. Note that "discrimination" is used in different contexts in different parts of the Act.

There are two conflicting theories with respect to the proper measure of inequality of price under the Robinson-Patman Act. The first of these is the *price difference theory,* based on the idea that the Act was designed to give competing purchasers of the same commodity equal competitive opportunities by permitting them to buy at the same price. Under this view, there can be no discrimination when the prices are the same to all purchasers. If there is a difference in price, that difference is the amount of the discrimination. Where the seller's costs differ, the statute *permits but does not require* price differences between competing purchasers. Where the cost of selling to A is 10¢ and to B 15¢, the seller is permitted but is not required to sell to A at 5¢ less than he sells to B, and presumably the same would hold true of 4¢, 3¢, 2¢, and 1¢ less than the price to B. Selling to A and B at the same price would not be a discrimination under the price difference theory. The Federal Trade Commission and the courts usually follow this theory.

The second is the *profit difference theory,* which is based on the idea that Section 2(a) does not require that competing purchasers be offered goods at the same price but that a purchaser is entitled to the benefit of any cost savings enjoyed by the seller as a result of the purchaser's location or his method or quantity of buying. Under this theory, a seller who does not reflect in full in the price his differences in cost in selling to different purchasers is discriminating. The amount of the discrimination is the amount by which the prices do not differ by the full amount of the cost differences. Discrimination is measured, then, by the difference in prices after deducting the seller's costs. The theory rests on interpreting the phrase "only due allowance," in the cost proviso of Section 2(a), to mean "no other than full allowance." Where the cost of selling to *A* is 10¢ and to *B* 15¢, the seller *must*, if he is not to discriminate, sell the goods to *A* at 5¢ less than to *B*. To offer them at a greater differential than 5¢ would be to discriminate in favor of *A*. To offer the goods at less than 5¢ under *B's* price would be to discriminate in favor of *B* and against the person who is actually paying the lower price, as where the sale to *A* was at 4¢ less than to *B*. This theory, if fully employed, would eliminate all zone, delivered, and basing point pricing. The Federal Trade Commission has applied, and the Supreme Court has approved, this theory in a few cases involving the sale of standardized goods delivered at varying distances from the seller's place of business where the non-transportation costs were more or less uniform.[48] The extension of this theory raises some interesting speculation. Recognizing the difficulties in proving most types of cost, the profit difference theory could, theoretically, lead to a situation where each seller would be limited to those customers who were geographically closer to him than to any of his competitors. It should be noted that the cases wherein the Supreme Court approved the profit difference theory involved the collusive use by several firms of such common pricing practices as basing point and delivered price systems with uniform prices as a result. In recent uniform zone pricing cases, the Commission has refused to apply this theory.

To illustrate the differences between the two theories, assume that *A* and *B* are competing purchasers of a particular commodity and that they are located at different distances from the seller's place of business. The seller's costs are exactly the same for *A* and *B* except that the freight cost to *A* is $2.00 per unit and to *B* $4.00 per unit. The seller's price to *A* is $10 per unit, delivered to *A's* place of business, and to *B*, $11 per unit on the same terms. Under the price difference theory, there is a discrimination of $1 in *A's* favor and against *B*, but the discrimination is justified by the difference in the cost of selling. The seller is not required to pass along all, or even part, of his cost saving to *A*. Under the profit difference theory, there is a discrimination of $1 in favor of *B* and against *A*, which is illegal if the stated effects on competition may result. The price to *A* is lower than the price to *B*, yet there is a discrimination against *A*.

B. Sales Below Cost

IN GENERAL. The Robinson-Patman Act was not the only depression-bred anti-chain store legislation enacted during the 1930's. The state legislatures were also interested in the problem, and wrote into law, during the depression years, a variety of statutes dealing with competitive practices.

---

[48] *Federal Trade Commission* v. *Cement Institute,* 333 U.S. 683 (1948); *Federal Trade Commission* v. *A. E. Staley Mfg. Co.,* 324 U.S. 746 (1945); *Corn Products Refining Co.* v. *Federal Trade Commission,* 324 U.S. 726 (1945).

Most of these statutes were concerned with price competition in one form or another. The two most common statutes were the Sales Below Cost Acts, which prohibited certain sales below cost, and the Fair Trade Acts, which were part of the movement to legalize resale price maintenance. The latter type of statute will be discussed in the next section. The same independent merchants and trade groups, especially the food, grocery, and drug trades, which fostered the Robinson-Patman Act were responsible for these state price control laws. The food and grocery trades were more interested in prohibiting sales below cost and in encouraging the establishment of minimum price levels than they were in the resale price maintenance, because a large portion of the food items offered for sale were not trade-marked or branded and were therefore not susceptible to the Fair Trade Laws. Furthermore, in the early years of the resale price maintenance laws, many manufacturers and distributors were reluctant to enter into fair trade contracts until their competitors had done likewise. The statutes prohibiting sales below cost provided a method by which price floors could be established and sometimes enforced at public expense. About two thirds of the states have such statutes.

The chief difficulty facing the draftsmen of the statutes prohibiting sales below cost was that of defining "cost." The difficulty has been met in two ways, generally speaking: the California statute,[49] which was the first of the current crop of statutes prohibiting sales below cost, and those statutes patterned after it attempt to set forth an itemized definition of cost, whereas the other method provides that any sale below invoice cost or manufacturer's list price plus a fixed mark-up is a violation. The California law was amended in 1953, incidentally, to impose a fixed mark-up where proof of the actual cost of doing business is absent. Neither method is entirely satisfactory. The "defined cost" system creates difficult problems of draftsmanship and of enforcement. Cost is almost impossible to define with any degree of accuracy, especially where the definitions must be made to serve all types of business. The "fixed mark-up" system is unrealistically arbitrary and may tend to favor the inefficient operator at the expense of the efficient. Whichever method is used, it must be recognized that these statutes are simply additional manifestations of increasing interest in protection *from* competition in contrast with the Sherman Act policy of protection *of* competition, though both types of statute are usually couched in terms of "unfair" competition.

In the food, grocery, and drug trades, the great paradox of competition becomes the most obvious. The small independent merchant feels that if only competition is protected, the large operators and the chains will soon drive the small independent out of business. The argument on the other side is that if you protect competitors from competition, then competition itself vanishes. No merchant argues publicly that all competition should be eliminated, but

---

[49] *Business and Professions Code,* Sections 17,000–101.

many do argue that price competition should be minimized or eliminated. This is the theory of the Fair Trade Laws and, to a somewhat lesser degree, the Sales Below Cost Acts. Whether the forms of competition remaining after competition in price is prohibited are sufficient to maintain the benefits normally expected to flow from competition is a question economists have not satisfactorily answered. The policy on which all can agree is that *unfair* competition should be prohibited. The problem is, of course, that there is no agreement on what is "unfair." There are many who feel that it is unfair for a competitor to sell at a lower price, whatever the justification, and there are those who think that this is unfair only where the competitor is selling below cost. Some feel that it is unfair for a competitor to sell below his own costs; but others say it is unfair to sell below some arbitrary cost figure even though it is higher than the seller's actual costs. The statutes will be examined here and in the next section to determine what policies they embody and what effects they have.

PROVISIONS OF THE STATUTES. Because the terms of the statutes prohibiting sales below cost vary from state to state, it will be necessary to speak somewhat generally about the provisions. It is suggested that the statutes of the reader's own state be compared with these general statements.

Definitions of "cost." The portions of the statutes dealing with "cost" are the ones most subject to attack because of the lack of certainty in the meaning of cost. Statutes of the California type define *cost* as "the cost of raw materials, labor and all overhead expenses," where applied to production, and as "invoice or replacement cost, whichever is lower, of the article or product to the distributor . . . , plus the cost of doing business," where applied to distribution. Invoice, replacement, raw material and labor costs are usually relatively easy to establish and allocate, but "overhead expense" and the "cost of doing business" still remain as difficult problems. The California Act defines *overhead expense* and *cost of doing business* as "all cost of doing business incurred in the conduct of the business" and then lists some of the factors to be included in such cost. Even if an exhaustive list of factors could be compiled in the statute, only the minor aspect of the problem would be solved. The major problem of allocation still remains, and has usually been dealt with by the courts by applying "any reasonable method." The period of time over which overhead expenses are to be determined is also subject to considerable variation in practice. A merchant operating under such a statute will usually resolve all doubts in favor of prices that avoid the dangers of litigation.

The mark-up statutes attempt to meet these cost problems by establishing a fixed percentage mark-up that is presumed to be the cost of doing business. *Cost* is defined as the invoice or replacement cost plus 6 percent, or higher percentages in some states, where a lower cost of doing business is not proved. A few states provide mark-up figures for wholesalers as well as for retailers.

Many statutes provide that goods acquired at bankrupt, forced, or close-out sales may not be used as a justification for a price lower than replacement cost unless the goods are advertised as having been purchased at such a sale. Some statutes require that the wages of persons working for less than the prevailing wage rate or for nothing must be figured into cost at the prevailing rate, thus effectively preventing lower prices explained by members of the family working in the business. Sales to retailers and wholesalers at prices that are not justified by existing market conditions within the state cannot be used, in some states, as a basis for computing cost, but such provisions have occasionally been struck down by the courts as being arbitrary.[50]

Goods may ordinarily be given away in combination with an article sold, but the cost of the free item must be included in the cost of the article that is sold.

The California Act exempts from its coverage any sale made in an "endeavor made in good faith to meet the legal prices of a competitor selling the same article or product, in the same locality or trade area and in the ordinary channels of trade." While, at first glance, this clause seems to require a seller to know the costs of his competitor as well as his own, all that is needed, presumably, is a reasonable belief that the competitor is not selling below cost, or if below cost, is not associated with an intent to injure competitors. Several other phrases in this clause are also troublesome.

Intent or effect.   Some of the statutes require an intent to injure competition; others look to the effect of sales below cost. The clause in the California Act, which is the more common variety, states that it is unlawful to sell below cost "for the purpose of injuring competitors or destroying competition." Note the significance of the word "or" as compared with "and" used in the same place. "And" is perfectly consistent with basic antitrust policy, which is concerned with the protection of competition, but "or" adds to this policy the policy of protecting competitors. "And" was changed to "or" in 1937. Some statutes say that a violation exists where there is either the intent or the effect of injuring competitors or destroying competition. A few statutes attempted to impose an absolute ban on sales below cost without regard to intent or effect, but these attempts have been held unconstitutional where they have come before the state courts.

Many of the "sales below cost" statutes contain provisions stating that proof of one or more acts of selling below cost, together with proof of the injurious effects of such acts, is presumptive evidence of intent to injure competitors or destroy competition, but it has been held that this presumption is rebutted by a showing that the primary purpose of the sale was not to injure competitors or to destroy competition. In those states where no proof of effect is required, a presumption of intent from the act of selling below cost reduces

---

[50] For example, *Kansas* v. *Consumer Warehouse Market, Inc.,* 183 Kan. 502, 329 P. 2d 638 (1958).

the requirement of intent to something almost completely meaningless and, in a statute imposing criminal penalties, would run directly contrary to the fundamental rule that where a criminal statute requires intent, that intent cannot be presumed from the commission of the unlawful act itself.

The whole theory of the Sales Below Cost Acts comes into question at this point. It would seem that some judicial relief should be provided for the merchant who is the victim of intentionally injurious practices, but, at the same time, it hardly seems right to punish the seller who sells his goods below cost for the purpose of attracting customers to himself and with no more than a casual disregard for his competitor's prices or the effect on the competitor. This is often the very heart of competition. Any other view might bring under the jurisdiction of "unfair practices" the seller who obtains better display cases or a newer building or who has a better location or a more attractive personality. If the purpose of the statutes is to eliminate price competition, then the statutes should be subjected to close and serious appraisal; but if the purpose is only to prohibit price competition which is unfair, in the stricter meanings of the word, then the statutes may play an important part in the enforcement of the basic antitrust policy of protecting competition. If the basic policy is to change to one of protecting from competition, there are many statutes which must be reappraised.

Enforcement. Most statutes provide for fines and imprisonment for violations, for injunctive relief, and for damages. The California Act says that "any person or trade association may bring an action to enjoin and restrain any violation of the chapter and, in addition thereto, for the recovery of damages." Some statutes provide for triple damages. Under some statutes it is not necessary to allege or prove actual damages; others require the person bringing the action to be damaged or threatened with damage.

The part played by trade associations in the original enactment of these statutes is matched in many states by the role the associations play in the enforcement. Under most of the statutes, a trade association may bring the action against the alleged violator. In some states, the Sales Below Cost Acts have been used as cloaks for price fixing, for compelling adherence to association policies, and for encouraging general price increases. The power of the association to bring an action under the statutes gives it a powerful weapon for conformance. The use of the "cost survey" has also facilitated the achievement of the illegal ends suggested above. The California Act contains a section providing that where "a particular trade or industry, of which the person, firm or corporation complained against is a member, has an established cost survey for the locality and vicinity in which the offense is committed, the said cost survey shall be deemed competent evidence to be used in proving the costs of the person, firm or corporation complained against within the provisions of this act." Some trade associations in California have been found guilty of violating the Sherman Act while purporting to be acting under the authority of the Sales Below Cost Act.[51]

CONSTITUTIONAL PROBLEMS. The Supreme Court of the United States has never passed upon the constitutionality of the statutes prohibiting sales below cost, but the state courts have, with few exceptions, held the statutes to be constitutional. The constitutionality of the statutes is subject to question in several areas. The most serious of these is whether the statute is sufficiently explicit to enable a person to ascertain with a fair degree of precision what acts the statute intends to prohibit and what conduct will render the person liable to its penalties. The great uncertainty with regard to intent and to the meaning of "cost" and "cost of doing business" makes the statutes somewhat vulnerable on this ground. Another constitutional issue on which a few of the state courts have based holdings of unconstitutionality is whether the statute is so arbitrary and unreasonable, so obviously unnecessary in its severity and comprehensiveness for the accomplishment of the object to be attained, as to amount to an unjustified interference with private business and property and to violate due process.

Another constitutional issue is whether the acts which the statutes seek to prevent are of sufficiently predatory and anti-social character to make the statutes a valid exercise of the police power of the state. On this sort of issue, the opinion of the legislature is usually bowed to by the courts. The issues raised by the omission of the requirement of intent have already been referred to.

EFFECT OF THE STATUTES. Section 17,001 of the California Act states that the "Legislature declares that the purpose of this chapter is to safeguard the public against the creation or perpetuation of monopolies and to foster and encourage competition, by prohibiting unfair, dishonest, deceptive, destructive, fraudulent and discriminatory practices by which fair and honest competition is destroyed or prevented." Few would argue with the objectives set forth in this section, but it is very doubtful if any of these ends has been accomplished by the statute, and many provisions of the statute appear to have been written without much regard for the purpose clause, unless the normal meanings of the words of that clause are unduly strained. Serious doubts have been raised with respect to the economic desirability of such statutes, and thirty years on the statute books have little served to solve the problems of enforcement. The conviction under the Sherman Act of trade associations which used the provisions of the Unfair Practices Act to cloak price-fixing and other activities is rather ironic in the light of the purpose clause. One threat to competition may simply have been substituted for another by the terms of

---

[51] *Food and Grocery Bureau of S. California* v. *United States*, 139 F. (2d) 973 (9th Cir. 1944); *Calif. Retail Grocers and Mfrs' Ass'n* v. *United States*, 139 F. (2d) 978 (9th Cir. 1944).

the statute. The statutes, as a whole, have made it difficult and risky for some merchants to compete vigorously in price with their rivals.

C. Resale Price Maintenance

In General. *Resale price maintenance* is a system of distribution under which the manufacturer or distributor of trade-marked or otherwise identified goods seeks to control the prices at which his products shall be resold by wholesalers and retailers. Its original purposes were to protect a manufacturer's or distributor's proprietary interest in the trade-marks and trade names his products bore, to facilitate national advertising of price, and to avoid the loss of a product's attractiveness as a result of widespread or continuous price-cutting. Resale price maintenance was largely an outgrowth of mass production and national advertising. Since 1930, however, almost the entire scope, initiative, and purpose of resale price maintenance have shifted from the manufacturer's point of view to that of the retailer and retailers' associations. Resale price maintenance has had a long and controversial legal history.

Many state courts held resale price maintenance contracts to be valid at common law, while others held them invalid as unreasonable restraints of trade. Before the Sherman Act was passed, federal courts had upheld resale price maintenance contracts as reasonable restraints of trade, but in 1911 the Supreme Court of the United States held them to be in violation of the Sherman Act.[52] This decision did not, of course, affect the validity of the contracts in intrastate commerce in those states which had found them not to be in violation of the common law. The law remained in this condition, almost unchanged, until 1931, although many attempts were made in the states and in Congress to legalize resale price maintenance contracts.

Pressure for changes in the law was not great until after 1930. Other devices, which were legal, could accomplish the same or similar ends as resale price maintenance contracts, and were reasonably satisfactory to manufacturers and distributors, the parties most interested. The agency device and consignments were perfectly adequate substitutes for some manufacturers, but they were not suitable in all trades. The use of different brands, one of which was sold to chain stores and to others who might be expected to cut prices, was another solution employed with good results by some manufacturers. Extensive advertising was used in some cases to create such a strong consumer demand that retailers were forced to carry the products in stock even though price-cutters had made them unprofitable.

Another rather common device was the refusal to sell to price-cutters, a primary boycott in bargaining, which was used rather effectively in some industries. The cases that tested the validity of this practice under the Sherman Act made it clear that a simple refusal by one manufacturer to sell was not

---

[52] *Dr. Miles Medical Co.* v. *John D. Park & Sons Co.,* 220 U.S. 373 (1911).

a violation of the Sherman Act and that a seller has an unqualified privilege to choose his customers and to refuse to sell whenever he wishes.[53] But the cases also made it clear that violations of the Sherman Act existed where several sellers entered into an agreement not to sell, where coercion, spying, and blacklisting were employed, and where there was active cooperation between a manufacturer and his distributors to enforce a price policy. The increasing erosion of the fair trade laws owing to trading stamp problems, enforcement difficulties, and unconstitutionality of non-signers clauses has caused much greater emphasis to be placed on the right of a manufacturer to suggest resale prices and to refuse to sell to those who do not take the suggestion. (See further discussion of individual refusals to sell under "Trade Boycott" below.)

It is interesting to note at this point that in the federal field resale price maintenance has usually been approached as a restraint-of-trade problem under the Sherman Act, whereas state courts and statutes have been primarily concerned with price-cutting as an unfair trade practice and with resale price maintenance as a means of prohibiting such price-cutting. This difference of approach is one of the ways of explaining the language of some of the statutes and decisions.

THE FAIR TRADE LAWS. The growth of the chains in the 1920's and the coming of the Great Depression in 1930 revived the attempts to legalize resale price maintenance contracts. The primary initiative this time, however, came not from the manufacturers and distributors but from retailers. Some manufacturers were involved in the fight, but they were not the prime movers. The most active group was the Retail Druggists Association, whose counsel actually drafted many of the early fair trade laws. California was again the first state in which pressures were brought sharply to bear, and these resulted in the passage of the first Fair Trade Law in 1931.[54] This statute legalized resale price maintenance contracts in California. It was enacted with very little opposition, probably because the statute was unnecessary in California, where such contracts were already legal at common law. It proved much easier to add teeth to an already existing statute by amendment than it would have been to get the teeth in when the statute was originally passed. The statute attracted little attention in the state or in the country, but the amendment of 1933 was a different story.

The weakness in the 1931 Act, from the standpoint of its proponents, was the fact that those who did not want to enter into price maintenance contracts refused to do so and went on setting their own prices as before. This problem did not bother the manufacturers, who could refuse to sell to those who would not sign the contracts, as much as it did the retailers who had

---

[53] *United States* v. *Colgate & Co.,* 250 U.S. 300 (1919).
[54] *Business and Professions Code,* Sections 16,900–5.

no direct means of enforcing their desires for price maintenance. The result was the addition to the California Act in 1933 of the so-called "non-signers clause," which bound retailers to the terms of resale price maintenance contracts whether they entered into them or not. The California clause read: "Wilfully and knowingly advertising, offering for sale or selling any commodity at less than the price stipulated in any contract entered into pursuant to this chapter, whether the person so advertising, offering for sale or selling is or is not a party to such contract, is unfair competition and is actionable at the suit of any person damaged thereby." This addition to the Act received a good deal of attention, but was not widely copied because of its doubtful constitutionality. However, in 1936, the Supreme Court of the United States upheld the constitutionality of the Fair Trade Acts of Illinois and of California, including the non-signers clauses.[55] Since that time, almost all states have adopted such laws, and many states still have them. In recent years, the courts of many states have declared the fair trade laws to be unconstitutional on a variety of grounds. By 1967, only sixteen states still had in force fair trade laws with effective non-signers clauses. Missouri, Texas, and Vermont have never had fair trade laws, nor has the District of Columbia.

The decision of the Supreme Court was based primarily on the argument that the manufacturer or distributor has a property interest in the trade-marks or brands and that the statute was a legitimate extension of the state's police power designed to protect that property interest. The non-signers clause was held valid on grounds that the violating retailer acquired the product knowing of the restrictions on its resale, did not have to acquire it, and could have removed the trade-mark or brand name and sold the product without it. There is no doubt that the Court considered the problem largely one of economic policy for the legislature and outside the proper jurisdiction of the judiciary.

MILLER-TYDINGS ACT. The advocates of fair trade laws had not yet achieved all of their ends because resale price maintenance contracts in interstate commerce still violated the Sherman Act. The next step in the almost complete reversal of public policy in this field was the passage by Congress of the Miller-Tydings Amendment to the Sherman Act in 1937. This amendment exempted from the Sherman Act and from the Federal Trade Commission Act resale price maintenance contracts that were lawful in the state where the resale was to be made. The Miller-Tydings Act went through Congress as a rider on the District of Columbia Revenue Bill, and was analyzed very little and debated less.

The law in 1937 appeared to authorize these contracts, including the effect of the non-signers clauses, in those states that had enacted fair trade laws and

---

[55] *Old Dearborn Distributing Co.* v. *Seagram Distillers Corp.,* 299 U.S. 183 (1936); *Pep Boys* v. *Pyroil Sales Co.,* and *Kunsman* v. *Max Factor & Co.,* 299 U.S. 198 (1936). See, however, discussion below.

in interstate commerce where the goods involved were to be resold in a state where the contracts were legal. The situation so remained until 1951 when the Supreme Court held that the Miller-Tydings Act exempted resale price maintenance contracts from the Sherman Act but that it did not permit distributors and retailers to impose price-fixing on persons who have not agreed to the resale price maintenance scheme.[56] In other words, the Miller-Tydings Act did not exempt the effect of the non-signers clauses from the Sherman Act. This decision, of course, destroyed the effect of the Miller-Tydings Act except with respect to the parties who had actually signed resale contracts. It did not make any difference in the long run, however, because Congress entered the picture in July, 1952, with the McGuire Act,[57] which restored the effect of the non-signers clause. The McGuire Act went further than this. It shifted the emphasis in the federal field from restraint of trade to unfair competition, and purported to give extraterritorial effect to minimum prices established under state fair trade laws. The wording of the McGuire Act in this latter regard was poor, and it is doubtful if the desired end was achieved.

OPERATION AND ENFORCEMENT OF THE FAIR TRADE LAWS. The California Act, which was the first one enacted, provides:

> No contract relating to the sale or resale of a commodity which bears, or the label or container of which bears, the trade-mark, brand, or name of the producer or owner of such commodity and which is in fair and open competition with commodities of the same general class produced by others violates any law of this state by reason of any of the following provisions which may be contained in such contract: (1) That the buyer will not resell such commodity except at the price stipulated by the vendor.

It is important to note that the statute applies only to trade-marked or branded items and only to those which are in fair and open competition with commodities of the same general class. In *Eastman Kodak Co.* v. *Federal Trade Commission*,[58] the court held that a particular type of film was not competitive; consequently, it was not properly the subject of a resale price maintenance contract. When competition later developed, the contracts were permitted.

The use of the word "stipulated" makes it possible for a price to be enforced both as a maximum and as a minimum. The Model Fair Trade Statute uses only the word "minimum," as the Miller-Tydings Act does. The McGuire Act uses both "minimum" and "stipulated." The California type statute permits the fixing of fair trade prices by any "vendor" whether or not he is the owner of the trade-mark or brand. This makes it possible for a wholesaler or other distributor who does not own the mark or brand to initiate fair trade contracts when a manufacturer does not, or to initiate contracts with higher

---

[56] *Schwegmann Bros.* v. *Calvert Distillers Corp.,* 341 U.S. 384 (1951).

[57] 66 Stat. 623; 15 U.S.C.A. 45.

[58] 158 F. (2d) 592 (2d Cir. 1946).

minimum prices than a manufacturer has set in his own fair trade contracts. The statute also would permit a manufacturer to be deprived of any price competition with other products in the same class. This could be done against his will and without his consent. This power of the wholesaler has not been widely used, and the Model Act removes the power of the non-owner of the mark or brand to enter into price maintenance contracts unless he has been authorized by the owner. All of the statutes exempt closing-out sales, sales of damaged or deteriorated goods, and sales under order of a court, but the Model Act provides that the dealer must give the producer or distributor of the goods an opportunity to repurchase before the goods are sold at a closing-out sale. Goods alleged to be damaged or deteriorated are a device used by some to avoid the statute. The California type law permits gifts, concessions, and combination sales in connection with price-maintained commodities, but the Model Act prohibits these devices, which are frequently used in avoidance of the law. The widespread use of trading stamps in recent years has raised many issues of interpretation and enforcement of the fair trade laws. Does the giving of stamps with goods sold at a fair trade price constitute a sale at less than the fair trade price? Most, though not all, courts have answered in the negative. A few courts have shown reasonable consistency, having upheld the fair trade laws on the basis of the manufacturer's property rights, in saying that trading stamps appeared to be no threat to the reputation or value of a trade-mark or a brand name.[59]

Enforcement of the fair trade laws takes several different forms. The statutes provide for suits by persons damaged by violation, but much of the enforcement is informal. Pressure is brought on manufacturers and distributors by retailers and retailers' associations to use fair trade contracts and to enforce them when they are violated. A severe depression or even a recession might very well create a demand for some sort of public enforcement. The McGuire Act may have made violations "unfair methods of competition" under the Federal Trade Commission Act.

EFFECTS OF THE FAIR TRADE LAWS.   Feelings sometimes run very high between the supporters of the fair trade laws and those who oppose them. Both groups correctly present evidence of effects of the laws which substantiate one view or the other. The supporters of the laws claim that cut-throat price-cutting, "bait," and loss-leader selling have been reduced, whereas the opponents allege that price competition is what has been reduced or eliminated, and the cut-throat activities have simply been shifted to other devices, such as trade-ins and advertising. The opposing group claims that prices are held artificially high under the fair trade laws and that sales promotion has taken the place of price competition. Supporters state that manufacturers' property interests in brand and trade names are protected and that the power of the

---

[59] For example: *Ramo* v. *Excel Pharmacy, Inc.,* 186 N.Y.S. 2d 548 (S.Ct.N.Y. 1959).

chains to drive out the independent merchant has been reduced. One of the strongest arguments which has been made against the fair trade laws is that the evils those laws purport to deal with can be dealt with much more effectively by other legislation that does not sanction price-fixing. The Attorney General's Report concluded that where "fair trade" is used "as a device for relieving distributors from the rigors of price competition" it "is at odds with the most elementary principles of a dynamic free enterprise system." The report also stated that the Committee regarded federal statutory exemption of fair trade pricing as "an unwarranted compromise of the basic tenets of National antitrust policy," and recommended that both the Miller-Tydings amendment to the Sherman Act and the McGuire Act be repealed.

To some degree, all of these statements are true. There are definitely arguments on both sides. The real difference of opinion is not on the effects of the fair trade laws but on basic competitive philosophy. If one's philosophy is aimed at the protection of competition in order that its free operation may bring about the desirable results claimed for it, then the fair trade laws appear to run contrary; but if one is interested in reducing some of the effects of competition in order to protect competitors, the laws are consistent with that philosophy. Neither view is totally right or wrong, but it should be noted that basically the views are incompatible. A visitor from a small planet examining the statute books today would have a great deal of trouble in determining which philosophy is being followed. Some statutes are founded on one view; whereas other statutes have a different premise. A reappraisal of our philosophies may well be in order.

The fair trade laws have, without partisan argument, encouraged private branding by the chains, which have thus avoided any real loss of general competitive position although their competitive position in nationally branded goods has been weakened. Retailers and wholesalers in some fields have lost control over their profit margins because the producer is the one generally authorized to fix the resale prices. The fair trade laws work a hardship on some small manufacturers and especially on new manufacturers attempting to enter a field where the products are widely "fair traded." Retailers and wholesalers may refuse to handle the product unless there is resale price maintenance, and if there is price maintenance at a level comparable with that of the established competitors, the new firm may find it difficult to build up its market. It must be pointed out that only about 10 per cent of the total volume of retail trade comes under the fair trade laws at present, and resale price maintenance has never invaded to any great extent the foodstuffs markets. The scope of the laws, as presently drawn, could be somewhat extended, and the basic philosophy could be extended very widely. For this reason, a reconsideration of the underlying theories on which our economic laws are to be founded may be justified. It will, of course, be difficult to achieve any sort of unanimity on a basic philosophy. One's philosophy is likely to be influenced by one's own interests, and it is obvious that all parties concerned, manufacturer, wholesaler, and consumer, do not have the same interests.

4. MISCELLANEOUS BUSINESS PRACTICES

A. Exclusive Dealing and Tying Arrangements

(1)

CASE. You are assistant to the president of the Gadget Production Company. For many years the company has required the independent retail gadget dealers who buy its products for resale to consumers to agree not to handle the products of any of Gadget Company's competitors. The president has called you into his office one Monday morning and asked you to do a little research on a problem that has been bothering him. It seems that at a cocktail party on Saturday he met an officer of the Standard Oil Company of California who, during the course of their conversation, told the Gadget president that Standard had once used similar arrangements with its retail gasoline dealers but that the Supreme Court had found them to be illegal, and Standard had been forced to give them up. What kind of data would you collect, and what would you put in your memorandum to the president?

(2)

CASE. In Case (1) above, the president also has asked you to look into the legality of the following proposal. While sales of most of Gadget Company's products have been lagging during the last quarter, the sales of one new gadget, on which the company holds a patent, have been larger than on any other single product since the company's formation 50 years ago and promise to become even larger. One of the company officers has suggested to the president that it might be a good idea to require the dealers and wholesalers who want to purchase the new gadget to purchase also two or three of the gadgets whose sales are not going very well. The president feels that the proposal has certain obvious attractions, but wants to get your views on the matter.

IN GENERAL. The phrase *exclusive dealing* describes the situation where a retailer agrees to refrain from dealing in the goods of a competitor of a manufacturer in consideration for the retailer being supplied with the manufacturer's products. Where carried too far, such arrangements not only could cut off competitors' access to consuming markets, but also deprive the consumer of a free choice from a variety of competing goods. It should not be confused with *exclusive representation,* which denotes an agreement whereby a manufacturer, in consideration of his products being carried by the merchant, promises to refrain from selling his products through competing merchants.

Under exclusive dealing contracts, a number of dealers in any particular area may be selling the manufacturer's product, but none of them would be handling the products of any competitor of the manufacturer. Under a policy of exclusive representation, only one dealer would be selling the product of the manufacturer in any particular area, but this dealer may also be handling the products of competitors of the manufacturer. It is not unusual to find the two combined. Our primary concern here is with "exclusive dealing." An arrangement closely associated with exclusive dealerships and included within the language of the Clayton Act is the *requirements contract,* whereby a buyer agrees to buy all of his requirements of a certain product from the seller.

The phrase *tying or tying arrangement* refers to the situation where a seller or lessor imposes as a condition of his sale or lease of a particular product to a buyer or lessee an agreement by the buyer or lessee to purchase or lease other products from the seller or lessor. It may also be an agreement that the buyer or lessee will not use the products of a competitor of the seller or lessor. Although tying is sometimes used in close association with "exclusive dealing," the two devices will be discussed separately here. The element which both practices have in common, however, is the exclusion of rival sellers, either by the terms of the arrangement or through its effects. Another closely related practice is *full line forcing,* whereby a dealer is required to handle the full lines of a manufacturer in order to obtain the items the dealer really wants.

Both exclusive dealing contracts and tying arrangements were valid at common law unless "effecting, or forming part of a plan to effect, a monopoly."[60] They were generally upheld under state antitrust legislation, except where the statutes expressly prohibited them, and received similar treatment under the Sherman Act. Section 3 of the Clayton Act made these devices unlawful where the effect "may be to substantially lessen competition or tend to create a monopoly in any line of commerce." It is primarily the legality of these devices under Section 3 that will be considered below. It is interesting to note that the qualifying phrase beginning with "where the effect . . . may be" was originally omitted from the House Bill, apparently with the intent to prohibit absolutely the use of the devices of exclusive dealing and tying. The devices have also been treated as "unfair methods of competition" under Section 5 of the Federal Trade Commission Act.

The economic effects and desirability of these practices have been investigated in some detail, and it is obvious from the results of the investigations that the economic factors should be of major importance in determining the legality of exclusive dealing and tying. Among the important economic factors are these: 1, the proportion of the business done by dealers participating in these arrangements; 2, the status within the industry of the supplier using these arrangements and the degree of competition within that industry;

---

[60] 2 Restatement, Contracts, Section 516.

3, the extent to which other suppliers are using the device; 4, the duration of the arrangement, and the rapidity of product and price changes within the industry; 5, the likelihood that other suppliers may be able to establish their own distribution outlets, or get new, independent dealers to handle their products; 6, the effect of the arrangement in reducing the costs of the supplier using it; 7, its effects on bringing additional dealers into the market; 8, the extent to which the arrangement significantly reduces dealer cost when accompanied by a requirements contract; 9, the extent to which an absolute prohibition of exclusive dealing would tend to lead to vertical integration in the industry. A consideration of the economic factors leads one to the conclusion that tying can satisfy few of the tests, and will be of benefit, in most cases, only to the supplier using it.

EXCLUSIVE DEALING. As the economic factors set forth above suggest, exclusive dealing has its desirable as well as its undesirable characteristics. The courts do not seem to have been much influenced by the kind of tests listed in the paragraph above. For many years, however, the courts did use a test phrased in terms of whether the defendant had a dominant position in his industry, a test not unlike several mentioned above. Where a manufacturer, for example, had achieved a dominant position and maintained it or sought to maintain or extend it through the use of exclusive dealing arrangements, the arrangements were usually held to be violations of Section 3. In *Standard Fashion Co.* v. *Magrane-Houston Co.*,[61] an exclusive dealing contract was held to be illegal where a supplier of dress patterns controlled 40 per cent of the 52,000 pattern outlets in the United States and had brought whole towns and areas into his exclusive dealing arrangements. In *Pearsall Butter Co.* v. *Federal Trade Commission*,[62] the exclusive dealing contracts of the manufacturer were upheld where he did only 1 per cent of the business in his particular industry. Section 3 of the Clayton Act has been held not to apply where the exclusive dealing contract exists between a manufacturer or supplier and dealers who are his agents.[63] On agency doctrines alone, it is clear that the principal may require his agents to handle only the products of the principal, but some doubt is cast on the result if a simple consignment arrangement is used by a dominant manufacturer to force dealer-consignees to give up competing lines. The apparent loophole here has not been widely taken advantage of, largely because the agency or consignment device is not suitable to all industries.

In establishing the criteria for violations of Section 3, the courts must look primarily at the phrase "may be substantially to lessen competition." The conclusions of the courts with regard to the meaning of this language where used in other portions of the Clayton Act are useful but not binding with

---

[61] 258 U.S. 346 (1922).

[62] 292 F. 720 (7th Cir. 1923).

[63] *Federal Trade Commission* v. *Curtis Publishing Co.,* 260 U.S. 568 (1923).

regard to the meaning when used in Section 3. The most important problems of interpretation have to do with the words "may be" and "substantially." While other views have been expressed and even followed, the courts are now in general agreement that "may be" was intended to prohibit arrangements which involve a *reasonable probability* that competition will be lessened or that an actual tendency toward monopoly will be created, and not intended to prohibit a mere "possibility" of the described consequences.

"Substantially" presents more difficult problems and a much less clear picture. Although originally approached in terms of dominant position in an industry or control of a market, an approach which makes possible the recognition of sound business reasons for using exclusive dealing contracts, the Supreme Court did not use that approach for many years, and almost no exclusive dealing arrangements survived the scrutiny of the courts or the Federal Trade Commission during that period. The high point of this era of judicial interpretation came in the *Standard Stations* case in 1949,[64] when, in a puzzling opinion, the Supreme Court upheld a principle laid down in the District Court to the effect that Section 3 is violated if a substantial *amount* of trade is *affected* by the arrangements. The Court further confounded its observers by expressing the fear that it was not qualified to conduct an economic inquiry to determine the probable effect of an exclusive dealing agreement on competition. There were several ways of viewing this decision, but sequel decisions, for a time, were consistent with the idea that the arrangements were to be tested only by the volume of sales affected. This view was referred to as "quantitative substantiality" and was in sharp contrast with the Supreme Court's own insistence on a factual showing of probable anticompetitive effects in proceedings under Section 7 of the Clayton Act.[65]

In 1961, however, the Court modified the *Standard Stations* rule and stated that consideration should be given to "the probable effect of the contract on the relevant area of effective competition, taking into account the relative strength of the parties, the proportionate volume of commerce involved . . . and the probable immediate and future effects . . . on effective competition therein." This change came about in the *Tampa Electric* case,[66] where the Court also called particular attention to the relevance of legitimate business goals and reasonable business practices in evaluating the use of certain arrangements. While the *Tampa* case involved a requirements contract and not an exclusive dealing contract, the two devices have received essentially the same treatment under Section 3. There is some evidence that the courts are a little more lenient with the requirements contract, perhaps because it relates to an ultimate user of a product rather than to a dealer who will resell. This slight difference of result does not mean that there is a difference in the application of Section 3,

---

[64] *Standard Oil Co. of California* v. *United States,* 337 U.S. 293 (1949).

[65] *United States* v. *E. I. du Pont de Nemours & Co.,* 353 U.S. 586 (1957).

[66] *Tampa Electric Co.* v. *Nashville Coal Co.,* 365 U.S. 320 (1961).

but rather that there is usually a different kind of business justification for the requirements contract than there is for the exclusive dealing arrangement. In fact, the former is probably just a special case of the latter.

TYING. The original approach to tying arrangements was almost the same as to exclusive dealing, i.e., in terms of dominant position. Virtually all of the tying contracts that have come before the courts have been held illegal on the ground that the contracts were being used to maintain or to extend dominant positions already attained. There seems to have been no realization for many years that the tying contract, unlike the exclusive dealing contract, is very unlikely to be used except by a manufacturer or supplier who has already achieved some sort of monopoly or dominant position either through a patent or through market control. Tying agreements, in other words, serve hardly any purpose beyond the suppression of competition, whereas exclusive dealing and requirements contracts are often of economic advantage to buyers and to the public as well as to the seller.

Most of the cases involving tying arrangements concerned defendants who had market control ranging from 62 to 95 per cent, so the cases were easily disposed of. Many of the cases also involved attempts to tie non-patented products to patented products, an activity now generally considered to be illegal *per se* under Section 1 of the Sherman Act. The nine economic factors discussed at the beginning of this section on exclusive dealing and tying cannot be applied very well to tying contracts, except to disclose that the economic benefits flowing from the use of these devices flow only to the seller and depend upon a suppression of competition for their attractiveness. Consequently, a quantitative substantiality test set up for tying arrangements in *International Salt Co.* v. *United States*[67] seems compatible with economic and business realities and does not raise the same issues that were raised by *Standard Stations*. Under very special circumstances, legitimate business needs have been accepted to protect a tying arrangement from being found illegal,[68] but, for general purposes, it must be assumed that tie-in sales are *per se* illegal and should be carefully avoided.

B. Advertising and Other Instruments of Demand Creation

IN GENERAL. The many ways in which the unwary customer is fooled by the dishonest advertiser or seller are well known today as a result of the exposures by the Federal Trade Commission, the Food and Drug Administration, consumer groups of many kinds, Better Business Bureaus, and many

---

[67] 332 U.S. 392 (1947).

[68] *United States* v. *Jerrold Electronics Corp.*, 187 F. Supp. 545 (E.D. Pa., 1960), *affirmed per curiam,* 365 U.S. 567 (1961) (tying held reasonable during developmental phase of highly sensitive electronic equipment).

private investigators. There is now a rather substantial body of literature devoted to the collection and analysis of the facts of false and misleading advertising, misbranding, adulteration of food and drugs, and of the many other practices coming within this general area. The field is a huge one, and only small portions of it will be discussed here, where our primary concern will be with the remedies available to the defrauded customer, remedies available to the competitor of a firm employing false and misleading practices in order to attract customers, and with legislative and administrative efforts to deal with the problem. It will be seen that the common law provides neither adequate remedies nor practical solutions, and that the administrative bodies, under their enabling legislation, have gained ground only in certain areas.

COMMON LAW. False and misleading advertising and related practices are actionable at common law under certain narrowly defined conditions required for the tort of deceit, for breach of express warranty, and for criminal liability, as for obtaining money under false pretenses. The latter sanction and its close relative, forbidding the use of the mails, have been used only against flagrant frauds, and are by nature applicable only to misrepresentations of fact. A clever advertiser need have no worry about these problems. Remedies in tort or warranty are not much more effective.

Remedies of the purchaser. The common law action of deceit or fraud is the principal remedy of a defrauded purchaser, but it is not a very satisfactory approach to the problem. The purchaser, in order to make his case, must show: 1, that the advertisement contained a misrepresentation of a material fact, not just an opinion, and not just a seller's puff or glowing exaggeration; 2, that the advertiser knew that the representation was false; 3, that the advertiser intended the reader of the advertisement to rely on the representation; 4, that the purchaser did rely on it; 5, that the purchaser was harmed. It is obvious that if the prevention of false and misleading advertising depended upon this tort action for enforcement, there would be little effect on advertising practices.

Any statement of fact or any promise in connection with the goods advertised, the natural tendency of which is to induce the buyer to purchase, constitutes an express warranty under the law of sales, but an action for breach of warranty is still subject to the circumscription of privity, which raises serious difficulties where the product is not bought directly from the person doing the advertising and where the person injured is not the person purchasing or relying on the representation. It is clear that the traditional actions of deceit and warranty are not and have not been of much use in the campaign against false advertising and related practices.

The chief difficulty with both of these remedies is that they were developed by the courts to deal with different types of situations from those with which false advertising confronts them. They are tied down to principles that really have no application to the kind of problem we are here concerned with, such things as knowledge of falsity, which is not of the slightest importance to the customer victim, privity, reasonable reliance, and materiality of the representation. If a "reasonable man" rule is applied to the false advertising cases, there would be few limits on what the advertiser could do or say. The reason that legislative protection is necessary is that consumers are unsophisticated —they do not always act wisely or reasonably, and are lured by baseless claims, half-truths, and appeals to the emotions. The laws must be designed to protect the fool, the gullible, the weak, and the "sucker" because most of us seem to fall into one or more of these categories when it comes to advertising. Would cigarette, soap, deodorant, and pink pill advertising influence a "reasonable man?" Any protection based on fraud, in the common law sense, on reasonable actions, on materiality, and on physical injury is doomed to failure.

Remedies of the competitor. The competitor is worse off than the purchaser at common law. His only available remedies are the injunction against an unfair trade practice and an accounting for profits. Originally, when a competitor felt that another was injuring him by the use of false and misleading advertising or its related activities, he had to show damage or interference with a property right. The courts became more liberal in this regard, but there are still two basic requirements the plaintiff must meet: he must usually demonstrate, first, that he has in fact lost customers, and, second, that he has lost them by a means which the law forbids. Both of these impose difficult burdens of proof on the plaintiff and miss the important fact that the consumer may also be injured.

LEGISLATION. Because of the shortcomings of the common law, some states and the federal government have enacted statutes seeking to reduce or prevent false advertising. Most of the state laws simply augment the availability of the traditional remedies, but a few state statutes and the Federal Trade Commission Act provide for administrative regulation of false advertising as one of the many varieties of unfair competition. For a time after the passage of the Federal Trade Commission Act, the key phrase "unfair methods of competition," now "unfair methods of competition . . . and unfair or deceptive acts or practices," was restricted to those practices already condemned by the common law; thus, it was not a very useful tool in seeking to prevent false and misleading advertising. The phrase is now interpreted to include many practices that were not illegal at common law. The Wheeler-Lea amendment to the FTC Act greatly increased the protection from the false advertising of foods, drugs, devices for the diagnosis and treatment of disease, and cosmetics, in which fields there is the greatest danger of physical harm. Labeling and packaging acts of recent years require correct and informative labeling and packaging of certain products.[69]

The power of the Federal Trade Commission and other agencies under

---

[69] For example: Wool Products Labeling Act 1939, 15 U.S.C.A. 68; Fur Products Labeling Act 1951, 15 U.S.C.A. 69; Textile Fiber Products Identification Act 1958, 15 U.S.C.A. 70; Fair Packaging and Labeling Act 1966, 15 U.S.C.A. 1451.

these statutes is largely preventive and not punitive. The Commission may issue cease and desist orders and may enforce these orders in the courts, but the primary purpose of the statutes is to protect the public and not to punish the offender. Under the FTC Act, the Federal Trade Commission has issued orders in a host of situations ranging from "Seals of Approval," representations that unsafe products were safe, and deceptions relating to quality, quantity, value, or condition of product to misleading or out-of-context endorsements or testimonials. The law with regard to food, drugs, cosmetics, and the like is much stricter than with regard to other products or services, but it is still not as stringent as it might be because only advertisements that are misleading in a "material respect" are included. Although a certain amount of puffing may do no harm in some fields, it is felt by many that where food, drugs, and therapeutic devices are concerned, an uncompromising standard of truth is not too much to require. There are those who would impose similar standards on all advertising.

The Pure Food and Drug Acts approach a similar problem in a similar fashion by prohibiting the shipment in interstate commerce of misbranded or adulterated drugs, food, cosmetics, and therapeutic devices. Labels of such items are required to contain the name and address of the manufacturer, the quantity in the container, the nature and amount of coloring matter, the presence of habit-forming or dangerous elements, and much other information.

C. Appropriation of Competitor's Trade Values

IN GENERAL. An important problem to any businessman is the extent of the protection afforded by the courts to ideas, to valuable trade information, such as trade secrets and customers lists, to styles and designs, and to other results of ingenuity and effort. The possible situations are infinite in number, and there is no convenient method of classification and certainly no general rule or formula which can be applied over a wide area of this field. The best that can be done in the short space available is to discuss briefly some of the more important problems and principles. It is important to note at the outset that common law remedies have long been available for this sort of unfair competition, and that statutory law has never achieved the importance in this area that it has achieved elsewhere. The Federal Trade Commission has included a few of these practices under Section 5 of the Trade Commission Act, and could probably include a great many more if the occasion arose or if this area suddenly came to be of major interest to the Commission. As it is, most of the law in this area is state law, and most of that is non-statutory.

TRADE SECRETS AND CUSTOMERS LISTS. Certain business information, devices, or processes that are not patented or copyrighted are kept as *trade secrets* of the user. It is sometimes said that the user has a property right in these secrets and that this property right is subject to protection. It is also said that the protection comes as a sort of reward for ingenuity and inventiveness as under a patent or copyright. Neither of these views is supportable, and the real explanation for the protection sometimes afforded is the general principle that intentionally inflicted harm is actionable unless it is privileged. The modern view is that, in the absence of copyright or patent, the ideas, devices, and information may be copied provided that it is done by proper means. Where they are kept secret by the user and are obtained improperly, a tort is committed. The protection is based not on the violation of property rights but on the intentional harm resulting from a breach of confidence or an induced breach of confidence. The desirability of competition has never been thought sufficient to justify extending it to types of confidential business information which are generally considered to be deserving of protection as against a user who has not independently arrived at the information.

Not all items of information are deemed worthy of such protection, and not all items deemed worthy of protection are entitled to protection against all types of acquisition. Items qualifying for some protection are usually called *trade secrets*. The courts have treated a wide variety of manufacturing and marketing procedures as trade secrets, including customers lists, blue prints, ingredients, secret pricing lists, and raw material sources. Unfortunately, the variety in the procedures protected is exceeded by the variety of judicial approaches to the problem and by the variety of grounds on which protection has been afforded or refused. Certain principles can be gleaned from the cases, however, and these principles are of use in most situations.

One element usually made a prerequisite to a finding that a particular piece of business information is a trade secret is that of "secrecy." A corollary of the requirement of secrecy is the lack of abandonment of the secrecy. The fact that information was once secret will not afford protection where that information has become widely known or where, even though not a matter of general knowledge, the possessor of the secret has manifested an intention to abandon the secret. Abandonment is largely a matter of intent, and where intent to abandon can be shown, the degree of secrecy is usually unimportant. Where there is no intent to abandon, the issue is determined by the amount of secrecy still remaining. In a few cases, applications for a patent are said to constitute abandonment or a destruction of the secrecy, but the better view is that the mere application, because it is processed in secret by the Patent Office, is not a public disclosure nor a manifestation of an intention to abandon. The intention would seem to be quite the contrary.

Some amount of secrecy is necessary in order to qualify information as a trade secret, but limited disclosure need not be the equivalent of general public knowledge. The degree of secrecy necessary for protection calls into consideration these four factors: 1, the measures taken to guard the secrecy; 2, the extent to which the information is known outside the business; 3, how readily the information can be acquired by others using only proper methods;

and 4, how extensively the information is known to persons who, because of a confidential or contractual relation with the possessor, are obligated not to disclose.

The following four factors, though not particularly relevant to the issue of secrecy, have been given weight by the courts in determining whether information is entitled to protection: 1, whether the information is of some competitive advantage to the possessor; 2, the value of the information; 3, the degree to which the conduct of the new user of the information violates general business ethics; and 4, the cost of development. No matter how ingenious, how costly, or how valuable, some business ideas cannot be protected because they have to be made public in order to be used, but even here, however, protection has been afforded, as where news gathered by a wire service has been protected until the commercial value of the news has been dissipated. It should be noted that the mere sale of a product resulting from a secret does not necessarily reveal the secret, and the information may still be entitled to protection.

Nature of protection. A preliminary issue in this area is: Against whom will a trade secret be protected? Section 757 of the Torts Restatement lays down the general principles:

> One who discloses or uses another's trade secret, without a privilege to do so, is liable to the other if (a) he discovered the secret by improper means, or (b) his disclosure or use constitutes a breach of confidence reposed in him by the other in disclosing the secret to him, or (c) he learned the secret from a third person with notice of the facts that it was a secret and that the third person discovered it by improper means or that the third person's disclosure of it was otherwise a breach of his duty to the other, or (d) he learned the secret with notice of the facts that it was a secret and that its disclosure was made to him by mistake.

It is clear that falling into these categories of persons against whom trade secrets may be protected are fiduciaries and contracting parties, shareholders and directors, parties agreeing not to reveal, purchasers, and even parties in no legal relation to the possessor of the secret. Difficult problems arise in all of these areas.

One of the most difficult and least well-understood situations occurs where the purpose of developing a trade secret is not the use of the secret but its sale to someone who will use it. The problem is, of course, that both the seller and the purchaser run risks in this area, and neither can be fully protected except at the expense of the other. It is sometimes suggested that an obligation should be put on the buyer either to buy the idea or not to reveal or use it. This approach, however, would seem to shift the balance too far in the seller's favor and to encourage the submission of unsolicited ideas that are easy to discover. Buyers might well be handicapped in their own research activities by such a rule, and might be subjected to many false claims. From the seller's point of view, it is difficult to know how best to market an idea. It has been suggested that the following formula is a useful one:

> a. Negotiate with the party authorized to contract in behalf of the firm. b. Express an unequivocal offer to sell. c. If possible, fix a sales price. d. Include a warning that the idea is being submitted in strict confidence to them alone; that if they do not desire to utilize it, it should not be released to others; that a violation of your property right therein will subject the violator to liability. e. Suggest various practical applications or uses for the idea but state that any utilization of the basic idea will be an acceptance of the offer. f. Keep the offer open. g. Retain proof of the submission of the idea.[70]

Under the modern approach of wrongful taking, protection of trade secrets, where they have been innocently acquired, cannot be very extensive. However, liability on the user is sometimes imposed after the user learns of the secrecy and of the mistake through which he acquired the secret information. Section 758 of the Torts Restatement provides that:

> One who learns another's trade secret from a third person without notice that it is secret and that the third person's disclosure is a breach of his duty to the other, or who learns the secret through a mistake without notice of the secrecy and the mistake, (a) is not liable to the other for a disclosure or use of the secret prior to receipt of such notice, and (b) is liable to the other for a disclosure or use of the secret after the receipt of such notice, unless prior thereto he has in good faith paid value for the secret or has so changed his position that to subject him to liability would be inequitable.

In addition to the parties against whom protection will be afforded, there is the question of what kind of protection is available. The remedies may include the following: 1, an injunction against wrongful use or disclosure; 2, an order for the return of copies of the secret; 3, destruction of the infringing product; 4, an accounting for profits; and 5, damages. Under the rule of mitigation of damages, losses will usually not be compensated for if they could have been averted by patenting the trade secret within the one year period after disclosure, which is allowed by the patent laws. This does not refer to any requirement to patent before disclosure. There are good reasons why the possessor of a secret might prefer to keep it as such rather than to patent it, and the law will not compel him to patent. Although a patent offers greater safety, the protection is only for seventeen years, and the possessors of a trade secret may prefer the opportunity to keep the secret indefinitely. The decision on whether to patent is an important one, and many pertinent factors must be considered. Keeping a secret may require extensive security measures. It is much more difficult to show that information is secret than it is to show that a patent is valid. The problem is further complicated where a competitor

---

[70] Note, 31 Cornell L.Q. 382 (1946).

acquires the secret and patents it for himself. Trade secrets are not readily saleable, and it is difficult to license their use to others without running serious risks of public disclosure. A patent, on the other hand, presupposes disclosure, and makes available information others may make use of in non-infringing ways and for improvement patents, but the patent procedure is expensive and time-consuming.

Customers lists are treated very much the same as other types of trade secrets, but, along with some other kinds of information, they present a few special problems because they are acquired by employees in the course of employment, and most of the difficulties arise as the result of use by former employees either for themselves or for competitors of the original possessor. Depending upon the trade, customers lists may range in importance: from little or no value to the most important of all the business assets; from information which is easy for anybody to acquire to information which required years of experience, money, and effort to accumulate; and from simple lists of names to detailed information on customers' requirements and methods of doing business. Some courts have protected all lists; whereas others have protected almost none. Some courts protect only retail customers lists, and other courts protect only those lists that are not easily duplicated by others. A few courts protect only written lists.

An employee, in the absence of express agreement, is under no duty not to compete with his former employer when he leaves his employ, but is under some duty not to use or disclose to third persons confidential information acquired while there employed. An employee who takes a copy of a secret customers list or makes his own copy and then uses the information in competition with his former employer is in a weaker defensive position than the employee who simply remembers the information. An employee who intentionally memorizes a list for use when he leaves should be no better off than the copier. A milk-route driver who remembers the customers on his own route usually may advise these customers of his new activities and even solicit their business, but where the employee has taken a list of customers on other routes or has gone out of his way to memorize those lists, there is likely to be a remedy for the former employer against him.

In California and New York, where rather elaborate rules have been evolved in connection with the use of customer lists, the line is frequently drawn on the basis of violation of duties while an employee and on whether the information gives the user a real competitive advantage. It can be said with certainty that the rules are not uniform. The use of an express contract with the employee is the best protection for the employer, where such contracts are valid, but must, of course, stay within the bounds of reasonable restraints of trade as discussed in a previous section. In a few states, statutes have entered the picture.

COMMERCIAL BRIBERY. Trade secrets were broadly enough defined above to include most of the areas usually dealt with in connection with the appropriation of a competitors' trade values, but there are a few areas outside the scope of "trade secret." *Commercial bribery,* now commonly called "payola," is the practice of sellers of secretly paying money or making gifts to employees or agents to induce them to promote purchases or use by their own employers of the goods and services of the sellers who offer the secret inducements. This definition makes it clear that a line should be drawn between innocent business courtesies and the secret and corrupting practice of bribery, but the line is sometimes hard to draw. There is little case law in the area. Most common law actions approach from the direction of an agent's violation of duties to his principal or as an interference with the agency relation. The Federal Trade Commission attacks the problem as an unfair method of competition. The public policy aspects of commercial bribery still remain to be clarified, and the principal difficulty is the widespread apathy among businessmen. As long as even the grosser types of commercial bribery are looked upon simply as methods of "oiling the wheels of commerce," it is unlikely that any clear-cut public policy will emerge.

STYLE AND DESIGN PIRACY. Styles and designs are extremely difficult to protect once they are put on the market. Little protection is afforded by the design patent statutes, and although many efforts have been made to improve the protection, little improvement has resulted. Some attempts at self-protection have been stricken down by the courts as boycotts and concerted refusals to deal.

D. Misrepresentation of Competitor's Products

IN GENERAL. The misrepresentation or disparagement of a competitor's product, sometimes called *trade libel,* is one of the numerous trade practices tending to injure competitors rather than the consuming public. This area has been reasonably adequately covered by the common law, and few statutes are found in connection with these or related issues. Disparagement activities have been the scene of cease and desist orders and complaints by the Federal Trade Commission.

In several important respects, the liability for disparaging product or property differs from that for defaming the personal reputation of another as follows:

1. In defamation, truth is a defense required to be proved by the defendant, but in disparagement the person whose ownership in goods or the quality of whose goods has been attacked must prove that the disparaging statement of fact is untrue or that the disparaging expression of opinion is incorrect.

2. In defamation, the defendant who seeks protection in a conditional privilege must prove the existence of the facts creating privilege; whereas in disparagement, the absence of privilege must be proved by the person who seeks to recover for financial loss caused by the disparagement.

3. In defamation, the publication of all libelous communications and of many types of slanderous communications subjects the publisher to liability even though no pecuniary loss or other harm results therefrom, but in disparagement, the defendant is not liable unless the disparaging matter has caused financial loss.

4. One of the most important purposes for which liability for the publication of matter derogatory to another's personal reputation is imposed is to enable the person defamed to force his accuser into open court so that the accusation, if untrue, may be branded as false by the verdict of the jury. The action for disparagement has no such purpose, and cannot be used merely to vindicate one's title to, or the quality of, one's possessions. Where, however, the disparaging statements also reflect on the business honesty or competence of the plaintiff, he may sue for defamation and not for disparagement. The basic element of damage for disparagement is the loss or impairment of ability to sell, as measured by the difference between the normal price and the depressed price or by the loss of business.

Injunctive relief is to some extent available for disparagement, but most courts only grant this equitable relief when the person making the disparaging statements acts in bad faith and where property rights are injured or threatened. There is, however, some indication of a trend toward handling misrepresentations of a competitor's goods as unfair competition, for which injunctive relief is readily available.

DEFENSES. Since untruth is an element in the plaintiff's cause of action, truth is not a defense in the same sense it is in defamation cases. It is, of course, a defense, but if the plaintiff fails to sustain the burden of proving an untruth, there is no burden on the defendant to prove the truth.

The important defense is that of the *conditional privilege* of a business competitor. A competitor may make a favorable comparison of his own goods with those of the plaintiff. Because this comparison, even if it involves intentional exaggerations and is not honestly believed by the person making the comparison, is an accepted practice, it is not actionable as long as it does not contain particular false statements of fact or, as Section 649 of the Torts Restatement puts it, "assertions of specific unfavorable facts." Conditional privileges are defeated by showing malice or lack of good faith.

There is also a recognized privilege where a person is interested in another person's protection, as, for example, a doctor, a member of the family, or any other person interested, who warns of danger of food or drugs thought to be impure. This privilege has been extended to research organizations on the theory that, though disinterested in a personal sense, these organizations are entitled to the privilege when warning about impure food and drugs. Truth of the statements is the greatest protection for the research organizations in most cases.

E. Interference with Trade Relations

IN GENERAL. There are many ways in which attacks may be made upon another's business relations: 1, physical violence, intimidation, coercion, and molestation of customers, none of which will be considered here; 2, disparagement of product or title, which has already been discussed; 3, commercial boycotts and interference with contractual relations, both of which will be examined in this section. Actually, almost all of the unfair trade practices and methods of competition could be brought under the heading of interference with trade relations, but, traditionally, the practices just mentioned are the ones considered under that label. As a whole, this is an area in which statutory law has not played a very important part. The Federal Trade Commission and the Attorney General have played important parts in the field of commercial boycotts, but they have seldom considered the problems of interference with contractual relations.

INDUCING BREACH OF CONTRACT.   The law in this area has been through several metamorphoses, and cannot yet be said to be settled. The original common law rule was that an inducement of the breach of an existing contractual relation is wrongful only when accomplished by such illegal means as violence, intimidation, or fraud. The Torts Restatement and some courts now go so far as to say that there is a general duty not to interfere purposely with another's reasonable expectancies of trade with third persons, whether or not the expectancies are secured by contract and whether or not the means used are themselves illegal.

The first break in the old common law rule came in 1853 when the Court of Queen's Bench decided the case of *Lumley* v. *Gye*.[71] In that case, an opera singer who had agreed to sing exclusively for the plaintiff was persuaded by the defendant, who knew of the contract with the plaintiff, to refuse to perform the contract. The court held that an action would lie for wilfully inducing the breach of contract. There has long been a conflict as to the extent of the decision in this case. In some jurisdictions, it is confined to its facts and only applies to the deliberate hiring away of employees or agents of a competitor. In other jurisdictions, the doctrine of the case has been extended to include the intentional inducement of the breach of any express contract. Some jurisdictions have repudiated it entirely and have fallen back on the older common law rule requiring illegal means. Even in those jurisdictions following the case, some uncertainty remains regarding the circumstances constituting adequate excuse or justification for interference with contractual relations. Vindictiveness or gratification of spite is not enough to justify interference, and the advancement of one's own trade interests is usually not enough by itself. The trend seems to be toward stricter liability in this area. The emphasis has gradually shifted through the years from malice and bad faith as criteria of liability to intentional interference, even in good faith.

If the protection has been extended to situations where contractual relations exist, problems immediately arise as to which interferences are privileged. It is obvious that the protection is not intended to extend to the ordinary rivalry

---

[71] Ellis & Blackburn 216, 118 Eng. Rep. 749 (1853).

of competitors for prospective customers. The inducement may also be privileged where there is a present, existing economic interest to protect, such as prior contract of his own or a financial interest in the affairs of the person persuaded. There may be privileges also to protect the public interest, as to remove a danger to public health or morals. Most of these privileges apply whether or not there is an existing contractual relation. Where there are no contractual relations, the interference is usually privileged unless there is an inducement of a refusal to do business. Prospective personal advantage is usually sufficient where there is no existing contract, but will not be enough for a privilege where a contract exists. (See discussion under "Inducement of Others Not to Deal" in next section.)

It has never been contended that there is any unfairness in offering to sell one's products, in the ordinary course of trade, to everyone who may deal in or consume such products, even though each particular transaction completed may tend to curtail by so much the potential demand for a competitor's goods. The Federal Trade Commission seems to take the approach that even where a private right of action may exist for interference, as it could in some states even within the terms of the sentence preceding, that is not enough by itself to constitute the interference an "unfair method of competition" and bring it under the jurisdiction of the Commission. In other words, the jurisdiction of the Commission is not co-extensive with the grounds for a private right of action. Bad faith or primary purpose of causing a loss to a competitor is probably necessary for Commission action. It can be argued, of course, that the existence of a common law action is enough to make the practice unfair competition.

TRADE BOYCOTT.   The term *boycott* in its broader and more general sense means an individual or concerted refusal by any person or persons to deal, or inducement of others not to deal, with a merchant. In the sense in which the term is to be used here, boycott will apply only to refusals or inducements by persons who are themselves merchants; it will not extend to labor boycotts and related problems. Even though the field has been narrowed, there is still a wide variety of situations covered by the term "boycott." There are individual refusals and concerted refusals and inducements of others to refuse to deal. There are boycotts in bargaining, and boycotts in competition. Some boycotts are treated as unfair competition in the tort field, but others are dealt with as restraints of trade. Not all of the permutations and combinations will be considered here, but the important problems will be raised and discussed.

Individual refusal to deal.   As was discussed briefly in the portion of this chapter devoted to resale price maintenance, there is no public policy against an individual refusal to deal, which is really not a boycott in any legal sense. A seller may pick his own customers, and no one violates the law who refuses to deal with a particular customer. There are, of course, exceptions under the Civil Rights Acts and in those trades that are strongly affected with a public interest, as, for example, the utilities, which do not have a broad right to refuse service to prospective customers. A special exception was created by the Automobile Dealers Franchise Act of 1956,[72] which establishes a federal cause of action for automobile dealers who have suffered injury as a result of the unwarranted termination of their franchises by the manufacturer. Other exceptions to the general rule are found where the refusal to deal is part of a larger plan or scheme to achieve monopoly or where the refusal to deal is accompanied by spying, blacklists, or persuasion of wholesalers and retailers to report to a manufacturer or distributor information on which a refusal to deal may be based. In general, the fact that harm is intended has no effect on the legality of the refusal to deal.

Concerted refusal to deal. Section 765 of the Torts Restatement sets forth the law in this area with accuracy and conciseness:

> (1) Persons who cause harm to another by a concerted refusal in their business to enter into or to continue business relations with him are liable to him for that harm, even though they would not be liable for similar conduct without concert, if their concerted refusal is not justified under the circumstances. (2) In the issue of justification under the rule stated in Subsection (1), the following are important factors: (a) the objects sought to be accomplished and the interests sought to be advanced by the actors' conduct; (b) the extent of the hardship caused to the person against whom the actors' conduct is directed and his opportunities for mitigating the hardship; (c) the appropriateness of the actors' conduct as a means of advancing their interests and the availability of less harmful means to that end; (d) the relations between the actors and the person against whom the conduct is directed and their relative economic power; (e) the effects of the actors' conduct and of its objects on the social interest in business enterprise and competition.

Group boycotts to maintain traditional channels of distribution through jobbers and retailers have been, as a whole, condemned under the Sherman Act and under comparable state laws. Group boycotts to correct through self-help alleged unfair competition and trade abuses have met a mixed reception in the courts. The group boycott used to correct style and design piracy was condemned in the federal courts[73] while a similar boycott to lessen credit risks was upheld.[74] A New York court upheld a combination boycott designed to terminate ruinous competitive bidding by small, "fly by night" firms in the building materials industry.[75] The Supreme Court decisions in *Associated Press* v. *United States*,[76] and in several other cases,[77] are viewed by some authorities

---

[72] 15 U.S.C. 1221.

[73] *Fashion Originators' Guild of America* v. *Federal Trade Commission,* 312 U.S. 457 (1941).

[74] *United States* v. *Dressers' and Fur Dyers' Ass'n,* 5 F.(2d) 869 (S.D.N.Y. 1925).

[75] *Arnold* v. *Burgess,* 241 App. Div. 364, 272 N.Y.S. 534 (1934).

[76] 326 U.S. 1 (1945).

[77] *Klor's, Inc.* v. *Broadway-Hale Stores, Inc.,* 359 U.S. 207 (1959); *Northern Pacific Railway Co.* v. *United States,* 356 U.S. 1 (1958); *Kiefer-Stewart Co.* v. *Seagram & Sons,* 340 U.S. 211 (1951); *Evening News Publishing Co.* v. *Allied Newspaper Carriers of New Jersey,* 263 F.(2d) 715 (3rd Cir. 1959), cert. den. 79 S.Ct. 1449 (1959).

to be a declaration that concerted refusals to deal are illegal *per se* under Section 1 of the Sherman Act.

Inducement of others not to deal. To a large extent, this area is overlapped by the extension of the doctrine of *Lumley* v. *Gye* to cover situations where no contractual relation exists. (See the preceding section on inducing breach of contract.) Section 768 of the Torts Restatement provides: "(1) One is privileged purposely to cause a third person not to enter into or continue a business relation with a competitor of the actor if (a) the relation concerns a matter involved in the competition between the actor and the competitor, and (b) the actor does not employ improper means, and (c) the actor does not intend thereby to create or continue an illegal restraint of competition, and (d) the actor's purpose is at least in part to advance his interest in his competition with the other." There is no privilege, under the conditions stated above, for a competitor to induce a third person to commit a breach of contract with the other.

Where the person seeking to induce another not to deal with a merchant is not a competitor of the merchant, the principles applied are somewhat different. One who, without a privilege to do so, induces or purposely causes a third person not to enter into or continue a business relation with another is liable for the harm caused. In determining the existence of a privilege, the following factors are important: 1, the nature of the actor's conduct; 2, the nature of the expectancy with which his conduct interferes; 3, the relations between the parties; 4, the interest sought to be advanced by the actor; and 5, the social interests in protecting the expectancy on the one hand and the actor's freedom of action on the other. Thus, where a railroad company threatened its employees with discharge if they patronized plaintiff's place of business, the railroad could claim no privilege, and the plaintiff was allowed recovery.[78] The railroad in this case paid its employees in scrip and did not want the scrip cashed at the plaintiff's place of business. If the railroad's instructions to its employees had been confined to the cashing of scrip, a privilege might have been found, but there was clearly no privilege to forbid patronage altogether. Where a school principal or teacher induces students to stay away from plaintiff's place of business on the ground that it is not a fit place for the children to go, there is no recovery because of the privilege to establish reasonable rules for the management of the school and for the protection of the children.[79] Malicious motives have seldom been held to be important in these cases, except as a basis for exemplary damages.

F. Infringement of Trade-Marks and Trade Names

IN GENERAL. The registration of trade-marks and the common law of trade-marks and trade names are all essentially parts of the much broader

---

[78] *International & G. N. Ry. Co.* v. *Greenwood,* 2 Tex. Civ. App. 76, 21 S.W. 559 (1893).
[79] *Guethler* v. *Altman,* 26 Ind. App. 587, 60 N.E. 355 (1901).

field of unfair competition, and are properly included here in connection with the miscellaneous business practices affecting competition. The statutory law dealing with infringement has not materially changed the common law principles, but it has added to the basic common law certain rights, benefits, and remedies that were not previously available. The field is a large one, and, if this discussion were to be an exhaustive one on the subject of trade-marks and trade names, its length would considerably exceed that of the remainder of the book. The only purpose of this discussion is to describe the nature of trade-marks and trade names and to explain briefly the protection afforded to them by the common law and by the more important statutes.

The use of distinguishing marks and names in the conduct of one's business is a very old practice. The marks have been used, however, for many different purposes, and the modern concept and use of the mark did not develop until the sixteenth century. Some of the earlier marks in England were used as a means of establishing ownership in property. This use was especially common where the goods were being transported by sea, because shipwrecked and pirated goods falling into the hands of public authorities were forfeited to the King unless their ownership was clear. Some early marks were compulsory, and these marks were required by guilds or by the government in order to show their origin. In this use the mark was more of a liability than an asset. The modern concept of a mark as having a value of its own and being more than just a means of identification appeared in England in the fifteenth century, but two of the elements of the modern mark were still absent: the marks themselves were not capable of legal ownership or possession, and they were afforded no particular protection. The missing elements developed first in the cutlery trade in England, and were well established there by the sixteenth century. As long as the producer and the consumer were not widely separated, the need for a trade-mark or trade name as a symbol of goodwill was not great in most trades. With the industrial revolution, however, and the growth of national markets and advertising, the use of distinguishing marks received its greatest boost, and problems of infringement became important. The first infringement cases did not appear until the nineteenth century, and distinguishing marks and names apparently had no nation-wide asset value until the latter half of that century. Since then the cases have been very numerous, and the law has developed rapidly.

DEFINITIONS AND REQUIREMENTS. Precise definitions of those devices that qualify as trade-marks or as trade names is very difficult. For our purposes here, though, the *trade-mark,* sometimes referred to as the *technical trade-mark,* may be defined as a distinctive mark, device, name or symbol which a manufacturer or seller affixes to the goods he manufacturers or sells in order to identify the goods in the market and to vouch for their origin. The *trade name,* or *non-technical trade-mark,* is best described as any designation which is adopted and used by a person to distinguish from those of other persons the goods he manufacturers or sells, or services he renders, or a business he conducts. The trade name need not be affixed to goods. A trade name is just a word or group of words, common or uncommon, which a person uses to denominate his goods, services, or business. A trade-mark, on the other hand, must be unique either in the words or devices used or in their arrangement. The trade-mark reaches a stage of being entitled to protection when a unique device or arrangement is selected, affixed to the goods, and put into the market. The trade name becomes entitled to protection only after it has been in use for a substantial period of time and has acquired a special market significance.

Ordinary words in their ordinary sense cannot be trade-marks for the simple reason that it would be against public policy to permit the removal of an ordinary word from the public domain for the exclusive use of such word by a merchant. Thus, the word "automobile" cannot be appropriated to the exclusive use of some manufacturer of motor vehicles. Ordinary words used in an arbitrary sense, such as "Eagle" in reference to a particular brand of pencil, or words invented by the trader, may qualify as trade-marks because they are not removed from the public domain and the public is not injured when a trader is granted the exclusive use of the invented word or of the word used in the arbitrary sense only. Trade names are less subject to these limitations. The word "California" could not be a trade-mark, except, possibly, where arranged in a unique design or device, because the word is an ordinary descriptive word in common use by the public. The use of the word would be protected, however, as part of a trade name or mark, such as *California Rubber Company,* against another trader attempting to use *California Rubber Company* or the confusing similar *California Rubber Products Company.* Once the trade name comes into existence, the protection afforded it is much the same as that afforded the trade-mark.

PROTECTION OF TRADE-MARKS AGAINST INFRINGEMENT. Before one can deal with the question of protection, one must first deal with the question of what constitutes an infringement. In general, the issue is whether the resemblance between the allegedly infringing mark and the established mark is so close as to cause confusion in the minds of the public. Of course, if it turns out that the allegedly infringing mark actually has a prior claim to the particular trade-mark, the infringement may be reversed. Whichever way the infringement runs, the problem resolves itself into one of psychology. If the average buyer examined trade-marks closely, the infringement problem and the problem of psychology would be simple. There would be no infringement unless the marks were exactly or almost exactly the same. Unfortunately, the average buyer is not attentive to details; instead, he relies to a large extent on general impressions. This fact means that the test of infringement is not just one of identity but also of sufficient similarity to confuse the buying public. The test may be one of sound or appearance, of an idea conveyed, or of total impression. Note that it is not necessary to show that buyers have actually been confused or deceived or, except with regard to the remedy, that the infringing seller intended to deceive. The borderline cases require a great deal of cautious analysis and the ability of the court or a jury to project itself into the ordinary purchaser's position. Some examples of close decisions follow:

1. *Curative Soap* infringes *Cuticura,* but *Cuticle* does not infringe *Cuticura.*

2. *Rinex* infringes *Pinex.*

3. *Rexall* infringes *Rex.*

4. *Liberty Bell* infringes *Old Liberty Bell.*

5. *Nevermiss* infringes *Notamiss.*

6. *Hava* does not infringe *Uneeda.*

7. *Dixie-Cola* does not infringe *Coca-Cola.*

8. *Muffler* does not infringe *Mufflet.*

9. *Emery* does not infringe *Emerald.*

Another element that must be considered in connection with infringements is the effect of the use of same or similar marks on different types of products or in different territories. It is obvious that this factor is important in determining the existence or non-existence of confusion. The general rule is that a party has no right to protection of a trade-mark that is used in a different territory or on a different type of product unless confusion is likely to occur. The designation *Beech-Nut* as used in connection with tobacco was held not to infringe the same designation when used with baby food, candy, and chewing gum. *Tea Rose* was held not to infringe, even though used on the same type of product, where used in different parts of the country. The designation *PM* has been used at the same time to refer to milk, whiskey, and a newspaper. Use in different parts of the country is not a complete bar to infringement proceedings, however. Where the second or junior use is in an area of legitimate trade expansion for the senior user, there may be infringement, as the case may also be where there is bad faith in the junior use.

Nature of the protection. As with other types of unfair competition, a variety of remedies is available for the infringement of trade-marks. The owner of the infringed mark may sue for damages. Actual damages to business and to reputation must be proved, but the court may award additional amounts in the form of punitive damages where the infringer acted wilfully and maliciously. Under the Federal Trade-Mark Acts, a court may award triple damages for trade-mark infringement. The action for damages arose out of the common law action for false representation, which required a showing of fraudulent intent on the part of the defendant. Although the difference between an ordinary fraud and a trade-mark infringement is substantial, many courts still require as a prerequisite to recovery of damages a showing of fraudulent intent.

It must be pointed out, however, that most of these courts have no difficulty in finding the necessary intent in the similarity of the marks. English courts and some American courts hold that the ability of the plaintiff to recover damages is determined, not by the defendant's intent, but by the result of the defendant's actions.

In addition to the common law remedy of damages, equitable relief is also available, and is much more frequently used. The common law remedy pays the injured party for losses, but does nothing to prevent the continued use of the infringing mark by the defendant. Equity supplies injunctive relief, which is available, in general, whether the infringing party intended to infringe or not, but the presence of such intent aids the complaining party's case where the imitation and infringement are not clearly established. The defendant may be compelled to account to the complaining party for profits resulting from his infringement. Proof may be difficult in these situations, especially where some of the resulting profits flowed from the inherent quality of the defendant's product. Damages, measured by the plaintiff's loss, are also available at equity. Some courts require the complainant to elect whether to take profits or damages on the theory that to get both would award him double compensation. But profits and damages do not necessarily overlap, and other courts give the injured party both damages and profits, especially where the defendant is shown to have acted wilfully and fraudulently.

PROTECTION OF TRADE NAMES AGAINST INFRINGEMENT. As has already been pointed out, the problems of infringement and protection of trade names are very similar to those of trade-marks although the two devices come into existence in different ways. It is often said that there is a difference between the infringement of the trade-mark and the infringement of the trade name, however. Because the user of the technical trade-mark has a property interest in the mark itself, he may exclude others from using that or similar marks for goods in the same general class. But the user of a trade name has no property in the name; thus, he is entitled to protection only where an imitation enables another to pass off his goods as those of the user. The distinction, if it still exists, is disappearing. It would be extremely difficult to find any difference between the infringement of a trade-mark and the infringement of a trade name which has been in long use and is affixed to the goods. The Torts Restatement draws little distinction between them, except with respect to origin and to the fact that a trade name does not have to be affixed to goods and may be identified with services or the conduct of a business. A trade-mark comes into existence as soon as it is adopted and used; the trade name does not become a trade name until it has acquired a special market significance through use. After this has been accomplished, it is the substantial equivalent of the trade-mark. Not every designation is entitled to immediate protection as a trade-mark, and many designations acquire their rights to protection only through the channel of the trade name.

A large proportion of the litigation in the trade name area has grown out of the use of family names, which, by themselves, are not capable of becoming trade-marks. On many occasions, the long use of a family name has resulted in its acquiring a special significance in the market, thus entitling it to protection against those who seek to infringe it. A person with the same name may, ordinarily, use that name only in such a manner as not to cause confusion with a prior use of the same name already established as a trade name.

REGISTRATION. *Federal law.* In order to simplify the proof of trade-marks and to secure greater protection for them, federal and state laws make provision for their registration and for some changes in the common law. Until 1947, when the latest of the Federal Trade Mark Acts, known as the Lanham Act,[80] went into effect, the principal advantages of registration under the federal law were procedural in character. The registration created a rebuttable presumption in favor of the registrant's right to the mark and gave the prospective registrant the benefit of expert advice from the Patent Office on the availability of the selected mark. The registrant was granted access to the federal courts for the protection of his marks and was entitled to triple damages. The Act also gave public notice of the appropriation of the particular mark; thus, it reduced the possibility of innocent infringement. The protection of the federal law extends for a period of twenty years, and is renewable for similar periods without limitation.

The Lanham Act made some changes both in the common law as it has been discussed above and in the antecedent federal law. Prior to the Lanham Act, the owner of a trade-mark was the one who first used the mark in commerce, and the registration was only *prima facie* evidence of such ownership, which could be rebutted by proof of prior commercial use. Under the new Act, after a mark has been registered for five years, the ownership of the registered owner purports to be final and incontestable. The incontestability is not absolute, however, and is subject to certain limitations set forth in the Act. The circumstances under which the registration is not conclusive evidence of the registrant's rights are:

1. If it is shown that the registrant was not entitled to registration under the Lanham Act at the time of registration, or that he obtained his registration fraudulently.

2. If the registered mark was abandoned by its registrant.

3. If the registered mark was assigned and is being used by the assignee so as to deceive the public as to the source of the articles or services to which it is applied.

4. If the right to use the mark concurrently is preserved.

5. If the registered mark is being or has been used to violate the antitrust laws.

---

[80] 15 U.S.C.A., Sections 1051–1127.

The changes worked by the Lanham Act in the direction of incontestability seem not to have been great and consist almost entirely of a codification of the law as it already existed. Codification does serve a useful purpose here, however, in that it adds a considerable measure of certainty to forecasting the outcome of trade-mark litigation.

The old law refused to recognize as trade-marks designations consisting of descriptive, geographical, or personal names. These designations could be protected as trade names, as has already been pointed out, provided that the name had acquired special significance through long use, but could not be registered no matter how long they had been in use or how special the significance they had acquired. The Lanham Act permits the registration of such designations where evidence is furnished that they have been in substantial and continuous use for five years prior to the request for registration. The granting of the registration, however, is discretionary with the Patent Office. Other marks may be registered as a matter of right if they do not infringe on any prior registered mark.

Prior to 1947, the sale or assignment of a trade-mark was invalid unless the entire business in which the mark was used was sold or assigned also. The new Act permits the transfer of the mark accompanied only by that portion of the business to which it relates.

A mark, in order to qualify for immediate registration, must be a true trade-mark in the sense that the trade-mark was defined in the first portion of this discussion. This requirement excludes the descriptive or geographical words and phrases and personal names that usually can qualify for registration only after five years of use. Where one of these unqualified words or phrases or names is combined with others or put into a unique design or symbol, they may be converted into trade-marks immediately registerable. The following are some of the types of trade-marks that are entitled to immediate registration: 1, a coined word; 2, a portrait; 3, words suggestive but not descriptive of an article, such as *Realsilk* for hosiery; 4, historical, famous, mythological, or fictitious names; 5, arbitrary or fanciful words, such as *Swansdown* for cake flour; 6, letters or initials when arbitrarily used, such as *B.V.D.* or *RPM* or *PM;* 7, symbols, such as a red cross; 8, personal names in combinations with other words or symbols, such as *DU PONT* enclosed by an oval. Whether the registration is immediate or after five years continuous use, the mark is classified according to the type of product with which it is being used, and the same mark is left available for others in connection with goods of a different class if that latter use is not likely to cause confusion as to the reputation of the maker or source of the product.

The Lanham Act expressly authorizes the registration of the same or similar marks to different users in cases where the users have in good faith used the mark in different parts of the country prior to the date of registration by any such user. Thus, the Act recognizes for registration purposes the general common law rule with regard to infringement where the same or similar marks are used in different parts of the country.

Literal physical affixation of the mark to goods has never been required for registration. Until 1947, however, marks that were not used on or in connection with "goods" were not registerable. The Lanham Act, on the other hand, provides for the registration of *service marks,* which are marks used in the sale or advertising of services to identify the services of one person and distinguish them from the services of others. This portion of the Act is of particular importance to those individuals and corporations that do not manufacture or sell any goods or tangible products to which a mark could be affixed or in connection with which a mark could be used.

Another improvement worked by the new Act is that it makes the registration constructive notice of the registrant's claim of ownership of the marks on a nation-wide basis. Except where an alleged infringer had actual notice of the registration there can be no recovery of damages or profits unless notice of registration accompanies the trademark as used, as by "Registered in U.S. Patent Office," "Reg. U.S. Pat. Off.," or the letter R enclosed by a circle.

The status of trade-marks registered before the new Act became effective is important. Section 46(b) of the Lanham Act provides that old registrants have the option of renewing their registrations when they expire or claiming the benefits of the new Act by filing an affidavit at any time prior to the expiration of the previous registration.

State trade-mark acts. Many states have trade-mark statutes of their own, but these statutes, of course, apply only to intrastate commerce. Few of these statutes add anything of a substantive nature to the common law protection of trade-marks, and there are not many advantages in registration, except possibly to avoid some innocent infringement. Some of the state laws permit registration only after a period of use; whereas others permit immediate registration. Most of the states having trade-mark acts are quite lenient on registration, and require only the filing of an application blank, together with facsimile of the mark, and a small fee. Since the protection afforded by the statutes is generally not great, no need arises for imposing strict rules on registration. Some states will register labels, package designs, and even slogans.

OTHER PROTECTION. The simulation of trade names is one of the areas of unfair competition that has been considered by the Federal Trade Commission.

5. PATENTS AND THE ANTITRUST LAWS

A. History

A *patent* is an exclusive privilege given by the government to inventors whereby the inventor has the sole right to make, use, and sell his invention for a certain period of time. In this country, the patenting power is possessed by the federal government alone, and the period of time during which protection is afforded to the inventor is seventeen years. The foundation of the English patent system, from which ours is an offshoot, was the Statute of Monopolies enacted by Parliament in 1624. Prior to the enactment of this statute, the Crown granted many monopolistic privileges, as has been discussed above, and, as a result of these grants of monopoly, came into conflict with Parliament and the common law. In 1624, Parliament prohibited such royal grants of monopoly. Because it recognized the desirability of encouraging and stimulating invention and progress in the development of the useful arts, Parliament excepted from its ban letters patent and limited grants of privilege to inventors. Our Constitution assigned to Congress the power "to promote the progress of science and useful arts, by securing for limited times to authors and inventors the exclusive right to their respective writings and discoveries."

In exercise of this authority granted by the Constitution, Congress has enacted and amended patent laws from time to time; prescribed the terms under which a person may obtain a patent; and set up a Patent Office in the Department of Commerce to receive and consider applications for patents, to issue patents, and to maintain books and records pertaining to patents. In 1952, Congress enacted the Patent Code, which codifies many existing patent statutes and makes certain changes in patent law, particularly with regard to the conditions necessary for patentability.[81]

B. Patents and Monopoly

There is no doubt that a patent gives to the *patentee,* the person to whom a patent is granted, a monopoly. It gives to him greater rights than he would have without the patent. An inventor, in the absence of any patent statute, can exclude others from the use or sale of an invention only as long as he can keep it a trade secret. The patent makes it possible for the inventor to exclude others from the use or sale of an invention even where the invention and its details are a matter of public record. How can this specific grant of monopoly be justified in the light of a general statutory and common law policy against monopoly? The answer to the question lies in the distinction made by Parliament in 1624, and by the delegates to our Constitutional Convention, between the temporary exclusive rights granted to an inventor and the detrimental industrial monopolies that deprive the public of the benefits of a competitive economic order and add nothing new or useful to the sum of human knowledge. The primary purpose of the patent is said to be the promotion of science and industry and only secondarily, the reward of the inventor. The patent monopoly is limited in time to seventeen years and in scope to the particular new invention or discovery. It is given only on some-

---

[81] 35 U.S.C.A. 1.

thing which is new and thus does not directly involve a monopoly on existing channels of commerce. This is not to say that the effective time and scope of the patent monopoly cannot be extended by taking advantage of defects in the patent laws. The defects, however, are in the laws and not in the basic concept of the patent.

The patent has been characterized as a "property right," as a "franchise," and as a "privilege conditioned by a public purpose." A great deal has been said for and against each of these views in books and articles and in court decisions. Probably the best way to describe the patent is as a special kind of property, which description may carry with it the connotation that the exclusive rights of the patentee may be subject to greater restrictions than other forms of property when the public interest so requires. This is not a unique idea in our law anyway, because all property rights are subject to the overriding authority of the public good, as exemplified by the police power of the states, the power of eminent domain, and the unusual powers based on war or economic emergency. In another sense, the patent may be described as a contract whereby the patentee makes full disclosure of all of the important features of his invention in consideration of the grant of a temporary monopoly in the exploitation and use of the invention. The purposes of the disclosure are to assure dedication to the public on the expiration of the period of exclusive right, to define the limits of the patent grant, and to aid the Patent Office in determining whether the invention is patentable.

C. Functioning of the Patent System

It has been asserted rather widely that many discrepancies exist between the patent system in theory and the patent system in practice. Some of the specific charges follow:

1. The details of many patents never become part of the public domain because of insufficient disclosure. In many cases, the details of the invention itself are not nearly as important to the manufacture or use of the invention as the know-how or technique necessary to utilize the invention. The grant of monopoly may thus be extended with regard to both time and scope.

2. The chief benefit of the patent system goes to those large corporations that maintain extensive research facilities. The small "basement workshop" inventor cannot compete.

3. Large corporations can extend the scope of their patent monopolies by threatening long, drawn out, expensive infringement suits.

4. The use of "improvement" and "blocking" patents makes it possible, especially where there is a large research staff, to extend the practical patent monopoly over an indefinite period of time. By the time the original patent expires, the invention is obsolete, but the improvements are, themselves, now protected by patents.

5. Patent monopoly can be extended in scope by: pools of patents, pur-

chase of related patents or of competitors owning related patents, price and marketing clauses in patent licenses, tying clauses, and by many other devices.

There are elements of truth in all of these allegations, but none of these allegations is really an argument for abolishing the patent system. Many of the present problems would only be aggravated by the elimination of the patent monopoly, and the advantage of the large corporation would be increased. There would, for example, be no disclosure at all as long as the details could be kept secret, and many inventions would never come into the public domain. Abuses have crept into the patent system. Changes in the law or in the enforcement are probably desirable. Many who favor changes in the law feel that the real problem is not the patent law itself but the antitrust laws, which should be improved and better enforced in order to eliminate the more serious abuses in the patent system. We have already seen how the tying of non-patented items to patented items has been dealt with by the courts. A number of suggestions have been made for technical and procedural improvements in the patent laws that would eliminate some of the difficulties and some of the objections set forth above. For example, the applicant is entitled to considerable protection during the pendency of an application for a patent, and many applicants take advantage of this fact to extend the time of patent protection by deliberate delay in the prosecution of an application. Some delays have exceeded fifty years. One proposal to solve this problem limits the total protection to twenty years from the date the application is filed.

D. Conflict with Antitrust Laws

Conflict between the patent laws and the antitrust laws is, of course, inevitable. As pointed out above, a distinction can be made between the type of monopoly the antitrust laws seek to eliminate and the type of monopoly the patent laws grant in order to encourage invention. Some take the view that the two policies are perfectly consistent and that conflict occurs only when the patentee steps outside the scope of his grant. Others say that the two policies not only are consistent but also are the same in that they are both aimed at the preservation of competition. This view can be supported by the argument that the entry of new and temporarily protected inventions into commerce provides competition for those already established in a particular field. Another view is that the policies of the patent laws and of the antitrust laws are basically opposed, and that the patent monopoly is a special case, based on sound reasons, which is allowed to run contrary to the fundamental policy against monopoly. Whatever the view, conflicts do occur and must be resolved. In general, their resolution is based on the public interest which both policies are designed to further. The translation of this broad and indisputable statement into methods and procedures and techniques is a difficult thing, indeed, to accomplish.

The important problem of how to treat the patentee who extends his patent beyond the claimed invention has not been satisfactorily solved. One may say that when the patentee exceeds his grant and finds himself in those areas of commerce where he is on the same level as any other property owner and subject to the general laws, the patentee's extra-patent conduct is contrary to the public policy of the patent laws, and the protection against infringement may be lost or reduced. The extra-patent activity should then be considered under the antitrust laws just as any other activity would be considered where patents were not involved. This view, which is the prevailing view, takes the approach that a violation of the public policy of patents does not necessarily violate the public policy of the antitrust laws. Another view, expressed in some recent Supreme Court decisions, including *International Salt* v. *United States*,[82] is based on the theory that every extension of the patent monopoly beyond the scope of the grant is necessarily a violation of the policies of both the patent laws and the antitrust laws. Any extension, then, is a *per se* violation of the antitrust laws. If this view is followed, the *per se* doctrine is considerably enlarged, and the presently prevailing view is substantially changed.

PROBLEMS

1. Trace the development of the competitive system.

2. Assume that you are living in England in 1630. You and two other persons, representing all of the widget manufacturers and sellers in England, have just entered into an agreement to fix the prices of your product, divide up the market, keep out competition, and pool management, manufacturing, and selling activities. Have you violated the Statute of Monopolies? Or the common law?

3. What are the legal characteristics of competition?

4. Albert owned and operated a retail fish store in the city of Grantland where there were several other retail fish stores but only one wholesaler of fish, Salty Sam. Albert and Sam had never got along very well, partly because Sam was a practical joker who took pleasure in tormenting Albert, and partly because, in Albert's opinion, Sam's prices were too high. After one particularly disagreeable practical joke, Albert told Sam that if Sam ever played another joke on him, he, Albert, would establish his own wholesale fish business and drive Sam into bankruptcy. Sam did not stop his joking, and Albert started his own wholesaling business. He sold for less than Sam did; he advertised: "Don't be just half safe. Demand sanitary fresh fish from Aquatic Albert. Protect your family's health." As soon as Albert had forced Sam out of business, he sold his wholesale operation to a man from Boston and went back to his retail store. Sam has brought an action against Albert and is demanding rather substantial damages for the loss of his business. What are the rights of the parties?

5. In connection with the sale of a builders' supply and lumber business to Hans, Henry promised that he would not enter into the same business anywhere in the states of Washington, Oregon, California, Nevada, Idaho, Montana, Utah,

---

[82] 332 U.S. 392 (1947).

Arizona, and New Mexico. The headquarters of the business were in Portland, Oregon, and the firm actually did make sales in all the states listed in the agreement, except Arizona and New Mexico, where the buyer planned to expand at some time in the future. No mention was made in the agreement of the duration of this restraint. Six months after the sale, Henry started a new business of the same type with its main office in Los Angeles and solicited customers in Southern California, Arizona, New Mexico, Nevada, and Utah. Hans is now suing to compel Henry to stop his competition and perform his agreement. What issues are likely to arise in the trial of this suit?

6. What is the meaning of the terms "ancillary" and "non-ancillary" when used with respect to restraints of trade?

7. What is the general nature of the substantive provisions (Sections 1 and 2) of the Sherman Act?

8. "The adoption of the 'rule of reason' was simply a change in theory and did not make any difference as far as the outcome of the cases was concerned. No important Sherman Act decision would have been any different had the 'rule of reason' been rejected by the Supreme Court."

    a. What is the "rule of reason?" What is its origin? Why was there so much uncertainty and disagreement about it before 1911?

    b. Is the quotation above accurate?

    c. Could the person who made the above statement have been misled by the fact that the rule has had much greater effect in some types of situations than in others or that ways may have been found to get around the rule or to minimize its effects?

    d. Do you believe that a restraint of trade should be held unreasonable if the defendants can prove that they did not intend to restrain trade unreasonably or to violate the law and that they were simply trying to improve chaotic conditions in their industry and that the public was really benefited by their activities?

9. Describe briefly the remedies available to the Government and to private parties under the federal antitrust laws.

10. What do the terms "close-knit combinations" and "loose-knit combinations" mean?

11. The Oakbirch Lumber Company (hereafter referred to as *OLC*) is in the business of cutting and curing hardwoods for use in the furniture industry. The lumber is purchased from *OLC* by the furniture manufacturers, who in turn make furniture from it and sell the furniture to distributors. *OLC* produces approximately 64% of the hardwood used by furniture manufacturers in the United States. The oak and birch which *OLC* processes comes from its own timber land, but the company must purchase its supplies of walnut and other hardwoods. *OLC* sells oak and birch logs to other lumber companies. Including *OLC*, there are ten lumber companies in the United States which sell hardwood to the furniture industry. Prior to 1936, conditions in the hardwood lumber industry could best be described as chaotic, but in 1936, five lumber companies organized an association for the purpose of bringing some order out of the chaos, and they succeeded in doing so by 1940. In that year, however, a Sherman Act suit against the association was successful and the association dissolved. In 1942, the five companies which had been members of the association consolidated to form *OLC*, which is now the largest hardwood lumber producer; the nearest competitor does about 10% of the business. In spite of the great relative size of *OLC*, there is competition in the industry, and small operators

frequently underbid *OLC* for the business of the furniture companies. Assume that you are Assistant to the President of *OLC*. The President has just called you into his office and told you that *OLC* has an opportunity to acquire controlling interests in two of the largest hardwood furniture manufacturing firms that between them produce about 17% of the hardwood furniture produced in the United States. These companies have been customers of *OLC* in the past but have also bought substantial quantities of hardwood from other lumber companies. The President wants you to prepare for him a memorandum appraising the position of *OLC* with regard to the antitrust laws. The President is interested both in the present position of the company and in its position should it acquire the manufacturing firms. Prepare the memorandum.

12. There are in the United States nine manufacturers of widgets, a more or less standardized product. There are large, small, medium-sized, efficient and inefficient producers in the group, but the *X* Company is the largest and most efficient. The nine companies organized an association to disseminate certain price, production, and market information among the members. Whereas before the formation of the association, the widget business had been in turmoil, with rapid and severe fluctuations in price and production, the industry seemed to stabilize after the association was formed. Prices became almost identical, and acute fluctuations in price and production vanished. Changes in prices and other policies seem to come first in the *X* Company and are quickly adopted by the others. Consider the status of this association with regard to the antitrust laws.

13. What do the following have in common?

    a. *United States* v. *Trenton Potteries Co.*

    b. Market allocation.

    c. Output control.

    d. License of patented device on condition that unpatented products of licensor be used also.

    e. Agreements not to deal.

14. Compare, in the light of possible changes in effect, the language of the old Section 7 of the Clayton Act with the language of the amendment of 1950.

15. In what way does the approach of the Clayton Act to antitrust problems differ from the approach of the Sherman Act?

16. Assume that you were carrying on an interstate business prior to 1936 and were taking advantage of the alleged loopholes afforded by Section 2 of the Clayton Act. What changes might you have to make in your business conduct after the enactment of the Robinson-Patman Act?

17. Describe briefly the nature, causes, current status, and significance of the controversy over the meaning of the "good faith to meet competition" clause in Section 2(b) of the Clayton Act as amended by the Robinson-Patman Act.

18. Assume that you are Assistant to the President of the North American Rubber Company, a corporation engaged in the manufacture and sale of automobile tires and related products. The President has asked you to prepare for him a memorandum setting forth your ideas on the following problem: The Montgomery-Roebuck Company, a large mail-order house, has offered to purchase all of its automobile and truck tires from North American; Montgomery-Roebuck will purchase in very large quantities, and the tires will be the same as those sold to other customers of North American but will bear the Montgomery-Roebuck brand name; the price offered by

Montgomery-Roebuck is substantially lower than that paid by any other buyer but is sufficient to return a good profit on the large volume sale; the Goodstone Rubber Company, a competitor of North American, is willing to enter into a deal with Montgomery-Roebuck at this low price, but Montgomery-Roebuck would prefer the North American tire if it can get the tire at this price. Write the memorandum, indicating whether you think the offer should be accepted.

19. Two theories have been advanced as to the proper way to measure discrimination in price: the price difference theory and the profit difference theory. Compare the two theories giving a practical example of the effect of the differences between them. Is there a better way to measure price discrimination than either of these ways?

20. What are the difficulties inherent in the enforcement of "sales below cost" statutes?

21. Trace briefly the legal and legislative history of resale price maintenance. What is a "non-signers clause?" Are there any devices, other than resale price maintenance, by which a manufacturer or distributor may control resale prices?

22. Compare "sales below cost" statutes and "resale price maintenance" statutes as methods of controlling cutthroat price competition.

23. Compare tying arrangements and exclusive dealing contracts with respect to their nature and legality.

24. You are Assistant to the President of a company which manufactures farm machinery; most of the company's products are sold through independent dealers in all parts of the country. The President has asked you to submit a memorandum reviewing the legal status of the contracts that the company requires its dealers to sign. Among other things, these contracts compel the dealers to sell only the products of your company. The President also asks you to consider the legality of the contracts that the company requires of purchasers who buy certain farm equipment directly from the company; most of the machinery so purchased cannot be obtained elsewhere, but the contract requires the purchaser to purchase from the company certain other equipment that is available elsewhere. The President is interested also in knowing what economic information might be of importance in defending these contracts. Write the memorandum.

25. Compare the remedies available to a competitor who has been injured by the false advertising of one of his rivals with the remedies available to a purchaser of the falsely advertised products.

26. Describe the legal protections afforded to trade secrets and customers' lists. What course of conduct does the nature of this protection suggest for a person attempting to preserve his trade secrets?

27. What is commercial bribery?

28. Compare the liability for disparaging product or property with liability for defaming the personal reputation of another person. What defenses are available against charges of disparagement?

29. What legal protection does the owner of a big league baseball club have against a rival club's inducement of star players to leave one club to play for the other?

30. Describe the various kinds of trade boycotts. With reference to liability and protection, compare concerted refusals to deal with the inducement of others not to deal.

31. Describe the protection which the common law affords to trade-marks and trade names.

32. What changes did the Lanham Act make in the antecedent law of trade-mark registration and protection?

33. Consider the ways in which the protection and use of trade-marks and trade names may conflict with the policies of the antitrust laws.

34. Some of the antitrust legislation in effect today is aimed at protecting competition, on the theory that the public welfare is furthered by the operation of a competitive economy. Other legislation appears to be directed at protecting competitors from competition, usually by defining broadly, and then prohibiting, "unfair competition." List and discuss briefly the statues that fall into each of these categories. State the approach you think is the proper one and explain why.

35. What is the function of the Federal Trade Commission in the enforcement of the antitrust laws?

36. What changes would you recommend in the present regulation of competitive practices? Explain.

37. List all the ways that you can think of where the organization and operation of a business is affected by governmental regulation.

38. "Conflicts between the patent laws and the antitrust laws are inevitable." Is this statement true? How can the public policies behind these two sets of laws be reconciled?

part V

Terminating a Business

THE NATURE OF THE LEGAL PROBLEMS IN THIS PART

The stage of the discussion has now been reached where we no longer have any concern for the creation or operation of a business enterprise, but this is not to say that our examination of the legal aspects of business administration has come to an end. We simply shift our attention to the problems of termination and insolvency, problems which not all businesses must face, but with which all businessmen should be familiar. It is pointed out here that insolvency and termination do not always go together. Many business enterprises terminate without insolvency ever having been an issue at all. This is especially true of partnerships, which are brought to termination by many events other than the failure of the business. By the same token, insolvency is not always accompanied by termination, although that is usually the case.

The termination of a business is an activity over which business managers have considerably more control than many people seem to realize. Short of bankruptcy and corporate reorganizations under Chapter X of the Bankruptcy Act, proprietors and managers of business have extensive discretion with regard to termination even where the cause of the termination is the insolvency of the business. The winding up of a partnership, for example, is carried out by the partners, and the skill with which this task is accomplished is often determinative of the loss or gain the partners will incur.

What kind of problem do businessmen face in connection with the termination of a business? The first important problem is that having to do with the cause of the termination. The cause may be simply the proprietors' own decision, or the necessity for termination may have been forced upon the proprietors by events such as insolvency, a partner's death, or the business becoming illegal. As will be seen below, there are circumstances where less than all of the proprietors may bring about a termination even over the objections of a majority. The method of termination may become important, as where a decision is made as to whether the business will be liquidated or sold as a going concern. Of major importance in all cases of termination is the effect of a decision to terminate, or of the first steps toward termination, on the rights and duties of the proprietors both with regard to outsiders and among themselves.

Problems of priorities between creditors and proprietors and among the proprietors themselves arise even where insolvency is not a factor. There may be questions as to how the business property is to be distributed—whether in cash or in kind—and as to how proprietors shall share in losses or in surpluses that may exist. Issues frequently arise over the extent to which a court may be asked to participate in or take over the processes of termination or over how the services of a court may be enlisted in order to bring about a termination. Different forms of business organization present these same problems in different ways, and time must be devoted to the problems peculiar to one form or another.

When insolvency is an issue, many additional problems raise their heads. A proprietor must decide which of the many insolvency procedures should be followed: whether he should voluntarily submit himself to bankruptcy or let his creditors take the initiative; whether he should make a general assignment for his creditors or attempt to negotiate a composition agreement. A creditor also has important issues facing him: whether he should force the debtor into bankruptcy, and the circumstances under which he may do this; the nature and extent of the creditor's security; the risks he runs either by taking or not taking the initiative; and a host of other problems that may plague a creditor of an insolvent or potentially insolvent debtor.

Some of the issues mentioned above have been considered elsewhere in the book, but here, for the first time, these issues are raised in the atmosphere in which they most commonly occur.

chapter 15

Terminating
the Partnership

1. DISSOLUTION, WINDING
UP, AND TERMINATION DEFINED

The problems of termination probably play a larger part in the law of partnership than in any other form of business organization. There are several reasons for this. The partnership is a very unstable device by comparison with the corporation, the joint stock company, or the business trust. It is very much like the sole-proprietorship in this regard. The life of any one partner, as the life of the sole-proprietor, generally measures the life of the firm, and, even under the best of conditions, the death or withdrawal of a partner causes the partnership severe stress. Unlike the sole-proprietorship, however, the partnership consists of several persons, and the coming-to-an-end of the firm calls into issue the rights, obligations, and claims of these persons among themselves. The partnership, then, is very unstable, like the sole-proprietorship, yet it is a much more complicated and sophisticated form of business organization, and the combination of these two characteristics makes the partnership's terminal problems proportionately more important than the terminal problems of other business forms.

Even today, these terminal problems are complicated

because of a confusion in terminology, and the terms least understood, least well-delineated, and most confused are the basic terms: dissolution, winding up, and termination. Oddly enough, much of this confusion still exists in states that have adopted the Uniform Partnership Act, a statute that seems to explain these terms in rather obvious language. In order to avoid confusion in the discussion here, the definitions and explanations of the basic terms are set forth in some detail, largely in the language of the Uniform Act.

Section 29 of the Act provides that "The dissolution of a partnership is the change in the relation of the partners caused by any partner ceasing to be associated in the carrying on as distinguished from the winding up of the business," and Section 30 says: "on dissolution the partnership is not terminated, but continues until the winding up of partnership affairs is completed." This language makes it clear that "dissolution" is simply the change in the relationship among the partners when they cease, for any reason, to do business together. Although dissolution is usually followed by "winding up" and "termination," it does not include these terms and is separate from them. *Winding up* is the process of settling partnership affairs, and follows dissolution. This process includes: (1) the performing of outstanding contracts and obligations; (2) the gathering together of the partnership property; (3) the determination of rights and claims by outsiders and among the partners themselves; (4) the paying of the partnership's debts to its creditors; and (5) the dividing of what property is left among the partners or the payment by the partners personally of any creditor obligations for the payment of which partnership property is not sufficient.

Termination takes place when winding up is completed, and is the end of the firm's life. Before termination, the firm continues to exist for certain purposes: It may still own property; the partners may still sue and be sued in connection with partnership business; each partner retains some of his power to act for the other members of the firm.

Many partnership agreements, in spite of the clear language of the statute, provide that the death or withdrawal of a partner shall not result in "dissolution." Since the partners have "ceased to do business together," there is a dissolution no matter what the agreement may say. The draftsmen of such agreements undoubtedly mean that winding up and termination are to be suspended and not that dissolution is to be avoided. If there is no dissolution, the old partnership exists as before, but this is impossible after the death or withdrawal of a partner, because the partners have ceased to do business together. There is in effect and in law a new partnership. The partners are usually not as interested in preventing dissolution as they are in providing some means by which the shock of dissolution on the partnership may be lessened.

Avoiding liquidation. All causes of dissolution have profound effects on partnerships. Some of the effect can be minimized or avoided; some cannot. Careful planning for eventual or possible dissolution is necessary if the harmful effects of dissolution are to be kept to a minimum, and this planning should begin at the very earliest stages of the business. The cause of dissolution most important for us to discuss is the death of a partner. Here, as with many of the other causes, forced liquidation of the business at a painful economic sacrifice often is the price that is paid for inadequate planning. However, there are numerous methods available today for the purpose of alleviating this problem.

The sacrifice liquidation could be entirely avoided if each partner would only bequeath his partnership interest to his fellow partners at his death or if the partnership contract provided that a partner's interest should exist only during his lifetime. But it would be a rare partner who would agree to anything like this. The easy convenience of this technique is attractive but it overlooks the fact that each partner probably has another objective that is even more important than avoiding liquidation: providing for his own family or enhancing his own estate on his death. Where a partner does have this objective, the technique of bequeathing the interest or terminating it on death is completely unsatisfactory.

Liquidation may also be avoided by providing in the partnership contract that the heirs shall become partners, but in many situations this prospect is even more objectionable to all concerned than liquidation. The original partners probably do not want the heirs in the firm, and the heirs probably do not want to be forced into being partners in order to preserve inherited property.

Liquidation may be postponed by a provision in the partnership agreement that the deceased partner's interest shall be continued in the business for a period after his death. This method usually is not satisfactory either, because it is no guaranty against liquidation and may be very unfair or even disastrous as far as the heirs are concerned. Most courts will not enforce these suspended distributions to the heirs for more than a very few years.

The best solutions to these problems lie in the direction of reciprocal agreements to purchase a deceased partner's interest or in granting to the survivors an option to purchase a partner's interest at his death. The most common type of arrangement, though others may be used successfully, is an agreement by the surviving associates to purchase the interest at some fixed or formula price. The most common method of funding such agreements is life insurance. These methods have certain obvious advantages: they assure a buyer for what otherwise might be an unmarketable property; they avoid forced liquidation of the business; they free the deceased partner's estate or heirs from the necessity of choosing between a forced sale and an unwilling participation in the business; they provide a ready supply of cash for the decedent's estate; they may simplify estate tax problems by providing a basis for valuation; they give the surviving associates an assurance of continuity and harmony of management without outside interference; they exert a stabilizing effect during the lifetime of the parties by dispelling the fears of creditors and key employees that the business may be forced to liquidate on the death of a partner.

There are disadvantages also: fluctuations in the value of the interest may result in great disparity between the agreed price and the actual value at the time of death; the mere existence of the scheme may prevent a change if another method of disposition becomes more desirable; the agreement may cause undesirable tax consequences in some cases, especially in a family partnership where the temptation to fix very low valuations in order to minimize estate taxes may lead tax authorities to adopt a suspicious attitude and to fix much higher valuations for tax purposes; other disadvantages may arise in certain cases. It should be noted that where the partners are of disparate ages or states of health, life insurance may not prove to be a satisfactory method of funding the agreements.

It should be noted also that much of what has been said here about the "buy-sell" agreement among partners is equally applicable to close corporations, where the desire to keep outsiders out of the business and yet to provide adequately for a deceased associate's family may dictate similar arrangements.

The use of the life insurance method for funding a buy-sell agreement among partners raises some special problems of its own, especially with regard to whether the proceeds of the policies are separate or partnership property. A life insurance policy issued to, and paid for by, a partner for the benefit of his estate or a relative is, of course, his separate property, and if a partner insures his own life for the benefit of another partner and pays his own premiums, there is not much question but that the proceeds are the separate property of the partner who is the beneficiary. In community property states the wife of the insured partner may have a claim to one-half of the proceeds if community funds were used to pay the premiums. Other problems are raised, however, if the partnership pays the premiums and the policy is made payable to the surviving partner or partners or to the partnership. You will recall that Section 8 of the Uniform Act states that property purchased with partnership funds is presumed to be partnership property. Consequently, the payment of the premiums on the policy out of partnership funds would lead to the presumption that the proceeds were also partnership property. Only a strong contrary showing could overcome this presumption. If the proceeds are partnership property, the legal representative of the deceased partner may have a claim to a share of them as a part of the value of the deceased partner's interest; thus, the amount due the partner's estate would be increased. Many other problems are raised by the question of whether the proceeds are partnership or separate property, and extreme care should be used, and expert advice obtained, in drafting these insurance agreements among the partners.

In addition to the problems of partnership property, problems of insurable interest also arise when a partner or a partnership seeks to insure a partner's life. For obvious reasons of public policy, the law will not permit a person to insure the life of another unless the person who does the insuring has an insurable interest. The decision whether or not the insuring party has the requisite interest is usually dealt with in terms of the loss he, the insuring party, might suffer on the death of the other party. The partnership problem is not so much one of whether there is an insurable interest as it is a problem of the *extent* of the insurable interest. It certainly would cover the amount of obligations owed to the partnership by the partner whose life is insured, and it may include a reasonable amount for the earning capacity of that partner. Beyond that the law is uncertain. A debtor has no insurable interest in the life of his creditor; thus, there is real doubt about the insurable interest of a partnership in the life of a partner to the extent that the proceeds are intended to cover the value of the partner's "interest" payable on dissolution. These insurable interest problems do not arise where a partner insures his own life for the benefit of the firm or fellow partner. Consequently, that method is one of the most common solutions to the issues raised above. The law of one's own state should be checked for details.

2. THE CAUSES OF DISSOLUTION

A. In General

Unlike the corporation, whose causes of dissolution are few, the events and acts that may cause the dissolution of a partnership are many. The cause may be a partner's act, voluntary or involuntary, or some event completely external to the partnership, such as the business becoming illegal. It may be a wrongful act or an act within the rights of the individual partner. There are many possible ways of categorizing the causes of dissolution, but the most useful way is that used by the Uniform Act itself: 1, dissolution caused without violation of the partnership agreement; 2, dissolution caused in contravention of the agreement; 3, dissolution by decree of court; and 4, a category which can only be listed as "miscellaneous." There is neither space nor need to discuss all of the possibilities in each of these categories. Illustrative examples will suffice.

B. Without Violation of the Agreement

COMPLETION OF TERM OR UNDERTAKING. The partners may consent in advance to dissolution at a particular time or on the completion of a particular undertaking. The dissolution will take place automatically when the time is reached or the undertaking completed. A partnerhip agreement specifying that the firm is to last for five years or until a definite date, or a partnership agreement describing the objectives of the business in terms of particular tasks or undertakings, would be examples. Where the business is continued after the expiration of the time or the completion of the undertaking, there is an implied in fact agreement for a new partnership to be carried on under the original terms, as far as they then apply. This new partnership would be what is called a *partnership at will,* which signifies that there is no fixed time of dissolution.

WITHDRAWAL OF ANY PARTNER. Unless a partner has agreed, expressly or impliedly, to remain in the business for a particular period of time, he may withdraw at any time without violating the partnership agreement. The partnership is a voluntary association, and where the partner has not voluntarily given up his right to do so, he may withdraw whenever he pleases without liability. Nor, by the majority view, may his motives be questioned. A few authorities have held that if the withdrawal is in bad faith, there may be liability on the withdrawing partner for harm done to his fellow partners. The ease with which the individual member may bring an end to the partnership is one of the chief factors accounting for its instability.

AGREEMENT OF ALL OF THE PARTNERS.   Even where all of the partners have agreed to remain in business for a particular length of time or until the completion of a particular undertaking, the oral or written unanimous agreement of the partners may in effect amend the partnership agreement to call for earlier dissolution. This result is nothing more than the application of the well-established rule of contracts that permits a mutual release to discharge a contract. But the consent must be unanimous. A majority, unless specifically given that authority, cannot dissolve a fixed term partnership without breaching the agreement.

C. In Violation of the Agreement

A partner may have agreed to remain with the firm for a certain time, but this agreement is no more a matter of specific compulsion than most other contractual obligations are. A partner may withdraw at any time, but, if he has agreed to stay for a longer time, he is breaching his contract by his withdrawal, and is subject to liability for the harm he has caused. It is usually a hardship on the remaining partners to have their business brought to a premature end, and they may recover damages from the wrongfully withdrawing partner either by an action at law or by charging them against him in the course of settling his account with the firm.

The Uniform Act extends the protection of the innocent partners even further by permitting them to buy out the interest of the withdrawing partner by paying him the net amount due him. This net amount would take into consideration the partner's capital contribution, any undivided profits, and the damages for his breach of contract. The withdrawing partner's share of goodwill is not included in this calculation, as it would be had he withdrawn rightfully. Further protection is provided by the Act in permitting the innocent partners to retain the withdrawing partner's interest in the business until the agreed upon term or undertaking has been completed. The innocent partners must post a bond to secure payment of the "net amount" to the wrongful partner at the later date and must indemnify him against all present or future partnership liabilities. Apparently, under Section 42 of the Act, if the withdrawing partner's account is not settled at the time of withdrawal, he is entitled to interest on the amounts retained in the business or else to that portion of the profits attributable to the use of his net capital.

D. By Decree of Court

APPLICATION BY A PARTNER. The death, withdrawal, or bankruptcy of a partner and the expiration of the agreed period are definite events not subject to equivocation, but there are many other events that may be just as valid reasons for dissolution; yet they are so uncertain and so subject to dispute that they cannot be the grounds for automatic dissolution. In most of the latter situations, the Uniform Act provides for dissolution by decree of court on the application of a partner. Note that granting the decree is mandatory on the court if the application states and the evidence supports any of the grounds set forth in the statute. The Uniform Partnership Act, Section 32, lists the following as grounds for the decree: 1, a partner has been declared insane in any judicial proceeding or is shown to be of unsound mind; 2, a partner becomes in some other way incapable of performing his part of the partnership contract; 3, a partner has been guilty of conduct that tends to affect prejudicially the carrying on of the business; 4, a partner wilfully or persistently commits a breach of the partnership agreement, or so conducts himself in matters relating to the partnership business that it is not reasonably practicable to carry on the business with him; 5, the business of the partnership can only be carried on at a loss; 6, other circumstances rendering a dissolution equitable. In some states the insanity of a partner causes an automatic dissolution, but the Uniform Act only makes it a ground for a partner's application.

Why does a partner not withdraw and bring about the dissolution in that way instead of going to court? The primary explanation is that the partner may have agreed to stay for a particular period, and premature withdrawal may subject him to liability.

APPLICATION BY THE PURCHASER OF A PARTNER'S INTEREST. It appears that under the Uniform Act a partner's sale of his interest to an outsider does not, of itself, cause a dissolution. The purchaser, obviously, does not become a partner and does not acquire any rights to participate in the management or to possess or use partnership property, but he does acquire the incidents of the assigning partner's interest, such as his share of the profits. The nonassigning partners may, however, dissolve by agreement among themselves even though the partnership contract provides for a fixed period not yet expired. The assigning partner gets no vote on the issue. The purchaser of the partner's interest may apply to the court for immediate dissolution of the firm, if it is a partnership at will, but he may not apply if a portion of the partnership term is still unexpired. He may apply at the end of the term. Here, as with the application by a partner, the decree is mandatory on the court if the prerequisites are satisfied. A purchaser of a partner's interest in connection with a court order qualifies as an applicant under this portion of the Act.

E. Miscellaneous Causes of Dissolution

DEATH OF A PARTNER.   Under the Uniform Partnership Act, there is no doubt that the death of a partner causes a dissolution even though, by agreement, the winding up and termination may be suspended. A few courts have erroneously held, however, that agreement may prevent dissolution although the Uniform Act is applicable.

EVENT MAKING IT ILLEGAL TO CARRY ON BUSINESS.   Dissolution takes place automatically where the business itself becomes unlawful or where it becomes unlawful to carry on a particular business by means of the partnership device. As with ordinary contracts, only future performance is discharged. Examples would be: 1, a declaration of war turns one of the partners into an enemy alien; 2, a partnership is conducting a liquor business at the time "prohibition" goes into effect; 3, a partner in a law firm becomes a judge; 4, a partnership is conducting a banking business at the time the corporate form becomes compulsory for that business.

BANKRUPTCY OF A PARTNER OR OF A PARTNERSHIP.   The bankruptcy of a partner removes his property from his control and puts it into the hands of the trustee. (See Chapter 17.) He no longer has the enjoyment of his interest in the firm, and the practical effect is much the same as though he had withdrawn from the firm. The bankruptcy of the partnership results in its property being removed from the partners' control and in the partners' inability to continue the business. Under the Uniform Act, the effect in both cases is an automatic dissolution.

Bankruptcy and insolvency problems will be discussed in the last chapter of this book, but it is important to note at this time that the two conditions, though related, are not the same. *Bankruptcy* is a formal legal status under the bankruptcy laws; whereas *insolvency* is just an informal reference to a person's condition when he cannot pay his debts. It is only a simple matter of deduction to arrive at the conclusion that a partnership is not really insolvent and cannot file in bankruptcy unless all of the partners are insolvent.

MARRIED WOMEN.   In those few jurisdictions where a married woman lacks capacity to become a partner or to become a partner with her husband, marriage may result in dissolution of the partnership.

3.   EFFECT OF DISSOLUTION

A. Cases

(1)

Porter and Wyman were partners in the real estate business. They employed Bell as a salesman and paid him a salary of $100 a month plus a percentage of the net profits of the business. The firm was voluntarily dissolved by the partners. After the dissolution, Bell went to see Wyman and told him that he thought he had $8500 still coming to him from the firm. Wyman agreed and made a notation to this effect in the books of the firm. Wyman died, and Bell filed suit against Porter, who denies that Bell had anything coming from the firm and also denies that Wyman had the power after dissolution to make a binding admission with regard to this claim. What are the rights of Bell against Porter?

[See *Bell* v. *Porter,* 261 Mich. 97, 246 N.W. 93 (1932)]

(2)

While Al Able was in New York on a buying trip, the other four partners in SIMUCO Toyland decided to dissolve the firm, which was a partnership at will. Two of the partners were in failing health; one wanted to get his money out so that he could invest it in a family lumber business in Oregon; one had received his partnership interest from his father and had been made a partner after the death of his father and had never really been interested in the toy business. The actual dissolution took place by vote of the partners shortly before noon on July 15. A registered letter was sent to Able informing him of this fact. Because Able had changed hotels, he did not receive the letter until 2 P.M. on the 18th. Between noon on the 15th and 2 P.M. on the 18th, Able had entered into the following contracts on behalf of SIMUCO: placed a $1,200 order for bicycles with the Schwink Corporation, from which SIMUCO bought most of its bicycles; contracted to buy $800 worth of novelty toys from Acey Toy Company, a firm that had long sought the SIMUCO business but had never had a contract with SIMUCO before; ordered $500 worth of stuffed animals from Fuzzy Wuzzy, Inc., a new importer of toys manufactured in South America. The four partners in Berkland have refused to perform any of these contracts. What are the rights of the parties?

(3)

When the other partners in Vosler, Hicks, and Wilson, an Anosmian partnership engaged in the grocery business, bought out John Vosler, who wanted to retire from the business, they promised Vosler that they would be responsible for Vosler's share of any partnership debts then outstanding. The business deteriorated rapidly after Vosler's retirement and finally failed. Among the unpaid creditors were several whose claims were already in existence when Vosler retired. These creditors have sued the partners and Vosler to recover their claims. What are their rights against Vosler?

B. In General

If dissolution is not followed by winding up and termination, the practical effects of dissolution usually are small. In effect the old partnership is gone, but a new one with the same prerogatives has taken its place. Creditors of the old firm are creditors of the new firm and of the individual partners, just as before. Creditors of the new firm are not affected, and their claims run against the new firm and against the partners in that new firm. Of course, the new partnership may have an obligation to a retired partner or to the estate of a deceased partner, which must be discharged at some time in the future, or the obligation may have been discharged by life insurance or some other device. Where winding up and termination are to follow dissolution, the effects of the dissolution are extensive and important. The Uniform Partnership Act is the principal source of information in regard to the effect of dissolution.

C. Effect on Authority of Partners

IN GENERAL. The best approach to this question is probably that which starts from the premise that dissolution terminates all of the authority of the individual partner to act for the partnership, and then proceeds to the exceptions, of which there are several. The first exception is an obvious one that requires little mention. The individual partner may still act to bind the partnership within the scope of winding up the business. As long as he acts reasonably within that area, he has much the same authority he had before dissolution, and the liability created for the firm and for the other partners is, likewise, the same. The process of winding up includes the performance of transactions left unfinished at dissolution, arranging for the auditing of partnership accounts, the sale of partnership property preparatory to paying off creditors, and even the making of new contracts where necessary for the performance of the other duties.

SECTION 35 OF UPA. Another important, though not as obvious, exception the to general rule grows out of a semi-estoppel doctrine provided for in Section 35 of the Uniform Partnership Act. This section is designed to protect certain third persons who had no notice of the dissolution, and does so by stating that a partner may bind the partnership after dissolution

> by any transaction which would bind the partnership if dissolution had not taken place, provided the other party to the transaction (I) Had extended credit to the partnership prior to dissolution and had no knowledge or notice of the dissolution; or (II) Though he had not so extended credit, had nevertheless known of the partnership prior to dissolution, and, having no knowledge or notice of dissolution, the fact of dissolution had not been advertised in a newspaper of general circulation in the place (or in each place if more than one) at which the partnership business was regularly carried on.

The phrase "extended credit" has been treated very liberally in some courts, and comes out meaning about the same as "dealt with."

In order to avoid the liability that the individual partner may impose upon the others under Section 35, the partners must give actual notice to the first group of third persons and must publish notice to take care of the second group. "*Actual notice*" means that the third person actually knows of the dissolution. A personal letter that never arrives does not constitute actual notice. Since the purpose of the section is to protect third persons who rely on the continued existence of the firm and authority of the partners, third persons who know of the dissolution or who are complete strangers to the partnership until after dissolution are not protected under this section. Knowledge of the dissolution by the partner who transacts the business with the third person is immaterial. With two exceptions, the cause of dissolution is also immaterial. The exceptions occur where the cause of dissolution is either the business becoming illegal or the bankruptcy of *the* partner with whom the third person deals. In either case, the cause of dissolution is looked upon as a matter of public knowledge, and the third person is presumed to know about the illegality of the business or the bankruptcy of the person with whom he deals and is entitled to no protection under Section 35. Where a partner is generally unknown as a partner and is unknown as a partner by the third person, his share of the liability under Section 35 must be satisfied out of partnership assets alone.

Section 34 of UPA. While not strictly an exception to the general rule, because partnership liability is not involved, liability may be imposed upon individual partners under Section 34; consequently, that section should be discussed here. This section is designed to protect a partner who becomes personally liable as a result of having entered into a transaction with a third person after dissolution without the partner's having known of the dissolution. The coverage, however, is quite narrow compared with that of Section 35. Where the dissolution is caused by the act, death, or bankruptcy of a partner, each partner is liable to his fellow partners for his share of any contractual liability incurred by any partner acting for the partnership as if the partnership had not been dissolved, unless the contracting partner had knowledge of the dissolution. Section 34 cannot apply where Section 35 creates partnership liability, on the grounds that where there is firm liability, all of the individual partners are liable anyway. But where the third person does not get a partnership claim under Section 35, either because he knew of the dissolution or because he had been a stranger before dissolution, the partner with whom he deals will become personally liable, a result which would be manifestly unjust if that partner did not know of the dissolution at the time the transaction was entered into. If the partner comes under the terms of Section 34, his loss is shared by the other partners. Note that Section 34 applies only to those dissolutions that would presumably be known to at least one partner or to his legal representative. A duty is imposed upon that partner or his representative to notify the other partners of the dissolution. The "act" of a partner generally refers to his withdrawal.

Albeit these two sections of the Uniform Act are rather indirect methods of requiring the partners to give notice of dissolution to third persons or to each other, the particular statutory device of imposing liability frequently gets the point across much more clearly than would otherwise be the case. There is no need to make reference here to the sometimes technical meanings of such words as *notice* and *knowledge*. The commonly understood meanings are sufficient for our purposes. References should be made to Section 3 of the UPA for details.

D. Effect on Title to Partnership Property

Dissolution has no direct effect on the title to partnership property either under the common law or the Uniform Partnership Act. In common law, the title to property could not be held by the firm but had to be held in the name or names of individual partners. Under these circumstances, a dissolution could and frequently did cause a great deal of confusion in connection with the title to partnership property, but the effect was indirect. On the death of a partner, the title to the property he held in his name went immediately to his heirs unless other arrangements were made by will or by the method in which the property was held. The partners might hold title to property as joint tenants, in which case the property went to the survivors on the death of one of the tenants. Even though the title went to the heirs of the deceased partner, the surviving partners had rights in the property, rights which might or might not be easy to enforce. Under the Uniform Partnership Act, the property is normally held in the name of the firm and remains that way after dissolution until the property is disposed of in connection with the winding up. The partners who are participating in the winding up have easy access to it without extensive lawsuits for the purpose of establishing their rights.

E. Effect on Existing Liabilities

In General.   The dissolution does not of itself discharge the existing liabilities of the partnership or of the partners, and has little effect on such liabilities, although the cause of dissolution may discharge some executory contract obligations under general principles of contract law. Where a contractual duty requires performance only by the promisor, the death or incapacity of the promisor will serve to discharge the contractual duty. Thus, a contract calling for the personal services of a particular partner would be discharged by the death or incapacity of that partner. This same result would be true of most employment contracts and most personal service contracts. Again, where the cause of dissolution of a partnership is the business becoming illegal, some of the pending contract obligations may have become illegal too, and their performance discharged. As has already been noted, where the business is continued after dissolution, the obligations existing prior to dissolution are still binding on both the retired partners and on the continuing partners.

Agreements to Discharge Partner from Liability.   It should surprise no one to learn that agreements among the partners to discharge one of their number from liability, usually in connection with the retirement of that partner, are binding on the partners but not on the creditors. Of course, if there is a novation, and consideration is present to support the creditor's promise to release the retiring partner, the result will be different, and the retiring partner will be released. The cases seem to show that the consideration is fairly easy to demonstrate, but the Uniform Partnership Act goes even further, and in Section 36(2) finds consideration in the promise of the continuing partners to the creditor to assume their fellow partner's obligations even though they are already obligated because they are partners. The consent of the creditor to the novation is sometimes express, but probably more often it is implied from his conduct. In the words of the Uniform Act, "such agreement may be inferred from the course of dealing between the creditor having knowledge of the dissolution and the person or partnership continuing the business." An agreement among the partners to discharge one of their number from liability may actually create a suretyship relation making the assuming partners the principal debtors and the retiring partner the surety. A majority of the courts have taken the view that if this is the result, the creditor with notice of the assumption agreement must take cognizance of the nature of the relation created and must first seek his remedies against the principal debtors.

DECEASED PARTNER'S ESTATE. Contrary to the common law rule, the Uniform Partnership Act provides that "the individual property of a deceased partner shall be liable for all obligations of the partnership incurred while he was a partner but subject to the prior payment of his separate debts." Under the common law rule the decedent's estate was not liable, although some relief for creditors was available in equity.

F. Rights of Partners to Participate in Winding Up

All partners, except those who have caused a wrongful dissolution or who are bankrupt, have a right to participate in the winding up of partnership affairs. In some states the representatives of deceased partners are, by statute, permitted to participate in the winding up. In the absence of such a statute, the representative of a deceased partner will participate in the winding up of the partnership only where he is the representative of the last surviving partner. In any case, a partner, his legal representative, or his assignee may obtain a winding up by the court where the winding up is not being pursued diligently and in good faith. The surviving partner in winding up occupies a fiduciary relation to the estate of a deceased partner. The surviving partner is not allowed to purchase the deceased's interest for himself except under the terms of the partnership contract or with the consent of the deceased partner's representative. If the surviving partner carries on the business without authority and uses partnership property, he is accountable for the profits thus made.

4. LIABILITY OF THE INCOMING PARTNER

To the incoming partner there is an important question as to his liability for partnership debts and obligations that existed before he became a partner.

Since that problem would most frequently arise at the firm's dissolution, it is discussed in connection with that stage of the partnership business.

The incoming partner, at common law, is not liable on debts existing before he became a partner, unless, in consideration of his being made a partner, he agrees to become liable on the old debts; in which case, under the rights of third party beneficiaries, the creditors would have claims against the new partner. The Uniform Partnership Act makes a change in the rule in that the incoming partner is liable on old debts to the extent of his capital contribution but, unless he specifically assumes these debts, is not personally liable. Presumably, the effect of the assumption is the same as under the common law rules. Obviously, the liability of the incoming partner for the new debts is the same as that of any other partner.

The Uniform Partnership Act does not state that the addition of a new partner causes a dissolution of the firm, and, inasmuch as the old partners have not ceased to do business together, it is doubtful if there is a dissolution in these circumstances, as far as the Uniform Act is concerned. The fact remains, however, that a new partnership arises when a new partner is added, whether or not any of the old partners withdraws; but the newness of the firm has no particular significance where the business is carried on without change, and where there is no formal transfer of property from the old firm to the new.

Where partnership property is transferred to a new firm, to a single continuing partner, or to a third person, some important legal issues arise. Under common law rules, such a transfer destroys the power of old firm creditors to reach the former firm property by attachment, execution, or bankruptcy proceedings, in priority to the new creditors, and the old creditors are neither creditors of the new firm nor separate creditors of the former partners. They are only partnership creditors of a now defunct partnership. Only a novation or an assumption by the person or persons conducting the new firm business would do the old creditors very much good. The Uniform Act has made important changes in these rules.

When the business of a dissolved partnership is continued by a former partner or partners, with or without new partners, the creditors of the old firm are also creditors of the new firm. When the business is purchased by third persons, the creditors of the dissolved partnership do not become creditors of the person or partnership continuing the business unless the persons acquiring the business promise to pay the debts of the dissolved partnership. The latter rule is not really as broad as it sounds because in most jurisdictions the promise to pay the debts is rather freely inferred from the circumstances surrounding the purchase. Furthermore, the old creditors still have their claims against the old partners, and bulk sales or fraudulent conveyance acts may be applicable.

The problems referred to above occur frequently where a business has been carried on by means of the partnership device and where, in order to get the advantages of the corporate form, a corporation is organized by the partners and the partnership property transferred to it. As a protection for the former partners, the transaction usually includes an express assumption by the corporation of the partnership obligations. Under these circumstances, the partnership creditors become creditors of the corporation, either under the Uniform Partnership Act or as third party beneficiaries at common law.

5. DISTRIBUTION OF FIRM ASSETS

A. Case

Bourne, Holler, and Arnet are partners. The partnership has dissolved and all of its assets have been converted into cash and paid out to the partnership creditors. $25,000 in partnership debts still remain to be paid. The partnership contract provides that profits are to be shared in proportion to capital contributions but says nothing about losses. What was the total loss suffered by each of the partners as a result of his participation in the partnership?

	Capital Contribution	*Separate Assets*	*Separate Debts*
Bourne	$10,000	$35,000	$ 5,000
Holler	20,000	25,000	36,000
Arnet	20,000	14,000	2,000

B. In General

The last steps in winding up a dissolved partnership include a conversion of the partnership property into cash and the distribution of the proceeds among creditors of the firm and among the partners. In connection with these steps there must also be a formal or informal accounting to determine the amounts of the claims and obligations of the various parties involved. It is not uncommon to find that the return of partners' capital is agreed by the partners to be on a basis different from their contributions. In the absence of agreement among the partners to the contrary, the distribution will always be in cash and not in kind. A partner who wants the return of specific property on winding up should make it clear in the partnership agreement that the property is only being loaned or that he is entitled to the return of the specific property which was his capital contribution. Distribution of cash is, of course, much more convenient, and would probably have to be used in paying the outside creditors anyhow.

C. Rules for Distribution

SOLVENT FIRM. Section 40 of the Uniform Partnership Act sets up the priorities by which the various claims and claimants against the partnership are to participate in the distribution. The liabilities of the partnership rank as follows: 1, those owing to outside creditors; 2, those owing to partners other than for capital and profits; 3, those owing to partners for capital; 4, those owing to partners for profits. It is obvious that if the firm is solvent to the extent of being able to cover the first three items on the priority list, the priority problem is of no particular importance. The firm will not distribute funds to the partners in three different groups but will, no doubt, give to the partner a single sum, which will include his capital, profit, and noncapital items. The noncapital items are the advances and loans to the firm and all other claims not based on contribution, capital, or profits. The surplus left over after distribution on the first three priorities will be divided as profits and in the proportions in which the partners have been accustomed to sharing profits, in the absence of contrary agreement.

INSOLVENT FIRM. The priority list becomes significant when the partnership property is insufficient to cover the claims of both creditors and partners. If outside creditors can be paid, then the remaining funds are distributed to the partners according to the ranking of their claims on the priority list; but if outside creditors cannot be paid, the partners will face a loss sharing problem. If the partnership property is not sufficient even to pay the outside creditors, the problem becomes almost exclusively one of loss sharing.

The Uniform Partnership Act continues the legal entity concept of the partnership to the extent that the assets of the firm include not only the partnership property but also the contributions of the partners necessary for the payment of all the liabilities specified in the priority list. Because of the approach taken by the Act, a partnership cannot really be insolvent, in the sense that its assets are exceeded by its debts, unless all of the partners, with partnership debts included, are also insolvent. This raises another priority issue. The partners and the partnership each have two sets of creditors: 1, the partnership creditors and 2, the separate creditors of the partners. The priorities of these two groups of creditors, both in the partnership property and in the separate property of the partners, become important where either a partner or a partnership is unable to pay his own debts out of his own property. The rules are simple and obvious. In partnership property the partnership creditors have priority over separate creditors of the partners except where there is only one active partner. In separate property the separate creditors have priority over the partnership creditors except where there are no partnership assets and no living solvent partners or where a partner has fraudulently converted firm assets to his own use.

Permitting separate creditors to reach partnership property in connection with the winding up of a firm is not a contradiction of the principle of the Uniform Act, discussed in Part IV, which prevents the separate creditors of the individual partner from reaching directly the partnership property. It should be clear that the reason behind the protection of the firm during the operation of its business does not exist when the firm is dissolved and is being wound up preparatory to termination. The priority of the partnership creditors in partnership property is sufficient protection for them at the latter stage.

ILLUSTRATION.   *A, B, C,* and *D* are partners. The partnership has been dissolved and all of its property is converted into cash and paid out to the partnership creditors. But $2,000 in partnership debts still remains to be paid. The partnership contract contains no provisions relative to the sharing of profits and losses. What was the total loss of each partner as a result of his participation in the firm? The partners' contributions, separate assets, and separate debts are shown below.

	Capital Contribution	*Separate Assets*	*Separate Debts*
A	$2,000	$6,500	$6,000
B	4,000	3,500	5,500
C	6,000	5,000	500
D	8,000	1,000	600

The problem is obviously one of loss sharing. The loss that must be shared consists of the total capital contributions, which will not be returned to the partners, and the $2,000 still owing to outside creditors, or $22,000. In the absence of contrary provision in the partnership agreement, profits and losses are shared equally, so each of these partners should lose $5,500.

Since separate creditors of the partners have priority over partnership creditors in separate property, only the net amount is available for partnership creditors, as follows:

A	$ 500
B	insolvent
C	4,500
D	400

Were all the partners solvent and possessed of adequate separate property, *A* would put in $3,500 to bring his loss up to $5,500, *B* would put in $1,500; *C* would take out $500; and *D* would take out $2,500. Out of a total of $5,000 additional put in by the partners, the creditors would receive $2,000, and *C* and *D* would take out a total of $3,000. Unfortunately, *B* is insolvent as regards his separate creditors, and *A* has insufficient assets to make his required contribution. After *A* puts in his remaining $500, *C* and *D* will have to share equally in the additional burden placed on them by the insolvency of *A* and *B*. This would be accomplished by a contribution of $1,750 by *C*, bringing his total loss up to $7,750, and a payment to *D* of $250, bringing his loss down to $7,750. Out of the $2,250 contributed by *A* and *C*, $2,000 would go to pay off the outside creditors. The total losses of the partners, as a result of participation in the firm, would be:

A	$2,500
B	4,000
C	7,750
D	7,750

or a total of $22,000 for the four partners.

PROBLEMS

1. What do the following terms mean when used in connection with the Uniform Partnership Act: dissolution, winding up, termination?

2. Assume that you are a partner in Berkland Labs, an Anosmian partnership. Your partners are Al and Bert. The three of you are approximately the same age. The firm manufactures highly complicated mechanical and electronic sub-assemblies for the Centaur rocket and for other specialized uses. The nature of the firm's business is such that the prospects for the future are excellent. All three partners are skillful and experienced managers and Bert is an outstanding electronics engineer. The firm owes its success, however, not only to the partners but also to two extremely capable employees: a tool and die maker and an electronics technician. Although the firm has made substantial profits during the three years since its organization, most of the profits have been put back into the business for the purpose of acquiring certain expensive equipment and of expanding to meet the increasing flow of orders. None of the partners has any source of income or any substantial property outside the business.

Al has been working too hard and, on his doctor's advice, has just taken a two-week vacation. On his return, he told you and Bert that he has been thinking about the future and wondering if it wouldn't be a good idea for you and Bert to do the same thing. Al is concerned about what would happen to the business if one of the partners should die or become unable to work and particularly worried about what his family would have to live on if something happened to him. Shortly after this little talk with Al, the tool and die maker comes to you and says he is planning to quit Berkland Labs and go to work for Lockheed. When you ask him for his reason he says that he and the technician, after they had heard about Al's overwork problem, suddenly realized how insecure their positions with Berkland Labs were. They are afraid that, if anything happened to one of the partners, the firm might have to be liquidated and that they would then be out of jobs. He said that he was not getting any younger and wanted a position with more security.

In order to maintain its production schedules and also to undertake a substantial contract for equipment to be used in the Pluto rocket, the firm will have to buy some very expensive machinery in the near future. All three of you are opposed to bringing anyone else into the firm, either as a partner or as a stockholder if you should decide to incorporate. You are a bit surprised when the bank loan officer seems a bit reluctant to lend the amount of money you request. He also seems concerned about the lack of security and the threat of liquidation and suggests that you give some attention to that issue before pressing him for an answer on the loan.

It suddenly dawns on all three of you partners that most of the current difficulties and uncertainty are really part of the same problem. Al and Bert ask you to draw up a proposal for dealing with this problem. They are interested not only in your recommendation but also in the pros and cons of the various alternatives. Draft a memorandum for your partners.

3. What may cause the dissolution of a partnership?

4. *P, D,* and *Q* are partners in the Rapid Action Company in a state which has adopted the Uniform Partnership Act. The partnership agreement specifies that the partners are to remain in business together for 10 years. *Q* put up most of the capital, but the unusual success of the business has been due largely to *P*'s sales ability and to *D*'s long hours devoted to improvements and economies in production. After

the business had been operating for $3\frac{1}{2}$ years, Q notified P and D that he was leaving the business and intended to invest his capital in some oil leases acquired by his brother-in-law. P and D insist that the partnership contract prevents Q from withdrawing; Q insists that he can withdraw any time he pleases because the partnership relation is a voluntary one. The three partners have come to you for advice. Give it to them.

5. Gow, a partner in the firm of Gow, Limp, and Ping, has just entered into a contract with Therd Pursen on behalf of the firm. Under what circumstances will Pursen *not* get a claim good against Limp, Ping, and the firm? Explain.

6. Able has withdrawn from his partnership with the consent of his fellow partners, who have also agreed to assume all of Able's partnership obligations. What effect does this agreement have on partnership creditors who had claims against the firm before Able's withdrawal?

7. What is the liability of an incoming partner to old and new creditors of the firm he has joined?

chapter 16

Terminating the Corporation

1. In General

Where a corporation sells all of its assets and distributes the proceeds among the shareholders, the corporation has accomplished a liquidation, but it has not, under most modern corporation statutes, brought about a dissolution. The reason is that the sale of the assets, the distribution among the shareholders, and cessation of the business do not, by themselves, terminate corporate existence. Consequently, no dissolution in law has taken place, although practical or *de facto* dissolution has occurred. Under modern corporation laws, a corporation is dissolved and corporate existence is terminated by compliance with procedures set forth in the statutes, by expiration of a specific term limiting the life of a particular corporation, or by forfeiture. Ordinarily, in order to accomplish the desired end, the corporate existence must be terminated and the affairs of the corporation wound up. For convenience's sake, the corporate existence continues for limited purposes during the course of the winding up, but is terminated as regards the conduct of the ordinary business.

Under some of the older corporation laws, corporate existence terminated before winding up. This brought about some rather odd and certainly inconvenient results: The title to the corporation's property passed to the shareholders; the directors became trustees to wind up the business; creditors had to sue the trustees; and a judgment against the corporation was void. The continuation of corporate existence for the limited purpose of winding up does away with these impractical methods of corporate dissolution.

Speaking very generally, the dissolution and winding up process of the corporation is much like that of the partnership, if the causes of dissolution are ignored. The process is essentially one of winding up the affairs of the corporation, performing unperformed contracts, converting the property into cash, paying off the creditors, and distributing whatever is left among the shareholders. It is in connection with the bringing about of the dissolution that the corporation and the partnership contrast so sharply. The corporation is a very stable form of business organization, and the acts and fates of individual shareholders have little effect on the company. Its dissolution cannot be brought about directly by the death or withdrawal of a member. Even the voluntary dissolution of a corporation usually requires the acts and consent of many persons as well as the passage of considerable time.

Dissolutions of corporations are either *voluntary* or *involuntary*. In the latter type, the court compels the dissolution; in the former, the shareholders or directors bring it about without court intervention. In some states dissolution takes place automatically on termination of the period for which the corporation was organized. In other states, the directors or others must still take action to dissolve. Since the laws of the various states differ so much in detail, the discussion here will be confined to general statements, except where detail becomes sufficiently important to justify its consideration.

2. VOLUNTARY DISSOLUTION

A. By the Shareholders

In all states the shareholders may dissolve the corporation, but some state laws are much stricter in this regard than others. Some require the unanimous vote of all shares and a resolution of the board of directors; whereas others require only 50 per cent of the voting shares of the corporation to approve. The variations between these extremes are many. Whether dissolution by the shareholders is difficult or easy to achieve, the power of the majority to dissolve may not be used to abuse or oppress the minority.

B. By Directors or Incorporators

Many statutes provide for dissolution by a majority vote of the directors or incorporators when the corporation has not begun the business for which it was organized and has issued no shares. Even where business has been begun and shares issued, the directors may dissolve the corporation, under some state laws, where the corporation has been adjudged bankrupt or has disposed of all of its operating assets and has done no business for a specified time. Under some laws, the directors must dissolve if the corporate term of existence has expired. Ordinarily, the directors must wind up if the corporation has been dissolved.

C. Winding Up by the Court

On the petition of the corporation, of a small portion of the shares, or of a few creditors, the court may take over control of the winding up proceedings following voluntary dissolution. The purpose is to protect the creditors of the corporation, a minority of the shareholders, the shareholders as a whole, and even the corporation from careless or fraudulent winding up by the directors. The dissolution does not lose its voluntary character on the grounds that the court has taken over the proceedings. The dissolution remains voluntary even in those states where some formal confirmation by the court is required of dissolutions initiated from within the corporation itself.

3. INVOLUNTARY DISSOLUTION

A. On Petition of Shareholders or Directors

In almost all states, including those that have not expressly granted statutory jurisdiction to the courts, a petition may be filed by the directors or by a portion of the shareholders asking the court to dissolve the corporation. The portion of shareholders is commonly less than one-half, and the right to petition is not confined to voting shares. Some statutes provide that one-half of the directors may petition the court for dissolution, the purpose being to facilitate the breaking of a deadlock in an evenly divided board of directors.

Where the dissolution is involuntary, it may usually be brought about only when certain grounds exist. A representative list of grounds would include the following: 1, abandonment of the business for a specified period of time; 2, inability of directors to act because evenly split and there is danger of loss of property or business; 3, division of voting shares into factions so that an uneven number of directors cannot be selected; 4, internal dissension and deadlock among the shareholders; 5, persistent fraud or mismanagement by directors or officers; 6, necessity of liquidation to protect rights and interests of a substantial number of shareholders; 7, necessity to terminate corporate existence. Because of the harm a minority may do to a majority through the use of the involuntary dissolution, many statutes give the court discretionary authority whether to grant the petition for dissolution even where grounds exist. You will recall that the court had no such discretion in comparable partnership situations under the UPA, owing largely to the fiduciary and close personal relation existing among partners.

B. By the State

The decision to include dissolution at the initiative of the state with the other forms of involuntary dissolution is debatable. The compulsory dissolution as a result of state action is a last resort remedy where the corporation has been guilty of serious misconduct. The court will not award such relief unless unusual grounds are present, such as intentional or fraudulent illegal acts, transactions of grave public concern, situations where the dissolution will serve some good purpose, or where it is expressly provided as a punishment. Furthermore, the court will be as concerned with the interests of the public as with the welfare of shareholders and creditors. The reason for this is that the suit by the state for compulsory dissolution is usually based on grounds of violation of a statute or abuse of power affecting the public. If only private interests are affected, remedies other than suit by the state are available, and the state will not be much concerned.

The proceedings by which the state seeks to oust the corporation from its corporate prerogatives are generally called "proceedings in *quo warranto*," although some states do have statutory substitutes which do not bear this title. They are sometimes referred to as "proceedings in the nature of *quo warranto*," in order to encompass all such proceedings. A proceeding in *quo warranto* asks the defendant corporation "by what authority" it is doing business as a corporation when it has failed to comply with the law or has abused its powers. Several remedies are available in these proceedings. The corporation may be ousted either from its corporate existence or from some specific power or privilege it has been exercising without authority. Fines and other penalties are also available in some states.

4. CORPORATE REORGANIZATION

A. In General

There are many reasons why a corporation might want to change its capital structure. The reason may be simply that, 1, the corporation desires to provide more funds for itself by the issue of new securities; 2, it may become advisable to substitute a new security for an old one; or 3, it may have become necessary to reorganize, in situations of financial distress, in order to preserve the going concern value of the enterprise. Changes in the capital structure resulting from the first and second reasons given above, and similar ones, are usually referred to as *recapitalizations,* but will not be our concern here because they are more clearly within the scope of the field of corporation finance. Those changes associated with financial distress are properly within the scope of corporation law, and will be examined in some detail. They are usually referred to as *reorganizations*.

A properly organized, capitalized, and managed corporation will probably never have to concern itself with reorganization. There are situations, however, brought on by severe depression or unusual obsolescence of equipment, process, or product, where even the well-planned and well-managed corporation may be faced with the necessity of reorganizing in order to protect its value as a going business. A corporation that has no inherent value as a going concern should not reorganize; it should get out of business. Unfortunately, many such corporations manage to use the reorganization device to keep themselves going through many years and through the pocketbooks of many investors. If a corporation does have value as an operating business appreciably in excess of the proceeds of an outright liquidation of the corporation's assets, then creditors, stockholders, and the public alike have an interest in the continuation of the enterprise. Whether a corporation has such value is of course largely a matter of judgment. Although this exercise of judgment was once almost exclusively in the hands of the creditors of the corporation, under modern statutes and procedures, discretion, judgment, and supervision are exercised by others as well. It is not absolutely necessary to obtain court action for a reorganization, but the reorganization of a financially distressed corporation without court proceedings is very unusual.

The corporate reorganizations prior to 1934 were accomplished through the cumbersome device of *equity receivership*. This procedure was usually initiated by the creditors, most frequently bondholders, and involved the transfer of the corporation's assets into the custody of the court and into the hands of an operating receiver, who was usually an officer or director of the corporation and friendly to the creditors. While the business was being operated by the receiver, a committee of creditors formulated a plan of reorganization. This plan would call for the organization of a new corporation and the purchase by this corporation of the assets of the old corporation at a judicial sale held by the receiver under the supervision of the court. Creditors or bondholders who did not approve the plan of reorganization were entitled to their proportionate share of the cash proceeds of the sale. Those who went along with the plan received securities, usually shares of stock, in the new corporation. The shareholders in the old corporation generally got nothing. This device was not only cumbersome, but also inefficient, unfair, and very much subject to abuse by the creditors.

Under the stimulus of the depression of the 1930's and the need for better techniques of reorganization, Congress enacted rather hastily, in 1934, Section 77B of the Bankruptcy Act. The attributes of Section 77B were: (1) elimination of the need for a foreclosure sale and the necessity of raising cash to pay off the dissenting creditors; (2) provision for administrative as well as court supervision of the procedure; and (3) better opportunity for various interested parties to make their views known. Section 77B was not as radical a change as many "experts" at the time thought, and, furthermore, it was subject to abuses of its own, in addition to being inadequate to solve the problems for which it was designed. After a long study and investigation by the Securities and Exchange Commission, a report was submitted to Congress. The Chandler Act, embodying this report, was written into law in 1938. The Chandler Act, like Section 77B, was enacted as an amendment to the Bankruptcy Act and now appears as Chapter X of that Act. Chapter X supersedes the old Section 77B.

B. Reorganization under Chapter X
of Bankruptcy Act

IN GENERAL. Although the older methods of reorganization gave lip service to the objective of affording the corporation the advantages of continued existence and the retention of whatever goodwill it may have acquired, the equity receivership, and even Section 77B, were more in the nature of a liquidation for the benefit of creditors only. The proceedings under Chapter X are carried on under much stricter judicial and administrative supervision than was the case with the older methods, and the basic objectives of protecting the interested parties while getting the corporation back into profitable operation are somewhat more likely to be achieved under Chapter X.

The reorganization under Chapter X is begun by filing a petition in the United States District Court. The petition may be voluntary, as when filed by the corporation, or involuntary. The board of directors must authorize the filing of the voluntary petition. An involuntary petition may be filed on behalf of the bondholders or by three or more creditors who have liquidated and non-contingent claims totalling $5,000 or more. It is important to note that the shareholders, except indirectly through the directors, do not have the right to file a petition for reorganization under Chapter X.

THE TRUSTEE. The discretion that the courts had under Section 77B to appoint a disinterested trustee or leave the debtor in possession of the assets is lost under Chapter X, except where the debts are $250,000 or less. Under Chapter X, where the debts are greater than $250,000, a trustee *must* be appointed. As soon as the court finds that the petition is properly filed and in good faith, the trustee will be appointed by the court. Title to all the assets of the debtor corporation is then vested in the trustee, and he is given the responsibility of operating the business. The trustee must be disinterested. If he is in any way connected with the debtors or the creditors or has any interest substantially contrary to that of any class of shareholder or creditor, he is disqualified. The emphasis on a disinterested trustee is the result of one of the lessons learned from experience with equity reorganization and Section 77B.

The trustee ordinarily retains most or all of the debtor corporation's payroll, but the payroll is subject to the approval of the court with regard to compensation for the officers who are retained. The duties of the trustee are many and varied, and the following is only a sample of his obligations: 1, to conduct an investigation of the assets, liabilities, and financial condition of the debtor, of the operation of its business, and of the desirability of its continued operation; 2, to prepare lists of creditors and shareholders; 3, to prepare a report for submission to the Securities and Exchange Commission, to creditors, and to shareholders setting forth the results of the investigation; 4, to determine whether legal actions against the officers or directors of the debtor corporation are justified and to pursue those actions; 5, to formulate a plan of reorganization.

REORGANIZATION PLAN.   The preparation of the plan of reorganization is perhaps the most important duty of the trustee. He is required to ask for suggestions from the shareholders and creditors. After the plan has been prepared, it is submitted to the court for approval; a hearing is held; and the creditors and shareholders are given an opportunity to present their objections. On the basis of this hearing, the court attempts to determine whether the plan is fair, equitable, and feasible. It is this determination which causes the most heat and the greatest controversy. The court must preserve the relative priorities among the interested parties, and it is fairly obvious that no one is ever really satisfied with his own relative priority. If, for instance, the claims of the creditors exceed the assets of the debtor corporation, the shareholders should not and will not be entitled to participation under the plan, but where the assets exceed creditor claims, it would be unfair to leave the shareholders out of consideration. All of this would be simple if the valuations, of assets in particular, were dictated by some infallible, super-human authority. Unfortunately, men have to do the job, and the valuations are the key to the whole problem. Unfortunately also, the valuations are not only of physical assets but also of going concern value in connection with which prospective earnings are more important than the value of the physical plant. Prospective earnings are frequently very difficult to estimate, and, after they have been estimated, are subject to the variable factor of capitalization in order to determine the value of the assets. All of these uncertainties, variables, and exercises of discretion leave a great deal of room for argument and for dilatory tactics by interested parties who feel they are aggrieved.

The details of the plan of reorganization will vary with the estimates of future earnings and the rate of capitalization of these estimated earnings. In general, the capital structure of the corporation will be very substantially altered. Bonded indebtedness may be scaled down or eliminated. Bondholders may become shareholders in a plan that provides for exchanging bonds for shares. Interest rates, maturity dates, and sinking fund provisions are commonly changed. Where a corporation has been through several reorganizations, it is not unusual to find that a person who was a bondholder before the first reorganization became a shareholder after the first reorganization and was dropped off the end with nothing in the second reorganization. Everybody has to give up something in a reorganization. A common shareholder in a corporation with heavy bonded indebtedness and large preferred share dividend arrearages does not have very much to give and, after his sacrifice, will sometimes end up with nothing.

APPROVAL OF THE PLAN. When the court has approved the reorganization plan and found it fair, equitable, and feasible, it is submitted by the trustee to the shareholders and creditors for their approval. The plan must receive the written acceptance of creditors holding two thirds of the amount of claims filed and allowed for each class of creditors. If the corporation's debts exceed its assets, this is all the approval required, but if the corporation is not insolvent, the plan must also receive the written approval of a majority of the shares in each class of shares for which proof has been filed and allowed. Following acceptance by the creditors and shareholders, the plan is confirmed by the court and goes into operation.

If the debts of the corporation are in excess of $3,000,000, the court must send the plan to the Securities and Exchange Commission for an advisory report before submitting it to the creditors and shareholders. The report, as its name indicates, is purely advisory, and is not binding on any of the parties, but if the Commission files a report, copies of it must go to the shareholders and creditors along with copies of the plan itself. The Securities and Exchange Commission may, under the law, make itself a party to any reorganization proceeding.

It is well to note that not all corporations go through precisely the same type of reorganization discussed above. Railroads and utilities, for example, are subject to special statutory provisions and to more extensive administrative supervision than are corporations in general.

5. TERMINATING THE OTHER FORMS OF ORGANIZATION

A. In General

The joint stock company and the business trust are so little used that time and space devoted to the termination of these forms cannot be justified. In some states, one or both of these forms of business organization may be treated as corporations for purposes of termination. Where not so treated, the procedure would still not be vastly different from that already outlined for corporations and for partnerships. Both the joint stock company and the business trust are stable forms of organization, and the causes of dissolution and the events leading up to dissolution are much like those of the corporation.

Certain aspects of the termination of the limited partnership do deserve brief examination.

B. Terminating the Limited Partnership

As a rule, and certainly as far as the general partners are concerned, the dissolution, winding up, and termination of the limited partnership are virtually the same as with the general partnership. The presence of the limited partners and the fact that the limited partnership is a creature of statute alter in some respects the causes and procedure.

The first and most important difference, and also the explanation for most of the other differences, is that the limited partner does not share the losses of the firm, except to the extent of his investment. Flowing from this basic difference are other differences. The act, death, or bankruptcy of a limited partner does not cause a dissolution of the partnership. Limited partners participate on the same level of priority as outside creditors where the limited partner's claim is based on a loan or advance to the firm. Limited partners have their capital returned from the business before general partners even get the return of their loans and advances.

Because of the formal nature of the limited partnership device, dissolution and termination require some formal steps. The limited partnership certificate must be canceled when the partnership is dissolved or when all of the limited partners cease to be such. The cancellation must be in writing and must be signed by all the members. If the firm dissolves voluntarily before the expiration date specified in the certificate, some state laws require public notice of the earlier dissolution. The written cancellation of the certificate must, ordinarily, be filed in the same places as those specified for the certificate itself. Since the legal entity concept does not apply to the limited partnership any more than it does to the general partnership, the problem of bringing an end to the existence of the firm is not as important in connection with the termination of the limited partnership device as it is with the corporation.

PROBLEMS

1. What are the methods by which a corporation may be dissolved? Give details. Compare with partnership dissolution.

2. Trace the development of the law with regard to corporate reorganizations. Describe the operation of the present law. Why have changes in the law been considered necessary?

3. What functions are performed by the Securities and Exchange Commission other than giving advisory reports under Chapter X of the Bankruptcy Act?

chapter 17

Problems of

Insolvency

1. BANKRUPTCY

A. In General

A businessman is not likely to be able to engage in business very long without coming into contact with bankruptcy law. The Bankruptcy Act exerts a profound influence upon debtor and creditor relationships, and ever must be taken into consideration by businessmen. It is to be hoped that the persons who have occasion to read this book will come into contact with bankruptcy law only as creditors and not as bankrupts. Be that as it may, every businessman should have a rudimentary knowledge of bankruptcy law, a very complicated field. The statute is a complex one, and much technical law surrounds this bankruptcy area. No attempt will be made to present a detailed or technical analysis of the entire field. The following discussion is intended merely to be a summary of some of the basic principles worthy of mention.

FEDERAL LAW CONTROLS. The first thing which might be noted about the Bankruptcy Act is that it is a federal statute substantially affecting debtor and creditor relationships that are ordinarily determined by state law. By what authority does the federal government presume to legislate in this field? The answer to this question is that under the Constitution this power is expressly delegated to the federal government; consequently, we do not need to strain notions of interstate commerce or anything else in order to uphold the power of the Congress of the United States to legislate in this area. Congress has passed a number of bankruptcy laws, the present statute being basically the Bankruptcy Act of 1898 as amended, notably by the Chandler Act of 1938. Any references to the "Act" or to the "statute" will mean the Bankruptcy Act.

PURPOSES OF ACT. The Bankruptcy Act is generally conceived to have two broad basic purposes: to aid the debtor, i. e., give the debtor a new start in life, if he is an honest debtor and deserving of this new start; and to protect creditors so that one does not obtain an unfair advantage over the other. Under ordinary state law, one general creditor may obtain a preference merely by being the first to proceed and obtain a lien on the debtor's property. The Bankruptcy Act tends to place general creditors on an equal footing and to give each a pro-rata share of the bankrupt's estate. Keep these two purposes in mind when considering the following general discussion of some of the provisions of the Bankruptcy Act.

WHO MAY BECOME A BANKRUPT. Any person, natural or artificial, may become a bankrupt under the Act, except certain types of corporations, namely: railway, banking, insurance, building and loan, and municipal corporations. Because the excluded corporations are quasi-public utilities, they are generally closely controlled by special statutes that take care of their reorganization upon insolvency. In addition to these exceptions, certain other classes of persons may not be *forced* involuntarily into bankruptcy. These groups include non-commercial organizations, farmers, and wage earners. A *wage earner* is defined as "an individual who works for wages, salary, or hire, at a rate of compensations not exceeding $1500 per year." It is readily appearent that wage earners do not constitute a large class at the present time. Why should farmers be accorded special exemption from involuntary bankruptcy under the Act? Apparently, there is no inherent reason why farmers should receive this special treatment. The provision is doubtless merely an extension of congressional policy of encouraging agriculture.

The term *a bankrupt* has a very special meaning. No one is a bankrupt unless a court of competent jurisdiction has so declared. In popular usage, the term may be used to indicate a person who is insolvent. Technically, however, a person may be hopelessly insolvent without being a bankrupt.

FILING OF PETITION. A bankruptcy proceeding is commenced by filing a petition with the proper court. The bankruptcy court of original jurisdiction is designated by the Act as the United States District Court, and the petition is generally filed with the Clerk of that court. The bankruptcy petition may be either a voluntary or an involuntary petition.

Voluntary petition.   A *voluntary petition* is one made by the bankrupt himself. Any person may voluntarily elect to become a bankrupt, except the five special classes of corporations mentioned above. There is no requirement in the case of a voluntary petition that the petitioner be insolvent. As a practical matter, however, persons do not voluntarily pursue the status of a bankrupt unless they are seeking a discharge and relief from certain claims of their creditors, which the petitioners find themselves unable to pay.

Involuntary petition.   An *involuntary petition* is a petition filed by the creditors of a particular debtor seeking to have that debtor declared a bankrupt by the court. Before the court will entertain an involuntary petition, it must appear that the debtor has debts totaling at least $1,000. In addition, the petitioning creditors must have unsecured claims in excess of $500. If the debtor has more than 12 creditors, 3 creditors must join in the petition; but if there are 12 or less creditors, one creditor alone may petition the court, asking that the debtor be declared a bankrupt.

ACTS OF BANKRUPTCY.   In addition to meeting the foregoing requirements, the creditors must be able to point to an act of bankruptcy committed by the debtor within the four-months period immediately preceding the filing of the petition. In general, the *acts of bankruptcy* consist of active or passive conduct on the part of the debtor, which causes his assets to be generally unavailable for equitable distribution among his creditors. The acts of bankruptcy should be noted briefly.

Fraudulent conevyance.   The first act of bankruptcy is generally referred to as a *fraudulent conveyance.* According to the statute, if the bankrupt has "conveyed, transferred, concealed, removed, or permitted to be concealed or removed, any part of his property with intent to hinder, delay, or defraud his creditors, or any of them," he has committed an act of bankruptcy. Creditors should be on the alert in the case of a debtor who is going downhill financially to make certain that the latter does not try to salvage some of his assets for later use after the storm caused by his insolvency has subsided. Oftentimes a debtor, in an attempt to salvage something will convey some of his property to a relative or friend, with the understanding that the relative or friend will later convey the property back to the debtor. Such a transaction is a fraudulent conveyance, and can always be set aside under state law. Also, because the making of a fraudulent conveyance, as we have seen, is an act of bankruptcy, it may form the basis of an involuntary petition. (See discussion of fraudulent conveyances in a later section of this chapter.)

Preference.   The second act of bankruptcy is often referred to as a *preference.* A debtor who has "transferred while insolvent any portion of his property to one or more of his creditors with intent to prefer such creditiors over his other creditors" has committed an act of bankruptcy. Generally, under ordinary state law, a debtor who has an excess of liabilities over assets may devote these assets to the satisfaction of any of the liabilities as he chooses. We have seen, however, that it is the general policy of the Bankruptcy Act to treat the general creditors more or less equally. Consequently, if it appears that the debtor is giving one or some of his creditors more than their equitable share in whatever assets he has available, this preferential transfer is made an act of bankruptcy, which may be the basis for the filing of an involuntary petition by the other creditors.

Failure to discharge judicial lien. A situation analogous to the second act of bankruptcy arises in an involuntary manner if one or more of the creditors takes action under state law against the debtor and obtains a lien against some of his property. Under ordinary legal principles, the creditors who attach or otherwise obtain a lien against certain assets are entitled to preference under state law. If this situation is allowed to persist, some of these creditors will obtain a greater share of the bankrupt's assets than that to which they would equitably be entitled. To forestall this possibility, the Bankruptcy Act designates as the third act of bankruptcy the following situation: If the debtor has "suffered or permitted while insolvent any creditor to obtain a lien upon any of his property through legal proceedings and not having vacated or discharged such lien within 30 days from the date thereof, or at least five days before the date set for any sale or other disposition of such property," the debtor has committed an act of bankruptcy. Note that in the usual case there is nothing the debtor can do about the situation. There is usually no way that he can obtain money to discharge this lien. However, if this condition is allowed to persist, one or more of the creditors may obtain an effective preference over the others. Consequently, this act forms the basis for the filing of an involuntary petition in bankruptcy. The mere fact that such a provision exists in the bankruptcy statute may tend, as a practical matter, to prevent various creditors from taking hasty and ill-timed action against a debtor in precarious financial position. The creditors realize that if they attempt to move in against the debtor's assets the other creditors may throw the debtor into bankruptcy, and that the amount realized may be less than if an attempt is made to work out the problems of the debtor outside of the bankruptcy court.

General assignment. The fourth act of bankruptcy is usually referred to as the making of a *general assignment.* In the words of the statute, if the bankrupt has "made a general assignment for the benefit of his creditors," he has committed an act of bankruptcy. In making a general assignment, the bankrupt transfers all his assets to someone for the purpose of liquidating and distributing them to his creditors. If any of the creditors are dissatisfied with such an arrangement, they have the right, by virtue of the statute, to have such liquidation carried out under the Bankruptcy Act.

Appointment of receiver. Another act of bankruptcy consists of the bankrupt's having "while insolvent or unable to pay his debts as they mature, procured, permitted, or suffered voluntarily or involuntarily, the appointment of a receiver or trustee to take charge of his property." Under certain state statutes, a court of equity may sometimes take charge of an insolvent business, or one in a precarious financial condition, and appoint a trustee or receiver to manage the business for the creditors' benefit. This state court proceeding can be superseded by proceedings in the United States District Court if any of the creditors who comply with the conditions mentioned above wish to take action and throw the debtor into bankruptcy.

Admission in writing. The sixth act of bankruptcy consists of the debtor's having "admitted in writing his inability to pay his debts, and his willingness to be adjudged a bankrupt." It may occasionally happen that an insolvent debtor is perfectly willing to go through bankruptcy, but he is unable or unwilling to undertake voluntary proceedings. If he admits in writing his inability to pay his debts and his willingness to be adjudged a bankrupt, the creditors themselves may proceed with bankruptcy proceedings of the involuntary type.

TESTS OF INSOLVENCY. As has been discussed elsewhere in this book, there are two basic tests of insolvency. The first and more familiar test is met when the debtor has an excess of liabilities over assets. This test is called the *balance sheet* or *bankruptcy test*. The second test, the *equity test,* is met when the debtor is simply unable to meet his obligations when they come due, although his assets may exceed his liabilities. Four of the six acts of bankruptcy refer to the debtor's insolvency as part of the required conditions for establishing the occurrence of the act. In the second, third, and fifth acts of bankruptcy, the balance sheet test is intended. In the fifth act, the equity test may also be used, and the sixth act calls for the debtor's admission of insolvency in the equity sense.

The acts of bankruptcy are rather technical in nature, and a detailed study of their meaning is far beyond the scope of this presentation. It is believed that all that is required of the average businessman is that he have some knowledge of the type of events which would permit the creditors of a debtor to proceed with the filing of an involuntary petition.

FILING OF SCHEDULES. Once a petition in bankruptcy has been filed, it becomes incumbent upon the debtor to cooperate with the court in straightening out his affairs. He is placed under the duty of filing certain schedules and listing his assets and his creditors. He is also given an opportunity to file a schedule showing his exempt assets. This a very important schedule as far as a debtor is concerned, for he may be able to claim a considerable amount of property free from the claims of his creditors. The federal bankruptcy statute bows to state law in this respect and permits the debtor to hold, free from the claims of his creditors and free from seizure by the trustee in bankruptcy, whatever property is exempt under state law. Debtor exemption statutes differ in detail from state to state, but there is usually a provision under which a bankrupt may keep a home or an equity in a home free from involuntary seizure by the creditors. Most exemption statutes also exempt miscellaneous personal property, and often substantial amounts of life insurance.

B. Administration of the Estate

Once a debtor has been duly adjudged a bankrupt, his assets, called his *estate,* pass into the control of the court for the purpose of being liquidated in an orderly manner. The proceeds ultimately are distributed to the creditors. There is elaborate machinery under the Bankruptcy Act for implementing the liquidation of the estate and its distribution among its various creditors.

OFFICERS OF THE COURT. Mention should be made of the officers of the court responsible for the administration of the bankrupt's estate. The proceedings will, of course, be under the control of some District Judge. Since bankruptcy is a very technical proposition, however, the judge generally refers the matter to another court officer known as the *referee in bankruptcy.* As a practical matter, this officer is generally in almost complete charge of the bankruptcy proceedings and exercises virtually all the powers of the court during the course of administration. The creditors are given an opportunity at the first meeting of the creditors to elect a *trustee in bankruptcy.* The creditors elect either one of their own members or a professional trustee who makes a business of acting as a trustee in bankruptcy. It is the function of the trustee in bankruptcy to assume control of the bankrupt's assets and to proceed to liquidate these assets in an orderly manner under proper court procedure and authority. In other words, the trustee in bankruptcy generally represents the creditors, and is charged with the actual physical administration of the estate. The referee exercises the authority of the court, and the court generally oversees the activity of the trustee. In some cases where immediate action is urgent, the court may appoint a receiver to assume the trustee's duties until a trustee can be elected and qualified. A receiver is usually appointed only when required to conserve the assets of the estate or dispose of perishable property, or the like.

STATUS OF THE ESTATE. As soon as the debtor has been adjudged a bankrupt, title to his assets, as of the time of filing the petition, passes to the trustee in bankruptcy. It is generally the duty of the trustee to attempt to locate all property belonging to the debtor (except exempt property) and get the greatest possible realization from the disposal of this property.

Recoverable preferences. In order to enlarge the estate available for distribution to the creditors, the trustee may take steps to recover preferences that have been made by the debtor within the four-month period immediately preceding the filing of the petition. Not all preferences made by the debtor are necessarily recoverable by the trustee, however. It must be shown that the creditor who received the preference was aware or reasonably should have been aware that he was receiving a preference before the amount of the preference is recoverable by the trustee for the general benefit of all the creditors. Consequently, it follows that a preference that was an act of bankruptcy is not necessarily recoverable. As a practical matter, however, most preferences occurring within the four-month period are recovered by the trustee.

Judicial liens. Liens obtained on property of the bankrupt by legal proceedings within the four months immediately preceding the filing of the petition are automatically set aside, if at the time the lien was obtained the debtor was insolvent, and if at the time of the filing of the petition, the lien has not been executed. Certain statutory liens, such as mechanic's liens, may be valid, and may entitle the lienholder to special priority.

Fraudulent conveyance. If the debtor has made a fraudulent conveyance within the one-year period immediately preceding the filing of a petition, the property may be retaken from the transferee by the trustee in bankruptcy for the benefit of the estate. It should also be noted that creditors acting outside of the bankruptcy statute may in many cases be able to have such fraudulent conveyances set aside even though they occurred beyond the one-year period mentioned.

Secured creditors.   Those creditors who obtained a security interest either at the time the obligation arose or later by contract, are generally unaffected by the bankruptcy proceedings. The creditors are allowed to enjoy their automatic priority, and the trustee in bankruptcy may either simply discharge these claims in order to secure the property free of the lien, or may permit the secured creditors to exercise their security interests outside the bankruptcy proceedings. It is not the intent or purpose of the Bankruptcy Act to deny secured creditors their rights. If, upon the exercise of his security rights, a creditor is unable to obtain full satisfaction of his claim, he usually becomes a general creditor for the deficiency, and is permitted to share, along with other creditors, in the distribution of the estate.

New property of debtor.   Once a debtor is adjudicated a bankrupt, he begins a new life, retroactive to the time of the filing of the petition, assuming that he gets his discharge in bankruptcy. New property that the bankrupt can acquire by his own efforts or otherwise, after the filing of the petition, is his own to keep, free from the claims of those old creditors whose claims are discharged by a discharge in bankruptcy. An exception to this rule occurs in the case of inherited property in which the bankrupt obtains an interest within six months after the filing of the petition. This property may be seized by the trustee in bankruptcy for the use of the old creditors. The apparent purpose of this provision is to prevent some person, without assets of his own, but who is an heir-apparent to a wealthy person, from filing a bankruptcy petition in anticipation of the death of the person from whom he expects to inherit.

Claims of creditors.   The creditors of a bankrupt are given an opportunity to present their claims to the court for approval and allowance and for an eventual share of the bankrupt's estate. Claims that may be presented and allowed are called *provable claims*. Generally, these claims must be filed within six months after the first creditors' meeting. Claims founded on contract, whether liquidated or unliquidated, are provable claims, and may be presented for allowance. Tort claims are generally provable only if liquidated, i. e., if they are reduced to a dollar value before the date of the filing of the petition in bankruptcy. With respect to a creditor who has a claim against the bankrupt based on the latter's negligence, however, it is sufficient if suit has been commenced prior to the date of the filing of the petition in bankruptcy for this claim to constitute a provable claim. Claims that may not be presented to the court for allowance and approval are generally referred to as *nonprovable claims*. As we shall see, nonprovable claims are not discharged by a discharge in bankruptcy.

Priorities in distribution.   It was earlier noted that one of the general purposes of the Bankruptcy Act was to prevent some of the general creditors from obtaining a preference at the expense of the others. In spite of this general purpose, however, the Act does set up certain priorities as among the creditors. After the assets of the estate have been liquidated, the proceeds are distributed under proper court order among certain groups with priority before any are made available to general creditors. The priorities specified by the Act are these:

1. The costs of administration.

2. Claims of wage earners earned within three months before the petition was filed and not exceeding $600 for each claimant.

3. Certain expenses and court costs of creditors incurred in the bankruptcy proceedings, such as in attempting to prevent the bankrupt's discharge or in securing evidence causing the conviction of the bankrupt for violation of certain provisions of the Bankruptcy Act.

4. Taxes due to the United States or any state or political subdivision thereof.

5. Debts which, by federal statute, are entitled to certain priority, or rent which is entitled to priority under state law.

6. General creditors.

It can be seen from the priorities listed that in many cases the expenses of administration, and perhaps the tax claims of the federal and state governments, may substantially dissipate the estate before anything is available to general creditors. The percentage of recovery among general creditors, may, in any particular case, of course, range anywhere from 0 to 100 per cent. In one particular district, the general creditors recover on an average of 17 per cent of their claims through bankruptcy proceedings. This figure is just an average; it does not constitute the percentage of recovery, necessarily, in any given case.

C. Discharge of Bankrupt

PROVABLE CLAIMS.   The principal benefit derived by the bankrupt from the proceedings will be his discharge in bankruptcy. This discharge, with few exceptions, releases him from virtually all his debts that are provable in bankruptcy. It is the general philosophy of the Bankruptcy Act, as has been previously mentioned, to afford the honest debtor a new start in life without the crushing burden of his old debts. The general rule is that all provable claims are discharged whether or not actually presented by the creditor and proved, if the creditor was properly notified of the proceedings. To this general rule there are some exceptions. There are some claims that are provable claims, but nonetheless they are not discharged by a discharge in bankruptcy. These exceptions include:

1. Taxes.

2. Losses occasioned by the bankrupt's fraudulent misconduct or breach of trust.

3. Claims based on a wilful or malicious tort committed by the bankrupt.

4. Claims of wage earners arising out of service during the three-months period immediately preceding the filing of the petition.

5. Claims of a former spouse for alimony.

With regard to tax liability, the federal government and most state governments have special statutes whereunder it may be possible for a debtor to compromise or otherwise secure a release of his tax liability under certain circumstances. However, these matters are taken care of by the Internal Revenue Code and special state laws, and the claims for taxes are unaffected by a discharge in bankruptcy.

NONPROVABLE CLAIMS. Claims that are nonprovable claims are not discharged by a discharge in bankruptcy. Because the creditor is given no opportunity to present his claim and participate in the distribution of the estate, he is not bound in any way by the bankruptcy proceedings, and may immediately proceed against the debtor and attach whatever property the debtor acquires. The same may be true with respect to any creditor, even though he had a provable claim, who is not properly notified of the bankruptcy proceedings. If creditors of this latter type exist, it is often the fault of the bankrupt himself who is not careful to list all the possible creditors on the schedule of his liabilities.

DENIAL OF DISCHARGE. It is not to be assumed that a discharge in bankruptcy is granted automatically by the court. No separate application for discharge need be filed, however, as the adjudication of an individual debtor as a bankrupt operates automatically as an application for a discharge. But the creditors are given an opportunity to present themselves before the court at a hearing and object to the bankrupt's discharge. Denial of a discharge to the bankrupt is a serious matter as far as he is concerned. It means that his assets have been seized, distributed, and administered at some expense, but that the claims of the creditors to the extent that they are not satisfied by the proceedings will remain and may be asserted against him even after the bankruptcy proceedings. The court may deny the bankrupt a discharge if he has committed any of various acts, which are generally summarized as follows:

1. Committed an offense punishable by imprisonment under the Bankruptcy Act.

2. Failed to keep or preserve books of account or records of his financial condition, unless such failure is justified in the opinion of the court.

3. Obtained money or property on credit by a materially false financial statement.

4. Made a fraudulent conveyance within the one-year period immediately preceding the filing of the petition.

5. Obtained a discharge in bankruptcy within the six-year period immediately preceding the filing of the petition.

6. Refused to obey a lawful order of the court, or to answer a material question put to him during a proceeding under the act.

7. Failed to explain satisfactorily any losses of assets or deficiency of assets.

Notice that the above reasons for a denial of a discharge are generally aimed at the dishonest or uncooperative debtor, or one who brings himself within an area of suspicion that he may be dishonest.

OTHER SPECIAL PROVISIONS OF THE ACT.   In addition to a general bankruptcy proceeding, which we have considered, there are important chapters of the Bankruptcy Act dealing with compositions, corporate reorganizations, various debtor arrangements, and wage-earner plans. While we forego a detailed discussion of all of these technical fields, every businessman should realize that the Bankruptcy Act does provide elaborate machinery for obtaining judicial sanction of many types of debtor-creditor arrangements. Some of these fields covered by the Act, as well as some others not covered, are discussed in the remainder of this chapter.

2. COMPOSITIONS AND OTHER CREDITOR ARRANGEMENTS

A. In General

Debtors throughout history have occasionally found themselves unable to pay their debts. The treatment of these insolvent debtors by the law has varied considerably, and there have been times when the only concern of the law was with protecting the creditor's rights. Imprisonment, being sold along with their families into slavery, even mutilation and death are penalties that debtors unable to pay their debts have faced at one time or another. The realization gradually dawned, however, that such treatment of debtors really did the creditor no good and that it often deprived society of a useful member.

Furthermore, the emergence of business competition and the appearance of severe economic fluctuations made it clear that most insolvent debtors were in that condition not because of any culpable acts on their part but because of circumstances beyond their control. Society came to recognize a genuine conflict between the rights of creditors and the relief of debtors, but the ordinary legal remedies of suit, judgment, and execution proved inadequate to the task of assisting either the creditor or the failing debtor. Bankruptcy legislation was enacted, and other formal and informal methods of assisting both creditor and debtor developed. Most of the legislation and other innovations had the two-fold objective of bringing about a fair distribution of the debtor's assets among his creditors and of permitting deserving debtors to discharge their debts and make a fresh start.

It is obvious that neither the creditor nor the debtor can have all of the doubts resolved in his favor. Concessions must be made by both in order to bring about a result which is fair and just to both. Out of this situation have come a number of compromises ranging from the informal, non-legal functions performed by credit adjustment bureaus to the formal and technical procedure known as bankruptcy. In between the two extremes are several different types of machinery, three of which are discussed below: compositions, arrangements under the Bankruptcy Act, and assignments for the benefit of creditors.

B. Compositions

The term *composition* is used here to refer to an agreement, outside of the Bankruptcy Act, under which a distressed debtor agrees to divide his assets, or part of them, among his creditors who are parties to the arrangement and who agree to release the debtor completely from the debts he owes them. Unlike an accord, which is an agreement between one debtor and one creditor whereby the creditor agrees to accept something less or something different than the original agreed-upon performance, the composition is an agreement between a debtor and all or most of his creditors. Because of the social desirability of giving a debtor a fresh start, encouraging the settlement of debts, and protecting creditors without resorting to formal legal steps, many states have special administrative machinery that gives aid to debtors and their creditors in working out composition agreements. Being a contract, the composition is voluntary.

Composition agreements are valid and enforceable, but the explanation for their enforceability is not always the same. The difficulty is one of consideration. It will be remembered from Chapter 3 that the promise of a creditor, in exchange for part payment, to forgive the remainder of a matured debt which is not in dispute is ordinarily not binding, because of the lack of consideration. Several explanations are offered for the binding effect of the composition. One is that there is in this case an exception to the general requirement of consideration based on the social desirability of composition agreements. Another view is that the debtor's promise not to prefer one creditor over another is the consideration for the creditors' promises to accept less than the amount owed in full satisfaction. A third view is that the mutual promises of the creditors are consideration for each other. This latter view is based on the argument that each creditor is really bargaining for the promises of the other creditors as much as he is for the debtor's promise. As a practical matter, composition agreements are not very likely to be entered into by a creditor unless all or substantially all of the other creditors agree to go in also. It really does not make any difference which explanation is taken. The agreements are binding on those who become parties to them. In some states this result is set forth expressly in legislation.

C. Arrangements under the Bankruptcy Act

Arrangements under the Bankruptcy Act are sometimes called compositions, but here they are differentiated for purposes of discussion. The Act encourages debtors, before they are actually adjudged bankrupt, to offer to settle or to compromise with their creditors. The arrangement, under these circumstances, is entered into with the supervision of the court after the debtor has been examined in open court or at a meeting of his creditors and after he has filed the schedule of assets and liabilities required by the Bankruptcy Act. The proposed arrangement must be presented at a creditors' meeting, and must be approved by a majority of the creditors representing a majority of the total amount of debts owed and allowed by the court. If such approval is secured and if the debtor has deposited an amount sufficient to cover the compromised claims, the arrangement is submitted to the court for its confirmation.

If all of the creditors have approved in writing, the court must confirm the arrangement if it is satisfied that the parties are in good faith. If less than all of the creditors approve, providing that a majority do approve, the court will confirm only if it is satisfied that the arrangement is for the best interests of the creditors, that the debtor has not committed any acts which would be a bar to his discharge, and that the arrangement and its component parts were entered into in good faith. If the court does not confirm the arrangement, the bankruptcy proceedings continue as though there had been no arrangement. If the court does confirm the arrangement, the assets deposited by the debtor are distributed under the direction of the court. Even a confirmed arrangement may be set aside by the court, however, if a creditor, within six months after confirmation, complains that the arrangement was procured by fraud and that he did not know of the fraud until after the confirmation. The confirmation of the arrangement discharges the debtor from those debts and obligations represented in the arrangement, except as provided therein or in the order of confirmation and except for those debts which are not dischargeable in an ordinary bankruptcy proceeding.

The Bankruptcy Act also provides for other types of composition and arrangement, such as agricultural compositions and extensions, corporate reorganizations, real property arrangements, and wage-earner plans.

D. Assignments for the Benefit of Creditors

An *assignment for the benefit of creditors* is a transaction whereby a debtor, usually an insolvent, transfers his property to another person in trust for the purpose of paying the debtor's debts or applying the property to the payment of debts. The transfer is voluntary on the part of the debtor. The assignment usually is accomplished by means of a written instrument that lists the property being transferred, names the assignee, and specifies how the property is to be disposed of by him among the creditors. The assignment itself is valid in most jurisdictions without the consent of the creditors, but in a few states, the assignment becomes effective only on the consent of the creditors. It must be remembered, however, that only after all of the creditors have consented is the assignment safe from being superseded by the filing of bankruptcy petitions. It will be recalled that the assignment constitutes an act of bankruptcy.

The duties of the assignee are to collect, preserve, and distribute the assets that have been assigned, without preferences, except for those preferences prescribed by law or specified in the assigning instrument. Certain types of unsecured claim, such as unpaid wages, have legal priority over ordinary claims of creditors. Those priorities are generally much the same as those listed in the section on bankruptcy. It is the duty of the assignee, usually imposed by statute, to give notice to the creditors of the assignment and to invite them to file claims on or before a certain date. The assignee is entitled to compensation for the performance of his acts, and that compensation is usually set by statute.

Generally speaking, the assignment for the benefit of creditors must meet five tests in order to be valid:

1. The assignment must provide for liquidation; it must not provide for any conservation of assets for the purpose of rehabilitating the debtor's estate.

2. The debtor must not reserve any control over the trust. If he does reserve control, the transaction is one of agency, not trust, and with respect to creditors it may be a fraudulent conveyance.

3. The assignment must be for the benefit of all of the creditors and not just for the benefit of certain groups or classes of creditors. In some states, however, the assignment may still give some preferences to one creditor over another.

4. The assignment must not provide that the creditors' benefits be conditioned on their granting releases, though it may be conditioned on their consenting to preferences.

5. The assignment must convey all of the debtor's property, reserving only exempt property.

3. CREDITORS' RIGHTS

A. In General

SCOPE OF DISCUSSION.   Specific rights of creditors have been examined in varying degrees of detail in other portions of the book and in the preceding portions of this chapter, but no great attention up to this point has been paid to the rights of unsecured creditors outside of bankruptcy and the other formal procedures utilized on insolvency of the debtor. Although many of the rights of creditors have nothing to do in particular with insolvency, that area provides a convenient orientation for the discussion of creditors' rights in general. The type of creditor with whom we will be primarily concerned here is the unsecured creditor who has no specific rights in any of the debtor's property and no priority over any other creditors. The debtor with whom we are concerned may be solvent or insolvent. Our interest will be centered on the debtor's assets that are available to his creditors and on the various methods the creditor has for realizing on those available assets.

PRIVILEGES OF DEBTORS.   No discussion of the rights of creditors can be properly introduced without at least briefly considering the privileges of debtors. Of course, many of the debtor's privileges and protections are simply limitations on particular rights of the creditor, and will be discussed in those connections, as, for example, the property of the debtor which is exempt from the creditor's claims, but inasmuch as some debtors' privileges are general in nature, they should be examined apart from creditors' rights.

The debtor has the privilege, as well as the duty, to pay his debts when they are due and by this act to bring an end to any rights the creditor may have had. Payment consists of delivering to the debtor something which the creditor accepts in full satisfaction of the debt. Ordinarily, the thing delivered to the creditor is money, or, more properly, legal tender, and the creditor has the right to insist on payment in legal tender unless the agreement between the parties specifies otherwise. As has already been learned, the promise by the creditor to accept less than the full amount of the debt in full satisfaction of the debt is not payment because consideration is lacking, but the promise is binding if the creditor agrees to take something different in satisfaction of the debt or if the amount of the debt is in dispute.

It is very important to bear in mind that delivery by the debtor to the creditor of a check or some other negotiable instrument in the full amount of the debt is not "payment" of the debt unless the creditor agrees to accept it as such. In the absence of this agreement by the creditor, a debt paid by check is not actually payment of the debt until the check has been converted into legal tender by the creditor when he cashes it.

The right of a debtor to pay his debt and thus to destroy the creditor's rights is augmented by the rule that a creditor cannot, with impunity, refuse to accept a valid tender of payment by the debtor. If the debtor's performance is something other than the payment of money, the refusal of the creditor to accept a valid tender of that performance may discharge the debtor's obligation entirely. Where the performance is the payment of money, the creditor's refusal does not discharge the debt, but it does bring an end to the accumulation of interest, and imposes on the creditor the duty to pay the costs of any action he may later bring against the debtor to enforce the debt. In general, a *valid tender* consists of an absolute and unconditional offer on the part of the debtor to pay the debt in legal tender, such offer being made at or after the maturity of the debt and under circumstances indicating that the debtor has the present ability to pay. Some courts require the debtor actually to show the money to the creditor.

Limitations of actions. Another privilege of the debtor is the right to defend himself by showing that the creditor waited too long to enforce the payment of the debt. It has been seen elsewhere that the law encourages the prompt and diligent pursuit of causes of action by requiring that the actions be brought within certain periods of time. If the creditor waits until the period of time has expired before he brings his action to collect the debt, he may find that his action has been barred. The relevant periods of time are specified in what are called *statutes of limitations,* which provide different periods of time for different types of action. These statutes have been discussed previously, however, and the details will not be reviewed here, except to remind the reader that under the general rule, the debt is not usually discharged by the running of the statute, but action on the debt is barred. The bar may be removed by the new promise of the debtor to pay or by his acknowledgment of the debt. Statutes of limitations protect the debtor, lulled into a sense of security by long delay on the part of the creditor in bringing his action, from being suddenly confronted with an action on the debt when evidence is lost or witnesses are no longer reliable or available.

B. Debtors' Assets Available to Creditors

IN GENERAL. As far as the type of property is concerned, it can safely be said that all types of a debtor's property are available to his creditors in satisfaction of their claims. Real property and personal property, as well as tangible and intangible property, are available. As a practical matter, almost anything that can be classified as property may be reached by the creditors. The subject of property available to creditors cannot be left there, however, because all states have statutes exempting certain property of the debtor on the basis of the use to which it is put. Other statutes make it possible for a creditor to reach property no longer in the hands of the debtor at all. These latter phases of the problem are the ones discussed below.

FRAUDULENT CONVEYANCES. Frequently, a debtor will try to remove nonexempt property from the reach of his creditors, by giving the property away or by purporting to sell it. The law has always frowned on such dishonest attempts to avoid one's debts, but until the intervention of statutory law in the field, the creditor had very little protection. The first such statute was enacted by the English Parliament in the year 1570, but this statute only protected the creditor who had already obtained a judgment. While this and other early statutes are generally held simply to have reenacted the common law, the protection for creditors seems to have been much more extensive after the statutes were passed than it was before. Since 1570, many changes and modifications have been worked in the law relative to fraudulent conveyances, and statutes have been passed in all states to protect creditors against such conveyances. The Commissioners for Uniform State Laws have drafted a Uniform Fraudulent Conveyances Act, which has been adopted by about one-half of the states. Under all of the statutes, conveyances violating the requirements of the statute are void.

When is a conveyance fraudulent? The Uniform Act recognizes several different types of situations where a conveyance may be fraudulent. Section 4 states that "Every conveyance made and every obligation incurred by a person who is or will be thereby rendered insolvent is fraudulent as to creditors without regard to his actual intent if the conveyance is made or the obligation is incurred without a fair consideration." Note that actual intent to defraud is not needed in this situation. It is sufficient if the creditor shows that the debtor was insolvent and that the debtor made the conveyance or incurred the obligation without fair consideration. For the purposes of the law, a person is deemed to be insolvent when the present saleable value of his assets is less than the amount that will be required to pay his probable liability on his existing debts as they become due. Section 3 of the Uniform Act states that "fair consideration" is given for property or an obligation in the following circumstances: "(a) When in exchange for such property, or obligation, as a fair equivalent therefor, and in good faith, property is conveyed or an antecedent debt is satisfied, or (b) When such property, or obligation is received in good faith to secure a present advance or antecedent debt in amount not disproportionately small as compared with the value of the property, or obligation obtained." Section 4 applies only to those who were creditors at the time the conveyance was made or the obligation incurred.

Section 7 of the Act provides: "Every conveyance made and every obligation incurred with actual intent, as distinguished from intent presumed in law, to hinder, delay, or defraud either present or future creditors, is fraudulent as to both present and future creditors." This section is designed to deal with the debtor who is not insolvent or in danger of insolvency but who makes a conveyance for the purpose of hindering or delaying his creditors. Note that actual intent must be shown, but that there is no requirement of a showing of lack of fair consideration. Thus, a debtor who makes a conveyance or incurs an obligation with actual intent to defraud his creditors has committed a fraudulent act whether he receives fair consideration or not. It has been held that subsequent creditors may attack the transaction as a fraudulent conveyance although made only with the intent to defraud existing creditors. As would be logically expected, a conveyance by a debtor of property exempt from the claims of the creditors is not fraudulent even though the debtor was insolvent at the time or actually intended to commit a fraud.

Section 6 of the Uniform Act makes special provision for the situation where the debtor conveys his property or incurs an obligation before he has any debts or creditors: "Every conveyance made and every obligation incurred without fair consideration when the person making the conveyance or entering into the obligation intends or believes that he will incur debts beyond his ability to pay as they mature, is fraudulent as to both present and future creditors." The Act, in Section 5, states that "every conveyance made without fair consideration when the person making it is engaged or is about to engage in a business or transaction for which the property remaining in his hands after the conveyance is an unreasonably small capital, is fraudulent as to creditors and as to other persons who become creditors during the continuance of such business or transaction without regard to his actual intent."

Remedies of the creditor. Where a conveyance or obligation is fraudulent as to a particular creditor, that creditor, if his claim has matured, may have the conveyance set aside or the obligation annulled to the extent necessary to satisfy his claim. The creditor may also ignore a conveyance by the debtor and attach or levy execution directly upon the property conveyed. The creditor may take these steps against any person except one who has purchased property or obtained an obligation for fair consideration *and* who is without knowledge of the fraud at the time of the transaction, or one who derived his rights directly or indirectly from such a purchaser. An additional remedy is recognized by the courts where the purchaser knowingly participated in the fraudulent transaction with the intention of defrauding creditors, or wrongfully sold or disposed of property, or refused to surrender possession to the creditor after the sale had been declared void. The additional remedy is a personal judgment against the purchaser. Where a purchaser gave less than fair consideration but did so without actual fraudulent intent, he is entitled to retain the property or the obligation of the debtor as security for his repayment, the creditor being entitled only to the excess.

A creditor whose debt has not matured does not have the same alternatives that the creditor with the matured debt has. While he may proceed against any person he could have proceeded against had his claim been matured, he must do so by court action. The court may 1, restrain the defendant from disposing of his property; 2, appoint a receiver to take charge of the property; 3, set aside the conveyance or annul the obligation; or 4, make any order the circumstances of the case may require.

Even in those states that have not adopted the Uniform Act, the rules are very similar to those discussed above. If there is no actual intent on the debtor's part to defraud his creditors, only those creditors existing at the time a conveyance is made or an obligation is incurred have standing to attack the transaction. This was the common law rule whether or not there was actual intent to defraud. Where there is actual intent to defraud, the transaction is void as to both existing and future creditors, although some courts do require a showing of an intent to defraud future creditors before the transaction is void as to them.

Miscellaneous. It should be remembered that, although a fraudulent conveyance is void as to the defrauded creditors, it is not void as between the parties to the transaction. Neither the debtor nor the purchaser may avoid the transaction, but must treat it as being valid. This result would be true, as far as the debtor is concerned, even if the courts did hold the transaction void as between the parties to it. The reason is that the seller is the moving party in an illegal transaction, and he cannot get relief from the courts.

A debtor has the right, it will be recalled, to prefer one creditor over another. While in bankruptcy proceeding certain preferences are voidable by the trustee in bankruptcy, these preferences do not constitute fraudulent conveyances. To permit one creditor to recall the payment by a debtor to another creditor would amount to the second creditor's being substituted for the first one to be paid. Where, however, the payment to one creditor is made with actual intent on the part of the parties to defraud other creditors, the transaction will be considered as a fraudulent conveyance.

BULK SALES. When a debtor who is carrying on a business enters into a transaction outside the ordinary course of his business, suspicion may be aroused that the debtor is trying to avoid or to embarrass his creditors. Such acts by the debtor are known as *badges of fraud*. To designate a particular act as a badge of fraud is not to say that it *is* a fraud on the creditors, but it is to say that it is outside the ordinary course of business and, consequently, is subject to suspicion and close scrutiny. It is not conclusive, and it may be explained. One of the most important badges of fraud is the sale by a merchant debtor of all or substantially all of his stock in trade. Although, under the common law, such bulk sales were suspicious acts from which fraud could be inferred, the practice of making bulk sales became so general that the common law approach was no more than a matter of locking the barn door after the horse is stolen. The result was that all states enacted special bulk sales statutes. These statutes were designed to protect those creditors who extend credit to persons engaged in business from the sudden conversion of the merchant's stock in trade into cash and other liquid assets that are easy to conceal and difficult for a creditor to seize.

The statutes varied considerably in detail. Some of them required personal notice to all of the creditors before the sale was made. Others simply required the recording of notice in some public place. Some made a sale in violation of the statute absolutely void with respect to existing creditors of the seller, whereas others made the sale only presumptively void. A typical Bulk Sales Act provided:

> The sale, transfer or assignment of a stock in trade, in bulk, or a substantial part thereof, other than in the ordinary course of trade and in the regular and usual practice and method of business of the vendor, transferor, or assignor, and the sale, transfer, assignment, or mortgage of the fixtures or store equipment of a baker, cafe or restaurant owner, garage owner, machinist, cleaner and dyer, or retail or wholesale merchant, is conclusively presumed fraudulent and void as against the existing creditors of the vendor, transferor, assignor, or mortgagor, unless at least 10 days before the consummation of the sale, transfer, assignment, or mortgage, the vendor, transferor, assignor, or mortgagor, or the intended vendee, transferee, assignee, or mortgagee does all of the following:

> (a) records in the office of the county recorder a notice of the intended transaction containing the names and addresses of the parties to the transaction, the general nature of the property affected, and the date of the intended transaction, and

> (b) publishes within five days of the intended transaction a copy of the recorded notice in a newspaper of general circulation in the district where the affected property is situated.

Uniform Commercial Code.   Because of the close association between bulk sales and other matters covered by the Uniform Commercial Code, and because no uniform legislation in the field of bulk sales had previously been proposed or enacted, the draftsmen of the Code, in order to achieve uniformity in this area, included a short article on the subject. Code provisions on bulk sales resemble precode law in most respects but vary considerably in certain details. Article 6, the shortest article in the Code, uses the term *bulk transfers* rather than "bulk sales" but defines the term in traditional fashion: "any transfer in bulk and not in the ordinary course of the transferor's business of a substantial part of the materials, supplies, merchandise, or other inventory. . . . " The Code also includes the transfer of equipment in this definition if it is made in connection with a bulk transfer of inventory. The enterprises subject to Code provisions are all those whose principal business is the sale of merchandise, including those who manufacture what they sell. Certain transactions, such as sales under court order, are exempt from Code provisions. Unfortunately for purposes of uniformity, many states have changed substantially the Code provisions on bulk sales or have retained their precode statutes. The law of one's own state should be examined carefully before relying on general descriptions of Code rules.

The Code provides that a bulk transfer is ineffective against creditors of the transferor unless the transferor furnishes the transferee with a signed and sworn list of all the transferor's existing creditors and claimants, including business addresses and amounts owed or claimed. The transferor is responsible for the accuracy of the lists, and the transferee may rely on it unless he knows of errors or omissions. The parties must also prepare a schedule of the property transferred sufficient to identify it.

The list and the schedule are retained by the transferee for six months following the transfer and are made available for inspection and copying at all reasonable hours by any creditors of the transferor; or, the transferee may file the list and schedule with the appropriate public officer. In addition, the transferee is required to delivery personally or send by registered mail to all creditors on the list detailed notice of the impending transfer. This notice must be given at least ten days before the goods are moved or the transferee pays for them and must contain the following: 1, a statement that a bulk transfer is about to be made or, where the transfer is made to secure an existing debt or debts, has been made; 2, the names and addresses of the transferor and the transferee; and 3, a full statement as to how and when the creditors are to be paid. The Code contains other detailed requirements with respect to the notice. These should be inspected in one's own state before a notice is drafted.

The Code goes much farther than most precode statutes in imposing duties and responsibilities upon the transferee. Generally speaking, this is appropriate, inasmuch as the transferee is the one most likely to suffer under a bulk sales act if the transferor's creditors are not sufficiently protected. An optional provision of the Code, which many states have not adopted with the rest of the Code, actually puts the burden on the transferee in certain situations to see that the creditors are paid from the consideration given for the transferred property. The Code contains special provisions governing procedures for sales at auction.

If the procedures required by the Code are followed, the creditors of the transferor have a generous opportunity to take steps to protect their interests. If the procedures are not complied with, the transfer is ineffective as regards the creditors, and they may proceed with appropriate remedies to obtain payment of their claims. Under the Code, the creditors have six months after the transferee takes possession of the property to bring their actions, unless the transfer was concealed, in which case the creditors have six months after learning of the transfer. As with most pre-existing law, a purchaser for value from the transferee takes the property free of any defects of title resulting from lack of full compliance with the Code, unless he knew of the noncompliance.

PROPERTY EXEMPT FROM CREDITORS' CLAIMS.   Deeply ingrained in our legal system is the idea that certain portions and types of a debtor's property should be exempt from claims of his creditors. So strong is the idea in some states that the debtor's rights to these exemptions cannot even be waived by the debtor himself. In most states, the rights may be waived by the debtor, or by the debtor and his spouse, but formalities of one type and another are usually required.

Typcially, real property used by the debtor as a homestead is exempt from the creditors. A *homestead* is usually defined as the dwelling-house in which the debtor resides, together with the land on which it is situated. Some states require that property be declared a homestead before the exemption takes effect, whereas other states grant the exemption automatically. Some states impose maximum limits on the value of property exempt as a homestead. These maximum figures range from $500 to $25,000. A few states impose no maximum at all. Some limit the exemption by acreage or by size of lot.

Certain items of personal property are generally exempt also. Included among these items are clothing, books, household furnishings, tools of the debtor's trade, insurance, family portaits, and even automobiles. In most states the maximum value of such property exempted is fixed at reasonable levels. Certain portions of a debtor's wages or salary are usually exempt also, and the exemption is commonly higher where the debtor has a family to support or where the wages are needed for the necessaries of life. The law of one's own state should be examined for details.

The state law relative to property exemptions is important in bankruptcy proceedings, although those proceedings are largely controlled by federal law. Section 6 of the Bankruptcy Act states that the Act shall not affect the exemptions allowed the debtor under state law, provided of course that the exemptions were applicable at the time the bankruptcy petition was filed and that the debtor had been a bona fide resident of the particular state for six months prior to the filing of the petition.

SOLDIERS' AND SAILORS' RELIEF ACT. Most states, as well as the federal government, have enacted statutes suspending the enforcement of certain civil liabilities against persons serving in the armed forces of the United States. Among the provisions of the statute enacted by Congress are the following:

1. If a defendant defaults in appearing in any action or proceeding commenced in any court, the plaintiff must file an affidavit to the effect that the defendant is not in the armed forces before he can secure his default judgment.

2. A court may stay any action or proceeding at any stage where either the plaintiff or the defendant is in military service. The stay is for the period of the service and three months thereafter.

3. A court may prevent the eviction of a member of the armed forces for the nonpayment of rent where the premises are occupied by the wife, children, or other dependents of the serviceman.

C. Methods of Realizing on Debtors' Assets

IN GENERAL. The discussion above has been confined almost entirely to the types and classifications of a debtor's assets that may be reached by the creditors or that are exempted, permanently or temporarily, from the creditors' reach. The discussion of creditors' rights will be completed with a consideration of the methods by which the creditors may utilize the amenable assets to satisfy the claims against the debtor. Four of these methods are discussed below: judgment, execution, garnishment, and attachment. It will be noted that in most cases the various methods are used in combinations, not singly.

One reason for this is that the judgment is usually a necessary prerequisite to the use of any of the other remedial devices.

JUDGMENT.   The right of a creditor to bring an action against a debtor and to have the court declare, through the judgment, that the debtor owes the creditor a certain fixed amount is the most important and the most common of creditors' remedies. The judgment transforms a creditor's original claim into a formal declaration by the court. Because the judgment is a much higher order of obligation than was the original claim, the original claim merges into the judgment and disappears as a separate right. The judgment is the final determination of the matter which was brought before the court. After the time allowed for appeals and reviews of judgments has expired or after the judgment has actually been reviewed, the judgment becomes binding on all of the parties thereto. A fundamental principle of the law is that matters that have been litigated and finally determined by a valid judgment should not be open to further litigation between the same parties. This principle goes by the name of *res judicata,* which means simply that the "matter has been decided." The principle of *res judicata* does not prevent the judgment from being challenged on grounds of lack of jurisdiction by the court, or the fraud or collusion of witnesses, parties, or officers of the court.

A valid judgment is binding only in the jurisdiction in which it was handed down. What this means is that a creditor who gets a judgment against a debtor in one jurisdiction cannot have the judgment enforced against the debtor in any other jurisdiction. This is not to say, however, that the judgment has no value in any jurisdiction except the one where it originated. As a practical matter, as among the states of the United States, a judgment has considerable value in other jurisdictions than its own. (See discussion of "full faith and credit clause" in Chapter 2.) Even among foreign countries the judgments of one may be of value in another, although the rules do vary as to just how much effect the foreign judgment will have. At least as among the states, a judgment of one state may, in effect, be exchanged for the judgment of the state where it is sought to be enforced, and the original judgment cannot be challenged in the new state except on the issue of whether the court which rendered the judgment had jurisdiction to do so.

Types of Judgments.   Although all judgments in cases involving debtors and creditors conform to a certain basic pattern, there are different kinds of judgments worthy of brief description here. Judgments may be personal, *quasi-in-rem,* or *in rem.* A *personal judgment* is binding on and imposes a personal obligation on a specific person or on specific persons. This kind of judgment results when the court handing down the judgment had jurisdiction over the person or persons who are obligated by the judgment. A judgment *quasi-in-rem* affects the interests of specific persons in some particular thing. Whereas in the personal judgment a court has the power to impose a personal obligation on a certain person to pay money or to do or refrain from doing something or other, the *quasi-in-rem* judgment cannot impose these obligations on a person because the court lacked jurisdiction over the person. The *quasi-in-rem* judgment, for example, may affect or destroy a person's interest in a piece of property but cannot impose a burden on the person to pay something or to do something. A judgment *in rem* affects the interests of all persons in a specific thing. Where a court has jurisdiction over the thing, it may hand down a judgment *in rem* determining the interest of all persons. Such a judgment determines the status of some subject matter, rather than rights between or among parties, and is binding as against the whole world, instead of just among the parties actually involved.

Judgment lien. As has been mentioned elsewhere, when a money judgment becomes effective, it also becomes a lien on the debtor's real property or so much of it as is within the jurisdiction of the court handing down the judgment. Thus, the person with a judgment also has a priority over other persons who may subsequently obtain interests in the debtor's property. The lien, depending upon the various statutes, continues to run for a considerable period of time, specified by statute. It is terminated by the lapse of time and by satisfaction of the judgment. (See discussion of judgment liens under Acts of Bankruptcy, above.) Frequently, state law requires that an abstract of the judgment be recorded in the public office where real property transactions are recorded. This is done for the purpose of protecting third persons who may purchase the affected property or accept it as security on a loan without knowledge of the prior judgment lien.

EXECUTION. *Execution* is the process by which a creditor actually enforces his claim and realizes on the debtor's assets in satisfaction of the claim. If the creditor is an unsecured creditor, a judgment is absolutely necessary before the creditor may realize on the debtor's assets. It will be remembered that a secured creditor, such as a mortgagee, does not need a judgment before satisfying his claim out of the debtor's property given as security. The unsecured creditor cannot simply seize his debtor's property; he must follow the procedure prescribed by statute in the particular state. A necessary first step is bringing an action and reducing the claim to a judgment. If the debtor does not pay the creditor, even after judgment, the creditor must ask the court for a *writ of execution,* which directs a sheriff, or other proper officer, to seize property of the debtor in sufficient quantity to satisfy the judgment, to sell the property at a public sale, to deliver to the creditor enough of the proceeds to pay his claim, and to deliver the surplus, if any, to the debtor. It should be noted also that a judgment usually bears interest until paid. A debtor normally has a statutory right to redeem his real property which is sold at such an execution sale. Actual seizure of the debtor's property is generally required, where physically possible. Although real property was originally exempt from execution, the law now permits the seizure and sale of real as well as personal property. Real property is seized by posting notice on the property that it has been levied upon by the sheriff or marshal. By the better view, the seizure itself is not the satisfaction of the judgment.

ATTACHMENT. Where there is danger before judgment that a debtor may remove property from the state, or conceal it, or put it out of the creditor's reach, an extraordinary statutory remedy known as *attachment* is available to the creditor. It is also available where the defendant is a nonresident of the state, where he has concealed himself or has absented himself from the state so as to avoid service of process, and when the defendant's whereabouts have been unknown for a period of time prescribed by statute. Attachment is available in some states even before an action is filed against the debtor. In order to protect the debtor from any loss he may suffer as a result of a wrongful attachment, the plaintiff is required to post a bond. The attachment is a proceeding *in rem* against the property.

Although the attached property is subject to execution after the judgment is obtained even though the court never acquired personal jurisdiction over the defendant, the plaintiff must make a diligent effort to serve process on the defendant so as to bring him within the jurisdiction of the court. If no personal jurisdiction is ever acquired, the judgment may be executed only against the attached property. If, on the other hand, personal service is accomplished, the judgment resulting from the action may be executed against the attached property and also against any of the debtor's property subject to execution.

The attachment itself involves an order by the court to the sheriff or other proper officer to levy upon and seize property of the debtor. Generally, any property that could be seized in execution of a judgment may be seized by attachment. The property is brought within the custody of the court while the action goes on to judgment. The debtor may usually get the property released from attachment by putting up a bond to cover the claim of the creditor.

GARNISHMENT. The term *garnishment* is used in several different ways. It may be used to describe the process by which an attachment is made of a debtor's property that is in the hands of a third person or by which the creditor reaches a debt that is owing to his debtor by a third person. In many states, both of these uses of the term are treated as attachments. In many states, a debtor's property in the hands of a third person or a debt owed to the debtor by a third person cannot be reached by ordinary attachment or by execution; hence, a separate garnishment proceeding is necessary. Garnishment is essentially a statutory matter, and the statutes of one's own state should be examined. Some states restrict the use of garnishment to contract situations, whereas others permit its use in tort actions as well.

When a third person receives notice that property in his possession belonging to the debtor or debts owed by him to the debtor have been garnished or attached, he becomes liable to the attaching party for the amount of such property or debts. He may terminate his liability by paying the debt or delivering the debtor's property to the sheriff or other officer carrying out the attachment. The liability of the garnishee is also terminated when the attachment is discharged or the creditor's judgment is satisfied.

PROBLEMS

1. How does it happen that bankruptcies are administered by federal courts acting under federal laws?

2. What are the purposes of the Bankruptcy Act?

3. What is a bankrupt? Who may become a bankrupt? Must a person be insolvent in order to become a bankrupt? May a deceased person be a bankrupt?

4. Outline the steps involved in bankruptcy procedure.

5. May a debtor be forced into bankruptcy against his will? Describe briefly the various acts of bankruptcy.

6. What is the function of the referee in bankruptcy? Of the trustee in bankruptcy?

7. Do all creditors have the same rights in the property of the bankrupt? Explain. List in order the priority of claims against the bankrupt's estate.

8. What is meant by the phrase "discharge in bankruptcy"? List and describe briefly the types of claims which are not discharged in bankruptcy, giving examples of each.

9. Under what circumstances may discharge be denied by the court?

10. Describe the operation of a composition.

11. Compare arrangements under the Bankruptcy Act with compositions and with assignments for the benefit of creditors.

12. What factors will determine which of the following procedures will be followed in a given situation: voluntary bankruptcy, involuntary bankruptcy, composition, arrangement under the Bankruptcy Act, assignment for the benefit of creditors?

13. List and describe briefly the privileges of a debtor who faces the claim of an unsecured creditor.

14. What protection has a creditor whose debtor is rapidly dissipating the property out of which the creditor expects satisfaction of his claim?

15. When is a conveyance considered to be fraudulent? What remedies has a creditor whose debtor has made a fraudulent conveyance?

16. What is the function of the bulk sales laws? What changes does the Uniform Commercial Code make in precode law?

17. List the types of property that are commonly exempt from the claims of creditors.

18. Describe four methods by which a creditor may realize on the assets of his debtor. Explain the particular usefulness of each.

19. Of what significance to a creditor is the fact that there are several types of judgments available: personal, *quasi-in-rem, in rem?*

20. As a result of the negligent operation of his automobile, Detur struck and seriously injured Victum, who has now filed suit for $60,000. Detur had no insurance, and his only assets at the time of the accident were $12,000 in cash and an oil lease

worth $2,000. Detur owed $3,000 to Cred One and $4,000 to Cred Two. Not long after the accident, Detur transferred the oil lease to Oncle without consideration; Oncle agreed secretly to return the lease to Detur whenever Detur wanted it. Detur made a $10,000 down payment on a $25,000 house and gave a mortgage to Selir to secure the balance. Detur then filed a voluntary petition in bankruptcy and was duly declared a bankrupt. Three weeks after being declared a bankrupt, Detur won $20,000 on a television program; four months after being declared a bankrupt, Detur inherited $15,000 from his grandfather. What are the rights of the parties in the bankruptcy proceeding and how much may the various creditors expect to receive? (Assume the costs of administration to be $3,000.)

Supplementary Reading List

Chapters 1 and 2

Berman, Harold J., and William R. Greiner, *The Nature and Functions of Law,* 2nd ed. Brooklyn: The Foundation Press, Inc., 1966.

Cardozo, Benjamin N., *The Nature of the Judicial Process.* New Haven: Yale University Press, 1921.

—————, *The Growth of the Law.* New Haven: Yale University Press, 1924.

Frank, Jerome, *Courts on Trial.* Princeton: Princeton University Press, 1949.

—————, *Law and the Modern Mind.* New York: Coward-McCann, 1949.

Friedman, W., *Law in a Changing Society.* Berkeley: University of California Press, 1959.

Levi, Edward H., *An Introduction to Legal Reasoning.* Chicago: University of Chicago Press, 1949.

Llewellyn, Karl N., *The Bramble Bush.* New York: Oceana Publications, 1960.

Maitland, F. W., and F. C. Montague, *A Sketch of English Legal History,* J. F. Colby, editor. New York: G. P. Putnam's Sons, 1915.

Mayer, Lewis, *The American Legal System,* rev. ed. New York: Harper and Row, Publishers, 1964.

Pound, Roscoe, *An Introduction to the Philosophy of Law.* New Haven: Yale University Press, 1922.

Shartel, Burke, *Our Legal System and How it Operates*. Ann Arbor: University of Michigan Law School, 1951.

Weissman, Jacob, *Law in a Business Society*. Englewood Cliffs, N.J.: Prentice-Hall, Inc., 1964.

Zelermyer, William, *The Process of Legal Reasoning*. Englewood Cliffs, N.J.: Prentice-Hall, Inc., 1963.

Chapter 3

American Law Institute, *Restatement: Contracts*. 1932.

Corbin, Arthur L., *Corbin on Contracts,* one volume ed. St. Paul: West Publishing Co., 1952.

Jones, Harry, E. A. Farnsworth, and W. F. Young, Jr., *Cases and Materials on Contracts*. Brooklyn: The Foundation Press, Inc., 1965.

Shepherd, Harold, and Byron D. Sher, *Law in Society: An Introduction to Freedom of Contract*. Brooklyn: The Foundation Press, Inc., 1960.

Williston, Samuel, *A Treatise on the Law of Contracts,* 3rd ed., Walter H. E. Jaeger, editor. New York: Baker, Voorhis & Co., 1957.

Chapters 4, 5, 6, 9, 15, 16

Ballantine, Henry W., *Corporations*. Chicago: Callaghan & Co., 1946.

Berle, Adolf A., and Gardiner C. Means, *The Modern Corporation and Private Property*. New York: The Macmillan Co., 1933.

Berle, Adolf A., *20th Century Capitalist Revolution*. New York: Harcourt Brace & World Co., 1954.

——————, *Power Without Property*. New York: Harcourt Brace & World Co., 1959.

Choka, Allen D., *Buying, Selling, and Merging Businesses*. Philadelphia: American Law Institute, 1965.

Crane, Judson A., *Handbook of the Law of Partnership,* 2nd ed. St. Paul: West Publishing Co., 1952.

Drucker, Peter F., *Concept of the Corporation*. Boston: Beacon Press, 1960.

Grunewald, Donald, and Henry L. Bass, editors, *Public Policy and the Modern Corporation*. New York: Appleton-Century-Crofts, 1966.

Hacker, Andrew, editor, *The Corporation Take-Over*. Garden City: Anchor Books, 1965.

Henn, Harry G., *Handbook on the Law of Corporations and Other Business Enterprises*. St. Paul: West Publishing Co., 1961.

Livingston, J. A., *The American Stockholder*. New York: Collier Books, 1963.

Mason, Edward S., editor, *The Corporation in Modern Society*. Cambridge: Harvard University Press, 1960.

Moore, Wilbert E., *The Conduct of the Corporation*. New York: Random House, 1962.

Mulder, John E., M. M. Volz, and A. L. Berger, *The Drafting of Partnership Agreements*. Philadelphia: American Law Institute, 1967.

Sarner, Leonard, *Organizational Problems of Small Businesses*. Philadelphia: American Law Institute, 1956.

Seward, George C., *Basic Corporate Practice*. Philadelphia: American Law Institute, 1966.

Thomas, Eliot B., *Federal Securities Act Handbook*. Philadelphia: American Law Institute, 1960.

Votaw, Dow, *Modern Corporations*. Englewood Cliffs, N.J.: Prentice-Hall, Inc., 1965.

Walton, Clarence C., *Corporate Social Responsibilities*. Belmont, Calif.: Wadsworth Publishing Company, Inc., 1967.

Chapter 7

American Law Institute, *Restatement: Property*. 1936.

Brown, Ray A., *A Treatise on the Law of Personal Property*. Chicago: Callaghan & Co., 1936.

Casner, A. James, editor, *American Law of Property*. Boston: Little, Brown & Company, 1952.

Kratovil, Robert, *Real Estate Law,* 4th ed. Englewood Cliffs, N.J.: Prentice-Hall, Inc., 1964.

Chapter 8

American Law Institute, *Restatement: Agency*. 1933.

Falcone, Nicholas S., *Labor Law*. New York: John Wiley and Sons, Inc., 1962.

Livengood, Charles H. Jr., *The Federal Wage and Hour Law*. Philadelphia: American Law Institute, 1951.

Manoff, Marcus, *Labor Relations Law*. Philadelphia: American Law Institute, 1959.

Seavey, Warren A., *Handbook of the Law of Agency*. St. Paul: West Publishing Co., 1964.

Chapter 10

Hawkland, William D., *Sales and Bulk Sales*. Philadelphia: American Law Institute, 1958.

Vold, Lawrence, *Handbook on the Law of Sales,* 2nd ed. St. Paul: West Publishing Co., 1959.

Chapter 11

Baxter, Nevins D., *The Commercial Paper Market*. Boston: Bankers Publishing Co., 1966.

Britton, William E., *Handbook of the Law of Bills and Notes,* 2nd ed. St. Paul: West Publishing Co., 1961.

Clarke, John J., H. J. Bailey, and Robert Young, *Bank Deposits and Collections.* (Philadelphia: American Law Institute, 1963.

Hawkland, William D., *Commercial Paper.* Philadelphia: American Law Institute, 1959.

Chapter 12

Braucher, Robert, *Documents of Title.* Philadelphia: American Law Institute, 1958.

Goddard, Edwin C., *Outlines of the Law of Bailments and Carriers,* 2nd ed. Chicago: Callaghan & Co., 1928.

Chapter 13

Davenport, William B., and Ray D. Henson, *Secured Transactions.* Philadelphia: American Law Institute, 1966.

Gilmore, Grant, *Security Interests in Personal Property,* 2 vols. Boston: Little, Brown, and Company, 1965.

Spivack, Oscar, *Secured Transactions.* Philadelphia: American Law Institute, 1963.

Chapter 14

Adams, Walter, editor, *The Structure of American Industry,* 3rd ed. New York: The Macmillan Co., 1961.

Areeda, Phillip, *Antitrust Analysis.* Boston: Little, Brown, and Company, 1967.

Arnold, Thurman W., *The Folklore of Capitalism.* New Haven: Yale University Press, 1937.

Bain, Joe S., *Industrial Organization,* 2nd ed. New York: John Wiley & Sons, 1967.

————, *Barriers to New Competition.* Cambridge: Harvard University Press, 1956.

Callmann, Rudolf, *The Law of Unfair Competition, Trademarks, and Monopolies,* 3rd ed. Chicago: Callaghan & Co., 1967.

Caves, Richard, *American Industry: Structure, Conduct, Performance.* Englewood Cliffs, N.J.: Prentice-Hall, Inc., 1964.

Dirlam, Joel B., and Alfred E. Kahn, *Fair Competition.* Ithaca: Cornell University Press, 1954.

Edwards, Corwin D., *The Price Discrimination Law.* Washington, D.C.: The Brookings Institution, 1959.

Galbraith, John Kenneth, *American Capitalism.* Boston: Houghton Mifflin Company, 1956.

————, *The New Industrial State.* Boston: Houghton Mifflin Company, 1967.

Kintner, Earl W., *An Antitrust Primer.* New York: The Macmillan Company, 1964.

Oppenheim, S. Chesterfield, *Federal Antitrust Laws,* 3rd ed. St. Paul: West Publishing Co., 1968.

——————, *Unfair Trade Practices,* 2nd ed. St. Paul: West Publishing Co., 1965.

Rowe, Frederick M., *Price Discrimination Under the Robinson-Patman Act.* Boston: Little, Brown and Company, 1962.

Schwartz, Louis B., *Free Enterprise and Economic Organization,* 2 vols. Brooklyn: The Foundation Press, Inc., 1966.

Thorelli, Hans B., *The Federal Antitrust Policy.* Baltimore: The Johns Hopkins Press, 1955.

Chapter 17

Mulder, John E., and Leon S. Forman, *Bankruptcy and Arrangement Proceedings.* Philadelphia: American Law Institute, 1964.

Nadler, Charles E., *The Law of Creditor and Debtor Relations.* St. Paul: West Publishing Co., 1956.

——————, *The Law of Debtor Relief.* Atlanta: Harrison Co., 1954.

Appendix

1. UNIFORM COMMERCIAL CODE: AN ACT

To be known as the Uniform Commercial Code, Relating to Certain Commercial Transactions in or regarding Personal Property and Contracts and other Documents concerning them, including Sales, Commercial Paper, Bank Deposits and Collections, Letters of Credit, Bulk Transfers, Warehouse Receipts, Bills of Lading, other Documents of Title, Investment Securities, and Secured Transactions, including certain Sales of Accounts, Chattel Paper, and Contract Rights; Providing for Public Notice to Third Parties in Certain Circumstances; Regulating Procedure, Evidence and Damages in Certain Court Actions Involving such Transactions, Contracts or Documents; to Make Uniform the Law with Respect Thereto; and Repealing Inconsistent Legislation.

ARTICLE 1

GENERAL PROVISIONS

PART 1

SHORT TITLE, CONSTRUCTION, APPLICATION AND SUBJECT MATTER OF THE ACT

SECTION 1—101.   SHORT TITLE. This Act shall be known and may be cited as Uniform Commercial Code.

SECTION 1—102.   PURPOSES; RULES OF CONSTRUCTION; VARIATION BY AGREEMENT. (1) This Act shall be liberally construed and applied to promote its underlying purposes and policies.

(2) Underlying purposes and policies of this Act are
    (a) to simplify, clarify and modernize the law governing commercial transactions;
    (b) to permit the continued expansion of commercial practices through custom, usage and agreement of the parties;
    (c) to make uniform the law among the various jurisdictions.

(3) The effect of provisions of this Act may be varied by agreement, except as otherwise provided in this Act and except that the obligations of good faith, diligence, reasonableness and care prescribed by this Act may not be disclaimed by agreement but the parties may by agreement determine the standards by which the performance of such obligations is to be measured if such standards are not manifestly unreasonable.

(4) The presence in certain provisions of this Act of the words "unless otherwise agreed" or words of similar import does not imply that the effect of other provisions may not be varied by agreement under subsection (3).

(5) In this Act unless the context otherwise requires
    (a) words in the singular number include the plural, and in the plural include the singular;
    (b) words of the masculine gender include the feminine and the neuter, and when the sense so indicates words of the neuter gender may refer to any gender.

SECTION 1—103.   SUPPLEMENTARY GENERAL PRINCIPLES OF LAW APPLICABLE. Unless displaced by the particular provisions of this Act, the principles of law and equity, including the law merchant and the law relative to capacity to contract, principal and agent, estoppel, fraud, misrepresentation, duress, coercion, mistake, bankruptcy, or other validating or invalidating cause shall supplement its provisions.

SECTION 1—104. CONSTRUCTION AGAINST IMPLICIT REPEAL. This Act being a general act intended as a unified coverage of its subject matter, no part of it shall be deemed to be impliedly repealed by subsequent legislation if such construction can reasonably be avoided.

SECTION 1—105. TERRITORIAL APPLICATION OF THE ACT; PARTIES' POWER TO CHOOSE APPLICABLE LAW. (1) Except as provided hereafter in this section, when a transaction bears a reasonable relation to this state and also to another state or nation the parties may agree that the law either of this state or of such other state or nation shall govern their rights and duties. Failing such agreement this Act applies to transactions bearing an appropriate relation to this state.

(2) Where one of the following provisions of this Act specifies the applicable law, that provision governs and a contrary agreement is effective only to the extent permitted by the law (including the conflict of laws rules) so specified:

Rights of creditors against sold goods. Section 2—402.

Applicability of the Article on Bank Deposits and Collections. Section 4—102.

Bulk transfers subject to the Article on Bulk Transfers. Section 6—102.

Applicability of the Article on Investment Securities. Section 8—106.

Policy and scope of the Article on Secured Transactions. Sections 9—102 and 9—103.

SECTION 1—106. REMEDIES TO BE LIBERALLY ADMINISTERED. (1) The remedies provided by this Act shall be liberally administered to the end that the aggrieved party may be put in as good a position as if the other party had fully performed but neither consequential or special nor penal damages may be had except as specifically provided in this Act or by other rule of law.

(2) Any right or obligation declared by this Act is enforceable by action unless the provision declaring it specifies a different and limited effect.

SECTION 1—107. WAIVER OR RENUNCIATION OF CLAIM OR RIGHT AFTER BREACH. Any claim or right arising out of an alleged breach can be discharged in whole or in part without consideration by a written waiver or renunciation signed and delivered by the aggrieved party.

SECTION 1—108. SEVERABILITY. If any provision or clause of this Act or application thereof to any person or circumstances is held invalid, such invalidity shall not affect other provisions or applications of the Act which can be given effect without the invalid provision or application, and to this end the provisions of this Act are declared to be severable.

PART 2

GENERAL DEFINITIONS AND PRINCIPLES OF INTERPRETATION

SECTION 1—201. GENERAL DEFINITION. Subject to additional definitions contained in the subsequent Articles of this Act which are applicable to specific Articles or Parts thereof, and unless the context otherwise requires, in this Act:

(1) "Action" in the sense of a judicial proceeding includes recoupment, counterclaim, set-off, suit in equity and any other proceedings in which rights are determined.

(2) "Aggrieved party" means a party entitled to resort to a remedy.

(3) "Agreement" means the bargain of the parties in fact as found in their language or by implication from other circumstances including course of dealing or usage of trade or course of performance as provided in this Act (Sections 1—205 and 2—208). Whether an agreement has legal consequences is determined by the provisions of this Act, if applicable; otherwise by the law of contracts (Section 1—103). (Compare "Contract".)

(4) "Bank" means any person engaged in the business of banking.

(5) "Bearer" means the person in possession of an instrument, document of title, or security payable to bearer or indorsed in blank.

(6) "Bill of lading" means a document evidencing the receipt of goods for shipment issued by a person engaged in the business of transporting or forwarding goods, and includes an airbill. "Airbill" means a document serving for air transportation as a bill of lading does for marine or rail transportation, and includes an air consignment note or air waybill.

(7) "Branch" includes a separately incorporated foreign branch of a bank.

(8) "Burden of establishing" a fact means the burden of persuading the triers of fact that the existence of the fact is more probable than its non-existence.

(9) "Buyer in ordinary course of business" means a person who in good faith and without knowledge that the sale to him is in violation of the ownership rights or security interest of a third party in the goods buys in ordinary course from a person in the business of selling goods of that kind but does not include a pawnbroker. "Buying" may be for cash or by exchange of other property or on secured or unsecured credit and includes receiving goods or documents of title under a pre-existing contract for sale but does not include a transfer in bulk or as security for or in total or partial satisfaction of a money debt.

(10) "Conspicuous": A term or clause is conspicuous when it is so written that a reasonable person against whom it is to operate ought to have noticed it. A printed heading in capitals (as: NON-NEGOTIABLE BILL OF LADING) is conspicuous. Language in the body of a form is "conspicuous" if it is in larger or other contrasting type or color. But in a telegram any stated term is "conspicuous". Whether a term or clause is "conspicuous" or not is for decision by the court.

(11) "Contract" means the total legal obligation which results from the parties' agreement as affected by this Act and any other applicable rules of law. (Compare "Agreement".)

(12) "Creditor" includes a general creditor, a secured creditor, a lien creditor and any representative of creditors, including an assignee for the benefit of creditors, a trustee in bankruptcy, a receiver in equity and an executor or administrator of an insolvent debtor's or assignor's estate.

(13) "Defendant" includes a person in the position of defendant in a cross-action or counterclaim.

(14) "Delivery" with respect to instruments, documents of title, chattel paper or securities means voluntary transfer of possession.

(15) "Document of title" includes bill of lading, dock warrant, dock receipt, warehouse receipt or order for the delivery of goods, and also any other document which in the regular course of business or financing is treated as adequately evidencing that the person in possession of it is entitled to receive, hold and dispose of the document and the goods it covers. To be a document of title a document must purport to be issued by or addressed to a bailee and purport to cover goods in the bailee's possession which are either identified or are fungible portions of an identified mass.

(16) "Fault" means wrongful act, omission or breach.

(17) "Fungible" with respect to goods or securities means goods or securities of which any unit is, by nature or usage of trade, the equivalent of any other like unit. Goods which are not fungible shall be deemed fungible for the purposes of this Act to the extent that under a particular agreement or document unlike units are treated as equivalents.

(18) "Genuine" means free of forgery or counterfeiting.

(19) "Good faith" means honesty in fact in the conduct or transaction concerned.

(20) "Holder" means a person who is in possession of a document of title or an instrument or an investment security drawn, issued or indorsed to him or to his order or to bearer or in blank.

(21) To "honor" is to pay or to accept and pay, or where a credit so engages to purchase or discount a draft complying with the terms of the credit.

(22) "Insolvency proceedings" includes any assignment for the benefit of creditors or other proceedings intended to liquidate or rehabilitate the estate of the person involved.

(23) A person is "insolvent" who either has ceased to pay his debts in the ordinary course of business or cannot pay his debts as they become due or is insolvent within the meaning of the federal bankruptcy law.

(24) "Money" means a medium of exchange authorized or adopted by a domestic or foreign government as a part of its currency.

(25) A person has "notice" of a fact when
    (a) he has actual knowledge of it; or
    (b) he has received a notice or notification of it; or

    (c) from all the facts and circumstances known to him at the time in question he has reason to know that it exists.

A person "knows" or has "knowledge" of a fact when he has actual knowledge of it. "Discover" or "learn" or a word or phrase of similar import refers to knowledge rather than to reason to know. The time and circumstances under which a notice or notification may cease to be effective are not determined by this Act.

    (26) A person "notifies" or "gives" a notice or notification to another by taking such steps as may be reasonably required to inform the other in ordinary course whether or not such other actually comes to know of it. A person "receives" a notice or notification when

    (a) it comes to his attention; or

    (b) it is duly delivered at the place of business through which the contract was made or at any other place held out by him as the place for receipt of such communications.

    (27) Notice, knowledge or a notice or notification received by an organization is effective for a particular transaction from the time when it is brought to the attention of the individual conducting that transaction, and in any event from the time when it would have been brought to his attention if the organization had exercised due diligence. An organization exercises due diligence if it maintains reasonable routines for communicating significant information to the person conducting the transaction and there is reasonable compliance with the routines. Due diligence does not require an individual acting for the organization to communicate information unless such communication is part of his regular duties or unless he has reason to know of the transaction and that the transaction would be materially affected by the information.

    (28) "Organization" includes a corporation, government or governmental subdivision or agency, business trust, estate, trust, partnership or association, two or more persons having a joint or common interest, or any other legal or commercial entity.

    (29) "Party", as distinct from "third party", means a person who has engaged in a transaction or made an agreement within this Act.

    (30) "Person" includes an individual or an organization (See Section 1—102).

    (31) "Presumption" or "presumed" means that the trier of fact must find the existence of the fact presumed unless and until evidence is introduced which would support a finding of its non-existence.

    (32) "Purchase" includes taking by sale, discount, negotiation, mortgage, pledge, lien, issue or re-issue, gift or any other voluntary transaction creating an interest in property.

    (33) "Purchaser" means a person who takes by purchase.

    (34) "Remedy" means any remedial right to which an aggrieved party is entitled with or without resort to a tribunal.

    (35) "Representative" includes an agent, an officer of a corporation or association, and a trustee, executor or administrator of an estate, or any other person empowered to act for another.

    (36) "Rights" includes remedies.

    (37) "Security interest" means an interest in personal property or fixtures which secures payment or performance of an obligation. The retention or reservation of title by a seller of goods notwithstanding shipment or delivery to the buyer (Section 2—401) is limited in effect to a reservation of a "security interest". The term also includes any interest of a buyer of accounts, chattel paper, or contract rights which is subject to Article 9. The special property interest of a buyer of goods on identification of such goods to a contract for sale under Section 2—401 is not a "security interest", but a buyer may also acquire a "security interest" by complying with Article 9. Unless a lease or consignment is intended as security, reservation of title thereunder is not a "security interest" but a consignment is in any event subject to the provisions on consignment sales (Section 2—326). Whether a lease is intended as security is to be determined by the facts of each case; however, (a) the inclusion of an option to purchase does not of itself make the lease one intended for security, and (b) an agreement that upon compliance with the terms of the lease the lessee shall become or has the option to become the owner of the property for no additional consideration or for a nominal consideration does make the lease one intended for security.

(38) "Send" in connection with any writing or notice means to deposit in the mail or deliver for transmission by any other usual means of communication with postage or cost of transmission provided for and properly addressed and in the case of an instrument to an address specified thereon or otherwise agreed, or if there be none to any address reasonable under the circumstances. The receipt of any writing or notice within the time at which it would have arrived if properly sent has the effect of a proper sending.

(39) "Signed" includes any symbol executed or adopted by a party with present intention to authenticate a writing.

(40) "Surety" includes guarantor.

(41) "Telegram" includes a message transmitted by radio, teletype, cable, any mechanical method of transmission, or the like.

(42) "Term" means that portion of an agreement which relates to a particular matter.

(43) "Unauthorized" signature or indorsement means one made without actual, implied or apparent authority and includes a forgery.

(44) "Value". Except as otherwise provided with respect to negotiable instruments and bank collections (Sections 3—303, 4—208 and 4—209) a person gives "value" for rights if he acquires them

> (a) in return for a binding commitment to extend credit or for the extension of immediately available credit whether or not drawn upon and whether or not a charge-back is provided for in the event of difficulties in collection; or
>
> (b) as security for or in total or partial satisfaction of a pre-existing claim; or
>
> (c) by accepting delivery pursuant to a pre-existing contract for purchase; or
>
> (d) generally, in return for any consideration sufficient to support a simple contract.

(45) "Warehouse receipt" means a receipt issued by a person engaged in the business of storing goods for hire.

(46) "Written" or "writing" includes printing, typewriting or any other intentional reduction to tangible form.

SECTION 1—202. PRIMA FACIE EVIDENCE BY THIRD PARTY DOCUMENTS. A document in due form purporting to be a bill of lading, policy or certificate of insurance, official weigher's or inspector's certificate, consular invoice, or any other document authorized or required by the contract to be issued by a third party shall be prima facie evidence of its own authenticity and genuineness and of the facts stated in the document by the third party.

SECTION 1—203. OBLIGATION OF GOOD FAITH. Every contract or duty within this Act imposes an obligation of good faith in its performance or enforcement.

SECTION 1—204. TIME; REASONABLE TIME; "SEASONABLY". (1) Whenever this Act requires any action to be taken within a reasonable time, any time which is not manifestly unreasonable may be fixed by agreement.

(2) What is a reasonable time for taking any action depends on the nature, purpose and circumstances of such action.

(3) An action is taken "seasonably" when it is taken at or within the time agreed or if no time is agreed at or within a reasonable time.

SECTION 1—205. COURSE OF DEALING AND USAGE OF TRADE. (1) A course of dealing is a sequence of previous conduct between the parties to a particular transaction which is fairly to be regarded as establishing a common basis of understanding for interpreting their expressions and other conduct.

(2) A usage of trade is any practice or method of dealing having such regularity of observance in a place, vocation or trade as to justify an expectation that it will be observed with respect to the transaction in question. The existence and scope of such a usage are to be proved as facts. If it is established that such a usage is embodied in a written trade code or similar writing the interpretation of the writing is for the court.

(3) A course of dealing between parties and any usage of trade in the vocation or trade in which they are engaged or of which they are or should be aware give particular meaning to and supplement or qualify terms of an agreement.

(4) The express terms of an agreement and an applicable course of dealing or usage of trade shall be construed wherever reasonable as consistent with each other; but when such construction is unreasonable express terms control both course of dealing and usage of trade and course of dealing controls usage of trade.

(5) An applicable usage of trade in the place where any part of performance is to occur shall be used in interpreting the agreement as to that part of the performance.

(6) Evidence of a relevant usage of trade offered by one party is not admissible unless and until he has given the other party such notice as the court finds sufficient to prevent unfair surprise to the latter.

SECTION 1—206. STATUTE OF FRAUDS FOR KINDS OF PERSONAL PROPERTY NOT OTHER-WISE COVERED. (1) Except in the cases described in subsection (2) of this section a contract for the sale of personal property is not enforceable by way of action or defense beyond five thousand dollars in amount or value of remedy unless there is some writing which indicates that a contract for sale has been made between the parties at a defined or stated price, reasonably identifies the subject matter, and is signed by the party against whom enforcement is sought or by his authorized agent.

(2) Subsection (1) of this section does not apply to contracts for the sale of goods (Section 2—201) nor of securities (Section 8—319) nor to security agreements (Section 9—203).

SECTION 1—207. PERFORMANCE OR ACCEPTANCE UNDER RESERVATION OF RIGHTS. A party who with explicit reservation of rights performs or promises performance or assents to performance in a manner demanded or offered by the other party does not thereby prejudice the rights reserved. Such words as "without prejudice", "under protest" or the like are sufficient.

SECTION 1—208. OPTION TO ACCELERATE AT WILL. A term providing that one party or his successor in interest may accelerate payment or performance or require collateral or additional collateral "at will" or "when he deems himself insecure" or in words of similar import shall be construed to mean that he shall have power to do so only if he in good faith believes that the prospect of payment or performance is impaired. The burden of establishing lack of good faith is on the party against whom the power has been exercised.

ARTICLE 2

SALES

PART 1

SHORT TITLE, GENERAL CONSTRUCTION AND SUBJECT MATTER

SECTION 2—101. SHORT TITLE. This Article shall be known and may be cited as Uniform Commercial Code—Sales.

SECTION 2—102. SCOPE; CERTAIN SECURITY AND OTHER TRANSACTIONS EXCLUDED FROM THIS ARTICLE. Unless the context otherwise requires, this Article applies to transactions in goods; it does not apply to any transaction which although in the form of an unconditional contract to sell or present sale is intended to operate only as a security transaction nor does this Article impair or repeal any statute regulating sales to consumers, farmers or other specified classes of buyers.

SECTION 2—103. DEFINITIONS AND INDEX OF DEFINITIONS. (1) In this Article unless the context otherwise requires

    (a) "Buyer" means a person who buys or contracts to buy goods.

    (b) "Good faith" in the case of a merchant means honesty in fact and the observance of reasonable commercial standards of fair dealing in the trade.

    (c) "Receipt" of goods means taking physical possession of them.

    (d) "Seller" means a person who sells or contracts to sell goods.

(2) Other definitions applying to this Article or to specified Parts thereof, and the sections in which they appear are:

"Acceptance". Section 2—606.

"Banker's credit". Section 2—325.

"Between merchants". Section 2—104.
"Cancellation". Section 2—106(4).
"Commercial unit". Section 2—105.
"Confirmed credit". Section 2—325.
"Conforming to contract". Section 2—106.
"Contract for sale". Section 2—106.
"Cover". Section 2—712.
"Entrusting". Section 2—403.
"Financing agency". Section 2—104.
"Future goods". Section 2—105.
"Goods". Section 2—105.
"Identification". Section 2—501.
"Installment contract". Section 2—612.
"Letter of Credit". Section 2—325.
"Lot". Section 2—105.
"Merchant". Section 2—104.
"Overseas". Section 2—323.
"Person in position of seller". Section 2—707.
"Present sale". Section 2—106.
"Sale". Section 2—106.
"Sale on approval". Section 2—326.
"Sale or return". Section 2—326.
"Termination". Section 2—106.

(3) The following definitions in other Articles apply to this Article:
"Check". Section 3—104.
"Consignee". Section 7—102.
"Consignor". Section 7—102.
"Consumer goods". Section 9—109.
"Dishonor". Section 3—507.
"Draft". Section 3—104.

(4) In addition Article 1 contains general definitions and principles of construction and interpretation applicable throughout this Article.

SECTION 2—104. DEFINITIONS: "MERCHANT"; "BETWEEN MERCHANTS"; "FINANCING AGENCY". (1) "Merchant" means a person who deals in goods of the kind or otherwise by his occupation holds himself out as having knowledge or skill peculiar to the practices or goods involved in the transaction or to whom such knowledge or skill may be attributed by his employment of an agent or broker or other intermediary who by his occupation holds himself out as having such knowledge or skill.

(2) "Financing agency" means a bank, finance company or other person who in the ordinary course of business makes advances against goods or documents of title or who by arrangement with either the seller or the buyer intervenes in ordinary course to make or collect payment due or claimed under the contract for sale, as by purchasing or paying the seller's draft or making advances against it or by merely taking it for collection whether or not documents of title accompany the draft. "Financing agency" includes also a bank or other person who similarly intervenes between persons who are in the position of seller and buyer in respect to the goods (Section 2—707).

(3) "Between merchants" means in any transaction with respect to which both parties are chargeable with the knowledge or skill of merchants.

SECTION 2—105. DEFINITIONS: TRANSFERABILITY; "GOODS"; "FUTURE" GOODS; "LOT"; "COMMERCIAL UNIT". (1) "Goods" means all things (including specially manufactured goods) which are movable at the time of identification to the contract for sale other than the money in which the price is to be paid, investment securities (Article 8) and things in action. "Goods" also includes the unborn young of animals and growing crops and other identified things attached to realty as described in the section on goods to be severed from realty (Section 2—107).

(2) Goods must be both existing and identified before any interest in them can pass. Goods which are not both existing and identified are "future" goods. A purported present sale of future goods or of any interest therein operates as a contract to sell.

(3) There may be a sale of a part interest in existing identified goods.

(4) An undivided share in an identified bulk of fungible goods is sufficiently iden-

tified to be sold although the quantity of the bulk is not determined. Any agreed proportion of such a bulk or any quantity thereof agreed upon by number, weight or other measure may to the extent of the seller's interest in the bulk be sold to the buyer who then becomes an owner in common.

(5) "Lot" means a parcel or a single article which is the subject matter of a separate sale or delivery, whether or not it is sufficient to perform the contract.

(6) "Commercial unit" means such a unit of goods as by commercial usage is a single whole for purposes of sale and division of which materially impairs its character or value on the market or in use. A commercial unit may be a single article (as a machine) or a set of articles (as a suite of furniture or an assortment of sizes) or a quantity (as a bale, gross, or carload) or any other unit treated in use or in the relevant market as a single whole.

SECTION 2—106. DEFINITIONS: "CONTRACT"; "AGREEMENT"; "CONTRACT FOR SALE"; "SALE"; "PRESENT SALE"; "CONFORMING" TO CONTRACT; "TERMINATION"; "CANCELLATION". (1) In this Article unless the context otherwise requires "contract" and "agreement" are limited to those relating to the present or future sale of goods. "Contract for sale" includes both a present sale of goods and a contract to sell goods at a future time. A "sale" consists in the passing of title from the seller to the buyer for a price (Section 2—401). A "present sale" means a sale which is accomplished by the making of the contract.

(2) Goods or conduct including any part of a performance are "conforming" or conform to the contract when they are in accordance with the obligations under the contract.

(3) "Termination" occurs when either party pursuant to a power created by agreement or law puts an end to the contract otherwise than for its breach. On "termination" all obligations which are still executory on both sides are discharged but any right based on prior breach or performance survives.

(4) "Cancellation" occurs when either party puts an end to the contract for breach by the other and its effect is the same as that of "termination" except that the cancelling party also retains any remedy for breach of the whole contract or any unperformed balance.

SECTION 2—107. GOODS TO BE SEVERED FROM REALTY: RECORDING. (1) A contract for the sale of timber, minerals or the like or a structure or its materials to be removed from realty is a contract for the sale of goods within this Article if they are to be severed by the seller but until severance a purported present sale thereof which is not effective as a transfer of an interest in land is effective only as a contract to sell.

(2) A contract for the sale apart from the land of growing crops or other things attached to realty and capable of severance without material harm thereto but not described in subsection (1) is a contract for the sale of goods within this Article whether the subject matter is to be severed by the buyer or by the seller even though it forms part of the realty at the time of contracting, and the parties can by identification effect a present sale before severance.

(3) The provisions of this section are subject to any third party rights provided by the law relating to realty records, and the contract for sale may be executed and recorded as a document transferring an interest in land and shall then constitute notice to third parties of the buyer's rights under the contract for sale.

PART 2

FORM, FORMATION AND READJUSTMENT OF CONTRACT

SECTION 2—201. FORMAL REQUIREMENTS; STATUTE OF FRAUDS. (1) Except as otherwise provided in this section a contract for the sale of goods for the price of $500 or more is not enforceable by way of action or defense unless there is some writing sufficient to indicate that a contract for sale has been made between the parties and signed by the party against whom enforcement is sought or by his authorized agent or broker. A writing is not insufficient because it omits or incorrectly states a term agreed upon but the contract is not enforceable under this paragraph beyond the quantity of goods shown in such writing.

(2) Between merchants if within a reasonable time a writing in confirmation of the contract and sufficient against the sender is received and the party receiving it has reason to know its contents, it satisfies the requirements of subsection (1) against such party unless written notice of objection to its contents is given within ten days after it is received.

(3) A contract which does not satisfy the requirements of subsection (1) but which is valid in other respects is enforceable

    (a) if the goods are to be specially mainufactured for the buyer and are not suitable for sale to others in the ordinary course of the seller's business and the seller, before notice of repudiation is received and under circumstances which reasonably indicate that the goods are for the buyer, has made either a substantial beginning of their manufacture or commitments for their procurement; or

    (b) if the party against whom enforcement is sought admits in his pleading, testimony or otherwise in court that a contract for sale was made, but the contract is not enforceable under this provision beyond the quantity of goods admitted; or

    (c) with respect to goods for which payment has been made and accepted or which have been received and accepted (Sec. 2—606).

SECTION 2—202. FINAL WRITTEN EXPRESSION: PAROL OR EXTRINSIC EVIDENCE. Terms with respect to which the confirmatory memoranda of the parties agree or which are otherwise set forth in a writing intended by the parties as a final expression of their agreement with respect to such terms as are included therein may not be contradicted by evidence of any prior agreement or of a contemporaneous oral agreement but may be explained or supplemented

    (a) by course of dealing or usage of trade (Section 1—205) or by course of performance (Section 2—208); and

    (b) by evidence of consistent additional terms unless the court finds the writing to have been intended also as a complete and exclusive statement of the terms of the agreement.

SECTION 2—203. SEALS INOPERATIVE. The affixing of a seal to a writing evidencing a contract for sale or an offer to buy or sell goods does not constitute the writing a sealed instrument and the law with respect to sealed instruments does not apply to such a contract or offer.

SECTION 2—204. FORMATION IN GENERAL. (1) A contract for sale of goods may be made in any manner sufficient to show agreement, including conduct by both parties which recognizes the existence of such a contract.

(2) An agreement sufficient to constitute a contract for sale may be found even though the moment of its making is undetermined.

(3) Even though one or more terms are left open a contract for sale does not fail for indefiniteness if the parties have intended to make a contract and there is a reasonably certain basis for giving an appropriate remedy.

SECTION 2—205. FIRM OFFERS. An offer by a merchant to buy or sell goods in a signed writing which by its terms gives assurance that it will be held open is not revocable, for lack of consideration, during the time stated or if no time is stated for a reasonable time, but in no event may such period of irrevocability exceed three months; but any such term of assurance on a form supplied by the offeree must be separately signed by the offeror.

SECTION 2—206. OFFER AND ACCEPTANCE IN FORMATION OF CONTRACT. (1) Unless otherwise unambiguously indicated by the language or circumstances

    (a) an offer to make a contract shall be construed as inviting acceptance in any manner and by any medium reasonable in the circumstances;

    (b) an order or other offer to buy goods for prompt or current shipment shall be construed as inviting acceptance either by a prompt promise to ship or by the prompt or current shipment of conforming or non-conforming goods, but such a shipment of non-conforming goods does not constitute an acceptance if the seller seasonably notifies the buyer that the shipment is offered only as an accommodation to the buyer.

(2) Where the beginning of a requested performance is a reasonable mode of ac-

ceptance an offeror who is not notified of acceptance within a reasonable time may treat the offer as having lapsed before acceptance.

SECTION 2—207. ADDITIONAL TERMS IN ACCEPTANCE OR CONFIRMATION. (1) A definite and seasonable expression of acceptance or a written confirmation which is sent within a reasonable time operates as an acceptance even though it states terms additional to or different from those offered or agreed upon, unless acceptance is expressly made conditional on assent to the additional or different terms.

(2) The additional terms are to be construed as proposals for addition to the contract. Between merchants such terms become part of the contract unless:

    (a) the offer expressly limits acceptance to the terms of the offer;

    (b) they materially alter it; or

    (c) notification of objection to them has already been given or is given within a reasonable time after notice of them is received.

(3) Conduct by both parties which recognizes the existence of a contract is sufficient to establish a contract for sale although the writings of the parties do not otherwise establish a contract. In such case the terms of the particular contract consist of those terms on which the writings of the parties agree, together with any supplementary terms incorporated under any other provisions of this Act.

SECTION 2—208. COURSE OF PERFORMANCE OR PRACTICAL CONSTRUCTION. (1) Where the contract for sale involves repeated occasions for performance by either party with knowledge of the nature of the performance and opportunity for objection to it by the other, any course of performance accepted or acquiesced in without objection shall be relevant to determine the meaning of the agreement.

(2) The express terms of the agreement and any such course of performance, as well as any course of dealing and usage of trade, shall be construed whenever reasonable as consistent with each other; but when such construction is unreasonable, express terms shall control course of performance and course of performance shall control both course of dealing and usage of trade (Section 1—205).

(3) Subject to the provisions of the next section on modification and waiver, such course of performance shall be relevant to show a waiver or modification of any term inconsistent with such course of performance.

SECTION 2—209. MODIFICATION, RESCISSION AND WAIVER. (1) An agreement modifying a contract within this Article needs no consideration to be binding.

(2) A signed agreement which excludes modification or rescission except by a signed writing cannot be otherwise modified or rescinded, but except as between merchants such a requirement on a form supplied by the merchant must be separately signed by the other party.

(3) The requirements of the statute of frauds section of this Article (Section 2—201) must be satisfied if the contract as modified is within its provisions.

(4) Although an attempt at modification or rescission does not satisfy the requirements of subsection (2) or (3) it can operate as a waiver.

(5) A party who has made a waiver affecting an executory portion of the contract may retract the waiver by reasonable notification received by the other party that strict performance will be required of any term waived, unless the retraction would be unjust in view of a material change of position in reliance on the waiver.

SECTION 2—210. DELEGATION OF PERFORMANCE; ASSIGNMENT OF RIGHTS. (1) A party may perform his duty through a delegate unless otherwise agreed or unless the other party has a substantial interest in having his original promisor perform or control the acts required by the contract. No delegation of performance relieves the party delegating of any duty to perform or any liability for breach.

(2) Unless otherwise agreed all rights of either seller or buyer can be assigned except where the assignment would materially change the duty of the other party, or increase materially the burden or risk imposed on him by his contract, or impair materially his chance of obtaining return performance. A right to damages for breach of the whole contract or a right arising out of the assignor's due performance of his entire obligation can be assigned despite agreement otherwise.

(3) Unless the circumstances indicate the contrary a prohibition of assignment of "the contract" is to be construed as barring only the delegation to the assignee of the assignor's performance.

(4) An assignment of "the contract" or of "all my rights under the contract" or an assignment in similar general terms is an assignment of rights and unless the language or the circumstances (as in an assignment for security) indicate the contrary, it is a delegation of performance of the duties of the assignor and its acceptance by the assignee constitutes a promise by him to perform those duties. This promise is enforceable by either the assignor or the other party to the original contract.

(5) The other party may treat any assignment which delegates performance as creating reasonable grounds for insecurity and may without prejudice to his rights against the assignor demand assurances from the assignee (Section 2—609).

PART 3

GENERAL OBLIGATION AND CONSTRUCTION OF CONTRACT

SECTION 2—301. GENERAL OBLIGATIONS OF PARTIES. The obligation of the seller is to transfer and deliver and that of the buyer is to accept and pay in accordance with the contract.

SECTION 2—302. UNCONSCIONABLE CONTRACT OR CLAUSE. (1) If the court as a matter of law finds the contract or any clause of the contract to have been unconscionable at the time it was made the court may refuse to enforce the contract, or it may enforce the remainder of the contract without the unconscionable clause, or it may so limit the application of any unconscionable clause as to avoid any unconscionable result.

(2) When it is claimed or appears to the court that the contract or any clause thereof may be unconscionable the parties shall be afforded a reasonable opportunity to present evidence as to its commercial setting, purpose and effect to aid the court in making the determination.

SECTION 2—303. ALLOCATION OR DIVISION OF RISKS. Where this Article allocates a risk or a burden as between the parties "unless otherwise agreed", the agreement may not only shift the allocation but may also divide the risk or burden.

SECTION 2—304. PRICE PAYABLE IN MONEY, GOODS, REALTY, OR OTHERWISE. (1) The price can be made payable in money or otherwise. If it is payable in whole or in part in goods each party is a seller of the goods which he is to transfer.

(2) Even though all or part of the price is payable in an interest in realty the transfer of the goods and the seller's obligations with reference to them are subject to this Article, but not the transfer of the interest in realty or the transferor's obligations in connection therewith.

SECTION 2—305. OPEN PRICE TERM. (1) The parties if they so intend can conclude a contract for sale even though the price is not settled. In such a case the price is a reasonable price at the time for delivery if
  (a) nothing is said as to price; or
  (b) the price is left to be agreed by the parties and they fail to agree; or
  (c) the price is to be fixed in terms of some agreed market or other standard as set or recorded by a third person or agency and it is not so set or recorded.

(2) A price to be fixed by the seller or by the buyer means a price for him to fix in good faith.

(3) When a price left to be fixed otherwise than by agreement of the parties fails to be fixed through fault of one party the other may at his option treat the contract as cancelled or himself fix a reasonable price.

(4) Where, however, the parties intend not to be bound unless the price be fixed or agreed and it is not fixed or agreed there is no contract. In such a case the buyer must return any goods already received or if unable so to do must pay their reasonable value at the time of delivery and the seller must return any portion of the price paid on account.

SECTION 2—306. OUTPUT, REQUIREMENTS AND EXCLUSIVE DEALINGS. (1) A term which measures the quantity by the output of the seller or the requirements of the buyer means such actual output or requirements as may occur in good faith, except that no quantity unreasonably disproportionate to any stated estimate or in the absence of a stated estimate to any normal or otherwise comparable prior output or requirements may be tendered or demanded.

(2) A lawful agreement by either the seller or the buyer for exclusive dealing in the kind of goods concerned imposes unless otherwise agreed an obligation by the seller to use best efforts to supply the goods and by the buyer to use best efforts to promote their sale.

SECTION 2—307. DELIVERY IN SINGLE LOT OR SEVERAL LOTS. Unless otherwise agreed all goods called for by a contract for sale must be tendered in a single delivery and payment is due only on such tender but where the circumstances give either party the right to make or demand delivery in lots the price if it can be apportioned may be demanded for each lot.

SECTION 2—308. ABSENCE OF SPECIFIED PLACE FOR DELIVERY. Unless otherwise agreed

    (a) the place for delivery of goods is the seller's place of business or if he has none his residence; but

    (b) in a contract for sale of identified goods which to the knowledge of the parties at the time of contracting are in some other place, that place is the place for their delivery; and

    (c) documents of title may be delivered through customary banking channels.

SECTION 2—309. ABSENCE OF SPECIFIC TIME PROVISIONS; NOTICE OF TERMINATION.

(1) The time for shipment or delivery or any other action under a contract if not provided in this Article or agreed upon shall be a reasonable time.

(2) Where the contract provides for successive performances but is indefinite in duration it is valid for a reasonable time but unless otherwise agreed may be terminated at any time by either party.

(3) Termination of a contract by one party except on the happening of an agreed event requires that reasonable notification be received by the other party and an agreement dispensing with notification is invalid if its operation would be unconscionable.

SECTION 2—310. OPEN TIME FOR PAYMENT OR RUNNING OF CREDIT; AUTHORITY TO SHIP UNDER RESERVATION. Unless otherwise agreed

    (a) payment is due at the time and place at which the buyer is to receive the goods even though the place of shipment is the place of delivery; and

    (b) if the seller is authorized to send the goods he may ship them under reservation, and may tender the documents of title, but the buyer may inspect the goods after their arrival before payment is due unless such inspection is inconsistent with the terms of the contract (Section 2—513); and

    (c) if delivery is authorized and made by way of documents of title otherwise than by subsection (b) then payment is due at the time and place at which the buyer is to receive the documents regardless of where the goods are to be received; and

    (d) where the seller is required or authorized to ship the goods on credit the credit period runs from the time of shipment but post-dating the invoice or delaying its dispatch will correspondingly delay the starting of the credit period.

SECTION 2—311. OPTIONS AND COOPERATION RESPECTING PERFORMANCE. (1) An agreement for sale which is otherwise sufficiently definite (subsection (3) of Section 2—204) to be a contract is not made invalid by the fact that it leaves particulars of performance to be specified by one of the parties. Any such specification must be made in good faith and within limits set by commercial reasonableness.

(2) Unless otherwise agreed specifications relating to assortment of the goods are at the buyer's option and except as otherwise provided in subsections (1) (c) and (3) of Section 2—319 specifications or arrangements relating to shipment are at the seller's option.

(3) Where such specification would materially affect the other party's performance but is not seasonably made or where one party's cooperation is necessary to the agreed performance of the other but is not seasonably forthcoming, the other party in addition to all other remedies

    (a) is excused for any resulting delay in his own performance; and

    (b) may also either proceed to perform in any reasonable manner or after the time for a material part of his own performance treat the failure to specify or to cooperate as a breach by failure to deliver or accept the goods.

Section 2—312. Warranty of Title and Against Infringement; Buyer's Obligation Against Infringement. (1) Subject to subsection (2) there is in a contract for sale a warranty by the seller that

(a) the title conveyed shall be good, and its transfer rightful; and

(b) the goods shall be delivered free from any security interest or other lien or encumbrance of which the buyer at the time of contracting has no knowledge.

(2) A warranty under subsection (1) will be excluded or modified only by specific language or by circumstances which give the buyer reason to know that the person selling does not claim title in himself or that he is purporting to sell only such right or title as he or a third person may have.

(3) Unless otherwise agreed a seller who is a merchant regularly dealing in goods of the kind warrants that the goods shall be delivered free of the rightful claim of any third person by way of infringement or the like but a buyer who furnishes specifications to the seller must hold the seller harmless against any such claim which arises out of compliance with the specifications.

Section 2—313. Express Warranties by Affirmation, Promise, Description, Sample. (1) Express warranties by the seller are created as follows:

(a) Any affirmation of fact or promise made by the seller to the buyer which relates to the goods and becomes part of the basis of the bargain creates an express warranty that the goods shall conform to the affirmation or promise.

(b) Any description of the goods which is made part of the basis of the bargain creates an express warranty that the goods shall conform to the description.

(c) Any sample or model which is made part of the basis of the bargain creates an express warranty that the whole of the goods shall conform to the sample or model.

(2) It is not necessary to the creation of an express warranty that the seller use formal words such as "warrant" or "guarantee" or that he have a specific intention to make a warranty, but an affirmation merely of the value of the goods or a statement purporting to be merely the seller's opinion or commendation of the goods does not create a warranty.

Section 2—314. Implied Warranty: Merchantability; Usage of Trade. (1) Unless excluded or modified (Section 2—316), a warranty that the goods shall be merchantable is implied in a contract for their sale if the seller is a merchant with respect to goods of that kind. Under this section the serving for value of food or drink to be consumed either on the premises or elsewhere is a sale.

(2) Goods to be merchantable must be at least such as

(a) pass without objection in the trade under the contract description; and

(b) in the case of fungible goods, are of fair average quality within the description; and

(c) are fit for the ordinary purposes for which such goods are used; and

(d) run, within the variations permitted by the agreement, of even kind, quality and quantity within each unit and among all units involved; and

(e) are adequately contained, packaged, and labeled as the agreement may require; and

(f) conform to the promises or affirmations of fact made on the container or label if any.

(3) Unless excluded or modified (Section 2—316) other implied warranties may arise from course of dealing or usage of trade.

Section 2—315. Implied Warranty: Fitness for Particular Purpose. Where the seller at the time of contracting has reason to know any particular purpose for which the goods are required and that the buyer is relying on the seller's skill or judgment to select or furnish suitable goods, there is unless excluded or modified under the next section an implied warranty that the goods shall be fit for such purpose.

Section 2—316. Exclusion or Modification of Warranties. (1) Words or conduct relevant to the creation of an express warranty and words or conduct tending to negate or limit warranty shall be construed wherever reasonable as consistent with each other; but subject to the provisions of this Article on parol or extrinsic evidence

(Section 2—202) negation or limitation is inoperative to the extent that such construction is unreasonable.

(2) Subject to subsection (3), to exclude or modify the implied warranty of merchantability or any part of it the language must mention merchantability and in case of a writing must be conspicuous, and to exclude or modify any implied warranty of fitness the exclusion must be by a writing and conspicuous. Language to exclude all implied warranties of fitness is sufficient if it states, for example, that "There are no warranties which extend beyond the description on the face hereof."

(3) Notwithstanding subsection (2)

(a) unless the circumstances indicate otherwise, all implied warranties are excluded by expressions like "as is", "with all faults" or other language which in common understanding calls the buyer's attention to the exclusion of warranties and makes plain that there is no implied warranty; and

(b) when the buyer before entering into the contract has examined the goods or the sample or model as fully as he desired or has refused to examine the goods there is no implied warranty with regard to defects which an examination ought in the circumstances to have revealed to him; and

(c) an implied warranty can also be excluded or modified by course of dealing or course of performance or usage of trade.

(4) Remedies for breach of warranty can be limited in accordance with the provisions of this Article on liquidation or limitation of damages and on contractual modification of remedy (Sections 2—718 and 2—719).

SECTION 2—317. CUMULATION AND CONFLICT OF WARRANTIES EXPRESS OR IMPLIED. Warranties whether express or implied shall be construed as consistent with each other and as cumulative, but if such construction is unreasonable the intention of the parties shall determine which warranty is dominant. In ascertaining that intention the following rules apply:

(a) Exact or technical specifications displace an inconsistent sample or model or general language of description.

(b) A sample from an existing bulk displaces inconsistent general language of description.

(c) Express warranties displace inconsistent implied warranties other than an implied warranty of fitness for a particular purpose.

SECTION 2—318. THIRD PARTY BENEFICIARIES OF WARRANTIES EXPRESS OR IMPLIED. A seller's warranty whether express or implied extends to any natural person who is in the family or household of his buyer or who is a guest in his home if it is reasonable to expect that such person may use, consume or be affected by the goods and who is injured in person by breach of the warranty. A seller may not exclude or limit the operation of this section.

SECTION 2—319. F.O.B. AND F.A.S. TERMS. (1) Unless otherwise agreed the term F.O.B. (which means "free on board") at a named place, even though used only in connection with the stated price, is a delivery term under which

(a) when the term is F.O.B. the place of shipment, the seller must at that place ship the goods in the manner provided in this article (Section 2—504) and bear the expense and risk of putting them into the possession of the carrier; or

(b) when the term is F.O.B. the place of destination, the seller must at his own expense and risk transport the goods to that place and there tender delivery of them in the manner provided in this Article (Section 2—503);

(c) when under either (a) or (b) the term is also F.O.B. vessel, car or other vehicle, the seller must in addition at his own expense and risk load the goods on board. It the term is F.O.B. vessel the buyer must name the vessel and in an appropriate case the seller must comply with the provisions of this Article on the form of bill of lading (Section 2—323).

(2) Unless otherwise agreed the term F.A.S. vessel (which means "free alongside") at a named port, even though used only in connection with the stated price, is a delivery term under which the seller must

(a) at his own expense and risk deliver the goods alongside the vessel in the manner usual in that port or on a dock designated and provided by the buyer; and

(b) obtain and tender a receipt for the goods in exchange for which the carrier is under a duty to issue a bill of lading.

(3) Unless otherwise agreed in any case falling within subsection (1)(a) or (c) or subsection (2) the buyer must seasonably give any needed instructions for making delivery, including when the term is F.A.S. or F.O.B. the loading berth of the vessel and in an appropriate case its name and sailing date. The seller may treat the failure of needed instructions as a failure of cooperation under this Article (Section 2–311). He may also at his option move the goods in any reasonable manner preparatory to delivery or shipment.

(4) Under the term F.O.B. vessel or F.A.S. unless otherwise agreed the buyer must make payment against tender of the required documents and the seller may not tender nor the buyer demand delivery of the goods in substitution for the documents.

SECTION 2–320. C.I.F. AND C. & F. TERMS. (1) The term C.I.F. means that the price includes in a lump sum the cost of the goods and the insurance and freight to the named destination. The term C. & F. or C.F. means that the price so includes cost and freight to the named destination.

(2) Unless otherwise agreed and even though used only in connection with the stated price and destination, the term C.I.F. destination or its equivalent requires the seller at his own expense and risk to

(a) put the goods into the possession of a carrier at the port for shipment and obtain a negotiable bill or bills of lading covering the entire transportation to the named destination; and

(b) load the goods and obtain a receipt from the carrier (which may be contained in the bill of lading) showing that the freight has been paid or provided for; and

(c) obtain a policy or certificate of insurance, including any war risk insurance, of a kind and on terms then current at the port of shipment in the usual amount, in the currency of the contract, shown to cover the same goods covered by the bill of lading and providing for payment of loss to the order of the buyer or for the account of whom it may concern; but the seller may add to the price the amount of the premium for any such war risk insurance; and

(d) prepare an invoice of the goods and procure any other documents required to effect shipment or to comply with the contract; and

(e) forward and tender with commercial promptness all the documents in due form and with any indorsement necessary to perfect the buyer's rights.

(3) Unless otherwise agreed the term C. & F. or its equivalent has the same effect and imposes upon the seller the same obligations and risks as a C.I.F. term except the obligation as to insurance.

(4) Under the term C.I.F. or C. & F. unless otherwise agreed the buyer must make payment against tender of the required documents and the seller may not tender nor the buyer demand delivery of the goods in substitution for the documents.

SECTION 2–321. C.I.F. OR C. & F.: "NET LANDED WEIGHTS"; "PAYMENT ON ARRIVAL"; WARRANTY OF CONDITION ON ARRIVAL. Under a contract containing a term C.I.F. or C. & F.

(1) Where the price is based on or is to be adjusted according to "net landed weights", "delivered weights", "out turn" quantity or quality or the like, unless otherwise agreed the seller must reasonably estimate the price. The payment due on tender of the documents called for by the contract is the amount so estimated, but after final adjustment of the price a settlement must be made with commercial promptness.

(2) An agreement described in subsection (1) or any warranty of quality or condition of the goods on arrival places upon the seller the risk of ordinary deterioration, shrinkage and the like in transportation but has no effect on the place or time of identification to the contract for sale or delivery or on the passing of the risk of loss.

(3) Unless otherwise agreed where the contract provides for payment on or after arrival of the goods the seller must before payment allow such preliminary inspection

as is feasible; but if the goods are lost delivery of the documents and payment are due when the goods should have arrived.

SECTION 2—322. DELIVERY "EX-SHIP". (1) Unless otherwise agreed a term for delivery of goods "ex-ship" (which means from the carrying vessel) or in equivalent language is not restricted to a particular ship and requires delivery from a ship which has reached a place at the named port of destination where goods of the kind are usually discharged.

(2) Under such a term unless otherwise agreed

    (a) the seller must discharge all liens arising out of the carriage and furnish the buyer with a direction which puts the carrier under a duty to deliver the goods; and

    (b) the risk of loss does not pass to the buyer until the goods leave the ship's tackle or are otherwise properly unloaded.

SECTION 2—323. FORM OF BILL OF LADING REQUIRED IN OVERSEAS SHIPMENT; "OVERSEAS". (1) Where the contract contemplates overseas shipment and contains a term C.I.F. or C. & F. or F.O.B. vessel, the seller unless otherwise agreed must obtain a negotiable bill of lading stating that the goods have been loaded on board or, in the case of a term C.I.F. or C. & F., received for shipment.

(2) Where in a case within subsection (1) a bill of lading has been issued in a set of parts, unless otherwise agreed if the documents are not to be sent from abroad the buyer may demand tender of the full set; otherwise only one part of the bill of lading need be tendered. Even if the agreement expressly requires a full set

    (a) due tender of a single part is acceptable within the provisions of this Article on cure of improper delivery (subsection (1) of Section 2—508); and

    (b) even though the full set is demanded, if the documents are sent from abroad the person tendering an incomplete set may nevertheless require payment upon furnishing an indemnity which the buyer in good faith deems adequate.

(3) A shipment by water or by air or a contract contemplating such shipment is "overseas" insofar as by usage of trade or agreement it is subject to the commercial, financing or shipping practices characteristic of international deep water commerce.

SECTION 2—324. "NO ARRIVAL, NO SALE" TERM. Under a term "no arrival, no sale" or terms of like meaning, unless otherwise agreed,

    (a) the seller must properly ship conforming goods and if they arrive by any means he must tender them on arrival but he assumes no obligation that the goods will arrive unless he has caused the non-arrival; and

    (b) where without fault of the seller the goods are in part lost or have so deteriorated as no longer to conform to the contract or arrive after the contract time, the buyer may proceed as if there had been casualty to identified goods (Section 2—613).

SECTION 2—325. "LETTER OF CREDIT" TERM; "CONFIRMED CREDIT". (1) Failure of the buyer seasonably to furnish an agreed letter of credit is a breach of the contract for sale.

(2) The delivery to seller of a proper letter of credit suspends the buyer's obligation to pay. If the letter of credit is dishonored, the seller may on seasonable notification to the buyer require payment directly from him.

(3) Unless otherwise agreed the term "letter of credit" or "banker's credit" in a contract for sale means an irrevocable credit issued by a financing agency of good repute and, where the shipment is overseas, of good international repute. The term "confirmed credit" means that the credit must also carry the direct obligation of such an agency which does business in the seller's financial market.

SECTION 2—326. SALE ON APPROVAL AND SALE OR RETURN; CONSIGNMENT SALES AND RIGHTS OF CREDITORS. (1) Unless otherwise agreed, if delivered goods may be returned by the buyer even though they conform to the contract, the transaction is.

    (a) a "sale on approval" if the goods are delivered primarily for use, and

    (b) a "sale or return" if the goods are delivered primarily for resale.

(2) Except as provided in subsection (3), goods held on approval are not subject to the claims of the buyer's creditors until acceptance; goods held on sale or return are subject to such claims while in the buyer's possession.

(3) Where goods are delivered to a person for sale and such person maintains a place of business at which he deals in goods of the kind involved, under a name other than the name of the person making delivery, then with respect to claims of creditors of the person conducting the business the goods are deemed to be on sale or return. The provisions of this subsection are applicable even though an agreement purports to reserve title to the person making delivery until payment or resale or uses such words as "on consignment" or "on memorandum". However, this subsection is not applicable if the person making delivery

    (a) complies with an applicable law providing for a consignor's interest or the like to be evidenced by a sign, or

    (b) establishes that the person conducting the business is generally known by his creditors to be substantially engaged in selling the goods of others, or

    (c) complies with the filing provisions of the Article on Secured Transactions (Article 9).

(4) Any "or return" term of a contract for sale is to be treated as a separate contract for sale within the statute of frauds section of this Article (Section 2—201) and as contradicting the sale aspect of the contract within the provisions of this Article on parol or extrinsic evidence (Section 2—202).

SECTION 2—327. SPECIAL INCIDENTS OF SALE ON APPROVAL AND SALE OR RETURN. (1) Under a sale on approval unless otherwise agreed

    (a) although the goods are identified to the contract the risk of loss and the title do not pass to the buyer until acceptance; and

    (b) use of the goods consistent with the purpose of trial is not acceptance but failure seasonably to notify the seller of election to return the goods is acceptance, and if the goods conform to the contract acceptance of any part is acceptance of the whole; and

    (c) after due notification of election to return, the return is at the seller's risk and expense but a merchant buyer must follow any reasonable instructions.

(2) Under a sale or return unless otherwise agreed

    (a) the option to return extends to the whole or any commercial unit of the goods while in substantially their original condition, but must be exercised seasonably; and

    (b) the return is at the buyer's risk and expense.

SECTION 2—328. SALE BY AUCTION. (1) In a sale by auction if goods are put up in lots each lot is the subject of a separate sale.

(2) A sale by auction is complete when the auctioneer so announces by the fall of the hammer or in other customary manner. Where a bid is made while the hammer is falling in acceptance of a prior bid the auctioneer may in his discretion reopen the bidding or declare the goods sold under the bid on which the hammer was falling.

(3) Such a sale is with reserve unless the goods are in explicit terms put up without reserve. In an auction with reserve the auctioneer may withdraw the goods at any time until he announces completion of the sale. In an auction without reserve, after the auctioneer calls for bids on an article or lot, that article or lot cannot be withdrawn unless no bid is made within a reasonable time. In either case a bidder may retract his bid until the auctioneer's announcement of completion of the sale, but a bidder's retraction does not revive any previous bid.

(4) If the auctioneer knowingly receives a bid on the seller's behalf or the seller makes or procures such a bid, and notice has not been given that liberty for such bidding is reserved, the buyer may at his option avoid the sale or take the goods at the price of the last good faith bid prior to the completion of the sale. This subsection shall not apply to any bid at a forced sale.

PART 4

TITLE, CREDITORS AND GOOD FAITH PURCHASERS

SECTION 2—401. PASSING OF TITLE; RESERVATION FOR SECURITY; LIMITED APPLICATION OF THIS SECTION. Each provision of this Article with regard to the rights, obligations and remedies of the seller, the buyer, purchasers or other third parties applies irrespective of title to the goods except where the provision refers to such title. Insofar as situations are not covered by the other provisions of this Article and matters concerning title become material the following rules apply:

(1) Title to goods cannot pass under a contract for sale prior to their identification to the contract (Section 2—501), and unless otherwise explicitly agreed the buyer acquires by their identification a special property as limited by this Act. Any retention or reservation by the seller of the title (property) in goods shipped or delivered to the buyer is limited in effect to a reservation of a security interest. Subject to these provisions and to the provisions of the Article on Secured Transactions (Article 9), title to goods passes from the seller to the buyer in any manner and on any conditions explicitly agreed on by the parties.

(2) Unless otherwise explicitly agreed title passes to the buyer at the time and place at which the seller completes his performance with reference to the physical delivery of the goods, despite any reservation of a security interest and even though a document of title is to be delivered at a different time or place; and in particular and despite any reservation of a security interest by the bill of lading

    (a) if the contract requires or authorizes the seller to send the goods to the buyer but does not require him to deliver them at destination, title passes to the buyer at the time and place of shipment; but

    (b) if the contract requires delivery at destination, title passes on tender there.

(3) Unless otherwise explicitly agreed where delivery is to be made without moving the goods,

    (a) if the seller is to deliver a document of title, title passes at the time when and the place where he delivers such documents; or

    (b) if the goods are at the time of contracting already identified and no documents are to be delivered, title passes at the time and place of contracting.

(4) A rejection or other refusal by the buyer to receive or retain the goods, whether or not justified, or a justified revocation of acceptance revests title to the goods in the seller. Such revesting occurs by operation of law and is not a "sale".

SECTION 2—402. RIGHTS OF SELLER'S CREDITORS AGAINST SOLD GOODS. (1) Except as provided in subsections (2) and (3), rights of unsecured creditors of the seller with respect to goods which have been identified to a contract for sale are subject to the buyer's rights to recover the goods under this Article (Sections 2—502 and 2—716).

(2) A creditor of the seller may treat a sale or an identification of goods to a contract for sale as void if as against him a retention of possession by the seller is fraudulent under any rule of law of the state where the goods are situated, except that retention of possession in good faith and current course of trade by a merchant-seller for a commercially reasonable time after a sale or identification is not fraudulent.

(3) Nothing in this Article shall be deemed to impair the rights of creditors of the seller

    (a) under the provisions of the Article on Secured Transactions (Article 9); or

    (b) where identification to the contract or delivery is made not in current course of trade but in satisfaction of or as security for a pre-existing claim for money, security or the like and is made under circumstances which under any rule of law of the state where the goods are situated would apart from this Article constitute the transaction a fraudulent transfer or voidable preference.

SECTION 2—403. POWER TO TRANSFER; GOOD FAITH PURCHASE OF GOODS; "ENTRUSTING". (1) A purchaser of goods acquires all title which his transferor had or had power to transfer except that a purchaser of a limited interest acquires rights only to the extent of the interest purchased. A person with voidable title has power to transfer a good title to a good faith purchaser for value. When goods have been delivered under a transaction of purchase the purchaser has such power even though

    (a) the transferor was deceived as to the identity of the purchaser, or

    (b) the delivery was in exchange for a check which is later dishonored, or

    (c) it was agreed that the transaction was to be a "cash sale", or

    (d) the delivery was procured through fraud punishable as larcenous under the criminal law.

(2) Any entrusting of possession of goods to a merchant who deals in goods of that

kind gives him power to transfer all rights of the entruster to a buyer in ordinary course of business.

(3) "Entrusting" includes any delivery and any acquiescence in retention of possession regardless of any condition expressed between the parties to the delivery or acquiescence and regardless of whether the procurement of the entrusting or the possessor's disposition of the goods have been such as to be larcenous under the criminal law.

(4) The rights of other purchasers of goods and of lien creditors are governed by the Articles on Secured Transactions (Article 9), Bulk Transfers (Article 6) and Documents of Title (Article 7).

PART 5

PERFORMANCE

SECTION 2—501. INSURABLE INTEREST IN GOODS; MANNER OF IDENTIFICATION OF GOODS. (1) The buyer obtains a special property and an insurable interest in goods by identification of existing goods as goods to which the contract refers even though the goods so identified are non-conforming and he has an option to return or reject them. Such identification can be made at any time and in any manner explicitly agreed to by the parties. In the absence of explicit agreement identification occurs

(a) when the contract is made if it is for the sale of goods already existing and identified;

(b) if the contract is for the sale of future goods other than those described in paragraph (c), when goods are shipped, marked or otherwise designated by the seller as goods to which the contract refers;

(c) when the crops are planted or otherwise become growing crops or the young are conceived if the contract is for the sale of unborn young to be born within twelve months after contracting or for the sale of crops to be harvested within twelve months or the next normal harvest season after contracting whichever is longer.

(2) The seller retains an insurable interest in goods so long as title to or any security interest in the goods remains in him and where the identification is by the seller alone he may until default or insolvency or notification to the buyer that the identification is final substitute other goods for those identified.

(3) Nothing in this section impairs any insurable interest recognized under any other statute or rule of law.

SECTION 2—502. BUYER'S RIGHT TO GOODS ON SELLER'S INSOLVENCY. (1) Subject to subsection (2) and even though the goods have not been shipped a buyer who has paid a part or all of the price of goods in which he has a special property under the provisions of the immediately preceding section may on making and keeping good a tender of any unpaid portion of their price recover them from the seller if the seller becomes insolvent within ten days after receipt of the first installment on their price.

(2) If the identification creating his special property has been made by the buyer he acquires the right to recover the goods only if they conform to the contract for sale.

SECTION 2—503. MANNER OF SELLER'S TENDER OF DELIVERY. (1) Tender of delivery requires that the seller put and hold conforming goods at the buyer's disposition and give the buyer any notification reasonably necessary to enable him to take delivery. The manner, time and place for tender are determined by the agreement and this Article, and in particular

(a) tender must be at a reasonable hour, and if it is of goods they must be kept available for the period reasonably necessary to enable the buyer to take possession; but

(b) unless otherwise agreed the buyer must furnish facilities reasonably suited to the receipt of the goods.

(2) Where the case is within the next section respecting shipment tender requires that the seller comply with its provisions.

(3) Where the seller is required to deliver at a particular destination tender requires that he comply with subsection (1) and also in any appropriate case tender documents as described in subsections (4) and (5) of this section.

(4) Where goods are in the possession of a bailee and are to be delivered without being moved

    (a) tender requires that the seller either tender a negotiable document of title covering such goods or procure acknowledgment by the bailee of the buyer's right to possession of the goods; but

    (b) tender to the buyer of a non-negotiable document of title or of a written direction to the bailee to deliver is sufficient tender unless the buyer seasonably objects, and receipt by the bailee of notification of the buyer's rights fixes those rights as against the bailee and all third persons; but risk of loss of the goods and of any failure by the bailee to honor the non-negotiable document of title or to obey the direction remains on the seller until the buyer has had a reasonable time to present the document or direction, and a refusal by the bailee to honor the document or to obey the direction defeats the tender.

(5) Where the contract requires the seller to deliver documents

    (a) he must tender all such documents in correct form, except as provided in this Article with respect to bills of lading in a set (subsection (2) of Section 2–323); and

    (b) tender through customary banking channels is sufficient and dishonor of a draft accompanying the documents constitutes non-acceptance or rejection.

SECTION 2–504. SHIPMENT BY SELLER. Where the seller is required or authorized to send the goods to the buyer and the contract does not require him to deliver them at a particular destination, then unless otherwise agreed he must

    (a) put the goods in the possession of such a carrier and make such a contract for their transportation as may be reasonable having regard to the nature of the goods and other circumstances of the case; and

    (b) obtain and promptly deliver or tender in due form any document necessary to enable the buyer to obtain possession of the goods or otherwise required by the agreement or by usage of trade; and

    (c) promptly notify the buyer of the shipment.

Failure to notify the buyer under paragraph (c) or to make a proper contract under paragraph (a) is a ground for rejection only if material delay or loss ensues.

SECTION 2–505. SELLER'S SHIPMENT UNDER RESERVATION. (1) Where the seller has identified goods to the contract by or before shipment:

    (a) his procurement of a negotiable bill of lading to his own order or otherwise reserves in him a security interest in the goods. His procurement of the bill to the order of a financing agency or of the buyer indicates in addition only the seller's expectation of transferring that interest to the person named.

    (b) a non-negotiable bill of lading to himself or his nominee reserves possession of the goods as security but except in a case of conditional delivery (subsection (2) of Section 2–507) a non-negotiable bill of lading naming the buyer as consignee reserves no security interest even though the seller retains possession of the bill of lading.

(2) When shipment by the seller with reservation of a security interest is in violation of the contract for sale it constitutes an improper contract for transportation within the preceding section but impairs neither the rights given to the buyer by shipment and identification of the goods to the contract nor the seller's powers as a holder of a negotiable document.

SECTION 2–506. RIGHTS OF FINANCING AGENCY. (1) A financing agency by paying or purchasing for value a draft which relates to a shipment of goods acquires to the extent of the payment or purchase and in addition to its own rights under the draft and any document of title securing it any rights of the shipper in the goods including the right to stop delivery and the shipper's right to have the draft honored by the buyer.

(2) The right to reimbursement of a financing agency which has in good faith honored or purchased the draft under commitment to or authority from the buyer is not impaired by subsequent discovery of defects with reference to any relevant document which was apparently regular on its face.

SECTION 2–507. EFFECT OF SELLER'S TENDER; DELIVERY ON CONDITION. (1) Tender of delivery is a condition to the buyer's duty to accept the goods and, unless otherwise agreed, to his duty to pay for them. Tender entitles the seller to acceptance of the goods and to payment according to the contract.

(2) Where payment is due and demanded on the delivery to the buyer of goods or documents of title, his right as against the seller to retain or dispose of them is conditional upon his making the payment due.

SECTION 2—508. CURE BY SELLER OF IMPROPER TENDER OR DELIVERY; REPLACEMENT. (1) Where any tender or delivery by the seller is rejected because non-conforming and the time for performance has not yet expired, the seller may seasonably notify the buyer of his intention to cure and may then within the contract time make a conforming delivery.

(2) Where the buyer rejects a non-conforming tender which the seller had reasonable grounds to believe would be acceptable with or without money allowance the seller may if he seasonably notifies the buyer have a further reasonable time to substitute a conforming tender.

SECTION 2—509. RISK OF LOSS IN THE ABSENCE OF BREACH. (1) Where the contract requires or authorizes the seller to ship the goods by carrier

    (a) if it does not require him to deliver them at a particular destination, the risk of loss passes to the buyer when the goods are duly delivered to the carrier even though the shipment is under reservation (Section 2—505); but

    (b) if it does require him to deliver them at a particular destination and the goods are there duly tendered while in the possession of the carrier, the risk of loss passes to the buyer when the goods are there duly so tendered as to enable the buyer to take delivery.

(2) Where the goods are held by a bailee to be delivered without being moved, the risk of loss passes to the buyer

    (a) on his receipt of a negotiable document of title covering the goods; or

    (b) on acknowledgment by the bailee of the buyer's right to possession of the goods; or

    (c) after his receipt of a non-negotiable document of title or other written direction to deliver, as provided in subsection (4) (b) of Section 2—503.

(3) In any case not within subsection (1) or (2), the risk of loss passes to the buyer on his receipt of the goods if the seller is a merchant; otherwise the risk passes to the buyer on tender of delivery.

(4) The provisions of this section are subject to contrary agreement of the parties and to the provisions of this Article on sale on approval (Section 2—327) and on effect of breach on risk of loss (Section 2—510).

SECTION 2—510. EFFECT OF BREACH ON RISK OF LOSS. (1) Where a tender or delivery of goods so fails to conform to the contract as to give a right of rejection the risk of their loss remains on the seller until cure or acceptance.

(2) Where the buyer rightfully revokes acceptance he may to the extent of any deficiency in his effective insurance coverage treat the risk of loss as having rested on the seller from the beginning.

(3) Where the buyer as to conforming goods already identified to the contract for sale repudiates or is otherwise in breach before risk of their loss has passed to him, the seller may to the extent of any deficiency in his effective insurance coverage treat the risk of loss as resting on the buyer for a commercially reasonable time.

SECTION 2—511. TENDER OF PAYMENT BY BUYER; PAYMENT BY CHECK. (1) Unless otherwise agreed tender of payment is a condition to the seller's duty to tender and complete any delivery.

(2) Tender of payment is sufficient when made by any means or in any manner current in the ordinary course of business unless the seller demands payment in legal tender and gives any extension of time reasonably necessary to procure it.

(3) Subject to the provisions of this Act on the effect of an instrument on an obligation (Section 3—802), payment by check is conditional and is defeated as between the parties by dishonor of the check on due presentment.

SECTION 2—512. PAYMENT BY BUYER BEFORE INSPECTION. (1) Where the contract requires payment before inspection non-conformity of the goods does not excuse the buyer from so making payment unless

(a) the non-conformity appears without inspection; or

(b) despite tender of the required documents the circumstances would justify injunction against honor under the provisions of this Act (Section 5—114).

(2) Payment pursuant to subsection (1) does not constitute an acceptance of goods or impair the buyer's right to inspect or any of his remedies.

SECTION 2—513. BUYER'S RIGHT TO INSPECTION OF GOODS. (1) Unless otherwise agreed and subject to subsection (3), where goods are tendered or delivered or identified to the contract for sale, the buyer has a right before payment or acceptance to inspect them at any reasonable place and time and in any reasonable manner. When the seller is required or authorized to send the goods to the buyer, the inspection may be after their arrival.

(2) Expenses of inspection must be borne by the buyer but may be recovered from the seller if the goods do not conform and are rejected.

(3) Unless otherwise agreed and subject to the provisions of this Article on C.I.F. contracts (subsection (3) of Section 2—321), the buyer is not entitled to inspect the goods before payment of the price when the contract provides

(a) for delivery "C.O.D." or on other like terms; or

(b) for payment against documents of title, except where such payment is due only after the goods are to become available for inspection.

(4) A place or method of inspection fixed by the parties is presumed to be exclusive but unless otherwise expressly agreed it does not postpone identification or shift the place for delivery or for passing the risk of loss. If compliance becomes impossible, inspection shall be as provided in this section unless the place or method fixed was clearly intended as an indispensable condition failure of which avoids the contract.

SECTION 2—514. WHEN DOCUMENTS DELIVERABLE ON ACCEPTANCE; WHEN ON PAYMENT. Unless otherwise agreed documents against which a draft is drawn are to be delivered to the drawee on acceptance of the draft if it is payable more than three days after presentment; otherwise, only on payment.

SECTION 2—515. PRESERVING EVIDENCE OF GOODS IN DISPUTE. In furtherance of the adjustment of any claim or dispute

(a) either party on reasonable notification to the other and for the purpose of ascertaining the facts and preserving evidence has the right to inspect, test and sample the goods including such of them as may be in the possession or control of the other; and

(b) the parties may agree to a third party inspection or survey to determine the conformity or condition of the goods and may agree that the findings shall be binding upon them in any subsequent litigation or adjustment.

PART 6

BREACH, REPUDIATION AND EXCUSE

SECTION 2—601. BUYER'S RIGHTS ON IMPROPER DELIVERY. Subject to the provisions of this Article on breach in installment contracts (Section 2—612) and unless otherwise agreed under the sections on contractual limitations of remedy (Sections 2—718 and 2—719), if the goods or the tender of delivery fail in any respect to conform to the contract, the buyer may

(a) reject the whole; or

(b) accept the whole; or

(c) accept any commercial unit or units and reject the rest.

SECTION 2—602. MANNER AND EFFECT OF RIGHTFUL REJECTION. (1) Rejection of goods must be within a reasonable time after their delivery or tender. It is ineffective unless the buyer seasonably notifies the seller.

(2) Subject to the provisions of the two following sections on rejected goods (Sections 2—603 and 2—604),

(a) after rejection any exercise of ownership by the buyer with respect to any commercial unit is wrongful as against the seller; and

(b) if the buyer has before rejection taken physical possession of goods in which he does not have a security interest under the provisions of this Article (subsection (3) of Section 2–711), he is under a duty after rejection to hold them with reasonable care at the seller's disposition for a time sufficient to permit the seller to remove them; but

(c) the buyer has no further obligations with regard to goods rightfully rejected.

(3) The seller's rights with respect to goods wrongfully rejected are governed by the provisions of this Article on Seller's remedies in general (Section 2–703).

SECTION 2–603. MERCHANT BUYER'S DUTIES AS TO RIGHTFULLY REJECTED GOODS. (1) Subject to any security interest in the buyer (subsection (3) of Section 2–711), when the seller has no agent or place of business at the market of rejection a merchant buyer is under a duty after rejection of goods in his possession or control to follow any reasonable instructions received from the seller with respect to the goods and in the absence of such instructions to make reasonable efforts to sell them for the seller's account if they are perishable or threaten to decline in value speedily. Instructions are not reasonable if on demand indemnity for expenses is not forthcoming.

(2) When the buyer sells goods under subsection (1), he is entitled to reimbursement from the seller or out of the proceeds for reasonable expenses of caring for and selling them, and if the expenses include no selling commission then to such commission as is usual in the trade or if there is none to a reasonable sum not exceeding ten per cent on the gross proceeds.

(3) In complying with this section the buyer is held only to good faith and good faith conduct hereunder is neither acceptance nor conversion nor the basis of an action for damages.

SECTION 2–604. BUYER'S OPTIONS AS TO SALVAGE OF RIGHTFULLY REJECTED GOODS. Subject to the provisions of the immediately preceding section on perishables if the seller gives no instructions within a reasonable time after notification of rejection the buyer may store the rejected goods for the seller's account or reship them to him or resell them for the seller's account with reimbursement as provided in the preceding section. Such action is not acceptance or conversion.

SECTION 2–605. WAIVER OF BUYER'S OBJECTIONS BY FAILURE TO PARTICULARIZE. (1) The buyer's failure to state in connection with rejection a particular defect which is ascertainable by reasonable inspection precludes him from relying on the unstated defect to justify rejection or to establish breach

(a) where the seller could have cured it if stated seasonably; or

(b) between merchants when the seller has after rejection made a request in writing for a full and final written statement of all defects on which the buyer proposes to rely.

(2) Payment against documents made without reservation of rights precludes recovery of the payment for defects apparent on the face of the documents.

SECTION 2–606. WHAT CONSTITUTES ACCEPTANCE OF GOODS. (1) Acceptance of goods occurs when the buyer

(a) after a reasonable opportunity to inspect the goods signifies to the seller that the goods are conforming or that he will take or retain them in spite of their non-conformity; or

(b) fails to make an effective rejection (subsection (1) of Section 2–602), but such acceptance does not occur until the buyer has had a reasonable opportunity to inspect them; or

(c) does any act inconsistent with the seller's ownership; but if such act is wrongful as against the seller it is an acceptance only if ratified by him.

(2) Acceptance of a part of any commercial unit is acceptance of that entire unit.

SECTION 2–607. EFFECT OF ACCEPTANCE; NOTICE OF BREACH; BURDEN OF ESTABLISHING BREACH AFTER ACCEPTANCE; NOTICE OF CLAIM OR LITIGATION TO PERSON ANSWERABLE OVER. (1) The buyer must pay at the contract rate for any goods accepted.

(2) Acceptance of goods by the buyer precludes rejection of the goods accepted and if made with knowledge of a non-conformity cannot be revoked because of it unless the acceptance was on the reasonable assumption that the non-conformity would be seasonably cured but acceptance does not of itself impair any other remedy provided by this Article for non-conformity.

(3) Where a tender has been accepted

(a) the buyer must within a reasonable time after he discovers or should have discovered any breach notify the seller of breach or be barred from any remedy; and

(b) if the claim is one for infringement or the like (subsection (3) of Section 2—312) and the buyer is sued as a result of such a breach he must so notify the seller within a reasonable time after he receives notice of the litigation or be barred from any remedy over for liability established by the litigation.

(4) The burden is on the buyer to establish any breach with respect to the goods accepted.

(5) Where the buyer is used for breach of a warranty or other obligation for which his seller is answerable over

(a) he may give his seller written notice of the litigation. If the notice states that the seller may come in and defend and that if the seller does not do so he will be bound in any action against him by his buyer by any determination of fact common to the two litigations, then unless the seller after seasonable receipt of the notice does come in and defend he is so bound.

(b) if the claim is one for infringement or the like (subsection (3) of Section 2—312) the original seller may demand in writing that his buyer turn over to him control of the litigation including settlement or else be barred from any remedy over and if he also agrees to bear all expense and to satisfy any adverse judgment, then unless the buyer after seasonable receipt of the demand does turn over control the buyer is so barred.

(6) The provisions of subsections (3), (4) and (5) apply to any obligation of a buyer to hold the seller harmless against infringement or the like (subsection (3) of Section 2—312).

SECTION 2—608. REVOCATION OF ACCEPTANCE IN WHOLE OR IN PART. (1) The buyer may revoke his acceptance of a lot or commercial unit whose non-conformity substantially impairs its value to him if he has accepted it

(a) on the reasonable assumption that its non-conformity would be cured and it has not been seasonably cured; or

(b) without discovery of such non-conformity if his acceptance was reasonably induced either by the difficulty of discovery before acceptance or by the seller's assurances.

(2) Revocation of acceptance must occur within a reasonable time after the buyer discovers or should have discovered the ground for it and before any substantial change in condition of the goods which is not caused by their own defects. It is not effective until the buyer notifies the seller of it.

(3) A buyer who so revokes has the same rights and duties with regard to the goods involved as if he had rejected them.

SECTION 2—609. RIGHT TO ADEQUATE ASSURANCE OF PERFORMANCE. (1) A contract for sale imposes an obligation on each party that the other's expectation of receiving due performance will not be impaired. When reasonable grounds for insecurity arise with respect to the performance of either party the other may in writing demand adequate assurance of due performance and until he receives such assurance may if commercially reasonable suspend any performance for which he has not already received the agreed return.

(2) Between merchants the reasonableness of grounds for insecurity and the adequacy of any assurance offered shall be determined according to commercial standards.

(3) Acceptance of any improper delivery or payment does not prejudice the aggrieved party's right to demand adequate assurance of future performance.

(4) After receipt of a justified demand failure to provide within a reasonable time not exceeding thirty days such assurance of due performance as is adequate under the circumstances of the particular case is a repudiation of the contract.

SECTION 2—610. ANTICIPATORY REPUDIATION. When either party repudiates the contract with respect to a performance not yet due the loss of which will substantially impair the value of the contract to the other, the aggrieved party may

(a) for a commercially reasonable time await performance by the repudiating party; or

(b) resort to any remedy for breach (Section 2—703 or Section 2—711), even though he has notified the repudiating party that he would await the latter's performance and has urged retraction; and

(c) in either case suspend his own performance or proceed in accordance with the provisions of this Article on the seller's right to identify goods to the contract notwithstanding breach or to salvage unfinished goods (Section 2—704).

SECTION 2—611. RETRACTION OF ANTICIPATORY REPUDIATION. (1) Until the repudiating party's next performance is due he can retract his repudiation unless the aggrieved party has since the repudiation cancelled or materially changed his position or otherwise indicated that he considers the repudiation final.

(2) Retraction may be by any method which clearly indicates to the aggrieved party that the repudiating party intends to perform, but must include any assurance justifiably demanded under the provisions of this Article (Section 2—609).

(3) Retraction reinstates the repudiating party's rights under the contract with due excuse and allowance to the aggrieved party for any delay occasioned by the repudiation.

SECTION 2—612. "INSTALLMENT CONTRACT"; BREACH. (1) An "installment contract" is one which requires or authorizes the delivery of goods in separate lots to be separately accepted, even though the contract contains a clause "each delivery is a separate contract" or its equivalent.

(2) The buyer may reject any installment which is non-conforming if the non-conformity substantially impairs the value of that installment and cannot be cured or if the non-conformity is a defect in the required documents; but if the non-conformity does not fall within subsection (3) and the seller gives adequate assurance of its cure the buyer must accept that installment.

(3) Whenever non-conformity or default with respect to one or more installments substantially impairs the value of the whole contract there is a breach of the whole. But the aggrieved party reinstates the contract if he accepts a non-conforming installment without seasonably notifying of cancellation or if he brings an action with respect only to past installments or demands performance as to future installments.

SECTION 2—613. CASUALTY TO IDENTIFIED GOODS. Where the contract requires for its performance goods identified when the contract is made, and the goods suffer casualty without fault of either party before the risk of loss passes to the buyer, or in a proper case under a "no arrival, no sale" term (Section 2—324) then

(a) if the loss is total the contract is avoided; and

(b) if the loss is partial or the goods have so deteriorated as no longer to conform to the contract the buyer may nevertheless demand inspection and at his option either treat the contract as avoided or accept the goods with allowance from the contract price for the deterioration or the deficiency in quantity but without further right against the seller.

SECTION 2—614. SUBSTITUTED PERFORMANCE. (1) Where without fault of either party the agreed berthing, loading, or unloading facilities fail or an agreed type of carrier becomes unavailable or the agreed manner of delivery otherwise becomes commercially impracticable but a commercially reasonable substitute is available, such substitute performance must be tendered and accepted.

(2) If the agreed means or manner of payment fails because of domestic or foreign governmental regulation, the seller may withhold or stop delivery unless the buyer provides a means or manner of payment which is commercially a substantial equivalent. If delivery has already been taken, payment by the means or in the manner provided by the regulation discharges the buyer's obligation unless the regulation is discriminatory, oppressive or predatory.

SECTION 2—615. EXCUSE BY FAILURE OF PRESUPPOSED CONDITIONS. Except so far as a seller may have assumed a greater obligation and subject to the preceding section on substituted performance:

(a) Delay in delivery or non-delivery in whole or in part by a seller who complies with paragraphs (b) and (c) is not a breach of his duty under a contract for sale if performance as agreed has been made impracticable by the occurrence of a contingency the non-occurrence of which was a basic assumption on which the contract was made or by compliance in good faith with any applicable foreign or domestic governmental regulation or order whether or not it later proves to be invalid.

(b) Where the causes mentioned in paragraph (a) affect only a part of the seller's capacity to perform, he must allocate production and deliveries among his customers but may at his option include regular customers not then under contract as well as his own requirements for further manufacture. He may so allocate in any manner which is fair and reasonable.

(c) The seller must notify the buyer seasonably that there will be delay or non-delivery and, when allocation is required under paragraph (b), of the estimated quota thus made available for the buyer.

SECTION 2—616. PROCEDURE ON NOTICE CLAIMING EXCUSE. (1) Where the buyer receives notification of a material or indefinite delay or an allocation justified under the preceding section he may by written notification to the seller as to any delivery concerned, and where the prospective deficiency substantially impairs the value of the whole contract under the provisions of this Article relating to breach of installment contracts (Sections 2—612), then also as to the whole,

(a) terminate and thereby discharge any unexecuted portion of the contract; or

(b) modify the contract by agreeing to take his available quota in substitution.

(2) If after receipt of such notification from the seller the buyer fails so to modify the contract within a reasonable time not exceeding thirty days the contract lapses with respect to any deliveries affected.

(3) The provisions of this section may not be negated by agreement except in so far as the seller has assumed a greater obligation under the preceding section.

PART 7

REMEDIES

SECTION 2—701. REMEDIES FOR BREACH OF COLLATERAL CONTRACTS NOT IMPAIRED. Remedies for breach of any obligation or promise collateral or ancillary to a contract for sale are not impaired by the provisions of this Article.

SECTION 2—702. SELLER'S REMEDIES ON DISCOVERY OF BUYER'S INSOLVENCY. (1) Where the seller discovers the buyer to be insolvent he may refuse delivery except for cash including payment for all goods theretofore delivered under the contract, and stop delivery under this Article (Section 2—705).

(2) Where the seller discovers that the buyer has received goods on credit while insolvent he may reclaim the goods upon demand made within ten days after the receipt, but if misrepresentation of solvency has been made to the particular seller in writing within three months before delivery the ten day limitation does not apply. Except as provided in this subsection the seller may not base a right to reclaim goods on the buyer's fraudulent or innocent misrepresentation of solvency or of intent to pay.

(3) The seller's right to reclaim under subsection (2) is subject to the rights of a buyer in ordinary course or other good faith purchaser or lien creditor under this Article (Section 2—403). Successful reclamation of goods excludes all other remedies with respect to them.

SECTION 2—703. SELLER'S REMEDIES IN GENERAL. Where the buyer wrongfully rejects or revokes acceptance of goods or fails to make a payment due on or before delivery or repudiates with respect to a part or the whole, then with respect to any goods directly affected and, if the breach is of the whole contract (Section 2—612), then also with respect to the whole undelivered balance, the aggrieved seller may

(a) withhold delivery of such goods;

(b) stop delivery by any bailee as hereafter provided (Section 2—705);

(c) proceed under the next section respecting goods still unidentified to the contract;

(d) resell and recover damages as hereafter provided (Section 2—706);

(e) recover damages for non-acceptance (Section 2—708) or in a proper case the price (Section 2—709);

(f) cancel.

Section 2—704. Seller's Right to Identify Goods to the Contract Notwithstanding Breach or to Salvage Unfinished Goods. (1) An aggrieved seller under the preceding section may

    (a) identify to the contract conforming goods not already identified if at the time he learned of the breach they are in his possession or control;

    (b) treat as the subject of resale goods which have demonstrably been intended for the particular contract even though those goods are unfinished.

(2) Where the goods are unfinished an aggrieved seller may in the exercise of reasonable commercial judgment for the purposes of avoiding loss and of effective realization either complete the manufacture and wholly identify the goods to the contract or cease manufacture and resell for scrap or salvage value or proceed in any other reasonable manner.

Section 2—705. Seller's Stoppage of Delivery in Transit or Otherwise. (1) The seller may stop delivery of goods in the possession of a carrier or other bailee when he discovers the buyer to be insolvent (Section 2—702) and may stop delivery of carload, truckload, planeload or larger shipments of express or freight when the buyer repudiates or fails to make a payment due before delivery or if for any other reason the seller has a right to withhold or reclaim the goods.

(2) As against such buyer the seller may stop delivery until

    (a) receipt of the goods by the buyer; or

    (b) acknowledgment to the buyer by any bailee of the goods except a carrier that the bailee holds the goods for the buyer; or

    (c) such acknowledgment to the buyer by a carrier by reshipment or as warehouseman; or

    (d) negotiation to the buyer of any negotiable document of title covering the goods.

(3) (a) To stop delivery the seller must so notify as to enable the bailee by reasonable diligence to prevent delivery of the goods.

    (b) After such notification the bailee must hold and deliver the goods according to the directions of the seller but the seller is liable to the bailee for any ensuing charges or damages.

    (c) If a negotiable document of title has been issued for goods the bailee is not obliged to obey a notification to stop until surrender of the document.

    (d) A carrier who has issued a non-negotiable bill of lading is not obliged to obey a notification to stop received from a person other than the consignor.

Section 2—706. Seller's Resale Including Contract for Resale. (1) Under the conditions stated in Section 2—703 on seller's remedies, the seller may resell the goods concerned or the undelivered balance thereof. Where the resale is made in good faith and in a commercially reasonable manner the seller may recover the difference between the resale price and the contract price together with any incidental damages allowed under the provisions of this Article (Section 2—710), but less expenses saved in consequence of the buyer's breach.

(2) Except as otherwise provided in subsection (3) or unless otherwise agreed resale may be at public or private sale including sale by way of one or more contracts to sell or of identification to an existing contract of the seller. Sale may be as a unit or in parcels and at any time and place and on any terms but every aspect of the sale including the method, manner, time, place and terms must be commercially reasonable. The resale must be reasonably identified as referring to the broken contract, but it is not necessary that the goods be in existence or that any or all of them have been identified to the contract before the breach.

(3) Where the resale is at private sale the seller must give the buyer reasonable notification of his intention to resell.

(4) Where the resale is at public sale

    (a) only identified goods can be sold except where there is a recognized market for a public sale of futures in goods of the kind; and

    (b) it must be made at a usual place or market for public sale if one is reasonably available and except in the case of goods which are perishable or threaten to decline in value speedily the seller must give the buyer reasonable notice of the time and place of the resale; and

(c) if the goods are not to be within the view of those attending the sale the notification of sale must state the place where the goods are located and provide for their reasonable inspection by prospective bidders; and

(d) the seller may buy.

(5) A purchaser who buys in good faith at a resale takes the goods free of any rights of the original buyer even though the seller fails to comply with one or more of the requirements of this section.

(6) The seller is not accountable to the buyer for any profit made on any resale. A person in the position of a seller (Section 2—707) or a buyer who has rightfully rejected or justifiably revoked acceptance must account for any excess over the amount of his security interest, as hereinafter defined (subsection (3) of Section 2—711).

SECTION 2—707. "PERSON IN THE POSITION OF A SELLER". (1) A "person in the position of a seller" includes as against a principal an agent who has paid or become responsible for the price of goods on behalf of his principal or anyone who otherwise holds a security interest or other right in goods similar to that of a seller.

(2) A person in the position of a seller may as provided in this Article withhold or stop delivery (Section 2—705) and resell (Section 2—706) and recover incidental damages (Section 2—710).

SECTION 2—708. SELLER'S DAMAGES FOR NON-ACCEPTANCE OR REPUDIATION. (1) Subject to subsection (2) and to the provisions of this Article with respect to proof of market price (Section 2—723), the measure of damages for non-acceptance or repudiation by the buyer is the difference between the market price at the time and place for tender and the unpaid contract price together with any incidental damages provided in this Article (Section 2—710), but less expenses saved in consequence of the buyer's breach.

(2) If the measure of damages provided in subsection (1) is inadequate to put the seller in as good a position as performance would have done then the measure of damages is the profit (including reasonable overhead) which the seller would have made from full performance by the buyer, together with any incidental damages provided in this Article (Section 2—710), due allowance for costs reasonably incurred and due credit for payments or proceeds of resale.

SECTION 2—709. ACTION FOR THE PRICE. (1) When the buyer fails to pay the price as it becomes due the seller may recover, together with any incidental damages under the next section, the price

(a) of goods accepted or of conforming goods lost or damaged within a commercially reasonable time after risk of their loss has passed to the buyer; and

(b) of goods identified to the contract if the seller is unable after reasonable effort to resell them at a reasonable price or the circumstances reasonably indicate that such effort will be unavailing.

(2) Where the seller sues for the price he must hold for the buyer any goods which have been identified to the contract and are still in his control except that if resale becomes possible he may resell them at any time prior to the collection of the judgment. The net proceeds of any such resale must be credited to the buyer and payment of the judgment entitles him to any goods not resold.

(3) After the buyer has wrongfully rejected or revoked acceptance of the goods or has failed to make a payment due or has repudiated (Section 2—610), a seller who is held not entitled to the price under this section shall nevertheless be awarded damages for non-acceptance under the preceding section.

SECTION 2—710. SELLER'S INCIDENTAL DAMAGES. Incidental damages to an aggrieved seller include any commercially reasonable charges, expenses or commissions incurred in stopping delivery, in the transportation, care and custody of goods after the buyer's breach, in connection with return or resale of the goods or otherwise resulting from the breach.

SECTION 2—711. BUYER'S REMEDIES IN GENERAL; BUYER'S SECURITY INTEREST IN REJECTED GOODS. (1) Where the seller fails to make delivery or repudiates or the buyer rightfully rejects or justifiably revokes acceptance then with respect to any goods involved, and with respect to the whole if the breach goes to the whole contract (Section 2—612), the buyer may cancel and whether or not he has done so may in addition to recovering so much of the price as has been paid

(a) "cover" and have damages under the next section as to all the goods affected whether or not they have been identified to the contract; or

(b) recover damages for non-delivery as provided in this Article (Section 2—713).

(2) Where the seller fails to deliver or repudiates the buyer may also

(a) if the goods have been identified recover them as provided in this Article (Section 2—502); or

(b) in a proper case obtain specific performance or replevy the goods as provided in this Article (Section 2—716).

(3) On rightful rejection or justifiable revocation of acceptance a buyer has a security interest in goods in his possession or control for any payments made on their price and any expenses reasonably incurred in their inspection, receipt, transportation, care and custody and may hold such goods and resell them in like manner as an aggrieved seller (Section 2—706).

SECTION 2—712. "COVER"; BUYER'S PROCUREMENT OF SUBSTITUTE GOODS. (1) After a breach within the preceding section the buyer may "cover" by making in good faith and without unreasonable delay any reasonable purchase of or contract to purchase goods in substitution for those due from the seller.

(2) The buyer may recover from the seller as damages the difference between the cost of cover and the contract price together with any incidental or consequential damages as hereinafter defined (Section 2—715), but less expenses saved in consequence of the seller's breach.

(3) Failure of the buyer to effect cover within this section does not bar him from any other remedy.

SECTION 2—713. BUYER'S DAMAGES FOR NON-DELIVERY OR REPUDIATION. (1) Subject to the provisions of this Article with respect to proof of market price (Section 2—723), the measure of damages for non-delivery or repudiation by the seller is the difference between the market price at the time when the buyer learned of the breach and the contract price together with any incidental and consequential damages provided in this Article (Section 2—715), but less expenses saved in consequence of the seller's breach.

(2) Market price is to be determined as of the place for tender or, in cases of rejection after arrival or revocation of acceptance, as of the place of arrival.

SECTION 2—714. BUYER'S DAMAGES FOR BREACH IN REGARD TO ACCEPTED GOODS. (1) Where the buyer has accepted goods and given notification (subsection (3) of Section 2—607) he may recover as damages for any non-conformity of tender the loss resulting in the ordinary course of events from the seller's breach as determined in any manner which is reasonable.

(2) The measure of damages for breach of warranty is the difference at the time and place of acceptance between the value of the goods accepted and the value they would have had if they had been as warranted, unless special circumstances show proximate damages of a different amount.

(3) In a proper case any incidental and consequential damages under the next section may also be recovered.

SECTION 2—715. BUYER'S INCIDENTAL AND CONSEQUENTIAL DAMAGES. (1) Incidental damages resulting from the seller's breach include expenses reasonably incurred in inspection, receipt, transportation and care and custody of goods rightfully rejected, any commercially reasonable charges, expenses or commissions in connection with effecting cover and any other reasonable expense incident to the delay or other breach.

(2) Consequential damages resulting from the seller's breach include

(a) any loss resulting from general or particular requirements and needs of which the seller at the time of contracting had reason to know and which could not reasonably be prevented by cover or otherwise; and

(b) injury to person or property proximately resulting from any breach of warranty.

SECTION 2—716. BUYER'S RIGHT TO SPECIFIC PERFORMANCE OR REPLEVIN. (1) Specific performance may be decreed where the goods are unique or in other proper circumstances.

(2) The decree for specific performance may include such terms and conditions as to payment of the price, damages, or other relief as the court may deem just.

(3) The buyer has a right of replevin for goods identified to the contract if after reasonable effort he is unable to effect cover for such goods or the circumstances reasonably indicate that such effort will be unavailing or if the goods have been shipped under reservation and satisfaction of the security interest in them has been made or tendered.

SECTION 2—717. DEDUCTION OF DAMAGES FROM THE PRICE. The buyer on notifying the seller of his intention to do so may deduct all or any part of the damages resulting from any breach of the contract from any part of the price still due under the same contract.

SECTION 2—718. LIQUIDATION OR LIMITATION OF DAMAGES; DEPOSITS. (1) Damages for breach by either party may be liquidated in the agreement but only at an amount which is reasonable in the light of the anticipated or actual harm caused by the breach, the difficulties of proof of loss, and the inconvenience or non-feasibility of otherwise obtaining an adequate remedy. A term fixing unreasonably large liquidated damages is void as a penalty.

(2) Where the seller justifiably withholds delivery of goods because of the buyer's breach, the buyer is entitled to restitution of any amount by which the sum of his payments exceeds

    (a) the amount to which the seller is entitled by virtue of terms liquidating the seller's damages in accordance with subsection (1), or

    (b) in the absence of such terms, twenty per cent of the value of the total performance for which the buyer is obligated under the contract or $500, whichever is smaller.

(3) The buyer's right to restitution under subsection (2) is subject to offset to the extent that the seller establishes

    (a) a right to recover damages under the provisions of this Article other than subsection (1), and

    (b) the amount or value of any benefits received by the buyer directly or indirectly by reason of the contract.

(4) Where a seller has received payment in goods their reasonable value or the proceeds of their resale shall be treated as payments for the purposes of subsection (2); but if the seller has notice of the buyer's breach before reselling goods received in part performance, his resale is subject to the conditions laid down in this Article on resale by an aggrieved seller (Section 2—706).

SECTION 2—719. CONTRACTUAL MODIFICATION OR LIMITATION OF REMEDY. (1) Subject to the provisions of subsections (2) and (3) of this section and of the preceding section on liquidation and limitation of damages,

    (a) the agreement may provide for remedies in addition to or in substitution for those provided in this Article and may limit or alter the measure of damages recoverable under this Article, as by limiting the buyer's remedies to return of the goods and repayment of the price or to repair and replacement of non-conforming goods or parts; and

    (b) resort to a remedy as provided is optional unless the remedy is expressly agreed to be exclusive, in which case it is the sole remedy.

(2) Where circumstances cause an exclusive or limited remedy to fail of its essential purpose, remedy may be had as provided in this Act.

(3) Consequential damages may be limited or excluded unless the limitation or exclusion is unconscionable. Limitation of consequential damages for injury to the person in the case of consumer goods is prima facie unconscionable but limitation of damages where the loss is commercial is not.

SECTION 2—720. EFFECT OF "CANCELLATION" OR "RESCISSION" ON CLAIMS FOR ANTECEDENT BREACH. Unless the contrary intention clearly appears, expressions of "cancellation" or "rescission" of the contract or the like shall not be construed as a renunciation or discharge of any claim in damages for an antecedent breach.

SECTION 2—721. REMEDIES FOR FRAUD. Remedies for material misrepresentation or fraud include all remedies available under this Article for non-fraudulent breach. Neither rescission or a claim for rescission of the contract for sale nor rejection or return of the goods shall bar or be deemed inconsistent with a claim for damages or other remedy.

SECTION 2—722. WHO CAN SUE THIRD PARTIES FOR INJURY TO GOODS. Where a third party so deals with goods which have been identified to a contract for sale as to cause actionable injury to a party to that contract

    (a) a right of action against the third party is in either party to the contract for sale who has title to or a security interest or a special property or an insurable interest in the goods; and if the goods have been destroyed or converted a right of action is also in the party who either bore the risk of loss under the contract for sale or has since the injury assumed that risk as against the other;

    (b) if at the time of the injury the party plaintiff did not bear the risk of loss as against the other party to the contract for sale and there is no arrangement between them for disposition of the recovery, his suit or settlement is, subject to his own interest, as a fiduciary for the other party to the contract;

    (c) either party may with the consent of the other sue for the benefit of whom it may concern.

SECTION 2—723. PROOF OF MARKET PRICE: TIME AND PLACE. (1) If an action based on anticipatory repudiation comes to trial before the time for performance with respect to some or all of the goods, any damages based on market price (Section 2—708 or Section 2—713) shall be determined according to the price of such goods prevailing at the time when the aggrieved party learned of the repudiation.

(2) If evidence of a price prevailing at the times or places described in this Article is not readily available the price prevailing within any reasonable time before or after the time described or at any other place which in commercial judgment or under usage of trade would serve as a reasonable substitute for the one described may be used, making any proper allowance for the cost of transporting the goods to or from such other place.

(3) Evidence of a relevant price prevailing at a time or place other than the one described in this Article offered by one party is not admissible unless and until he has given the other party such notice as the court finds sufficient to prevent unfair surprise.

SECTION 2—724. ADMISSIBILITY OF MARKET QUOTATIONS. Whenever the prevailing price or value of any goods regularly bought and sold in any established commodity market is in issue, reports in official publications or trade journals or in newspapers or periodicals of general circulation published as the reports of such market shall be admissible in evidence. The circumstances of the preparation of such a report may be shown to affect its weight but not its admissibility.

SECTION 2—725. STATUTE OF LIMITATIONS IN CONTRACTS FOR SALE. (1) An action for breach of any contract for sale must be commenced within four years after the cause of action has accrued. By the original agreement the parties may reduce the period of limitation to not less than one year but may not extend it.

(2) A cause of action accrues when the breach occurs, regardless of the aggrieved party's lack of knowledge of the breach. A breach of warranty occurs when tender of delivery is made, except that where a warranty explicitly extends to future performance of the goods and discovery of the breach must await the time of such performance the cause of action accrues when the breach is or should have been discovered.

(3) Where an action commenced within the time limited by subsection (1) is so terminated as to leave available a remedy by another action from the same breach such other action may be commenced after the expiration of the time limited and within six months after the termination of the first action unless the termination resulted from voluntary discontinuance or from dismissal for failure or neglect to prosecute.

(4) This section does not alter the law on tolling of the statute of limitations nor does it apply to causes of action which have accrued before this Act becomes effective.

ARTICLE 3

COMMERCIAL PAPER

PART 1

SHORT TITLE, FORM AND INTERPRETATION

SECTION 3—101. SHORT TITLE. This Article shall be known and may be cited as Uniform Commercial Code—Commercial Paper.

SECTION 3—102. DEFINITIONS AND INDEX OF DEFINITIONS. (1) In this Article unless the context otherwise requires

    (a) "Issue" means the first delivery of an instrument to a holder or a remitter.

    (b) An "order" is a direction to pay and must be more than an authorization or request. It must identify the person to pay with reasonable certainty. It may be addressed to one or more such persons jointly or in the alternative but not in succession.

    (c) A "promise" is an undertaking to pay and must be more than an acknowledgment of an obligation.

    (d) "Secondary party" means a drawer or endorser.

    (e) "Instrument" means a negotiable instrument.

(2) Other definitions applying to this Article and the sections in which they appear are:

"Acceptance". Section 3—410.
"Accommodation party". Section 3—415.
"Alteration". Section 3—407.
"Certificate of deposit". Section 3—104.
"Certification". Section 3—411.
"Check". Section 3—104.
"Definite time". Section 3—109.
"Dishonor". Section 3—507.
"Draft". Section 3—104.
"Holder in due course". Section 3—302.
"Negotiation". Section 3—202.
"Note". Section 3—104.
"Notice of dishonor". Section 3—508.
"On demand". Section 3—108.
"Presentment". Section 3—504.
"Protest". Section 3—509.
"Restrictive Indorsement". Section 3—205.
"Signature". Section 3—401.

(3) The following definitions in other Articles apply to this Article:

"Account". Section 4—104.
"Banking Day". Section 4—104.
"Clearing house". Section 4—104.
"Collecting bank". Section 4—105.
"Customer". Section 4—104.
"Depositary Bank". Section 4—105.
"Documentary Draft". Section 4—104.
"Intermediary Bank". Section 4—105.
"Item". Section 4—104.
"Midnight deadline". Section 4—104.
"Payor bank". Section 4—105.

(4) In addition Article 1 contains general definitions and principles of construction and interpretation applicable throughout this Article.

SECTION 3—103. LIMITATIONS ON SCOPE OF ARTICLE. (1) This Article does not apply to money, documents of title or investment securities.

(2) The provisions of this Article are subject to the provisions of the Article on Bank Deposits and Collections (Article 4) and Secured Transactions (Article 9).

SECTION 3—104. FORM OF NEGOTIABLE INSTRUMENTS; "DRAFT"; "CHECK"; "CERTIFICATE OF DEPOSIT"; "NOTE". (1) Any writing to be a negotiable instrument within this Article must

    (a) be signed by the maker or drawer; and

    (b) contain an unconditional promise or order to pay a sum certain in money and no other promise, order, obligation or power given by the maker or drawer except as authorized by this Article; and

    (c) be payable on demand or at a definite time; and

    (d) be payable to order or to bearer.

(2) A writing which complies with the requirements of this section is

    (a) a "draft" ("bill of exchange") if it is an order;

    (b) a "check" if it is a draft drawn on a bank and payable on demand;

    (c) a "certificate of deposit" if it is an acknowledgment by a bank of receipt of money with an engagement to repay it;

    (d) a "note" if it is a promise other than a certificate of deposit.

(3) As used in other Articles of this Act, and as the context may require, the terms "draft", "check", "certificate of deposit" and "note" may refer to instruments which are not negotiable within this Article as well as to instruments which are so negotiable.

SECTION 3—105. WHEN PROMISE OR ORDER UNCONDITIONAL. (1) A promise or order otherwise unconditional is not made conditional by the fact that the instrument

    (a) is subject to implied or constructive conditions; or

    (b) states its consideration, whether performed or promised, or the transaction which gave rise to the instrument, or that the promise or order is made or the instrument matures in accordance with or "as per" such transaction; or

    (c) refers to or states that it arises out of a separate agreement or refers to a separate agreement for rights as to prepayment or acceleration; or

    (d) states that it is drawn under a letter of credit; or

    (e) states that it is secured, whether by mortgage, reservation of title or otherwise; or

    (f) indicates a particular account to be debited or any other fund or source from which reimbursement is expected; or

    (g) is limited to payment out of a particular fund or the proceeds of a particular source, if the instrument is issued by a government or governmental agency or unit; or

    (h) is limited to payment out of the entire assets of a partnership, unincorporated association, trust or estate by or on behalf of which the instrument is issued.

(2) A promise or order is not unconditional if the instrument

    (a) states that it is subject to or governed by any other agreement; or

    (b) states that it is to be paid only out of a particular fund or source except as provided in this section.

SECTION 3—106. SUM CERTAIN. (1) The sum payable is a sum certain even though it is to be paid

    (a) with stated interest or by stated installments; or

    (b) with stated different rates of interest before and after default or a specified date; or

    (c) with a stated discount or addition if paid before or after the date fixed for payment; or

    (d) with exchange or less exchange, whether at a fixed rate or at the current rate; or

    (e) with costs of collection or an attorney's fee or both upon default.

(2) Nothing in this section shall validate any term which is otherwise illegal.

SECTION 3—107. MONEY. (1) An instrument is payable in money if the medium of exchange in which it is payable is money at the time the instrument is made. An instrument payable in "currency" or "current funds" is payable in money.

(2) A promise or order to pay a sum stated in a foreign currency is for a sum certain in money and, unless a different medium of payment is specified in the instru-

ment, may be satisfied by payment of that number of dollars which the stated foreign currency will purchase at the buying sight rate for that currency on the day on which the instrument is payable or, if payable on demand, on the day of demand. If such an instrument specifies a foreign currency as the medium of payment the instrument is payable in that currency.

SECTION 3—108. PAYABLE ON DEMAND. Instruments payable on demand include those payable at sight or on presentation and those in which no time for payment is stated.

SECTION 3—109. DEFINITE TIME. (1) An instrument is payable at a definite time if by its terms it is payable

    (a) on or before a stated date or at a fixed period after a stated date; or

    (b) at a fixed period after sight; or

    (c) at a definite time subject to any acceleration; or

    (d) at a definite time subject to extension at the option of the holder, or to extension to a further definite time at the option of the maker or acceptor or automatically upon or after a specified act or event.

(2) An instrument which by its terms is otherwise payable only upon an act or event uncertain as to time of occurrence is not payable at a definite time even though the act or event has occurred.

SECTION 3—110. PAYABLE TO ORDER. (1) An instrument is payable to order when by its terms it is payable to the order or assigns of any person therein specified with reasonable certainty, or to him or his order, or when it is conspicuously designated on its face as "exchange" or the like and names a payee. It may be payable to the order of

    (a) the maker or drawer; or

    (b) the drawee; or

    (c) a payee who is not maker, drawer or drawee; or

    (d) two or more payees together or in the alternative; or

    (e) an estate, trust or fund, in which case it is payable to the order of the representative of each estate, trust or fund or his successors; or

    (f) an office, or an officer by his title as such in which case it is payable to the principal but the incumbent of the office or his successors may act as if he or they were the holder; or

    (g) a partnership or unincorporated association, in which case it is payable to the partnership or association and may be indorsed or transferred by any person thereto authorized.

(2) An instrument not payable to order is not made so payable by such words as "payable upon return of this instrument properly indorsed."

(3) an instrument made payable both to order and to bearer is payable to order unless the bearer words are handwritten or typewritten.

SECTION 3—111. PAYABLE TO BEARER. An instrument is payable to bearer when by its terms it is payable to

    (a) bearer or the order of bearer; or

    (b) a specified person or bearer; or

    (c) "cash" or the order of "cash", or any other indication which does not purport to designate a specific payee.

SECTION 3—112. TERMS AND OMISSIONS NOT AFFECTING NEGOTIABILITY. (1) The negotiability of an instrument is not affected by

    (a) the omission of a statement of any consideration or of the place where the instrument is drawn or payable; or

    (b) a statement that collateral has been given to secure obligations either on the instrument or otherwise of an obligor on the instrument or that in case of default on those obligations the holder may realize on or dispose of the collateral; or

    (c) a promise or power to maintain or protect collateral or to give additional collateral; or

    (d) a term authorizing a confession of judgment on the instrument if it is not paid when due; or

    (e) a term purporting to waive the benefit of any law intended for the advantage or protection of any obligor; or

(f) a term in a draft providing that the payee by indorsing or cashing it acknowledges full satisfaction of an obligation of the drawer; or

(g) a statement in a draft drawn in a set of parts (Section 3—801) to the effect that the order is effective only if no other part has been honored.

(2) Nothing in this section shall validate any term which is otherwise illegal.

SECTION 3—113. SEAL. An instrument otherwise negotiable is within this Article even though it is under a seal.

SECTION 3—114. DATE, ANTEDATING, POSTDATING. (1) The negotiability of an instrument is not affected by the fact that it is undated, antedated or postdated.

(2) Where an instrument is antedated or postdated the time when it is payable is determined by the stated date if the instrument is payable on demand or at a fixed period after date.

(3) Where the instrument or any signature thereon is dated, the date is presumed to be correct.

SECTION 3—115. INCOMPLETE INSTRUMENTS. (1) When a paper whose contents at the time of signing show that it is intended to become an instrument is signed while still incomplete in any necessary respect it cannot be enforced until completed, but when it is completed in accordance with authority given it is effective as completed.

(2) It the completion is unauthorized the rules as to material alteration apply (Section 3—407), even though the paper was not delivered by the maker or drawer; but the burden of establishing that any completion is unauthorized is on the party so asserting.

SECTION 3—116. INSTRUMENTS PAYABLE TO TWO OR MORE PERSONS. An instrument payable to the order of two or more persons

(a) if in the alternative is payable to any one of them and may be negotiated, discharged or enforced by any of them who has possession of it;

(b) if not in the alternative is payable to all of them and may be negotiated, discharged or enforced only by all of them.

SECTION 3—117. INSTRUMENTS PAYABLE WITH WORDS OF DESCRIPTION. An instrument made payable to a named person with the addition of words describing him

(a) as agent or officer of a specified person is payable to his principal but the agent or officer may act as if he were the holder;

(b) as any other fiduciary for a specified person or purpose is payable to the payee and may be negotiated, discharged or enforced by him;

(c) in any other manner is payable to the payee unconditionally and the additional words are without effect on subsequent parties.

SECTION 3—318. AMBIGUOUS TERMS AND RULES OF CONSTRUCTION. The following rules apply to every instrument:

(a) Where there is doubt whether the instrument is a draft or a note the holder may treat it as either. A draft drawn on the drawer is effective as a note.

(b) Handwritten terms control typewritten and printed terms, and typewritten control printed.

(c) Words control figures except that if the words are ambiguous figures control.

(d) Unless otherwise specified a provision for interest means interest at the judgment rate at the place of payment from the date of the instrument, or if it is undated from the date of issue.

(e) Unless the instrument otherwise specifies two or more persons who sign as maker, acceptor or drawer or indorser and as a part of the same transaction are jointly and severally liable even though the instrument contains such words as "I promise to pay."

(f) Unless otherwise specified consent to extension authorizes a single extention for not longer than the original period. A consent to extension, expressed in the instrument, is binding on secondary parties and accommodation makers. A holder may not exercise his option to extend an instrument over the objection of a maker or acceptor or other party who in accordance with Section 3—604 tenders full payment when the instrument is due.

SECTION 3—119. OTHER WRITINGS AFFECTING INSTRUMENT. (1) As between the obligor and his immediate obligee or any transferee the terms of an instrument may be modified or affected by any other written agreement executed as a part of the same transaction, except that a holder in due course is not affected by any limitation of his rights arising out of the separate written agreement if he had no notice of the limitation when he took the instrument.

(1) A separate agreement does not affect the negotiability of an instrument.

SECTION 3—120. INSTRUMENTS "PAYABLE THROUGH" BANK. An instrument which states that it is "payable through" a bank or the like designates that bank as a collecting bank to make presentment but does not of itself authorize the bank to pay the instrument.

SECTION 3—121. INSTRUMENTS PAYABLE AT BANK.

NOTE: *If this Act is introduced in the Congress of the United States this section should be omitted.*

(States to select either alternative)

ALTERNATIVE A—

A note or acceptance which states that it is payable at a bank is the equivalent of a draft drawn on the bank payable when it falls due out of any funds of the maker or acceptor in current account or otherwise available for such payment.

ALTERNATIVE B—

A note or acceptance which states that it is payable at a bank is not of itself an order or authorization to the bank to pay it.

SECTION 3—122. ACCRUAL OF CAUSE OF ACTION. (1) A cause of action against a maker or an acceptor accrues

    (a) in the case of a time instrument on the day after maturity;

    (b) in the case of a demand instrument upon its date or, if no date is stated, on the date of issue.

(2) A cause of action against the obligor of a demand or time certificate of deposit accrues upon demand, but demand on a time certificate may not be made until on or after the date of maturity.

(3) A cause of action against a drawer of a draft or an indorser of any instrument accrues upon demand following dishonor of the instrument. Notice of dishonor is a demand.

(4) Unless an instrument provides otherwise, interest runs at the rate provided by law for a judgment.

    (a) in the case of a maker, acceptor or other primary obligor of a demand instrument, from the date of demand;

    (b) in all other cases from the date of accrual of the cause of action.

PART 2

TRANSFER AND NEGOTIATION

SECTION 3—201. TRANSFER: RIGHT TO INDORSEMENT. (1) Transfer of an instrument vests in the transferee such rights as the transferor has therein, except that a transferee who has himself been a party to any fraud or illegality affecting the instrument or who as a prior holder had notice of a defense or claim against it cannot improve his position by taking from a later holder a due course.

(2) A transfer of a security interest in an instrument vests the foregoing rights in the transferee to the extent of the interest transferred.

(3) Unless otherwise agreed any transfer for value of an instrument not then payable to bearer gives the transferee the specifically enforceable right to have the unqualified indorsement of the transferor. Negotiation takes effect only when the indorsement is made and until that time there is no presumption that the transferee is the owner.

SECTION 3—202. NEGOTIATION. (1) Negotiation is the transfer of an instrument in such form that the transferee becomes a holder. If the instrument is payable to order it is negotiated by delivery with any necessary indorsement; if payable to bearer it is negotiated by delivery.

(2) An indorsement must be writted by or on behalf of the holder and on the instrument or on a paper so firmly affixed thereto as to become a part thereof.

(3) An indorsement is effective for negotiation only when it conveys the entire instrument or any unpaid residue. If it purports to be of less it operates only as a partial assignment.

(4) Words of assignment, condition, waiver, guaranty, limitation or disclaimer of liability and the like accompanying an indorsement do not affect its character as an indorsement.

SECTION 3—203. WRONG OR MISSPELLED NAME. Where an instrument is made payable to a person under a misspelled name or one other than his own he may indorse in that name or his own or both; but signature in both names may be required by a person paying or giving value for the instrument.

SECTION 3—204. SPECIAL INDORSEMENT; BLANK INDORSEMENT. (1) A special indorsement specifies the person to whom or to whose order it makes the instrument payable. Any instrument specially indorsed becomes payable to the order of the special indorsee and may be further negotiated only by his indorsement.

(2) An indorsement in blank specifies no particular indorsee and may consist of a mere signature. An instrument payable to order and indorsed in blank becomes payable to bearer and may be negotiated by delivery alone until specially indorsed.

(3) The holder may convert a blank indorsement into a special indorsement by writing over the signature of the indorser in blank any contract consistent with the character of the indorsement.

SECTION 3—205. RESTRICTIVE INDORSEMENTS. An indorsement is restrictive which either

(a) is conditional; or

(b) purports to prohibit further transfer of the instrument; or

(c) includes the words "for collection", "for deposit", "pay any bank" or like terms signifying a purpose of deposit or collection; or

(d) otherwise states that it is for the benefit or use of the indorser or of another person.

SECTION 3—206. EFFECT OF RESTRICTIVE INDORSEMENT. (1) No restrictive indorsement prevents further transfer or negotiation of the instrument.

(2) An intermediary bank, or a payor bank which is not the depositary bank, is neither given notice nor otherwise affected by a restrictive indorsement of any person except the bank's immediate transferor or the person presenting for payment.

(3) Except for an intermediary bank, any transferee under an indorsement which is conditional or includes the words "for collection", "for deposit", "pay any bank", or like terms (subparagraphs (a) and (c) of Section 3—205) must pay or apply any value given by him for or on the security of the instrument consistently with the indorsement and to the extent that he does so he becomes a holder for value. In addition such transferee is a holder in due course if he otherwise complies with the requirements of Section 3—302 on what constitutes a holder in due course.

(4) The first taker under an indorsement for the benefit of the indorser or another person (subparagraph (d) of Section 3—205) must pay or apply any value given by him for or on the security of the instrument consistently with the indorsement and to the extent that he does so he becomes a holder for value. In addition such taker is a holder in due course if he otherwise complies with the requirements of Section 3—302 on what constitutes a holder in due course. A later holder for value is neither given notice nor otherwise affected by such restrictive indorsement unless he has knowledge that a fiduciary or other person has negotiated the instrument in any transaction for his own benefit or otherwise in breach of duty (subsection (2) of Section 3—304).

SECTION 3—207. NEGOTIATION EFFECTIVE ALTHOUGH IT MAY BE RESCINDED. (1) Negotiation is effective to transfer the instrument although the negotiation is

(a) made by an infant, a corporation exceeding its powers, or any other person without capacity; or

(b) obtained by fraud, duress or mistake of any kind; or

(c) part of an illegal transaction; or

(d) made in breach of duty.

(2) Except as against a subsequent holder in due course such negotiation is in an appropriate case subject to rescission, the declaration of a constructive trust or any other remedy permitted by law.

SECTION 3—208. REACQUISITION. Where an instrument is returned to or reacquired by a prior party he may cancel any indorsement which is not necessary to his title and reissue or further negotiate the instrument, but any intervening party is discharged as against the reacquiring party and subsequent holders not in due course and if his indorsement has been cancelled is discharged as against subsequent holders in due course as well.

PART 3

RIGHTS OF A HOLDER

SECTION 3—301. RIGHTS OF A HOLDER. The holder of an instrument whether or not he is the owner may transfer or negotiate it and, except as otherwise provided in Section 3—603 on payment or satisfaction, discharge it or enforce payment in his own name.

SECTION 3—302. HOLDER IN DUE COURSE. (1) A holder in due course is a holder who takes the instrument

    (a) for value; and

    (b) in good faith; and

    (c) without notice that it is overdue or has been dishonored or of any defense against or claim to it on the part of any person.

(2) A payee may be a holder in due course.

(3) A holder does not become a holder in due course of an instrument:

    (a) by purchase of it at judicial sale or by taking it under legal process; or

    (b) by acquiring it in taking over an estate; or

    (c) by purchasing it as part of a bulk transaction not in regular course of business of the transferor.

(4) A purchaser of a limited interest can be a holder in due course only to the extent of the interest purchased.

SECTION 3—303. TAKING FOR VALUE. A holder takes the instrument for value

    (a) to the extent that the agreed consideration has been performed or that he acquires a security interest in or a lien on the instrument otherwise than by legal process; or

    (b) when he takes the instrument in payment of or as security for an antecedent claim against any person whether or not the claim is due; or

    (c) when he gives a negotiable instrument for it or makes an irrevocable commitment to a third person.

SECTION 3—304. NOTICE TO PURCHASER. (1) The purchaser has notice of a claim or defense if

    (a) the instrument is so incomplete, bears such visible evidence of forgery or alteration, or is otherwise so irregular as to call into question its validity, terms or ownership or to create an ambiguity as to the party to pay; or

    (b) the purchaser has notice that the obligation of any party is voidable in whole or in part, or that all parties have been discharged.

(2) The purchaser has notice of a claim against the instrument when he has knowledge that a fiduciary has negotiated the instrument in payment of or as security for his own debt or in any transaction for his own benefit or otherwise in breach of duty.

(3) The purchaser has notice that an instrument is overdue if he has reason to know

    (a) that any part of the principal amount is overdue or that there is an uncured default in payment of another instrument of the same series; or

    (b) that acceleration of the instrument has been made; or

    (c) that he is taking a demand instrument after demand has been made or more than a reasonable length of time after its issue. A reasonable time for a check drawn and payable within the states and territories of the United States and the District of Columbia is presumed to be thirty days.

(4) Knowledge of the following facts does not of itself give the purchaser notice of a defense or claim

    (a) that the instrument is antedated or postdated;

    (b) that it was issued or negotiated in return for an executory promise or accompanied by a separate agreement, unless the purchaser has notice that a defense or claim has arisen from the terms thereof;

    (c) that any party has signed for accommodation;

    (d) that an incomplete instrument has been completed, unless the purchaser has notice of any improper completion;

(e) that any person negotiating the instrument is or was a fiduciary;

(f) that there has been default in payment of interest on the instrument or in payment of any other instrument, except one of the same series.

(5) The filing or recording of a document does not of itself constitute notice within the provisions of this Article to a person who would otherwise be a holder in due course.

(6) To be effective notice must be received at such time and in such manner as to give a reasonable opportunity to act on it.

SECTION 3—305. RIGHTS OF A HOLDER IN DUE COURSE. To the extent that a holder is a holder in due course he takes the instrument free from

(1) all claims to it on the part of any person; and

(2) all defenses of any party to the instrument with whom the holder has not dealt except

(a) infancy, to the extent that it is a defense to a simple contract; and

(b) such other incapacity, or duress, or illegality of the transaction, as renders the obligation of the party a nullity; and

(c) such misrepresentation as has induced the party to sign the instrument with neither knowledge nor reasonable opportunity to obtain knowledge of its character or its essential terms; and

(d) discharge in insolvency proceedings; and

(e) any other discharge of which the holder has notice when he takes the instrument.

SECTION 3—306. RIGHTS OF ONE NOT HOLDER IN DUE COURSE. Unless he has the rights of a holder in due course any person takes the instrument subject to

(a) all valid claims to it on the part of any person; and

(b) all defenses of any party which would be available in an action on a simple contract; and

(c) the defenses of want or failure of consideration, non-performance of any condition precedent, non-delivery, or delivery for a special purpose (Section 3—408); and

(d) the defense that he or a person through whom he holds the instrument acquired it by theft, or that payment or satisfaction to such holder would be inconsistent with the terms of a restrictive indorsement. The claim of any third person to the instrument is not otherwise available as a defense to any party liable thereon unless the third person himself defends the action for such party.

SECTION 3—307. BURDEN OF ESTABLISHING SIGNATURES, DEFENSES AND DUE COURSE. (1) Unless specifically denied in the pleadings each signature on an instrument is admitted. When the effectiveness of a signature is put in issue

(a) the burden of establishing it is on the party claiming under the signature; but

(b) the signature is presumed to be genuine or authorized except where the action is to enforce the obligation of a purported signer who has died or become incompetent before proof is required.

(2) When signatures are admitted or established, production of the instrument entitles a holder to recover on it unless the defendant establishes a defense.

(3) After it is shown that a defense exists a person claiming the rights of a holder in due course has the burden of establishing that he or some person under whom he claims is in all respects a holder in due course.

PART 4

LIABILITY OF PARTIES

SECTION 3—401. SIGNATURE. (1) No person is liable on an instrument unless his signature appears thereon.

(2) A signature is made by use of any name, including any trade or assumed name, upon an instrument, or by any word or mark used in lieu of a written signature.

SECTION 3—402. SIGNATURE IN AMBIGUOUS CAPACITY. Unless the instrument clearly indicates that a signature is made in some other capacity it is an indorsement.

SECTION 3—403. SIGNATURE BY AUTHORIZED REPRESENTATIVE. (1) A signature may be made by an agent or other representative, and his authority to make it may be established as in other cases of representation. No particular form of appointment is necessary to establish such authority.

(2) An authorized representative who signs his own name to an instrument

    (a) is personally obligated if the instrument neither names the person represented nor shows that the representative signed in a representative capacity;

    (b) except as otherwise established between the immediate parties, is personally obligated if the instrument names the person represented but does not show that the representative signed in a representative capacity, or if the instrument does not name the person represented but does show that the representative signed in a representative capacity.

(3) Except as otherwise established the name of an organization preceded or followed by the name and office of an authorized individual is a signature made in a representative capacity.

SECTION 3—404. UNAUTHORIZED SIGNATURES. (1) Any unauthorized signature is wholly inoperative as that of the person whose name is signed unless he ratifies it or is precluded from denying it; but it operates as the signature of the unauthorized signer in favor of any person who in good faith pays the instrument or takes it for value.

(2) Any unauthorized signature may be ratified for all purposes of this Article. Such ratification does not of itself affect any rights of the person ratifying against the actual signer.

SECTION 3—405. IMPOSTORS; SIGNATURE IN NAME OF PAYEE. (1) An indorsement by any person in the name of a named payee is effective if

    (a) an impostor by use of the mails or otherwise has induced the maker or drawer to issue the instrument to him or his confederate in the name of the payee; or

    (b) a person signing as or on behalf of a maker or drawer intends the payee to have no interest in the instrument; or

    (c) an agent or employee of the maker or drawer has supplied him with the name of the payee intending the latter to have no such interest.

(2) Nothing in this section shall affect the criminal or civil liability of the person so indorsing.

SECTION 3—406. NEGLIGENCE CONTRIBUTING TO ALTERATION OR UNAUTHORIZED SIGNATURE. Any person who by his negligence substantially contributes to a material alteration of the instrument or to the making of an unauthorized signature is precluded from asserting the alteration or lack of authority against a holder in due course or against a drawee or other payor who pays the instrument in good faith and in accordance with the reasonable commercial standards of the drawee's or payor's business.

SECTION 3—407. ALTERATION. (1) Any alteration of an instrument is material which changes the contract of any party thereto in any respect, including any such change in

    (a) the number or relations of the parties; or

    (b) an incomplete instrument, by completing it otherwise than as authorized; or

    (c) the writing as signed, by adding to it or by removing any part of it.

(2) As against any person other than a subsequent holder in due course

    (a) alteration by the holder which is both fraudulent and material discharges any party whose contract is thereby changed unless that party assents or is precluded from asserting the defense;

    (b) no other alteration discharges any party and the instrument may be enforced according to its original tenor, or as to incomplete instruments according to the authority given.

(3) A subsequent holder in due course may in all cases enforce the instrument according to its original tenor, and when an incomplete instrument has been completed, he may enforce it as completed.

SECTION 3—408. CONSIDERATION. Want or failure of consideration is a defense as against any person not having the rights of a holder in due course (Section 3—305), except that no consideration is necessary for an instrument or obligation thereon given in payment of or as security for an antecedent obligation of any kind. Nothing in this section shall be taken to displace any statute outside this Act under which a promise is enforceable notwithstanding lack or failure of consideration. Partial failure of consideration is a defense pro tanto whether or not the failure is in an ascertained or liquidated amount.

SECTION 3—409. DRAFT NOT AN ASSIGNMENT. (1) A check or other draft does not of itself operate as an assignment of any funds in the hands of the drawee available for its payment, and the drawee is not liable on the instrument until he accepts it.

(2) Nothing in this section shall affect any liability in contract, tort or otherwise arising from any letter of credit or other obligation or representation which is not an acceptance.

SECTION 3—410. DEFINITION AND OPERATION OF ACCEPTANCE. (1) Acceptance is the drawee's signed engagement to honor the draft as presented. It must be written on the draft, and may consist of his signature alone. It becomes operative when completed by delivery or notification.

(2) A draft may be accepted although it has not been signed by the drawer or is otherwise incomplete or is overdue or has been dishonored.

(3) Where the draft is payable at a fixed period after sight and the acceptor fails to date his acceptance the holder may complete it by supplying a date in good faith.

SECTION 3—411. CERTIFICATE OF A CHECK. (1) Certification of a check is acceptance. Where a holder procures certification the drawer and all prior indorsers are discharged.

(2) Unless otherwise agreed a bank has no obligation to certify a check.

(3) A bank may certify a check before returning it for lack of proper indorsement. If it does so the drawer is discharged.

SECTION 3—412. ACCEPTANCE VARYING DRAFT. (1) Where the drawee's proffered acceptance in any manner varies the draft as presented the holder may refuse the acceptance and treat the draft as dishonored in which case the drawee is entitled to have his acceptance cancelled.

(2) The terms of the draft are not varied by an acceptance to pay at any particular bank or place in the United States, unless the acceptance states that the draft is to be paid only at such bank or place.

(3) Where the holder assents to an acceptance varying the terms of the draft each drawer and indorser who does not affirmatively assent is discharged.

SECTION 3—413. CONTRACT OF MAKER, DRAWER AND ACCEPTOR. (1) The maker or acceptor engages that he will pay the instrument according to its tenor at the time of his engagement or as completed pursuant to Section 3—115 on incomplete instruments.

(2) The drawer engages that upon dishonor of the draft and any necessary notice of dishonor or protest he will pay the amount of the draft to the holder or to any indorser who takes it up. The drawer may disclaim this liability by drawing without recourse.

(3) By making, drawing or accepting the party admits as against all subsequent parties including the drawee the existence of the payee and his then capacity to indorse.

SECTION 3—414. CONTRACT OF INDORSER; ORDER OF LIABILITY. (1) Unless the indorsement otherwise specifies (as by such words as "without recourse") every indorser engages that upon dishonor and any necessary notice of dishonor and protest he will pay the instrument according to its tenor at the time of his indorsement to the holder or to any subsequent indorser who takes it up, even though the indorser who takes it up was not obligated to do so.

(2) Unless they otherwise agree indorsers are liable to one another in the order in which they indorse, which is presumed to be the order in which their signatures appear on the instrument.

SECTION 3—415. CONTRACT OF ACCOMMODATION PARTY. (1) An accommodation party is one who signs the instrument in any capacity for the purpose of lending his name to another party to it.

(2) When the instrument has been taken for value before it is due the accommodation party is liable in the capacity in which he has signed even though the taker knows of the accommodation.

(3) As against a holder in due course and without notice of the accommodation oral proof of the accommodation is not admissible to give the accommodation party the benefit of discharges dependent on his character as such. In other cases the accommodation character may be shown by oral proof.

(4) An indorsement which shows that it is not in the chain of title is notice of its accommodation character.

(5) An accommodation party is not liable to the party accommodated, and if he pays the instrument has a right of recourse on the instrument against such party.

SECTION 3—416. CONTRACT OF GUARANTOR. (1) "Payment guaranteed" or equivalent words added to a signature mean that the signer engages that if the instrument is not paid when due he will pay it according to its tenor without resort by the holder to any other party.

(2) "Collection guaranteed" or equivalent words added to a signature mean that the signer engages that if the instrument is not paid when due he will pay it according to its tenor, but only after the holder has reduced his claim against the maker or acceptor to judgment and execution has been returned unsatisfied, or after the maker or acceptor has become insolvent or it is otherwise apparent that it is useless to proceed against him.

(3) Words of guaranty which do not otherwise specify guarantee payment.

(4) No words of guaranty added to the signature of a sole maker or acceptor affect his liability on the instrument. Such words added to the signature of one of two or more makers or acceptors create a presumption that the signature is for the accommodation of the others.

(5) When words of guaranty are used presentment, notice of dishonor and protest are not necessary to charge the user.

(6) Any guaranty written on the instrument is enforcible notwithstanding any statute of frauds.

SECTION 3—417. WARRANTIES ON PRESENTMENT AND TRANSFER. (1) Any person who obtains payment or acceptance and any prior transferor warrants to a person who in good faith pays or accepts that

    (a) he has a good title to the instrument or is authorized to obtain payment or acceptance on behalf of one who has a good title; and

    (b) he has no knowledge that the signature of the maker or drawer is unauthorized, except that this warranty is not given by a holder in due course acting in good faith

        (i) to a maker with respect to the maker's own signature; or

        (ii) to a drawer with respect to the drawer's own signature, whether or not the drawer is also the drawee; or

        (iii) to an acceptor of a draft if the holder in due course took the draft after the acceptance or obtained the acceptance without knowledge that the drawer's signature was unauthorized; and

    (c) the instrument has not been materially altered, except that this warranty is not given by a holder in due course acting in good faith

        (i) to the maker of a note; or

        (ii) to the drawer of a draft whether or not the drawer is also the drawee; or

        (iii) to the acceptor of a draft with respect to an alteration made prior to the acceptance if the holder in due course took the draft after the acceptance, even though the acceptance provided "payable as originally drawn" or equivalent terms; or

        (iv) to the acceptor of a draft with respect to an alteration made after the acceptance.

(2) Any person who transfers an instrument and receives consideration warrants to his transferee and if the transfer is by indorsement to any subsequent holder who takes the instrument in good faith that

    (a) he has a good title to the instrument or is authorized to obtain payment or acceptance on behalf of one who has a good title and the transfer is otherwise rightful; and

    (b) all signatures are genuine or authorized; and

    (c) the instrument has not been materially altered; and

    (d) no defense of any party is good against him; and

    (e) he has no knowledge of any insolvency proceeding instituted with respect to the maker or acceptor or the drawer of an unaccepted instrument.

(3) By transferring "without recourse" the transferor limits the obligation stated in subsection (2) (d) to a warranty that he has no knowledge of such a defense.

(4) A selling agent or broker who does not disclose the fact that he is acting only as such gives the warranties provided in this section, but if he makes such disclosure warrants only his good faith and authority.

SECTION 3—418. FINALITY OF PAYMENT OR ACCEPTANCE. Except for recovery of bank payments as provided in the Article on Bank Deposits and Collections (Article 4) and except for liability for breach of warranty on presentment under the preceding section, payment or acceptance of any instrument is final in favor of a holder in due course, or a person who has in good faith changed his position in reliance on the payment.

SECTION 3—419. CONVERSION OF INSTRUMENT; INNOCENT REPRESENTATIVE. (1) An instrument is converted when

    (a) a drawee to whom it is delivered for acceptance refuses to return it on demand; or

    (b) any person to whom it is delivered for payment refuses on demand either to pay or to return it; or

    (c) it is paid on a forged indorsement.

(2) In an action against a drawee under subsection (1) the measure of the drawee's liability is the face amount of the instrument. In any other action under subsection (1) the measure of liability is presumed to be the face amount of the instrument.

(3) Subject to the provisions of this Act concerning restrictive indorsements a representative, including a depositary or collecting bank, who has in good faith and in accordance with the reasonable commercial standards applicable to the business of such representative dealt with an instrument or its proceeds on behalf of one who was not the true owner is not liable in conversion or otherwise to the true owner beyond the amount of any proceeds remaining in his hands.

(4) An intermediary bank or payor bank which is not a depositary bank is not liable in conversion solely by reason of the fact that proceeds of an item indorsed restrictively (Sections 3—205 and 3—206) are not paid or applied consistently with the restrictive indorsement of an indorser other than its immediate transferor.

PART 5

PRESENTMENT, NOTICE OF DISHONOR AND PROTEST

SECTION 3—501. WHEN PRESENTMENT, NOTICE OF DISHONOR, AND PROTEST NECESSARY OR PERMISSIBLE. (1) Unless excused (Section 3—511) presentment is necessary to charge secondary parties as follows:

    (a) presentment for acceptance is necessary to charge the drawer and indorsers of a draft where the draft so provides, or is payable elsewhere than at the residence or place of business of the drawee, or its date of payment depends upon such presentment. The holder may at his option present for acceptance any other draft payable at a stated date;

    (b) presentment for payment is necessary to charge any indorser;

    (c) in the case of any drawer, the acceptor of a draft payable at a bank or the maker of a note payable at a bank, presentment for payment is necessary, but failure to make presentment discharges such drawer, acceptor or maker only as stated in Section 3—502(1) (b).

(2) Unless excused (Section 3—511)

    (a) notice of any dishonor is necessary to charge any indorser;

    (b) in the case of any drawer, the acceptor of a draft payable at a bank or the maker of a note payable at a bank, notice of any dishonor is necessary, but failure to give such notice discharges such drawer, acceptor or maker only as stated in Section 3—502(1) (b).

(3) Unless excused (Section 3—511) protest of any dishonor is necessary to charge the drawer and indorsers of any draft which on its face appears to be drawn or payable outside of the states and territories of the United States and the District of Columbia. The holder may at his option make protest of any dishonor of any other

instrument and in the case of a foreign draft may on insolvency of the acceptor before maturity make protest for better security.

(4) Notwithstanding any provision of this section, neither presentment nor notice of dishonor nor protest is necessary to charge an indorser who has indorsed an instrument after maturity.

SECTION 3—502. UNEXCUSED DELAY; DISCHARGE. (1) Where without excuse any necessary presentment or notice of dishonor is delayed beyond the time when it is due

    (a) any indorser is discharged; and

    (b) any drawer or the acceptor of a draft payable at a bank or the maker of a note payable at a bank who because the drawee or payor bank becomes insolvent during the delay is deprived of funds maintained with the drawee or payor bank to cover the instrument may discharge his liability by written assignment to the holder of his rights against the drawee or payor bank in respect of such funds, but such drawer, acceptor or maker is not otherwise discharged.

(2) Where without excuse a necessary protest is delayed beyond the time when it is due any drawer or indorser is discharged.

SECTION 3—503. TIME OF PRESENTMENT. (1) Unless a different time is expressed in the instrument the time for any presentment is determined as follows:

    (a) where an instrument is payable at or a fixed period after a stated date any presentment for acceptance must be made on or before the date it is payable;

    (b) where an instrument is payable after sight it must either be presented for acceptance or negotiated within a reasonable time after date or issue whichever is later;

    (c) where an instrument shows the date on which it is payable presentment for payment is due on that date;

    (d) where an instrument is accelerated presentment for payment is due within a reasonable time after the acceleration;

    (e) with respect to the liability of any secondary party presentment for acceptance or payment of any other instrument is due within a reasonable time after such party becomes liable thereon.

(2) A reasonable time for presentment is determined by the nature of the instrument, any usage of banking or trade and the facts of the particular case. In the case of an uncertified check which is drawn and payable within the United States and which is not a draft drawn by a bank the following are presumed to be reasonable periods within which to present for payment or to initiate bank collection:

    (a) with respect to the liability of the drawer, thirty days after date or issue which ever is later; and

    (b) with respect to the liability of an indorser, seven days after his indorsement.

(3) Where any presentment is due on a day which is not a full business day for either the person making presentment or the party to pay or accept, presentment is due on the next following day which is a full business day for both parties.

(4) Presentment to be sufficient must be made at a reasonable hour, and if at a bank during its banking day.

SECTION 3—504. HOW PRESENTMENT MADE. (1) Presentment is a demand for acceptance or payment made upon the maker, acceptor, drawee or other payor by or on behalf of the holder.

(2) Presentment may be made

    (a) by mail, in which event the time of presentment is determined by the time of receipt of the mail; or

    (b) through a clearing house; or

    (c) at the place of acceptance or payment specified in the instrument or if there be none at the place of business or residence of the party to accept or pay. If neither the party to accept or pay nor anyone authorized to act for him is present or accessible at such place presentment is excused.

(3) It may be made

    (a) to any one of two or more makers, acceptors, drawees or other payors; or

(b) to any person who has authority to make or refuse the acceptance or payment.

(4) A draft accepted or a note made payable at a bank in the United States must be presented at such bank.

(5) In the cases described in Section 4—210 presentment may be made in the manner and with the result stated in that section.

SECTION 3—505. RIGHTS OF PARTY TO WHOM PRESENTMENT IS MADE. (1) The party to whom presentment is made may without dishonor require

(a) exhibition of the instrument; and

(b) reasonable identification of the person making presentment and evidence of his authority to make it if made for another; and

(c) that the instrument be produced for acceptance or payment at a place specified in it, or if there be none at any place reasonable in the circumstances; and

(d) a signed receipt on the instrument for any partial or full payment and its surrender upon full payment.

(2) Failure to comply with any such requirement invalidates the presentment but the person presenting has a reasonable time in which to comply and the time for acceptance or payment runs from the time of compliance.

SECTION 3—506. TIME ALLOWED FOR ACCEPTANCE OR PAYMENT. (1) Acceptance may be deferred without dishonor until the close of the next business day following presentment. The holder may also in a good faith effort to obtain acceptance and without either dishonor of the instrument or discharge of secondary parties allow postponement of acceptance for an additional business day.

(2) Except as a longer time is allowed in the case of documentary drafts drawn under a letter of credit, and unless an earlier time is agreed to by the party to pay, payment of an instrument may be deferred without dishonor pending reasonable examination to determine whether it is properly payable, but payment must be made in any event before the close of business on the day of presentment.

SECTION 3—507. DISHONOR; HOLDER'S RIGHT OF RECOURSE; TERM ALLOWING RE-PRESENTMENT. (1) An instrument is dishonored when

(a) a necessary or optional presentment is duly made and due acceptance or payment is refused or cannot be obtained within the prescribed time or in case of bank collections the instrument is seasonably returned by the midnight deadline (Section 4—301); or

(b) presentment is excused and the instrument is not duly accepted or paid.

(2) Subject to any necessary notice of dishonor and protest, the holder has upon dishonor an immediate right of recourse against the drawers and indorsers.

(3) Return of an instrument for lack of proper indorsement is not dishonor.

(4) A term in a draft or an indorsement thereof allowing a stated time for re-presentment in the event of any dishonor of the draft by nonacceptance if a time draft or by nonpayment if a sight draft gives the holder as against any secondary party bound by the term an option to waive the dishonor without affecting the liability of the secondary party and he may present again up to the end of the stated time.

SECTION 3—508. NOTICE OF DISHONOR. (1) Notice of dishonor may be given to any person who may be liable on the instrument by or on behalf of the holder or any party who has himself received notice, or any other party who can be compelled to pay the instrument. In addition an agent or bank in whose hands the instrument is dishonored may give notice to his principal or customer or to another agent or bank from which the instrument was received.

(2) Any necessary notice must be given by a bank before its midnight deadline and by any other person before midnight of the third business day after dishonor or receipt of notice of dishonor.

(3) Notice may be given in any reasonable manner. It may be oral or written and in any terms which identify the instrument and state that it has been dishonored. A misdescription which does not mislead the party notified does not vitiate the notice. Sending the instrument bearing a stamp, ticket or writing stating that acceptance or payment has been refused or sending a notice of debit with respect to the instrument is sufficient.

(4) Written notice is given when sent although it is not received.

(5) Notice to one partner is notice to each although the firm has been dissolved.

(6) When any party is in insolvency proceedings instituted after the issue of the instrument notice may be given either to the party or to the representative of his estate.

(7) When any party is dead or incompetent notice may be sent to his last known address or given to his personal representative.

(8) Notice operates for the benefit of all parties who have rights on the instrument against the party notified.

SECTION 3—509. PROTEST; NOTING FOR PROTEST. (1) A protest is a certificate of dishonor made under the hand and seal of a United States consul or vice consul or a notary public or other person authorized to certify dishonor by the law of the place where dishonor occurs. It may be made upon information satisfactory to such person.

(2) The protest must identify the instrument and certify either that due presentment has been made or the reason why it is excused and that the instrument has been dishonored by nonacceptance or nonpayment.

(3) The protest may also certify that notice of dishonor has been given to all parties or to specified parties.

(4) Subject to subsection (5) any necessary protest is due by the time that notice of dishonor is due.

(5) If, before protest is due, an instrument has been noted for protest by the officer to make protest, the protest may be made at any time thereafter as of the date of the noting.

SECTION 3—510. EVIDENCE OF DISHONOR AND NOTICE OF DISHONOR. The following are admissible as evidence and create a presumption of dishonor and of any notice of dishonor therein shown:

(a) a document regular in form as provided in the preceding section which purports to be a protest;

(b) the purported stamp or writing of the drawee, payor bank or presenting bank on the instrument or accompanying it stating that acceptance or payment has been refused for reasons consistent with dishonor;

(c) any book or record of the drawee, payor bank, or any collecting bank kept in the usual course of business which shows dishonor, even though there is no evidence of who made the entry.

SECTION 3—511. WAIVED OR EXCUSED PRESENTMENT, PROTEST OR NOTICE OF DISHONOR OR DELAY THEREIN. (1) Delay in presentment, protest or notice of dishonor is excused when the party is without notice that it is due or when the delay is caused by circumstances beyond his control and he exercises reasonable diligence after the cause of the delay ceases to operate.

(2) Presentment or notice or protest as the case may be is entirely excused when

(a) the party to be charged has waived it expressly or by implication either before or after it is due; or

(b) such party has himself dishonored the instrument or has countermanded payment or otherwise has no reason to expect or right to require that the instrument be accepted or paid; or

(c) by reasonable diligence the presentment or protest cannot be made or the notice given.

(3) Presentment is also entirely excused when

(a) the maker, acceptor or drawee of any instrument except a documentary draft is dead or in insolvency proceedings instituted after the issue of the instrument; or

(b) acceptance or payment is refused but not for want of proper presentment.

(4) Where a draft has been dishonored by nonacceptance a later presentment for payment and any notice of dishonor and protest for nonpayment are excused unless in the meantime the instrument has been accepted.

(5) A waiver of protest is also a waiver of presentment and of notice of dishonor even though protest is not required.

(6) Where a waiver of presentment or notice or protest is embodied in the instrument itself it is binding upon all parties; but where it is written above the signature of an indorser it binds him only.

PART 6

SECTION 3—601. DISCHARGE OF PARTIES. (1) The extent of the discharge of any party from liability on an instrument is governed by the section on

(a) payment or satisfaction (Section 3—603); or

(b) tender of payment (Section 3—604); or

(c) cancellation or renunciation (Section 3—605); or

(d) impairment of right of recourse or of collateral (Section 3—606); or

(e) reacquisition of the instrument by a prior party (Section 3—208); or

(f) fraudulent and material alteration (Section 3—407); or

(g) certification of a check (Section 3—411); or

(h) acceptance varying a draft (Section 3—412); or

(i) unexcused delay in presentment or notice of dishonor or protest (Section 3—502).

(2) Any party is also discharged from his liability on an instrument to another party by any other act or agreement with such party which would discharge his simple contract for the payment of money.

(3) The liability of all parties is discharged when any party who has himself no right of action or recourse on the instrument

(a) reacquires the instrument in his own right; or

(b) is discharged under any provision of this Article, except as otherwise provided with respect to discharge for impairment of recourse or of collateral (Section 3—606).

SECTION 3—602. EFFECT OF DISCHARGE AGAINST HOLDER IN DUE COURSE. No discharge of any party provided by this Article is effective against a subsequent holder in due course unless he has notice thereof when he takes the instrument.

SECTION 3—603. PAYMENT OR SATISFACTION. (1) The liability of any party is discharged to the extent of his payment or satisfaction to the holder even though it is made with knowledge of a claim of another person to the instrument unless prior to such payment or satisfaction the person making the claim either supplies indemnity deemed adequate by the party seeking the discharge or enjoins payment or satisfaction by order of a court of competent jurisdiction in an action in which the adverse claimant and the holder are parties. This subsection does not, however, result in the discharge of the liability

(a) of a party who in bad faith pays or satisfies a holder who acquired the instrument by theft or who (unless having the rights of a holder in due course) holds through one who so acquired it; or

(b) of a party (other than an intermediary bank or a payor bank which is not a depositary bank) who pays or satisfies the holder of an instrument which has been restrictively indorsed in a manner not consistent with the terms of such restrictive indorsement.

(2) Payment or satisfaction may be made with the consent of the holder by any person including a stranger to the instrument. Surrender of the instrument to such a person gives him the rights of a transferee (Section 3—201).

SECTION 3—604. TENDER OF PAYMENT. (1) Any party making tender of full payment to a holder when or after it is due is discharged to the extent of all subsequent liability for interest, costs and attorney's fees.

(2) The holder's refusal of such tender wholly discharges any party who has a right of recourse against the party making the tender.

(3) Where the maker or acceptor of an instrument payable otherwise than on demand is able and ready to pay at every place of payment specified in the instrument when it is due, it is equivalent to tender.

SECTION 3—605. CANCELLATION AND RENUNCIATION. (1) The holder of an instrument may even without consideration discharge any party

(a) in any manner apparent on the face of the instrument or the indorsement, as by intentionally cancelling the instrument or the party's signature by destruction or mutilation, or by striking out the party's signature; or

(b) by renouncing his rights by a writing signed and delivered or by surrender of the instrument to the party to be discharged.

(2) Neither cancellation nor renunciation without surrender of the instrument affects the title thereto.

SECTION 3—606. IMPAIRMENT OF RECOURSE OR OF COLLATERAL. (1) The holder discharges any party to the instrument to the extent that without such party's consent the holder

(a) without express reservation of rights releases or agrees not to sue any person against whom the party has to the knowledge of the holder a right of recourse or agrees to suspend the right to enforce against such person the instrument or collateral or otherwise discharges such person, except that failure or delay in effecting any required presentment, protest or notice of dishonor with respect to any such person does not discharge any party as to whom presentment, protest or notice of dishonor is effective or unnecessary; or

(b) unjustifiably impairs any collateral for the instrument given by or on behalf of the party or any person against whom he has a right of recourse.

(2) By express reservation of rights against a party with a right of recourse the holder preserves

(a) all his rights against such party as of the time when the instrument was originally due; and

(b) the right of the party to pay the instrument as of that time; and

(c) all rights of such party to recourse against others.

PART 7

ADVICE OF INTERNATIONAL SIGHT DRAFT

SECTION 3—701. LETTER OF ADVICE OF INTERNATIONAL SIGHT DRAFT. (1) A "letter of advice" is a drawer's communication to the drawee that a described draft has been drawn.

(2) Unless otherwise agreed when a bank receives from another bank a letter of advice of an international sight draft the drawee bank may immediately debit the drawer's account and stop the running of interest pro tanto. Such a debit and any resulting credit to any account covering outstanding drafts leaves in the drawer full power to stop payment or otherwise dispose of the amount and creates no trust or interest in favor of the holder.

(3) Unless otherwise agreed and except where a draft is drawn under a credit issued by the drawee, the drawee of an international sight draft owes the drawer no duty to pay an unadvised draft but if it does so and the draft is genuine, may appropriately debit the drawer's account.

PART 8

MISCELLANEOUS

SECTION 3—801. DRAFTS IN A SET. (1) Where a draft is drawn in a set of parts, each of which is numbered and expressed to be an order only if no other part has been honored, the whole of the parts constitutes one draft but a taker of any part may become a holder in due course of the draft.

(2) Any person who negotiates, indorses or accepts a single part of a draft drawn in a set thereby becomes liable to any holder in due course of that part as if it were the whole set, but as between different holders in due course to whom different parts have been negotiated the holder whose title first accrues has all rights to the draft and its proceeds.

(3) As against the drawee the first presented part of a draft drawn in a set is the part entitled to payment, or if a time draft to acceptance and payment. Acceptance of

any subsequently presented part renders the drawee liable thereon under subsection (2). With respect both to a holder and to the drawer payment of a subsequently presented part of a draft payable at sight has the same effect as payment of a check notwithstanding an effective stop order (Section 4—407).

(4) Except as otherwise provided in this section, where any part of a draft in a set is discharged by payment or otherwise the whole draft is discharged.

SECTION 3—802. EFFECT OF INSTRUMENT ON OBLIGATION FOR WHICH IT IS GIVEN. (1) Unless otherwise agreed where an instrument is taken for an underlying obligation

    (a) the obligation is pro tanto discharged if a bank is drawer, maker or acceptor of the instrument and there is no recourse on the instrument against the underlying obligor; and

    (b) in any other case the obligation is suspended pro tanto until the instrument is due or if it is payable on demand until its presentment. If the instrument is dishonored action may be maintained on either the instrument or the obligation; discharge of the underlying obligor on the instrument also discharges him on the obligation.

(2) The taking in good faith of a check which is not postdated does not of itself so extend the time on the original obligation as to discharge a surety.

SECTION 3—803. NOTICE TO THIRD PARTY. Where a defendant is sued for breach of an obligation for which a third person is answerable over under this Article he may give the third person written notice of the litigation, and the person notified may then give similar notice to any other person who is answerable over to him under this Article. If the notice states that the person notified may come in and defend and that if the person notified does not do so he will in any action against him by the person giving the notice be bound by any determination of fact common to the two litigations, then unless after seasonable receipt of the notice the person notified does come in and defend he is so bound.

SECTION 3—804. LOST, DESTROYED OR STOLEN INSTRUMENTS. The owner of an instrument which is lost, whether by destruction, theft or otherwise, may maintain an action in his own name and recover from any party liable thereon upon due proof of his ownership, the facts which prevent his production of the instrument and its terms. The court may require security indemnifying the defendant against loss by reason of further claims on the instrument.

SECTION 3—805. INSTRUMENTS NOT PAYABLE TO ORDER OR TO BEARER. This Article applies to any instrument whose terms do not preclude transfer and which is otherwise negotiable within this Article but which is not payable to order or to bearer, except that there can be no holder in due course of such an instrument.

ARTICLE 4

BANK DEPOSITS AND COLLECTIONS

PART 1

GENERAL PROVISIONS AND DEFINITIONS

SECTION 4—101. SHORT TITLE. This Article shall be known and may be cited as Uniform Commercial Code—Bank Deposits and Collections.

SECTION 4—102. APPLICABILITY. (1) To the extent that items within this Article are also within the scope of Articles 3 and 8, they are subject to the provisions of those Articles. In the event of conflict the provisions of this Article govern those of Article 3 but the provisions of Article 8 govern those of this Article.

(2) The liability of a bank for action or non-action with respect to any item handled by it for purposes of presentment, payment or collection is governed by the law of the place where the bank is located. In the case of action or non-action by or at a branch or separate office of a bank, its liability is governed by the law of the place where the branch or separate office is located.

SECTION 4—103. VARIATION BY AGREEMENT; MEASURE OF DAMAGES; CERTAIN ACTION CONSTITUTING ORDINARY CARE. (1) The effect of the provisions of this Article may be varied by agreement except that no agreement can disclaim a bank's responsibility for its own lack of good faith or failure to exercise ordinary care or can limit the measure of damages for such lack or failure; but the parties may by agreement determine the standards by which such responsibility is to be measured if such standards are not manifestly unreasonable.

(2) Federal Reserve regulations and operating letters, clearing house rules, and the like, have the effect of agreements under subsection (1), whether or not specifically assented to by all parties interested in items handled.

(3) Action or non-action approved by this Article or pursuant to Federal Reserve regulations or operating letters constitutes the exercise of ordinary care and, in the absence of special instructions, action or non-action consistent with clearing house rules and the like or with a general banking usage not disapproved by this Article, prima facie constitutes the exercise of ordinary care.

(4) The specification or approval of certain procedures by this Article does not constitute disapproval of other procedures which may be reasonable under the circumstances.

(5) The measure of damages for failure to exercise ordinary care in handling an item is the amount of the item reduced by an amount which could not have been realized by the use of ordinary care, and where there is bad faith it includes other damages, if any, suffered by the party as a proximate consequence.

SECTION 4—104. DEFINITIONS AND INDEX OF DEFINITIONS. (1) In this Article unless the context otherwise requires

    (a) "Account" means any account with a bank and includes a checking, time, interest or savings account;

    (b) "Afternoon" means the period of a day between noon and midnight;

    (c) "Banking day" means that part of any day on which a bank is open to the public for carrying on substantially all of its banking functions;

    (d) "Clearing house" means any association of banks or other payors regularly clearing items;

    (e) "Customer" means any person having an account with a bank or for whom a bank has agreed to collect items and includes a bank carrying an account with another bank;

    (f) "Documentary draft" means any negotiable or non-negotiable draft with accompanying documents, securities or other papers to be delivered against honor of the draft;

    (g) "Item" means any instrument for the payment of money even though it is not negotiable but does not include money;

    (h) "Midnight deadline" with respect to a bank is midnight on its next banking day following the banking day on which it receives the relevant item or notice or from which the time for taking action commences to run, whichever is later;

    (i) "Properly payable" includes the availability of funds for payment at the time of decision to pay or dishonor;

    (j) "Settle" means to pay in cash, by clearing house settlement, in a charge or credit or by remittance, or otherwise as instructed. A settlement may be either provisional or final;

    (k) "Suspends payments" with respect to a bank means that it has been closed by order of the supervisory authorities, that a public officer has been appointed to take it over or that it ceases or refuses to make payments in the ordinary course of business.

(2) Other definitions applying to this Article and the sections in which they appear are:

"Collecting bank"	Section 4—105.
"Depositary bank"	Section 4—105.
"Intermediary bank"	Section 4—105.
"Payor bank"	Section 4—105.
"Presenting bank"	Section 4—105.
"Remitting bank"	Section 4—105.

(3) The following definitions in other Articles apply to this Article:

"Acceptance"	Section 3—410.
"Certificate of deposit"	Section 3—104.
"Certification"	Section 3—411.
"Check"	Section 3—104.
"Draft"	Section 3—104.
"Holder in due course"	Section 3—302.
"Notice of dishonor"	Section 3—508.
"Presentment"	Section 3—504.
"Protest"	Section 3—509.
"Secondary party"	Section 3—102.

(4) In addition Article 1 contains general definitions and principles of construction and interpretation applicable throughout this Article.

SECTION 4—105. "DEPOSITARY BANK"; "INTERMEDIARY BANK"; "COLLECTING BANK"; "PAYOR BANK"; "PRESENTING BANK"; "REMITTING BANK". In this Article unless the context otherwise requires:

(a) "Depositary bank" means the first bank to which an item is transferred for collection even though it is also the payor bank;

(b) "Payor bank" means a bank by which an item is payable as drawn or accepted;

(c) "Intermediary bank" means any bank to which an item is transferred in course of collection except the depositary or payor bank;

(d) "Collecting bank" means any bank handling the item for collection except the payor bank;

(e) "Presenting bank" means any bank presenting an item except a payor bank;

(f) "Remitting bank" means any payor or intermediary bank remitting for an item.

SECTION 4—106. SEPARATE OFFICE OF A BANK. A branch or separate office of a bank [maintaining its own deposit ledgers] is a separate bank for the purpose of computing the time within which and determining the place at or to which action may be taken or notices or orders shall be given under this Article and under Article 3.

NOTE: *The words in brackets are optional.*

SECTION 4—107. TIME OF RECEIPT OF ITEMS. (1) For the purpose of allowing time to process items, prove balances and make the necessary entries on its books to determine its position for the day, a bank may fix an afternoon hour of two P.M. or later as a cut-off hour for the handling of money and items and the making of entries on its books:

(2) Any item or deposit of money received on any day after a cut-off hour so fixed or after the close of the banking day may be treated as being received at the opening of the next banking day.

SECTION 4—108. DELAYS. (1) Unless otherwise instructed, a collecting bank in a good faith effort to secure payment may, in the case of specific items and with or without the approval of any person involved, waive, modify or extend time limits imposed or permitted by this Act for a period not in excess of an additional banking day without discharge of secondary parties and without liability to its transferor or any prior party.

(2) Delay by a collecting bank or payor bank beyond time limits prescribed or permitted by this Act or by instructions is excused if caused by interruption of communication facilities, suspension of payments by another bank, war, emergency conditions or other circumstances beyond the control of the bank provided it exercises such diligence as the circumstances require.

SECTION 4—109. PROCESS OF POSTING. The "process of posting" means the usual procedure followed by a payor bank in determining to pay an item and in recording the payment including one or more of the following or other steps as determined by the bank:

(a) verification of any signature;

(b) ascertaining that sufficient founds are available;

(c) affixing a "paid" or other stamp;

(d) entering a charge or entry to a customer's account;

(e) correcting or reversing an entry or erroneous action with respect to the item.

PART 2

COLLECTION OF ITEMS: DEPOSITARY AND COLLECTING BANKS

SECTION 4—201. PRESUMPTION AND DURATION OF AGENCY STATUS OF COLLECTING BANKS AND PROVISIONAL STATUS OF CREDITS; APPLICABILITY OF ARTICLE; ITEM INDORSED "PAY ANY BANK". (1) Unless a contrary intent clearly appears and prior to the time that a settlement given by a collecting bank for an item is or becomes final (subsection (3) of Section 4—211 and Sections 4—212 and 4—213) the bank is an agent or sub-agent of the owner of the item and any settlement given for the item is provisional. This provision applies regardless of the form of indorsement or lack of indorsement and even though credit given for the item is subject to immediate withdrawal as of right or is in fact withdrawn; but the continuance of ownership of an item by its owner and any rights of the owner to proceeds of the item are subject to rights of a collecting bank such as those resulting from outstanding advances on the item and valid rights of setoff. When an item is handled by banks for purposes of presentment, payment and collection, the relevant provisions of this Article apply even though action of parties clearly establishes that a particular bank has purchased the item and is the owner of it.

(2) After an item has been indorsed with the words "pay any bank" or the like, only a bank may acquire the rights of a holder

    (a) until the item has been returned to the customer initiating collection; or

    (b) until the item has been specially indorsed by a bank to a person who is not a bank.

SECTION 4—202. RESPONSIBILITY FOR COLLECTION; WHEN ACTION SEASONABLE. (1) A collecting bank must use ordinary care in

    (a) presenting an item or sending it for presentment; and

    (b) sending notice of dishonor or non-payment or returning an item other than a documentary draft to the bank's transferor [or directly to the depositary bank under subsection (2) of Section 4—212] *(see note to Section 4—212)* after learning that the item has not been paid or accepted, as the case may be; and

    (c) settling for an item when the bank receives final settlement; and

    (d) making or providing for any necessary protest; and

    (e) notifying its transferor of any loss or delay in transit within a reasonable time after discovery thereof.

(2) A collecting bank taking proper action before its midnight deadline following receipt of an item, notice or payment acts seasonably; taking proper action within a reasonably longer time may be seasonable but the bank has the burden of so establishing.

(3) Subject to subsection (1) (a), a bank is not liable for the insolvency, neglect, misconduct, mistake or default of another bank or person or for loss or destruction of an item in transit or in the possession of others.

SECTION 4—203. EFFECT OF INSTRUCTIONS. Subject to the provisions of Article 3 concerning conversion of instruments (Section 3—419) and the provisions of both Article 3 and this Article concerning restrictive indorsements only a collecting bank's transferor can give instructions which affect the bank or constitute notice to it and a collecting bank is not liable to prior parties for any action taken pursuant to such instructions or in accordance with any agreement with its transferor.

SECTION 4—204. METHODS OF SENDING AND PRESENTING; SENDING DIRECT TO PAYOR BANK. (1) A collecting bank must send items by reasonably prompt method taking into consideration any relevant instructions, the nature of the item, the number of such items on hand, and the cost of collection involved and the method generally used by it or others to present such items.

(2) A collecting bank may send

    (a) any item direct to the payor bank;

    (b) any item to any non-bank payor if authorized by its transferor; and

    (c) any item other than documentary drafts to any non-bank payor, if authorized by Federal Reserve regulation or operating letter, clearing house rule or the like.

(3) Presentment may be made by a presenting bank at a place where the payor bank has requested that presentment be made.

SECTION 4—205. SUPPLYING MISSING INDORSEMENT; NO NOTICE FROM PRIOR INDORSEMENT. (1) A depositary bank which has taken an item for collection may supply any indorsement of the customer which is necessary to title unless the item contains the words "payee's indorsement required" or the like. In the absence of such a requirement a statement placed on the item by the depositary bank to the effect that the item was deposited by a customer or credited to his account is effective as the customer's indorsement.

(2) An intermediary bank, or payor bank which is not a depositary bank, is neither given notice nor otherwise affected by a restrictive indorsement of any person except the bank's immediate transferor.

SECTION 4—206. TRANSFER BETWEEN BANKS. Any agreed method which identifies the transferor bank is sufficient for the item's further transfer to another bank.

SECTION 4—207. WARRANTIES OF CUSTOMER AND COLLECTING BANK ON TRANSFER OR PRESENTMENT OF ITEMS; TIME FOR CLAIMS. (1) Each customer or collecting bank who obtains payment or acceptance of an item and each prior customer and collecting bank warrants to the payor bank or other payor who in good faith pays or accepts the item that

(a) he has a good title to the item or is authorized to obtain payment or acceptance on behalf of one who has a good title; and

(b) he has no knowledge that the signature of the maker or drawer is unauthorized, except that this warranty is not given by any customer or collecting bank that is a holder in due course and acts in good faith
  (i) to a maker with respect to the maker's own signature; or
  (ii) to a drawer with respect to the drawer's own signature, whether or not the drawer is also the drawee; or
  (iii) to an acceptor of an item if the holder in due course took the item after the acceptance or obtained the acceptance without knowledge that the drawer's signature was unauthorized; and

(c) the item has not been materially altered, except that this warranty is not given by any customer or collecting bank that is a holder in due course and acts in good faith
  (i) to the maker of a note; or
  (ii) to the drawer of a draft whether or not the drawer is also the drawee; or
  (iii) to the acceptor of an item with respect to an alteration made prior to the acceptance if the holder in due course took the item after the acceptance provided "payable as originally drawn" or equivalent terms; or
  (iv) to the acceptor of an item with respect to an alteration made after the acceptance.

(2) Each customer and collecting bank who transfers an item and receives a settlement or other consideration for it warrants to his transferee and to any subsequent collecting bank who takes the item in good faith that

(a) he has a good title to the item or is authorized to obtain payment or acceptance on behalf of one who has a good title and the transfer is otherwise rightful; and

(b) all signatures are genuine or authorized; and

(c) the item has not been materially altered; and

(d) no defense of any party is good against him; and

(e) he has no knowledge of any insolvency proceeding instituted with respect to the maker or acceptor or the drawer of an unaccepted item.

In addition each customer and collecting bank so transferring an item and receiving a settlement or other consideration engages that upon dishonor and any necessary notice of dishonor and protest he will take up the item.

(3) The warranties and the engagement to honor set forth in the two preceding subsections arise notwithstanding the absence of indorsement or words of guaranty or warranty in the transfer or presentment and a collecting bank remains liable for their

breach despite remittance to its transferor. Damages for breach of such warranties or engagement to honor shall not exceed the consideration received by the customer or collecting bank responsible plus finance charges and expenses related to the item, if any.

(4) Unless a claim for breach of warranty under this section is made within a reasonable time after the person claiming learns of the breach, the person liable is discharged to the extent of any loss caused by the delay in making claim.

SECTION 4—208. SECURITY INTEREST OF COLLECTING BANK IN ITEMS, ACCOMPANYING DOCUMENTS AND PROCEEDS. (1) A bank has a security interest in an item and any accompanying documents or the proceeds of either

    (a) in case of an item deposited in an account to the extent to which credit given for the item has been withdrawn or applied;

    (b) in case of an item for which it has given cerdit available for withdrawal as of right, to the extent of the credit given whether or not the credit is drawn upon and whether or not there is a right of charge-back; or

    (c) if it makes an advance on or against the item.

(2) When credit which has been given for several items received at one time or pursuant to a single agreement is withdrawn or applied in part the security interest remains upon all the items, any accompanying documents or the proceeds of either. For the purpose of this section, credits first given are first withdrawn.

(3) Receipt by a collecting bank of a final settlement for an item is a realization on its security interest in the item, accompanying documents and proceeds. To the extent and so long as the bank does not receive final settlment for the item or give up possession of the item or accompanying documents for purposes other than collection, the security interest continues and is subject to the provisions of Article 9 except that

    (a) no security agreement is necessary to make the security interest enforceable (subsection (1) (b) of Section 9—203); and

    (b) no filing is required to perfect the security interest; and

    (c) the security interest has priority over conflicting perfected security interests in the item, accompanying documents or proceeds.

SECTION 4—209. WHEN BANK GIVES VALUE FOR PURPOSES OF HOLDER IN DUE COURSE. For purposes of determining its status as a holder in due course, the bank has given value to the extent that it has a security interest in an item provided that the bank otherwise complies with the requirements of Section 3—302 on what constitutes a holder in due course.

SECTION 4—210. PRESENTMENT BY NOTICE OF ITEM NOT PAYABLE BY, THROUGH OR AT A BANK; LIABILITY OF SECONDARY PARTIES. (1) Unless otherwise instructed, a collecting bank may present an item not payable by, through or at a bank by sending to the party to accept or pay a written notice that the bank holds the item for acceptance or payment. The notice must be sent in time to be received on or before the day when presentment is due and the bank must meet any requirement of the party to accept or pay under Section 3—505 by the close of the bank's next banking day after it knows of the requirement.

(2) Where presentment is made by notice and neither honor nor request for compliance with a requirement under Section 3—505 is received by the close of business on the day after maturity or in the case of demand items by the close of business on the third banking day after notice was sent, the presenting bank may treat the item as dishonored and charge any secondary party by sending him notice of the facts.

SECTION 4—211. MEDIA OF REMITTANCE; PROVISIONAL AND FINAL SETTLEMENT IN REMITTANCE CASES. (1) A collecting bank may take in settlment of an item

    (a) a check of the remitting bank or of another bank on any bank except the remitting bank; or

    (b) a cashier's check or similar primary obligation of a remitting bank which is a member of or clears through a member of the same clearing house or group as the collecting bank; or

    (c) appropriate authority to charge an account of the remitting bank or of another bank with the collecting bank; or

(d) if the item is drawn upon or payable by a person other than a bank, a cashier's check, certified check or other bank check or obligation.

(2) If before its midnight deadline the collecting bank properly dishonors a remittance check or authorization to charge on itself or presents or forwards for collection a remittance instrument of or on another bank which is of a kind approved by subsection (1) or has not been authorized by it, the collecting bank is not liable to prior parties in the event of the dishonor of such check, instrument or authorization.

(3) A settlement for an item by means of a remittance instrument or authorization to charge is or becomes a final settlment as to both the person making and the person receiving the settlement

(a) if the remittance instrument or authorization to charge is of a kind approved by subsection (1) or has not been authorized by the person receiving the settlement and in either case the person receiving the settlement acts seasonably before its midnight deadline in presenting, forwarding for collection or paying the instrument or authorization,—at the time the remittance intrument or authorization is finally paid by the payor by which it is payable;

(b) if the person receiving the settlement has authorized remittance by a non-bank check or obligation or by a cashier's check or similar primary obligation of or a check upon the payor or other remitting bank which is not of a kind approved by subsection (1) (b),—at the time of the receipt of such remittance check or obligation; or

(c) if in a case not covered by sub-paragraphs (a) or (b) the person receiving the settlment fails to seasonably present, forward for collection, pay or return a remittance instrument or authorization to it to charge before its midnight deadline,—at such midnight deadline.

SECTION 4—212. RIGHT OF CHARGE-BACK OR REFUND. (1) If a collecting bank has made provisional settlement with its customer for an item and itself fails by reason of dishonor, suspension of payments by a bank or otherwise to receive a settlement for the item which is or becomes final, the bank may revoke the settlement given by it, charge back the amount of any credit given for the item to its customer's account or obtain refund from its customer whether or not it is able to return the items if by its midnight deadline or within a longer reasonable time after it learns the facts it returns the item or sends notification of the facts. These rights to revoke, charge-back and obtain refund terminate if and when a settlement for the item received by the bank is or becomes final (subsection (3) of Section 4—211 and subsections (2) and (3) of Section 4—213).

[(2) Within the time and manner prescribed by this section and Section 4—301, an intermediary or payor bank, as the case may be, may return an unpaid item directly to the depositary bank and may send for collection a draft on the depositary bank and obtain reimbursement. In such case, if the depositary bank has received provisional settlement for the item, it must reimburse the bank drawing the draft and any provisional credits for the item between banks shall become and remain final.]

NOTE: *Direct returns is recognized as an innovation that is not yet established bank practice, and therefore, Paragraph 2 has been bracketed. Some lawyers have doubted whether it should be included in legislation or left to development by agreement.*

(3) A depositary bank which is also the payor may charge-back the amount of an item to its customer's account or obtain refund in accordance with the section governing return of an item received by a payor bank for credit on its books (Section 4—301).

(4) The right to charge-back is not affected by

(a) prior use of the credit given for the item; or

(b) failure by any bank to exercise ordinary care with respect to the item but any bank so failing remains liable.

(5) A failure to charge-back or claim refund does not affect other rights of the bank against the customer or any other party.

(6) If credit is given in dollars as the equivalent of the value of an item payable in

a foreign currency the dollar amount of any charge-back or refund shall be calculated on the basis of the buying sight rate for the foreign currency prevailing on the day when the person entitled to the charge-back or refund learns that it will not receive payment in ordinary course.

SECTION 4—213. FINAL PAYMENT OF ITEM BY PAYOR BANK; WHEN PROVISIONAL DEBITS AND CREDITS BECOME FINAL; WHEN CERTAIN CREDITS BECOME AVAILABLE FOR WITHDRAWAL. (1) An item is finally paid by a payor bank when the bank has done any of the following, whichever happens first:

(a) paid the item in cash; or

(b) settled for the item without reserving a right to revoke the settlement and without having such right under statute, clearing house rule or agreement; or

(c) completed the process of posting the item to the indicated account of the drawer, maker or other person to be charged therewith; or

(d) made a provisional settlement for the item and failed to revoke the settlement in the time and manner permitted by statute, clearing house rule or agreement.

Upon a final payment under subparagraphs (b), (c) or (d) the payor bank shall be accountable for the amount of the item.

(2) If provisional settlement for an item between the presenting and payor banks is made through a clearing house or by debits or credits in an account between them, then to the extent that provisional debits or credits for the item are entered in accounts between the presenting and payor banks or between the presenting and successive prior collecting banks seriatim, they become final upon final payment of the item by the payor bank.

(3) If a collecting bank receives a settlement for an item which is or becomes final (subsection (3) of Section 4—211, subsection (2) of Section 4—213) the bank is accountable to its customer for the amount of the item and any provisional credit given for the item in an account with its customer becomes final.

(4) Subject to any right of the bank to apply the credit to an obligation of the customer, credit given by a bank for an item in an account with its customer becomes available for withdrawal as of right

(a) in any case where the bank has received a provisional settlement for the item,—when such settlement becomes final and the bank has had a reasonable time to learn that the settlement is final;

(b) in any case where the bank is both a depositary bank and a payor bank and the item is finally paid,—at the opening of the bank's second banking day following receipt of the item.

(5) A deposit of money in a bank is final when made but, subject to any right of the bank to apply the deposit to an obligation of the customer, the deposit becomes available for withdrawal as of right at the opening of the bank's next banking day following receipt of the deposit.

SECTION 4—214. INSOLVENCY AND PREFERENCE. (1) Any item in or coming into the possession of a payor or collecting bank which suspends payment and which item is not finally paid shall be returned by the receiver, trustee or agent in charge of the closed bank to the presenting bank or the closed bank's customer.

(2) If a payor bank finally pays an item and suspends payments without making a settlement for the item with its customer or the presenting bank which settlement is or becomes final, the owner of the item has a preferred claim against the payor bank.

(3) If a payor bank gives or a collecting bank gives or receives a provisional settlement for an item and thereafter suspends payments, the suspension does not prevent or interfere with the settlement becoming final if such finality occurs automatically upon the lapse of certain time or the happening of certain events (subsection (3) of Section 4—211, subsections (1) (d), (2) and (3) of Section 4—213).

(4) If a collecting bank receives from subsequent parties settlement for an item which settlement is or becomes final and suspends payments without making a settlement for the item with its customer which is or becomes final, the owner of the item has a preferred claim against such collecting bank.

PART 3

COLLECTION OF ITEMS: PAYOR BANKS

SECTION 4—301. DEFERRED POSTING; RECOVERY OF PAYMENT BY RETURN OF ITEMS; TIME OF DISHONOR. (1) Where an authorized settlement for a demand item (other than a documentary draft) received by a payor bank otherwise than for immediate payment over the counter has been made before midnight of the banking day of receipt the payor bank may revoke the settlement and recover any payment if before it has made final payment (subsection (1) of Section 4—213) and before its midnight deadline it

(a) returns the item; or

(b) sends written notice of dishonor or nonpayment if the item is held for protest or is otherwise unavailable for return

(2) If a demand item is received by a payor bank for credit on its books it may return such item or send notice of dishonor and may revoke any credit given or recover the amount thereof withdrawn by its customer, if it acts within the time limit and in the manner specified in the preceding subsection.

(3) Unless previous notice of dishonor has been sent an item is dishonored at the time when for purposes of dishonor it is returned or notice sent in accordance with this section.

(4) An item is returned:

(a) as to an item received through a clearing house, when it is delivered to the presenting or last collecting bank or to the clearing house or is sent or delivered in accordance with its rules; or

(b) in all other cases, when it is sent or delivered to the bank's customer or transferor or pursuant to his instructions.

SECTION 4—302. PAYOR BANK'S RESPONSIBILITY FOR LATE RETURN OF ITEM. In the absence of a valid defense such as breach of a presentment warranty (subsection (1) of Section 4—207), settlement effected or the like, if an item is presented on and received by a payor bank the bank is accountable for the amount of

(a) a demand item other than a documentary draft whether properly payable or not if the bank, in any case where it is not also the depositary bank, retains the item beyond midnight of the banking day of receipt without settling for it or, regardless of whether it is also the depositary bank, does not pay or return the item or send notice of dishonor until after its midnight deadline; or

(b) any other properly payable item unless within the time allowed for acceptance or payment of that item the bank either accepts or pays the item or returns it and accompanying documents.

SECTION 4—303. WHEN ITEMS SUBJECT TO NOTICE, STOP-ORDER, LEGAL PROCESS OR SETOFF; ORDER IN WHICH ITEMS MAY BE CHARGED OR CERTIFIED. (1) Any knowledge, notice or stop-order received by, legal process served upon or setoff exercised by a payor bank, whether or not effective under other rules of law to terminate, suspend or modify the bank's right or duty to pay an item or to charge its customer's account for the item, comes too late to so terminate, suspend or modify such right or duty if the knowledge, notice, stop-order or legal process is received or served and a reasonable time for the bank to act thereon expires or the setoff is exercised after the bank has done any of the following:

(a) accepted or certified the item;

(b) paid the item in cash;

(c) settled for the item without reserving the right to revoke the settlement and without having such right under statute, clearing house rule or agreement;

(d) completed the process of posting the item to the indicated account of the drawer, maker or other person to be charged therewith or otherwise has evidenced by examination of such indicated account and by action its decision to pay the item; or

(e) become accountable for the amount of the item under subsection (1) (d) of

Section 4—213 and Section 4—302 dealing with the payor bank's responsibility for late return of items.

(2) Subject to the provisions of subsection (1) items may be accepted, paid, certified or charged to the indicated account of its customer in any order convenient to the bank.

PART 4

RELATIONSHIP BETWEEN PAYOR BANK AND ITS CUSTOMER

SECTION 4—401. WHEN BANK MAY CHARGE CUSTOMER'S ACCOUNT. (1) As against its customer, a bank may charge against his account any item which is otherwise properly payable from that account even though the charge creates an overdraft.

(2) A bank which in good faith makes payment to a holder may charge the indicated account of its customer according to

(a) the original tenor of his altered item; or

(b) the tenor of his completed item, even though the bank knows the item has been completed unless the bank has notice that the completion was improper.

SECTION 4—402. BANK'S LIABILITY TO CUSTOMER FOR WRONGFUL DISHONOR. A payor bank is liable to its customer for damages proximately caused by the wrongful dishonor of an item. When the dishonor occurs through mistake liability is limited to actual damages proved. If so proximately caused and proved damages may include damages for an arrest or prosecution of the customer or other consequential damages. Whether any consequential damages are proximately caused by the wrongful dishonor is a question of fact to be determined in each case.

SECTION 4—403. CUSTOMER'S RIGHT TO STOP PAYMENT; BURDEN OF PROOF OF LOSS. (1) A customer may by order to his bank stop payment of any item payable for his account but the order must be received at such time and in such manner as to afford the bank a reasonable opportunity to act on it prior to any action by the bank with respect to the item described in Section 4—303.

(2) An oral order is binding upon the bank only for fourteen calendar days unless confirmed in writing within that period. A written order is effective for only six months unless renewed in writing.

(3) The burden of establishing the fact and amount of loss resulting from the payment of an item contrary to a binding stop payment order is on the customer.

SECTION 4—404. BANK NOT OBLIGATED TO PAY CHECK MORE THAN SIX MONTHS OLD. A bank is under no obligation to a customer having a checking account to pay a check, other than a certified check, which is presented more than six months after its date, but it may charge its customer's account for a payment made thereafter in good faith.

SECTION 4—405. DEATH OR INCOMPETENCE OF CUSTOMER. (1) A payor or collecting bank's authority to accept, pay or collect an item or to account for proceeds of its collection if otherwise effective is not rendered ineffective by incompetence of a customer of either bank existing at the time the item is issued or its collection is undertaken if the bank does not know of an adjudication of incompetence. Neither death nor incompetence of a customer revokes such authority to accept, pay, collect or account until the bank knows of the fact of death or of an adjudication of incompetence and has reasonable opportunity to act on it.

(2) Even with knowledge a bank may for ten days after the date of death pay or certify checks drawn on or prior to that date unless ordered to stop payment by a person claiming an interest in the account.

SECTION 4—406. CUSTOMER'S DUTY TO DISCOVER AND REPORT UNAUTHORIZED SIGNATURE OR ALTERATION. (1) When a bank sends to its customer a statement of account accompanied by items paid in good faith in support of the debit entries or holds the statement and items pursuant to a request or instructions of its customer or otherwise in a reasonable manner makes the statement and items available to the customer, the customer must exercise reasonable care and promptness to examine the statement and items to discover his unauthorized signature or any alteration on an item and must notify the bank promptly after discovery thereof.

(2) If the bank establishes that the customer failed with respect to an item to comply with the duties imposed on the customer by subsection (1) the customer is precluded from asserting against the bank

- (a) his unauthorized signature or any alteration on the item of the bank also establishes that it suffered a loss by reason of such failure; and
- (b) an unauthorized signature or alteration by the same wrongdoer on any other item paid in good faith by the bank after the first item and statement was available to the customer for a reasonable period not exceeding fourteen calendar days and before the bank receives notification from the customer of any such unauthorized signature or alteration.

(3) The preclusion under subsection (2) does not apply if the customer establishes lack of ordinary care on the part of the bank in paying the item(s).

(4) Without regard to care or lack of care of either the customer or the bank a customer who does not within one year from the time the statement and items are made available to the customer (subsection (1)) discover and report his unauthorized signature or any alteration on the face or back of the item or does not within three years from that time discover and report any unauthorized indorsement is precluded from asserting against the bank such unauthorized signature or indorsement or such alteration.

(3) If under this section a payor bank has a valid defense against a claim of a customer upon or resulting from payment of an item and waives or fails upon request to assert the defense the bank may not assert against any collecting bank or other prior party presenting or transferring the item a claim based upon the unauthorized signature or alteration giving rise to the customer's claim.

SECTION 4—407. PAYOR BANK'S RIGHT TO SUBROGATION ON IMPROPER PAYMENT. If a payor bank has paid an item over the stop payment order of the drawer or maker or otherwise under circumstances giving a basis for objection by the drawer or maker, to prevent unjust enrichment and only to the extent necessary to prevent loss to the bank by reason of its payment of the item, the payor bank shall be subrogated to the rights

- (a) of any holder in due course on the item against the drawer or maker; and
- (b) of the payee or any other holder of the item against the drawer or maker either on the item or under the transaction out of which the item arose; and
- (c) of the drawer or maker against the payee or any other holder of the item with respect to the transaction out of which the item arose.

PART 5

COLLECTION OF DOCUMENTARY DRAFTS

SECTION 4—501. HANDLING OF DOCUMENTARY DRAFTS; DUTY TO SEND FOR PRESENTMENT AND TO NOTIFY CUSTOMER OF DISHONOR. A bank which takes a documentary draft for collection must present or send the draft and accompanying documents for presentment and upon learning that the draft has not been paid or accepted in due course must seasonably notify its customer of such fact even though it may have discounted or bought the draft or extended credit available for withdrawal as if right.

SECTION 4—502. PRESENTMENT OF "ON ARRIVAL" DRAFTS. When a draft or the relevant instructions require presentment "on arrival", "when goods arrive" or the like, the collecting bank need not present until in its judgment a reasonable time for arrival of the goods has expired. Refusal to pay or accept because the goods have not arrived is not dishonor; the bank must notify its transferor of such refusal but need not present the draft again until it is instructed to do so or learns of the arrival of the goods.

SECTION 4—503. RESPONSIBILITY OF PRESENTING BANK FOR DOCUMENTS AND GOODS; REPORT OF REASONS FOR DISHONOR; REFEREE IN CASE OF NEED. Unless otherwise instructed and except as provided in Article 5 a bank presenting a documentary draft

- (a) must deliver the documents to the drawee on acceptance of the draft if it is payable more than three days after presentment; otherwise, only on payment; and
- (b) upon dishonor, either in the case of presentment for acceptance or present-

ment for payment, may seek and follow instructions from any referee in case of need designated in the draft or if the presenting bank does not choose to utilize his services it must use diligence and good faith to ascertain the reason for dishonor, must notify its transferor of the dishonor and of the results of its effort to ascertain the reasons therefor and must request instructions.

But the presenting bank is under no obligation with respect to goods represented by the documents except to follow any reasonable instructions seasonably received; it has a right to reimbursement for any expense incurred in following instructions and to prepayment of or indemnity for such expenses.

SECTION 4—504. PRIVILEGE OF PRESENTING BANK TO DEAL WITH GOODS; SECURITY INTEREST FOR EXPENSES. (1) A presenting bank which, following the dishonor of a documentary draft, has seasonably requested instructions but does not receive them within a reasonable time may store, sell, or otherwise deal with the goods in any reasonable manner.

(2) For its reasonable expenses incurred by action under subsection (1) the presenting bank has a lien upon the goods or their proceeds, which may be foreclosed in the same manner as an unpaid seller's lien.

ARTICLE 5

LETTERS OF CREDIT

SECTION 5—101. SHORT TITLE. This Article shall be known and may be cited as Uniform Commercial Code—Letters of Credit.

SECTION 5—102. SCOPE. (1) This Article applies

(a) to a credit issued by a bank if the credit requires a documentary draft or a documentary demand for payment; and

(b) to a credit issued by a person other than a bank if the credit requires that the draft or demand for payment be accompanied by a document of title; and

(c) to a credit issued by a bank or other person if the credit is not within subparagraphs (a) or (b) but conspicuously states that it is a letter of credit or is conspicuously so entitled.

(2) Unless the engagement meets the requirements of subsection (1), this Article does not apply to engagements to make advances or to honor drafts or demands for payment, to authorities to pay or purchase, to guarantees or to general agreements.

(3) This Article deals with some but not all of the rules and concepts of letters of credit as such rules or concepts have developed prior to this act or may hereafter develop. The fact that this Article states a rule does not by itself require, imply or negate application of the same or a converse rule to a situation not provided for or to a person not specified by this Article.

SECTION 5—103. DEFINITIONS. (1) In this Article unless the context otherwise requires

(a) "Credit" or "letter of credit" means an engagement by a bank or other person made at the request of a customer and of a kind within the scope of this Article (Section 5—102) that the issuer will honor drafts or other demands for payment upon compliance with the conditions specified in the credit. A credit may be either revocable or irrevocable. The engagement may be either an agreement to honor or a statement that the bank or other person is authorized to honor.

(b) A "documentary draft" or a "documentary demand for payment" is one honor of which is conditioned upon the presentation of a document or documents. "Document" means any paper including document of title, security, invoice, certificate, notice of default and the like.

(c) An "issuer" is a bank or other person issuing a credit.

(d) A "beneficiary" of a credit is a person who is entitled under its terms to draw or demand payment.

(e) An "advising bank" is a bank which gives notification of the issuance of a credit by another bank.

(f) A "confirming bank" is a bank which engages either that it will itself honor a credit already issued by another bank or that such a credit will be honored by the issuer or a third bank.

(g) A "customer" is a buyer or other person who causes an issuer to issue a credit. The term also includes a bank which procures issuance or confirmation on behalf of that bank's customer.

(2) Other definitions applying to this Article and the sections in which they appear are:

"Notation of Credit".	Section 5—108.
"Presenter".	Section 5—112(3).

(3) Definitions in other Articles applying to this Article and the sections in which they appear are:

"Accept" or "Acceptance".	Section 3—410.
"Contract for sale".	Section 2—106.
"Draft".	Section 3—104.
"Holder in due course".	Section 3—302.
"Midnight deadline".	Section 4—104.
"Security".	Section 8—102.

(4) In addition, Article 1 contains general definitions and principles of construction and interpretation applicable throughout this Article.

SECTION 5—104. FORMAL REQUIREMENTS; SIGNING. (1) Except as otherwise required in subsection (1) (c) of Section 5—102 on scope, no particular form of phrasing is required for a credit. A credit must be in writing and signed by the issuer and a confirmation must be in writing and signed by the confirming bank. A modification of the terms of a credit or confirmation must be signed by the issuer or confirming bank.

(2) A telegram may be a sufficient signed writing if it identifies its sender by an authorized authentication. The authentication may be in code and the authorized naming of the issuer in an advice of credit is a sufficient signing.

SECTION 5—106. TIME AND EFFECT OF ESTABLISHMENT OF CREDIT. (1) Unless otherwise agreed a credit is established

(a) as regards the customer as soon as a letter of credit is sent to him or the letter of credit or an authorized written advice of its issuance is sent to the beneficiary; and

(b) as regards the beneficiary when he receives a letter of credit or an authorized written advice of its issuance.

(2) Unless otherwise agreed once an irrevocable credit is established as regards the customer it can be modified or revoked only with the consent of the customer and once it is established as regards the beneficiary it can be modified or revoked only with his consent.

(3) Unless otherwise agreed after a revocable credit is established it may be modified or revoked by the issuer without notice to or consent from the customer or beneficiary.

(4) Notwithstanding any modification or revocation of a revocable credit any person authorized to honor or negotiate under the terms of the original credit is entitled to reimbursement for or honor of any draft or demand for payment duly honored or negotiated before receipt of notice of the modification or revocation and the issuer in turn is entitled to reimbursement from its customer.

SECTION 5—107. ADVICE OF CREDIT; CONFIRMATION; ERROR IN STATEMENT OF TERMS. (1) Unless otherwise specified an advising bank by advising a credit issued by another bank does not assume any obligation to honor drafts drawn or demands for payment made under the credit but it does assume obligation for the accuracy of its own statement.

(2) A confirming bank by confirming a credit becomes directly obligated on the credit to the extent of its confirmation as though it were its issuer and acquires the rights of an issuer.

(3) Even though an advising bank incorrectly advises the terms of a credit it has been authorized to advise the credit is established as against the issuer to the extent of its original terms.

(4) Unless otherwise specified the customer bears as against the issuer all risks of transmission and reasonable translation or interpretation of any message relating to a credit.

SECTION 5—108. "NOTATION CREDIT"; EXHAUSTION OF CREDIT. (1) A credit which specifies that any person purchasing or paying drafts drawn or demands for payment made under it must note the amount of the draft or demand on the letter or advice of credit is a "notation credit".

(2) Under a notation credit

    (a) a person paying the beneficiary or purchasing a draft or demand for payment from him acquires a right to honor only if the appropriate notation is made and by transferring or forwarding for honor the documents under the credit such a person warrants to the issuer that the notation has been made; and

    (b) unless the credit or a signed statement that an appropriate notation has been made accompanies the draft or demand for payment the issuer may delay honor until evidence of notation has been procured which is satisfactory to it but its obligation and that of its customer continue for a reasonable time not exceeding thirty days to obtain such evidence.

(3) If the credit is not a notation credit

    (a) the issuer may honor complying drafts or demands for payment presented to it in the order in which they are presented and is discharged pro tanto by honor of any such draft or demand;

    (b) as between competing good faith purchasers of complying drafts or demands the person first purchasing has priority over a subsequent purchaser even though the later purchased draft or demand has been first honored.

SECTION 5—109. ISSUER'S OBLIGATION TO ITS CUSTOMER. (1) An issuer's obligation to its customer includes good faith and observance of any general banking usage but unless otherwise agreed does not include liability or responsibility

    (a) for performance of the underlying contract for sale or other transaction between the customer and the beneficiary; or

    (b) for any act or omission of any person other than itself or its own branch or for loss or destruction of a draft, demand or document in transit or in the possession of others; or

    (c) based on knowledge or lack of knowledge of any usage of any particular trade.

(2) An issuer must examine documents with care so as to ascertain that on their face they appear to comply with the terms of the credit but unless otherwise agreed assumes no liability or responsibility for the genuineness, falsification or effect of any document which appears on such examination to be regular on its face.

(3) A non-bank issuer is not bound by any banking usage of which it has no knowledge.

SECTION 5—110. AVAILABILITY OF CREDIT IN PORTIONS; PRESENTER'S RESERVATION OF LIEN OR CLAIM. (1) Unless otherwise specified a credit may be used in portions in the discretion of the beneficiary.

(2) Unless otherwise specified a person by presenting a documentary draft or demand for payment under a credit relinquishes upon its honor all claims to the documents and a person by transferring such draft or demand or causing such presentment authorizes such relinquishment. An explicit reservation of claim makes the draft or demand non-complying.

SECTION 5—111. WARRANTIES ON TRANSFER AND PRESENTMENT. (1) Unless otherwise agreed the beneficiary by transferring or presenting a documentary draft or demand for payment warrants to all interested parties that the necessary conditions of the credit have been complied with. This is in addition to any warranties arising under Articles 3, 4, 7 and 8.

(2) Unless otherwise agreed a negotiating, advising, confirming, collecting or issuing bank presenting or transferring a draft or demand for payment under a credit warrants only the matters warranted by a collecting bank under Article 4 and any such bank transferring a document warrants only the matters warranted by an intermediary under Articles 7 and 8.

SECTION 5—112. TIME ALLOWED FOR HONOR OR REJECTION; WITHHOLDING HONOR OR REJECTION BY CONSENT; "PRESENTER". (1) A bank to which a documentary draft or demand for payment is presented under a credit may without dishonor of the draft, demand or credit

 (a) defer honor until the close of the third banking day following receipt of the documents; and

 (b) further defer honor if the presenter has expressly or impliedly consented thereto.

Failure to honor within the time here specified constitutes dishonor of the draft or demand and of the credit [except as otherwise provided in subsection (4) of Section 5—114 on conditional payment].

 NOTE: *The bracketed language in the last sentence of subsection (1) should be included only if the optional provisions of Section 5—114(4) and (5) are included.*

(2) Upon dishonor the bank may unless otherwise instructed fulfill its duty to return the draft or demand and the documents by holding them at the disposal of the presenter and sending him an advice to that effect.

(3) "Presenter" means any person presenting a draft or demand for payment for honor under a credit even though that person is a confirming bank or other correspondent which is acting under an issuer's authorization.

SECTION 5—113. INDEMNITIES. (1) A bank seeking to obtain (whether for itself or another) honor, negotiation or reimbursement under a credit may give an indemnity to induce such honor, negotiation or reimbursement.

(2) An indemnity agreement inducing honor, negotiation or reimbursement

 (a) unless otherwise explicitly agreed applies to defects in the documents but not in the goods; and

 (b) unless a longer time is explicitly agreed expires at the end of ten business days following receipt of the documents by the ultimate customer unless notice of objection is sent before such expiration date. The ultimate customer may send notice of objection to the person from whom he received the documents and any bank receiving such notice is under a duty to send notice to its transferor before its midnight deadline.

SECTION 5—114. ISSUER'S DUTY AND PRIVILEGE TO HONOR; RIGHT TO REIMBURSEMENT. (1) An issuer must honor a draft or demand for payment which complies with the terms of the relevant credit regardless of whether the goods or documents conform to the underlying contract for sale or other contract between the customer and the beneficiary. The issuer is not excused from honor of such a draft or demand by reason of an additional general term that all documents must be satisfactory to the issuer, but an issuer may require that specified documents must be satisfactory to it.

(2) Unless otherwise agreed when documents appear on their face to comply with the terms of a credit but a required document does not in fact conform to the warranties made on negotiation or transfer of a document of title (Section 7—507) or of a security (Section 8—306) or is forged or fraudulent or there is fraud in the transaction

 (a) the issuer must honor the draft or demand for payment if honor is demanded by a negotiating bank or other holder of the draft or demand which has taken the draft or demand under the credit and under circumstances which would make it a holder in due course (Section 3—302) and in an appropriate case would make it a person to whom a document of title has been duly negotiated (Section 7—502) or a bona fide purchaser of a security (Section 8—302); and

 (b) in all other cases as against its customer, an issuer acting in good faith may honor the draft or demand for payment despite notification from the customer of fraud, forgery or other defect not apparent on the face of the documents but a court of appropriate jurisdiction may enjoin such honor.

(3) Unless otherwise agreed an issuer which has duly honored a draft or demand for payment is entitled to immediate reimbursement of any payment made under the credit and to be put in effectively available funds not later than the day before maturity of any acceptance made under the credit.

[(4) When a credit provides for payment by the issuer on receipt of notice that the required documents are in the possession of a correspondent or other agent of the issuer

    (a) any payment made on receipt of such notice is conditional; and

    (b) ˙the issuer may reject documents which do not comply with the credit if it does so within three banking days following its receipt of the documents; and

    (c) in the event of such rejection, the issuer is entitled by charge back or otherwise to return of the payment made.]

  [(5) In the case covered by subsection (4) failure to reject documents within the time specified in sub-paragraph (b) constitutes acceptance of the documents and makes the payment final in favor of the beneficiary.]

  NOTE: *Subsections (4) and (5) are bracketed as optional. If they are included the bracketed language in the last sentence of Section 5—112(1) should also be included.*

SECTION 5—115. REMEDY FOR IMPROPER DISHONOR OR ANTICIPATORY REPUDIATION. (1) When an issuer wrongfully dishonors a draft or demand for payment under a credit the person entitled to honor has with respect to any documents the rights of a person in the position of a seller (Section 2—707) and may recover from the issuer the face amount of the draft or demand together with incidental damages under Section 2—710 on seller's incidental damages and interest but less any amount realized by resale or other use or disposition of the subject matter of the transaction. In the event no resale or other utilization is made the documents, goods or other subject matter involved in the transaction must be turned over to the issuer on payment of judgment.

  (2) When an issuer wrongfully cancels or otherwise repudiates a credit before presentment of a draft or demand for payment drawn under it the beneficiary has the rights of a seller after anticipatory repudiation by the buyer under Section 2—610 if he learns of the repudiation in time reasonably to avoid procurement of the required documents. Otherwise the beneficiary has an immediate right of action for wrongful dishonor.

SECTION 5—116. TRANSFER AND ASSIGNMENT. (1) The right to draw under a credit can be transferred or assigned only when the credit is expressly designated as transferable or assignable.

  (2) Even though the credit specifically states that it is nontransferable or nonassignable the beneficiary may before performance of the conditions of the credit assign his right to proceeds. Such an assignment is an assignment of a contract right under Article 9 on Secured Transactions and is governed by that Article except that

    (a) the assignment is ineffective until the letter of credit or advice of credit is delivered to the assignee which delivery constitutes perfection of the security interest under Article 9; and

    (b) the issuer may honor drafts or demands for payment drawn under the credit until it receives a notification of the assignment signed by the beneficiary which reasonably identifies the credit involved in the assignment and contains a request to pay the assignee; and

    (c) after what reasonably appears to be such a notification has been received the issuer may without dishonor refuse to accept or pay even to a person otherwise entitled to honor until the letter of credit or advice of credit is exhibited to the issuer.

  (3) Except where the beneficiary has effectively assigned his right to draw or his right to proceeds, nothing in this section limits his right to transfer or negotiate drafts or demands drawn under the credit.

SECTION 5—117. INSOLVENCY OF BANK HOLDING FUNDS FOR DOCUMENTARY CREDIT. (1) Where an issuer or an advising or confirming bank or a bank which has for a customer procured issuance of a credit by another bank becomes insolvent before final payment under the credit and the credit is one to which this Article is made applicable by paragraphs (a) or (b) of Section 5—102(1) on scope, the receipt or allocation of funds or collateral to secure or meet obligations under the credit shall have the following results:

    (a) to the extent of any funds or collateral turned over after or before the insolvency as indemnity against or specifically for the purpose of payment of drafts or demands for payment drawn under the designated credit, the drafts or demands are entitled to payment in preference over depositors or other general creditors of the issuer or bank; and

(b) on expiration of the credit or surrender of the beneficiary's rights under it unused any person who has given such funds or collateral is similarly entitled to return thereof; and

(c) a change to a general or current account with a bank if specifically consented to for the purpose of indemnity against or payment of drafts or demands for payment drawn under the designated credit falls under the same rules as if the funds had been drawn out in cash and then turned over with specific instructions.

(2) After honor or reimbursement under this section the customer or other person for whose account the insolvent bank has acted is entitled to receive the documents involved.

ARTICLE 6

BULK TRANSFERS

SECTION 6—101. SHORT TITLE. This Article shall be known and may be cited as Uniform Commercial Code—Bulk Transfers.

SECTION 6—102. "BULK TRANSFERS"; TRANSFERS OF EQUIPMENT; ENTERPRISES SUBJECT TO THIS ARTICLE; BULK TRANSFERS SUBJECT TO THIS ARTICLE. (1) A "bulk transfer" is any transfer in bulk and not in the ordinary course of the transferor's business of a major part of the materials, supplies, merchandise or other inventory (Section 9—109) of an enterprise subject to this Article.

(2) A transfer of a substantial part of the equipment (Section 9—109) of such an enterprise is a bulk transfer if it is made in connection with a bulk transfer of inventory, but not otherwise.

(3) The enterprises subject to this Article are all those whose principal business is the sale of merchandise from stock, including those who manufacture what they sell.

(4) Except as limited by the following section all bulk transfers of goods located within this state are subject to this Article.

SECTION 6—103. TRANSFERS EXCEPTED FROM THIS ARTICLE. The following transfers are not subject to this Article:

(1) Those made to give security for the performance of an obligation;

(2) General assignments for the benefit of all the creditors of the transferor, and subsequent transfers by the assignee thereunder;

(3) Transfers in settlement or realization of a lien or other security interest;

(4) Sales by executors, administrators, receivers, trustees in bankruptcy, or any public officer under judicial process;

(5) Sales made in the course of judicial or administrative proceedings for the dissolution or reorganization of a corporation and of which notice is sent to the creditors of the corporation to order of the court or administrative agency;

(6) Transfers to a person maintaining a known place of business in this State who becomes bound to pay the debts of the transferor in full and gives public notice of that fact, and who is solvent after becoming so bound;

(7) A transfer to a new business enterprise organized to take over and continue the business, if public notice of the transaction is given and the new enterprise assumes the debts of the transferor and he receives nothing from the transaction except an interest in the new enterprise junior to the claims of creditors;

(8) Transfers of property which is exempt from execution.

Public notice under subsection (6) or subsection (7) may be given by publishing once a week for two consecutive weeks in a newspaper of general circulation where the transferor had its principal place of business in this state an advertisement including the names and addresses of the transferor and transferee and the effective date of the transfer.

SECTION 6—104. SCHEDULE OF PROPERTY, LIST OF CREDITORS. (1) Except as provided with respect to auction sales (Section 6—108), a bulk transfer subject to this Article is ineffective against any creditor of the transferor unless:

    (a) The transferee requires the transferor to furnish a list of his existing creditors prepared as stated in this section; and

    (b) The parties prepare a schedule of the property transferred sufficient to identify it; and

    (c) The transferee preserves the list and schedule for six months next following the transfer and permits inspection of either or both and copying therefrom at all reasonable hours by any creditor of the transferor, or files the list and schedule in (a public office to be here identified).

(2) The list of creditors must be signed and sworn to or affirmed by the transferor or his agent. It must contain the names and business addresses of all creditors of the transferor, with the amounts when known, and also the names of all persons who are known to the transferor to assert claims against him even though such claims are disputed. If the transferor is the obligor of an outstanding issue of bonds, debentures or the like as to which there is an indenture trustee, the list of creditors need include only the name and address of the indenture trustee and the aggregate outstanding principal amount of the issue.

(3) Responsibility for the completeness and accuracy of the list of creditors rests on the transferor, and the transfer is not rendered ineffective by errors or omissions therein unless the transferee is shown to have had knowledge.

SECTION 6—105. NOTICE TO CREDITORS. In addition to the requirements of the preceding section, any bulk transfer subject to this Article except one made by auction sale (Section 6—108) is ineffective against any creditor of the transferor unless at least ten days before he takes possession of the goods or pays for them, whichever happens first, the transferee gives notice of the transfer in the manner and to the persons hereafter provided (Section 6—107).

[SECTION 6—106. APPLICATION OF THE PROCEEDS. In addition to the requirements of the two preceding sections:

(1) Upon every bulk transfer subject to this Article for which new consideration becomes payable except those made by sale at auction it is the duty of the transferee to assure that such consideration is applied so far as necessary to pay those debts of the transferor which are either shown on the list furnished by the transferor (Section 6—104) or filed in writing in the place stated in the notice (Section 6—107) within thirty days after the mailing of such notice. This duty of the transferee runs to all the holders of such debts, and may be enforced by any of them for the benefit of all.

(2) If any of said debts are in dispute the necessary sum may be withheld from distribution until the dispute is settled or adjudicated.

(3) If the consideration payable is not enough to pay all of the said debts in full distribution shall be made pro rata.]

    NOTE: *This section is bracketed to indicate division of opinion as to whether or not it is a wise provision, and to suggest that this is a point on which State enactments may differ without serious damage to the principle of uniformity.*

    In any State where this section is omitted, the following parts of sections, also bracketed in the text, should also be omitted, namely:

    Section 6—107(2)(e).

        6—108(3)(c).

        6—109(2).

    In any State where this section is enacted, these other provisions should be also.

OPTIONAL SUBSECTION (4) [(4) The transferee may within ten days after he takes possession of the goods pay the consideration into the (specify court) in the county where the transferor had its principal place of business in this state and thereafter may discharge his duty under this section by giving notice by registered or certified mail to all the persons to whom the duty runs that the consideration has been paid into that court and that they should file their claims there. On motion of any interested party, the court may order the distribution of the consideration to the persons entitled to it.]

NOTE: *Optional subsection (4) is recommended for those states which do not have a general statute providing for payment of money into court.*

SECTION 6—107. THE NOTICE. (1) The notice to creditors (Section 6—105) shall state:

(a) that a bulk transfer is about to be made; and

(b) the names and business addresses of the transferor and transferee, and all other business names and addresses used by the tranferor within three years last past so far as known to the transferee; and

(c) whether or not all the debts of the transferor are to be paid in full as they fall due as a result of the transaction, and if so, the address to which creditors should send their bills.

(2) If the debts of the transferor are not to be paid in full as they fall due or if the transferee is in doubt on that point then the notice shall state further:

(a) the location and general description of the property to be transferred and the estimated total of the transferor's debts;

(b) the address where the schedule of property and list of creditors (Section 6—104) may be inspected;

(c) whether the transfer is to pay existing debts and if so the amount of such debts and to whom owing;

(d) whether the transfer is for new consideration and if so the amount of such consideration and the time and place of payment; [and]

[(e) if for new consideration the time and place where creditors of the transferor are to file their claims.]

(3) The notice in any case shall be delivered personally or sent by registered mail to all the persons shown on the list of creditors furnished by the transferor (Section 6—104) and to all other persons who are known to the transferee to hold or assert claims against the transferor.

NOTE: *The words in brackets are optional.*

SECTION 6—108. AUCTION SALES; "AUCTIONEER". (1) A bulk transfer is subject to this Article even though it is by sale at auction, but only in the manner and with the results stated in this section.

(2) The transferor shall furnish a list of his creditors and assist in the preparation of a schedule of the property to be sold, both prepared as before stated (Section 6—104).

(3) The person or persons other than the transferor who direct, control or are responsible for the auction are collectively called the "auctioneer". The auctioneer shall:

(a) receive and retain the list of creditors and prepare and retain the schedule of property for the period stated in this Article (Section 6—104);

(b) give notice of the auction personally or by registered or certified mail at least ten days before it occurs to all persons shown on the list of creditors and to all other persons who are known to him to hold or assert claims against the transferor; [and]

[(c) assure that the net proceeds of the auction are applied as provided in this Article (Section 6—106).]

(4) Failure of the auctioneer to perform any of these duties does not affect the validity of the sale or the title of the purchasers, but if the auctioneer knows that the auction constitutes a bulk transfer such failure renders the auctioneer liable to the creditors of the transferor as a class for the sums owing to them from the transferor up to but not exceeding the net proceeds of the auction. If the auctioneer consists of several persons their liability is joint and several.

NOTE: *The words in brackets are optional.*

SECTION 6—109. WHAT CREDITORS PROTECTED; [CREDIT FOR PAYMENT TO PARTICULAR CREDITORS]. (1) The creditors of the transferor mentioned in this Article are those holding claims based on transactions or events occurring before the bulk transfer, but creditors who become such after notice to creditors is given (Sections 6—105 and 6—107) are not entitled to notice.

[(2) Against the aggregate obligation imposed by the provisions of this Article concerning the application of the proceeds (Section 6—106 and subsection (3) (c) of 6—108) the transferee or auctioneer is entitled to credit for sums paid to particular creditors of the transferor, not exceeding the sums believed in good faith at the time of the payment to be properly payable to such creditors.]

SECTION 6—110. SUBSEQUENT TRANSFERS. When the title of a transferee to property is subject to a defect by reason of his non-compliance with the requirements of this Article, then:

(1) a purchaser of any of such property from such transferee who pays no value or who takes with notice of such non-compliance takes subject to such defect, but

(2) a purchaser for value in good faith and without such notice takes free of such defect.

SECTION 6—111. LIMITATION OF ACTIONS AND LEVIES. No action under this Article shall be brought nor levy made more than six months after the date on which the transferee took possession of the goods unless the transfer has been concealed. If the transfer has been concealed, actions may be brought or levies made within six months after its discovery.

NOTE TO ARTICLE 6: *Section 6—106 is bracketed to indicate division of opinion as to whether or not it is a wise provision, and to suggest that this is a point on which State enactments may differ without serious damage to the principle of uniformity.*

In any State where Section 6—106 is not enacted, the following parts of sections, also bracketed in the text, should also be omitted, namely:

   Sec. 6—107(2)(e).

    6—108(3)(c).

    6—109(2).

In any State where Section 6—106 is enacted, these other provisions should be also.

ARTICLE 7

WAREHOUSE RECEIPTS, BILLS OF LADING AND OTHER DOCUMENTS OF TITLE

PART 1

GENERAL

SECTION 7—101. SHORT TITLE. This Article shall be known and may be cited as Uniform Commercial Code—Documents of Title.

SECTION 7—102. DEFINITIONS AND INDEX OF DEFINITIONS. (1) In this Article, unless the context otherwise requires:

(a) "Bailee" means the person who by a warehouse receipt, bill of lading or other document of title acknowledges possession of goods and contracts to deliver them.

(b) "Consignee" means the person named in a bill to whom or to whose order the bill promises delivery.

(c) "Consignor" means the person named in a bill as the person from whom the goods have been received for shipment.

(d) "Delivery order" means a written order to deliver goods directed to a warehouseman, carrier or other person who in the ordinary course of business issues warehouse receipts or bills of lading.

(e) "Document" means document of title as defined in the general definitions in Article 1 (Section 1—201).

(f) "Goods" means all things which are treated as movable for the purposes of a contract of storage or transportation.

(g) "Issuer" means a bailee who issues a document except that in relation to an unaccepted delivery order it means the person who orders the possessor of goods to deliver. Issuer includes any person for whom an agent or employee purports to act in issuing a document if the agent or employee has real or apparent authority to issue documents, notwithstanding that the issuer received no goods or that the goods were misdescribed or that in any other respect the agent or employee violated his instructions.

(h) "Warehouseman" is a person engaged in the business of storing goods for hire.

(2) Other definitions applying to this Article or to specified Parts thereof, and the sections in which they appear are:

"Duly negotiate". Section 7—501.

"Person entitled under the document". Section 7—403(4).

(3) Definitions in other Articles applying to this Article and the sections in which they appear are:

"Contract for sale". Section 2—106.

"Overseas". Section 2—323.

"Receipt" of goods. Section 2—103.

(4) In addition Article 1 contains general definitions and principles of construction and interpretation applicable throughout this Article.

SECTION 7—103. RELATION OF ARTICLE TO TREATY, STATUTE, TARIFF, CLASSIFICATION OR REGULATION. To the extent that any treaty or statute of the United States, regulatory statute of this State or tariff, classification or regulation filed or issued pursuant thereto is applicable, the provisions of this Article are subject thereto.

SECTION 7—104. NEGOTIABLE AND NON-NEGOTIABLE WAREHOUSE RECEIPT, BILL OF LADING OR OTHER DOCUMENT OF TITLE. (1) A warehouse receipt, bill of lading or other document of title is negotiable

(a) if by its terms the goods are to be delivered to bearer or to the order of a named person; or

(b) where recognized in overseas trade, if it runs to a named person or assigns.

(2) Any other document is non-negotiable. A bill of lading in which it is stated that the goods are consigned to a named person is not made negotiable by a provision that the goods are to be delivered only against a written order signed by the same or another named person.

SECTION 7—105. CONSTRUCTION AGAINST NEGATIVE IMPLICATION. The omission from either Part 2 or Part 3 of this Article of a provision corresponding to a provision made in the other Part does not imply that a corresponding rule of law is not applicable.

PART 2

WAREHOUSE RECEIPTS: SPECIAL PROVISIONS

SECTION 7—201. WHO MAY ISSUE A WAREHOUSE RECEIPT; STORAGE UNDER GOVERNMENT BOND. (1) A warehouse receipt may be issued by any warehouseman.

(2) Where goods including distilled spirits and agricultural commodities are stored under a statute requiring a bond against withdrawal or a license for the issuance of receipts in the nature of warehouse receipts, a receipt for the goods has like effect as a warehouse receipt even though issued by a person who is the owner of the goods and is not a warehouseman.

SECTION 7—202. FORM OF WAREHOUSE RECEIPT; ESSENTIAL TERMS; OPTIONAL TERMS. (1) A warehouse receipt need not be in any particular form.

(2) Unless a warehouse receipt embodies within its written or printed terms each of the following, the warehouseman is liable for damages caused by the omission to a person injured thereby:

(a) the location of the warehouse where the goods are stored;

(b) the date of issue of the receipt;

(c) the consecutive number of the receipt;

(d) a statement whether the goods received will be delivered to the bearer, to a specified person, or to a specified person or his order;

(e) the rate of storage and handling charges, except that where goods are stored under a field warehousing arrangement a statement of that fact is sufficient on a non-negotiable receipt;

(f) a description of the goods or of the packages containing them;

(g) the signature of the warehouseman, which may be made by his authorized agent;

(h) if the receipt is issued for goods of which the warehouseman is owner, either solely or jointly or in common with others, the fact of such ownership; and

(i) a statement of the amount of advances made and of liabilities incurred for which the warehouseman claims a lien or security interest (Section 7—209). If the precise amount of such advances made or of such liabilities incurred is, at the time of the issue of the receipt, unknown to the warehouseman or to his agent who issues it, a statement of the fact that advances have been made or liabilities incurred and the purpose thereof is sufficient.

(3) A warehouseman may insert in his receipt any other terms which are not contrary to the provisions of this Act and do not impair his obligation of delivery (Section 7—403) or his duty of care (Section 7—204). Any contrary provisions shall be ineffective.

SECTION 7—203. LIABILITY FOR NON-RECEIPT OR MISDESCRIPTION. A party to or purchaser for value in good faith of a document of title other than a bill of lading relying in either case upon the description therein of the goods may recover from the issuer damages caused by the non-receipt or misdescription of the goods, except to the extent that the document conspicuously indicates that the issuer does not know whether any part or all of the goods in fact were received or conform to the description, as where the description is in terms of marks or labels or kind, quantity or condition, or the receipt or description is qualified by "contents, condition and quality unknown", "said to contain" or the like, if such indication be true, or the party or purchaser otherwise has notice.

SECTION 7—204. DUTY OF CARE; CONTRACTUAL LIMITATION OF WAREHOUSEMAN'S LIABILITY. (1) A warehouseman is liable for damages for loss of or injury to the goods caused by his failure to exercise such care in regard to them as a reasonably careful man would exercise under like circumstances but unless otherwise agreed he is not liable for damages which could not have been avoided by the exercise of such care.

(2) Damages may be limited by a term in the warehouse receipt or storage agreement limiting the amount of liability in case of loss or damage, and setting forth a specific liability per article or item, or value per unit of weight, beyond which the warehouseman shall not be liable; provided, however, that such liability may on written request of the bailor at the time of signing such storage agreement or within a reasonable time after receipt of the warehouse receipt be increased on part or all of the goods thereunder, in which event increased rates may be charged based on such increased valuation, but that no such increase shall be permitted contrary to a lawful limitation of liability contained in the warehouseman's tariff, if any. No such limitation is effective with respect to the warehouseman's liability for conversion to his own use.

(3) Reasonable provisions as to the time and manner of presenting claims and instituting actions based on the bailment may be included in the warehouse receipt or tariff.

(4) This section does not impair or repeal . .

NOTE: *Insert in subsection (4) a reference to any statute which imposes a higher responsibility upon the warehouseman or invalidates contractual limitations which would be permissible under this Article.*

SECTION 7—205. TITLE UNDER WAREHOUSE RECEIPT DEFEATED IN CERTAIN CASES. A buyer in the ordinary course of business of fungible goods sold and delivered by a warehouseman who is also in the business of buying and selling such goods takes free of any claim under a warehouse receipt even though it has been duly negotiated.

SECTION 7—206. TERMINATION OF STORAGE AT WAREHOUSEMAN'S OPTION. (1) A warehouseman may on notifying the person on whose account the goods are held and any other person known to claim an interest in the goods require payment of any charges and removal of the goods from the warehouse at the termination of the period of storage fixed by the document, or, if no period is fixed, within a stated period not less than thirty days after the notification. If the goods are not removed before the date specified in the notification, the warehouseman may sell them in accordance with the provisions of the section on enforcement of a warehouseman's lien (Section 7–210).

(2) If a warehouseman in good faith believes that the goods are about to deteriorate or decline in value to less than the amount of his lien within the time prescribed in subsection (1) for notification, advertisement and sale, the warehouseman may specify in the notification any reasonable shorter time for removal of the goods and in case the goods are not removed, may sell them at public sale held not less than one week after a single advertisement or posting.

(3) If as a result of a quality or condition of the goods of which the warehouseman had no notice at the time of deposit the goods are a hazard to other property or to the warehouse or to persons, the warehouseman may sell the goods at public or private sale without advertisement on reasonable notification to all persons known to claim an interest in the goods. If the warehouseman after a reasonable effort is unable to sell the goods he may dispose of them in any lawful manner and shall incur no liability by reason of such disposition.

(4) The warehouseman must deliver the goods to any person entitled to them under this Article upon due demand made at any time prior to sale or other disposition under this section.

(5) The warehouseman may satisfy his lien from the proceeds of any sale or disposition under this section but must hold the balance for delivery on the demand of any person to whom he would have been bound to deliver the goods.

SECTION 7–207. GOODS MUST BE KEPT SEPARATE; FUNGIBLE GOODS. (1) Unless the warehouse receipt otherwise provides, a warehouseman must keep separate the goods covered by each receipt so as to permit at all times identification and delivery of those goods except that different lots of fungible goods may be commingled.

(2) Fungible goods so commingled are owned in common by the persons entitled thereto and the warehouseman is severally liable to each owner for that owner's share. Where because of overissue a mass of fungible goods is insufficient to meet all the receipts which the warehouseman has issued against it, the persons entitled include all holders to whom overissued receipts have been duly negotiated.

SECTION 7–208. ALTERED WAREHOUSE RECEIPTS. Where a blank in a negotiable warehouse receipt has been filled in without authority, a purchaser for value and without notice of the want of authority may treat the insertion as authorized. Any other unauthorized alteration leaves any receipt enforceable against the issuer according to its original tenor.

SECTION 7–209. LIEN OF WAREHOUSEMAN. (1) A warehouseman has a lien against the bailor on the goods covered by a warehouse receipt or on the proceeds thereof in his possession for charges for storage or transportation (including demurrage and terminal charges), insurance, labor, or charges present or future in relation to the goods, and for expenses necessary for preservation of the goods or reasonably incurred in their sale pursuant to law. If the person on whose account the goods are held is liable for like charges or expenses in relation to other goods whenever deposited and it is stated in the receipt that a lien is claimed for charges and expenses in relation to other goods, the warehouseman also has a lien against him for such charges and expenses whether or not the other goods have been delivered by the warehouseman. But against a person to whom a negotiable warehouse receipt is duly negotiated a warehouseman's lien is limited to charges in an amount or at a rate specified on the receipt or if no charges are so specified then to a reasonable charge for storage of the goods covered by the receipt subsequent to the date of the receipt.

(2) The warehouseman may also reserve a security interest against the bailor for a maximum amount specified on the receipt for charges other than those specified in subsection (1), such as for money advanced and interest. Such a security interest is governed by the Article on Secured Transactions (Article 9).

(3) A warehouseman's lien for charges and expenses under subsection (1) or a security interest under subsection (2) is also effective against any person who so entrusted the bailor with possession of the goods that a pledge of them by him to a

good faith purchaser for value would have been valid but is not effective against a person as to whom the document confers no right in the goods covered by it under Section 7—503.

(4) A warehouseman loses his lien on any goods which he voluntarily delivers or which he unjustifiably refuses to deliver.

SECTION 7—210. ENFORCEMENT OF WAREHOUSEMAN'S LIEN. (1) Except as provided in subsection (2), a warehouseman's lien may be enforced by public or private sale of the goods in block or in parcels, at any time or place and on any terms which are commercially reasonable, after notifying all persons known to claim an interest in the goods. Such notification must include a statement of the amount due, the nature of the proposed sale and the time and place of any public sale. The fact that a better price could have been obtained by a sale at a different time or in a different method from that selected by the warehouseman is not of itself sufficient to establish that the sale was not made in a commercially reasonable manner. If the warehouseman either sells the goods in the usual manner in any recognized market therefor, or if he sells at the price current in such market at the time of his sale, or if he has otherwise sold in conformity with commercially reasonable practices among dealers in the type of goods sold, he has sold in a commercially reasonable manner. A sale of more goods than apparently necessary to be offered to insure satisfaction of the obligation is not commercially reasonable except in cases covered by the preceding sentence.

(2) A warehouseman's lien on goods other than goods stored by a merchant in the course of his business may be enforced only as follows:

(a) All persons known to claim an interest in the goods must be notified.

(b) The notification must be delivered in person or sent by registered or certified letter to the last known address of any person to be notified.

(c) The notification must include an itemized statement of the claim, a description of the goods subject to the lien, a demand for payment within a specified time not less than ten days after receipt of the notification, and a conspicuous statement that unless the claim is paid within that time the goods will be advertised for sale and sold by auction at a specified time and place.

(d) The sale must conform to the terms of the notification.

(e) The sale must be held at the nearest suitable place to that where the goods are held or stored.

(f) After the expiration of the time given in the notification, an advertisement of the sale must be published once a week for two weeks consecutively in a newspaper of general circulation where the sale is to be held. The advertisement must include a description of the goods, the name of the person on whose account they are being held, and the time and place of the sale. The sale must take place at least fifteen days after the first publication. If there is no newspaper of general circulation where the sale is to be held, the advertisement must be posted at least ten days before the sale in not less than six conspicuous places in the neighborhood of the proposed sale.

(3) Before any sale pursuant to this section any person claiming a right in the goods may pay the amount necessary to satisfy the lien and the reasonable expenses incurred under this section. In that event the goods must not be sold, but must be retained by the warehouseman subject to the terms of the receipt and this Article.

(4) The warehouseman may buy at any public sale pursuant to this section.

(5) A purchaser in good faith of goods sold to enforce a warehouseman's lien takes the goods free of any rights of persons against whom the lien was valid, despite non-compliance by the warehouseman with the requirements of this section.

(6) The warehouseman may satisfy his lien from the proceeds of any sale pursuant to this section but must hold the balance, if any, for delivery on demand to any person to whom he would have been bound to deliver the goods.

(7) The rights provided by this section shall be in addition to all other rights allowed by law to a creditor against his debtor.

(8) Where a lien is on goods stored by a merchant in the course of his business the lien may be enforced in accordance with either subsection (1) or (2).

(9) The warehouseman is liable for damages caused by failure to comply with the

requirements for sale under this section and in case of willful violation is liable for conversion.

PART 3

BILLS OF LADING: SPECIAL PROVISIONS

SECTION 7—301. LIABILITY FOR NON-RECEIPT OR MISDESCRIPTION; "SAID TO CONTAIN"; "SHIPPER'S LOAD AND COUNT"; IMPROPER HANDLING. (1) A consignee of a non-negotiable bill who has given value in good faith or a holder to whom a negotiable bill has been duly negotiated relying in either case upon the description therein of the goods, or upon the date therein shown, may recover from the issuer damages caused by the misdating of the bill or the nonreceipt or misdescription of the goods, except to the extent that the document indicates that the issuer does not know whether any part or all of the goods in fact were received or conform to the description, as where the description is in terms of marks or labels or kind, quantity, or condition or the receipt or description is qualified by "contents or condition of contents of packages unknown", "said to contain", "shipper's weight, load and count" or the like, if such indication be true.

(2) When goods are loaded by an issuer who is a common carrier, the issuer must count the packages of goods if package freight and ascertain the kind and quantity if bulk freight. In such cases "shipper's weight, load and count" or other words indicating that the description was made by the shipper are ineffective except as to freight concealed by packages.

(3) When bulk freight is loaded by a shipper who makes available to the issuer adequate facilities for weighing such freight, an issuer who is a common carrier must ascertain the kind and quantity within a reasonable time after receiving the written request of the shipper to do so. In such cases "shipper's weight" or other words of like purport are ineffective.

(4) The issuer may by inserting in the bill the words "shipper's weight, load and count" or other words of like purport indicate that the goods were loaded by the shipper; and if such statement be true the issuer shall not be liable for damages caused by the improper loading. But their omission does not imply liability for such damages.

(5) The shipper shall be deemed to have guaranteed to the issuer the accuracy at the time of shipment of the description, marks, labels, number, kind, quantity, condition and weight, as furnished by him; and the shipper shall indemnify the issuer against damage caused by inaccuracies in such particulars. The right of the issuer to such indemnity shall in no way limit his responsibility and liability under the contract of carriage to any person other than the shipper.

SECTION 7—302. THROUGH BILLS OF LADING AND SIMILAR DOCUMENTS. (1) The issuer of a through bill of lading or other document embodying an undertaking to be performed in part by persons acting as its agents or by connecting carriers is liable to anyone entitled to recover on the document for any breach by such other persons or by a connecting carrier of its obligation under the document but to the extent that the bill covers an undertaking to be performed overseas or in territory not contiguous to the continental United States or an undertaking including matters other than transportation this liability may be varied by agreement of the parties.

(2) Where goods covered by a through bill of lading or other document embodying an undertaking to be performed in part by persons other than the issuer are received by any such person, he is subject with respect to his own performance while the goods are in his possession to the obligation of the issuer. His obligation is discharged by delivery of the goods to another such person pursuant to the document, and does not include liability for breach by any other such persons or by the issuer.

(3) The issuer of such through bill of lading or other document shall be entitled to recover from the connecting carrier or such other person in possession of the goods when the breach of the obligation under the document occurred, the amount it may be required to pay to anyone entitled to recover on the document therefor, as may be evidenced by any receipt, judgment, or transcript thereof, and the amount of any

expense reasonably incurred by it in defending any action brought by anyone entitled to recover on the document therefor.

SECTION 7—303. DIVERSION; RECONSIGNMENT; CHANGE OF INSTRUCTIONS. (1) Unless the bill of lading otherwise provides, the carrier may deliver the goods to a person or destination other than that stated in the bill or may otherwise dispose of the goods on instructions from

(a) the holder of a negotiable bill; or

(b) the consignor on a non-negotiable bill notwithstanding contrary instructions from the consignee; or

(c) the consignee on a non-negotiable bill in the absence of contrary instructions from the consignor, if the goods have arrived at the billed destination or if the consignee is in possession of the bill; or

(d) the consignee on a non-negotiable bill if he is entitled as against the consignor to dispose of them.

(2) Unless such instructions are noted on a negotiable bill of lading, a person to whom the bill is duly negotiated can hold the bailee according to the original terms.

SECTION 7—304. BILLS OF LADING IN A SET. (1) Except where customary in overseas transportation, a bill of lading must not be issued in a set of parts. The issuer is liable for damages caused by violation of this subsection.

(2) Where a bill of lading is lawfully drawn in a set of parts, each of which is numbered and expressed to be valid only if the goods have not been delivered against any other part, the whole of the parts constitute one bill.

(3) Where a bill of lading is lawfully issued in a set of parts and different parts are negotiated to different persons, the title of the holder to whom the first due negotiation is made prevails as to both the document and the goods even though any later holder may have received the goods from the carrier in good faith and discharged the carrier's obligation by surrender of his part.

(4) Any person who negotiates or transfers a single part of a bill of lading drawn in a set is liable to holders of that part as if it were the whole set.

(5) The bailee is obliged to deliver in accordance with Part 4 of this Article against the first presented part of a bill of lading lawfully drawn in a set. Such delivery discharges the bailee's obligation on the whole bill.

SECTION 7—305. DESTINATION BILLS. (1) Instead of issuing a bill of lading to the consignor at the place of shipment a carrier may at the request of the consignor procure the bill to be issued at destination or at any other place designated in the request.

(2) Upon request of anyone entitled as against the carrier to control the goods while in transit and on surrender of any outstanding bill of lading or other receipt covering such goods, the issuer may procure a substitute bill to be issued at any place designated in the request.

SECTION 7—306. ALTERED BILLS OF LADING. An unauthorized alteration or filling in of a blank in a bill of lading leaves the bill enforceable according to its original tenor.

SECTION 7—307. LIEN OF CARRIER. (1) A carrier has a lien on the goods covered by a bill of lading for charges subsequent to the date of its receipt of the goods for storage or transportation (including demurrage and terminal charges) and for expenses necessary for preservation of the goods incident to their transportation or reasonably incurred in their sale pursuant to law. But against a purchaser for value of a negotiable bill of lading a carrier's lien is limited to charges stated in the bill or the applicable tariffs, or if no charges are stated then to a reasonable charge.

(2) A lien for charges and expenses under subsection (1) on goods which the carrier was required by law to receive for transportation is effective against the consignor or any person entitled to the goods unless the carrier had notice that the consignor lacked authority to subject the goods to such charges and expenses. Any other lien under subsection (1) is effective against the consignor and any person who permitted the bailor to have control or possession of the goods unless the carrier had notice that the bailor lacked such authority.

(3) A carrier loses his lien on any goods which he voluntarily delivers or which he unjustifiably refuses to deliver.

SECTION 7—308. ENFORCEMENT OF CARRIER'S LIEN. (1) A carrier's lien may be enforced by public or private sale of the goods, in bloc or in parcels, at any time or place and on any terms which are commercially reasonable, after notifying all persons known to claim an interest in the goods. Such notification must include a statement of the amount due, the nature of the proposed sale and the time and place of any public sale. The fact that a better price could have been obtained by a sale at a different time or in a different method from that selected by the carrier is not of itself sufficient to establish that the sale was not made in a commercially reasonable manner. If the carrier either sells the goods in the usual manner in any recognized market therefor or if he sells at the price current in such market at the time of his sale or if he has otherwise sold in conformity with commercially reasonable practices among dealers in the type of goods sold he has sold in a commercially reasonable manner. A sale of more goods than apparently necessary to be offered to ensure satisfaction of the obligation is not commercially reasonable except in cases covered by the preceding sentence.

(2) Before any sale pursuant to this section any person claiming a right in the goods may pay the amount necessary to satisfy the lien and the reasonable expenses incurred under this section. In that event the goods must not be sold, but must be retained by the carrier subject to the terms of the bill and this Article.

(3) The carrier may buy at any public sale pursuant to this section.

(4) A purchaser in good faith of goods sold to enforce a carrier's lien takes the goods free of any rights of persons against whom the lien was valid, despite noncompliance by the carrier with the requirements of this section.

(5) The carrier may satisfy his lien from the proceeds of any sale pursuant to this section but must hold the balance, if any, for delivery on demand to any person to whom he would have been bound to deliver the goods.

(6) The rights provided by this section shall be in addition to all other rights allowed by law to a creditor against his debtor.

(7) A carrier's lien may be enforced in accordance with either subsection (1) or the procedure set forth in subsection (2) of Section 7—210.

(8) The carrier is liable for damages caused by failure to comply with the requirements for sale under this section and in case of willful violation is liable for conversion.

SECTION 7—309. DUTY OF CARE; CONTRACTUAL LIMITATION OF CARRIER'S LIABILITY. (1) A carrier who issues a bill of lading whether negotiable or non-negotiable must exercise the degree of care in relation to the goods which a reasonably careful man would exercise under like circumstances. This subsection does not repeal or change any law or rule of law which imposes liability upon a common carrier for damages not caused by its negligence.

(2) Damages may be limited by a provision that the carrier's liability shall not exceed a value stated in the document if the carrier's rates are dependent upon value and the consignor by the carrier's tariff is afforded an opportunity to declare a higher value or a value as lawfully provided in the tariff, or where no tariff is filed he is otherwise advised of such opportunity; but no such limitation is effective with respect to the carrier's liability for conversion to its own use.

(3) Reasonable provisions as to the time and manner of presenting claims and instituting actions based on the shipment may be included in a bill of lading or tariff.

PART 4

WAREHOUSE RECEIPTS AND BILLS OF LADING: GENERAL OBLIGATIONS

SECTION 7—401. IRREGULARITIES IN ISSUE OF RECEIPT OR BILL OR CONDUCT OF ISSUER. The obligations imposed by this Article on an issuer apply to a document of title regardless of the fact that

    (a) the document may not comply with the requirements of this Article or of any other law or regulation regarding its issue, form or content; or

    (b) the issuer may have violated laws regulating the conduct of his business; or

    (c) the goods covered by the document were owned by the bailee at the time the document was issued; or

    (d) the person issuing the document does not come within the definition of warehouseman if it purports to be a warehouse receipt.

SECTION 7—402. DUPLICATE RECEIPT OR BILL; OVERISSUE. Neither a duplicate nor any other document of title purporting to cover goods already represented by an outstanding document of the same issuer confers any right in the goods, except as provided in the case of bills in a set, overissue of documents for fungible goods and substitutes for lost, stolen or destroyed documents. But the issuer is liable for damages caused by his overissue or failure to identify a duplicate document as such by conspicuous notation on its face.

SECTION 7—403. OBLIGATION OF WAREHOUSEMAN OR CARRIER TO DELIVER; EXCUSE. (1) The bailee must deliver the goods to a person entitled under the document who complies with subsections (2) and (3), unless and to the extent that the bailee establishes any of the following:

    (a) delivery of the goods to a person whose receipt was rightful as against the claimant;

    (b) damage to or delay, loss or destruction of the goods for which the bailee is not liable [, but the burden of establishing negligence in such cases is on the person entitled under the document];

NOTE: *The brackets in (1) (b) indicate that State enactments may differ on this point without serious damage to the principle of uniformity.*

    (c) previous sale or other disposition of the goods in lawful enforcement of a lien or on warehouseman's lawful termination of storage;

    (d) the exercise by a seller of his right to stop delivery pursuant to the provisions of the Article on Sales (Section 2—705);

    (e) a diversion, reconsignment or other disposition pursuant to the provisions of this Article (Section 7—303) or tariff regulating such right;

    (f) release, satisfaction or any other fact affording a personal defense against the claimant;

    (g) any other lawful excuse.

(2) A person claiming goods covered by a document of title must satisfy the bailee's lien where the bailee so requests or where the bailee is prohibited by law from delivering the goods until the charges are paid.

(3) Unless the person claiming is one against whom the document confers no right under Sec. 7—503 (1), he must surrender for cancellation or notation of partial deliveries any outstanding negotiable document covering the goods, and the bailee must cancel the document or conspicuously note the partial delivery thereon or be liable to any person to whom the document is duly negotiated.

(4) "Person entitled under the document" means holder in the case of a negotiable document, or the person to whom delivery is to be made by the terms of or pursuant to written instructions under a non-negotiable document.

SECTION 7—404. NO LIABILITY FOR GOOD FAITH DELIVERY PURSUANT TO RECEIPT OR BILL. A bailee who in good faith including observance of reasonable commercial standards has received goods and delivered or otherwise disposed of them according to the terms of the document of title or pursuant to this Article is not liable therefor. This rule applies even though the person from whom he received the goods had no authority to procure the document or to dispose of the goods and even though the person to whom he delivered the goods had no authority to receive them.

PART 5

WAREHOUSE RECEIPTS AND BILLS OF LADING: NEGOTIATION AND TRANSFER

SECTION 7—501. FORM OF NEGOTIATION AND REQUIREMENTS OF "DUE NEGOTIATION". (1) A negotiable document of title running to the order of a named person is negotiated by his indorsement and delivery. After his indorsement in blank or to bearer any person can negotiate it by delivery alone.

(2) (a) A negotiable document of title is also negotiated by delivery alone when by its original terms it runs to bearer.

    (b) When a document running to the order of a named person is delivered to him the effect is the same as if the document had been negotiated.

(3) Negotiation of a negotiable document of title after it has been indorsed to a specified person requires indorsement by the special indorsee as well as delivery.

(4) A negotiable document of title is "duly negotiated" when it is negotiated in the manner stated in this section to a holder who purchases it in good faith without notice of any defense against or claim to it on the part of any person and for value, unless it is established that the negotiation is not in the regular course of business or financing or involves receiving the document in settlement or payment of a money obligation.

(5) Indorsement of a non-negotiable document neither makes it negotiable nor adds to the transferee's rights.

(6) The naming in a negotiable bill of a person to be notified of the arrival of the goods does not limit the negotiability of the bill nor constitute notice to a purchaser thereof of any interest of such person in the goods.

SECTION 7—502. RIGHTS ACQUIRED BY DUE NEGOTIATION. (1) Subject to the following section and to the provisions of Section 7—205 on fungible goods, a holder to whom a negotiable document of title has been duly negotiated acquires thereby:

    (a) title to the document;

    (b) title to the goods;

    (c) all rights accruing under the law of agency or estoppel, including rights to goods delivered to the bailee after the document was issued; and

    (d) the direct obligation of the issuer to hold or deliver the goods according to the terms of the document free of any defense or claim by him except those arising under the terms of the document or under this Article. In the case of a delivery order the bailee's obligation accrues only upon acceptance and the obligation acquired by the holder is that the issuer and any indorser will procure the acceptance of the bailee.

(2) Subject to the following section, title and rights so acquired are not defeated by any stoppage of the goods represented by the document or by surrender of such goods by the bailee, and are not impaired even though the negotiation or any prior negotiation constituted a breach of duty or even though any person has been deprived of possession of the document by misrepresentation, fraud, accident, mistake, duress, loss, theft or conversion, or even though a previous sale or other transfer of the goods has been made to a third person.

SECTION 7—503. DOCUMENTS OF TITLE TO GOODS DEFEATED IN CERTAIN CASES. (1) A document of title confers no right in goods against a person who before issuance of the document had a legal interest or a perfected security interest in them and who neither

    (a) delivered or entrusted them or any document of title covering them to the bailor or his nominee with actual or apparent authority to ship, store or sell or with power to obtain delivery under this Article (Section 7—403) or with power of disposition under this Act (Sections 2—403 and 9—307) or other statute or rule of law; nor

    (b) acquiesced in the procurement by the bailor or his nominee of any document of title.

(2) Title to goods based upon an unaccepted delivery order is subject to the rights of anyone to whom a negotiable warehouse receipt or bill of lading covering the goods has been duly negotiated. Such a title may be defeated under the next section to the same extent as the rights of the issuer or a transferee from the issuer.

(3) Title to goods based upon a bill of lading issued to a freight forwarder is subject to the rights of anyone to whom a bill issued by the freight forwarder is duly negotiated; but delivery by the carrier in accordance with Part 4 of this Article pursuant to its own bill of lading discharges the carrier's obligation to deliver.

SECTION 7—504. RIGHTS ACQUIRED IN THE ABSENCE OF DUE NEGOTIATION; EFFECT OF DIVERSION; SELLER'S STOPPAGE OF DELIVERY. (1) A transferee of a document, whether negotiable or non-negotiable, to whom the document has been delivered but not duly negotiated, acquires the title and rights which his transferor had or had actual authority to convey.

(2) In the case of a non-negotiable document, until but not after the bailee receives notification of the transfer, the rights of the transferee may be defeated

 (a) by those creditors of the transferor who could treat the sale as void under Section 2—402; or

 (b) by a buyer from the transferor in ordinary course of business if the bailee has delivered the goods to the buyer or received notification of his rights; or

 (c) as against the bailee by good faith dealings of the bailee with the transferor.

(3) A diversion or other change of shipping instructions by the consignor in a non-negotiable bill of lading which causes the bailee not to deliver to the consignee defeats the consignee's title to the goods if they have been delivered to a buyer in ordinary course of business and in any event defeats the consignee's rights against the bailee.

(4) Delivery pursuant to a non-negotiable document may be stopped by a seller under Section 2—705, and subject to the requirement of due notification there provided. A bailee honoring the seller's instructions is entitled to be indemnified by the seller against any resulting loss or expense.

SECTION 7—505. INDORSER NOT A GUARANTOR FOR OTHER PARTIES. The indorsement of a document of title issued by a bailee does not make the indorser liable for any default by the bailee or by previous indorsers.

SECTION 7—506. DELIVERY WITHOUT INDORSEMENT: RIGHT TO COMPEL INDORSEMENT. The transferee of a negotiable document of title has a specifically enforceable right to have his transferor supply any necessary indorsement but the transfer becomes a negotiation only as of the time the indorsement is supplied.

SECTION 7—507. WARRANTIES ON NEGOTIATION OR TRANSFER OF RECEIPT OR BILL. Where a person negotiates or transfers a document of title for value otherwise than as a mere intermediary under the next following section, then unless otherwise agreed he warrants to his immediate purchaser only in addition to any warranty made in selling the goods

 (a) that the document is genuine; and

 (b) that he has no knowledge of any fact which would impair its validity or worth; and

 (c) that his negotiation or transfer is rightful and fully effective with respect to the title to the document and the goods it represents.

SECTION 7—508. WARRANTIES OF COLLECTING BANK AS TO DOCUMENTS. A collecting bank or other intermediary known to be entrusted with documents on behalf of another or with collection of a draft or other claim against delivery of documents warrants by such delivery of the documents only its own good faith and authority. This rule applies even though the intermediary has purchased or made advances against the claim or draft to be collected.

SECTION 7—509. RECEIPT OR BILL: WHEN ADEQUATE COMPLIANCE WITH COMMERCIAL CONTRACT. The question whether a document is adequate to fulfill the obligations of a contract for sale or the conditions of a credit is governed by the Articles on Sales (Article 2) and on Letters of Credit (Article 5).

PART 6

WAREHOUSE RECEIPTS AND BILLS OF LADING: MISCELLANEOUS PROVISIONS

SECTION 7—601. LOST AND MISSING DOCUMENTS. (1) If a document has been lost, stolen or destroyed, a court may order delivery of the goods or issuance of a substitute document and the bailee may without liability to any person comply with such order. If the document was negotiable the claimant must post security approved by the court to indemnify any person who may suffer loss as a result of non-surrender of the document. If the document was not negotiable, such security may be required at the discretion of the court. The court may also in its discretion order payment of the bailee's reasonable costs and counsel fees.

(2) A bailee who without court order delivers goods to a person claiming under a missing negotiable document is liable to any person injured thereby, and if the delivery is not in good faith becomes liable for conversion. Delivery in good faith is not conversion if made in accordance with a filed classification or tariff or, where no classification or tariff is filed, if the claimant posts security with the bailee in an amount at least double the value of the goods at the time of posting to indemnify any person injured by the delivery who files a notice of claim within one year after the delivery.

Section 7—602. Attachment of Goods Covered by a Negotiable Document. Except where the document was originally issued upon delivery of the goods by a person who had no power to dispose of them, no lien attaches by virtue of any judicial process to goods in the possession of a bailee for which a negotiable doucment of title is outstanding unless the document be first surrendered to the bailee or its negotiation enjoined, and the bailee shall not be compelled to deliver the goods pursuant to process until the document is surrendered to him or impounded by the court. One who purchases the document for value without notice of the process or injunction takes free of the lien imposed by judicial process.

Section 7—603. Conflecting Claims; Interpleader. If more than one person claims title or possession of the goods, the bailee is excused from delivery until he has had a reasonable time to ascertain the validity of the adverse claims or to bring an action to compel all claimants to interplead and may compel such interpleader, either in defending an action for non-delivery of the goods, or by original action, whichever is appropriate.

ARTICLE 8

Investment Securities

PART 1

SHORT TITLE AND GENERAL MATTERS

Section 8—101. Short Title. This Article shall be known and may be cited as Uniform Commercial Code—Investment Securities.

Section 8—102. Definitions and Index of Definitions (1) In this Article unless the context otherwise requires

    (a) A "security" is an instrument which
        (i) is issued in bearer or registered form; and
        (ii) is of a type commonly dealt in upon securities exchanges or markets or commonly recognized in any area in which it is issued or dealt in as a medium for investment; and
        (iii) is either one of a class or series or by its terms is divisible into a class or series of instruments; and
        (iv) evidences a share, participation or other interest in property or in an enterprise or evidences an obligation of the issuer.
    (b) A writing which is a security is governed by this Article and not by Uniform Commercial Code-Commercial Paper even though it also meets the requirements of that Article. This Article does not apply to money.
    (c) A security is in "registered form" when it specifies a person entitled to the security or to the rights it evidences and when its transfer may be registered upon books maintained for that purpose by or on behalf of an issuer or the security so states.
    (d) A security is in "bearer form" when it runs to bearer according to its terms and not by reason of any indorsement.
(2) A "subsequent purchaser" is a person who takes other than by original issue.
(3) A "clearing corporation" is a corporation all of the capital stock of which is held

by or for a national security exchange or association registered under a statute of the United States such as the Securities Exchange Act of 1934.

(4) A "custodian bank" is any bank or trust company which is supervised and examined by state or federal authority having supervision over banks and which is acting as custodian for a clearing corporation.

(5) Other definitions applying to this Article or to specified Parts thereof and the sections in which they appear are:

"Adverse claim".	Section 8—301.
"Bona fide purchaser".	Section 8—302.
"Broker".	Section 8—303.
"Guarantee of the signature".	Section 8—402.
"Intermediary bank".	Section 4—105.
"Issuer".	Section 8—201.
"Overissue".	Section 8—104.

(6) In addition Article 1 contains general definitions and principles of construction and interpretation applicable throughout this Article.

SECTION 8—103. ISSUER'S LIEN. A lien upon a security in favor of an issuer thereof is valid against a purchaser only if the right of the issuer to such lien is noted conspicuously on the security.

SECTION 8—104. EFFECT OF OVERISSUE; "OVERISSUE." (1) The provisions of this Article which validate a security or compel its issue or reissue do not apply to the extent that validation, issue or reissue would result in overissue; but

   (a) if an identical security which does not constitute an overissue is reasonably available for purchase, the person entitled to issue or validation may compel the issuer to purchase and deliver such a security to him against surrender of the security, if any, which he holds; or

   (b) if a security is not so available for purchase, the person entitled to issue or validation may recover from the issuer the price he or the last purchaser for value paid for it with interest from the date of his demand.

(2) "Overissue" means the issue of securities in excess of the amount which the issuer has corporate power to issue.

SECTION 8—105. SECURITIES NEGOTIABLE; PRESUMPTIONS. (1) Securities governed by this Article are negotiable instruments.

(2) In any action on a security

   (a) unless specifically denied in the pleadings, each signature on the security or in a necessary indorsement is admitted;

   (b) when the effectiveness of a signature is put in issue the burden of establishing it is on the party claiming under the signature but the signature is presumed to be genuine or authorized;

   (c) when signatures are admitted or established production of the instrument entitles a holder to recover on it unless the defendant establishes a defense or a defect going to the validity of the security; and

   (d) after it is shown that a defense or defect exists the plaintiff has the burden of establishing that he or some person under whom he claims is a person against whom the defense or defect is ineffective (Section 8—202).

SECTION 8—106. APPLICABILITY. The validity of a security and the rights and duties of the issuer with respect to registration of transfer are governed by the law (including the conflict of laws rules) of the jurisdiction of organization of the issuer.

SECTION 8—107. SECURITIES DELIVERABLE; ACTION FOR PRICE. (1) Unless otherwise agreed and subject to any applicable law or regulation respecting short sales, a person obligated to deliver securities may deliver any security of the specified issue in bearer form or registered in the name of the transferee or indorsed to him or in blank.

(2) When the buyer fails to pay the price as it comes due under a contract of sale the seller may recover the price

   (a) of securities accepted by the buyer; and

   (b) of other securities if efforts at their resale would be unduly burdensome or if there is no readily available market for their resale.

PART 2

ISSUE—ISSUER

SECTION 8—201. "ISSUER." (1) With respect to obligations on or defenses to a security "issuer" includes a person who

    (a) places or authorizes the placing of his name on a security (otherwise than as authenticating trustee, registrar, transfer agent or the like) to evidence that it represents a share, participation or other interest in his property or in an enterprise or to evidence his duty to perform an obligation evidenced by the security; or

    (b) directly or indirectly creates fractional interests in his rights or property which fractional interests are evidenced by securities; or

    (c) becomes responsible for or in place of any other person described as an issuer in this section.

(2) With respect to obligations on or defenses to a security a guarantor is an issuer to the extent of his guaranty whether or not his obligation is noted on the security.

(3) With respect to registration of transfer (Part 4 of this Article) "issuer" means a person on whose behalf transfer books are maintained.

SECTION 8—202. ISSUER'S RESPONSIBILITY AND DEFENSES; NOTICE OF DEFECT OR DEFENSE. (1) Even against a purchaser for value and without notice, the terms of a security include those stated on the security and those made part of the security by reference to another instrument, indenture or document or to a constitution, statute, ordinance, rule, regulation, order or the like to the extent that the terms so referred to do not conflict with the stated terms. Such a reference does not of itself charge a purchaser for value with notice of a defect going to the validity of the security even though the security expressly states that a person accepting it admits such notice.

    (2) (a) A security other than one issued by a government or governmental agency or unit even though issued with a defect going to its validity is valid in the hands of a purchaser for value and without notice of the particular defect unless the defect involves a violation of constitutional provisions in which case the security is valid in the hands of a subsequent purchaser for value and without notice of the defect.

        (b) The rule of subparagraph (a) applies to an issuer which is a government or governmental agency or unit only if either there has been substantial compliance with the legal requirements governing the issue or the issuer has received a substantial consideration for the issue as a whole or for the particular security and a stated purpose of the issue is one for which the issuer has power to borrow money or issue the security.

(3) Except as otherwise provided in the case of certain unauthorized signatures on issue (Section 8—205), lack of genuineness of a security is a complete defense even against a purchaser for value and without notice.

(4) All other defenses of the issuer including nondelivery and conditional delivery of the security are ineffective against a purchaser for value who has taken without notice of the particular defense.

(5) Nothing in this section shall be construed to affect the right of a party to a "when, as and if issued" or a "when distributed" contract to cancel the contract in the event of a material change in the character of the security which is the subject of the contract or in the plan or arrangement pursuant to which such security is to be issued or distributed.

SECTION 8—203. STALENESS AS NOTICE OF DEFECTS OR DEFENSES. (1) After an act or event which creates a right to immediate performance of the principal obligation evidenced by the security or which sets a date on or after which the security is to be presented or surrendered for redemption or exchange, a purchaser is charged with notice of any defect in its issue or defense of the issuer

    (a) if the act or event is one requiring the payment of money or the delivery of securities or both on presentation or surrender of the security and such funds or securities are available on the date set for payment or exchange and he takes the security more than one year after that date; and

(b) if the act or event is not covered by paragraph (a) and he takes the security more than two years after the date set for surrender or presentation or the date on which such performance became due.

(2) A call which has been revoked is not within subsection (1).

SECTION 8—204. EFFECT OF ISSUER'S RESTRICTIONS ON TRANSFER. Unless noted conspicuously on the security a restriction on transfer imposed by the issuer even though otherwise lawful is ineffective except against a person with actual knowledge of it.

SECTION 8—205. EFFECT OF UNAUTHORIZED SIGNATURE ON ISSUE. An unauthorized signature placed on a security prior to or in the course of issue is ineffective except that the signature is effective in favor of a purchaser for value and without notice of the lack of authority if the signing has been done by

(a) an authenticating trustee, registrar, transfer agent or other person entrusted by the issuer with the signing of the security or of similar securities or their immediate preparation for signing; or

(b) an employee of the issuer or of any of the foregoing entrusted with responsible handling of the security.

SECTION 8—206. COMPLETION OR ALTERATION OF INSTRUMENT. (1) Where a security contains the signatures necessary to its issue or transfer but is incomplete in any other respect

(a) any person may complete it by filling in the blanks as authorized; and

(b) even though the blanks are incorrectly filled in, the security as completed is enforceable by a purchaser who took it for value and without notice of such incorrectness.

(2) A complete security which has been improperly altered even though fraudulently remains enforceable but only according to its original terms.

SECTION 8—207. RIGHTS OF ISSUER WITH RESPECT TO REGISTERED OWNERS. (1) Prior to due presentment for registration of transfer of a security in registered form the issuer or indenture trustee may treat the registered owner as the person exclusively entitled to vote, to receive notifications and otherwise to exercise all the rights and powers of an owner.

(2) Nothing in this Article shall be construed to affect the liability of the registered owner of a security for calls, assessments or the like.

SECTION 8—208. EFFECT OF SIGNATURE OF AUTHENTICATING TRUSTEE, REGISTRAR OR TRANSFER AGENT. (1) A person placing his signature upon a security as authenticating trustee, registrar, transfer agent or the like warrants to a purchaser for value without notice of the particular defect that

(a) the security is genuine; and

(b) his own participation in the issue of the security is within his capacity and within the scope of the authorization received by him from the issuer; and

(c) he has reasonable grounds to believe that the security is in the form and within the amount the issuer is authorized to issue.

(2) Unless otherwise agreed, a person by so placing his signature does not assume responsibility for the validity of the security in other respects.

PART 3

PURCHASE

SECTION 8—301. RIGHTS ACQUIRED BY PURCHASER; "ADVERSE CLAIM"; TITLE ACQUIRED BY BONA FIDE PURCHASER. (1) Upon delivery of a security the purchaser acquires the rights in the security which his transferor had or had actual authority to convey except that a purchaser who has himself been a party to any fraud or illegality affecting the security or who as a prior holder had notice of an adverse claim cannot improve his position by taking from a later bona fide purchaser. "Adverse claim" includes a claim that a transfer was or would be wrongful or that a particular adverse person is the owner of or has an interest in the security.

(2) A bona fide purchaser in addition to acquiring the rights of a purchaser also acquires the security free of any adverse claim.

(3) A purchaser of a limited interest acquires rights only to the extent of the interest purchased.

SECTION 8—302. "BONA FIDE PURCHASER." A "bona fide purchaser" is a purchaser for value in good faith and without notice of any adverse claim who takes delivery of a security in bearer form or of one in registered form issued to him or indorsed to him or in blank.

SECTION 8—303. "BROKER." "Broker" means a person engaged for all or part of his time in the business of buying and selling securities, who in the transaction concerned acts for, or buys a security from or sells a security to a customer. Nothing in this Article determines the capacity in which a person acts for purposes of any other statute or rule to which such person is subject.

SECTION 8—304. NOTICE TO PURCHASER OF ADVERSE CLAIMS. (1) A purchaser (including a broker for the seller or buyer but excluding an intermediary bank) of a security is charged with notice of adverse claims if

(a) the security whether in bearer or registered form has been indorsed "for collection" or "for surrender" or for some other purpose not involving transfer; or

(b) the security is in bearer form and has on it an unambiguous statement that it is the property of a person other than the transferor. The mere writing of a name on a security is not such a statement.

(2) The fact that the purchaser (including a broker for the seller or buyer) has notice that the security is held for a third person or is registered in the name of or indorsed by a fiduciary does not create a duty of inquiry into the rightfulness of the transfer or constitute notice of adverse claims. If, however, the purchaser (excluding an intermediary bank) has knowledge that the proceeds are being used or that the transaction is for the individual benefit of the fiduciary or otherwise in breach of duty, the purchaser is charged with notice of adverse claims.

SECTION 8—305. STALENESS AS NOTICE OF ADVERSE CLAIMS. An act or event which creates a right to immediate performance of the principal obligation evidenced by the security or which sets a date on or after which the security is to be presented or surrendered for redemption or exchange does not of itself constitute any notice of adverse claims except in the case of a purchase

(a) after one year from any date set for such presentment or surrender for redemption or exchange; or

(b) after six months from any date set for payment of money against presentation or surrender of the security if funds are available for payment on that date.

SECTION 8—306. WARRANTIES ON PRESENTMENT AND TRANSFER. (1) A person who presents a security for registration on transfer or for payment or exchange warrants to the issuer that he is entitled to the registration, payment or exchange. But a purchaser for value without notice of adverse claims who receives a new, reissued or reregistered security on registration of transfer warrants only that he has no knowledge of any unauthorized signature (Section 8—311) in a necessary indorsement.

(2) A person by transferring a security to a purchaser for value warrants only that

(a) his transfer is effective and rightful; and

(b) the security is genuine and has not been materially altered; and

(c) he knows no fact which might impair the validity of the security.

(3) Where a security is delivered by an intermediary known to be entrusted with delivery of the security on behalf of another or with collection of a draft or other claim against such delivery, the intermediary by such delivery warrants only his own good faith and authority even though he has purchased or made advances against the claim to be collected against the delivery.

(4) A pledgee or other holder for security who redelivers the security received, or after payment and on order of the debtor delivers that security to a third person makes only the warranties of an intermediary under subsection (3).

(5) A broker gives to his customer and to the issuer and a purchaser the warranties provided in this section and has the rights and privileges of a purchaser under this section. The warranties of and in favor of the broker acting as an agent are in addition to applicable warranties given by and in favor of his customer.

Section 8—307. Effect of Delivery Without Indorsement; Right to Compel Indorsement. Where a security in registered form has been delivered to a purchaser without a necessary indorsement he may become a bona fide purchaser only as of the time the indorsement is supplied, but against the transferor the transfer is complete upon delivery and the purchaser has a specifically enforceable right to have any necessary indorsement supplied.

Section 8—308. Indorsement, How Made; Special Indorsement; Indorser Not a Guarantor; Partial Assignment. (1) An indorsement of a security in registered form is made when an appropriate person signs on it or on a separate document an assignment or transfer of the security or a power to assign or transfer it or when the signature of such person is written without more upon the back of the security.

(2) An indorsement may be in blank or special. An indorsement in blank includes an indorsement to bearer. A special indorsement specifies the person to whom the security is to be transferred, or who has power to transfer it. A holder may convert a blank indorsement into a special indorsement.

(3) "An appropriate person" in subsection (1) means
   (a) the person specified by the security or by special indorsement to be entitled to the security; or
   (b) where the person so specified is described as a fiduciary but is no longer serving in the described capacity,—either that person or his successor; or
   (c) where the security or indorsement so specifies more than one person as fiduciaries and one or more are no longer serving in the described capacity, —the remaining fiduciary or fiduciaries, whether or not a successor has been appointed or qualified; or
   (d) where the person so specified is an individual and is without capacity to act by virtue of death, incompetence, infancy or otherwise,—his executor, administrator, guardian or like fiduciary; or
   (e) where the security or indorsement so specifies more than one person as tenants by the entirety or with right of survivorship and by reason of death all cannot sign,—the survivor or survivors; or
   (f) a person having power to sign under applicable law or controlling instrument; or
   (g) to the extent that any of the foregoing persons may act through an agent,— his authorized agent.

(4) Unless otherwise agreed the indorser by his indorsement assumes no obligation that the security will be honored by the issuer.

(5) An indorsement purporting to be only of part of a security representing units intended by the issuer to be separately transferable is effective to the extent of the indorsement.

(6) Whether the person signing is appropriate is determined as of the date of signing and an indorsement by such a person does not become unauthorized for the purposes of this Article by virtue of any subsequent change of circumstances.

(7) Failure of a fiduciary to comply with a controlling instrument or with the law of the state having jurisdiction of the fiduciary relationship, including any law requiring the fiduciary to obtain court approval of the transfer, does not render his indorsement unauthorized for the purposes of this Article.

Section 8—309. Effect of Indorsement Without Delivery. An indorsement of a security whether special or in blank does not constitute a transfer until delivery of the security on which it appears or if the indorsement is on a separate document until delivery of both the document and the security.

Section 8—310. Indorsement of Security in Bearer Form. An indorsement of a security in bearer form may give notice of adverse claims (Section 8—304) but does not otherwise affect any right to registration the holder may possess.

Section 8—311. Effect of Unauthorized Indorsement. Unless the owner has ratified an unauthorized indorsement or is otherwise precluded from asserting its ineffectiveness
   (a) he may assert its ineffectiveness against the issuer or any purchaser other than a purchaser for value and without notice of adverse claims who has in good faith received a new, reissued or re-registered security on registration of transfer; and

(b) an issuer who registers the transfer of a security upon the unauthorized indorsement is subject to liability for improper registration (Section 8–404).

SECTION 8–312. EFFECT OF GUARANTEEING SIGNATURE OR INDORSEMENT. (1) Any person guaranteeing a signature of an indorser of a security warrants that at the time of signing

(a) the signature was genuine; and

(b) the signer was an appropriate person to indorse (Section 8–308); and

(c) the signer had legal capacity to sign.

But the guarantor does not otherwise warrant the rightfulness of the particular transfer.

(2) Any person may guarantee an indorsement of a security and by so doing warrants not only the signature (subsection 1) but also the rightfulness of the particular transfer in all respects. But no issuer may require a guarantee of indorsement as a condition to registration of transfer.

(3) The foregoing warranties are made to any person taking or dealing with the security in reliance on the guarantee and the guarantor is liable to such person for any loss resulting from breach of the warranties.

SECTION 8–313. WHEN DELIVERY TO THE PURCHASER OCCURS; PURCHASER'S BROKER AS HOLDER. (1) Delivery to a purchaser occurs when

(a) he or a person designated by him acquires possession of a security; or

(b) his broker acquires possession of a security specially indorsed to or issued in the name of the purchaser; or

(c) his broker sends him confirmation of the purchase and also by book entry or otherwise identifies a specific security in the broker's possession as belonging to the purchaser; or

(d) with respect to an identified security to be delivered while still in the possession of a third person when that person acknowledges that he holds for the purchaser; or

(e) appropriate entries on the books of a clearing corporation are made under Section 8–320.

(2) The purchaser is the owner of a security held for him by his broker, but is not the holder except as specified in subparagraphs (b), (c) and (e) of subsection (1). Where a security is part of a fungible bulk the purchaser is the owner of a proportionate property interest in the fungible bulk.

(3) Notice of an adverse claim received by the broker or by the purchaser after the broker takes delivery as a holder for value is not effective either as to the broker or as to the purchaser. However, as between the broker and the purchaser the purchaser may demand delivery of an equivalent security as to which no notice of an adverse claim has been received.

SECTION 8–314. DUTY TO DELIVER, WHEN COMPLETED. (1) Unless otherwise agreed where a sale of a security is made on an exchange or otherwise through brokers

(a) the selling customer fulfills his duty to deliver when he places such a security in the possession of the selling broker or of a person designated by the broker or if requested causes an acknowledgment to be made to the selling broker that it is held for him; and

(b) the selling broker including a correspondent broker acting for a selling customer fulfills his duty to deliver by placing the security or a like security in the possession of the buying broker or a person designated by him or by effecting clearance of the sale in accordance with the rules of the exchange on which the transaction took place.

(2) Except as otherwise provided in this section and unless otherwise agreed, a transferor's duty to deliver a security under a contract of purchase is not fulfilled until he places the security in form to be negotiated by the purchaser in the possession of the purchaser or of a person designated by him or at the purchaser's request causes an acknowledgment to be made to the purchaser that it is held for him. Unless made on an exchange a sale to a broker purchasing for his own account is within this subsection and not within subsection (1).

SECTION 8–315. ACTION AGAINST PURCHASER BASED UPON WRONGFUL TRANSFER. (1) Any person against whom the transfer of a security is wrongful for any reason, including his incapacity, may against anyone except a bona fide purchaser reclaim possession of the security or obtain possession of any new security evidencing all or part of the same rights or have damages.

(2) If the transfer is wrongful because of an unauthorized indorsement, the owner may also reclaim or obtain possession of the security or new security even from a bona fide purchaser if the ineffectiveness of the purported indorsement can be asserted against him under the provisions of this Article on unauthorized indorsements (Section 8–311).

(3) The right to obtain or reclaim possession of a security may be specifically enforced and its transfer enjoined and the security impounded pending the litigation.

SECTION 8–316. PURCHASER'S RIGHT TO REQUISITES FOR REGISTRATION OF TRANSFER ON BOOKS. Unless otherwise agreed the transferor must on due demand supply his purchaser with any proof of his authority to transfer or with any other requisite which may be necessary to obtain registration of the transfer of the security but if the transfer is not for value a transferor need not do so unless the purchaser furnishes the necessary expenses. Failure to comply with a demand made within a reasonable time gives the purchaser the right to reject or rescind the transfer.

SECTION 8–317. ATTACHMENT OR LEVY UPON SECURITY. (1) No attachment or levy upon a security or any share or other interest evidenced thereby which is outstanding shall be valid until the security is actually seized by the officer making the attachment or levy but a security which has been surrendered to the issuer may be attached or levied upon at the source.

(2) A creditor whose debtor is the owner of a security shall be entitled to such aid from courts of appropriate jurisdiction, by injunction or otherwise, in reaching such security or in satisfying the claim by means thereof as is allowed at law or in equity in regard to property which cannot readily be attached or levied upon by ordinary legal process.

SECTION 8–318. NO CONVERSION BY GOOD FAITH DELIVERY. An agent or bailee who in good faith (including observance of reasonable commercial standards if he is in the business of buying, selling or otherwise dealing with securities) has received securities and sold, pledged or delivered them according to the instructions of his principal is not liable for conversion or for participation in breach of fiduciary duty although the principal had no right to dispose of them.

SECTION 8–319. STATUTE OF FRAUDS. A contract for the sale of securities is not enforceable by way of action or defense unless

(a) there is some writing signed by the party against whom enforcement is sought or by his authorized agent or broker sufficient to indicate that a contract has been made for sale of a stated quantity of described securities at a defined or stated price; or

(b) delivery of the security has been accepted or payment has been made but the contract is enforceable under this provision only to the extent of such delivery or payment; or

(c) within a reasonable time a writing in confirmation of the sale or purchase and sufficient against the sender under paragraph (a) has been received by the party against whom enforcement is sought and he has failed to send written objection to its contents within ten days after its receipt; or

(d) the party against whom enforcement is sought admits in his pleading, testimony or otherwise in court that a contract was made for sale of a stated quantity of described securities at a defined or stated price.

SECTION 8–320. TRANSFER OR PLEDGE WITHIN A CENTRAL DEPOSITORY SYSTEM. (1) If a security

(a) is in the custody of a clearing corporation or of a custodian bank or a nominee of either subject to the instructions of the clearing corporation; and

(b) is in bearer form or indorsed in blank by an appropriate person or registered in the name of the clearing corporation or custodian bank or a nominee of either; and

(c) is shown on the account of a transferor or pledgor on the books of the clearing corporation;

then, in addition to other methods, a transfer or pledge of the security or any interest therein may be effected by the making of appropriate entries on the books of the clearing corporation reducing the account of the transferor or pledgor and increasing the account of the transferee or pledgee by the amount of the obligation or the number of shares or rights transferred or pledged.

(2) Under this section entries may be with respect to like securities or interests therein as a part of a fungible bulk and may refer merely to a quantity of a particular security without reference to the name of the registered owner, certificate or bond number or the like and, in appropriate cases, may be on a net basis taking into account other transfers or pledges of the same security.

(3) A transfer or pledge under this section has the effect of a delivery of a security in bearer form or duly indorsed in blank (Section 8—301) representing the amount of the obligation or the number of shares or rights transferred or pledged. If a pledge or the creation of a security interest is intended, the making of entries has the effect of a taking of delivery by the pledgee or a secured party (Sections 9—304 and 9—305). A transferee or pledgee under this section is a holder.

(4) A transfer or pledge under this section does not constitute a registration of transfer under Part 4 of this Article.

(5) That entries made on the books of the clearing corporation as provided in subsection (1) are not appropriate does not affect the validity or effect of the entries nor the liabilities or obligations of the clearing corporation to any person adversely affected thereby.

PART 4

REGISTRATION

SECTION 8—401. DUTY OF ISSUER TO REGISTER TRANSFER. (1) Where a security in registered form is presented to the issuer with a request to register transfer, the issuer is under a duty to register the transfer as requested if

    (a) the security is indorsed by the appropriate person or persons (Section 8—308); and

    (b) reasonable assurance is given that those indorsements are genuine and effective (Section 8—402); and

    (c) the issuer has no duty to inquire into adverse claims or has discharged any such duty (Section 8—403); and

    (d) any applicable law relating to the collection of taxes has been complied with; and

    (e) the transfer is in fact rightful or is to a bona fide purchaser.

(2) Where an issuer is under a duty to register a transfer of a security the issuer is also liable to the person presenting it for registration or his principal for loss resulting from any unreasonable delay in registration or from failure or refusal to register the transfer.

SECTION 8—402. ASSURANCE THAT INDORSEMENTS ARE EFFECTIVE. (1) The issuer may require the following assurance that each necessary indorsement (Section 8—308) is genuine and effective

    (a) in all cases, a guarantee of the signature (subsection (1) of Section 8—312) of the person indorsing; and

    (b) where the indorsement is by an agent, appropriate assurance of authority to sign;

    (c) where the indorsement is by a fiduciary, appropriate evidence of appointment or incumbency;

    (d) where there is more than one fiduciary, reasonable assurance that all who are required to sign have done so;

    (e) where the indorsement is by a person not covered by any of the foregoing, assurance appropriate to the case corresponding as nearly as may be to the foregoing.

(2) A "guarantee of the signature" in subsection (1) means a guarantee signed by or on behalf of a person reasonably believed by the issuer to be responsible. The issuer may adopt standards with respect to responsibility provided such standards are not manifestly unreasonable.

(3) "Appropriate evidence of appointment or incumbency" in subsection (1) means
- (a) in the case of a fiduciary appointed or qualified by a court, a certificate issued by or under the direction or supervision of that court or an officer thereof and dated within sixty days before the date of presentation for transfer; or
- (b) in any other case, a copy of a document showing the appointment or a certificate issued by or on behalf of a person reasonably believed by the issuer to be responsible or, in the absence of such a document or certificate, other evidence reasonably deemed by the issuer to be appropriate. The issuer may adopt standards with respect to such evidence provided such standards are not manifestly unreasonable. The issuer is not charged with notice of the contents of any document obtained pursuant to this paragraph (b) except to the extent that the contents relate directly to the appoinment or incumbency.

(4) The issuer may elect to require reasonable assurance beyond that specified in this section but if it does so and for a purpose other than that specified in subsection 3 (b) both requires and obtains a copy of a will, trust, indenture, articles of co-partnership, by-laws or other controlling instrument it is charged with notice of all matters contained therein affecting the transfer.

Section 8—403. Limited Duty of Inquiry. (1) An issuer to whom a security is presented for registration is under a duty to inquire into adverse claims if
- (a) a written notification of an adverse claim is received at a time and in a manner which affords the issuer a reasonable opportunity to act on it prior to the issuance of a new, reissued or re-registered security and the notification identifies the claimant, the registered owner and the issue of which the security is a part and provides an address for communications directed to the claimant; or
- (b) the issuer is charged with notice of an adverse claim from a controlling instrument which it has elected to require under subsection (4) of Section 8—402.

(2) The issuer may discharge any duty of inquiry by any reasonable means, including notifying an adverse claimant by registered or certified mail at the address furnished by him or if there be no such address at his residence or regular place of business that the security has been presented for registration of transfer by a named person, and that the transfer will be registered unless within thirty days from the date of mailing the notification, either
- (a) an appropriate restraining order, injunction or other process issues from a court of competent jurisdiction; or
- (b) an indemnity bond sufficient in the issuer's judgment to protect the issuer and any transfer agent, registrar or other agent of the issuer involved, from any loss which it or they may suffer by complying with the adverse claim is filed with the issuer.

(3) Unless an issuer is charged with notice of an adverse claim from a controlling instrument which it has elected to require under subsection (4) of Section 8—402 or receives notification of an adverse claim under subsection (1) of this section, where a security presented for registration is indorsed by the appropriate person or persons the issuer is under no duty to inquire into adverse claims. In particular
- (a) an issuer registering a security in the name of a person who is a fiduciary or who is described as a fiduciary is not bound to inquire into the existence, extent, or correct description of the fiduciary relationship and thereafter the issuer may assume without inquiry that the newly registered owner continues to be the fiduciary until the issuer receives written notice that the fiduciary is no longer acting as such with respect to the particular security;
- (b) an issuer registering transfer on an indorsement by a fiduciary is not bound to inquire whether the transfer is made in compliance with a controlling instrument or with the law of the state having jurisdiction of the fiduciary relationship, including any law requiring the fiduciary to obtain court approval of the transfer; and

(c) the issuer is not charged with notice of the contents of any court record or file or other recorded or unrecorded documents even though the document is in its possession and even though the transfer is made on the indorsement of a fiduciary to the fiduciary himself or to his nominee.

SECTION 8—404. LIABILITY AND NON-LIABILITY FOR REGISTRATION. (1) Except as otherwise provided in any law relating to the collection of taxes, the issuer is not liable to the owner or any other person suffering loss as a result of the registration of a transfer of a security if

(a) there were on or with the security the necessary indorsements (Section 8—308); and

(b) the issuer had no duty to inquire into adverse claims or has discharged any such duty (Section 8—403).

(2) Where an issuer has registered a transfer of a security to a person not entitled to it the issuer on demand must deliver a like security to the true owner unless

(a) the registration was pursuant to subsection (1); or

(b) the owner is precluded from asserting any claim for registering the transfer under subsection (1) of the following section; or

(c) such delivery would result in overissue, in which case the issuer's liability is governed by Section 8—104.

SECTION 8—405. LOST, DESTROYED AND STOLEN SECURITIES. (1) Where a security has been lost, apparently destroyed or wrongfully taken and the owner fails to notify the issuer of that fact within a reasonable time after he has notice of it and the issuer registers a transfer of the security before receiving such a notification, the owner is precluded from asserting against the issuer any claim for registering the transfer under the preceding section or any claim to a new security under this section.

(2) Where the owner of a security claims that the security has been lost, destroyed or wrongfully taken, the issuer must issue a new security in place of the original security if the owner

(a) so requests before the issuer has notice that the security has been acquired by a bona fide purchaser; and

(b) files with the issuer a sufficient indemnity bond; and

(c) satisfies any other reasonable requirements imposed by the issuer.

(3) If, after the issue of the new security, a bona fide purchaser of the original security presents it for registration of transfer, the issuer must register the transfer unless registration would result in overissue, in which event the issuer's liability is governed by Section 8—104. In addition to any rights on the indemnity bond, the issuer may recover the new security from the person to whom it was issued or any person taking under him except a bona fide purchaser.

SECTION 8—406. DUTY OF AUTHENTICATING TRUSTEE, TRANSFER AGENT OR REGISTRAR. (1) Where a person acts as authenticating trustee, transfer agent, registrar, or other agent for an issuer in the registration of transfers of its securities or in the issue of new securities or in the cancellation of surrendered securities.

(a) he is under a duty to the issuer to exercise good faith and due diligence in performing his functions; and

(b) he has with regard to the particular functions he performs the same obligation to the holder or owner of the security and has the same rights and privileges as the issuer has in regard to those functions.

(2) Notice to an authenticating trustee, transfer agent, registrar or other such agent is notice to the issuer with respect to the functions performed by the agent.

ARTICLE 9

SECURED TRANSACTIONS; SALES OF ACCOUNTS, CONTRACT RIGHTS
AND CHATTEL PAPER

PART 1

SHORT TITLE, APPLICABILITY AND DEFINITIONS

SECTION 9—101. SHORT TITLE. This Article shall be known and may be cited as Uniform Commercial Code—Secured Transactions.

SECTION 9—102. POLICY AND SCOPE OF ARTICLE. (1) Except as otherwise provided in Section 9—103 on multiple state transactions and in Section 9—104 on excluded transactions, this Article applies so far as concerns any personal property and fixtures within the jurisdiction of this state

(a) to any transaction (regardless of its form) which is intended to create a security interest in personal property or fixtures including goods, documents, instruments, general intangibles, chattel paper, accounts or contract rights; and also

(b) to any sale of accounts, contract rights or chattel paper.

(2) This Article applies to security interests created by contract including pledge, assignment, chattel mortgage, chattel trust, trust deed, factor's lien, equipment trust, conditional sale, trust receipt, other lien or title retention contract and lease or consignment intended as security. This Article does not apply to statutory liens except as provided in Section 9—310.

(3) The application of this Article to a security interest in a secured obligation is not affected by the fact that the obligation is itself secured by a transaction or interest to which this Article does not apply.

NOTE: *The adoption of this Article should be accompanied by the repeal of existing statutes dealing with conditional sales, trust receipts, factor's liens where the factor is given a non-possessory lien, chattel mortgages, crop mortgages, mortgages on railroad equipment, assignment of accounts and generally statutes regulating security interests in personal property.*

Where the state has a retail installment selling act or small loan act, that legislation should be carefully examined to determine what changes in those acts are needed to conform them to this Article. This Article primarily sets out rules defining rights of a secured party against persons dealing with the debtor; it does not prescribe regulations and controls which may be necessary to curb abuses arising in the small loan business or in the financing of consumer purchases on credit. Accordingly there is no intention to repeal existing regulatory acts in those fields. See Section 9—203(2) and the Note thereto.

SECTION 9—103. ACCOUNTS, CONTRACT RIGHTS, GENERAL INTANGIBLES AND EQUIPMENT RELATING TO ANOTHER JURISDICTION; AND INCOMING GOODS ALREADY SUBJECT TO A SECURITY INTEREST. (1) If the office where the assignor accounts or contract rights keeps his records concerning them is in this state, the validity and perfection of a security interest therein and the possibility and effect of proper filing is governed by this Article; otherwise by the law (including the conflict of laws rules) of the jurisdiction where such office is located.

(2) If the chief place of business of a debtor is in this state, this Article governs the validity and perfection of a security interest and the possibility and effect of proper filing with regard to general intangibles or with regard to goods of a type which are normally used in more than one jurisdiction (such as automotive equipment, rolling stock, airplanes, road building equipment, commercial harvesting equipment, construction machinery and the like) if such goods are classified as equipment or classified as inventory by reason of their being leased by the debtor to others. Otherwise, the law (including the conflict of laws rules) of the jurisdiction where

such chief place of business is located shall govern. If the chief place of business is located in a jurisdiction which does not provide for perfection of the security interest by filing or recording in that jurisdiction, then the security interest may be perfected by filing in this state. [For the purpose of determining the validity and perfection of a security interest in an airplane, the chief place of business of a debtor who is a foreign air carrier under the Federal Aviation Act of 1958, as amended, is the designated office of the agent upon whom service of process may be made on behalf of the debtor.]

(3) If personal property other than that governed by subsections (1) and (2) is already subject to a security interest when it is brought into this state, the validity of the security interest in this state is to be determined by the law (including the conflict of laws rules) of the jurisdiction where the property was when the security interest attached. However, if the parties to the transaction understood at the time that the security interest attached that the property would be kept in this state and it was brought into this state within 30 days after the security interest attached for purposes other than transportation through this state, then the validity of the security interest in this state is to be determined by the law of this state. If the security interest was already perfected under the law of the jurisdiction where the property was when the security interest attached and before being brought into this state, the security interest continues perfected in this state for four months and also thereafter if within the four month period it is perfected in this state. The security interest may also be perfected in this state after the expiration of the four month period; in such case perfection dates from the time of perfection in this state. If the security interest was not perfected under the law of the jurisdiction where the property was when the security interest attached and before being brought into this state, it may be perfected in this state; in such case perfection dates from the time of perfection in this state.

(4) Notwithstanding subsections (2) and (3), if personal property is covered by a certificate of title issued under a statute of this state or any other jurisdiction which requires indication on a certificate of title of any security interest in the property as a condition of perfection, then the perfection is governed by the law of the jurisdiction which issued the certificate.

[(5) Notwithstanding subsection (1) and Section 9–302, if the office where the assignor of accounts or contract rights keeps his records concerning them is not located in a jurisdiction which is a part of the United States, its territories or possessions, and the accounts or contract rights are within the jurisdiction of this state or the transaction which creates the security interest otherwise bears an appropriate relation to this state, this Article governs the validiy and perfection of the security interest and the security interest may only be perfected by notification to the account debtor.]

NOTE: *The last sentence of subsection (2) and subsection (5) are bracketed to indicate optional enactment. In states engaging in financing of airplanes of foreign carriers and of international open accounts receivable, bracketed language will be of value. In other states not engaging in financing of this type, the bracketed language may not be considered neecessary.*

SECTION 9–104.　TRANSACTIONS EXCLUDED FROM ARTICLE.　This Article does not apply

  (a) to a security interest subject to any statute of the United States such as the Ship Mortgage Act, 1920, to the extent that such statute governs the rights of parties to and third parties affected by transactions in particular types of property; or

  (b) to a landlord's lien; or

  (c) to a lien given by statute or other rule of law for services or materials except as provided in Section 9–310 on priority of such liens; or

  (d) to a transfer of a claim for wages, salary or other compensation of an employee; or

  (e) to an equipment trust covering railway rolling stock; or

  (f) to a sale of accounts, contract rights or chattel paper as part of a sale of the business out of which they arose, or an assignment of accounts, contract rights or chattel paper which is for the purpose of collection only, or a transfer of a contract right to an assignee who is also to do the performance under the contract; or

(g) to a transfer of an interest or claim in or under any policy of insurance; or

(h) to a right represented by a judgment; or

(i) to any right of set-off; or

(j) except to the extent that provision is made for fixtures in Section 9—313, to the creation or transfer of an interest in or lien on real estate, including a lease or rents thereunder; or

(k) to a transfer in whole or in part of any of the following: any claim arising out of tort; any deposit, savings, passbook or like account maintained with a bank, savings and loan association, credit union or like organization.

SECTION 9—105. DEFINITIONS AND INDEX OF DEFINITIONS. (1) In this Article unless the context otherwise requires:

(a) "Account debtor" means the person who is obligated on an account, chattel paper, contract right or general intangible;

(b) "Chattel paper" means a writing or writings which evidence both a monetary obligation and a security interest in or a lease of specific goods. When a transaction is evidenced both by such a security agreement or a lease and by an instrument or a series of instruments, the group of writings taken together constitutes chattel paper;

(c) "Collateral" means the property subject to a security interest, and includes accounts, contract rights and chattel paper which have been sold;

(d) "Debtor" means the person who owes payment or other performance of the obligation secured, whether or not he owns or has rights in the collateral, and includes the seller of accounts, contract rights or chattel paper. Where the debtor and the owner of the collateral are not the same person, the term "debtor" means the owner of the collateral in any provision of the Article dealing with the collateral, the obligor in any provision dealing with the obligation, and may include both where the context so requires;

(e) "Document" means document of title as defined in the general definitions of Article 1 (Section 1—201);

(f) "Goods" includes all things which are movable at the time the security interest attaches or which are fixtures (Section 9—313), but does not include money, documents, instruments, accounts, chattel paper, general intangibles, contract rights and other things in action. "Goods" also include the unborn young of animals and growing crops;

(g) "Instrument" means a negotiable instrument (defined in Section 3—104), or a security (defined in Section 8—102) or any other writing which evidences a right to the payment of money and is not itself a security agreement or lease and is of a type which is in ordinary course of business transferred by delivery with any necessary indorsement or assignment;

(h) "Security agreement" means an agreement which creates or provides for a security interest;

(i) "Secured party" means a lender, seller or other person in whose favor there is a security interest, including a person to whom accounts, contract rights or chattel paper have been sold. When the holders of obligations issued under an indenture of trust, equipment trust agreement or the like are represented by a trustee or other person, the representative is the secured party.

(2) Other definitions applying to this Article and the sections in which they appear are:

"Account".	Section 9—106.
"Consumer goods".	Section 9—109(1).
"Contract right".	Section 9—106.
"Equipment".	Section 9—109(2).
"Farm products".	Section 9—109(3).
"General intangibles".	Section 9—106.
"Inventory".	Section 9—109(4).
"Lien creditor".	Section 9—301(3).
"Proceeds".	Section 9—306(1).
"Purchase money security interest".	Section 9—107.

(3) The following definitions in other Articles apply to this Article:

"Check".	Section 3—104.
"Contract for sale".	Section 2—106.
"Holder in due course".	Section 3—302.
"Note".	Section 3—104.
"Sale".	Section 2—106.

(4) In addition Article 1 contains general definitions and principles of construction and interpretation applicable throughout this Article.

SECTION 9—106. DEFINITIONS: "ACCOUNT"; "CONTRACT RIGHT"; "GENERAL INTANGIBLES". "Account" means any right to payment for goods sold or leased or for services rendered which is not evidenced by an instrument or chattel paper. "Contract right" means any right to payment under a contract not yet earned by performance and not evidenced by an instrument or chattel paper. "General intangibles" means any personal property (including things in action) other than goods, accounts, contract rights, chattel paper, documents and instruments.

SECTION 9—107. DEFINITIONS: "PURCHASE MONEY SECURITY INTEREST". A security interest is a "purchase money security interest" to the extent that it is

(a) taken or retained by the seller of the collateral to secure all or part of i⁺ price; or

(b) taken by a person who by making advances or incurring an obligation gives value to enable the debtor to acquire rights in or the use of collateral if such value is in fact so used.

SECTION 9—108. WHEN AFTER-ACQUIRED COLLATERAL NOT SECURITY FOR ANTECEDENT DEBT. Where a secured party makes an advance, incurs an obligation, releases a perfected security interest, or otherwise gives new value which is to be secured in whole or in part by after-acquired property his security interest in the after-acquired collateral shall be deemed to be taken for new value and not as security for an antecedent debt if the debtor acquires his rights in such collateral either in the ordinary course of his business or under a contract of purchase made pursuant to the security agreement within a reasonable time after new value is given.

SECTION 9—109. CLASSIFICATION OF GOODS; "CONSUMER GOODS"; "EQUIPMENT"; "FARM PRODUCTS"; "INVENTORY". Goods are

(1) "consumer goods" if they are used or bought for use primarily for personal, family or household purposes;

(2) "equipment" if they are used or bought for use primarily in business (including farming or a profession) or by a debtor who is a non-profit organization or a governmental subdivision or agency or if the goods are not included in the definitions of inventory, farm products or consumer goods;

(3) "farm products" if they are crops or livestock or supplies used or produced in farming operations or if they are products of crops or livestock in their unmanufactured states (such as ginned cotton, wool-clip, maple syrup, milk and eggs), and if they are in the possession of a debtor engaged in raising, fattening, grazing or other farming operations. If goods are farm products they are neither equipment nor inventory;

(4) "inventory" if they are held by a person who holds them for sale or lease or to be furnished under contracts of service or if he has so furnished them, or if they are raw materials, work in process or materials used or consumed in a business. Inventory of a person is not to be classified as his equipment.

SECTION 9—110. SUFFICIENCY OF DESCRIPTION. For the purposes of this Article any description of personal property or real estate is sufficient whether or not it is specific if it reasonably identifies what is described.

SECTION 9—111. APPLICABILITY OF BULK TRANSFER LAWS. The creation of a security interest is not a bulk transfer under Article 6 (see Section 6—103).

SECTION 9—112. WHERE COLLATERAL IS NOT OWNED BY DEBTOR. Unless otherwise agreed, when a secured party knows that collateral is owned by a person who is not the debtor, the owner of the collateral is entitled to receive from the secured party any surplus under Section 9—502(2) or under Section 9—504(1), and is not liable for the debt or for any deficiency after resale, and he has the same right as the debtor

(a) to receive statements under Section 9—208;

(b) to receive notice of and to object to a secured party's proposal to retain the collateral in satisfaction of the indebtedness under Section 9—505;

(c) to redeem the collateral under Section 9—506;

(d) to obtain injunctive or other relief under Section 9—507(1); and

(e) to recover losses caused to him under Section 9—208(2).

SECTION 9—113. SECURITY INTERESTS ARISING UNDER ARTICLE ON SALES. A security interest arising solely under the Article on Sales (Article 2) is subject to the provisions of this Article except that to the extent that and so long as the debtor does not have or does not lawfully obtain possession of the goods

(a) no security agreement is necessary to make the security interest enforceable; and

(b) no filing is required to perfect the security interest; and

(c) the rights of the secured party on default by the debtor are governed by the Article on Sales (Article 2).

PART 2

VALIDITY OF SECURITY AGREEMENT AND RIGHTS OF PARTIES THERETO

SECTION 9—201. GENERAL VALIDITY OF SECURITY AGREEMENT. Except as otherwise provided by this Act a security agreement is effective according to its terms between the parties, against purchasers of the collateral and against creditors. Nothing in this Article validates any charge or practice illegal under any statute or regulation thereunder governing usury, small loans, retail installment sales, or the like, or extends the application of any such statute or regulation to any transaction not otherwise subject thereto.

SECTION 9—202. TITLE TO COLLATERAL IMMATERIAL. Each provision of this Article with regard to rights, obligations and remedies applies whether title to collateral is in the secured party or in the debtor.

SECTION 9—203. ENFORCEABILITY OF SECURITY INTEREST; PROCEEDS, FORMAL REQUISITES. (1) Subject to the provisions of Section 4—208 on the security interest of a collecting bank and Section 9—113 on a security interest arising under the Article on Sales, a security interest is not enforceable against the debtor or third parties unless

(a) the collateral is in the possession of the secured party; or

(b) the debtor has signed a security agreement which contains a description of the collateral and in addition, when the security interest covers crops or oil, gas or minerals to be extracted or timber to be cut, a description of the land concerned. In describing collateral, the word "proceeds" is sufficient without further description to cover proceeds of any character.

(2) A transaction, although subject to this Article, is also subject to ....*, and in the case of conflict between the provisions of this Article and any such statute, the provisions of such statute control. Failure to comply with any applicable statute has only the effect which is specified therein.

NOTE: *At* * *in subsection (2) insert reference to any local statute regulating small loans, retail installments sales and the like.*

The foregoing subsection (2) is designed to make it clear that certain transactions, although subject to this Article, must also comply with other applicable legislation.

This Article is designed to regulate all the "security" aspects of transactions within its scope. There is, however, much regulatory legislation, particularly in the consumer field, which supplements this Article and should not be repealed by its enactment. Examples are small loan acts, retail installment selling acts and the like. Such acts may provide for licensing and rate regulation and may prescribe particular forms of contract. Such provisions should remain in force despite the enactment of this Article. On the other hand if a Retail Installment Selling Act contains provisions on filing, rights on default, etc., such provisions should be repealed as inconsistent with this Article.

SECTION 9—204. WHEN SECURITY INTEREST ATTACHES; AFTER-ACQUIRED PROPERTY; FUTURE ADVANCES. (1) A security interest cannot attach until there is agreement (subsection (3) of Section 1—201) that it attach and value is given and the debtor has rights in the collateral. It attaches as soon as all of the events in the preceding sentence have taken place unless explicit agreement postpones the time of attaching.

(2) For the purposes of this section the debtor has no rights

    (a) in crops until they are planted or otherwise become growing crops, in the young of livestock until they are conceived;

    (b) in fish until caught, in oil, gas or minerals until they are extracted, in timber until it is cut;

    (c) in a contract right until the contract has been made;

    (d) in an account until it comes into existence.

(3) Except as provided in subsection (4) a security agreement may provide that collateral, whenever acquired, shall secure all obligations covered by the security agreement.

(4) No security interest attaches under an after-acquired property clause

    (a) to crops which become such more than one year after the security agreement is executed except that a security interest in crops which is given in conjunction with a lease or a land purchase or improvement transaction evidenced by a contract, mortgage or deed of trust may if so agreed attach to crops to be grown on the land concerned during the period of such real estate transaction;

    (b) to consumer goods other than accessions (Section 9—314) when given as additional security unless the debtor acquires rights in them within ten days after the secured party gives value.

(5) Obligations covered by a security agreement may include future advances or other value whether or not the advances or value are given pursuant to commitment.

SECTION 9—205. USE OR DISPOSITION OF COLLATERAL WITHOUT ACCOUNTING PERMISSIBLE. A security interest is not invalid or fraudulent against creditors by reason of liberty in the debtor to use, commingle or dispose of all or part of the collateral (including returned or repossessed goods) or to collect or compromise accounts, contract rights or chattel paper, or to accept the return of goods or make repossessions, or to use, commingle or dispose of proceeds, or by reason of the failure of the secured party to require the debtor to account for proceeds or replace collateral. This section does not relax the requirements of possession where perfection of a security interest depends upon possession of the collateral by the secured party or by a bailee.

SECTION 9—206. AGREEMENT NOT TO ASSERT DEFENSES AGAINST ASSIGNEE; MODIFICATION OF SALES WARRANTIES WHERE SECURITY AGREEMENT EXISTS. (1) Subject to any statute or decision which establishes a different rule for buyers or lessees of consumer goods, an agreement by a buyer or lessee that he will not assert against an assignee any claim or defense which he may have against the seller or lessor is enforceable by an assignee who takes his assignment for value, in good faith and without notice of a claim or defense, except as to defenses of a type which may be asserted against a holder in due course of a negotiable instrument under the Article on Commercial Paper (Article 3). A buyer who as part of one transaction signs both a negotiable instrument and a security agreement makes such an agreement.

(2) When a seller retains a purchase money security interest in goods the Article on Sales (Article 2) governs the sale and any disclaimer, limitation or modification of the seller's warranties.

SECTION 9—207. RIGHTS AND DUTIES WHEN COLLATERAL IS IN SECURED PARTY'S POSSESSION. (1) A secured party must use reasonable care in the custody and preservation of collateral in his possession. In the case of an instrument or chattel paper reasonable care includes taking necessary steps to preserve rights against prior parties unless otherwise agreed.

(2) Unless otherwise agreed, when collateral is in the secured party's possession

    (a) reasonable expenses (including the cost of any insurance and payment of taxes or other charges) incurred in the custody, preservation, use or operation of the collateral are chargeable to the debtor and are secured by the collateral;

    (b) the risk of accidental loss or damage is on the debtor to the extent of any deficiency in any effective insurance coverage;

(c) the secured party may hold as additional security any increase or profits (except money) received from the collateral, but money so received, unless remitted to the debtor, shall be applied in reduction of the secured obligation;

(d) the secured party must keep the collateral identifiable but fungible collateral may be commingled;

(e) the secured party may repledge the collateral upon terms which do not impair the debtor's right to redeem it.

(3) A secured party is liable for any loss caused by his failure to meet any obligation imposed by the preceding subsections but does not lose his security interest.

(4) A secured party may use or operate the collateral for the purpose of preserving the collateral or its value or pursuant to the order of a court of appropriate jurisdiction or, except in the case of consumer goods, in the manner and to the extent provided in the security agreement.

SECTION 9—208. REQUEST FOR STATEMENT OF ACCOUNTS OR LIST OF COLLATERAL. (1) A debtor may sign a statement indicating what he believes to be the aggregate amount of unpaid indebtedness as of a specified date and may send it to the secured party with a request that the statement be approved or corrected and returned to the debtor. When the security agreement or any other record kept by the secured party identifies the collateral a debtor may similarly request the secured party to approve or correct a list of the collateral.

(2) The secured party must comply with such a request within two weeks after receipt by sending a written correction or approval. If the secured party claims a security interest in all of a particular type of collateral owned by the debtor he may indicate that fact in his reply and need not approve or correct an itemized list of such collateral. If the secured party without reasonable excuse fails to comply he is liable for any loss caused to the debtor thereby; and if the debtor has properly included in his request a good faith statement of the obligation or a list of the collateral or both the secured party may claim a security interest only as shown in the statement against persons misled by his failure to comply. If he no longer has an interest in the obligation or collateral at the time the request is received he must disclose the name and address of any successor in interest known to him and he is liable for any loss caused to the debtor as a result of failure to disclose. A successor in interest is not subject to this section until a request is received by him.

(3) A debtor is entitled to such a statement once every six months without charge. The secured party may require payment of a charge not exceeding $10 for each additional statement furnished.

PART 3

RIGHTS OF THIRD PARTIES; PERFECTED AND UNPERFECTED SECURITY INTERESTS;
RULES OF PRIORITY

SECTION 9—301. PERSONS WHO TAKE PRIORITY OVER UNPERFECTED SECURITY INTERESTS; "LIEN CREDITOR". (1) Except as otherwise provided in subsection (2), an unperfected security interest is subordinate to the rights of

(a) persons entitled to priority under Section 9—312;

(b) a person who becomes a lien creditor without knowledge of the security interest and before it is perfected;

(c) in the case of goods, instruments, documents, and chattel paper, a person who is not a secured party and who is a transferee in bulk or other buyer not in ordinary course of business to the extent that he gives value and receives delivery of the collateral without knowledge of the security interest and before it is perfected;

(d) in the case of accounts, contract rights, and general intangibles, a person who is not a secured party and who is a transferee to the extent that he gives value without knowledge of the security interest and before it is perfected.

(2) If the secured party files with respect to a purchase money security interest

before or within ten days after the collateral comes into possession of the debtor, he takes priority over the rights of a transferee in bulk or of a lien creditor which arise between the time the security interest attaches and the time of filing.

(3) A "lien creditor" means a creditor who has acquired a lien on the property involved by attachment, levy or the like and includes an assignee for benefit of creditors from the time of assignment, and a trustee in bankruptcy from the date of the filing of the petition or a receiver in equity from the time of appointment. Unless all the creditors represented had knowledge of the security interest such a representative of creditors is a lien creditor without knowledge even though he personally has knowledge of the security interest.

Section 9—302. When Filing Is Required to Perfect Security Interest; Security Interests to Which Filing Provisions of This Article Do Not Apply. (1) A financing statement must be filed to perfect all security interests except the following:

(a) a security interest in collateral in possession of the secured party under Section 9—305;

(b) a security interest temporarily perfected in instruments or documents without delivery under Section 9—304 or in proceeds for a 10 day period under Section 9—306;

(c) a purchase money security interest in farm equipment having a purchase price not in excess of $2500; but filing is required for a fixture under Section 9—313 or for a motor vehicle required to be licensed;

(d) a purchase money security interest in consumer goods; but filing is required for a fixture under Section 9—313 or for a motor vehicle required to be licensed;

(e) an assignment of accounts or contract rights which does not alone or in conjunction with other assignments to the same assignee transfer a significant part of the outstanding accounts or contract rights of the assignor;

(f) a security interest of a collecting bank (Section 4—208) or arising under the Article on Sales (see Section 9—113) or covered in subsection (3) of this section.

(2) If a secured party assigns a perfected security interest, no filing under this Article is required in order to continue the perfected status of the security interest against creditors of and transferees from the original debtor.

(3) The filing provisions of this Article do not apply to a security interest in property subject to a statute

(a) of the United States which provides for a national registration or filing of all security interests in such property; or

Note: *States to select either Alternative A or Alternative B.*

Alternative A—

(b) of this state which provides for central filing of, or which requires indication on a certificate of title of, such security interests in such property.

Alternative B—

(b) of this state which provides for central filing of security interests in such property, or in a motor vehicle which is not inventory held for sale for which a certificate of title is required under the statutes of this state if a notation of such a security interest can be indicated by a public official on a certificate or a duplicate thereof.

(4) A security interest in property covered by a statute described in subsection (3) can be perfected only by registration or filing under that statute or by indication of the security interest on a certificate of title or a duplicate thereof by a public official.

Section 9—303. When Security Interest Is Perfected; Continuity of Perfection. (1) A security interest is perfected when it has attached and when all of the applicable steps required for perfection have been taken. Such steps are specified in Sections 9—302, 9—304, 9—305 and 9—306. If such steps are taken before the security interest attaches, it is perfected at the time when it attaches.

(2) If a security interest is originally perfected in any way permitted under this Article and is subsequently perfected in some other way under this Article, without an intermediate period when it was unperfected, the security interest shall be deemed to be perfected continuously for the purposes of this Article.

SECTION 9—304. PERFECTION OF SECURITY INTERESTS IN INSTRUMENTS, DOCUMENTS, AND GOODS COVERED BY DOCUMENTS; PERFECTION BY PERMISSIVE FILING; TEMPORARY PERFECTION WITHOUT FILING OR TRANSFER OF POSSESSION. (1) A security interest in chattel paper or negotiable documents may be perfected by filing. A security interest in instruments (other than instruments which constitute part of chattel paper) can be perfected only by the secured party's taking possession, except as provided in subsections (4) and (5).

(2) During the period that goods are in the possession of the issuer of a negotiable document therefor, a security interest in the goods is perfected by perfecting a security interest in the document, and any security interest in the goods otherwise perfected during such period is subject thereto.

(3) A security interest in goods in the possession of a bailee other than one who has issued a negotiable document therefor is perfected by issuance of a document in the name of the secured party or by the bailee's receipt of notification of the secured party's interest or by filing as to the goods.

(4) A security interest in instruments or negotiable documents is perfected without filing or the taking of possession for a period of 21 days from the time it attaches to the extent that it arises for new value given under a written security agreement.

(5) A security interest remains perfected for a period of 21 days without filing where a secured party having a perfected security interest in an instrument, a negotiable document or goods in possession of a bailee other than one who has issued a negotiable document therefor

    (a) makes available to the debtor the goods or documents representing the goods for the purpose of ultimate sale or exchange or for the purpose of loading, unloading, storing, shipping, transshipping, manufacturing, processing or otherwise dealing with them in a manner preliminary to their sale or exchange; or

    (b) delivers the instrument to the debtor for the purpose of ultimate sale or exchange or of presentation, collection, renewal or registration of transfer.

(6) After the 21 day period in subsections (4) and (5) perfection depends upon compliance with applicable provisions of this Article.

SECTION 9—305. WHEN POSSESSION BY SECURED PARTY PERFECTS SECURITY INTEREST WITHOUT FILING. A security interest in letters of credit and advices of credit (subsection (2)(a) of Section 5—116), goods, instruments, negotiable documents or chattel paper may be perfected by the secured party's taking possession of the collateral. If such collateral other than goods covered by a negotiable document is held by a bailee, the secured party is deemed to have possession from the time the bailee receives notification of the secured party's interest. A security interest is perfected by possession from the time possession is taken without relation back and continues only so long as possession is retained, unless otherwise specified in this Article. The security interest may be otherwise perfected as provided in this Article before or after the period of possession by the secured party.

SECTION 9—306. "PROCEEDS"; SECURED PARTY'S RIGHTS ON DISPOSITION OF COLLATERAL. (1) "Proceeds" includes whatever is received when collateral or proceeds is sold, exchanged, collected or otherwise disposed of. The term also includes the account arising when the right to payment is earned under a contract right. Money, checks and the like are "cash proceeds". All other proceeds are "non-cash proceeds".

(2) Except where this Article otherwise provides, a security interest continues in collateral notwithstanding sale, exchange or other disposition thereof by the debtor unless his action was authorized by the secured party in the security agreement or otherwise, and also continues in any identifiable proceeds including collections received by the debtor.

(3) The security interest in proceeds is a continuously perfected security interest if the interest in the original collateral was perfected but it ceases to be a perfected security interest and becomes unperfected ten days after receipt of the proceeds by the debtor unless

    (a) a filed financing statement covering the original collateral also covers proceeds; or

    (b) the security interest in the proceeds is perfected before the expiration of the ten day period.

(4) In the event of insolvency proceedings instituted by or against a debtor, a secured party with a perfected security interest in proceeds has a perfected security interest

(a) in identifiable non-cash proceeds;

(b) in identifiable cash proceeds in the form of money which is not commingled with other money or deposited in a bank account prior to the insolvency proceedings;

(c) in identifiable cash proceeds in the form of checks and the like which are not deposited in a bank account prior to the insolvency proceedings; and

(d) in all cash and bank accounts of the debtor, if other cash proceeds have been commingled or deposited in a bank account, but the perfected security interest under this paragraph (d) is

(i) subject to any right of set-off; and

(ii) limited to an amount not greater than the amount of any cash proceeds received by the debtor within ten days before the institution of the insolvency proceedings and commingled or deposited in a bank account prior to the insolvency proceedings less the amount of cash proceeds received by the debtor and paid over to the secured party during the ten day period.

(5) If a sale of goods results in an account or chattel paper which is transferred by the seller to a secured party, and if the goods are returned to or are repossessed by the seller or the secured party, the following rules determine priorities:

(a) If the goods were collateral at the time of sale for an indebtedness of the seller which is still unpaid, the original security interest attaches again to the goods and continues as a perfected security interest if it was perfected at the time when the goods were sold. If the security interest was originally perfected by a filing which is still effective, nothing further is required to continue the perfected status; in any other case, the secured party must take possession of the returned or repossessed goods or must file.

(b) An unpaid transferee of the chattel paper has a security interest in the goods against the transferor. Such security interest is prior to a security interest asserted under paragraph (a) to the extent that the transferee of the chattel paper was entitled to priority under Section 9–308.

(c) An unpaid transferee of the account has a security interest in the goods against the transferor. Such security interest is subordinate to a security interest asserted under paragraph (a).

(d) A security interest of an unpaid transferee asserted under paragraph (b) or (c) must be perfected for protection against creditors of the transferor and purchasers of the returned or repossessed goods.

SECTION 9–307. PROTECTION OF BUYERS OF GOODS. (1) A buyer in ordinary course of business (subsection (9) of Section 1–201) other than a person buying farm products from a person engaged in farming operations takes free of a security interest created by his seller even though the security interest is perfected and even though the buyer knows of its existence.

(2) In the case of consumer goods and in the case of farm equipment having an original purcase price not in excess of $2500 (other than fixtures, see Section 9–313), a buyer takes free of a security interest even though perfected if he buys without knowledge of the security interest, for value and for his own personal, family or household purposes or his own farming operations unless prior to the purchase the secured party has filed a financing statement covering such goods.

SECTION 9–308. PURCHASE OF CHATTEL PAPER AND NON-NEGOTIABLE INSTRUMENTS. A purchaser of chattel paper or a non-negotiable instrument who gives new value and takes possession of it in the ordinary course of his business and without knowledge that the specific paper or instrument is subject to a security interest has priority over a security interest which is perfected under Section 9–304 (permissive filing and temporary perfection). A purchaser of chattel paper who gives new value and takes possession of it in the ordinary course of his business has priority over a security interest in chattel paper which is claimed merely as proceeds of inventory subject to a security interest (Section 9–306), even though he knows that the specific paper is subject to the security interest.

(a) in the order of filing if both are perfected by filing, regardless of which security interest attached first under Section 9—204(1) and whether it attached before or after filing;

(b) in the order of perfection unless both are perfected by filing, regardless of which security interest attached first under Section 9—204(1) and, in the case of a filed security interest, whether it attached before or after filing; and

(c) in the order of attachment under Section 9—204(1) so long as neither is perfected.

(6) For the purpose of the priority rules of the immediately preceding subsection, a continuously perfected security interest shall be treated at all times as if perfected by filing if it was originally so perfected and it shall be treated at all times as if perfected otherwise than by filing if it was originally perfected otherwise than by filing.

SECTION 9—313. PRIORITY OF SECURITY INTERESTS IN FIXTURES. (1) The rules of this section do not apply to goods incorporated into a structure in the manner of lumber, bricks, tile, cement, glass, metal work and the like and no security interest in them exists under this Article unless the structure remains personal property under applicable law. The law of this state other than this Act determines whether and when other goods become fixtures. This Act does not prevent creation of an encumbrance upon fixtures or real estate pursuant to the law applicable to real estate.

(2) A security interest which attaches to goods before they become fixtures takes priority as to the goods over the claims of all persons who have an interest in the real estate except as stated in subsection (4).

(3) A security interest which attaches to goods after they become fixtures is valid against all persons subsequently acquiring interests in the real estate except as stated in subsection (4) but is invalid against any person with an interest in the real estate at the time the security interest attaches to the goods who has not in writing consented to the security interest or disclaimed an interest in the goods as fixtures.

(4) The security interests described in subsections (2) and (3) do not take priority over

(a) a subsequent purchaser for value of any interest in the real estate; or

(b) a creditor with a lien on the real estate subsequently obtained by judicial proceedings; or

(c) a creditor with a prior encumbrance of record on the real estate to the extent that he makes subsequent advances

if the subsequent purchase is made, the lien by judicial proceedings is obtained, or the subsequent advance under the prior encumbrance is made or contracted for without knowledge of the security interest and before it is perfected. A purchaser of the real estate at a foreclosure sale other than an encumbrancer, purchasing at his own foreclosure sale is a subsequent purchaser within this section.

(5) When under subsections (2) or (3) and (4) a secured party has priority over the claims of all persons who have interests in the real estate, he may, on default, subject to the provisions of Part 5, remove his collateral from the real estate but he must reimburse any encumbrancer or owner of the real estate who is not the debtor and who has not otherwise agreed for the cost of repair of any physical injury, but not for any diminution in value of the real estate caused by the absence of the goods removed or by any necessity for replacing them. A person entitled to reimbursement may refuse permission to remove until the secured party gives adequate security for the performance of this obligation.

SECTION 9—314. ACCESSIONS. (1) A security interest in goods which attaches before they are installed in or affixed to other goods takes priority as to the goods installed or affixed (called in this section "accessions") over the claims of all persons to the whole except as stated in subsection (3) and subject to Section 9—315(1).

(2) A security interest which attaches to goods after they become part of a whole is valid against all persons subsequently acquiring interests in the whole except as stated in subsection (3) but is invalid against any person with an interest in the whole at the time the security interest attaches to the goods who has not in writing consented to the security interest or disclaimed an interest in the goods as part of the whole.

Uniform Commercial Code

SECTION 9—309. PROTECTION OF PURCHASERS OF INSTRUMENTS AND DOCUMENTS. ing in this Article limits the rights of a holder in due course of a negotiable ment (Section 3—302) or a holder to whom a negotiable document of title h; duly negotiated (Section 7—501) or a bona fide purchaser of a security (, 8—301) and such holders or purchasers take priority over an earlier security i\ even though perfected. Filing under this Article does not constitute notice (security interest to such holders or purchasers.

SECTION 9—310. PRIORITY OF CERTAIN LIENS ARISING BY OPERATION OF LAW. \ a person in the ordinary course of his business furnishes services or materials respect to goods subject to a security interest, a lien upon goods in the possessio such person given by statute or rule of law for such materials or services takes \ ority over a perfected security interest unless the lien is statutory and the sta\ expressly provides otherwise.

SECTION 9—311. ALIENABILITY OF DEBTOR'S RIGHTS: JUDICIAL PROCESS. The debt(rights in collateral may be voluntarily or involuntarily transferred (by way of s; creation of a security interest, attachment, levy, garnishment or other judici process) notwithstanding a provision in the security agreement prohibiting a1 transfer or making the transfer constitute a default.

SECTION 9—312. PRIORITIES AMONG CONFLICTING SECURITY INTERESTS IN THE SAM COLLATERAL. (1) The rules of priority stated in the following sections shall gover1 where applicable: Section 4—208 with respect to the security interest of collecting banks in items being collected, accompanying documents and proceeds; Section 9—301 on certain priorities; Section 9—304 on goods covered by documents; Section 9—306 on proceeds and repossessions; Section 9—307 on buyers of goods; Section 9—308 on possessory against non-possessory interests in chattel paper or non-negotiable instruments; Section 9—309 on security interests in negotiable instruments, documents or securities; Section 9—310 on priorities between perfected security interests and liens by operation of law; Section 9—313 on security interests in fixtures as against interests in real estate; Section 9—314 on security interests in accessions as against interest in goods; Section 9—315 on conflicting security interests where goods lose their identity or become part of a product; and Section 9—316 on contractual subordination.

(2) A perfected security interest in crops for new value given to enable the debtor to produce the crops during the production season and given not more than three months before the crops become growing crops by planting or otherwise takes priority over an earlier perfected security interest to the extent that such earlier interest secures obligations due more than six months before the crops become growing crops by planting or otherwise, even though the person giving new value had knowledge of the earlier security interest.

(3) A purchase money security interest in inventory collateral has priority over a conflicting security interest in the same collateral if

(a) the purchase money security interest is perfected at the time the debtor receives possession of the collateral; and

(b) any secured party whose security interest is known to the holder of the purchase money security interest or who, prior to the date of the filing made by the holder of the purchase money security interest, had filed a financing statement covering the same items or type of inventory, has received notification of the purchase money security interest before the debtor receives possession of the collateral covered by the purchase money security interest; and

(c) such notification states that the person giving the notice has or expects to acquire a purchase money security interest in inventory of the debtor, describing such inventory by item or type.

(4) A purchase money security interest in collateral other than inventory has priority over a conflicting security interest in the same collateral if the purchase money security interest is perfected at the time the debtor receives possession of the collateral or within ten days thereafter.

(5) In all cases not governed by other rules stated in this section (including cases of purchase money security interests which do not qualify for the special priorities set forth in subsections (3) and (4) of this section), priority between conflicting security interests in the same collateral shall be determined as follows:

(3) The security interests described in subsections (1) and (2) do not take priority over
  (a) a subsequent purchaser for value of any interest in the whole; or
  (b) a creditor with a lien on the whole subsequently obtained by judicial proceedings; or
  (c) a creditor with a prior perfected security interest in the whole to the extent that he makes subsequent advances

if the subsequent purchase is made, the lien by judicial proceedings obtained or the subsequent advance under the prior perfected security interest is made or contracted for without knowledge of the security interest and before it is perfected. A purchaser of the whole at a foreclosure sale other than the holder of a perfected security interest purchasing at his own foreclosure sale is a subsequent purchaser within this section.

(4) When under subsections (1) or (2) and (3) a secured party has an interest in accessions which has priority over the claims of all persons who have interests in the whole, he may on default subject to the provisions of Part 5 remove his collateral from the whole but he must reimburse any encumbrancer or owner of the whole who is not the debtor and who has not otherwise agreed for the cost of repair of any physical injury but not for any diminution in value of the whole caused by the absence of the goods removed or by any necessity for replacing them. A person entitled to reimbursement may refuse permission to remove until the secured party gives adequate security for the performance of this obligation.

SECTION 9–315. PRIORITY WHEN GOODS ARE COMMINGLED OR PROCESSED. (1) If a security interest in goods was perfected and subsequently the goods or a part thereof have become part of a product or mass, the security interest continues in the product or mass if
  (a) the goods are so manufactured, processed, assembled or commingled that their identity is lost in the product or mass; or
  (b) a financing statement covering the original goods also covers the product into which the goods have been manufactured, processed or assembled.

In a case to which paragraph (b) applies, no separate security interest in that part of the original goods which has been manufactured, processed or assembled into the product may be claimed under Section 9–314.

(2) When under subsection (1) more than one security interest attaches to the product or mass, they rank equally according to the ratio that the cost of the goods to which each interest originally attached bears to the cost of the total product or mass.

SECTION 9–316. PRIORITY SUBJECT TO SUBORDINATION. Nothing in this Article prevents subordination by agreement by any person entitled to priority.

SECTION 9–317. SECURED PARTY NOT OBLIGATED ON CONTRACT OF DEBTOR. The mere existence of a security interest or authority given to the debtor to dispose of or use collateral does not impose contract or tort liability upon the secured party for the debtor's acts or omissions.

SECTION 9–318. DEFENSES AGAINST ASSIGNEE; MODIFICATION OF CONTRACT AFTER NOTIFICATION OF ASSIGNMENT; TERM PROHIBITING ASSIGNMENT INEFFECTIVE; IDENTIFICATION AND PROOF OF ASSIGNMENT. (1) Unless an account debtor has made an enforceable agreement not to assert defenses or claims arising out of a sale as provided in Section 9–206 the rights of an assignee are subject to
  (a) all the terms of the contract between the account debtor and assignor and any defense or claim arising therefrom; and
  (b) any other defense or claim of the account debtor against the assignor which accrues before the account debtor receives notification of the assignment.

(2) So far as the right to payment under an assigned contract right has not already become an account, and notwithstanding notification of the assignment, any modification of or substitution for the contract made in good faith and in accordance with reasonable commercial standards is effective against an assignee unless the account debtor has otherwise agreed but the assignee acquires corresponding rights under the modified or substituted contract. The assignment may provide that such modification or substitution is a breach by the assignor.

(3) The account debtor is authorized to pay the assignor until the account debtor receives notification that the account has been assigned and that payment is to be made to the assignee. A notification which does not reasonably identify the rights

assigned is ineffective. If requested by the account debtor, the assignee must season-ably furnish reasonable proof that the assignment has been made and unless he does so the account debtor may pay the assignor.

(4) A term in any contract between an account debtor and an assignor which pro-hibits assignment of an account or contract right to which they are parties is ineffec-tive.

PART 4

FILING

Section 9—401. Place of Filing; Erroneous Filing; Removal of Collateral.

First Alternative Subsection (1)

(1) The proper place to file in order to perfect a security interest is as follows:
  (a) when the collateral is goods which at the time the security interest attaches are or are to become fixtures, then in the office where a mortgage on the real estate concerned would be filed or recorded;
  (b) in all other cases, in the office of the [Secretary of State].

Second Alternative Subsection (1)

(1) The proper place to file in order to perfect a security interest is as follows:
  (a) when the collateral is equipment used in farming operations, or farm products, or accounts, contract rights or general intangibles arising from or relating to the sale of farm products by a farmer, or consumer goods, then in the office of the .... in the county of the debtor's residence or if the debtor is not a resident of this state then in the office of the .... in the county where the goods are kept, and in addition when the collateral is crops in the office of the .... in the county where the land on which the crops are growing or to be grown is located;
  (b) when the collateral is goods which at the time the security interest attaches are or are to become fixtures, then in the office where a mortgage on the real estate concerned would be filed or recorded;
  (c) in all other cases, in the office of the [Secretary of State].

Third Alternative Subsection (1)

(1) The proper place to file in order to perfect a security interest is as follows:
  (a) when the collateral is equipment used in farming operations, or farm products, or accounts, contract rights or general intangibles arising from or relating to the sale of farm products by a farmer, or consumer goods, then in the office of the .... in the county of the debtor's residence or if the debtor is not a resident of this state then in the office of the .... in the county where the goods are kept, and in addition when the collateral is crops in the office of the .... in the county where the land on which the crops are growing or to be grown is located;
  (b) when the collateral is goods which at the time the security interest attaches are or are to become fixtures, then in the office where a mortgage on the real estate concerned would be filed or recorded;
  (c) in all other cases, in the office of the [Secretary of State] and in addition, if the debtor has a place of business in only one county of this state, also in the office of .... of such county, or, if the debtor has no place of business in this state, but resides in the state, also in the office of .... of the county in which he resides.

Note: *One of the three alternatives should be selected as subsection (1).*

(2) A filing which is made in good faith in an improper place or not in all of the places required by this section is nevertheless effective with regard to any collateral as to which the filing complied with the requirements of this Article and is also effective with regard to collateral covered by the financing statement against any person who has knowledge of the contents of such financing statement.

(3) A filing which is made in the proper place in this state continues effective even

though the debtor's residence or place of business or the location of the collateral or its use, whichever controlled the original filing, is thereafter changed.

Alternative Subsection (3).

[(3) A filing which is made in the proper county continues effective for four months after a change to another county of the debtor's residence or place of business or the location of the collateral, whichever controlled the original filing. It becomes ineffective thereafter unless a copy of the financing statement signed by the secured party is filed in the new county within said period. The security interest may also be perfected in the new county after the expiration of the four-month period; in such case perfection dates from the time of perfection in the new county. A change in the use of the collateral does not impair the effectiveness of the original filing.]

(4) If collateral is brought into this state from another jurisdiction, the rules stated in Section 9–103 determine whether filing is necessary in this state.

SECTION 9–402. FORMAL REQUISITES OF FINANCING STATEMENT; AMENDMENTS. (1) A financing statement is sufficient if it is signed by the debtor and the secured party, gives an address of the secured party from which information concerning the security interest may be obtained, gives a mailing address of the debtor and contains a statement indicating the types, or describing the items, of collateral. A financing statement may be filed before a security agreement is made or a security interest otherwise attaches. When the financing statement covers crops growing or to be grown or goods which are or are to become fixtures, the statement must also contain a description of the real estate concerned. A copy of the security agreement is sufficient as a financing statement if it contains the above information and is signed by both parties.

(2) A financing statement which otherwise complies with subsection (1) is sufficient although it is signed only by the secured party when it is filed to perfect a security interest in

(a) collateral already subject to a security interest in another jurisdiction when it is brought into this state. Such a financing statement must state that the collateral was brought into this state under such circumstances.

(b) proceeds under Section 9–306 if the security interest in the original collateral was perfected. Such a financing statement must describe the original collateral.

(3) A form substantially as follows is sufficient to comply with subsection (1):

Name of debtor (or assignor) ....

Address ....

Name of secured party (or assignee) ....

Address ....

1. This financing statement covers the following types (or items) of property:

    (Describe) ....

2. (If collateral is crops) The above described crops are growing or are to be grown on:

    (Describe Real Estate) ....

3. (If collateral is goods which are or are to become fixtures) The above described goods are affixed or to be affixed to:

    (Describe Real Estate) ....

4. (If proceeds or products of collateral are claimed) Proceeds—Products of the collateral are also covered.

    Signature of Debtor (or Assignor) ....

    Signature of Secured Party (or Assignee) ....

(4) The term "financing statement" as used in this Article means the original financing statement and any amendments but if any amendment adds collateral, it is effective as to the added collateral only from the filing date of the amendment.

(5) A financing statement substantially complying with the requirements of this section is effective even though it contains minor errors which are not seriously misleading.

SECTION 9–403. WHAT CONSTITUTES FILING; DURATION OF FILING; EFFECT OF LAPSED FILING; DUTIES OF FILING OFFICER. (1) Presentation for filing of a financing statement and tender of the filing fee or acceptance of the statement by the filing officer constitutes filing under this Article.

(2) A filed financing statement which states a maturity date of the obligation secured of five years or less is effective until such maturity date and thereafter for a period of sixty days. Any other filed financing statement is effective for a period of five years from the date of filing. The effectiveness of a filed financing statement lapses on the expiration of such sixty day period after a stated maturity date or on the expiration of such five year period, as the case may be, unless a continuation statement is filed prior to the lapse. Upon such lapse the security interest becomes unperfected. A filed financing statement which states that the obligation secured is payable on demand is effective for five years from the date of filing.

(3) A continuation statement may be filed by the secured party (i) within six months before and sixty days after a stated maturity date of five years or less, and (ii) otherwise within six months prior to the expiration of the five year period specified in subsection (2). Any such continuation statement must be signed by the secured party, identify the original statement by file number and state that the original statement is still effective. Upon timely filing of the continuation statement, the effectiveness of the original statement is continued for five years after the last date to which the filing was effective whereupon it lapses in the same manner as provided in subsection (2) unless another continuation statement is filed prior to such lapse. Succeeding continuation statements may be filed in the same manner to continue the effectiveness of the original statement. Unless a statute on disposition of public records provides otherwise, the filing officer may remove a lapsed statement from the files and destroy it.

(4) A filing officer shall mark each statement with a consecutive file number and with the date and hour of filing and shall hold the statement for public inspection. In addition the filing officer shall index the statements according to the name of the debtor and shall note in the index the file number and the address of the debtor given in the statement.

(5) The uniform fee for filing, indexing and furnishing filing data for an original or a continuation statement shall be $. . . . .

SECTION 9—404. TERMINATION STATEMENT. (1) Whenever there is no outstanding secured obligation and no commitment to make advances, incur obligations or otherwise give value, the secured party must on written demand by the debtor send the debtor a statement that he no longer claims a security interest under the financing statement, which shall be identified by file number. A termination statement signed by a person other than the secured party of record must include or be accompanied by the assignment or a statement by the secured party of record that he has assigned the security interest to the signer of the termination statement. The uniform fee for filing and indexing such an assignment or statement thereof shall be $. . . . . If the affected secured party fails to send such a termination statement within ten days after proper demand therefor he shall be liable to the debtor for one hundred dollars, and in addition for any loss caused to the debtor by such failure.

(2) On presentation to the filing officer of such a termination statement he must note it in the index. The filing officer shall remove from the files, mark "terminated" and send or deliver to the secured party the financing statement and any continuation statement, statement of assignment or statemet of release pertaining thereto.

(3) The uniform fee for filing and indexing a termination statement including sending or delivering the financing statement shall be $. . . . .

SECTION 9—405. ASSIGNMENT OF SECURITY INTEREST; DUTIES OF FILING OFFICER; FEES. (1) A financing statement may disclose an assignment of a security interest in the collateral described in the statement by indication in the statement of the name and address of the assignee or by an assignment itself or a copy thereof on the face or back of the statement. Either the original secured party or the assignee may sign this statement as the secured party. On presentation to the filing officer of such a financing statement the filing officer shall mark the same as provided in Section 9—403(4). The uniform fee for filing, indexing and furnishing filing data for a financing statement so indicating an assignment shall be $. . . . .

(2) A secured party may assign of record all or a part of his rights under a financing statement by the filing of a separate written statement of assignment signed by the secured party of record and setting forth the name of the secured party of record and the debtor, the file number and the date of filing of the financing statement and

the name and address of the assignee and containing a description of the collateral assigned. A copy of the assignment is sufficient as a separate statement if it complies with the preceding sentence. On presentation to the filing officer of such a separate statement, the filing officer shall mark such separate statement with the date and hour of the filing. He shall note the assignment on the index of the financing statement. The uniform fee for filing, indexing and furnishing filing data about such a separate statement of assignment shall be $............

(3) After the disclosure or filing of an assignment under this section, the assignee is the secured party of record.

SECTION 9—406. RELEASE OF COLLATERAL; DUTIES OF FILING OFFICER; FEES. A secured party of record may by his signed statement release all or a part of any collateral described in a filed financing statement. The statement of release is sufficient if it contains a description of the collateral being released, the name and address of the debtor, the name and address of the secured party, and the file number of the financing statement. Upon presentation of such a statement to the filing officer he shall mark the statement with the hour and date of filing and shall note the same upon the margin of the index of the filing of the financing statement. The uniform fee for filing and noting such a statement of release shall be $............

SECTION 9—407. INFORMATION FROM FILING OFFICER. (1) If the person filing any financing statement, termination statement, statement of assignment, or statement of release, furnishes the filing officer a copy thereof, the filing officer shall upon request note upon the copy the file number and date and hour of the filing of the original and deliver or send the copy to such person.

(2) Upon request of any person, the filing officer shall issue his certificate showing whether there is on file on the date and hour stated therein, any presently effective financing statement naming a particular debtor and any statement of assignment thereof and if there is, giving the date and hour of filing of each such statement and the names and addresses of each secured party therein. The uniform fee for such a certificate shall be $.......... plus $.......... for each financing statement and for each statement of assignment reported therein. Upon request the filing officer shall furnish a copy of any filed financing statement or statement of assignment for a uniform fee of $.......... per page.

NOTE: *This new section is proposed as an optional provision to require filing officers to furnish certificates. Local law and practices should be consulted with regard to the advisability of adoption.*

PART 5

DEFAULT

SECTION 9—501. DEFAULT; PROCEDURE WHEN SECURITY AGREEMENT COVERS BOTH REAL AND PERSONAL PROPERTY. (1) When a debtor is in default under a security agreement, a secured party has the rights and remedies provided in this Part and except as limited by subsection (3) those provided in the security agreement. He may reduce his claim to judgment, foreclose or otherwise enforce the security interest by any available judicial procedure. If the collateral is documents the secured party may proceed either as to the documents or as to the goods covered thereby. A secured party in possession has the rights, remedies and duties provided in Section 9—207. The rights and remedies referred to in this subsection are cumulative.

(2) After default, the debtor has the rights and remedies provided in this Part, those provided in the security agreement and those provided in Section 9—207.

(3) To the extent that they give rights to the debtor and impose duties on the secured party, the rules stated in the subsections referred to below may not be waived or varied except as provided with respect to compulsory disposition of collateral (subsection (1) of Section 9—505) and with respect to redemption of collateral (Section 9—506) but the parties may by agreement determine the standards by which the fulfillment of these rights and duties is to be measured if such standards are not manifestly unreasonable:

    (a) subsection (2) of Section 9—502 and subsection (2) of Section 9—504 insofar as they require accounting for surplus proceeds of collateral;

(b) subsection (3) of Section 9—504 and subsection (1) of Section 9—505 which deal with disposition of collaterial;

(c) subsection (2) of Section 9—505 which deals with acceptance of collateral as discharge of obligation;

(d) Section 9—506 which deals with redemption of collateral; and

(e) subsection (1) of Section 9—507 which deals with the secured party's liability for failure to comply with this Part.

(4) If the security agreement covers both real and personal property, the secured party may proceed under this Part as to the personal property or he may proceed as to both the real and the personal property in accordance with his rights and remedies in respect of the real property in which case the provisions of this Part do not apply.

(5) When a secured party has reduced his claim to judgment the lien of any levy which may be made upon his collateral by virtue of any execution based upon the judgment shall relate back to the date of the perfection of the security interest in such collateral. A judicial sale, pursuant to such execution, is a foreclosure of the security interest by judicial procedure within the meaning of this section, and the secured party may purchase at the sale and thereafter hold the collateral free of any other requirements of this Article.

SECTION 9—502. COLLECTION RIGHTS OF SECURED PARTY. (1) When so agreed and in any event on default the secured party is entitled to notify an account debtor or the obligor on an instrument to make payment to him whether or not the assignor was theretofore making collections on the collateral, and also to take control of any proceeds to which he is entitled under Section 9—306.

(2) A secured party who by agreement is entitled to charge back uncollected collateral or otherwise to full or limited recourse against the debtor and who undertakes to collect from the account debtors or obligors must proceed in a commercially reasonable manner and may deduct his reasonable expenses of realization from the collections. If the security agreement secures an indebtedness, the secured party must account to the debtor for any surplus, and unless otherwise agreed, the debtor is liable for any deficiency. But, if the underlying transaction was a sale of accounts, contract rights, or chattel paper, the debtor is entitled to any surplus or is liable for any deficiency only if the security agreement so provides.

SECTION 9—503. SECURED PARTY'S RIGHT TO TAKE POSSESSION AFTER DEFAULT. Unless otherwise agreed a secured party has on default the right to take possession of the collateral. In taking possession a secured party may proceed without judicial process if this can be done without breach of the peace or many proceed by action. If the security agreement so provides the secured party may require the debtor to assemble the collateral and make it available to the secured party at a place to be designated by the secured party which is reasonably convenient to both parties. Without removal a secured party may render equipment unusuable, and may dispose of collateral on the debtor's premises under Section 9—504.

SECTION 9—504. SECURED PARTY'S RIGHT TO DISPOSE OF COLLATERAL AFTER DEFAULT; EFFECT OF DISPOSITION. (1) A secured party after default may sell, lease or otherwise dispose of any or all of the collateral in its then condition or following any commercially reasonable preparation or processing. Any sale of goods is subject to the Article on Sales (Article 2). The proceeds of disposition shall be applied in the order following to

(a) the reasonable expenses of retaking, holding, preparing for sale, selling and the like and, to the extent provided for in the agreement and not prohibited by law, the reasonable attorney's fees and legal expenses incurred by the secured party;

(b) the satisfaction of indebtedness secured by the security interest under which the disposition is made;

(c) the satisfaction of indebtedness secured by any subordinate security interest in the collateral if written notification of demand therefor is received before distribution of the proceeds is completed. If requested by the secured party, the holder of a subordinate security interest must seasonably furnish reasonable proof of his interest, and unless he does so, the secured party need not comply with his demand.

(2) If the security interest secures an indebtedness, the secured party must account

to the debtor for any surplus, and, unless otherwise agreed, the debtor is liable for any deficiency. But if the underlying transaction was a sale of accounts, contract rights, or chattel paper, the debtor is entitled to any surplus or is liable for any deficiency only if the security agreement so provides.

(3) Disposition of the collateral may be by public or private proceedings and may be made by way of one or more contracts. Sale or other disposition may be as a unit or in parcels and at any time and place and on any terms but every aspect of the disposition including the method, manner, time, place and terms must be commercially reasonable. Unless collateral is perishable or threatens to decline speedily in value or is of a type customarily sold on a recognized market, reasonable notification of the time and place of any public sale or reasonable notification of the time after which any private sale or other intended disposition is to be made shall be sent by the secured party to the debtor, and except in the case of consumer goods to any other person who has a security interest in the collateral and who has duly filed a financing statement indexed in the name of the debtor in this state or who is known by the secured party to have a security interest in the collateral. The secured party may buy at any public sale and if the collateral is of a type customarily sold in a recognized market or is of a type which is the subject of widely distributed standard price quotations he may buy at private sale.

(4) When collateral is disposed of by a secured party after default, the disposition transfers to a purchaser for value all of the debtor's rights therein, discharges the security interest under which it is made and any security interest or lien subordinate thereto. The purchaser takes free of all such rights and interests even though the secured party fails to comply with the requirements of this Part or of any judicial proceedings

    (a) in the case of a public sale, if the purchaser has no knowledge of any defects in the sale and if he does not buy in collusion with the secured party, other bidders or the person conducting the sale; or

    (b) in any other case, if the purchaser acts in good faith.

(5) A person who is liable to a secured party under a guaranty, indorsement, repurchase agreement or the like and who receives a transfer of collateral from the secured party or is subrogated to his rights has thereafter the rights and duties of the secured party. Such a transfer of collateral is not a sale or disposition of the collateral under this Article.

SECTION 9–505. COMPULSORY DISPOSITION OF COLLATERAL; ACCEPTANCE OF THE COLLATERAL AS DISCHARGE OF OBLIGATION. (1) If the debtor has paid sixty per cent of the cash price in the case of a purchase money security interest in consumer goods or sixty per cent of the loan in the case of another security interest in consumer goods, and has not signed after default a statement renouncing or modifying his rights under this Part a secured party who has taken possession of collateral must dispose of it under Section 9–504 and if he fails to do so within ninety days after he takes possession the debtor at his option may recover in conversion or under Section 9–507(1) on secured party's liability.

(2) In any other case involving consumer goods or any other collateral a secured party in possession may, after default, propose to retain the collateral in satisfaction of the obligation. Written notice of such proposal shall be sent to the debtor and except in the case of consumer goods to any other secured party who has a security interest in the collateral and who has duly filed a financing statement indexed in the name of the debtor in this state or is known by the secured party in possession to have a security interest in it. If the debtor or other person entitled to receive notification objects in writing within thirty days from the receipt of the notification or if any other secured party objects in writing within thirty days after the secured party obtains possession the secured party must dispose of the collateral under Section 9–504. In the absence of such written objection the secured party may retain the collateral in satisfaction of the debtor's obligation.

SECTION 9–506. DEBTOR'S RIGHT TO REDEEM COLLATERAL. At any time before the secured party has disposed of collateral or entered into a contract for its disposition under Section 9–504 or before the obligation has been discharged under Section 9–505(2) the debtor or any other secured party may unless otherwise agreed in writing after default redeem the collateral by tendering fulfillment of all obligations secured by the collateral as well as the expenses reasonably incurred by the secured party in retaking, holding and preparing the collateral for disposition, in arranging for the sale, and to the extent provided in the agreement and not prohibited by law, his reasonable attorney's fees and legal expenses.

SECTION 9—507. SECURED PARTY'S LIABILITY FOR FAILURE TO COMPLY WITH THIS PART. (1) If it is established that the secured party is not proceeding in accordance with the provisions of this Part disposition may be ordered or restrained on appropriate terms and conditions. If the disposition has occurred the debtor or any person entitled to notification or whose security interest has been made known to the secured party prior to the disposition has a right to recover from the secured party any loss caused by a failure to comply with the provisions of this Part. If the collateral is consumer goods, the debtor has a right to recover in any event an amount not less than the credit service charge plus ten per cent of the principal amount of the debt or the time price differential plus ten per cent of the cash price.

(2) The fact that a better price could have been obtained by a sale at a different time or in a different method from that selected by the secured party is not of itself sufficient to establish that the sale was not made in a commercially reasonable manner. If the secured party either sells the collateral in the usual manner in any recognized market therefor or if he sells at the price current in such market at the time of his sale or if he has otherwise sold in conformity with reasonable commercial practices among dealers in the type of property sold he has sold in a commercially reasonable manner. The principles stated in the two preceding sentences with respect to sales also apply as may be appropriate to other types of disposition. A disposition which has been approved in any judicial proceeding or by any bona fide creditors' committee or representative of creditors shall conclusively be deemed to be commercially reasonable, but this sentence does not indicate that any such approval must be obtained in any case nor does it indicate that any disposition not so approved is not commercially reasonable.

ARTICLE 10

EFFECTIVE DATE AND REPEALER

SECTION 10—101. EFFECTIVE DATE. This Act shall become effective at midnight on December 31st following its enactment. It applies to transactions entered into and events occurring after that date.

SECTION 10—102. SPECIFIC REPEALER; PROVISION FOR TRANSITION. (1) The following acts and all other acts and parts of acts inconsistent herewith are hereby repealed:
   (Here should follow the acts to be specifically repealed including the following:
   Uniform Negotiable Instruments Act
   Uniform Warehouse Receipts Act
   Uniform Sales Act
   Uniform Bills of Lading Act
   Uniform Stock Transfer Act
   Uniform Conditional Sales Act
   Uniform Trust Receipts Act
Also any acts regulating:
   Bank collections
   Bulk sales
   Chattel mortgages
   Conditional sales
   Factor's lien acts
   Farm storage of grain and similar acts
   Assignment of accounts receivable)

(2) Transactions validly entered into before the effective date specified in Section 10—101 and the rights, duties and interests flowing from them remain valid thereafter and may be terminated, completed, consummated or enforced as required or permitted

by any statute or other law amended or repealed by this Act as though such repeal or amendment had not occurred.

NOTE: *Subsection (1) should be separately prepared for each state. The foregoing is a list of statutes to be checked.*

SECTION 10—103. GENERAL REPEALER. Except as provided in the following section, all acts and parts of acts inconsistent with this Act are hereby repealed.

SECTION 10—104. LAWS NOT REPEALED. [(1)] The Article on Documents of Title (Article 7) does not repeal or modify any laws prescribing the form or contents of documents of title or the services or facilities to be afforded by bailees, or otherwise regulating bailees' businesses in respects not specifically dealt with herein; but the fact that such laws are violated does not affect the status of a document of title which otherwise complies with the definition of a document of title (Section 1—201).

[(2) This Act does not repeal ....
....*, cited as the Uniform Act for the Simplification of Fiduciary Security Transfers, and if in any respect there is any inconsistency between that Act and the Article of this Act on investment securities (Article 8) the provisions of the former Act shall control.]

NOTE: *At * in subsection (2) insert the statutory reference to the Uniform Act for the Simplification of Fiduciary Security Transfers if such Act has previously been enacted. If it has not been enacted, omit subsection (2).*

2. UNIFORM PARTNERSHIP ACT

PART 1

PRELIMINARY PROVISIONS

SECTION 1. NAME OF ACT. This act may be cited as Uniform Partnership Act.

SECTION 2. DEFINITION OF TERMS. In this act, "Court" includes every court and judge having jurisdiction in the case.

"Business" includes every trade, occupation, or profession.

"Person" includes individuals, partnerships, corporations, and other associations.

"Bankrupt" includes bankrupt under the Federal Bankruptcy Act or insolvent under any state insolvent act.

"Conveyance" includes every assignment, lease, mortgage, or encumbrance.

"Real property" includes land and any interest or estate in land.

SECTION 3. INTERPRETATION OF KNOWLEDGE AND NOTICE. (1) A person has "knowledge" of a fact within the meaning of this act not only when he has actual knowledge thereof, but also when he has knowledge of such other facts as in the circumstances shows bad faith.

(2) A person has "notice" of a fact within the meaning of this act when the person who claims the benefit of the notice:

    (a) States the fact to such person, or

    (b) Delivers through the mail, or by other means of communication, a written statement of the fact to such person or to a proper person at his place of business or residence.

SECTION 4. RULES OF CONSTRUCTION. (1) The rule that statutes in derogation of the common law are to be strictly construed shall have no application to this act.

(2) The law of estoppel shall apply under this act.

(3) The law of agency shall apply under this act.

(4) This act shall be so interpreted and construed as to effect its general purpose to make uniform the law of those states which enact it.

(5) This act shall not be construed so as to impair the obligations of any contract existing when the act goes into effect, nor to affect any action or proceedings begun or right accrued before this act takes effect.

SECTION 5. RULES FOR CASES NOT PROVIDED FOR IN THIS ACT. In any case not provided for in this act the rules of law and equity, including the law merchant, shall govern.

PART 2

NATURE OF A PARTNERSHIP

SECTION 6. PARTNERSHIP DEFINED. (1) A partnership is an association of two or more persons to carry on as co-owners a business for profit.

(2) But any association formed under any other statute of this state, or any statute adopted by authority, other than the authority of this state, is not a partnership under this act, unless such association would have been a partnership in this state prior to the adoption of this act; but this act shall apply to limited partnerships except in so far as the statutes relating to such partnerships are inconsistent herewith.

SECTION 7. RULES FOR DETERMINING THE EXISTENCE OF A PARTNERSHIP. In determining whether a partnership exists, these rules shall apply:

(1) Except as provided by section 16 persons who are not partners as to each other are not partners as to third persons.

(2) Joint tenancy, tenancy in common, tenancy by the entireties, joint property, common property, or part ownership does not of itself establish a partnership, whether such co-owners do or do not share any profits made by the use of the property.

(3) The sharing of gross returns does not of itself establish a partnership, whether or not the persons sharing them have a joint or common right or interest in any property from which the returns are derived.

(4) The receipt by a person of a share of the profits of a business is *prima facie* evidence that he is a partner in the business, but no such inference shall be drawn if such profits were received in payment:

    (a) As a debt by installments or otherwise,

    (b) As wages of an employee or rent to a landlord,

    (c) As an annuity to a widow or representative of a deceased partner,

    (d) As interest on a loan, though the amount of payment vary with the profits of the business,

    (e) As the consideration for the sale of a good-will of a business or other property by installments or otherwise.

SECTION 8. PARTNERSHIP PROPERTY. (1) All property originally brought into the partnership stock or subsequently acquired by purchase or otherwise, on account of the partnership, is partnership property.

(2) Unless the contrary intention appears, property acquired with partnership funds is partnership property.

(3) Any estate in real property may be acquired in the partnership name. Title so acquired can be conveyed only in the partnership name.

(4) A conveyance to a partnership in the partnership name, though without words of inheritance, passes the entire estate of the grantor unless a contrary intent appears.

PART 3

RELATIONS OF PARTNERS TO PERSONS DEALING WITH THE PARTNERSHIP

SECTION 9. PARTNER AGENT OF PARTNERSHIP AS TO PARTNERSHIP BUSINESS. (1) Every partner is an agent of the partnership for the purpose of its business, and the act of every partner, including the execution in the partnership name of any instrument, for apparently carrying on in the usual way the business of the partnership of which he is a member binds the partnership, unless the partner so acting has in fact no authority to act for the partnership in the particular matter, and the person with whom he is dealing has knowledge of the fact that he has no such authority.

(2) An act of a partner which is not apparently for the carrying on of the business of the partnership in the usual way does not bind the partnership unless authorized by the other partners.

(3) Unless authorized by the other partners or unless they have abandoned the business, one or more but less than all the partners have no authority to:

    (a) Assign the partnership property in trust for creditors or on the assignee's promise to pay the debts of the partnership,

    (b) Dispose of the good-will of the business,

    (c) Do any other act which would make it impossible to carry on the ordinary business of a partnership,

    (d) Confess a judgment,

    (e) Submit a partnership claim or liability to arbitration or reference.

(4) No act of a partner in contravention of a restriction on authority shall bind the partnership to persons having knowledge of the restriction.

SECTION 10. CONVEYANCE OF REAL PROPERTY OF THE PARTNERSHIP. (1) Where title to real property is in the partnership name, any partner may convey title to such property by a conveyance executed in the partnership name; but the partnership may recover such property unless the partner's act binds the partnership under the provisions of paragraph (1) of section 9, or unless such property has been conveyed by the grantee or a person claiming through such grantee to a holder for value without knowledge that the partner, in making the conveyance, has exceeded his authority.

(2) Where title to real property is in the name of the partnership, a conveyance executed by a partner, in his own name, passes the equitable interest of the partnership, provided the act is one within the authority of the partner under the provisions of paragraph (1) of section 9.

(3) Where title to real property is in the name of one or more but not all the partners, and the record does not disclose the right of the partnership, the partners in whose name the title stands may convey title to such property, but the partnership may recover such property if the partners' act does not bind the partnership under the provisions of paragraph (1) of section 9, unless the purchaser or his assignee, is a holder for value, without knowledge.

(4) Where the title to real property is in the name of one or more or all the partners, or in a third person in trust for the partnership, a conveyance executed by a partner in the partnership name, or in his own name, passes the equitable interest of the partnership, provided the act is one within the authority of the partner under the provisions of paragraph (1) of section 9.

(5) Where the title to real property is in the names of all the partners a conveyance executed by all the partners passes all their rights in such property.

Section 11. Partnership Bound by Admission of Partner. An admission or representation made by any partner concerning partnership affairs within the scope of his authority as conferred by this act is evidence against the partnership.

Section 12. Partnership Charged with Knowledge of or Notice to Partner. Notice to any partner of any matter relating to partnership affairs, and the knowledge of the partner acting in the particular matter, acquired while a partner or then present to his mind, and the knowledge of any other partner who reasonably could and should have communicated it to the acting partner, operate as notice to or knowledge of the partnership, except in the case of a fraud on the partnership committed by or with the consent of that partner.

Section 13. Partnership Bound by Partner's Wrongful Act. Where, by any wrongful act or omission of any partner acting in the ordinary course of the business of the partnership or with the authority of his co-partners, loss or injury is caused to any person, not being a partner in the partnership, or any penalty is incurred, the partnership is liable therefor to the same extent as the partner so acting or omitting to act.

Section 14. Partnership Bound by Partner's Breach of Trust. The partnership is bound to make good the loss:

(a) Where one partner acting within the scope of his apparent authority receives money or property of a third person and misapplies it; and

(b) Where the partnership in the course of its business receives money or property of a third person and the money or property so received is misapplied by any partner while it is in the custody of the partnership.

Section 15. Nature of Partner's Liability. All partners are liable

(a) Jointly and severally for everything chargeable to the partnership under sections 13 and 14.

(b) Jointly for all other debts and obligations of the partnership; but any partner may enter into a separate obligation to perform a partnership contract.

Section 16. Partner by Estoppel. (1) When a person, by words spoken or written or by conduct, represents himself, or consents to another representing him to any one, as a partner in an existing partnership or with one or more persons not actual partners, he is liable to any such person to whom such representation has been made, who has, on the faith of such representation, given credit to the actual or apparent partnership, and if he has made such representation or consented to its being made in a public manner he is liable to such person, whether the representation has or has not been made or communicated to such person so giving credit by or with the knowledge of the apparent partner making the representation or consenting to its being made.

(a) When a partnership liability results, he is liable as though he were an actual member of the partnership.

(b) When no partnership liability results, he is liable jointly with the other persons, if any, so consenting to the contract or representation as to incur liability, otherwise separately.

(2) When a person has been thus represented to be a partner in an existing partnership, or with one or more persons not actual partners, he is an agent of the persons consenting to such representation to bind them to the same extent and in the same manner as though he were a partner in fact, with respect to persons who rely upon the representation. Where all the members of the existing partnership consent to the representation, a partnership act or obligation results; but in all other cases it is the joint act or obligation of the person acting and the persons consenting to the representation.

SECTION 17. LIABILITY OF INCOMING PARTNER. A person admitted as a partner into an existing partnership is liable for all the obligations of the partnership arising before his admission as though he had been a partner when such obligations were incurred, except that this liability shall be satisfied only out of partnership property.

PART 4

RELATIONS OF PARTNERS TO ONE ANOTHER

SECTION 18. RULES DETERMINING RIGHTS AND DUTIES OF PARTNERS. The rights and duties of the partners in relation to the partnership shall be determined, subject to any agreement between them, by the following rules:

(a) Each partner shall be repaid his contributions, whether by way of capital or advances to the partnership property and share equally in the profits and surplus remaining after all liabilities, including those to partners, are satisfied; and must contribute toward the losses, whether of capital or otherwise, sustained by the partnership according to his share in the profits.

(b) The partnership must indemnify every partner in respect of payments made and personal liabilities reasonably incurred by him in the ordinary and proper conduct of its business, or for the preservation of its business or property.

(c) A partner, who in aid of the partnership makes any payment or advance beyond the amount of captial which he agreed to contribute, shall be paid interest from the date of the payment or advance.

(d) A partner shall receive interest on the capital contributed by him only from the date when repayment should be made.

(e) All partners have equal rights in the management and conduct of the partnership business.

(f) No partner is entitled to remuneration for acting in the partnership business, except that a surviving partner is entitled to reasonable compensation for his services in winding up the partnership affairs.

(g) No person can become a member of a partnership without the consent of all the partners.

(h) Any difference arising as to ordinary matters connected with the partnership business may be decided by a majority of the partners; but no act in contravention of any agreement between the partners may be done rightfully without the consent of all the partners.

SECTION 19. PARTNERSHIP BOOKS. The partnership books shall be kept, subject to any agreement between the partners, at the principal place of business of the partnership, and every partner shall at all times have access to and may inspect and copy any of them.

SECTION 20. DUTY OF PARTNERS TO RENDER INFORMATION. Partners shall render on demand true and full information of all things affecting the partnership to any partner or the legal representative of any deceased partner or partner under legal disability.

SECTION 21. PARTNER ACCOUNTABLE AS A FIDUCIARY. (1) Every partner must account to the partnership for any benefit, and hold as trustee for it any profits derived by him without the consent of the other partners from any transaction connected with the formation, conduct, or liquidation of the partnership or from any use by him of its property.

(2) This section applies also to the representatives of a deceased partner engaged in the liquidation of the affairs of the partnership as the personal representatives of the last surviving partner.

SECTION 22. RIGHT TO AN ACCOUNT. Any partner shall have the right to a formal account as to partnership affairs:

    (a) If he is wrongfully excluded from the partnership business or possession of its property by his co-partners,

    (b) If the right exists under the terms of any agreement,

    (c) As provided by section 21,

    (d) Whenever other circumstances render it just and reasonable.

SECTION 23. CONTINUATION OF PARTNERSHIP BEYOND FIXED TERM. (1) When a partnership for a fixed term or particular undertaking is continued after the termination of such term or particular undertaking without any express agreement, the rights and duties of the partners remain the same as they were at such termination, so far as is consistent with a partnership at will.

(2) A continuation of the business by the partners or such of them as habitually acted therein during the term, without any settlement or liquidation of the partnership affairs, is *prima facie* evidence of a continuation of the partnership.

PART 5

PROPERTY RIGHTS OF A PARTNER

SECTION 24. EXTENT OF PROPERTY RIGHTS OF A PARTNER. The property rights of a partner are (1) his rights in specific partnership property, (2) his interest in the partnership, and (3) his right to participate in the management.

SECTION 25. NATURE OF A PARTNER'S RIGHT IN SPECIFIC PARTNERSHIP PROPERTY. (1) A partner is co-owner with his partners of specific partnership property holding as a tenant in partnership.

(2) The incidents of this tenancy are such that:

    (a) A partner, subject to the provisions of this act and to any agreement between the partners, has an equal right with his partners to possess specific partnership property for partnership purposes; but he has no right to possess such property for any other purpose without the consent of his partners.

    (b) A partner's right in specific partnership property is not assignable except in connection with the assignment of rights of all the partners in the same property.

    (c) A partner's right in specific partnership property is not subject to attachment or execution, except on a claim against the partnership. When partnership property is attached for a partnership debt the partners, or any of them, or the representatives of a deceased partner, cannot claim any right under the homestead or exemption laws.

    (d) On the death of a partner his right in specific partnership property vests in the surviving partner or partners, except where the deceased was the last surviving partner, when his right in such property vests in his legal representative. Such surviving partner or partners, or the legal representative of the last surviving partner, has no right to possess the partnership property for any but a partnership purpose.

    (e) A partner's right in specific partnership property is not subject to dower, curtesy, or allowances to widows, heirs, or next of kin.

SECTION 26. NATURE OF PARTNER'S INTEREST IN THE PARTNERSHIP. A partner's interest in the partnership is his share of the profits and surplus, and the same is personal property.

SECTION 27. ASSIGNMENT OF PARTNER'S INTEREST. (1) A conveyance by a partner of his interest in the partnership does not of itself dissolve the partnership, nor, as

against the other partners in the absence of agreement, entitle the assignee, during the continuance of the partnership, to interfere in the management or administration of the partnership business or affairs, or to require any information or account of partnership transactions, or to inspect the partnership books; but it merely entitles the assignee to receive in accordance with his contract the profits to which the assigning partner would otherwise be entitled.

(2) In case of a dissolution of the partnership, the assignee is entitled to receive his assignor's interest and may require an account from the date only of the last account agreed to by all the partners.

SECTION 28. PARTNER'S INTEREST SUBJECT TO CHARGING ORDER. (1) On due application to a competent court by any judgment creditor of a partner, the court which entered the judgment, order, or decree, or any other court, may charge the interest of the debtor partner with payment of the unsatisfied amount of such judgment debt with interest thereon; and may then or later appoint a receiver of his share of the profits, and of any other money due or to fall due to him in respect of the partnership, and make all other orders, directions, accounts and inquiries which the debtor partner might have made, or which the circumstances of the case may require.

(2) The interest charged may be redeemed at any time before foreclosure, or in case of a sale being directed by the court may be purchased without thereby causing a dissolution:

(a) With separate property, by any one or more of the partners, or
(b) With partnership property, by any one or more of the partners with the consent of all the partners whose interests are not so charged or sold.

(3) Nothing in this act shall be held to deprive a partner of his right, if any, under the exemption laws, as regards his interest in the partnership.

PART 6

DISSOLUTION AND WINDING UP

SECTION 29. DISSOLUTION DEFINED. The dissolution of a partnership is the change in the relation of the partners caused by any partner ceasing to be associated in the carrying on as distinguished from the winding up of the business.

SECTION 30. PARTNERSHIP NOT TERMINATED BY DISSOLUTION. On dissolution the partnership is not terminated, but continues until the winding up of partnership affairs is completed.

SECTION 31. CAUSES OF DISSOLUTION. Dissolution is caused: (1) Without violation of the agreement between the partners,

(a) By the termination of the definite term or particular undertaking specified in the agreement,
(b) By the express will of any partner when no definite term or particular undertaking is specified,
(c) By the express will of all the partners who have not assigned their interests or suffered them to be charged for their separate debts, either before or after the termination of any specified term or particular undertaking,
(d) By the expulsion of any partner from the business *bona fide* in accordance with such a power conferred by the agreement between the partners;

(2) In contravention of the agreement between the partners, where the circumstances do not permit a dissolution under any other provision of this section, by the express will of any partner at any time;

(3) By any event which makes it unlawful for the business of the partnership to be carried on or for the members to carry it on in partnership;

(4) By the death of any partner;

(5) By the bankruptcy of any partner or the partnership;

(6) By decree of court under section 32.

SECTION 32. DISSOLUTION BY DECREE OF COURT. (1) On application by or for a partner the court shall decree a dissolution whenever:

(a) A partner has been declared a lunatic in any judicial proceeding or is shown to be of unsound mind,

(b) A partner becomes in any other way incapable of performing his part of the partnership contract,

(c) A partner has been guilty of such conduct as tends to affect prejudicially the carrying on of the business.

(d) A partner wilfully or persistently commits a breach of the partnership agreement, or otherwise so conducts himself in matters relating to the partnership business that it is not reasonably practicable to carry on the business in partnership with him,

(e) The business of the partnership can only be carried on at a loss,

(f) Other circumstances render a dissolution equitable.

(2) On the application of the purchaser of a partner's interest under sections 27 and 28:

(a) After the termination of the specified term or particular undertaking,

(b) At any time if the partnership was a partnership at will when the interest was assigned or when the charging order was issued.

SECTION 33. GENERAL EFFECT OF DISSOLUTION ON AUTHORITY OF PARTNER. Except so far as may be necessary to wind up partnership affairs or to complete transactions begun but not then finished, dissolution terminates all authority of any partner to act for the partnership,

(1) With respect to the partners,

(a) When the dissolution is not by the act, bankruptcy or death of a partner; or

(b) When the dissolution is by such act, bankruptcy or death of a partner, in cases where section 34 so requires.

(2) With respect to persons not partners, as declared in section 35.

SECTION 34. RIGHT OF PARTNER TO CONTRIBUTION FROM CO-PARTNERS AFTER DISSOLUTION. Where the dissolution is caused by the act, death or bankruptcy of a partner, each partner is liable to his co-partners for his share of any liability created by any partner acting for the partnership as if the partnership had not been dissolved unless

(a) The dissolution being by act of any partner, the partner acting for the partnership had knowledge of the dissolution, or

(b) The dissolution being by the death or bankruptcy of a partner, the partner acting for the partnership had knowledge or notice of the death or bankruptcy.

SECTION 35. POWER OF PARTNER TO BIND PARTNERSHIP TO THIRD PERSONS AFTER DISSOLUTION. (1) After dissolution a partner can bind the partnership except as provided in Paragraph (3).

(a) By any act appropriate for winding up partnership affairs or completing transactions unfinished at dissolution;

(b) By any transaction which would bind the partnership if dissolution had not taken place, provided the other party to the transaction

(i) Had extended credit to the partnership prior to dissolution and had no knowledge or notice of the dissolution; or

(ii) Though he had not so extended credit, had nevertheless known of the partnership prior to dissolution, and, having no knowledge or notice of dissolution, the fact of dissolution had not been advertised in a newspaper of general circulation in the place (or in each place if more than one) at which the partnership business was regularly carried on.

(2) The liability of a partner under Paragraph (1b) shall be satisfied out of partnership assets alone when such partner had been prior to dissolution

(a) Unknown as a partner to the person with whom the contract is made; and

(b) So far unknown and inactive in partnership affairs that the business reputation of the partnership could not be said to have been in any degree due to his connection with it.

(3) The partnership is in no case bound by any act of a partner after dissolution

(a) Where the partnership is dissolved because it is unlawful to carry on the business, unless the act is appropriate for winding up partnership affairs; or

(b) Where the partner has become bankrupt; or

(c) Where the partner has no authority to wind up partnership affairs; except by a transaction with one who

    (i) Had an extended credit to the partnership prior to dissolution and had no knowledge or notice of his want of authority; or

    (ii) Had not extended credit to the partnership prior to dissolution, and, having no knowledge or notice of his want of authority, the fact of his want of authority has not been advertised in the manner provided for advertising the fact of dissolution in Paragraph (1bii).

(4) Nothing in this section shall affect the liability under Section 16 of any person who after dissolution represents himself or consents to another representing him as a partner in a partnership engaged in carrying on business.

SECTION 36. EFFECT OF DISSOLUTION ON PARTNER'S EXISTING LIABILITY. (1) The dissolution of the partnership does not of itself discharge the existing liability of any partner.

(2) A partner is discharged from any existing liability upon dissolution of the partnership by an agreement to that effect between himself, the partnership creditor and the person or partnership continuing the business; and such agreement may be inferred from the course of dealing between the creditor having knowledge of the dissolution and the person or partnership continuing the business.

(3) Where a person agrees to assume the existing obligations of a dissolved partnership, the partners whose obligations have been assumed shall be discharged from any liability to any creditor of the partnership who, knowing of the agreement, consents to a material alteration in the nature or time of payment of such obligations.

(4) The individual property of a deceased partner shall be liable for all obligations of the partnership incurred while he was a partner but subject to the prior payment of his separate debts.

SECTION 37. RIGHT TO WIND UP. Unless otherwise agreed the partners who have not wrongfully dissolved the partnership or the legal representative of the last surviving partner, not bankrupt, has the right to wind up the partnership affairs; provided, however, that any partner, his legal representative or his assignee, upon cause shown, may obtain winding up by the court.

SECTION 38. RIGHTS OF PARTNERS TO APPLICATION OF PARTNERSHIP PROPERTY. (1) When dissolution is caused in any way, except in contravention of the partnership agreement, each partner, as against his co-partners and all persons claiming through them in respect of their interests in the partnership, unless otherwise agreed, may have the partnership property applied to discharge its liabilities, and the surplus applied to pay in cash the net amount owing to the respective partners. But if dissolution is caused by expulsion of a partner, *bona fide* under the partnership agreement and if the expelled partner is discharged from all partnership liabilities, either by payment or agreement under section 36(2), he shall receive in cash only the net amount due him from the partnership.

(2) When dissolution is caused in contravention of the partnership agreement the rights of the partners shall be as follows:

    (a) Each partner who has not caused dissolution wrongfully shall have,

        (i) All the rights specified in paragraph (1) of this section, and

        (ii) The right, as against each partner who has caused the dissolution wrongfully, to damages for breach of the agreement.

    (b) The partners who have not caused the dissolution wrongfully, if they all desire to continue the business in the same name, either by themselves or jointly with others, may do so, during the agreed term for the partnership and for that purpose may possess the partnership property, provided they secure the payment by bond approved by the court, or pay to any partner who has caused the dissolution wrongfully, the value of his interest in the partnership at the dissolution, less any damages recoverable under clause (2aii) of this section, and in like manner indemnify him against all present or future partnership liabilities.

    (c) A partner who has caused the dissolution wrongfully shall have:

        (i) If the business is not continued under the provisions of paragraph (2b) all the rights of a partner under paragraph (1), subject to clause (2aii), of this section,

        (ii) If the business is continued under paragraph (2b) of this section the right as against his co-partners and all claiming through them in respect of their interests in the partnership, to have the value of his interest in the partnership, less any damages caused to his co-partners by the dissolution, ascertained and paid to him in cash, or the payment secured by bond approved by the court, and to be released from all existing liabilities of the partnership; but in ascertaining the value of the partner's interest the value of the good-will of the business shall not be considered.

SECTION 39. RIGHTS WHERE PARTNERSHIP IS DISSOLVED FOR FRAUD OR MISREPRESENTATION. Where a partnership contract is rescinded on the ground of the fraud or misrepresentation of one of the parties thereto, the party entitled to rescind is, without prejudice to any other right, entitled,

(a) To a lien on, or right of retention of, the surplus of the partnership property after satisfying the partnership liabilities to third persons for any sum of money paid by him for the purchase of an interest in the partnership and for any capital or advances contributed by him; and

(b) To stand, after all liabilities to third persons have been satisfied, in the place of the creditors of the partnership for any payments made by him in respect of the partnership liabilities; and

(c) To be indemnified by the person guilty of the fraud or making the representation against all debts and liabilities of the partnership.

SECTION 40. RULES FOR DISTRIBUTION. In settling accounts between the partners after dissolution, the following rules shall be observed, subject to any agreement to the contrary:

(a) The assets of the partnership are:
  (i) The partnership property,
  (ii) The contributions of the partners necessary for the payment of all the liabilities specified in clause (b) of this paragraph.

(b) The liabilities of the partnership shall rank in order of payment, as follows:
  (i) Those owing to creditors other than partners,
  (ii) Those owing to partners other than for capital and profits,
  (iii) Those owning to partners in respect of capital,
  (iv) Those owing to partners in respect of profits.

(c) The assets shall be applied in the order of their declaration in clause (a) of this paragraph to the satisfaction of the liabilities.

(d) The partners shall contribute, as provided by section 18(a) the amount necessary to satisfy the liabilities; but if any, but not all, of the partners are insolvent, or, not being subject to process, refuse to contribute, the other partners shall contribute their share of the liabilities, and, in the relative proportions in which they share the profits, the additional amount necessary to pay the liabilities.

(e) An assignee for the benefit of creditors or any person appointed by the court shall have the right to enforce the contributions specified in clause (d) of this paragraph.

(f) Any partner or his legal representative shall have the right to enforce the contributions specified in clause (d) of this paragraph, to the extent of the amount which he has paid in excess of his share of the liability.

(g) The individual property of a deceased partner shall be liable for the contributions specified in clause (d) of this paragraph.

(h) When partnership property and the individual properties of the partners are in possession of a court for distribution, partnership creditors shall have priority on partnership property and separate creditors on individual property, saving the rights of lien or secured creditors as heretofore.

(i) Where a partner has become bankrupt or his estate is insolvent the claims against his separate property shall rank in the following order:
  (i) Those owing to separate creditors,
  (ii) Those owing to partnership creditors,
  (iii) Those owing to partners by way of contribution.

SECTION 41. LIABILITY OF PERSONS CONTINUING THE BUSINESS IN CERTAIN CASES.

(1) When any new partner is admitted into an existing partnership, or when any partner retires and assigns (or the representative of the deceased partner assigns) his rights in partnership property to two or more of the partners, or to one or more of the partners and one or more third persons, if the business is continued without liquidation of the partnership affairs, creditors of the first or dissolved partnership are also creditors of the partnership so continuing the business.

(2) When all but one partner retire and assign (or the representative of a deceased partner assigns) their rights in partnership property to the remaining partner, who continues the business without liquidation of partnership affairs, either alone or with others, creditors of the dissolved partnership are also creditors of the person or partnership so continuing the business.

(3) When any partner retires or dies and the business of the dissolved partnership is continued as set forth in paragraphs (1) and (2) of this section, with the consent of the retired partners or the representative of the deceased partner, but without any assignment of his right in partnership property, rights of creditors of the dissolved partnership and of the creditors of the person or partnership continuing the business shall be as if such assignment had been made.

(4) When all the partners or their representatives assign their rights in partnership property to one or more third persons who promise to pay the debts and who continue the business of the dissolved partnership, creditors of the dissolved partnership are also creditors of the person or partnership continuing the business.

(5) When any partner wrongfully causes a dissolution and the remaining partners continue the business under the provisions of section 38(2b), either alone or with others, and without liquidation of the partnership affairs, creditors of the dissolved partnership are also creditors of the person or partnership continuing the business.

(6) When a partner is expelled and the remaining partners continue the business either alone or with others, without liquidation of the partnership affairs, creditors of the dissolved partnership are also creditors of the person or partnership continuing the business.

(7) The liability of a third person becoming a partner in the partnership continuing the business, under this section, to the creditors of the dissolved partnership shall be satisfied out of partnership property only.

(8) When the business of a partnership after dissolution is continued under any conditions set forth in this section the creditors of the dissolved partnership, as against the separate creditors of the retiring or deceased partner or the representative of the deceased partner, have a prior right to any claim of the retired partner or the representative of the deceased partner against the person or partnership continuing the business, on account of the retired or deceased partner's interest in the dissolved partnership or on account of any consideration promised for such interest or for his right in partnership property.

(9) Nothing in this section shall be held to modify any right of creditors to set aside any assignment on the ground of fraud.

(10) The use by the person or partnership continuing the business of the partnership name, or the name of a deceased partner as part thereof, shall not of itself make the individual property of the deceased partner liable for any debts contracted by such person or partnership.

SECTION 42. RIGHTS OF RETIRING OR ESTATE OF DECEASED PARTNER WHEN THE BUSINESS IS CONTINUED. When any partner retires or dies, and the business is continued under any of the conditions set forth in section 41 (1, 2, 3, 5, 6), or section 38(2b), without any settlement of accounts as between him or his estate and the person or partnership continuing the business, unless otherwise agreed, he or his legal representative as against such persons or partnership may have the value of his interest at the date of dissolution ascertained, and shall receive as an ordinary creditor an amount equal to the value of his interest in the dissolved partnership with interest, or, at his option or at the option of his legal representative, in lieu of interest, the profits attributable to the use of his right in the property of the dissolved partnership; provided that the creditors of the dissolved partnership as against the separate creditors, or the representative of the retired or deceased partner, shall have priority on any claim arising under this section, as provided by section 41(8) of this act.

Section 43. Accrual of Actions. The right to an account of his interest shall accrue to any partner, or his legal representative, as against the winding up partners or the surviving partners or the person or partnership continuing the business, at the date of dissolution, in the absence of any agreement to the contrary.

PART 7

MISCELLANEOUS PROVISIONS

Section 44. When Act Takes Effect. This act shall take effect on the .... day of .... one thousand nine hundred and ....

Section 45. Legislation Repealed. All acts or parts of acts inconsistent with this act are hereby repealed.

3. UNIFORM LIMITED PARTNERSHIP ACT

AN ACT TO MAKE UNIFORM THE LAW RELATING TO LIMITED PARTNERSHIPS

Be it enacted, etc., as follows:

. . .

SECTION 1. LIMITED PARTNERSHIP DEFINED. A limited partnership is a partnership formed by two or more persons under the provisions of Section 2, having as members one or more general partners and one or more limited partners. The limited partners as such shall not be bound by the obligations of the partnership.

SECTION 2. FORMATION. (1) Two or more persons desiring to form a limited partnership shall

(a) Sign and swear to a certificate, which shall state

(i) The name of the partnership,

(ii) The character of the business,

(iii) The location of the principal place of business,

(iv) The name and place of residence of each member; general and limited partners being respectively designated.

(v) The term for which the partnership is to exist,

(vi) The amount of cash and a description of and the agreed value of the other property contributed by each limited partner,

(vii) The additional contributions, if any, agreed to be made by each limited partner and the times at which or events on the happening of which they shall be made,

(viii) The time, if agreed upon, when the contribution of each limited partner is to be returned.

(ix) The share of the profits or the other compensation by way of income which each limited partner shall receive by reason of his contribution,

(x) The right, if given, of a limited partner to substitute an assignee as contributor in his place, and the terms and conditions of the substitution,

(xi) The right, if given, of the partners to admit additional limited partners,

(xii) The right, if given, of one or more of the limited partners to priority over other limited partners, as to contributions or as to compensation by way of income, and the nature of such priority,

(xiii) The right, if given, of the remaining general partner or partners to continue the business on the death, retirement or insanity of a general partner, and

(xiv) The right, if given, of a limited partner to demand and receive property other than cash in return for his contribution.

(b) File for record the certificate in the office of [here designate the proper office].

(2) A limited partnership is formed if there has been substantial compliance in good faith with the requirements of paragraph (1).

SECTION 3. BUSINESS WHICH MAY BE CARRIED ON. A limited partnership may carry on any business which a partnership without limited partners may carry on, except [here designate the business to be prohibited].

SECTION 4. CHARACTER OF LIMITED PARTNER'S CONTRIBUTION. The contributions of a limited partner may be cash or other property, but not services.

SECTION 5. A NAME NOT TO CONTAIN SURNAME OF LIMITED PARTNER; EXCEPTIONS. (1) The surname of a limited partner shall not appear in the partnership name, unless

(a) It is also the surname of a general partner, or

(b) Prior to the time when the limited partner became such the business had been carried on under a name in which his surname appeared.

(2) A limited partner whose name appears in a partnership name contrary to the provisions of paragraph (1) is liable as a general partner to partnership creditors who extend credit to the partnership without actual knowledge that he is not a general partner.

SECTION 6. LIABILITY FOR FALSE STATEMENTS IN CERTIFICATE. If the certificate contains a false statement, one who suffers loss by reliance on such statement may hold liable any party to the certificate who knew the statement to be false.

(a) At the time he signed the certificate, or

(b) Subsequently, but within a sufficient time before the statement was relied upon to enable him to cancel or amend the certificate, or to file a petition for its cancellation or amendment as provided in Section 25(3).

SECTION 7. LIMITED PARTNER NOT LIABLE TO CREDITORS. A limited partner shall not become liable as a general partner unless, in addition to the exercise of his rights and powers as a limited partner, he takes part in the control of the business.

SECTION 8. ADMISSION OF ADDITIONAL LIMITED PARTNERS. After the formation of a limited partnership, additional limited partners may be admitted upon filing an amendment to the original certificate in accordance with the requirements of Section 25.

SECTION 9. RIGHTS, POWERS AND LIABILITIES OF A GENERAL PARTNER. (1) A general partner shall have all the rights and powers and be subject to all the restrictions and liabilities of a partner in a partnership without limited partners, except that without the written consent or ratification of the specific act by all the limited partners, a general partner or all of the general partners have no authority to

(a) Do any act in contravention of the certificate,

(b) Do any act which would make it impossible to carry on the ordinary business of the partnership,

(c) Confess a judgment against the partnership,

(d) Possess partnership property, or assign their rights in specific partnership property, for other than a partnership purpose,

(e) Admit a person as a general partner,

(f) Admit a person as a limited partner, unless the right so to do is given in the certificate,

(g) Continue the business with partnership property on the death, retirement or insanity of a general partner, unless the right so to do is given in the certificate.

SECTION 10. RIGHTS OF A LIMITED PARTNER. (1) A limited partner shall have the same rights as a general partner to

(a) Have the partnership books kept at the principal place of business of the partnership, and at all times to inspect and copy any of them,

(b) Have on demand true and full information of all things affecting the partnership, and a formal account of partnership affairs whenever circumstances render it just and reasonable, and

(c) Have dissolution and winding up by decree of court.

(2) A limited partner shall have the right to receive a share of the profits or other compensation by way of income, and to the return of his contribution as provided in Sections 15 and 16.

SECTION 11. STATUS OF PERSON ERRONEOUSLY BELIEVING HIMSELF A LIMITED PARTNER. A person who has contributed to the capital of a business conducted by a person or partnership erroneously believing that he has become a limited partner in a limited partnership, is not, by reason of his exercise of the rights of a limited partner, a general partner with the person or in the partnership carrying on the business, or bound by the obligations of such person or partnership; provided that on ascertaining the mistake he promptly renounces his interest in the profits of the business, or other compensation by way of income.

SECTION 12. ONE PERSON BOTH GENERAL AND LIMITED PARTNER. (1) A person may be a general partner and a limited partner in the same partnership at the same time.

(2) A person who is a general, and also at the same time a limited partner, shall

have all the rights and powers and be subject to all the restrictions of a general partner; except that, in respect to his contribution, he shall have the rights against the other members which he would have had if he were not also a general partner.

SECTION 13. LOANS AND OTHER BUSINESS TRANSACTIONS WITH LIMITED PARTNER. (1) A limited partner also may loan money to and transact other business with the partnership, and, unless he is also a general partner, receive on account of resulting claims against the partnership, with general creditors, a pro rata share of the assets. No limited partner shall in respect to any such claim

(a) Receive or hold as collateral security any partnership property, or

(b) Receive from a general partner or the partnership any payment, conveyance, or release from liability, if at the time the assets of the partnership are not sufficient to discharge partnership liabilities to persons not claiming as general or limited partners,

(2) The receiving of collateral security, or a payment, conveyance, or release in violation of the provisions of paragraph (1) is a fraud on the creditors of the partnership.

SECTION 14. RELATION OF LIMITED PARTNERS INTER SE. Where there are several limited partners the members may agree that one or more of the limited partners shall have a priority over other limited partners as to the return of their contributions, as to their compensation by way of income, or as to any other matter. If such an agreement is made it shall be stated in the certificate, and in the absence of such a statement all the limited partners shall stand upon equal footing.

SECTION 15. COMPENSATION OF LIMITED PARTNER. A limited partner may receive from the partnership the share of the profits or the compensation by way of income stipulated for in the certificate; provided, that after such payment is made, whether from the property of the partnership or that of a general partner, the partnership assets are in excess of all liabilities of the partnership except liabilities to limited partners on account of their contributions and to general partners.

SECTION 16. WITHDRAWAL OR REDUCTION OF LIMITED PARTNER'S CONTRIBUTION. (1) A limited partner shall not receive from a general partner or out of partnership property any part of his contribution until

(a) All liabilities of the partnership, except liabilities to general partners and to limited partners on account of their contributions, have been paid or there remains property of the partnership sufficient to pay them,

(b) The consent of all members is had, unless the return of the contribution may be rightfully demanded under the provisions of paragraph (2), and

(c) The certificate is cancelled or so amended as to set forth the withdrawal or reduction.

(2) Subject to the provisions of paragraph (1) a limited partner may rightfully demand the return of his contribution

(a) On the dissolution of a partnership, or

(b) When the date specified in the certificate for its return has arrived, or

(c) After he has given six months' notice in writing to all other members, if no time is specified in the certificate either for the return of the contribution or for the dissolution of the partnership,

(3) In the absence of any statement in the certificate to the contrary or the consent of all members, a limited partner, irrespective of the nature of his contribution, has only the right to demand and receive cash in return for his contribution.

(4) A limited partner may have the partnership dissolved and its affairs wound up when

(a) He rightfully but unsuccessfully demands the return of his contribution, or

(b) The other liabilities of the partnership have not been paid, or the partnership property is insufficient for their payment as required by paragraph (1a) and the limited partner would otherwise be entitled to the return of his contribution.

SECTION 17. LIABILITY OF LIMITED PARTNER TO PARTNERSHIP. (1) A limited partner is liable to the partnership

(a) For the difference between his contribution as actually made and that stated in the certificate as having been made, and

    (b) For any unpaid contribution which he agreed in the certificate to make in the future at the time and on the conditions stated in the certificate.

  (2) A limited partner holds as trustee for the partnership

    (a) Specific property stated in the certificate as contributed by him, but which was not contributed or which has been wrongfully returned, and

    (b) Money or other property wrongfully paid or conveyed to him on account of his contribution.

  (3) The liabilities of a limited partner as set forth in this section can be waived or compromised only by the consent of all members; but a waiver or compromise shall not affect the right of a creditor of a partnership, who extended credit or whose claim arose after the filing and before a cancellation or amendment of the certificate, to enforce such liabilities.

  (4) When a contributor has rightfully received the return in whole or in part of the capital of his contribution, he is nevertheless liable to the partnership for any sum, not in excess of such return with interest, necessary to discharge its liabilities to all creditors who extended credit or whose claims arose before such return.

  Section 18. Nature of Limited Partner's Interest in Partnership. A limited partner's interest in the partnership is personal property.

  Section 19. Assignment of Limited Partner's Interest. (1) A limited partner's interest is assignable.

  (2) A substituted limited partner is a person admitted to all the rights of a limited partner who has died or has assigned his interest in a partnership.

  (3) An assignee, who does not become a substituted limited partner, has no right to require any information or account of the partnership transactions or to inspect the partnership books; he is only entitled to receive the share of the profits or other compensation by way of income, or the return of his contribution, to which his assignor would otherwise be entitled.

  (4) An assignee shall have the right to become a substituted limited partner if all the members (except the assignor) consent thereto or if the assignor, being thereunto empowered by the certificate, gives the assignee that right.

  (5) An assignee becomes a substituted limited partner when the certificate is appropriately amended in accordance with Section 25.

  (6) The substituted limited partner has all the rights and powers, and is subject to all the restrictions and liabilities of his assignor, except those liabilities of which he was ignorant at the time he became a limited partner and which could not be ascertained from the certificate.

  (7) The substitution of the assignee as a limited partner does not release the assignor from liability to the partnership under Sections 6 and 17.

  Section 20. Effect of Retirement, Death or Insanity of a General Partner. The retirement, death or insanity of a general partner dissolves the partnership, unless the business is continued by the remaining general partners

    (a) Under a right so to do stated in the certificate, or

    (b) With the consent of all members.

  Section 21. Death of Limited Partner. (1) On the death of a limited partner his executor or administrator shall have all the rights of a limited partner for the purpose of settling his estate, and such power as the deceased had to constitute his assignee a substituted limited partner.

  (2) The estate of a deceased limited partner shall be liable for all his liabilities as a limited partner.

  Section 22. Rights of Creditors of Limited Partner.[1] (1) On due application to a court of competent jurisdiction by any judgment creditor of a limited partner,

---

[1] In those states where a creditor on beginning an action can attach debts due the defendant before he has obtained a judgment against the defendant it is recommended that paragraph (1) of this section read as follows:

On due application to a court of competent jurisdiction by any creditor of a limited partner, the court may charge the interest of the indebted limited partner with payment of the unsatisfied amount of such claim; and may appoint a receiver, and make all other orders, directions, and inquires which the circumstances of the case may require.

the court may charge the interest of the indebted limited partner with payment of the unsatisfied amount of the judgment debt; and may appoint a receiver, and make all other orders, directions, and inquiries which the circumstances of the case may require.

(2) The interest may be redeemed with the separate property of any general partner, but may not be redeemed with partnership property.

(3) The remedies conferred by paragraph (1) shall not be deemed exclusive of others which may exist.

(4) Nothing in this act shall be held to deprive a limited partner of his statutory exemption.

Section 23. Distribution of Assets. (1) In settling accounts after dissolution the liabilities of the partnership shall be entitled to payment in the following order:

(a) Those to creditors, in the order of priority as provided by law, except those to limited partners on account of their contributions, and to general partners,

(b) Those to limited partners in respect to their share of the profits and other compensation by way of income on their contributions,

(c) Those to limited partners in respect to the capital of their contributions,

(d) Those to general partners other than for capital and profits,

(e) Those to general partners in respect to profits,

(f) Those to general partners in respect to capital.

(2) Subject to any statement in the certificate or to subsequent agreement, limited partners share in the partnership assets in respect to their claims for capital, and in respect to their claims for profits or for compensation by way of income on their contributions respectively, in proportion to the respective amounts of such claims.

Section 24. When Certificate Shall be Cancelled or Amended (1) The certificate shall be cancelled when the partnership is dissolved or all limited partners cease to be such.

(2) A certificate shall be amended when

(a) There is a change in the name of the partnership or in the amount of character of the contribution of any limited partner,

(b) A person is substituted as a limited partner,

(c) An additional limited partner is admitted,

(d) A person is admitted as a general partner,

(e) A general partner retires, dies or becomes insane, and the business is continued under Section 20.

(f) There is a change in the character of the business of the partnership,

(g) There is a false or erroneous statement in the certificate,

(h) There is a change in the time as stated in the certificate for the dissolution of the partnership or for the return of a contribution,

(i) A time is fixed for the dissolution of the partnership, or the return of a contribution, no time having been specified in the certificate, or

(j) The members desire to make a change in any other statement in the certificate in order that it shall accurately represent the agreement between them.

Section 25. Requirements for Amendment and for Cancellation of Certificate. (1) The writing to amend a certificate shall

(a) Conform to the requirements of Section 2(1a) as far as necessary to set forth clearly the change in the certificate which it is desired to make, and

(b) Be signed and sworn to by all members, and an amendement substituting a limited partner or adding a limited or general partner shall be signed also by the member to be substituted or added, and when a limited partner is to be substituted, the amendment shall also be signed by the assigning limited partner.

(2) The writing to cancel a certificate shall be signed by all members.

(3) A person desiring the cancellation or amendment of a certificate, if any person designated in paragraph (1) and (2) as a person who must execute the writing refuses to do so, may petition the [here designate the proper court] to direct a cancellation or amendment thereof.

(4) If the court finds that the petitioner has a right to have the writing executed by

a person who refuses to do so, it shall order the [here designate the responsible official in the office designated in Section 2] in the office where the certificate is recorded to record the cancellation or amendment of the certificate; and where the certificate is to be amended, the court shall also cause to be filed for record in said office a certified copy of its decree setting forth the amendment.

(5) A certificate is amended or cancelled when there is filed for record in the office [here designate the office designated in Section 2] where the certificate is recorded

   (a) A writing in accordance with the provisions of paragraph (1), or (2) or

   (b) A certified copy of the order of court in accordance with the provisions of paragraph (4).

(6) After the certificate is duly amended in accordance with this section, the amended certificate shall thereafter be for all purposes the certificate provided for by this act.

SECTION 26. PARTIES TO ACTIONS. A contributor, unless he is a general partner, is not a proper party to proceedings by or against a partnership, except where the object is to enforce a limited partner's right against or liability to the partnership.

SECTION 27. NAME OF ACT. This act may be cited as The Uniform Limited Partnership Act.

SECTION 28. RULES OF CONSTRUCTION. (1) The rule that statutes in derogation of the common law are to be strictly construed shall have no application to this act.

(2) This act shall be so interpreted and construed as to effect its general purpose to make uniform the law of those states which enact it.

(3) This act shall not be so construed as to impair the obligations of any contract existing when the act goes into effect, nor to affect any action on proceedings begun or right accrued before this act takes effect.

SECTION 29. RULES FOR CASES NOT PROVIDED FOR IN THIS ACT. In any case not provided for in this act the rules of law and equity, including the law merchant, shall govern.

SECTION 30.[2] PROVISIONS FOR EXISTING LIMITED PARTNERSHIPS. (1) A limited partnership formed under any statute of this state prior to the adoption of this act, may become a limited partnership under this act by complying with the provisions of Section 2; provided the certificate sets forth

   (a) The amount of the original contribution of each limited partner, and the time when the contribution was made, and

   (b) That the property of the partnership exceeds the amount sufficient to discharge its liabilities to persons not claiming as general or limited partners by an amount greater than the sum of the contributions of its limited partners.

(2) A limited partnership formed under any statute of this state prior to the adoption of this act, until or unless it becomes a limited partnership under this act, shall continue to be governed by the provisions of [here insert proper reference to the existing limited partnership act or acts], except that such partnership shall not be renewed unless so provided in the original agreement.

SECTION 31.[2] ACT (ACTS) REPEALED. Except as affecting existing limited partnerships to the extent set forth in Section 30, the act (acts) of [here designate the existing limited partnership act or acts] is (are) hereby repealed.

---

[2] Sections 30, 31, will be omitted in any state which has not a limited partnership act.

Index